Business Statistics

KEN BLACK

UMASS–Boston

MSIS 111 / Managerial Statistics

WILEY *Custom*
LEARNING SOLUTIONS

www.wileyplus.com

WileyPLUS is a research-based online environment for effective teaching and learning.

WileyPLUS builds students' confidence because it takes the guesswork out of studying by providing students with a clear roadmap:

- what to do
- how to do it
- if they did it right

It offers interactive resources along with a complete digital textbook that help students learn more. With *WileyPLUS*, students take more initiative so you'll have greater impact on their achievement in the classroom and beyond.

7TH EDITION

Business Statistics
For Contemporary
Decision Making

7TH EDITION

Business Statistics
For Contemporary
Decision Making

Ken Black

University of Houston—Clear Lake

WILEY

John Wiley & Sons, Inc.

Vice President & Executive Publisher   *George Hoffman*
Senior Acquisitions Editor   *Franny Kelly*
Senior Content Editor   *Brian Kamins*
Assistant Editor   *Emily McGee*
Senior Content Manager   *Dorothy Sinclair*
Senior Production Editor   *Erin Bascom*
Marketing Manager   *Kelly Simmons*
Marketing Assistant   *Ashley Tomeck*
Design Director   *Harry Nolan*
Senior Designer   *Wendy Lai*
Production Management Services   *Aptara*
Senior Illustration Editor   *Anna Melhorn*
Senior Photo Editor   *Jennifer MacMillan*
Editorial Assistant   *Melissa Solarz*
Executive Media Editor   *Allison Morris*
Media Specialists   *Elena Santa Maria and Thomas Caruso*
Cover Photo   *Yagi Studio/Digital Vision/Getty Images*
Back Cover   *iStock*

This book was set in 10/12 Minion by Aptara®, and printed and bound by Courier/Kendallville.
The cover was printed by Lehigh Phoenix.

This book is printed on acid free paper. ∞

Founded in 1807, John Wiley & Sons, Inc. has been a valued source of knowledge and understanding for more than 200 years, helping people around the world meet their needs and fulfill their aspirations. Our company is built on a foundation of principles that include responsibility to the communities we serve and where we live and work. In 2008, we launched a Corporate Citizenship Initiative, a global effort to address the environmental, social, economic, and ethical challenges we face in our business. Among the issues we are addressing are carbon impact, paper specifications and procurement, ethical conduct within our business and among our vendors, and community and charitable support. For more information, please visit our website: www.wiley.com/go/citizenship.

ISBN 13   978-0-470-93146-2
ISBN 13   978-1-118-02411-9

Printed in the United States of America.

10 9 8 7 6 5 4 3 2 1

For Carolyn, Caycee, and Wendi

BRIEF CONTENTS

CONTENTS

UNIT III
MAKING INFERENCES ABOUT POPULATION PARAMETERS

PREFACE

The seventh edition of *Business Statistics for Contemporary Decision Making* continues the tradition of presenting and explaining the wonders of business statistics through the use of clear, complete, student-friendly pedagogy. With the seventh edition, the author and Wiley have expanded the vast ancillary resources available through WileyPLUS with which to complement the text in helping instructors effectively deliver this subject matter and in assisting students in their learning. With the seventh edition, WileyPLUS has been significantly updated to allow instructors far greater latitude in developing and delivering their course than ever before.

In this edition, several changes have been made in an effort to improve the delivery and completeness of the text. Two new chapter sections have been added, including a new section in Chapter 1 entitled Variables and Data, and a new section in Chapter 14 on Logistic Regression. In Variables and Data, students are introduced to the concepts of variable, measurement, and data to help prepare them for studying levels of data measurement and to help them attain an introductory understanding of what is a variable. Logistic regression was added to the seventh edition because of its growing importance and use in business statistics.

In the seventh edition, all of the features of the sixth edition have been updated and changed as needed to reflect today's business world. A new Decision Dilemma, "Container Shipping Companies," a timely topic given the high visibility of international transportation, has been added to Chapter 2. The seventh edition contains two new cases, "Whole Foods Market Grows Through Mergers and Acquisitions" and "The Container Store." In addition, there has been a major refocusing of another case, "Coca-Cola Develops the African Market."

In an effort to place more emphasis on critical thinking, the Statistics in Business feature has been changed to Thinking Critically about Statistics in Business and questions to ponder have been added to each. In the seventh edition, there are seven new Thinking Critically about Statistics in Business features including "Consumer Attitudes Toward Food in the U.S.," "Beverage Consumption: America vs. Europe," "Are Facial Characteristics Correlated with CEO Traits?," "Assessing Property Values Using Multiple Regression," "Can Scrap Metal Prices Forecast the Economy?" (a complete rewrite), "City Images of Cruise Destinations in the Taiwan Strait," and "Does an Iranian Auto Parts Manufacturer's Orientation Impact Innovation?"

Five new video tutorials of the author explaining key difficult topics and demonstrating how to work problems from challenging sections of the text have been added to the 17 already available making a total of 22 videos to accompany the text. There is now at least one video to accompany each of the first 12 chapters. New videos include Levels of Data Measurement, Stem-and-Leaf Plot, Solving for Probabilities of Sample Means Using the z Statistic, Hypothesis Tests of the Difference in Means of Two Independent Populations Using the t Statistic, and Computing and Interpreting a One-Way ANOVA.

This edition is written and designed for a two-semester introductory undergraduate business statistics course or an MBA-level introductory course. In addition, with 19 chapters, the seventh edition lends itself nicely to adaptation for a one-semester introductory business statistics course. The text is written with the assumption that the student has a college algebra mathematical background. No calculus is used in the presentation of material in the text.

An underlying philosophical approach to the text is that every statistical tool presented in the book has some business application. While the text contains statistical rigor, it is written so that the student can readily see that the proper application of statistics in the business world goes hand-in-hand with good decision making. In this edition, statistics are presented as a means for converting data into useful information that can be used to assist the business decision maker in making more thoughtful, information-based decisions. Thus, the text presents business statistics as "value added" tools in the process of converting data into useful information.

CHANGES FOR THE SEVENTH EDITION

Units and Chapters

In the seventh edition, the unit and chapter organization remains the same as it was in the sixth edition—there are 19 chapters organized into five units. Unit I, Introduction, contains the first four chapters of the text. In this unit, students learn some important foundational tools for understanding topics presented in the rest of the course. In Unit II, Distributions and Sampling, consisting of chapters 5 through 7, students are presented with six population distributions and two sampling distributions. In Unit III, Making Inferences About Population Parameters, which includes chapters 8 through 11, students learn about estimating and testing population parameters. Unit IV, chapters 12 through 15, is called Regression Analysis and Forecasting. In this unit, students explore relationships between variables including developing models to predict a variable by other variables and developing models to forecast. Unit V, Nonparametric Statistics and Quality, includes chapters 16 through 18. In these chapters, students are presented with a series of well-known nonparametric techniques along with a number of quality-improvement concepts and techniques. Chapter 19, Decision Analysis, is available only through WileyPLUS or custom versions of the text.

Topical Changes

Sections and topics from the sixth edition remain virtually unchanged in the seventh edition, with two exceptions. In Chapter 1, there is a new section 1.3 entitled, Variables and Data. In this section, students are introduced to the concepts of variable, measurement, and data. A discussion of these three concepts is important early in the course so that students have a better understanding of where data come from, why it is important to study levels of data measurement, and what are variables in business. The old section 1.3, Data Measurement, has been retained and is now section 1.4 in this edition.

A second new section in the seventh edition is section 14.5, Logistic Regression. Until now, no edition of the text has included a presentation of logistic regression. Logistic regression was added to the seventh edition because of its growing importance and use in business statistics. In this section, the approach is to give the student an introduction to the concepts and importance of logistic regression along with presenting an explanation of the basic computer output from a logistic regression analysis.

Decision Dilemma and the Decision Dilemma Solved

Each chapter of the seventh edition begins with a Decision Dilemma. Decision Dilemmas are real business vignettes that set the tone for each chapter by presenting a business dilemma and asking a number of managerial or statistical questions, the solutions to which require the use of techniques presented in the chapter. At the end of each chapter, there is a Decision Dilemma Solved feature, which discusses and answers the managerial and statistical questions posed in the Decision Dilemma using techniques from the chapter, thus bringing closure to the chapter. In the seventh edition, all decision dilemmas have been revised and updated. Solutions given in the Decision Dilemma Solved features have been revised for new data and for new versions of computer output.

In addition, one new Decision Dilemma has been added in the seventh edition, located in Chapter 2. The title of this Decision Dilemma is "Container Shipping Companies," a current and timely topic given international commerce and the high volumes of products and goods being shipped. In this Decision Dilemma, students are presented with a brief history of how the current size of the more efficient standard shipping containers evolved from the wide variety of shapes and sizes in the past that created substantially more work thereby consuming additional expense and time. This Decision Dilemma displays total container capacity and fleet size of the top five shipping companies in the world and asks such questions as, "Suppose you are a shipping container industry analyst, and you are asked to prepare a brief report showing the leading shipping companies both in TEU shipping capacity and in number of ships. What is the best way to display this shipping container company information? Are the raw data enough? Can you effectively display the data graphically?"

Thinking Critically About Statistics in Business Today

In previous editions, every chapter has included one or two Statistics in Business Today features that present real-life examples of how the statistics presented in that chapter apply in the business world today. In the seventh edition, this feature has been renamed Thinking Critically About Statistics in Business Today because thought-provoking questions called Things to Ponder have been added to the feature. The objective is to change the feature from an informative article to a feature that can effect critical thinking on behalf of the student and perhaps generate discussion involving critical thinking in the classroom. This approach to learning is in sync with various accreditation organizations and their current emphasis on developing critical thinking in our students.

In addition to these changes, seven new Thinking Critically About Statistics in Business Today features have been added to the seventh edition across seven chapters. These new features are "Consumer Attitudes Toward Food in the U.S.," "Beverage Consumption: America vs. Europe," "Are Facial Characteristics Correlated with CEO Traits?," "Assessing Property Values Using Multiple Regression," "Can Scrap Metal Prices Forecast the Economy?" (a complete rewrite), "City Images of Cruise Destinations in the Taiwan Strait," and "Does an Iranian Auto Parts Manufacturer's Orientation Impact Innovation?" As an example, from "Beverage Consumption: America vs. Europe," Americans drink nearly five times as much soda as do Europeans and almost twice as much beer. On the other hand, Europeans drink more than twice as much tea (hot or cold), more than three times as much wine, and over four times as much tap water as Americans. Statistics show that the average American consumes forty-eight 12 oz. containers of carbonated soda per month compared to only 10 for Europeans. Europeans consume an average of sixteen 4 oz. containers of wine per month compared to an average of only five for Americans. One of the Things to Ponder questions is, "Can you think of some reasons why Americans consume more carbonated soda pop and beer than Europeans, but less wine, hot or iced tea, or tap water? Do you think that these outcomes may change in time?"

Cases

Every chapter in this text contains a unique business case at the end of the chapter presenting a different company. All cases in the seventh edition have been updated and edited for today's market. These business cases are more than just long problems, and in the discussion that follows the business scenario, several issues and questions are posed that can be addressed using techniques presented in the chapter. Two new cases have been added to the seventh edition, and one previously used case has been given a major new rewrite. The case with the major rewrite is in Chapter 3, where a new twist has been made on Coca-Cola's international efforts with "Coca-Cola Develops the African Market." The two new cases are "Whole Foods Market Grows Through Mergers and Acquisitions" in Chapter 5 and "The Container Store" in Chapter 8. Both of these cases present exciting companies relevant to present-day markets. Here are some excerpts from the new case, "The Container Store"?

"In the late 1970s, Kip Tindell (chairman and CEO), Garrett Boone (Chairman Emeritus), and John Mullen (architect) drew up plans for a first-of-a-kind retail store specializing in storage solutions for both the home and the office. The vision that they created was realized when on July 1, 1978, the Container Store opened its doors in a small 1,600 square foot retail space in Dallas. The store was stocked with products that were devoted to simplifying people's lives, such as commercial parts bins, wire drawers, mailboxes, milk crates, wire leaf burners, and many others. Some critics even questioned that a store selling "empty boxes" could survive. However, the concept took off, and in the past 33 years, the company has expanded coast to coast in the United States with stores in 49 locations. Now headquartered in Coppell, Texas, the Container Store has 4,000 employees and annual revenues of over $650 million. Besides their innovative product mix, one of the keys to the success of the Container Store is the enthusiasm with which their employees work, the care that employees give to the customer, and employee knowledge of their products."

New Problems

Every problem in the sixth edition has been examined for timeliness, appropriateness, and logic before inclusion in the seventh edition. Those that fell short were replaced or rewritten. In the seventh edition, there are 25 new problems for a net gain of 15 additional problems, bringing the total number of practice problems in the text to about 965. Over 35 percent of the new problems are in Chapter 2, where more emphasis has been placed on interpreting graphical output. In addition, with the inclusion of a new section in Chapter 14 on logistic regression, there are five additional problems in that chapter.

All demonstration problems and example problems were thoroughly reviewed and edited for effectiveness. A demonstration problem is an extra example containing both a problem and its solution and is used as an additional pedagogical tool to supplement explanations and examples in the chapters. Virtually all example and demonstration problems in the seventh edition are business oriented and contain the most current data available.

As with the previous edition, problems are located at the end of most sections in the chapters. A significant number of additional problems are provided at the end of each chapter in the Supplementary Problems. The Supplementary Problems are "scrambled"—problems using the various techniques in the chapter are mixed—so that students can test themselves on their ability to discriminate and differentiate ideas and concepts.

Databases

Available with the seventh edition are nine databases that provide additional opportunities for students to apply the statistics presented in this text. These nine databases represent a wide variety of business areas, such as agribusiness, consumer spending, energy, finance, healthcare, international labor, manufacturing, and the stock market. Altogether, these databases contain 61 variables and 7,722 observations. The data are gathered from such reliable sources as the U.S. government's Bureau of Labor, the U.S. Department of Agriculture, the American Hospital Association, the Energy Information Administration, *Moody's Handbook of Common Stocks,* and the U.S. Census Bureau. Five of the nine databases contain time-series data. The databases are 12-Year Gasoline Database, Consumer Food Database, Manufacturing Database, International Labor Database, Financial Database, Energy Database, U.S. and International Stock Market Database, Hospital Database, and Agribusiness Time-Series Database.

VIDEOTAPE TUTORIALS BY KEN BLACK

An exciting feature of the seventh edition package that will impact the effectiveness of student learning in business statistics and significantly enhance the presentation of course material is the series of videotape tutorials by Ken Black. With the advent of online business statistics courses, increasingly large class sizes, and the number of commuter students who have very limited access to educational resources on business statistics, it is often difficult for students to get the learning assistance that they need to bridge the gap between theory and application on their own. There are now 22 videotaped tutorial sessions on key difficult topics in business statistics delivered by Ken Black and available for all adopters on WileyPLUS. In addition, these tutorials can easily be uploaded for classroom usage to augment lectures and enrich classroom presentations. Because there is at least one video for each of the first 12 chapters, the instructor has the option to include at least one video in the template of each chapter's plan for most, if not all, of the course. While the video tutorials vary in length, a typical video is about 10 minutes in length. The 22 video tutorials are:

1. Chapter 1: Levels of Data Measurement
2. Chapter 2: Stem-and-Leaf Plot

3. Chapter 3: Computing Variance and Standard Deviation
4. Chapter 3: Understanding and Using the Empirical Rule
5. Chapter 4: Constructing and Solving Joint Probability Tables
6. Chapter 4: Solving Probability Word Problems
7. Chapter 5: Solving Binomial Distribution Problems, Part I
8. Chapter 5: Solving Binomial Distribution Problems, Part II
9. Chapter 6: Solving Problems Using the Normal Curve
10. Chapter 7: Solving for Probabilities of Sample Means Using the z Statistic
11. Chapter 8: Confidence Intervals
12. Chapter 8: Determining Which Inferential Technique to Use, Part I, Confidence Intervals
13. Chapter 9: Hypothesis Testing Using the z Statistic
14. Chapter 9: Establishing Hypotheses
15. Chapter 9: Understanding p-Values
16. Chapter 9: Type I and Type II errors
17. Chapter 9: Two-Tailed Tests
18. Chapter 9: Determining Which Inferential Technique to Use, Part II, Hypothesis Tests
19. Chapter 10: Hypothesis Tests of the Difference in Means of Two Independent Populations Using the t Statistic
20. Chapter 11: Computing and Interpreting a One-Way ANOVA
21. Chapter 12: Testing the Regression Model I—Predicted Values, Residuals, and Sum of Squares of Error
22. Chapter 12: Testing the Regression Model II—Standard Error of the Estimate and r^2

FEATURES AND BENEFITS

Each chapter of the seventh edition contains sections called Learning Objectives, a Decision Dilemma, Demonstration Problems, Section Problems, Thinking Critically About Statistics in Business Today, Decision Dilemma Solved, Chapter Summary, Key Terms, Formulas, Ethical Considerations, Supplementary Problems, Analyzing the Databases, Case, Using the Computer, and Computer Output from both Excel 2010 and Minitab Release 16.

- **Learning Objectives.** Each chapter begins with a statement of the chapter's main learning objectives. This statement gives the reader a list of key topics that will be discussed and the goals to be achieved from studying the chapter.
- **Decision Dilemma.** At the beginning of each chapter, a short case describes a real company or business situation in which managerial and statistical questions are raised. In most Decision Dilemmas, actual data are given and the student is asked to consider how the data can be analyzed to answer the questions.
- **Demonstration Problems.** Virtually every section of every chapter in the seventh edition contains demonstration problems. A demonstration problem contains both an example problem and its solution, and is used as an additional pedagogical tool to supplement explanations and examples.
- **Section Problems.** There are over 960 problems in the text. Problems for practice are found at the end of almost every section of the text. Most problems utilize real data gathered from a plethora of sources. Included here are a few brief excerpts from some of the real-life problems in the text: "*The Wall Street Journal* reported that 40% of all workers say they would change jobs for 'slightly higher pay.' In

addition, 88% of companies say that there is a shortage of qualified job candidates." "In a study by Peter D. Hart Research Associates for the Nasdaq Stock Market, it was determined that 20% of all stock investors are retired people. In addition, 40% of all U.S. adults have invested in mutual funds." "A survey conducted for the Northwestern National Life Insurance Company revealed that 70% of American workers say job stress caused frequent health problems." "According to Padgett Business Services, 20% of all small-business owners say the most important advice for starting a business is to prepare for long hours and hard work. Twenty-five percent say the most important advice is to have good financing ready."

- **Thinking Critically About Statistics in Business Today.** Every chapter in the seventh edition contains at least one Thinking Critically About Statistics in Business Today feature. These focus boxes contain an interesting application of how techniques of that particular chapter are used in the business world today and ask probing questions of the student. They are usually based on real companies, surveys, or published research.

- **Decision Dilemma Solved.** Situated at the end of the chapter, the Decision Dilemma Solved feature addresses the managerial and statistical questions raised in the Decision Dilemma. Data given in the Decision Dilemma are analyzed computationally and by computer using techniques presented in the chapter. Answers to the managerial and statistical questions raised in the Decision Dilemma are arrived at by applying chapter concepts, thus bringing closure to the chapter.

- **Chapter Summary.** Each chapter concludes with a summary of the important concepts, ideas, and techniques of the chapter. This feature can serve as a preview of the chapter as well as a chapter review.

- **Key Terms.** Important terms are bolded and their definitions italicized throughout the text as they are discussed. At the end of the chapter, a list of the key terms from the chapter is presented. In addition, these terms appear with their definitions in the end-of-book glossary.

- **Formulas.** Important formulas in the text are highlighted to make it easy for a reader to locate them. At the end of the chapter, most of the chapter's formulas are listed together as a handy reference.

- **Ethical Considerations.** Each chapter contains an Ethical Considerations feature that is very timely, given the serious breach of ethics and lack of moral leadership of some business executives in recent years. With the abundance of statistical data and analysis, there is considerable potential for the misuse of statistics in business dealings. The important Ethical Considerations feature underscores this potential misuse by discussing such topics as lying with statistics, failing to meet statistical assumptions, and failing to include pertinent information for decision makers. Through this feature, instructors can begin to integrate the topic of ethics with applications of business statistics. Here are a few excerpts from Ethical Considerations features: "It is unprofessional and unethical to draw cause-and-effect conclusions just because two variables are correlated." "The business researcher needs to conduct the experiment in an environment such that as many concomitant variables are controlled as possible. To the extent that this is not done, the researcher has an ethical responsibility to report that fact in the findings." "The reader is warned that the value lambda is assumed to be constant in a Poisson distribution experiment. Business researchers may produce spurious results if the value of lambda is used throughout a study; but because the study is conducted during different time periods, the value of lambda is actually changing." "In describing a body of data to an audience, it is best to use whatever statistical measures it takes to present a 'full' picture of the data. By limiting the descriptive measures used, the business researcher may give the audience only part of the picture and skew the way the receiver understands the data."

- **Supplementary Problems.** At the end of each chapter is an extensive set of additional problems. The Supplementary Problems are divided into three groups: Calculating the Statistics, which are strictly computational problems; Testing Your

Understanding, which are problems for application and understanding; and Interpreting the Output, which are problems that require the interpretation and analysis of software output.

- **Analyzing the Databases.** There are nine major databases located on the student companion Web site that accompanies the seventh edition and in WileyPLUS. The end-of-chapter Analyzing the Databases section contains several questions/problems that require the application of techniques from the chapter to data in the variables of the databases. It is assumed that most of these questions/problems will be solved using a computer.

- **Case.** Each chapter has an end-of-chapter case based on a real company. These cases give the student an opportunity to use statistical concepts and techniques presented in the chapter to solve a business dilemma. Some cases feature very large companies—such as Shell Oil, Coca-Cola, or Colgate Palmolive. Others pertain to small businesses—such as Virginia Semiconductor, Delta Wire, or DeBourgh—that have overcome obstacles to survive and thrive. Most cases include raw data for analysis and questions that encourage the student to use several of the techniques presented in the chapter. In many cases, the student must analyze software output in order to reach conclusions or make decisions.

- **Using the Computer.** The Using the Computer section contains directions for producing the Excel 2010 and Minitab Release 16 software output presented in the chapter. It is assumed that students have a general understanding of a Microsoft Windows environment. Directions include specifics about menu bars, drop-down menus, and dialog boxes. Not every detail of every dialog box is discussed; the intent is to provide enough information for students to produce the same statistical output analyzed and discussed in the chapter. The seventh edition has a strong focus on both Excel and Minitab software packages. More than 250 Excel 2010 or Minitab Release 16 computer-generated outputs are displayed.

WILEYPLUS

WileyPLUS is a powerful online tool that provides instructors and students with an integrated suite of teaching and learning resources, including an online version of the text, in one easy-to-use Web site. To learn more about WileyPLUS, and view a demo, please visit www.wiley.com/college/WileyPLUS.

WileyPLUS Tools for Instructors

WileyPLUS enables you to:

- Assign automatically graded homework, practice, and quizzes from the end of chapter and test bank.
- Track your students' progress in an instructor's grade book.
- Access all teaching and learning resources, including an online version of the text, and student and instructor supplements, in one easy-to-use Web site. These include full color PowerPoint slides, teaching videos, case files, and answers and animations.
- Create class presentations using Wiley-provided resources, with the ability to customize and add your own materials.

WileyPLUS Resources for Students Within WileyPLUS

In WileyPLUS, students will find various helpful tools, such as an ebook, the student study manual, videos with tutorials by the author, applets, Decision Dilemma and Decision Dilemma Solved animations, learning activities, flash cards for key terms, demonstration problems, databases in both Excel and Minitab, case data in both Excel and Minitab, and problem data in both Excel and Minitab.

- **Ebook.** The complete text is available on WileyPLUS with learning links to various features and tools to assist students in their learning.
- **Videos.** There are 22 videos of the author explaining concepts and demonstrating how to work problems for some of the more difficult topics.
- **Applets.** Statistical applets are available, affording students the opportunity to learn concepts by iteratively experimenting with various values of statistics and parameters and observing the outcomes.
- **Learning Activities.** There are numerous learning activities to help the student better understand concepts and key terms. These activities have been developed to make learning fun, enjoyable, and challenging.
- **Data Sets.** Virtually all problems in the text along with the case problems and the databases are available to students in both Excel and Minitab format.
- **Animations.** To aid students in understanding complex interactions, selected figures from the text that involve dynamic activity have been animated using Flash technology. Students can download these animated figures and run them to improve their understanding of dynamic processes.
- **Flash Cards.** Key terms will be available to students in a flash card format along with their definition.
- **Student Study Manual.** Complete solutions to all odd-numbered questions.
- **Demo Problems.** Step-by-step solved problems for each chapter.

ANCILLARY TEACHING AND LEARNING MATERIALS
www.wiley.com/college/black

Students' Companion Site

The student companion Web site contains:

- All databases in both Excel and Minitab formats for easy access and use.
- Excel and Minitab files of data from all text problems and all cases. Instructors and students now have the option of analyzing any of the data sets using the computer.
- Full and complete version of Chapter 19, Decision Analysis, in PDF format. This allows an instructor the option of covering the material in this chapter in the normal manner, while keeping the text manageable in size and length.
- A section on Advanced Exponential Smoothing Techniques (from Chapter 15), which offers the instructor an opportunity to delve deeper into exponential smoothing if so desired, and derivation of the slope and intercept formulas from Chapter 12.
- A tutorial on summation theory.

Instructor's Resource Kit

All instructor ancillaries are provided on the Instructor Resource Site. Included in this convenient format are:

- **Instructor's Manual.** Prepared by Ken Black, this manual contains the worked out solutions to virtually all problems in the text. In addition, this manual contains chapter objectives, chapter outlines, chapter teaching strategies, and solutions to the cases.
- **PowerPoint Presentation Slides.** The presentation slides, prepared by Michael Posner of Villanova University, contain graphics to help instructors create stimulating lectures. The PowerPoint slides may be adapted using PowerPoint software to facilitate classroom use.
- **Test Bank.** Prepared by Osnat Stramer of the University of Iowa, The Test Bank includes multiple-choice questions for each chapter. The Test Bank is provided in Microsoft Word format.

ACKNOWLEDGMENTS

John Wiley & Sons and I would like to thank the reviewers and advisors who cared enough and took the time to provide us with their excellent insights and advice, which was used to reshape and mold the text into the seventh edition. These colleagues include: Lihui Bai, Valparaiso University; Pam Boger, Ohio University; Parag Dhumal, Winona State University; Bruce Ketler, Grove City College; Peter Lenk, University of Michigan—Ann Arbor; Robert Montague, Southern Adventist University; Robert Patterson, Penn State University—Behrend; Victor Prybutok, University of North Texas; Nikolai Pulchritudoff, California State University—Los Angeles; Ahmad Saranjam, Northeastern University; Vijay Shah, West Virginia University; Daniel Shimshak, University of Massachusetts—Boston; Cheryl Staley, Lake Land College—Mattoon; Debbie Stiver, University of Nevada—Reno; Minghe Sun, University of Texas—San Antonio; Osnat Stramer, University of Iowa; Eric Howington, Valdosta State University; Michael Posner, Villanova University; Charu Sinha, Chapman University; Lloyd Jaisingh, Morehead State University; Linda Dawson, University of Washington; Lee Revere, University of Houston—Clear Lake; Thomas Vadakkeveetil, George Washington University & Johns Hopkins University; Courtney Pham, Missouri State University; Rick Szal, Northern Arizona University.

As always, I wish to recognize my colleagues at the University of Houston–Clear Lake for their continued interest and support of this project. In particular, I want to thank William Staples, president; Carl Stockton, provost; and Ted Cummings, dean of the School of Business for their personal interest in the book and their administrative support. A special thanks goes to Brent Goucher, my videographer, for his guidance, artistic direction, and patience in filming the videos.

There are several people within the John Wiley & Sons publishing group whom I would like to thank for their invaluable assistance on this project. These include: Franny Kelly, Emily McGee, and Allie Morris.

I want to express a special appreciation to my wife of 43 years, Carolyn, who is the love of my life and continues to provide both professional and personal support in my writing. Thanks also to my daughters, Wendi and Caycee, for their patience, love, and support.

—Ken Black

Ken Black is currently professor of decision sciences in the School of Business at the University of Houston–Clear Lake. Born in Cambridge, Massachusetts, and raised in Missouri, he earned a bachelor's degree in mathematics from Graceland University, a master's degree in math education from the University of Texas at El Paso, a Ph.D. in business administration in management science, and a Ph.D. in educational research from the University of North Texas.

Since joining the faculty of UHCL in 1979, Professor Black has taught all levels of statistics courses, forecasting, management science, market research, and production/operations management. In 2005, he was awarded the President's Distinguished Teaching Award for the university. He has published over 20 journal articles and 20 professional papers, as well as two textbooks: *Business Statistics: An Introductory Course* and *Business Statistics for Contemporary Decision Making*. Black has consulted for many different companies, including Aetna, the city of Houston, NYLCare, AT&T, Johnson Space Center, Southwest Information Resources, Connect Corporation, and Eagle Engineering.

Ken Black and his wife, Carolyn, have two daughters, Caycee and Wendi. His hobbies include playing the guitar, participating in track-and-field events, reading, and traveling.

UNIT I

INTRODUCTION

The study of business statistics is important, valuable, and interesting. However, because it involves a new language of terms, symbols, logic, and application of mathematics, it can be at times overwhelming. For many students, this text is their first and only introduction to business statistics, which instructors often teach as a "survey course." That is, the student is presented with an overview of the subject, including a waterfront of techniques, concepts, and formulas. It can be overwhelming! One of the main difficulties in studying business statistics in this way is to be able to see "the forest for the trees," that is, sorting out the myriad of topics so they make sense. With this in mind, the 18 chapters of this text have been organized into five units with each unit containing chapters that tend to present similar material. At the beginning of each unit, there is an introduction presenting the overlying themes to those chapters.

Unit I is titled Introduction because the four chapters (1–4) contained therein "introduce" the study of business statistics. In Chapter 1, students will learn what statistics are, the concepts of descriptive and inferential statistics, and levels of data measurement. In Chapter 2, students will see how raw data can be organized using various graphical and tabular techniques to facilitate their use in making better business decisions. Chapter 3 introduces some essential and basic statistics that will be used to both summarize data and as tools for techniques introduced later in the text. There will also be discussion of distribution shapes. In Chapter 4, the basic laws of probability are presented. The notion of probability underlies virtually every business statistics topic, distribution, and technique, thereby making it important to acquire an appreciation and understanding of probability. In Unit I, the first four chapters, we are developing "building blocks" that will enable students to understand and apply statistical concepts to analyze data that can assist present and future business managers in making better decisions.

CHAPTER 1

Introduction to Statistics

LEARNING OBJECTIVES

The primary objective of Chapter 1 is to introduce you to the world of statistics, thereby enabling you to:

1. List quantitative and graphical examples of statistics within a business context

2. Define important statistical terms, including population, sample, and parameter, as they relate to descriptive and inferential statistics

3. Explain the difference between variables, measurement, and data

4. Compare the four different levels of data: nominal, ordinal, interval, and ratio

Lindsay Hebberd/Corbis

Statistics Describe the State of Business in India's Countryside

India is the second largest country in the world, with more than a billion people. Nearly three-quarters of the people live in rural areas scattered about the countryside in 6,000,000 villages. In fact, it may be said that 1 in every 10 people in the world live in rural India. Presently, the population in rural India can be described as poor and semi-illiterate. With an annual per capita income of less than $1 (U.S.) per day, rural India accounts for only about one-third of total national product sales. Less than 50% of households in rural India have electricity, and many of the roads are not paved. The annual per capita consumption for toothpaste is only 30 grams per person in rural India compared to 160 grams in urban India and 400 grams in the United States.

Besides the impressive size of its population, there are other compelling reasons for companies to market their goods and services to rural India. The market of rural India has been growing at five times the rate of the urban India market. There is increasing agricultural productivity, leading to growth in disposable income, and there is a reduction in the gap between the tastes of urban and rural customers. The literacy level is increasing, and people are becoming more conscious about their lifestyles and opportunities for a better life.

Nearly two-thirds of all middle-income households in India are in rural areas, with the number of middle- and high-income households in rural India expected to grow from 80 million to 111 million over the next three years. More than one-third of all rural households now have a main source of income other than farming. Virtually every home has a radio, almost 20% have a television, and more than 30% have at least one bank account.

In the early 1990s, toothpaste consumption in rural India doubled, and the consumption of shampoo increased fourfold. Recently, other products have done well in rural India, accounting for nearly one-half of all of the country's sales of televisions, fans, bicycles, bath soap, and other products. According to MART, a New Delhi–based research organization, rural India buys 46% of all soft drinks and 49% of motorcycles sold in India. In one year alone, the market for Coca-Cola in rural India grew by 37%, accounting for 80% of new Coke drinkers in India. Because of such factors, many U.S. and Indian firms, such as Microsoft, General Electric, Kellogg's, Colgate-Palmolive, Hindustan Lever, Godrej, Nirma Chemical Works, and Mahotra Marketing, have entered the rural Indian market with enthusiasm. Marketing to rural customers often involves building categories by persuading them to try and adopt products that they may not have used before. Rural India is a huge, relatively untapped market for businesses. However, entering such a market is not without risks and obstacles. The dilemma facing companies is whether to enter this marketplace and, if so, to what extent and how.

Managerial and Statistical Questions

1. Are the statistics presented in this report exact figures or estimates?
2. How and where could the researchers have gathered such data?
3. In measuring the potential of the rural India marketplace, what other statistics could have been gathered?
4. What levels of data measurement are represented by data on rural India?
5. How can managers use these and other statistics to make better decisions about entering this marketplace?

Source: Adapted from Raja Ramachandran, "Understanding the Market Environment of India," *Business Horizons,* January 2000; P. Balakrishna and B. Sidharth, "Selling in Rural India," *The Hindu Business Line*—Internet Edition, February 16, 2004; Rohit Bansal and Srividya Easwaran, "Creative Marketing for Rural India," research paper, http://www.indiainfoline.com; Alex Steffen, "Rural India Ain't What It Used to Be," *WorldChanging,* http://www.worldchanging.com/archives/001235.html; "Corporates Turn to Rural India for Growth," BS Corporate Bureau in New Delhi, August 21, 2003, http://www.rediff.com/money/2003/aug/21rural.htm; Rajesh Jain, "Tech Talk: The Discovery of India: Rural India," June 20, 2003, http://www.emergic.org/archives/indi/005721.php; "Marketing to Rural India: Making the Ends Meet," March 8, 2007, in *India Knowledge@Wharton,* http://knowledge.wharton.upenn.edu/india/article.cfm?articleid=4172; "Rural Economy in India," businessmapsofindia.com, http://business.mapsofindia.com/rural-economy/.

Every minute of the working day, decisions are made by businesses around the world that determine whether companies will be profitable and growing or whether they will stagnate and die. Most of these decisions are made with the assistance of information gathered about the marketplace, the economic and financial environment, the workforce, the competition, and other factors. Such information usually comes in the form of data or is accompanied by data.

Business statistics provides the tool through which such data are collected, analyzed, summarized, and presented to facilitate the decision-making process, and business statistics plays an important role in the ongoing saga of decision making within the dynamic world of business.

1.1 STATISTICS IN BUSINESS

Virtually every area of business uses statistics in decision making. Here are some recent examples:

- According to a TNS Retail Forward ShopperScape survey, the average amount spent by a shopper on electronics in a three-month period is $629 at Circuit City, $504 at Best Buy, $246 at Wal-Mart, $172 at Target, and $120 at RadioShack.
- A survey of 1465 workers by Hotjobs reports that 55% of workers believe that the quality of their work is perceived the same when they work remotely as when they are physically in the office.
- A survey of 477 executives by the Association of Executive Search Consultants determined that 48% of men and 67% of women say they are more likely to negotiate for less business travel compared with five years ago.
- A survey of 1007 adults by RBC Capital Markets showed that 37% of adults would be willing to drive 5 to 10 miles to save 20 cents on a gallon of gas.
- A Deloitte Retail "Green" survey of 1080 adults revealed that 54% agreed that plastic, non-compostable shopping bags should be banned.
- A recent Household Economic Survey by Statistic New Zealand determined that the average weekly household net expenditure in New Zealand was $956 and that households in the Wellington region averaged $120 weekly on recreation and culture. In addition, 75% of all households were satisfied or very satisfied with their material standard of living.
- The Experience's Life After College survey of 320 recent college graduates showed that 58% moved back home after college. Thirty-two percent then remained at home for more than a year.

You can see from these few examples that there is a wide variety of uses and applications of statistics in business. Note that in most of these examples, business researchers have conducted a study and provided us rich and interesting information.

In this text we will examine several types of graphs for depicting data as we study ways to arrange or structure data into forms that are both meaningful and useful to decision makers. We will learn about techniques for sampling from a population that allow studies of the business world to be conducted more inexpensively and in a more timely manner. We will explore various ways to forecast future values and examine techniques for predicting trends. This text also includes many statistical tools for testing hypotheses and for estimating population values. These and many other exciting statistics and statistical techniques await us on this journey through business statistics. Let us begin.

1.2 BASIC STATISTICAL CONCEPTS

Business statistics, like many areas of study, has its own language. It is important to begin our study with an introduction of some basic concepts in order to understand and communicate about the subject. We begin with a discussion of the word *statistics*. The word *statistics* has many different meanings in our culture. *Webster's Third New International Dictionary* gives a comprehensive definition of **statistics** as *a science dealing with the collection, analysis, interpretation, and presentation of numerical data.* Viewed from this perspective, statistics includes all the topics presented in this text.

Photodisc/Getty Images, Inc.

The study of statistics can be organized in a variety of ways. One of the main ways is to subdivide statistics into two branches: descriptive statistics and inferential statistics. To understand the difference between descriptive and inferential statistics, definitions of *population* and *sample* are helpful. *Webster's Third New International Dictionary* defines **population** as *a collection of persons, objects, or items of interest.* The population can be a widely defined category, such as "all automobiles," or it can be narrowly defined, such as "all Ford Mustang cars produced from 2008 to 2010." A population can be a group of people, such as "all workers presently employed by Microsoft," or it can be a set of objects, such as "all dishwashers produced on February 3, 2009, by the General Electric Company at the Louisville plant." The researcher defines the population to be whatever he or she is studying. When researchers *gather data from the whole population for a given measurement of interest,* they call it a **census.** Most people are familiar with the U.S. Census. Every 10 years, the government attempts to measure all persons living in this country.

A **sample** is *a portion of the whole* and, if properly taken, is representative of the whole. For various reasons (explained in Chapter 7), researchers often prefer to work with a sample of the population instead of the entire population. For example, in conducting quality-control experiments to determine the average life of lightbulbs, a lightbulb manufacturer might randomly sample only 75 lightbulbs during a production run. Because of time and money limitations, a human resources manager might take a random sample of 40 employees instead of using a census to measure company morale.

If a business analyst is *using data gathered on a group to describe or reach conclusions about that same group,* the statistics are called **descriptive statistics.** For example, if an instructor produces statistics to summarize a class's examination effort and uses those statistics to reach conclusions about that class only, the statistics are descriptive.

Many of the statistical data generated by businesses are descriptive. They might include number of employees on vacation during June, average salary at the Denver office, corporate sales for 2011, average managerial satisfaction score on a company-wide census of employee attitudes, and average return on investment for the Lofton Company for the years 1990 through 2010.

Another type of statistics is called **inferential statistics**. If a researcher *gathers data from a sample and uses the statistics generated to reach conclusions about the population from which the sample was taken,* the statistics are inferential statistics. The data gathered from the sample are used to infer something about a larger group. Inferential statistics are sometimes referred to as *inductive statistics.* The use and importance of inferential statistics continue to grow.

One application of inferential statistics is in pharmaceutical research. Some new drugs are expensive to produce, and therefore tests must be limited to small samples of patients. Utilizing inferential statistics, researchers can design experiments with small randomly selected samples of patients and attempt to reach conclusions and make inferences about the population.

Market researchers use inferential statistics to study the impact of advertising on various market segments. Suppose a soft drink company creates an advertisement depicting a dispensing machine that talks to the buyer, and market researchers want to measure the impact of the new advertisement on various age groups. The researcher could stratify the population into age categories ranging from young to old, randomly sample each stratum, and use inferential statistics to determine the effectiveness of the advertisement for the various age groups in the population. The advantage of using inferential statistics is that they enable the researcher to study effectively a wide range of phenomena without having to conduct a census. Most of the topics discussed in this text pertain to inferential statistics.

A *descriptive measure of the population* is called a **parameter**. Parameters are usually denoted by Greek letters. Examples of parameters are population mean (μ), population variance (σ^2), and population standard deviation (σ). A *descriptive measure of a sample* is called a **statistic**. Statistics are usually denoted by Roman letters. Examples of statistics are sample mean ($\overline{x}$), sample variance (s^2), and sample standard deviation (s).

Differentiation between the terms *parameter* and *statistic* is important only in the use of inferential statistics. A business researcher often wants to estimate the value of a parameter or conduct tests about the parameter. However, the calculation of parameters is usually either impossible or infeasible because of the amount of time and money required to take a census. In such cases, the business researcher can take a random sample of the population, calculate a statistic on the sample, and infer by estimation the value of the parameter. The basis for inferential statistics, then, is the ability to make decisions about parameters without having to complete a census of the population.

For example, a manufacturer of washing machines would probably want to determine the average number of loads that a new machine can wash before it needs repairs. The parameter is the population mean or average number of washes per machine before repair. A company researcher takes a sample of machines, computes the number of washes before repair for each machine, averages the numbers, and estimates the population value or parameter by using the statistic, which in this case is the sample average. Figure 1.1 demonstrates the inferential process.

Inferences about parameters are made under uncertainty. Unless parameters are computed directly from the population, the statistician never knows with certainty whether the estimates or inferences made from samples are true. In an effort to estimate the level of confidence in the result of the process, statisticians use probability statements. For this and other reasons, part of this text is devoted to probability (Chapter 4).

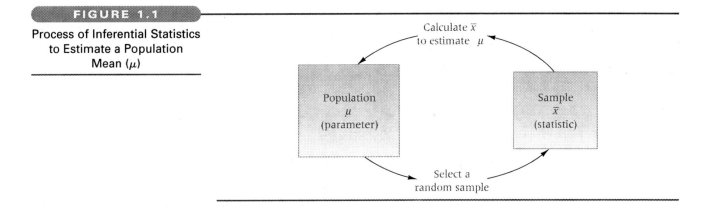

FIGURE 1.1

Process of Inferential Statistics
to Estimate a Population
Mean (μ)

1.3 VARIABLES AND DATA

Business statistics is about measuring phenomena in the business world and organizing, analyzing, and presenting the resulting numerical information in such a way such that better, more informed business decisions can be made. Most business statistics studies contain variables, measurements, and data.

In business statistics, a **variable** is *a characteristic of any entity being studied that is capable of taking on different values*. Some examples of variables in business might include return on investment, advertising dollars, labor productivity, stock price, historic cost, total sales, market share, age of worker, earnings per share, miles driven to work, time spent in store shopping, and many, many others. In business statistics studies, most variables produce a measurement that can be used for analysis. A **measurement** is *when a standard process is used to assign numbers to particular attributes or characteristics of a variable*. Many measurements are obvious, such as time spent in a store shopping by a customer, age of the worker, or the number of miles driven to work. However, some measurements, such as labor productivity, customer satisfaction, and return on investment, have to be defined by the business researcher or by experts within the field. Once such measurements are recorded and stored, they can be denoted as "data." It can be said that **data** are *recorded measurements*. The processes of measuring and data gathering are basic to all that we do in business statistics. It is data that are analyzed by a business statistician in order to learn more about the variables being studied. Sometimes, sets of data are organized into databases as a way to store data or as a means for more conveniently analyzing data or comparing variables. Valid data are the lifeblood of business statistics, and it is important that the business researcher give thoughtful attention to the creation of meaningful, valid data before embarking on analysis and reaching conclusions.

1.4 DATA MEASUREMENT

Millions of numerical data are gathered in businesses every day, representing myriad items. For example, numbers represent dollar costs of items produced, geographical locations of retail outlets, weights of shipments, and rankings of subordinates at yearly reviews. All such data should not be analyzed the same way statistically because the entities represented by the numbers are different. For this reason, the business researcher needs to know the *level of data measurement* represented by the numbers being analyzed.

The disparate use of numbers can be illustrated by the numbers 40 and 80, which could represent the weights of two objects being shipped, the ratings received on a consumer test by two different products, or football jersey numbers of a fullback and a wide receiver. Although 80 pounds is twice as much as 40 pounds, the wide receiver is probably not twice as big as the fullback! Averaging the two weights seems reasonable, but averaging the football jersey numbers makes no sense. The appropriateness of the data analysis depends on the level of measurement of the data gathered. The phenomenon represented by the numbers determines the level of data measurement. Four common levels of data measurement follow.

1. Nominal
2. Ordinal
3. Interval
4. Ratio

Nominal Level

The *lowest level of data measurement* is the **nominal level**. Numbers representing nominal-level data (the word *level* often is omitted) can be *used only to classify or categorize.* Employee identification numbers are an example of nominal data. The numbers are used only to differentiate employees and not to make a value statement about them. Many demographic questions in surveys result in data that are nominal because the questions are used for classification only. The following is an example of such a question that would result in nominal data:

Which of the following employment classifications best describes your area of work?

1. Educator
2. Construction worker
3. Manufacturing worker
4. Lawyer
5. Doctor
6. Other

Suppose that, for computing purposes, an educator is assigned a 1, a construction worker is assigned a 2, a manufacturing worker is assigned a 3, and so on. These numbers should be used only to classify respondents. The number 1 does not denote the top classification. It is used only to differentiate an educator (1) from a lawyer (4).

Some other types of variables that often produce nominal-level data are sex, religion, ethnicity, geographic location, and place of birth. Social Security numbers, telephone numbers, employee ID numbers, and ZIP code numbers are further examples of nominal data. Statistical techniques that are appropriate for analyzing nominal data are limited. However, some of the more widely used statistics, such as the chi-square statistic, can be applied to nominal data, often producing useful information.

Ordinal Level

Ordinal-level data measurement is higher than the nominal level. In addition to the nominal-level capabilities, ordinal-level measurement can be used to rank or order objects. For example, using ordinal data, a supervisor can evaluate three employees by ranking their productivity with the numbers 1 through 3. The supervisor could identify one employee as the most productive, one as the least productive, and one as somewhere between by using ordinal data. However, the supervisor could not use ordinal data to establish that the intervals between the employees ranked 1 and 2 and between the employees ranked 2 and 3 are equal; that is, she could not say that the differences in the amount of productivity between workers ranked 1, 2, and 3 are necessarily the same. With ordinal data, the distances or spacing represented by consecutive numbers are not always equal.

Some questionnaire Likert-type scales are considered by many researchers to be ordinal in level. The following is an example of one such scale:

This computer tutorial is	___	___	___	___	___
	not helpful	somewhat helpful	moderately helpful	very helpful	extremely helpful
	1	2	3	4	5

When this survey question is coded for the computer, only the numbers 1 through 5 will remain, not the adjectives. Virtually everyone would agree that a 5 is higher than a 4 on this scale and that ranking responses is possible. However, most respondents would not consider the differences between not helpful, somewhat helpful, moderately helpful, very helpful, and extremely helpful to be equal.

Mutual funds as investments are sometimes rated in terms of risk by using measures of default risk, currency risk, and interest rate risk. These three measures are applied to investments by rating them as having high, medium, and low risk. Suppose high risk is assigned a 3, medium risk a 2, and low risk a 1. If a fund is awarded a 3 rather than a 2, it carries more risk, and so on. However, the differences in risk between categories 1, 2, and 3 are not necessarily equal. Thus, these measurements of risk are only ordinal-level measurements. Another example of the use of ordinal numbers in business is the ranking of the top 50 most admired companies in *Fortune* magazine. The numbers ranking the companies are only ordinal in measurement. Certain statistical techniques are specifically suited to ordinal data, but many other techniques are not appropriate for use on ordinal data. For example, it does not make sense to say that the average of "moderately helpful" and "very helpful" is "moderately helpful and a half."

Because nominal and ordinal data are often derived from imprecise measurements such as demographic questions, the categorization of people or objects, or the ranking of items, *nominal and ordinal data* are **nonmetric data** and are sometimes referred to as *qualitative data.*

Interval Level

Interval-level data measurement is the *next to the highest level of data in which the distances between consecutive numbers have meaning and the data are always numerical.* The distances represented by the differences between consecutive numbers are equal; that is, interval data have equal intervals. An example of interval measurement is Fahrenheit temperature. With Fahrenheit temperature numbers, the temperatures can be ranked, and the amounts of heat between consecutive readings, such as 20°, 21°, and 22°, are the same.

In addition, with interval-level data, the zero point is a matter of convention or convenience and not a natural or fixed zero point. Zero is just another point on the scale and does not mean the absence of the phenomenon. For example, zero degrees Fahrenheit is not the lowest possible temperature. Some other examples of interval-level data are the percentage change in employment, the percentage return on a stock, and the dollar change in stock price.

Ratio Level

Ratio-level data measurement is *the highest level of data measurement.* Ratio data *have the same properties as interval data,* but ratio data have an *absolute zero,* and *the ratio of two numbers is meaningful.* The notion of absolute zero means that zero is fixed, and *the zero value in the data represents the absence of the characteristic being studied.* The value of zero cannot be arbitrarily assigned because it represents a fixed point. This definition enables the statistician to create *ratios* with the data.

Examples of ratio data are height, weight, time, volume, and Kelvin temperature. With ratio data, a researcher can state that 180 pounds of weight is twice as much as 90 pounds or, in other words, make a ratio of 180:90. Many of the data gathered by machines in industry are ratio data.

Other examples in the business world that are ratio level in measurement are production cycle time, work measurement time, passenger miles, number of trucks sold, complaints per 10,000 fliers, and number of employees.

Because interval- and ratio-level data are usually gathered by precise instruments often used in production and engineering processes, in national standardized testing, or in standardized accounting procedures, they are called **metric data** and are sometimes referred to as *quantitative* data.

Comparison of the Four Levels of Data

FIGURE 1.2

Usage Potential of Various
Levels of Data

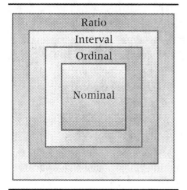

Figure 1.2 shows the relationships of the usage potential among the four levels of data measurement. The concentric squares denote that each higher level of data can be analyzed by any of the techniques used on lower levels of data but, in addition, can be used in other statistical techniques. Therefore, ratio data can be analyzed by any statistical technique applicable to the other three levels of data plus some others.

Nominal data are the most limited data in terms of the types of statistical analysis that can be used with them. Ordinal data allow the researcher to perform any analysis that can be done with nominal data and some additional analyses. With ratio data, a statistician can make ratio comparisons and appropriately do any analysis that can be performed on nominal, ordinal, or interval data. Some statistical techniques require ratio data and cannot be used to analyze other levels of data.

Statistical techniques can be separated into two categories: parametric statistics and nonparametric statistics. **Parametric statistics** require that data be interval or ratio. If the data are nominal or ordinal, **nonparametric statistics** must be used. Nonparametric statistics can also be used to analyze interval or ratio data. This text focuses largely on parametric statistics, with the exception of Chapter 16 and Chapter 17, which contain nonparametric techniques. Thus much of the material in this text requires that data be interval or ratio data.

**DEMONSTRATION
PROBLEM 1.1**

**Demonstration
Problem**

Many changes continue to occur in the healthcare industry. Because of increased competition for patients among providers and the need to determine how providers can better serve their clientele, hospital administrators sometimes administer a quality satisfaction survey to their patients after the patient is released. The following types of questions are sometimes asked on such a survey. These questions will result in what level of data measurement?

1. How long ago were you released from the hospital?
2. Which type of unit were you in for most of your stay?
   __Coronary care
   __Intensive care
   __Maternity care
   __Medical unit
   __Pediatric/children's unit
   __Surgical unit
3. In choosing a hospital, how important was the hospital's location?

   (circle one)

   | Very Important | Somewhat Important | Not Very Important | Not at All Important |

4. How serious was your condition when you were first admitted to the hospital?
   __Critical   __Serious   __Moderate   __Minor
5. Rate the skill of your doctor:
   __Excellent   __Very Good   __Good   __Fair   __Poor

Solution

Question 1 is a time measurement with an absolute zero and is therefore ratio-level measurement. A person who has been out of the hospital for two weeks has been out twice as long as someone who has been out of the hospital for one week.

Question 2 yields nominal data because the patient is asked only to categorize the type of unit he or she was in. This question does not require a hierarchy or ranking of the type of unit. Questions 3, 4, and 5 are likely to result in ordinal-level data. Suppose a number is assigned the descriptors in each of these three questions. For question 3, "very important" might be assigned a 4, "somewhat important" a 3, "not very important" a 2, and "not at all important" a 1. Certainly, the higher the number, the more important is the hospital's location. Thus, these responses can be ranked by selection. However, the increases in importance from 1 to 2 to 3 to 4 are not necessarily equal. This same logic applies to the numeric values assigned in questions 4 and 5.

THINKING CRITICALLY ABOUT STATISTICS IN BUSINESS TODAY

Cellular Phone Use in Japan

The Communications and Information Network Association of Japan (CIAJ) conducts an annual study of cellular phone use in Japan. A recent survey was taken as part of this study using a sample of 600 cell phone users split evenly between men and women and almost equally distributed over six age brackets. The survey was administered in the greater Tokyo and Osaka metropolitan areas. The study produced several interesting findings. It was determined that 62.2% had replaced their handsets in the previous 10 months. A little more than 6% owned a second cell phone. Of these, the objective of about two-thirds was to own one for business use and a second one for personal use. Of all those surveyed, 18.2% used their handsets to view videos, and another 17.3% were not currently using their handsets to view videos but were interested in doing so. Some of the everyday uses of cell phones included e-mailing (91.7% of respondents), camera functions (77.7%), Internet searching (46.7%), and watching TV (28.0%). In the future, respondents hoped there would be cell phones with high-speed data trans-

mission that could be used to send and receive PC files (47.7%), for video services such as YouTube (46.9%), for downloading music albums (45.3%) and music videos (40.8%), and for downloading long videos such as movies (39.2%).

Things to Ponder

1. In what way was this study an example of inferential statistics?
2. What is the population of this study?
3. What are some of the variables being studied?
4. How might a study such as this yield information that is useful to business decision makers?

Source: "CIAJ Releases Report on the Study of Cellular Phone Use," Results of an annual study of cellular phone use in Japan conducted by the Communications and Information Network Association of Japan (CIAJ), July 30, 2008, http://www.wirelesswatch.jp/docs/CIAJ_0808.doc.

Statistical Analysis Using the Computer: Excel and Minitab

The advent of the modern computer opened many new opportunities for statistical analysis. The computer allows for storage, retrieval, and transfer of large data sets. Furthermore, computer software has been developed to analyze data by means of sophisticated statistical techniques. Some widely used statistical techniques, such as multiple regression, are so tedious and cumbersome to compute manually that they were of little practical use to researchers before computers were developed.

Business statisticians use many popular statistical software packages, including Minitab, SAS, and SPSS. Many computer spreadsheet software packages also have the capability of analyzing data statistically. In this text, the computer statistical output presented is from both the Minitab and the Microsoft Excel software.

Statistics Describe the State of Business in India's Countryside

Several statistics were reported in the Decision Dilemma about rural India, including the average annual consumption of toothpaste per person, the percentage of households having electricity, and the percentage of households that have at least one bank account. The authors of the sources from which the Decision Dilemma was drawn never stated whether the reported statistics were based on actual data drawn from a census of rural India households or were based on estimates taken from a sample of rural households. If the data came from a census, then the totals, averages, and percentages presented in the Decision Dilemma are parameters. If, on the other hand, the data were gathered from samples, then they are statistics. Although governments especially do conduct censuses and at least some of the reported numbers could be parameters, more often than not, such data are gathered from samples of people or items. For example, in rural India, the government, academicians, or business researchers could have taken random samples of households, gathering consumer statistics that are then used to estimate population parameters, such as percentage of households with televisions, and so forth.

In conducting research on a topic like consumer consumption in rural India, there is potential for a wide variety of statistics to be gathered that represent several levels of data. For example, ratio-level measurements on items such as income, number of children, age of household heads, number of livestock, and grams of toothpaste consumed per year might be obtained. On the other hand, if researchers use a Likert scale (1-to-5 measurements) to gather responses about the interests, likes, and preferences of rural India consumers, an ordinal-level measurement would be obtained, as would the ranking of products or brands in market research studies. Other variables, such as geographic location, sex, occupation, or religion, are usually measured with nominal data.

The decision to enter the rural India market is not just a marketing decision. It involves production capacity and schedule issues, transportation challenges, financial commitments, managerial growth or reassignment, accounting issues (accounting for rural India may differ from techniques used in traditional markets), information systems, and other related areas. With so much on the line, company decision makers need as much relevant information available as possible. In this Decision Dilemma, it is obvious to the decision maker that rural India is still quite poor and illiterate. Its capacity as a market is great. The statistics on the increasing sales of a few personal-care products look promising. What are the future forecasts for the earning power of people in rural India? Will major cultural issues block the adoption of the types of products that companies want to sell there? The answers to these and many other interesting and useful questions can be obtained by the appropriate use of statistics. The 750 million people living in rural India represent the second largest group of people in the world. It certainly is a market segment worth studying further.

ETHICAL CONSIDERATIONS

With the abundance and proliferation of statistical data, potential misuse of statistics in business dealings is a concern. It is, in effect, unethical business behavior to use statistics out of context. Unethical business people might use only selective data from studies to underscore their point, omitting statistics from the same studies that argue against their case. The results of statistical studies can be misstated or overstated to gain favor.

This chapter noted that if data are nominal or ordinal, then only nonparametric statistics are appropriate for analysis. The use of parametric statistics to analyze nominal and/or ordinal data is wrong and could be considered under some circumstances to be unethical.

In this text, each chapter contains a section on ethics that discusses how businesses can misuse the techniques presented in the chapter in an unethical manner. As both users and producers, business students need to be aware of the potential ethical pitfalls that can occur with statistics.

SUMMARY

Statistics is an important decision-making tool in business and is used in virtually every area of business. In this course, the word *statistics* is defined as the science of gathering, analyzing, interpreting, and presenting numerical data.

The study of statistics can be subdivided into two main areas: *descriptive statistics* and *inferential statistics*. Descriptive statistics result from gathering data from a body, group, or population and reaching conclusions only about that group. Inferential statistics are generated from the process of gathering sample data from a group, body, or population and reaching conclusions about the larger group from which the sample was drawn.

Most business statistics studies contain variables, measurements, and data. A *variable* is a characteristic of any entity being studied that is capable of taking on different values. Examples of variables might include monthly household food spending, time between arrivals at a restaurant, and patient satisfaction rating. A *measurement* is when a standard process is used to assign numbers to particular attributes or characteristics of a variable. Measurements on monthly household food spending might be taken in dollars, time between arrivals might be measured in minutes, and patient satisfaction might be measured using a 5-point scale. *Data* are recorded measurements. It is data that are analyzed

by business statisticians in order to learn more about the variables being studied.

The appropriate type of statistical analysis depends on the level of data measurement, which can be (1) *nominal,* (2) *ordinal,* (3) *interval,* or (4) *ratio.* Nominal is the lowest level, representing classification only of such data as geographic location, sex, or Social Security number. The next level is ordinal, which provides rank ordering measurements in which the intervals between consecutive numbers do not necessarily represent equal distances. Interval is the next to highest level of data measurement in which the distances represented by consecutive numbers are equal. The highest level of data measurement is ratio, which has all the qualities of interval measurement, but ratio data contain an absolute zero and ratios between numbers are meaningful. Interval and ratio data sometimes are called *metric* or *quantitative* data. Nominal and ordinal data sometimes are called *nonmetric* or *qualitative* data.

Two major types of inferential statistics are (1) *parametric statistics* and (2) *nonparametric statistics.* Use of parametric statistics requires interval or ratio data and certain assumptions about the distribution of the data. The techniques presented in this text are largely parametric. If data are only nominal or ordinal in level, nonparametric statistics must be used.

KEY TERMS

Flash Cards

census
data

descriptive statistics
inferential statistics
interval-level data
measurement
metric data
nominal-level data

nonmetric data
nonparametric statistics
ordinal-level data
parameter
parametric statistics
population

ratio-level data
sample
statistic
statistics
variable

SUPPLEMENTARY PROBLEMS

1.1 Give a specific example of data that might be gathered from each of the following business disciplines: accounting, finance, human resources, marketing, information systems, production, and management. An example in the marketing area might be "number of sales per month by each salesperson."

1.2 State examples of data that can be gathered for decision making purposes from each of the following industries: manufacturing, insurance, travel, retailing, communications, computing, agriculture, banking, and healthcare. An example in the travel industry might be the cost of business travel per day in various European cities.

1.3 Give an example of *descriptive* statistics in the recorded music industry. Give an example of how

inferential statistics could be used in the recorded music industry. Compare the two examples. What makes them different?

1.4 Suppose you are an operations manager for a plant that manufactures batteries. Give an example of how you could use *descriptive* statistics to make better managerial decisions. Give an example of how you could use *inferential* statistics to make better managerial decisions.

1.5 There are many types of information that might help the manager of a large department store run the business more efficiently and better understand how to improve sales. Think about this in such areas as sales, customers, human resources, inventory, suppliers, etc., and list five variables that might produce information that could aid the manager in his or her job. Write a sentence or two describing each variable, and briefly discuss some numerical observations that might be generated for each variable.

1.6 Suppose you are the owner of a medium-sized restaurant in a small city. What are some variables associated with different aspects of the business that might be helpful to you in making business decisions about the restaurant? Name four of these variables, and for each variable, briefly describe a numerical observation that might be the result of measuring the variable.

1.7 Classify each of the following as nominal, ordinal, interval, or ratio data.
   a. The time required to produce each tire on an assembly line
   b. The number of quarts of milk a family drinks in a month
   c. The ranking of four machines in your plant after they have been designated as excellent, good, satisfactory, and poor
   d. The telephone area code of clients in the United States
   e. The age of each of your employees
   f. The dollar sales at the local pizza shop each month
   g. An employee's identification number
   h. The response time of an emergency unit

1.8 Classify each of the following as nominal, ordinal, interval, or ratio data.
   a. The ranking of a company by *Fortune* 500
   b. The number of tickets sold at a movie theater on any given night
   c. The identification number on a questionnaire
   d. Per capita income

e. The trade balance in dollars
f. Profit/loss in dollars
g. A company's tax identification
h. The Standard & Poor's bond ratings of cities based on the following scales:

Rating	Grade
Highest quality	AAA
High quality	AA
Upper medium quality	A
Medium quality	BBB
Somewhat speculative	BB
Low quality, speculative	B
Low grade, default possible	CCC
Low grade, partial recovery possible	CC
Default, recovery unlikely	C

1.9 The Rathburn Manufacturing Company makes electric wiring, which it sells to contractors in the construction industry. Approximately 900 electric contractors purchase wire from Rathburn annually. Rathburn's director of marketing wants to determine electric contractors' satisfaction with Rathburn's wire. He developed a questionnaire that yields a satisfaction score between 10 and 50 for participant responses. A random sample of 35 of the 900 contractors is asked to complete a satisfaction survey. The satisfaction scores for the 35 participants are averaged to produce a mean satisfaction score.
   a. What is the population for this study?
   b. What is the sample for this study?
   c. What is the statistic for this study?
   d. What would be a parameter for this study?

ANALYZING THE DATABASES

see www.wiley.com/college/black

Nine databases are available with this text, providing additional opportunities to apply the statistics presented in this course. These databases are located in WileyPLUS, and each is available in either Minitab or Excel format for your convenience. These nine databases represent a wide variety of business areas, such as agribusiness, consumer spending, energy, finance, healthcare, international labor, manufacturing, and the stock market. Altogether, these databases contain 61 variables and 7722 observations. The data are gathered from such reliable sources as the U.S. government's Bureau of Labor, the U.S. Department of Agriculture, the American Hospital Association, the Energy Information Administration, *Moody's Handbook of Common Stocks*, and the U.S. Census Bureau. Five of the nine databases contain time-series data. These databases are:

12-YEAR GASOLINE DATABASE

The 12-year time-series gasoline database contains monthly data for four variables: U.S. Gasoline Prices, OPEC Spot Price,

U.S. Finished Motor Gasoline Production, and U.S. Natural Gas Wellhead Price. There are 137 data entries for each variable. U.S. Gasoline Prices are given in cents, the OPEC Spot Price is given in dollars per barrel, U.S. Finished Motor Gasoline Production is given in 1000 barrels per day, and U.S. Natural Gas Wellhead Price is given in dollars per 1000 cubic feet.

CONSUMER FOOD DATABASE

The consumer food database contains five variables: Annual Food Spending per Household, Annual Household Income, Non-Mortgage Household Debt, Geographic Region of the U.S. of the Household, and Household Location. There are 200 entries for each variable in this database representing 200 different households from various regions and locations in the United States. Annual Food Spending per Household, Annual Household Income, and Non-Mortgage Household Debt are all given in dollars. The variable Region tells in which one of four regions the household resides. In this variable, the Northeast is coded as 1, the Midwest is coded 2, the South is coded as 3, and the West is coded as 4. The variable Location is coded as 1 if the household is in a metropolitan area and 2 if the household is outside a metro area. The data in this database were randomly derived and developed based on actual national norms.

MANUFACTURING DATABASE

This database contains eight variables taken from 20 industries and 140 subindustries in the United States. Some of the industries are food products, textile mill products, furniture, chemicals, rubber products, primary metals, industrial machinery, and transportation equipment. The eight variables are Number of Employees, Number of Production Workers, Value Added by Manufacture, Cost of Materials, Value of Industry Shipments, New Capital Expenditures, End-of-Year Inventories, and Industry Group. Two variables, Number of Employees and Number of Production Workers, are in units of 1000. Four variables, Value Added by Manufacture, Cost of Materials, New Capital Expenditures, and End-of-Year Inventories, are in million-dollar units. The Industry Group variable consists of numbers from 1 to 20 to denote the industry group to which the particular subindustry belongs. Value of Industry Shipments has been recoded to the following 1-to-4 scale.

1 = $0 to $4.9 billion
2 = $5 billion to $13.9 billion
3 = $14 billion to $28.9 billion
4 = $29 billion or more

INTERNATIONAL LABOR DATABASE

This time-series database contains the civilian unemployment rates in percent from seven countries presented yearly over a 49-year period. The data are published by the Bureau of Labor Statistics of the U.S. Department of Labor. The countries are the United States, Canada, Australia, Japan, France, Germany, and Italy.

FINANCIAL DATABASE

The financial database contains observations on eight variables for 100 companies. The variables are Type of Industry, Total Revenues ($ millions), Total Assets ($ millions), Return on Equity (%), Earnings per Share ($), Average Yield (%), Dividends per Share ($), and Average Price per Earnings (P/E) ratio. The companies represent seven different types of industries. The variable Type displays a company's industry type as:

1 = apparel
2 = chemical
3 = electric power
4 = grocery
5 = healthcare products
6 = insurance
7 = petroleum

ENERGY DATABASE

The time-series energy database consists of data on five energy variables over a period of 26 years. The five variables are U.S. Energy Consumption, World Crude Oil Production, U.S. Nuclear Electricity Generation, U.S. Coal Production, and U.S. Natural Dry Gas Production. U.S. Energy Consumption

is given in quadrillion BTUs per year, World Crude Oil Production is given in million barrels per day, U.S. Nuclear Electricity Generation is given in billion kilowatt-hours, U.S. Coal Production is given in million short tons, and U.S. Natural Dry Gas Production is given in million cubic feet.

U.S. AND INTERNATIONAL STOCK MARKET DATABASE

This database contains seven variables—three from the U.S. stock market and four from international stock markets—with data representing monthly averages of each over a period of five years resulting in 60 data points per variable. The U.S. stock market variables include the Dow Jones Industrial Average, the NASDAQ, and Standard & Poor's 500. The four international stock market variables of Nikkei 225, Hang Seng, FTSE 100, and IPC represent Japan, Hong Kong, United Kingdom, and Mexico.

HOSPITAL DATABASE

This database contains observations for 11 variables on U.S. hospitals. These variables include Geographic Region, Control, Service, Number of Beds, Number of Admissions, Census, Number of Outpatients, Number of Births, Total Expenditures, Payroll Expenditures, and Personnel.

The region variable is coded from 1 to 7, and the numbers represent the following regions:

1 = South
2 = Northeast
3 = Midwest
4 = Southwest
5 = Rocky Mountain
6 = California
7 = Northwest

Control is a type of ownership. Four categories of control are included in the database:

1 = government, nonfederal
2 = nongovernment, not-for-profit
3 = for-profit
4 = federal government

Service is the type of hospital. The two types of hospitals used in this database are:

1 = general medical
2 = psychiatric

The total expenditures and payroll variables are in units of $1000.

AGRIBUSINESS TIME-SERIES DATABASE

The agribusiness time-series database contains the monthly weight (in 1000 lbs.) of cold storage holdings for six different vegetables and for total frozen vegetables over a 14-year period. Each of the seven variables represents 168 months of data. The six vegetables are green beans, broccoli, carrots, sweet corn, onions, and green peas. The data are published by the National Agricultural Statistics Service of the U.S. Department of Agriculture.

ASSIGNMENT

Use the databases to answer the following questions.

1. In the manufacturing database, what is the level of data for each of the following variables?
   a. Number of Production Workers
   b. Cost of Materials
   c. Value of Industry Shipments
   d. Industry Group

2. In the hospital database, what is the level of data for each of the following variables?

   a. Region
   b. Control
   c. Number of Beds
   d. Personnel

3. In the financial database, what is the level of data for each of the following variables?
   a. Type of Industry
   b. Total Assets
   c. P/E Ratio

CASE

DIGIORNO PIZZA: INTRODUCING A FROZEN PIZZA TO COMPETE WITH CARRY-OUT

Kraft Foods successfully introduced DiGiorno Pizza into the marketplace in 1996, with first year sales of $120 million, followed by $200 million in sales in 1997. It was neither luck nor coincidence that DiGiorno Pizza was an instant success. Kraft conducted extensive research about the product and the marketplace before introducing this product to the public. Many questions had to be answered before Kraft began production. For example, why do people eat pizza? When do they eat pizza? Do consumers believe that carry-out pizza is always more tasty?

SMI-Alcott conducted a research study for Kraft in which they sent out 1000 surveys to pizza lovers. The results indicated that people ate pizza during fun social occasions or at home when no one wanted to cook. People used frozen pizza mostly for convenience but selected carry-out pizza for a variety of other reasons, including quality and the avoidance of cooking. The Loran Marketing Group conducted focus groups for Kraft with women aged 25 to 54. Their findings showed that consumers used frozen pizza for convenience but wanted carry-out pizza taste. Kraft researchers realized that if they were to launch a successful frozen pizza that could compete with carry-out pizza, they had to develop a frozen pizza that (a) had restaurant takeout quality, (b) possessed flavor variety, (c) was fast and easy to prepare, and (d) had the convenience of freezer storage. To satisfy these seemingly divergent goals, Kraft developed DiGiorno Pizza, which rises in the oven as it cooks. This impressed focus group members, and in a series of blind taste tests conducted by Product Dynamics, DiGiorno Pizza beat out all frozen pizzas and finished second overall behind one carry-out brand.

DiGiorno Pizza has continued to grow in sales and market share over the years. By 2005, sales had topped the $600 million mark, and DiGiorno Pizza held nearly a quarter of the market share of frozen pizza sales. In each of the last two quarters of 2009, DiGiorno sales increased 20%. On January 6, 2010, Kraft agreed to sell its North American frozen pizza business, including its DiGiorno products, to Nestlé for $3.7 billion.

Discussion

Think about the market research that was conducted by Kraft and the fact that they used several companies.

1. What are some of the populations that Kraft might have been interested in measuring for these studies? Did Kraft actually attempt to contact entire populations? What samples were taken? In light of these two questions, how was the inferential process used by Kraft in their market research? Can you think of any descriptive statistics that might have been used by Kraft in their decision-making process?

2. In the various market research efforts made by Kraft for DiGiorno, some of the possible measurements appear in the following list. Categorize these by level of data. Think of some other measurements that Kraft researchers might have made to help them in this research effort, and categorize them by level of data.

   a. Number of pizzas consumed per week per household
   b. Age of pizza purchaser
   c. Zip code of the survey respondent
   d. Dollars spent per month on pizza per person
   e. Time in between purchases of pizza
   f. Rating of taste of a given pizza brand on a scale from 1 to 10, where 1 is very poor tasting and 10 is excellent taste
   g. Ranking of the taste of four pizza brands on a taste test
   h. Number representing the geographic location of the survey respondent
   i. Quality rating of a pizza brand as excellent, good, average, below average, poor
   j. Number representing the pizza brand being evaluated
   k. Sex of survey respondent

Source: Adapted from "Upper Crust," *American Demographics,* March 1999, p. 58; *Marketwatch—News That Matters* Web sites, "What's in a Name? Brand Extension Potential" and "DiGiorno Rising Crust Delivers $200 Million," formerly at http://www.foodexplorer.com/BUSINESS/Products/MarketAnalysis/PF02896b.htm, last accessed in 1999; Web site for Kraft's 2005 Investor Meeting: Changing Consumers, Changing Kraft, May 25, http://media.corporateir.net/media_files/nys/kft/presentations/kft_050510c.pdf; "Kraft Trading Pizza for Chocolate," *MarketWatch,* October 25, 1010, http://www.marketwatch.com/story/kraft-trading-pizza-for-chocolate-2010-01-05.

Charts and Graphs

LEARNING OBJECTIVES

The overall objective of Chapter 2 is for you to master several techniques for summarizing and depicting data, thereby enabling you to:

1. Construct a frequency distribution from a set of data
2. Construct different types of quantitative data graphs, including histograms, frequency polygons, ogives, dot plots, and stem-and-leaf plots, in order to interpret the data being graphed
3. Construct different types of qualitative data graphs, including pie charts, bar graphs, and Pareto charts, in order to interpret the data being graphed
4. Recognize basic trends in two-variable scatter plots of numerical data

Alberto Biscaro/Masterfile

Container Shipping Companies

For decades, business people in many countries around the world wrestled with the issue of how to store and ship goods via trucks, trains, and ships. Various sizes and shapes of containers were developed to ship goods even within a country. The lack of consistent containers created a lot of extra work, as products were relocated from one container to another. Fortunately, in 1955 a former trucking company executive teamed up with an engineer to develop a version of the modern intermodal container that is widely used today. Because it is a standard size, this container in various forms can be moved from trucks to trains to ships without being opened, thereby eliminating the work of loading and unloading its contents multiple times. The International Organization for Standardization (ISO) has set up standards for the modern day container, and perhaps the most commonly used container is 20 feet long and 8 feet wide. The container capacity of a ship is often measured in the number of 20-foot equivalent units or TEUs that can be loaded or unloaded from the vessel. Containerization has revolutionized cargo shipping, and today approximately 90% of non-bulk cargo worldwide moves by containers stacked on transport ships.

Shown in the next column are TEU capacities available on board operated ships for the top five companies in the world as of October 25, 2010. Also included in the data is the total number of ships operated by each company.

Company	Total TEU Capacity	Number of Ships
APM-Maersk	2,128,651	568
Mediterranean Shipping Co.	1,833,795	445
CMA CGM Group	1,210,179	396
Evergreen Line	606,900	159
Hapag-Lloyd	589,563	136

Managerial and Statistical Questions

Suppose you are a shipping container industry analyst, and you are asked to prepare a brief report showing the leading shipping companies both in TEU shipping capacity and in number of ships.

1. What is the best way to display this shipping container company information? Are the raw data enough? Can you effectively display the data graphically?

2. Because some of the data are close together in size, is there a preferred graphical technique for differentiating between two or more similar numbers?

Source: "Shipping Containers," October 25, 2010, http://www.emase.co.uk/data/cont.html; "Alphaliner—TOP 100—Existing Fleet on October 2010," October 25, 2010, http://www.alphaliner.com/top100/index.php.

In Chapters 2 and 3 many techniques are presented for reformatting or reducing data so that the data are more manageable and can be used to assist decision makers more effectively. Two techniques for grouping data are the frequency distribution and the stem-and-leaf plot presented in this chapter. In addition, Chapter 2 discusses and displays several graphical tools for summarizing and presenting data, including histogram, frequency polygon, ogive, dot plot, bar chart, pie chart, and Pareto chart for one-variable data and the scatter plot for two-variable numerical data.

Raw data, or data that have not been summarized in any way, are sometimes referred to as **ungrouped data.** Table 2.1 contains 60 years of raw data of the unemployment rates for Canada. *Data that have been organized into a frequency distribution* are called **grouped data.** Table 2.2 presents a frequency distribution for the data displayed in Table 2.1. The distinction between ungrouped and grouped data is important because the calculation of statistics differs between the two types of data. This chapter focuses on organizing ungrouped data into grouped data and displaying them graphically.

TABLE 2.1
60 Years of Canadian Unemployment Rates (ungrouped data)

2.3	7.0	6.3	11.3	9.6
2.8	7.1	5.6	10.6	9.1
3.6	5.9	5.4	9.7	8.3
2.4	5.5	7.1	8.8	7.6
2.9	4.7	7.1	7.8	6.8
3.0	3.9	8.0	7.5	7.2
4.6	3.6	8.4	8.1	7.7
4.4	4.1	7.5	10.3	7.6
3.4	4.8	7.5	11.2	7.2
4.6	4.7	7.6	11.4	6.8
6.9	5.9	11.0	10.4	6.3
6.0	6.4	12.0	9.5	6.0

TABLE 2.2
Frequency Distribution of 60 Years of Unemployment Data for Canada (grouped data)

Class Interval	Frequency
1–under 3	4
3–under 5	12
5–under 7	13
7–under 9	19
9–under 11	7
11–under 13	5

2.1 FREQUENCY DISTRIBUTIONS

One particularly useful tool for grouping data is the **frequency distribution,** which is *a summary of data presented in the form of class intervals and frequencies.* How is a frequency distribution constructed from raw data? That is, how are frequency distributions like the one displayed in Table 2.2 constructed from raw data like those presented in Table 2.1? Frequency distributions are relatively easy to construct. Although some guidelines and rules of thumb help in their construction, frequency distributions vary in final shape and design, even when the original raw data are identical. In a sense, frequency distributions are constructed according to individual business researchers' taste.

When constructing a frequency distribution, the business researcher should first determine the range of the raw data. The **range** often is defined as *the difference between the largest and smallest numbers.* The range for the data in Table 2.1 is 9.7 (12.0–2.3).

The second step in constructing a frequency distribution is to determine how many classes it will contain. One rule of thumb is to select between *5 and 15 classes.* If the frequency distribution contains too few classes, the data summary may be too general to be useful. Too many classes may result in a frequency distribution that does not aggregate the data enough to be helpful. The final number of classes is arbitrary. The business researcher arrives at a number by examining the range and determining a number of classes that will span the range adequately and also be meaningful to the user. The data in Table 2.1 were grouped into six classes for Table 2.2.

After selecting the number of classes, the business researcher must determine the width of the class interval. An approximation of the class width can be calculated by dividing the range by the number of classes. For the data in Table 2.1, this approximation would be 9.7/6 = 1.62. Normally, the number is rounded up to the next whole number, which in this case is 2. The frequency distribution must start at a value equal to or lower than the lowest number of the ungrouped data and end at a value equal to or higher than the highest number. The lowest unemployment rate is 2.3 and the highest is 12.0, so the business researcher starts the frequency distribution at 1 and ends it at 13. Table 2.2 contains the completed frequency distribution for the data in Table 2.1. Class endpoints are selected so that no value of the data can fit into more than one class. The class interval expression "under" in the distribution of Table 2.2 avoids such a problem.

Class Midpoint

The *midpoint of each class interval* is called the **class midpoint** and is sometimes referred to as the **class mark**. It is *the value halfway across the class interval* and can be calculated as *the average of the two class endpoints.* For example, in the distribution of Table 2.2, the midpoint of the class interval 3–under 5 is 4, or (3 + 5)/2.

	TABLE 2.3				
Interval	**Frequency**	**Class Midpoint**	**Relative Frequency**	**Cumulative Frequency**	

Class Midpoints, Relative Frequencies, and Cumulative Frequencies for Unemployment Data

Interval	Frequency	Class Midpoint	Relative Frequency	Cumulative Frequency
1–under 3	4	2	.0667	4
3–under 5	12	4	.2000	16
5–under 7	13	6	.2167	29
7–under 9	19	8	.3167	48
9–under 11	7	10	.1167	55
11–under 13	5	12	.0833	60
Total	60			

The class midpoint is important, because it becomes the representative value for each class in most group statistics calculations. The third column in Table 2.3 contains the class midpoints for all classes of the data from Table 2.2.

Relative Frequency

Relative frequency is *the proportion of the total frequency that is in any given class interval in a frequency distribution.* Relative frequency is the individual class frequency divided by the total frequency. For example, from Table 2.3, the relative frequency for the class interval 5–under 7 is 13/60 = .2167. Consideration of the relative frequency is preparatory to the study of probability in Chapter 4. Indeed, if values were selected randomly from the data in Table 2.1, the probability of drawing a number that is "5–under 7" would be .2167, the relative frequency for that class interval. The fourth column of Table 2.3 lists the relative frequencies for the frequency distribution of Table 2.2.

Cumulative Frequency

The **cumulative frequency** is *a running total of frequencies through the classes of a frequency distribution.* The cumulative frequency for each class interval is the frequency for that class interval added to the preceding cumulative total. In Table 2.3 the cumulative frequency for the first class is the same as the class frequency: 4. The cumulative frequency for the second class interval is the frequency of that interval (12) plus the frequency of the first interval (4), which yields a new cumulative frequency of 16. This process continues through the last interval, at which point the cumulative total equals the sum of the frequencies (60). The concept of cumulative frequency is used in many areas, including sales cumulated over a fiscal year, sports scores during a contest (cumulated points), years of service, points earned in a course, and costs of doing business over a period of time. Table 2.3 gives cumulative frequencies for the data in Table 2.2.

DEMONSTRATION PROBLEM 2.1

Demonstration Problem

The following data are the average weekly mortgage interest rates for a 40-week period.

7.29	7.23	7.11	6.78	7.47
6.69	6.77	6.57	6.80	6.88
6.98	7.16	7.30	7.24	7.16
7.03	6.90	7.16	7.40	7.05
7.28	7.31	6.87	7.68	7.03
7.17	6.78	7.08	7.12	7.31
7.40	6.35	6.96	7.29	7.16
6.97	6.96	7.02	7.13	6.84

Construct a frequency distribution for these data. Calculate and display the class midpoints, relative frequencies, and cumulative frequencies for this frequency distribution.

Solution

How many classes should this frequency distribution contain? The range of the data is 1.33 (7.68–6.35). If 7 classes are used, each class width is approximately:

$$\text{Class Width} = \frac{\text{Range}}{\text{Number of Classes}} = \frac{1.33}{7} = 0.19$$

If a class width of .20 is used, a frequency distribution can be constructed with endpoints that are more uniform looking and allow presentation of the information in categories more familiar to mortgage interest rate users.

The first class endpoint must be 6.35 or lower to include the smallest value; the last endpoint must be 7.68 or higher to include the largest value. In this case the frequency distribution begins at 6.30 and ends at 7.70. The resulting frequency distribution, class midpoints, relative frequencies, and cumulative frequencies are listed in the following table.

Interval	Frequency	Class Midpoint	Relative Frequency	Cumulative Frequency
6.30–under 6.50	1	6.40	.025	1
6.50–under 6.70	2	6.60	.050	3
6.70–under 6.90	7	6.80	.175	10
6.90–under 7.10	10	7.00	.250	20
7.10–under 7.30	13	7.20	.325	33
7.30–under 7.50	6	7.40	.150	39
7.50–under 7.70	1	7.60	.025	40
Total	40			

The frequencies and relative frequencies of these data reveal the mortgage interest rate classes that are likely to occur during the period. Most of the mortgage interest rates (36 of the 40) are in the classes starting with 6.70–under 6.90 and going through 7.30–under 7.50. The rates with the greatest frequency, 13, are in the 7.10–under 7.30 class.

2.1 PROBLEMS

2.1 The following data represent the afternoon high temperatures for 50 construction days during a year in St. Louis.

42	70	64	47	66	69	73	38	48	25
55	85	10	24	45	31	62	47	63	84
16	40	81	15	35	17	40	36	44	17
38	79	35	36	23	64	75	53	31	60
31	38	52	16	81	12	61	43	30	33

a. Construct a frequency distribution for the data using five class intervals.

b. Construct a frequency distribution for the data using 10 class intervals.

c. Examine the results of (a) and (b) and comment on the usefulness of the frequency distribution in terms of temperature summarization capability.

2.2 A packaging process is supposed to fill small boxes of raisins with approximately 50 raisins so that each box will weigh the same. However, the number of raisins in each box will vary. Suppose 100 boxes of raisins are randomly sampled, the raisins counted, and the following data are obtained.

57	51	53	52	50	60	51	51	52	52
44	53	45	57	39	53	58	47	51	48
49	49	44	54	46	52	55	54	47	53
49	52	49	54	57	52	52	53	49	47
51	48	55	53	55	47	53	43	48	46
54	46	51	48	53	56	48	47	49	57
55	53	50	47	57	49	43	58	52	44
46	59	57	47	61	60	49	53	41	48
59	53	45	45	56	40	46	49	50	57
47	52	48	50	45	56	47	47	48	46

a. Construct a frequency distribution for these data.

b. What does the frequency distribution reveal about the box fills?

2.3 The owner of a fast-food restaurant ascertains the ages of a sample of customers. From these data, the owner constructs the frequency distribution shown. For each class interval of the frequency distribution, determine the class midpoint, the relative frequency, and the cumulative frequency.

Class Interval	Frequency
0–under 5	6
5–under 10	8
10–under 15	17
15–under 20	23
20–under 25	18
25–under 30	10
30–under 35	4

What does the relative frequency tell the fast-food restaurant owner about customer ages?

2.4 The human resources manager for a large company commissions a study in which the employment records of 500 company employees are examined for absenteeism during the past year. The business researcher conducting the study organizes the data into a frequency distribution to assist the human resources manager in analyzing the data. The frequency distribution is shown. For each class of the frequency distribution, determine the class midpoint, the relative frequency, and the cumulative frequency.

Class Interval	Frequency
0–under 2	218
2–under 4	207
4–under 6	56
6–under 8	11
8–under 10	8

2.5 List three specific uses of cumulative frequencies in business.

2.2 QUANTITATIVE DATA GRAPHS

Interactive Applet

One of the most effective mechanisms for presenting data in a form meaningful to decision makers is graphical depiction. Through graphs and charts, the decision maker can often get an overall picture of the data and reach some useful conclusions merely by studying the chart or graph. Converting data to graphics can be creative and artful. Often the most difficult step in this process is to reduce important and sometimes expensive data to a graphic picture that is both clear and concise and yet consistent with the message of the original data. One of the most important uses of graphical depiction in statistics is to help the researcher determine the shape of a distribution. Data graphs can generally be classified as quantitative or qualitative. Quantitative data graphs are plotted along a numerical scale, and qualitative graphs are plotted using non-numerical categories. In this section, we will examine five types of quantitative data graphs: (1) histogram, (2) frequency polygon, (3) ogive, (4) dot plot, and (5) stem-and-leaf plot.

Histograms

One of the more widely used types of graphs for quantitative data is the **histogram**. A histogram is a series of contiguous rectangles that represent the frequency of data in given class intervals. If the class intervals used along the horizontal axis are equal, then the heights of the rectangles represent the frequency of values in a given class interval. If the class intervals are unequal, then the areas of the rectangles can be used for relative comparisons of class frequencies. Construction of a histogram involves labeling the x-axis (abscissa) with the class endpoints and the y-axis (ordinate) with the frequencies, drawing a horizontal line segment from class endpoint to class endpoint at each frequency value,

FIGURE 2.1

Minitab Histogram of Canadian Unemployment Data

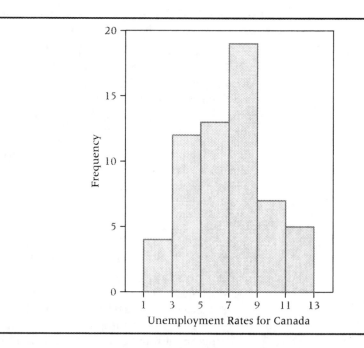

and connecting each line segment vertically from the frequency value to the *x*-axis to form a series of rectangles. Figure 2.1 is a histogram of the frequency distribution in Table 2.2 produced by using the software package Minitab.

A histogram is a useful tool for differentiating the frequencies of class intervals. A quick glance at a histogram reveals which class intervals produce the highest frequency totals. Figure 2.1 clearly shows that the class interval 7–under 9 yields by far the highest frequency count (19). Examination of the histogram reveals where large increases or decreases occur between classes, such as from the 1–under 3 class to the 3–under 5 class, an increase of 8, and from the 7–under 9 class to the 9–under 11 class, a decrease of 12.

Note that the scales used along the *x*- and *y*-axes for the histogram in Figure 2.1 are almost identical. However, because ranges of meaningful numbers for the two variables being graphed often differ considerably, the graph may have different scales on the two axes. Figure 2.2 shows what the histogram of unemployment rates would look like if the scale on the *y*-axis were more compressed than that on the *x*-axis. Notice that less difference in the length of the rectangles appears to represent the frequencies in Figure 2.2. It is important that the user of the graph clearly understands the scales used for the axes of a histogram. Otherwise, a graph's creator can "lie with statistics" by stretching or compressing a graph to make a point.*

FIGURE 2.2

Minitab Histogram of Canadian Unemployment Data (*y*-axis compressed)

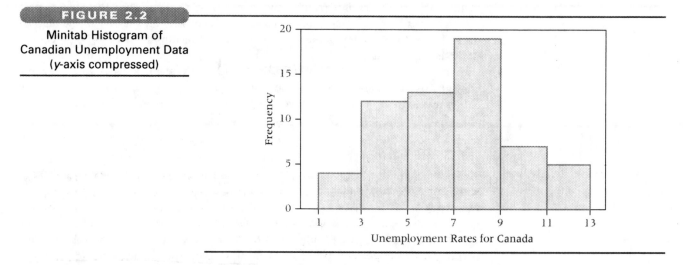

*It should be pointed out that the software package Excel uses the term *histogram* to refer to a frequency distribution. However, by checking Chart Output in the Excel histogram dialog box, a graphical histogram is also created.

FIGURE 2.3

Histogram of Stock Volumes

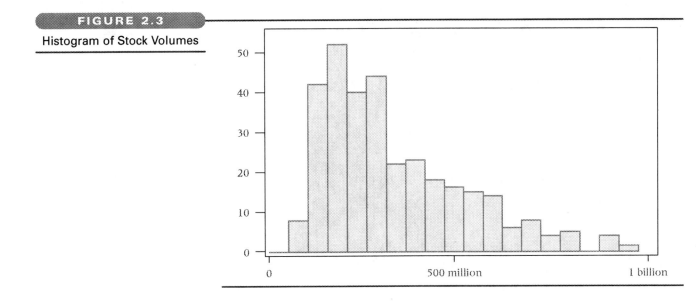

Using Histograms to Get an Initial Overview of the Data

Because of the widespread availability of computers and statistical software packages to business researchers and decision makers, the histogram continues to grow in importance in yielding information about the shape of the distribution of a large database, the variability of the data, the central location of the data, and outlier data. Although most of these concepts are presented in Chapter 3, the notion of histogram as an initial tool to access these data characteristics is presented here.

A business researcher measured the volume of stocks traded on Wall Street three times a month for nine years resulting in a database of 324 observations. Suppose a financial decision maker wants to use these data to reach some conclusions about the stock market. Figure 2.3 shows a Minitab-produced histogram of these data. What can we learn from this histogram? Virtually all stock market volumes fall between zero and 1 billion shares. The distribution takes on a shape that is high on the left end and tapered to the right. In Chapter 3 we will learn that the shape of this distribution is skewed toward the right end. In statistics, it is often useful to determine whether data are approximately normally distributed (bell-shaped curve) as shown in Figure 2.4. We can see by examining the histogram in Figure 2.3 that the stock market volume data are not normally distributed. Although the center of the histogram is located near 500 million shares, a large portion of stock volume observations falls in the lower end of the data somewhere between 100 million and 400 million shares. In addition, the histogram shows some outliers in the upper end of the distribution. Outliers are data points that appear outside of the main body of observations and may represent phenomena that differ from those represented by other data points. By observing the histogram, we notice a few data observations near 1 billion. One could conclude that on a few stock market days an unusually large volume of shares are traded. These and other insights can be gleaned by examining the histogram and show that histograms play an important role in the initial analysis of data.

Frequency Polygons

FIGURE 2.4

Normal Distribution

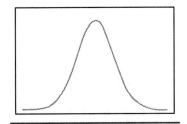

A **frequency polygon**, like the histogram, is a graphical display of class frequencies. However, instead of using rectangles like a histogram, in a frequency polygon each class frequency is plotted as a dot at the class midpoint, and the dots are connected by a series of line segments. Construction of a frequency polygon begins by scaling class midpoints along the horizontal axis and the frequency scale along the vertical axis. A dot is plotted for the associated frequency value at each class midpoint. Connecting these midpoint dots completes the graph. Figure 2.5 shows a frequency polygon of the distribution data from Table 2.2 produced by using the software package Excel. The information gleaned from frequency polygons and histograms is similar. As with the histogram, changing the scales of the axes can compress or stretch a frequency polygon, which affects the user's impression of what the graph represents.

FIGURE 2.5

Excel-Produced Frequency
Polygon of the Unemployment
Data

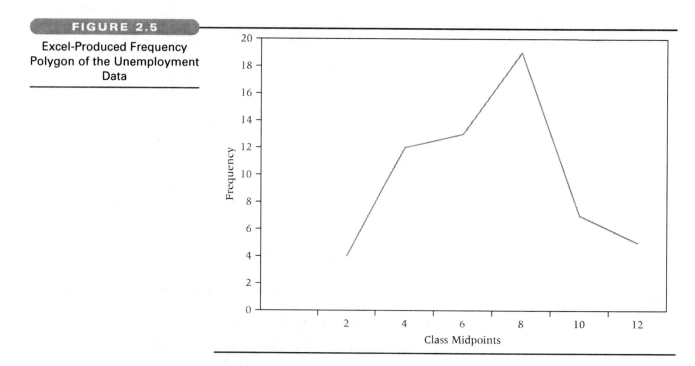

Ogives

An **ogive** (o-jive) is *a cumulative frequency polygon.* Construction begins by labeling the
x-axis with the class endpoints and the y-axis with the frequencies. However, the use of
cumulative frequency values requires that the scale along the y-axis be great enough to
include the frequency total. A dot of zero frequency is plotted at the beginning of the first
class, and construction proceeds by marking a dot at the *end* of each class interval for the
cumulative value. Connecting the dots then completes the ogive. Figure 2.6 presents an
ogive produced by using Excel for the data in Table 2.2.

Ogives are most useful when the decision maker wants to see *running totals.* For example, if a comptroller is interested in controlling costs, an ogive could depict cumulative
costs over a fiscal year.

Steep slopes in an ogive can be used to identify sharp increases in frequencies. In
Figure 2.6, a particularly steep slope occurs in the 7–under 9 class, signifying a large jump
in class frequency totals.

FIGURE 2.6

Excel Ogive of the
Unemployment Data

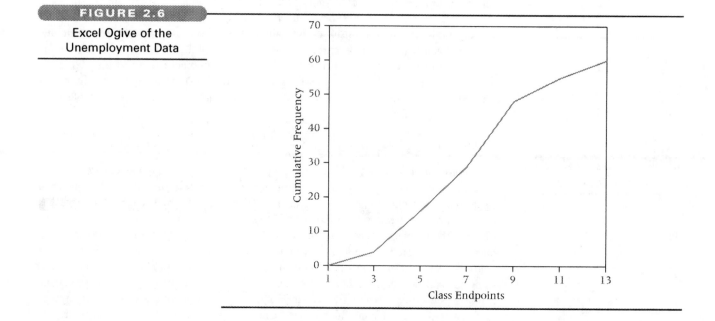

FIGURE 2.7

A Minitab-Produced Dot Plot
of the Canadian
Unemployment Data

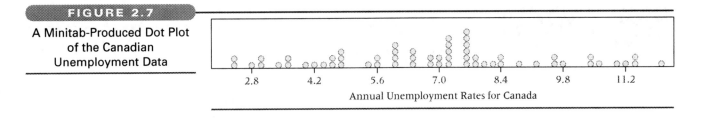

Annual Unemployment Rates for Canada

Dot Plots

A relatively simple statistical chart that is generally used to display continuous, quantitative data is the **dot plot**. In a dot plot, each data value is plotted along the horizontal axis and is represented on the chart by a dot. If multiple data points have the same values, the dots will stack up vertically. If there are a large number of close points, it may not be possible to display all of the data values along the horizontal axis. Dot plots can be especially useful for observing the overall shape of the distribution of data points along with identifying data values or intervals for which there are groupings and gaps in the data. Figure 2.7 displays a minitab-produced dot plot for the Canadian unemployment data shown in Table 2.1. Note that the distribution is relatively balanced with a peak near the center. There are a few gaps to note, such as from 4.9 to 5.3, from 9.9 to 10.2, and from 11.5 to 11.9. In addition, there are groupings around 6.0, 7.1, and 7.5.

Stem-and-Leaf Plots

Another way to organize raw data into groups besides using a frequency distribution is a **stem-and-leaf plot**. This technique is simple and provides a unique view of the data. A stem-and-leaf plot is constructed by separating the digits for each number of the data into two groups, *a stem and a leaf*. The leftmost digits are the stem and consist of the higher valued digits. The rightmost digits are the leaves and contain the lower values. If a set of data has only two digits, the stem is the value on the left and the leaf is the value on the right. For example, if 34 is one of the numbers, the stem is 3 and the leaf is 4. For numbers with more than two digits, division of stem and leaf is a matter of researcher preference.

Table 2.4 contains scores from an examination on plant safety policy and rules given to a group of 35 job trainees. A stem-and-leaf plot of these data is displayed in Table 2.5. One advantage of such a distribution is that the instructor can readily see whether the scores are in the upper or lower end of each bracket and also determine the spread of the scores. A second advantage of stem-and-leaf plots is that the values of the original raw data are retained (whereas most frequency distributions and graphic depictions use the class midpoint to represent the values in a class).

TABLE 2.4

Safety Examination Scores
for Plant Trainees

86	77	91	60	55
76	92	47	88	67
23	59	72	75	83
77	68	82	97	89
81	75	74	39	67
79	83	70	78	91
68	49	56	94	81

TABLE 2.5

Stem-and-Leaf Plot for Plant Safety
Examination Data

Stem	Leaf								
2	3								
3	9								
4	7	9							
5	5	6	9						
6	0	7	7	8	8				
7	0	2	4	5	5	6	7	7	8	9
8	1	1	2	3	3	6	8	9	
9	1	1	2	4	7				

DEMONSTRATION PROBLEM 2.2

The following data represent the costs (in dollars) of a sample of 30 postal mailings by a company.

3.67	2.75	9.15	5.11	3.32	2.09
1.83	10.94	1.93	3.89	7.20	2.78
6.72	7.80	5.47	4.15	3.55	3.53
3.34	4.95	5.42	8.64	4.84	4.10
5.10	6.45	4.65	1.97	2.84	3.21

Using dollars as a stem and cents as a leaf, construct a stem-and-leaf plot of the data.

Solution

Stem	Leaf						
1	83	93	97				
2	09	75	78	84			
3	21	32	34	53	55	67	89
4	10	15	65	84	95		
5	10	11	42	47			
6	45	72					
7	20	80					
8	64						
9	15						
10	94						

2.2 PROBLEMS

2.6 Assembly times for components must be understood in order to "level" the stages of a production process. Construct both a histogram and a frequency polygon for the following assembly time data and comment on the key characteristics of the distribution.

Class Interval	Frequency
30–under 32	5
32–under 34	7
34–under 36	15
36–under 38	21
38–under 40	34
40–under 42	24
42–under 44	17
44–under 46	8

2.7 A call center is trying to better understand staffing requirements. It investigates the number of calls received during the evening shift and obtains the information given below. Construct a histogram of the data and comment on the key characteristics of the distribution. Construct a frequency polygon and compare it to the histogram. Which do you prefer, and why?

Class Interval	Frequency
10–under 20	9
20–under 30	7
30–under 40	10
40–under 50	6
50–under 60	13
60–under 70	18
70–under 80	15

2.8 Construct an ogive for the following data.

Class Interval	Frequency
3–under 6	2
6–under 9	5
9–under 12	10
12–under 15	11
15–under 18	17
18–under 21	5

2.9 A real estate group is investigating the price of condominiums for a given size (sq ft). The following sales prices ($1,000) were obtained in one region of a city. Construct a stem-and-leaf plot for the following data using two digits for the stem. Comment on the key characteristics of the distribution. Construct a dot plot of the data and comment on how it differs from the stem-and-leaf plot in providing information about the data.

212	239	240	218	222	249	265	224
257	271	266	234	239	219	255	260
243	261	249	230	246	263	235	229
218	238	254	249	250	263	229	221
253	227	270	257	261	238	240	239
273	220	226	239	258	259	230	262
255	226						

2.10 The following data represent the number of passengers per flight in a sample of 50 flights from Wichita, Kansas, to Kansas City, Missouri.

23	46	66	67	13	58	19	17	65	17
25	20	47	28	16	38	44	29	48	29
69	34	35	60	37	52	80	59	51	33
48	46	23	38	52	50	17	57	41	77
45	47	49	19	32	64	27	61	70	19

a. Construct a dot plot for these data.

b. Construct a stem-and-leaf plot for these data. What does the stem-and-leaf plot tell you about the number of passengers per flight?

2.11 The Airports Council International (ACI) publishes data on the world's busiest airports. Shown below is a Minitab-produced histogram constructed from ACI data on the number of passengers that enplaned and deplaned in 2008. As an example, Atlanta's Hartsfield-Jackson International Airport was the busiest airport in the world, with 90,039,280 passengers. What are some observations that you can make from the graph? Describe the top 30 airports in the world using this histogram.

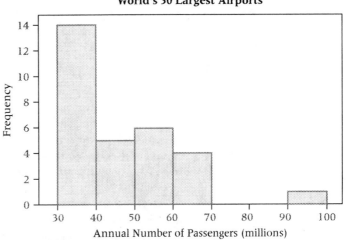

World's 30 Largest Airports

2.12 Study the Minitab-produced dot plot shown below of the number of farms per state in the United States. Comment on any observations that you make from the graph. What does this graph tell you about the number of farms per state? The average number of farms per state calculated from the raw data (not given here and sourced from the USDA) is 41,500. Reconcile this number with the dotplot.

Dotplot of Farms Per State in the U.S.

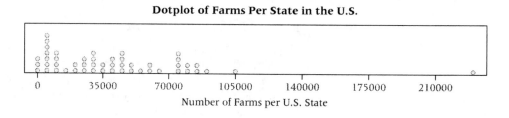

Number of Farms per U.S. State

2.13 A full-service car wash has an automated exterior conveyor car wash system that does the initial cleaning in a few minutes. However, once the car is through the system, car wash workers hand clean the inside and the outside of the car for approximately 15 to 25 additional minutes. There are enough workers to handle four cars at once during this stage. On a busy day with good weather, the car wash can handle up to 150 cars in a 12-hour time period. However, on rainy days or on certain days of the year, business is slow. Suppose 50 days of work are randomly sampled from the car wash's records and the number of cars washed each day is recorded. A stem-and-leaf plot of this output is constructed and is given below. Study the plot and write a few sentences describing the number of cars washed per day over this period of work. Note that the stem-and-leaf display is from Minitab, the stems are in the middle column, each leaf is only one digit and is shown in the right column, and the numbers in the left column are cumulative frequencies up to the median and then decumulative thereafter.

STEM-AND-LEAF DISPLAY: CARS WASHED PER DAY

Stem-and-leaf of Cars Washed Per Day N = 50
Leaf Unit = 1.0

	Stem	Leaf
3	2	599
9	3	344778
15	4	015689
18	5	378
21	6	223
24	7	457
(3)	8	112
23	9	05
21	10	1234578
14	11	466
11	12	01467
6	13	37
4	14	1457

2.14 A hundred or so boats go fishing every year for three or four weeks off of the Bering Strait for Alaskan king crabs. To catch these king crabs, large pots are baited and left on the sea bottom, often several hundred feet deep. Because of the investment in boats, equipment, personnel, and supplies, fishing for such crabs can be financially risky if not enough crabs are caught. Thus, as pots are pulled and emptied, there is great interest in how many legal king crabs (males of a certain size) there are in any given pot. Suppose the number of legal king crabs is reported for each pot during a season and recorded. In addition, suppose that 200 of these are randomly selected and the numbers per pot are used to create the ogive shown below. Study the ogive and comment on the number of legal king crabs per pot.

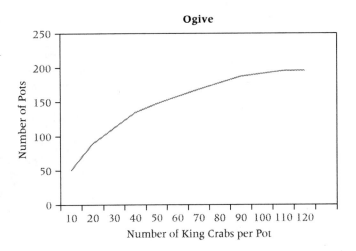

Ogive

2.3 QUALITATIVE DATA GRAPHS

In contrast to quantitative data graphs that are plotted along a numerical scale, qualitative graphs are plotted using non-numerical categories. In this section, we will examine three types of qualitative data graphs: (1) pie charts, (2) bar charts, and (3) Pareto charts.

Pie Charts

A **pie chart** is *a circular depiction of data where the area of the whole pie represents 100% of the data and slices of the pie represent a percentage breakdown of the sublevels.* Pie charts show the relative magnitudes of the parts to the whole. They are widely used in business, particularly to depict such things as budget categories, market share, and time/resource allocations. However, the use of pie charts is minimized in the sciences and technology because pie charts can lead to less accurate judgments than are possible with other types of graphs.* Generally, it is more difficult for the viewer to interpret the relative size of angles in a pie chart than to judge the length of rectangles in a bar chart. In the feature Thinking Critically about Statistics in Business Today, "Where Are Soft Drinks Sold?" graphical depictions of the percentage of sales by place are displayed by both a pie chart and a vertical bar chart.

Construction of the pie chart begins by determining the proportion of the subunit to the whole. Table 2.6 contains annual sales for the top petroleum refining companies in the

TABLE 2.6

Leading Petroleum Refining Companies

Company	Annual Sales ($ millions)	Proportion	Degrees
ExxonMobil	442,851	.3752	135.07
Chevron	263,159	.2230	80.28
Conoco Phillips	230,764	.1955	70.38
Valero Energy	118,298	.1002	36.07
Marathon Oil	73,504	.0623	22.43
Sunoco	51,652	.0438	15.77
Totals	1,180,228	1.0000	360.00

*William S. Cleveland, *The Elements of Graphing Data.* Monterey, CA: Wadsworth Advanced Books and Software, 1985.

FIGURE 2.8

Minitab Pie Chart of Petroleum
Refining Sales by Brand

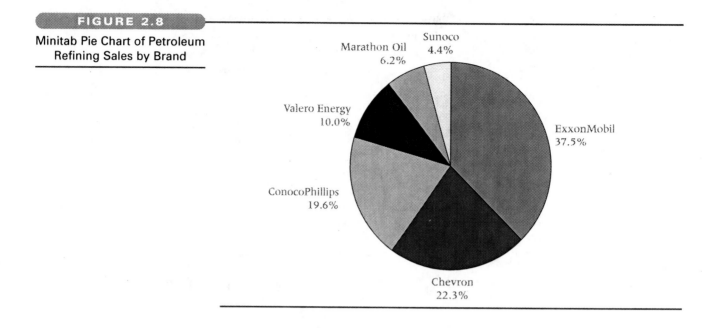

United States in a recent year. To construct a pie chart from these data, first convert the raw
sales figures to proportions by dividing each sales figure by the total sales figure. This proportion is analogous to relative frequency computed for frequency distributions. Because a
circle contains 360°, each proportion is then multiplied by 360 to obtain the correct number of degrees to represent each item. For example, Exxon Mobil sales of $442,851 million
represent a .3752 proportion of the total sales $\left(\dfrac{442,851}{1,180,228} = .3752 \right)$. Multiplying this value
by 360° results in an angle of 135.07°. The pie chart is then completed by determining each
of the other angles and using a compass to lay out the slices. The pie chart in Figure 2.8,
constructed by using Minitab, depicts the data from Table 2.6.

Bar Graphs

Another widely used qualitative data graphing technique is the **bar graph** or **bar chart**. A
bar graph or chart contains two or more categories along one axis and a series of bars, one
for each category, along the other axis. Typically, the length of the bar represents the magnitude of the measure (amount, frequency, money, percentage, etc.) for each category. The
bar graph is qualitative because the categories are non-numerical, and it may be either
horizontal or vertical. In Excel, horizontal bar graphs are referred to as **bar charts**, and vertical bar graphs are referred to as **column charts**. A bar graph generally is constructed from
the same type of data that is used to produce a pie chart. However, an advantage of using
a bar graph over a pie chart for a given set of data is that for categories that are close in
value, it is considered easier to see the difference in the bars of bar graph than discriminat-
ing between pie slices.

  As an example, consider the data in Table 2.7 regarding how much the average college
student spends on back-to-college spending. Constructing a bar graph from these data, the

TABLE 2.7

How Much is Spent on Back-
to-College Shopping by the
Average Student

Category	Amount Spent ($ US)
Electronics	$211.89
Clothing and Accessories	134.40
Dorm Furnishings	90.90
School Supplies	68.47
Misc.	93.72

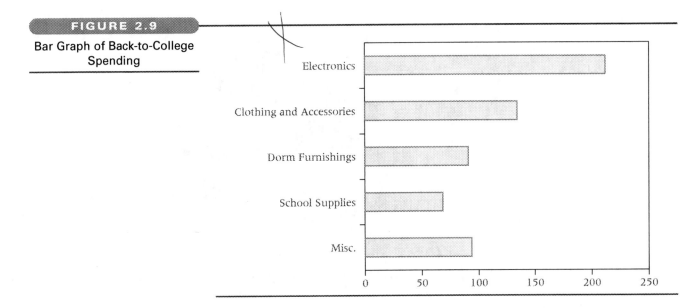

FIGURE 2.9

Bar Graph of Back-to-College Spending

categories are Electronics, Clothing and Accessories, Dorm Furnishings, School Supplies, and misc. Bars for each of these categories are made using the dollar figures given in the table. The resulting bar graph is shown in Figure 2.9 produced by Excel.

DEMONSTRATION PROBLEM 2.3

According to the National Retail Federation and Center for Retailing Education at the University of Florida, the four main sources of inventory shrinkage are employee theft, shoplifting, administrative error, and vendor fraud. The estimated annual dollar amount in shrinkage ($ millions) associated with each of these sources follows:

Employee theft	$17,918.6
Shoplifting	15,191.9
Administrative error	7,617.6
Vendor fraud	2,553.6
Total	$43,281.7

Construct a pie chart and a bar chart to depict these data.

Solution

To produce a pie chart, convert each raw dollar amount to a proportion by dividing each individual amount by the total.

Employee theft	17,918.6/43,281.7 =	.414
Shoplifting	15,191.9/43,281.7 =	.351
Administrative error	7,617.6/43,281.7 =	.176
Vendor fraud	2,553.6/43,281.7 =	.059
Total		1.000

Convert each proportion to degrees by multiplying each proportion by 360°.

Employee theft	.414 · 360° =	149.0°
Shoplifting	.351 · 360° =	126.4°
Administrative error	.176 · 360° =	63.4°
Vendor fraud	.059 · 360° =	21.2°
Total		360.0°

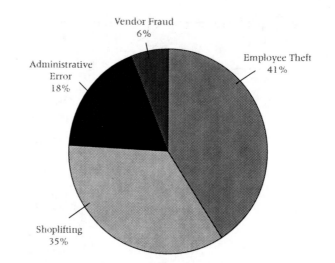

Using the raw data above, we can produce the following bar chart.

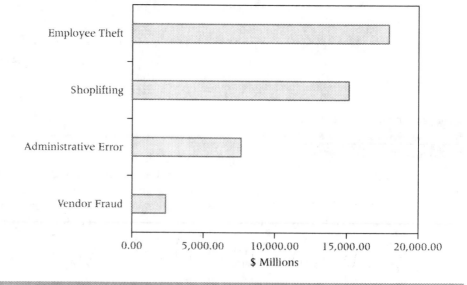

Pareto Charts

A third type of qualitative data graph is a Pareto chart, which could be viewed as a particular application of the bar graph. An important concept and movement in business is total quality management (see Chapter 18). One of the important aspects of total quality management is the constant search for causes of problems in products and processes. A graphical technique for displaying problem causes is Pareto analysis. Pareto analysis is a quantitative tallying of the number and types of defects that occur with a product or service. Analysts use this tally to produce *a vertical bar chart that displays the most common types of defects, ranked in order of occurrence from left to right.* The bar chart is called a **Pareto chart**.

Pareto charts were named after an Italian economist, Vilfredo Pareto, who observed more than 100 years ago that most of Italy's wealth was controlled by a few families who were the major drivers behind the Italian economy. Quality expert J. M. Juran applied this notion to the quality field by observing that poor quality can often be addressed by attacking a few major causes that result in most of the problems. A Pareto chart enables quality-management decision makers to separate the most important defects from trivial defects, which helps them to set priorities for needed quality improvement work.

Suppose the number of electric motors being rejected by inspectors for a company has been increasing. Company officials examine the records of several hundred of the motors in which at least one defect was found to determine which defects occurred more frequently. They find that 40% of the defects involved poor wiring, 30% involved a short in the coil, 25%

THINKING CRITICALLY ABOUT STATISTICS IN BUSINESS TODAY

Where Are Soft Drinks Sold?

The soft drink market is an extremely large and growing market in the United States and worldwide. In a recent year, 9.6 billion cases of soft drinks were sold in the United States alone. Where are soft drinks sold? The following data from Sanford C. Bernstein research indicate that the four leading places for soft drink sales are super-markets, fountains, convenience/gas stores, and vending machines.

Place of Sales	Percentage
Supermarket	44
Fountain	24
Convenience/gas stations	16
Vending	11
Mass merchandisers	3
Drugstores	2

These data can be displayed graphically several ways. Displayed here is an Excel pie chart and a Minitab bar chart of the data. Some statisticians prefer the histogram or the bar chart over the pie chart because they believe it is easier to compare categories that are similar in size with the histogram or the bar chart rather than the pie chart.

Things to Ponder

1. How might this information be useful to large soft drink companies?
2. How might the packaging of soft drinks differ according to the top four places where soft drinks are sold?

3. How might the distribution of soft drinks differ between the various places where soft drinks are sold?

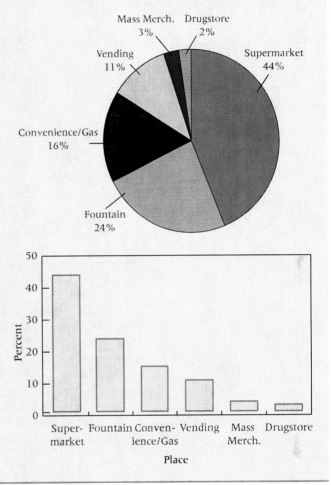

involved a defective plug, and 5% involved cessation of bearings. Figure 2.10 is a Pareto chart constructed from this information. It shows that the main three problems with defective motors—poor wiring, a short in the coil, and a defective plug—account for 95% of the problems. From the Pareto chart, decision makers can formulate a logical plan for reducing the number of defects.

FIGURE 2.10

Pareto Chart for Electric Motor Problems

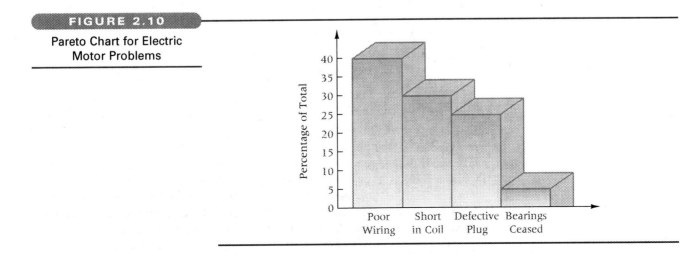

FIGURE 2.11

Minitab Pareto Chart for
Electric Motor Problems

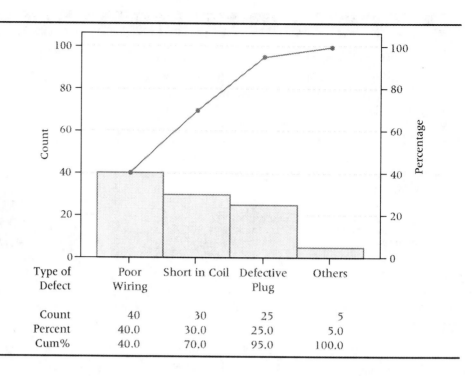

Type of Defect	Poor Wiring	Short in Coil	Defective Plug	Others
Count	40	30	25	5
Percent	40.0	30.0	25.0	5.0
Cum%	40.0	70.0	95.0	100.0

Company officials and workers would probably begin to improve quality by examining the segments of the production process that involve the wiring. Next, they would study the construction of the coil, then examine the plugs used and the plug-supplier process.

Figure 2.11 is a Minitab rendering of this Pareto chart. In addition to the bar chart analysis, the Minitab Pareto analysis contains a cumulative percentage line graph. Observe the slopes on the line graph. The steepest slopes represent the more frequently occurring problems. As the slopes level off, the problems occur less frequently. The line graph gives the decision maker another tool for determining which problems to solve first.

2.3 PROBLEMS

2.15 Shown here is a list of the top five industrial and farm equipment companies in the United States, along with their annual sales ($ millions).

Firm	Revenue ($ million)
Caterpillar	30,251
Deere	19,986
Illinois Tool Works	11,731
Eaton	9,817
American Standard	9,509

a. Construct a bar chart to display these data.

b. Construct a pie chart from these data and label the slices with the appropriate percentages.

c. Comment on the effectiveness of using a pie chart to display the revenue of these top industrial and farm equipment companies.

2.16 According to T-100 Domestic Market, the top seven airlines in the United States by domestic boardings in a recent year were Southwest Airlines with 81.1 million, Delta Airlines with 79.4 million, American Airlines with 72.6 million, United Airlines with 56.3 million, Northwest Airlines with 43.3 million, US Airways with 37.8 million, and Continental Airlines with 31.5 million. Construct a pie chart and a bar graph to depict this information.

2.17 The following list shows the top six pharmaceutical companies in the United States and their sales figures ($ millions) for a recent year. Use this information to construct a pie chart and a bar graph to represent these six companies and their sales.

Pharmaceutical Company	Sales
Pfizer	52,921
Johnson & Johnson	47,348
Merck	22,939
Bristol-Myers Squibb	21,886
Abbott Laboratories	20,473
Wyeth	17,358

2.18 How do various currencies around the world stack up to the U.S. dollar? Shown below is a bar chart of the value of the currency of various countries in U.S. dollars as of April 2010. The currencies represented here are the Malaysia ringgit, United Arab Emirates dirham, New Zealand dollar, China yuan, Mexico peso, India rupee, Canada dollar, European euro, and U.S. dollar. Study the bar chart and discuss the various currencies as they relate to each other in value and as they compare to the U.S. dollar.

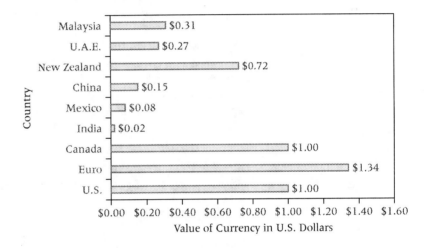

2.19 An airline company uses a central telephone bank and a semiautomated telephone process to take reservations. It has been receiving an unusually high number of customer complaints about its reservation system. The company conducted a survey of customers, asking them whether they had encountered any of the following problems in making reservations: busy signal, disconnection, poor connection, too long a wait to talk to someone, could not get through to an agent, connected with the wrong person. Suppose a survey of 744 complaining customers resulted in the following frequency tally.

Number of Complaints	Complaint
184	Too long a wait
10	Transferred to the wrong person
85	Could not get through to an agent
37	Got disconnected
420	Busy signal
8	Poor connection

Construct a Pareto diagram from this information to display the various problems encountered in making reservations.

2.4 CHARTS AND GRAPHS FOR TWO VARIABLES

It is very common in business statistics to want to analyze two variables simultaneously in an effort to gain insight into a possible relationship between them. For example, business researchers might be interested in the relationship between years of experience and amount of productivity in a manufacturing facility or in the relationship between a person's technology usage and their age. Business statistics has many techniques for exploring such relationships. Two of the more elementary tools for observing the relationships between two variables are cross tabulation and scatter plot.

Cross Tabulation

Cross tabulation is *a process for producing a two-dimensional table that displays the frequency counts for two variables simultaneously.* As an example, suppose a job satisfaction survey of a randomly selected sample of 177 bankers is taken in the banking industry. The bankers are asked how satisfied they are with their job using a 1 to 5 scale where 1 denotes very dissatisfied, 2 denotes dissatisfied, 3 denotes neither satisfied nor dissatisfied, 4 denotes satisfied, and 5 denotes very satisfied. In addition, each banker is asked to report his/her age by using one of the three categories: under 30 years, 30 to 50 years, and over 50 years. Table 2.8 displays how some of the data might look as they are gathered. Note that for each banker the level of their job satisfaction and their age are recorded. By tallying the frequency of responses for each combination of categories between the two variables, the data are cross tabulated according to the two variables. For instance, in this example, there is a tally of how many bankers rated their level of satisfaction as 1 and were under 30 years of age, there is a tally of how many bankers rated their level of satisfaction as 2 and were under 30 years of age, and so on until frequency tallies are determined for each possible combination of the two variables. Table 2.9 shows the completed cross-tabulation table for the banker survey. A cross-tabulation table is sometimes referred to as a contingency table, and Excel refers to such a table as a Pivot Table.

Scatter Plot

A **scatter plot** is *a two-dimensional graph plot of pairs of points from two numerical variables.* The scatter plot is a graphical tool that is often used to examine possible relationships between two variables.

TABLE 2.8

Banker Data Observations by Job Satisfaction and Age

Banker	Level of Job Satisfaction	Age
1	4	53
2	3	37
3	1	24
4	2	28
5	4	46
6	5	62
7	3	41
8	3	32
9	4	29
.		
.		
.		
177	3	51

TABLE 2.9

Cross-Tabulation Table of Banker Data

		Age Category			
		Under 30	30–50	Over 50	Total
	1	7	3	0	10
	2	19	14	3	36
Level of Job Satisfaction	3	28	17	12	57
	4	11	22	16	49
	5	2	9	14	25
Total		67	65	45	177

TABLE 2.10	
Value of New Construction Over a 35-Year Period	

Residential	Nonresidential
169635	96497
155113	115372
149410	96407
175822	129275
162706	140569
134605	145054
195028	131289
231396	155261
234955	178925
266481	163740
267063	160363
263385	164191
252745	169173
228943	167896
197526	135389
232134	120921
249757	122222
274956	127593
251937	139711
281229	153866
280748	166754
297886	177639
315757	175048

Source: U.S. Census Bureau, *Current Construction Reports* (in millions of constant dollars).

FIGURE 2.12
Minitab Scatter Plot of New Residential and New Nonresidential Construction

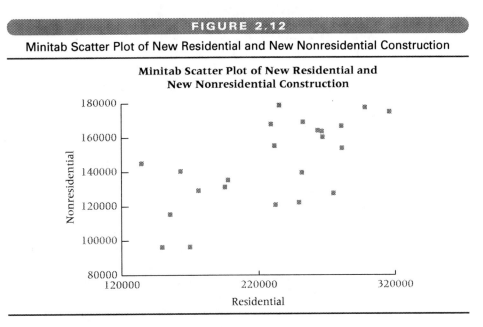

Observe the data in Table 2.10. Displayed are the values of new residential and new nonresidential buildings in the United States for various years over a 35-year period. Do these two numerical variables exhibit any relationship? It might seem logical when new construction booms that it would boom in both residential building and in nonresidential building at the same time. However, the Minitab scatter plot of these data displayed in Figure 2.12 shows somewhat mixed results. The apparent tendency is that more new residential building construction occurs when more new nonresidential building construction is also taking place and less new residential building construction when new nonresidential building construction is also at lower levels. The scatter plot also shows that in some years more new residential building and less new nonresidential building happened at the same time, and vice versa.

2.4 PROBLEMS

2.20 The U.S. National Oceanic and Atmospheric Administration, National Marine Fisheries Service, publishes data on the quantity and value of domestic fishing in the United States. The quantity (in millions of pounds) of fish caught and used for human food and for industrial products (oil, bait, animal food, etc.) over a decade follows. Is a relationship evident between the quantity used for human food and the quantity used for industrial products for a given year? Construct a scatter plot of the data. Examine the plot and discuss the strength of the relationship of the two variables.

Human Food	Industrial Product
3654	2828
3547	2430
3285	3082
3238	3201
3320	3118
3294	2964
3393	2638
3946	2950
4588	2604
6204	2259

2.21 Are the advertising dollars spent by a company related to total sales revenue? The following data represent the advertising dollars and the sales revenues for various companies in a given industry during a recent year. Construct a scatter plot of the data from the two variables and discuss the relationship between the two variables.

Advertising (in $ millions)	Sales (in $ millions)
4.2	155.7
1.6	87.3
6.3	135.6
2.7	99.0
10.4	168.2
7.1	136.9
5.5	101.4
8.3	158.2

2.22 It seems logical that the number of days per year that an employee is tardy is at least somewhat related to the employee's job satisfaction. Suppose 10 employees are asked to record how satisfied they are with their job on a scale of from 0 to 10, with 0 denoting completely unsatisfied and 10 denoted completely satisfied. Suppose also that through human resource records, it is determined how many days each of these employees was tardy last year. The scatter plot below graphs the job satisfaction scores of each employee against the number of days he/she was tardy. What information can you glean from the scatter plot? Does there appear to be any relationship between job satisfaction and tardiness? If so, how might they appear to be related?

Scatter Plot of Job Satisfaction vs. Tardiness

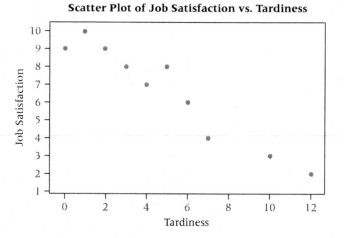

2.23 The human resources manager of a large chemical plant was interested in determining what factors might be related to the number of non-vacation days that workers were absent during the past year. One of the factors that the manager considered was the distance that the person commutes to work, wondering if longer commutes resulting in such things as stress on the worker and/or increases in the likelihood of transportation failure might result in more worker absences. The manager studied company records, randomly selected 532 plant workers, and recorded the number of non-vacation days that the workers were absent last year and how far their place of residence is from the plant. The manager then recoded the raw data in categories and created the cross-tabulation table shown below. Study the table and comment on any relationship that may exist between distance to the plant and number of absences.

		One-Way Commute Distance (in miles)		
		0–3	4–10	More than 10
Number of Annual Non-Vacation-Day Absences	0–2	95	184	117
	3–5	21	40	53
	more than 5	3	7	12

2.24 A customer relations expert for a retail tire company is interested in determining if there is any relationship between a customer's level of education and his or her rating of the quality of the tire company's service. The tire company administers a very brief survey to each customer who buys a pair of tires and has them installed at the store. The customer is asked to respond to the quality of the service rendered as either "acceptable" or "unacceptable." In addition, each respondent is asked the level of education attained from the categories of "high school only" or "college degree." These data are gathered on 25 customers and are given below. Use this information to construct a cross-tabulation table. Comment on any relationships that may exist in the table.

Customer	Level of Education	Rating of Service
1	high school only	acceptable
2	college degree	unacceptable
3	college degree	acceptable
4	high school only	acceptable
5	college degree	unacceptable
6	high school only	acceptable
7	high school only	unacceptable
8	college degree	acceptable
9	college degree	unacceptable
10	college degree	unacceptable
11	high school only	acceptable
12	college degree	acceptable
13	college degree	unacceptable
14	high school only	acceptable
15	college degree	acceptable
16	high school only	acceptable
17	high school only	acceptable
18	high school only	unacceptable
19	college degree	unacceptable
20	college degree	acceptable
21	college degree	unacceptable
22	high school only	acceptable
23	college degree	acceptable
24	high school only	acceptable
25	college degree	unacceptable

Container Shipping Companies

The raw values as shown in the table in the Decision Dilemma are relatively easy to read and interpret. However, these numbers could also be displayed graphically in different ways to create interest and discussion among readers and to allow for more ease of comparisons. For example, shown here is a Minitab pie chart displaying the TEU capacities for the five companies. In addition, there is an Excel-produced bar chart for the number of ships for these companies. Note that some of the slices in the pie chart are so close together in size that it is difficult to determine which company has the greater TEU capacity. Some statisticians prefer to use a bar chart in examining data that are similar in size and value because they believe that it is easier to differentiate between categories with close values when using a bar chart as compared to a pie chart. Since the number of ships is close together for two companies, determine for yourself if you prefer the bar chart to the pie chart in such instances.

Minitab Pie Chart of Total TEU Capacity   Excel-Produced Bar Chart of Number of Ships

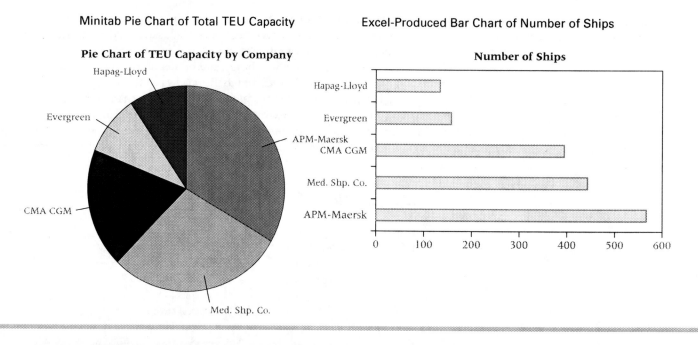

Ethical considerations for techniques learned in Chapter 2 begin with the data chosen for representation. With the abundance of available data in business, the person constructing the data summary must be selective in choosing the reported variables. The potential is great for the analyst to select variables or even data within variables that are favorable to his or her own situation or that are perceived to be well received by the listener.

Section 2.1 noted that the number of classes and the size of the intervals in frequency distributions are usually selected by the researcher. The researcher should be careful to select values and sizes that will give an honest, accurate reflection of the situation and not a biased over- or under-stated case.

Sections 2.2, 2.3, and 2.4 discussed the construction of charts and graphs. It pointed out that in many instances, it makes sense to use unequal scales on the axes. However, doing so opens the possibility of "cheating with statistics" by stretching or compressing of the axes to underscore the researcher's or analyst's point. It is imperative that frequency distributions and charts and graphs be constructed in a manner that most reflects actual data and not merely the researcher's own agenda.

SUMMARY

The two types of data are grouped and ungrouped. Grouped data are data organized into a frequency distribution. Differentiating between grouped and ungrouped data is important, because statistical operations on the two types are computed differently.

Constructing a frequency distribution involves several steps. The first step is to determine the range of the data, which is the difference between the largest value and the smallest value. Next, the number of classes is determined, which is an arbitrary choice of the researcher. However, too few classes overaggregate the data into meaningless categories, and too many classes do not summarize the data enough to be useful. The third step in constructing the frequency distribution is to determine the width of the class interval. Dividing the range of values by the number of classes yields the approximate width of the class interval.

The class midpoint is the midpoint of a class interval. It is the average of the class endpoints and represents the halfway point of the class interval. Relative frequency is a value computed by dividing an individual frequency by the sum of the frequencies. Relative frequency represents the proportion of total values that is in a given class interval. The cumulative frequency is a running total frequency tally that starts with the first frequency value and adds each ensuing frequency to the total.

Two types of graphical depictions are quantitative data graphs and qualitative data graphs. Quantitative data graphs presented in this chapter are histogram, frequency polygon, ogive, dot plot, and stem-and-leaf plot. Qualitative data graphs presented are pie chart, bar chart, and Pareto chart. In addition, two-dimensional scatter plots are presented. A histogram is a vertical bar chart in which a line segment connects class endpoints at the value of the frequency. Two vertical lines connect this line segment down to the x-axis, forming a rectangle. A frequency polygon is constructed by plotting a dot at the midpoint of each class interval for the value of each frequency and then connecting the dots. Ogives are cumulative frequency polygons. Points on an ogive are plotted at the class endpoints. A dot plot is a graph that displays frequency counts for various data points as dots graphed above the data point. Dot plots are especially useful for observing the overall shape of the distribution and determining both gaps in the data and high concentrations of data. Stem-and-leaf plots are another way to organize data. The numbers are divided into two parts, a stem and a leaf. The stems are the leftmost digits of the numbers and the leaves are the rightmost digits. The stems are listed individually, with all leaf values corresponding to each stem displayed beside that stem.

A pie chart is a circular depiction of data. The amount of each category is represented as a slice of the pie proportionate to the total. The researcher is cautioned in using pie charts because it is sometimes difficult to differentiate the relative sizes of the slices.

The bar chart or bar graph uses bars to represent the frequencies of various qualitative categories. The bar chart can be displayed horizontally or vertically.

A Pareto chart is a vertical bar chart that is used in total quality management to graphically display the causes of problems. The Pareto chart presents problem causes in descending order to assist the decision maker in prioritizing problem causes. Cross tabulation is a process for producing a two-dimensional table that displays the frequency counts for two variables simultaneously. The scatter plot is a two-dimensional plot of pairs of points from two numerical variables. It is used to graphically determine whether any apparent relationship exists between the two variables.

KEY TERMS

Flash Cards

bar graph
class mark

class midpoint
cross tabulation
cumulative frequency
dot plot
frequency distribution
frequency polygon

grouped data
histogram
ogive
Pareto chart
pie chart
range

relative frequency
scatter plot
stem-and-leaf plot
ungrouped data

SUPPLEMENTARY PROBLEMS

CALCULATING THE STATISTICS

2.25 For the following data, construct a frequency distribution with six classes.

57	23	35	18	21
26	51	47	29	21
46	43	29	23	39
50	41	19	36	28
31	42	52	29	18
28	46	33	28	20

2.26 For each class interval of the frequency distribution given, determine the class midpoint, the relative frequency, and the cumulative frequency.

Class Interval	Frequency
20–under 25	17
25–under 30	20
30–under 35	16
35–under 40	15
40–under 45	8
45–under 50	6

2.27 Construct a histogram, a frequency polygon, and an ogive for the following frequency distribution.

Class Interval	Frequency
50–under 60	13
60–under 70	27
70–under 80	43
80–under 90	31
90–under 100	9

2.28 Construct a dot plot from the following data.

16	15	17	15	15
15	14	9	16	15
13	10	8	18	20
17	17	17	18	23
7	15	20	10	14

2.29 Construct a stem-and-leaf plot for the following data. Let the leaf contain one digit.

312	324	289	335	298
314	309	294	326	317
290	311	317	301	316
306	286	308	284	324

2.30 Construct a pie chart from the following data.

Label	Value
A	55
B	121
C	83
D	46

2.31 Construct a bar graph from the following data.

Category	Frequency
A	7
B	12
C	14
D	5
E	19

2.32 An examination of rejects shows at least 7 problems. A frequency tally of the problems follows. Construct a Pareto chart for these data.

Problem	Frequency
1	673
2	29
3	108
4	202
5	73
6	564
7	402

2.33 Construct a scatter plot for the following two numerical variables.

x	y
12	5
17	3
9	10
6	15
10	8
14	9
8	8

TESTING YOUR UNDERSTANDING

2.34 The Whitcomb Company manufactures a metal ring for industrial engines that usually weighs about 50 ounces. A random sample of 50 of these metal rings produced the following weights (in ounces).

51	53	56	50	44	47
53	53	42	57	46	55
41	44	52	56	50	57
44	46	41	52	69	53
57	51	54	63	42	47
47	52	53	46	36	58
51	38	49	50	62	39
44	55	43	52	43	42
57	49				

a. Construct a dot plot for these data and comment on any observations you make about the data from the plot.

b. Construct a frequency distribution and histogram for these data using eight classes. What can you observe about the data from the histogram?

c. Construct a frequency polygon and an ogive from the frequency distribution created in b and note any information gleaned from these graphs.

2.35 A northwestern distribution company surveyed 53 of its midlevel managers. The survey obtained the ages of these managers, which later were organized into the frequency distribution shown. Determine the class midpoint, relative frequency, and cumulative frequency for these data.

Class Interval	Frequency
20–under 25	8
25–under 30	6
30–under 35	5
35–under 40	12
40–under 45	15
45–under 50	7

2.36 Suppose 1000 commuters in New York City submit their typical daily commute time to a transportation research company who then organizes the data into the histogram shown below. Study the histogram and comment on information gleaned from the graph. Describe commuter times in New York City based on what you see here.

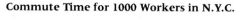

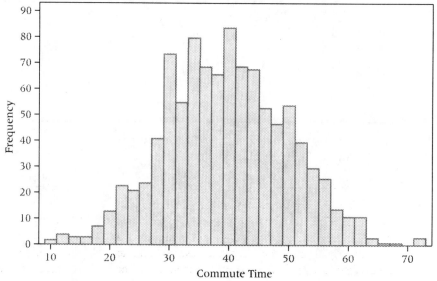

2.37 The following data are shaped roughly like a normal distribution (discussed in Chapter 6).

61.4	27.3	26.4	37.4	30.4	47.5
63.9	46.8	67.9	19.1	81.6	47.9
73.4	54.6	65.1	53.3	71.6	58.6
57.3	87.8	71.1	74.1	48.9	60.2
54.8	60.5	32.5	61.7	55.1	48.2
56.8	60.1	52.9	60.5	55.6	38.1
76.4	46.8	19.9	27.3	77.4	58.1
32.1	54.9	32.7	40.1	52.7	32.5
35.3	39.1				

Construct a frequency distribution starting with 10 as the lowest class beginning point and use a class width of 10. Construct a histogram and a frequency polygon for this frequency distribution and observe the shape of a normal distribution. On the basis of your results from these graphs, what does a normal distribution look like?

2.38 In a medium-sized southern city, 86 houses are for sale, each having about 2000 square feet of floor space. The asking prices vary. The frequency distribution shown contains the price categories for the 86 houses. Construct a histogram, a frequency polygon, and an ogive from these data.

Asking Price	Frequency
$ 80,000–under $100,000	21
100,000–under 120,000	27
120,000–under 140,000	18
140,000–under 160,000	11
160,000–under 180,000	6
180,000–under 200,000	3

2.39 Shipping a 40-foot container by boat from Shanghai to Chicago via the port of Los Angeles takes, on average, 16 days. However, due to several possible mitigating circumstances, shipping times can vary. Suppose a transportation researcher randomly selects 20 different shipments over a yearly period and records the number of days that it takes for a container to travel from Shanghai to Chicago. The resulting data in number of days is given below.

25	12	23	16	27	19	32	20	32	13
17	18	26	19	18	28	18	31	30	24

a. Construct a stem-and-leaf plot for the data.
b. Construct a dot plot for the data.
c. Comment on any observations that you glean from these two plots.

2.40 Good, relatively inexpensive prenatal care often can prevent a lifetime of expense owing to complications resulting from a baby's low birth weight. A survey of a random sample of 57 new mothers asked them to estimate how much they spent on prenatal care. The researcher tallied the results and presented them in the frequency distribution shown. Use these data to construct a histogram, a frequency polygon, and an ogive.

Amount Spent on Prenatal Care	Frequency of New Mothers
$ 0–under $100	3
100–under 200	6
200–under 300	12
300–under 400	19
400–under 500	11
500–under 600	6

2.41 A consumer group surveyed food prices at 87 stores on the East Coast. Among the food prices being measured was that of sugar. From the data collected, the group constructed the frequency distribution of the prices of 5 pounds of Domino's sugar in the stores surveyed. Compute a histogram, a frequency polygon, and an ogive for the following data.

Price	Frequency
$1.75–under $1.90	9
1.90–under 2.05	14
2.05–under 2.20	17
2.20–under 2.35	16
2.35–under 2.50	18
2.50–under 2.65	8
2.65–under 2.80	5

2.42 The top music genres according to SoundScan for a recent year are R&B, Alternative (Rock), Rap, and Country. These and other music genres along with the number of albums sold in each (in millions) are shown.

Genre	Albums Sold
R&B	146.4
Alternative	102.6
Rap	73.7
Country	64.5
Soundtrack	56.4
Metal	26.6
Classical	14.8
Latin	14.5

a. Construct a pie chart for these data displaying the percentage of the whole that each of these genres represents.
b. Construct a bar chart for these data.
c. Compare and contrast the displays of the pie chart and the bar chart.

2.43 The following figures for U.S. imports of agricultural products and manufactured goods were taken from selected years over a 30-year period (in $ billions). The source of the data is the U.S. International Trade

Administration. Construct a scatter plot for these data and determine whether any relationship is apparent between the U.S. imports of agricultural products and the U.S. imports of manufactured goods during this time period.

Agricultural Products	Manufactured Goods
5.8	27.3
9.5	54.0
17.4	133.0
19.5	257.5
22.3	388.8
29.3	629.7

2.44 Shown here is a list of the industries with the largest total release of toxic chemicals in a recent year according to the U.S. Environmental Protection Agency. Construct both a bar chart and a pie chart to depict this information and comment on the advantages of each type of chart in depicting these data.

Industry	Total Release (pounds)
Chemicals	737,100,000
Primary metals	566,400,000
Paper	229,900,000
Plastics and rubber	109,700,000
Transportation equipment	102,500,000
Food	89,300,000
Fabricated metals	85,900,000
Petroleum	63,300,000
Electrical equipment	29,100,000

2.45 A manufacturing company produces plastic bottles for the dairy industry. Some of the bottles are rejected because of poor quality. Causes of poor-quality bottles include faulty plastic, incorrect labeling, discoloration, incorrect thickness, broken handle, and others. The following data for 500 plastic bottles that were rejected include the problems and the frequency of the problems. Use these data to construct a Pareto chart. Discuss the implications of the chart.

Problem	Number
Discoloration	32
Thickness	117
Broken handle	86
Fault in plastic	221
Labeling	44

2.46 A research organization selected 50 U.S. towns with Census 2010 populations between 4000 and 6000 as a sample to represent small towns for survey purposes. The populations of these towns follow.

4420	5221	4299	5831	5750
5049	5556	4361	5737	4654
4653	5338	4512	4388	5923
4730	4963	5090	4822	4304
4758	5366	5431	5291	5254
4866	5858	4346	4734	5919
4216	4328	4459	5832	5873
5257	5048	4232	4878	5166
5366	4212	5669	4224	4440
4299	5263	4339	4834	5478

Construct a stem-and-leaf plot for the data, letting each leaf contain two digits.

INTERPRETING THE OUTPUT

2.47 Suppose 150 shoppers at an upscale mall are interviewed and one of the questions asked is the household income. Study the Minitab histogram of the following data and discuss what can be learned about the shoppers.

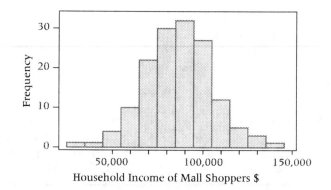

2.48 Study the following dot plot and comment on the general shape of the distribution. Discuss any gaps or heavy concentrations in the data.

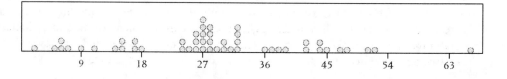

2.49 Shown here is an Excel-produced pie chart representing physician specialties. What does the chart tell you about the various specialties?

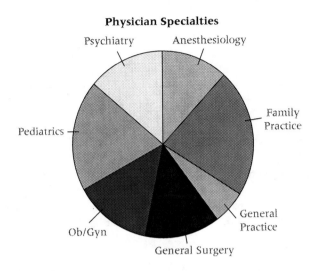

Physician Specialties

2.50 Suppose 100 CPA firms are surveyed to determine how many audits they perform over a certain time. The data are summarized using the Minitab stem-and-leaf plot shown in the next column. What can you learn about the number of audits being performed by these firms from this plot?

Stem-and-Leaf Display: Audits

Stem-and-leaf of Audits		N = 100

Leaf Unit = 1.0

9	1	222333333
16	1	4445555
26	1	6666667777
35	1	888899999
39	2	0001
44	2	22333
49	2	55555
(9)	2	677777777
42	2	8888899
35	3	000111
29	3	223333
23	3	44455555
15	3	67777
10	3	889
7	4	0011
3	4	222

2.51 Shown below is a scatter plot of the NASDAQ–100 Index versus the Dow Jones Industrial Average on Friday closings over a period of one year (May 1, 2009, to April 23, 2010). What does the graph tell you about the relationship of the NASDAQ-100 Index to the DJIA? Explain what you observe in the graph and share any conclusions that you reach.

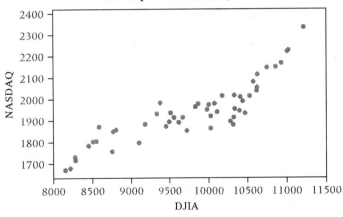

Scatter plot of NASDAQ vs. DJIA

see www.wiley.com/college/black

ANALYZING THE DATABASES

Database

1. Using the manufacturer database, construct a frequency distribution for the variable Number of Production Workers. What does the frequency distribution reveal about the number of production workers?

2. Using the Consumer Food database, construct a histogram for the variable Annual Food Spending. How is the histogram shaped? Is it high in the middle or high near one or both ends of the data? Is it relatively constant in size across the class (uniform), or does it appear to have no shape? Does it appear to be nearly "normally" distributed?

3. Construct an ogive for the variable Type in the financial database. The 100 companies in this database are each categorized into one of seven types of companies. These types are listed at the end of Chapter 1. Construct a pie chart of these types and discuss the output. For example, which type is most prevalent in the database and which is the least?

4. Using the international unemployment database, construct a stem-and-leaf plot for Italy. What does the plot show about unemployment for Italy over the past 40 years? What does the plot fail to show?

CASE

SOAP COMPANIES DO BATTLE

Procter & Gamble has been the leading soap manufacturer in the United States since 1879, when it introduced Ivory soap. However, late in 1991, its major rival, Lever Bros. (Unilever), overtook it by grabbing 31.5% of the $1.6 billion personal soap market, of which Procter & Gamble had a 30.5% share. Lever Bros. had trailed Procter & Gamble since it entered the soap market with Lifebuoy in 1895. In 1990, Lever Bros. introduced a new soap, Lever 2000, into its product mix as a soap for the entire family. A niche for such a soap had been created because of the segmentation of the soap market into specialty soaps for children, women, and men. Lever Bros. felt that it could sell a soap for everyone in the family. Consumer response was strong; Lever 2000 rolled up $113 million in sales in 1991, putting Lever Bros. ahead of Procter & Gamble for the first time in the personal-soap revenue contest. Procter & Gamble still sells more soap, but Lever's brands cost more, thereby resulting in greater overall sales.

Needless to say, Procter & Gamble was quick to search for a response to the success of Lever 2000. Procter & Gamble looked at several possible strategies, including repositioning Safeguard, which has been seen as a male soap. Ultimately, Procter & Gamble responded to the challenge by introducing its Oil of Olay Moisturizing Bath Bar. In its first year of national distribution, this product was backed by a $24 million media effort. The new bath bar was quite successful and helped Procter & Gamble regain market share.

These two major companies continue to battle it out for domination in the personal soap market, along with the Dial Corporation (a subsidiary of Henkel, AG) and Colgate-Palmolive. While liquid soaps have made great strides in the marketplace in the past few years, bar soaps are still popular, particularly among men. Shown below are the year 2009 sales figures for both deodorant and nondeodorant bar soaps at supermarkets, drug stores, and mass merchandisers, excluding Wal-Mart in the United States.

Soap	Manufacturer	Sales ($ millions)
Dial (all brands)	Dial	73.4
Dove (all brands)	Unilever	57.7
Irish Spring	Colgate Palmolive	49.2
Lever 2000	Unilever	35.7
Ivory	Proctor & Gamble	7.8
Caress	Unilever	4.6
Olay	Proctor & Gamble	4.3
Zest	Proctor & Gamble	3.1
Others		120.4

In 1983, the market shares for soap were Procter & Gamble with 37.1%, Lever Bros. (Unilever) with 24%, Dial with 15%, Colgate-Palmolive with 6.5%, and all others with 17.4%. By 1991, the market shares for soap were Lever Bros. (Unilever) with 31.5%, Procter & Gamble with 30.5%, Dial with 19%, Colgate-Palmolive with 8%, and all others with 11%.

Discussion

1. Suppose you are making a report for Procter & Gamble displaying their share of the market along with the share of other companies for the years 1983, 1991, and the latest figures. Using either Excel or Minitab, produce graphs for the market shares of personal soap for each of these years. What do you observe about the market shares of the various companies by studying the graphs? In particular, how is Procter & Gamble doing relative to previous years?

2. Suppose Procter & Gamble sells about 20 million bars of soap per week, but the demand is not constant and production management would like to get a better handle on how sales are distributed over the year. Let the following sales figures given in units of million bars represent the sales of bars per week over one year. Construct a histogram to represent these data. What do you see in the graph that might be helpful to the production (and sales) people?

17.1	19.6	15.4	17.4	15.0	18.5	20.6	18.4
20.0	20.9	19.3	18.2	14.7	17.1	12.2	19.9
18.7	20.4	20.3	15.5	16.8	19.1	20.4	15.4
20.3	17.5	17.0	18.3	13.6	39.8	20.7	21.3
22.5	21.4	23.4	23.1	22.8	21.4	24.0	25.2
26.3	23.9	30.6	25.2	26.2	26.9	32.8	26.3
26.6	24.3	26.2	23.8				

Construct a stem-and-leaf plot using the whole numbers as the stems. What advantages does the stem-and-leaf plot of these sales figures offer over the histogram? What are some disadvantages? Which would you use in discussions with production people, and why?

3. A random sample of finished soap bars in their packaging is tested for quality. All defective bars are examined for problem causes. Among the problems found were improper packaging, poor labeling, bad seal, shape of bar wrong, bar surface marred, wrong color in bar, wrong bar fragrance, wrong soap consistency, and others. Some of the leading problem causes and the number of each are given here. Use a Pareto chart to analyze these problem

causes. Based on your findings, what would you recommend to the company?

Problem Cause	Frequency
Bar surface	89
Color	17
Fragrance	2
Label	32
Shape	8
Seal	47
Labeling	5
Soap consistency	3

Source: Adapted from Valerie Reitman, "Buoyant Sales of Lever 2000 Soap Bring Sinking Sensation to Procter & Gamble," *The Wall Street Journal*, March 19, 1992, p. B1. Reprinted by permission of *The Wall Street Journal* © 1992, Dow Jones & Company, Inc. All rights reserved worldwide; Pam Weisz, "$40 M Extends Lever 2000 Family," *Brandweek*, vol. 36, no. 32 (August 21, 1995), p. 6; Laurie Freeman, "P&G Pushes Back Against Unilever in Soap," *Advertising Age*, vol. 65, no. 41 (September 28, 1994), p. 21; Jeanne Whalen and Pat Sloan, "Intros Help Boost Soap Coupons," *Advertising Age*, vol. 65, no. 19 (May 2, 1994), p. 30; and "P&G Places Coast Soap up for Sale," *The Post*, World Wide Web Edition of *The Cincinnati Post*, February 2, 1999, http://www.cincypost.com.business/pg022599.html; Robert S. Lazich, Editor, *Market Share Reporter, Volume 1*. Detroit: Gale Cengage Learning, 2011, pp. 299–300.

USING THE COMPUTER

EXCEL

- Excel offers the capability of producing many of the charts and graphs presented in this chapter. Most of these can be accessed by clicking on the **Insert** tab found along the top of an Excel worksheet (second tab from the left next to **Home**). In addition, Excel can generate frequency distributions and histograms using the **Data Analysis** feature.

- Many of the statistical techniques presented in this text can be performed in Excel using a tool called **Data Analysis**. To access this feature, select the **Data** tab along the top of an Excel worksheet. The **Data** tab is the fifth tab over from the left. If the **Data Analysis** feature has been uploaded into your Excel package, it will be found in the **Analysis** section at the top right of the **Data** tab page on the far right. If **Data Analysis** does not appear in the **Analysis** section, it must be added in. To add in **Data Analysis**: 1.) Click on the **File** tab (leftmost tab at top of page). 2.) Now click on **options** located in the menu on the left next to the bottom. 3.) In the **Excel options** dialog box, click on **Add-Ins** next to the bottom of the left menu. A screen of add-ins will appear. 4.) Click on **Analysis ToolPak** near the top of the dialog box and then click on **Go…** at the bottom of the page. 5.) In the dialog box **Add Ins**, check the box to the left of **Analysis ToolPak** and click **OK**. Your **Data Analysis** feature is now uploaded onto your computer, and you need not add it in again. Now you can bring up the **Analysis ToolPak** feature at any time by going to the **Data** tab at the top of the Excel worksheet and clicking on **Data Analysis**.

- In Excel, frequency distributions are referred to as histograms, and the classes of a frequency distribution are referred to as bins. If you do not specify bins (classes), Excel will automatically determine the number of bins and assign class endpoints based on a formula. If you want to specify bins, load the class endpoints that you want to use into a column. To construct a frequency distribution, select the **Data** tab in the Excel worksheet and then select the **Data Analysis** feature (upper right). If this feature does not appear, you may need to add it (see above). Clicking on **Data Analysis**, the dialog box features a pulldown menu of many of the statistical analysis tools presented and used in this text. From this list, select **Histogram**. In the **Histogram** dialog box, place the location of the raw data values in the space beside **Input Range**. Place the location of the class endpoints (optional) in the space beside **Bin Range**. Leave this blank if you want Excel to determine the bins (classes). If you have labels, check **Labels**. If you want a histogram graph, check **Chart Output**. If you want an ogive, select **Cumulative Percentage** along with **Chart Output**. If you opt for this, Excel will yield a histogram graph with an ogive overlaid on it.

- Excel has excellent capability of constructing many different types of charts, including column charts, line charts, pie charts, bar charts, area charts, and XY (scatter) charts. To begin the process of producing these charts, select the **Insert** tab from the top of the Excel worksheet. In the **Charts** section, which is the middle section shown at the top of the **Insert** worksheet, there are icons for column, line, pie, bar, area, scatter, and other charts. Click on the icon representing the desired chart to begin construction. Each of these types of charts allow for several versions of the chart shown in the dropdown menu. For example, the pie chart menu contains four types of two-dimensional pie charts and two types of three-dimensional pie charts. To select a particular version of a type of chart, click on the type of chart and then the version of that chart that is desired.

- To construct a pie chart, enter the categories in one column and the data values of each category in another column in the Excel worksheet. Categories and data values could also be entered in rows instead of columns. Click and drag over the data for which the pie chart is to be constructed. From the **Insert** tab, select **Pie** from the **Charts** section and the select the type of pie chart to be constructed. The result is a pie chart from the data. Once the chart has been constructed, a set of three new tabs appear at the top of the worksheet under the general area of **Chart Tools** (see top upper right corner of worksheet). The three new tabs are **Design**, **Layout**, and **Format**. There are many options available for changing the design of the pie chart that can be accessed by clicking on the up and down arrow on the right end of the **Design** tab in the section called **Chart Styles**. On the far right end of the **Design** menu bar is a feature called **Move Chart Location**, which can be used to move the chart to another location or to a new sheet. On the far left end of the **Design** menu bar, there is a **Change Chart Type** feature that allows for changing the type of chart that has been constructed. The second group of features from the left at the top of the **Design** menu bar makes it possible to switch to another set of data (**Select Data**) or switch rows and columns (**Switch Row/Column**). There is a useful feature in the middle of the Design menu bar called **Chart Layouts** that offers several different layouts for the given chart type. For example, for pie charts, there are seven different possible layouts using titles, labels, and legends in different ways. Right-clicking on the pie chart brings up a menu that includes **Add Data Labels** and **Format Data Series…** Clicking on **Add Data Labels** adds data labels to your pie chart. If you then right-click on the pie chart, another menu opens up, and one of the features in this menu is **Format Data Labels…** Clicking on this feature brings up another menu that allows you to modify or edit various features of your graph, including **Label Options, Number, Fill, Border Color, Shadow, Glow and Soft Edges, 3-D Format,** and **Alignment.** Under **Label Options**, there are several different types of labels for pie charts and there are other various chart options available, such as **Series Name, Category Name, Value, Percentage,** and **Show Leader Lines**. In addition, it offers various options for the label location, such as **Center, Inside End, Outside End,** and **Best Fit**. It also offers the opportunity to include the legend key in the label. The **Number** option under **Format Data Labels…** allows for the usual Excel options in using numbers. The **Fill** option allows you to determine what type of fill you want to have for the chart. Options include **No fill, Solid fill, Gradient fill, Picture or texture fill,** and **Automatic**. Other options under **Format Data Labels…** allow you to manipulate the border colors and styles, shadow, Soft and Glow Edges, and 3-D format, and text alignment or layout. The **Layout** tab at the top of the worksheet page has a **Labels** panel located at the top of the worksheet page just to the left of the center. In this section, you can further specify the location of the chart title by selecting **Chart Title**, the location of the legend by selecting **Legend**, or the location of the labels by selecting **Data Labels**. The **Format** tab at the top of the worksheet page contains a **Shape Styles** panel just to the left of center at the top of the worksheet. This panel contains options for visual styles of the graph (for more options, use the up and down arrow) and options for **Shape Fill, Shape Outline,** and **Shape Effects**. Other formatting options are available through the use of the **Format Selection** option on the far upper left of the **Current Selection** panel on the **Format** tab page.

▨ Frequency polygons can be constructed in Excel 2010 by using the **Histogram** feature. Follow the directions shown above to construct a histogram. Once the histogram is constructed, right-click on one of the "bars" of the histogram. From the dropdown menu, select **Change Series Chart Type**. Next select a line chart type. The result will be a frequency polygon.

▨ An ogive can be constructed at least two ways. One way is to cumulate the data manually. Enter the cumulated data in one column and the class endpoints in another column. Click and drag over both columns. Go to the **Insert** tab at the top of the Excel worksheet. Select **Scatter** as the type of chart. Under the **Scatter** options, select the option with the solid lines. The result is an ogive. A second way is to construct a frequency distribution first using the **Histogram** feature in the **Data Analysis** tool. In the **Histogram** dialog box, enter the location of the data and enter the location of the class endpoints as bin numbers. Check **Cumulative Percentage** and **Chart Output** in the **Histogram** dialog box. Once the chart is constructed, right-click on one of the bars and select the **Delete** option. The result will be an ogive chart with just the ogive line graph (and bars eliminated).

▨ Bar charts and column charts are constructed in a manner similar to that of a pie chart. Begin by entering the categories in one column and the data values of each category in another column in the Excel worksheet. Categories and data values could also be entered in rows instead of columns. Click and drag over the data and categories for which the chart is to be constructed. Go to the **Insert** tab at the top of the worksheet. Select **Column** or **Bar** from the **Charts** section and the select the version of the chart to be constructed. The result is a chart from the data. Once the bar chart or column chart has been constructed, there are many options available to you. By right-clicking on the bars or columns, a menu appears that allows you, among other things, to label the columns or bars. This command is **Add Data Labels**. Once data labels are added, clicking on the bars or columns will allow you to modify the labels and the characteristics of the bars or columns by selecting **Format Data Labels…** or **Format Data Series…** Usage of these commands is the same as when constructing or modifying pie charts (see above). Various options are also available under **Chart Tools** (see pie charts above).

▨ Pareto charts, as presented in the text, have categories and numbers of defects. As such, Pareto charts can be constructed as **Column** charts in Excel using the same commands (see above). However, the user will first need to order the categories and their associated frequencies in descending order. In addition, in constructing a histogram in Excel (see above), there is an option in the **Histogram** dialog box called **Pareto (sorted histogram)** in which Excel takes histogram data and presents the data with categories organized from highest frequency to lowest. However, to do this, you must also check **Chart Output** in the Histogram dialog box.

▨ Scatter diagrams can be constructed in Excel. Begin by entering the data for the two variables to be graphed in two separate rows or columns. You may either use a label for each variable or not. Click and drag over the data (and labels). Go to the **Insert** tab. From the **Charts** panel (upper middle), select **Scatter**. From the ensuing pulldown menu of scatter plot options, select one of the versions from the five presented. The result is the scatter chart. By right-clicking on the chart, various other chart options are available including, **Format Plot Area....** The resulting menu associated with this command offers the usual chart options regarding fill, border color, border styles, shadow, Glow and Soft Edges, and 3-D format (see pie charts above). In addition, if you want to fit a line or curve to the data, right-click on one of the chart points. A menu pops up containing, among other options, **Add Trendline....** From the **Trendline Options**, select the type of line or curve that you want to fit to the data. The result is a line or curve shown on the scatter plot attempting to fit to the points. Various other options are available regarding the line color, style, and shadow.

MINITAB

▨ Minitab has the capability of constructing histograms, dot plots, stem-and-leaf charts, pie charts, bar charts, and Pareto charts. With the exception of Pareto charts, which are accessed through **Stat**, all of these other charts and graphs are accessed by selecting **Graph** on the menu bar.

▨ To construct a histogram, select **Graph** on the Minitab menu bar, and then select **Histogram.** The first dialog box offers four histogram options: **Simple, With Fit, With Outline and Groups**, and **With Fit and Groups.** Select the **Simple** option, which is also the default option. In the dialog box that follows beside **Graph variables**, insert the column location (or columns) containing the data for which you want to create a histogram. There are several options from which to modify the histogram. Select **Scale** to adjust or modify the axes, ticks, and gridlines. Select **Labels** to title the graph and label the axes. Select **Data view** for optional ways to present the data, including bars, symbols, project lines, and areas in addition to presenting other options such as smoothing the data. Select **Multiple graphs** to create multiple separate graphs or to combine several graphs on one. Select **Data options** for several options in grouping data.

▨ To construct a dot plot, select **Graph** on the Minitab menu bar, and then select **Dotplot.** The first dialog box offers seven different ways to configure the plot. Select **Simple** to produce a dot plot like those shown in this chapter. In the dialog box that follows, insert the column location(s) containing the data for which you want to create the dot plot in **Graph variables.** There are several options available. Select **Scale** to adjust or modify the axes and ticks. Select **Labels** to title the graph and add footnotes. Select **Multiple graphs** to create multiple separate graphs or to combine several graphs on one. Select **Data options** for options in grouping data, frequencies, and subsets.

▨ To construct a stem-and-leaf chart, select **Stem-and-Leaf** from the **Graph** pulldown menu. In the **Stem-and-Leaf** dialog box, place the name of the column(s) containing the data in the **Graph variables** space. Click **OK** and the stem-and-leaf plot is generated. If you have a grouping variable in another column and want to use it, enter the location or

name of the column into the **By variable** space. You can trim outliers from the plot by checking **Trim outliers.**

▨ To construct a pie chart, select **Graph** on the Minitab menu bar, and then select **PieChart** on the **Graph** pulldown menu. In the **Pie Chart** dialog box, there are two options to consider: **Chart counts of unique values** and **Chart values from a table.** If you have raw data and you want Minitab to group them for you into a pie chart, select **Chart counts of unique values.** You can also use this command even if you have text data. On the other hand, if your data are in one column and your categories are in another column, select **Chart values from a table.** The dialog box will ask for the name of the **Categorical variable** and the name of the **Summary variables.** Several options are available to modify the pie chart, including **Labels, Multiple graphs**, and **Data options.** Several **Pie Options** are available, including how the pie slices are ordered, the starting angle, and the option of combining small categories.

▨ To construct a bar chart, select **Graph** on the Minitab menu bar, then select **Bar Chart.** In the **Bar Chart** dialog box, there are three options available. To construct a bar chart like those presented in the chapter, select **Simple.** In the dialog box that follows, enter the column(s) containing the data in **Categorical variables.** Several options are available to modify the bar chart, including **Chart Options, Labels, Scale, Data View, Multiple Graphs**, and **Data Options.**

▨ To construct a Pareto chart, select **Stat** from the menu bar, and then from the pulldown menu that appears, select **Quality Tools.** From the **Quality Tools** pulldown menu, select **Pareto Chart.** From the **Pareto Chart** dialog box, select **Chart defects table** if you have a summary of the defects with the reasons (**Labels in**) in one column and the frequency of occurrence (**Frequencies in**) in another column. Enter the location of the reasons in **Labels in** and the location of the frequencies in **Frequencies in.** If you have unsummarized data, you can select **Chart defects data in.** In the space provided, give the location of the column with all the defects that occurred. It is possible to have the defects either by name or with some code. If you want to have the labels in one column and the defects in another, then select **By variable in** and place the location of the labels there.

▨ To construct a scatter plot, select **Graph**, then select **Scatterplot.** In the **Scatterplot** dialog box, select the type of scatter plot you want from **Simple, With Groups, With Regression, With Regression and Groups, With Connect Line**, and **With Connect and Groups.** In the second dialog box, enter the x and y variable names/locations. There are several options from which to modify the scatter plot. Select **Scale** to adjust or modify the axes, ticks, and gridlines. Select **Labels** to title the graph and label the axes. Select **Data view** for optional ways to present the data, including bars, symbols, project lines, and areas in addition to presenting other options such as smoothing the data. Select **Multiple graphs** to create multiple separate graphs or to combine several graphs on one. Select **Data options** for several options in grouping data.

Descriptive Statistics

LEARNING OBJECTIVES

The focus of Chapter 3 is the use of statistical techniques to describe data, thereby enabling you to:

1. Apply various measures of central tendency—including the mean, median, and mode—to a set of ungrouped data

2. Apply various measures of variability—including the range, interquartile range, mean absolute deviation, variance, and standard deviation (using the empirical rule and Chebyshev's theorem)—to a set of ungrouped data

3. Compute the mean, median, mode, standard deviation, and variance of grouped data

4. Describe a data distribution statistically and graphically using skewness, kurtosis, and box-and-whisker plots

5. Use computer packages to compute various measures of central tendency, variation, and shape on a set of data, as well as to describe the data distribution graphically

Emmanuel Faure/Digital Vision/Getty Images

Laundry Statistics

According to Procter & Gamble, 35 billion loads of laundry are run in the United States each year. Every second 1,100 loads are started. Statistics show that one person in the United States generates a quarter of a ton of dirty clothing each year. Americans appear to be spending more time doing laundry than they did 40 years ago. Today, the average American woman spends seven to nine hours a week on laundry. However, industry research shows that the result is dirtier laundry than in other developed countries. Various companies market new and improved versions of washers and detergents. Yet, Americans seem to be resistant to manufacturers' innovations in this area. In the United States, the average washing machine uses about 16 gallons of water. In Europe, the figure is about 4 gallons. The average wash cycle of an American wash is about 35 minutes compared to 90 minutes in Europe. Americans prefer top loading machines because they do not have to bend over, and the top loading machines are larger. Europeans use the smaller front-loading machines because of smaller living spaces.

Managerial and Statistical Questions

Virtually all of the statistics cited here are gleaned from studies or surveys.

1. Suppose a study of laundry usage is done in 50 U.S. households that contain washers and dryers. Water measurements are taken for the number of gallons of water used by each washing machine in completing a cycle. The following data are the number of gallons used by each washing machine during the washing cycle. Summarize the data so that study findings can be reported.

15	17	16	15	16	17	18	15	14	15
16	16	17	16	15	15	17	14	15	16
16	17	14	15	12	15	16	14	14	16
15	13	16	17	17	15	16	16	16	14
17	16	17	14	16	13	16	15	16	15

2. The average wash cycle for an American wash is 35 minutes. Suppose the standard deviation of a wash cycle for an American wash is 5 minutes. Within what range of time do most American wash cycles fall?

Source: Adapted from Emily Nelson, "In Doing Laundry, Americans Cling to Outmoded Ways," *The Wall Street Journal*, May 16, 2002, pp. A1 & A10.

Chapter 2 presented graphical techniques for organizing and displaying data. Even though such graphical techniques allow the researcher to make some general observations about the shape and spread of the data, a more complete understanding of the data can be attained by summarizing the data using statistics. This chapter presents such statistical measures, including measures of central tendency, measures of variability, and measures of shape. The computation of these measures is different for ungrouped and grouped data. Hence we present some measures for both ungrouped and grouped data.

3.1 MEASURES OF CENTRAL TENDENCY: UNGROUPED DATA

Interactive Applet

One type of measure that is used to describe a set of data is the **measure of central tendency**. Measures of central tendency *yield information about the center, or middle part, of a group of numbers.* Table 3.1 displays offer price for the 20 largest U.S. initial public offerings in a recent year according to Securities Data. For these data, measures of central tendency can yield such information as the average offer price, the middle offer price, and the most frequently occurring offer price. Measures of central tendency do not focus on the span of the data set or how far values are from the middle numbers. The measures of central tendency presented here for ungrouped data are the mode, the median, the mean, percentiles, and quartiles.

TABLE 3.1			
Offer Prices for the 20 Largest U.S. Initial Public Offerings in a Recent Year			
$14.25	$19.00	$11.00	$28.00
24.00	23.00	43.25	19.00
27.00	25.00	15.00	7.00
34.22	15.50	15.00	22.00
19.00	19.00	27.00	21.00

Mode

The **mode** is *the most frequently occurring value in a set of data.* For the data in Table 3.1 the mode is $19.00 because the offer price that recurred the most times (four) was $19.00. Organizing the data into an ordered array (an ordering of the numbers from smallest to largest) helps to locate the mode. The following is an ordered array of the values from Table 3.1.

7.00	11.00	14.25	15.00	15.00	15.50	19.00	19.00	19.00	19.00
21.00	22.00	23.00	24.00	25.00	27.00	27.00	28.00	34.22	43.25

This grouping makes it easier to see that 19.00 is the most frequently occurring number.

In the case of a tie for the most frequently occurring value, two modes are listed. Then the data are said to be **bimodal**. If a set of data is not exactly bimodal but contains two values that are more dominant than others, some researchers take the liberty of referring to the data set as bimodal even without an exact tie for the mode. Data sets with more than two modes are referred to as **multimodal**.

In the world of business, the concept of mode is often used in determining sizes. As an example, manufacturers who produce cheap rubber flip-flops that are sold for as little as $1.00 around the world might only produce them in one size in order to save on machine setup costs. In determining the one size to produce, the manufacturer would most likely produce flip-flops in the modal size. The mode is an appropriate measure of central tendency for nominal-level data.

Median

The **median** is *the middle value in an ordered array of numbers.* For an array with an odd number of terms, the median is the middle number. For an array with an even number of terms, the median is the average of the two middle numbers. The following steps are used to determine the median.

STEP 1. Arrange the observations in an ordered data array.

STEP 2. For an odd number of terms, find the middle term of the ordered array. It is the median.

STEP 3. For an even number of terms, find the average of the middle two terms. This average is the median.

Suppose a business researcher wants to determine the median for the following numbers.

15   11   14   3   21   17   22   16   19   16   5   7   19   8   9   20   4

The researcher arranges the numbers in an ordered array.

3   4   5   7   8   9   11   14   15   16   16   17   19   19   20   21   22

Because the array contains 17 terms (an odd number of terms), the median is the middle number, or 15.

If the number 22 is eliminated from the list, the array would contain only 16 terms.

3   4   5   7   8   9   11   14   15   16   16   17   19   19   20   21

Now, for an even number of terms, the statistician determines the median by averaging the two middle values, 14 and 15. The resulting median value is 14.5.

Another way to locate the median is by finding the $(n + 1)/2$ term in an ordered array. For example, if a data set contains 77 terms, the median is the 39th term. That is,

$$\frac{n + 1}{2} = \frac{77 + 1}{2} = \frac{78}{2} = 39\text{th term}$$

This formula is helpful when a large number of terms must be manipulated.

Consider the offer price data in Table 3.1. Because this data set contains 20 values, or $n = 20$, the median for these data is located at the $(20 + 1)/2$ term, or the 10.5th term. This equation indicates that the median is located halfway between the 10th and 11th terms or the average of 19.00 and 21.00. Thus, the median offer price for the largest 20 U.S. initial public offerings is $20.00.

The median is unaffected by the magnitude of extreme values. This characteristic is an advantage, because large and small values do not inordinately influence the median. For this reason, the median is often the best measure of location to use in the analysis of variables such as house costs, income, and age. Suppose, for example, that a real estate broker wants to determine the median selling price of 10 houses listed at the following prices.

$67,000	$105,000	$148,000	$5,250,000
91,000	116,000	167,000	
95,000	122,000	189,000	

The median is the average of the two middle terms, $116,000 and $122,000, or $119,000. This price is a reasonable representation of the prices of the 10 houses. Note that the house priced at $5,250,000 did not enter into the analysis other than to count as one of the 10 houses. If the price of the tenth house were $200,000, the results would be the same. However, if all the house prices were averaged, the resulting average price of the original 10 houses would be $635,000, higher than 9 of the 10 individual prices.

A disadvantage of the median is that not all the information from the numbers is used. For example, information about the specific asking price of the most expensive house does not really enter into the computation of the median. The level of data measurement must be at least ordinal for a median to be meaningful.

Mean

The **arithmetic mean** is *the average of a group of numbers* and is computed by summing all numbers and dividing by the number of numbers. Because the arithmetic mean is so widely used, most statisticians refer to it simply as the *mean.*

The population mean is represented by the Greek letter mu (μ). The sample mean is represented by $\bar{x}$. The formulas for computing the population mean and the sample mean are given in the boxes that follow.

POPULATION MEAN	$\mu = \dfrac{\Sigma x_i}{N} = \dfrac{x_1 + x_2 + x_3 + \cdots + x_N}{N}$

SAMPLE MEAN	$\bar{x} = \dfrac{\Sigma x_i}{n} = \dfrac{x_1 + x_2 + x_3 + \cdots + x_n}{n}$

The capital Greek letter sigma (Σ) is commonly used in mathematics to represent a summation of all the numbers in a grouping.* Also, N is the number of terms in the population, and n is the number of terms in the sample. The algorithm for computing a mean is to sum all the numbers in the population or sample and divide by the number of terms. It is inappropriate to use the mean to analyze data that are not at least interval level in measurement.

Suppose a company has five departments with 24, 13, 19, 26, and 11 workers each. The *population mean* number of workers in each department is 18.6 workers. The computations follow.

$$
\begin{array}{r}
24 \\
13 \\
19 \\
26 \\
\underline{11} \\
\Sigma x_i = 93
\end{array}
$$

*The mathematics of summations is not discussed here. A more detailed explanation is given in WileyPLUS, Chapter 3.

and

$$\mu = \frac{\Sigma x_i}{N} = \frac{93}{5} = 18.6$$

The calculation of a sample mean uses the same algorithm as for a population mean and will produce the same answer if computed on the same data. However, it is inappropriate to compute a sample mean for a population or a population mean for a sample. Because both populations and samples are important in statistics, a separate symbol is necessary for the population mean and for the sample mean.

DEMONSTRATION PROBLEM 3.1

Shown below is a list of the 11 largest motor vehicle producers in the world and the number of vehicles produced by each in 2009 according to the OICA (Organisation Internationale des Constructeurs d'Automobiles).[1]

Auto Manufacturer	Production (millions)
Toyota	7.2
General Motors	6.5
Volkswagen Group	6.1
Ford	4.7
Hyundai	4.6
PSA Peugeot Citroën	3.0
Honda	3.0
Nissan	2.7
Fiat	2.5
Suzuki	2.4
Renault	2.3

[1] *Source:* http//oica.net/wp-content/uploads/ranking-2009.pdf.

Solution

Mode: There are two companies that produce 3.0 (million) which is the mode.

Median: With 11 different companies in this group, $N = 11$. The median is located at the $(11 + 1)/2 = $ 6th position. Because the data are already ordered, the 6th term is 3.0 (million) which is the median.

Mean: The total number of vehicles produced by these 11 companies is $45 = \Sigma x_i$

$$\mu = \frac{\Sigma x_i}{N} = \frac{45}{11} = 4.1$$

The mean is affected by each and every value, which is an advantage. The mean uses all the data, and each data item influences the mean. It is also a disadvantage because extremely large or small values can cause the mean to be pulled toward the extreme value. Recall the preceding discussion of the 10 house prices. If the mean is computed for the 10 houses, the mean price is higher than the prices of 9 of the houses because the $5,250,000 house is included in the calculation. The total price of the 10 houses is $6,350,000, and the mean price is $635,000.

The mean is the most commonly used measure of central tendency because it uses each data item in its computation, it is a familiar measure, and it has mathematical properties that make it attractive to use in inferential statistics analysis.

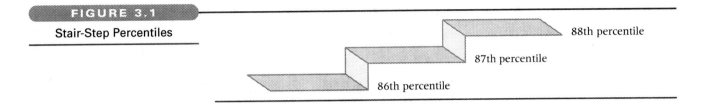

FIGURE 3.1

Stair-Step Percentiles

88th percentile

87th percentile

86th percentile

Percentiles

Percentiles are *measures of central tendency that divide a group of data into 100 parts.* There are 99 percentiles because it takes 99 dividers to separate a group of data into 100 parts. The *n*th percentile is the value such that at least *n* percent of the data are below that value and at most $(100 - n)$ percent are above that value. Specifically, the 87th percentile is a value such that at least 87% of the data are below the value and no more than 13% are above the value. Percentiles are "stair-step" values, as shown in Figure 3.1, because there is no percentile between the 87th percentile and the 88th percentile. If a plant operator takes a safety examination and 87.6% of the safety exam scores are below that person's score, he or she still scores at only the 87th percentile, even though more than 87% of the scores are lower.

Percentiles are widely used in reporting test results. Almost all college or university students have taken the SAT, ACT, GRE, or GMAT examination. In most cases, the results for these examinations are reported in percentile form and also as raw scores. Shown next is a summary of the steps used in determining the location of a percentile.

Steps in Determining the Location of a Percentile

1. Organize the numbers into an ascending-order array.
2. Calculate the percentile location (i) by:

$$i = \frac{P}{100}(N)$$

where

P = the percentile of interest
i = percentile location
N = number in the data set

3. Determine the location by either (a) or (b).
   a. If i is a whole number, the Pth percentile is the average of the value at the ith location and the value at the $(i + 1)^{st}$ location.
   b. If i is not a whole number, the Pth percentile value is located at the whole number part of $i + 1$.

For example, suppose you want to determine the 80th percentile of 1240 numbers. P is 80 and N is 1240. First, order the numbers from lowest to highest. Next, calculate the location of the 80th percentile.

$$i = \frac{80}{100}(1240) = 992$$

Because $i = 992$ is a whole number, follow the directions in step 3(a). The 80th percentile is the average of the 992nd number and the 993rd number.

$$P_{80} = \frac{(992\text{nd number} + 993\text{rd number})}{2}$$

DEMONSTRATION PROBLEM 3.2

Determine the 30th percentile of the following eight numbers: 14, 12, 19, 23, 5, 13, 28, 17.

Solution

For these eight numbers, we want to find the value of the 30th percentile, so $N = 8$ and $P = 30$.

First, organize the data into an ascending-order array.

5	12	13	14	17	19	23	28

Next, compute the value of i.

$$i = \frac{30}{100}(8) = 2.4$$

Because i is not a whole number, step 3(b) is used. The value of $i + 1$ is $2.4 + 1$, or 3.4. The whole-number part of 3.4 is 3. The 30th percentile is located at the third value. The third value is 13, so 13 is the 30th percentile. Note that a percentile may or may not be one of the data values.

Quartiles

Quartiles are *measures of central tendency that divide a group of data into four subgroups or parts.* The three quartiles are denoted as Q_1, Q_2, and Q_3. The first quartile, Q_1, separates the first, or lowest, one-fourth of the data from the upper three-fourths and is equal to the 25th percentile. The second quartile, Q_2, separates the second quarter of the data from the third quarter. Q_2 is located at the 50th percentile and equals the median of the data. The third quartile, Q_3, divides the first three-quarters of the data from the last quarter and is equal to the value of the 75th percentile. These three quartiles are shown in Figure 3.2.

Suppose we want to determine the values of Q_1, Q_2, and Q_3 for the following numbers.

106	109	114	116	121	122	125	129

The value of Q_1 is found at the 25th percentile, P_{25}, by:

$$\text{For } N = 8, i = \frac{25}{100}(8) = 2$$

Because i is a whole number, P_{25} is found as the average of the second and third numbers.

$$P_{25} = \frac{(109 + 114)}{2} = 111.5$$

The value of Q_1 is $P_{25} = 111.5$. Notice that one-fourth, or two, of the values (106 and 109) are less than 111.5.

The value of Q_2 is equal to the median. Because the array contains an even number of terms, the median is the average of the two middle terms.

$$Q_2 = \text{median} = \frac{(116 + 121)}{2} = 118.5$$

Notice that exactly half of the terms are less than Q_2 and half are greater than Q_2.

FIGURE 3.2

Quartiles

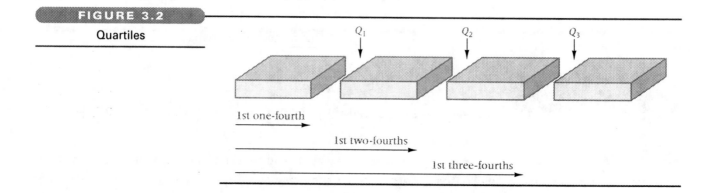

Q_1 Q_2 Q_3

1st one-fourth

1st two-fourths

1st three-fourths

The value of Q_3 is determined by P_{75} as follows.

$$i = \frac{75}{100}(8) = 6$$

Because i is a whole number, P_{75} is the average of the sixth and the seventh numbers.

$$P_{75} = \frac{(122 + 125)}{2} = 123.5$$

The value of Q_3 is $P_{75} = 123.5$. Notice that three-fourths, or six, of the values are less than 123.5 and two of the values are greater than 123.5.

DEMONSTRATION PROBLEM 3.3

The following shows the top 16 global marketing categories for advertising spending for a recent year according to *Advertising Age*. Spending is given in millions of U.S. dollars. Determine the first, the second, and the third quartiles for these data.

Category	Ad Spending
Automotive	$22,195
Personal Care	19,526
Entertainment & Media	9,538
Food	7,793
Drugs	7,707
Electronics	4,023
Soft Drinks	3,916
Retail	3,576
Cleaners	3,571
Restaurants	3,553
Computers	3,247
Telephone	2,488
Financial	2,433
Beer, Wine & Liquor	2,050
Candy	1,137
Toys	699

Solution

For 16 marketing organizations, $N = 16$. $Q_1 = P_{25}$ is found by

$$i = \frac{25}{100}(16) = 4$$

Because i is a whole number, Q_1 is found to be the average of the fourth and fifth values from the bottom.

$$Q_1 = \frac{2433 + 2488}{2} = 2460.5$$

$Q_2 = P_{50} =$ median; with 16 terms, the median is the average of the eighth and ninth terms.

$$Q_2 = \frac{3571 + 3576}{2} = 3573.5$$

$Q_3 = P_{75}$ is solved by

$$i = \frac{75}{100}(16) = 12$$

Q_3 is found by averaging the 12th and 13th terms.

$$Q_3 = \frac{7707 + 7793}{2} = 7750$$

3.1 PROBLEMS

3.1 Determine the median and the mode for the following numbers.

2   4   8   4   6   2   7   8   4   3   8   9   4   3   5

3.2 Determine the median for the following numbers.

213   345   609   073   167   243   444   524   199   682

3.3 Compute the mean for the following numbers.

17.3   44.5   31.6   40.0   52.8   38.8   30.1   78.5

3.4 Compute the mean for the following numbers.

7   −2   5   9   0   −3   −6   −7   −4   −5   2   −8

3.5 Compute the 35th percentile, the 55th percentile, Q_1, Q_2, and Q_3 for the following data.

16   28   29   13   17   20   11   34   32   27   25   30   19   18   33

3.6 Compute P_{20}, P_{47}, P_{83}, Q_1, Q_2, and Q_3 for the following data.

120	138	97	118	172	144
138	107	94	119	139	145
162	127	112	150	143	80
105	116	142	128	116	171

3.7 On a certain day, the average closing price of a group of stocks on the New York Stock Exchange (to the nearest dollar) is shown.

21   21   21   22   23   25   28   29   33   35   38   56   61

What are the mean, the median, and the mode for these data?

3.8 The following list shows the 15 largest banks in the world by assets according to EagleTraders.com. Compute the median and the mean assets from this group. Which of these two measures do think is most appropriate for summarizing these data, and why? What is the value of Q_2? Determine the 63rd percentile for the data. Determine the 29th percentile for the data.

Bank	Assets ($ billions)
Deutsche Bank AG (Frankfurt)	842
BNP Paribas SA (Paris)	700
Bank of Tokyo-Mitsubishi Ltd (Tokyo)	700
UBS AG (Zurich)	687
Bank of America NA (Charlotte)	572
The Sumitomo Bank Ltd (Tokyo)	524
Bayerische Hypo-und Vereinsbank AG (Munich)	504
The Norinchukin Bank (Tokyo)	485
The Dai-Ichi Kangyo Bank Ltd (Tokyo)	481
The Sakura Bank Ltd (Tokyo)	473
ABN AMRO Holding NV (Amsterdam)	459
The Fuji Bank Ltd (Tokyo)	458
Credit Agricole (Paris)	441
Industrial & Commercial Bank of China (Beijing)	428
Societe Generale (Paris)	407

3.9 The number of cars in service by the top 10 U.S. car rental companies in 2009 according to *Auto Rental News* follows. Compute the median, Q_3, P_{20}, P_{60}, P_{80}, and P_{93} on these data.

Company	Number of Cars in Service
Enterprise	842,376
Avis Budget	300,000
Hertz	286,000
Dollar Thrifty	106,425
Independents	53,500
U-Save	11,000
Payless	9,000
ACE	8,500
Fox	7,700
Rent-A-Wreck	5,075

3.10 The following lists the number of fatal accidents by scheduled commercial airlines over a 17-year period according to the Air Transport Association of America. Using these data, compute the mean, median, and mode. What is the value of the third quartile? Determine P_{11}, P_{35}, P_{58}, and P_{67}.

$$4 \quad 4 \quad 4 \quad 1 \quad 4 \quad 2 \quad 4 \quad 3 \quad 8 \quad 6 \quad 4 \quad 4 \quad 1 \quad 4 \quad 2 \quad 3 \quad 3$$

3.2 MEASURES OF VARIABILITY: UNGROUPED DATA

Measures of central tendency yield information about the center or middle part of a data set. However, business researchers can use another group of analytic tools, **measures of variability**, to *describe the spread or the dispersion of a set of data.* Using measures of variability in conjunction with measures of central tendency makes possible a more complete numerical description of the data.

For example, a company has 25 salespeople in the field, and the median annual sales figure for these people is $1.2 million. Are the salespeople being successful as a group or not? The median provides information about the sales of the person in the middle, but what about the other salespeople? Are all of them selling $1.2 million annually, or do the sales figures vary widely, with one person selling $5 million annually and another selling only $150,000 annually? Measures of variability provide the additional information necessary to answer that question.

Figure 3.3 shows three distributions in which the mean of each distribution is the same ($\mu = 50$) but the variabilities differ. Observation of these distributions shows that a measure of variability is necessary to complement the mean value in describing the data. Methods of computing measures of variability differ for ungrouped data and grouped data. This section focuses on seven measures of variability for ungrouped data: range, interquartile range, mean absolute deviation, variance, standard deviation, z scores, and coefficient of variation.

Range

The **range** is *the difference between the largest value of a data set and the smallest value of a set.* Although it is usually a single numeric value, some business researchers define the range of data as the ordered pair of smallest and largest numbers (smallest, largest). It is a crude measure of variability, describing the distance to the outer bounds of the data set. It reflects those extreme values because it is constructed from them. An advantage of the range is its ease of computation. One important use of the range is in quality assurance, where the range is used to construct control charts. A disadvantage of the range is that, because it is computed with the values that are on the extremes of the data, it is affected by extreme values, and its application as a measure of variability is limited.

The data in Table 3.1 represent the offer prices for the 20 largest U.S. initial public offerings in a recent year. The lowest offer price was $7.00 and the highest price was $43.25. The range of the offer prices can be computed as the difference of the highest and lowest values:

$$\text{Range} = \text{Highest} - \text{Lowest} = \$43.25 - \$7.00 = \$36.25$$

FIGURE 3.3

Three Distributions with the Same Mean but Different Dispersions

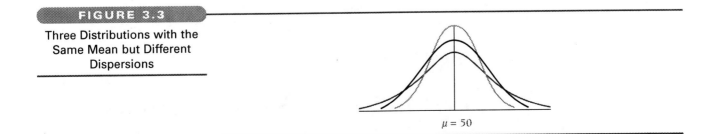

$\mu = 50$

Interquartile Range

Another measure of variability is the **interquartile range**. The interquartile range is *the range of values between the first and third quartile*. Essentially, it is the range of the middle 50% of the data and is determined by computing the value of $Q_3 - Q_1$. The interquartile range is especially useful in situations where data users are more interested in values toward the middle and less interested in extremes. In describing a real estate housing market, Realtors might use the interquartile range as a measure of housing prices when describing the middle half of the market for buyers who are interested in houses in the midrange. In addition, the interquartile range is used in the construction of box-and-whisker plots.

INTERQUARTILE RANGE	$Q_3 - Q_1$

The following data indicate the top 15 trading partners of the United States in exports in 2008 according to the U.S. Census Bureau.

Country	Exports ($ billions)
Canada	261.1
Mexico	151.2
China	69.7
Japan	65.1
Germany	54.5
United Kingdom	53.6
Netherlands	39.7
South Korea	34.7
Brazil	32.3
Belgium	28.9
France	28.8
Singapore	27.9
Taiwan	24.9
Australia	22.2
India	17.7

What is the interquartile range for these data? The process begins by computing the first and third quartiles as follows.

Solving for $Q_1 = P_{25}$ when $N = 15$:

$$i = \frac{25}{100}(15) = 3.75$$

Because i is not a whole number, P_{25} is found as the fourth term from the bottom.

$$Q_1 = P_{25} = 27.9$$

Solving for $Q_3 = P_{75}$:

$$i = \frac{75}{100}(15) = 11.25$$

Because i is not a whole number, P_{75} is found as the 12th term from the bottom.

$$Q_3 = P_{75} = 65.1$$

The interquartile range is:

$$Q_3 - Q_1 = 65.1 - 27.9 = 37.2$$

The middle 50% of the exports for the top 15 U.S. trading partners spans a range of 37.2 ($ billions).

THINKING CRITICALLY ABOUT STATISTICS IN BUSINESS TODAY

Recycling Statistics

There are many interesting statistics with regard to recycling. Recycling one aluminum can saves enough energy, the equivalent of a half gallon of gasoline, to run a television for three hours. Because Americans have done such a good job of recycling aluminum cans, they account for less than 1% of the total U.S. waste stream. Recycling 1 pound of steel saves enough energy to run a 60-watt light bulb for over a day. On average, one American uses seven trees a year in paper, wood, and other products made from trees. In addition, Americans use 680 pounds of paper per year. Each ton of recycled paper saves about 17 trees, 380 gallons of oil, three cubic yards of landfill space, 4000 kilowatts of energy, and 7000 gallons of water. Americans use 2.5 million plastic bottles every hour and throw away 25 billion Styrofoam cups every year. The energy saved from recycling one glass bottle can run a 100-watt light bulb for four hours.

Every year, each American throws out about 1200 pounds of organic garbage that could be composted. The U.S. is number one in the world in producing trash, with an average of 1609 pounds per person per year.

Things to Ponder

1. The average person in the United States produces 1609 pounds of trash per year. What additional information could be gleaned by also knowing a measure of variability on these data (pounds of trash).
2. On average, one American uses seven trees a year in products. What different information might a median yield on these data, and how might it help decision makers?

Sources: http://www.recycling-revolution.com/recycling-facts.html, National Recycling Coalition, the Environmental Protection Agency, Earth911.org.

Mean Absolute Deviation, Variance, and Standard Deviation

Three other measures of variability are the variance, the standard deviation, and the mean absolute deviation. They are obtained through similar processes and are, therefore, presented together. These measures are not meaningful unless the data are at least interval-level data. The variance and standard deviation are widely used in statistics. Although the standard deviation has some stand-alone potential, the importance of variance and standard deviation lies mainly in their role as tools used in conjunction with other statistical devices.

Suppose a small company started a production line to build computers. During the first five weeks of production, the output is 5, 9, 16, 17, and 18 computers, respectively. Which descriptive statistics could the owner use to measure the early progress of production? In an attempt to summarize these figures, the owner could compute a mean.

$$\frac{x_i}{\begin{array}{c} 5 \\ 9 \\ 16 \\ 17 \\ 18 \end{array}}$$

$$\Sigma x_i = 65 \qquad \mu = \frac{\Sigma x_i}{N} = \frac{65}{5} = 13$$

What is the variability in these five weeks of data? One way for the owner to begin to look at the spread of the data is to subtract the mean from each data value. *Subtracting the mean from each value of data* yields the **deviation from the mean** $(x_i - \mu)$. Table 3.2 shows

	TABLE 3.2
	Deviations from the Mean for Computer Production

Number (x_i)	Deviations from the Mean ($x_i - \mu$)
5	$5 - 13 = -8$
9	$9 - 13 = -4$
16	$16 - 13 = +3$
17	$17 - 13 = +4$
18	$18 - 13 = +5$
$\Sigma x_i = 65$	$\Sigma(x_i - \mu) = 0$

FIGURE 3.4

Geometric Distances from the
Mean (from Table 3.2)

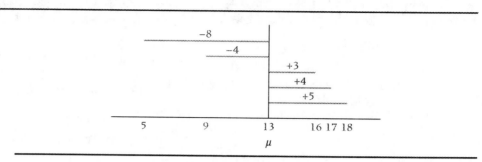

these deviations for the computer company production. Note that some deviations from the mean are positive and some are negative. Figure 3.4 shows that geometrically the negative deviations represent values that are below (to the left of) the mean and positive deviations represent values that are above (to the right of) the mean.

An examination of deviations from the mean can reveal information about the variability of data. However, the deviations are used mostly as a tool to compute other measures of variability. Note that in both Table 3.2 and Figure 3.4 these deviations total zero. This phenomenon applies to all cases. For a given set of data, the sum of all deviations from the arithmetic mean is always zero.

SUM OF DEVIATIONS FROM THE ARITHMETIC MEAN IS ALWAYS ZERO	$\Sigma(x_i - \mu) = 0$

This property requires considering alternative ways to obtain measures of variability.

One obvious way to force the sum of deviations to have a nonzero total is to take the absolute value of each deviation around the mean. Utilizing the absolute value of the deviations about the mean makes solving for the mean absolute deviation possible.

Mean Absolute Deviation

The **mean absolute deviation (MAD)** is *the average of the absolute values of the deviations around the mean for a set of numbers.*

MEAN ABSOLUTE DEVIATION	$\text{MAD} = \dfrac{\Sigma|x_i - \mu|}{N}$

Using the data from Table 3.2, the computer company owner can compute a mean absolute deviation by taking the absolute values of the deviations and averaging them, as shown in Table 3.3. The mean absolute deviation for the computer production data is 4.8.

TABLE 3.3

MAD for Computer
Production Data

x_i	$x_i - \mu$	$|x_i - \mu|$
5	−8	+8
9	−4	+4
16	+3	+3
17	+4	+4
18	+5	+5
$\Sigma x_i = 65$	$\Sigma(x_i - \mu) = 0$	$\Sigma|x_i - \mu| = 24$

$$\text{MAD} = \frac{\Sigma|x_i - \mu|}{N} = \frac{24}{5} = 4.8$$

Because it is computed by using absolute values, the mean absolute deviation is less useful in statistics than other measures of dispersion. However, in the field of forecasting, it is used occasionally as a measure of error.

Variance

Because absolute values are not conducive to easy manipulation, mathematicians developed an alternative mechanism for overcoming the zero-sum property of deviations from the mean. This approach utilizes the square of the deviations from the mean. The result is the variance, an important measure of variability.

The **variance** is *the average of the squared deviations about the arithmetic mean for a set of numbers.* The population variance is denoted by σ^2.

POPULATION VARIANCE	$\sigma^2 = \dfrac{\Sigma(x_i - \mu)^2}{N}$

Table 3.4 shows the original production numbers for the computer company, the deviations from the mean, and the squared deviations from the mean.

The sum of the squared deviations about the mean of a set of values—called the **sum of squares of x** and sometimes abbreviated as SS_x—is used throughout statistics. For the computer company, this value is 130. Dividing it by the number of data values (5 weeks) yields the variance for computer production.

$$\sigma^2 = \frac{130}{5} = 26.0$$

Because the variance is computed from squared deviations, the final result is expressed in terms of squared units of measurement. Statistics measured in squared units are problematic to interpret. Consider, for example, Mattel Toys attempting to interpret production costs in terms of squared dollars or Troy-Bilt measuring production output variation in terms of squared lawn mowers. Therefore, when used as a descriptive measure, variance can be considered as an intermediate calculation in the process of obtaining the standard deviation.

	TABLE 3.4	

Computing a Variance and a Standard Deviation from the Computer Production Data

x_i	$x_i - \mu$	$(x_i - \mu)^2$
5	−8	64
9	−4	16
16	+3	9
17	+4	16
18	+5	25
$\Sigma x_i = 65$	$\Sigma(x_i - \mu) = 0$	$\Sigma(x_i - \mu)^2 = 130$

$$SS_x = \Sigma(x_i - \mu)^2 = 130$$

$$\text{Variance} = \sigma^2 = \frac{SS_x}{N} = \frac{\Sigma(x_i - \mu)^2}{N} = \frac{130}{5} = 26.0$$

$$\text{Standard Deviation} = \sigma = \sqrt{\frac{\Sigma(x_i - \mu)^2}{N}} = \sqrt{\frac{130}{5}} = 5.1$$

Standard Deviation

The standard deviation is a popular measure of variability. It is used both as a separate entity and as a part of other analyses, such as computing confidence intervals and in hypothesis testing (see Chapters 8, 9, and 10).

POPULATION STANDARD DEVIATION	$$\sigma = \sqrt{\frac{\Sigma(x_i - \mu)^2}{N}}$$

The **standard deviation** is *the square root of the variance.* The population standard deviation is denoted by σ.

Like the variance, the standard deviation utilizes the sum of the squared deviations about the mean (SS_x). It is computed by averaging these squared deviations (SS_x/N) and taking the square root of that average. One feature of the standard deviation that distinguishes it from a variance is that the standard deviation is expressed in the same units as the raw data, whereas the variance is expressed in those units squared. Table 3.4 shows the standard deviation for the computer production company: $\sqrt{26}$, or 5.1.

What does a standard deviation of 5.1 mean? The meaning of standard deviation is more readily understood from its use, which is explored in the next section. Although the standard deviation and the variance are closely related and can be computed from each other, differentiating between them is important, because both are widely used in statistics.

Meaning of Standard Deviation

What is a standard deviation? What does it do, and what does it mean? The most precise way to define standard deviation is by reciting the formula used to compute it. However, insight into the concept of standard deviation can be gleaned by viewing the manner in which it is applied. Two ways of applying the standard deviation are the **empirical rule** and **Chebyshev's theorem**.

Empirical Rule

The empirical rule is an important rule of thumb that *is used to state the approximate percentage of values that lie within a given number of standard deviations from the mean of a set of data if the data are normally distributed.*

The empirical rule is used only for three numbers of standard deviations: 1σ, 2σ, and 3σ. More detailed analysis of other numbers of σ values is presented in Chapter 6. Also discussed in further detail in Chapter 6 is the normal distribution, a unimodal, symmetrical distribution that is bell (or mound) shaped. The requirement that the data be normally distributed contains some tolerance, and the empirical rule generally applies as long as the data are approximately mound shaped.

EMPIRICAL RULE*	Distance from the Mean	Values Within Distance
	$\mu \pm 1\sigma$	68%
	$\mu \pm 2\sigma$	95%
	$\mu \pm 3\sigma$	99.7%

*Based on the assumption that the data are approximately normally distributed.

FIGURE 3.5

Empirical Rule for One and
Two Standard Deviations
of Gasoline Prices

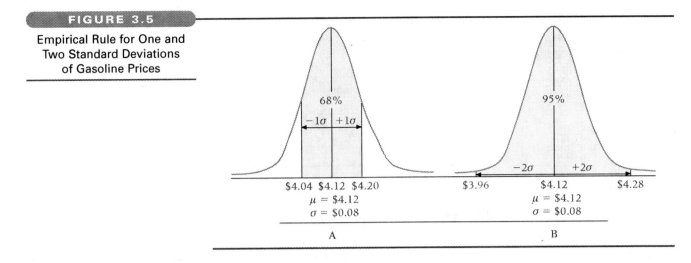

$4.04 $4.12 $4.20 $3.96 $4.12 $4.28
$\mu = \$4.12$ $\mu = \$4.12$
$\sigma = \$0.08$ $\sigma = \$0.08$

A   B

If a set of data is normally distributed, or bell shaped, approximately 68% of the data values are within one standard deviation of the mean, 95% are within two standard deviations, and almost 100% are within three standard deviations.

Suppose a recent report states that for California, the average statewide price of a gallon of regular gasoline is $4.12. Suppose regular gasoline prices vary across the state with a standard deviation of $0.08 and are normally distributed. According to the empirical rule, approximately 68% of the prices should fall within $\mu \pm 1\sigma$, or $4.12 ± 1($0.08). Approximately 68% of the prices should be between $4.04 and $4.20, as shown in Figure 3.5A. Approximately 95% should fall within $\mu \pm 2\sigma$ or $4.12 ± 2($0.08) = $4.12 ± $0.16, or between $3.96 and $4.28, as shown in Figure 3.5B. Nearly all regular gasoline prices (99.7%) should fall between $3.88 and $4.36($\mu \pm 3\sigma$).

Note that with 68% of the gasoline prices falling within one standard deviation of the mean, approximately 32% are outside this range. Because the normal distribution is symmetrical, the 32% can be split in half such that 16% lie in each tail of the distribution. Thus, approximately 16% of the gasoline prices should be less than $4.04 and approximately 16% of the prices should be greater than $4.20.

Many phenomena are distributed approximately in a bell shape, including most human characteristics such as height and weight; therefore the empirical rule applies in many situations and is widely used.

**DEMONSTRATION
PROBLEM 3.4**

A company produces a lightweight valve that is specified to weigh 1365 grams. Unfortunately, because of imperfections in the manufacturing process not all of the valves produced weigh exactly 1365 grams. In fact, the weights of the valves produced are normally distributed with a mean weight of 1365 grams and a standard deviation of 294 grams. Within what range of weights would approximately 95% of the valve weights fall? Approximately 16% of the weights would be more than what value? Approximately 0.15% of the weights would be less than what value?

Solution

Because the valve weights are normally distributed, the empirical rule applies. According to the empirical rule, approximately 95% of the weights should fall within $\mu \pm 2\sigma = 1365 \pm 2(294) = 1365 \pm 588$. Thus, approximately 95% should fall between 777 and 1953. Approximately 68% of the weights should fall within $\mu \pm 1\sigma$, and 32% should fall outside this interval. Because the normal distribution is symmetrical, approximately 16% should lie above $\mu + 1\sigma = 1365 + 294 = 1659$. Approximately 99.7% of the weights should fall within $\mu \pm 3\sigma$, and .3% should fall outside this interval. Half of these, or .15%, should lie below $\mu - 3\sigma = 1365 - 3(294) = 1365 - 882 = 483$.

FIGURE 3.6

Application of Chebyshev's Theorem for Two Standard Deviations

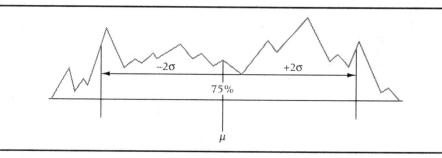

Chebyshev's Theorem

The empirical rule applies only when data are known to be approximately normally distributed. What do researchers use when data are not normally distributed or when the shape of the distribution is unknown? Chebyshev's theorem applies to all distributions regardless of their shape and thus can be used whenever the data distribution shape is unknown or is nonnormal. Even though Chebyshev's theorem can in theory be applied to data that are normally distributed, the empirical rule is more widely known and is preferred whenever appropriate. Chebyshev's theorem is not a rule of thumb, as is the empirical rule, but rather it is presented in formula format and therefore can be more widely applied. Chebyshev's theorem states that *at least* $1 - 1/k^2$ *values will fall within* $\pm k$ *standard deviations of the mean regardless of the shape of the distribution.*

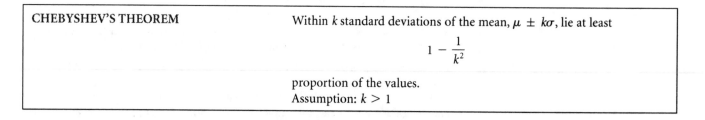

CHEBYSHEV'S THEOREM

Within k standard deviations of the mean, $\mu \pm k\sigma$, lie at least

$$1 - \frac{1}{k^2}$$

proportion of the values.
Assumption: $k > 1$

Specifically, Chebyshev's theorem says that at least 75% of all values are within $\pm 2\sigma$ of the mean regardless of the shape of a distribution because if $k = 2$, then $1 - 1/k^2 = 1 - 1/2^2 = 3/4 = .75$. Figure 3.6 provides a graphic illustration. In contrast, the empirical rule states that if the data are normally distributed 95% of all values are within $\mu \pm 2\sigma$. According to Chebyshev's theorem, the percentage of values within three standard deviations of the mean is at least 89%, in contrast to 99.7% for the empirical rule. Because a formula is used to compute proportions with Chebyshev's theorem, any value of k greater than $1 (k > 1)$ can be used. For example, if $k = 2.5$, at least .84 of all values are within $\mu \pm 2.5\sigma$, because $1 - 1/k^2 = 1 - 1/(2.5)^2 = .84$.

DEMONSTRATION PROBLEM 3.5

In the computing industry the average age of professional employees tends to be younger than in many other business professions. Suppose the average age of a professional employed by a particular computer firm is 28 with a standard deviation of 6 years. A histogram of professional employee ages with this firm reveals that the data are not normally distributed but rather are amassed in the 20s and that few workers are over 40. Apply Chebyshev's theorem to determine within what range of ages would at least 80% of the workers' ages fall.

Solution

Because the ages are not normally distributed, it is not appropriate to apply the empirical rule; and therefore Chebyshev's theorem must be applied to answer the question.

Chebyshev's theorem states that at least $1 - 1/k^2$ proportion of the values are within $\mu \pm k\sigma$. Because 80% of the values are within this range, let

$$1 - \frac{1}{k^2} = .80$$

Solving for k yields

$$.20 = \frac{1}{k^2}$$
$$k^2 = 5.000$$
$$k = 2.24$$

Chebyshev's theorem says that at least .80 of the values are within ± 2.24 of the mean.

For $\mu = 28$ and $\sigma = 6$, at least .80, or 80%, of the values are within $28 \pm 2.24(6) = 28 \pm 13.4$ years of age or between 14.6 and 41.4 years old.

Population Versus Sample Variance and Standard Deviation

The sample variance is denoted by s^2 and the sample standard deviation by s. The main use for sample variances and standard deviations is as estimators of population variances and standard deviations. Because of this, computation of the sample variance and standard deviation differs slightly from computation of the population variance and standard deviation. Both the sample variance and sample standard deviation use $n - 1$ in the denominator instead of n because using n in the denominator of a sample variance results in a statistic that tends to underestimate the population variance. While discussion of the properties of *good estimators* is beyond the scope of this text, one of the properties of a good estimator is being *unbiased*. Whereas using n in the denominator of the sample variance makes it a *biased* estimator, using $n - 1$ allows it to be an *unbiased* estimator, which is a desirable property in inferential statistics.

SAMPLE VARIANCE	$s^2 = \dfrac{\Sigma(x_i - \bar{x})^2}{n - 1}$

SAMPLE STANDARD DEVIATION	$s = \sqrt{\dfrac{\Sigma(x_i - \bar{x})^2}{n - 1}}$

Shown here is a sample of six of the largest accounting firms in the United States and the number of partners associated with each firm as reported by the *Public Accounting Report*.

Firm	Number of Partners
Deloitte & Touche	2654
Ernst & Young	2108
PricewaterhouseCoopers	2069
KPMG	1664
RSM McGladrey	720
Grant Thornton	309

The sample variance and sample standard deviation can be computed by:

x_i	$(x_i - \bar{x})^2$
2654	1,137,784.89
2108	271,097.25
2069	232,005.99
1664	5,878.29
720	752,261.33
309	1,634,127.59
$\Sigma x_i = 9524$	$\Sigma(x_i - \bar{x})^2 = 4,033,155.34$

$$\bar{x} = \frac{9524}{6} = 1587.33$$

$$s^2 = \frac{\Sigma(x_i - \bar{x})^2}{n-1} = \frac{4,033,155.34}{5} = 806,631.07$$

$$s = \sqrt{s^2} = \sqrt{806,631.07} = 898.13$$

The sample variance is 806,631.07, and the sample standard deviation is 898.13.

Computational Formulas for Variance and Standard Deviation

An alternative method of computing variance and standard deviation, sometimes referred to as the computational method or shortcut method, is available. Algebraically,

$$\Sigma(x_i - \mu)^2 = \Sigma x_i^2 - \frac{(\Sigma x_i)^2}{N}$$

and

$$\Sigma(x_i - \bar{x})^2 = \Sigma x_i^2 - \frac{(\Sigma x_i)^2}{n}$$

Substituting these equivalent expressions into the original formulas for variance and standard deviation yields the following computational formulas.

COMPUTATIONAL FORMULA FOR POPULATION VARIANCE AND STANDARD DEVIATION	$\sigma^2 = \dfrac{\Sigma x_i^2 - \dfrac{(\Sigma x_i)^2}{N}}{N}$ $\sigma = \sqrt{\sigma^2}$

COMPUTATIONAL FORMULA FOR SAMPLE VARIANCE AND STANDARD DEVIATION	$s^2 = \dfrac{\Sigma x_i^2 - \dfrac{(\Sigma x_i)^2}{n}}{n-1}$ $s = \sqrt{s^2}$

These computational formulas utilize the sum of the x values and the sum of the x^2 values instead of the difference between the mean and each value and computed deviations. In the precalculator/computer era, this method usually was faster and easier than using the original formulas.

TABLE 3.5

TABLE 3.5

Computational Formula
Calculations of Variance and
Standard Deviation for
Computer Production Data

x_i	x_i^2
5	25
9	81
16	256
17	289
18	324
$\Sigma x_i = 65$	$\Sigma x_i^2 = 975$

$$\sigma^2 = \frac{975 - \dfrac{(65)^2}{5}}{5} = \frac{975 - 845}{5} = \frac{130}{5} = 26$$

$$\sigma = \sqrt{26} = 5.1$$

For situations in which the mean is already computed or is given, alternative forms of these formulas are

$$\sigma^2 = \frac{\Sigma x_i^2 - N\mu^2}{N}$$

$$s^2 = \frac{\Sigma x_i^2 - n(\bar{x})^2}{n - 1}$$

Using the computational method, the owner of the start-up computer production company can compute a population variance and standard deviation for the production data, as shown in Table 3.5. (Compare these results with those in Table 3.4.)

DEMONSTRATION PROBLEM 3.6

Demonstration Problem

The effectiveness of district attorneys can be measured by several variables, including the number of convictions per month, the number of cases handled per month, and the total number of years of conviction per month. A researcher uses a sample of five district attorneys in a city and determines the total number of years of conviction that each attorney won against defendants during the past month, as reported in the first column in the following tabulations. Compute the mean absolute deviation, the variance, and the standard deviation for these figures.

Solution

The researcher computes the mean absolute deviation, the variance, and the standard deviation for these data in the following manner.

x_i	$|x_i - \bar{x}|$	$(x_i - \bar{x})^2$
55	41	1681
100	4	16
125	29	841
140	44	1936
60	36	1296
$\Sigma x_i = 480$	$\Sigma |x_i - \bar{x}| = 154$	$\Sigma(x_i - \bar{x})^2 = 5770$

$$\bar{x} = \frac{\Sigma x_i}{n} = \frac{480}{5} = 96$$

$$MAD = \frac{154}{5} = 30.8$$

$$s^2 = \frac{5770}{4} = 1442.5 \text{ and } s = \sqrt{s^2} = 37.98$$

She then uses computational formulas to solve for s^2 and s and compares the results.

x_i	x_i^2
55	3,025
100	10,000
125	15,625
140	19,600
60	3,600
$\Sigma x_i = 480$	$\Sigma x_i^2 = 51,850$

$$s^2 = \frac{51,850 - \frac{(480)^2}{5}}{4} = \frac{51,850 - 46,080}{4} = \frac{5,770}{4} = 1,442.5$$

$$s = \sqrt{1,442.5} = 37.98$$

The results are the same. The sample standard deviation obtained by both methods is 37.98, or 38, years.

z Scores

A **z score** represents the number of standard deviations a value (x) is above or below the mean of a set of numbers when the data are normally distributed. Using z scores allows translation of a value's raw distance from the mean into units of standard deviations.

z SCORE	$$z = \frac{x_i - \mu}{\sigma}$$

For samples,

$$z = \frac{x_i - \bar{x}}{s}$$

If a z score is negative, the raw value (x) is below the mean. If the z score is positive, the raw value (x) is above the mean.

For example, for a data set that is normally distributed with a mean of 50 and a standard deviation of 10, suppose a statistician wants to determine the z score for a value of 70. This value ($x = 70$) is 20 units above the mean, so the z value is

$$z = \frac{70 - 50}{10} = +2.00$$

This z score signifies that the raw score of 70 is two standard deviations above the mean. How is this z score interpreted? The empirical rule states that 95% of all values are within two standard deviations of the mean if the data are approximately normally distributed. Figure 3.7 shows that because the value of 70 is two standard deviations above the mean ($z = +2.00$), 95% of the values are between 70 and the value ($x = 30$), that is two standard

FIGURE 3.7

Percentage Breakdown of Scores Two Standard Deviations from the Mean

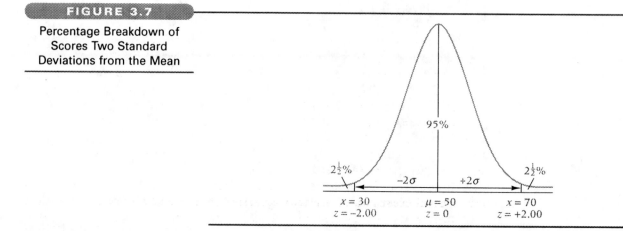

deviations below the mean, or $z = (30 - 50)/10 = -2.00$. Because 5% of the values are outside the range of two standard deviations from the mean and the normal distribution is symmetrical, 2½% ($\frac{1}{2}$ of the 5%) are below the value of 30. Thus 97½% of the values are below the value of 70. Because a z score is the number of standard deviations an individual data value is from the mean, the empirical rule can be restated in terms of z scores.

> Between $z = -1.00$ and $z = +1.00$ are approximately 68% of the values.
> Between $z = -2.00$ and $z = +2.00$ are approximately 95% of the values.
> Between $z = -3.00$ and $z = +3.00$ are approximately 99.7% of the values.

The topic of z scores is discussed more extensively in Chapter 6.

Coefficient of Variation

The **coefficient of variation** is a statistic that *is the ratio of the standard deviation to the mean expressed in percentage* and is denoted CV.

COEFFICIENT OF VARIATION	$$CV = \frac{\sigma}{\mu}(100)$$

The coefficient of variation essentially is a relative comparison of a standard deviation to its mean. The coefficient of variation can be useful in comparing standard deviations that have been computed from data with different means.

Suppose five weeks of average prices for stock A are 57, 68, 64, 71, and 62. To compute a coefficient of variation for these prices, first determine the mean and standard deviation: $\mu = 64.40$ and $\sigma = 4.84$. The coefficient of variation is:

$$CV_A = \frac{\sigma_A}{\mu_A}(100) = \frac{4.84}{64.40}(100) = .075 = 7.5\%$$

The standard deviation is 7.5% of the mean.

Sometimes financial investors use the coefficient of variation or the standard deviation or both as measures of risk. Imagine a stock with a price that never changes. An investor bears no risk of losing money from the price going down because no variability occurs in the price. Suppose, in contrast, that the price of the stock fluctuates wildly. An investor who buys at a low price and sells for a high price can make a nice profit. However, if the price drops below what the investor buys it for, the stock owner is subject to a potential loss. The greater the variability is, the more the potential for loss. Hence, investors use measures of variability such as standard deviation or coefficient of variation to determine the risk of a stock. What does the coefficient of variation tell us about the risk of a stock that the standard deviation does not?

Suppose the average prices for a second stock, B, over these same five weeks are 12, 17, 8, 15, and 13. The mean for stock B is 13.00 with a standard deviation of 3.03. The coefficient of variation can be computed for stock B as:

$$CV_B = \frac{\sigma_B}{\mu_B}(100) = \frac{3.03}{13}(100) = .233 = 23.3\%$$

The standard deviation for stock B is 23.3% of the mean.

With the standard deviation as the measure of risk, stock A is more risky over this period of time because it has a larger standard deviation. However, the average price of stock A is almost five times as much as that of stock B. Relative to the amount invested in stock A, the standard deviation of $4.84 may not represent as much risk as the standard deviation of $3.03 for stock B, which has an average price of only $13.00. The coefficient of variation reveals the risk of a stock in terms of the size of standard deviation relative to the size of the mean (in percentage). Stock B has a coefficient of variation that is nearly three times as much as the coefficient of variation for stock A. Using coefficient of variation as a measure of risk indicates that stock B is riskier.

The choice of whether to use a coefficient of variation or raw standard deviations to compare multiple standard deviations is a matter of preference. The coefficient of variation also provides an optional method of interpreting the value of a standard deviation.

THINKING CRITICALLY ABOUT STATISTICS IN BUSINESS TODAY

Business Travel

Findings from the Bureau of Transportation Statistics' National Household Travel Survey revealed that more than 405 million long-distance business trips are taken each year in the United States. Over 80% of these business trips are taken by personal vehicle. Almost three out of four business trips are for less than 250 miles, and only about 7% are for more than 1000 miles. The mean one-way distance for a business trip in the United States is 123 miles. Air travel accounts for 16% of all business travel. The average per diem cost of business travel to New York City is about $450, to Beijing is about $282, to Moscow is about $376, and to Paris is about $305. Seventy-seven percent of all business travelers are men, and 55% of business trips are taken by people in the 30-to-49-year-old age bracket. Forty-five percent of business trips are taken by people who have a household income of more than $75,000.

Things to Ponder

1. In light of the fact that 7% of business trips are for more than 1000 miles, why is the mean distance 123 miles? How do the 1000+ mile trips impact the mean?

2. It is reported here that the average per diem cost of business travel to New York City is about $450. Would the median or even the mode be more representative here? How might a measure of variability add insight?

Sources: U.S. Department of Transportation site at http://www.dot.gov/affairs/bts2503.htm and Expansion Management.com site at http://www.expansionmanagement.com/cmd/articledetail/articleid/15602/default.asp.

3.2 PROBLEMS

3.11 A data set contains the following seven values.

6   2   4   9   1   3   5

a. Find the range.
b. Find the mean absolute deviation.
c. Find the population variance.
d. Find the population standard deviation.
e. Find the interquartile range.
f. Find the z score for each value.

3.12 A data set contains the following eight values.

4   3   0   5   2   9   4   5

a. Find the range.
b. Find the mean absolute deviation.
c. Find the sample variance.
d. Find the sample standard deviation.
e. Find the interquartile range.

3.13 A data set contains the following six values.

12   23   19   26   24   23

a. Find the population standard deviation using the formula containing the mean (the original formula).
b. Find the population standard deviation using the computational formula.
c. Compare the results. Which formula was faster to use? Which formula do you prefer? Why do you think the computational formula is sometimes referred to as the "shortcut" formula?

3.14 Use your calculator or computer to find the sample variance and sample standard deviation for the following data.

57	88	68	43	93
63	51	37	77	83
66	60	38	52	28
34	52	60	57	29
92	37	38	17	67

3.15 Use your calculator or computer to find the population variance and population standard deviation for the following data.

123	090	546	378
392	280	179	601
572	953	749	075
303	468	531	646

3.16 The following sample data represent the time (in minutes) required by business executives to complete an expense report. Determine the interquartile range on these data and comment on what it means.

44	18	39	40	59
46	59	37	15	73
23	19	90	58	35
82	14	38	27	24
71	25	39	84	70

3.17 According to Chebyshev's theorem, at least what proportion of the data will be within $\mu \pm k\sigma$ for each value of k?

a. $k = 2$
b. $k = 2.5$
c. $k = 1.6$
d. $k = 3.2$

3.18 Compare the variability of the following two sets of data by using both the population standard deviation and the population coefficient of variation.

Data Set 1	Data Set 2
49	159
82	121
77	138
54	152

3.19 A sample of 12 small accounting firms reveals the following numbers of professionals per office.

7	10	9	14	11	8
5	12	8	3	13	6

a. Determine the mean absolute deviation.
b. Determine the variance.
c. Determine the standard deviation.
d. Determine the interquartile range.
e. What is the z score for the firm that has six professionals?
f. What is the coefficient of variation for this sample?

3.20 Shown below are the top food and drug stores in the United States in a recent year according to *Supermarket News and Chain Drug Review*.

Company	Revenues ($ billions)
Wal-Mart	258.5
Kroger	77.2
Costco	72.5
Walgreens	63.3
CVS Caremark	49.0
Supervalu	45.0
Safeway	44.8
Loblaw	31.5
Rite Aid	26.3

Assume that the data represent a population.

a. Find the range.
b. Find the mean absolute deviation.
c. Find the population variance.
d. Find the population standard deviation.

e. Find the interquartile range.

f. Find the z score for Walgreen.

g. Find the coefficient of variation.

3.21 A distribution of numbers is approximately bell shaped. If the mean of the numbers is 125 and the standard deviation is 12, between what two numbers would approximately 68% of the values fall? Between what two numbers would 95% of the values fall? Between what two values would 99.7% of the values fall?

3.22 Some numbers are not normally distributed. If the mean of the numbers is 38 and the standard deviation is 6, what proportion of values would fall between 26 and 50? What proportion of values would fall between 14 and 62? Between what two values would 89% of the values fall?

3.23 According to Chebyshev's theorem, how many standard deviations from the mean would include at least 80% of the values?

3.24 The time needed to assemble a particular piece of furniture with experience is normally distributed with a mean time of 43 minutes. If 68% of the assembly times are between 40 and 46 minutes, what is the value of the standard deviation? Suppose 99.7% of the assembly times are between 35 and 51 minutes and the mean is still 43 minutes. What would the value of the standard deviation be now? Suppose the time needed to assemble another piece of furniture is not normally distributed and that the mean assembly time is 28 minutes. What is the value of the standard deviation if at least 77% of the assembly times are between 24 and 32 minutes?

3.25 Environmentalists are concerned about emissions of sulfur dioxide into the air. The average number of days per year in which sulfur dioxide levels exceed 150 milligrams per cubic meter in Milan, Italy, is 29. The number of days per year in which emission limits are exceeded is normally distributed with a standard deviation of 4.0 days. What percentage of the years would average between 21 and 37 days of excess emissions of sulfur dioxide? What percentage of the years would exceed 37 days? What percentage of the years would exceed 41 days? In what percentage of the years would there be fewer than 25 days with excess sulfur dioxide emissions?

3.26 Shown below are the per diem business travel expenses in 11 international cities listed by Business Affairs of Oregon State University. Use this list to calculate the z scores for Moscow, Beijing, and Paris. Treat the list as a sample.

City	Per Diem Expense ($)
Beijing	381
Hong Kong	479
London	503
Mexico City	300
Moscow	420
New Delhi	486
Paris	487
Rio de Janeiro	363
Rome	576
Sydney	395
Tokyo	478

3.3 MEASURES OF CENTRAL TENDENCY AND VARIABILITY: GROUPED DATA

Grouped data do not provide information about individual values. Hence, measures of central tendency and variability for grouped data must be computed differently from those for ungrouped or raw data.

Measures of Central Tendency

Three measures of central tendency are presented here for grouped data: the mean, the median, and the mode.

Mean

For ungrouped data, the mean is computed by summing the data values and dividing by the number of values. With grouped data, the specific values are unknown. What can be used to represent the data values? The midpoint of each class interval is used to represent all the values in a class interval. This midpoint is weighted by the frequency of values in that class interval. The mean for grouped data is then computed by summing the products of the class midpoint and the class frequency for each class and dividing that sum by the total number of frequencies. The formula for the mean of grouped data follows.

MEAN OF GROUPED DATA	
	$$\mu_{grouped} = \frac{\Sigma f_i M_i}{N} = \frac{\Sigma f_i M_i}{\Sigma f_i}$$

where
$$f_i = \text{class frequency}$$
$$N = \text{total frequencies}$$
$$M_i = \text{class midpoint}$$

Table 3.6 gives the frequency distribution of the unemployment rates of Canada from Table 2.2. To find the mean of these data, we need Σf_i and $\Sigma f_i M_i$. The value of Σf_i can be determined by summing the values in the frequency column. To calculate $\Sigma f_i M_i$, we must first determine the values of M, or the class midpoints. Next we multiply each of these class midpoints by the frequency in that class interval, f_i, resulting in $f_i M_i$. Summing these values of $f_i M_i$ yields the value of $\Sigma f_i M_i$.

Table 3.7 contains the calculations needed to determine the group mean. The group mean for the unemployment data is 6.93. Remember that because each class interval was represented by its class midpoint rather than by actual values, the group mean is only approximate.

Median

The median for ungrouped or raw data is the middle value of an ordered array of numbers. For grouped data, solving for the median is considerably more complicated. The calculation of the median for grouped data is done by using the following formula.

MEDIAN OF GROUPED DATA	
	$$Median = L + \frac{\frac{N}{2} - cf_p}{f_{med}}(W)$$

where:
$$L = \text{the lower limit of the median class interval}$$
$$cf_p = \text{a cumulative total of the frequencies up to but not including the frequency of the median class}$$
$$f_{med} = \text{the frequency of the median class}$$
$$W = \text{the width of the median class interval}$$
$$N = \text{total number of frequencies}$$

The first step in calculating a grouped median is to determine the value of $N/2$, which is the location of the median term. Suppose we want to calculate the median for the frequency distribution data in Table 3.6. Since there are 60 values (N), the value of $N/2$ is $60/2 = 30$.

TABLE 3.6

Frequency Distribution of 60 Years of Unemployment Data for Canada (Grouped Data)

Class Interval	Frequency	Cumulative Frequency
1–under 3	4	4
3–under 5	12	16
5–under 7	13	29
7–under 9	19	48
9–under 11	7	55
11–under 13	5	60

TABLE 3.7
Calculation of Grouped Mean

Class Interval	Frequency (f_i)	Class Midpoint (M_i)	f_iM_i
1–under 3	4	2	8
3–under 5	12	4	48
5–under 7	13	6	78
7–under 9	19	8	152
9–under 11	7	10	70
11–under 13	5	12	60
	$\Sigma f_i = N = 60$		$\Sigma f_iM_i = 416$

$$\mu = \frac{\Sigma f_iM_i}{\Sigma f_i} = \frac{416}{60} = 6.93$$

The median is the 30th term. The question to ask is where does the 30th term fall? This can be answered by determining the cumulative frequencies for the data, as shown in Table 3.6.

An examination of these cumulative frequencies reveals that the 30th term falls in the fourth class interval because there are only 29 values in the first three class intervals. Thus, the median value is in the fourth class interval somewhere between 7 and 9. The class interval containing the median value is referred to as the *median class interval*.

Since the 30th value is between 7 and 9, the value of the median must be at least 7. How much more than 7 is the median? The difference between the location of the median value, $N/2 = 30$, and the cumulative frequencies up to but not including the median class interval, $cf_p = 29$, tells how many values into the median class interval lies the value of the median. This is determined by solving for $N/2 - cf_p = 30 - 29 = 1$. The median value is located one value into the median class interval. However, there are 19 values in the median interval (denoted in the formula as f_{med}). The median value is 1/19 of the way through this interval.

$$\frac{\frac{N}{2} - cf_p}{f_{med}} = \frac{30 - 29}{19} = \frac{1}{19}$$

Thus, the median value is at least 7, the value of L, and is 1/19 of the way across the median interval. How far is it across the median interval? Each class interval is 2 units wide (w). Taking 1/19 of this distance tells us how far the median value is into the class interval.

$$\frac{\frac{N}{2} - cf_p}{f_{med}}(W) = \frac{\frac{60}{2} - 29}{19}(2) = \frac{1}{19}(2) = .105$$

Adding this distance to the lower endpoint of the median class interval yields the value of the median.

$$\text{Median} = 7 + \frac{\frac{60}{2} - 29}{19}(2) = 7 + \frac{1}{19}(2) = 7 + .105 = 7.105$$

The median value of unemployment rates for Canada is 7.105. Keep in mind that like the grouped mean, this median value is merely approximate. The assumption made in these calculations is that the actual values fall uniformly across the median class interval—which may or may not be the case.

Mode

The *mode* for grouped data is *the class midpoint of the modal class. The modal class is the class interval with the greatest frequency.* Using the data from Table 3.7, the 7–under 9 class interval contains the greatest frequency, 19. Thus, the modal class is 7–under 9. The class midpoint of this modal class is 8. Therefore, the mode for the frequency distribution shown in Table 3.7 is 8. The modal unemployment rate is 8%.

Measures of Variability

Two measures of variability for grouped data are presented here: the variance and the standard deviation. Again, the standard deviation is the square root of the variance. Both measures have original and computational formulas.

FORMULAS FOR POPULATION VARIANCE AND STANDARD DEVIATION OF GROUPED DATA	**Original Formula**	**Computational Version**

$$\sigma^2 = \frac{\Sigma f_i (M_i - \mu)^2}{N} \qquad \sigma^2 = \frac{\Sigma f_i M_i^2 - \frac{(\Sigma f_i M_i)^2}{N}}{N}$$

$$\sigma = \sqrt{\sigma^2}$$

where:

f_i = frequency

M_i = class midpoint

$N = \Sigma f_i$, or total frequencies of the population

μ = grouped mean for the population

TABLE 3.8

Calculating Grouped Variance and Standard Deviation with the Original Formula

Class Interval	f_i	M_i	$f_i M_i$	$(M_i - \mu)$	$(M_i - \mu)^2$	$f_i(M_i - \mu)^2$
1–under 3	4	2	8	−4.93	24.305	97.220
3–under 5	12	4	48	−2.93	8.585	103.020
5–under 7	13	6	78	−0.93	0.865	11.245
7–under 9	19	8	152	1.07	1.145	21.755
9–under 11	7	10	70	3.07	9.425	65.975
11–under 13	5	12	60	5.07	25.705	128.525
$\Sigma f_i = N = 60$			$\Sigma f_i M_i = 416$			$\Sigma f_i(M_i - \mu)^2 = 427.740$

$$\mu = \frac{\Sigma f_i M_i}{\Sigma f_i} = \frac{416}{60} = 6.93$$

$$\sigma^2 = \frac{\Sigma f_i (M_i - \mu)^2}{N} = \frac{427.74}{60} = 7.129$$

$$\sigma = \sqrt{7.129} = 2.670$$

FORMULAS FOR SAMPLE VARIANCE AND STANDARD DEVIATION OF GROUPED DATA	**Original Formula**	**Computational Version**

$$s^2 = \frac{\Sigma f_i (M_i - \bar{x})^2}{n - 1} \qquad s^2 = \frac{\Sigma f_i M_i^2 - \frac{(\Sigma f_i M_i)^2}{n}}{n - 1}$$

$$s = \sqrt{s^2}$$

where:

f_i = frequency

M_i = class midpoint

$n = \Sigma f_i$, or total of the frequencies of the sample

$\bar{x}$ = grouped mean for the sample

For example, let us calculate the variance and standard deviation of the Canadian unemployment data grouped as a frequency distribution in Table 3.6. If the data are treated as a population, the computations are as follows.

For the original formula, the computations are given in Table 3.8. The method of determining σ^2 and σ by using the computational formula is shown in Table 3.9. In either case, the variance of the unemployment data is 7.129 (squared percent), and the standard deviation is 2.67%. As with the computation of the grouped mean, the class midpoint is used to represent all values in a class interval. This approach may or may not be appropriate, depending on whether the average value in a class is at the midpoint. If this situation does not occur, then the variance and the standard deviation are only approximations. Because grouped statistics are usually computed without knowledge of the actual data, the statistics computed potentially may be only approximations.

TABLE 3.9				
Class Interval	f_i	M_i	f_iM_i	$f_iM_i^2$
1–under 3	4	2	8	16
3–under 5	12	4	48	192
5–under 7	13	6	78	468
7–under 9	19	8	152	1216
9–under 11	7	10	70	700
11–under 13	5	12	60	720
	$\Sigma f_i = N = 60$		$\Sigma f_iM_i = 416$	$\Sigma f_iM_i^2 = 3312$

Calculating Grouped Variance and Standard Deviation with the Computational Formula

$$\sigma^2 = \frac{\Sigma f_iM_i^2 - \frac{(\Sigma f_iM_i)^2}{N}}{N} = \frac{3312 - \frac{416^2}{60}}{60} = \frac{3312 - 2884.27}{60} = \frac{427.73}{60} = 7.129$$

$$\sigma = \sqrt{7.129} = 2.670$$

DEMONSTRATION PROBLEM 3.7

Compute the mean, median, mode, variance, and standard deviation on the following sample data.

Class Interval	Frequency	Cumulative Frequency
10–under 15	6	6
15–under 20	22	28
20–under 25	35	63
25–under 30	29	92
30–under 35	16	108
35–under 40	8	116
40–under 45	4	120
45–under 50	2	122

Solution

The mean is computed as follows.

Class	f_i	M_i	f_iM_i
10–under 15	6	12.5	75.0
15–under 20	22	17.5	385.0
20–under 25	35	22.5	787.5
25–under 30	29	27.5	797.5
30–under 35	16	32.5	520.0
35–under 40	8	37.5	300.0
40–under 45	4	42.5	170.0
45–under 50	2	47.5	95.0
	$\Sigma f_i = n = 122$		$\Sigma f_iM_i = 3130.0$

$$\bar{x} = \frac{\Sigma f_iM_i}{\Sigma f_i} = \frac{3130}{122} = 25.66$$

The grouped mean is 25.66.

The grouped median is located at the 61st value (122/2). Observing the cumulative frequencies, the 61st value falls in the 20-under 25 class, making it the median class interval; and thus, the grouped median is at least 20. Since there are 28 cumulative values before the median class interval, 33 more (61 − 28) are needed to reach the grouped median. However, there are 35 values in the median class. The grouped median is located 33/35 of the way across the class interval which has a width of 5. The grouped median is $20 + \frac{33}{35}(5) = 20 + 4.71 = 24.71$.

The grouped mode can be determined by finding the class midpoint of the class interval with the greatest frequency. The class with the greatest frequency is 20–under 25 with a frequency of 35. The midpoint of this class is 22.5, which is the grouped mode.

The variance and standard deviation can be found as shown next. First, use the original formula.

Class	f_i	M_i	$M_i - \bar{x}$	$(M_i - \bar{x})^2$	$f_i(M_i - \bar{x})^2$
10–under 15	6	12.5	−13.16	173.19	1039.14
15–under 20	22	17.5	−8.16	66.59	1464.98
20–under 25	35	22.5	−3.16	9.99	349.65
25–under 30	29	27.5	1.84	3.39	98.31
30–under 35	16	32.5	6.84	46.79	748.64
35–under 40	8	37.5	11.84	140.19	1121.52
40–under 45	4	42.5	16.84	283.59	1134.36
45–under 50	2	47.5	21.84	476.99	953.98
$\Sigma f_i = n = 122$					$\Sigma f_i(M_i - \bar{x})^2 = 6910.58$

$$s^2 = \frac{\Sigma f_i(M_i - \bar{x})^2}{n - 1} = \frac{6910.58}{121} = 57.11$$

$$s = \sqrt{57.11} = 7.56$$

Next, use the computational formula.

Class	f_i	M_i	f_iM_i	$f_iM_i^2$
10–under 15	6	12.5	75.0	937.50
15–under 20	22	17.5	385.0	6,737.50
20–under 25	35	22.5	787.5	17,718.75
25–under 30	29	27.5	797.5	21,931.25
30–under 35	16	32.5	520.0	16,900.00
35–under 40	8	37.5	300.0	11,250.00
40–under 45	4	42.5	170.0	7,225.00
45–under 50	2	47.5	95.0	4,512.50
$\Sigma f_i = n = 122$			$\Sigma f_iM_i = 3,130.0$	$\Sigma f_iM_i^2 = 87,212.50$

$$s^2 = \frac{\Sigma f_iM_i^2 - \dfrac{(\Sigma f_iM_i)^2}{n}}{n - 1} = \frac{87,212.5 - \dfrac{(3,130)^2}{122}}{121} = \frac{6,910.04}{121} = 57.11$$

$$s = \sqrt{57.11} = 7.56$$

The sample variance is 57.11 and the standard deviation is 7.56.

3.3 PROBLEMS

3.27 Compute the mean, the median, and the mode for the following data.

Class	f
0–under 2	39
2–under 4	27
4–under 6	16
6–under 8	15
8–under 10	10
10–under 12	8
12–under 14	6

3.28 Compute the mean, the median, and the mode for the following data.

Class	f
1.2–under 1.6	220
1.6–under 2.0	150
2.0–under 2.4	90
2.4–under 2.8	110
2.8–under 3.2	280

3.29 Determine the population variance and standard deviation for the following data by using the original formula.

Class	f
20–under 30	7
30–under 40	11
40–under 50	18
50–under 60	13
60–under 70	6
70–under 80	4

3.30 Determine the sample variance and standard deviation for the following data by using the computational formula.

Class	f
5–under 9	20
9–under 13	18
13–under 17	8
17–under 21	6
21–under 25	2

3.31 A random sample of voters in Nashville, Tennessee, is classified by age group, as shown by the following data.

Age Group	Frequency
18–under 24	17
24–under 30	22
30–under 36	26
36–under 42	35
42–under 48	33
48–under 54	30
54–under 60	32
60–under 66	21
66–under 72	15

a. Calculate the mean of the data.
b. Calculate the mode.
c. Calculate the median.
d. Calculate the variance.
e. Calculate the standard deviation.

3.32 The following data represent the number of appointments made per 15-minute interval by telephone solicitation for a lawn-care company. Assume these are population data.

Number of Appointments	Frequency of Occurrence
0–under 1	31
1–under 2	57
2–under 3	26
3–under 4	14
4–under 5	6
5–under 6	3

a. Calculate the mean of the data.
b. Calculate the mode.
c. Calculate the median.
d. Calculate the variance.
e. Calculate the standard deviation.

3.33 The Air Transport Association of America publishes figures on the busiest airports in the United States. The following frequency distribution has been constructed from these figures for a recent year. Assume these are population data.

Number of Passengers Arriving and Departing (millions)	Number of Airports
20–under 30	8
30–under 40	7
40–under 50	1
50–under 60	0
60–under 70	3
70–under 80	1

a. Calculate the mean of these data.

b. Calculate the mode.

c. Calculate the median.

d. Calculate the variance.

e. Calculate the standard deviation.

3.34 The frequency distribution shown represents the number of farms per state for the 50 United States, based on information from the U.S. Department of Agriculture. Determine the average number of farms per state from these data. The mean computed from the original ungrouped data was 41,796 and the standard deviation was 38,856. How do your answers for these grouped data compare? Why might they differ?

Number of Farms per State	f
0–under 20,000	16
20,000–under 40,000	11
40,000–under 60,000	11
60,000–under 80,000	6
80,000–under 100,000	4
100,000–under 120,000	2

3.4 MEASURES OF SHAPE

Measures of shape are *tools that can be used to describe the shape of a distribution of data.* In this section, we examine two measures of shape, skewness and kurtosis. We also look at box-and-whisker plots.

Skewness

A distribution of data in which the right half is a mirror image of the left half is said to be *symmetrical*. One example of a symmetrical distribution is the normal distribution, or bell curve, shown in Figure 3.8 and presented in more detail in Chapter 6.

Skewness is when *a distribution is asymmetrical or lacks symmetry.* The distribution in Figure 3.8 has no skewness because it is symmetric. Figure 3.9 shows a distribution that is skewed left, or negatively skewed, and Figure 3.10 shows a distribution that is skewed right, or positively skewed.

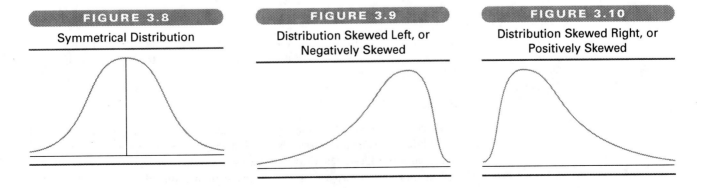

FIGURE 3.8
Symmetrical Distribution

FIGURE 3.9
Distribution Skewed Left, or Negatively Skewed

FIGURE 3.10
Distribution Skewed Right, or Positively Skewed

FIGURE 3.11

Relationship of Mean, Median, and Mode

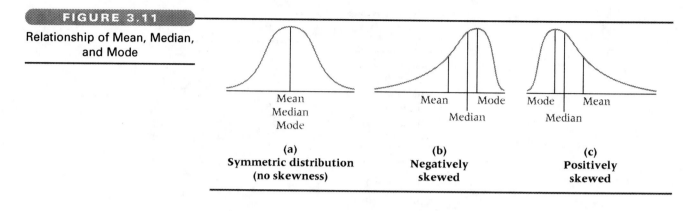

(a)
Symmetric distribution (no skewness)

(b)
Negatively skewed

(c)
Positively skewed

The skewed portion is the long, thin part of the curve. Many researchers use skewed distribution to denote that the data are sparse at one end of the distribution and piled up at the other end. Instructors sometimes refer to a grade distribution as skewed, meaning that few students scored at one end of the grading scale, and many students scored at the other end.

Skewness and the Relationship of the Mean, Median, and Mode

The concept of skewness helps to understand the relationship of the mean, median, and mode. In a unimodal distribution (distribution with a single peak or mode) that is skewed, the mode is the apex (high point) of the curve and the median is the middle value. The mean tends to be located toward the tail of the distribution, because the mean is particularly affected by the extreme values. A bell-shaped or normal distribution with the mean, median, and mode all at the center of the distribution has no skewness. Figure 3.11 displays the relationship of the mean, median, and mode for different types of skewness.

Coefficient of Skewness

Statistician Karl Pearson is credited with developing at least two coefficients of skewness that can be used to determine the degree of skewness in a distribution. We present one of these coefficients here, referred to as a Pearsonian **coefficient of skewness**. This coefficient *compares the mean and median in light of the magnitude of the standard deviation.* Note that if the distribution is symmetrical, the mean and median are the same value and hence the coefficient of skewness is equal to zero.

COEFFICIENT OF SKEWNESS

$$S_k = \frac{3(\mu - M_d)}{\sigma}$$

where

S_k = coefficient of skewness
M_d = median

Suppose, for example, that a distribution has a mean of 29, a median of 26, and a standard deviation of 12.3. The coefficient of skewness is computed as

$$S_k = \frac{3(29 - 26)}{12.3} = +0.73$$

Because the value of S_k is positive, the distribution is positively skewed. If the value of S_k is negative, the distribution is negatively skewed. The greater the magnitude of S_k, the more skewed is the distribution.

Kurtosis

Kurtosis *describes the amount of peakedness of a distribution.* Distributions that are high and thin are referred to as **leptokurtic** distributions. Distributions that are flat and spread out are referred to as **platykurtic** distributions. Between these two types are distributions that are more "normal" in shape, referred to as **mesokurtic** distributions. These three types of kurtosis are illustrated in Figure 3.12.

FIGURE 3.12

Types of Kurtosis

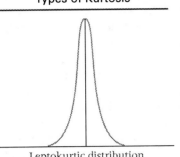

Leptokurtic distribution

Platykurtic distribution

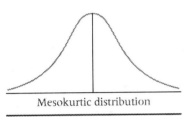

Mesokurtic distribution

Box-and-Whisker Plots and Five-Number Summary

Interactive Applet

Another way to describe a distribution of data is by using a box and whisker plot. A **box-and-whisker plot**, sometimes called a *box plot*, is *a diagram that utilizes the upper and lower quartiles along with the median and the two most extreme values to depict a distribution graphically*. The plot is constructed by using a box to enclose the median. This *box* is extended outward from the median along a continuum to the lower and upper quartiles, enclosing not only the median but also the middle 50% of the data. From the lower and upper quartiles, lines referred to as *whiskers* are extended out from the box toward the outermost data values. The box-and-whisker plot is determined from five specific numbers sometimes referred to as the **five-number summary**.

1. The median (Q_2)
2. The lower quartile (Q_1)
3. The upper quartile (Q_3)
4. The smallest value in the distribution
5. The largest value in the distribution

The box of the plot is determined by locating the median and the lower and upper quartiles on a continuum. A box is drawn around the median with the lower and upper quartiles (Q_1 and Q_3) as the box endpoints. These box endpoints (Q_1 and Q_3) are referred to as the *hinges* of the box.

Next the value of the interquartile range (IQR) is computed by $Q_3 - Q_1$. The interquartile range includes the middle 50% of the data and should equal the length of the box. However, here the interquartile range is used outside of the box also. At a distance of $1.5 \cdot \text{IQR}$ outward from the lower and upper quartiles are what are referred to as *inner fences*. A *whisker*, a line segment, is drawn from the lower hinge of the box outward to the smallest data value. A second whisker is drawn from the upper hinge of the box outward to the largest data value. The inner fences are established as follows.

$$Q_1 - 1.5 \cdot \text{IQR}$$
$$Q_3 + 1.5 \cdot \text{IQR}$$

If data fall beyond the inner fences, then *outer* fences can be constructed:

$$Q_1 - 3.0 \cdot \text{IQR}$$
$$Q_3 + 3.0 \cdot \text{IQR}$$

Figure 3.13 shows the features of a box-and-whisker plot.

Data values outside the mainstream of values in a distribution are viewed as *outliers.* Outliers can be merely the more extreme values of a data set. However, sometimes outliers occur due to measurement or recording errors. Other times they are values so unlike the other values that they should not be considered in the same analysis as the rest of the distribution. Values in the data distribution that are outside the inner fences but within the outer fences are referred to as *mild outliers.* Values that are outside the outer fences are called *extreme outliers.* Thus, one of the main uses of a box-and-whisker plot is to identify outliers. In some computer-produced box-and-whisker plots (such as in Minitab), the whiskers are drawn to the largest and smallest data values within the inner fences. An asterisk is then printed for each

FIGURE 3.13

Box-and-Whisker Plot

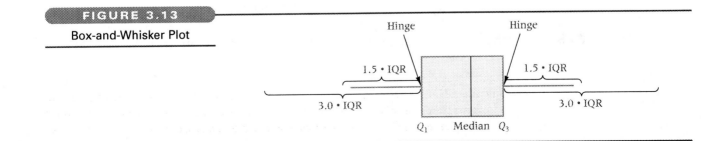

TABLE 3.10							
Data for Box-and-Whisker Plot							
71	87	82	64	72	75	81	69
76	79	65	68	80	73	85	71
70	79	63	62	81	84	77	73
82	74	74	73	84	72	81	65
74	62	64	68	73	82	69	71

data value located between the inner and outer fences to indicate a mild outlier. Values outside the outer fences are indicated by a zero on the graph. These values are extreme outliers.

Another use of box-and-whisker plots is to determine whether a distribution is skewed. The location of the median in the box can relate information about the skewness of the middle 50% of the data. If the median is located on the right side of the box, then the middle 50% are skewed to the left. If the median is located on the left side of the box, then the middle 50% are skewed to the right. By examining the length of the whiskers on each side of the box, a business researcher can make a judgment about the skewness of the outer values. If the longest whisker is to the right of the box, then the outer data are skewed to the right and vice versa. We shall use the data given in Table 3.10 to construct a box-and-whisker plot.

After organizing the data into an ordered array, as shown in Table 3.11, it is relatively easy to determine the values of the lower quartile (Q_1), the median, and the upper quartile (Q_3). From these, the value of the interquartile range can be computed.

The hinges of the box are located at the lower and upper quartiles, 69 and 80.5. The median is located within the box at distances of 4 from the lower quartile and 7.5 from the upper quartile. The distribution of the middle 50% of the data is skewed right, because the median is nearer to the lower or left hinge. The inner fence is constructed by

$$Q_1 - 1.5 \cdot IQR = 69 - 1.5(11.5) = 69 - 17.25 = 51.75$$

and

$$Q_3 + 1.5 \cdot IQR = 80.5 + 1.5(11.5) = 80.5 + 17.25 = 97.75$$

The whiskers are constructed by drawing a line segment from the lower hinge outward to the smallest data value and a line segment from the upper hinge outward to the largest data value. An examination of the data reveals that no data values in this set of numbers are outside the inner fence. The whiskers are constructed outward to the lowest value, which is 62, and to the highest value, which is 87.

To construct an outer fence, we calculate $Q_1 - 3 \cdot IQR$ and $Q_3 + 3 \cdot IQR$, as follows.

$$Q_1 - 3 \cdot IQR = 69 - 3(11.5) = 69 - 34.5 = 34.5$$
$$Q_3 + 3 \cdot IQR = 80.5 + 3(11.5) = 80.5 + 34.5 = 115.0$$

Figure 3.14 is the Minitab computer printout for this box-and-whisker plot.

TABLE 3.11									
Data in Ordered Array with Quartiles and Median									
87	85	84	84	82	82	82	81	81	81
80	79	79	77	76	75	74	74	74	73
73	73	73	72	72	71	71	71	70	69
69	68	68	65	65	64	64	63	62	62

$$Q_1 = 69$$
$$Q_2 = \text{median} = 73$$
$$Q_3 = 80.5$$
$$IQR = Q_3 - Q_1 = 80.5 - 69 = 11.5$$

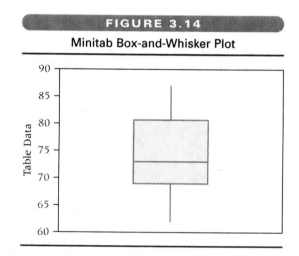

FIGURE 3.14

Minitab Box-and-Whisker Plot

3.4 PROBLEMS

3.35 On a certain day the average closing price of a group of stocks on the New York Stock Exchange is $35 (to the nearest dollar). If the median value is $33 and the mode is $21, is the distribution of these stock prices skewed? If so, how?

3.36 A local hotel offers ballroom dancing on Friday nights. A researcher observes the customers and estimates their ages. Discuss the skewness of the distribution of ages if the mean age is 51, the median age is 54, and the modal age is 59.

3.37 The sales volumes for the top real estate brokerage firms in the United States for a recent year were analyzed using descriptive statistics. The mean annual dollar volume for these firms was $5.51 billion, the median was $3.19 billion, and the standard deviation was $9.59 billion. Compute the value of the Pearsonian coefficient of skewness and discuss the meaning of it. Is the distribution skewed? If so, to what extent?

3.38 Suppose the following data are the ages of Internet users obtained from a sample. Use these data to compute a Pearsonian coefficient of skewness. What is the meaning of the coefficient?

41	15	31	25	24
23	21	22	22	18
30	20	19	19	16
23	27	38	34	24
19	20	29	17	23

3.39 Construct a box-and-whisker plot on the following data. Do the data contain any outliers? Is the distribution of data skewed?

540	690	503	558	490	609
379	601	559	495	562	580
510	623	477	574	588	497
527	570	495	590	602	541

3.40 Suppose a consumer group asked 18 consumers to keep a yearly log of their shopping practices and that the following data represent the number of coupons used by each consumer over the yearly period. Use the data to construct a box-and-whisker plot. List the median, Q_1, Q_3, the endpoints for the inner fences, and the endpoints for the outer fences. Discuss the skewness of the distribution of these data and point out any outliers.

| 81 | 68 | 70 | 100 | 94 | 47 | 66 | 70 | 82 |
| 110 | 105 | 60 | 21 | 70 | 66 | 90 | 78 | 85 |

3.5 DESCRIPTIVE STATISTICS ON THE COMPUTER

Both Minitab and Excel yield extensive descriptive statistics. Even though each computer package can compute individual statistics such as a mean or a standard deviation, they can also produce multiple descriptive statistics at one time. Figure 3.15 displays a Minitab output for the descriptive statistics associated with the computer production data presented earlier in this section. The Minitab output contains, among other things, the mean, the median, the sample standard deviation, the minimum and maximum (which can then be used to compute the range), and Q_1 and Q_3 (from which the interquartile range can be computed). Excel's descriptive statistics output for the same computer production data is displayed in Figure 3.16. The Excel output contains the mean, the median, the mode, the sample standard deviation, the sample variance, and the range. The descriptive statistics feature on either of these computer packages yields a lot of useful information about a data set.

FIGURE 3.15

Minitab Output for the Computer Production Problem

DESCRIPTIVE STATISTICS

Variable	N	N*	Mean	SE Mean	StDev	Minimum	Q_1
Computers Produced	5	0	13.00	2.55	5.70	5.00	7.00

	Median	Q_3	Maximum
	16.00	17.50	18.00

FIGURE 3.16

Excel Output for the Computer Production Problem

COMPUTER PRODUCTION DATA

Mean	13
Standard error	2.54951
Median	16
Mode	#N/A
Standard deviation	5.700877
Sample variance	32.5
Kurtosis	−1.71124
Skewness	−0.80959
Range	13
Minimum	5
Maximum	18
Sum	65
Count	5

Decision Dilemma SOLVED

Decision Dilemma SOLVED

Laundry Statistics

The descriptive statistics presented in this chapter are excellent for summarizing and presenting data sets in more concise formats. For example, question 1 of the managerial and statistical questions in the Decision Dilemma reports water measurements for 50 U.S. households. Using Excel and/or Minitab, many of the descriptive statistics presented in this chapter can be applied to these data. The results are shown in Figures 3.17 and 3.18.

These computer outputs show that the average water usage is 15.48 gallons with a standard deviation of about 1.233 gallons. The median is 16 gallons with a range of 6 gallons (12 to 18). The first quartile is 15 gallons and the third quartile is 16 gallons. The mode is also 16 gallons. The Minitab graph and the skewness measures show that the data are slightly skewed to the left. Applying Chebyshev's theorem to the mean and standard deviation shows that at least 88.9% of

FIGURE 3.17

Excel Descriptive Statistics

GALLONS OF WATER

Mean	15.48
Standard error	0.174356
Median	16
Mode	16
Standard deviation	1.232883
Sample variance	1.52
Kurtosis	0.263785
Skewness	−0.53068
Range	6
Minimum	12
Maximum	18
Sum	774
Count	50

FIGURE 3.18

Minitab Descriptive Statistics

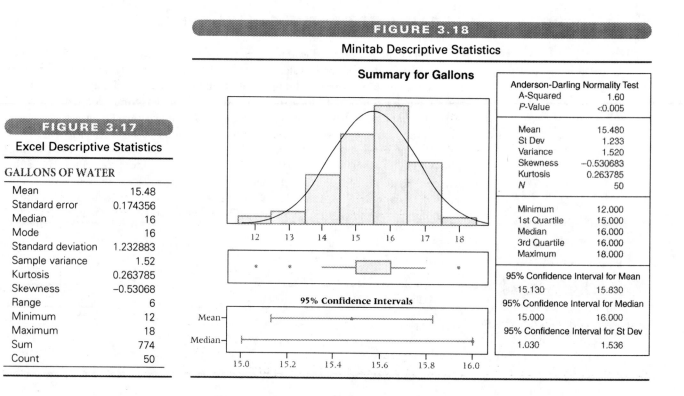

the measurements should fall between 11.78 gallons and 19.18 gallons. An examination of the data and the minimum and maximum reveals that 100% of the data actually fall within these limits.

According to the Decision Dilemma, the mean wash cycle time is 35 minutes with a standard deviation of 5 minutes. If the wash cycle times are approximately normally distributed,

we can apply the empirical rule. According to the empirical rule, 68% of the times would fall within 30 and 40 minutes, 95% of the times would fall within 25 and 45 minutes, and 99.7% of the wash times would fall within 20 and 50 minutes. If the data are not normally distributed, Chebyshev's theorem reveals that at least 75% of the times should fall between 25 and 45 minutes and 88.9% should fall between 20 and 50 minutes.

ETHICAL CONSIDERATIONS

In describing a body of data to an audience, it is best to use whatever measures it takes to present a "full" picture of the data. By limiting the descriptive measures used, the business researcher may give the audience only part of the picture and can skew the way the receiver understands the data. For example, if a researcher presents only the mean, the audience will have no insight into the variability of the data; in addition, the mean might be inordinately large or small because of extreme values. Likewise, the choice of the median precludes a picture that includes the extreme values.

Using the mode can cause the receiver of the information to focus only on values that occur often.

At least one measure of variability is usually needed with at least one measure of central tendency for the audience to begin to understand what the data look like. Unethical researchers might be tempted to present only the descriptive measure that will convey the picture of the data that they want the audience to see. Ethical researchers will instead use any and all methods that will present the fullest, most informative picture possible from the data.

SUMMARY

Statistical descriptive measures include measures of central tendency, measures of variability, and measures of shape. Measures of central tendency and measures of variability are computed differently for ungrouped and grouped data. Measures of central tendency are useful in describing data because they communicate information about the more central portions of the data. The most common measures of central tendency are the three Ms': mode, median, and mean. In addition, percentiles and quartiles are measures of central tendency.

The mode is the most frequently occurring value in a set of data. Among other things, the mode is used in business for determining sizes.

The median is the middle term in an ordered array of numbers containing an odd number of terms. For an array with an even number of terms, the median is the average of the two middle terms. A median is unaffected by the magnitude of extreme values. This characteristic makes the median a most useful and appropriate measure of location in reporting such things as income, age, and prices of houses.

The arithmetic mean is widely used and is usually what researchers are referring to when they use the word *mean*. The arithmetic mean is the average. The population mean and the sample mean are computed in the same way but are denoted by different symbols. The arithmetic mean is affected by every value and can be inordinately influenced by extreme values.

Percentiles divide a set of data into 100 groups, which means 99 percentiles are needed. Quartiles divide data into

four groups. The three quartiles are Q_1, which is the lower quartile; Q_2, which is the middle quartile and equals the median; and Q_3, which is the upper quartile.

Measures of variability are statistical tools used in combination with measures of central tendency to describe data. Measures of variability provide information about the spread of the data values. These measures include the range, mean absolute deviation, variance, standard deviation, interquartile range, z scores, and coefficient of variation for ungrouped data.

One of the most elementary measures of variability is the range. It is the difference between the largest and smallest values. Although the range is easy to compute, it has limited usefulness. The interquartile range is the difference between the third and first quartile. It equals the range of the middle 50% of the data.

The mean absolute deviation (MAD) is computed by averaging the absolute values of the deviations from the mean. The mean absolute deviation has limited usage in statistics, but interest is growing for the use of MAD in the field of forecasting.

Variance is widely used as a tool in statistics but is used little as a stand-alone measure of variability. The variance is the average of the squared deviations about the mean.

The square root of the variance is the standard deviation. It also is a widely used tool in statistics, but it is used more often than the variance as a stand-alone measure. The standard deviation is best understood by examining its applications in determining where data are in relation to the mean. The empirical rule and Chebyshev's theorem are statements about the proportions of data values that are within various numbers of standard deviations from the mean.

The empirical rule reveals the percentage of values that are within one, two, or three standard deviations of the mean for a set of data. The empirical rule applies only if the data are in a bell-shaped distribution.

Chebyshev's theorem also delineates the proportion of values that are within a given number of standard deviations from the mean. However, it applies to any distribution. The z score represents the number of standard deviations a value is from the mean for normally distributed data.

The coefficient of variation is a ratio of a standard deviation to its mean, given as a percentage. It is especially useful in comparing standard deviations or variances that represent data with different means.

Some measures of central tendency and some measures of variability are presented for grouped data. These measures include mean, median, mode, variance, and standard deviation. Generally, these measures are only approximate for grouped data because the values of the actual raw data are unknown.

Two measures of shape are skewness and kurtosis. Skewness is the lack of symmetry in a distribution. If a distribution is skewed, it is stretched in one direction or the other. The skewed part of a graph is its long, thin portion. One measure of skewness is the Pearsonian coefficient of skewness.

Kurtosis is the degree of peakedness of a distribution. A tall, thin distribution is referred to as leptokurtic. A flat distribution is platykurtic, and a distribution with a more normal peakedness is said to be mesokurtic.

A box-and-whisker plot is a graphical depiction of a distribution. The plot is constructed by using the median, the lower quartile, the upper quartile, the smallest value, and the largest value. It can yield information about skewness and outliers.

KEY TERMS

Flash Cards

arithmetic mean
bimodal
box-and-whisker plot
Chebyshev's theorem
coefficient of skewness

coefficient of variation (CV)
deviation from the mean
empirical rule
five-number summary
interquartile range
kurtosis
leptokurtic
mean absolute deviation (MAD)

measures of central tendency
measures of shape
measures of variability
median
mesokurtic
mode
multimodal
percentiles

platykurtic
quartiles
range
skewness
standard deviation
sum of squares of x
variance
z score

FORMULAS

Population mean (ungrouped)

$$\mu = \frac{\Sigma x_i}{N}$$

Sample mean (ungrouped)

$$\bar{x} = \frac{\Sigma x_i}{n}$$

Mean absolute deviation

$$\text{MAD} = \frac{\Sigma |x_i - \mu|}{N}$$

Population variance (ungrouped)

$$\sigma^2 = \frac{\Sigma (x_i - \mu)^2}{N}$$

$$\sigma^2 = \frac{\Sigma x_i^2 - \frac{(\Sigma x_i)^2}{N}}{N}$$

$$\sigma^2 = \frac{\Sigma x_i^2 - N\mu^2}{N}$$

Population standard deviation (ungrouped)

$$\sigma = \sqrt{\sigma^2}$$

$$\sigma = \sqrt{\frac{\Sigma (x_i - \mu)^2}{N}}$$

$$\sigma = \sqrt{\frac{\Sigma x_i^2 - \frac{(\Sigma x_i)^2}{N}}{N}}$$

$$\sigma = \sqrt{\frac{\Sigma x_i^2 - N\mu^2}{N}}$$

Grouped mean

$$\mu_{\text{grouped}} = \frac{\Sigma f_i M_i}{N}$$

Grouped Median

$$Median = L + \frac{\frac{N}{2} - cf_p}{f_{med}}(W)$$

Population variance (grouped)

$$\sigma^2 = \frac{\Sigma f_i(M_i - \mu)^2}{N} = \frac{\Sigma f_i M_i^2 - \frac{(\Sigma f_i M_i)^2}{N}}{N}$$

Population standard deviation (grouped)

$$\sigma = \sqrt{\frac{\Sigma f_i(M_i - \mu)^2}{N}} = \sqrt{\frac{\Sigma f_i M_i^2 - \frac{(\Sigma f_i M_i)^2}{N}}{N}}$$

Sample variance

$$s^2 = \frac{\Sigma(x_i - \bar{x})^2}{n - 1}$$

$$s^2 = \frac{\Sigma x_i^2 - \frac{(\Sigma x_i)^2}{n}}{n - 1}$$

$$s^2 = \frac{\Sigma x_i^2 - n(\bar{x})^2}{n - 1}$$

Sample standard deviation

$$s = \sqrt{s^2}$$

$$s = \sqrt{\frac{\Sigma(x_i - \bar{x})^2}{n - 1}}$$

$$s = \sqrt{\frac{\Sigma x_i^2 - \frac{(\Sigma x_i)^2}{n}}{n - 1}}$$

$$s = \sqrt{\frac{\Sigma x_i^2 - n(\bar{x})^2}{n - 1}}$$

Chebyshev's theorem

$$1 - \frac{1}{k^2}$$

z score

$$z = \frac{x_i - \mu}{\sigma}$$

Coefficient of variation

$$CV = \frac{\sigma}{\mu}(100)$$

Interquartile range

$$IQR = Q_3 - Q_1$$

Sample variance (grouped)

$$s^2 = \frac{\Sigma f_i(M_i - \bar{x})^2}{n - 1} = \frac{\Sigma f_i M_i^2 - \frac{(\Sigma f_i M_i)^2}{n}}{n - 1}$$

Sample standard deviation (grouped)

$$s = \sqrt{\frac{\Sigma f_i(M_i - \bar{x})^2}{n - 1}} = \sqrt{\frac{\Sigma f_i M_i^2 - \frac{(\Sigma f_i M_i)^2}{n}}{n - 1}}$$

Pearsonian coefficient of skewness

$$S_k = \frac{3(\mu - M_d)}{\sigma}$$

SUPPLEMENTARY PROBLEMS

CALCULATING THE STATISTICS

3.41 The 2010 U.S. Census asked every household to report information on each person living there. Suppose for a sample of 30 households selected, the number of persons living in each was reported as follows.

2 3 1 2 6 4 2 1 5 3 2 3 1 2 2
1 3 1 2 2 4 2 1 2 8 3 2 1 1 3

Compute the mean, median, mode, range, lower and upper quartiles, and interquartile range for these data.

3.42 The 2010 U.S. Census also asked for each person's age. Suppose that a sample of 40 households taken from the census data showed the age of the first person recorded on the census form to be as follows.

42 29 31 38 55 27 28
33 49 70 25 21 38 47
63 22 38 52 50 41 19
22 29 81 52 26 35 38
29 31 48 26 33 42 58
40 32 24 34 25

Compute P_{10}, P_{80}, Q_1, Q_3, the interquartile range, and the range for these data.

3.43 Shown below are the top 15 market research firms in the United States in 2008 according to *Marketing News*. Compute the mean, median, P_{30}, P_{60}, P_{90}, Q_1, Q_3, range, and the interquartile range on these data.

Company	Sales ($ millions)
The Nielsen Co.	2,231.0
Kantar Group	918.5
IMS Health Inc.	842.0
Westat Inc.	469.5
Information Resources Inc.	454.0
Arbitron Inc.	364.4
Gfk USA	313.1
Ipsos	307.6
Synovate	245.0
Maritz Research	197.4
J.D. Power & Associates	188.6
The NPD Group Inc.	168.5
Opinion Research Corp.	145.3
Harris Interactive Inc.	137.1
comScore Inc.	100.9

3.44 Shown in left column are the top 10 companies receiving the largest dollar volume of contract awards from the U.S. Department of Defense in 2009. Use this population data to compute a mean and a standard deviation for these top 10 companies.

Company	Amount of Contracts ($ billions)
Lockheed Martin	21.03
Boeing	15.94
General Dynamics	9.90
Northrop Grumman	9.89
Raytheon	8.51
United Technologies	4.93
L-3 Communications	4.15
BAE Systems	3.71
Humana	2.89
KBR	2.80

3.45 Shown here are the U.S. oil refineries with the largest capacity in terms of barrels per day according to the U.S. Energy Information Administration. Use these as population data and answer the questions.

Refinery Location	Company	Capacity
Baytown, Texas	ExxonMobil	560,640
Baton Rouge, Louisiana	ExxonMobil	504,500
Texas City, Texas	BP	437,080
Garyville, Louisiana	Marathon Oil	436,000
Lake Charles, Louisiana	Citgo	429,500
Whiting, Indiana	BP	405,000
Wood River, Illinois	WRB	362,000
Beaumont, Texas	ExxonMobil	344,500
Philadelphia, Pennsylvania	Sunoco	335,000
Pascagoula, Mississippi	Chevron	330,000

a. What are the values of the mean and the median? Compare the answers and state which you prefer as a measure of location for these data and why.
b. What are the values of the range and interquartile range? How do they differ?
c. What are the values of variance and standard deviation for these data?
d. What is the z score for Pascagoula, Mississippi? What is the z score for Texas City, Texas? Interpret these z scores.
e. Calculate the Pearsonian coefficient of skewness and comment on the skewness of this distribution.

3.46 The U.S. Department of the Interior releases figures on mineral production. Following are the 15 leading states in nonfuel mineral production in the United States in 2008.

State	Value ($ billions)
Arizona	7.84
Nevada	6.48
Florida	4.20
Utah	4.17
California	4.00
Texas	3.30
Minnesota	3.21
Alaska	2.74
Missouri	2.08
Colorado	2.05
Michigan	2.05
Wyoming	1.89
Georgia	1.85
New Mexico	1.81
Pennsylvania	1.68

a. Calculate the mean, median, and mode.
b. Calculate the range, interquartile range, mean absolute deviation, sample variance, and sample standard deviation.
c. Compute the Pearsonian coefficient of skewness for these data.
d. Sketch a box-and-whisker plot.

3.47 The radio music listener market is diverse. Listener formats might include adult contemporary, album rock, top 40, oldies, rap, country and western, classical, and jazz. In targeting audiences, market researchers need to be concerned about the ages of the listeners attracted to particular formats. Suppose a market researcher surveyed a sample of 170 listeners of country music radio stations and obtained the following age distribution.

Age	Frequency
15–under 20	9
20–under 25	16
25–under 30	27
30–under 35	44
35–under 40	42
40–under 45	23
45–under 50	7
50–under 55	2

a. What are the mean and modal ages of country music listeners?
b. What are the variance and standard deviation of the ages of country music listeners?

3.48 A research agency administers a demographic survey to 90 telemarketing companies to determine the size of their operations. When asked to report how many employees now work in their telemarketing operation, the companies gave responses ranging from 1 to 100. The agency's analyst organizes the figures into a frequency distribution.

Number of Employees Working in Telemarketing	Number of Companies
0–under 20	32
20–under 40	16
40–under 60	13
60–under 80	10
80–under 100	19

a. Compute the mean, median, and mode for this distribution.
b. Compute the sample standard deviation for these data.

TESTING YOUR UNDERSTANDING

3.49 Financial analysts like to use the standard deviation as a measure of risk for a stock. The greater the deviation in a stock price over time, the more risky it is to invest in the stock. However, the average prices of some stocks are considerably higher than the average price of others, allowing for the potential of a greater standard deviation of price. For example, a standard deviation of $5.00 on a $10.00 stock is considerably different from a $5.00 standard deviation on a $40.00 stock. In this situation, a coefficient of variation might provide insight into risk. Suppose stock X costs an average of $32.00 per share and showed a standard deviation of $3.45 for the past 60 days. Suppose stock Y costs an average of $84.00 per share and showed a standard deviation of $5.40 for the past 60 days. Use the coefficient of variation to determine the variability for each stock.

3.50 The Polk Company reported that the average age of a car on U.S. roads in a recent year was 7.5 years. Suppose the distribution of ages of cars on U.S. roads is approximately bellshaped. If 99.7% of the ages are between 1 year and 14 years, what is the standard deviation of car age? Suppose the standard deviation is 1.7 years and the mean is 7.5 years. Between what two values would 95% of the car ages fall?

3.51 According to a *Human Resources* report, a worker in the industrial countries spends on average 419 minutes a day on the job. Suppose the standard deviation of time spent on the job is 27 minutes.

    a. If the distribution of time spent on the job is approximately bell shaped, between what two times would 68% of the figures be? 95%? 99.7%?

    b. If the shape of the distribution of times is unknown, approximately what percentage of the times would be between 359 and 479 minutes?

    c. Suppose a worker spent 400 minutes on the job. What would that worker's z score be, and what would it tell the researcher?

3.52 During the 1990s, businesses were expected to show a lot of interest in Central and Eastern European countries. As new markets began to open, American business people needed a better understanding of the market potential there. The following are the per capita GDP figures for eight of these European countries published by the *World Almanac*. **Note:** The per capita GDP for the United States is $46,900.

Country	Per Capita GDP (U.S. $)
Albania	6,000
Bulgaria	12,900
Croatia	18,300
Czech Republic	25,900
Hungary	19,800
Poland	17,300
Romania	12,200
Bosnia/Herzegovina	6,500

    a. Compute the mean and standard deviation for Albania, Bulgaria, Croatia, and Czech Republic.

    b. Compute the mean and standard deviation for Hungary, Poland, Romania, and Bosnia/Herzegovina.

    c. Use a coefficient of variation to compare the two standard deviations. Treat the data as population data.

3.53 According to the Bureau of Labor Statistics, the average annual salary of a worker in Detroit, Michigan, is $35,748. Suppose the median annual salary for a worker in this group is $31,369 and the mode is $29,500. Is the distribution of salaries for this group skewed? If so, how and why? Which of these measures of central tendency would you use to describe these data? Why?

3.54 According to the U.S. Army Corps of Engineers, the top 20 U.S. ports, ranked by total tonnage (in million tons), were as follows.

Port	Total Tonnage
South Louisiana, LA	229.0
Houston, TX	216.1
New York, NY and NJ	157.2
Long Beach, CA	85.9
Beaumont, TX	81.4
Corpus Christi, TX	81.1
Huntington, WV, KY, and OH	76.5
New Orleans, LA	76.0
Los Angeles, CA	65.5
Mobile, AL	64.5
Lake Charles, LA	64.2
Plaquemines, LA	58.5
Texas City, TX	56.8
Baton Rouge, LA	54.6
Tampa, FL	46.9
Duluth-Superior, MN and WI	46.5
Baltimore, MD	41.3
Norfolk Harbor, VA	39.7
Pittsburgh, PA	38.1
Paulsboro, NJ	38.0

    a. Construct a box-and-whisker plot for these data.

    b. Discuss the shape of the distribution from the plot.

    c. Are there outliers?

    d. What are they and why do you think they are outliers?

3.55 *Runzheimer International* publishes data on overseas business travel costs. They report that the average per diem total for a business traveler in Paris, France, is $349. Suppose the shape of the distribution of the per diem costs of a business traveler to Paris is unknown, but that 53% of the per diem figures are between $317 and $381. What is the value of the standard deviation? The average per diem total for a business traveler in Moscow is $415. If the shape of the distribution of per diem costs of a business traveler in Moscow is unknown and if 83% of the per diem costs in Moscow lie between $371 and $459, what is the standard deviation?

INTERPRETING THE OUTPUT

3.56 Netvalley.com compiled a list of the top 100 banks in the United States according to total assets. Leading the list was Bank of America, followed by JPMorgan Chase and Citibank. Following is an Excel analysis of total assets ($ billions) of these banks using the descriptive statistics feature. Study the output and describe in your own words what you can learn about the assets of these top 100 banks.

Top 100 Banks in U.S.	
Mean	76.5411
Standard error	17.93374
Median	21.97
Mode	13.01
Standard deviation	179.3374
Sample variance	32161.9
Kurtosis	22.2632
Skewness	4.586275
Range	1096.01
Minimum	8.99
Maximum	1105
Sum	7654.11
Count	100

3.57 *Hispanic Business* magazine publishes a list of the top 50 advertisers in the Hispanic market. The advertising spending for each of these 50 advertisers (in $ millions) was entered into a Minitab spreadsheet and the data were analyzed using Minitab's Graphical Summary. Study the output from this analysis and describe the advertising expenditures of these top Hispanic market advertisers.

3.58 Excel was used to analyze the number of employees for the top 60 employers with headquarters around the world outside of the United States. The data was compiled by myglobalcareer.com, extracted from *My Global Career 500*, and was analyzed using Excel's descriptive statistics feature. Summarize what you have learned about the number of employees for these companies by studying the output.

Top 60 Employers Outside of the U.S.	
Mean	211942.9
Standard error	12415.31
Median	175660
Mode	150000
Standard deviation	96168.57
Sample variance	9.25E+09
Kurtosis	1.090976
Skewness	1.356847
Range	387245
Minimum	115300
Maximum	502545
Sum	12716575
Count	60

3.59 The Nielsen Company compiled a list of the top 25 advertisers in African American media. Shown below are a Minitab descriptive statistics analysis of the annual advertising spending in $ million by these companies in African American media and a box plot of these data. Study this output and summarize the expenditures of these top 25 advertisers in your own words.

Top 50 Advertisers in the Hispanic Market

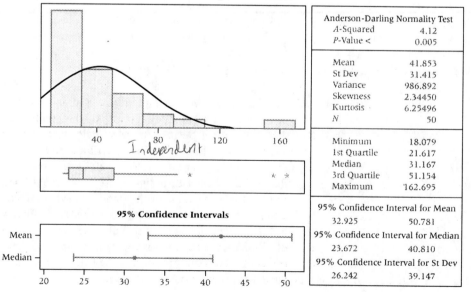

Anderson-Darling Normality Test	
A-Squared	4.12
P-Value <	0.005

Mean	41.853
St Dev	31.415
Variance	986.892
Skewness	2.34450
Kurtosis	6.25496
N	50

Minimum	18.079
1st Quartile	21.617
Median	31.167
3rd Quartile	51.154
Maximum	162.695

95% Confidence Interval for Mean	
32.925	50.781

95% Confidence Interval for Median	
23.672	40.810

95% Confidence Interval for St Dev	
26.242	39.147

Variable	N	N*	Mean	SE Mean	StDev	Minimum	Q_1
Advertisers	25	0	27.24	2.84	14.19	16.20	21.25

Variable	Median	Q_3	Maximum
Advertisers	24.00	27.50	89.70

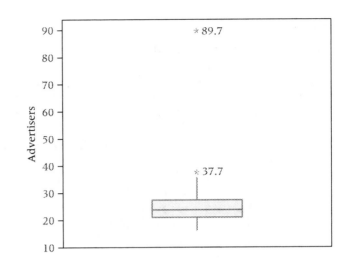

see www.wiley.com/college/black

ANALYZING THE DATABASES

1. What are the mean and the median amounts of new capital expenditures for industries in the Manufacturing database? Comparing the mean and the median for these data, what do these statistics tell you about the data?

2. Analyze U.S. finished motor gasoline production in the 12-Year Gasoline database using a descriptive statistics feature of either Excel or Minitab. By examining such statistics as the mean, median, mode, range, standard deviation, and a measure of skewness, describe U.S. motor gasoline production over this period of time.

3. Using measures of central tendency including the mean, median, and mode, describe annual food spending and annual household income for the 200 households in the Consumer Food database. Compare the two results by determining approximately what percent of annual household income is spent on food.

4. Using the Financial database, study earnings per share for Type 2 and Type 7 companies (chemical and petrochemical) using statistics. Compute a coefficient of variation for both Type 2 and Type 7. Compare the two coefficients and comment on them.

5. Using the Hospital database, construct a box-and-whisker plot for births. Thinking about hospitals and birthing facilities, comment on why the box-and-whisker plot looks like it does.

CASE

COCA-COLA DEVELOPS THE AFRICAN MARKET

The Coca-Cola Company is the number-one seller of soft drinks in the world. Every day an average of more than 1.6 billion servings of Coca-Cola, Diet Coke, Sprite, Fanta, and other products of Coca-Cola are enjoyed around the world. The company has the world's largest production and distribution system for soft drinks and sells more than twice as many soft drinks as its nearest competitor. Coca-Cola products are sold in more than 200 countries around the globe.

For a variety of reasons in developing countries, sales have been flat or growing slowly. For example, in 1989, North Americans bought $2.6 billion worth of Coke, but in 2009, the figure had only grown to $2.9 billion. Looking for attractive, newer, growing markets, Coca-Cola has turned its attention to Africa. The potential is great there, with 59 million African households earning enough in the year 2000 to be able to spend half their income on nonfood items. This figure is expected to increase to 106 million by the year 2014. Africa has very little debt and a positive trade balance, which can add to its attraction as a place to invest. While Coke has been in Africa since 1929, more recently it has made substantial efforts to significantly increase sales there, building on its current presence. At present, Coke is Africa's largest employer, with 65,000 employees and 160 plants. Its market share in Africa and the Middle East is 29%, and 9.1 billion liters of beverage are sold by Coca-Cola there annually. Building on techniques learned in Latin America, Coke is trying to earn new customers in Africa by winning over small stores. Moving throughout villages and towns, Coca-Cola is distributing Coke signage and drink coolers to shop after shop. In an effort to distribute their products in areas with poor roads and to reach remote areas, Coca-Cola is establishing Manual Distribution Centers like they used in Vietnam and Thailand. Such centers currently employ more than 12,000 Africans and generate $500 million in annual revenue.

Discussion

1. In several countries of Africa, a common size for a Coke can is 340 milliliters (mL). Because of the variability of bottling machinery, it is likely that every 340-mL bottle of Coca-Cola does not contain exactly 340 milliliters of fluid. Some bottles may contain more fluid and others less. Because of this variation, a production engineer wants to test some of the bottles from a production run to determine how close they are to the 340-mL specification. Suppose the following data are the fill measurements from a random sample of 50 cans. Use the techniques presented in this chapter to describe the sample. Consider measures of central tendency, variability, and skewness. Based on this analysis, how is the bottling process working on this production run?

340.1	339.9	340.2	340.2	340.0
340.1	340.9	340.1	340.3	340.5
339.7	340.4	340.3	339.8	339.3
340.1	339.4	339.6	339.2	340.2
340.4	339.8	339.9	340.2	339.6
339.6	340.4	340.4	340.6	340.6
340.1	340.8	339.9	340.0	339.9
340.3	340.5	339.9	341.1	339.7
340.2	340.5	340.2	339.7	340.9
340.2	339.5	340.6	340.3	339.8

2. Suppose that at another plant Coca-Cola is filling bottles with 20 ounces of fluid. A lab randomly samples 150 bottles and tests the bottles for fill volume. The descriptive statistics are given in both Minitab and Excel computer output. Write a brief report to supervisors summarizing what this output is saying about the process.

Minitab Output

Descriptive Statistics: Bottle Fills

Variable	Total Count	Mean	SE Mean	StDev	Variance	CoefVar	Minimum	Q_1
Bottle Fills	150	20.008	0.00828	0.101	0.0103	0.51	19.706	19.940

Variable	Median	Q_3	Maximum	Range	IQR
Bottle Fills	19.997	20.079	20.263	0.557	0.139

Summary for Bottle Fills

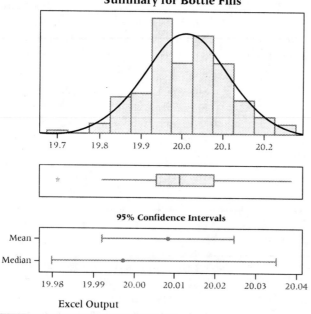

Anderson-Darling Normality Test	
A-Squared	0.32
P-Value	0.531
Mean	20.008
St Dev	0.101
Variance	0.010
Skewness	0.080479
Kurtosis	−0.116220
N	150
Minimum	19.706
1st Quartile	19.940
Median	19.997
3rd Quartile	20.079
Maximum	20.263
95% Confidence Interval for Mean	
19.992 20.025	
95% Confidence Interval for Median	
19.980 20.035	
95% Confidence Interval for St Dev	
0.091 0.114	

Excel Output

Bottle Fills	
Mean	20.00817
Standard error	0.008278
Median	19.99697
Mode	#N/A
Standard deviation	0.101388
Sample variance	0.010279
Kurtosis	−0.11422
Skewness	0.080425
Range	0.557666
Minimum	19.70555
Maximum	20.26322
Sum	3001.225
Count	150

Sources: Duane D. Stanford, "Coke's Last Round," *Bloomberg Businessweek*, November 1–7, 2010, pp. 54–61; "Dimensions of a Standard Coke Can," Dimensionsguide, http://www.dimensionsguide.com/dimensions-of-a-standard-coke-can. View Coca-Cola Company's 2009 annual report at http://www.thecoca-colacompany.com/investors/pdfs/10-K_2009/03_Coca-Cola_Item1.pdf.

USING THE COMPUTER

EXCEL

◾ While Excel has the capability of producing many of the statistics in this chapter piecemeal, there is one Excel feature, **Descriptive Statistics**, that produces many of these statistics in one output.

◾ To use the **Descriptive Statistics** feature, begin by selecting the **Data** tab on the Excel worksheet. From the **Analysis** panel at the right top of the **Data** tab worksheet, click on **Data Analysis**. If your Excel worksheet does not show the **Data Analysis** option, then you can load it as an add-in following directions given in Chapter 2. From the **Data Analysis** pulldown menu, select **Descriptive Statistics**. In the **Descriptive Statistics** dialog box, enter the location of the data to be analyzed in **Input Range**. Check **Labels in the First Row** if your data contains a label in the first row (cell). Check the box beside **Summary statistics**. The **Summary statistics** feature computes a wide variety of descriptive statistics. The output includes the mean, the median, the mode, the standard deviation, the sample variance, a measure of kurtosis, a measure of skewness, the range, the minimum, the maximum, the sum and the count.

◾ The **Rank and Percentile** feature of the **Data Analysis** tool of Excel has the capability of ordering the data, assigning ranks to the data, and yielding the percentiles of the data. To access this command, click on **Data Analysis** (see above) and select **Rank and Percentile** from the menu. In the **Rank and Percentile** dialog box, enter the location of the data to be analyzed in **Input Range**. Check **Labels in the First Row** if your data contains a label in the first row (cell).

◾ Many of the individual statistics presented in this chapter can be computed using the **Insert Function** (f_x) of Excel. To access the **Insert Function**, go to the **Formulas** tab on an Excel worksheet (top center tab). The **Insert Function** is on the far left of the menu bar. In the **Insert Function** dialog box at the top, there is a pulldown menu where it says **Or select a category**. From the pulldown menu associated with this command, select **Statistical**. There are 83 different statistics that can be computed using one of these commands. Select the one that you want to compute and enter the location of the data. Some of the more useful commands in this menu are **AVERAGE, MEDIAN, MODE.SNGL, SKEW, STDEV.S,** and **VAR.S.**

MINITAB

◾ Minitab is capable of performing many of the tasks presented in this chapter, including descriptive statistics and box plots. To begin Descriptive Statistics, select **Stat** on the menu bar, and then from the pulldown menu select **Basic Statistics**. From the **Basic Statistics** menu, select either **Display Descriptive Statistics** or **Graphical Summary**. If you select **DisplayDescriptiveStatistics** in the dialog box that appears, input the column(s) to be analyzed in the box labeled **Variables**. If you click **OK**, then your output will include the sample size, mean, median, standard deviation, minimum, the first quartile, and the third quartile. If in the **Display Descriptive Statistics** dialog box you select the option **Graphs**, you will have several other output options that are relatively self-explanatory. The options include **Histogram of data; Histogram of data, with normal curve; Individual value plot;** and **Boxplot of data**. If in the **Display Descriptive Statistics** dialog box you select the option **Statistics**, you have the option of selecting any of 24 statistics offered to appear in your output.

◾ On the other hand, you may opt to use the **Graphical Summary** option under **Basic Statistics**. If you use this option, in the dialog box that appears input the column(s) to be analyzed in the box labeled **Variables**. If you click **OK**, then your output will include a histogram graph of the data with the normal curve superimposed, a box plot of the data, the same descriptive statistics listed above for the output from **Display Descriptive Statistics**, along with skewness and kurtosis statistics and other output that pertain to Chapter 8 topics.

◾ A variety of descriptive statistics can be obtained through the use of **Column Statistics** or **Row Statistics**. To begin, select **Calc** from the menu bar. From the pulldown menu, select either **Column Statistics** or **Row Statistics**, depending on where the data are located. For **Column Statistics**, in the space below **Input variable**, enter the column to be analyzed. For **Row Statistics**, in the space below **Input variables**, enter the rows to be analyzed. Check which **Statistic** you want to compute from **Sum, Mean, Standard deviation, Minimum, Maximum, Range, Median,** and **N total**. Minitab will only allow you to select one statistic at a time.

◾ Minitab can produce box-and-whisker plots. To begin, select **Graph** from the menu bar, and then select **Boxplot** from the pulldown menu.

In the Boxplot dialog box, there are four options: **One Y Simple, One Y With Groups, Multiple Y's Simple,** and **Multiple Y's With Groups;** and you must select one.

After you select one of these types of box plots, another dialog box appears with several options to select, including: **Scale..., Labels..., Data View..., Multiple Graphs...,** and **Data Options...**

Enter the location of the variables to be graphed in the top box labeled **Graph variables**, and click **OK**.

CHAPTER 4

Probability

LEARNING OBJECTIVES

The main objective of Chapter 4 is to help you understand the basic principles of probability, thereby enabling you to:

1. Describe what probability is and when one would use it
2. Differentiate among three methods of assigning probabilities: the classical method, relative frequency of occurrence, and subjective probability
3. Deconstruct the elements of probability by defining experiments, sample spaces, and events, classifying events as mutually exclusive, collectively exhaustive, complementary, or independent, and counting possibilities
4. Compare marginal, union, joint, and conditional probabilities by defining each one
5. Calculate probabilities using the general law of addition, along with a joint probability table, the complement of a union, or the special law of addition if necessary
6. Calculate joint probabilities of both independent and dependent events using the general and special laws of multiplication
7. Calculate conditional probabilities with various forms of the law of conditional probability, and use them to determine if two events are independent.
8. Calculate conditional probabilities using Bayes' rule

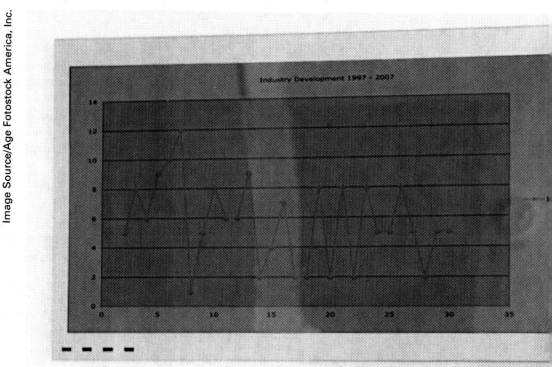

Image Source/Age Fotostock America, Inc.

Equity of the Sexes in the Workplace

The Civil Rights Act was signed into law in the United States in 1964 by President Lyndon Johnson. This law, which was amended in 1972, resulted in several "titles" that addressed discrimination in American society at various levels. One is Title VII, which pertains specifically to employment discrimination. It applies to all employers with more than 15 employees, along with other institutions. One of the provisions of Title VII makes it illegal to refuse to hire a person on the basis of the person's sex.

Today, company hiring procedures must be within the purview and framework of the Equal Employment Opportunity Commission (EEOC) guidelines and Title VII. How does a company defend its hiring practices or know when they are within acceptable bounds? How can individuals or groups who feel they have been the victims of illegal hiring practices "prove" their case? How can a group demonstrate that they have been "adversely impacted" by a company's discriminatory hiring practices?

Statistics are widely used in employment discrimination actions and by companies in attempting to meet EEOC guidelines. Substantial quantities of human resources data are logged and analyzed on a daily basis.

Managerial and Statistical Questions

Assume that a small portion of the human resource data was gathered on a client company.

1. Suppose some legal concern has been expressed that a disproportionate number of managerial people at the client company are men. If a worker is randomly selected from the client company, what is the probability that the worker is a woman? If a managerial person is randomly selected, what is the probability that the person is a woman? What factors might enter into the apparent discrepancy between probabilities?

2. Suppose a special bonus is being given to one person in the technical area this year. If the bonus is randomly awarded, what is the probability that it will go to a woman, given that worker is in the technical area? Is this discrimination against male technical workers? What factors might enter into the awarding of the bonus other than random selection?

3. Suppose that at the annual holiday party the name of an employee of the client company will be drawn randomly to win a trip to Hawaii. What is the probability that a professional person will be the winner? What is the probability that the winner will be either a man or a clerical worker? What is the probability that the winner will be a woman and in management? Suppose the winner is a man. What is the probability that the winner is from the technical group, given that the winner is a man?

Source: EEOC information adapted from Richard D. Arvey and Robert H. Faley, *Fairness in Selecting Employees*, 2nd ed. Reading, MA: Addison-Wesley Publishing Company, 1992.

Client Company Human Resource Data by Sex

| Type of Position | Sex | | |
	Male	Female	Total
Managerial	8	3	11
Professional	31	13	44
Technical	52	17	69
Clerical	9	22	31
Total	100	55	155

In business, most decision making involves uncertainty. For example, an operations manager does not know definitely whether a valve in the plant is going to malfunction or continue to function—or, if it continues, for how long. When should it be replaced? What is the chance that the valve will malfunction within the next week? In the banking industry, what are the new vice president's prospects for successfully turning a department around? The answers to these questions are uncertain.

In the case of a high-rise building, what are the chances that a fire-extinguishing system will work when needed if redundancies are built in? Business people must address these and thousands of similar questions daily. Because most such questions do not have definite answers, the decision making is based on uncertainty. In many of these situations, a probability can be assigned to the likelihood of an outcome. This chapter is about learning how to determine or assign probabilities.

FIGURE 4.1

Probability in the Process of
Inferential Statistics

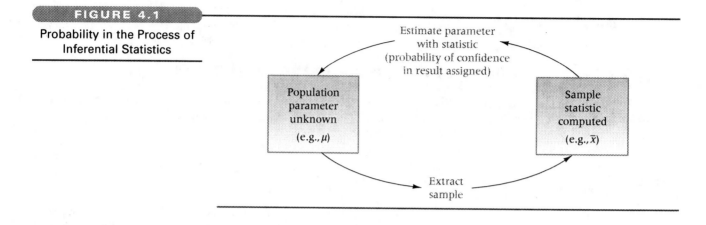

4.1 INTRODUCTION TO PROBABILITY

Chapter 1 discussed the difference between descriptive and inferential statistics. Much statistical analysis is inferential, and probability is the basis for inferential statistics. Recall that inferential statistics involves taking a sample from a population, computing a statistic on the sample, and inferring from the statistic the value of the corresponding parameter of the population. The reason for doing so is that the value of the parameter is unknown. Because it is unknown, the analyst conducts the inferential process under uncertainty. However, by applying rules and laws, the analyst can often assign a probability of obtaining the results. Figure 4.1 depicts this process.

Suppose a quality control inspector selects a random sample of 40 lightbulbs from a population of brand X bulbs and computes the average number of hours of luminance for the sample bulbs. By using techniques discussed later in this text, the specialist estimates the average number of hours of luminance for the *population* of brand X lightbulbs from this sample information. Because the lightbulbs being analyzed are only a sample of the population, the average number of hours of luminance for the 40 bulbs may or may not accurately estimate the average for all bulbs in the population. The results are uncertain. By applying the laws presented in this chapter, the inspector can assign a value of probability to this estimate.

In addition, probabilities are used directly in certain industries and industry applications. For example, the insurance industry uses probabilities in actuarial tables to determine the likelihood of certain outcomes in order to set specific rates and coverages. The gaming industry uses probability values to establish charges and payoffs. One way to determine whether a company's hiring practices meet the government's EEOC guidelines mentioned in the Decision Dilemma is to compare various proportional breakdowns of their employees (by ethnicity, gender, age, etc.) to the proportions in the general population from which the employees are hired. In comparing the company figures with those of the general population, the courts could study the probabilities of a company randomly hiring a certain profile of employees from a given population. In other industries, such as manufacturing and aerospace, it is important to know the life of a mechanized part and the probability that it will malfunction at any given length of time in order to protect the firm from major breakdowns.

4.2 METHODS OF ASSIGNING PROBABILITIES

The three general methods of assigning probabilities are (1) the classical method, (2) the relative frequency of occurrence method, and (3) subjective probabilities.

Classical Method of Assigning Probabilities

When probabilities are assigned based on laws and rules, the method is referred to as the **classical method of assigning probabilities**. This method involves an experiment, which is *a process that produces outcomes*, and an event, *which is an outcome of an experiment.*

When we assign probabilities using the classical method, the probability of an individual event occurring is determined as the ratio of the number of items in a population containing the event (n_e) to the total number of items in the population (N). That is, $P(E) = n_e/N$. For example, if a company has 200 workers and 70 are female, the probability of randomly selecting a female from this company is $70/200 = .35$.

CLASSICAL METHOD OF ASSIGNING PROBABILITIES	$$P(E) = \frac{n_e}{N}$$ where N = total possible number of outcomes of an experiment n_e = the number of outcomes in which the event occurs out of N outcomes

Based on experiment (handwritten annotation)

Suppose, in a particular plant, three machines make a given product. Machine A always produces 40% of the total number of this product. Ten percent of the items produced by machine A are defective. If the finished products are well mixed with regard to which machine produced them and if one of these products is randomly selected, the classical method of assigning probabilities tells us that the probability that the part was produced by machine A and is defective is .04. This probability can be determined even before the part is sampled because with the classical method, the probabilities can be determined **a priori**; that is, *they can be determined prior to the experiment.*

Because n_e can never be greater than N (no more than N outcomes in the population could possibly have attribute e), the highest value of any probability is 1. If the probability of an outcome occurring is 1, the event is certain to occur. The smallest possible probability is 0. If none of the outcomes of the N possibilities has the desired characteristic, e, the probability is $0/N = 0$, and the event is certain not to occur.

RANGE OF POSSIBLE PROBABILITIES	$$0 \leq P(E) \leq 1$$

Thus, probabilities are nonnegative proper fractions or nonnegative decimal values greater than or equal to 0 and less than or equal to 1.

Probability values can be converted to percentages by multiplying by 100. Meteorologists often report weather probabilities in percentage form. For example, when they forecast a 60% chance of rain for tomorrow, they are saying that the probability of rain tomorrow is .60.

Relative Frequency of Occurrence

The **relative frequency of occurrence method** of assigning probabilities is based on cumulated historical data. With this method, *the probability of an event occurring is equal to the number of times the event has occurred in the past divided by the total number of opportunities for the event to have occurred.*

Based on the past (handwritten annotation)

PROBABILITY BY RELATIVE FREQUENCY OF OCCURRENCE	Number of Times an Event Occurred ———————————————————————— Total Number of Opportunities for the Event to Have Occurred

Relative frequency of occurrence is not based on rules or laws but on what has occurred in the past. For example, a company wants to determine the probability that its inspectors are going to reject the next batch of raw materials from a supplier. Data gathered from company record books show that the supplier sent the company 90 batches in the past, and inspectors rejected 10 of them. By the method of relative frequency of occurrence, the probability of the inspectors rejecting the next batch is 10/90, or .11. If the next batch is rejected, the relative frequency of occurrence probability for the subsequent shipment would change to $11/91 = .12$.

Based on feeling

Subjective Probability

The **subjective method** of *assigning probability is based on the feelings or insights of the person determining the probability.* Subjective probability comes from the person's intuition or reasoning. Although not a scientific approach to probability, the subjective method often is based on the accumulation of knowledge, understanding, and experience stored and processed in the human mind. At times it is merely a guess. At other times, subjective probability can potentially yield accurate probabilities. Subjective probability can be used to capitalize on the background of experienced workers and managers in decision making.

Suppose a director of transportation for an oil company is asked the probability of getting a shipment of oil out of Saudi Arabia to the United States within three weeks. A director who has scheduled many such shipments, has a knowledge of Saudi politics, and has an awareness of current climatological and economic conditions may be able to give an accurate probability that the shipment can be made on time.

Subjective probability also can be a potentially useful way of tapping a person's experience, knowledge, and insight and using them to forecast the occurrence of some event. An experienced airline mechanic can usually assign a meaningful probability that a particular plane will have a certain type of mechanical difficulty. Physicians sometimes assign subjective probabilities to the life expectancy of people who have cancer.

4.3 STRUCTURE OF PROBABILITY

In the study of probability, developing a language of terms and symbols is helpful. The structure of probability provides a common framework within which the topics of probability can be explored.

Experiment

As previously stated, an **experiment** is *a process that produces outcomes.* Examples of business-oriented experiments with outcomes that can be statistically analyzed might include the following.

- Interviewing 20 randomly selected consumers and asking them which brand of appliance they prefer
- Sampling every 200th bottle of ketchup from an assembly line and weighing the contents
- Testing new pharmaceutical drugs on samples of cancer patients and measuring the patients' improvement
- Auditing every 10th account to detect any errors
- Recording the Dow Jones Industrial Average on the first Monday of every month for 10 years

Event

Because an **event** is *an outcome of an experiment,* the experiment defines the possibilities of the event. If the experiment is to sample five bottles coming off a production line, an event could be to get one defective and four good bottles. In an experiment to roll a die, one event could be to roll an even number and another event could be to roll a number greater than two. Events are denoted by uppercase letters; italic capital letters (e.g., A and E_1, E_2, . . .) represent the general or abstract case, and roman capital letters (e.g., H and T for heads and tails) denote specific things and people.

Elementary Events

Events that cannot be decomposed or broken down into other events are called **elementary events.** Elementary events are denoted by lowercase letters (e.g., e_1, e_2, e_3, . . .). Suppose the experiment is to roll a die. The elementary events for this experiment are to roll a 1 or roll a 2 or roll a 3, and so on. Rolling an even number is an event, but it is not an elementary event because the even number can be broken down further into events 2, 4, and 6.

Possible Outcomes for the
Roll of a Pair of Dice

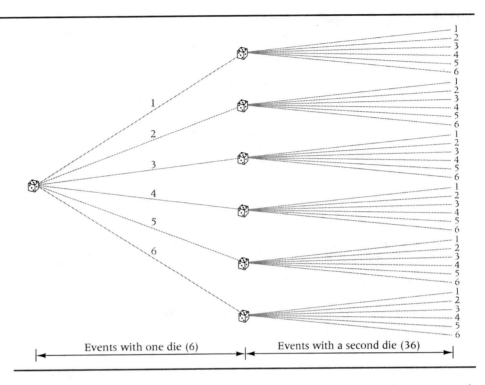

In the experiment of rolling a die, there are six elementary events {1, 2, 3, 4, 5, 6}. Rolling a pair of dice results in 36 possible elementary events (outcomes). For each of the six elementary events possible on the roll of one die, there are six possible elementary events on the roll of the second die, as depicted in the tree diagram in Figure 4.2. Table 4.1 contains a list of these 36 outcomes.

In the experiment of rolling a pair of dice, other events could include outcomes such as two even numbers, a sum of 10, a sum greater than five, and others. However, none of these events is an elementary event because each can be broken down into several of the elementary events displayed in Table 4.1.

Sample Space

A **sample space** is *a complete roster or listing of all elementary events for an experiment*. Table 4.1 is the sample space for the roll of a pair of dice. The sample space for the roll of a single die is {1, 2, 3, 4, 5, 6}.

Sample space can aid in finding probabilities. Suppose an experiment is to roll a pair of dice. What is the probability that the dice will sum to 7? An examination of the sample space shown in Table 4.1 reveals that there are six outcomes in which the dice sum to 7—{(1,6), (2,5), (3,4), (4,3), (5,2), (6,1)}—in the total possible 36 elementary events in the sample space. Using this information, we can conclude that the probability of rolling a pair of dice that sum to 7 is 6/36, or .1667. However, using the sample space to determine probabilities is unwieldy and cumbersome when the sample space is large. Hence, statisticians usually use other more effective methods of determining probability.

Unions and Intersections

Set notation, the use of braces to group numbers, is used as *a symbolic tool for unions and intersections* in this chapter. The **union** of X, Y is *formed by combining elements from each of the sets*

All Possible Elementary
Events in the Roll of a Pair
of Dice (Sample Space)

(1,1)	(2,1)	(3,1)	(4,1)	(5,1)	(6,1)
(1,2)	(2,2)	(3,2)	(4,2)	(5,2)	(6,2)
(1,3)	(2,3)	(3,3)	(4,3)	(5,3)	(6,3)
(1,4)	(2,4)	(3,4)	(4,4)	(5,4)	(6,4)
(1,5)	(2,5)	(3,5)	(4,5)	(5,5)	(6,5)
(1,6)	(2,6)	(3,6)	(4,6)	(5,6)	(6,6)

FIGURE 4.3

A Union

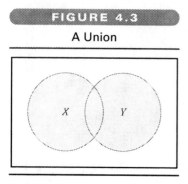

and is denoted $X \cup Y$. An element qualifies for the union of X, Y if it is in either X or Y or in both X and Y. The union expression $X \cup Y$ can be translated to "X or Y." For example, if

$$A = \{1, 4, 7, 9\} \quad \text{and} \quad B = \{2, 3, 4, 5, 6\}$$
$$A \cup B = \{1, 2, 3, 4, 5, 6, 7, 9\}$$

Note that all the values of A and all the values of B qualify for the union. However, none of the values is listed more than once in the union. In Figure 4.3, the shaded region of the Venn diagram denotes the union.

An intersection is denoted $X \cap Y$. To qualify for intersection, an element must be in both X and Y. The **intersection** *contains the elements common to both sets.* Thus the intersection symbol, $\cap$, is often read as *and.* The intersection of X, Y is referred to as X and Y. For example, if

$$A = \{1, 4, 7, 9\} \quad \text{and} \quad B = \{2, 3, 4, 5, 6\}$$
$$A \cap B = \{4\}$$

FIGURE 4.4

An Intersection

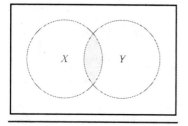

Note that only the value 4 is common to both sets A and B. The intersection is more exclusive than and hence equal to or (usually) smaller than the union. Elements must be characteristic of both X and Y to qualify. In Figure 4.4, the shaded region denotes the intersection.

Mutually Exclusive Events

Two or more events are **mutually exclusive events** if *the occurrence of one event precludes the occurrence of the other event(s).* This characteristic means that mutually exclusive events cannot occur simultaneously and therefore can have no intersection.

A manufactured part is either defective or okay: The part cannot be both okay and defective at the same time because "okay" and "defective" are mutually exclusive categories. In a sample of the manufactured products, the event of selecting a defective part is mutually exclusive with the event of selecting a nondefective part. Suppose an office building is for sale and two different potential buyers have placed bids on the building. It is not possible for both buyers to purchase the building; therefore, the event of buyer A purchasing the building is mutually exclusive with the event of buyer B purchasing the building. In the toss of a single coin, heads and tails are mutually exclusive events. The person tossing the coin gets either a head or a tail but never both.

The probability of two mutually exclusive events occurring at the same time is zero.

MUTUALLY EXCLUSIVE EVENTS X AND Y	$P(X \cap Y) = 0$

Independent Events

Two or more events are **independent events** if *the occurrence or nonoccurrence of one of the events does not affect the occurrence or nonoccurrence of the other event(s).* Certain experiments, such as rolling dice, yield independent events; each die is independent of the other. Whether a 6 is rolled on the first die has no influence on whether a 6 is rolled on the second die. Coin tosses always are independent of each other. The event of getting a head on the first toss of a coin is independent of getting a head on the second toss. It is generally believed that certain human characteristics are independent of other events. For example, left-handedness is probably independent of the possession of a credit card. Whether a person wears glasses or not is probably independent of the brand of milk preferred.

Many experiments using random selection can produce either independent or nonindependent event, depending on how the experiment is conducted. In these experiments, the outcomes are independent if sampling is done with replacement; that is, after each item is selected and the outcome is determined, the item is restored to the population and the population is shuffled. This way, each draw becomes independent of the previous draw. Suppose an inspector is randomly selecting bolts from a bin that contains 5% defects. If the inspector samples a defective bolt and returns it to the bin, on the second draw there are still 5% defects in the bin regardless of the fact that the first outcome was a defect. If the inspector does not replace the first draw, the second draw is not independent of the first; in this case, fewer than 5% defects remain in the population. Thus the probability of the second outcome is dependent on the first outcome.

If X and Y are independent, the following symbolic notation is used.

INDEPENDENT EVENTS X AND Y	$P(X|Y) = P(X)$ and $P(Y|X) = P(Y)$

$P(X|Y)$ denotes the probability of X occurring given that Y has occurred. If X and Y are independent, then the probability of X occurring given that Y has occurred is just the probability of X occurring. Knowledge that Y has occurred does not impact the probability of X occurring because X and Y are independent. For example, P (prefers Pepsi|person is right-handed) = P (prefers Pepsi) because a person's handedness is independent of brand preference.

Collectively Exhaustive Events

A list of **collectively exhaustive events** contains *all possible elementary events for an experiment.* Thus, all sample spaces are collectively exhaustive lists. The list of possible outcomes for the tossing of a pair of dice contained in Table 4.1 is a collectively exhaustive list. The sample space for an experiment can be described as a list of events that are mutually exclusive and collectively exhaustive. Sample space events do not overlap or intersect, and the list is complete.

FIGURE 4.5

The Complement of Event X

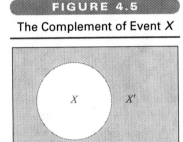

Complementary Events

The **complement** of event X is denoted X', pronounced "not X." All *the elementary events of an experiment not in X comprise its complement.* For example, if in rolling one die, event X is getting an even number, the complement of X is getting an odd number. If event X is getting a 5 on the roll of a die, the complement of X is getting a 1, 2, 3, 4, or 6. The complement of event X contains whatever portion of the sample space that event X does not contain, as the Venn diagram in Figure 4.5 shows.

Using the complement of an event sometimes can be helpful in solving for probabilities because of the following rule.

PROBABILITY OF THE COMPLEMENT OF X	$P(X') = 1 - P(X)$

Suppose 32% of the employees of a company have a college degree. If an employee is randomly selected from the company, the probability that the person does not have a college degree is $1 - .32 = .68$. Suppose 42% of all parts produced in a plant are molded by machine A and 31% are molded by machine B. If a part is randomly selected, the probability that it was molded by neither machine A nor machine B is $1 - .73 = .27$. (Assume that a part is only molded on one machine.)

Counting the Possibilities

In statistics, a collection of techniques and rules for counting the number of outcomes that can occur for a particular experiment can be used. Some of these rules and techniques can delineate the size of the sample space. Presented here are three of these counting methods.

The *mn* Counting Rule

Suppose a customer decides to buy a certain brand of new car. Options for the car include two different engines, five different paint colors, and three interior packages. If each of these options is available with each of the others, how many different cars could the customer choose from? To determine this number, we can use the ***mn* counting rule.**

THE *mn* COUNTING RULE	For an operation that can be done *m* ways and a second operation that can be done *n* ways, the two operations then can occur, in order, in *mn* ways. This rule can be extended to cases with three or more operations.

Using the *mn* counting rule, we can determine that the automobile customer has $(2)(5)(3) = 30$ different car combinations of engines, paint colors, and interiors available.

Suppose a scientist wants to set up a research design to study the effects of sex (M, F), marital status (single never married, divorced, married), and economic class (lower, middle, and upper) on the frequency of airline ticket purchases per year. The researcher would set up a design in which 18 different samples are taken to represent all possible groups generated from these customer characteristics.

$$\text{Number of Groups} = (\text{Sex})(\text{Marital Status})(\text{Economic Class})$$
$$= (2)(3)(3) = 18 \text{ Groups}$$

Sampling from a Population with Replacement

In the second counting method, sampling *n* items from a population of size *N* *with replacement* would provide

$$(N)^n \text{ possibilities}$$

where

N = population size
n = sample size

For example, each time a die, which has six sides, is rolled, the outcomes are independent (with replacement) of the previous roll. If a die is rolled three times in succession, how many different outcomes can occur? That is, what is the size of the sample space for this experiment? The size of the population, N, is 6, the six sides of the die. We are sampling three dice rolls, $n = 3$. The sample space is

$$(N)^n = (6)^3 = 216$$

Suppose in a lottery six numbers are drawn from the digits 0 through 9, with replacement (digits can be reused). How many different groupings of six numbers can be drawn? N is the population of 10 numbers (0 through 9) and n is the sample size, six numbers.

$$(N)^n = (10)^6 = 1,000,000$$

That is, a million six-digit numbers are available!

Combinations: Sampling from a Population Without Replacement

The third counting method uses **combinations**, sampling *n* items from a population of size *N* without replacement provides

$$_{N}C_{n} = \binom{N}{n} = \frac{N!}{n!(N-n)!}$$

possibilities.

For example, suppose a small law firm has 16 employees and three are to be selected randomly to represent the company at the annual meeting of the American Bar Association. How many different combinations of lawyers could be sent to the meeting? This situation does not allow sampling with replacement because three *different* lawyers will be selected to go. This problem is solved by using combinations. $N = 16$ and $n = 3$, so

$$_{N}C_{n} = {_{16}C_{3}} = \frac{16!}{3!13!} = 560$$

A total of 560 combinations of three lawyers could be chosen to represent the firm.

4.3 PROBLEMS

4.1 A supplier shipped a lot of six parts to a company. The lot contained three defective parts. Suppose the customer decided to randomly select two parts and test them for defects. How large a sample space is the customer potentially working with? List the sample space. Using the sample space list, determine the probability that the customer will select a sample with exactly one defect.

4.2 Given A = {1, 3, 5, 7, 8, 9}, B = {2, 4, 7, 9}, and C = {1, 2, 3, 4, 7}, solve the following.

a. $A \cup C =$ _____

b. $A \cap B =$ _____

c. $A \cap C =$ _____

d. $A \cup B \cup C =$ _____

e. $A \cap B \cap C =$ _____

f. $(A \cup B) \cap C =$ _____

g. $(B \cap C) \cup (A \cap B) =$ _____

h. A or B = _____

i. B and A = _____

4.3 If a population consists of the positive even numbers through 30 and if A = {2, 6, 12, 24}, what is A′?

4.4 A company's customer service 800 telephone system is set up so that the caller has six options. Each of these six options leads to a menu with four options. For each of these four options, three more options are available. For each of these three options, another three options are presented. If a person calls the 800 number for assistance, how many total options are possible?

4.5 A bin contains six parts. Two of the parts are defective and four are acceptable. If three of the six parts are selected from the bin, how large is the sample space? Which counting rule did you use, and why? For this sample space, what is the probability that exactly one of the three sampled parts is defective?

4.6 A company places a seven-digit serial number on each part that is made. Each digit of the serial number can be any number from 0 through 9. Digits can be repeated in the serial number. How many different serial numbers are possible?

4.7 A small company has 20 employees. Six of these employees will be selected randomly to be interviewed as part of an employee satisfaction program. How many different groups of six can be selected?

4.4 MARGINAL, UNION, JOINT, AND CONDITIONAL PROBABILITIES

Four particular types of probability are presented in this chapter. The first type is **marginal probability**. Marginal probability is denoted $P(E)$, where E is some event. A marginal probability is usually *computed by dividing some subtotal by the whole*. An example of marginal probability is the probability that a person owns a Ford car. This probability is computed by dividing the number of Ford owners by the total number of car owners. The probability of a person wearing glasses is also a marginal probability. This probability is computed by dividing the number of people wearing glasses by the total number of people.

A second type of probability is the union of two events. Union probability is de- $P(E_1 \cup E_2)$, where E_1 and E_2 are two events. $P(E_1 \cup E_2)$ is the probability that E_1 wi that E_2 will occur or that both E_1 and E_2 will occur. An example of union pro probability that a person owns a Ford or a Chevrolet. To qualify for the unio has to have at least one of these cars. Another example is the probabili glasses or having red hair. All people wearing glasses are included redheads and all redheads who wear glasses. In a company, the r or a clerical worker is a union probability. A person qualifi being a clerical worker or by being both (a male cleri

A third type of probability is the intersecti joint probability of events E_1 and E_2 occurrir is read as the probability of E_1 and E_2. To occur. An example of joint probability is the and a Chevrolet. Owning one type of car is not ability is the probability that a person is a redheac

The fourth type is conditional probability. Condi This expression is read: the probability that E_1 will o occurred. Conditional probabilities involve knowledge

Marginal, Union, Joint, and
Conditional Probabilities

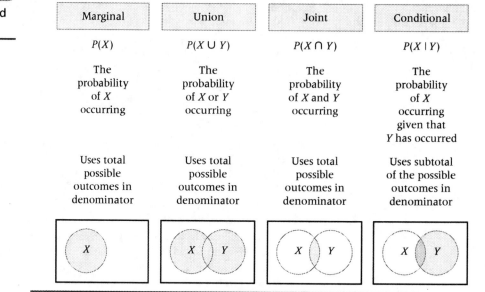

Marginal	Union	Joint	Conditional
$P(X)$	$P(X \cup Y)$	$P(X \cap Y)$	$P(X \mid Y)$
The probability of X occurring	The probability of X or Y occurring	The probability of X and Y occurring	The probability of X occurring given that Y has occurred
Uses total possible outcomes in denominator	Uses total possible outcomes in denominator	Uses total possible outcomes in denominator	Uses subtotal of the possible outcomes in denominator

information that is known or given is written to the right of the vertical line in the probability statement. An example of conditional probability is the probability that a person owns a Chevrolet given that she owns a Ford. This conditional probability is only a measure of the proportion of Ford owners who have a Chevrolet—not the proportion of total car owners who own a Chevrolet. Conditional probabilities are computed by determining the number of items that have an outcome out of some subtotal of the population. In the car owner example, the possibilities are reduced to Ford owners, and then the number of Chevrolet owners out of those Ford owners is determined. Another example of a conditional probability is the probability that a worker in a company is a professional given that he is male. Of the four probability types, only conditional probability does not have the population total as its denominator. Conditional probabilities have a population subtotal in the denominator. Figure 4.6 summarizes these four types of probability.

THINKING CRITICALLY ABOUT STATISTICS IN BUSINESS TODAY

Probabilities in the Dry Cleaning Business

According to the International Fabricare Institute, about two-thirds or 67% of all dry cleaning customers are female, and 65% are married. Thirty-seven percent of dry cleaning customers use a cleaner that is within a mile of their home. Do dry cleaning customers care about coupons? Fifty-one percent of dry cleaning customers say that coupons or discounts are important, and in fact, 57% would try another cleaner if a discount were offered. Converting these percentages to proportions, each could be considered to be a marginal probability. For example, if a customer is randomly selected from the dry-cleaning industry, there is a probability that he/she uses a dry cleaner within a mile of her home, $P(\leq 1 \text{ mile}) = .37$.

Suppose further analysis shows that 55% of dry-cleaning customers are female and married. Converting this figure to results in the joint probability: $P(F \cap M) = .55$. Subtracting this value from the .67 who are female, we find that 11% of dry cleaning customers are female and not married: $P(F \cap \text{not } M) = .11$. Suppose 90% of those who say coupons or discounts are important would

try another cleaner if a discount were offered. This can be restated as a conditional probability: $P(\text{try another} \mid \text{coupons important}) = .90$.

Each of the four types of probabilities discussed in this chapter can be applied to the data on consumers in the dry-cleaner industry. Further breakdowns of these statistics using probabilities can offer insights into how to better serve dry-cleaning customers and how to better market dry-cleaning services and products.

Things to Ponder

1. Why do you think it is that two-thirds of all dry-cleaning customers are female? What are some of the factors? What could dry cleaners do to increase the number of male customers?

2. Sixty-five percent of customers at dry-cleaning establishments are married. Can you think of reasons why a smaller percentage of dry-cleaning customers are single? What could dry cleaners do to increase the number of single customers?

4.5 ADDITION LAWS

Several tools are available for use in solving probability problems. These tools include sample space, tree diagrams, the laws of probability, joint probability tables, and insight. Because of the individuality and variety of probability problems, some techniques apply more readily in certain situations than in others. No best method is available for solving all probability problems. In some instances, the joint probability table lays out a problem in a readily solvable manner. In other cases, setting up the joint probability table is more difficult than solving the problem in another way. The probability laws almost always can be used to solve probability problems.

Four laws of probability are presented in this chapter: The addition laws, conditional probability, the multiplication laws, and Bayes' rule. The addition laws and the multiplication laws each have a general law and a special law.

The general law of addition is used to find the probability of the union of two events, $P(X \cup Y)$. The expression $P(X \cup Y)$ denotes the probability of X occurring or Y occurring or both X and Y occurring.

GENERAL LAW OF ADDITION

$$P(X \cup Y) = P(X) + P(Y) - P(X \cap Y)$$

where X, Y are events and $(X \cap Y)$ is the intersection of X and Y.

Yankelovich Partners conducted a survey for the American Society of Interior Designers in which workers were asked which changes in office design would increase productivity. Respondents were allowed to answer more than one type of design change. The number one change that 70% of the workers said would increase productivity was reducing noise. In second place was more storage/filing space, selected by 67%. If one of the survey respondents was randomly selected and asked what office design changes would increase worker productivity, what is the probability that this person would select reducing noise *or* more storage/filing space?

Let N represent the event "reducing noise." Let S represent the event "more storage/filing space." The probability of a person responding with N or S can be symbolized statistically as a union probability by using the law of addition.

$$P(N \cup S)$$

FIGURE 4.7

Solving for the Union in the Office Productivity Problem

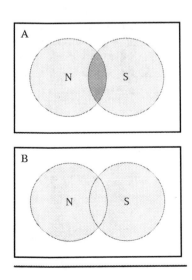

To successfully satisfy the search for a person who responds with reducing noise *or* more storage/filing space, we need only find someone who wants *at least one* of those two events. Because 70% of the surveyed people responded that reducing noise would create more productivity, $P(N) = .70$. In addition, because 67% responded that increased storage space would improve productivity, $P(S) = .67$. Either of these would satisfy the requirement of the union. Thus, the solution to the problem seems to be

$$P(N \cup S) = P(N) + P(S) = .70 + .67 = 1.37$$

However, we already established that probabilities cannot be more than 1. What is the problem here? Notice that all people who responded that *both* reducing noise *and* increasing storage space would improve productivity are included in *each* of the marginal probabilities $P(N)$ and $P(S)$. Certainly a respondent who recommends both of these improvements should be included as favoring at least one. However, because they are included in the $P(N)$ *and* the $P(S)$, the people who recommended both improvements are *double counted*. For that reason, the general law of addition subtracts the intersection probability, $P(N \cap S)$.

In Figure 4.7, Venn diagrams illustrate this discussion. Notice that the intersection area of N and S is double shaded in diagram A, indicating that it has been counted twice. In diagram B, the shading is consistent throughout N and S because the intersection area has been subtracted out. Thus diagram B illustrates the proper application of the general law of addition.

So what is the answer to Yankelovich Partners' union probability question? Suppose 56% of all respondents to the survey had said that *both* noise reduction *and* increased

TABLE 4.2

Joint Probability Table for the
Office Design Problem

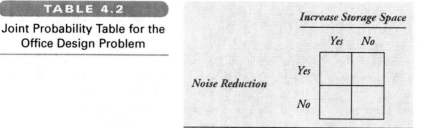

storage/filing space would improve productivity: $P(N \cap S) = .56$. Then we could use the general law of addition to solve for the probability that a person responds that *either* noise reduction *or* increased storage space would improve productivity.

$$P(N \cup S) = P(N) + P(S) - P(N \cap S) = .70 + .67 - .56 = .81$$

Hence, 81% of the workers surveyed responded that *either* noise reduction *or* increased storage space would improve productivity.

Joint Probability Tables

In addition to the formulas, another useful tool in solving probability problems is using a joint probability table. A **joint probability table** *displays the intersection (joint) probabilities along with the marginal probabilities of a given problem.* Union probabilities or conditional probabilities are not directly displayed in a joint probability table but can be computed using values from the table. Generally, a joint probability table is constructed as a two-dimensional table with one variable on each side of the table. For example, in the office design problem, noise reduction would be on one side of the table and increased storage space on the other. In this problem, a Yes row and a No row would be created for one variable and a Yes column and a No column would be created for the other variable, as shown in Table 4.2.

Once the joint probability table is created, we can enter the marginal probabilities. $P(N) = .70$ is the marginal probability that a person responds yes to noise reduction. This value is placed in the "margin" in the row of Yes to noise reduction, as shown in Table 4.3. If $P(N) = .70$, then 30% of the people surveyed did not think that noise reduction would increase productivity. Thus, $P(\text{not } N) = 1 - .70 = .30$. This value, also a marginal probability, goes in the row indicated by No under noise reduction. In the column under Yes for increased storage space, the marginal probability $P(S) = .67$ is recorded. Finally, the marginal probability of No for increased storage space, $P(\text{not } S) = 1 - .67 = .33$, is placed in the No column.

In this joint probability table, all four marginal probabilities are given or can be computed simply by using the probability of a complement rule, $P(\text{not } S) = 1 - P(S)$. The intersection of noise reduction and increased storage space is given as $P(N \cap S) = .56$. This value is entered into the joint probability table in the cell under Yes Yes, as shown in Table 4.3. The rest of the table can be determined by subtracting the cell values from the marginal probabilities. For example, subtracting .56 from .70 and getting .14 yields the value for the cell under Yes for noise reduction and No for increased storage space. In other words, 14% of all respondents said that noise reduction would improve productivity but

TABLE 4.3

Joint Probability Table for
the Office Design Problem

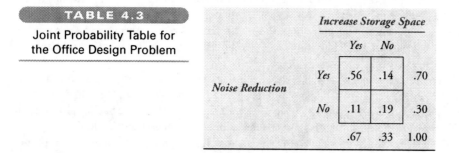

TABLE 4.4

Yes Row and Yes Column for the Joint Probability Table of the Office Design Problem

	Increase Storage Space		
	Yes	No	
Noise Reduction Yes	.56	.14	.70
No	.11		
	.67		

increased storage space would not. Filling out the rest of the table results in the probabilities shown in Table 4.3.

Now we can solve the union probability, $P(N \cup S)$, in at least two different ways using the joint probability table. The focus is on the Yes row for noise reduction and the Yes column for increase storage space, as displayed in Table 4.4. The probability of a person suggesting noise reduction *or* increased storage space as a solution for improving productivity, $P(N \cup S)$, can be determined from the joint probability table by adding the marginal probabilities of Yes for noise reduction and Yes for increased storage space and then subtracting the Yes Yes cell, following the pattern of the general law of probabilities.

$$P(N \cup S) = .70\,(\text{from Yes row}) + .67\,(\text{from Yes column})$$
$$- .56\,(\text{From Yes Yes cell}) = .81$$

Another way to solve for the union probability from the information displayed in the joint probability table is to sum all cells in any of the Yes rows or columns. Observe the following from Table 4.4.

$P(N \cup S) = .56$ (from Yes Yes cell)
$\qquad\qquad + .14$ (from Yes on noise reduction and No on increase storage space)
$\qquad\qquad + .11$ (from No on noise reduction and Yes on increase storage space)
$\qquad = .81$

DEMONSTRATION PROBLEM 4.1

The client company data from the Decision Dilemma reveal that 155 employees worked one of four types of positions. Shown here again is the cross-tabulation table (also called a contingency table) with the frequency counts for each category and for subtotals and totals containing a breakdown of these employees by type of position and by sex. If an employee of the company is selected randomly, what is the probability that the employee is female or a professional worker?

COMPANY HUMAN RESOURCE DATA

		Sex		
		Male	Female	
	Managerial	8	3	11
Type of Position	Professional	31	13	44
	Technical	52	17	69
	Clerical	9	22	31
		100	55	155

Solution

Let F denote the event of female and P denote the event of professional worker. The question is

$$P(F \cup P) = ?$$

By the general law of addition,

$$P(F \cup P) = P(F) + P(P) - P(F \cap P)$$

Of the 155 employees, 55 are women. Therefore, $P(F) = 55/155 = .355$. The 155 employees include 44 professionals. Therefore, $P(P) = 44/155 = .284$. Because 13 employees are both female and professional, $P(F \cap P) = 13/155 = .084$. The union probability is solved as

$$P(F \cup P) = .355 + .284 - .084 = .555.$$

To solve this probability using a joint probability table, you can either use the cross-tabulation table shown previously or convert the cross-tabulation table to a joint probability table by dividing every value in the table by the value of N, 155. The cross-tabulation table is used in a manner similar to that of the joint probability table. To compute the union probability of selecting a person who is either female or a professional worker from the cross-tabulation table, add the number of people in the Female column (55) to the number of people in the Professional row (44), then subtract the number of people in the intersection cell of Female and Professional (13). This step yields the value $55 + 44 - 13 = 86$. Dividing this value (86) by the value of N (155) produces the union probability.

$$P(F \cup P) = 86/155 = .555$$

A second way to produce the answer from the cross-tabulation table is to add all the cells one time that are in either the Female column or the Professional row

$$3 + 13 + 17 + 22 + 31 = 86$$

and then divide by the total number of employees, $N = 155$, which gives

$$P(F \cup P) = 86/155 = .555$$

DEMONSTRATION PROBLEM 4.2

Demonstration Problem

Shown here are the cross-tabulation table and corresponding joint probability table for the results of a national survey of 200 executives who were asked to identify the geographic locale of their company and their company's industry type. The executives were only allowed to select one locale and one industry type.

CROSS-TABULATION TABLE

		Geographic Location				
		Northeast D	Southeast E	Midwest F	West G	
Industry Type	Finance A	24	10	8	14	56
	Manufacturing B	30	6	22	12	70
	Communications C	28	18	12	16	74
		82	34	42	42	200

By dividing every value of the cross-tabulation table by the total (200), the corresponding joint probability table (shown at top of next page) can be constructed.

JOINT PROBABILITY TABLE

		Geographic Location				
		Northeast D	Southeast E	Midwest F	West G	
	Finance A	.12	.05	.04	.07	.28
Industry Type	Manufacturing B	.15	.03	.11	.06	.35
	Communications C	.14	.09	.06	.08	.37
		.41	.17	.21	.21	1.00

Suppose a respondent is selected randomly from these data.

a. What is the probability that the respondent is from the Midwest (F)?

b. What is the probability that the respondent is from the communications industry (C) or from the Northeast (D)?

c. What is the probability that the respondent is from the Southeast (E) or from the finance industry (A)?

Solution

a. $P(\text{Midwest}) = P(F) = .21$

b. $P(C \cup D) = P(C) + P(D) - P(C \cap D) = .37 + .41 - .14 = .64$

c. $P(E \cup A) = P(E) + P(A) - P(E \cap A) = .17 + .28 - .05 = .40$

The X or Y but Not Both Case

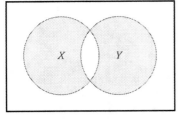

In computing the union by using the general law of addition, the intersection probability is subtracted because it is already included in both marginal probabilities. This adjusted probability leaves a union probability that properly includes both marginal values and the intersection value. If the intersection probability is subtracted out a second time, the intersection is removed, leaving the probability of X or Y but *both*.

$$P(X \text{ or } Y \text{ but not both}) = P(X) + P(Y) - P(X \cap Y) - P(X \cap Y)$$
$$= P(X \cup Y) - P(X \cap Y)$$

Figure 4.8 is the Venn diagram for this probability.

Complement of a Union

The probability of the union of two events X and Y represents the probability that the outcome is *either X or* it is Y or it is *both X and* Y. The union includes everything except the possibility that it is neither (X or Y). Another way to state it is as *neither X nor Y*, which can symbolically be represented as $P(\text{not } X \cap \text{not } Y)$. Because it is the only possible case other than the union of X or Y, it is the **complement of a union**. Stated more formally,

$$P(\text{neither } X \text{ nor } Y) = P(\text{not } X \cap \text{not } Y) = 1 - P(X \cup Y).$$

Examine the Venn diagram in Figure 4.9. Note that the complement of the union of X, Y is the shaded area outside the circles. This area represents the neither X nor Y region.

In the survey about increasing worker productivity by changing the office design discussed earlier, the probability that a randomly selected worker would respond with noise reduction *or* increased storage space was determined to be

The Complement of a Union: The Neither/Nor Region

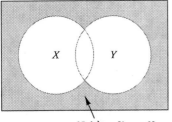

Neither X nor Y

$$P(N \cup S) = P(N) + P(S) - P(N \cap S) = .70 + .67 - .56 = .81$$

The probability that a worker would respond with *neither* noise reduction *nor* increased storage space is calculated as the complement of this union.

$$P(\text{neither N nor S}) = P(\text{not N} \cap \text{not S}) = 1 - P(\text{N} \cup \text{S}) = 1 - .81 = .19$$

Thus 19% of the workers selected neither noise reduction nor increased storage space as solutions to increasing productivity. In Table 4.3, this *neither/nor* probability is found in the No No cell of the table, .19.

Special Law of Addition

If two events are mutually exclusive, the probability of the union of the two events is the probability of the first event plus the probability of the second event. Because mutually exclusive events do not intersect, nothing has to be subtracted.

SPECIAL LAW OF ADDITION If X, Y are mutually exclusive, $P(X \cup Y) = P(X) + P(Y)$.

The special law of addition is a special case of the general law of addition. In a sense, the general law fits all cases. However, when the events are mutually exclusive, a zero is inserted into the general law formula for the intersection, resulting in the special law formula.

In the survey about improving productivity by changing office design, the respondents were allowed to choose more than one possible office design change. Therefore, it is most likely that virtually none of the change choices were mutually exclusive, and the special law of addition would not apply to that example.

In another survey, however, respondents were allowed to select only one option for their answer, which made the possible options mutually exclusive. In this survey, conducted by Yankelovich Partners for William M. Mercer, Inc., workers were asked what most hinders their productivity and were given only the following selections from which to choose only one answer.

- Lack of direction
- Lack of support
- Too much work
- Inefficient process
- Not enough equipment/supplies
- Low pay/chance to advance

Lack of direction was cited by the most workers (20%), followed by lack of support (18%), too much work (18%), inefficient process (8%), not enough equipment/supplies (7%), low pay/chance to advance (7%), and a variety of other factors added by respondents. If a worker who responded to this survey is selected (or if the survey actually reflects the views of the working public and a worker in general is selected) and that worker is asked which of the given selections most hinders his or her productivity, what is the probability that the worker will respond that it is either too much work or inefficient process?

Let M denote the event "too much work" and I denote the event "inefficient process." The question is:

$$P(\text{M} \cup \text{I}) = ?$$

Because 18% of the survey respondents said "too much work,"

$$P(\text{M}) = .18$$

Because 8% of the survey respondents said "inefficient process,"

$$P(\text{I}) = .08$$

Because it was not possible to select more than one answer,

$$P(\text{M} \cap \text{I}) = .0000$$

Implementing the special law of addition gives

$$P(\text{M} \cup \text{I}) = P(\text{M}) + P(\text{I}) = .18 + .08 = .26$$

DEMONSTRATION PROBLEM 4.3

If a worker is randomly selected from the company described in Demonstration Problem 4.1, what is the probability that the worker is either technical or clerical? What is the probability that the worker is either a professional or a clerical?

Solution

Examine the cross-tabulation table of the company's human resources data shown in Demonstration Problem 4.1. In many cross-tabulation tables like this one, the rows are nonoverlapping or mutually exclusive, as are the columns. In this matrix, a worker can be classified as being in only one type of position and as either male or female but not both. Thus, the categories of type of position are mutually exclusive, as are the categories of sex, and the special law of addition can be applied to the human resource data to determine the union probabilities.

Let T denote technical, C denote clerical, and P denote professional. The probability that a worker is either technical or clerical is

$$P(T \cup C) = P(T) + P(C) = \frac{69}{155} + \frac{31}{155} = \frac{100}{155} = .645$$

The probability that a worker is either professional or clerical is

$$P(P \cup C) = P(P) + P(C) = \frac{44}{155} + \frac{31}{155} = \frac{75}{155} = .484$$

DEMONSTRATION PROBLEM 4.4

Use the data from the matrices in Demonstration Problem 4.2. What is the probability that a randomly selected respondent is from the Southeast or the West?

$$P(E \cup G) = ?$$

Solution

Because geographic location is mutually exclusive (the work location is either in the Southeast or in the West but not in both),

$$P(E \cup G) = P(E) + P(G) = .17 + .21 = .38$$

4.5 PROBLEMS

4.8 Given $P(A) = .10$, $P(B) = .12$, $P(C) = .21$, $P(A \cap C) = .05$, and $P(B \cap C) = .03$, solve the following.
  a. $P(A \cup C) = $ _____
  b. $P(B \cup C) = $ _____
  c. If A and B are mutually exclusive, $P(A \cup B) = $ _____

4.9 Use the values in the cross-tabulation table to solve the equations given.

	D	E	F	
A	5	8	12	25
B	10	6	4	20
C	8	2	5	15
	23	18	21	60

  a. $P(A \cup D) = $ _____
  b. $P(E \cup B) = $ _____
  c. $P(D \cup E) = $ _____
  d. $P(C \cup F) = $ _____

4.10 Use the values in the joint probability table to solve the equations given.

	E	F
A	.10	.03
B	.04	.12
C	.27	.06
D	.31	.07

a. $P(A \cup F) =$ _____
b. $P(E \cup B) =$ _____
c. $P(B \cup C) =$ _____
d. $P(E \cup F) =$ _____

4.11 Suppose that 47% of all Americans have flown in an airplane at least once and that 28% of all Americans have ridden on a train at least once. What is the probability that a randomly selected American has either ridden on a train or flown in an airplane? Can this problem be solved? Under what conditions can it be solved? If the problem cannot be solved, what information is needed to make it solvable?

4.12 According to the U.S. Bureau of Labor Statistics, 75% of the women 25 through 49 years of age participate in the labor force. Suppose 78% of the women in that age group are married. Suppose also that 61% of women 25 through 49 years of age are married and are participating in the labor force.

a. What is the probability that a randomly selected woman in that age group is married or is participating in the labor force?

b. What is the probability that a randomly selected woman in that age group is married or is participating in the labor force but not both?

c. What is the probability that a randomly selected woman in that age group is neither married nor participating in the labor force?

4.13 According to Nielsen Media Research, approximately 67% of all U.S. households with television have cable TV. Seventy-four percent of all U.S. households with television have two or more TV sets. Suppose 55% of all U.S. households with television have cable TV and two or more TV sets. A U.S. household with television is randomly selected.

a. What is the probability that the household has cable TV or two or more TV sets?

b. What is the probability that the household has cable TV or two or more TV sets but not both?

c. What is the probability that the household has neither cable TV nor two or more TV sets?

d. Why does the special law of addition not apply to this problem?

4.14 A survey conducted by the Northwestern University Lindquist-Endicott Report asked 320 companies about the procedures they use in hiring. Only 54% of the responding companies review the applicant's college transcript as part of the hiring process, and only 44% consider faculty references. Assume that these percentages are true for the population of companies in the United States and that 35% of all companies use both the applicant's college transcript and faculty references.

a. What is the probability that a randomly selected company uses either faculty references or college transcript as part of the hiring process?

b. What is the probability that a randomly selected company uses either faculty references or college transcript but not both as part of the hiring process?

c. What is the probability that a randomly selected company uses neither faculty references nor college transcript as part of the hiring process?

d. Construct a joint probability table for this problem and indicate the locations of your answers for parts (a), (b), and (c) on the table.

4.6 MULTIPLICATION LAWS

General Law of Multiplication

As stated in Section 4.4, the probability of the intersection of two events $(X \cap Y)$ is called the joint probability. The general law of multiplication is used to find the joint probability.

GENERAL LAW OF MULTIPLICATION	$P(X \cap Y) = P(X) \cdot P(Y|X) = P(Y) \cdot P(X|Y)$

The notation $X \cap Y$ means that both X and Y must *happen*. The general law of multiplication gives the probability that *both* event X and event Y will occur at the same time.

According to the U.S. Bureau of Labor Statistics, 46% of the U.S. labor force is female. In addition, 25% of the women in the labor force work part time. What is the probability that a randomly selected member of the U.S. labor force is a woman *and* works part-time? This question is one of joint probability, and the general law of multiplication can be applied to answer it.

Let W denote the event that the member of the labor force is a woman. Let T denote the event that the member is a part-time worker. The question is:

$$P(W \cap T) = ?$$

According to the general law of multiplication, this problem can be solved by

$$P(W \cap T) = P(W) \cdot P(T|W)$$

Since 46% of the labor force is women, $P(W) = .46$. $P(T|W)$ is a conditional probability that can be stated as the probability that a worker is a part-time worker given that the worker is a woman. This condition is what was given in the statement that 25% *of the women in the labor force* work part time. Hence, $P(T|W) = .25$. From there it follows that

$$P(W \cap T) = P(W) \cdot P(T|W) = (.46)(.25) = .115$$

It can be stated that 11.5% of the U.S. labor force are women *and* work part-time. The Venn diagram in Figure 4.10 shows these relationships and the joint probability.

Determining joint probabilities from joint probability tables is easy because every cell of these matrices is a joint probability, hence the name "joint probability table." For example, suppose the cross-tabulation table of the client company data from Demonstration Problem 4.1 and the Decision Dilemma is converted to a joint probability table by dividing by the total number of employees ($N = 155$), resulting in Table 4.5. Each value in the cell of Table 4.5 is an intersection, and the table contains all possible intersections (joint probabilities) for the events of sex and type of position. For example, the probability that a randomly selected worker is male *and* a technical worker, $P(M \cap T)$, is .335. The probability that a randomly selected worker is female *and* a professional worker,

FIGURE 4.10

Joint Probability that a Woman Is in the Labor Force and Is a Part-Time Worker

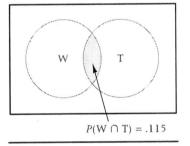

$P(W \cap T) = .115$

TABLE 4.5

Joint Probability Table of Company Human Resource Data

		Sex		
		Male	*Female*	
	Managerial	.052	.019	.071
Type of Position	*Professional*	.200	.084	.284
	Technical	.335	.110	.445
	Clerical	.058	.142	.200
		.645	.355	1.000

$P(F \cap P)$, is .084. Once a joint probability table is constructed for a problem, usually the easiest way to solve for the joint probability is to find the appropriate cell in the table and select the answer. However, sometimes because of what is given in a problem, using the formula is easier than constructing the table.

DEMONSTRATION PROBLEM 4.5

A company has 140 employees, of which 30 are supervisors. Eighty of the employees are married, and 20% of the married employees are supervisors. If a company employee is randomly selected, what is the probability that the employee is married and is a supervisor?

Solution

Let M denote married and S denote supervisor. The question is:

$$P(M \cap S) = ?$$

First, calculate the marginal probability.

$$P(M) = \frac{80}{140} = .5714$$

Then, note that 20% of the married employees are supervisors, which is the conditional probability, $P(S|M) = .20$. Finally, applying the general law of multiplication gives

$$P(M \cap S) = P(M) \cdot P(S|M) = (.5714)(.20) = .1143$$

Hence, 11.43% of the 140 employees are married and are supervisors.

DEMONSTRATION PROBLEM 4.6

From the data obtained from the interviews of 200 executives in Demonstration Problem 4.2, find:

   a. $P(B \cap E)$
   b. $P(G \cap A)$
   c. $P(B \cap C)$

JOINT PROBABILITY TABLE

		Northeast D	Southeast E	Midwest F	West G	
	Finance A	.12	.05	.04	.07	.28
Industry Type	Manufacturing B	.15	.03	.11	.06	.35
	Communications C	.14	.09	.06	.08	.37
		.41	.17	.21	.21	1.00

(Geographic Location header spans Northeast D, Southeast E, Midwest F, West G)

Solution

   a. From the cell of the joint probability table, $P(B \cap E) = .03$. To solve by the formula, $P(B \cap E) = P(B) \cdot P(E|B)$, first find $P(B)$:

$$P(B) = .35$$

The probability of E occurring given that B has occurred, $P(E|B)$, can be determined from the joint probability table as $P(E|B) = .03/.35$. Therefore,

$$P(B \cap E) = P(B) \cdot P(E|B) = (.35)\left(\frac{.03}{.35}\right) = .03$$

Although the formula works, finding the joint probability in the cell of the joint probability table is faster than using the formula.

An alternative formula is $P(B \cap E) = P(E) \cdot P(B|E)$, but $P(E) = .17$. Then $P(B|E)$ means the probability of B if E is given. There are .17 Es in the probability matrix and .03 Bs in these Es. Hence,

$$P(B|E) = \frac{.03}{.17} \quad \text{and} \quad P(B \cap E) = P(E) \cdot P(B|E) = (.17)\left(\frac{.03}{.17}\right) = .03$$

b. To obtain $P(G \cap A)$, find the intersecting cell of G and A in the probability matrix, .07, or use one of the following formulas:

$$P(G \cap A) = P(G) \cdot P(A|G) = (.21)\left(\frac{.07}{.21}\right) = .07$$

or

$$P(G \cap A) = P(A) \cdot P(G|A) = (.28)\left(\frac{.07}{.28}\right) = .07$$

c. The probability $P(B \cap C)$ means that one respondent would have to work both in the manufacturing industry and the communications industry. The survey used to gather data from the 200 executives, however, requested that each respondent specify only one industry type for his or her company. The joint probability table shows no intersection for these two events. Thus B and C are mutually exclusive. None of the respondents is in both manufacturing and communications. Hence,

$$P(B \cap C) = .0$$

Special Law of Multiplication

If events X and Y are independent, a special law of multiplication can be used to find the intersection of X and Y. This special law utilizes the fact that when two events X, Y are independent, $P(X|Y) = P(X)$ and $P(Y|X) = P(Y)$. Thus, the general law of multiplication, $P(X \cap Y) = P(X) \cdot P(Y|X)$, becomes $P(X \cap Y) = P(X) \cdot P(Y)$ when X and Y are independent.

SPECIAL LAW OF MULTIPLICATION	If X, Y are independent, $P(X \cap Y) = P(X) \cdot P(Y)$

A study released by Bruskin-Goldring Research for SEIKO found that 28% of American adults believe that the automated teller has had a most significant impact on everyday life. Another study by David Michaelson & Associates for Dale Carnegie & Associates examined employee views on team spirit in the workplace and discovered that 72% of all employees believe that working as a part of a team lowers stress. Are people's views on automated tellers independent of their views on team spirit in the workplace? If they are independent, then the probability of a person being randomly selected who believes that the automated teller has had a most significant impact on everyday life *and* that working as part of a team lowers stress is found as follows. Let A denote automated teller and S denote teamwork lowers stress.

$$P(A) = .28$$
$$P(S) = .72$$
$$P(A \cap S) = P(A) \cdot P(S) = (.28)(.72) = .2016$$

Therefore, 20.16% of the population believes that the automated teller has had a most significant impact on everyday life *and* that working as part of a team lowers stress.

DEMONSTRATION PROBLEM 4.7

A manufacturing firm produces pads of bound paper. Three percent of all paper pads produced are improperly bound. An inspector randomly samples two pads of paper, one at a time. Because a large number of pads are being produced during the inspection, the sampling being done, in essence, is with replacement. What is the probability that the two pads selected are both improperly bound?

Solution

Let I denote improperly bound. The problem is to determine

$$P(I_1 \cap I_2) = ?$$

The probability of I = .03, or 3% are improperly bound. Because the sampling is done with replacement, the two events are independent. Hence,

$$P(I_1 \cap I_2) = P(I_1) \cdot P(I_2) = (.03)(.03) = .0009$$

TABLE 4.6

Cross-Tabulation Table of Data from Independent Events

	D	E	
A	8	12	20
B	20	30	50
C	6	9	15
	34	51	85

Most cross-tabulation tables contain variables that are not independent. If a cross-tabulation table contains independent events, the special law of multiplication can be applied. If not, the special law cannot be used. In Section 4.7 we explore a technique for determining whether events are independent. Table 4.6 contains data from independent events.

DEMONSTRATION PROBLEM 4.8

Use the data from Table 4.6 and the special law of multiplication to find $P(B \cap D)$.

Solution

$$P(B \cap D) = P(B) \cdot P(D) = \frac{50}{85} \cdot \frac{34}{85} = .2353$$

This approach works *only* for cross-tabulation and joint probability tables in which the variable along one side of the table is *independent* of the variable along the other side of the table. Note that the answer obtained by using the formula is the same as the answer obtained by using the cell information from Table 4.6.

$$P(B \cap D) = \frac{20}{85} = .2353$$

4.6 PROBLEMS

4.15 Use the values in the cross-tabulation table to solve the equations given.

	C	D	E	F	
A	5	11	16	8	40
B	2	3	5	7	17
	7	14	21	15	57

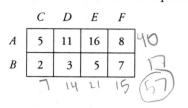

a. $P(A \cap E) = $ _____
b. $P(D \cap B) = $ _____
c. $P(D \cap E) = $ _____
d. $P(A \cap B) = $ _____

4.16 Use the values in the joint probability table to solve the equations given.

	D	E	F
A	.12	.13	.08
B	.18	.09	.04
C	.06	.24	.06

  a. $P(E \cap B) =$ _____
  b. $P(C \cap F) =$ _____
  c. $P(E \cap D) =$ _____

4.17 a. A batch of 50 parts contains six defects. If two parts are drawn randomly one at a time without replacement, what is the probability that both parts are defective?

  b. If this experiment is repeated, with replacement, what is the probability that both parts are defective?

4.18 According to the nonprofit group Zero Population Growth, 78% of the adult U.S. population now lives in urban areas. Scientists at Princeton University and the University of Wisconsin report that about 15% of all American adults care for ill relatives. Suppose that 11% of American adults living in urban areas care for ill relatives.

  a. Use the general law of multiplication to determine the probability of randomly selecting an adult from the U.S. population who lives in an urban area and is caring for an ill relative.

  b. What is the probability of randomly selecting an adult from the U.S. population who lives in an urban area and does not care for an ill relative?

  c. Construct a joint probability table and show where the answer to this problem lies in the matrix.

  d. From the joint probability table, determine the probability that an adult lives in a nonurban area and cares for an ill relative.

4.19 A study by Peter D. Hart Research Associates for the Nasdaq Stock Market revealed that 43% of all American adults are stockholders. In addition, the study determined that 75% of all American adult stockholders have some college education. Suppose 37% of all American adults have some college education. An American adult is randomly selected.

  a. What is the probability that the adult does not own stock?

  b. What is the probability that the adult owns stock and has some college education?

  c. What is the probability that the adult owns stock or has some college education?

  d. What is the probability that the adult has neither some college education nor owns stock?

  e. What is the probability that the adult does not own stock or has no college education?

  f. What is the probability that the adult has some college education and owns no stock?

4.20 According to Reuters, a survey undertaken by the National Center for Health Statistics revealed that about 25% of U.S. households have only a cell phone (no land line). According to the FCC, 65% of U.S. households have high-speed Internet. Suppose of U.S. households having only a cell phone, 80% have high-speed Internet. A U.S. household is randomly selected.

  a. What is the probability that the household has only a cell phone and has high-speed Internet?

  b. What is the probability that the household has only a cell phone or has high-speed Internet?

  c. What is the probability that the household has only a cell phone and does not have high-speed Internet?

  d. What is the probability that the household does not have just a cell phone and does not have high-speed Internet?

  e. What is the probability that the household does not have just a cell phone and does have high-speed Internet?

4.21 A study by Becker Associates, a San Diego travel consultant, found that 30% of the traveling public said that their flight selections are influenced by perceptions of airline safety. Thirty-nine percent of the traveling public wants to know the age of the aircraft. Suppose 87% of the traveling public who say that their flight selections are influenced by perceptions of airline safety wants to know the age of the aircraft.

a. What is the probability of randomly selecting a member of the traveling public and finding out that she says that flight selection is influenced by perceptions of airline safety and she does not want to know the age of the aircraft?

b. What is the probability of randomly selecting a member of the traveling public and finding out that she says that flight selection is neither influenced by perceptions of airline safety nor does she want to know the age of the aircraft?

c. What is the probability of randomly selecting a member of the traveling public and finding out that he says that flight selection is not influenced by perceptions of airline safety and he wants to know the age of the aircraft?

4.22 The U.S. Energy Department states that 60% of all U.S. households have ceiling fans. In addition, 29% of all U.S. households have an outdoor grill. Suppose 13% of all U.S. households have both a ceiling fan and an outdoor grill. A U.S. household is randomly selected.

a. What is the probability that the household has a ceiling fan or an outdoor grill?

b. What is the probability that the household has neither a ceiling fan nor an outdoor grill?

c. What is the probability that the household does not have a ceiling fan and does have an outdoor grill?

d. What is the probability that the household does have a ceiling fan and does not have an outdoor grill?

4.7 CONDITIONAL PROBABILITY

Conditional probabilities are computed based on the prior knowledge that a business researcher has on one of the two events being studied. If X, Y are two events, the conditional probability of X occurring given that Y is known or has occurred is expressed as $P(X|Y)$ and is given in the *law of conditional probability*.

LAW OF CONDITIONAL PROBABILITY	
	$$P(X|Y) = \frac{P(X \cap Y)}{P(Y)} = \frac{P(X) \cdot P(Y|X)}{P(Y)}$$

The conditional probability of $(X|Y)$ is the probability that X will occur given Y. The formula for conditional probability is derived by dividing both sides of the general law of multiplication by $P(Y)$.

In the study by Yankelovich Partners to determine what changes in office design would improve productivity, 70% of the respondents believed noise reduction would improve productivity and 67% said increased storage space would improve productivity. In addition, suppose 56% of the respondents believed both noise reduction and increased storage space would improve productivity. A worker is selected randomly and asked about changes in office design. This worker believes that noise reduction would improve productivity. What is the probability that this worker believes increased storage space would improve productivity? That is, what is the probability that a randomly selected person believes storage space would improve productivity *given that* he or she believes noise reduction improves productivity? In symbols, the question is

$$P(S|N) = ?$$

Note that the given part of the information is listed to the right of the vertical line in the conditional probability. The formula solution is

$$P(S|N) = \frac{P(S \cap N)}{P(N)}$$

but

$$P(N) = .70 \quad \text{and} \quad P(S \cap N) = .56$$

therefore

$$P(S|N) = \frac{P(S \cap N)}{P(N)} = \frac{.56}{.70} = .80$$

Eighty percent of workers who believe noise reduction would improve productivity believe increased storage space would improve productivity.

Note in Figure 4.11 that the area for N in the Venn diagram is completely shaded because it is given that the worker believes noise reduction will improve productivity. Also notice that the intersection of N and S is more heavily shaded. This portion of noise reduction includes increased storage space. It is the only part of increased storage space that is in noise reduction, and because the person is known to favor noise reduction, it is the only area of interest that includes increased storage space.

Examine the joint probability table in Table 4.7 for the office design problem. None of the probabilities given in the table are conditional probabilities. To reiterate what has been previously stated, a joint probability table contains only two types of probabilities, marginal and joint. The cell values are all joint probabilities and the subtotals in the margins are marginal probabilities. How are conditional probabilities determined from a joint probability table? The law of conditional probabilities shows that a conditional probability is computed by dividing the joint probability by the marginal probability. Thus, the joint probability table has all the necessary information to solve for a conditional probability.

What is the probability that a randomly selected worker believes noise reduction would not improve productivity given that the worker does believe increased storage space would improve productivity? That is,

$$P(\text{not } N|S) = ?$$

The law of conditional probability states that

$$P(\text{not } N|S) = \frac{P(\text{not } N \cap S)}{P(S)}$$

Notice that because S is given, we are interested only in the column that is shaded in Table 4.7, which is the Yes column for increased storage space. The marginal probability, $P(S)$, is the total of this column and is found in the margin at the bottom of the table as .67. $P(\text{not } N \cap S)$ is found as the intersection of No for noise and Yes for storage. This value is .11. Hence, $P(\text{not } N \cap S)$ is .11. Therefore,

$$P(\text{not } N|S) = \frac{P(\text{not } N \cap S)}{P(S)} = \frac{.11}{.67} = .164$$

FIGURE 4.11

Conditional Probability of Increased Storage Space Given Noise Reduction

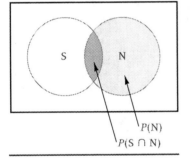

$P(N)$
$P(S \cap N)$

TABLE 4.7

Office Design Problem Joint Probability Table

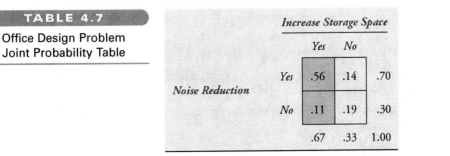

		Increase Storage Space		
		Yes	No	
Noise Reduction	Yes	.56	.14	.70
	No	.11	.19	.30
		.67	.33	1.00

The second version of the conditional probability law formula is

$$P(X|Y) = \frac{P(X) \cdot P(Y \cdot X)}{P(Y)}$$

This version is more complex than the first version, $P(X \cap Y)/P(Y)$. However, sometimes the second version must be used because of the information given in the problem—for example, when solving for $P(X|Y)$ but $P(Y|X)$ is given. The second version of the formula is obtained from the first version by substituting the formula for $P(X \cap Y) = P(X) \cdot P(Y|X)$ into the first version.

As an example, in Section 4.6, data relating to women in the U.S. labor force were presented. Included in this information was the fact that 46% of the U.S. labor force is female and that 25% of the females in the U.S. labor force work part-time. In addition, 17.4% of all American laborers are known to be part-time workers. What is the probability that a randomly selected American worker is a woman if that person is known to be a part-time worker? Let W denote the event of selecting a woman and T denote the event of selecting a part-time worker. In symbols, the question to be answered is

$$P(W|T) = ?$$

The first form of the law of conditional probabilities is

$$P(W|T) = \frac{P(W \cap T)}{P(T)}$$

Note that this version of the law of conditional probabilities requires knowledge of the joint probability, $P(W \cap T)$, which is not given here. We therefore try the second version of the law of conditional probabilities, which is

$$P(W|T) = \frac{P(W) \cdot P(T|W)}{P(T)}$$

For this version of the formula, everything is given in the problem.

$$P(W) = .46$$
$$P(T) = .174$$
$$P(T|W) = .25$$

The probability of a laborer being a woman given that the person works part-time can now be computed.

$$P(W|T) = \frac{P(W) \cdot P(T|W)}{P(T)} = \frac{(.46)(.25)}{(.174)} = .661$$

Hence, 66.1% of the part-time workers are women.

In general, this second version of the law of conditional probabilities is likely to be used for solving $P(X|Y)$ when $P(X \cap Y)$ is unknown but $P(Y|X)$ is known.

DEMONSTRATION PROBLEM 4.9

The data from the executive interviews given in Demonstration Problem 4.2 are repeated here. Use these data to find:

a. $P(B|F)$

b. $P(G|C)$

c. $P(D|F)$

JOINT PROBABILITY TABLE

		Geographic Location				
		Northeast D	Southeast E	Midwest F	West G	
Industry Type	Finance A	.12	.05	.04	.07	.28
	Manufacturing B	.15	.03	.11	.06	.35
	Communications C	.14	.09	.06	.08	.37
		.41	.17	.21	.21	1.00

Solution

a.
$$P(B|F) = \frac{P(B \cap F)}{P(F)} = \frac{.11}{.21} = .524$$

Determining conditional probabilities from a joint probability table by using the formula is a relatively painless process. In this case, the joint probability, $P(B \cap F)$, appears in a cell of the table (.11); the marginal probability, $P(F)$, appears in a margin (.21). Bringing these two probabilities together by formula produces the answer, $.11/.21 = .524$. This answer means that 52.4% of the Midwest executives (the F values) are in manufacturing (the B values).

b.
$$P(G|C) = \frac{P(G \cap C)}{P(C)} = \frac{.08}{.37} = .216$$

This result means that 21.6% of the responding communications industry executives, (C) are from the West (G).

c.
$$P(D|F) = \frac{P(D \cap F)}{P(F)} = \frac{.00}{.21} = .00$$

Because D and F are mutually exclusive, $P(D \cap F)$ is zero and so is $P(D|F)$. The rationale behind $P(D|F) = 0$ is that, if F is given (the respondent is known to be located in the Midwest), the respondent could not be located in D (the Northeast).

Independent Events

INDEPENDENT EVENTS X, Y	To test to determine if X and Y are independent events, the following must be true. $P(X|Y) = P(X)$ and $P(Y|X) = P(Y)$

In each equation, it does not matter that X or Y is given because X and Y are *independent*. When X and Y are independent, the conditional probability is solved as a marginal probability.

Sometimes, it is important to test a cross-tabulation table of raw data to determine whether events are independent. If *any* combination of two events from the different sides of the table fail the test, $P(X|Y) = P(X)$, the table does not contain independent events.

DEMONSTRATION PROBLEM 4.10

Test the cross-tabulation table for the 200 executive responses to determine whether industry type is independent of geographic location.

THINKING CRITICALLY ABOUT STATISTICS IN BUSINESS TODAY

Newspaper Advertising Reading Habits of Canadians

A national survey by Ipsos Reid for the Canadian Newspaper Association reveals some interesting statistics about newspaper advertising reading habits of Canadians. Sixty-six percent of Canadians say that they enjoy reading the page advertising and the product inserts that come with a newspaper. The percentage is higher for women (70%) than men (62%), but 73% of households with children enjoy doing so. While the percentage of those over 55 years of age who enjoy reading such ads is 71%, the percentage is only 55% for those in the 18-to-34-year-old category. These percentages decrease with increases in education as revealed by the fact that while 70% of those with a high school education enjoy reading such ads, only 55% of those having a university degree do so. Canadians living in the Atlantic region lead the country in this regard with 74%, in contrast to those living in British Columbia (63%) and Quebec (62%).

These facts can be converted to probabilities: The probability that a Canadian enjoys reading such ads is .66. Many of the other statistics represent conditional probabilities. For example, the probability that a Canadian enjoys such ads given that the Canadian is a woman is .70; and the probability that a Canadian enjoys such ads given that the Canadian has a college degree is .55. About 13% of the Canadian population resides in British Columbia. From this and from the conditional probability that a Canadian enjoys such ads given that they live in British Columbia (.63), one can compute the joint probability that a randomly selected Canadian enjoys such ads and lives in British Columbia (.13)(.63) = .0819. That is, 8.19% of all Canadians live in British Columbia and enjoy such ads.

Things to Ponder

1. It is plain from the information given here that many Canadians enjoy reading newspaper ads. If you are a business in Canada, what implications might this have on your marketing plan?

2. What do you think might be some factors that contribute to fact that about 10% more of Canadians in the Atlantic region than in other regions of the country enjoy reading newspaper ads?

CROSS-TABULATION TABLE

		Geographic Location				
		Northeast D	Southeast E	Midwest F	West G	
Industry Type	Finance A	24	10	8	14	56
	Manufacturing B	30	6	22	12	70
	Communications C	28	18	12	16	74
		82	34	42	42	200

Solution

Select one industry and one geographic location (say, A—Finance and G—West). Does $P(A|G) = P(A)$?

$$P(A|G) = \frac{14}{42} \text{ and } P(A) = \frac{56}{200}$$

Does 14/42 = 56/200? No, .33 ≠ .28. Industry and geographic location are not independent because at least one exception to the test is present.

DEMONSTRATION PROBLEM 4.11

Determine whether the cross-tabulation table shown as Table 4.6 and repeated here contains independent events.

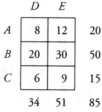

	D	E	
A	8	12	20
B	20	30	50
C	6	9	15
	34	51	85

Solution

Check the first cell in the table to find whether $P(A|D) = P(A)$.

$$P(A|D) = \frac{8}{34} = .2353$$

$$P(A) = \frac{20}{85} = .2353$$

The checking process must continue until all the events are determined to be independent. In this table, all the possibilities check out. Thus, Table 4.6 contains independent events.

4.7 PROBLEMS

4.23 Use the values in the cross-tabulation table to solve the equations given.

	E	F	G	
A	15	12	8	35
B	11	17	19	47
C	21	32	27	80
D	18	13	12	43
	65	74	66	205

a. $P(G|A) = $ _____
b. $P(B|F) = $ _____
c. $P(C|E) = $ _____
d. $P(E|G) = $ _____

4.24 Use the values in the joint probability table to solve the equations given.

	C	D
A	.36	.44
B	.11	.09

a. $P(C|A) = $ _____
b. $P(B|D) = $ _____
c. $P(A|B) = $ _____

4.25 The results of a survey asking, "Do you have a calculator and/or a computer in your home?" follow.

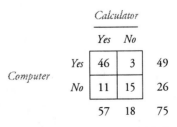

		Calculator		
		Yes	No	
Computer	Yes	46	3	49
	No	11	15	26
		57	18	75

Is the variable "calculator" independent of the variable "computer"? Why or why not?

4.26 In a recent year, business failures in the United States numbered 83,384, according to Dun & Bradstreet. The construction industry accounted for 10,867 of these business failures. The South Atlantic states accounted for 8,010 of the business failures. Suppose that 1,258 of all business failures were construction businesses located in the South Atlantic states. A failed business is randomly selected from this list of business failures.

a. What is the probability that the business is located in the South Atlantic states?

b. What is the probability that the business is in the construction industry or located in the South Atlantic states?

c. What is the probability that the business is in the construction industry if it is known that the business is located in the South Atlantic states?

d. What is the probability that the business is located in the South Atlantic states if it is known that the business is a construction business?

e. What is the probability that the business is not located in the South Atlantic states if it is known that the business is not a construction business?

f. Given that the business is a construction business, what is the probability that the business is not located in the South Atlantic states?

4.27 Arthur Andersen Enterprise Group/National Small Business United, Washington, conducted a national survey of small-business owners to determine the challenges for growth for their businesses. The top challenge, selected by 46% of the small-business owners, was the economy. A close second was finding qualified workers (37%). Suppose 15% of the small-business owners selected both the economy and finding qualified workers as challenges for growth. A small-business owner is randomly selected.

a. What is the probability that the owner believes the economy is a challenge for growth if the owner believes that finding qualified workers is a challenge for growth?

b. What is the probability that the owner believes that finding qualified workers is a challenge for growth if the owner believes that the economy is a challenge for growth?

c. Given that the owner does not select the economy as a challenge for growth, what is the probability that the owner believes that finding qualified workers is a challenge for growth?

d. What is the probability that the owner believes neither that the economy is a challenge for growth nor that finding qualified workers is a challenge for growth?

4.28 According to a survey published by ComPsych Corporation, 54% of all workers read e-mail while they are talking on the phone. Suppose that 20% of those who read e-mail while they are talking on the phone write personal "to-do" lists during meetings. Assuming that these figures are true for all workers, if a worker is randomly selected, determine the following probabilities:

a. The worker reads e-mail while talking on the phone and writes personal "to-do" lists during meetings.

b. The worker does not write personal "to-do" lists given that he reads e-mail while talking on the phone.

c. The worker does not write personal "to-do" lists and does read e-mail while talking on the phone.

4.29 *Accounting Today* reported that 37% of accountants purchase their computer hardware by mail order direct and that 54% purchase their computer software by mail order direct. Suppose that 97% of the accountants who purchase their computer hardware by mail order direct purchase their computer software by mail order direct. If an accountant is randomly selected, determine the following probabilities:

a. The accountant does not purchase his computer software by mail order direct given that he does purchase his computer hardware by mail order direct.

b. The accountant does purchase his computer software by mail order direct given that he does not purchase his computer hardware by mail order direct.

c. The accountant does not purchase his computer hardware by mail order direct if it is known that he does purchase his computer software by mail order direct.

d. The accountant does not purchase his computer hardware by mail order direct if it is known that he does not purchase his computer software by mail order direct.

4.30 In a study undertaken by Catalyst, 43% of women senior executives agreed or strongly agreed that a lack of role models was a barrier to their career development. In addition, 46% agreed or strongly agreed that gender-based stereotypes were barriers to their career advancement. Suppose 77% of those who agreed or strongly agreed that gender-based stereotypes were barriers to their career advancement agreed or strongly agreed that the lack of role models was a barrier to their career development. If one of these female senior executives is randomly selected, determine the following probabilities:

a. What is the probability that the senior executive does not agree or strongly agree that a lack of role models was a barrier to her career development given that she does agree or strongly agree that gender-based stereotypes were barriers to her career development?

b. What is the probability that the senior executive does not agree or strongly agree that gender-based stereotypes were barriers to her career development given that she does agree or strongly agree that the lack of role models was a barrier to her career development?

c. If it is known that the senior executive does not agree or strongly agree that gender-based stereotypes were barriers to her career development, what is the probability that she does not agree or strongly agree that the lack of role models was a barrier to her career development?

4.8 ## REVISION OF PROBABILITIES: BAYES' RULE

An extension to the conditional law of probabilities is Bayes' rule, which was developed by and named for Thomas Bayes (1702–1761). **Bayes' rule** is *a formula that extends the use of the law of conditional probabilities to allow revision of original probabilities with new information.*

BAYES' RULE	$$P(X_i|Y) = \frac{P(X_i) \cdot P(Y|X_i)}{P(X_1) \cdot P(Y|X_1) + P(X_2) \cdot P(Y|X_2) + \cdots + P(X_n) \cdot P(Y|X_n)}$$

Recall that the law of conditional probability for

$$P(X_i|Y)$$

is

$$P(X_i|Y) = \frac{P(X_i) \cdot P(Y|X_i)}{P(Y)}$$

Compare Bayes' rule to this law of conditional probability. The numerators of Bayes' rule and the law of conditional probability are the same—the intersection of X_i and Y shown in the form of the general rule of multiplication. The new feature that Bayes' rule uses is found in the denominator of the rule:

$$P(X_1) \cdot P(Y|X_1) + P(X_2) \cdot P(Y|X_2) + \cdots + P(X_n) \cdot P(Y|X_n)$$

The denominator of Bayes' rule includes a product expression (intersection) for every partition in the sample space, Y, including the event (X_i) itself. The denominator is thus a collective exhaustive listing of mutually exclusive outcomes of Y. This denominator is sometimes referred to as the "total probability formula." It represents a weighted average of the conditional probabilities, with the weights being the prior probabilities of the corresponding event.

	TABLE 4.8			
	Bayesian Table for Revision of Ribbon Problem Probabilities			

Event	Prior Probability $P(E_i)$	Conditional Probability $P(d|E_i)$	Joint Probability $P(E_i \cap d)$	Posterior or Revised Probability
Alamo	.65	.08	.052	$\dfrac{.052}{.094} = .553$
South Jersey	.35	.12	.042	$\dfrac{.042}{.094} = .447$
			$P(\text{defective}) = .094$	

By expressing the law of conditional probabilities in this new way, Bayes' rule enables the statistician to make new and different applications using conditional probabilities. In particular, statisticians use Bayes' rule to "revise" probabilities in light of new information.

A particular type of printer ribbon is produced by only two companies, Alamo Ribbon Company and South Jersey Products. Suppose Alamo produces 65% of the ribbons and that South Jersey produces 35%. Eight percent of the ribbons produced by Alamo are defective and 12% of the South Jersey ribbons are defective. A customer purchases a new ribbon. What is the probability that Alamo produced the ribbon? What is the probability that South Jersey produced the ribbon? The ribbon is tested, and it is defective. Now what is the probability that Alamo produced the ribbon? That South Jersey produced the ribbon?

The probability was .65 that the ribbon came from Alamo and .35 that it came from South Jersey. These are called *prior* probabilities because they are based on the original information.

The new information that the ribbon is defective changes the probabilities because one company produces a higher percentage of defective ribbons than the other company does. How can this information be used to update or revise the original probabilities? Bayes' rule allows such updating. One way to lay out a revision of probabilities problem is to use a table. Table 4.8 shows the analysis for the ribbon problem.

The process begins with the prior probabilities: .65 Alamo and .35 South Jersey. These prior probabilities appear in the second column of Table 4.8. Because the product is found to be defective, the conditional probabilities, $P(\text{defective}|\text{Alamo})$ and $P(\text{defective}|\text{South Jersey})$ should be used. Eight percent of Alamo's ribbons are defective: $P(\text{defective}|\text{Alamo}) = .08$. Twelve percent of South Jersey's ribbons are defective: $P(\text{defective}|\text{South Jersey}) = .12$. These two conditional probabilities appear in the third column. Eight percent of Alamo's 65% of the ribbons are defective: $(.08)(.65) = .052$, or 5.2% of the total. This figure appears in the fourth column of Table 4.8; it is the joint probability of getting a ribbon that was made by Alamo and is defective. Because the purchased ribbon is defective, these are the only Alamo ribbons of interest. Twelve percent of South Jersey's 35% of the ribbons are defective. Multiplying these two percentages yields the joint probability of getting a South Jersey ribbon that is defective. This figure also appears in the fourth column of Table 4.8: $(.12)(.35) = .042$; that is, 4.2% of all ribbons are made by South Jersey and are defective. This percentage includes the only South Jersey ribbons of interest because the ribbon purchased is defective.

Column 4 is totaled to get .094, indicating that 9.4% of all ribbons are defective (Alamo and defective = .052 + South Jersey and defective = .042). The other 90.6% of the ribbons, which are acceptable, are not of interest because the ribbon purchased is defective. To compute the fifth column, the posterior or revised probabilities, involves dividing each value in column 4 by the total of column 4. For Alamo, .052 of the total ribbons are Alamo and defective out of the total of .094 that are defective. Dividing .052 by .094 yields .553 as a revised probability that the purchased ribbon was made by Alamo. This probability is lower than the prior or original probability of .65 because fewer of Alamo's ribbons (as a percentage) are defective than those produced by South Jersey. The defective ribbon is now less likely to have come from Alamo than before the knowledge of the defective ribbon. South Jersey's probability is revised by dividing the .042 joint probability of the ribbon being made by South Jersey and defective by the total probability of the ribbon being defective (.094).

FIGURE 4.12

Tree Diagram for Ribbon
Problem Probabilities

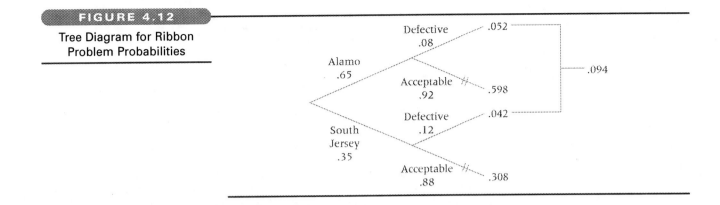

The result is .042/.094 = .447. The probability that the defective ribbon is from South Jersey increased because a higher percentage of South Jersey ribbons are defective.

Tree diagrams are another common way to solve Bayes' rule problems. Figure 4.12 shows the solution for the ribbon problem. Note that the tree diagram contains all possibilities, including both defective and acceptable ribbons. When new information is given, only the pertinent branches are selected and used. The joint probability values at the end of the appropriate branches are used to revise and compute the posterior probabilities. Using the total number of defective ribbons, .052 + .042 = .094, the calculation is as follows.

$$\text{Revised Probability: Alamo} = \frac{.052}{.094} = .553$$

$$\text{Revised Probability: South Jersey} = \frac{.042}{.094} = .447$$

DEMONSTRATION PROBLEM 4.12

Machines A, B, and C all produce the same two parts, X and Y. Of all the parts produced, machine A produces 60%, machine B produces 30%, and machine C produces 10%. In addition,

40% of the parts made by machine A are part X.

50% of the parts made by machine B are part X.

70% of the parts made by machine C are part X.

A part produced by this company is randomly sampled and is determined to be an X part. With the knowledge that it is an X part, revise the probabilities that the part came from machine A, B, or C.

Solution

The prior probability of the part coming from machine A is .60, because machine A produces 60% of all parts. The prior probability is .30 that the part came from B and .10 that it came from C. These prior probabilities are more pertinent if nothing is known about the part. However, the part is known to be an X part. The conditional probabilities show that different machines produce different proportions of X parts. For example, .40 of the parts made by machine A are X parts, but .50 of the parts made by machine B and .70 of the parts made by machine C are X parts. It makes sense that the probability of the part coming from machine C would increase and that the probability that the part was made on machine A would decrease because the part is an X part.

The following table shows how the prior probabilities, conditional probabilities, joint probabilities, and marginal probability, $P(X)$, can be used to revise the prior probabilities to obtain posterior probabilities.

Event	Prior $P(E_i)$	Conditional $P(X \mid E_i)$	Joint $P(X \cap E_i)$	Posterior
A	.60	.40	$(.60)(.40) = .24$	$\dfrac{.24}{.46} = .52$
B	.30	.50	.15	$\dfrac{.15}{.46} = .33$
C	.10	.70	.07	$\dfrac{.07}{.46} = .15$
			$P(X) = .46$	

After the probabilities are revised, it is apparent that the probability of the part being made at machine A decreased and that the probabilities that the part was made at machines B and C increased. A tree diagram presents another view of this problem.

Revised Probabilities: Machine A: $\dfrac{.24}{.46} = .52$

Machine B: $\dfrac{.15}{.46} = .33$

Machine C: $\dfrac{.07}{.46} = .15$

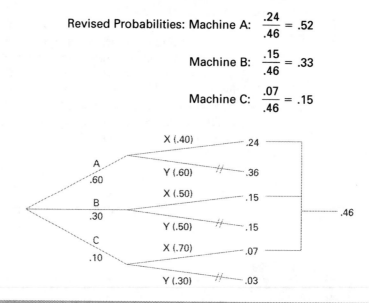

4.8 PROBLEMS

4.31 In a manufacturing plant, machine A produces 10% of a certain product, machine B produces 40% of this product, and machine C produces 50% of this product. Five percent of machine A products are defective, 12% of machine B products are defective, and 8% of machine C products are defective. The company inspector has just sampled a product from this plant and has found it to be defective. Determine the revised probabilities that the sampled product was produced by machine A, machine B, or machine C.

4.32 Alex, Alicia, and Juan fill orders in a fast-food restaurant. Alex incorrectly fills 20% of the orders he takes. Alicia incorrectly fills 12% of the orders she takes. Juan incorrectly fills 5% of the orders he takes. Alex fills 30% of all orders, Alicia fills 45% of all orders, and Juan fills 25% of all orders. An order has just been filled.

   a. What is the probability that Alicia filled the order?

   b. If the order was filled by Juan, what is the probability that it was filled correctly?

   c. Who filled the order is unknown, but the order was filled incorrectly. What are the revised probabilities that Alex, Alicia, or Juan filled the order?

   d. Who filled the order is unknown, but the order was filled correctly. What are the revised probabilities that Alex, Alicia, or Juan filled the order?

4.33 In a small town, two lawn companies fertilize lawns during the summer. Tri-State Lawn Service has 72% of the market. Thirty percent of the lawns fertilized by Tri-State could be rated as very healthy one month after service. Greenchem has the other 28% of the market. Twenty percent of the lawns fertilized by Greenchem could be rated as very healthy one month after service. A lawn that has been treated with fertilizer by one of these companies within the last month is selected randomly. If the lawn is rated as very healthy, what are the revised probabilities that Tri-State or Greenchem treated the lawn?

4.34 Suppose 70% of all companies are classified as small companies and the rest as large companies. Suppose further, 82% of large companies provide training to employees, but only 18% of small companies provide training. A company is randomly selected without knowing if it is a large or small company; however, it is determined that the company provides training to employees. What are the prior probabilities that the company is a large company or a small company? What are the revised probabilities that the company is large or small? Based on your analysis, what is the overall percentage of companies that offer training?

Equity of the Sexes in the Workplace

The client company data given in the Decision Dilemma are displayed in a cross-tabulation table. Using the techniques presented in this chapter, it is possible to statistically answer the managerial questions. If a worker is randomly selected from the 155 employees, the probability that the worker is a woman, $P(W)$, is 55/155, or .355. This marginal probability indicates that roughly 35.5% of all employees of the client company are women. Given that the employee has a managerial position, the probability that the employee is a woman, $P(W|M)$ is 3/11, or .273. The proportion of managers at the company who are women is lower than the proportion of all workers at the company who are women. Several factors might be related to this discrepancy, some of which may be defensible by the company—including experience, education, and prior history of success—and some may not.

Suppose a technical employee is randomly selected for a bonus. What is the probability that a female would be selected given that the worker is a technical employee? That is, $P(F|T) = ?$ Applying the law of conditional probabilities to the cross-tabulation table given in the Decision Dilemma, $P(F|T) =$ 17/69 = .246. Using the concept of complementary events, the probability that a man is selected given that the employee is a technical person is $1 - .246 = .754$. It is more than three times as likely that a randomly selected technical person is a male. If a woman were the one chosen for the bonus, a man could argue discrimination based on the mere probabilities. However, the company decision makers could then present documentation of the choice criteria based on productivity, technical suggestions, quality measures, and others.

Suppose a client company employee is randomly chosen to win a trip to Hawaii. The marginal probability that the winner

is a professional is $P(P) = 44/155 = .284$. The probability that the winner is either a male or is a clerical worker, a union probability, is:

$$P(M \cup C) = P(M) + P(C) - P(M \cap C)$$
$$= \frac{100}{155} + \frac{31}{155} - \frac{9}{155} = \frac{122}{155} = .787$$

The probability of a male or clerical employee at the client company winning the trip is .787. The probability that the winner is a woman *and* a manager, a joint probability, is

$$P(F \cap M) = 3/155 = .019$$

There is less than a 2% chance that a female manager will be selected randomly as the trip winner.

What is the probability that the winner is from the technical group if it is known that the employee is a male? This conditional probability is as follows:

$$P(T|M) = 52/100 = .52.$$

Many other questions can be answered about the client company's human resource situation using probabilities.

The probability approach to a human resource pool is a factual, numerical approach to people selection taken without regard to individual talents, skills, and worth to the company. Of course, in most instances, many other considerations go into the hiring, promoting, and rewarding of workers besides the random draw of their name. However, company management should be aware that attacks on hiring, promotion, and reward practices are sometimes made using statistical analyses such as those presented here. It is not being argued here that management should base decisions merely on the probabilities within particular categories. Nevertheless, being aware of the probabilities, management can proceed to undergird their decisions with documented evidence of worker productivity and worth to the organization.

ETHICAL CONSIDERATIONS

One of the potential misuses of probability occurs when subjective probabilities are used. Most subjective probabilities are based on a person's feelings, intuition, or experience. Almost everyone has an opinion on something and is willing to share it. Although such probabilities are not strictly unethical to report, they can be misleading and disastrous to other decision makers. In addition, subjective probabilities leave the door open for unscrupulous people to overemphasize their point of view by manipulating the probability.

The decision maker should remember that the laws and rules of probability are for the "long run." If a coin is tossed, even though the probability of getting a head is .5, the result will be either a head or a tail. It isn't possible to get a half head. The probability of getting a head (.5) will probably work out in the long run, but in the short run an experiment might produce 10 tails in a row. Suppose the probability of

striking oil on a geological formation is .10. This probability means that, in the long run, if the company drills enough holes on this type of formation, it should strike oil in about 10% of the holes. However, if the company has only enough money to drill one hole, it will either strike oil or have a dry hole. The probability figure of .10 may mean something different to the company that can afford to drill only one hole than to the company that can drill many hundreds. Classical probabilities could be used unethically to lure a company or client into a potential short-run investment with the expectation of getting at least something in return, when in actuality the investor will either win or lose. The oil company that drills only one hole will not get 10% back from the hole. It will either win or lose on the hole. Thus, classical probabilities open the door for unsubstantiated expectations, particularly in the short run.

SUMMARY

The study of probability addresses ways of assigning probabilities, types of probabilities, and laws of probabilities. Probabilities support the notion of inferential statistics. Using sample data to estimate and test hypotheses about population parameters is done with uncertainty. If samples are taken at random, probabilities can be assigned to outcomes of the inferential process.

Three methods of assigning probabilities are (1) the classical method, (2) the relative frequency of occurrence method, and (3) subjective probabilities. The classical method can assign probabilities a priori, or before the experiment takes place. It relies on the laws and rules of probability. The relative frequency of occurrence method assigns probabilities based on historical data or empirically derived data. Subjective probabilities are based on the feelings, knowledge, and experience of the person determining the probability.

Certain special types of events necessitate amendments to some of the laws of probability: mutually exclusive events and independent events. Mutually exclusive events are events that cannot occur at the same time, so the probability of their intersection is zero. With independent events, the occurrence of one has no impact or influence on the occurrence of the other. Certain experiments, such as those involving coins or dice, naturally produce independent events. Other experiments

produce independent events when the experiment is conducted with replacement. If events are independent, the joint probability is computed by multiplying the marginal probabilities, which is a special case of the law of multiplication.

Three techniques for counting the possibilities in an experiment are the mn counting rule, the N^n possibilities, and combinations. The mn counting rule is used to determine how many total possible ways an experiment can occur in a series of sequential operations. The N^n formula is applied when sampling is being done with replacement or events are independent. Combinations are used to determine the possibilities when sampling is being done without replacement.

Four types of probability are marginal probability, conditional probability, joint probability, and union probability. The general law of addition is used to compute the probability of a union. The general law of multiplication is used to compute joint probabilities. The conditional law is used to compute conditional probabilities.

Bayes' rule is a method that can be used to revise probabilities when new information becomes available; it is a variation of the conditional law. Bayes' rule takes prior probabilities of events occurring and adjusts or revises those probabilities on the basis of information about what subsequently occurs.

KEY TERMS

Flash Cards

a priori
Bayes' rule
classical method of assigning probabilities

collectively exhaustive events
combinations
complement of a union
complement
conditional probability
cross-tabulation table
elementary events

event
experiment
independent events
intersection
joint probability
joint probability table
marginal probability
mn counting rule

mutually exclusive events
relative frequency of occurrence
sample space
set notation
subjective probability
union
union probability

FORMULAS

Counting rule

$$mn$$

Sampling with replacement

$$N^n$$

Sampling without replacement

$$_NC_n$$

Combination formula

$$_NC_n = \binom{N}{n} = \frac{N!}{n!(N-n)!}$$

General law of addition

$$P(X \cup Y) = P(X) + P(Y) - P(X \cap Y)$$

Special law of addition

$$P(X \cup Y) = P(X) + P(Y)$$

General law of multiplication

$$P(X \cap Y) = P(X) \cdot P(Y|X) = P(Y) \cdot P(X|Y)$$

Special law of multiplication

$$P(X \cap Y) = P(X) \cdot P(Y)$$

Law of conditional probability

$$P(X|Y) = \frac{P(X \cap Y)}{P(Y)} = \frac{P(X) \cdot P(Y|X)}{P(Y)}$$

Bayes' rule

$$P(X_i|Y) = \frac{P(X_i) \cdot P(Y|X_i)}{P(X_1) \cdot P(Y|X_1) + P(X_2) \cdot P(Y|X_2) + \cdots + P(X_n) \cdot P(Y|X_n)}$$

SUPPLEMENTARY PROBLEMS

CALCULATING THE STATISTICS

4.35 Use the values in the cross-tabulation table to solve the equations given.

		Variable 1	
		D	*E*
	A	10	20
Variable 2	*B*	15	5
	C	30	15

a. P(E) = _____
b. P(B ∪ D) = _____
c. P(A ∩ E) = _____
d. P(B|E) = _____
e. P(A ∪ B) = _____
f. P(B ∩ C) = _____
g. P(D|C) = _____
h. P (A|B) = _____
i. Are variables 1 and 2 independent? Why or why not?

4.36 Use the values in the cross-tabulation table to solve the equations given.

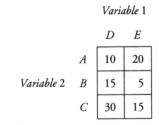

	D	*E*	*F*	*G*
A	3	9	7	12
B	8	4	6	4
C	10	5	3	7

a. P(F ∩ A) = _____
b. P(A|B) = _____
c. P(B) = _____
d. P(E ∩ F) = _____
e. P(D|B) = _____
f. P(B|D) = _____
g. P(D ∪ C) = _____
h. P(F) = _____

4.37 The following joint probability table contains a breakdown on the age and gender of U.S. physicians in a recent year, as reported by the American Medical Association.

U.S. PHYSICIANS IN A RECENT YEAR

		Age (years)					
		<35	*35–44*	*45–54*	*55–64*	*>65*	
Gender	*Male*	.11	.20	.19	.12	.16	.78
	Female	.07	.08	.04	.02	.01	.22
		.18	.28	.23	.14	.17	1.00

a. What is the probability that one randomly selected physician is 35–44 years old?
b. What is the probability that one randomly selected physician is both a woman and 45–54 years old?
c. What is the probability that one randomly selected physician is a man or is 35–44 years old?
d. What is the probability that one randomly selected physician is less than 35 years old or 55–64 years old?
e. What is the probability that one randomly selected physician is a woman if she is 45–54 years old?
f. What is the probability that a randomly selected physician is neither a woman nor 55–64 years old?

TESTING YOUR UNDERSTANDING

4.38 Purchasing Survey asked purchasing professionals what sales traits impressed them most in a sales representative. Seventy-eight percent selected "thoroughness." Forty percent responded "knowledge of your own product." The purchasing professionals were allowed to list more than one trait. Suppose 27% of the purchasing professionals listed both "thoroughness" and "knowledge of your own product" as sales traits that impressed them most. A purchasing professional is randomly sampled.
  a. What is the probability that the professional selected "thoroughness" or "knowledge of your own product"?
  b. What is the probability that the professional selected neither "thoroughness" nor "knowledge of your own product"?
  c. If it is known that the professional selected "thoroughness," what is the probability that the professional selected "knowledge of your own product"?
  d. What is the probability that the professional did not select "thoroughness" and did select "knowledge of your own product"?

4.39 The U.S. Bureau of Labor Statistics publishes data on the benefits offered by small companies to their employees. Only 42% offer retirement plans while 61% offer life insurance. Suppose 33% offer both retirement plans and life insurance as benefits. If a small company is randomly selected, determine the following probabilties:
  a. The company offers a retirement plan given that they offer life insurance.
  b. The company offers life insurance given that they offer a retirement plan.
  c. The company offers life insurance or a retirement plan.
  d. The company offers a retirement plan and does not offer life insurance.
  e. The company does not offer life insurance if it is known that they offer a retirement plan.

4.40 An Adweek Media/Harris Poll revealed that 44% of U.S. adults in the 18–34 years category think that "Made in America" ads boost sales. A different Harris Interactive poll showed that 78% of U.S. adults in the 18–34 years category use social media online. Suppose that 85% of U.S. adults in the 18–34 years category think that "Made in America" ads boost sales or use social media online. If a U.S. adult in the 18–34 years category is randomly selected,
  a. What is the probability that the person thinks that "Made in America" ads boost sales and uses social media online?
  b. What is the probability that the person neither thinks that "Made in America" ads boost sales nor uses social media online?
  c. What is the probability that the person thinks that "Made in America" ads boost sales and does not use social media online?
  d. What is the probability that the person thinks that "Made in America" ads boost sales given that the person does not use social media online?

  e. What is the probability that the person either does not think that "Made in America" ads boost sales or does use social media online?

4.41 In a certain city, 30% of the families have a MasterCard, 20% have an American Express card, and 25% have a Visa card. Eight percent of the families have both a MasterCard and an American Express card. Twelve percent have both a Visa card and a MasterCard. Six percent have both an American Express card and a Visa card.
  a. What is the probability of selecting a family that has either a Visa card or an American Express card?
  b. If a family has a MasterCard, what is the probability that it has a Visa card?
  c. If a family has a Visa card, what is the probability that it has a MasterCard?
  d. Is possession of a Visa card independent of possession of a MasterCard? Why or why not?
  e. Is possession of an American Express card mutually exclusive of possession of a Visa card?

4.42 A few years ago, a survey commissioned by *The World Almanac* and *Maturity News* Service reported that 51% of the respondents did not believe the Social Security system will be secure in 20 years. Of the respondents who were age 45 or older, 70% believed the system will be secure in 20 years. Of the people surveyed, 57% were under age 45. One respondent is selected randomly.
  a. What is the probability that the person is age 45 or older?
  b. What is the probability that the person is younger than age 45 and believes that the Social Security system will be secure in 20 years?
  c. If the person selected believes the Social Security system will be secure in 20 years, what is the probability that the person is 45 years old or older?
  d. What is the probability that the person is younger than age 45 or believes the Social Security system will not be secure in 20 years?

4.43 A telephone survey conducted by the Maritz Marketing Research company found that 43% of Americans expect to save more money next year than they saved last year. Forty-five percent of those surveyed plan to reduce debt next year. Of those who expect to save more money next year, 81% plan to reduce debt next year. An American is selected randomly.
  a. What is the probability that this person expects to save more money next year and plans to reduce debt next year?
  b. What is the probability that this person expects to save more money next year or plans to reduce debt next year?
  c. What is the probability that this person neither expects to save more money next year nor plans to reduce debt next year?
  d. What is the probability that this person expects to save more money next year and does not plan to reduce debt next year?

4.44 The Steelcase Workplace Index studied the types of work-related activities that Americans did while on vacation in the summer. Among other things, 40% read work-related material. Thirty-four percent checked in with the boss. Respondents to the study were allowed to select more than one activity. Suppose that of those who read work-related material, 78% checked in with the boss. One of these survey respondents is selected randomly.

    a. What is the probability that while on vacation this respondent checked in with the boss and read work-related material?

    b. What is the probability that while on vacation this respondent neither read work-related material nor checked in with the boss?

    c. What is the probability that while on vacation this respondent read work-related material given that the respondent checked in with the boss?

    d. What is the probability that while on vacation this respondent did not check in with the boss given that the respondent read work-related material?

    e. What is the probability that while on vacation this respondent did not check in with the boss given that the respondent did not read work-related material?

    f. Construct a joint probability table for this problem.

4.45 A study on ethics in the workplace by the Ethics Resource Center and Kronos, Inc., revealed that 35% of employees admit to keeping quiet when they see coworker misconduct. Suppose 75% of employees who admit to keeping quiet when they see coworker misconduct call in sick when they are well. In addition, suppose that 40% of the employees who call in sick when they are well admit to keeping quiet when they see coworker misconduct. If an employee is randomly selected, determine the following probabilities:

    a. The employee calls in sick when well and admits to keeping quiet when seeing coworker misconduct.

    b. The employee admits to keeping quiet when seeing coworker misconduct or calls in sick when well.

    c. Given that the employee calls in sick when well, he or she does not keep quiet when seeing coworker misconduct.

    d. The employee neither keeps quiet when seeing coworker misconduct nor calls in sick when well.

    e. The employee admits to keeping quiet when seeing coworker misconduct and does not call in sick when well.

4.46 Health Rights Hotline published the results of a survey of 2,400 people in Northern California in which consumers were asked to share their complaints about managed care. The number one complaint was denial of care, with 17% of the participating consumers selecting it. Several other complaints were noted, including inappropriate care (14%), customer service (14%), payment disputes (11%), specialty care (10%), delays in getting care

(8%), and prescription drugs (7%). These complaint categories are mutually exclusive. Assume that the results of this survey can be inferred to all managed care consumers. If a managed care consumer is randomly selected, determine the following probabilities:

    a. The consumer complains about payment disputes or specialty care.

    b. The consumer complains about prescription drugs and customer service.

    c. The consumer complains about inappropriate care given that the consumer complains about specialty care.

    d. The consumer does not complain about delays in getting care nor does the consumer complain about payment disputes.

4.47 Companies use employee training for various reasons, including employee loyalty, certification, quality, and process improvement. In a national survey of companies, BI Learning Systems reported that 56% of the responding companies named employee retention as a top reason for training. Suppose 36% of the companies replied that they use training for process improvement and for employee retention. In addition, suppose that of the companies that use training for process improvement, 90% use training for employee retention. A company that uses training is randomly selected.

    a. What is the probability that the company uses training for employee retention and not for process improvement?

    b. If it is known that the company uses training for employee retention, what is the probability that it uses training for process improvement?

    c. What is the probability that the company uses training for process improvement?

    d. What is the probability that the company uses training for employee retention or process improvement?

    e. What is the probability that the company neither uses training for employee retention nor uses training for process improvement?

    f. Suppose it is known that the company does not use training for process improvement. What is the probability that the company does use training for employee retention?

4.48 Pitney Bowes surveyed 302 directors and vice presidents of marketing at large and midsized U.S. companies to determine what they believe is the best vehicle for educating decision makers on complex issues in selling products and services. The highest percentage of companies chose direct mail/catalogs, followed by direct sales/sales rep. Direct mail/catalogs was selected by 38% of the companies. None of the companies selected both direct mail/catalogs and direct sales/sales rep. Suppose also that 41% selected neither direct mail/catalogs nor direct sales/sales rep. If one of these companies is selected randomly and their top marketing person interviewed about this matter, determine the following probabilities:

a. The marketing person selected direct mail/catalogs and did not select direct sales/sales rep.

b. The marketing person selected direct sales/sales rep.

c. The marketing person selected direct sales/sales rep given that the person selected direct mail/catalogs.

d. The marketing person did not select direct mail/catalogs given that the person did not select direct sales/sales rep.

4.49 In a study of incentives used by companies to retain mature workers by The Conference Board, it was reported that 41% use flexible work arrangements. Suppose that of those companies that do not use flexible work arrangements, 10% give time off for volunteerism. In addition, suppose that of those companies that use flexible work arrangements, 60% give time off for volunteerism. If a company is randomly selected, determine the following probabilities:

a. The company uses flexible work arrangements or gives time off for volunteerism.

b. The company uses flexible work arrangements and does not give time off for volunteerism.

c. Given that the company does not give time off for volunteerism, the company uses flexible work arrangements.

d. The company does not use flexible work arrangements given that the company does give time off for volunteerism.

e. The company does not use flexible work arrangements or the company does not give time off for volunteerism.

4.50 A small independent physicians' practice has three doctors. Dr. Sarabia sees 41% of the patients, Dr. Tran sees 32%, and Dr. Jackson sees the rest. Dr. Sarabia requests blood tests on 5% of her patients, Dr. Tran requests blood tests on 8% of his patients, and Dr. Jackson requests blood tests on 6% of her patients. An auditor randomly selects a patient from the past week and discovers that the patient had a blood test as a result of the physician visit. Knowing this information, what is the probability that the patient saw Dr. Sarabia? For what percentage of all patients at this practice are blood tests requested?

4.51 A survey by the Arthur Andersen Enterprise Group/National Small Business United attempted to determine what the leading challenges are for the growth and survival of small businesses. Although the economy and finding qualified workers were the leading challenges, several others were listed in the results of the study, including regulations, listed by 30% of the companies, and the tax burden, listed by 35%. Suppose that 71% of the companies listing regulations as a challenge listed the tax burden as a challenge. Assume these percentages hold for all small businesses. If a

small business is randomly selected, determine the following probabilities:

a. The small business lists both the tax burden and regulations as a challenge.

b. The small business lists either the tax burden or regulations as a challenge.

c. The small business lists either the tax burden or regulations but not both as a challenge.

d. The small business lists regulations as a challenge given that it lists the tax burden as a challenge.

e. The small business does not list regulations as a challenge given that it lists the tax burden as a challenge.

f. The small business does not list regulations as a challenge given that it does not list the tax burden as a challenge.

4.52 According to U.S. Census Bureau figures, 35.3% of all Americans are in the 0–24 age bracket, 14.2% are in the 25–34 age bracket, 16.0% are in the 35–44 age bracket, and 34.5 are in the 45 and older age bracket. A study by Jupiter Media Metrix determined that Americans use their leisure time in different ways according to age. For example, of those who are in the 45 and older age bracket, 39% read a book or a magazine more than 10 hours per week. Of those who are in the 0–24 age bracket, only 11% read a book or a magazine more than 10 hours per week. The percentage figures for reading a book or a magazine for more than 10 hours per week are 24% for the 25–34 age bracket and 27% the 35–44 age bracket. Suppose an American is randomly selected and it is determined that he or she reads a book or a magazine more than 10 hours per week. Revise the probabilities that he or she is in any given age category. Using these figures, what is the overall percentage of the U.S. population that reads a book or a magazine more than 10 hours per week?

4.53 A retail study by Deloitte revealed that 54% of adults surveyed believed that plastic, noncompostable shopping bags should be banned. Suppose 41% of adults regularly recycle aluminum cans and believe that plastic, noncompostable shopping bags should be banned. In addition, suppose that 60% of adults who do not believe that plastic, noncompostable shopping bags should be banned do recycle. If an adult is randomly selected,

a. What is the probability that the adult recycles and does not believe that plastic, noncompostable shopping bags should be banned?

b. What is the probability that the adult does recycle?

c. What is the probability that the adult does recycle or does believe that plastic, noncompostable shopping bags should be banned?

d. What is the probability that the adult does not recycle or does not believe that plastic, noncompostable shopping bags should be banned?

e. What is the probability that the adult does not believe that plastic, noncompostable shopping bags should be banned given that the adult does recycle?

ANALYZING THE DATABASES

1. In the Manufacturing database, what is the probability that a randomly selected SIC Code industry is in industry group 13? What is the probability that a randomly selected SIC Code industry has a value of industry shipments of 4 (see Chapter 1 for coding)? What is the probability that a randomly selected SIC Code industry is in industry group 13 and has a value of industry shipments of 2? What is the probability that a randomly selected SIC Code industry is in industry group 13 or has a value of industry shipments of 2? What is the probability that a randomly selected SIC Code industry neither is in industry group 13 nor has a value of industry shipments of 2?

2. Use the Hospital database. Construct a cross-tabulation table for region and for type of control. You should have a 7×4 table. Using this table, answer the following questions. (Refer to Chapter 1 for category members.) What is the probability that a randomly selected hospital is in the Midwest if the hospital is known to be for-profit? If the hospital is known to be in the South, what is the probability that it is a government, nonfederal hospital? What is the probability that a hospital is in the Rocky Mountain region or a not-for-profit, nongovernment hospital? What is the probability that a hospital is a for-profit hospital located in California?

CASE

COLGATE-PALMOLIVE MAKES A "TOTAL" EFFORT

In the mid-1990s, Colgate-Palmolive developed a new toothpaste for the U.S. market, Colgate Total, with an antibacterial ingredient that was already being successfully sold overseas. However, the word *antibacterial* was not allowed for such products by the Food and Drug Administration rules. So Colgate-Palmolive had to come up with another way of marketing this and other features of their new toothpaste to U.S. consumers. Market researchers told Colgate-Palmolive that consumers were weary of trying to discern among the different advantages of various toothpaste brands and wanted simplification in their shopping lives. In response, the name "Total" was given to the product in the United States: The one word would convey that the toothpaste is the "total" package of various benefits.

Young & Rubicam developed several commercials illustrating Total's benefits and tested the commercials with focus groups. One commercial touting Total's long-lasting benefits was particularly successful. Meanwhile, in 1997, Colgate-Palmolive received FDA approval for Total, five years after the company had applied for it. The product was launched in the United States in January of 1998 using commercials that were designed from the more successful ideas of the focus group tests. Total was introduced with a $100 million advertising campaign. Ten months later, 21% of all United States households had purchased Total for the first time. During this same time period, 43% of those who initially tried Total purchased it again. A year after its release, Total was the number one toothpaste in the United States. Total is advertised as not just a toothpaste but as a protective shield that protects you for a full range of oral health problems for up to 12 hours. Total is now offered in a variety of forms, including Colgate Total Enamel Strength, Colgate Total Advanced Whitening, Colgate Total Advanced Clean, Colgate Total Advanced Fresh, Colgate Total Clean Mint, Colgate Total Whitening, and Colgate Total Mint Stripe. In the United States, market share for Colgate Total toothpaste was 16.2% in the second quarter of 2008, which was its highest quarterly share ever.

Discussion

1. What probabilities are given in this case? Use these probabilities and the probability laws to determine what percentage of U.S. households purchased Total at least twice in the first 10 months of its release.

2. Is age category independent of willingness to try new products? According to the U.S. Census Bureau, approximately 20% of all Americans are in the 45–64 age category. Suppose 24% of the consumers who purchased Total for the first time during the initial 10-month period were in the 45–64 age category. Use this information to determine whether age is independent of the initial purchase of Total during the introductory time period. Explain your answer.

3. Using the probabilities given in Question 2, calculate the probability that a randomly selected U.S. consumer is either in the 45–64 age category or purchased Total during the initial 10-month period. What is the probability that a randomly selected person purchased Total in the first 10 months given that the person is in the 45–64 age category?

4. Suppose 32% of all toothpaste consumers in the United States saw the Total commercials. Of those who saw the commercials, 40% purchased Total at least once in the first 10 months of its introduction. Of those who did not see the commercials, 12.06% purchased Total at least once in the first 10 months of its introduction. Suppose a toothpaste consumer is randomly selected and it is learned that they purchased Total during the first 10 months of its introduction. Revise the probability that this person saw the Total commercials and the probability that the person did not see the Total commercials.

Source: Colgate-Palmolive's home page at http://www.colgate.com/app/Colgate/US/HomePage.cvsp, Total's homepage at http://www.colgate.com/app/ColgateTotal/US/EN/Products.cvsp, and at http://www.colgate.com/app/ColgateTotal/ US/EN/HomePage.cwsp, 2010.

UNIT II

DISTRIBUTIONS AND SAMPLING

Unit II of this textbook introduces you to the concept of statistical distribution. In lay terms, a statistical distribution is a numerical or graphical depiction of frequency counts or probabilities for various values of a variable that can occur. Distributions are important because most of the analyses done in business statistics are based on the characteristics of a particular distribution. In Unit II, you will study eight distributions: six population distributions and two sampling distributions.

Six population distributions are presented in Chapters 5 and 6. These population distributions can be categorized as discrete distributions or continuous distributions. Discrete distributions are introduced in Chapter 5, and they include the binomial distribution, the Poisson distribution, and the hypergeometric distribution. Continuous distributions are presented in Chapter 6, and they include the uniform distribution, the normal distribution, and the exponential distribution. Information about sampling is discussed in Chapter 7 along with two sampling distributions, the sampling distribution of $\bar{x}$ and the sampling distribution of $\hat{p}$. Three more population distributions are introduced later in the text in Unit III. These include the t distribution and the chi-square distribution in Chapter 8 and the F distribution in Chapter 10.

CHAPTER 5

Discrete Distributions

LEARNING OBJECTIVES

The overall learning objective of Chapter 5 is to help you understand a category of probability distributions that produces only discrete outcomes, thereby enabling you to:

1. Define a random variable in order to differentiate between a discrete distribution and a continuous distribution
2. Determine the mean, variance, and standard deviation of a discrete distribution
3. Solve problems involving the binomial distribution using the binomial formula and the binomial table
4. Solve problems involving the Poisson distribution using the Poisson formula and the Poisson table
5. Solve problems involving the hypergeometric distribution using the hypergeometric formula

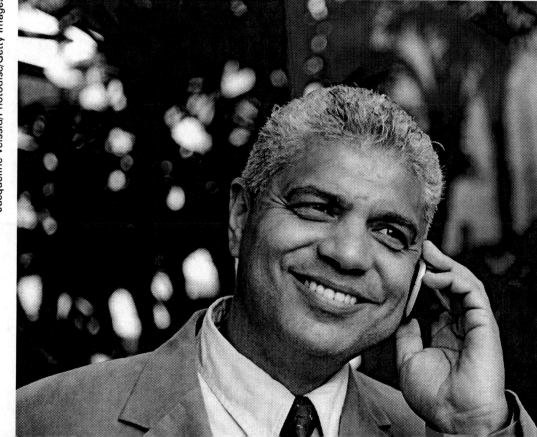

Jacqueline Veissid/Photodisc/Getty Images

Life with a Cell Phone

As early as 1947, scientists understood the basic concept of a cell phone as a type of two-way radio. Seeing the potential of crude mobile car phones, researchers understood that by using a small range of service areas (cells) with frequency reuse, they could increase the capacity for mobile phone usage significantly even though the technology was not then available. During that same year, AT&T proposed the allocation of a large number of radio-spectrum frequencies by the FCC that would thereby make widespread mobile phone service feasible. At the same time, the FCC decided to limit the amount of frequency capacity available such that only 23 phone conversations could take place simutaneously. In 1968, the FCC reconsidered its position and freed the airwaves for more phones. About this time, AT&T and Bell Labs proposed to the FCC a system in which they would construct a series of many small, low-powered broadcast towers, each of which would broadcast to a "cell" covering a few miles. Taken as a whole, such "cells" could be used to pass phone calls from cell to cell, thereby reaching a large area.

The first company to actually produce a cell phone was Motorola, and Dr. Martin Cooper, then of Motorola and considered the inventor of the first modern portable handset, made his first call on the portable cell phone in 1973. By 1977,

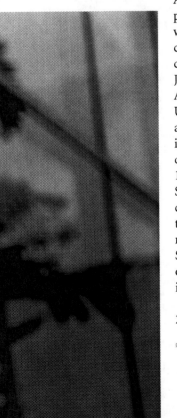

AT&T and Bell Labs had developed a prototype cellular phone system that was tested in Chicago by 2,000 trial customers. After the first commercial cell phone system began operation in Japan in 1979, and Motorola and American Radio developed a second U.S. cell system in 1981, the FCC authorized commerical cellular service in the United States in 1982. By 1987, cell phone subscribers had exceeded 1 million customers in the United States, and as frequencies were getting crowded, the FCC authorized alternative cellular technologies, opening up new opportunities for development. Since that time, researchers have developed a number of advances that have increased capacity exponentially.

Today in the United States, nearly 25% of cell phone owners use only cellular phones, and the trend is rising. According to a Harris Poll of 9132 surveyed adults, 89% of adults have a cell phone. In an Associated Press/America Online Pew Poll of 1,200 cell phone users, it was discovered that two-thirds of all cell phone users said that it would be hard to give up their cell phones, and 26% responded that they cannot imagine life without their cell phones. In spite of American's growing dependence on their cell phones, not everyone is happy about their usage. Almost 9 out of 10 cell users encounter others using their phones in an annoying way. In addition, 28% claim that sometimes they do not drive as safely as they should because they are using cell phones. Now, there are multiple uses for the cell phone, including picture taking, text messaging, game playing, and others. According to the study, two-thirds of cell phone owners in the 18 to 29 age bracket sent text messages using their cell phones, 55% take pictures with their phones, 47% play games on the phones, and 28% use the Internet through their cell phones.

Managerial and Statistical Questions

1. One study reports that nearly 25% of cell phone owners in the United States use only cellular phones (no land line). Suppose you randomly select 20 Americans, what is the probability that more than 10 of the sample use only cell phones?

2. The study also reports that 9 out of 10 cell users encounter others using their phones in an annoying way. Based on this, if you were to randomly select 25 cell phone users, what is the probability that fewer than 20 report that they encounter others using their phones in an annoying way?

3. Suppose a survey of cell phone users shows that, on average, a cell phone user receives 3.6 calls per day. If this figure is true, what is the probability that a cell phone user receives no calls in a day? What is the probability that a cell phone user receives five or more calls in a day?

Sources: Mary Bellis, "Selling the Cell Phone, Part 1: History of Cellular Phones," in *About Business & Finance.* An America Online site, Selling the Cell Phone—History of Cellular Phones at: http://inventors.about.com/library/weekly/aa070899.htm; *USA Today* Tech, "For Many, Their Cell Phone Has Become Their Only Phone," at: http://www.usatoday.com/tech/news/2003-03-24-cell-phones x.htm; and Will Lester, "A Love-Hate Relationship," *Houston Chronicle.* April 4, 2006, p. D4. http://www.harrisinteractive.com/harris_poll/index.asp?PID=890; "Nearly a Quarter of U.S. Homes Only Use Cellphones," Reuters, at: http://www.reuters.com/assets/print?aid=USTRE64B6F620100512, May 12, 2010.

TABLE 5.1

All Possible Outcomes for the
Battery Experiment

$G_1 \, G_2 \, G_3$
$D_1 \, G_2 \, G_3$
$G_1 \, D_2 \, G_3$
$G_1 \, G_2 \, D_3$
$D_1 \, D_2 \, G_3$
$D_1 \, G_2 \, D_3$
$G_1 \, D_2 \, D_3$
$D_1 \, D_2 \, D_3$

In statistical experiments involving chance, outcomes occur randomly. As an example of such an experiment, a battery manufacturer randomly selects three batteries from a large batch of batteries to be tested for quality. Each selected battery is to be rated as good or defective. The batteries are numbered from 1 to 3, a defective battery is designated with a D, and a good battery is designated with a G. All possible outcomes are shown in Table 5.1. The expression $D_1 \, G_2 \, D_3$ denotes one particular outcome in which the first and third batteries are defective and the second battery is good. In this chapter, we examine the probabilities of events occurring in experiments that produce such discrete distributions. In particular, we will study the binomial distribution, the Poisson distribution, and the hypergeometric distribution.

5.1 DISCRETE VERSUS CONTINUOUS DISTRIBUTIONS

A **random variable** is *a variable that contains the outcomes of a chance experiment*. For example, suppose an experiment is to measure the arrivals of automobiles at a turnpike tollbooth during a 30-second period. The possible outcomes are: 0 cars, 1 car, 2 cars, . . . , n cars. These numbers $(0, 1, 2, \ldots, n)$ are the values of a random variable. Suppose another experiment is to measure the time between the completion of two tasks in a production line. The values will range from 0 seconds to n seconds. These time measurements are the values of another random variable. The two categories of random variables are (1) discrete random variables and (2) continuous random variables.

A random variable is a **discrete random variable** *if the set of all possible values is at most a finite or a countably infinite number of possible values*. In most statistical situations, discrete random variables produce values that are nonnegative whole numbers. For example, if six people are randomly selected from a population and how many of the six are left-handed is to be determined, the random variable produced is discrete. The only possible numbers of left-handed people in the sample of six are 0, 1, 2, 3, 4, 5, and 6. There cannot be 2.75 left-handed people in a group of six people; obtaining nonwhole number values is impossible. Other examples of experiments that yield discrete random variables include the following:

1. Randomly selecting 25 people who consume soft drinks and determining how many people prefer diet soft drinks
2. Determining the number of defects in a batch of 50 items
3. Counting the number of people who arrive at a store during a five-minute period
4. Sampling 100 registered voters and determining how many voted for the president in the last election

The battery experiment described at the beginning of the chapter produces a distribution that has discrete outcomes. Any one trial of the experiment will contain 0, 1, 2, or 3 defective batteries. It is not possible to get 1.58 defective batteries. It could be said that discrete random variables are usually generated from experiments in which things are "counted" not "measured."

Continuous random variables *take on values at every point over a given interval.* Thus continuous random variables have no gaps or unassumed values. It could be said that continuous random variables are generated from experiments in which things are "measured" not "counted." For example, if a person is assembling a product component, the time it takes to accomplish that feat could be any value within a reasonable range such as 3 minutes 36.4218 seconds or 5 minutes 17.5169 seconds. A list of measures for which continuous random variables might be generated would include time, height, weight, and volume. Other examples of experiments that yield continuous random variables include the following:

1. Sampling the volume of liquid nitrogen in a storage tank
2. Measuring the time between customer arrivals at a retail outlet
3. Measuring the lengths of newly designed automobiles
4. Measuring the weight of grain in a grain elevator at different points of time

Once continuous data are measured and recorded, they become discrete data because the data are rounded off to a discrete number. Thus in actual practice, virtually all business data are discrete. However, for practical reasons, data analysis is facilitated greatly by using continuous distributions on data that were continuous originally.

The outcomes for random variables and their associated probabilities can be organized into distributions. The two types of distributions are **discrete distributions**, *constructed from discrete random variables*, and **continuous distributions**, *based on continuous random variables*.

In this text, three discrete distributions are presented:

1. binomial distribution
2. Poisson distribution
3. hypergeometric distribution

All three of these distributions are presented in this chapter.

In addition, six continuous distributions are discussed later in this text:

1. uniform distribution
2. normal distribution
3. exponential distribution
4. *t* distribution
5. chi-square distribution
6. *F* distribution

Discrete

Continuous

5.2 DESCRIBING A DISCRETE DISTRIBUTION

How can we describe a discrete distribution? One way is to construct a graph of the distribution and study the graph. The histogram is probably the most common graphical way to depict a discrete distribution.

Observe the discrete distribution in Table 5.2. An executive is considering out-of-town business travel for a given Friday. She recognizes that at least one crisis could occur on the day that she is gone and she is concerned about that possibility. Table 5.2 shows a discrete distribution that contains the number of crises that could occur during the day that she is gone and the probability that each number will occur. For example, there is a .37 probability that no crisis will occur, a .31 probability of one crisis, and so on. The histogram in Figure 5.1 depicts the distribution given in Table 5.2. Notice that the *x*-axis of the histogram contains the possible outcomes of the experiment (number of crises that might occur) and that the *y*-axis contains the probabilities of these occurring.

It is readily apparent from studying the graph of Figure 5.1 that the most likely number of crises is 0 or 1. In addition, we can see that the distribution is discrete in that no probabilities are shown for values in between the whole-number crises.

TABLE 5.2

Discrete Distribution of Occurrence of Daily Crises

Number of Crises	Probability
0	.37
1	.31
2	.18
3	.09
4	.04
5	.01

Minitab Histogram of Discrete
Distribution of Crises Data

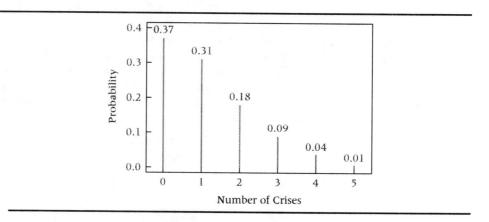

Mean, Variance, and Standard Deviation of Discrete Distributions

What additional mechanisms can be used to describe discrete distributions besides depicting them graphically? The measures of central tendency and measures of variability discussed in Chapter 3 for grouped data can be applied to discrete distributions to compute a mean, a variance, and a standard deviation. Each of those three descriptive measures (mean, variance, and standard deviation) is computed on grouped data by using the class midpoint as the value to represent the data in the class interval. With discrete distributions, using the class midpoint is not necessary because the discrete value of an outcome (0, 1, 2, 3, . . .) is used to represent itself. Thus, instead of using the value of the class midpoint (M) in computing these descriptive measures for grouped data, the discrete experiment's outcomes (x) are used. In computing these descriptive measures on grouped data, the frequency of each class interval is used to weight the class midpoint. With discrete distribution analysis, the probability of each occurrence is used as the weight.

TABLE 5.3

Computing the Mean of the
Crises Data

x	$P(x)$	$x \cdot P(x)$
0	.37	.00
1	.31	.31
2	.18	.36
3	.09	.27
4	.04	.16
5	.01	.05
		$\Sigma[x \cdot P(x)] = 1.15$
		$\mu = 1.15$ crises

Mean or Expected Value

The **mean** or **expected value** of a discrete distribution is *the long-run average of occurrences.* We must realize that any one trial using a discrete random variable yields only one outcome. However, if the process is repeated long enough, the average of the outcomes are most likely to approach a long-run average, expected value, or mean value. This mean, or expected, value is computed as follows.

MEAN OR EXPECTED VALUE OF A DISCRETE DISTRIBUTION

$$\mu = E(x) = \Sigma[x \cdot P(x)]$$

where

$E(x) =$ long-run average
$x =$ an outcome
$P(x) =$ probability of that outcome

As an example, let's compute the mean or expected value of the distribution given in Table 5.2. See Table 5.3 for the resulting values. In the long run, the mean or expected number of crises on a given Friday for this executive is 1.15 crises. Of course, the executive will never have 1.15 crises.

Variance and Standard Deviation of a Discrete Distribution

The variance and standard deviation of a discrete distribution are solved for by using the outcomes (x) and probabilities of outcomes [$P(x)$] in a manner similar to that of computing a

TABLE 5.4

Calculation of Variance
and Standard Deviation on
Crises Data

x	P(x)	$(x - \mu)^2$	$(x - \mu)^2 \cdot P(x)$
0	.37	$(0 - 1.15)^2 = 1.32$	$(1.32)(.37) = .49$
1	.31	$(1 - 1.15)^2 = .02$	$(0.02)(.31) = .01$
2	.18	$(2 - 1.15)^2 = .72$	$(0.72)(.18) = .13$
3	.09	$(3 - 1.15)^2 = 3.42$	$(3.42)(.09) = .31$
4	.04	$(4 - 1.15)^2 = 8.12$	$(8.12)(.04) = .32$
5	.01	$(5 - 1.15)^2 = 14.82$	$(14.82)(.01) = .15$
			$\Sigma[(x - \mu)^2 \cdot P(x)] = 1.41$

The variance of $\sigma^2 = \Sigma[(x - \mu)^2 \cdot P(x)] = 1.41$

The standard deviation is $\sigma = \sqrt{1.41} = 1.19$ crises.

mean. In addition, the computations for variance and standard deviations use the mean of the discrete distribution. The formula for computing the variance follows.

VARIANCE OF A DISCRETE DISTRIBUTION

$$\sigma^2 = \Sigma[(x - \mu)^2 \cdot P(x)]$$

where

x = an outcome
$P(x)$ = probability of a given outcome
μ = mean

The standard deviation is then computed by taking the square root of the variance.

STANDARD DEVIATION OF A DISCRETE DISTRIBUTION

$$\sigma = \sqrt{\Sigma[(x - \mu)^2 \cdot P(x)]}$$

The variance and standard deviation of the crisis data in Table 5.2 are calculated and shown in Table 5.4. The mean of the crisis data is 1.15 crises. The standard deviation is 1.19 crises, and the variance is 1.41.

DEMONSTRATION PROBLEM 5.1

During one holiday season, the Texas lottery played a game called the Stocking Stuffer. With this game, total instant winnings of $34.8 million were available in 70 million $1 tickets, with ticket prizes ranging from $1 to $1,000. Shown here are the various prizes and the probability of winning each prize. Use these data to compute the expected value of the game, the variance of the game, and the standard deviation of the game.

Prize (x)	Probability P(x)
$1,000	.00002
100	.00063
20	.00400
10	.00601
4	.02403
2	.08877
1	.10479
0	.77175

Solution

The mean is computed as follows.

Prize (x)	Probability $P(x)$	$x \cdot P(x)$
$1,000	.00002	.02000
100	.00063	.06300
20	.00400	.08000
10	.00601	.06010
4	.02403	.09612
2	.08877	.17754
1	.10479	.10479
0	.77175	.00000
		$\Sigma[x \cdot P(x)] = .60155$

$$\mu = E(x) = \Sigma[x \cdot P(x)] = .60155$$

The expected payoff for a $1 ticket in this game is 60.2 cents. If a person plays the game for a long time, he or she could expect to average about 60 cents in winnings. In the long run, the participant will lose about $1.00 − .602 = .398, or about 40 cents a game. Of course, an individual will never win 60 cents in any one game.

Using this mean, $\mu = .60155$, the variance and standard deviation can be computed as follows.

x	$P(x)$	$(x - \mu)^2$	$(x - \mu)^2 \cdot P(x)$
$1,000	.00002	998797.26190	19.97595
100	.00063	9880.05186	6.22443
20	.00400	376.29986	1.50520
10	.00601	88.33086	0.53087
4	.02403	11.54946	0.27753
2	.08877	1.95566	0.17360
1	.10479	0.15876	0.01664
0	.77175	0.36186	0.27927
			$\Sigma[(x - \mu)^2 \cdot P(x)] = 28.98349$

$$\sigma^2 = \Sigma[(x - \mu)^2 \cdot P(x)] = 28.98349$$
$$\sigma = \sqrt{\sigma^2} = \sqrt{\Sigma[(x - \mu)^2 \cdot P(x)]} = \sqrt{28.98349} = 5.38363$$

The variance is 28.98349 (dollars)^2 and the standard deviation is $5.38.

5.2 PROBLEMS

5.1 Determine the mean, the variance, and the standard deviation of the following discrete distribution.

x	$P(x)$
1	.238
2	.290
3	.177
4	.158
5	.137

5.2 Determine the mean, the variance, and the standard deviation of the following discrete distribution.

x	$P(x)$
0	.103
1	.118
2	.246
3	.229
4	.138
5	.094
6	.071
7	.001

5.3 The following data are the result of a historical study of the number of flaws found in a porcelain cup produced by a manufacturing firm. Use these data and the associated probabilities to compute the expected number of flaws and the standard deviation of flaws.

Flaws	Probability
0	.461
1	.285
2	.129
3	.087
4	.038

5.4 Suppose 20% of the people in a city prefer Pepsi-Cola as their soft drink of choice. If a random sample of six people is chosen, the number of Pepsi drinkers could range from zero to six. Shown here are the possible numbers of Pepsi drinkers in a sample of six people and the probability of that number of Pepsi drinkers occurring in the sample. Use the data to determine the mean number of Pepsi drinkers in a sample of six people in the city, and compute the standard deviation.

Number of Pepsi Drinkers	Probability
0	.262
1	.393
2	.246
3	.082
4	.015
5	.002
6	.000

5.3 BINOMIAL DISTRIBUTION

Perhaps the most widely known of all discrete distributions is the **binomial distribution**. The binomial distribution has been used for hundreds of years. Several assumptions underlie the use of the binomial distribution:

ASSUMPTIONS OF THE BINOMIAL DISTRIBUTION	• The experiment involves n identical trials. • Each trial has only two possible outcomes denoted as success or as failure. • Each trial is independent of the previous trials. • The terms p and q remain constant throughout the experiment, where the term p is the probability of getting a success on any one trial and the term $q = (1 - p)$ is the probability of getting a failure on any one trial.

As the word *binomial* indicates, any single trial of a binomial experiment contains only two possible outcomes. These two outcomes are labeled *success* or *failure*. Usually the outcome of interest to the researcher is labeled a success. For example, if a quality control analyst is looking for defective products, he would consider finding a defective product a success even though the company would not consider a defective product a success. If researchers are studying left-handedness, the outcome of getting a left-handed person in a trial of an experiment is a success. The other possible outcome of a trial in a binomial experiment is called a failure. The word *failure* is used only in opposition to success. In the preceding experiments, a failure could be to get an acceptable part (as opposed to a defective part) or to get a right-handed person (as opposed to a left-handed person). In a binomial distribution experiment, any one trial can have only two possible, mutually exclusive outcomes (right-handed/left-handed, defective/good, male/female, etc.).

The binomial distribution is a discrete distribution. In n trials, only x successes are possible, where x is a whole number between 0 and n inclusive. For example, if five parts are randomly selected from a batch of parts, only 0, 1, 2, 3, 4, or 5 defective parts are possible in that sample. In a sample of five parts, getting 2.714 defective parts is not possible, nor is getting eight defective parts possible.

In a binomial experiment, the trials must be independent. This constraint means that either the experiment is by nature one that produces independent trials (such as tossing coins or rolling dice) or the experiment is conducted with replacement. The effect of the independent trial requirement is that p, the probability of getting a success on one trial, remains constant from trial to trial. For example, suppose 5% of all parts in a bin are defective. The probability of drawing a defective part on the first draw is $p = .05$. If the first part drawn is not replaced, the second draw is not independent of the first, and the p value will change for the next draw. The binomial distribution does not allow for p to change from trial to trial within an experiment. However, if the population is large in comparison with the sample size, the effect of sampling without replacement is minimal, and the independence assumption essentially is met, that is, p remains relatively constant.

Generally, if the sample size, n, is less than 5% of the population, the independence assumption is not of great concern. Therefore the acceptable sample size for using the binomial distribution with samples taken *without* replacement is

$$n < 5\% \, N$$

where

$n =$ sample size
$N =$ population size

For example, suppose 10% of the population of the world is left-handed and that a sample of 20 people is selected randomly from the world's population. If the first person selected is left-handed—and the sampling is conducted without replacement—the value of $p = .10$ is virtually unaffected because the population of the world is so large. In addition, with many experiments the population is continually being replenished even as the sampling is being done. This condition often is the case with quality control sampling of products from large production runs. Some examples of binomial distribution problems follow.

1. Suppose a machine producing computer chips has a 6% defective rate. If a company purchases 30 of these chips, what is the probability that none is defective?
2. One ethics study suggested that 84% of U.S. companies have an ethics code. From a random sample of 15 companies, what is the probability that at least 10 have an ethics code?
3. A survey found that nearly 67% of company buyers stated that their company had programs for preferred buyers. If a random sample of 50 company buyers is taken, what is the probability that 40 or more have companies with programs for preferred buyers?

Solving a Binomial Problem

A survey of relocation administrators by Runzheimer International revealed several reasons why workers reject relocation offers. Included in the list were family considerations, financial reasons, and others. Four percent of the respondents said they rejected relocation offers because they received too little relocation help. Suppose five workers who just rejected relocation offers are randomly selected and interviewed. Assuming the 4% figure holds for all workers rejecting relocation, what is the probability that the first worker interviewed rejected the offer because of too little relocation help and the next four workers rejected the offer for other reasons?

Let T represent too little relocation help and R represent other reasons. The sequence of interviews for this problem is as follows:

$$T_1, R_2, R_3, R_4, R_5$$

The probability of getting this sequence of workers is calculated by using the special rule of multiplication for independent events (assuming the workers are independently selected from a large population of workers). If 4% of the workers rejecting relocation offers do so for too little relocation help, the probability of one person being randomly selected from workers rejecting relocation offers who does so for that reason is .04, which is the value of p. The other 96% of the workers who reject relocation offers do so for other reasons. Thus the probability of randomly selecting a worker from those who reject relocation offers who does so for other reasons is $1 - .04 = .96$, which is the value for q. The probability of obtaining this sequence of five workers who have rejected relocation offers is

$$P(T_1 \cap R_2 \cap R_3 \cap R_4 \cap R_5) = (.04)(.96)(.96)(.96)(.96) = .03397$$

Obviously, in the random selection of workers who rejected relocation offers, the worker who did so because of too little relocation help could have been the second worker or the third or the fourth or the fifth. All the possible sequences of getting one worker who rejected relocation because of too little help and four workers who did so for other reasons follow.

$$T_1, R_2, R_3, R_4, R_5$$
$$R_1, T_2, R_3, R_4, R_5$$
$$R_1, R_2, T_3, R_4, R_5$$
$$R_1, R_2, R_3, T_4, R_5$$
$$R_1, R_2, R_3, R_4, T_5$$

The probability of each of these sequences occurring is calculated as follows:

$$(.04)(.96)(.96)(.96)(.96) = .03397$$
$$(.96)(.04)(.96)(.96)(.96) = .03397$$
$$(.96)(.96)(.04)(.96)(.96) = .03397$$
$$(.96)(.96)(.96)(.04)(.96) = .03397$$
$$(.96)(.96)(.96)(.96)(.04) = .03397$$

Note that in each case the final probability is the same. Each of the five sequences contains the product of .04 and four .96s. The commutative property of multiplication allows for the reordering of the five individual probabilities in any one sequence. The probabilities in each of the five sequences may be reordered and summarized as $(.04)^1 (.96)^4$. Each sequence contains the same five probabilities, which makes recomputing the probability of each sequence unnecessary. What *is* important is to determine how many different ways the sequences can be formed and multiply that figure by the probability of one sequence occurring. For the five sequences of this problem, the total probability of getting exactly one worker who rejected relocation because of too little relocation help in a random sample of five workers who rejected relocation offers is

$$5(.04)^1(.96)^4 = .16987$$

An easier way to determine the number of sequences than by listing all possibilities is to use *combinations* to calculate them. (The concept of combinations was introduced in Chapter 4.) Five workers are being sampled, so $n = 5$, and the problem is to get one worker who rejected a relocation offer because of too little relocation help, $x = 1$. Hence $_nC_x$ will yield the number of possible ways to get x successes in n trials. For this problem, $_5C_1$ tells the number of sequences of possibilities.

$$_5C_1 = \frac{5!}{1!(5 - 1)!} = 5$$

Weighting the probability of one sequence with the combination yields

$$_5C_1(.04)^1(.96)^4 = .16987$$

Using combinations simplifies the determination of how many sequences are possible for a given value of x in a binomial distribution.

As another example, suppose 70% of all Americans believe cleaning up the environment is an important issue. What is the probability of randomly sampling four Americans and having exactly two of them say that they believe cleaning up the environment is an important issue? Let E represent the success of getting a person who believes cleaning up the environment is an important issue. For this example, $p = .70$. Let N represent the failure of not getting a person who believes cleaning up is an important issue (N denotes not important). The probability of getting one of these persons is $q = .30$.

The various sequences of getting two E's in a sample of four follow.

$$E_1, E_2, N_3, N_4$$
$$E_1, N_2, E_3, N_4$$
$$E_1, N_2, N_3, E_4$$
$$N_1, E_2, E_3, N_4$$
$$N_1, E_2, N_3, E_4$$
$$N_1, N_2, E_3, E_4$$

Two successes in a sample of four can occur six ways. Using combinations, the number of sequences is

$$_4C_2 = 6 \text{ ways}$$

The probability of selecting any individual sequence is

$$(.70)^2(.30)^2 = .0441$$

Thus the overall probability of getting exactly two people who believe cleaning up the environment is important out of four randomly selected people, when 70% of Americans believe cleaning up the environment is important, is

$$_4C_2(.70)^2(.30)^2 = .2646$$

Generalizing from these two examples yields the binomial formula, which can be used to solve binomial problems.

BINOMIAL FORMULA

$$P(x) = \,_nC_x \cdot p^x \cdot q^{n-x} = \frac{n!}{x!(n-x)!} \cdot p^x \cdot q^{n-x}$$

where

n = the number of trials (or the number being sampled)
x = the number of successes desired
p = the probability of getting a success in one trial
$q = 1 - p$ = the probability of getting a failure in one trial

---

The binomial formula summarizes the steps presented so far to solve binomial problems. The formula allows the solution of these problems quickly and efficiently.

DEMONSTRATION PROBLEM 5.2

A Gallup survey found that 65% of all financial consumers were very satisfied with their primary financial institution. Suppose that 25 financial consumers are sampled and if the Gallup survey result still holds true today, what is the probability that exactly 19 are very satisfied with their primary financial institution?

Solution

The value of p is .65 (very satisfied), the value of $q = 1 - p = 1 - .65 = .35$ (not very satisfied), $n = 25$, and $x = 19$. The binomial formula yields the final answer.

$$_{25}C_{19}(.65)^{19}(.35)^6 = (177,100)(.00027884)(.00183827) = .0908$$

If 65% of all financial consumers are very satisfied, about 9.08% of the time the researcher would get exactly 19 out of 25 financial consumers who are very satisfied with their financial institution. How many very satisfied consumers would one expect to get in 25 randomly selected financial consumers? If 65% of the financial consumers are very satisfied with their primary financial institution, one would expect to get about 65% of 25 or $(.65)(25) = 16.25$ very satisfied financial consumers. While in any individual sample of 25 the number of financial consumers who are very satisfied cannot be 16.25, business researchers understand the x values near 16.25 are the most likely occurrences.

DEMONSTRATION PROBLEM 5.3

According to the U.S. Census Bureau, approximately 6% of all workers in Jackson, Mississippi, are unemployed. In conducting a random telephone survey in Jackson, what is the probability of getting two or fewer unemployed workers in a sample of 20?

Solution

This problem must be worked as the union of three problems: (1) zero unemployed, $x = 0$; (2) one unemployed, $x = 1$; and (3) two unemployed, $x = 2$. In each problem, $p = .06$, $q = .94$, and $n = 20$. The binomial formula gives the following result.

$$
\begin{array}{ccccccc}
x=0 & & x=1 & & x=2 & \\
{}_{20}C_0(.06)^0(.94)^{20} & + & {}_{20}C_1(.06)^1(.94)^{19} & + & {}_{20}C_2(.06)^2(.94)^{18} & = \\
.2901 & + & .3703 & + & .2246 & = .8850
\end{array}
$$

If 6% of the workers in Jackson, Mississippi, are unemployed, the telephone surveyor would get zero, one, or two unemployed workers 88.5% of the time in a random sample of 20 workers. The requirement of getting two or fewer is satisfied by getting zero, one, or two unemployed workers. Thus this problem is the union of three probabilities. Whenever the binomial formula is used to solve for cumulative success (not an exact number), the probability of each x value must be solved and the probabilities summed. If an actual survey produced such a result, it would serve to validate the census figures.

Using the Binomial Table

Anyone who works enough binomial problems will begin to recognize that the probability of getting $x = 5$ successes from a sample size of $n = 18$ when $p = .10$ is the same no matter whether the five successes are left-handed people, defective parts, brand X purchasers, or any other variable. Whether the sample involves people, parts, or products does not matter in terms of the final probabilities. The essence of the problem is the same: $n = 18$, $x = 5$, and $p = .10$. Recognizing this fact, mathematicians constructed a set of binomial tables containing presolved probabilities.

Two parameters, n and p, describe or characterize a binomial distribution. Binomial distributions actually are a family of distributions. Every different value of n and/or every different value of p gives a different binomial distribution, and tables are available for various combinations of n and p values. Because of space limitations, the binomial tables presented in this text are limited. Table A.2 in Appendix A contains binomial tables. Each table is headed by a value of n. Nine values of p are presented in each table of size n. In the column below each value of p is the binomial distribution for that combination of n and p. Table 5.5 contains a segment of Table A.2 with the binomial probabilities for $n = 20$.

DEMONSTRATION PROBLEM 5.4

Solve the binomial probability for $n = 20$, $p = .40$, and $x = 10$ by using Table A.2, Appendix A.

Solution

To use Table A.2, first locate the value of n. Because $n = 20$ for this problem, the portion of the binomial tables containing values for $n = 20$ presented in Table 5.5 can be used. After locating the value of n, search horizontally across the top of the table for the appropriate value of p. In this problem, $p = .40$. The column under .40 contains the probabilities for the binomial distribution of $n = 20$ and $p = .40$. To get the probability of $x = 10$, find the value of x in the leftmost column and locate the probability in the table at the intersection of $p = .40$ and $x = 10$. The answer is .117. Working this problem by the binomial formula yields the same result.

$$
{}_{20}C_{10}(.40)^{10}(.60)^{10} = .1171
$$

TABLE 5.5

Excerpt from Table A.2,
Appendix A

$n = 20$					Probability				
x	.1	.2	.3	.4	.5	.6	.7	.8	.9
0	.122	.012	.001	.000	.000	.000	.000	.000	.000
1	.270	.058	.007	.000	.000	.000	.000	.000	.000
2	.285	.137	.028	.003	.000	.000	.000	.000	.000
3	.190	.205	.072	.012	.001	.000	.000	.000	.000
4	.090	.218	.130	.035	.005	.000	.000	.000	.000
5	.032	.175	.179	.075	.015	.001	.000	.000	.000
6	.009	.109	.192	.124	.037	.005	.000	.000	.000
7	.002	.055	.164	.166	.074	.015	.001	.000	.000
8	.000	.022	.114	.180	.120	.035	.004	.000	.000
9	.000	.007	.065	.160	.160	.071	.012	.000	.000
10	.000	.002	.031	.117	.176	.117	.031	.002	.000
11	.000	.000	.012	.071	.160	.160	.065	.007	.000
12	.000	.000	.004	.035	.120	.180	.114	.022	.000
13	.000	.000	.001	.015	.074	.166	.164	.055	.002
14	.000	.000	.000	.005	.037	.124	.192	.109	.009
15	.000	.000	.000	.001	.015	.075	.179	.175	.032
16	.000	.000	.000	.000	.005	.035	.130	.218	.090
17	.000	.000	.000	.000	.001	.012	.072	.205	.190
18	.000	.000	.000	.000	.000	.003	.028	.137	.285
19	.000	.000	.000	.000	.000	.000	.007	.058	.270
20	.000	.000	.000	.000	.000	.000	.001	.012	.122

**DEMONSTRATION
PROBLEM 5.5**

**Decision
Dilemma**

According to Information Resources, which publishes data on market share for various products, Oreos control about 10% of the market for cookie brands. Suppose 20 purchasers of cookies are selected randomly from the population. What is the probability that fewer than four purchasers choose Oreos?

Solution

For this problem, $n = 20$, $p = .10$, and $x < 4$. Because $n = 20$, the portion of the binomial tables presented in Table 5.5 can be used to work this problem. Search along the row of p values for .10. Determining the probability of getting $x < 4$ involves summing the probabilities for $x = 0, 1, 2,$ and 3. The values appear in the x column at the intersection of each x value and $p = .10$.

x Value	Probability
0	.122
1	.270
2	.285
3	.190
$(x < 4) =$	.867

If 10% of all cookie purchasers prefer Oreos and 20 cookie purchasers are randomly selected, about 86.7% of the time fewer than four of the 20 will select Oreos.

Using the Computer to Produce a Binomial Distribution

Both Excel and Minitab can be used to produce the probabilities for virtually any binomial distribution. Such computer programs offer yet another option for solving binomial problems besides using the binomial formula or the binomial tables. Actually, the

TABLE 5.6

Minitab Output for the
Binomial Distribution of
$n = 23$, $p = .64$

PROBABILITY DENSITY FUNCTION	
Binomial with n = 23 and p = 0.64	
x	$P(X = x)$
0	0.000000
1	0.000000
2	0.000000
3	0.000001
4	0.000006
5	0.000037
6	0.000199
7	0.000858
8	0.003051
9	0.009040
10	0.022500
11	0.047273
12	0.084041
13	0.126420
14	0.160533
15	0.171236
16	0.152209
17	0.111421
18	0.066027
19	0.030890
20	0.010983
21	0.002789
22	0.000451
23	0.000035

computer packages in effect print out what would be a column of the binomial table. The advantages of using statistical software packages for this purpose are convenience (if the binomial tables are not readily available and a computer is) and the potential for generating tables for many more values than those printed in the binomial tables.

For example, a study of bank customers stated that 64% of all financial consumers believe banks are more competitive today than they were five years ago. Suppose 23 financial consumers are selected randomly and we want to determine the probabilities of various x values occurring. Table A.2 in Appendix A could not be used because only nine different p values are included and $p = .64$ is not one of those values. In addition, $n = 23$ is not included in the table. Without the computer, we are left with the binomial formula as the only option for solving binomial problems for $n = 23$ and $p = .64$. Particularly if the cumulative probability questions are asked (for example, $x \leq 10$), the binomial formula can be a tedious way to solve the problem.

Shown in Table 5.6 is the Minitab output for the binomial distribution of $n = 23$ and $p = .64$. With this computer output, a researcher could obtain or calculate the probability of any occurrence within the binomial distribution of $n = 23$ and $p = .64$. Table 5.7 contains Minitab output for the particular binomial problem, $P(x \leq 10)$ when $n = 23$ and $p = .64$, solved by using Minitab's cumulative probability capability.

Shown in Table 5.8 is Excel output for all values of x that have probabilities greater than .000001 for the binomial distribution discussed in Demonstration Problem 5.3 ($n = 20$, $p = .06$) and the solution to the question posed in Demonstration Problem 5.3.

Mean and Standard Deviation of a Binomial Distribution

A binomial distribution has an expected value or a long-run average, which is denoted by μ. The value of μ is determined by $n \cdot p$. For example, if $n = 10$ and $p = .4$, then $\mu = n \cdot p = (10)(.4) = 4$. The long-run average or expected value means that, if n items are sampled over and over for a long time and if p is the probability of getting a success on one trial, the average number of successes per sample is expected to be $n \cdot p$. If 40% of all graduate business students at a large university are women and if random samples of 10 graduate business students are selected many times, the expectation is that, on average, four of the 10 students would be women.

MEAN AND STANDARD DEVIATION OF A BINOMIAL DISTRIBUTION	$\mu = n \cdot p$ $\sigma = \sqrt{n \cdot p \cdot q}$

Examining the mean of a binomial distribution gives an intuitive feeling about the likelihood of a given outcome.

According to one study, 64% of all financial consumers believe banks are more competitive today than they were five years ago. If 23 financial consumers are selected randomly, what is the expected number who believe banks are more competitive today than they were five years ago? This problem can be described by the binomial distribution of $n = 23$ and $p = .64$ given in Table 5.6. The mean of this binomial distribution yields the expected value for this problem.

TABLE 5.7

Minitab Output for the
Binomial Problem,
$P(x \leq 10 | n = 23$ and $p = .64$

Cumulative Distribution Function	
Binomial with n = 23 and p = 0.64	
x	$P(X \Leftarrow x)$
10	0.0356916

TABLE 5.8

Excel Output for Demonstration Problem 5.3 and the Binomial Distribution of $n = 20$, $p = .06$

x	Prob(x)	
0	0.2901	
1	0.3703	
2	0.2246	The probability $x \leq 2$ when $n = 20$ and $p = .06$ is .8850
3	0.0860	
4	0.0233	
5	0.0048	
6	0.0008	
7	0.0001	
8	0.0000	
9	0.0000	

$$\mu = n \cdot p = 23(.64) = 14.72$$

In the long run, if 23 financial consumers are selected randomly over and over and if indeed 64% of all financial consumers believe banks are more competitive today, then the experiment should average 14.72 financial consumers out of 23 who believe banks are more competitive today. Realize that because the binomial distribution is a discrete distribution you will never actually get 14.72 people out of 23 who believe banks are more competitive today. The mean of the distribution does reveal the relative likelihood of any individual occurrence. Examine Table 5.6. Notice that the highest probabilities are those near $x = 14.72$: $P(x = 15) = .1712$, $P(x = 14) = .1605$, and $P(x = 16) = .1522$. All other probabilities for this distribution are less than these probabilities.

The standard deviation of a binomial distribution is denoted σ and is equal to $\sqrt{n \cdot p \cdot q}$. The standard deviation for the financial consumer problem described by the binomial distribution in Table 5.6 is

$$\sigma = \sqrt{n \cdot p \cdot q} = \sqrt{(23)(.64)(.36)} = 2.30$$

Chapter 6 shows that some binomial distributions are nearly bell shaped and can be approximated by using the normal curve. The mean and standard deviation of a binomial distribution are the tools used to convert these binomial problems to normal curve problems.

Graphing Binomial Distributions

The graph of a binomial distribution can be constructed by using all the possible x values of a distribution and their associated probabilities. The x values usually are graphed along the x-axis and the probabilities are graphed along the y-axis.

Table 5.9 lists the probabilities for three different binomial distributions: $n = 8$ and $p = .20$, $n = 8$ and $p = .50$, and $n = 8$ and $p = .80$. Figure 5.2 displays Excel graphs for each of these three binomial distributions. Observe how the shape of the distribution changes as the value of p increases. For $p = .50$, the distribution is symmetrical. For $p = .20$ the distribution is skewed right and for $p = .80$ the distribution is skewed left. This pattern makes sense because the mean of the binomial distribution $n = 8$ and $p = .50$ is 4, which is in the middle of the distribution. The mean of the distribution $n = 8$ and $p = .20$ is 1.6, which results in the highest probabilities being near $x = 2$ and $x = 1$. This graph peaks early and stretches toward the higher values of x. The mean of the distribution $n = 8$ and $p = .80$ is 6.4, which results in the highest probabilities being near $x = 6$ and $x = 7$. Thus the peak of the distribution is nearer to 8 than to 0 and the distribution stretches back toward $x = 0$.

In any binomial distribution the largest x value that can occur is n and the smallest value is zero. Thus the graph of any binomial distribution is constrained by zero and n. If the p value of the distribution is not .50, this constraint will result in the graph "piling up" at one end and being skewed at the other end.

TABLE 5.9

Probabilities for Three Binomial Distributions with $n = 8$

	Probabilities for		
x	p = .20	p = .50	p = .80
0	.1678	.0039	.0000
1	.3355	.0312	.0001
2	.2936	.1094	.0011
3	.1468	.2187	.0092
4	.0459	.2734	.0459
5	.0092	.2187	.1468
6	.0011	.1094	.2936
7	.0001	.0312	.3355
8	.0000	.0039	.1678

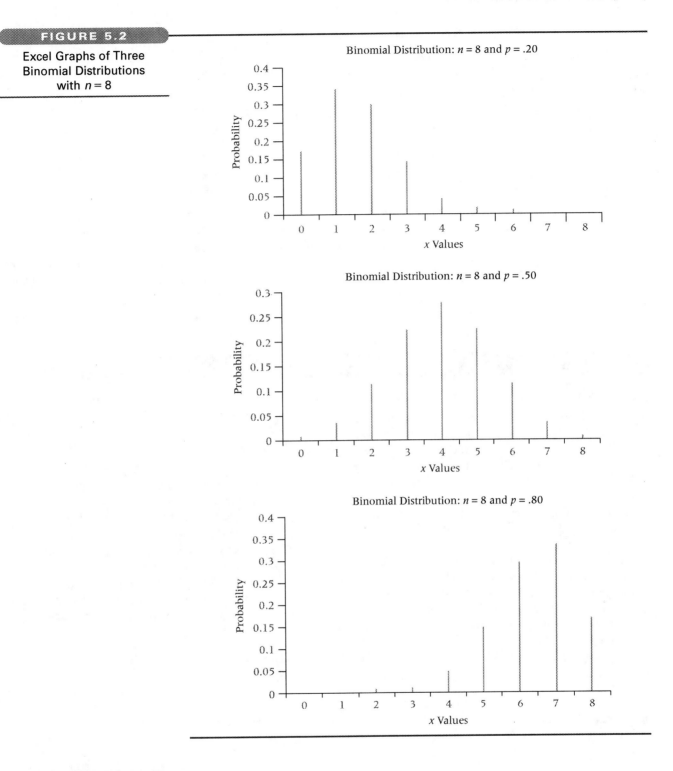

FIGURE 5.2

Excel Graphs of Three
Binomial Distributions
with *n* = 8

**DEMONSTRATION
PROBLEM 5.6**

A manufacturing company produces 10,000 plastic mugs per week. This company
supplies mugs to another company, which packages the mugs as part of picnic sets.
The second company randomly samples 10 mugs sent from the supplier. If two or
fewer of the sampled mugs are defective, the second company accepts the lot. What
is the probability that the lot will be accepted if the mug manufacturing company
actually is producing mugs that are 10% defective? 20% defective? 30% defective?
40% defective?

Solution

In this series of binomial problems, $n = 10$, $x \leq 2$, and p ranges from .10 to .40. From Table A.2—and cumulating the values—we have the following probability of $x \leq 2$ for each p value and the expected value ($\mu = n \cdot p$).

p	Lot Accepted P($x \leq 2$)	Expected Number of Defects (μ)
.10	.930	1.0
.20	.677	2.0
.30	.382	3.0
.40	.167	4.0

These values indicate that if the manufacturing company is producing 10% defective mugs, the probability is relatively high (.930) that the lot will be accepted by chance. For higher values of p, the probability of lot acceptance by chance decreases. In addition, as p increases, the expected value moves away from the acceptable values, $x \leq 2$. This move reduces the chances of lot acceptance.

THINKING CRITICALLY ABOUT STATISTICS IN BUSINESS TODAY

Plastic Bags vs. Bringing Your Own in Japan

In a move to protect and improve the environment, governments and companies around the world are making an effort to reduce the use of plastic bags by shoppers for transporting purchased food and goods. Specifically, in Yamagata City in northern Japan, the city concluded an agreement with seven local food supermarket chains to reduce plastic bag use in May of 2008 by having them agree to charge for the use of such bags. Before the agreement, in April of 2008, the average percentage of shoppers bringing their own shopping bags was about 35%. By the end of June, with some of the supermarket chains participating, the percentage had risen to almost 46%. However, by August, when 39 stores of the nine supermarket chains (two other chains joined the agreement) were charging for the use of plastic bags, the percentage rose to nearly 90%. It is estimated that the reduction of carbon dioxide emissions by this initiative is about 225 tons during July and August alone.

Things to Ponder

1. Do you think that this strategy would work in your country? For example, in the United States, do you think that consumers would reduce their use of plastic bags if they were charged for them?

2. Do you believe that a country's cultural value systems have anything to do with the success of such programs? That is, do you believe that it is the extra money that consumers have to spend to purchase the plastic bags that drives the decrease in usage, or are there other factors in addition to the added cost?

Source: http://www.japanfs.org/en/pages/028631.html.

5.3 PROBLEMS

5.5 Solve the following problems by using the binomial formula.

a. If $n = 4$ and $p = .10$, find $P(x = 3)$.

b. If $n = 7$ and $p = .80$, find $P(x = 4)$.

c. If $n = 10$ and $p = .60$, find $P(x \geq 7)$.

d. If $n = 12$ and $p = .45$, find $P(5 \leq x \leq 7)$.

5.6 Solve the following problems by using the binomial tables (Table A.2).

a. If $n = 20$ and $p = .50$, find $P(x = 12)$.

b. If $n = 20$ and $p = .30$, find $P(x > 8)$.

c. If $n = 20$ and $p = .70$, find $P(x < 12)$.

d. If $n = 20$ and $p = .90$, find $P(x \leq 16)$.

e. If $n = 15$ and $p = .40$, find $P(4 \leq x \leq 9)$.

f. If $n = 10$ and $p = .60$, find $P(x \geq 7)$.

5.7 Solve for the mean and standard deviation of the following binomial distributions.

    a. $n = 20$ and $p = .70$

    b. $n = 70$ and $p = .35$

    c. $n = 100$ and $p = .50$

5.8 Use the probability tables in Table A.2 and sketch the graph of each of the following binomial distributions. Note on the graph where the mean of the distribution falls.

    a. $n = 6$ and $p = .70$

    b. $n = 20$ and $p = .50$

    c. $n = 8$ and $p = .80$

5.9 What is the first big change that American drivers made due to higher gas prices? According to an Access America survey, 30% said that it was cutting recreational driving. However, 27% said that it was consolidating or reducing errands. If these figures are true for all American drivers, and if 20 such drivers are randomly sampled and asked what is the first big change they made due to higher gas prices,

    a. What is the probability that exactly 8 said that it was consolidating or reducing errands?

    b. What is the probability that none of them said that it was cutting recreational driving?

    c. What is the probability that more than 7 said that it was cutting recreational driving?

5.10 *The Wall Street Journal* reported some interesting statistics on the job market. One statistic is that 40% of all workers say they would change jobs for "slightly higher pay." In addition, 88% of companies say that there is a shortage of qualified job candidates. Suppose 16 workers are randomly selected and asked if they would change jobs for "slightly higher pay."

    a. What is the probability that nine or more say yes?

    b. What is the probability that three, four, five, or six say yes?

    c. If 13 companies are contacted, what is the probability that exactly 10 say there is a shortage of qualified job candidates?

    d. If 13 companies are contacted, what is the probability that all of the companies say there is a shortage of qualified job candidates?

    e. If 13 companies are contacted, what is the expected number of companies that would say there is a shortage of qualified job candidates?

5.11 An increasing number of consumers believe they have to look out for themselves in the marketplace. According to a survey conducted by the Yankelovich Partners for *USA WEEKEND* magazine, 60% of all consumers have called an 800 or 900 telephone number for information about some product. Suppose a random sample of 25 consumers is contacted and interviewed about their buying habits.

    a. What is the probability that 15 or more of these consumers have called an 800 or 900 telephone number for information about some product?

    b. What is the probability that more than 20 of these consumers have called an 800 or 900 telephone number for information about some product?

    c. What is the probability that fewer than 10 of these consumers have called an 800 or 900 telephone number for information about some product?

5.12 Studies have shown that about half of all workers who change jobs cash out their 401(k) plans rather than leaving the money in the account to grow. The percentage is much higher for workers with small 401(k) balances. In fact, 87% of workers with 401(k) accounts less than $5,000 opt to take their balance in cash rather than roll it over into individual retirement accounts when they change jobs.

    a. Assuming that 50% of all workers who change jobs cash out their 401(k) plans, if 16 workers who have recently changed jobs that had 401(k) plans are randomly sampled, what is the probability that more than 10 of them cashed out their 401(k) plan?

b. If 10 workers who have recently changed jobs and had 401(k) plans with accounts less than $5,000 are randomly sampled, what is the probability that exactly 6 of them cashed out?

5.13 In the past few years, outsourcing overseas has become more frequently used than ever before by U.S. companies. However, outsourcing is not without problems. A recent survey by *Purchasing* indicates that 20% of the companies that outsource overseas use a consultant. Suppose 15 companies that outsource overseas are randomly selected.

a. What is the probability that exactly five companies that outsource overseas use a consultant?

b. What is the probability that more than nine companies that outsource overseas use a consultant?

c. What is the probability that none of the companies that outsource overseas use a consultant?

d. What is the probability that between four and seven (inclusive) companies that outsource overseas use a consultant?

e. Construct a graph for this binomial distribution. In light of the graph and the expected value, explain why the probability results from parts (a) through (d) were obtained.

5.14 According to Cerulli Associates of Boston, 30% of all CPA financial advisors have an average client size between $500,000 and $1 million. Thirty-four percent have an average client size between $1 million and $5 million. Suppose a complete list of all CPA financial advisors is available and 18 are randomly selected from that list.

a. What is the expected number of CPA financial advisors that have an average client size between $500,000 and $1 million? What is the expected number with an average client size between $1 million and $5 million?

b. What is the probability that at least eight CPA financial advisors have an average client size between $500,000 and $1 million?

c. What is the probability that two, three, or four CPA financial advisors have an average client size between $1 million and $5 million?

d. What is the probability that none of the CPA financial advisors have an average client size between $500,000 and $1 million? What is the probability that none have an average client size between $1 million and $5 million? Which probability is higher and why?

5.4 POISSON DISTRIBUTION

Interactive Applet

The Poisson distribution is another discrete distribution. It is named after Simeon-Denis Poisson (1781–1840), a French mathematician, who published its essentials in a paper in 1837. The Poisson distribution and the binomial distribution have some similarities but also several differences. The binomial distribution describes a distribution of two possible outcomes designated as successes and failures from a given number of trials. The **Poisson distribution** *focuses only on the number of discrete occurrences over some interval or continuum.* A Poisson experiment does not have a given number of trials (n) as a binomial experiment does. For example, whereas a binomial experiment might be used to determine how many U.S.-made cars are in a random sample of 20 cars, a Poisson experiment might focus on the number of cars randomly arriving at an automobile repair facility during a 10-minute interval.

The Poisson distribution describes the occurrence of *rare events*. In fact, the Poisson formula has been referred to as the *law of improbable events*. For example, serious accidents at a chemical plant are rare, and the number per month might be described by the Poisson distribution. The Poisson distribution often is used to describe the number of random arrivals per some time interval. If the number of arrivals per interval is too frequent, the time interval can be reduced enough so that a rare number of occurrences is expected. Another example of a Poisson distribution is the number of random customer arrivals per five-minute interval at a small boutique on weekday mornings.

The Poisson distribution also has an application in the field of management science. The models used in queuing theory (theory of waiting lines) usually are based on the assumption that the Poisson distribution is the proper distribution to describe random arrival rates over a period of time.

The Poisson distribution has the following characteristics:

- It is a discrete distribution.
- It describes rare events.
- Each occurrence is independent of the other occurrences.
- It describes discrete occurrences over a continuum or interval.
- The occurrences in each interval can range from zero to infinity.
- The expected number of occurrences must hold constant throughout the experiment.

Examples of Poisson-type situations include the following:

1. Number of telephone calls per minute at a small business
2. Number of hazardous waste sites per county in the United States
3. Number of arrivals at a turnpike tollbooth per minute between 3 A.M. and 4 A.M. in January on the Kansas Turnpike
4. Number of sewing flaws per pair of jeans during production
5. Number of times a tire blows on a commercial airplane per week

Each of these examples represents a rare occurrence of events for some interval. Note that, although time is a more common interval for the Poisson distribution, intervals can range from a county in the United States to a pair of jeans. Some of the intervals in these examples might have zero occurrences. Moreover, the average occurrence per interval for many of these examples is probably in the single digits (1–9).

If a Poisson-distributed phenomenon is studied over a long period of time, a *long-run average* can be determined. This average is denoted **lambda (λ)**. Each Poisson problem contains a lambda value from which the probabilities of particular occurrences are determined. Although n and p are required to describe a binomial distribution, a Poisson distribution can be described by λ alone. The Poisson formula is used to compute the probability of occurrences over an interval for a given lambda value.

POISSON FORMULA

$$P(x) = \frac{\lambda^x e^{-\lambda}}{x!} \quad \frac{(n \cdot p)\, e^{-(n \cdot p)}}{x!}$$

where

$x = 0, 1, 2, 3, \ldots$
$\lambda = \text{long-run average} = n \cdot p$
$e = 2.718282$

Here, x is the number of occurrences per interval for which the probability is being computed, λ is the long-run average, and $e = 2.718282$ is the base of natural logarithms.

A word of caution about using the Poisson distribution to study various phenomena is necessary. The λ value must hold constant throughout a Poisson experiment. The researcher must be careful not to apply a given lambda to intervals for which lambda changes. For example, the average number of customers arriving at a Sears store during a one-minute interval will vary from hour to hour, day to day, and month to month. Different times of the day or week might produce different lambdas. The number of flaws per pair of jeans might vary from Monday to Friday. The researcher should be specific in describing the interval for which λ is being used.

Working Poisson Problems by Formula

Suppose bank customers arrive randomly on weekday afternoons at an average of 3.2 customers every 4 minutes. What is the probability of exactly 5 customers arriving in a 4-minute interval on a weekday afternoon? The lambda for this problem is 3.2 customers per 4 minutes. The value of x is 5 customers per 4 minutes. The probability of 5 customers randomly arriving during a 4-minute interval when the long-run average has been 3.2 customers per 4-minute interval is

$$\frac{(3.2^5)(e^{-3.2})}{5!} = \frac{(335.54)(.0408)}{120} = .1141$$

If a bank averages 3.2 customers every 4 minutes, the probability of 5 customers arriving during any one 4-minute interval is .1141.

DEMONSTRATION PROBLEM 5.7

Bank customers arrive randomly on weekday afternoons at an average of 3.2 customers every 4 minutes. What is the probability of having more than 7 customers in a 4-minute interval on a weekday afternoon?

Solution

$$\lambda = 3.2 \text{ customers/minutes}$$

$$x > 7 \text{ customers/4 minutes}$$

In theory, the solution requires obtaining the values of x = 8, 9, 10, 11, 12, 13, 14, . . . ∞. In actuality, each x value is determined until the values are so far away from $\lambda = 3.2$ that the probabilities approach zero. The exact probabilities are then summed to find $x > 7$.

$$P(x = 8 | \lambda = 3.2) = \frac{(3.2^8)(e^{-3.2})}{8!} = .0111$$

$$P(x = 9 | \lambda = 3.2) = \frac{(3.2^9)(e^{-3.2})}{9!} = .0040$$

$$P(x = 10 | \lambda = 3.2) = \frac{(3.2^{10})(e^{-3.2})}{10!} = .0013$$

$$P(x = 11 | \lambda = 3.2) = \frac{(3.2^{11})(e^{-3.2})}{11!} = .0004$$

$$P(x = 12 | \lambda = 3.2) = \frac{(3.2^{12})(e^{-3.2})}{12!} = .0001$$

$$P(x = 13 | \lambda = 3.2) = \frac{(3.2^{13})(e^{-3.2})}{13!} = .0000$$

$$P(x > 7) = P(x \geq 8) = .0169$$

If the bank has been averaging 3.2 customers every 4 minutes on weekday afternoons, it is unlikely that more than 7 people would randomly arrive in any one 4-minute period. This answer indicates that more than 7 people would randomly arrive in a 4-minute period only 1.69% of the time. Bank officers could use these results to help them make staffing decisions.

DEMONSTRATION PROBLEM 5.8

A bank has an average random arrival rate of 3.2 customers every 4 minutes. What is the probability of getting exactly 10 customers during an 8-minute interval?

Solution

$$\lambda = 3.2 \text{ customers/4 minutes}$$
$$x = 10 \text{ customers/8 minutes}$$

This example is different from the first two Poisson examples in that the intervals for lambda and the sample are different. The intervals must be the same in order to use λ and x together in the probability formula. The right way to approach this dilemma is to adjust the interval for lambda so that it and x have the same interval. The interval for x is 8 minutes, so lambda should be adjusted to an 8-minute interval. Logically, if the bank averages 3.2 customers every 4 minutes, it should average twice as many, or 6.4 customers, every 8 minutes. If x were for a 2-minute interval, the value of lambda would be halved from 3.2 to 1.6 customers per 2-minute interval. The wrong approach to this dilemma is to equalize the intervals by changing the x value. Never adjust or change x in a problem. Just because 10 customers arrive in one 8-minute interval does not mean that there would necessarily have been five customers in a 4-minute interval. There is no guarantee how the 10 customers are spread over the 8-minute interval. Always adjust the lambda value. After lambda has been adjusted for an 8-minute interval, the solution is

$$\lambda = 6.4 \text{ customers/8 minutes}$$
$$x = 10 \text{ customers/8 minutes}$$
$$\frac{(6.4)^{10}e^{-6.4}}{10!} = .0528$$

TABLE 5.10

Poisson Table for $\lambda = 1.6$

x	Probability
0	.2019
1	.3230
2	.2584
3	.1378
4	.0551
5	.0176
6	.0047
7	.0011
8	.0002
9	.0000

Using the Poisson Tables

Every value of lambda determines a different Poisson distribution. Regardless of the nature of the interval associated with a lambda, the Poisson distribution for a particular lambda is the same. Table A.3, Appendix A, contains the Poisson distributions for selected values of lambda. Probabilities are displayed in the table for each x value associated with a given lambda if the probability has a nonzero value to four decimal places. Table 5.10 presents a portion of Table A.3 that contains the probabilities of $x \leq 9$ if lambda is 1.6.

DEMONSTRATION PROBLEM 5.9

If a real estate office sells 1.6 houses on an average weekday and sales of houses on weekdays are Poisson distributed, what is the probability of selling exactly 4 houses in one day? What is the probability of selling no houses in one day? What is the probability of selling more than five houses in a day? What is the probability of selling 10 or more houses in a day? What is the probability of selling exactly 4 houses in two days?

Solution

$$\lambda = 1.6 \text{ houses/day}$$
$$P(x = 4|\lambda = 1.6) = ?$$

Table 5.10 gives the probabilities for $\lambda = 1.6$. The left column contains the x values. The line $x = 4$ yields the probability .0551. If a real estate firm has been averaging 1.6 houses sold per day, only 5.51% of the days would it sell exactly 4 houses and still maintain the lambda value. Line 1 of Table 5.10 shows the probability of selling no houses in a day (.2019). That is, on 20.19% of the days, the firm would sell no houses if sales are Poisson distributed with $\lambda = 1.6$ houses per day. Table 5.10 is not cumulative. To determine $P(x > 5)$, more than 5 houses, find the probabilities of $x = 6$, $x = 7$, $x = 8$, $x = 9$, . . . $x = ?$. However, at $x = 9$, the probability to four decimal places is zero, and Table 5.10 stops when an x value zeros out at four decimal places. The answer for $x > 5$ follows.

x	Probability
6	.0047
7	.0011
8	.0002
9	.0000
$x > 5 =$	.0060

What is the probability of selling 10 or more houses in one day? As the table zeros out at $x = 9$, the probability of $x \geq 10$ is essentially .0000—that is, if the real estate office has been averaging only 1.6 houses sold per day, it is virtually impossible to sell 10 or more houses in a day. What is the probability of selling exactly 4 houses in two days? In this case, the interval has been changed from one day to two days. Lambda is for one day, so an adjustment must be made: A lambda of 1.6 for one day converts to a lambda of 3.2 for two days. Table 5.10 no longer applies, so Table A.3 must be used to solve this problem. The answer is found by looking up $\lambda = 3.2$ and $x = 4$ in Table A.3: the probability is .1781.

Mean and Standard Deviation of a Poisson Distribution

The mean or expected value of a Poisson distribution is λ. It is the long-run average of occurrences for an interval if many random samples are taken. Lambda usually is not a whole number, so most of the time actually observing lambda occurrences in an interval is impossible.

For example, suppose $\lambda = 6.5$/interval for some Poisson-distributed phenomenon. The resulting numbers of x occurrences in 20 different random samples from a Poisson distribution with $\lambda = 6.5$ might be as follows.

$$6 \quad 9 \quad 7 \quad 4 \quad 8 \quad 7 \quad 6 \quad 6 \quad 10 \quad 6 \quad 5 \quad 5 \quad 8 \quad 4 \quad 5 \quad 8 \quad 5 \quad 4 \quad 9 \quad 10$$

Computing the mean number of occurrences from this group of 20 intervals gives 6.6. In theory, for infinite sampling the long-run average is 6.5. Note from the samples that,

---

THINKING CRITICALLY ABOUT STATISTICS IN BUSINESS TODAY

Air Passengers' Complaints

In recent months, airline passengers have expressed much more dissatisfaction with airline service than ever before. Complaints include flight delays, lost baggage, long runway delays with little or no onboard service, overbooked flights, cramped space due to fuller flights, canceled flights, and grumpy airline employees. A majority of dissatisfied fliers merely grin and bear it. In fact, in the mid-1990s, the average number of complaints per 100,000 passengers boarded was only 0.66. For several years, the average number of complaints increased to 0.74, 0.86, 1.08, and 1.21. More recently, the figure has leveled off at 1.19 in the year 2010.

In 2010, according to the Department of Transportation, Mesa Airlines had the fewest average number of complaints per 100,000 with 0.12, followed by Alaska Airlines with 0.23, and Southwest Airlines with 0.26. Within the top 10 largest U.S. airlines by number of enplanements, Delta Airlines (includes merging with Northwest Airlines) had the highest number of complaints logged against it— 1.94 complaints per 100,000 passengers.

Because these average numbers are relatively small, it appears that the actual number of complaints per 100,000 is rare and may follow a Poisson distribution. In this case, λ represents the average number of complaints and the interval is 100,000 passengers. For example, using $\lambda = 1.19$ complaints (average for all airlines), if 100,000 boarded passengers were contacted, the probability that exactly three of them logged a complaint to the Department of Transportation could be computed as

$$\frac{(1.19)^3 e^{-1.19}}{3!} = .0854$$

That is, if 100,000 boarded passengers were contacted over and over, 8.54% of the time exactly three would have logged complaints with the Department of Transportation.

Things to Ponder

1. Based on the figures given in this feature, can you reach any conclusions about the rate of passenger complaints in general?

2. Passenger complaints appear to be rare occurrences. Can you suggest some reasons why this is the case?

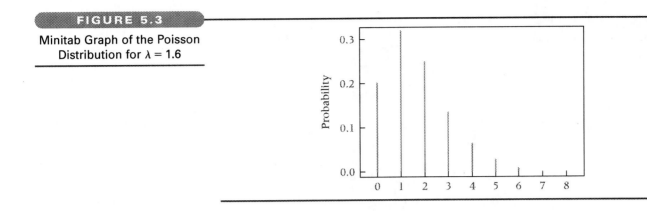

FIGURE 5.3

Minitab Graph of the Poisson Distribution for $\lambda = 1.6$

when λ is 6.5, several 5s and 6s occur. Rarely would sample occurrences of 1, 2, 3, 11, 12, 13, . . . occur when $\lambda = 6.5$. Understanding the mean of a Poisson distribution gives a feel for the actual occurrences that are likely to happen.

The variance of a Poisson distribution also is λ. The standard deviation is $\sqrt{\lambda}$. Combining the standard deviation with Chebyshev's theorem indicates the spread or dispersion of a Poisson distribution. For example, if $\lambda = 6.5$, the variance also is 6.5, and the standard deviation is 2.55. Chebyshev's theorem states that at least $1 - 1/k^2$ values are within k standard deviations of the mean. The interval $\mu \pm 2\sigma$ contains at least $1 - (1/2^2) = .75$ of the values. For $\mu = \lambda = 6.5$ and $\sigma = 2.55$, 75% of the values should be within the $6.5 \pm 2(2.55) = 6.5 \pm 5.1$ range. That is, the range from 1.4 to 11.6 should include at least 75% of all the values. An examination of the 20 values randomly generated for a Poisson distribution with $\lambda = 6.5$ shows that actually 100% of the values are within this range.

Graphing Poisson Distributions

The values in Table A.3, Appendix A, can be used to graph a Poisson distribution. The x values are on the x-axis and the probabilities are on the y-axis. Figure 5.3 is a Minitab graph for the distribution of values for $\lambda = 1.6$.

The graph reveals a Poisson distribution skewed to the right. With a mean of 1.6 and a possible range of x from zero to infinity, the values obviously will "pile up" at 0 and 1. Consider, however, the Minitab graph of the Poisson distribution for $\lambda = 6.5$ in Figure 5.4. Note that with $\lambda = 6.5$, the probabilities are greatest for the values of 5, 6, 7, and 8. The graph has less skewness, because the probability of occurrence of values near zero is small, as are the probabilities of large values of x.

Using the Computer to Generate Poisson Distributions

Using the Poisson formula to compute probabilities can be tedious when one is working problems with cumulative probabilities. The Poisson tables in Table A.3, Appendix A, are faster to use than the Poisson formula. However, Poisson tables are limited by the amount

FIGURE 5.4

Minitab Graph of the Poisson Distribution for $\lambda = 6.5$

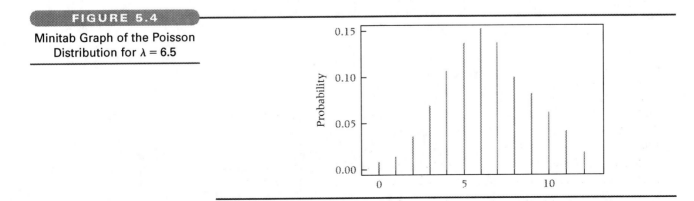

TABLE 5.11

Minitab Output for the Poisson
Distribution $\lambda = 1.9$

PROBABILITY DENSITY FUNCTION	
Poisson with mean = 1.9	
x	$P(X = x)$
0	0.149569
1	0.284180
2	0.269971
3	0.170982
4	0.081216
5	0.030862
6	0.009773
7	0.002653
8	0.000630
9	0.000133
10	0.000025

TABLE 5.12

Excel Output for the Poisson
Distribution $\lambda = 1.6$

x	Probability
0	0.2019
1	0.3230
2	0.2584
3	0.1378
4	0.0551
5	0.0176
6	0.0047
7	0.0011
8	0.0002
9	0.0000

of space available, and Table A.3 only includes probability values for Poisson distributions with lambda values to the tenths place in most cases. For researchers who want to use lambda values with more precision or who feel that the computer is more convenient than textbook tables, some statistical computer software packages are an attractive option.

Minitab will produce a Poisson distribution for virtually any value of lambda. For example, one study by the National Center for Health Statistics claims that, on average, an American has 1.9 acute illnesses or injuries per year. If these cases are Poisson distributed, lambda is 1.9 per year. What does the Poisson probability distribution for this lambda look like? Table 5.11 contains the Minitab computer output for this distribution.

Excel can also generate probabilities of different values of x for any Poisson distribution. Table 5.12 displays the probabilities produced by Excel for the real estate problem from Demonstration Problem 5.9 using a lambda of 1.6.

Approximating Binomial Problems by the Poisson Distribution

Certain types of binomial distribution problems can be approximated by using the Poisson distribution. Binomial problems with large sample sizes and small values of p, which then generate rare events, are potential candidates for use of the Poisson distribution. As a rule of thumb, if $n > 20$ and $n \cdot p \leq 7$, the approximation is close enough to use the Poisson distribution for binomial problems.

If these conditions are met and the binomial problem is a candidate for this process, the procedure begins with computation of the mean of the binomial distribution, $\mu = n \cdot p$. Because μ is the expected value of the binomial, it translates to the expected value, λ, of the Poisson distribution. Using μ as the λ value and using the x value of the binomial problem allows approximation of the probability from a Poisson table or by the Poisson formula.

Large values of n and small values of p usually are not included in binomial distribution tables thereby precluding the use of binomial computational techniques. Using the Poisson distribution as an approximation to such a binomial problem in such cases is an attractive alternative; and indeed, when a computer is not available, it can be the only alternative.

As an example, the following binomial distribution problem can be worked by using the Poisson distribution: $n = 50$ and $p = .03$. What is the probability that $x = 4$? That is, $P(x = 4 \mid n = 50 \text{ and } p = .03) = ?$

To solve this equation, first determine lambda:

$$\lambda = \mu = n \cdot p = (50)(.03) = 1.5$$

As $n > 20$ and $n \cdot p \leq 7$, this problem is a candidate for the Poisson approximation. For $x = 4$, Table A.3 yields a probability of .0471 for the Poisson approximation. For comparison, working the problem by using the binomial formula yields the following results:

$$_{50}C_4(.03)^4(.97)^{46} = .0459$$

The Poisson approximation is .0012 different from the result obtained by using the binomial formula to work the problem.

A Minitab graph of this binomial distribution follows.

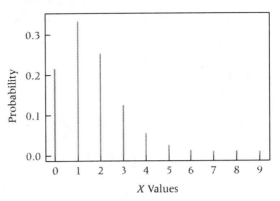

With $\lambda = 1.5$, the Poisson distribution can be generated. A Minitab graph of this Poisson distribution follows.

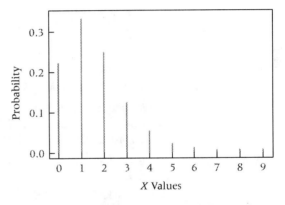

In comparing the two graphs, it is difficult to tell the difference between the binomial distribution and the Poisson distribution because the approximation of the binomial distribution by the Poisson distribution is close.

DEMONSTRATION PROBLEM 5.10

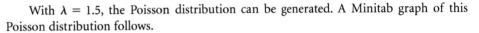

Suppose the probability of a bank making a mistake in processing a deposit is .0003. If 10,000 deposits (n) are audited, what is the probability that more than 6 mistakes were made in processing deposits?

Solution

$$\lambda = \mu = n \cdot p = (10{,}000)(.0003) = 3.0$$

Because $n > 20$ and $n \cdot p \leq 7$, the Poisson approximation is close enough to analyze $x > 6$. Table A.3 yields the following probabilities for $\lambda = 3.0$ and $x \geq 7$.

$\lambda = 3.0$	
x	**Probability**
7	.0216
8	.0081
9	.0027
10	.0008
11	.0002
12	.0001
	$x > 6 = .0335$

To work this problem by using the binomial formula requires starting with $x = 7$.

$$_{10{,}000}C_7(.0003)^7(.9997)^{9993}$$

This process would continue for x values of 8, 9, 10, 11, . . . , until the probabilities approach zero. Obviously, this process is impractical, making the Poisson approximation an attractive alternative.

5.4 PROBLEMS

5.15 Find the following values by using the Poisson formula.

a. $P(x = 5 | \lambda = 2.3)$

b. $P(x = 2 | \lambda = 3.9)$

c. $P(x \leq 3 | \lambda = 4.1)$

d. $P(x = 0 | \lambda = 2.7)$

e. $P(x = 1 | \lambda = 5.4)$

f. $P(4 < x < 8 | \lambda = 4.4)$

5.16 Find the following values by using the Poisson tables in Appendix A.

a. $P(x = 6 | \lambda = 3.8)$

b. $P(x > 7 | \lambda = 2.9)$

c. $P(3 \leq x \leq 9 | \lambda = 4.2)$

d. $P(x = 0 | \lambda = 1.9)$

e. $P(x \leq 6 | \lambda = 2.9)$

f. $P(5 < x \leq 8 | \lambda = 5.7)$

5.17 Sketch the graphs of the following Poisson distributions. Compute the mean and standard deviation for each distribution. Locate the mean on the graph. Note how the probabilities are graphed around the mean.

a. $\lambda = 6.3$

b. $\lambda = 1.3$

c. $\lambda = 8.9$

d. $\lambda = 0.6$

5.18 On Monday mornings, the First National Bank only has one teller window open for deposits and withdrawals. Experience has shown that the average number of arriving customers in a four-minute interval on Monday mornings is 2.8, and each teller can serve more than that number efficiently. These random arrivals at this bank on Monday mornings are Poisson distributed.

a. What is the probability that on a Monday morning exactly six customers will arrive in a four-minute interval?

b. What is the probability that no one will arrive at the bank to make a deposit or withdrawal during a four-minute interval?

c. Suppose the teller can serve no more than four customers in any four-minute interval at this window on a Monday morning. What is the probability that, during any given four-minute interval, the teller will be unable to meet the demand? What is the probability that the teller will be able to meet the demand? When demand cannot be met during any given interval, a second window is opened. What percentage of the time will a second window have to be opened?

d. What is the probability that exactly three people will arrive at the bank during a two-minute period on Monday mornings to make a deposit or a withdrawal? What is the probability that five or more customers will arrive during an eight-minute period?

5.19 A restaurant manager is interested in taking a more statistical approach to predicting customer load. She begins the process by gathering data. One of the restaurant hosts or hostesses is assigned to count customers every five minutes from 7 P.M. until 8 P.M. every Saturday night for three weeks. The data are shown here. After the data are gathered, the manager computes lambda using the data from all three weeks as one data set as a basis for probability analysis. What value of lambda did she find? Assume that these customers randomly arrive and that the arrivals are Poisson distributed. Use the value of lambda computed by the manager and help the manager calculate the probabilities in parts (a) through (e) for any given five-minute interval between 7 P.M. and 8 P.M. on Saturday night.

Number of Arrivals

Week 1	Week 2	Week 3
3	1	5
6	2	3
4	4	5
6	0	3
2	2	5
3	6	4
1	5	7
5	4	3
1	2	4
0	5	8
3	3	1
3	4	3

a. What is the probability that no customers arrive during any given five-minute interval?

b. What is the probability that six or more customers arrive during any given five-minute interval?

c. What is the probability that during a 10-minute interval fewer than four customers arrive?

d. What is the probability that between three and six (inclusive) customers arrive in any 10-minute interval?

e. What is the probability that exactly eight customers arrive in any 15-minute interval?

5.20 According to the United National Environmental Program and World Health Organization, in Mumbai, India, air pollution standards for particulate matter are exceeded an average of 5.6 days in every three-week period. Assume that the distribution of number of days exceeding the standards per three-week period is Poisson distributed.

a. What is the probability that the standard is not exceeded on any day during a three-week period?

b. What is the probability that the standard is exceeded exactly six days of a three-week period?

c. What is the probability that the standard is exceeded 15 or more days during a three-week period? If this outcome actually occurred, what might you conclude?

5.21 The average number of annual trips per family to amusement parks in the United States is Poisson distributed, with a mean of 0.6 trips per year. What is the probability of randomly selecting an American family and finding the following?

a. The family did not make a trip to an amusement park last year.

b. The family took exactly one trip to an amusement park last year.

c. The family took two or more trips to amusement parks last year.

d. The family took three or fewer trips to amusement parks over a three-year period.

e. The family took exactly four trips to amusement parks during a six-year period.

5.22 Ship collisions in the Houston Ship Channel are rare. Suppose the number of collisions are Poisson distributed, with a mean of 1.2 collisions every four months.

a. What is the probability of having no collisions occur over a four-month period?

b. What is the probability of having exactly two collisions in a two-month period?

c. What is the probability of having one or fewer collisions in a six-month period? If this outcome occurred, what might you conclude about ship channel conditions during this period? What might you conclude about ship channel safety awareness during this period? What might you conclude about weather conditions during this period? What might you conclude about lambda?

5.23 A pen company averages 1.2 defective pens per carton produced (200 pens). The number of defects per carton is Poisson distributed.

    a. What is the probability of selecting a carton and finding no defective pens?

    b. What is the probability of finding eight or more defective pens in a carton?

    c. Suppose a purchaser of these pens will quit buying from the company if a carton contains more than three defective pens. What is the probability that a carton contains more than three defective pens?

5.24 A medical researcher estimates that .00004 of the population has a rare blood disorder. If the researcher randomly selects 100,000 people from the population,

    a. What is the probability that seven or more people will have the rare blood disorder?

    b. What is the probability that more than 10 people will have the rare blood disorder?

    c. Suppose the researcher gets more than 10 people who have the rare blood disorder in the sample of 100,000 but that the sample was taken from a particular geographic region. What might the researcher conclude from the results?

5.25 A data firm records a large amount of data. Historically, .9% of the pages of data recorded by the firm contain errors. If 200 pages of data are randomly selected,

    a. What is the probability that six or more pages contain errors?

    b. What is the probability that more than 10 pages contain errors?

    c. What is the probability that none of the pages contain errors?

    d. What is the probability that fewer than five pages contain errors?

5.26 A high percentage of people who fracture or dislocate a bone see a doctor for that condition. Suppose the percentage is 99%. Consider a sample in which 300 people are randomly selected who have fractured or dislocated a bone.

    a. What is the probability that exactly five of them did not see a doctor?

    b. What is the probability that fewer than four of them did not see a doctor?

    c. What is the expected number of people who would not see a doctor?

5.5 HYPERGEOMETRIC DISTRIBUTION

Another discrete statistical distribution is the hypergeometric distribution. Statisticians often use the **hypergeometric distribution** to complement the types of analyses that can be made by using the binomial distribution. Recall that the binomial distribution applies, in theory, only to experiments in which the trials are done with replacement (independent events). The hypergeometric distribution applies only to experiments in which the trials are done without replacement.

The hypergeometric distribution, like the binomial distribution, consists of two possible outcomes: success and failure. However, the user must know the size of the population and the proportion of successes and failures in the population to apply the hypergeometric distribution. In other words, because the hypergeometric distribution is used when sampling is done without replacement, information about population makeup must be known in order to redetermine the probability of a success in each successive trial as the probability changes.

The hypergeometric distribution has the following characteristics:

    ▓ It is discrete distribution.

    ▓ Each outcome consists of either a success or a failure.

▦ Sampling is done without replacement.

▦ The population, N, is finite and known.

▦ The number of successes in the population, A, is known.

HYPERGEOMETRIC FORMULA	$$P(x) = \frac{{}_AC_x \cdot {}_{N-A}C_{n-x}}{{}_NC_n}$$

where

N = size of the population
n = sample size
A = number of successes in the population
x = number of successes in the sample; sampling is done *without* replacement

A hypergeometric distribution is characterized or described by three parameters: N, A, and n. Because of the multitude of possible combinations of these three parameters, creating tables for the hypergeometric distribution is practically impossible. Hence, the researcher who selects the hypergeometric distribution for analyzing data must use the hypergeometric formula to calculate each probability. Because this task can be tedious and time-consuming, most researchers use the hypergeometric distribution as a fallback position when working binomial problems without replacement. Even though the binomial distribution theoretically applies only when sampling is done with replacement and p stays constant, recall that, if the population is large enough in comparison with the sample size, the impact of sampling without replacement on p is minimal. Thus the binomial distribution can be used in some situations when sampling is done without replacement. Because of the tables available, using the binomial distribution instead of the hypergeometric distribution whenever possible is preferable. As a rule of thumb, if the sample size is less than 5% of the population, use of the binomial distribution rather than the hypergeometric distribution is acceptable when sampling is done without replacement. The hypergeometric distribution yields the exact probability, and the binomial distribution yields a good approximation of the probability in these situations.

In summary, the hypergeometric distribution should be used instead of the binomial distribution when the following conditions are present:

1. Sampling is being done without replacement.
2. $n \geq 5\%\ N$.

Hypergeometric probabilities are calculated under the assumption of equally likely sampling of the remaining elements of the sample space.

As an application of the hypergeometric distribution, consider the following problem. Twenty-four people, of whom eight are women, apply for a job. If five of the applicants are sampled randomly, what is the probability that exactly three of those sampled are women?

This problem contains a small, finite population of 24, or $N = 24$. A sample of five applicants is taken, or $n = 5$. The sampling is being done without replacement, because the five applicants selected for the sample are five different people. The sample size is 21% of the population, which is greater than 5% of the population ($n/N = 5/24 = .21$). The hypergeometric distribution is the appropriate distribution to use. The population breakdown is $A = 8$ women (successes) and $N - A = 24 - 8 = 16$ men. The probability of getting $x = 3$ women in the sample of $n = 5$ is

$$\frac{{}_8C_3 \cdot {}_{16}C_2}{{}_{24}C_5} = \frac{(56)(120)}{42,504} = .1581$$

Conceptually, the combination in the denominator of the hypergeometric formula yields all the possible ways of getting n samples from a population, N, including the ones with the desired outcome. In this problem, there are 42,504 ways of selecting 5 people from 24 people. The numerator of the hypergeometric formula computes all the possible ways of getting x successes from the A successes available and $n - x$ failures from the $N - A$ available failures in the population. There are 56 ways of getting three women from a pool of eight, and there are 120 ways of getting 2 men from a pool of 16. The combinations of each are multiplied in the numerator because the joint probability of getting x successes and $n - x$ failures is being computed.

DEMONSTRATION PROBLEM 5.11

Suppose 18 major computer companies operate in the United States and that 12 are located in California's Silicon Valley. If three computer companies are selected randomly from the entire list, what is the probability that one or more of the selected companies are located in the Silicon Valley?

Solution

$$N = 18, n = 3, A = 12, \text{ and } x \geq 1$$

This problem is actually three problems in one: $x = 1$, $x = 2$, and $x = 3$. Sampling is being done without replacement, and the sample size is 16.6% of the population. Hence this problem is a candidate for the hypergeometric distribution. The solution follows.

$$
\begin{array}{ccc}
x = 1 & x = 2 & x = 3 \\[4pt]
\dfrac{_{12}C_1 \cdot {_6}C_2}{_{18}C_3} + & \dfrac{_{12}C_2 \cdot {_6}C_1}{_{18}C_3} + & \dfrac{_{12}C_3 \cdot {_6}C_0}{_{18}C_3} = \\[10pt]
.2206 \quad + & .4853 \quad + & .2696 \quad = .9755
\end{array}
$$

An alternative solution method using the law of complements would be one minus the probability that none of the companies is located in Silicon Valley, or

$$1 - P(x = 0 | N = 18, n = 3, A = 12)$$

Thus,

$$1 - \frac{_{12}C_0 \cdot {_6}C_3}{_{18}C_3} = 1 - .0245 = .9755$$

Using the Computer to Solve for Hypergeometric Distribution Probabilities

Using Minitab or Excel, it is possible to solve for hypergeometric distribution probabilities on the computer. Both software packages require the input of N, A, n, and x. In either package, the resulting output is the exact probability for that particular value of x. The Minitab output for the example presented in this section, where $N = 24$ people of whom $A = 8$ are women, $n = 5$ are randomly selected, and $x = 3$ are women, is displayed in Table 5.13. Note that Minitab represents successes in the population as "M." The Excel output for this same problem is presented in Table 5.14.

TABLE 5.13

Minitab Output for Hypergeometric Problem

```
PROBABILITY DENSITY FUNCTION

Hypergeometric with N = 24,
M = 8 and n = 5

x            P(X = x)
3            0.158103
```

TABLE 5.14

Excel Output for a Hypergeometric Problem

The probability of $x = 3$ when $N = 24$, $n = 5$, and $A = 8$ is: 0.158103

5.5 PROBLEMS

5.27 Compute the following probabilities by using the hypergeometric formula.

a. The probability of $x = 3$ if $N = 11$, $A = 8$, and $n = 4$

b. The probability of $x < 2$ if $N = 15$, $A = 5$, and $n = 6$

c. The probability of $x = 0$ if $N = 9$, $A = 2$, and $n = 3$

d. The probability of $x > 4$ if $N = 20$, $A = 5$, and $n = 7$

5.28 Shown here are the top 19 companies in the world in terms of oil refining capacity. Some of the companies are privately owned and others are state owned. Suppose six companies are randomly selected.

a. What is the probability that exactly one company is privately owned?

b. What is the probability that exactly four companies are privately owned?

c. What is the probability that all six companies are privately owned?

d. What is the probability that none of the companies is privately owned?

Company	Ownership Status
ExxonMobil	Private
Royal Dutch/Shell	Private
Sinopec	Private
British Petroleum	Private
ConocoPhillips	Private
Petroleos de Venezuela	State
Total	Private
Valero Energy	Private
China National	State
Saudi Arabian	State
Petroleo Brasilerio	State
Chevron	Private
Petroleos Mexicanos	State
National Iranian	State
Nippon	Private
Rosneft (Russia)	State
OAO Lukoil	Private
Repsol YPF	Private
Kuwait National	State

5.29 *Catalog Age* lists the top 17 U.S. firms in annual catalog sales. Dell Computer is number one followed by IBM and W. W. Grainger. Of the 17 firms on the list, 8 are in some type of computer-related business. Suppose four firms are randomly selected.

a. What is the probability that none of the firms is in some type of computer-related business?

b. What is the probability that all four firms are in some type of computer-related business?

c. What is the probability that exactly two are in non-computer-related business?

5.30 W. Edwards Deming in his red bead experiment had a box of 4,000 beads, of which 800 were red and 3,200 were white.* Suppose a researcher were to conduct a modified version of the red bead experiment. In her experiment, she has a bag of 20 beads, of which 4 are red and 16 are white. This experiment requires a participant to reach into the bag and randomly select five beads without replacement.

a. What is the probability that the participant will select exactly four white beads?

b. What is the probability that the participant will select exactly four red beads?

c. What is the probability that the participant will select all red beads?

*Mary Walton, "Deming's Parable of Red Beads," *Across the Board* (February 1987): 43–48.

5.31 Shown here are the top 10 U.S. cities ranked by number of rooms sold in a recent year.

Rank	City	Number of Rooms Sold
1	Las Vegas (NV)	40,000,000
2	Orlando (FL)	27,200,000
3	Los Angeles (CA)	25,500,000
4	Chicago (IL)	24,800,000
5	New York City (NY)	23,900,000
6	Washington (DC)	22,800,000
7	Atlanta (GA)	21,500,000
8	Dallas (TX)	15,900,000
9	Houston (TX)	14,500,000
10	San Diego (CA)	14,200,000

Suppose four of these cities are selected randomly.

a. What is the probability that exactly two cities are in California?

b. What is the probability that none of the cities is east of the Mississippi River?

c. What is the probability that exactly three of the cities are ones with more than 24 million rooms sold?

5.32 A company produces and ships 16 personal computers knowing that 4 of them have defective wiring. The company that purchased the computers is going to thoroughly test three of the computers. The purchasing company can detect the defective wiring. What is the probability that the purchasing company will find the following?

a. No defective computers

b. Exactly three defective computers

c. Two or more defective computers

d. One or fewer defective computer

5.33 A western city has 18 police officers eligible for promotion. Eleven of the 18 are Hispanic. Suppose only five of the police officers are chosen for promotion and that one is Hispanic. If the officers chosen for promotion had been selected by chance alone, what is the probability that one or fewer of the five promoted officers would have been Hispanic? What might this result indicate?

Life with a Cell Phone

Suppose that 25% of cell phone owners in the United States use only cellular phones. If 20 Americans are randomly selected, what is the probability that more than 10 use only cell phones? Converting the 25% to a proportion, the value of p is .25, and this is a classic binomial distribution problem with $n = 20$ and $x > 10$. Because the binomial distribution probability tables (Appendix A, Table A.2) do not include $p = .25$, the problem will have to be solved using the binomial formula for each of $x = 11, 12, 13, \ldots, 20$.

For $x = 11$: $_{20}C_{11}(.25)^{11}(.75)^9 = .0030$

Solving for $x = 12, 13,$ and 14 in a similar manner results in probabilities of .0008, .0002, and .0000, respectively. Since

the probabilities "zero out" (four decimal places) at $x = 14$, we need not proceed on to $x = 15, 16, 17, \ldots, 20$. Summing these four probabilities ($x = 11$, $x = 12$, $x = 13$, and $x = 14$) results in a total probability of .0040 as the answer to the posed question. To further understand these probabilities, we calculate the expected value of this distribution as:

$$\mu = n \cdot p = 20(.25) = 5.0$$

In the long run, one would expect to average about 5.0 Americans out of every 20 who consider their cell phone as their primary phone number. In light of this, there is a very small probability that more than 10 Americans would do so.

The study also stated that 9 out of 10 cell users encounter others using their phones in an annoying way. Converting this to $p = .90$ and using $n = 25$ and $x < 20$, this, too, is a binomial problem, but it can be solved by using the binomial tables obtaining the values shown below:

x	Probability
19	.024
18	.007
17	.002
16	.000

The total of these probabilities is .033. Probabilities for all other values ($x \leq 15$) are displayed as .000 in the binomial probability table and are not included here. If 90% of all cell phone users encounter others using their phones in an annoying way, the probability is very small (.033) that out of 25 randomly selected cell phone users less than 20 encounter others using their phones in an annoying way. The expected number in any random sample of 25 is $(25)(.90) = 22.5$.

Suppose, on average, cell phone users receive 3.6 calls per day. Given that information, what is the probability that a cell phone user receives no calls per day? Since random telephone calls are generally thought to be Poisson distributed, this problem can be solved by using either the Poisson probability formula or the Poisson tables (A.3, Appendix A). In this problem, $\lambda = 3.6$ and $x = 0$; and the probability associated with this is:

$$\frac{\lambda^x e^{-\lambda}}{x!} = \frac{(3.6)^0 e^{-3.6}}{0!} = .0273$$

What is the probability that a cell phone user receives 5 or more calls in a day? Since this is a cumulative probability question ($x \geq 5$), the best option is to use the Poisson probability tables (A.3, Appendix A) to obtain:

x	Probability
5	.1377
6	.0826
7	.0425
8	.0191
9	.0076
10	.0028
11	.0009
12	.0003
13	.0001
14	.0000
total	.2936

There is a 29.36% chance that a cell phone user will receive 5 or more calls per day if, on average, such a cell phone user averages 3.6 calls per day.

SUMMARY

Probability experiments produce random outcomes. A variable that contains the outcomes of a random experiment is called a random variable. Random variables such that the set of all possible values is at most a finite or countably infinite number of possible values are called discrete random variables. Random variables that take on values at all points over a given interval are called continuous random variables. Discrete distributions are constructed from discrete random variables. Continuous distributions are constructed from continuous random variables. Three discrete distributions are the binomial distribution, Poisson distribution, and hypergeometric distribution.

The binomial distribution fits experiments when only two mutually exclusive outcomes are possible. In theory, each trial in a binomial experiment must be independent of the other trials. However, if the population size is large enough in relation to the sample size ($n < 5\% \, N$), the binomial distribution can be used where applicable in cases where the trials are not independent. The probability of getting a desired outcome on any one trial is denoted as p, which is the probability of getting a success. The binomial formula is used to determine the probability of obtaining x

outcomes in n trials. Binomial distribution problems can be solved more rapidly with the use of binomial tables than by formula. Table A.2 of Appendix A contains binomial tables for selected values of n and p.

The Poisson distribution usually is used to analyze phenomena that produce rare occurrences. The only information required to generate a Poisson distribution is the long-run average, which is denoted by lambda (λ). The Poisson distribution pertains to occurrences over some interval. The assumptions are that each occurrence is independent of other occurrences and that the value of lambda remains constant throughout the experiment. Poisson probabilities can be determined by either the Poisson formula or the Poisson tables in Table A.3 of Appendix A. The Poisson distribution can be used to approximate binomial distribution problems when n is large ($n > 20$), p is small, and $n \cdot p \leq 7$.

The hypergeometric distribution is a discrete distribution that is usually used for binomial-type experiments when the population is small and finite and sampling is done without replacement. Because using the hypergeometric distribution is a tedious process, using the binomial distribution whenever possible is generally more advantageous.

KEY TERMS

Flash Cards

binomial distribution
continuous distributions
continuous random
variables

discrete distributions
discrete random variables
hypergeometric distribution
lambda (λ)

mean or expected value
Poisson distribution
random variable

FORMULAS

Mean (expected) value of a discrete distribution

$$\mu = E(x) = \Sigma[x \cdot P(x)]$$

Variance of a discrete distribution

$$\sigma^2 = \Sigma[(x - \mu)^2 \cdot P(x)]$$

Standard deviation of a discrete distribution

$$\sigma = \sqrt{\Sigma[(x - \mu)^2 \cdot P(x)]}$$

Binomial formula

$$_nC_x \cdot p^x \cdot q^{n-x} = \frac{n!}{x!(n - x)!} \cdot p^x \cdot q^{n-x}$$

Mean of a binomial distribution

$$\mu = n \cdot p$$

Standard deviation of a binomial distribution

$$\sigma = \sqrt{n \cdot p \cdot q}$$

Poisson Formula

$$P(x) = \frac{\lambda^x e^{-\lambda}}{x!}$$

Hypergeometric formula

$$P(x) = \frac{_AC_x \cdot {_{N-A}C_{n-x}}}{_NC_n}$$

ETHICAL CONSIDERATIONS

Several points must be emphasized about the use of discrete distributions to analyze data. The independence and/or size assumptions must be met in using the binomial distribution in situations where sampling is done without replacement. Size and λ assumptions must be satisfied in using the Poisson distribution to approximate binomial problems. In either case, failure to meet such assumptions can result in spurious conclusions.

As n increases, the use of binomial distributions to study exact x-value probabilities becomes questionable in decision making. Although the probabilities are mathematically correct, as n becomes larger, the probability of any particular x value becomes lower because there are more values among which to split the probabilities. For example, if $n = 100$ and $p = .50$, the probability of $x = 50$ is .0796. This probability of occurrence appears quite low, even though $x = 50$ is the expected value of this distribution and is also the value most likely to occur. It is more useful to decision makers and, in a sense, probably more ethical to present cumulative values for larger sizes of n. In this example, it is probably more useful to examine $P(x > 50)$ than $P(x = 50)$.

The reader is warned in the chapter that the value of λ is assumed to be constant in a Poisson distribution experiment. Researchers may produce spurious results because the λ value changes during a study. For example, suppose the value of λ is obtained for the number of customer arrivals at a toy store between 7 P.M. and 9 P.M. in the month of December. Because December is an active month in terms of traffic volume through a toy store, the use of such a λ to analyze arrivals at the same store between noon and 2 P.M. in February would be inappropriate and, in a sense, unethical.

Errors in judgment such as these are probably more a case of misuse than lack of ethics. However, it is important that statisticians and researchers adhere to assumptions and appropriate applications of these techniques. The inability or unwillingness to do so opens the way for unethical decision making.

SUPPLEMENTARY PROBLEMS

CALCULATING THE STATISTICS

5.34 Solve for the probabilities of the following binomial distribution problems by using the binomial formula.
   a. If $n = 11$ and $p = .23$, what is the probability that $x = 4$?
   b. If $n = 6$ and $p = .50$, what is the probability that $x \geq 1$?
   c. If $n = 9$ and $p = .85$, what is the probability that $x > 7$?
   d. If $n = 14$ and $p = .70$, what is the probability that $x \leq 3$?

5.35 Use Table A.2, Appendix A, to find the values of the following binomial distribution problems.
   a. $P(x = 14 | n = 20$ and $p = .60)$
   b. $P(x < 5 | n = 10$ and $p = .30)$
   c. $P(x \geq 12 | n = 15$ and $p = .60)$
   d. $P(x > 20 | n = 25$ and $p = .40)$

5.36 Use the Poisson formula to solve for the probabilities of the following Poisson distribution problems.
    a. If $\lambda = 1.25$, what is the probability that $x = 4$?
    b. If $\lambda = 6.37$, what is the probability that $x \leq 1$?
    c. If $\lambda = 2.4$, what is the probability that $x > 5$?

5.37 Use Table A.3, Appendix A, to find the following Poisson distribution values.
    a. $P(x = 3 \mid \lambda = 1.8)$
    b. $P(x < 5 \mid \lambda = 3.3)$
    c. $P(x \geq 3 \mid \lambda = 2.1)$
    d. $P(2 < x \leq 5 \mid \lambda = 4.2)$

5.38 Solve the following problems by using the hypergeometric formula.
    a. If $N = 6$, $n = 4$, and $A = 5$, what is the probability that $x = 3$?
    b. If $N = 10$, $n = 3$, and $A = 5$, what is the probability that $x \leq 1$?
    c. If $N = 13$, $n = 5$, and $A = 3$, what is the probability that $x \geq 2$?

TESTING YOUR UNDERSTANDING

5.39 In a study by Peter D. Hart Research Associates for the Nasdaq Stock Market, it was determined that 20% of all stock investors are retired people. In addition, 40% of all U.S. adults invest in mutual funds. Suppose a random sample of 25 stock investors is taken.
    a. What is the probability that exactly seven are retired people?
    b. What is the probability that 10 or more are retired people?
    c. How many retired people would you expect to find in a random sample of 25 stock investors?
    d. Suppose a random sample of 20 U.S. adults is taken. What is the probability that exactly eight adults invested in mutual funds?
    e. Suppose a random sample of 20 U.S. adults is taken. What is the probability that fewer than six adults invested in mutual funds?
    f. Suppose a random sample of 20 U.S. adults is taken. What is the probability that none of the adults invested in mutual funds?
    g. Suppose a random sample of 20 U.S. adults is taken. What is the probability that 12 or more adults invested in mutual funds?
    h. For parts e–g, what exact number of adults would produce the highest probability? How does this compare to the expected number?

5.40 A service station has a pump that distributes diesel fuel to automobiles. The station owner estimates that only about 3.2 cars use the diesel pump every 2 hours. Assume the arrivals of diesel pump users are Poisson distributed.
    a. What is the probability that three cars will arrive to use the diesel pump during a one-hour period?
    b. Suppose the owner needs to shut down the diesel pump for half an hour to make repairs. However, the owner hates to lose any business. What is the probability that no cars will arrive to use the diesel pump during a half-hour period?
    c. Suppose five cars arrive during a one-hour period to use the diesel pump. What is the probability of five or more cars arriving during a one-hour period to use the diesel pump? If this outcome actually occurred, what might you conclude?

5.41 In a particular manufacturing plant, two machines (A and B) produce a particular part. One machine (B) is newer and faster. In one five-minute period, a lot consisting of 32 parts is produced. Twenty-two are produced by machine B and the rest by machine A. Suppose an inspector randomly samples a dozen of the parts from this lot.
    a. What is the probability that exactly three parts were produced by machine A?
    b. What is the probability that half of the parts were produced by each machine?
    c. What is the probability that all of the parts were produced by machine B?
    d. What is the probability that seven, eight, or nine parts were produced by machine B?

5.42 Suppose that, for every lot of 100 computer chips a company produces, an average of 1.4 are defective. Another company buys many lots of these chips at a time, from which one lot is selected randomly and tested for defects. If the tested lot contains more than three defects, the buyer will reject all the lots sent in that batch. What is the probability that the buyer will accept the lots? Assume that the defects per lot are Poisson distributed.

5.43 The National Center for Health Statistics reports that 25% of all Americans between the ages of 65 and 74 have a chronic heart condition. Suppose you live in a state where the environment is conducive to good health and low stress and you believe the conditions in your state promote healthy hearts. To investigate this theory, you conduct a random telephone survey of 20 persons 65 to 74 years of age in your state.
    a. On the basis of the figure from the National Center for Health Statistics, what is the expected number of persons 65 to 74 years of age in your survey who have a chronic heart condition?
    b. Suppose only one person in your survey has a chronic heart condition. What is the probability of getting one or fewer people with a chronic heart condition in a sample of 20 if 25% of the population in this age bracket has this health problem? What do you conclude about your state from the sample data?

5.44 A survey conducted for the Northwestern National Life Insurance Company revealed that 70% of American workers say job stress caused frequent health problems. One in three said they expected to burn out in the job in the near future. Thirty-four percent said they thought seriously about quitting their job last year because of work-place stress. Fifty-three percent said they were required to work more than 40 hours a week very often or somewhat often.

a. Suppose a random sample of 10 American workers is selected. What is the probability that more than seven of them say job stress caused frequent health problems? What is the expected number of workers who say job stress caused frequent health problems?

b. Suppose a random sample of 15 American workers is selected. What is the expected number of these sampled workers who say they will burn out in the near future? What is the probability that none of the workers say they will burn out in the near future?

c. Suppose a sample of seven workers is selected randomly. What is the probability that all seven say they are asked very often or somewhat often to work more than 40 hours a week? If this outcome actually happened, what might you conclude?

5.45 According to Padgett Business Services, 20% of all small-business owners say the most important advice for starting a business is to prepare for long hours and hard work. Twenty-five percent say the most important advice is to have good financing ready. Nineteen percent say having a good plan is the most important advice; 18% say studying the industry is the most important advice; and 18% list other advice. Suppose 12 small business owners are contacted, and assume that the percentages hold for all small-business owners.

a. What is the probability that none of the owners would say preparing for long hours and hard work is the most important advice?

b. What is the probability that six or more owners would say preparing for long hours and hard work is the most important advice?

c. What is the probability that exactly five owners would say having good financing ready is the most important advice?

d. What is the expected number of owners who would say having a good plan is the most important advice?

5.46 According to a recent survey, the probability that a passenger files a complaint with the Department of Transportation about a particular U.S. airline is .000014. Suppose 100,000 passengers who flew with this particular airline are randomly contacted.

a. What is the probability that exactly five passengers filed complaints?

b. What is the probability that none of the passengers filed complaints?

c. What is the probability that more than six passengers filed complaints?

5.47 A hair stylist has been in business one year. Sixty percent of his customers are walk-in business. If he randomly samples eight of the people from last week's list of customers, what is the probability that three or fewer were walk-ins? If this outcome actually occurred, what would be some of the explanations for it?

5.48 A Department of Transportation survey showed that 60% of U.S. residents over 65 years of age oppose use of cell phones in flight even if there were no issues with the phones interfering with aircraft communications systems. If this information is correct and if a researcher randomly selects 25 U.S. residents who are over 65 years of age,

a. What is the probability that exactly 12 oppose the use of cell phones in flight?

b. What is the probability that more than 17 oppose the use of cell phones in flight?

c. What is the probability that less than eight oppose the use of cell phones in flight? If the researcher actually got less than eight, what might she conclude about the Department of Transportation survey?

5.49 A survey conducted by the Consumer Reports National Research Center reported, among other things, that women spend an average of 1.2 hours per week shopping online. Assume that hours per week shopping online are Poisson distributed. If this survey result is true for all women and if a woman is randomly selected,

a. What is the probability that she did not shop at all online over a one-week period?

b. What is the probability that a woman would shop three or more hours online during a one-week period?

c. What is the probability that a woman would shop fewer than five hours in a three-week period?

5.50 According to the Audit Bureau of Circulations, the top 25 city newspapers in the United States ranked according to circulation are:

Rank	Newspaper
1	New York Times (NY)
2	Los Angeles Times (CA)
3	Washington Post (DC)
4	New York Daily News (NY)
5	New York Post (NY)
6	San Jose Mercury News (CA)
7	Chicago Tribune (IL)
8	Houston Chronicle (TX)
9	Philadelphia Inquirer (PA)
10	Long Island Newsday (NY)
11	Denver Post (CO)
12	Phoenix Arizona Republic (AZ)
13	Minneapolis Star Tribune (MN)
14	Dallas Morning News (TX)
15	Cleveland Plain Dealer (OH)
16	Seattle Times (WA)
17	Chicago Sun-Times (IL)
18	Detroit Free Press (MI)
19	St. Petersburg Times (FL)
20	Portland Oregonian (OR)
21	San Diego Union-Tribune (CA)
22	San Francisco Chronicle (CA)
23	Newark Star-Ledger (NJ)
24	Boston Globe (MA)
25	St. Louis Post-Dispatch (MO)

Suppose a researcher wants to sample a portion of these newspapers and compare the sizes of the business sections of the Sunday papers. She randomly samples eight of these newspapers.

a. What is the probability that the sample contains exactly one newspaper located in New York state?

b. What is the probability that half of the sampled newspapers are ranked in the top 10 by circulation?

c. What is the probability that none of the newspapers is located in California?

d. What is the probability that exactly three of the newspapers are located in states that begin with the letter *M*?

5.51 An office in Albuquerque has 24 workers including management. Eight of the workers commute to work from the west side of the Rio Grande River. Suppose six of the office workers are randomly selected.

a. What is the probability that all six workers commute from the west side of the Rio Grande?

b. What is the probability that none of the workers commute from the west side of the Rio Grande?

c. Which probability from parts (a) and (b) was greatest? Why do you think this is?

d. What is the probability that half of the workers do not commute from the west side of the Rio Grande?

5.52 According to the U.S. Census Bureau, 20% of the workers in Atlanta use public transportation. If 25 Atlanta workers are randomly selected, what is the expected number to use public transportation? Graph the binomial distribution for this sample. What are the mean and the standard deviation for this distribution? What is the probability that more than 12 of the selected workers use public transportation? Explain conceptually and from the graph why you would get this probability. Suppose you randomly sample 25 Atlanta workers and actually get 14 who use public transportation. Is this outcome likely? How might you explain this result?

5.53 One of the earliest applications of the Poisson distribution was in analyzing incoming calls to a telephone switchboard. Analysts generally believe that random phone calls are Poisson distributed. Suppose phone calls to a switchboard arrive at an average rate of 2.4 calls per minute.

a. If an operator wants to take a one-minute break, what is the probability that there will be no calls during a one-minute interval?

b. If an operator can handle at most five calls per minute, what is the probability that the operator will be unable to handle the calls in any one-minute period?

c. What is the probability that exactly three calls will arrive in a two-minute interval?

d. What is the probability that one or fewer calls will arrive in a 15-second interval?

5.54 A survey by Frank N. Magid Associates revealed that 3% of Americans are not connected to the Internet at home. Another researcher randomly selects 70 Americans.

a. What is the expected number of these who would not be connected to the Internet at home?

b. What is the probability that eight or more are not connected to the Internet at home?

c. What is the probability that between three and six (inclusive) are not connected to the Internet at home?

5.55 Suppose that in the bookkeeping operation of a large corporation the probability of a recording error on any one billing is .005. Suppose the probability of a recording error from one billing to the next is constant, and 1,000 billings are randomly sampled by an auditor.

a. What is the probability that fewer than four billings contain a recording error?

b. What is the probability that more than 10 billings contain a billing error?

c. What is the probability that all 1,000 billings contain no recording errors?

5.56 According to the American Medical Association, about 36% of all U.S. physicians under the age of 35 are women. Your company has just hired eight physicians under the age of 35 and none is a woman. If a group of women physicians under the age of 35 want to sue your company for discriminatory hiring practices, would they have a strong case based on these numbers? Use the binomial distribution to determine the probability of the company's hiring result occurring randomly, and comment on the potential justification for a lawsuit.

5.57 The following table lists the 25 largest U.S. universities according to enrollment figures from *The World Almanac*. The state of location is given in parentheses.

University	Enrollment
University of Phoenix (AZ)	292,797
Arizona State University (AZ)	68,064
Ohio State University (OH)	55,014
University of Central Florida (FL)	53,537
University of Minnesota (MN)	51,659
University of Texas at Austin (TX)	50,995
University of Florida (FL)	50,691
Texas A&M University (TX)	48,703
Michigan State University (MI)	47,278
University of South Florida (FL)	47,024
University of Washington (WA)	45,943
Penn State, University Park (PA)	45,185
University of Illinois (IL)	43,881
New York University (NY)	43,404
Indiana University (IN)	42,347
University of Wisconsin (WI)	42,099
University of Michigan (MI)	41,674
University of California, Los Angeles (CA)	39,984
Florida State University (FL)	39,785
Florida International University (FL)	39,718
Purdue University (IN)	39,697
University of Arizona (AZ)	38,767
Rutgers, The State University of New Jersey (NJ)	37,364
University of Maryland, College Park (MD)	37,146
University of Houston (TX)	37,000

a. If five different universities are selected randomly from the list, what is the probability that three of them have enrollments of 40,000 or more?

b. If eight different universities are selected randomly from the list, what is the probability that two or fewer are universities in Florida?

c. Suppose universities are being selected randomly from this list with replacement. If five universities are sampled, what is the probability that the sample will contain exactly two universities in Texas?

5.58 In one midwestern city, the government has 14 repossessed houses, which are evaluated to be worth about the same. Ten of the houses are on the north side of town and the rest are on the west side. A local contractor submitted a bid to purchase four of the houses. Which houses the contractor will get is subject to a random draw.

a. What is the probability that all four houses selected for the contractor will be on the north side of town?

b. What is the probability that all four houses selected for the contractor will be on the west side of town?

c. What is the probability that half of the houses selected for the contractor will be on the west side and half on the north side of town?

5.59 The Public Citizen's Health Research Group studied the serious disciplinary actions that were taken during a recent year on nonfederal medical doctors in the United States. The national average was 3.05 serious actions per 1000 doctors. The state with the lowest number was Minnesota with only 1.07 serious actions per 1000 doctors. Assume that the numbers of serious actions per 1000 doctors in both the United States and in South Carolina are Poisson distributed.

a. What is the probability of randomly selecting 1000 U.S. doctors and finding no serious actions taken?

b. What is the probability of randomly selecting 2000 U.S. doctors and finding six serious actions taken?

c. What is the probability of randomly selecting 3000 Minnesota doctors and finding fewer than seven serious actions taken?

INTERPRETING THE OUTPUT

5.60 Study the Minitab output. Discuss the type of distribution, the mean, standard deviation, and why the probabilities fall as they do.

```
Probability Density Function

Binomial with n = 15 and n = 0.36

x            P(X = x)
0            0.001238
1            0.010445
2            0.041128
3            0.100249
4            0.169170
5            0.209347
6            0.196263
7            0.141940
```

8	0.079841
9	0.034931
10	0.011789
11	0.003014
12	0.000565
13	0.000073
14	0.000006
15	0.000000

5.61 Study the Excel output. Explain the distribution in terms of shape and mean. Are these probabilities what you would expect? Why or why not?

x Values	Poisson Probabilities: $\lambda = 2.78$
0	0.0620
1	0.1725
2	0.2397
3	0.2221
4	0.1544
5	0.0858
6	0.0398
7	0.0158
8	0.0055
9	0.0017
10	0.0005
11	0.0001

5.62 Study the graphical output from Excel. Describe the distribution and explain why the graph takes the shape it does.

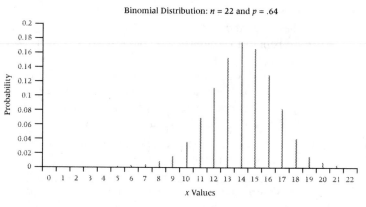

Binomial Distribution: $n = 22$ and $p = .64$

5.63 Study the Minitab graph. Discuss the distribution including type, shape, and probability outcomes.

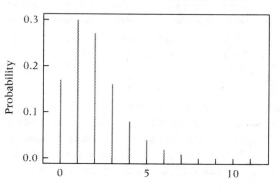

Poisson Distribution: Lambda = 1.784

ANALYZING THE DATABASES

1. Use the Consumer Food database. What proportion of the database households are in the Metro area? Use this as the value of p in a binomial distribution. If you were to randomly select 12 of these households, what is the probability that fewer than 3 would be households in the Metro area? If you were to randomly select 25 of these households, what is the probability that exactly 8 would be in the Metro area?

2. Use the Hospital database. What is the breakdown between hospitals that are general medical hospitals and those that are psychiatric hospitals in this database of 200 hospitals? (Hint: In Service, 1 = general medical and 2 = psychiatric). Using these figures and the hypergeometric distribution, determine the probability of randomly selecting 16 hospitals from the database and getting exactly 9 that are psychiatric hospitals. Now, determine the number of hospitals in this database that are for-profit (Hint: In Control, 3 = for-profit). From this number, calculate p, the proportion of hospitals that are for-profit. Using this value of p and the binomial distribution, determine the probability of randomly selecting 30 hospitals and getting exactly 10 that are for-profit.

CASE

WHOLE FOODS MARKET GROWS THROUGH MERGERS AND ACQUISITIONS

Over three decades ago, four businesspeople who had experience in retailing natural foods through food stores believed that there was a demand for a supermarket for natural foods. As a result, in 1980 in Austin, Texas, they founded the first Whole Foods Market store in a building that had around 10,000 square feet and with a staff of 19. This store was quite large compared to health food stores at the time. By 1984, the company was successful enough to expand to Houston and Dallas. In 1988, they purchased the Whole Food Company in New Orleans and expanded there. The next year, they moved into the West Coast with a store in Palo Alto, California. Even though the company has built a number of its own stores, much of the company growth has come through mergers and acquisitions, many of which came in the 1990s in such places as North Carolina, Massachusetts, Rhode Island, both Northern and Southern California, and Michigan. After the turn of the century, Whole Foods Market established a presence in Manhattan (NY), followed by a move into Canada and later into the United Kingdom.

Presently, Whole Foods Market has 297 stores in 38 U.S. states, the District of Columbia, Canada, and the United Kingdom with 44 more in development. There are over 57,000 team members, 82% of whom are full-time employees. Existing stores now average 43,000 square feet in size, about four times as large as the original "supermarket." Whole Foods Market is the ninth largest food and drug store in the United States with almost $2 billion in sales last year and is number 284 on the list of Fortune 500 companies.

Whole Food Markets is the largest retailer of natural and organic foods and prides itself in doing the research necessary to assure customers that offered products are free of artificial flavors, colors, sweeteners, preservatives, or hydrogenated fats. The company attempts to customize each store by stocking it with products that are most in demand in any given community. Whole Foods Market management cares about their employees, and the company has been named by *Fortune* magazine as one of the "100 Best Companies to Work For" in the

United States every year since the list was first compiled 13 years ago. The company attempts to be a good community citizen, and it gives back at least 5% of after-tax profits to the communities in which they operate. In January 2008, Whole Foods Market was the first U.S. supermarket to commit to completely eliminating disposable plastic bags. The Core Values of the company are "Whole Foods, Whole People, and Whole Planet." The Whole Foods Market searches "for the highest quality, least processed, most flavorful and natural foods possible . . ." The company attempts to "create a respectful workplace where people are treated fairly and are highly motivated to succeed." In addition, the company is committed to the world around us and protecting the planet.

Discussion

1. Whole Foods Market has shown steady growth at a time when traditional supermarkets have been flat. This could be attributed to a growing awareness of and demand for more natural foods. According to a study by Mintel in 2006, 30% of consumers have a high level of concern about the safety of the food they eat. Suppose we want to test this figure to determine if consumers have changed since then. Assuming that the 30% figure still holds, what is the probability of randomly sampling 25 consumers and having 12 or more respond that they have a high level of concern about the safety of the food they eat? What would the expected number be? If a researcher actually got 12 or more out of 25 to respond that they have a high level of concern about the safety of the food they eat, what might this mean?

2. Suppose that, on average, in a Whole Foods Market in Dallas, 3.4 customers want to check out every minute. Based on this figure, store management wants to staff "checkout" lines such that less than 1% of the time demand for checkout cannot be met. In this case, store management would have to staff for what number of customers? Based

on the 3.4 customer average per minute, what percentage of the time would the store have 12 or more customers who want to check out in any two-minute period?

3. Suppose a survey is taken of 30 managers of Whole Foods Market stores and it is determined that 17 are at least 40 years old. If another researcher randomly selects 10 of these 30 managers to interview, what is the probability that 3 or fewer are at least 40 years old? Suppose 9 of the

30 surveyed managers are female. What is the probability of randomly selecting 10 managers from the 30 and finding out that 7 of the 10 are female?

Adapted from: Information found at Whole Foods Market Web site at http://www.wholefoodsmarket.com, 2010, and William A. Knudson, "The Organic Food Market," a working paper from the Strategic Marketing Institute, Michigan State University, 2007.

USING THE COMPUTER

EXCEL

* Excel can be used to compute exact or cumulative probabilities for particular values of discrete distributions including the binomial, Poisson, and hypergeometric distributions.

* Calculation of probabilities from each of these distributions begins with the **Insert Function** (f_x). To access the **Insert Function**, go to the **Formulas** tab on an Excel worksheet (top center tab). The **Insert Function** is on the far left of the menu bar. In the **Insert Function** dialog box at the top, there is a pulldown menu where it says **Or select a category**. From the pulldown menu associated with this command, select **Statistical**.

* To compute probabilities from a binomial distribution, select **BINOM.DIST** from the **Insert Function's Statistical** menu. In the **BINOM.DIST** dialog box, there are four lines to which you must respond. On the first line, **Number_s**, enter the value of x, the number of successes. On the second line, **Trials**, enter the number of trials (sample size, n). On the third line, **Probability_s**, enter the value of p. The fourth line, **Cumulative**, requires a logical response of either TRUE or FALSE. Place TRUE in the slot to get the cumulative probabilities for all values from 0 to x. Place FALSE in the slot to get the exact probability of getting x successes in n trials.

* To compute probabilities from a Poisson distribution, select **POISSON.DIST** from the **Insert Function's Statistical** menu. In the **POISSON.DIST** dialog box, there are three lines to which you must respond. On the first line, **X**, enter the value of x, the number of events. On the second line, **Mean**, enter the expected number, λ. The third line, **Cumulative**, requires a logical response of either TRUE or FALSE. Place TRUE in the slot to get the cumulative probabilities for all values from 0 to x. Place FALSE in the slot to get the exact probability of getting x successes when λ is the expected number.

* To compute probabilities from a hypergeometric distribution, select **HYPGEOM.DIST** from the **Insert Function's Statistical** menu. In the **HYPGEOM.DIST** dialog box, there are five lines to which you must respond. On the first

line, **Sample_s**, enter the value of x, the number of successes in the sample. On the second line, **Number_sample**, enter the size of the sample, n. On the third line, **Population_s**, enter the number of successes in the population. The fourth line, **Number_pop**, enter the size of the population, N. The fifth line, **Cumulative**, requires a logical response of either TRUE or FALSE. Place TRUE in the slot to get the cumulative probabilities for all values from 0 to x. Place FALSE in the slot to get the exact probability of getting x successes in n trials.

MINITAB

* Probabilities can be computed using Minitab for the binomial distribution, the Poisson distribution, and the hypergeometric distribution.

* To begin binomial distribution probabilities, select **Calc** on the menu bar. Select **Probability Distributions** from the pulldown menu. From the long second pulldown menu, select **Binomial**. From the dialog box, check how you want the probabilities to be calculated from **Probability**, **Cumulative probability**, or **Inverse cumulative probability**. **Probability** yields the exact probability n, p, and x. **Cumulative probability** produces the cumulative probabilities for values less than or equal to x. **Inverse probability** yields the inverse of the cumulative probabilities. If you want to compute probabilities for several values of x, place them in a column, and list the column location in **Input column**. If you want to compute the probability for a particular value of x, check **Input constant**, and enter the value of x.

* To begin Poisson distribution probabilities, select **Calc** on the menu bar. Select **Probability Distributions** from the pulldown menu. From the long second pulldown menu, select **Poisson**. From the dialog box, check how you want the probabilities to be calculated from **Probability**, **Cumulative probability**, or **Inverse cumulative probability**. **Probability** yields the exact probability of a particular λ, and x. **Cumulative probability** produces the cumulative probabilities for values less than or equal to x. **Inverse probability** yields the inverse of the cumulative probabilities. If you want to compute probabilities for several values of x, place them

in a column, and list the column location in **Input column**. If you want to compute the probability for a particular value of x, check **Input constant**, and enter the value of x.

■ To begin hypergeometric distribution probabilities, select **C**alc on the menu bar. Select **Probability** **D**istributions from the pulldown menu. From the long second pull-down menu, select **H**ypergeometric. From the dialog box, check how you want the probabilities to be calculated from **Probability**, **Cumulative probability**, or **Inverse cumulative probability**. **Probability** yields the exact probability of a particular combination of N, A, n, and x. Note that Minitab uses M for number of successes in the population instead of A. **Cumulative probability** produces the cumulative probabilities for values less than or equal to x. **Inverse probability** yields the inverse of the cumulative probabilities. If you want to compute probabilities for several values of x, place them in a column, and list the column location in **Input column**. If you want to compute the probability for a particular value of x, check **Input constant**, and enter the value of x.

Continuous Distributions

LEARNING OBJECTIVES

The primary learning objective of Chapter 6 is to help you understand continuous distributions, thereby enabling you to:

1. Solve for probabilities in a continuous uniform distribution
2. Solve for probabilities in a normal distribution using z scores and for the mean, the standard deviation, or a value of x in a normal distribution when given information about the area under the normal curve
3. Solve problems from the discrete binomial distribution using the continuous normal distribution and correcting for continuity
4. Solve for probabilities in an exponential distribution and contrast the exponential distribution to the discrete Poisson distribution

Comstock/Getty Images

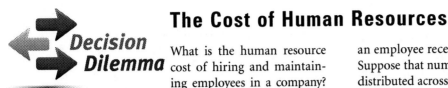

The Cost of Human Resources

What is the human resource cost of hiring and maintaining employees in a company? Studies conducted by Saratoga Institute, Pricewaterhouse-Coopers Human Resource Services, determined that the average cost of hiring an employee is $3,270, and the average annual human resource expenditure per employee is $1,554. The average health benefit payment per employee is $6,393, and the average employer 401(k) cost per participant is $2,258. According to a survey conducted by the American Society for Training and Development, companies annually spend an average of $955 per employee on training, and, on average, an employee receives 32 hours of training annually. Business researchers have attempted to measure the cost of employee absenteeism to an organization. A survey conducted by CCH, Inc., showed that the average annual cost of unscheduled absenteeism per employee is $660. According to this survey, 35% of all unscheduled absenteeism is caused by personal illness.

Managerial and Statistical Questions

1. The survey conducted by the American Society for Training and Development reported that, on average, an employee receives 32 hours of training per year. Suppose that number of hours of training is uniformly distributed across all employees varying from 0 hours to 64 hours. What percentage of employees receive between 20 and 40 hours of training? What percentage of employees receive 50 hours or more of training?

2. As the result of another survey, it was estimated that, on average, it costs $3,270 to hire an employee. Suppose such costs are normally distributed with a standard deviation of $400. Based on these figures, what is the probability that a randomly selected hire costs more than $4,000? What percentage of employees is hired for less than $3,000?

3. The absenteeism survey determined that 35% of all unscheduled absenteeism is caused by personal illness. If this is true, what is the probability of randomly sampling 120 unscheduled absences and finding out that more than 50 were caused by personal illness?

Sources: Adapted from: "Human Resources Is Put on Notice," *Workforce Management*, vol. 84, no. 14 (December 12, 2005), pp. 44–48. Web sites for data sources: www.pwcservices.com/, www.astd.org, and www.cch.com.

Whereas Chapter 5 focused on the characteristics and applications of discrete distributions, Chapter 6 concentrates on information about continuous distributions. Continuous distributions are constructed from continuous random variables in which values are taken on for every point over a given interval and are usually generated from experiments in which things are "measured" as opposed to "counted." With continuous distributions, probabilities of outcomes occurring between particular points are determined by calculating the area under the curve between those points. In addition, the entire area under the whole curve is equal to 1. The many continuous distributions in statistics include the uniform distribution, the normal distribution, the exponential distribution, the *t* distribution, the chi-square distribution, and the *F* distribution. This chapter presents the uniform distribution, the normal distribution, and the exponential distribution.

6.1 THE UNIFORM DISTRIBUTION

The **uniform distribution**, sometimes referred to as the **rectangular distribution**, is *a relatively simple continuous distribution in which the same height, or f(x), is obtained over a range of values.* The following probability density function defines a uniform distribution.

185

FIGURE 6.1

Uniform Distribution

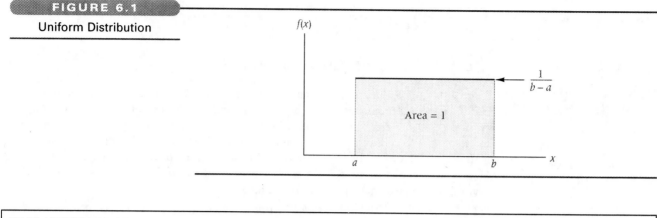

PROBABILITY DENSITY FUNCTION OF A UNIFORM DISTRIBUTION

$$f(x) = \begin{cases} \dfrac{1}{b-a} & \text{for } a \leq x \leq b \\ 0 & \text{for all other values} \end{cases}$$

Figure 6.1 is an example of a uniform distribution. In a uniform, or rectangular, distribution, the total area under the curve is equal to the product of the length and the width of the rectangle and equals 1. Because the distribution lies, by definition, between the x values of a and b, the length of the rectangle is $(b - a)$. Combining this area calculation with the fact that the area equals 1, the height of the rectangle can be solved as follows.

$$\text{Area of Rectangle} = (\text{Length})(\text{Height}) = 1$$

But

$$\text{Length} = (b - a)$$

Therefore,

$$(b - a)(\text{Height}) = 1$$

and

$$\text{Height} = \frac{1}{(b - a)}$$

These calculations show why, between the x values of a and b, the distribution has a constant height of $1/(b - a)$.

The mean and standard deviation of a uniform distribution are given as follows.

MEAN AND STANDARD DEVIATION OF A UNIFORM DISTRIBUTION

$$\mu = \frac{a + b}{2}$$

$$\sigma = \frac{b - a}{\sqrt{12}}$$

Many possible situations arise in which data might be uniformly distributed. As an example, suppose a production line is set up to manufacture machine braces in lots of five per minute during a shift. When the lots are weighed, variation among the weights is detected, with lot weights ranging from 41 to 47 grams in a uniform distribution. The height of this distribution is

$$f(x) = \text{Height} = \frac{1}{(b - a)} = \frac{1}{(47 - 41)} = \frac{1}{6}$$

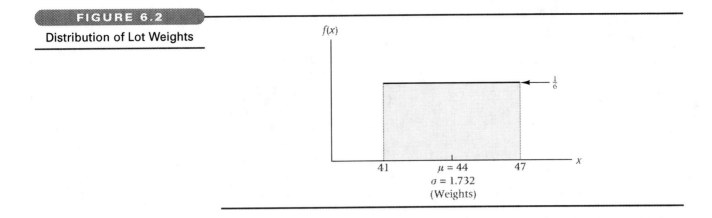

FIGURE 6.2

Distribution of Lot Weights

The mean and standard deviation of this distribution are

$$\text{Mean} = \frac{a + b}{2} = \frac{41 + 47}{2} = \frac{88}{2} = 44$$

$$\text{Standard Deviation} = \frac{b - a}{\sqrt{12}} = \frac{47 - 41}{\sqrt{12}} = \frac{6}{3.464} = 1.732$$

Figure 6.2 provides the uniform distribution for this example, with its mean, standard deviation, and the height of the distribution.

Determining Probabilities in a Uniform Distribution

With discrete distributions, the probability function yields the value of the probability. For continuous distributions, probabilities are calculated by determining the area over an interval of the function. With continuous distributions, there is no area under the curve for a single point. The following equation is used to determine the probabilities of x for a uniform distribution between a and b.

PROBABILITIES IN A UNIFORM DISTRIBUTION	$P(x) = \dfrac{x_2 - x_1}{b - a}$

where

$$a \le x_1 \le x_2 \le b$$

Remember that the area between a and b is equal to 1. The probability for any interval that includes a and b is 1. The probability of $x \ge b$ or of $x \le a$ is zero because there is no area above b or below a.

Suppose that on the machine braces problem we want to determine the probability that a lot weighs between 42 and 45 grams. This probability is computed as follows:

$$P(x) = \frac{x_2 - x_1}{b - a} = \frac{45 - 42}{47 - 41} = \frac{3}{6} = .5000$$

Figure 6.3 displays this solution.

The probability that a lot weighs more than 48 grams is zero, because $x = 48$ is greater than the upper value, $x = 47$, of the uniform distribution. A similar argument gives the probability of a lot weighing less than 40 grams. Because 40 is less than the lowest value of the uniform distribution range, 41, the probability is zero.

FIGURE 6.3

Solved Probability in a
Uniform Distribution

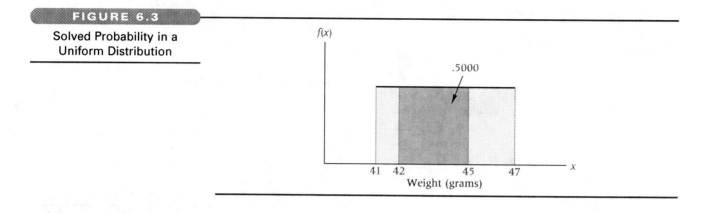

**DEMONSTRATION
PROBLEM 6.1**

Suppose the amount of time it takes to assemble a plastic module ranges from 27 to 39 seconds and that assembly times are uniformly distributed. Describe the distribution. What is the probability that a given assembly will take between 30 and 35 seconds? Fewer than 30 seconds?

Solution

$$f(x) = \frac{1}{39 - 27} = \frac{1}{12}$$

$$\mu = \frac{a + b}{2} = \frac{39 + 27}{2} = 33$$

$$\sigma = \frac{b - a}{\sqrt{12}} = \frac{39 - 27}{\sqrt{12}} = \frac{12}{\sqrt{12}} = 3.464$$

The height of the distribution is 1/12. The mean time is 33 seconds with a standard deviation of 3.464 seconds.

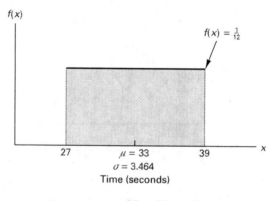

$$P(30 \le x \le 35) = \frac{35 - 30}{39 - 27} = \frac{5}{12} = .4167$$

There is a .4167 probability that it will take between 30 and 35 seconds to assemble the module.

$$P(x < 30) = \frac{30 - 27}{39 - 27} = \frac{3}{12} = .2500$$

There is a .2500 probability that it will take less than 30 seconds to assemble the module. Because there is no area less than 27 seconds, $P(x < 30)$ is determined by using only the interval $27 \le x < 30$. In a continuous distribution, there is no area at any one point (only over an interval). Thus the probability $x < 30$ is the same as the probability of $x \le 30$.

DEMONSTRATION PROBLEM 6.2

According to the National Association of Insurance Commissioners, the average annual cost for automobile insurance in the United States in a recent year was $691. Suppose automobile insurance costs are uniformly distributed in the United States with a range of from $200 to $1,182. What is the standard deviation of this uniform distribution? What is the height of the distribution? What is the probability that a person's annual cost for automobile insurance in the United States is between $410 and $825?

Solution

The mean is given as $691. The value of a is $200 and b is $1,182.

$$\sigma = \frac{b - a}{\sqrt{12}} = \frac{1,182 - 200}{\sqrt{12}} = 283.5$$

The height of the distribution is $\dfrac{1}{1,182 - 200} = \dfrac{1}{982} = .001$

$$x_1 = 410 \text{ and } x_2 = 825$$

$$P(410 \le x \le 825) = \frac{825 - 410}{1,182 - 200} = \frac{415}{982} = .4226$$

The probability that a randomly selected person pays between $410 and $825 annually for automobile insurance in the United States is .4226. That is, about 42.26% of all people in the United States pay in that range.

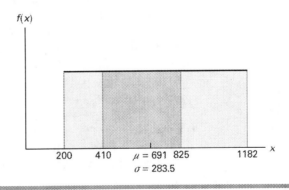

Using the Computer to Solve for Uniform Distribution Probabilities

Using the values of a, b, and x, Minitab has the capability of computing probabilities for the uniform distribution. The resulting computation is a cumulative probability from the left end of the distribution to each x value. As an example, the probability question, $P(410 \le x \le 825)$, from Demonstration Problem 6.2 can be worked using Minitab. Minitab computes the probability of $x \le 825$ and the probability of $x \le 410$, and these results are shown in Table 6.1. The final answer to the probability question from Demonstration Problem 6.2 is obtained by subtracting these two probabilities:

$$P(410 \le x \le 825) = .636456 - .213849 = .422607$$

TABLE 6.1

Minitab Output for Uniform Distribution

CUMULATIVE DISTRIBUTION FUNCTION	
Continuous uniform on 200 to 1182	
x	P(X <= x)
825	0.636456
410	0.213849

Excel does not have the capability of directly computing probabilities for the uniform distribution.

6.1 PROBLEMS

6.1 Values are uniformly distributed between 200 and 240.
   a. What is the value of $f(x)$ for this distribution?
   b. Determine the mean and standard deviation of this distribution.
   c. Probability of $(x > 230) = ?$
   d. Probability of $(205 \leq x \leq 220) = ?$
   e. Probability of $(x \leq 225) = ?$

6.2 x is uniformly distributed over a range of values from 8 to 21.
   a. What is the value of $f(x)$ for this distribution?
   b. Determine the mean and standard deviation of this distribution.
   c. Probability of $(10 \leq x < 17) = ?$
   d. Probability of $(x < 22) = ?$
   e. Probability of $(x \geq 7) = ?$

6.3 The retail price of a medium-sized box of a well-known brand of cornflakes ranges from \$2.80 to \$3.14. Assume these prices are uniformly distributed. What are the average price and standard deviation of prices in this distribution? If a price is randomly selected from this list, what is the probability that it will be between \$3.00 and \$3.10?

6.4 The average fill volume of a regular can of soft drink is 12 ounces. Suppose the fill volume of these cans ranges from 11.97 to 12.03 ounces and is uniformly distributed. What is the height of this distribution? What is the probability that a randomly selected can contains more than 12.01 ounces of fluid? What is the probability that the fill volume is between 11.98 and 12.01 ounces?

6.5 According to the U.S. Department of Labor, the average American household spends \$639 on household supplies per year. Suppose annual expenditures on household supplies per household are uniformly distributed between the values of \$253 and \$1,025. What are the standard deviation and the height of this distribution? What proportion of households spend more than \$850 per year on household supplies? What proportion of households spend more than \$1,200 per year on household supplies? What proportion of households spend between \$350 and \$480 on household supplies?

6.2 NORMAL DISTRIBUTION

Video

Interactive Applet

FIGURE 6.4

The Normal Curve

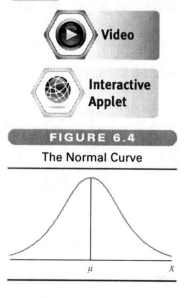

Probably the most widely known and used of all distributions is the **normal distribution**. It fits many human characteristics, such as height, weight, length, speed, IQ, scholastic achievement, and years of life expectancy, among others. Like their human counterparts, living things in nature, such as trees, animals, insects, and others, have many characteristics that are normally distributed.

Many variables in business and industry also are normally distributed. Some examples of variables that could produce normally distributed measurements include the annual cost of household insurance, the cost per square foot of renting warehouse space, and managers' satisfaction with support from ownership on a five-point scale. In addition, most items produced or filled by machines are normally distributed.

Because of its many applications, the normal distribution is an extremely important distribution. Besides the many variables mentioned that are normally distributed, the normal distribution and its associated probabilities are an integral part of statistical process control (see Chapter 18). When large enough sample sizes are taken, many statistics are normally distributed regardless of the shape of the underlying distribution from which they are drawn (as discussed in Chapter 7). Figure 6.4 is the graphic representation of the normal distribution: the normal curve.

History of the Normal Distribution

Discovery of the normal curve of errors is generally credited to mathematician and astronomer Karl Gauss (1777–1855), who recognized that the errors of repeated measurement of objects are often normally distributed.* Thus the normal distribution is sometimes referred to as the *Gaussian distribution* or the *normal curve of error.* A modern-day analogy of Gauss's work might be the distribution of measurements of machine-produced parts, which often yield a normal curve of error around a mean specification.

To a lesser extent, some credit has been given to Pierre-Simon de Laplace (1749–1827) for discovering the normal distribution. However, many people now believe that Abraham de Moivre (1667–1754), a French mathematician, first understood the normal distribution. De Moivre determined that the binomial distribution approached the normal distribution as a limit. De Moivre worked with remarkable accuracy. His published table values for the normal curve are only a few ten-thousandths off the values of currently published tables.[†]

The normal distribution exhibits the following characteristics.

- It is a continuous distribution.
- It is a symmetrical distribution about its mean.
- It is asymptotic to the horizontal axis.
- It is unimodal.
- It is a family of curves.
- Area under the curve is 1.

The normal distribution is symmetrical. Each half of the distribution is a mirror image of the other half. Many normal distribution tables contain probability values for only one side of the distribution because probability values for the other side of the distribution are identical because of symmetry.

In theory, the normal distribution is asymptotic to the horizontal axis. That is, it does not touch the *x*-axis, and it goes forever in each direction. The reality is that most applications of the normal curve are experiments that have finite limits of potential outcomes. For example, even though GMAT scores are analyzed by the normal distribution, the range of scores on the GMAT is from 200 to 800.

The normal curve sometimes is referred to as the *bell-shaped curve.* It is unimodal in that values *mound up* in only one portion of the graph—the center of the curve. The normal distribution actually is a family of curves. Every unique value of the mean and every unique value of the standard deviation result in a different normal curve. In addition, *the total area under any normal distribution is 1.* The area under the curve yields the probabilities, so the total of all probabilities for a normal distribution is 1. Because the distribution is symmetric, the area of the distribution on each side of the mean is 0.5.

Probability Density Function of the Normal Distribution

The normal distribution is described or characterized by two parameters: the mean, μ, and the standard deviation, σ. The values of μ and σ produce a normal distribution. The density function of the normal distribution is

$$f(x) = \frac{1}{\sigma\sqrt{2\pi}}e^{-1/2[(x-\mu)/\sigma]^2}$$

where

μ = mean of x
σ = standard deviation of x
π = 3.14159 . . . , and
e = 2.71828. . . .

---

*John A. Ingram and Joseph G. Monks, *Statistics for Business and Economics.* San Diego: Harcourt Brace Jovanovich, 1989.
[†]Roger E. Kirk, *Statistical Issues: A Reader for the Behavioral Sciences.* Monterey, CA: Brooks/Cole, 1972.

FIGURE 6.5

Normal Curves for Three
Different Combinations of
Means and Standard
Deviations

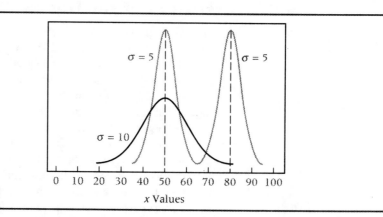

Using Integral Calculus to determine areas under the normal curve from this function is difficult and time-consuming, therefore, virtually all researchers use table values to analyze normal distribution problems rather than this formula.

Standardized Normal Distribution

Every unique pair of μ and σ values defines a different normal distribution. Figure 6.5 shows the Minitab graphs of normal distributions for the following three pairs of parameters.

1. $\mu = 50$ and $\sigma = 5$
2. $\mu = 80$ and $\sigma = 5$
3. $\mu = 50$ and $\sigma = 10$

Note that every change in a parameter (μ or σ) determines a different normal distribution. This characteristic of the normal curve (a family of curves) could make analysis by the normal distribution tedious because volumes of normal curve tables—one for each different combination of μ and σ—would be required. Fortunately, a mechanism was developed by which all normal distributions can be converted into a single distribution: the z distribution. This process yields the **standardized normal distribution** (or curve). The conversion formula for any x value of a given normal distribution follows.

z FORMULA	$$z = \frac{x - \mu}{\sigma}, \qquad \sigma \neq 0$$

A **z score** is *the number of standard deviations that a value, x, is above or below the mean.* If the value of x is less than the mean, the z score is negative; if the value of x is more than the mean, the z score is positive; and if the value of x equals the mean, the associated z score is zero. This formula allows conversion of the distance of any x value from its mean into standard deviation units. A standard z score table can be used to find probabilities for any normal curve problem that has been converted to z scores. The **z distribution** is *a normal distribution with a mean of 0 and a standard deviation of 1.* Any value of x at the mean of a normal curve is zero standard deviations from the mean. Any value of x that is one standard deviation above the mean has a z value of 1. The empirical rule, introduced in Chapter 3, is based on the normal distribution in which about 68% of all values are within one standard deviation of the mean regardless of the values of μ and σ. In a z distribution, about 68% of the z values are between $z = -1$ and $z = +1$.

The z distribution probability values are given in Table A.5. Because it is so frequently used, the z distribution is also printed inside the cover of this text. For discussion purposes, a list of z distribution values is presented in Table 6.2.

Table A.5 gives the total area under the z curve between 0 and any point on the positive z-axis. Since the curve is symmetric, the area under the curve between z and 0 is the same whether z is positive or negative (the sign on the z value designates whether the z score is above or below the mean). The table areas or probabilities are always positive.

TABLE 6.2

z Distribution

SECOND DECIMAL PLACE IN *z*

z	0.00	0.01	0.02	0.03	0.04	0.05	0.06	0.07	0.08	0.09
0.0	.0000	.0040	.0080	.0120	.0160	.0199	.0239	.0279	.0319	.0359
0.1	.0398	.0438	.0478	.0517	.0557	.0596	.0636	.0675	.0714	.0753
0.2	.0793	.0832	.0871	.0910	.0948	.0987	.1026	.1064	.1103	.1141
0.3	.1179	.1217	.1255	.1293	.1331	.1368	.1406	.1443	.1480	.1517
0.4	.1554	.1591	.1628	.1664	.1700	.1736	.1772	.1808	.1844	.1879
0.5	.1915	.1950	.1985	.2019	.2054	.2088	.2123	.2157	.2190	.2224
0.6	.2257	.2291	.2324	.2357	.2389	.2422	.2454	.2486	.2517	.2549
0.7	.2580	.2611	.2642	.2673	.2704	.2734	.2764	.2794	.2823	.2852
0.8	.2881	.2910	.2939	.2967	.2995	.3023	.3051	.3078	.3106	.3133
0.9	.3159	.3186	.3212	.3238	.3264	.3289	.3315	.3340	.3365	.3389
1.0	.3413	.3438	.3461	.3485	.3508	.3531	.3554	.3577	.3599	.3621
1.1	.3643	.3665	.3686	.3708	.3729	.3749	.3770	.3790	.3810	.3830
1.2	.3849	.3869	.3888	.3907	.3925	.3944	.3962	.3980	.3997	.4015
1.3	.4032	.4049	.4066	.4082	.4099	.4115	.4131	.4147	.4162	.4177
1.4	.4192	.4207	.4222	.4236	.4251	.4265	.4279	.4292	.4306	.4319
1.5	.4332	.4345	.4357	.4370	.4382	.4394	.4406	.4418	.4429	.4441
1.6	.4452	.4463	.4474	.4484	.4495	.4505	.4515	.4525	.4535	.4545
1.7	.4554	.4564	.4573	.4582	.4591	.4599	.4608	.4616	.4625	.4633
1.8	.4641	.4649	.4656	.4664	.4671	.4678	.4686	.4693	.4699	.4706
1.9	.4713	.4719	.4726	.4732	.4738	.4744	.4750	.4756	.4761	.4767
2.0	.4772	.4778	.4783	.4788	.4793	.4798	.4803	.4808	.4812	.4817
2.1	.4821	.4826	.4830	.4834	.4838	.4842	.4846	.4850	.4854	.4857
2.2	.4861	.4864	.4868	.4871	.4875	.4878	.4881	.4884	.4887	.4890
2.3	.4893	.4896	.4898	.4901	.4904	.4906	.4909	.4911	.4913	.4916
2.4	.4918	.4920	.4922	.4925	.4927	.4929	.4931	.4932	.4934	.4936
2.5	.4938	.4940	.4941	.4943	.4945	.4946	.4948	.4949	.4951	.4952
2.6	.4953	.4955	.4956	.4957	.4959	.4960	.4961	.4962	.4963	.4964
2.7	.4965	.4966	.4967	.4968	.4969	.4970	.4971	.4972	.4973	.4974
2.8	.4974	.4975	.4976	.4977	.4977	.4978	.4979	.4979	.4980	.4981
2.9	.4981	.4982	.4982	.4983	.4984	.4984	.4985	.4985	.4986	.4986
3.0	.4987	.4987	.4987	.4988	.4988	.4989	.4989	.4989	.4990	.4990
3.1	.4990	.4991	.4991	.4991	.4992	.4992	.4992	.4992	.4993	.4993
3.2	.4993	.4993	.4994	.4994	.4994	.4994	.4994	.4995	.4995	.4995
3.3	.4995	.4995	.4995	.4996	.4996	.4996	.4996	.4996	.4996	.4997
3.4	.4997	.4997	.4997	.4997	.4997	.4997	.4997	.4997	.4997	.4998
3.5	.4998									
4.0	.49997									
4.5	.499997									
5.0	.4999997									
6.0	.499999999									

FIGURE 6.6

Graphical Depiction of the Area Between a Score of 660 and a Mean on a GMAT

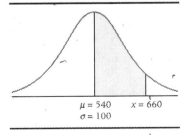

$\mu = 540$ $x = 660$
$\sigma = 100$

Solving Normal Curve Problems

The mean and standard deviation of a normal distribution and the *z* formula and table enable a researcher to determine the probabilities for intervals of any particular values of a normal curve. One example is the many possible probability values of GMAT scores examined next.

The Graduate Management Aptitude Test (GMAT), produced by the Princeton Review in Princeton, New Jersey, is widely used by graduate schools of business in the United States

FIGURE 6.7

Graphical Solutions to the
GMAT Problem

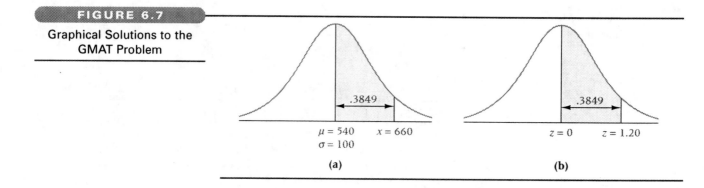

as an entrance requirement. Assuming that the scores are normally distributed, probabilities of achieving scores over various ranges of the GMAT can be determined. In a recent year, the mean GMAT score was 540 and the standard deviation was about 100. What is the probability that a randomly selected score from this administration of the GMAT is between 660 and the mean? That is,

$$P(540 \leq x \leq 660 \,|\, \mu = 540 \text{ and } \sigma = 100) = ?$$

Figure 6.6 is a graphical representation of this problem.

The z formula yields the number of standard deviations that the x value, 660, is away from the mean.

$$z = \frac{x - \mu}{\sigma} = \frac{660 - 540}{100} = \frac{120}{100} = 1.20$$

The z value of 1.20 reveals that the GMAT score of 660 is 1.2 standard deviations more than the mean. The z distribution values in Table 6.2 give the probability of a value being between this value of x and the mean. The whole-number and tenths-place portion of the z score appear in the first column of Table 6.2 (the 1.0 portion of this z score). Across the top of the table are the values of the hundredths-place portion of the z score. For this z score, the hundredths-place value is 0. The probability value in Table 6.2 for $z = 1.20$ is .3849. The shaded portion of the curve at the top of the table indicates that the probability value given *always* is the probability or area between an x value and the mean. In this particular example, that is the desired area. Thus the answer is that .3849 of the scores on the GMAT are between a score of 660 and the mean of 540. Figure 6.7(a) depicts graphically the solution in terms of x values. Figure 6.7(b) shows the solution in terms of z values.

**DEMONSTRATION
PROBLEM 6.3**

What is the probability of obtaining a score greater than 750 on a GMAT test that has a mean of 540 and a standard deviation of 100? Assume GMAT scores are normally distributed.

$$P(x > 750 \,|\, \mu = 540 \text{ and } \sigma = 100) = ?$$

Solution

Examine the following diagram.

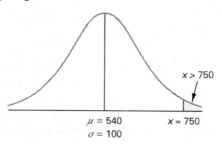

This problem calls for determining the area of the upper tail of the distribution. The z score for this problem is

$$z = \frac{x - \mu}{\sigma} = \frac{750 - 540}{100} = \frac{210}{100} = 2.10$$

Table 6.2 gives a probability of .4821 for this z score. This value is the probability of randomly drawing a GMAT with a score between the mean and 750. Finding the probability of getting a score greater than 750, which is the tail of the distribution, requires subtracting the probability value of .4821 from .5000, because each half of the distribution contains .5000 of the area. The result is .0179. Note that an attempt to determine the area of $x \geq 750$ instead of $x > 750$ would have made no difference because, in continuous distributions, the area under an exact number such as $x = 750$ is zero. A line segment has no width and hence no area.

$$
\begin{array}{ll}
.5000 & \text{(probability of } x \text{ greater than the mean)} \\
-.4821 & \text{(probability of } x \text{ between 750 and the mean)} \\
\hline
.0179 & \text{(probability of } x \text{ greater than 750)}
\end{array}
$$

The solution is depicted graphically in (a) for x values and in (b) for z values.

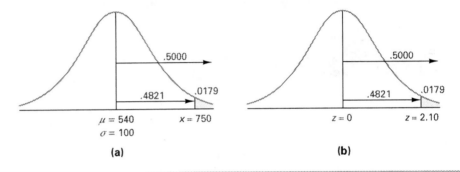

(a)　　　　　　　　　　　**(b)**

DEMONSTRATION PROBLEM 6.4

For the same GMAT examination, what is the probability of randomly drawing a score that is 590 or less?

$$P(x \leq 590 \mid \mu = 540 \text{ and } \sigma = 100) = ?$$

Solution

A sketch of this problem is shown here. Determine the area under the curve for all values less than or equal to 590.

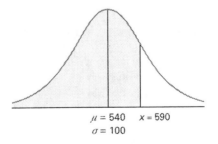

The z value for the area between 590 and the mean is equal to:

$$z = \frac{x - \mu}{\sigma} = \frac{590 - 540}{100} = \frac{50}{100} = 0.50$$

The area under the curve for $z = 0.50$ is .1915, which is the probability of getting a score between 590 and the mean. However, obtaining the probability for all values less than or equal to 590 also requires including the values less than the mean.

Because one-half or .5000 of the values are less than the mean, the probability of $x \leq 590$ is found as follows.

.5000	(probability of values less than the mean)
+.1915	(probability of values between 590 and the mean)
.6915	(probability of values ≤590)

This solution is depicted graphically in (a) for x values and in (b) for z values.

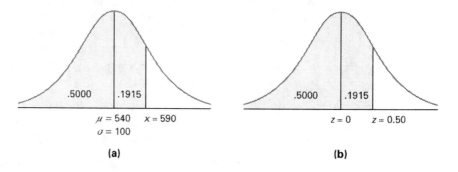

(a)   (b)

DEMONSTRATION PROBLEM 6.5

What is the probability of randomly obtaining a score between 350 and 630 on the GMAT exam?

$$P(350 < x < 630 \,|\, \mu = 540 \text{ and } \sigma = 100) = ?$$

Solution

The following sketch depicts the problem graphically: determine the area between $x = 350$ and $x = 630$, which spans the mean value. Because areas in the z distribution are given in relation to the mean, this problem must be worked as two separate problems and the results combined.

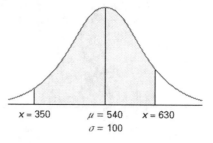

A z score is determined for each x value.

$$z = \frac{x - \mu}{\sigma} = \frac{630 - 540}{100} = \frac{90}{100} = 0.90$$

and

$$z = \frac{x - \mu}{\sigma} = \frac{350 - 540}{100} = \frac{-190}{100} = -1.90$$

Note that this z value ($z = -1.90$) is negative. A negative z value indicates that the x value is below the mean and the z value is on the left side of the distribution. None of the z values in Table 6.2 is negative. However, because the normal distribution is symmetric, probabilities for z values on the left side of the distribution are the same as the values on the right side of the distribution. The negative sign in the z value merely indicates that the area is on the left side of the distribution. The probability is always positive.

The probability for $z = 0.90$ is .3159; the probability for $z = -1.90$ is .4713. The solution of $P(350 < x < 630)$ is obtained by summing the probabilities.

.3159   (probability of a value between the mean and 630)
+.4713   (probability of a value between the mean and 350)
.7872   (probability of a value between 350 and 630)

Graphically, the solution is shown in (a) for x values and in (b) for z values.

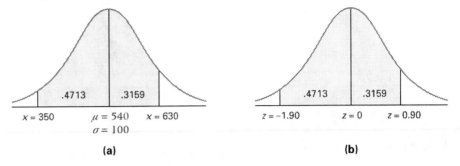

(a)   (b)

DEMONSTRATION PROBLEM 6.6

What is the probability of getting a score between 400 and 500 on the same GMAT exam?

$$P(400 < x < 500 \mid \mu = 540 \text{ and } \sigma = 100) = ?$$

Solution

The following sketch reveals that the solution to the problem involves determining the area of the shaded slice in the lower half of the curve.

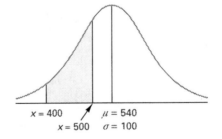

In this problem, the two x values are on the same side of the mean. The areas or probabilities of each x value must be determined and the final probability found by determining the difference between the two areas.

$$z = \frac{x - \mu}{\sigma} = \frac{400 - 540}{100} = \frac{-140}{100} = -1.40$$

and

$$z = \frac{x - \mu}{\sigma} = \frac{500 - 540}{100} = \frac{-40}{100} = -0.40$$

The probability associated with $z = -1.40$ is .4192.
The probability associated with $z = -0.40$ is .1554.

Subtracting gives the solution.

.4192   (probability of a value between 400 and the mean)
−.1554   (probability of a value between 500 and the mean)
.2638   (probability of a value between 400 and 500)

Graphically, the solution is shown in (a) for x values and in (b) for z values.

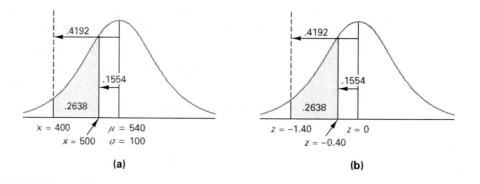

.4192 .1554 .2638

$x = 400$ $\mu = 540$
$x = 500$ $\sigma = 100$

(a)

.4192 .1554 .2638

$z = -1.40$ $z = 0$
$z = -0.40$

(b)

DEMONSTRATION PROBLEM 6.7

Runzheimer International publishes business travel costs for various cities throughout the world. In particular, they publish per diem totals, which represent the average costs for the typical business traveler including three meals a day in business-class restaurants and single-rate lodging in business-class hotels and motels. If 86.65% of the per diem costs in Buenos Aires, Argentina, are less than $449 and if the standard deviation of per diem costs is $36, what is the average per diem cost in Buenos Aires? Assume that per diem costs are normally distributed.

Solution

In this problem, the standard deviation and an x value are given; the object is to determine the value of the mean. Examination of the z score formula reveals four variables: x, μ, σ, and z. In this problem, only two of the four variables are given. Because solving one equation with two unknowns is impossible, one of the other unknowns must be determined. The value of z can be determined from the normal distribution table (Table 6.2).

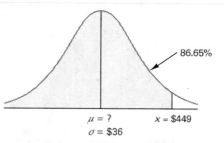

86.65%

$\mu = ?$ $x = \$449$
$\sigma = \$36$

Because 86.65% of the values are less than $x = \$449$, 36.65% of the per diem costs are between $449 and the mean. The other 50% of the per diem costs are in the lower half of the distribution. Converting the percentage to a proportion yields .3665 of the values between the x value and the mean. What z value is associated with this area? This area, or probability, of .3665 in Table 6.2 is associated with the z value of 1.11. This z value is positive, because it is in the upper half of the distribution. Using the z value of 1.11, the x value of $449, and the σ value of $36 allows solving for the mean algebraically.

$$z = \frac{x - \mu}{\sigma}$$

$$1.11 = \frac{\$449 - \mu}{\$36}$$

and

$$\mu = \$449 - (\$36)(1.11) = \$449 - \$39.96 = \$409.04$$

The mean per diem cost for business travel in Buenos Aires is $409.04.

DEMONSTRATION PROBLEM 6.8

The U.S. Environmental Protection Agency publishes figures on solid waste generation in the United States. One year, the average number of waste generated per person per day was 3.58 pounds. Suppose the daily amount of waste generated per person is normally distributed, with a standard deviation of 1.04 pounds. Of the daily amounts of waste generated per person, 67.72% would be greater than what amount?

Solution

The mean and standard deviation are given, but x and z are unknown. The problem is to solve for a specific x value when .6772 of the x values are greater than that value.

If .6772 of the values are greater than x, then .1772 are between x and the mean (.6772 − .5000). Table 6.2 shows that the probability of .1772 is associated with a z value of 0.46. Because x is less than the mean, the z value actually is − 0.46. Whenever an x value is less than the mean, its associated z value is negative and should be reported that way.

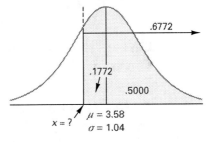

Solving the z equation yields

$$z = \frac{x - \mu}{\sigma}$$

$$-0.46 = \frac{x - 3.58}{1.04}$$

and

$$x = 3.58 + (-0.46)(1.04) = 3.10$$

Thus 67.72% of the daily average amount of solid waste per person weighs more than 3.10 pounds.

THINKING CRITICALLY ABOUT STATISTICS IN BUSINESS TODAY

Warehousing

Tompkins Associates conducted a national study of warehousing in the United States. The study revealed many interesting facts. Warehousing is a labor-intensive industry that presents considerable opportunity for improvement in productivity. What does the "average" warehouse look like? The construction of new warehouses is restricted by prohibitive expense. Perhaps for that reason, the average age of a warehouse is 19 years. Warehouses vary in size, but the average size is about 50,000 square feet. To visualize such an "average" warehouse, picture one that is square with about 224 feet on each side or a rectangle that is 500 feet by 100 feet. The average clear height of a warehouse in the United States is 22 feet.

Suppose the ages of warehouses, the sizes of warehouses, and the clear heights of warehouses are normally distributed. Using the mean values already given and the

standard deviations, techniques presented in this section could be used to determine, for example, the probability that a randomly selected warehouse is less than 15 years old, is larger than 60,000 square feet, or has a clear height between 20 and 25 feet.

Things to Ponder

1. The feature states that "Warehousing is a labor-intensive industry that presents considerable opportunity for improvement in productivity." How might there be opportunities for improvement in productivity of warehousing?

2. What are some reasons why new warehouses might be prohibitively expensive?

3. With current technology, what are some ways that warehousing may be changing?

TABLE 6.3	
Excel and Minitab Normal Distribution Output for Demonstration Problem 6.6	

Excel Output

x Value	probability
500	0.344578
400	0.080757
400 < x < 500	**0.263821**

Minitab Output

CUMULATIVE DISTRIBUTION FUNCTION

Normal with mean = 540 and standard deviation = 100

x	P(X <= x)
500	0.344578
400	0.080757

Prob (400 < x < 500) = .263821

Using the Computer to Solve for Normal Distribution Probabilities

Both Excel and Minitab can be used to solve for normal distribution probabilities. In each case, the computer package uses μ, σ, and the value of x to compute a cumulative probability from the left. Shown in Table 6.3 are Excel and Minitab output for the probability question addressed in Demonstration Problem 6.6: $P(400 < x < 500 \mid \mu = 540$ and $\sigma = 100)$. Since both computer packages yield probabilities cumulated from the left, this problem is solved manually with the computer output by finding the difference in $P(x < 500)$ and $P(x < 400)$.

6.2 PROBLEMS

6.6 Determine the probabilities for the following normal distribution problems.
   a. $\mu = 604$, $\sigma = 56.8$, $x \leq 635$
   b. $\mu = 48$, $\sigma = 12$, $x < 20$
   c. $\mu = 111$, $\sigma = 33.8$, $100 \leq x < 150$
   d. $\mu = 264$, $\sigma = 10.9$, $250 < x < 255$
   e. $\mu = 37$, $\sigma = 4.35$, $x > 35$
   f. $\mu = 156$, $\sigma = 11.4$, $x \geq 170$

6.7 Tompkins Associates reports that the mean clear height for a Class A warehouse in the United States is 22 feet. Suppose clear heights are normally distributed and that the standard deviation is 4 feet. A Class A warehouse in the United States is randomly selected.
   a. What is the probability that the clear height is greater than 17 feet?
   b. What is the probability that the clear height is less than 13 feet?
   c. What is the probability that the clear height is between 25 and 31 feet?

6.8 According to a report by Scarborough Research, the average monthly household cellular phone bill is $73. Suppose local monthly household cell phone bills are normally distributed with a standard deviation of $11.35.
   a. What is the probability that a randomly selected monthly cell phone bill is more than $100?
   b. What is the probability that a randomly selected monthly cell phone bill is between $60 and $83?
   c. What is the probability that a randomly selected monthly cell phone bill is between $80 and $90?
   d. What is the probability that a randomly selected monthly cell phone bill is no more than $55?

6.9 According to the Internal Revenue Service, income tax returns one year averaged $1,332 in refunds for taxpayers. One explanation of this figure is that taxpayers would rather have the government keep back too much money during the year than to owe it money at the end of the year. Suppose the average amount of tax at the end of a year is a refund of $1,332, with a standard deviation of $725. Assume that amounts owed or due on tax returns are normally distributed.

   a. What proportion of tax returns show a refund greater than $2,000?

   b. What proportion of the tax returns show that the taxpayer owes money to the government?

   c. What proportion of the tax returns show a refund between $100 and $700?

6.10 Toolworkers are subject to work-related injuries. One disorder, caused by strains to the hands and wrists, is called carpal tunnel syndrome. It strikes as many as 23,000 workers per year. The U.S. Labor Department estimates that the average cost of this disorder to employers and insurers is approximately $30,000 per injured worker. Suppose these costs are normally distributed, with a standard deviation of $9,000.

   a. What proportion of the costs are between $15,000 and $45,000?

   b. What proportion of the costs are greater than $50,000?

   c. What proportion of the costs are between $5,000 and $20,000?

   d. Suppose the standard deviation is unknown, but 90.82% of the costs are more than $7,000. What would be the value of the standard deviation?

   e. Suppose the mean value is unknown, but the standard deviation is still $9,000. How much would the average cost be if 79.95% of the costs were less than $33,000?

6.11 Suppose you are working with a data set that is normally distributed, with a mean of 200 and a standard deviation of 47. Determine the value of x from the following information.

   a. 60% of the values are greater than x.

   b. x is less than 17% of the values.

   c. 22% of the values are less than x.

   d. x is greater than 55% of the values.

6.12 Suppose the annual employer 401(k) cost per participant is normally distributed with a standard deviation of $625, but the mean is unknown.

   a. If 73.89% of such costs are greater than $1,700, what is the mean annual employer 401(k) cost per participant?

   b. Suppose the mean annual employer 401(k) cost per participant is $2,258 and the standard deviation is $625. If such costs are normally distributed, 31.56% of the costs are greater than what value?

6.13 Based on annual driving of 15,000 miles and fuel efficiency of 20 mpg, a car in the United States uses, on average, 750 gallons of gasoline per year. If annual automobile fuel usage is normally distributed, and if 29.12% of cars in the United States use less than 500 gallons of gasoline per year, what is the standard deviation?

6.14 The U.S. national average door-to-doctor wait time for patients to see a doctor is now 21.3 minutes. Suppose such wait times are normally distributed with a standard deviation of 6.7 minutes. Some patients will have to wait much longer than the mean to see the doctor. In fact, based on this information, 3% of patients still have to wait more than how many minutes to see a doctor?

6.15 Suppose commute times in a large city are normally distributed and that 62.5% of commuters in this city take more than 21 minutes to commute one-way. If the standard deviation of such commutes is 6.2 minutes, what is the mean commute?

6.16 According to Student Monitor, a New Jersey research firm, the average cumulated college student loan debt for a graduating senior is $25,760. Assume that the standard deviation of such student loan debt is $5,684. Thirty percent of these graduating seniors owe more than what amount?

6.3 USING THE NORMAL CURVE TO APPROXIMATE BINOMIAL DISTRIBUTION PROBLEMS

Interactive Applet

For certain types of binomial distribution problems, the normal distribution can be used to approximate the probabilities. As sample sizes become large, binomial distributions approach the normal distribution in shape regardless of the value of p. This phenomenon occurs faster (for smaller values of n) when p is near .50. Figures 6.8 through 6.10 show three binomial distributions. Note in Figure 6.8 that even though the sample size, n, is only 10, the binomial graph bears a strong resemblance to a normal curve.

The graph in Figure 6.9 ($n = 10$ and $p = .20$) is skewed to the right because of the low p value and the small size. For this distribution, the expected value is only 2 and the probabilities pile up at $x = 0$ and 1. However, when n becomes large enough, as in the binomial distribution ($n = 100$ and $p = .20$) presented in Figure 6.10, the graph is relatively symmetric around the mean ($\mu = n \cdot p = 20$) because enough possible outcome values to the left of $x = 20$ allow the curve to fall back to the x-axis.

For large n values, the binomial distribution is cumbersome to analyze without a computer. Table A.2 goes only to $n = 25$. The normal distribution is a good approximation for binomial distribution problems for large values of n.

To work a binomial problem by the normal curve requires a translation process. The first part of this process is to convert the two parameters of a binomial distribution, n and p, to the two parameters of the normal distribution, μ and σ. This process utilizes formulas from Chapter 5:

$$\mu = n \cdot p \text{ and } \sigma = \sqrt{n \cdot p \cdot q}$$

After completion of this, a test must be made to determine whether the normal distribution is a good enough approximation of the binomial distribution:

Does the interval $\mu \pm 3\sigma$ lie between 0 and n?

Recall that the empirical rule states that approximately 99.7%, or almost all, of the values of a normal curve are within three standard deviations of the mean. For a normal curve approximation of a binomial distribution problem to be acceptable, all possible x values should be between 0 and n, which are the lower and upper limits, respectively, of a binomial distribution. If $\mu \pm 3\sigma$ is not between 0 and n, do *not* use the normal distribution to work a binomial problem because the approximation is not good enough. Upon demonstration that the normal curve is a good approximation for a binomial problem, the procedure continues. Another rule of thumb for determining when to use the normal curve to approximate a binomial problem is that the approximation is good enough if both $n \cdot p > 5$ and $n \cdot q > 5$.

The process can be illustrated in the solution of the binomial distribution problem.

$$P(x \geq 25 \mid n = 60 \text{ and } p = .30) = ?$$

Note that this binomial problem contains a relatively large sample size and that none of the binomial tables in Appendix A.2 can be used to solve the problem. This problem is a good candidate for use of the normal distribution.

Translating from a binomial problem to a normal curve problem gives

$$\mu = n \cdot p = (60)(.30) = 18 \text{ and } \sigma = \sqrt{n \cdot p \cdot q} = 3.55$$

The binomial problem becomes a normal curve problem.

$$P(x \geq 25 \mid \mu = 18 \text{ and } \sigma = 3.55) = ?$$

Next, the test is made to determine whether the normal curve sufficiently fits this binomial distribution to justify the use of the normal curve.

$$\mu \pm 3\sigma = 18 \pm 3(3.55) = 18 \pm 10.65$$

$$7.35 \leq \mu \pm 3\sigma \leq 28.65$$

This interval is between 0 and 60, so the approximation is sufficient to allow use of the normal curve. Figure 6.11 is a Minitab graph of this binomial distribution. Notice how

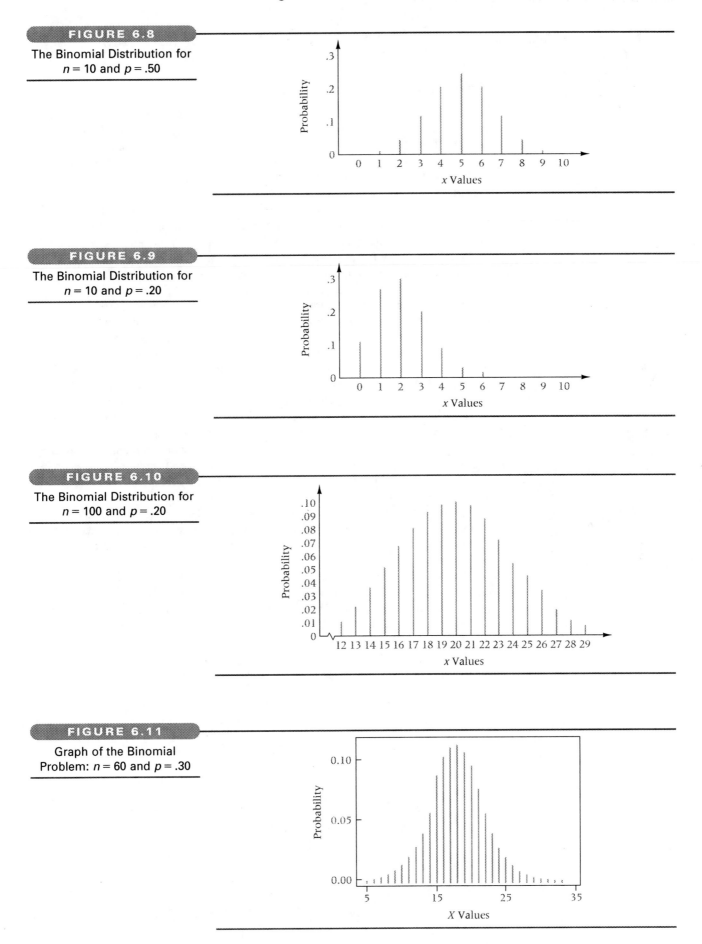

FIGURE 6.8

The Binomial Distribution for $n = 10$ and $p = .50$

FIGURE 6.9

The Binomial Distribution for $n = 10$ and $p = .20$

FIGURE 6.10

The Binomial Distribution for $n = 100$ and $p = .20$

FIGURE 6.11

Graph of the Binomial Problem: $n = 60$ and $p = .30$

FIGURE 6.12

Graph of Apparent Solution of Binomial Problem Worked by the Normal Curve

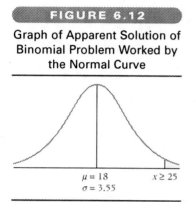

TABLE 6.4

Rules of Thumb for the Correction for Continuity

Values Being Determined	Corrections
$x >$	$+.50$
$x \geq$	$-.50$
$x <$	$-.50$
$x \leq$	$+.50$
$\leq x \leq$	$-.50$ and $+.50$
$< x <$	$+.50$ and $-.50$
$x =$	$-.50$ and $+.50$

closely it resembles the normal curve. Figure 6.12 is the apparent graph of the normal curve version of this problem.

Correcting for Continuity

The translation of a discrete distribution to a continuous distribution is not completely straightforward. A correction of $+.50$ or $-.50$ or $\pm.50$, depending on the problem, is required. This correction ensures that most of the binomial problem's information is correctly transferred to the normal curve analysis. This correction is called the **correction for continuity**, which is *made during conversion of a discrete distribution into a continuous distribution.*

Figure 6.13 is a portion of the graph of the binomial distribution, $n = 60$ and $p = .30$. Note that with a binomial distribution, all the probabilities are concentrated on the whole numbers. Thus, the answers for $x \geq 25$ are found by summing the probabilities for $x = 25$, 26, 27, . . . , 60. There are no values between 24 and 25, 25 and 26, . . . , 59, and 60. Yet, the normal distribution is continuous, and values are present all along the x-axis. A correction must be made for this discrepancy for the approximation to be as accurate as possible.

As an analogy, visualize the process of melting iron rods in a furnace. The iron rods are like the probability values on each whole number of a binomial distribution. Note that the binomial graph in Figure 6.13 looks like a series of iron rods in a line. When the rods are placed in a furnace, they melt down and spread out. Each rod melts and moves to fill the area between it and the adjacent rods. The result is a continuous sheet of solid iron (continuous iron) that looks like the normal curve. The melting of the rods is analogous to spreading the binomial distribution to approximate the normal distribution.

How far does each rod spread toward the others? A good estimate is that each rod goes about halfway toward the adjacent rods. In other words, a rod that was concentrated at $x = 25$ spreads to cover the area from 24.5 to 25.5; $x = 26$ becomes continuous from 25.5 to 26.5; and so on. For the problem $P(x \geq 25 \mid n = 60$ and $p = .30)$, conversion to a continuous normal curve problem yields $P(x \geq 24.5 \mid \mu = 18$ and $\sigma = 3.55)$. The correction for continuity was $-.50$ because the problem called for the inclusion of the value of 25 along with all greater values; the binomial value of $x = 25$ translates to the normal curve value of 24.5 to 25.5. Had the binomial problem been to analyze $P(x > 25)$, the correction would have been $+.50$, resulting in a normal curve problem of $P(x \geq 25.5)$. The latter case would begin at more than 25 because the value of 25 would not be included.

The decision as to how to correct for continuity depends on the equality sign and the direction of the desired outcomes of the binomial distribution. Table 6.4 lists some rules of thumb that can help in the application of the correction for continuity.

For the binomial problem $P(x \geq 25 \mid n = 60$ and $p = .30)$, the normal curve becomes $P(x \geq 24.5 \mid \mu = 18$ and $\sigma = 3.55)$, as shown in Figure 6.14, and

$$z = \frac{x - \mu}{\sigma} = \frac{24.5 - 18}{3.55} = 1.83$$

FIGURE 6.13

Graph of a Portion of the Binomial Problem: $n = 60$ and $p = .30$

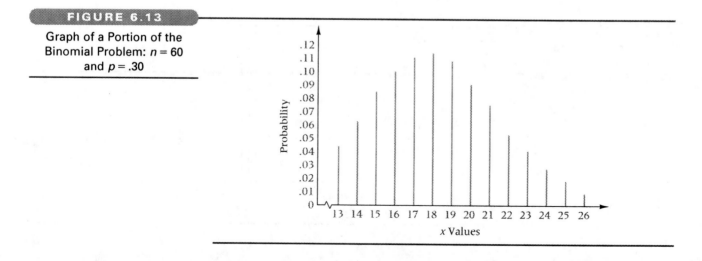

TABLE 6.5

Probability Values for the
Binomial Problem: $n = 60$,
$p = .30$, and $x \geq 25$

x Value	Probability
25	.0167
26	.0096
27	.0052
28	.0026
29	.0012
30	.0005
31	.0002
32	.0001
33	.0000
$x \geq 25$	.0361

FIGURE 6.14

Graph of the Solution to the
Binomial Problem Worked by
the Normal Curve

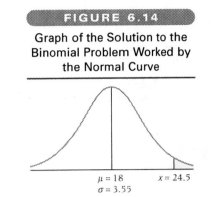

The probability (Table 6.2) of this z value is .4664. The answer to this problem lies in the tail of the distribution, so the final answer is obtained by subtracting.

$$\begin{array}{r} .5000 \\ -.4664 \\ \hline .0336 \end{array}$$

Had this problem been worked by using the binomial formula, the solution would have been as shown in Table 6.5. The difference between the normal distribution approximation and the actual binomial values is only .0025 (.0361 − .0336).

DEMONSTRATION PROBLEM 6.9

Work the following binomial distribution problem by using the normal distribution.

$$P(x = 12 \mid n = 25 \text{ and } p = .40) = ?$$

Solution

Find μ and σ.

$$\mu = n \cdot p = (25)(.40) = 10.0$$
$$\sigma = \sqrt{n \cdot p \cdot q} = \sqrt{(25)(.40)(.60)} = 2.45$$
$$\text{test: } \mu \pm 3\sigma = 10.0 \pm 3(2.45) = 2.65 \text{ to } 17.35$$

This range is between 0 and 25, so the approximation is close enough. Correct for continuity next. Because the problem is to determine the probability of x being exactly 12, the correction entails both −.50 and +.50. That is, a binomial probability at $x = 12$ translates to a continuous normal curve area that lies between 11.5 and 12.5. The graph of the problem follows:

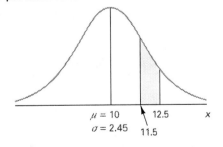

Then,

$$z = \frac{x - \mu}{\sigma} = \frac{12.5 - 10}{2.45} = 1.02$$

and

$$z = \frac{x - \mu}{\sigma} = \frac{11.5 - 10}{2.45} = 0.61$$

$z = 1.02$ produces a probability of .3461.
$z = 0.61$ produces a probability of .2291.

The difference in areas yields the following answer:

$$.3461 - .2291 = .1170$$

Had this problem been worked by using the binomial tables, the resulting answer would have been .114. The difference between the normal curve approximation and the value obtained by using binomial tables is only .003.

DEMONSTRATION PROBLEM 6.10

Solve the following binomial distribution problem by using the normal distribution.

$$P(x < 27 \mid n = 100 \text{ and } p = .37) = ?$$

Solution

Because neither the sample size nor the p value is contained in Table A.2, working this problem by using binomial distribution techniques is impractical. It is a good candidate for the normal curve. Calculating μ and σ yields

$$\mu = n \cdot p = (100)(.37) = 37.0$$
$$\sigma = \sqrt{n \cdot p \cdot q} = \sqrt{(100)(.37)(.63)} = 4.83$$

Testing to determine the closeness of the approximation gives

$$\mu \pm 3\sigma = 37 \pm 3(4.83) = 37 \pm 14.49$$

The range 22.51 to 51.49 is between 0 and 100. This problem satisfies the conditions of the test. Next, correct for continuity: $x < 27$ as a binomial problem translates to $x \le 26.5$ as a normal distribution problem. The graph of the problem follows.

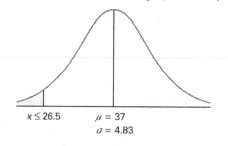

$x \le 26.5$ $\mu = 37$
$\sigma = 4.83$

Then,

$$z = \frac{x - \mu}{\sigma} = \frac{26.5 - 37}{4.83} = -2.17$$

Table 6.2 shows a probability of .4850. Solving for the tail of the distribution gives

$$.5000 - .4850 = .0150$$

which is the answer.

Had this problem been solved by using the binomial formula, the probabilities would have been the following.

x Value	Probability
26	.0059
25	.0035
24	.0019
23	.0010
22	.0005
21	.0002
20	.0001
$x < 27$	.0131

The answer obtained by using the normal curve approximation (.0150) compares favorably to this exact binomial answer. The difference is only .0019.

THINKING CRITICALLY ABOUT STATISTICS IN BUSINESS TODAY

Teleworking Facts

There are many interesting statistics about teleworkers. In a recent year, there were 45 million teleworkers in the United States, and more than 18% of employed adult Americans telework from home during business hours at least one day per month. Fifty-seven percent of HR professionals indicate that their organizations offer some form of telecommuting. The typical teleworker works an average of 5.5 days at home per month. The average commuting distance of a teleworker when he/she is not teleworking is 18 miles. Teleworkers save an average of 53 minutes commuting each day, saving them the equivalent of one extra day of work for every nine days of commuting. Thirty-three percent of Canadians would prefer to telework over a 10% wage increase, and 43% would change jobs to an employer allowing telework. Sixty-five percent of home teleworkers are males versus 44% of non-teleworkers. Among 20 United States, government agencies,

the average per-user cost of setting up telecommuting is $1,920. Telecommuting saves 840 million gallons of fuel annually in the United States, and telecommuting saves the equivalent of 9 to 14 billion kilowatt-hours of electricity per year—the same amount of energy used by roughly 1 million United States households every year.

Things to Ponder

1. What are some of the impacts of telecommuting on the company, the worker, and the product or service? That is, what are some of the pros and cons of telecommuting on the various constituencies?

2. What are some aspects of our culture that have facilitated the advent of telecommuting?

Source: Telecommuting and Remote Work Statistics site, http://www.suitecommute.com/Statistics.htm; and Telework Facts, http://www.telcoa.org/id33_m.htm.

6.3 PROBLEMS

6.17 Convert the following binomial distribution problems to normal distribution problems. Use the correction for continuity.
  a. $P(x \leq 16 \mid n = 30$ and $p = .70)$
  b. $P(10 < x \leq 20) \mid n = 25$ and $p = .50)$
  c. $P(x = 22 \mid n = 40$ and $p = .60)$
  d. $P(x > 14 \mid n = 16$ and $p = .45)$

6.18 Use the test $\mu \pm 3\sigma$ to determine whether the following binomial distributions can be approximated by using the normal distribution.
  a. $n = 8$ and $p = .50$
  b. $n = 18$ and $p = .80$
  c. $n = 12$ and $p = .30$
  d. $n = 30$ and $p = .75$
  e. $n = 14$ and $p = .50$

6.19 Where appropriate, work the following binomial distribution problems by using the normal curve. Also, use Table A.2 to find the answers by using the binomial distribution and compare the answers obtained by the two methods.
  a. $P(x = 8 \mid n = 25$ and $p = .40) = ?$
  b. $P(x \geq 13 \mid n = 20$ and $p = .60) = ?$
  c. $P(x = 7 \mid n = 15$ and $p = .50) = ?$
  d. $P(x < 3 \mid n = 10$ and $p = .70) = ?$

6.20 The Zimmerman Agency conducted a study for Residence Inn by Marriott of business travelers who take trips of five nights or more. According to this study, 37% of these travelers enjoy sightseeing more than any other activity that they do not get to do as much at home. Suppose 120 randomly selected business travelers who take trips of five nights or more are contacted. What is the probability that fewer than 40 enjoy sightseeing more than any other activity that they do not get to do as much at home?

6.21 One study on managers' satisfaction with management tools reveals that 59% of all managers use self-directed work teams as a management tool. Suppose 70 managers selected randomly in the United States are interviewed. What is the probability that fewer than 35 use self-directed work teams as a management tool?

6.22 According to the Yankee Group, 53% of all cable households rate cable companies as good or excellent in quality transmission. Sixty percent of all cable households rate cable companies as good or excellent in having professional personnel. Suppose 300 cable households are randomly contacted.

a. What is the probability that more than 175 cable households rate cable companies as good or excellent in quality transmission?

b. What is the probability that between 165 and 170 (inclusive) cable households rate cable companies as good or excellent in quality transmission?

c. What is the probability that between 155 and 170 (inclusive) cable households rate cable companies as good or excellent in having professional personnel?

d. What is the probability that fewer than 200 cable households rate cable companies as good or excellent in having professional personnel?

6.23 According to ars technica, HP is the leading company in the United States in PC sales with about 27% of the market share. Suppose a business researcher randomly selects 130 recent purchasers of PCs in the United States.

a. What is the probability that more than 39 PC purchasers bought an HP computer?

b. What is the probability that between 28 and 38 PC purchasers (inclusive) bought an HP computer?

c. What is the probability that fewer than 23 PC purchasers bought an HP computer?

d. What is the probability that exactly 33 PC purchasers bought an HP computer?

6.24 A study about strategies for competing in the global marketplace states that 52% of the respondents agreed that companies need to make direct investments in foreign countries. It also states that about 70% of those responding agree that it is attractive to have a joint venture to increase global competitiveness. Suppose CEOs of 95 manufacturing companies are randomly contacted about global strategies.

a. What is the probability that between 44 and 52 (inclusive) CEOs agree that companies should make direct investments in foreign countries?

b. What is the probability that more than 56 CEOs agree with that assertion?

c. What is the probability that fewer than 60 CEOs agree that it is attractive to have a joint venture to increase global competitiveness?

d. What is the probability that between 55 and 62 (inclusive) CEOs agree with that assertion?

6.4 EXPONENTIAL DISTRIBUTION

Another useful continuous distribution is the exponential distribution. It is closely related to the Poisson distribution. Whereas the Poisson distribution is discrete and describes random occurrences over some interval, the **exponential distribution** is *continuous and describes a probability distribution of the times between random occurrences.* The following are the characteristics of the exponential distribution.

- It is a continuous distribution.
- It is a family of distributions.
- It is skewed to the right.
- The *x* values range from zero to infinity.
- Its apex is always at $x = 0$.
- The curve steadily decreases as *x* gets larger.

The exponential probability distribution is determined by the following.

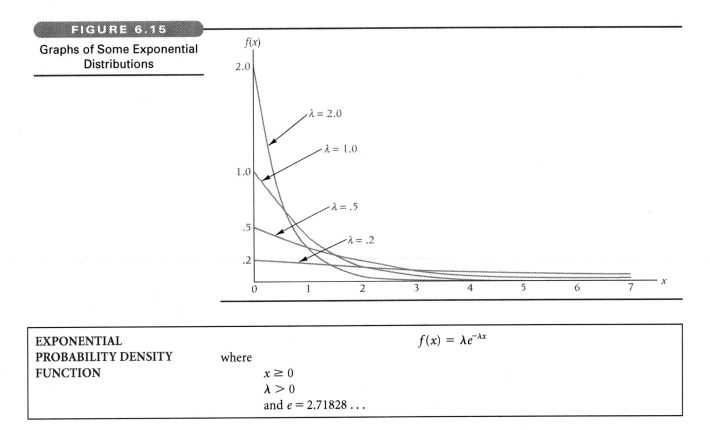

FIGURE 6.15

Graphs of Some Exponential Distributions

EXPONENTIAL PROBABILITY DENSITY FUNCTION	$$f(x) = \lambda e^{-\lambda x}$$

where

$x \geq 0$
$\lambda > 0$
and $e = 2.71828\ldots$

An exponential distribution can be characterized by the one parameter, λ. Each unique value of λ determines a different exponential distribution, resulting in a family of exponential distributions. Figure 6.15 shows graphs of exponential distributions for four values of λ. The points on the graph are determined by using λ and various values of x in the probability density formula. The mean of an exponential distribution is $\mu = 1/\lambda$, and the standard deviation of an exponential distribution is $\sigma = 1/\lambda$.

Probabilities of the Exponential Distribution

Probabilities are computed for the exponential distribution by determining the area under the curve between two points. Applying calculus to the exponential probability density function produces a formula that can be used to calculate the probabilities of an exponential distribution.

PROBABILITIES OF THE RIGHT TAIL OF THE EXPONENTIAL DISTRIBUTION	$$P(x \geq x_0) = e^{-\lambda x_0}$$

where

$x_0 \geq 0$

To use this formula requires finding values of e^{-x}. These values can be computed on most calculators or obtained from Table A.4, which contains the values of e^{-x} for selected values of x. x_0 is the fraction of the interval or the number of intervals between arrivals in the probability question and λ is the average arrival rate.

For example, arrivals at a bank are Poisson distributed with a λ of 1.2 customers every minute. What is the average time between arrivals and what is the probability that at least 2 minutes will elapse between one arrival and the next arrival? Since the interval for lambda is 1 minute and we want to know the probability that at least 2 minutes transpire between arrivals (twice the lambda interval), x_0 is 2.

Interarrival times of random arrivals are exponentially distributed. The mean of this exponential distribution is $\mu = 1/\lambda = 1/1.2 = .833$ minute (50 seconds). On average,

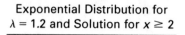

FIGURE 6.16

Exponential Distribution for
$\lambda = 1.2$ and Solution for $x \geq 2$

.833 minute, or 50 seconds, will elapse between arrivals at the bank. The probability of an interval of 2 minutes or more between arrivals can be calculated by

$$P(x \geq 2 \mid \lambda = 1.2) = e^{-1.2(2)} = .0907.$$

About 9.07% of the time when the rate of random arrivals is 1.2 per minute, 2 minutes or more will elapse between arrivals, as shown in Figure 6.16.

This problem underscores the potential of using the exponential distribution in conjunction with the Poisson distribution to solve problems. In operations research and management science, these two distributions are used together to solve queuing problems (theory of waiting lines). The Poisson distribution can be used to analyze the arrivals to the queue, and the exponential distribution can be used to analyze the interarrival time.

DEMONSTRATION PROBLEM 6.11

A manufacturing firm has been involved in statistical quality control for several years. As part of the production process, parts are randomly selected and tested. From the records of these tests, it has been established that a defective part occurs in a pattern that is Poisson distributed on the average of 1.38 defects every 20 minutes during production runs. Use this information to determine the probability that less than 15 minutes will elapse between any two defects.

Solution

The value of λ is 1.38 defects per 20-minute interval. The value of μ can be determined by

$$\mu = \frac{1}{\lambda} = \frac{1}{1.38} = .7246$$

On the average, it is .7246 of the interval, or (.7246)(20 minutes) = 14.49 minutes, between defects. The value of x_0 represents the desired number of intervals between arrivals or occurrences for the probability question. In this problem, the probability question involves 15 minutes and the interval is 20 minutes. Thus x_0 is 15/20, or .75 of an interval. The question here is to determine the probability of there being less than 15 minutes between defects. The probability formula always yields the right tail of the distribution—in this case, the probability of there being 15 minutes or more between arrivals. By using the value of x_0 and the value of λ, the probability of there being 15 minutes or more between defects can be determined.

$$P(x \geq x_0) = P(x \geq .75) = e^{-\lambda x_0} = e^{(-1.38)(.75)} = e^{-1.035} = .3552$$

The probability of .3552 is the probability that at least 15 minutes will elapse between defects. To determine the probability of there being less than 15 minutes between defects, compute $1 - P(x)$. In this case, $1 - .3552 = .6448$. There is a probability of .6448 that less than 15 minutes will elapse between two defects when there is an average of 1.38 defects per 20-minute interval or an average of 14.49 minutes between defects.

TABLE 6.6

Excel and Minitab Output for
Exponential Distribution

Excel Output

x Value	Probability < x Value
0.75	0.6448

Minitab Output

```
CUMULATIVE DISTRIBUTION FUNCTION

Exponential with mean = 0.7246
    x    P(X <= x)
 0.75    0.644793
```

Using the Computer to Determine Exponential Distribution Probabilities

Both Excel and Minitab can be used to solve for exponential distribution probabilities. Excel uses the value of λ and x_0, but Minitab requires μ (equals $1/\lambda$) and x_0. In each case, the computer yields the cumulative probability from the left (the complement of what the probability formula shown in this section yields). Table 6.6 provides Excel and Minitab output for the probability question addressed in Demonstration Problem 6.11.

6.4 PROBLEMS

6.25 Use the probability density formula to sketch the graphs of the following exponential distributions.
   a. $\lambda = 0.1$
   b. $\lambda = 0.3$
   c. $\lambda = 0.8$
   d. $\lambda = 3.0$

6.26 Determine the mean and standard deviation of the following exponential distributions.
   a. $\lambda = 3.25$
   b. $\lambda = 0.7$
   c. $\lambda = 1.1$
   d. $\lambda = 6.0$

6.27 Determine the following exponential probabilities.
   a. $P(x \geq 5 \mid \lambda = 1.35)$
   b. $P(x < 3 \mid \lambda = 0.68)$
   c. $P(x > 4 \mid \lambda = 1.7)$
   d. $P(x < 6 \mid \lambda = 0.80)$

6.28 The average length of time between arrivals at a turnpike tollbooth is 23 seconds. Assume that the time between arrivals at the tollbooth is exponentially distributed.
   a. What is the probability that a minute or more will elapse between arrivals?
   b. If a car has just passed through the tollbooth, what is the probability that no car will show up for at least 3 minutes?

6.29 A busy restaurant determined that between 6:30 P.M. and 9:00 P.M. on Friday nights, the arrivals of customers are Poisson distributed with an average arrival rate of 2.44 per minute.
   a. What is the probability that at least 10 minutes will elapse between arrivals?
   b. What is the probability that at least 5 minutes will elapse between arrivals?
   c. What is the probability that at least 1 minute will elapse between arrivals?
   d. What is the expected amount of time between arrivals?

6.30 During the summer at a small private airport in western Nebraska, the unscheduled arrival of airplanes is Poisson distributed with an average arrival rate of 1.12 planes per hour.

  a. What is the average interarrival time between planes?

  b. What is the probability that at least 2 hours will elapse between plane arrivals?

  c. What is the probability of two planes arriving less than 10 minutes apart?

6.31 The exponential distribution can be used to solve Poisson-type problems in which the intervals are not time. The Air Travel Consumer Report published by the U.S. Department of Transportation reported that in a recent year, Airtran led the nation in fewest occurrences of mishandled baggage, with a mean rate of 1.31 per 1,000 passengers. Assume mishandled baggage occurrences are Poisson distributed. Using the exponential distribution to analyze this problem, determine the average number of passengers between occurrences. Suppose baggage has just been mishandled.

  a. What is the probability that at least 500 passengers will have their baggage handled properly before the next mishandling occurs?

  b. What is the probability that the number will be fewer than 200 passengers?

6.32 The Foundation Corporation specializes in constructing the concrete foundations for new houses in the South. The company knows that because of soil types, moisture conditions, variable construction, and other factors, eventually most foundations will need major repair. On the basis of its records, the company's president believes that a new house foundation on average will not need major repair for 20 years. If she wants to guarantee the company's work against major repair but wants to have to honor no more than 10% of its guarantees, for how many years should the company guarantee its work? Assume that occurrences of major foundation repairs are Poisson distributed.

6.33 During the dry month of August, one U.S. city has measurable rain on average only two days per month. If the arrival of rainy days is Poisson distributed in this city during the month of August, what is the average number of days that will pass between measurable rain? What is the standard deviation? What is the probability during this month that there will be a period of less than two days between rain?

The Cost of Human Resources

The American Society for Training and Development reported that, on average, an employee receives 32 hours of training per year. Suppose that number of hours of training is uniformly distributed across all employees varying from 0 hours to 64 hours. Using techniques presented in Section 6.1, this uniform distribution can be described by $a = 0$, $b = 64$, and $\mu = 32$. The probability that an employee receives between 20 and 40 hours of training can be determined by the following calculation assuming that $x_1 = 20$ and $x_2 = 40$:

$$P(x) = \frac{x_2 - x_1}{b - a} = \frac{40 - 20}{64 - 0} = \frac{20}{64} = .3125$$

Thus, 31.25% of employees receive between 20 and 40 hours of training.

The probability that an employee receives 50 hours or more of training can be calculated as:

$$P(x) = \frac{x_2 - x_1}{b - a} = \frac{64 - 50}{64 - 0} = \frac{14}{64} = .21875$$

Almost 22% of employees receive 50 hours or more of training. Note that here, x_2 is 64 since 64 hours is the upper end of the distribution.

It is estimated by some studies that, on average, it costs $3,270 to hire an employee. If such costs are normally distributed with a standard deviation of $400, the probability that it costs more than $4,000 to hire an employee can be calculated using techniques from Section 6.2 as:

$$z = \frac{x - \mu}{\sigma} = \frac{4000 - 3270}{400} = 1.83$$

The area associated with this z value is .4664 and the tail of the distribution is $.5000 - .4664 = .0336$. That is, 3.36% of the time, it costs more than $4,000 to hire an employee. The probability that it costs less than $3,000 to hire an employee can be determined in a similar manner:

$$z = \frac{x - \mu}{\sigma} = \frac{3000 - 3270}{400} = 0.68$$

The area associated with this z value is .2517 and the tail of the distribution is $.5000 - .2517 = .2483$. That is, 24.83% of the time, it costs less than $3,000 to hire an employee.

Thirty-five percent of all unscheduled absenteeism is caused by personal illness. Using techniques presented in Section 6.3, the probability that more than 50 of 120 randomly selected unscheduled absences were caused by personal illness can be determined. With $n = 120$, $p = .35$ and $x > 50$, this binomial distribution problem can be converted into a normal distribution problem by:

$$\mu = n \cdot p = (120)(.35) = 42$$

and

$$\sigma = \sqrt{n \cdot p \cdot q} = \sqrt{(120)(.35)(.65)} = 5.225$$

Since $42 \pm 3(5.225)$ is between 0 and 120, it is appropriate to use the normal distribution to approximate this binomial problem. Applying the correction for continuity, $x \geq 50.5$. The z value is calculated as:

$$z = \frac{x - \mu}{\sigma} = \frac{50.5 - 42}{5.225} = 1.63$$

The area associated with this z value is .4484 and the tail of the distribution is $.5000 - .4484 = .0516$. That is, 5.16% of the time, more than 50 out of 120 unscheduled absences are due to personal illness.

ETHICAL CONSIDERATIONS

Several points must be considered in working with continuous distributions. Is the population being studied the same population from which the parameters (mean, standard deviation, λ) were determined? If not, the results may not be valid for the analysis being done. Invalid or spurious results can be obtained by using the parameters from one population to analyze another population. For example, a market study in New England may result in the conclusion that the amount of fish eaten per month by adults is normally distributed with the average of 2.3 pounds of fish per month. A market researcher in the Southwest should not assume that these figures apply to her population. People in the Southwest probably have quite different fish-eating habits than people in New England, and the application of New England population parameters to the Southwest probably will result in questionable conclusions.

As was true with the Poisson distribution in Chapter 5, the use of λ in the exponential distribution should be judicious because a λ for one interval in a given time period or situation may not be the same as the λ for the same interval in a different time period or situation. For example, the number of arrivals per five-minute time period at a restaurant on Friday night is not likely to be the same as the number of arrivals in a five-minute time period at that same restaurant from 2 P.M. to 4 P.M. on weekdays. In using established parameters such as μ and λ, a researcher should be certain that the population from which the parameter was determined is, indeed, the same population being studied.

Sometimes a normal distribution is used to analyze data when, in fact, the data are not normal. Such an analysis can contain bias and produce false results. Certain techniques for testing a distribution of data can determine whether they are distributed a certain way. Some of the techniques are presented in Chapter 16. In general, Chapter 6 techniques can be misused if the wrong type of distribution is applied to the data or if the distribution used for analysis is the right one but the parameters (μ, σ, λ) do not fit the data of the population being analyzed.

SUMMARY

This chapter discussed three different continuous distributions: the uniform distribution, the normal distribution, and the exponential distribution. With continuous distributions, the value of the probability density function does not yield the probability but instead gives the height of the curve at any given point. In fact, with continuous distributions, the probability at any discrete point is .0000. Probabilities are determined over an interval. In each case, the probability is the area under the curve for the interval being considered. In each distribution, the probability or total area under the curve is 1.

Probably the simplest of these distributions is the uniform distribution, sometimes referred to as the rectangular distribution. The uniform distribution is determined from a probability density function that contains equal values along some interval between the points a and b. Basically, the height of the curve is the same everywhere between these two points. Probabilities are determined by calculating the portion of the rectangle between the two points a and b that is being considered.

The most widely used of all distributions is the normal distribution. Many phenomena are normally distributed, including characteristics of most machine-produced parts, many measurements of the biological and natural environment, and many human characteristics such as height, weight, IQ, and achievement test scores. The normal curve is continuous, symmetrical, unimodal, and asymptotic to the axis; actually, it is a family of curves.

The parameters necessary to describe a normal distribution are the mean and the standard deviation. For convenience, data that are being analyzed by the normal curve should be standardized by using the mean and the standard deviation to compute z scores. A z score is the distance that an x value is from the mean, μ, in units of standard deviations. With the z score of an x value, the probability of that value occurring by chance from a given normal distribution can be determined by using a table of z scores and their associated probabilities.

The normal distribution can be used to work certain types of binomial distribution problems. Doing so requires converting the n and p values of the binomial distribution to μ and σ of the normal distribution. When worked by using the normal distribution, the binomial distribution solution is only an approximation. If the values of $\mu \pm 3\sigma$ are within a range from 0 to n, the approximation is reasonably accurate. Adjusting for the fact that a discrete distribution problem is being worked by using a continuous distribution requires a correction for continuity. The correction for continuity involves adding or subtracting .50 to the x value being analyzed. This correction usually improves the normal curve approximation.

Another continuous distribution is the exponential distribution. It complements the discrete Poisson distribution. The exponential distribution is used to compute the probabilities of times between random occurrences. The exponential distribution is a family of distributions described by one parameter, λ. The distribution is skewed to the right and always has its highest value at $x = 0$.

KEY TERMS

Flash Cards

correction for continuity
exponential distribution
normal distribution

rectangular distribution
standardized normal distribution

uniform distribution
z distribution
z score

FORMULAS

Probability density function of a uniform distribution

$$f(x) = \begin{cases} \dfrac{1}{b-a} & \text{for } a \leq x \leq b \\ 0 & \text{for all other values} \end{cases}$$

Mean and standard deviation of a uniform distribution

$$\mu = \frac{a+b}{2}$$

$$\sigma = \frac{b-a}{\sqrt{12}}$$

Probability density function of the normal distribution

$$f(x) = \frac{1}{\sigma\sqrt{2\pi}} e^{-(1/2)[(x-\mu)/\sigma]^2}$$

z formula

$$z = \frac{x-\mu}{\sigma}$$

Conversion of a binomial problem to the normal curve

$$\mu = n\cdot p \text{ and } \sigma = \sqrt{n\cdot p\cdot q}$$

Exponential probability density function

$$f(x) = \lambda e^{-\lambda x}$$

Probabilities of the right tail of the exponential distribution

$$P(x \geq x_0) = e^{-\lambda x_0}$$

SUPPLEMENTARY PROBLEMS

CALCULATING THE STATISTICS

6.34 Data are uniformly distributed between the values of 6 and 14. Determine the value of $f(x)$. What are the mean and standard deviation of this distribution? What is the probability of randomly selecting a value greater than 11? What is the probability of randomly selecting a value between 7 and 12?

6.35 Assume a normal distribution and find the following probabilities.

a. $P(x < 21 \mid \mu = 25 \text{ and } \sigma = 4)$
b. $P(x \geq 77 \mid \mu = 50 \text{ and } \sigma = 9)$
c. $P(x > 47 \mid \mu = 50 \text{ and } \sigma = 6)$
d. $P(13 < x < 29 \mid \mu = 23 \text{ and } \sigma = 4)$
e. $P(x \geq 105 \mid \mu = 90 \text{ and } \sigma = 2.86)$

6.36 Work the following binomial distribution problems by using the normal distribution. Check your answers by using Table A.2 to solve for the probabilities.

a. $P(x = 12 | n = 25$ and $p = .60)$
b. $P(x > 5 | n = 15$ and $p = .50)$
c. $P(x \leq 3 | n = 10$ and $p = .50)$
d. $P(x \geq 8 | n = 15$ and $p = .40)$

6.37 Find the probabilities for the following exponential distribution problems.

a. $P(x \geq 3 | \lambda = 1.3)$
b. $P(x < 2 | \lambda = 2.0)$
c. $P(1 \leq x \leq 3 | \lambda = 1.65)$
d. $P(x > 2 | \lambda = .405)$

TESTING YOUR UNDERSTANDING

6.38 The U.S. Bureau of Labor Statistics reports that of persons who usually work full-time, the average number of hours worked per week is 43.4. Assume that the number of hours worked per week for those who usually work full-time is normally distributed. Suppose 12% of these workers work more than 48 hours. Based on this percentage, what is the standard deviation of number of hours worked per week for these workers?

6.39 A U.S. Bureau of Labor Statistics survey showed that one in five people 16 years of age or older volunteers some of his or her time. If this figure holds for the entire population and if a random sample of 150 people 16 years of age or older is taken, what is the probability that more than 50 of those sampled do volunteer work?

6.40 An entrepreneur opened a small hardware store in a strip mall. During the first few weeks, business was slow, with the store averaging only one customer every 20 minutes in the morning. Assume that the random arrival of customers is Poisson distributed.

a. What is the probability that at least one hour would elapse between customers?
b. What is the probability that 10 to 30 minutes would elapse between customers?
c. What is the probability that less than five minutes would elapse between customers?

6.41 According to an NRF survey conducted by BIGresearch, the average family spends about $237 on electronics (computers, cell phones, etc.) in back-to-college spending per student. Suppose back-to-college family spending on electronics is normally distributed with a standard deviation of $54. If a family of a returning college student is randomly selected, what is the probability that:

a. They spend less than $150 on back-to-college electronics?
b. They spend more than $400 on back-to-college electronics?
c. They spend between $120 and $185 on back-to-college electronics?

6.42 According to the U.S. Department of Agriculture, Alabama egg farmers produce millions of eggs every year. Suppose egg production per year in Alabama is normally distributed, with a standard deviation of 83 million eggs. If during only 3% of the years Alabama egg farmers produce more than 2,655 million eggs, what is the mean egg production by Alabama farmers?

6.43 The U.S. Bureau of Labor Statistics releases figures on the number of full-time wage and salary workers with flexible schedules. The numbers of full-time wage and salary workers in each age category are almost uniformly distributed by age, with ages ranging from 18 to 65 years. If a worker with a flexible schedule is randomly drawn from the U.S. workforce, what is the probability that he or she will be between 25 and 50 years of age? What is the mean value for this distribution? What is the height of the distribution?

6.44 A business convention holds its registration on Wednesday morning from 9:00 A.M. until 12:00 noon. Past history has shown that registrant arrivals follow a Poisson distribution at an average rate of 1.8 every 15 seconds. Fortunately, several facilities are available to register convention members.

a. What is the average number of seconds between arrivals to the registration area for this conference based on past results?
b. What is the probability that 25 seconds or more would pass between registration arrivals?
c. What is the probability that less than five seconds will elapse between arrivals?
d. Suppose the registration computers went down for a one-minute period. Would this condition pose a problem? What is the probability that at least one minute will elapse between arrivals?

6.45 *M/PF Research, Inc.* lists the average monthly apartment rent in some of the most expensive apartment rental locations in the United States. According to their report, the average cost of renting an apartment in Minneapolis is $951. Suppose that the standard deviation of the cost of renting an apartment in Minneapolis is $96 and that apartment rents in Minneapolis are normally distributed. If a Minneapolis apartment is randomly selected, what is the probability that the price is:

a. $1,000 or more?
b. Between $900 and $1,100?
c. Between $825 and $925?
d. Less than $700?

6.46 According to *The Wirthlin Report*, 24% of all workers say that their job is very stressful. If 60 workers are randomly selected:

a. What is the probability that 17 or more say that their job is very stressful?
b. What is the probability that more than 22 say that their job is very stressful?

c. What is the probability that between 8 and 12 (inclusive) say that their job is very stressful?

6.47 The U.S. Bureau of Economic Statistics reports that the average annual salary in the metropolitan Boston area is $50,542. Suppose annual salaries in the metropolitan Boston area are normally distributed with a standard deviation of $4,246. A Boston worker is randomly selected.

a. What is the probability that the worker's annual salary is more than $60,000?

b. What is the probability that the worker's annual salary is less than $45,000?

c. What is the probability that the worker's annual salary is more than $40,000?

d. What is the probability that the worker's annual salary is between $44,000 and $52,000?

6.48 Suppose interarrival times at a hospital emergency room during a weekday are exponentially distributed, with an average interarrival time of nine minutes. If the arrivals are Poisson distributed, what would the average number of arrivals per hour be? What is the probability that less than five minutes will elapse between any two arrivals?

6.49 Suppose the average speeds of passenger trains traveling from Newark, New Jersey, to Philadelphia, Pennsylvania, are normally distributed, with a mean average speed of 88 miles per hour and a standard deviation of 6.4 miles per hour.

a. What is the probability that a train will average less than 70 miles per hour?

b. What is the probability that a train will average more than 80 miles per hour?

c. What is the probability that a train will average between 90 and 100 miles per hour?

6.50 The Conference Board published information on why companies expect to increase the number of part-time jobs and reduce full-time positions. Eighty-one percent of the companies said the reason was to get a flexible workforce. Suppose 200 companies that expect to increase the number of part-time jobs and reduce full-time positions are identified and contacted. What is the expected number of these companies that would agree that the reason is to get a flexible workforce? What is the probability that between 150 and 155 (not including the 150 or the 155) would give that reason? What is the probability that more than 158 would give that reason? What is the probability that fewer than 144 would give that reason?

6.51 According to the U.S. Bureau of the Census, about 75% of commuters in the United States drive to work alone. Suppose 150 U.S. commuters are randomly sampled.  **Demonstration Problem**

a. What is the probability that fewer than 105 commuters drive to work alone?

b. What is the probability that between 110 and 120 (inclusive) commuters drive to work alone?

c. What is the probability that more than 95 commuters drive to work alone?

6.52 According to figures released by the National Agricultural Statistics Service of the U.S. Department of Agriculture, the U.S. production of wheat over the past 20 years has been approximately uniformly distributed. Suppose the mean production over this period was 2.165 billion bushels. If the height of this distribution is .862 billion bushels, what are the values of *a* and *b* for this distribution?

6.53 The Federal Reserve System publishes data on family income based on its Survey of Consumer Finances. When the head of the household has a college degree, the mean before-tax family income is $85,200. Suppose that 60% of the before-tax family incomes when the head of the household has a college degree are between $75,600 and $94,800 and that these incomes are normally distributed. What is the standard deviation of before-tax family incomes when the head of the household has a college degree?

6.54 According to the Polk Company, a survey of households using the Internet in buying or leasing cars reported that 81% were seeking information about prices. In addition, 44% were seeking information about products offered. Suppose 75 randomly selected households who are using the Internet in buying or leasing cars are contacted.

a. What is the expected number of households who are seeking price information?

b. What is the expected number of households who are seeking information about products offered?

c. What is the probability that 67 or more households are seeking information about prices?

d. What is the probability that fewer than 23 households are seeking information about products offered?

6.55 Coastal businesses along the Gulf of Mexico from Texas to Florida worry about the threat of hurricanes during the season from June through October. Businesses become especially nervous when hurricanes enter the Gulf of Mexico. Suppose the arrival of hurricanes during this season is Poisson distributed, with an average of three hurricanes entering the Gulf of Mexico during the five-month season. If a hurricane has just entered the Gulf of Mexico:

a. What is the probability that at least one month will pass before the next hurricane enters the Gulf?

b. What is the probability that another hurricane will enter the Gulf of Mexico in two weeks or less?

c. What is the average amount of time between hurricanes entering the Gulf of Mexico?

6.56 With the growing emphasis on technology and the changing business environment, many workers are discovering that training such as reeducation, skill development, and personal growth are of great assistance in the job marketplace. A recent Gallup survey found that 80% of Generation Xers considered the availability of company-sponsored training as a factor to weigh in taking a job. If 50 Generation Xers are randomly sampled, what is the probability that fewer than 35 consider the availability of company-sponsored training as a factor to weigh in taking a job? What is the expected number? What is the probability that between 42 and 47 (inclusive) consider the availability of company-sponsored training as a factor to weigh in taking a job?

6.57 According to the Air Transport Association of America, the average operating cost of an MD-80 jet airliner is $2,087 per hour. Suppose the operating costs of an MD-80 jet airliner are normally distributed with a standard deviation of $175 per hour. At what operating cost would only 20% of the operating costs be less? At what operating cost would 65% of the operating costs be more? What operating cost would be more than 85% of operating costs?

6.58 Supermarkets usually become busy at about 5 P.M. on weekdays, because many workers stop by on the way home to shop. Suppose at that time arrivals at a supermarket's express checkout station are Poisson distributed, with an average of .8 person/minute. If the clerk has just checked out the last person in line, what is the probability that at least one minute will elapse before the next customer arrives? Suppose the clerk wants to go to the manager's office to ask a quick question and needs 2.5 minutes to do so. What is the probability that the clerk will get back before the next customer arrives?

6.59 In a recent year, the average daily circulation of the *Wall Street Journal* was 1,717,000. Suppose the standard deviation is 50,940. Assume the paper's daily circulation is normally distributed. On what percentage of days would circulation pass 1,800,000? Suppose the paper cannot support the fixed expenses of a full-production setup if the circulation drops below 1,600,000. If the probability of this even occurring is low, the production manager might try to keep the full crew in place and not disrupt operations. How often will this even happen, based on this historical information?

6.60 Incoming phone calls generally are thought to be Poisson distributed. If an operator averages 2.2 phone calls every 30 seconds, what is the expected (average) amount of time between calls? What is the probability that a minute or more would elapse between incoming calls? Two minutes?

INTERPRETING THE OUTPUT

6.61 Shown here is a Minitab output. Suppose the data represent the number of sales associates who are working in a department store in any given retail day. Describe the distribution including the mean and standard deviation. Interpret the shape of the distribution and the mean in light of the data being studied. What do the probability statements mean?

CUMULATIVE DISTRIBUTION FUNCTION

Continuous uniform on 11 to 32
x	$P(X <= x)$
28	0.80952
34	1.00000
16	0.23810
21	0.47619

6.62 A manufacturing company produces a metal rod. Use the Excel output shown here to describe the weight of the rod. Interpret the probability values in terms of the manufacturing process.

Normal Distribution
Mean = 227 mg.
Standard Deviation = 2.3 mg.

x Value	Probability < x Value
220	0.0012
225	0.1923
227	0.5000
231	0.9590
238	1.0000

6.63 Suppose the Minitab output shown here represents the analysis of the length of home-use cell phone calls in terms of minutes. Describe the distribution of cell phone call lengths and interpret the meaning of the probability statements.

CUMULATIVE DISTRIBUTION FUNCTION

Normal with mean = 2.35 and
standard deviation = 0.11
x	$P(X <= x)$
2.60	0.988479
2.45	0.818349
2.30	0.324718
2.00	0.000732

6.64 A restaurant averages 4.51 customers per 10 minutes during the summer in the late afternoon. Shown here are Excel and Minitab output for this restaurant. Discuss the type of distribution used to analyze the data and the meaning of the probabilities.

Exponential Distribution

x Value	Probability < x Value
0.1	0.3630
0.2	0.5942
0.5	0.8951
1.0	0.9890
2.4	1.0000

CUMULATIVE DISTRIBUTION FUNCTION

Exponential with mean = 0.221729
x	$P(X <= x)$
0.1	0.363010
0.2	0.594243
0.5	0.895127
1.0	0.989002
2.4	0.999980

ANALYZING THE DATABASES

Database

1. The Consumer Food database contains a variable, Annual Food Spending, which represents the amount spent per household on food for a year. Calculate the mean and standard deviation for this variable that is approximately normally distributed in this database. Using the mean and standard deviation, calculate the probability that a randomly selected household spends more than $10,000 annually on food. What is the probability that a randomly selected household spends less than $5,000 annually on food? What is the probability that a randomly selected household spends between $8,000 and $11,000 annually on food?

2. Select the Agribusiness time-series database. Create a histogram graph for onions and for broccoli. Each of these variables is approximately normally distributed. Compute the mean and the standard deviation for each distribution. The data in this database represent the monthly weight (in thousands of pounds) of each vegetable. In terms of monthly weight, describe each vegetable (onions and broccoli). If a month were randomly selected from the onion distribution, what is the probability that the weight would be more than 50,000? What is the probability that the weight would be between 25,000 and 35,000? If a month were randomly selected from the broccoli distribution, what is the probability that the weight would be more than 100,000? What is the probability that the weight would be between 135,000 and 170,000?

3. From the Hospital database, it can be determined that some hospitals admit around 50 patients per day. Suppose we select a hospital that admits 50 patients per day. Assuming that admittance only occurs within a 12-hour time period each day and that admittance is Poisson distributed, what is the value of lambda for per hour for this hospital? What is the interarrival time for admittance based on this figure? Suppose a person was just admitted to the hospital. What the probability that it would be more than 30 minutes before the next person was admitted? What is the probability that there would be less than 10 minutes before the next person was admitted?

CASE

MERCEDES GOES AFTER YOUNGER BUYERS

Mercedes and BMW have been competing head-to-head for market share in the luxury-car market for more than four decades. Back in 1959, BMW (Bayerische Motoren Werke) almost went bankrupt and nearly sold out to Daimler-Benz, the maker of Mercedes-Benz cars. BMW was able to recover to the point that in 1992 it passed Mercedes in worldwide sales. Among the reasons for BMW's success was its ability to sell models that were more luxurious than previous models but still focused on consumer quality and environmental responsibility. In particular, BMW targeted its sales pitch to the younger market, whereas Mercedes retained a more mature customer base.

In response to BMW's success, Mercedes has been trying to change their image by launching several products in an effort to attract younger buyers who are interested in sporty, performance-oriented cars. BMW, influenced by Mercedes, is pushing for more refinement and comfort. In fact, one automotive expert says that Mercedes wants to become BMW, and vice versa. However, according to one recent automotive expert, the focus is still on luxury and comfort for Mercedes while BMW focuses on performance and driving dynamics. Even though each company produces many different models, two relatively comparable coupe automobiles are the BMW 3 Series Coupe 335i and the Mercedes C350 Coupe. In a recent year, the national U.S. market price for the BMW 3 Series Coupe 335i was $41,022 and for the Mercedes C350 Coupe $45,493. Gas mileage for both of these cars is around 17 mpg in town and 25 mpg on the highway.

Discussion

1. Suppose Mercedes is concerned that dealer prices of the C350 Coupe are not consistent and that even though the average price is $45,493, actual prices are normally distributed with a standard deviation of $2,981. Suppose also that Mercedes believes that at $44,000, the C350 is priced out of the BMW 3 Series Coupe 335i market. What percentage of the dealer prices for the Mercedes C350 Coupe is more than $44,000 and hence priced out of the BMW 3 Series Coupe 335i market? The average price for a BMW 3 Series Coupe 335i is $41,022. Suppose these prices are also normally distributed with a standard deviation of $2,367. What percentage of BMW dealers is pricing the BMW 3 Series Coupe 335i at more than the average price of a Mercedes C350 Coupe? What might this mean to BMW if dealers were pricing the 3 Series Coupe 335i at this level? What percentage of Mercedes dealers is pricing the C350 Coupe at less than the average price of a BMW 3 Series Coupe 335i?

2. Suppose that highway gas mileage rates for both of these cares are uniformly distributed over a range of from 20 to 30 mpg. What proportion of these cars would fall into the 22 to 27 mpg range? Compute the proportion of cars that get more than 28 mpg. What proportion of cars would get less than 23 mpg?

3. Suppose that in one dealership an average of 1.37 CLKs is sold every 3 hours (during a 12-hour showroom day) and

that sales are Poisson distributed. The following Excel-produced probabilities indicate the occurrence of different intersales times based on this information. Study the output and interpret it for the salespeople. For example, what is the probability that less than an hour will elapse between sales? What is the probability that more than a day (12-hour day) will pass before the next sale after a car has been sold? What can the dealership managers do with such information? How can it help in staffing? How can such information be used as a tracking device for the impact of advertising? Is there a chance that these probabilities would change during the year? If so, why?

Portion of 3-Hour Time Frame	Cumulative Exponential Probabilities from Left
0.167	0.2045
0.333	0.3663
0.667	0.5990
1	0.7459
2	0.9354
3	0.9836
4	0.9958
5	0.9989

USING THE COMPUTER

EXCEL

- Excel can be used to compute cumulative probabilities for particular values of x from either a normal distribution or an exponential distribution.

- Calculation of probabilities from each of these distributions begins with the **Insert Function** (f_x). To access the **Insert Function**, go to the **Formulas** tab on an Excel worksheet (top center tab). The **Insert Function** is on the far left of the menu bar. In the **Insert Function** dialog box at the top, there is a pulldown menu where it says **Or select a category**. From the pulldown menu associated with this command, select **Statistical**.

- To compute probabilities from a normal distribution, select **NORM.DIST** from the **Insert Function's Statistical** menu. In the **NORM.DIST** dialog box, there are four lines to which you must respond. On the first line, **X**, enter the value of x. On the second line, **Mean**, enter the value of the mean. On the third line, **Standard_dev**, enter the value of the standard deviation. The fourth line, **Cumulative**, requires a logical response of either TRUE or FALSE. Place TRUE in the slot to get the cumulative probabilities for all values up to x. Place FALSE in the slot to get the value of the probability density function for that combination of x, the mean, and the standard deviation. In this chapter, we are more interested in the cumulative probabilities and will enter TRUE most of the time.

- To compute probabilities from an exponential distribution, select **EXPON.DIST** from the **Insert Function's Statistical** menu. In the **EXPON.DIST** dialog box, there are three lines to which you must respond. On the first line, **X**, enter the value of x. On the second line, **Lambda**, enter the value of lambda. The third line, **Cumulative**, requires a logical response of either TRUE or FALSE. Place TRUE in the slot to get the cumulative probabilities for all values up to x. Place FALSE in the slot to get the value of the probability density function for that combination of x and lambda. In this chapter, we are more interested in the cumulative probabilities and will enter TRUE most of the time.

MINITAB

- Probabilities can be computed using Minitab for many different distributions, including the uniform distribution, the normal distribution, and the exponential distribution.

- To begin uniform distribution probabilities, select **Calc** on the menu bar. Select **Probability Distributions** from the pulldown menu. From the long second pulldown menu, select **Uniform**. From the dialog box, check how you want the probabilities to be calculated from **Probability density**, **Cumulative probability**, or **Inverse cumulative probability**. **Probability density** yields the value of the probability density for a particular combination of a, b, and x. **Cumulative probability** produces the cumulative probabilites for values less than or equal to x. **Inverse cumulative probability** yields the inverse of the cumulative probabilites. Here we are mostly interested in **Cumulative probability**. On the line, **Lower endpoint:**, enter the value of a. On the line, **Upper endpoint:**, enter the value of b. If you want to compute probabilites for several values of x, place them in a column, list the column location in **Input column**. If you want to compute the probability for a particular value of x, check **Input constant**, and enter the value of x.

- To begin normal distribution probabilites, select **Calc** on the menu bar. Select **Probability Distributions** from the pulldown menu. From the long second pulldown menu, select **Normal**. From the dialog box, check how you want the probabilities to be calculated from **Probability density**, **Cumulative probability**, or **Inverse cumulative probability**. **Probability density** yields the value of the probability density for a particular combination of μ, σ and x. **Cumulative probability** produces the cumulative probabilities for values less than or equal to x. **Inverse cumulative probability** yields the inverse of the cumulative probabilities. Here we are mostly interested in **Cumulative probability**. In the space beside **Mean**, enter the value of the mean. In the space beside **Standard deviation**, enter the value of the standard deviation. If you want to compute probabilities for several values of x, place them in a column, list the column location in **Input column**. If you want to compute the probability for a particular value of x, check **Input constant**, and enter the value of x.

■ To begin exponential distribution probabilites, select **C**alc on the menu bar. Select **Probability** **D**istributions from the pulldown menu. From the long second pulldown menu, select **E**xponential. From the dialog box, check how you want the probabilities to be calculated from **Probability density**, **Cumulative probability**, or **Inverse cumulative probability**. **Probability density** yields the value of the probability density for a particular combination of x_0 and μ. **Cumulative probability** produces the cumulative probabilities for values less than or equal to x.

Inverse cumulative probability yields the inverse of the cumulative probabilities. Here we are mostly interested in **Cumulative probability**. In the space beside **Scale**, enter a scale value to define the exponential distribution. The scale parameter equals the mean, when the threshold parameter equals 0. *Note:* Minitab uses the mean, $\mu = 1/\lambda$, not the value of λ. In the space beside **Threshold**, enter a threshold number to define the exponential distribution. If you want to compute probabilities for several values of x, place them in a column, list the column location in **Input column**. If you want to compute the probability for a particular value of x, check **Input constant**, and enter the value of x.

CHAPTER 7

Sampling and Sampling Distributions

LEARNING OBJECTIVES

The two main objectives for Chapter 7 are to give you an appreciation for the proper application of sampling techniques and an understanding of the sampling distributions of two statistics, thereby enabling you to:

1. Contrast sampling to census and differentiate among different methods of sampling, which include simple, stratified, systematic, and cluster random sampling; and convenience, judgment, quota, and snowball nonrandom sampling, by assessing the advantages associated with each

2. Describe the distribution of a sample's mean using the central limit theorem, correcting for a finite population if necessary

3. Describe the distribution of a sample's proportion using the z formula for sample proportions

Keith Dannemiller/Alamy

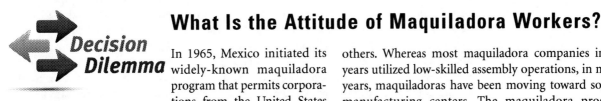

What Is the Attitude of Maquiladora Workers?

In 1965, Mexico initiated its widely-known maquiladora program that permits corporations from the United States and other countries to build manufacturing facilities inside the Mexican border, where the company can import supplies and materials from outside of Mexico free of duty, assemble or produce products, and then export the finished items back to the country of origin. Mexico's establishment of the maquiladora program was to promote foreign investment and jobs in the poverty-stricken country and, at the same time, provide a cheaper labor pool to the participating companies, thereby reducing labor costs so that companies could more effectively compete on the world market. After 2006, the Mexican government renamed the Maquila program as the INMEX program.

The maquiladora effort has been quite successful, with more than 3,500 registered companies participating and more than 1.1 million maquiladora workers employed in the program. It has been estimated that $50 billion has been spent by maquiladora companies with suppliers. Recently, industry exports were approaching $65 billion. About 1,600 of the maquiladora plants are located in the U.S.-Mexico border area, where about 40% manufacture electronic equipment, materials, and supplies. In recent years, the maquiladora program has spread to the interior of Mexico, where maquiladora employment growth has been nearly 30%. Maquiladora companies also manufacture and assemble products from the petroleum, metal, transportation, and medical industries, among

others. Whereas most maquiladora companies in the early years utilized low-skilled assembly operations, in more recent years, maquiladoras have been moving toward sophisticated manufacturing centers. The maquiladora program now encompasses companies from all over the world, including Japan, Korea, China, Canada, and European countries.

What are the Mexican maquiladora workers like? What are their attitudes toward their jobs and their companies? Are there cultural gaps between the company and the worker that must be bridged in order to utilize the human resources more effectively? What culture-based attitudes and expectations do the maquiladora laborers bring to the work situation? How does a business researcher go about surveying workers?

Managerial and Statistical Questions

Suppose researchers decide to survey maquiladora workers to ascertain the workers' attitudes toward and expectations of the work environment and the company.

1. Should the researchers take a census of all maquiladora workers or just a sample? What are reasons for each?
2. If a sample is used, what type of sampling technique would gain the most valid information? How can the researchers be certain that the sample of workers is representative of the population?
3. How can survey questions be analyzed quantitatively?

Sources: Adapted from Cheryl I. Noll, "Mexican Maquiladora Workers: An Attitude Toward Working," *Southwest Journal of Business and Economics,* vol. IX, no. 1 (Spring 1992), pp. 1–8; Steven B. Zisser, "Maquiladora 2001 Understanding and Preparing," Web site located at http://www.maqguide.com/zisser1.htm; Maquila Portal (2004). Maquila Census-June 2004, retrieved July 14, 2004, http://www.maquilaportal.com/cgibin/public/index.pl; Harlingen Economic Development Corporation, "Maquiladora Advantages to U.S. and Mexico Economics," January 4, 2011, http://www.harlingenedc.com/InternationalOpportunity/Maquiladoras.

This chapter explores the process of sampling and the sampling distributions of some statistics. How do we obtain the data used in statistical analysis? Why do researchers often take a sample rather than conduct a census? What are the differences between random and nonrandom sampling? This chapter addresses these and other questions about sampling.

In addition to sampling theory, the distributions of two statistics: the sample mean and the sample proportion are presented. It has been determined that statistics such as these are approximately normally distributed under certain conditions. Knowledge of the uses of the sample mean and sample proportion is important in the study of statistics and is basic to much of statistical analysis.

7.1 SAMPLING

Interactive Applet

Sampling is widely used in business as a means of gathering useful information about a population. Data are gathered from samples and conclusions are drawn about the population as a part of the inferential statistics process. In the Decision Dilemma on maquiladora workers, a random sample of workers could be taken from a wide selection of companies in several industries in many of the key border cities. A carefully constructed questionnaire that is culturally sensitive to Mexicans could be administered to the selected workers to determine work attitudes, expectations, and cultural differences between workers and companies. The researchers could compile and analyze the data gleaned from the responses. Summaries and observations could be made about worker outlook and culture in the maquiladora program. Management and decision makers could then attempt to use the results of the study to improve worker performance and motivation. Often, a sample provides a reasonable means for gathering such useful decision-making information that might be otherwise unattainable and unaffordable.

Reasons for Sampling

Taking a sample instead of conducting a census offers several advantages.

1. The sample can save money.
2. The sample can save time.
3. For given resources, the sample can broaden the scope of the study.
4. Because the research process is sometimes destructive, the sample can save product.
5. If accessing the population is impossible, the sample is the only option.

A sample can be cheaper to obtain than a census for a given magnitude of questions. For example, if an eight-minute telephone interview is being undertaken, conducting the interviews with a sample of 100 customers rather than with a population of 100,000 customers obviously is less expensive. In addition to the cost savings, the significantly smaller number of interviews usually requires less total time. Thus, if obtaining the results is a matter of urgency, sampling can provide them more quickly. With the volatility of some markets and the constant barrage of new competition and new ideas, sampling has a strong advantage over a census in terms of research turnaround time.

If the resources allocated to a research project are fixed, more detailed information can be gathered by taking a sample than by conducting a census. With resources concentrated on fewer individuals or items, the study can be broadened in scope to allow for more specialized questions. One organization budgeted $100,000 for a study and opted to take a census instead of a sample by using a mail survey. The researchers mass-mailed thousands of copies of a computer card that looked like a Major League Baseball all-star ballot. The card contained 20 questions to which the respondent could answer Yes or No by punching out a perforated hole. The information retrieved amounted to the percentages of respondents who answered Yes and No on the 20 questions. For the same amount of money, the company could have taken a random sample from the population, held interactive one-on-one sessions with highly trained interviewers, and gathered detailed information about the process being studied. By using the money for a sample, the researchers could have spent significantly more time with each respondent and thus increased the potential for gathering useful information.

Some research processes are destructive to the product or item being studied. For example, if light bulbs are being tested to determine how long they burn or if candy bars are being taste tested to determine whether the taste is acceptable, the product is destroyed. If a census was conducted for this type of research, no product would be left to sell. Hence, taking a sample is the only realistic option for testing such products.

Sometimes a population is virtually impossible to access for research. For example, some people refuse to answer sensitive questions, and some telephone numbers are unlisted. Some items of interest (like a 1957 Chevrolet) are so scattered that locating all of them would be extremely difficult. When the population is inaccessible for these or other reasons, sampling is the only option.

Reasons for Taking a Census

Sometimes it is preferable to conduct a census of the entire population rather than taking a sample. There are at least two reasons why a business researcher may opt to take a census rather than a sample, providing there is adequate time and money available to conduct

THINKING CRITICALLY ABOUT STATISTICS IN BUSINESS TODAY

Sampling Canadian Manufacturers

Statistics Canada, Canada's national statistical agency, administers a monthly survey of manufacturing for Canada. This Monthly Survey of Manufacturing (MSM) includes information on such variables as sales of goods manufactured, inventories, and orders. The MSM data are used as indicators of the economic condition of manufacturing industries in Canada along with inputs for Canada's gross domestic product, economic studies, and econometric models. The sampling frame for the MSM is the Business Register of Statistics Canada. The target population consists of all statistical establishments on the business register that are classified as being in the manufacturing sector. The frame is further reduced by eliminating the smallest units of the survey population. As a result, there are 27,000 establishments in the sampling frame, of which approximately 10,500 units are sampled. Before the sample is taken, the sampling frame is stratified by both industry and province. Further stratification is then made within each combination of industry and province by company size so that similar-sized companies are grouped together. Selected establishments are required to respond to the survey, and data are collected directly from survey respondents and extracted from administrative files. Sampled companies are contacted either by mail or telephone, whichever they prefer.

Things to Ponder

1. According to the information presented, the MSM sample is stratified by province, industry, and size. Do you think that these strata make sense? If so, why? Can you think of other strata that might be used in this survey?

2. Sampled companies are contacted either by mail or telephone. Do you think that survey responses might differ by whether they were obtained by mail or by telephone? Explain why or why not.

Source: Statistics Canada website at: http://www.statcan.gc.ca/cgibin/imdb/p2SV.pl?Function=getSurvey&SurvId=32686&SurvVer=2&InstaId=32690&InstaVer=98&DispYear=2008&SDDS=2101&lang=en&db=imdb&adm=8&dis=2.

---

such a census: 1) to eliminate the possibility that by chance a randomly selected sample may not be representative of the population and 2) for the safety of the consumer.

Even when proper sampling techniques are implemented in a study, there is the possibility a sample could be selected by chance that does not represent the population. For example, if the population of interest is all truck owners in the state of Colorado, a random sample of truck owners could yield mostly ranchers when, in fact, many of the truck owners in Colorado are urban dwellers. If the researcher or study sponsor cannot tolerate such a possibility, then taking a census may be the only option.

In addition, sometimes a census is taken to protect the safety of the consumer. For example, there are some products, such as airplanes or heart defibrillators, in which the performance of such is so critical to the consumer that 100% of the products are tested, and sampling is not a reasonable option.

Frame

Every research study has a target population that consists of the individuals, institutions, or entities that are the object of investigation. The sample is taken from a population *list, map, directory, or other source used to represent the population.* This list, map, or directory is called the **frame**, which can be school lists, trade association lists, or even lists sold by list brokers. Ideally, a one-to-one correspondence exists between the frame units and the population units. In reality, the frame and the target population are often different. For example, suppose the target population is all families living in Detroit. A feasible frame would be the residential pages of the Detroit telephone books. How would the frame differ from the target population? Some families have no telephone. Other families have unlisted numbers. Still other families might have moved and/or changed numbers since the directory was printed. Some families even have multiple listings under different names.

Frames that have *overregistration* contain the target population units plus some additional units. Frames that have *underregistration* contain fewer units than does the target population. Sampling is done from the frame, not the target population. In theory, the target population and the frame are the same. In reality, a business researcher's goal is to minimize the differences between the frame and the target population.

Random Versus Nonrandom Sampling

The two main types of sampling are random and nonrandom. In **random sampling** *every unit of the population has the same probability of being selected into the sample.* Random sampling implies that chance enters into the process of selection. For example, most Americans would like to believe that winners of nationwide magazine sweepstakes or numbers selected as state lottery winners are selected by some random draw of numbers, hence, random sampling.

In **nonrandom sampling** *not every unit of the population has the same probability of being selected into the sample.* Members of nonrandom samples are not selected by chance. For example, they might be selected because they are at the right place at the right time or because they know the people conducting the research.

Sometimes random sampling is called *probability sampling* and nonrandom sampling is called *nonprobability sampling.* Because every unit of the population is not equally likely to be selected, assigning a probability of occurrence in nonrandom sampling is impossible. The statistical methods presented and discussed in this text are based on the assumption that the data come from random samples. *Nonrandom sampling methods are not appropriate techniques for gathering data to be analyzed by most of the statistical methods presented in this text.* However, several nonrandom sampling techniques are described in this section, primarily to alert you to their characteristics and limitations.

Random Sampling Techniques

The four basic random sampling techniques are simple random sampling, stratified random sampling, systematic random sampling, and cluster (or area) random sampling. Each technique offers advantages and disadvantages. Some techniques are simpler to use, some are less costly, and others show greater potential for reducing sampling error.

Simple Random Sampling

The most elementary random sampling technique is **simple random sampling**. Simple random sampling can be viewed as the basis for other random sampling techniques. With simple random sampling, each unit of the frame is numbered from 1 to N (where N is the size of the population). Next, a table of random numbers or a random number generator is used to select n items into the sample. A random number generator is usually a computer program that allows computer-calculated output to yield random numbers. Table 7.1 contains a brief table of random numbers. Table A.1 in Appendix A contains a full table of random numbers. These numbers are random in all directions. The spaces in the table are there only for ease of reading the values. For each number, any of the 10 digits (0–9) is equally likely, so getting the same digit twice or more in a row is possible.

As an example, from the population frame of companies listed in Table 7.2, we will use simple random sampling to select a sample of six companies. First, we number every member of the population. We select as many digits for each unit sampled as there are in the largest number in the population. For example, if a population has 2,000 members, we select four-digit numbers. Because the population in Table 7.2 contains 30 members, only two digits need be selected for each number. The population is numbered from 01 to 30, as shown in Table 7.3.

TABLE 7.1							
A Brief Table of Random Numbers							
91567	42595	27958	30134	04024	86385	29880	99730
46503	18584	18845	49618	02304	51038	20655	58727
34914	63974	88720	82765	34476	17032	87589	40836
57491	16703	23167	49323	45021	33132	12544	41035
30405	83946	23792	14422	15059	45799	22716	19792
09983	74353	68668	30429	70735	25499	16631	35006
85900	07119	97336	71048	08178	77233	13916	47564

TABLE 7.2			
A Population Frame of 30 Companies	Alaska Airlines	DuPont	Lubrizol
	Alcoa	ExxonMobil	Mattel
	Ashland	General Dynamics	Merck
	Bank of America	General Electric	Microsoft
	BellSouth	General Mills	Occidental Petroleum
	Chevron	Halliburton	JCPenney
	Citigroup	IBM	Procter & Gamble
	Clorox	Kellogg's	Ryder
	Delta Air Lines	Kmart	Sears
	Disney	Lowe's	Time Warner

The object is to sample six companies, so six different two-digit numbers must be selected from the table of random numbers. Because this population contains only 30 companies, all numbers greater than 30 (31–99) must be ignored. If, for example, the number 67 is selected, we discard the number and continue the process until a value between 1 and 30 is obtained. If the same number occurs more than once, we proceed to another number. For ease of understanding, we start with the first pair of digits in Table 7.1 and proceed across the first row until $n = 6$ different values between 01 and 30 are selected. If additional numbers are needed, we proceed across the second row, and so on. Often a researcher will start at some randomly selected location in the table and proceed in a predetermined direction to select numbers.

In the first row of digits in Table 7.1, the first number is 91. This number is out of range so it is cast out. The next two digits are 56. Next is 74, followed by 25, which is the first usable number. From Table 7.3, we see that 25 is the number associated with Occidental Petroleum, so Occidental Petroleum is the first company selected into the sample. The next number is 95, unusable, followed by 27, which is usable. Twenty-seven is the number for Procter & Gamble, so this company is selected. Continuing the process, we pass over the numbers 95 and 83. The next usable number is 01, which is the value for Alaska Airlines. Thirty-four is next, followed by 04 and 02, both of which are usable. These numbers are associated with Bank of America and Alcoa, respectively. Continuing along the first row, the next usable number is 29, which is associated with Sears. Because this selection is the sixth, the sample is complete. The following companies constitute the final sample.

Alaska Airlines
Alcoa
Bank of America
Occidental Petroleum
Procter & Gamble
Sears

Best for small populations

Simple random sampling is easier to perform on small than on large populations. The process of numbering all the members of the population and selecting items is cumbersome for large populations.

TABLE 7.3			
Numbered Population of 30 Companies	01 Alaska Airlines	11 DuPont	21 Lubrizol
	02 Alcoa	12 ExxonMobil	22 Mattel
	03 Ashland	13 General Dynamics	23 Merck
	04 Bank of America	14 General Electric	24 Microsoft
	05 BellSouth	15 General Mills	25 Occidental Petroleum
	06 Chevron	16 Halliburton	26 JCPenney
	07 Citigroup	17 IBM	27 Procter & Gamble
	08 Clorox	18 Kellogg	28 Ryder
	09 Delta Air Lines	19 Kmart	29 Sears
	10 Disney	20 Lowe's	30 Time Warner

[Handwritten margin notes: "subpopulations = strata", "(2)", "main reason for use: potential for reducing error b/c portions from the sample are taken from diff. sub groups", "Disadvantage: - more costly"]

Stratified Random Sampling

A second type of random sampling is **stratified random sampling**, in which the population is divided into nonoverlapping subpopulations called strata. The researcher then extracts a random sample from each of the subpopulations (strata). The main reason for using stratified random sampling is that it has the potential for reducing sampling error. Sampling error occurs when, by chance, the sample does not represent the population. With stratified random sampling, the potential to match the sample closely to the population is greater than it is with simple random sampling because portions of the total sample are taken from different population subgroups. However, stratified random sampling is generally more costly than simple random sampling because each unit of the population must be assigned to a stratum before the random selection process begins.

Strata selection is usually based on available information. Such information may have been gleaned from previous censuses or surveys. Stratification benefits increase as the strata differ more. Internally, a stratum should be relatively homogeneous; externally, strata should contrast with each other. Stratification is often done by using demographic variables, such as sex, socioeconomic class, geographic region, religion, and ethnicity. For example, if a U.S. presidential election poll is to be conducted by a market research firm, what important variables should be stratified? The sex of the respondent might make a difference because a gender gap in voter preference has been noted in past elections; that is, men and women tended to vote differently in national elections. Geographic region also provides an important variable in national elections because voters are influenced by local cultural values that differ from region to region.

In FM radio markets, age of listener is an important determinant of the type of programming used by a station. Figure 7.1 contains a stratification by age with three strata, based on the assumption that age makes a difference in preference of programming. This stratification implies that listeners 20 to 30 years of age tend to prefer the same type of programming, which is different from that preferred by listeners 30 to 40 and 40 to 50 years of age. Within each age subgroup (stratum), *homogeneity* or alikeness is present; between each pair of subgroups a difference, or *heterogeneity*, is present.

Stratified random sampling can be either proportionate or disproportionate. **Proportionate stratified random sampling** occurs *when the percentage of the sample taken from each stratum is proportionate to the percentage that each stratum is within the whole population.* For example, suppose voters are being surveyed in Boston and the sample is being stratified by religion as Catholic, Protestant, Jewish, and others. If Boston's population is 90% Catholic and if a sample of 1,000 voters is taken, the sample would require inclusion of 900 Catholics to achieve proportionate stratification. Any other number of Catholics would be disproportionate stratification. The sample proportion of other religions would also have to follow population percentages. Or consider the city of El Paso, Texas, where the population is approximately 77% Hispanic. If a researcher is conducting a citywide poll in El Paso and if stratification is by ethnicity, a proportionate stratified random

---

FIGURE 7.1

Stratified Random Sampling of FM Radio Listeners

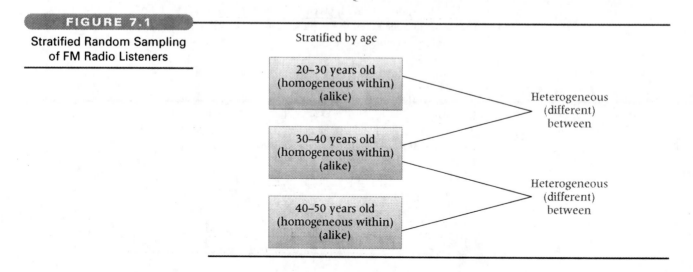

sample should contain 77% Hispanics. Hence, an ethnically proportionate stratified sample of 160 residents from El Paso's 660,000 residents should contain approximately 123 Hispanics. *Whenever the proportions of the strata in the sample are different from the proportions of the strata in the population,* **disproportionate stratified random sampling** occurs.

Systematic Sampling

Systematic sampling is a third random sampling technique. Unlike stratified random sampling, systematic sampling is not done in an attempt to reduce sampling error. Rather, systematic sampling is used because of its convenience and relative ease of administration. With **systematic sampling**, *every k^{th} item is selected to produce a sample of size n from a population of size N.* The value of k, sometimes called the sampling cycle, can be determined by the following formula. If k is not an integer value, the whole-number value should be used.

Handwritten margin notes: "Easy to administrate ③" and "④"

DETERMINING THE VALUE OF k	
	$$k = \frac{N}{n}$$

where

n = sample size
N = population size
k = size of interval for selection

As an example of systematic sampling, a management information systems researcher wanted to sample the manufacturers in Texas. He had enough financial support to sample 1,000 companies (n). The *Directory of Texas Manufacturers* listed approximately 17,000 total manufacturers in Texas (N) in alphabetical order. The value of k was 17 (17,000/1,000) and the researcher selected every 17th company in the directory for his sample.

Did the researcher begin with the first company listed or the 17th or one somewhere between? In selecting every kth value, a simple random number table should be used to select a value between 1 and k inclusive as a starting point. The second element for the sample is the starting point plus k. In the example, $k = 17$, so the researcher would have gone to a table of random numbers to determine a starting point between 1 and 17. Suppose he selected the number 5. He would have started with the 5th company, then selected the 22nd (5 + 17), and then the 39th, and so on.

Besides convenience, systematic sampling has other advantages. Because systematic sampling is evenly distributed across the frame, a knowledgeable person can easily determine whether a sampling plan has been followed in a study. However, a problem with systematic sampling can occur if the data are subject to any periodicity, and the sampling interval is in syncopation with it. In such a case, the sampling would be nonrandom. For example, if a list of 150 college students is actually a merged list of five classes with 30 students in each class and if each of the lists of the five classes has been ordered with the names of top students first and bottom students last, then systematic sampling of every 30th student could cause selection of all top students, all bottom students, or all mediocre students; that is, the original list is subject to a cyclical or periodic organization. Systematic sampling methodology is based on the assumption that the source of population elements is random.

Cluster (or Area) Sampling

Cluster (or area) sampling is a fourth type of random sampling. **Cluster (or area) sampling** involves dividing the population into nonoverlapping areas, or clusters. However, in contrast to stratified random sampling where strata are homogeneous within, cluster sampling identifies clusters that tend to be internally heterogeneous. In theory, each cluster contains a wide variety of elements, and the cluster is a miniature, or microcosm, of the population. Examples of clusters are towns, companies, homes, colleges, areas of a city, and geographic regions. Often clusters are naturally occurring groups of the population and are already identified, such as states or Standard Metropolitan Statistical Areas. Although area sampling usually refers to clusters that are areas of the population, such as geographic regions and cities, the terms *cluster sampling* and *area sampling* are used interchangeably in this text.

FIGURE 7.2

Some Top Rated Test Market
Cities in the United States

After randomly selecting clusters from the population, the business researcher either
selects all elements of the chosen clusters or randomly selects individual elements into the
sample from the clusters. One example of business research that makes use of clustering is
test marketing of new products. Often in test marketing, the United States is divided into
clusters of test market cities, and individual consumers within the test market cities are surveyed. Figure 7.2 shows some of the top U.S. cities that are used as clusters to test products.
The Thinking Critically about Statistics in Business Today feature on test market cities
elaborates more on the concept of test market cities and how they are selected.

Sometimes the clusters are too large, and a second set of clusters is taken from each
original cluster. This technique is called **two-stage sampling**. For example, a researcher
could divide the United States into clusters of cities. She could then divide the cities into
clusters of blocks and randomly select individual houses from the block clusters. The first
stage is selecting the test cities and the second stage is selecting the blocks.

Cluster or area sampling offers several advantages. Two of the foremost advantages are
convenience and cost. Clusters are usually convenient to obtain, and the cost of sampling
from the entire population is reduced because the scope of the study is reduced to the
clusters. The cost per element is usually lower in cluster or area sampling than in stratified
sampling because of lower element listing or locating costs. The time and cost of contacting elements of the population can be reduced, especially if travel is involved, because clustering reduces the distance to the sampled elements. In addition, administration of the
sample survey can be simplified. Sometimes cluster or area sampling is the only feasible
approach because the sampling frames of the individual elements of the population
are unavailable and therefore other random sampling techniques cannot be used.

Cluster or area sampling also has several disadvantages. If the elements of a cluster are
similar, cluster sampling may be statistically less efficient than simple random sampling. In an
extreme case—when the elements of a cluster are the same—sampling from the cluster may
be no better than sampling a single unit from the cluster. Moreover, the costs and problems of
statistical analysis are greater with cluster or area sampling than with simple random sampling.

Nonrandom Sampling

Sampling techniques used to select elements from the population by any mechanism that does
not involve a random selection process are called **nonrandom sampling techniques**. Because
chance is not used to select items from the samples, these techniques are non-probability
techniques and are not desirable for use in gathering data to be analyzed by the methods of

inferential statistics presented in this text. Sampling error cannot be determined objectively for these sampling techniques. Four nonrandom sampling techniques are presented here: convenenience sampling, judgment sampling, quota sampling, and snowball sampling.

Convenience Sampling

In **convenience sampling**, *elements for the sample are selected for the convenience of the researcher.* The researcher typically chooses elements that are readily available, nearby, or willing to participate. The sample tends to be less variable than the population because in many environments the extreme elements of the population are not readily available. The researcher will select more elements from the middle of the population. For example, a convenience sample of homes for door-to-door interviews might include houses where people are at home, houses with no dogs, houses near the street, first-floor apartments, and houses with friendly people. In contrast, a random sample would require the researcher to gather data only from houses and apartments that have been selected randomly, no matter how inconvenient or unfriendly the location. If a research firm is located in a mall, a convenience sample might be selected by interviewing only shoppers who pass the shop and look friendly.

THINKING CRITICALLY ABOUT STATISTICS IN BUSINESS TODAY

Test Market Cities

Companies that intend to introduce a new product across a country will often use test market cities to help determine how well the product will sell in the country and to gain insight into how to better market the product to consumers. Test market cities serve as a sample of the entire country, thereby reducing the cost of testing the product throughout the entire country and minimizing the time to do so. In the sense that test market cities are randomly selected areas from the country, such sampling could be viewed as a form of area or cluster sampling. However, there are other reasons (besides random selection) that test market cities are chosen, including demographics, familiarity, convenience, and psychographics. Sometimes a test market city is chosen because the company has used that city in a previous test and the product went on to be successful. Still, others are chosen because market researchers are comfortable there.

In cluster or area sampling, each area or cluster is ideally a miniature or microcosm of the population. This being the case for a test market city, a business researcher can gain the benefits of test marketing a product in an environment that closely resembles the population and, at the same time, realize cost and time savings benefits associated with sampling. According to Valerie Skala, Vice President of Analytic Product Management and Development at Information Resources, Inc., "To deliver accurate results, a test market must be representative of the United States in terms of sales development of the category and related products." Josh Herman, Product Manager of Acxiom Corp, reports that companies in the United States have begun utilizing life-stage-based consumer segmentation to identify test market cities that most effectively represent the market makeup of consumers in the United States. One of these systems suggests that the 110 million U.S. households consist of 70 different life-stage segments, including "getting married," "having children," "raising kids," "launching the kids out of the house," "retiring," etc. Since such life-stage changes greatly impact our consumer behavior, it is important that market researchers who are interested in test marketing products to the entire country select test market cities that most closely parallel the overall U.S. profile in life-stage segments.

According to one study, the Albany, New York, Metropolitan Statistical Area (MSA) is most closely correlated (with a correlation score of .91) in life-stage segments with the United States overall. Albany has almost the same proportion of consumers across the different life stages as one would find in the nation as a whole. Adopting such a test market city allows researchers to use multiple markets in their testing and, at the same time, have a consistent way to tie them together. Figure 7.2 displays some of the top-rated test market cities in the United States.

Things to Ponder

1. Think about your home city. What characteristics of it would lend themselves to making your city an effective test market for the entire country? What characteristics would hinder the use of your city as a test market?

2. Select a product or service and suppose that it is going to be test marketed in a test market city. What characteristics (demographics) would a test market city have to have in order to conduct a successful market test?

Source: Adapted from "Marketing News: Albany, N.Y. Reflects True Test Market," located at the Acxiom Corp's Web site: http://www.acxiom.com/default.aspx?ID=2428&DisplayID=18.

Judgment Sampling

Judgment sampling occurs when *elements selected for the sample are chosen by the judgment of the researcher.* Researchers often believe they can obtain a representative sample by using sound judgment, which will result in saving time and money. Sometimes ethical, professional researchers might believe they can select a more representative sample than the random process will provide. They might be right! However, some studies show that random sampling methods outperform judgment sampling in estimating the population mean even when the researcher who is administering the judgment sampling is trying to put together a representative sample. When sampling is done by judgment, calculating the probability that an element is going to be selected into the sample is not possible. The sampling error cannot be determined objectively because probabilities are based on *nonrandom* selection.

Other problems are associated with judgment sampling. The researcher tends to make errors of judgment in one direction. These systematic errors lead to what are called *biases*. The researcher also is unlikely to include extreme elements. Judgment sampling provides no objective method for determining whether one person's judgment is better than another's.

Quota Sampling

A third nonrandom sampling technique is **quota sampling**, which appears to be similar to stratified random sampling. Certain population subclasses, such as age group, gender, or geographic region, are used as strata. However, instead of randomly sampling from each stratum, the researcher uses a nonrandom sampling method to gather data from one stratum until the desired quota of samples is filled. Quotas are described by quota controls, which set the sizes of the samples to be obtained from the subgroups. Generally, a quota is based on the proportions of the subclasses in the population. In this case, the quota concept is similar to that of proportional stratified sampling.

Quotas often are filled by using available, recent, or applicable elements. For example, instead of randomly interviewing people to obtain a quota of Italian Americans, the researcher would go to the Italian area of the city and interview there until enough responses are obtained to fill the quota. In quota sampling, an interviewer would begin by asking a few filter questions; if the respondent represents a subclass whose quota has been filled, the interviewer would terminate the interview.

Quota sampling can be useful if no frame is available for the population. For example, suppose a researcher wants to stratify the population into owners of different types of cars but fails to find any lists of Toyota van owners. Through quota sampling, the researcher would proceed by interviewing all car owners and casting out non–Toyota van owners until the quota of Toyota van owners is filled.

Quota sampling is less expensive than most random sampling techniques because it essentially is a technique of convenience. However, cost may not be meaningful because the quality of nonrandom and random sampling techniques cannot be compared. Another advantage of quota sampling is the speed of data gathering. The researcher does not have to call back or send out a second questionnaire if he does not receive a response; he just moves on to the next element. Also, preparatory work for quota sampling is minimal.

The main problem with quota sampling is that, when all is said and done, it still is only a *nonrandom* sampling technique. Some researchers believe that if the quota is filled by *randomly* selecting elements and discarding those not from a stratum, quota sampling is essentially a version of stratified random sampling. However, most quota sampling is carried out by the researcher going where the quota can be filled quickly. The object is to gain the benefits of stratification without the high field costs of stratification. Ultimately, it remains a nonprobability sampling method.

Snowball Sampling

Another nonrandom sampling technique is **snowball sampling**, in which *survey subjects are selected based on referral from other survey respondents.* The researcher identifies a person who fits the profile of subjects wanted for the study. The researcher then asks this person for the names and locations of others who would also fit the profile of subjects wanted for the study. Through these referrals, survey subjects can be identified cheaply and efficiently, which is particularly useful when survey subjects are difficult to locate. It is the main advantage of snowball sampling; its main disadvantage is that it is nonrandom.

Sampling Error

Sampling error occurs *when the sample is not representative of the population.* When random sampling techniques are used to select elements for the sample, sampling error occurs by chance. Many times the statistic computed on the sample is not an accurate estimate of the population parameter because the sample was not representative of the population. This result is caused by sampling error. With random samples, sampling error can be computed and analyzed.

Nonsampling Errors

All errors other than sampling errors are **nonsampling errors**. The many possible nonsampling errors include missing data, recording errors, input processing errors, and analysis errors. Other nonsampling errors result from the measurement instrument, such as errors of unclear definitions, defective questionnaires, and poorly conceived concepts. Improper definition of the frame is a nonsampling error. In many cases, finding a frame that perfectly fits the population is impossible. Insofar as it does not fit, a nonsampling error has been committed.

Response errors are also nonsampling errors. They occur when people do not know, will not say, or overstate. Virtually no statistical method is available to measure or control for nonsampling errors. The statistical techniques presented in this text are based on the assumption that none of these nonsampling errors were committed. The researcher must eliminate these errors through carefully planning and executing the research study.

7.1 PROBLEMS

7.1 Develop a frame for the population of each of the following research projects.
  a. Measuring the job satisfaction of all union employees in a company
  b. Conducting a telephone survey in Utica, New York, to determine the level of interest in opening a new hunting and fishing specialty store in the mall
  c. Interviewing passengers of a major airline about its food service
  d. Studying the quality control programs of boat manufacturers
  e. Attempting to measure the corporate culture of cable television companies

7.2 Make a list of 20 people you know. Include men and women, various ages, various educational levels, and so on. Number the list and then use the random number list in Table 7.1 to select six people randomly from your list. How representative of the population is the sample? Find the proportion of men in your population and in your sample. How do the proportions compare? Find the proportion of 20-year-olds in your sample and the proportion in the population. How do they compare?

7.3 Use the random numbers in Table A.1 of Appendix A to select 10 of the companies from the 30 companies listed in Table 7.2. Compare the types of companies in your sample with the types in the population. How representative of the population is your sample?

7.4 For each of the following research projects, list three variables for stratification of the sample.
  a. A nationwide study of motels and hotels is being conducted. An attempt will be made to determine the extent of the availability of online links for customers. A sample of motels and hotels will be taken.
  b. A consumer panel is to be formed by sampling people in Michigan. Members of the panel will be interviewed periodically in an effort to understand current consumer attitudes and behaviors.
  c. A large soft drink company wants to study the characteristics of its U.S. bottlers, but the company does not want to conduct a census.
  d. The business research bureau of a large university is conducting a project in which the bureau will sample paper-manufacturing companies.

7.5 In each of the following cases, the variable represents one way that a sample can be stratified in a study. For each variable, list some strata into which the variable can be divided.

a. Age of respondent (person)

b. Size of company (sales volume)

c. Size of retail outlet (square feet)

d. Geographic location

e. Occupation of respondent (person)

f. Type of business (company)

7.6 A city's telephone book lists 100,000 people. If the telephone book is the frame for a study, how large would the sample size be if systematic sampling were done on every 200th person?

7.7 If every 11th item is systematically sampled to produce a sample size of 75 items, approximately how large is the population?

7.8 If a company employs 3500 people and if a random sample of 175 of these employees has been taken by systematic sampling, what is the value of k? The researcher would start the sample selection between what two values? Where could the researcher obtain a frame for this study?

7.9 For each of the following research projects, list at least one area or cluster that could be used in obtaining the sample.

a. A study of road conditions in the state of Missouri

b. A study of U.S. offshore oil wells

c. A study of the environmental effects of petrochemical plants west of the Mississippi River

7.10 Give an example of how judgment sampling could be used in a study to determine how district attorneys feel about attorneys advertising on television.

7.11 Give an example of how convenience sampling could be used in a study of *Fortune* 500 executives to measure corporate attitude toward paternity leave for employees.

7.12 Give an example of how quota sampling could be used to conduct sampling by a company test marketing a new personal computer.

7.2 SAMPLING DISTRIBUTION OF $\bar{x}$

Interactive Applet

In the inferential statistics process, a researcher selects a random sample from the population, computes a statistic on the sample, and reaches conclusions about the population parameter from the statistic. In attempting to analyze the sample statistic, it is essential to know the distribution of the statistic. So far we studied several distributions, including the binomial distribution, the Poisson distribution, the hypergeometric distribution, the uniform distribution, the normal distribution, and the exponential distribution.

In this section we explore the sample mean, $\bar{x}$, as the statistic. The sample mean is one of the more common statistics used in the inferential process. To compute and assign the probability of occurrence of a particular value of a sample mean, the researcher must know the distribution of the sample means. One way to examine the distribution possibilities is to take a population with a particular distribution, randomly select samples of a given size, compute the sample means, and attempt to determine how the means are distributed.

Suppose a small finite population consists of only $N = 8$ numbers:

$$54 \quad 55 \quad 59 \quad 63 \quad 64 \quad 68 \quad 69 \quad 70$$

Using an Excel-produced histogram, we can see the shape of the distribution of this population of data.

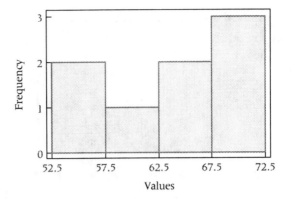

Suppose we take all possible samples of size $n = 2$ from this population with replacement. The result is the following pairs of data.

(54,54)	(55,54)	(59,54)	(63,54)
(54,55)	(55,55)	(59,55)	(63,55)
(54,59)	(55,59)	(59,59)	(63,59)
(54,63)	(55,63)	(59,63)	(63,63)
(54,64)	(55,64)	(59,64)	(63,64)
(54,68)	(55,68)	(59,68)	(63,68)
(54,69)	(55,69)	(59,69)	(63,69)
(54,70)	(55,70)	(59,70)	(63,70)
(64,54)	(68,54)	(69,54)	(70,54)
(64,55)	(68,55)	(69,55)	(70,55)
(64,59)	(68,59)	(69,59)	(70,59)
(64,63)	(68,63)	(69,63)	(70,63)
(64,64)	(68,64)	(69,64)	(70,64)
(64,68)	(68,68)	(69,68)	(70,68)
(64,69)	(68,69)	(69,69)	(70,69)
(64,70)	(68,70)	(69,70)	(70,70)

The means of each of these samples follow.

54	54.5	56.5	58.5	59	61	61.5	62
54.5	55	57	59	59.5	61.5	62	62.5
56.5	57	59	61	61.5	63.5	64	64.5
58.5	59	61	63	63.5	65.5	66	66.5
59	59.5	61.5	63.5	64	66	66.5	67
61	61.5	63.5	65.5	66	68	68.5	69
61.5	62	64	66	66.5	68.5	69	69.5
62	62.5	64.5	66.5	67	69	69.5	70

Again using an Excel-produced histogram, we can see the shape of the distribution of these sample means.

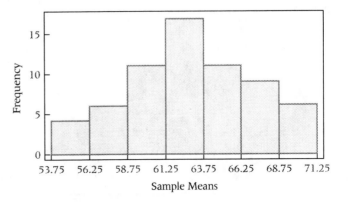

FIGURE 7.3

Minitab Histogram of a
Poisson Distributed
Population, $\lambda = 1.25$

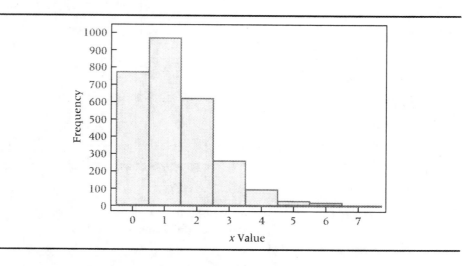

Notice that the shape of the histogram for sample means is quite unlike the shape of the histogram for the population. The sample means appear to "pile up" toward the middle of the distribution and "tail off" toward the extremes.

Figure 7.3 is a Minitab histogram of the data from a Poisson distribution of values with a population mean of 1.25. Note that the histogram is skewed to the right. Suppose 90 samples of size $n = 30$ are taken randomly from a Poisson distribution with $\lambda = 1.25$ and the means are computed on each sample. The resulting distribution of sample means is displayed in Figure 7.4. Notice that although the samples were drawn from a Poisson distribution, which is skewed to the right, the sample means form a distribution that approaches a symmetrical, nearly normal-curve-type distribution.

Suppose a population is uniformly distributed. If samples are selected randomly from a population with a uniform distribution, how are the sample means distributed? Figure 7.5 displays the Minitab histogram distributions of sample means from five different sample sizes. Each of these histograms represents the distribution of sample means from 90 samples generated randomly from a uniform distribution in which $a = 10$ and $b = 30$. Observe the shape of the distributions. Notice that even for small sample sizes, the distributions of sample means for samples taken from the uniformly distributed population begin to "pile up" in the middle. As sample sizes become much larger, the sample mean distributions begin to approach a normal distribution and the variation among the means decreases.

So far, we examined three populations with different distributions. However, the sample means for samples taken from these populations appear to be approximately normally distributed, especially as the sample sizes become larger. What would happen to the distribution of sample means if we studied populations with differently shaped distributions? The answer to that question is given in the **central limit theorem**.

FIGURE 7.4

Minitab Histogram of
Sample Means

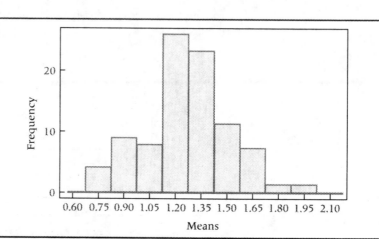

FIGURE 7.5

Minitab Outputs for Sample Means from 90 Samples Ranging in Size from $n = 2$ to $n = 30$ from a Uniformly Distributed Population with $a = 10$ and $b = 30$

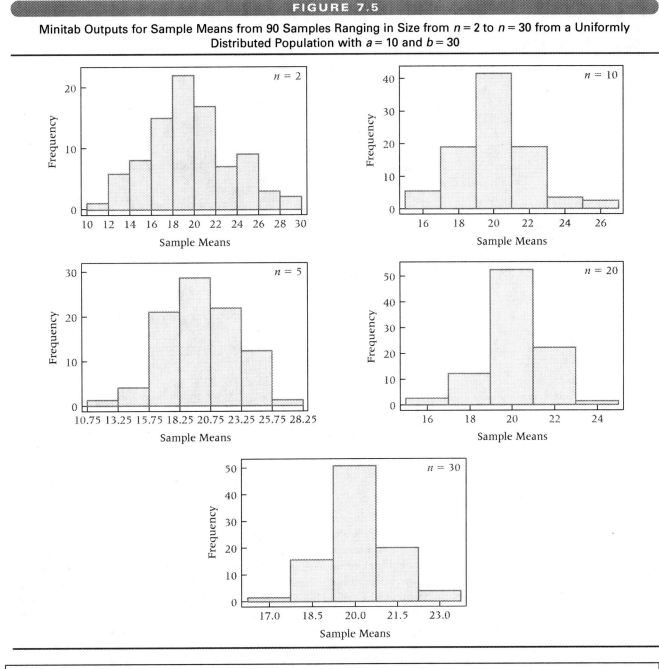

CENTRAL LIMIT THEOREM   If samples of size n are drawn randomly from a population that has a mean of μ and a standard deviation of σ, the sample means, $\bar{x}$, are approximately normally distributed for sufficiently large sample sizes ($n \geq 30$) regardless of the shape of the population distribution. If the population is normally distributed, the sample means are normally distributed for any size sample.

From mathematical expectation,* it can be shown that the mean of the sample means is the population mean.

$$\mu_{\bar{x}} = \mu$$

and the standard deviation of the sample means (called the standard error of the mean) is the standard deviation of the population divided by the square root of the sample size.

$$\sigma_{\bar{x}} = \frac{\sigma}{\sqrt{n}}$$

*The derivations are beyond the scope of this text and are not shown.

FIGURE 7.6

Shapes of the Distributions of Sample Means for Three Sample Sizes Drawn from Four Different Population Distributions

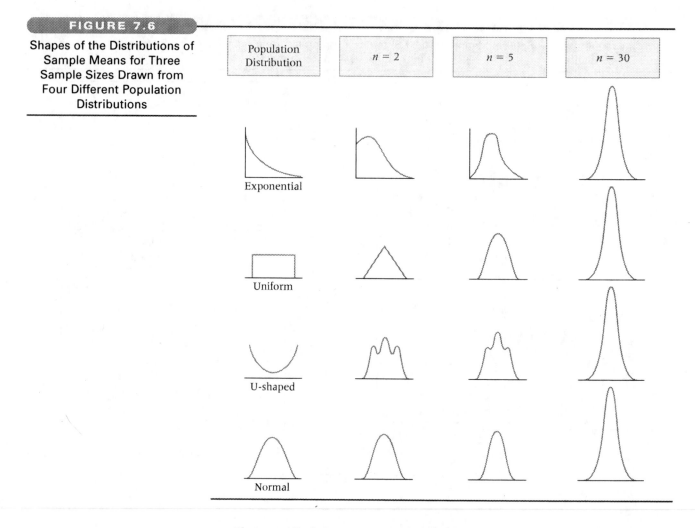

The central limit theorem creates the potential for applying the normal distribution to many problems when sample size is sufficiently large. Sample means that have been computed for random samples drawn from normally distributed populations are normally distributed. However, the real advantage of the central limit theorem comes when sample data drawn from populations not normally distributed or from populations of unknown shape also can be analyzed by using the normal distribution because the sample means are normally distributed for sufficiently large sample sizes.* Column 1 of Figure 7.6 shows four different population distributions. Each succeeding column displays the shape of the distribution of the sample means for a particular sample size. Note in the bottom row for the normally distributed population that the sample means are normally distributed even for $n = 2$. Note also that with the other population distributions, the distribution of the sample means begins to approximate the normal curve as n becomes larger. For all four distributions, the distribution of sample means is approximately normal for $n = 30$.

How large must a sample be for the central limit theorem to apply? The sample size necessary varies according to the shape of the population. However, in this text (as in many others), a sample of *size 30 or larger* will suffice. Recall that if the population is normally distributed, the sample means are normally distributed for sample sizes as small as $n = 1$.

The shapes displayed in Figure 7.6 coincide with the results obtained empirically from the random sampling shown in Figures 7.4 and 7.5. As shown in Figure 7.6, and as indicated in Figure 7.5, as sample size increases, the distribution narrows, or becomes more leptokurtic. This trend makes sense because the standard deviation of the mean is $\sigma/\sqrt{n}$. This value will become smaller as the size of n increases.

*The actual form of the central limit theorem is a limit function of calculus. As the sample size increases to infinity, the distribution of sample means literally becomes normal in shape.

	Sample Size	Mean of Sample Means	Standard Deviation of Sample Means	μ	$\dfrac{\sigma}{\sqrt{n}}$
TABLE 7.4	$n = 2$	19.92	3.87	20	4.08
$\mu_{\bar{x}}$ and $\sigma_{\bar{x}}$ of 90 Random Samples for Five Different Sizes*	$n = 5$	20.17	2.65	20	2.58
	$n = 10$	20.04	1.96	20	1.83
	$n = 20$	20.20	1.37	20	1.29
	$n = 30$	20.25	0.99	20	1.05

*Randomly generated by using Minitab from a uniform distribution with $a = 10$, $b = 30$.

In Table 7.4, the means and standard deviations of the means are displayed for random samples of various sizes ($n = 2$ through $n = 30$) drawn from the uniform distribution of $a = 10$ and $b = 30$ shown in Figure 7.5. The population mean is 20, and the standard deviation of the population is 5.774. Note that the mean of the sample means for each sample size is approximately 20 and that the standard deviation of the sample means for each set of 90 samples is approximately equal to $\sigma/\sqrt{n}$. A small discrepancy occurs between the standard deviation of the sample means and $\sigma/\sqrt{n}$, because not all possible samples of a given size were taken from the population (only 90). In theory, if all possible samples for a given sample size are taken exactly once, the mean of the sample means will equal the population mean and the standard deviation of the sample means will equal the population standard deviation divided by the square root of n.

The central limit theorem states that sample means are normally distributed regardless of the shape of the population for large samples and for any sample size with normally distributed populations. Thus, sample means can be analyzed by using z scores. Recall from Chapters 3 and 6 the formula to determine z scores for individual values from a normal distribution:

$$z = \frac{x - \mu}{\sigma}$$

If sample means are normally distributed, the z score formula applied to sample means would be

$$z = \frac{\bar{x} - \mu_{\bar{x}}}{\sigma_{\bar{x}}}$$

This result follows the general pattern of z scores: the difference between the statistic and its mean divided by the statistic's standard deviation. In this formula, the mean of the statistic of interest is $\mu_{\bar{x}}$, and *the standard deviation of the statistic of interest is* $\sigma_{\bar{x}}$, sometimes referred to as **the standard error of the mean**. To determine $\mu_{\bar{x}}$, the researcher would randomly draw out all possible samples of the given size from the population, compute the sample means, and average them. This task is virtually impossible to accomplish in any realistic period of time. Fortunately, $\mu_{\bar{x}}$ equals the population mean, μ, which is easier to access. Likewise, to determine directly the value of $\sigma_{\bar{x}}$, the researcher would take all possible samples of a given size from a population, compute the sample means, and determine the standard deviation of sample means. This task also is practically impossible. Fortunately, $\sigma_{\bar{x}}$ can be computed by using the population standard deviation divided by the square root of the sample size.

As sample size increases, the standard deviation of the sample means becomes smaller and smaller because the population standard deviation is being divided by larger and larger values of the square root of n. The ultimate benefit of the central limit theorem is a practical, useful version of the z formula for sample means.

z FORMULA FOR SAMPLE MEANS	$$z = \frac{\bar{x} - \mu}{\dfrac{\sigma}{\sqrt{n}}}$$

FIGURE 7.7

Graphical Solution to the Tire
Store Example

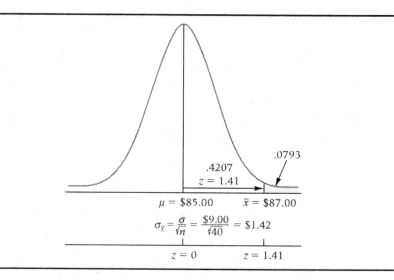

When the population is normally distributed and the sample size is 1, this formula for sample means becomes the z formula for individual values that we used in Chapter 6. The reason is that the mean of one value is that value, and when $n = 1$ the value of $\sigma/\sqrt{n} = \sigma$.

Suppose, for example, that the mean expenditure per customer at a tire store is $85.00, with a standard deviation of $9.00. If a random sample of 40 customers is taken, what is the probability that the sample average expenditure per customer for this sample will be $87.00 or more? Because the sample size is greater than 30, the central limit theorem can be used, and the sample means are normally distributed. With $\mu = \$85.00$, $\sigma = \$9.00$, and the z formula for sample means, z is computed as

$$z = \frac{\bar{x} - \mu}{\dfrac{\sigma}{\sqrt{n}}} = \frac{\$87.00 - \$85.00}{\dfrac{\$9.00}{\sqrt{40}}} = \frac{\$2.00}{\$1.42} = 1.41$$

From the z distribution (Table A.5), $z = 1.41$ produces a probability of .4207. This number is the probability of getting a sample mean between $87.00 and $85.00 (the population mean). Solving for the tail of the distribution yields

$$.5000 - .4207 = .0793$$

which is the probability of $\bar{x} \geq \$87.00$. That is, 7.93% of the time, a random sample of 40 customers from this population will yield a sample mean expenditure of $87.00 or more. Figure 7.7 shows the problem and its solution.

**DEMONSTRATION
PROBLEM 7.1**

Suppose that during any hour in a large department store, the average number of shoppers is 448, with a standard deviation of 21 shoppers. What is the probability that a random sample of 49 different shopping hours will yield a sample mean between 441 and 446 shoppers?

Solution

For this problem, $\mu = 448$, $\sigma = 21$, and $n = 49$. The problem is to determine $P(441 \leq \bar{x} \leq 446)$. The following diagram depicts the problem.

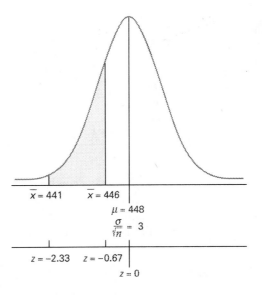

Solve this problem by calculating the z scores and using Table A.5 to determine the probabilities.

$$z = \frac{441 - 448}{\frac{21}{\sqrt{49}}} = \frac{-7}{3} = -2.33$$

and

$$z = \frac{446 - 448}{\frac{21}{\sqrt{49}}} = \frac{-2}{3} = -0.67$$

z Value	Probability
-2.33	.4901
-0.67	-.2486
	.2415

The probability of a value being between $z = -2.33$ and -0.67 is .2415; that is, there is a 24.15% chance of randomly selecting 49 hourly periods for which the sample mean is between 441 and 446 shoppers.

Sampling from a Finite Population

The example shown in this section and Demonstration Problem 7.1 was based on the assumption that the population was infinitely or extremely large. In cases of a finite population, *a statistical adjustment can be made to the z formula for sample means.* The adjustment is called the **finite correction factor**: $\sqrt{\dfrac{N - n}{N - 1}}$. It operates on the standard deviation of sample mean, $\sigma_{\bar{x}}$. Following is the z formula for sample means when samples are drawn from finite populations.

Z FORMULA FOR SAMPLE MEANS OF A FINITE POPULATION	$z = \dfrac{\bar{x} - \mu}{\dfrac{\sigma}{\sqrt{n}} \sqrt{\dfrac{N - n}{N - 1}}}$

TABLE 7.5
Finite Correction Factor for
Some Sample Sizes

Population Size	Sample Size	Value of Correction Factor
2000	30 (<5%N)	.993
2000	500	.866
500	30	.971
500	200	.775
200	30	.924
200	75	.793

If a random sample of size 35 were taken from a finite population of only 500, the sample mean would be less likely to deviate from the population mean than would be the case if a sample of size 35 were taken from an infinite population. For a sample of size 35 taken from a finite population of size 500, the finite correction factor is

$$\sqrt{\frac{500 - 35}{500 - 1}} = \sqrt{\frac{465}{499}} = .965$$

Thus the standard deviation of the mean—sometimes referred to as the standard error of the mean—is adjusted downward by using .965. As the size of the finite population becomes larger in relation to sample size, the finite correction factor approaches 1. In theory, whenever researchers are working with a finite population, they can use the finite correction factor. A rough rule of thumb for many researchers is that, if the sample size is less than 5% of the finite population size or $n/N < 0.05$, the finite correction factor does not significantly modify the solution. Table 7.5 contains some illustrative finite correction factors.

DEMONSTRATION PROBLEM 7.2

Demonstration Problem

A production company's 350 hourly employees average 37.6 years of age, with a standard deviation of 8.3 years. If a random sample of 45 hourly employees is taken, what is the probability that the sample will have an average age of less than 40 years?

Solution

The population mean is 37.6, with a population standard deviation of 8.3; that is, $\mu = 37.6$ and $\sigma = 8.3$. The sample size is 45, but it is being drawn from a finite population of 350; that is, $n = 45$ and $N = 350$. The sample mean under consideration is 40, or $\bar{x} = 40$. The following diagram depicts the problem on a normal curve.

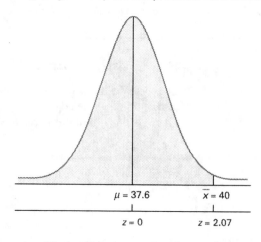

Using the z formula with the finite correction factor gives

$$z = \frac{40 - 37.6}{\dfrac{8.3}{\sqrt{45}}\sqrt{\dfrac{350 - 45}{350 - 1}}} = \frac{2.4}{1.157} = 2.07$$

This *z* value yields a probability (Table A.5) of .4808. Therefore, the probability of getting a sample average age of less than 40 years is .4808 + .5000 = .9808. Had the finite correction factor not been used, the *z* value would have been 1.94, and the final answer would have been .9738.

7.2 PROBLEMS

7.13 A population has a mean of 50 and a standard deviation of 10. If a random sample of 64 is taken, what is the probability that the sample mean is each of the following?
   a. Greater than 52
   b. Less than 51
   c. Less than 47
   d. Between 48.5 and 52.4
   e. Between 50.6 and 51.3

7.14 A population is normally distributed, with a mean of 23.45 and a standard deviation of 3.8. What is the probability of each of the following?
   a. Taking a sample of size 10 and obtaining a sample mean of 22 or more
   b. Taking a sample of size 4 and getting a sample mean of more than 26

7.15 Suppose a random sample of size 36 is drawn from a population with a mean of 278. If 86% of the time the sample mean is less than 280, what is the population standard deviation?

7.16 A random sample of size 81 is drawn from a population with a standard deviation of 12. If only 18% of the time a sample mean greater than 300 is obtained, what is the mean of the population?

7.17 Find the probability in each case.
   a. $N = 1000$, $n = 60$, $\mu = 75$, and $\sigma = 6$; $P(\bar{x} < 76.5) = ?$
   b. $N = 90$, $n = 36$, $\mu = 108$, and $\sigma = 3.46$; $P(107 < \bar{x} < 107.7) = ?$
   c. $N = 250$, $n = 100$, $\mu = 35.6$, and $\sigma = 4.89$; $P(\bar{x} \geq 36) = ?$
   d. $N = 5000$, $n = 60$, $\mu = 125$, and $\sigma = 13.4$; $P(\bar{x} \leq 123) = ?$

7.18 The Statistical Abstract of the United States published by the U.S. Census Bureau reports that the average annual consumption of fresh fruit per person is 99.9 pounds. The standard deviation of fresh fruit consumption is about 30 pounds. Suppose a researcher took a random sample of 38 people and had them keep a record of the fresh fruit they ate for one year.
   a. What is the probability that the sample average would be less than 90 pounds?
   b. What is the probability that the sample average would be between 98 and 105 pounds?
   c. What is the probability that the sample average would be less than 112 pounds?
   d. What is the probability that the sample average would be between 93 and 96 pounds?

7.19 Suppose a subdivision on the southwest side of Denver, Colorado, contains 1,500 houses. The subdivision was built in 1983. A sample of 100 houses is selected randomly and evaluated by an appraiser. If the mean appraised value of a house in this subdivision for all houses is $177,000, with a standard deviation of $8,500, what is the probability that the sample average is greater than $185,000?

7.20 Suppose the average checkout tab at a large supermarket is $65.12, with a standard deviation of $21.45. Twenty-three percent of the time when a random sample of 45 customer tabs is examined, the sample average should exceed what value?

7.21 According to Nielsen Media Research, the average number of hours of TV viewing per household per week in the United States is 50.4 hours. Suppose the standard deviation is 11.8 hours and a random sample of 42 U.S. households is taken.
   a. What is the probability that the sample average is more than 52 hours?
   b. What is the probability that the sample average is less than 47.5 hours?

c. What is the probability that the sample average is less than 40 hours? If the sample average actually is less than 40 hours, what would it mean in terms of the Nielsen Media Research figures?

d. Suppose the population standard deviation is unknown. If 71% of all sample means are greater than 49 hours and the population mean is still 50.4 hours, what is the value of the population standard deviation?

7.3 SAMPLING DISTRIBUTION OF $\hat{p}$

Sometimes in analyzing a sample, a researcher will choose to use the sample proportion, denoted $\hat{p}$. If research produces *measurable* data such as weight, distance, time, and income, the sample mean is often the statistic of choice. However, if research results in *countable* items such as how many people in a sample choose Dr. Pepper as their soft drink or how many people in a sample have a flexible work schedule, the sample proportion is often the statistic of choice. Whereas the mean is computed by averaging a set of values, the **sample proportion** is *computed by dividing the frequency with which a given characteristic occurs in a sample by the number of items in the sample.*

SAMPLE PROPORTION

$$\hat{p} = \frac{x}{n}$$

where

x = number of items in a sample that have the characteristic
n = number of items in the sample

For example, in a sample of 100 factory workers, 30 workers might belong to a union. The value of $\hat{p}$ for this characteristic, union membership, is 30/100 = .30. In a sample of 500 businesses in suburban malls, if 10 are shoe stores, then the sample proportion of shoe stores is 10/500 = .02. The sample proportion is a widely used statistic and is usually computed on questions involving Yes or No answers. For example, do you have at least a high school education? Are you predominantly right-handed? Are you female? Do you belong to the student accounting association?

How does a researcher use the sample proportion in analysis? The central limit theorem applies to sample proportions in that the normal distribution approximates the shape of the distribution of sample proportions if $n \cdot p > 5$ and $n \cdot q > 5$ (p is the population proportion and $q = 1 - p$). The mean of sample proportions for all samples of size n randomly drawn from a population is p (the population proportion) and the standard deviation of sample proportions is $\sqrt{\dfrac{p \cdot q}{n}}$ sometimes referred to as the **standard error of the proportion**. Sample proportions also have a z formula.

---

z FORMULA FOR SAMPLE PROPORTIONS FOR $n \cdot p > 5$ AND $n \cdot q > 5$

$$z = \frac{\hat{p} - p}{\sqrt{\dfrac{p \cdot q}{n}}}$$

where

$\hat{p}$ = sample proportion
n = sample size
p = population proportion
$q = 1 - p$

FIGURE 7.8

Graphical Solution to the
Electrical Contractor Example

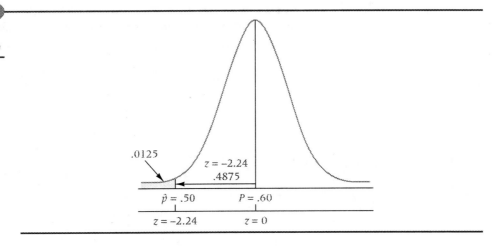

Suppose 60% of the electrical contractors in a region use a particular brand of wire. What is the probability of taking a random sample of size 120 from these electrical contractors and finding that .50 or less use that brand of wire? For this problem,

$$p = .60 \quad \hat{p} = .50 \quad n = 120$$

The z formula yields

$$z = \frac{.50 - .60}{\sqrt{\dfrac{(.60)(.40)}{120}}} = \frac{-.10}{.0447} = -2.24$$

From Table A.5, the probability corresponding to $z = -2.24$ is .4875. For $z < -2.24$ (the tail of the distribution), the answer is $.5000 - .4875 = .0125$. Figure 7.8 shows the problem and solution graphically.

This answer indicates that a researcher would have difficulty (probability of .0125) finding that 50% or less of a sample of 120 contractors use a given brand of wire if indeed the population market share for that wire is .60. If this sample result actually occurs, either it is a rare chance result, the .60 proportion does not hold for this population, or the sampling method may not have been random.

DEMONSTRATION PROBLEM 7.3

If 10% of a population of parts is defective, what is the probability of randomly selecting 80 parts and finding that 12 or more parts are defective?

Solution

Here, $p = .10$, $\hat{p} = 12/80 = .15$, and $n = 80$. Entering these values in the z formula yields

$$z = \frac{.15 - .10}{\sqrt{\dfrac{(.10)(.90)}{80}}} = \frac{.05}{.0335} = 1.49$$

Table A.5 gives a probability of .4319 for a z value of 1.49, which is the area between the sample proportion, .15, and the population proportion, .10. The answer to the question is

$$P(\hat{p} \geq .15) = .5000 - .4319 = .0681.$$

Thus, about 6.81% of the time, 12 or more defective parts would appear in a random sample of 80 parts when the population proportion is .10. If this result actually occurred, the 10% proportion for population defects would be open to question. The diagram shows the problem graphically.

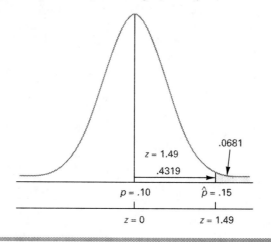

7.3 PROBLEMS

7.22 A given population proportion is .25. For the given value of n, what is the probability of getting each of the following sample proportions?

a. $n = 110$ and $\hat{p} \leq .21$

b. $n = 33$ and $\hat{p} > .24$

c. $n = 59$ and $.24 \leq \hat{p} < .27$

d. $n = 80$ and $\hat{p} < .30$

e. $n = 800$ and $\hat{p} < .30$

7.23 A population proportion is .58. Suppose a random sample of 660 items is sampled randomly from this population.

a. What is the probability that the sample proportion is greater than .60?

b. What is the probability that the sample proportion is between .55 and .65?

c. What is the probability that the sample proportion is greater than .57?

d. What is the probability that the sample proportion is between .53 and .56?

e. What is the probability that the sample proportion is less than .48?

7.24 Suppose a population proportion is .40, and 80% of the time when you draw a random sample from this population you get a sample proportion of .35 or more. How large a sample were you taking?

7.25 If a population proportion is .28 and if the sample size is 140, 30% of the time the sample proportion will be less than what value if you are taking random samples?

7.26 According to a study by Decision Analyst, 21% of the people who have credit cards are very close to the total limit on the card(s). Suppose a random sample of 600 credit card users is taken. What is the probability that more than 150 credit card users are very close to the total limit on their card(s)?

7.27 According to a survey by Accountemps, 48% of executives believe that employees are most productive on Tuesdays. Suppose 200 executives are randomly surveyed.

a. What is the probability that fewer than 90 of the executives believe employees are most productive on Tuesdays?

b. What is the probability that more than 100 of the executives believe employees are most productive on Tuesdays?

c. What is the probability that more than 80 of the executives believe employees are most productive on Tuesdays?

7.28 A Travel Weekly International Air Transport Association survey asked business travelers about the purpose for their most recent business trip. Nineteen percent responded that it was for an internal company visit. Suppose 950 business travelers are randomly selected.

a. What is the probability that more than 25% of the business travelers say that the reason for their most recent business trip was an internal company visit?

b. What is the probability that between 15% and 20% of the business travelers say that the reason for their most recent business trip was an internal company visit?

c. What is the probability that between 133 and 171 of the business travelers say that the reason for their most recent business trip was an internal company visit?

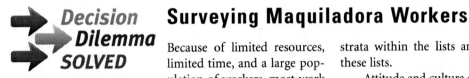

Surveying Maquiladora Workers

Because of limited resources, limited time, and a large population of workers, most work attitude and cultural studies of maquiladora workers are accomplished through the use of random sampling. To ensure the inclusion of certain groups and in an effort to reduce sampling error, a proportionate stratified sampling technique might be selected. Such a sampling plan could include as strata such things as geographic location of the plant in Mexico, type of industry, size of the plant, number of maquiladora workers at that facility, age of the worker, gender of the worker, level of responsibility of the worker, and other variables.

Lists of maquiladora companies and plants can be obtained for use as a company frame for the study. Each company is likely to have a complete list of all workers. These lists could serve as a frame for the sampling of workers. If granted permission to use the lists, the researcher could then identify strata within the lists and randomly sample workers from these lists.

Attitude and culture questions are not easy to formulate in a way that produces valid data. Experts on the measurement of such things should be consulted. However, if questions are asked in a way that produces numerical responses that can be averaged, sample means can be computed. If sample sizes are large enough, the central limit theorem can be invoked, enabling the business researcher to analyze mean sample responses as though they came from normally distributed populations.

Some of the questions asked might require only a Yes or No response. For example, the question: "Are working conditions in a U.S. company-owned maquiladora plant considerably different from those in a plant owned by an equivalent Mexican company?" requires only a Yes or No response. These responses, when tallied, can be used to compute sample proportions. If the sample sizes are large enough, the business researcher can assume from the central limit theorem that sample proportions come from a normal distribution, which can provide the basis for analysis.

ETHICAL CONSIDERATIONS

The art and science of sampling has potential for breeding unethical behavior. Considerable research is reported under the guise of random sampling when, in fact, nonrandom sampling is used. Remember, if nonrandom sampling is used, probability statements about sampling error are not appropriate. Some researchers purport to be using stratified random sampling when they are actually using quota sampling. Others claim to be using systematic random sampling when they are actually using convenience or judgment sampling.

In the process of inferential statistics, researchers use sample results to make conclusions about a population. These conclusions are disseminated to the interested public. The public often assumes that sample results truly reflect the state of the population. If the sample does not reflect the population because questionable sampling practices were used, it could be argued that unethical research behavior occurred. Valid, representative sampling is not an easy task. Researchers and statisticians should exercise extreme caution in taking samples to be sure the results obtained reflect the conditions in the population as nearly as possible.

The central limit theorem is based on large samples unless the population is normally distributed. In analyzing small-sample data, it is an unethical practice to assume a sample mean is from a normal distribution unless the population can be shown with some confidence to be normally distributed. Using the normal distribution to analyze sample proportions is also unethical if sample sizes are smaller than those recommended by the experts.

SUMMARY

For much business research, successfully conducting a census is virtually impossible and the sample is a feasible alternative. Other reasons for sampling include cost reduction, potential for broadening the scope of the study, and loss reduction when the testing process destroys the product.

To take a sample, a population must be identified. Often the researcher cannot obtain an exact roster or list of the population and so must find some way to identify the population as closely as possible. The final list or directory used to represent the population and from which the sample is drawn is called the frame.

The two main types of sampling are random and nonrandom. Random sampling occurs when each unit of the population has the same probability of being selected for the sample. Nonrandom sampling is any sampling that is not random. The four main types of random sampling discussed are simple random sampling, stratified sampling, systematic sampling, and cluster, or area, sampling.

In simple random sampling, every unit of the population is numbered. A table of random numbers or a random number generator is used to select n units from the population for the sample.

Stratified random sampling uses the researcher's prior knowledge of the population to stratify the population into subgroups. Each subgroup is internally homogeneous but different from the others. Stratified random sampling is an attempt to reduce sampling error and ensure that at least some of each of the subgroups appears in the sample. After the strata are identified, units can be sampled randomly from each stratum. If the proportions of units selected from each subgroup for the sample are the same as the proportions of the subgroups in the population, the process is called proportionate stratified sampling. If not, it is called disproportionate stratified sampling.

With systematic sampling, every kth item of the population is sampled until n units have been selected. Systematic sampling is used because of its convenience and ease of administration.

Cluster or area sampling involves subdividing the population into nonoverlapping clusters or areas. Each cluster or area is a microcosm of the population and is usually heterogeneous within. Individual units are then selected randomly from the clusters or areas to get the final sample. Cluster or area sampling is usually done to reduce costs. If a set of second clusters or areas is selected from the first set, the method is called two-stage sampling.

Four types of nonrandom sampling were discussed: convenience, judgment, quota, and snowball. In convenience sampling, the researcher selects units from the population to be in the sample for convenience. In judgment sampling, units are selected according to the judgment of the researcher. Quota sampling is similar to stratified sampling, with the researcher identifying subclasses or strata. However, the researcher selects units from each stratum by some nonrandom technique until a specified quota from each stratum is filled. With snowball sampling, the researcher obtains additional sample members by asking current sample members for referral information.

Sampling error occurs when the sample does not represent the population. With random sampling, sampling error occurs by chance. Nonsampling errors are all other research and analysis errors that occur in a study. They include recording errors, input errors, missing data, and incorrect definition of the frame.

According to the central limit theorem, if a population is normally distributed, the sample means for samples taken from that population also are normally distributed regardless of sample size. The central limit theorem also says that if the sample sizes are large ($n \geq 30$), the sample mean is approximately normally distributed regardless of the distribution shape of the population. This theorem is extremely useful because it enables researchers to analyze sample data by using the normal distribution for virtually any type of study in which means are an appropriate statistic, as long as the sample size is large enough. The central limit theorem states that sample proportions are normally distributed for large sample sizes.

KEY TERMS

Flash Cards

central limit theorem
cluster (or area) sampling
convenience sampling

disproportionate stratified
   random sampling
finite correction factor
frame
judgment sampling
nonrandom sampling
nonrandom sampling
   techniques

nonsampling errors
proportionate stratified
   random sampling
quota sampling
random sampling
sample proportion
sampling error
simple random sampling

snowball sampling
standard error of the mean
standard error of the
   proportion
stratified random sampling
systematic sampling
two-stage sampling

FORMULAS

Determining the value of k

$$k = \frac{N}{n}$$

z formula for sample means

$$z = \frac{\bar{x} - \mu}{\frac{\sigma}{\sqrt{n}}}$$

z formula for sample means when there is a finite population

$$z = \frac{\bar{x} - \mu}{\frac{\sigma}{\sqrt{n}}\sqrt{\frac{N-n}{N-1}}}$$

z formula for sample proportions

$$z = \frac{\hat{p} - p}{\sqrt{\frac{p \cdot q}{n}}}$$

Sample proportion

$$\hat{p} = \frac{x}{n}$$

SUPPLEMENTARY PROBLEMS

CALCULATING THE STATISTICS

7.29 The mean of a population is 76 and the standard deviation is 14. The shape of the population is unknown. Determine the probability of each of the following occurring from this population.
  a. A random sample of size 35 yielding a sample mean of 79 or more
  b. A random sample of size 140 yielding a sample mean of between 74 and 77
  c. A random sample of size 219 yielding a sample mean of less than 76.5

7.30 Forty-six percent of a population possesses a particular characteristic. Random samples are taken from this population. Determine the probability of each of the following occurrences.
  a. The sample size is 60 and the sample proportion is between .41 and .53.
  b. The sample size is 458 and the sample proportion is less than .40.
  c. The sample size is 1350 and the sample proportion is greater than .49.

TESTING YOUR UNDERSTANDING

7.31 Suppose the age distribution in a city is as follows.

Under 18	22%
18–25	18%
26–50	36%
51–65	10%
Over 65	14%

A researcher is conducting proportionate stratified random sampling with a sample size of 250. Approximately how many people should he sample from each stratum?

7.32 Candidate Jones believes she will receive .55 of the total votes cast in her county. However, in an attempt to validate this figure, her pollster contacts a random sample of 600 registered voters in the county. The poll results show that 298 of the voters say they are committed to voting for her. If she actually has .55 of the total vote, what is the probability of getting a sample proportion this small or smaller? Do you think she actually has 55% of the vote? Why or why not?

7.33 Determine a possible frame for conducting random sampling in each of the following studies.
  a. The average amount of overtime per week for production workers in a plastics company in Pennsylvania

  b. The average number of employees in all Ralphs super-markets in Southern California
  c. A survey of commercial lobster catchers in Maine

7.34 A particular automobile costs an average of $21,755 in the Pacific Northwest. The standard deviation of prices is $650. Suppose a random sample of 30 dealerships in Washington and Oregon is taken, and their managers are asked what they charge for this automobile. What is the probability of getting a sample average cost of less than $21,500? Assume that only 120 dealerships in the entire Pacific Northwest sell this automobile.

7.35 A company has 1,250 employees, and you want to take a simple random sample of $n = 60$ employees. Explain how you would go about selecting this sample by using the table of random numbers. Are there numbers that you cannot use? Explain.

7.36 Suppose the average client charge per hour for out-of-court work by lawyers in the state of Iowa is $125. Suppose further that a random telephone sample of 32 lawyers in Iowa is taken and that the sample average charge per hour for out-of-court work is $110. If the population variance is $525, what is the probability of getting a sample mean of $110 or larger? What is the probability of getting a sample mean larger than $135 per hour? What is the probability of getting a sample mean of between $120 and $130 per hour?

7.37 A survey of 2645 consumers by DDB Needham Worldwide of Chicago for public relations agency Porter/Novelli showed that how a company handles a crisis when at fault is one of the top influences in consumer buying decisions, with 73% claiming it is an influence. Quality of product was the number one influence, with 96% of consumers stating that quality influences their buying decisions. How a company handles complaints was number two, with 85% of consumers reporting it as an influence in their buying decisions. Suppose a random sample of 1100 consumers is taken and each is asked which of these three factors influence their buying decisions.
  a. What is the probability that more than 810 consumers claim that how a company handles a crisis when at fault is an influence in their buying decisions?
  b. What is the probability that fewer than 1030 consumers claim that quality of product is an influence in their buying decisions?
  c. What is the probability that between 82% and 84% of consumers claim that how a company handles complaints is an influence in their buying decisions?

7.38 Suppose you are sending out questionnaires to a randomly selected sample of 100 managers. The frame for this study is the membership list of the American Managers Association. The questionnaire contains demographic questions about the company and its top manager. In addition, it asks questions about the manager's leadership style. Research assistants are to score and enter the responses into the computer as soon as they are received. You are to conduct a statistical analysis of the data. Name and describe four nonsampling errors that could occur in this study.

7.39 A researcher is conducting a study of a *Fortune* 500 company that has factories, distribution centers, and retail outlets across the country. How can she use cluster or area sampling to take a random sample of employees of this firm?

7.40 A directory of personal computer retail outlets in the United States contains 12,080 alphabetized entries. Explain how systematic sampling could be used to select a sample of 300 outlets.

7.41 In an effort to cut costs and improve profits, many U.S. companies have been turning to outsourcing. In fact, according to *Purchasing* magazine, 54% of companies surveyed outsourced some part of their manufacturing process in the past two to three years. Suppose 565 of these companies are contacted.

    a. What is the probability that 339 or more companies outsourced some part of their manufacturing process in the past two to three years?

    b. What is the probability that 288 or more companies outsourced some part of their manufacturing process in the past two to three years?

    c. What is the probability that 50% or less of these companies outsourced some part of their manufacturing process in the past two to three years?

7.42 The average cost of a one-bedroom apartment in a town is $650 per month. What is the probability of randomly selecting a sample of 50 one-bedroom apartments in this town and getting a sample mean of less than $630 if the population standard deviation is $100?

7.43 The Aluminum Association reports that the average American uses 56.8 pounds of aluminum in a year. A random sample of 51 households is monitored for one year to determine aluminum usage. If the population standard deviation of annual usage is 12.3 pounds, what is the probability that the sample mean will be each of the following?

    a. More than 60 pounds

    b. More than 58 pounds

    c. Between 56 and 57 pounds

    d. Less than 55 pounds

    e. Less than 50 pounds

7.44 Use Table A.1 to select 20 three-digit random numbers. Did any of the numbers occur more than once? How is it possible for a number to occur more than once? Make a stem-and-leaf plot of the numbers with the stem being the left digit. Do the numbers seem to be equally distributed, or are they bunched together?

7.45 Direct marketing companies are turning to the Internet for new opportunities. A recent study by Gruppo, Levey, & Co. showed that 73% of all direct marketers conduct transactions on the Internet. Suppose a random sample of 300 direct marketing companies is taken.

    a. What is the probability that between 210 and 234 (inclusive) direct marketing companies are turning to the Internet for new opportunities?

    b. What is the probability that 78% or more of direct marketing companies are turning to the Internet for new opportunities?

    c. Suppose a random sample of 800 direct marketing companies is taken. Now what is the probability that 78% or more are turning to the Internet for new opportunities? How does this answer differ from the answer in part (b)? Why do the answers differ?

7.46 According to the U.S. Bureau of Labor Statistics, 20% of all people 16 years of age or older do volunteer work. In this age group, women volunteer slightly more than men, with 22% of women volunteering and 19% of men volunteering. What is the probability of randomly sampling 140 women 16 years of age or older and getting 35 or more who do volunteer work? What is the probability of getting 21 or fewer from this group? Suppose a sample of 300 men and women 16 years of age or older is selected randomly from the U.S. population. What is the probability that the sample proportion of those who do volunteer work is between 18% and 25%?

7.47 Suppose you work for a large firm that has 20,000 employees. The CEO calls you in and asks you to determine employee attitudes toward the company. She is willing to commit $100,000 to this project. What are the advantages of taking a sample versus conducting a census? What are the trade-offs?

7.48 In a particular area of the Northeast, an estimated 75% of the homes use heating oil as the principal heating fuel during the winter. A random telephone survey of 150 homes is taken in an attempt to determine whether this figure is correct. Suppose 120 of the 150 homes surveyed use heating oil as the principal heating fuel. What is the probability of getting a sample proportion this large or larger if the population estimate is true?

7.49 The U.S. Bureau of Labor Statistics released hourly wage figures for various countries for workers in the manufacturing sector. The hourly wage was $30.67 for Switzerland, $20.20 for Japan, and $23.82 for the U.S. Assume that in all three countries, the standard deviation of hourly labor rates is $3.00.

    a. Suppose 40 manufacturing workers are selected randomly from across Switzerland and asked what their hourly wage is . What is the probability that the sample average will be between $30.00 and $31.00?

    b. Suppose 35 manufacturing workers are selected randomly from across Japan. What is the probability that the sample average will exceed $21.00?

    c. Suppose 50 manufacturing workers are selected randomly from across the United States What is the probability that the sample average will be less than $22.75?

7.50 Give a variable that could be used to stratify the population for each of the following studies. List at least four subcategories for each variable.

a. A political party wants to conduct a poll prior to an election for the office of U.S. senator in Minnesota.

b. A soft drink company wants to take a sample of soft drink purchases in an effort to estimate market share.

c. A retail outlet wants to interview customers over a one-week period.

d. An eyeglasses manufacturer and retailer wants to determine the demand for prescription eyeglasses in its marketing region.

7.51 According to Runzheimer International, a typical business traveler spends an average of $281 per day in Chicago. This cost includes hotel, meals, car rental, and incidentals. A survey of 65 randomly selected business travelers who have been to Chicago on business recently is taken. For the population mean of $281 per day, what is the probability of getting a sample average of more than $273 per day if the population standard deviation is $47?

see www.wiley.com/college/black

ANALYZING THE DATABASES

Database

1. Let the Manufacturing database be the frame for a population of manufacturers to be studied. This database has 140 different SIC codes. Suppose you want to randomly sample six of these SIC codes from these using simple random sampling. Explain how you would take a systematic sample of size 10 from this frame. Examining the variables in the database, name two variables that could be used to stratify the population. Explain how these variables could be used in stratification and why each variable might produce important strata.

2. Consider the Consumer Food database. Compute the mean and standard deviation for annual food spending for this population. Now take a random sample of 32 of the households in this database and compute the sample mean.

Using techniques presented in this chapter, determine the probability of getting a mean this large or larger from the population. Work this problem both with and without the finite correction factor and compare the results by discussing the differences in answers.

3. Use the Hospital database and determine the proportion of hospitals that are under the control of nongovernment not-for-profit organizations (category 2). Assume that this proportion represents the entire population of all hospitals. If you randomly selected 500 hospitals from across the United States, what is the probability that 45% or more are under the control of nongovernment not-for-profit organizations? If you randomly selected 100 hospitals, what is the probability that less than 40% are under the control of nongovernment not-for-profit organizations?

CASE

SHELL ATTEMPTS TO RETURN TO PREMIERE STATUS

The Shell Oil Company, which began about 1912, had been for decades a household name as a quality oil company in the United States. However, by the late 1970s much of its prestige as a premiere company had disappeared. How could Shell regain its high status?

In the 1990s, Shell undertook an extensive research effort to find out what it needed to do to improve its image. As a first step, Shell hired Responsive Research and the Opinion Research Corporation to conduct a series of focus groups and personal interviews among various segments of the population. Included in these were youths, minorities, residents in neighborhoods near Shell plants, legislators, academics, and present and past employees of Shell. The researchers learned that people believe that top companies are integral parts of the communities in which the companies are located rather than separate entities. These studies and others led to the development of materials that Shell used to explain their core values to the general public.

Next, PERT Survey Research ran a large quantitative study to determine which values were best received by the target audience. Social issues emerged as the theme with the most support. During the next few months, the advertising agency of Ogilvy & Mather, hired by Shell, developed several campaigns with social themes. Two market research com-

panies were hired to evaluate the receptiveness of the various campaigns. The result was the "Count on Shell" campaign, which featured safety messages with useful information about what to do in various dangerous situations.

A public "Count on Shell" campaign was launched in February 1998 and met with considerable success: the ability to recall Shell advertising jumped from 20% to 32% among opinion influencers, and more than 1 million copies of Shell's free safety brochures were distributed. By promoting itself as a reliable company that cares, Shell seems to be regaining its premiere status.

Today, Shell initiates and supports several programs in which the company and employees are involved in community and civic activities. These programs range from local improvement projects to fundraising events for regional nonprofit organizations. According to company sources, "every year, more than 1,500 Shell employees, retirees and their family members contribute, on average, more than 40,000 hours for company-sponsored volunteer initiatives nationwide" in the United States. Some of these include America's WETLAND Campaign, Shell's Workforce Development Initiative, and United Way campaigns. Shell U.S. has been a strong supporter of the Points of Light Foundation; and each fall, Shell volunteers participate in the cleaning of beaches in Texas, Louisiana, and California. In addition, Shell sponsors the Shell Houston Open PGA golf tournament, which has raised $50 million since 1974 for various children's charity organizations.

Discussion

1. Suppose you were asked to develop a sampling plan to determine what a "premiere company" is to the general public. What sampling plan would you use? What is the target population? What would you use for a frame? Which of the four types of random sampling discussed in this chapter would you use? Could you use a combination of two or more of the types (two-stage sampling)? If so, how?

2. It appears that at least one of the research companies hired by Shell used some stratification in their sampling. What are some of the variables on which they are stratified? If you were truly interested in ascertaining opinions from a variety of segments of the population with regard to opinions on "premiere" companies or about Shell, what strata might make sense? Name at least five and justify why you would include them.

3. Suppose that in 1979 only 12% of the general adult U.S. public believed that Shell was a "premiere" company. Suppose further that you randomly selected 350 people from the general adult U.S. public this year and 25% said that Shell was a "premiere" company. If only 12% of the general adult U.S. public still believes that Shell is a "premiere" company, how likely is it that the 25% figure is a chance result in sampling 350 people? *Hint:* Use the techniques in this chapter to determine the probability of the 25% figure occurring by chance.

4. PERT Survey Research conducted quantitative surveys in an effort to measure the effectiveness of various campaigns. Suppose on their survey instrument, they used a continuous scale of from 0 to 10 where 0 denotes that the campaign is not effective at all, 10 denotes that the campaign is extremely effective, and other values fall in between to measure the effectiveness. Suppose also that a particular campaign received an average of 3.6 on the scale with a standard deviation of 1.4 early in the tests. Later, after the campaign had been critiqued and improved, a survey of 35 people was taken and a sample mean of 4.0 was recorded. What is the probability of this sample mean or one greater occurring if the actual population mean is still just 3.6? Based on this probability, do you think that a sample mean of 4.0 is just a chance fluctuation on the 3.6 population mean, or do you think that perhaps it indicates the population mean is now greater than 3.6? Support your conclusion. Suppose a sample mean of 5.0 is attained. What is the likelihood of this result occurring by chance when the population mean is 3.6? Suppose this higher mean value actually occurs after the campaign has been improved. What does it indicate?

Source: Adapted from "Count on It," *American Demographics* (March 1999), p. 60; Shell Oil Company information (2011), http://www.shell.us/home/content/usa/environment_society/shell_in_the_society/giving_back/, and Shell Oil Company's "Shell in the U.S." Web site at http://www.shell.us/.

USING THE COMPUTER

EXCEL

- Random numbers can be generated from Excel for several different distributions, including the binomial distribution, the Poisson distribution, the uniform distribution, and the normal distribution. To generate random numbers from a particular distribution, begin by selecting the **Data** tab on the Excel worksheet. From the **Analysis** panel at the right top of the **Data** tab worksheet, click on **Data Analysis**. If your Excel worksheet does not show the **Data Analysis** option, then you can load it as an add-in following directions given in Chapter 2. From the **Data Analysis** pulldown menu, select **Random Number Generation**.

- In the **Random Number Generation** dialog box, enter the number of columns of values you want to produce into **Number of Variables**.

- Next, enter the number of data points to be generated in each column into **Number of Random Numbers**.

- The third line of the dialog box, **Distribution**, contains the choices of distributions. Select from which one of the following distributions you want to generate random data: **discrete, uniform, normal, Bernoulli, binomial, Poisson,** and **patterned**.

- The options and required responses in the **Random Number Generation** dialog box will change with the chosen distribution.

MINITAB

- Random numbers can be generated from Minitab for many different distributions, including the binomial distribution, the Poisson distribution, the hypergeometric distribution, the uniform distribution, the normal distribution, and the exponential distribution. To generate random numbers from a particular distribution, select **Calc** on the menu bar. Select **Random Data** from the pulldown menu. From the long second pulldown menu, select the distribution from which you want to generate random numbers. A dialog box for the distribution selected will open, asking you to enter the number of rows of data that you want to generate. In this, it is asking you how many random numbers you want to generate. In the second space of the dialog box, **Store in column(s)**, enter the number of columns of random numbers you want to generate. Next, each individual distribution requires specific parameters. For example, the binomial distribution asks for **Number of trials:** (n) and **Event probability:** (p). The normal distribution asks for the value of the mean and the standard deviation. The Poisson distribution asks for the value of lambda in the box, **Mean**. The hypergeometric distribution requires the entry of three items, **Population size** (N), **Event count in population** (A), and the **Sample size** (n). The uniform distribution asks for the **Lower endpoint:** and the **Upper endpoint**. The exponential distribution requires a value for the **Scale:** and the **Threshold**.

MAKING INFERENCES ABOUT POPULATION PARAMETERS

The ability to estimate population parameters or to test hypotheses about population parameters using sample statistics is one of the main applications of statistics in improving decision making in business. Whether estimating parameters or testing hypotheses about parameters, the inferential process consists of taking a random sample from a group or body (the population), analyzing data from the sample, and reaching conclusions about the population using the sample data, as shown in Figure 1.1 of Chapter 1.

One widely used technique for estimating population measures (parameters) from a sample using statistics is the confidence interval. Confidence interval estimation is generally reserved for instances where a business researcher does not know what the population value is or does not have a very clear idea of it. For example, what is the mean dollar amount spent by families per month at the movies including concession expenditures, or what proportion of workers telecommute at least one day per week? Confidence intervals can be used to estimate these and many other useful and interesting population parameters, including means, proportions, and variances in the business world.

Sometimes, a business analyst already knows the value of a population parameter or has a good idea but would like to test to determine if the value has changed, if the value applies in other situations, or if the value is what other researchers say it is. In such cases, business researchers use hypothesis tests. In the hypothesis testing process, the known parameter is assumed to be true, data are gathered from random samples taken from the population, and the resulting data are analyzed to determine if the parameter value is still true or has changed in some way. For example, does the average worker still work 40 hours per week?

Are 65% of all workers unhappy with their job? Like with confidence intervals, hypothesis testing can be used to test hypotheses about means, proportions, variances, and other parameters.

Unit III of this textbook, from Chapter 8 through Chapter 11, contains a cadre of estimation and hypotheses testing techniques organized by usage and number of samples. Chapter 8 and Chapter 10 present confidence interval techniques for the estimation of parameters. Chapter 8 introduces the concept of a confidence interval and focuses on one-sample analyses, while Chapter 10 confidence intervals are for two-sample analyses. Chapter 9 introduces the concept of hypotheses testing and presents hypothesis tests for one sample. Chapter 10 contains hypothesis tests for two samples, while Chapter 11 presents hypothesis tests for three or more samples.

Because there is a plethora of confidence interval and hypothesis testing techniques presented in Unit III, it is easy to lose the big picture of when to use what technique. To assist you in sorting out these techniques, a taxonomy of techniques has been created and is presented in a tree diagram both here and inside the front cover for your convenience and consideration. Note that in determining which technique to use, there are several key questions that one should consider:

1. Are you estimating (using a confidence interval) or testing (using a hypothesis test)?
2. How many samples are you analyzing?
3. Are you analyzing means, proportions, or variances?
4. If you are analyzing means, is (are) the standard deviation(s) or variance(s) known or not?
5. If you are analyzing means from two samples, are the samples independent or related?
6. If you are analyzing three or more samples, are you studying one or two independent variables, and is there a blocking variable?

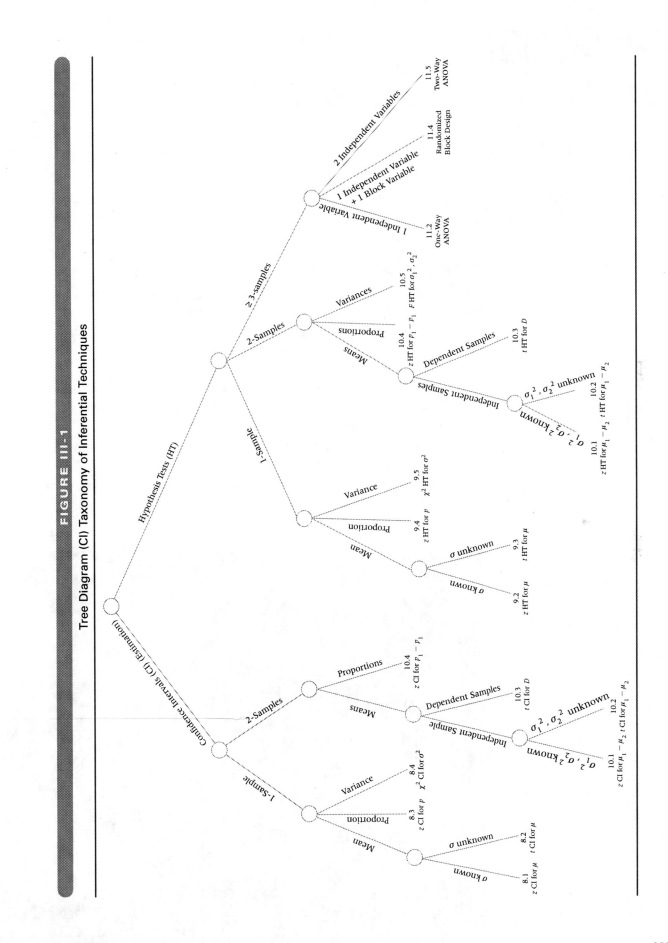

FIGURE III-1

Tree Diagram (CI) Taxonomy of Inferential Techniques

255

CHAPTER 8

Statistical Inference: Estimation for Single Populations

LEARNING OBJECTIVES

The overall learning objective of Chapter 8 is to help you understand estimating parameters of single populations, thereby enabling you to:

1. Estimate the population mean with a known population standard deviation with the z statistic, correcting for a finite population if necessary.
2. Estimate the population mean with an unknown population standard deviation using the t statistic and properties of the t distribution.
3. Estimate a population proportion using the z statistic.
4. Use the chi-square distribution to estimate the population variance given the sample variance.
5. Determine the sample size needed in order to estimate the population mean and population proportion.

Alamy Limited

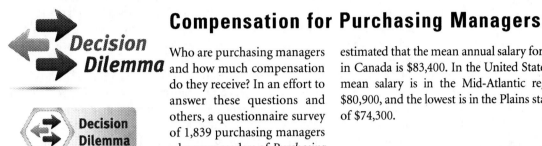

Compensation for Purchasing Managers

Decision Dilemma

Who are purchasing managers and how much compensation do they receive? In an effort to answer these questions and others, a questionnaire survey of 1,839 purchasing managers who were readers of *Purchasing* magazine or who were respondents on the *Purchasing* Web site was taken. Demographic questions about sex, age, years of experience, title, industry, company annual sales, location, and others were asked along with compensation questions.

The results of the survey indicated that the mean age of a purchasing manager is 46.2 years, and the mean years of experience in the field is 16. Sixty-five percent of purchasing managers are male, and 35% are female. Seventy-three percent of all respondents have a college degree or a certificate. College graduates hold the highest paying jobs, work for the biggest companies, and hold the highest ranking purchasing positions. Twenty-four percent of all the respondents are designated as a Certified Purchasing Manager (CPM).

Purchasing manager compensation varies with position, size of company, industry, and company location. Recent studies indicate that the mean salary for a purchasing manager is $89,160. However, salary varies considerably according to buying responsibilities, with purchasers who buy IT goods and services earning an average of $101,104 on the high end and purchasers who buy office equipment/supplies earning an average of $71,392 on the low end. Purchasing managers with the title of buyer receive a mean salary of $47,100 and supplier vice presidents earning a mean of $159,600. Sixty percent of all survey respondents receive bonuses as a part of their annual compensation, while 16% receive stock options.

Based on sample sizes as small as 25, mean annual salaries are broken down by U.S. region and Canada. It is estimated that the mean annual salary for a purchasing manager in Canada is $83,400. In the United States the highest reported mean salary is in the Mid-Atlantic region with a mean of $80,900, and the lowest is in the Plains states with a mean figure of $74,300.

Managerial and Statistical Questions

1. Can the mean national salary for a purchasing manager be estimated using sample data such as that reported in this study? If so, how much error is involved and how much confidence can we have in it?

2. The study reported that the mean age of a respondent is 46.2 years and that, on average, a purchasing manager has 16 years of experience. How can these sample figures be used to estimate a mean for the population? For example, is the population mean age for purchasing managers also 46.2 years, or is it different? If the population mean years of experience is estimated using such a study, then what is the error of the estimation?

3. This Decision Dilemma reports that 73% of the responding purchasing managers have a college degree or certificate. Does this figure hold for all purchasing managers? Are 65% of all purchasing managers male as reported in this study? How can population proportions be estimated using sample data? How much error is involved? How confident can decision makers be in the results?

4. When survey data are broken down by U.S. region and Canada, the sample size for each subgroup is as low as 25 respondents. Does sample size affect the results of the study? If the study reports that the mean salary for a Canadian purchasing manager is $83,400 based on 25 respondents, then is that information less valid than the overall mean salary of $78,500 reported by 1,839 respondents? How do business decision makers discern between study results when sample sizes vary?

Sources: Adapted from the *Purchasing* 2007 salary survey at: http://www.purchasing.com/article/CA6511754.html and Susan Avery, "2005 Salary Study: Applause Please," *Purchasing*, vol 134, no 20 (December 8, 2005), pp. 29–33; "Purchasing Manager Salary," 2010, http://www.highersalary.com/management/purchasing-manager/.

Unit III of this text (Chapters 8 to 11) presents, discusses, and applies various statistical techniques for making inferential estimations and hypothesis tests to enhance decision making in business. Figure III-1 displays a tree diagram taxonomy of these techniques, organizing them by usage, number of samples, and type of statistic. Chapter 8 contains the portion of these techniques that can be used for estimating a mean, a proportion, or

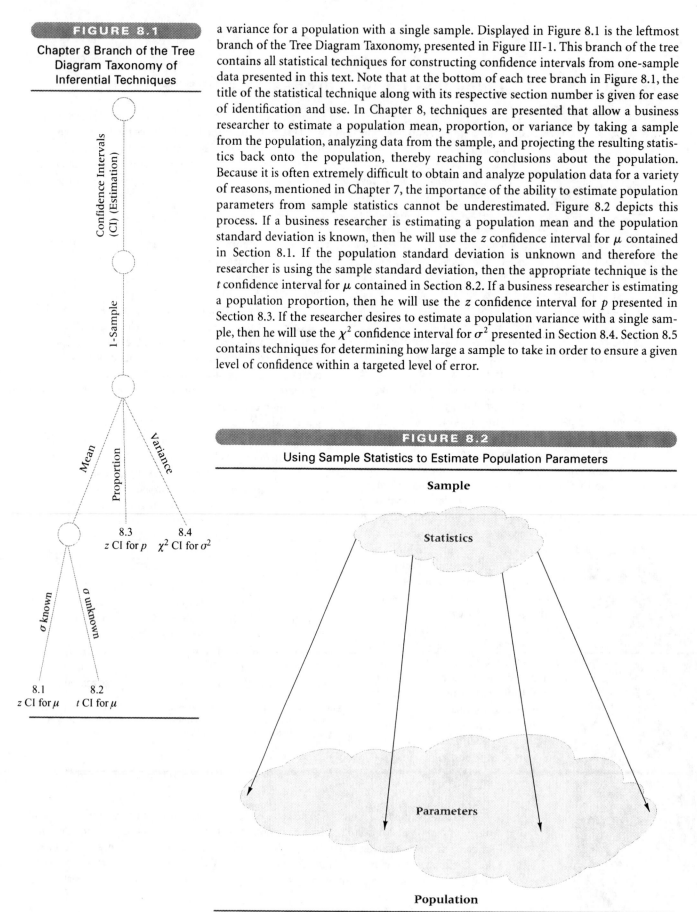

FIGURE 8.1

Chapter 8 Branch of the Tree Diagram Taxonomy of Inferential Techniques

a variance for a population with a single sample. Displayed in Figure 8.1 is the leftmost branch of the Tree Diagram Taxonomy, presented in Figure III-1. This branch of the tree contains all statistical techniques for constructing confidence intervals from one-sample data presented in this text. Note that at the bottom of each tree branch in Figure 8.1, the title of the statistical technique along with its respective section number is given for ease of identification and use. In Chapter 8, techniques are presented that allow a business researcher to estimate a population mean, proportion, or variance by taking a sample from the population, analyzing data from the sample, and projecting the resulting statistics back onto the population, thereby reaching conclusions about the population. Because it is often extremely difficult to obtain and analyze population data for a variety of reasons, mentioned in Chapter 7, the importance of the ability to estimate population parameters from sample statistics cannot be underestimated. Figure 8.2 depicts this process. If a business researcher is estimating a population mean and the population standard deviation is known, then he will use the z confidence interval for μ contained in Section 8.1. If the population standard deviation is unknown and therefore the researcher is using the sample standard deviation, then the appropriate technique is the t confidence interval for μ contained in Section 8.2. If a business researcher is estimating a population proportion, then he will use the z confidence interval for p presented in Section 8.3. If the researcher desires to estimate a population variance with a single sample, then he will use the χ^2 confidence interval for σ^2 presented in Section 8.4. Section 8.5 contains techniques for determining how large a sample to take in order to ensure a given level of confidence within a targeted level of error.

FIGURE 8.2

Using Sample Statistics to Estimate Population Parameters

8.1 ESTIMATING THE POPULATION MEAN USING THE *z* STATISTIC (*σ* KNOWN)

On many occasions estimating the population mean is useful in business research. For example, the manager of human resources in a company might want to estimate the average number of days of work an employee misses per year because of illness. If the firm has thousands of employees, direct calculation of a population mean such as this may be practically impossible. Instead, a random sample of employees can be taken, and the sample mean number of sick days can be used to estimate the population mean. Suppose another company developed a new process for prolonging the shelf life of a loaf of bread. The company wants to be able to date each loaf for freshness, but company officials do not know exactly how long the bread will stay fresh. By taking a random sample and determining the sample mean shelf life, they can estimate the average shelf life for the population of bread.

As the cellular telephone industry has grown and matured, it is apparent that the use of texting has increased dramatically. Suppose a large cellular phone company in wanting to meet the needs of cell phone users hires a business research company to estimate the average number of texts used per month by Americans in the 18-to-24-years-of-age category. The research company studies the phone records of 85 randomly sampled Americans in the 18-to-24-years-of-age category and computes a sample monthly mean of 1300 texts. This mean, which is a statistic, is used to estimate the population mean, which is a parameter. If the cellular phone company uses the sample mean of 1300 texts as an estimate for the population mean, the same sample mean is used as a *point estimate*.

A **point estimate** is *a statistic taken from a sample that is used to estimate a population parameter*. A point estimate is only as good as the representativeness of its sample. If other random samples are taken from the population, the point estimates derived from those samples are likely to vary. Because of variation in sample statistics, estimating a population parameter with an interval estimate is often preferable to using a point estimate. An **interval estimate** (confidence interval) is *a range of values within which the analyst can declare, with some confidence, the population parameter lies*. Confidence intervals can be two sided or one sided. This text presents only two-sided confidence intervals. How are confidence intervals constructed?

As a result of the central limit theorem, the following *z* formula for sample means can be used if the population standard deviation is known when sample sizes are large, regardless of the shape of the population distribution, or for smaller sizes if the population is normally distributed.

$$z = \frac{\bar{x} - \mu}{\dfrac{\sigma}{\sqrt{n}}}$$

Rearranging this formula algebraically to solve for μ gives

$$\mu = \bar{x} - z\frac{\sigma}{\sqrt{n}}$$

Because a sample mean can be greater than or less than the population mean, *z* can be positive or negative. Thus the preceding expression takes the following form.

$$\bar{x} \pm z\frac{\sigma}{\sqrt{n}}$$

Rewriting this expression yields the confidence interval formula for estimating μ with large sample sizes if the population standard deviation is known.

100(1 − α)% CONFIDENCE INTERVAL TO ESTIMATE μ: σ KNOWN (8.1)	$$\bar{x} \pm z_{\alpha/2}\frac{\sigma}{\sqrt{n}}$$ or $$\bar{x} - z_{\alpha/2}\frac{\sigma}{\sqrt{n}} \leq \mu \leq \bar{x} + z_{\alpha/2}\frac{\sigma}{\sqrt{n}}$$ where α = the area under the normal curve outside the confidence interval area $\alpha/2$ = the area in one end (tail) of the distribution outside the confidence interval

Alpha (α) is the area under the normal curve in the tails of the distribution outside the area defined by the confidence interval. We will focus more on α in Chapter 9. Here we use α to locate the z value in constructing the confidence interval as shown in Figure 8.3. Because the standard normal table is based on areas between a z of 0 and $z_{\alpha/2}$, the table z value is found by locating the area of $.5000 - \alpha/2$, which is the part of the normal curve between the middle of the curve and one of the tails. Another way to locate this z value is to change the confidence level from percentage to proportion, divide it in half, and go to the table with this value. The results are the same.

The confidence interval formula (8.1) yields a range (interval) within which we feel with some confidence that the population mean is located. It is not certain that the population mean is in the interval unless we have a 100% confidence interval that is infinitely wide. If we want to construct a 95% confidence interval, the level of confidence is 95%, or .95. If 100 such intervals are constructed by taking random samples from the population, it is likely that 95 of the intervals would include the population mean and 5 would not.

As an example, in the cellular telephone company's effort to estimate the population monthly mean number of texts in the 18-to-24-year-old age category, from a sample of 85 bills it is determined that the sample mean is 1300 texts. Using this sample mean, a confidence interval can be calculated within which the researcher is relatively confident that the actual population mean is located. To make this calculation using formula 8.1, the value of the population standard deviation and the value of z (in addition to the sample mean, 1300, and the sample size, 85) must be known. Suppose past history and similar studies indicate that the population standard deviation is about 160.

The value of z is driven by the level of confidence. An interval with 100% confidence is so wide that it is meaningless. Some of the more common levels of confidence used by business researchers are 90%, 95%, 98%, and 99%. Why would a business researcher not just select the highest confidence and always use that level? The reason is that trade-offs between sample size, interval width, and level of confidence must be considered. For example, as the level of confidence is increased, the interval gets wider, provided the sample size and standard deviation remain constant.

For the cellular telephone problem, suppose the business researcher decided on a 95% confidence interval for the results. Figure 8.4 shows a normal distribution of sample means about the population mean. When using a 95% level of confidence, the researcher selects an interval centered on μ within which 95% of all sample mean values will fall and then uses the width of that interval to create an interval around the *sample mean* within which he has some confidence the population mean will fall.

FIGURE 8.3

z Scores for Confidence Intervals in Relation to α

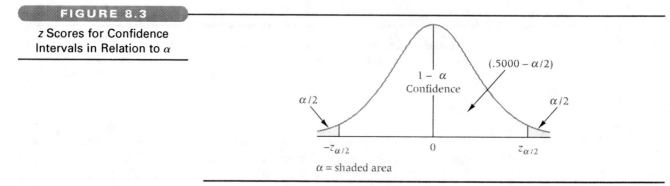

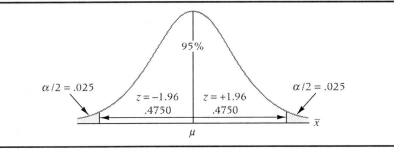

FIGURE 8.4

Distribution of Sample Means
for 95% Confidence

For 95% confidence, $\alpha = .05$ and $\alpha/2 = .025$. The value of $z_{\alpha/2}$ or $z_{.025}$ is found by looking in the standard normal table under $.5000 - .0250 = .4750$. This area in the table is associated with a z value of 1.96. Another way can be used to locate the table z value. Because the distribution is symmetric and the intervals are equal on each side of the population mean, $\frac{1}{2}(95\%)$, or .4750, of the area is on each side of the mean. Table A.5 yields a z value of 1.96 for this portion of the normal curve. Thus the z value for a 95% confidence interval is always 1.96. In other words, of all the possible $\bar{x}$ values along the horizontal axis of the diagram, 95% of them should be within a z score of 1.96 from the population mean.

The business researcher can now complete the cellular telephone problem. To determine a 95% confidence interval for $\bar{x} = 1300$, $\sigma = 160$, $n = 85$, and $z = 1.96$, the researcher estimates the average number of texts by including the value of z in formula 8.1.

FIGURE 8.5

Twenty 95% Confidence
Intervals of μ

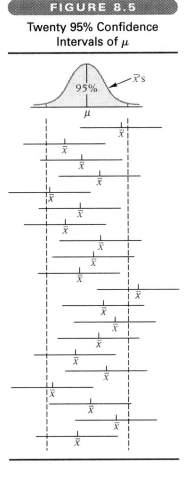

$$1300 - 1.96\frac{160}{\sqrt{85}} \leq \mu \leq 1300 + 1.96\frac{160}{\sqrt{85}}$$

$$1300 - 34.01 \leq \mu \leq 1300 + 34.01$$

$$1265.99 \leq \mu \leq 1334.01$$

The confidence interval is constructed from the point estimate, which in this problem is 1300 texts, and the error of this estimate, which is ± 34.01 texts. The resulting confidence interval is $1265.99 \leq \mu \leq 1334.01$. The cellular telephone company researcher is 95% confident that the average number of texts per month by an American in the 18-to-24-year-old category is between 1265.99 and 1334.01.

What does being 95% confident that the population mean is in an interval actually indicate? It indicates that, if the company researcher were to randomly select 100 samples of 85 bills and use the results of each sample to construct a 95% confidence interval, approximately 95 of the 100 intervals would contain the population mean. It also indicates that 5% of the intervals would not contain the population mean. The company researcher is likely to take only a single sample and compute the confidence interval from that sample information. That interval either contains the population mean or it does not. Figure 8.5 depicts the meaning of a 95% confidence interval for the mean. Note that if 20 random samples are taken from the population, 19 of the 20 are likely to contain the population mean if a 95% confidence interval is used ($19/20 = 95\%$). If a 90% confidence interval is constructed, only 18 of the 20 intervals are likely to contain the population mean.

**DEMONSTRATION
PROBLEM 8.1**

A survey was taken of U.S. companies that do business with firms in India. One of the questions on the survey was: Approximately how many years has your company been trading with firms in India? A random sample of 44 responses to this question yielded a mean of 10.455 years. Suppose the population standard deviation for this question is 7.7 years. Using this information, construct a 90% confidence interval for the mean number of years that a company has been trading in India for the population of U.S. companies trading with firms in India.

Solution

Here, $n = 44$, $\bar{x} = 10.455$, and $\sigma = 7.7$. To determine the value of $z_{\alpha/2}$, divide the 90% confidence in half, or take $.5000 - \alpha/2 = .5000 - .0500$ where $\alpha = 10\%$. *Note:* The z

distribution of $\bar{x}$ around μ contains .4500 of the area on each side of μ, or ½(90%). Table A.5 yields a z value of 1.645 for the area of .4500 (interpolating between .4495 and .4505). The confidence interval is

$$\bar{x} - z\frac{\sigma}{\sqrt{n}} \le \mu \le \bar{x} + z\frac{\sigma}{\sqrt{n}}$$

$$10.455 - 1.645\frac{7.7}{\sqrt{44}} \le \mu \le 10.455 + 1.645\frac{7.7}{\sqrt{44}}$$

$$10.455 - 1.910 \le \mu \le 10.455 + 1.910$$

$$8.545 \le \mu \le 12.365$$

The analyst is 90% confident that if a census of all U.S. companies trading with firms in India were taken at the time of this survey, the actual population mean number of years a company would have been trading with firms in India would be between 8.545 and 12.365. The point estimate is 10.455 years.

TABLE 8.1

Values of z for Common Levels of Confidence

Confidence Level	z Value
90%	1.645
95%	1.96
98%	2.33
99%	2.575

For convenience, Table 8.1 contains some of the more common levels of confidence and their associated z values.

Finite Correction Factor

Recall from Chapter 7 that if the sample is taken from a finite population, a finite correction factor may be used to increase the accuracy of the solution. In the case of interval estimation, the finite correction factor is used to reduce the width of the interval. As stated in Chapter 7, if the sample size is less than 5% of the population, the finite correction factor does not significantly alter the solution. If formula 8.1 is modified to include the finite correction factor, the result is formula 8.2.

CONFIDENCE INTERVAL TO ESTIMATE μ USING THE FINITE CORRECTION FACTOR (8.2)	$\bar{x} - z_{\alpha/2}\frac{\sigma}{\sqrt{n}}\sqrt{\frac{N-n}{N-1}} \le \mu \le \bar{x} + z_{\alpha/2}\frac{\sigma}{\sqrt{n}}\sqrt{\frac{N-n}{N-1}}$

Demonstration Problem 8.2 shows how the finite correction factor can be used.

DEMONSTRATION PROBLEM 8.2

A study is conducted in a company that employs 800 engineers. A random sample of 50 of these engineers reveals that the average sample age is 34.30 years. Historically, the population standard deviation of the age of the company's engineers is approximately 8 years. Construct a 98% confidence interval to estimate the average age of all the engineers in this company.

Solution

This problem has a finite population. The sample size, 50, is greater than 5% of the population, so the finite correction factor may be helpful. In this case $N = 800$, $n = 50$, $\bar{x} = 34.30$, and $\sigma = 8$. The z value for a 98% confidence interval is 2.33 (.98 divided into two equal parts yields .4900; the z value is obtained from Table A.5 by using .4900). Substituting into formula 8.2 and solving for the confidence interval gives

$$34.30 - 2.33\frac{8}{\sqrt{50}}\sqrt{\frac{750}{799}} \le \mu \le 34.30 + 2.33\frac{8}{\sqrt{50}}\sqrt{\frac{750}{799}}$$

$$34.30 - 2.55 \le \mu \le 34.30 + 2.55$$

$$31.75 \le \mu \le 36.85$$

Without the finite correction factor, the result would have been

$$34.30 - 2.64 \le \mu \le 34.30 + 2.64$$
$$31.66 \le \mu \le 36.94$$

The finite correction factor takes into account the fact that the population is only 800 instead of being infinitely large. The sample, $n = 50$, is a greater proportion of the 800 than it would be of a larger population, and thus the width of the confidence interval is reduced when using the finite correction factor.

Estimating the Population Mean Using the z Statistic when the Sample Size Is Small

In the formulas and problems presented so far in the section, sample size was large ($n \ge 30$). However, quite often in the business world, sample sizes are small. While the Central Limit theorem applies only when sample size is large, the distribution of sample means is approximately normal even for small sizes *if the population is normally distributed.* This is visually displayed in the bottom row of Figure 7.6 in Chapter 7. Thus, if it is known that the population from which the sample is being drawn is normally distributed and if σ is known, the z formulas presented in this section can still be used to estimate a population mean even if the sample size is small ($n < 30$).

As an example, suppose a U.S. car rental firm wants to estimate the average number of miles traveled per day by each of its cars rented in California. A random sample of 20 cars rented in California reveals that the sample mean travel distance per day is 85.5 miles, with a population standard deviation of 19.3 miles. Compute a 99% confidence interval to estimate μ.

Here, $n = 20, \bar{x} = 85.5,$ and $\sigma = 19.3$. For a 99% level of confidence, a z value of 2.575 is obtained. Assume that number of miles traveled per day is normally distributed in the population. The confidence interval is

$$\bar{x} - z_{\alpha/2}\frac{\sigma}{\sqrt{n}} \le \mu \le \bar{x} + z_{\alpha/2}\frac{\sigma}{\sqrt{n}}$$

$$85.5 - 2.575\frac{19.3}{\sqrt{20}} \le \mu \le 85.5 + 2.575\frac{19.3}{\sqrt{20}}$$

$$85.5 - 11.1 \le \mu \le 85.5 + 11.1$$

$$74.4 \le \mu \le 96.6$$

The point estimate indicates that the average number of miles traveled per day by a rental car in California is 85.5. With 99% confidence, we estimate that the population mean is somewhere between 74.4 and 96.6 miles per day.

FIGURE 8.6

Excel and Minitab Output for the Cellular Telephone Example

Excel Output

The sample mean is:	1300
The error of the interval is:	34.014
The confidence interval is:	1300 ± 34.014
The confidence interval is:	$1265.986 \le \mu \le 1334.014$

Minitab Output

One-Sample Z

The assumed standard deviation = 160

N	Mean	SE Mean	95% CI
85	1300.00	17.35	(1265.99, 1334.01)

Using the Computer to Construct z Confidence Intervals for the Mean

It is possible to construct a z confidence interval for the mean with either Excel or Minitab. Excel yields the $\pm$ error portion of the confidence interval that must be placed with the sample mean to construct the complete confidence interval. Minitab constructs the complete confidence interval. Figure 8.6 shows both the Excel output and the Minitab output for the cellular telephone example.

8.1 PROBLEMS

8.1 Use the following information to construct the confidence intervals specified to estimate μ.

a. 95% confidence for $\bar{x} = 25$, $\sigma = 3.5$, and $n = 60$

b. 98% confidence for $\bar{x} = 119.6$, $\sigma = 23.89$, and $n = 75$

c. 90% confidence for $\bar{x} = 3.419$, $\sigma = 0.974$, and $n = 32$

d. 80% confidence for $\bar{x} = 56.7$, $\sigma = 12.1$, $N = 500$, and $n = 47$

8.2 For a random sample of 36 items and a sample mean of 211, compute a 95% confidence interval for μ if the population standard deviation is 23.

8.3 A random sample of 81 items is taken, producing a sample mean of 47. The population standard deviation is 5.89. Construct a 90% confidence interval to estimate the population mean.

8.4 A random sample of size 70 is taken from a population that has a variance of 49. The sample mean is 90.4 What is the point estimate of μ? Construct a 94% confidence interval for μ.

8.5 A random sample of size 39 is taken from a population of 200 members. The sample mean is 66 and the population standard deviation is 11. Construct a 96% confidence interval to estimate the population mean. What is the point estimate of the population mean?

8.6 A candy company fills a 20-ounce package of Halloween candy with individually wrapped pieces of candy. The number of pieces of candy per package varies because the package is sold by weight. The company wants to estimate the number of pieces per package. Inspectors randomly sample 120 packages of this candy and count the number of pieces in each package. They find that the sample mean number of pieces is 18.72. Assuming a population standard deviation of .8735, what is the point estimate of the number of pieces per package? Construct a 99% confidence interval to estimate the mean number of pieces per package for the population.

8.7 A small lawnmower company produced 1,500 lawnmowers in 2003. In an effort to determine how maintenance-free these units were, the company decided to conduct a multiyear study of the 2003 lawnmowers. A sample of 200 owners of these lawnmowers was drawn randomly from company records and contacted. The owners were given an 800 number and asked to call the company when the first major repair was required for the lawnmowers. Owners who no longer used the lawnmower to cut their grass were disqualified. After many years, 187 of the owners had reported. The other 13 disqualified themselves. The average number of years until the first major repair was 5.3 for the 187 owners reporting. It is believed that the population standard deviation was 1.28 years. If the company wants to advertise an average number of years of repair-free lawn mowing for this lawnmower, what is the point estimate? Construct a 95% confidence interval for the average number of years until the first major repair.

8.8 The average total dollar purchase at a convenience store is less than that at a supermarket. Despite smaller-ticket purchases, convenience stores can still be

profitable because of the size of operation, volume of business, and the markup.
A researcher is interested in estimating the average purchase amount for convenience stores in suburban Long Island. To do so, she randomly sampled 24 purchases from several convenience stores in suburban Long Island and tabulated the amounts to the nearest dollar. Use the following data to construct a 90% confidence interval for the population average amount of purchases. Assume that the population standard deviation is 3.23 and the population is normally distributed.

$2	$11	$8	$7	$9	$3
5	4	2	1	10	8
14	7	6	3	7	2
4	1	3	6	8	4

8.9 A community health association is interested in estimating the average number of maternity days women stay in the local hospital. A random sample is taken of 36 women who had babies in the hospital during the past year. The following numbers of maternity days each woman was in the hospital are rounded to the nearest day.

3	3	4	3	2	5	3	1	4	3
4	2	3	5	3	2	4	3	2	4
1	6	3	4	3	3	5	2	3	2
3	5	4	3	5	4				

Use these data and a population standard deviation of 1.17 to construct a 98% confidence interval to estimate the average maternity stay in the hospital for all women who have babies in this hospital.

8.10 A meat-processing company in the Midwest produces and markets a package of eight small sausage sandwiches. The product is nationally distributed, and the company is interested in knowing the average retail price charged for this item in stores across the country. The company cannot justify a national census to generate this information. Based on the company information system's list of all retailers who carry the product, a researcher for the company contacts 36 of these retailers and ascertains the selling prices for the product. Use the following price data and a population standard deviation of 0.113 to determine a point estimate for the national retail price of the product. Construct a 90% confidence interval to estimate this price.

$2.23	$2.11	$2.12	$2.20	$2.17	$2.10
2.16	2.31	1.98	2.17	2.14	1.82
2.12	2.07	2.17	2.30	2.29	2.19
2.01	2.24	2.18	2.18	2.32	2.02
1.99	1.87	2.09	2.22	2.15	2.19
2.23	2.10	2.08	2.05	2.16	2.26

8.11 According to the U.S. Census Bureau, the average travel time to work in Philadelphia is 27.4 minutes. Suppose a business researcher wants to estimate the average travel time to work in Cleveland using a 95% level of confidence. A random sample of 45 Cleveland commuters is taken and the travel time to work is obtained from each. The data follow. Assuming a population standard deviation of 5.124, compute a 95% confidence interval on the data. What is the point estimate and what is the error of the interval? Explain what these results means in terms of Philadelphia commuters.

27	25	19	21	24	27	29	34	18	29	16	28
20	32	27	28	22	20	14	15	29	28	29	33
16	29	28	28	27	23	27	20	27	25	21	18
26	14	23	27	27	21	25	28	30			

8.12 Suppose a random sample of turkey prices is taken from across the nation in an effort to estimate the average turkey price per pound in the United States. Shown here is the Minitab output for such a sample. Examine the output. What is the point estimate? What is the value of the assumed population standard deviation? How large is the sample? What level of confidence is being used? What table value is associated with this level of confidence? What is the confidence interval? Often the portion of the confidence interval that is added and subtracted from the mean is referred to as the error of the estimate. How much is the error of the estimate in this problem?

One-Sample Z

```
The assumed standard deviation = 0.14
 N       Mean     SE Mean        95% CI
41     0.960000   0.021864   (0.917147, 1.002853)
```

8.2   ESTIMATING THE POPULATION MEAN USING THE t STATISTIC (σ UNKNOWN)

Video

Interactive Applet

In Section 8.1, we learned how to estimate a population mean by using the sample mean when the population standard deviation is known. In most instances, if a business researcher desires to estimate a population mean, the population standard deviation will be unknown and thus techniques presented in Section 8.1 will not be applicable. When the population standard deviation is unknown, the sample standard deviation must be used in the estimation process. In this section, a statistical technique is presented to estimate a population mean using the sample mean when the population standard deviation is unknown.

Suppose a business researcher is interested in estimating the average flying time of a 757 jet from New York to Los Angeles. Since the business researcher does not know the population mean or average time, it is likely that she also does not know the population standard deviation. By taking a random sample of flights, the researcher can compute a sample mean and a sample standard deviation from which the estimate can be constructed. Another business researcher wants to estimate the mean number of work hours lost annually per worker due to illness, using a random sample but the researcher has no idea what the population standard deviation is. He will have the sample mean and sample standard deviation available to perform this analysis.

The z formulas presented in Section 8.1 are inappropriate for use when the population standard deviation is unknown (and is replaced by the sample standard deviation). Instead, another mechanism to handle such cases was developed by a British statistician, William S. Gosset.

Gosset was born in 1876 in Canterbury, England. He studied chemistry and mathematics and in 1899 went to work for the Guinness Brewery in Dublin, Ireland. Gosset was involved in quality control at the brewery, studying variables such as raw materials and temperature. Because of the circumstances of his experiments, Gosset conducted many studies where the population standard deviation was unavailable. He discovered that using the standard z test with a sample standard deviation produced inexact and incorrect distributions. This finding led to his development of the distribution of the sample standard deviation and the t test.

Gosset was a student and close personal friend of Karl Pearson. When Gosset's first work on the t test was published, he used the pen name "Student." As a result, the t test is sometimes referred to as the Student's t test. Gosset's contribution was significant because it led to more exact statistical tests, which some scholars say marked the beginning of the modern era in mathematical statistics.*

*Adapted from Arthur L. Dudycha and Linda W. Dudycha, "Behavioral Statistics: An Historical Perspective," in *Statistical Issues: A Reader for the Behavioral Sciences,* Roger Kirk, ed. (Monterey, CA: Brooks/Cole, 1972).

The *t* Distribution

Gosset developed the **t distribution**, which is used instead of the *z* distribution for doing inferential statistics on the population mean when the population standard deviation is unknown and the population is normally distributed. The formula for the *t* statistic is

$$t = \frac{\bar{x} - \mu}{\dfrac{s}{\sqrt{n}}}$$

This formula is essentially the same as the *z* formula, but the distribution table values are different. The *t* distribution values are contained in Table A.6 and, for convenience, inside the front cover of the text.

The *t* distribution actually is a series of distributions because every sample size has a different distribution, thereby creating the potential for many *t* tables. To make these *t* values more manageable, only select key values are presented; each line in the table contains values from a different *t* distribution. An assumption underlying the use of the *t* statistic is that the population is normally distributed. If the population distribution is not normal or is unknown, nonparametric techniques (presented in Chapter 17) should be used.

Robustness

Most statistical techniques have one or more underlying assumptions. If a statistical technique is relatively insensitive to minor violations in one or more of its underlying assumptions, the technique is said to be **robust** to that assumption. The *t* statistic for estimating a population mean is relatively robust to the assumption that the population is normally distributed.

Some statistical techniques are not robust, and a statistician should exercise extreme caution to be certain that the assumptions underlying a technique are being met before using it or interpreting statistical output resulting from its use. A business analyst should always beware of statistical assumptions and the robustness of techniques being used in an analysis.

Characteristics of the *t* Distribution

Figure 8.7 displays two *t* distributions superimposed on the standard normal distribution. Like the standard normal curve, *t* distributions are symmetric, unimodal, and a family of curves. The *t* distributions are flatter in the middle and have more area in their tails than the standard normal distribution.

An examination of *t* distribution values reveals that the *t* distribution approaches the standard normal curve as *n* becomes large. The *t* distribution is the appropriate distribution to use any time the population variance or standard deviation is unknown, regardless of sample size.

Reading the *t* Distribution Table

To find a value in the *t* distribution table requires knowing the degrees of freedom; each different value of degrees of freedom is associated with a different *t* distribution. The *t* distribution table used here is a compilation of many *t* distributions, with each line of the

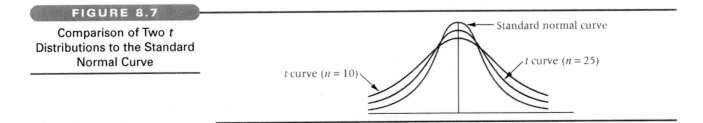

FIGURE 8.7

Comparison of Two *t* Distributions to the Standard Normal Curve

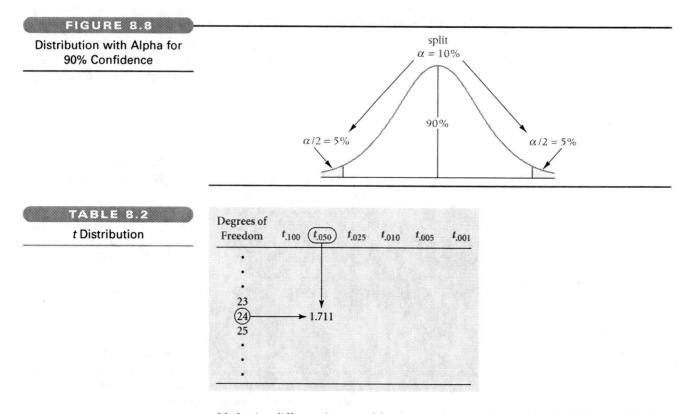

FIGURE 8.8

Distribution with Alpha for
90% Confidence

TABLE 8.2

t Distribution

table having different degrees of freedom and containing *t* values for different *t* distributions. The **degrees of freedom** for the *t* statistic presented in this section are computed by $n - 1$. The term **degrees of freedom** refers to *the number of independent observations for a source of variation minus the number of independent parameters estimated in computing the variation.*[*] In this case, one independent parameter, the population mean, μ, is being estimated by $\bar{x}$ in computing *s*. Thus, the degrees of freedom formula is *n* independent observations minus one independent parameter being estimated $(n - 1)$. Because the degrees of freedom are computed differently for various *t* formulas, a degrees of freedom formula is given along with each *t* formula in the text.

In Table A.6, the degrees of freedom are located in the left column. The *t* distribution table in this text does not use the area between the statistic and the mean as does the *z* distribution (standard normal distribution). Instead, the *t* table uses the area in the tail of the distribution. The emphasis in the *t* table is on α, and each tail of the distribution contains $\alpha/2$ of the area under the curve when confidence intervals are constructed. For confidence intervals, the table *t* value is found in the column under the value of $\alpha/2$ and in the row of the degrees of freedom (df) value.

For example, if a 90% confidence interval is being computed, the total area in the two tails is 10%. Thus, α is .10 and $\alpha/2$ is .05, as indicated in Figure 8.8. The *t* distribution table shown in Table 8.2 contains only six values of $\alpha/2$ (.10, .05, .025, .01, .005, .001). The *t* value is located at the intersection of the df value and the selected $\alpha/2$ value. So if the degrees of freedom for a given *t* statistic are 24 and the desired $\alpha/2$ value is .05, the *t* value is 1.711.

Confidence Intervals to Estimate the Population Mean Using the *t* Statistic

The *t* formula

$$t = \frac{\bar{x} - \mu}{\frac{s}{\sqrt{n}}}$$

*Roger E. Kirk. *Experimental Design: Procedures for the Behavioral Sciences.* Belmont, California: Brooks/Cole, 1968.

can be manipulated algebraically to produce a formula for estimating the population mean when α is unknown and the population is normally distributed. The results are the formulas given next.

CONFIDENCE INTERVAL TO ESTIMATE μ: POPULATION STANDARD DEVIATION UNKNOWN AND THE POPULATION NORMALLY DISTRIBUTED (8.3)	$$\bar{x} \pm t_{\alpha/2,\,n-1}\frac{s}{\sqrt{n}}$$ $$\bar{x} - t_{\alpha/2,\,n-1}\frac{s}{\sqrt{n}} \leq \mu \leq \bar{x} + t_{\alpha/2,\,n-1}\frac{s}{\sqrt{n}}$$ $$\mathrm{df} = n - 1$$

Formula 8.3 can be used in a manner similar to methods presented in Section 8.1 for constructing a confidence interval to estimate μ. For example, in the aerospace industry some companies allow their employees to accumulate extra working hours beyond their 40-hour week. These extra hours sometimes are referred to as *green* time, or *comp* time. Many managers work longer than the eight-hour workday preparing proposals, overseeing crucial tasks, and taking care of paperwork. Recognition of such overtime is important. Most managers are usually not paid extra for this work, but a record is kept of this time and occasionally the manager is allowed to use some of this comp time as extra leave or vacation time. Suppose a researcher wants to estimate the average amount of comp time accumulated per week for managers in the aerospace industry. He randomly samples 18 managers and measures the amount of extra time they work during a specific week and obtains the results shown (in hours).

6	21	17	20	7	0	8	16	29
3	8	12	11	9	21	25	15	16

He constructs a 90% confidence interval to estimate the average amount of extra time per week worked by a manager in the aerospace industry. He assumes that comp time is normally distributed in the population. The sample size is 18, so df = 17. A 90% level of confidence results in $\alpha/2 = .05$ area in each tail. The table *t* value is

$$t_{.05,17} = 1.740$$

The subscripts in the *t* value denote to other researchers the area in the right tail of the *t* distribution (for confidence intervals $\alpha/2$) and the number of degrees of freedom. The sample mean is 13.56 hours, and the sample standard deviation is 7.80 hours. The confidence interval is computed from this information as

$$\bar{x} \pm t_{\alpha/2,\,n-1}\frac{s}{\sqrt{n}}$$

$$13.56 \pm 1.740\frac{7.80}{\sqrt{18}} = 13.56 \pm 3.20$$

$$10.36 \leq \mu \leq 16.76$$

The point estimate for this problem is 13.56 hours, with an error of ±3.20 hours. The researcher is 90% confident that the average amount of comp time accumulated by a manager per week in this industry is between 10.36 and 16.76 hours.

From these figures, aerospace managers could attempt to build a reward system for such extra work or evaluate the regular 40-hour week to determine how to use the normal work hours more effectively and thus reduce comp time.

DEMONSTRATION PROBLEM 8.3

Demonstration Problem

The owner of a large equipment rental company wants to make a rather quick estimate of the average number of days a piece of ditchdigging equipment is rented out per person per time. The company has records of all rentals, but the amount of time required to conduct an audit of *all* accounts would be prohibitive. The owner decides to take a random sample of rental invoices. Fourteen different rentals of ditchdiggers are selected randomly from the files, yielding the following data. She uses these data to construct a 99% confidence interval to estimate the average number of days that a ditchdigger is rented and assumes that the number of days per rental is normally distributed in the population.

$$3 \quad 1 \quad 3 \quad 2 \quad 5 \quad 1 \quad 2 \quad 1 \quad 4 \quad 2 \quad 1 \quad 3 \quad 1 \quad 1$$

Solution

As $n = 14$, the df = 13. The 99% level of confidence results in $\alpha/2 = .005$ area in each tail of the distribution. The table t value is

$$t_{.005,13} = 3.012$$

The sample mean is 2.14 and the sample standard deviation is 1.29. The confidence interval is

$$\bar{x} \pm t\frac{s}{\sqrt{n}}$$

$$2.14 \pm 3.012\frac{1.29}{\sqrt{14}} = 2.14 \pm 1.04$$

$$1.10 \leq \mu \leq 3.18$$

The point estimate of the average length of time per rental is 2.14 days, with an error of ±1.04. With a 99% level of confidence, the company's owner can estimate that the average length of time per rental is between 1.10 and 3.18 days. Combining this figure with variables such as frequency of rentals per year can help the owner estimate potential profit or loss per year for such a piece of equipment.

Using the Computer to Construct t Confidence Intervals for the Mean

Both Excel and Minitab can be used to construct confidence intervals for μ using the t distribution. Figure 8.9 displays Excel output and Minitab output for the aerospace comp time problem. The Excel output includes the mean, the standard error, the sample standard deviation, and the error of the confidence interval, referred to by Excel as the "confidence level." The standard error of the mean is computed by dividing the standard deviation (7.8006) by the square root of n (4.243). When using the Excel output, the confidence interval must be computed from the sample mean and the confidence level (error of the interval).

The Minitab output yields the confidence interval endpoints (10.36, 16.75). The "SE Mean" is the standard error of the mean. The error of the confidence interval is computed by multiplying the standard error of the mean by the table value of t. Adding and subtracting this error from the mean yields the confidence interval endpoints produced by Minitab.

FIGURE 8.9

Excel and Minitab Output for the Comp Time Example

Excel Output

Comp Time	
Mean	13.560
Standard Error	1.839
Standard Deviation	7.801
Confidence Level (90.0%)	3.200

Minitab Output

One-Sample T: Comp Time

Variable	N	Mean	StDev	SE Mean	90% CI
Comp Time	18	13.56	7.80	1.84	(10.36, 16.75)

THINKING CRITICALLY ABOUT STATISTICS IN BUSINESS TODAY

Canadian Grocery Shopping Statistics

A study of 1,000 adult Canadians was conducted by the Environics Research Group in a recent year in behalf of Master Card Worldwide to ascertain information about Canadian shopping habits. Canadian shopping activities were divided into two core categories: 1.) the "quick" trip for traditional staples, convenience items, or snack foods, and 2.) the "stock-up" trip that generally occurs once per week and is approximately two and a half times longer than a quick trip. As a result, many interesting statistics were reported. Canadians take a mean of 37 stock-up trips per year, spending an average of 44 minutes in the store, and they take a mean of 76 quick trips per year, spending an average of 18 minutes in the store. Forty-six percent of households with kids usually take them on quick trips as do 51% on stock-up trips. On average, Canadians spend four times more money on a stock-up trip than on a quick trip. Some other interesting statistics from this survey include: 23% often buy items that are not on their list but catch their eye, 28% often go to a store to buy an item that is on sale, 24% often switch to another checkout lane to get out faster, and 45% often bring their own bag. Since these statistics are based on a sample of 1,000 shoppers, it is virtually certain that the statistics given here are point estimates.

Things to Ponder

1. Suppose a Canadian chain of large supermarkets wants to specifically appeal to customers making "quick" trips. What are some steps that the supermarkets could take to appeal more to customers making "quick trips"?

2. Since 23% of buyers in this survey buy items that are not on their lists, what are some things that a store can do to encourage even more buyers to purchase items not on their lists?

Source: 2008 MASTERINDEX Report: *Checking Out the Canadian Grocery Shopping Experience,* located at: http://www.mastercard.com/ca/wce/PDF/ TRANSACTOR_REPORT_E.pdf.

8.2 PROBLEMS

8.13 Suppose the following data are selected randomly from a population of normally distributed values.

40	51	43	48	44	57	54
39	42	48	45	39	43	

Construct a 95% confidence interval to estimate the population mean.

8.14 Assuming x is normally distributed, use the following information to compute a 90% confidence interval to estimate μ.

313	320	319	340	325	310
321	329	317	311	307	318

8.15 If a random sample of 41 items produces $\bar{x} = 128.4$ and $s = 20.6$, what is the 98% confidence interval for μ? Assume x is normally distributed for the population. What is the point estimate?

8.16 A random sample of 15 items is taken, producing a sample mean of 2.364 with a sample variance of .81. Assume x is normally distributed and construct a 90% confidence interval for the population mean.

8.17 Use the following data to construct a 99% confidence interval for μ.

16.4	17.1	17.0	15.6	16.2
14.8	16.0	15.6	17.3	17.4
15.6	15.7	17.2	16.6	16.0
15.3	15.4	16.0	15.8	17.2
14.6	15.5	14.9	16.7	16.3

Assume x is normally distributed. What is the point estimate for μ?

8.18 According to Runzheimer International, the average cost of a domestic trip for business travelers in the financial industry is $1,250. Suppose another travel industry research company takes a random sample of 51 business travelers in the financial industry and determines that the sample average cost of a domestic trip is $1,192, with a sample standard deviation of $279. Construct a 98% confidence interval for the population mean from these sample data. Assume that the data are normally distributed in the population. Now go back and examine the $1,250 figure published by Runzheimer International. Does it fall into the confidence interval computed from the sample data? What does it tell you?

8.19 A valve manufacturer produces a butterfly valve composed of two semicircular plates on a common spindle that is used to permit flow in one direction only. The semicircular plates are supplied by a vendor with specifications that the plates be 2.37 millimeters thick and have a tensile strength of five pounds per millimeter. A random sample of 20 such plates is taken. Electronic calipers are used to measure the thickness of each plate; the measurements are given here. Assuming that the thicknesses of such plates are normally distributed, use the data to construct a 95% level of confidence for the population mean thickness of these plates. What is the point estimate? How much is the error of the interval?

2.4066	2.4579	2.6724	2.1228	2.3238
2.1328	2.0665	2.2738	2.2055	2.5267
2.5937	2.1994	2.5392	2.4359	2.2146
2.1933	2.4575	2.7956	2.3353	2.2699

8.20 Some fast-food chains offer a lower-priced combination meal in an effort to attract budget-conscious customers. One chain test-marketed a burger, fries, and a drink combination for $1.71. The weekly sales volume for these meals was impressive. Suppose the chain wants to estimate the average amount its customers spent on a meal at their restaurant while this combination offer was in effect. An analyst gathers data from 28 randomly selected customers. The following data represent the sample meal totals.

$3.21	5.40	3.50	4.39	5.60	8.65	5.02	4.20	1.25	7.64
3.28	5.57	3.26	3.80	5.46	9.87	4.67	5.86	3.73	4.08
5.47	4.49	5.19	5.82	7.62	4.83	8.42	9.10		

Use these data to construct a 90% confidence interval to estimate the population mean value. Assume the amounts spent are normally distributed.

8.21 The marketing director of a large department store wants to estimate the average number of customers who enter the store every five minutes. She randomly selects five-minute intervals and counts the number of arrivals at the store. She obtains the figures 58, 32, 41, 47, 56, 80, 45, 29, 32, and 78. The analyst assumes the number of arrivals is normally distributed. Using these data, the analyst computes a 95% confidence interval to estimate the mean value for all five-minute intervals. What interval values does she get?

8.22 Suppose a company from the United States does considerable business in the city of Johannesburg, South Africa, and wishes to establish a per diem rate for employee travel to that city. The company researcher is assigned this task, and in an effort to determine this figure, she obtains a random sample of 14 business travelers staying in Johannesburg. The result is the data presented below. Use these data to construct a 98% confidence interval to estimate the average per diem expense for business people traveling to Johannesburg. What is the point estimate? Assume per diem rates for any locale are approximately normally distributed.

418.42	229.06	396.48	326.21	435.57	363.38	426.57
607.69	372.80	583.10	253.67	332.25	350.81	362.37

8.23 How much experience do supply-chain transportation managers have in their field? Suppose in an effort to estimate this, 41 supply-chain transportation managers are surveyed and asked how many years of managerial experience they have in transportation. Survey results (in years) are shown below. Use these data to construct a 99% confidence interval to estimate the mean number of years of experience in transportation. Assume that years of experience in transportation is normally distributed in the population.

5	8	10	21	20
25	14	6	19	3
1	9	11	2	3
13	2	4	9	4
5	4	21	7	6
3	28	17	32	2
25	8	13	17	27
7	3	15	4	16
6				

8.24 Cycle time in manufacturing can be viewed as the total time it takes to complete a product from the beginning of the production process. The concept of cycle time varies according to the industry and product or service being offered. Suppose a boat manufacturing company wants to estimate the mean cycle time it takes to produce a 16-foot skiff. A random sample of such skiffs is taken, and the cycle times (in hours) are recorded for each skiff in the sample. The data are analyzed using Minitab and the results are shown below in hours. What is the point estimate for cycle time? How large was the sample size? What is the level of confidence and what is the confidence interval? What is the error of the confidence interval?

One-Sample T

N	Mean	StDev	SE Mean	98% CI
26	25.41	5.34	1.05	(22.81, 28.01)

8.3   ESTIMATING THE POPULATION PROPORTION

Business decision makers and researchers often need to be able to estimate a population proportion. For most businesses, estimating market share (their proportion of the market) is important because many company decisions evolve from market share information. Companies spend thousands of dollars estimating the proportion of produced goods that are defective. Market segmentation opportunities come from a knowledge of the proportion of various demographic characteristics among potential customers or clients.

Methods similar to those in Section 8.1 can be used to estimate the population proportion. The central limit theorem for sample proportions led to the following formula in Chapter 7.

$$z = \frac{\hat{p} - p}{\sqrt{\dfrac{p \cdot q}{n}}}$$

where $q = 1 - p$. Recall that this formula can be applied only when $n \cdot p$ and $n \cdot q$ are greater than 5.

Algebraically manipulating this formula to estimate p involves solving for p. However, p is in both the numerator and the denominator, which complicates the resulting formula. For this reason—for confidence interval purposes only and for large sample sizes—$\hat{p}$ is substituted for p in the denominator, yielding

$$z = \frac{\hat{p} - p}{\sqrt{\dfrac{\hat{p} \cdot \hat{q}}{n}}}$$

where $\hat{q} = 1 - \hat{p}$. Solving for p results in the confidence interval in formula (8.4).*

CONFIDENCE INTERVAL TO ESTIMATE p (8.4)

$$\hat{p} - z_{\alpha/2}\sqrt{\frac{\hat{p} \cdot \hat{q}}{n}} \le p \le \hat{p} + z_{\alpha/2}\sqrt{\frac{\hat{p} \cdot \hat{q}}{n}}$$

where

$\hat{p} = $ sample proportion
$\hat{q} = 1 - \hat{p}$
$p = $ population proportion
$n = $ sample size

*Because we are not using the true standard deviation of $\hat{p}$, the correct divisor of the standard error of $\hat{p}$ is $n - 1$. However, for large sample sizes, the effect is negligible. Although technically the minimal sample size for the techniques presented in this section is $n \cdot p$ and $n \cdot q$ greater than 5, in actual practice sample sizes of several hundred are more commonly used. As an example, for $\hat{p}$ and $\hat{q}$ of .50 and $n = 300$, the standard error of $\hat{p}$ is .02887 using n and .02892 using $n - 1$, a difference of only .00005.

THINKING CRITICALLY ABOUT STATISTICS IN BUSINESS TODAY

Coffee Consumption in the United States

In 1969, more people drank coffee than soft drinks in the United States. In fact, according to Jack Maxwell of *Beverage Digest,* U.S. consumption of coffee in 1969 was close to 40 gallons per capita compared to about 20 gallons of soft drinks. However, by 1998, coffee consumption was down to about 20 gallons per capita annually compared to more than 50 gallons for soft drink consumption. Although coffee lost out to soft drinks as a beverage leader in the past three decades, it made a comeback recently with the increase in the popularity of coffee shops in the United States.

What is the state of coffee consumption in the United States now? A survey conducted by the National Coffee Association revealed that 80% of Americans now drink coffee at least occasionally, and over 50% drink coffee every day. Out-of-home consumption has grown to 39%. Daily consumption among 18-to-24-year-olds rose to 31% compared to 74% of the over-60-year-olds. The average consumption per drinker rose to 3.3 cups per day. However, the 18- to 24-year-olds who drink coffee average 4.6 cups per day, whereas the over-60-year-olds average only 2.8 cups. Coffee consumption also varies by geographic region. Fifty-three percent of Northeasterners surveyed had drunk coffee the previous day compared to 47% of Westerners. Only 16% of Northeasterners drink their coffee black compared to 33% of Westerners and 42% of people in the North Central region.

How does U.S. consumption of coffee compare to other countries? The U.S. per capita consumption of coffee is 4 kilograms, compared to 5.56 kilograms in Europe in general and 11 kilograms in Finland.

Because much of the information presented here was gleaned from some survey, virtually all of the percentages and means are sample statistics and not population parameters. Thus, what are presented as coffee population statistics are actually point estimates. Using the sample size (3,300) and a level of confidence, confidence intervals can be constructed for the proportions. Confidence intervals for means can be constructed from these point estimates if the value of the standard deviation can be determined.

Things to Ponder

1. What might be some reasons why a lower percentage of young adults drink coffee than do older adults? Of those young adults who do drink coffee, consumption is higher than for other groups. Why might this be?

2. The percentages of consumers who drink coffee black vary by region in the United States. How might that effect the marketing of various coffee cream products?

Source: Adapted from Nikhil Deogun, "Joe Wakes Up, Smells the Soda," *The Wall Street Journal* (June 8, 1999), p. B1; "Better Latte than Never," *Prepared Foods* (March 2001), p. 1; "Coffee Consumption on the Rise," *Nation's Restaurant News* (July 2, 2001), p. 1. "Coffee Consumption by Age," *Chain Leader* (January 7, 2008) at http://www.chainleader.com/coffee-trends/article/CA6524742.html. Other sources include the National Coffee Association, Jack Maxwell, the International Coffee Organization, and Datamonitor.

In this formula, $\hat{p}$ is the point estimate and $\pm z_{\alpha/2}\sqrt{\dfrac{\hat{p} \cdot \hat{q}}{n}}$ is the error of the estimation.

As an example, a study of 87 randomly selected companies with a telemarketing operation revealed that 39% of the sampled companies used telemarketing to assist them in order processing. Using this information, how could a researcher estimate the *population* proportion of telemarketing companies that use their telemarketing operation to assist them in order processing?

The sample proportion, $\hat{p} = .39$, is the *point estimate* of the population proportion, p. For $n = 87$ and $\hat{p} = .39$, a 95% confidence interval can be computed to determine the interval estimation of p. The z value for 95% confidence is 1.96. The value of $\hat{q} = 1 - \hat{p} = 1 - .39 = .61$. The confidence interval estimate is

$$.39 - 1.96\sqrt{\frac{(.39)(.61)}{87}} \le p \le .39 + 1.96\sqrt{\frac{(.39)(.61)}{87}}$$

$$.39 - .10 \le p \le .39 + .10$$

$$.29 \le p \le .49$$

This interval suggests that the population proportion of telemarketing firms that use their operation to assist order processing is somewhere between .29 and .49, based on the point estimate of .39 with an error of ±.10. This result has a 95% level of confidence.

DEMONSTRATION PROBLEM 8.4

Coopers & Lybrand surveyed 210 chief executives of fast-growing small companies. Only 51% of these executives had a management succession plan in place. A spokesperson for Cooper & Lybrand said that many companies do not worry about management succession unless it is an immediate problem. However, the unexpected exit of a corporate leader can disrupt and unfocus a company for long enough to cause it to lose its momentum.

Use the data given to compute a 92% confidence interval to estimate the proportion of *all* fast-growing small companies that have a management succession plan.

Solution

The point estimate is the sample proportion given to be .51. It is estimated that .51, or 51% of all fast-growing small companies have a management succession plan. Realizing that the point estimate might change with another sample selection, we calculate a confidence interval.

The value of n is 210; $\hat{p}$ is .51, and $\hat{q} = 1 - \hat{p} = .49$. Because the level of confidence is 92%, the value of $z_{.04} = 1.75$. The confidence interval is computed as

$$.51 - 1.75\sqrt{\frac{(.51)(.49)}{210}} \le p \le .51 + 1.75\sqrt{\frac{(.51)(.49)}{210}}$$

$$.51 - .06 \le p \le .51 + .06$$

$$.45 \le p \le .57$$

It is estimated with 92% confidence that the proportion of the population of fast-growing small companies that have a management succession plan is between .45 and .57.

DEMONSTRATION PROBLEM 8.5

A clothing company produces men's jeans. The jeans are made and sold with either a regular cut or a boot cut. In an effort to estimate the proportion of their men's jeans market in Oklahoma City that prefers boot-cut jeans, the analyst takes a random sample of 423 jeans sales from the company's two Oklahoma City retail outlets. Only 72 of the sales were for boot-cut jeans. Construct a 90% confidence interval to estimate the proportion of the population in Oklahoma City who prefer boot-cut jeans.

Solution

The sample size is 423, and the number preferring boot-cut jeans is 72. The sample proportion is $\hat{p} = 72/423 = .17$. A point estimate for boot-cut jeans in the population is .17, or 17%. The z value for a 90% level of confidence is 1.645, and the value of $\hat{q} = 1 - \hat{p} = 1 - .17 = .83$. The confidence interval estimate is

$$.17 - 1.645\sqrt{\frac{(.17)(.83)}{423}} \le p \le .17 + 1.645\sqrt{\frac{(.17)(.83)}{423}}$$

$$.17 - .03 \le p \le .17 + .03$$

$$.14 \le p \le .20$$

The analyst estimates that the population proportion of boot-cut jeans purchases is between .14 and .20. The level of confidence in this result is 90%.

FIGURE 8.10

Minitab Output for
Demonstration Problem 8.5

Minitab Output

Test and CI for One Proportion

Sample	X	N	Sample p	90% CI
1	72	423	0.170213	(0.140156, 0.200269)

Using the Computer to Construct Confidence Intervals of the Population Proportion

Minitab has the capability of producing confidence intervals for proportions, and Excel does not. Figure 8.10 contains Minitab output for Demonstration Problem 8.5. The Minitab output contains the sample size (labeled as N), the number in the sample containing the characteristic of interest (X), the sample proportion, the level of confidence, and the endpoints of the confidence interval. Note that the endpoints of the confidence interval are essentially the same as those computed in Demonstration Problem 8.5.

8.3 PROBLEMS

8.25 Use the information about each of the following samples to compute the confidence interval to estimate p.

a. $n = 44$ and $\hat{p} = .51$; compute a 90% confidence interval.

b. $n = 300$ and $\hat{p} = .82$; compute a 95% confidence interval.

c. $n = 1,150$ and $\hat{p} = .48$; compute a 90% confidence interval.

d. $n = 95$ and $\hat{p} = .32$; compute a 88% confidence interval.

8.26 Use the following sample information to calculate the confidence interval to estimate the population proportion. Let x be the number of items in the sample having the characteristic of interest.

a. $n = 116$ and $x = 57$, with 99% confidence

b. $n = 800$ and $x = 479$, with 97% confidence

c. $n = 240$ and $x = 106$, with 85% confidence

d. $n = 60$ and $x = 21$, with 90% confidence

8.27 Suppose a random sample of 85 items has been taken from a population and 40 of the items contain the characteristic of interest. Use this information to calculate a 90% confidence interval to estimate the proportion of the population that has the characteristic of interest. Calculate a 95% confidence interval. Calculate a 99% confidence interval. As the level of confidence changes and the other sample information stays constant, what happens to the confidence interval?

8.28 The Universal Music Group is the music industry leader worldwide in sales according to Nielsen Sound Scan. Suppose a researcher wants to determine what market share the company holds in the city of St. Louis by randomly selecting 1,003 people who purchased a CD last month. In addition, suppose 25.5% of the purchases made by these people were for products manufactured and distributed by the Universal Music Group.

a. Based on these data, construct a 99% confidence interval to estimate the proportion of the CD sales market in St. Louis that is held by the Universal Music Group.

b. Suppose that the survey had been taken with 10,000 people. Recompute the confidence interval and compare your results with the first confidence interval. How did they differ? What might you conclude from this about sample size and confidence intervals?

8.29 According to the Stern Marketing Group, 9 out of 10 professional women say that financial planning is more important today than it was five years ago. Where do these women go for help in financial planning? Forty-seven percent use a financial advisor (broker, tax consultant, financial planner). Twenty-eight percent use written sources such as magazines, books, and newspapers. Suppose these figures were obtained by taking a sample of 560 professional women who said that financial planning is more important today than it was five years ago.

a. Construct a 95% confidence interval for the proportion of professional women who use a financial advisor. Use the percentage given in this problem as the point estimate.

b. Construct a 90% confidence interval for the proportion of professional women who use written sources. Use the percentage given in this problem as the point estimate.

8.30 What proportion of pizza restaurants that are primarily for walk-in business have a salad bar? Suppose that, in an effort to determine this figure, a random sample of 1,250 of these restaurants across the United States based on the Yellow Pages is called. If 997 of the restaurants sampled have a salad bar, what is the 98% confidence interval for the population proportion?

8.31 The highway department wants to estimate the proportion of vehicles on Interstate 25 between the hours of midnight and 5:00 A.M. that are 18-wheel tractor trailers. The estimate will be used to determine highway repair and construction considerations and in highway patrol planning. Suppose researchers for the highway department counted vehicles at different locations on the interstate for several nights during this time period. Of the 3,481 vehicles counted, 927 were 18-wheelers.

a. Determine the point estimate for the proportion of vehicles traveling Interstate 25 during this time period that are 18-wheelers.

b. Construct a 99% confidence interval for the proportion of vehicles on Interstate 25 during this time period that are 18-wheelers.

8.32 What proportion of commercial airline pilots are more than 40 years of age? Suppose a researcher has access to a list of all pilots who are members of the Commercial Airline Pilots Association. If this list is used as a frame for the study, she can randomly select a sample of pilots, contact them, and ascertain their ages. From 89 of these pilots so selected, she learns that 48 are more than 40 years of age. Construct an 85% confidence interval to estimate the population proportion of commercial airline pilots who are more than 40 years of age.

8.33 According to Runzheimer International, in a survey of relocation administrators 63% of all workers who rejected relocation offers did so for family considerations. Suppose this figure was obtained by using a random sample of the files of 672 workers who had rejected relocation offers. Use this information to construct a 95% confidence interval to estimate the population proportion of workers who reject relocation offers for family considerations.

8.34 Suppose a survey of 275 executives is taken in an effort to determine what qualities are most important for an effective CEO to possess. The survey participants are offered several qualities as options, one of which is "communication." One hundred twenty-one of the surveyed respondents select "communicator" as the most important quality for an effective CEO. Use these data to construct a 98% confidence interval to estimate the population proportion of executives who believe that "communicator" is the most important quality of an effective CEO.

8.4 ESTIMATING THE POPULATION VARIANCE

At times in statistical analysis, the researcher is more interested in the population variance than in the population mean or population proportion. For example, in the total quality movement, suppliers who want to earn world-class supplier status or even those who want to maintain customer contracts are often asked to show continual reduction of variation on supplied parts. Tests are conducted with samples in efforts to determine lot variation and to determine whether variability goals are being met.

Estimating the variance is important in many other instances in business. For example, variations between airplane altimeter readings need to be minimal. It is not enough just to know that, on the average, a particular brand of altimeter produces the correct altitude. It is also important that the variation between instruments be small. Thus measuring the

FIGURE 8.11

Three Chi-Square Distributions

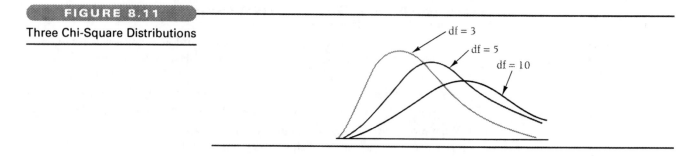

variation of altimeters is critical. Parts being used in engines must fit tightly on a consistent basis. A wide variability among parts can result in a part that is too large to fit into its slots or so small that it results in too much tolerance, which causes vibrations. How can variance be estimated?

You may recall from Chapter 3 that sample variance is computed by using the formula

$$s^2 = \frac{\sum(x - \bar{x})^2}{n - 1}$$

Because sample variances are typically used as estimators or estimations of the population variance, as they are here, a mathematical adjustment is made in the denominator by using $n - 1$ to make the sample variance an unbiased estimator of the population variance.

Suppose a researcher wants to estimate the population variance from the sample variance in a manner that is similar to the estimation of the population mean from a sample mean. The relationship of the sample variance to the population variance is captured by the **chi-square distribution** (χ^2). The ratio of the sample variance (s^2), multiplied by $n - 1$, to the population variance (σ^2) is approximately chi-square distributed, as shown in formula 8.5, if the population from which the values are drawn is normally distributed.

Caution: *Use of the chi-square statistic to estimate the population variance is extremely sensitive to violations of the assumption that the population is normally distributed. For that reason, some researchers do not include this technique among their statistical repertoire. Although the technique is still rather widely presented as a mechanism for constructing confidence intervals to estimate a population variance, you should proceed with extreme caution and apply the technique only in cases where the population is known to be normally distributed. We can say that this technique lacks robustness.*

Like the *t* distribution, the chi-square distribution varies by sample size and contains a degrees-of-freedom value. The number of degrees of freedom for the chi-square formula (8.5) is $n - 1$.

χ^2 **FORMULA FOR SINGLE VARIANCE (8.5)**	$\chi^2 = \dfrac{(n - 1)s^2}{\sigma^2}$ $df = n - 1$

The chi-square distribution is not symmetrical, and its shape will vary according to the degrees of freedom. Figure 8.11 shows the shape of chi-square distributions for three different degrees of freedom.

Formula 8.5 can be rearranged algebraically to produce a formula that can be used to construct confidence intervals for population variances. This new formula is shown as formula 8.6.

CONFIDENCE INTERVAL TO ESTIMATE THE POPULATION VARIANCE (8.6)	$\dfrac{(n - 1)s^2}{\chi^2_{\alpha/2}} \leq \sigma^2 \leq \dfrac{(n - 1)s^2}{\chi^2_{1-\alpha/2}}$ $df = n - 1$

The value of alpha (α) is equal to $1 -$ (level of confidence expressed as a proportion). Thus, if we are constructing a 90% confidence interval, alpha is 10% of the area and is expressed in proportion form: $\alpha = .10$.

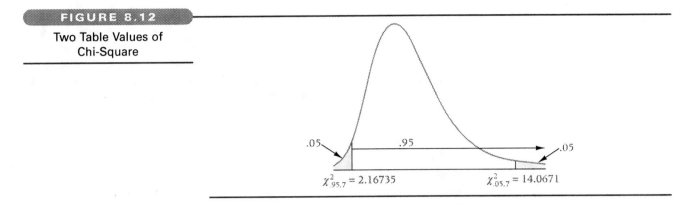

FIGURE 8.12

Two Table Values of Chi-Square

How can this formula be used to estimate the population variance from a sample variance? Suppose eight purportedly 7-centimeter aluminum cylinders in a sample are measured in diameter, resulting in the following values:

6.91 cm	6.93 cm	7.01 cm	7.02 cm
7.05 cm	7.00 cm	6.98 cm	7.01 cm

In estimating a population variance from these values, the sample variance must be computed. This value is $s^2 = .0022125$. If a point estimate is all that is required, the point estimate is the sample variance, .0022125. However, realizing that the point estimate will probably change from sample to sample, we want to construct an interval estimate. To do this, we must know the degrees of freedom and the table values of the chi-squares. Because $n = 8$, the degrees of freedom are df $= n - 1 = 7$. What are the chi-square values necessary to complete the information needed in formula 8.6? Assume the population of cylinder diameters is normally distributed.

Suppose we are constructing a 90% confidence interval. The value of α is $1 - .90 = .10$. It is the portion of the area under the chi-square curve that is outside the confidence interval. This outside area is needed because the chi-square table values given in Table A.8 are listed according to the area in the right tail of the distribution. In a 90% confidence interval, $\alpha/2$ or .05 of the area is in the right tail of the distribution and .05 is in the left tail of the distribution. The chi-square value for the .05 area on the right tail of the distribution can be obtained directly from the table by using the degrees of freedom, which in this case are 7. Thus the right-side chi-square, $\chi^2_{.05,7}$, is 14.0671. Because Table A.8 lists chi-square values for areas in the right tail, the chi-square value for the left tail must be obtained by determining how much area lies to the right of the left tail. If .05 is to the left of the confidence interval, then $1 - .05 = .95$ of the area is to the right of the left tail. This calculation is consistent with the $1 - \alpha/2$ expression used in formula (8.6). Thus the chi-square for the left tail is $\chi^2_{.95,7} = 2.16735$. Figure 8.12 shows the two table values of χ^2 on a chi-square distribution.

Incorporating these values into the formula, we can construct the 90% confidence interval to estimate the population variance of the 7-centimeter aluminum cylinders.

$$\frac{(n-1)s^2}{\chi^2_{\alpha/2}} \leq \sigma^2 \leq \frac{(n-1)s^2}{\chi^2_{1-\alpha/2}}$$

$$\frac{(7)(.0022125)}{14.0671} \leq \sigma^2 \leq \frac{(7)(.0022125)}{2.16735}$$

$$.001101 \leq \sigma^2 \leq .007146$$

The confidence interval says that with 90% confidence, the population variance is somewhere between .001101 and .007146.

DEMONSTRATION PROBLEM 8.6

The U.S. Bureau of Labor Statistics publishes data on the hourly compensation costs for production workers in manufacturing for various countries. The latest figures published for Greece show that the average hourly wage for a production worker in manufacturing is $19.58. Suppose the business council of Greece wants to know how consistent this figure is. They randomly select 25 production workers in manufacturing from across the country and determine that the standard deviation of hourly wages for such workers is $1.12. Use this information to develop a 95% confidence interval to estimate the population variance for the hourly wages of production workers in manufacturing in Greece. Assume that the hourly wages for production workers across the country in manufacturing are normally distributed.

Solution

By squaring the standard deviation, $s = 1.12$, we can obtain the sample variance, $s^2 = 1.2544$. This figure provides the point estimate of the population variance. Because the sample size, n, is 25, the degrees of freedom, $n - 1$, are 24. A 95% confidence means that alpha is $1 - .95 = .05$. This value is split to determine the area in each tail of the chi-square distribution: $\alpha/2 = .025$. The values of the chi-squares obtained from Table A.8 are

$$\chi^2_{.025,24} = 39.3641 \text{ and } \chi^2_{.975,24} = 12.40115$$

From this information, the confidence interval can be determined.

$$\frac{(n-1)s^2}{\chi^2_{\alpha/2}} \leq \sigma^2 \leq \frac{(n-1)s^2}{\chi^2_{1-\alpha/2}}$$

$$\frac{(24)(1.2544)}{39.3641} \leq \sigma^2 \leq \frac{(24)(1.2544)}{12.40115}$$

$$0.7648 \leq \sigma^2 \leq 2.4276$$

The business council can estimate with 95% confidence that the population variance of the hourly wages of production workers in manufacturing in Greece is between 0.7648 and 2.4276.

8.4 PROBLEMS

8.35 For each of the following sample results, construct the requested confidence interval. Assume the data come from normally distributed populations.

a. $n = 12, \bar{x} = 28.4, s^2 = 44.9$; 99% confidence for σ^2

b. $n = 7, \bar{x} = 4.37, s = 1.24$; 95% confidence for σ^2

c. $n = 20, \bar{x} = 105, s = 32$; 90% confidence for σ^2

d. $n = 17, s^2 = 18.56$; 80% confidence for σ^2

8.36 Use the following sample data to estimate the population variance. Produce a point estimate and a 98% confidence interval. Assume the data come from a normally distributed population.

27	40	32	41	45	29	33	39
30	28	36	32	42	40	38	46

8.37 The Interstate Conference of Employment Security Agencies says the average workweek in the United States is down to only 35 hours, largely because of a rise in part-time workers. Suppose this figure was obtained from a random sample of 20 workers and that the standard deviation of the sample was 4.3 hours. Assume hours worked per week are normally distributed in the population. Use this sample information to develop a 98% confidence interval for the population variance of the number of hours worked per week for a worker. What is the point estimate?

8.38 A manufacturing plant produces steel rods. During one production run of 20,000 such rods, the specifications called for rods that were 46 centimeters in length and 3.8 centimeters in width. Fifteen of these rods comprising a random sample were measured for length; the resulting measurements are shown here. Use these data to estimate the population variance of length for the rods. Assume rod length is normally distributed in the population. Construct a 99% confidence interval. Discuss the ramifications of the results.

44 cm	47 cm	43 cm	46 cm	46 cm
45 cm	43 cm	44 cm	47 cm	46 cm
48 cm	48 cm	43 cm	44 cm	45 cm

8.39 Suppose a random sample of 14 people 30–39 years of age produced the household incomes shown here. Use these data to determine a point estimate for the population variance of household incomes for people 30–39 years of age and construct a 95% confidence interval. Assume household income is normally distributed.

$37,500	44,800
33,500	36,900
42,300	32,400
28,000	41,200
46,600	38,500
40,200	32,000
35,500	36,800

8.5 ESTIMATING SAMPLE SIZE

In most business research that uses sample statistics to infer about the population, being able to *estimate the size of sample necessary to accomplish the purposes of the study* is important. The need for this **sample-size estimation** is the same for the large corporation investing tens of thousands of dollars in a massive study of consumer preference and for students undertaking a small case study and wanting to send questionnaires to local business people. In either case, such things as level of confidence, sampling error, and width of estimation interval are closely tied to sample size. If the large corporation is undertaking a market study, should it sample 40 people or 4,000 people? The question is an important one. In most cases, because of cost considerations, business researchers do not want to sample any more units or individuals than necessary.

Sample Size when Estimating μ

In research studies when μ is being estimated, the size of sample can be determined by using the z formula for sample means to solve for n. Consider,

$$z = \frac{\bar{x} - \mu}{\frac{\sigma}{\sqrt{n}}}$$

The difference between $\bar{x}$ and μ is the **error of estimation** resulting from the sampling process. Let $E = (\bar{x} - \mu)$ = the error of estimation. Substituting E into the preceding formula yields

$$z = \frac{E}{\frac{\sigma}{\sqrt{n}}}$$

Solving for n yields a formula that can be used to determine sample size.

SAMPLE SIZE WHEN ESTIMATING μ (8.7)	$n = \dfrac{z_{\alpha/2}^2 \sigma^2}{E^2} = \left(\dfrac{z_{\alpha/2}\sigma}{E}\right)^2$

Sometimes in estimating sample size the population variance is known or can be determined from past studies. Other times, the population variance is unknown and must be estimated to determine the sample size. In such cases, it is acceptable to use the following estimate to represent σ.

$$\sigma \approx \frac{1}{4} \, (range)$$

Using formula (8.7), the business researcher can estimate the sample size needed to achieve the goals of the study before gathering data. For example, suppose a researcher wants to estimate the average monthly expenditure on bread by a family in Chicago. She wants to be 90% confident of her results. How much error is she willing to tolerate in the results? Suppose she wants the estimate to be within $1.00 of the actual figure (error) and the standard deviation of average monthly bread purchases is $4.00. What is the sample size estimation for this problem? The value of z for a 90% level of confidence is 1.645. Using formula (8.7) with $E = \$1.00$, $\sigma = \$4.00$, and $z = 1.645$ gives

$$n = \frac{z_{\alpha/2}^2 \sigma^2}{E^2} = \frac{(1.645)^2(4)^2}{1^2} = 43.30$$

That is, at least $n = 43.3$ must be sampled randomly to attain a 90% level of confidence and produce an error within $1.00 for a standard deviation of $4.00. Sampling 43.3 units is impossible, so this result should be rounded up to $n = 44$ units.

In this approach to estimating sample size, we view the error of the estimation as the amount of difference between the statistic (in this case, $\bar{x}$) and the parameter (in this case, μ). The error could be in either direction; that is, the statistic could be over or under the parameter. Thus, the error, E, is actually $\pm E$ as we view it. So when a problem states that the researcher wants to be within $1.00 of the actual monthly family expenditure for bread, it means that the researcher is willing to allow a tolerance within $\pm \$1.00$ of the actual figure. Another name for this error is the **bounds** of the interval.

DEMONSTRATION PROBLEM 8.7

Suppose you want to estimate the average age of all Boeing 737-300 airplanes now in active domestic U.S. service. You want to be 95% confident, and you want your estimate to be within one year of the actual figure. The 737-300 was first placed in service about 24 years ago, but you believe that no active 737-300s in the U.S. domestic fleet are more than 20 years old. How large of a sample should you take?

Solution

Here, $E = 1$ year, the z value for 95% is 1.96, and σ is unknown, so it must be estimated by using $\sigma \approx (1/4) \cdot (range)$. As the range of ages is 0 to 20 years, $\sigma = (1/4)(20) = 5$. Use formula (8.7).

$$n = \frac{z^2 \sigma^2}{E^2} = \frac{(1.96)^2(5)^2}{1^2} = 96.04$$

Because you cannot sample 96.04 airplanes, the required sample size is 97. If you randomly sample 97 airplanes, you have an opportunity to estimate the average age of active 737-300s within one year and be 95% confident of the results.

Note: *Sample-size estimates for the population mean where σ is unknown using the t distribution are not shown here. Because a sample size must be known to determine the table value of t, which in turn is used to estimate the sample size, this procedure usually involves an iterative process.*

TABLE 8.3

$p \cdot q$ for Various Selected Values of p

p	$p \cdot q$
.9	.09
.8	.16
.7	.21
.6	.24
.5	.25
.4	.24
.3	.21
.2	.16
.1	.09

Determining Sample Size when Estimating p

Determining the sample size required to estimate the population proportion, p, also is possible. The process begins with the z formula for sample proportions.

$$z = \frac{\hat{p} - p}{\sqrt{\dfrac{p \cdot q}{n}}}$$

where $q = 1 - p$.

As various samples are taken from the population, $\hat{p}$ will rarely equal the population proportion, p, resulting in an error of estimation. The difference between $\hat{p}$ and p is the error of estimation, so $E = \hat{p} - p$.

$$z = \frac{E}{\sqrt{\dfrac{p \cdot q}{n}}}$$

Solving for n yields the formula for determining sample size.

SAMPLE SIZE WHEN ESTIMATING P (8.8)

$$n = \frac{z^2 pq}{E^2}$$

where

p = population proportion
$q = 1 - p$
E = error of estimation
n = sample size

How can the value of n be determined prior to a study if the formula requires the value of p and the study is being done to estimate p? Although the actual value of p is not known prior to the study, similar studies might have generated a good approximation for p. If no previous value is available for use in estimating p, some possible p values, as shown in Table 8.3, might be considered.

Note that, as $p \cdot q$ is in the numerator of the sample size formula, $p = .5$ will result in the largest sample sizes. Often *if p is unknown, researchers use .5 as an estimate of p* in formula 8.8. This selection results in the largest sample size that could be determined from formula 8.8 for a given z value and a given error value.

DEMONSTRATION PROBLEM 8.8

Hewitt Associates conducted a national survey to determine the extent to which employers are promoting health and fitness among their employees. One of the questions asked was, Does your company offer on-site exercise classes? Suppose it was estimated before the study that no more than 40% of the companies would answer Yes. How large a sample would Hewitt Associates have to take in estimating the population proportion to ensure a 98% confidence in the results and to be within .03 of the true population proportion?

Solution

The value of E for this problem is .03. Because it is estimated that no more than 40% of the companies would say Yes, $p = .40$ can be used. A 98% confidence interval results in a z value of 2.33. Inserting these values into formula (8.8) yields

$$n = \frac{(2.33)^2 (.40)(.60)}{(.03)^2} = 1447.7$$

Hewitt Associates would have to sample 1,448 companies to be 98% confident in the results and maintain an error of .03.

8.5 PROBLEMS

8.40 Determine the sample size necessary to estimate μ for the following information.

a. $\sigma = 36$ and $E = 5$ at 95% confidence

b. $\sigma = 4.13$ and $E = 1$ at 99% confidence

c. Values range from 80 to 500, error is to be within 10, and the confidence level is 90%

d. Values range from 50 to 108, error is to be within 3, and the confidence level is 88%

8.41 Determine the sample size necessary to estimate p for the following information.

a. $E = .02$, p is approximately .40, and confidence level is 96%

b. E is to be within .04, p is unknown, and confidence level is 95%

c. E is to be within 5%, p is approximately 55%, and confidence level is 90%

d. E is to be no more than .01, p is unknown, and confidence level is 99%

8.42 A bank officer wants to determine the amount of the average total monthly deposits per customer at the bank. He believes an estimate of this average amount using a confidence interval is sufficient. How large a sample should he take to be within $200 of the actual average with 99% confidence? He assumes the standard deviation of total monthly deposits for all customers is about $1,000.

8.43 Suppose you have been following a particular airline stock for many years. You are interested in determining the average daily price of this stock in a 10-year period and you have access to the stock reports for these years. However, you do not want to average all the daily prices over 10 years because there are several thousand data points, so you decide to take a random sample of the daily prices and estimate the average. You want to be 90% confident of your results, you want the estimate to be within $2.00 of the true average, and you believe the standard deviation of the price of this stock is about $12.50 over this period of time. How large a sample should you take?

8.44 A group of investors wants to develop a chain of fast-food restaurants. In determining potential costs for each facility, they must consider, among other expenses, the average monthly electric bill. They decide to sample some fast-food restaurants currently operating to estimate the monthly cost of electricity. They want to be 90% confident of their results and want the error of the interval estimate to be no more than $100. They estimate that such bills range from $600 to $2,500. How large a sample should they take?

8.45 Suppose a production facility purchases a particular component part in large lots from a supplier. The production manager wants to estimate the proportion of defective parts received from this supplier. She believes the proportion defective is no more than .20 and wants to be within .02 of the true proportion of defective parts with a 90% level of confidence. How large a sample should she take?

8.46 What proportion of secretaries of *Fortune* 500 companies has a personal computer at his or her workstation? You want to answer this question by conducting a random survey. How large a sample should you take if you want to be 95% confident of the results and you want the error of the confidence interval to be no more than .05? Assume no one has any idea of what the proportion actually is.

8.47 What proportion of shoppers at a large appliance store actually makes a large-ticket purchase? To estimate this proportion within 10% and be 95% confident of the results, how large a sample should you take? Assume you have no idea what proportion of all shoppers actually make a large-ticket purchase.

Decision Dilemma SOLVED

Compensation for Purchasing Managers

Published national management salary and demographic information, such as mean salary, mean age, and mean years experience, is mostly likely based on random samples of data. Such is the case in the Decision Dilemma where the salary, age, and experience parameters are actually point estimates based on a survey of 1,839 purchasing managers. For example, the study states that the average salary for a purchasing manager is $89,160. This is a point estimate of the population mean salary based on the sample mean of 1,839 purchasing managers. Suppose it is known that the population standard deviation for purchasing manager salaries is $6,000. From this information, a 95% confidence interval using the *z* statistic can be constructed as follows:

$$\$89,160 \pm 1.96\frac{\$6,000}{\sqrt{1,839}} = \$89,160 \pm \$274.23$$

$$\$88,885.77 \le \mu \le \$89,434.23$$

This confidence interval, constructed to estimate the mean annual salary for purchasing managers across the United States, shows that the estimated mean salary is $89,160 with an error of $274.23. The reason that this error is quite small is that the sample size is very large. In fact, the sample size is so large that if the $6,000 had actually been a sample standard deviation, the table *t* value would have been 1.961257 (compared to the *z* = 1.96), resulting in a confidence interval error of estimate of $274.41. Note that because of the large sample size, this *t* value is not found in Appendix Table A.6, and it was obtained using Excel's TINV function within the Paste function. Of course, in using the *t* statistic, one would have to assume that salaries are normally distributed in the population. Because the sample size is so large and the corresponding *t* table value is so close to the *z* value, the error using the *t* statistic is only 18¢ more than that produced using the *z* statistic. Confidence intervals for the population mean age and mean years of experience can be computed similarly.

The study also reports that the mean annual salary of a purchasing manager in Canada is $83,400 but is based on a sample of only 25 respondents. Suppose annual salaries of purchasing managers in Canada are normally distributed and that the sample standard deviation for such managers in this study is also $6,000. A 95% confidence interval for estimating the population mean annual salary for Canadian purchasing managers can be computed using the *t* statistic as follows:

$$\$83,400 \pm 2.064\frac{\$6,000}{\sqrt{25}} = \$83,400 \pm \$2,476.80$$

$$\$80,923.20 \le \mu \le \$85,876.80$$

Note that the point estimate mean annual salary for Canadian purchasing managers is $83,400 as reported in the study. However, the error of estimation in the interval is $2,476.80, indicating that the actual population mean annual salary could be as low as $80,923.20 or as high as $85,876.80. Observe that the error of this interval, $2,476.80, is nearly 10 times as big as the error in the confidence interval used to estimate the U.S. figure. This is due to the fact that the sample size used in the U.S. estimate is about 75 times as large. Since sample size is under the radical sign in confidence interval computation, taking the square root of this (75) indicates that the error in the Canadian estimate is almost 9 times as large as it is in the U.S. estimate (with a slight adjustment for the fact that a *t* value is used in the Canadian estimate).

The study reported that 73% of the respondents have a college degree or certificate. Using methods presented in Section 8.3, a 99% confidence interval can be computed assuming that the sample size is 1,839, the table *z* value for a 99% confidence interval is 2.575, and $\hat{p}$ is .73. The resulting confidence interval is:

$$.73 \pm 2.575\sqrt{\frac{(.73)(.27)}{1,839}} = .73 \pm .027$$

$$.703 \le p \le .757$$

While the point estimate is .73 or 73%, the error of the estimate is .027 or 2.7%, and therefore we are 99% confident that the actual population proportion of purchasing managers who have a college degree or certificate is between .703 and .757.

ETHICAL CONSIDERATIONS

Using sample statistics to estimate population parameters poses a couple of ethical concerns. Many survey reports and advertisers use point estimates as the values of the population parameter. Often, no error value is stated, as would have been the case if a confidence interval had been computed. These point estimates are subject to change if another sample is taken. It is probably unethical to state as a conclusion that a point estimate is the population parameter without some sort of disclaimer or explanation about what a point estimate is.

The misapplication of t formulas when data are not normally distributed in the population is also of concern. Although some studies have shown that the t formula analyses are robust, a researcher should be careful not to violate the assumptions underlying the use of the t formulas. An even greater potential for misuse lies in using the chi-square for the estimation of a population variance because this technique is highly sensitive to violations of the assumption that the data are normally distributed.

SUMMARY

Techniques for estimating population parameters from sample statistics are important tools for business research. These tools include techniques for estimating population means, techniques for estimating the population proportion and the population variance, and methodology for determining how large a sample to take.

At times in business research a product is new or untested or information about the population is unknown. In such cases, gathering data from a sample and making estimates about the population is useful and can be done with a point estimate or an interval estimate. A point estimate is the use of a statistic from the sample as an estimate for a parameter of the population. Because point estimates vary with each sample, it is usually best to construct an interval estimate. An interval estimate is a range of values computed from the sample within which the researcher believes with some confidence that the population parameter lies. Certain levels of confidence seem to be used more than others: 90%, 95%, 98%, and 99%.

If the population standard deviation is known, the z statistic is used to estimate the population mean. If the population standard deviation is unknown, the t distribution should be used instead of the z distribution. It is assumed when using the t distribution that the population from which the samples

are drawn is normally distributed. However, the technique for estimating a population mean by using the t test is robust, which means it is relatively insensitive to minor violations to the assumption. The population variance can be estimated by using sample variance and the chi-square distribution. The chi-square technique for estimating the population variance is not robust; it is sensitive to violations of the assumption that the population is normally distributed. Therefore, extreme caution must be exercised in using this technique.

The formulas in Chapter 7 resulting from the central limit theorem can be manipulated to produce formulas for estimating sample size for large samples. Determining the sample size necessary to estimate a population mean, if the population standard deviation is unavailable, can be based on one-fourth the range as an approximation of the population standard deviation. Determining sample size when estimating a population proportion requires the value of the population proportion. If the population proportion is unknown, the population proportion from a similar study can be used. If none is available, using a value of .50 will result in the largest sample size estimation for the problem if other variables are held constant. Sample size determination is used mostly to provide a ballpark figure to give researchers some guidance. Larger sample sizes usually result in greater costs.

KEY TERMS

bounds
chi-square distribution
degrees of freedom (df)
error of estimation

interval estimate
point estimate
robust
sample-size estimation

t distribution
t value

FORMULAS

$100(1-\alpha)\%$ confidence interval to estimate μ: population standard deviation known

$$\bar{x} - z_{\alpha/2}\frac{\sigma}{\sqrt{n}} \leq \mu \leq \bar{x} + z_{\alpha/2}\frac{\sigma}{\sqrt{n}}$$

Confidence interval to estimate μ using the finite correction factor

$$\bar{x} - z_{\alpha/2}\frac{\sigma}{\sqrt{n}}\sqrt{\frac{N-n}{N-1}} \leq \mu \leq \bar{x} + z_{\alpha/2}\frac{\sigma}{\sqrt{n}}\sqrt{\frac{N-n}{N-1}}$$

Confidence interval to estimate μ: population standard deviation unknown

$$\bar{x} - t_{\alpha/2,\,n-1}\frac{s}{\sqrt{n}} \le \mu \le \bar{x} + t_{\alpha/2,\,n-1}\frac{s}{\sqrt{n}}$$
$$df = n - 1$$

Confidence interval to estimate p

$$\hat{p} - z_{\alpha/2}\sqrt{\frac{\hat{p}\cdot\hat{q}}{n}} \le p \le \hat{p} + z_{\alpha/2}\sqrt{\frac{\hat{p}\cdot\hat{q}}{n}}$$

χ^2 formula for single variance

$$\chi^2 = \frac{(n-1)s^2}{\sigma^2}$$
$$df = n - 1$$

Confidence interval to estimate the population variance

$$\frac{(n-1)s^2}{\chi^2_{\alpha/2}} \le \sigma^2 \le \frac{(n-1)s^2}{\chi^2_{1-\alpha/2}}$$
$$df = n - 1$$

Sample size when estimating μ

$$n = \frac{z^2_{\alpha/2}\sigma^2}{E^2} = \left(\frac{z_{\alpha/2}\sigma}{E}\right)^2$$

Sample size when estimating p

$$n = \frac{z^2 pq}{E^2}$$

SUPPLEMENTARY PROBLEMS

CALCULATING THE STATISTICS

8.48 Use the following data to construct 80%, 94%, and 98% confidence intervals to estimate μ. Assume that σ is 7.75. State the point estimate.

44	37	49	30	56	48	53	42	51
38	39	45	47	52	59	50	46	34
39	46	27	35	52	51	46	45	58
51	37	45	52	51	54	39	48	

8.49 Construct 90%, 95%, and 99% confidence intervals to estimate μ from the following data. State the point estimate. Assume the data come from a normally distributed population.

12.3	11.6	11.9	12.8	12.5	11.4	12.0
11.7	11.8	12.3				

8.50 Use the following information to compute the confidence interval for the population proportion.
   a. $n = 715$ and $x = 329$, with 95% confidence
   b. $n = 284$ and $\hat{p} = .71$, with 90% confidence
   c. $n = 1250$ and $\hat{p} = .48$, with 95% confidence
   d. $n = 457$ and $x = 270$, with 98% confidence

8.51 Use the following data to construct 90% and 95% confidence intervals to estimate the population variance. Assume the data come from a normally distributed population.

212	229	217	216	223	219	208
214	232	219				

8.52 Determine the sample size necessary under the following conditions.
   a. To estimate μ with $\sigma = 44$, $E = 3$, and 95% confidence
   b. To estimate μ with a range of values from 20 to 88 with $E = 2$ and 90% confidence
   c. To estimate p with p unknown, $E = .04$, and 98% confidence

   d. To estimate p with $E = .03$, 95% confidence, and p thought to be approximately .70

TESTING YOUR UNDERSTANDING

8.53 In planning both market opportunity and production levels, being able to estimate the size of a market can be important. Suppose a diaper manufacturer wants to know how many diapers a one-month-old baby uses during a 24-hour period. To determine this usage, the manufacturer's analyst randomly selects 17 parents of one-month-olds and asks them to keep track of diaper usage for 24 hours. The results are shown. Construct a 99% confidence interval to estimate the average daily diaper usage of a one-month-old baby. Assume diaper usage is normally distributed.

12	8	11	9	13	14	10
10	9	13	11	8	11	15
10	7	12				

8.54 Suppose you want to estimate the proportion of cars that are sport utility vehicles (SUVs) being driven in Kansas City, Missouri, at rush hour by standing on the corner of I-70 and I-470 and counting SUVs. You believe the figure is no higher than .40. If you want the error of the confidence interval to be no greater than .03, how many cars should you randomly sample? Use a 90% level of confidence.

8.55 Use the data in Problem 8.53 to construct a 99% confidence interval to estimate the population variance for the number of diapers used during a 24-hour period for one-month-olds. How could information about the population variance be used by a manufacturer or marketer in planning?

8.56 What is the average length of a company's policy book? Suppose policy books are sampled from 45 medium-sized companies. The average number of pages in the sample books is 213, and the population standard deviation of 48. Use this information to construct a 98% confidence interval to estimate the mean number of pages for the population of medium-sized company policy books.

8.57 A random sample of small-business managers was given a leadership style questionnaire. The results were scaled so that each manager received a score for initiative. Suppose the following data are a random sample of these scores.

37	42	40	39	38	31	40
37	35	45	30	33	35	44
36	37	39	33	39	40	41
33	35	36	41	33	37	38
40	42	44	35	36	33	38
32	30	37	42			

Assuming σ is 3.891, use these data to construct a 90% confidence interval to estimate the average score on initiative for all small-business managers.

8.58 A national beauty salon chain wants to estimate the number of times per year a woman has her hair done at a beauty salon if she uses one at least once a year. The chain's researcher estimates that, of those women who use a beauty salon at least once a year, the standard deviation of number of times of usage is approximately 6. The national chain wants the estimate to be within one time of the actual mean value. How large a sample should the researcher take to obtain a 98% confidence level?

8.59 Is the environment a major issue with Americans? To answer that question, a researcher conducts a survey of 1255 randomly selected Americans. Suppose 714 of the sampled people replied that the environment is a major issue with them. Construct a 95% confidence interval to estimate the proportion of Americans who feel that the environment is a major issue with them. What is the point estimate of this proportion?

8.60 According to a survey by Topaz Enterprises, a travel auditing company, the average error by travel agents is $128. Suppose this figure was obtained from a random sample of 41 travel agents and the sample standard deviation is $21. What is the point estimate of the national average error for all travel agents? Compute a 98% confidence interval for the national average error based on these sample results. Assume the travel agent errors are normally distributed in the population. How wide is the interval? Interpret the interval.

8.61 A national survey on telemarketing was undertaken. One of the questions asked was: How long has your organization had a telemarketing operation? Suppose the following data represent some of the answers received to this question. Suppose further that only 300 telemarketing firms comprised the population when this survey was taken. Use the following data to compute a 98% confidence interval to estimate the average number of years a telemarketing organization has had a telemarketing operation. The population standard deviation is 3.06.

5	5	6	3	6	7	5
5	6	8	4	9	6	4
10	5	10	11	5	14	7
5	9	6	7	3	4	3
7	5	9	3	6	8	16
12	11	5	4	3	6	5
8	3	5	9	7	13	4
6	5	8	3	5	8	7
11	5	14	4			

8.62 An entrepreneur wants to open an appliance service repair shop. She would like to know about what the average home repair bill is, including the charge for the service call for appliance repair in the area. She wants the estimate to be within $20 of the actual figure. She believes the range of such bills is between $30 and $600. How large a sample should the entrepreneur take if she wants to be 95% confident of the results?

8.63 A national survey of insurance offices was taken, resulting in a random sample of 245 companies. Of these 245 companies, 189 responded that they were going to purchase new software for their offices in the next year. Construct a 90% confidence interval to estimate the population proportion of insurance offices that intend to purchase new software during the next year.

8.64 A national survey of companies included a question that asked whether the company had at least one bilingual telephone operator. The sample results of 90 companies follow (Y denotes that the company does have at least one bilingual operator; N denotes that it does not).

N	N	N	N	Y	N	Y	N	N
Y	N	N	N	Y	Y	N	N	N
N	N	Y	N	Y	N	Y	N	Y
Y	Y	N	Y	N	N	N	Y	N
N	Y	N	N	N	N	N	N	N
Y	N	Y	Y	N	N	Y	N	Y
N	N	Y	Y	N	N	N	N	N
Y	N	N	N	N	Y	N	N	N
Y	Y	Y	N	N	Y	N	N	N
N	N	N	Y	Y	N	N	Y	N

Use this information to estimate with 95% confidence the proportion of the population that does have at least one bilingual operator.

8.65 A movie theater has had a poor accounting system. The manager has no idea how many large containers of popcorn are sold per movie showing. She knows that the amounts vary by day of the week and hour of the day. However, she wants to estimate the overall average per movie showing. To do so, she randomly selects 12 movie performances and counts the number of large containers of popcorn sold between 30 minutes before the movie showing and 15 minutes after the movie showing. The sample average was 43.7 containers, with a variance of 228. Construct a 95% confidence interval to estimate the mean number of large containers of popcorn sold during a movie showing. Assume the number of large containers of popcorn sold per movie is normally distributed in the population. Use this information to construct a 98% confidence interval to estimate the population variance.

8.66 According to a survey by Runzheimer International, the average cost of a fast-food meal (quarter-pound cheeseburger, large fries, medium soft drink, excluding taxes) in Seattle is $4.82. Suppose this figure was based on a sample of 27 different establishments and the standard deviation was $0.37. Construct a 95% confidence interval for the population mean cost for all fast-food meals in Seattle. Assume the costs of a fast-food meal in Seattle are normally distributed. Using the interval as a guide, is it likely that the population mean is really $4.50? Why or why not?

8.67 A survey of 77 commercial airline flights of under 2 hours resulted in a sample average late time for a flight of 2.48 minutes. The population standard deviation was 12 minutes. Construct a 95% confidence interval for the average time that a commercial flight of under 2 hours is late. What is the point estimate? What does the interval tell about whether the average flight is late?

8.68 A regional survey of 560 companies asked the vice president of operations how satisfied he or she was with the software support received from the computer staff of the company. Suppose 33% of the 560 vice presidents said they were satisfied. Construct a 99% confidence interval for the proportion of the population of vice presidents who would have said they were satisfied with the software support if a census had been taken.

8.69 A research firm has been asked to determine the proportion of all restaurants in the state of Ohio that serve alcoholic beverages. The firm wants to be 98% confident of its results but has no idea of what the actual proportion is. The firm would like to report an error of no more than .05. How large a sample should it take?

8.70 A national magazine marketing firm attempts to win subscribers with a mail campaign that involves a contest using magazine stickers. Often when people subscribe to magazines in this manner they sign up for multiple magazine subscriptions. Suppose the marketing firm wants to estimate the average number of subscriptions per customer of those who purchase at least one subscription. To do so, the marketing firm's researcher randomly selects 65 returned contest entries. Twenty-seven contain subscription requests. Of the 27, the average number of subscriptions is 2.10, with a standard deviation of .86. The researcher uses this information to compute a 98% confidence interval to estimate μ and assumes that x is normally distributed. What does the researcher find?

8.71 A national survey showed that Hillshire Farm Deli Select cold cuts were priced, on the average, at $5.20 per pound. Suppose a national survey of 23 retail outlets was taken and the price per pound of Hillshire Farm Deli Select cold cuts was ascertained. If the following data represent these prices, what is a 90% confidence interval for the population variance of these prices? Assume prices are normally distributed in the population.

5.18	5.22	5.25	5.19	5.30
5.17	5.15	5.28	5.20	5.14
5.05	5.19	5.26	5.23	5.19
5.22	5.08	5.21	5.24	5.33
5.22	5.19	5.19		

8.72 The price of a head of iceberg lettuce varies greatly with the season and the geographic location of a store. During February a researcher contacts a random sample of 39 grocery stores across the United States and asks the produce manager of each to state the current price charged for a head of iceberg lettuce. Using the researcher's results that follow, construct a 99% confidence interval to estimate the mean price of a head of iceberg lettuce in February in the United States. Assume that σ is 0.205.

1.59	1.25	1.65	1.40	0.89
1.19	1.50	1.49	1.30	1.39
1.29	1.60	0.99	1.29	1.19
1.20	1.50	1.49	1.29	1.35
1.10	0.89	1.10	1.39	1.39
1.50	1.50	1.55	1.20	1.15
0.99	1.00	1.30	1.25	1.10
1.00	1.55	1.29	1.39	

INTERPRETING THE OUTPUT

8.73 A soft drink company produces a cola in a 12-ounce can. Even though their machines are set to fill the cans with 12 ounces, variation due to calibration, operator error, and other things sometimes precludes the cans having the correct fill. To monitor the can fills, a quality team randomly selects some filled 12-ounce cola cans and measures their fills in the lab. A confidence interval for the population mean is constructed from the data. Shown here is the Minitab output from this effort. Discuss the output.

One-Sample Z

The assumed standard deviation = 0.0536

N	Mean	SE Mean	99%	CI
58	11.9788	0.0070	(11.9607,	11.99691)

8.74 A company has developed a new light bulb that seems to burn longer than most residential bulbs. To determine how long these bulbs burn, the company randomly selects a sample of these bulbs and burns them in the laboratory. The Excel output shown here is a portion of the analysis from this effort. Discuss the output.

Bulb Burn	
Mean	2198.217
Standard deviation	152.9907
Count	84
Confidence level (90.0%)	27.76691

8.75 Suppose a researcher wants to estimate the average age of a person who is a first-time home buyer. A random sample of first-time home buyers is taken and their ages are ascertained. The Minitab output shown here is an analysis of that data. Study the output and explain its implication.

One-Sample T

N	Mean	StDev	SE Mean	99% CI
21	27.63	6.54	1.43	(23.57, 31.69)

8.76 What proportion of all American workers drive their cars to work? Suppose a poll of American workers is taken in an effort to answer that question, and the Minitab output shown here is an analysis of the data from the poll. Explain the meaning of the output in light of the question.

Test and CI for One Proportion

Sample	X	N	Sample p	95% CI
1	506	781	0.647887	(0.613240, 0.681413)

ANALYZING THE DATABASES

see www.wiley.com/college/black

Database

1. Construct a 95% confidence interval for the population mean number of production workers using the Manufacturing database as a sample. What is the point estimate? How much is the error of the estimation? Comment on the results.

2. Construct a 90% confidence interval to estimate the average census for hospitals using the Hospital database. State the point estimate and the error of the estimation. Change the level of confidence to 99%. What happened to the interval? Did the point estimate change?

3. The Financial database contains financial data on 100 companies. Use this database as a sample and estimate the earnings per share for all corporations from these data. Select several levels of confidence and compare the results.

4. Using the tally or frequency feature of the computer software, determine the sample proportion of the Hospital database under the variable "service" that are "general medical" (category 1). From this statistic, construct a 95% confidence interval to estimate the population proportion of hospitals that are "general medical." What is the point estimate? How much error is there in the interval?

CASE

THE CONTAINER STORE

In the late 1970s, Kip Tindell (chairman and CEO), Garrett Boone (Chairman Emeritus), and John Mullen (architect) drew up plans for a first of a kind retail store specializing in storage solutions for both the home and the office. The vision that they created was realized when on July 1, 1978, the Container Store opened its doors in a small 1600-square-foot retail space in Dallas. The store was stocked with products that were devoted to simplifying people's lives, such as commercial parts bins, wire drawers, mailboxes, milk crates, wire leaf burners, and many others. Some critics even questioned whether a store selling "empty boxes" could survive. However, the concept took off, and in the past 33 years, the company has expanded coast to coast in the United States with stores in 49 locations. Now headquartered in Coppell, Texas, the Container Store has 4000 employees and annual revenues of over $650 million.

Besides their innovative product mix, some of the keys to the success of the Container Store are the enthusiasm with which their employees work, the care that employees give to the customer, and employee knowledge of their products. For 12 straight years, the Container Store has made *Fortune* magazine's list of "100 Best Companies to Work For." Generally rated in the top 40 of this list each year, the company was number 1 for the first two years that they applied for consideration.

Their current president, Melissa Reiff, credits the company's devotion to recruiting and retaining a highly qualified workforce as one of the keys to its success. Company sources say that the Container Store offers more than 240 hours of formal training for full-time employees the first year of employment with the company and that this compares to about 8 hours of such training with other companies in the industry. According to company sources, the Container Store believes that their employees are their number one stakeholder and "The Container Store is an absolutely exhilarating and inspiring place to shop and an equally exciting place to work."

In addition to innovative products and motivated employees, the Container Store has embraced a commitment to the environment. Chairman Emeritus Garrett Boone says that they firmly believe that there is no conflict between economic prosperity and environmental stewardship. The Container Company is embracing sustainability as a key to their economic future. As part of this effort, they sell eco-friendly products, use highly efficient HVAC units in their stores and warehouses, sponsor an employee purchase program for compact fluorescent lights, are switching from neon to LED lighting in all exterior signage, and offer an employee battery and light bulb recycling program.

Discussion

1. Among other things, the Container Store has grown and flourished because of strong customer relationships, which include listening to customer needs, containing products that meet customer needs, having sales people who understand both customer needs and the products, and creating a store environment that is customer friendly both in layout and in culture. Suppose company management wants to formally measure customer satisfaction at least once a year and develops a brief survey that includes the following four questions. Suppose that the survey was administered to 115 customers with the following results. Use techniques presented in this chapter to analyze the data to estimate the population responses to these questions.

Question	Yes	No
1. Compared to most other stores that you shop in, is the Container Store more customer friendly?	73	42
2. Most of the time, this store has the number and type of home or office storage solution that I need.	81	34
3. The salespeople at this store appear the be particularly knowledgeable of their products.	88	27
4. Store hours are particularly convenient for me.	66	49

2. The Container Store is well known as a great company to work for. In addition, company management states that their employee is their number one stakeholder. Suppose in spite of their history as an employee-friendly company, management wants to measure employee satisfaction this year to determine if they are maintaining this culture. A researcher is hired by the company who randomly selects 21 employees and asks them to complete a satisfaction survey under the supervision of an independent testing organization. As part of this survey, employees are asked to respond to questions by providing a score of from 0 to 50 along a continuous scale, where 0 denotes no satisfaction and 50 denotes the utmost satisfaction. Assume that the data are normally distributed in the population. The questions and the results of the survey are shown below. Analyze the results by using techniques from this chapter. Discuss your findings.

Question	Mean	Standard Deviation
1. Are you treated fairly by the company as an employee?	42.4	5.2
2. Has the company given you the training that you need to do the job adequately?	44.9	3.1
3. Does management seriously consider your input in making decisions about the store?	38.7	7.5
4. Is your physical work environment acceptable?	35.6	9.2
5. Is the compensation for your work adequate and fair?	34.5	12.4
6. Overall, do you feel that company management really cares about you as a person?	41.8	6.3

Sources: The Container Store 2011 Web sites at http://www.containerstore.com/welcome.htm; http://www.containerstore.com/careers/index.html; http://standfor.containerstore.com/; http://en.wikipedia.org/wiki/The_Container_Store, January 23, 2011.

USING THE COMPUTER

EXCEL

- Excel has some capability to construct confidence intervals to estimate a population mean using the *z* statistic when σ is known and using the *t* statistic when σ is unknown.

- To construct confidence intervals of a single population mean using the *z* statistic (σ is known), begin with the **Insert Function** (f_x). To access the **Insert Function**, go to the **Formulas** tab on an Excel worksheet (top center tab). The **Insert Function** is on the far left of the menu bar. In the **Insert Function** dialog box at the top, there is a pulldown menu where it says **Or select a category**. From the pulldown menu associated with this command, select **Statistical**. Select **CONFIDENCE.NORM** from the **Insert Function's Statistical** menu. In the **CONFIDENCE.NORM** dialog box, place the value of alpha (a number between 0 and 1), which equals 1–level of confidence. (*Note:* level of confidence is given as a proportion and not as a percent.) For example, if the level of confidence is 95%, enter .05 as alpha. Insert the value of the population standard deviation in **Standard_dev**. Insert the size of the sample in **Size**. The output is the ± error of the confidence interval.

- To construct confidence intervals of a single population mean using the *t* statistic (σ is unknown), begin by selecting the **Data** tab on the Excel worksheet. From the **Analysis** panel at the right top of the **Data** tab worksheet, click on **Data Analysis**. If your Excel worksheet does not show the **Data Analysis** option, then you can load it as an add-in following directions given in Chapter 2. From the **Data Analysis** pulldown menu, select **Descriptive Statistics**. In the **Descriptive Statistics** dialog box, enter the location of the observations from the single sample in **Input Range**. Check **Labels** if you have a label for your data. Check **Summary Statistics**. Check **Confidence Level for Mean:** (required to get confidence interval output). If you want to change the level of confidence from the default value of 95%, enter it (in percent, between 0 and 100) in the box with the % sign beside it. The output is a single number that is the ± error portion of the confidence interval and is shown at the bottom of the **Descriptive Statistics** output as **Confidence Level.**

MINITAB

※ Minitab has the capability for constructing confidence intervals about a population mean either when σ is known or it is unknown and for constructing confidence intervals about a population proportion.

※ To begin constructing confidence intervals of a single population mean using z statistic (σ known), select **Stat** on the menu bar. Select **Basic Statistics** from the pulldown menu. From the second pulldown menu, select **1-sample Z**. Check **Samples in columns:** if you have raw data and enter the location of the column containing the observations. Check **Summarized data** if you wish to use the summarized statistics of the sample mean and the sample size rather than raw data. Enter the size of the sample in the box beside **Sample size.** Enter the sample mean in the box beside **Mean.** Enter the value of the population standard deviation in the box beside **Standard deviation.** Click on **Options** if you want to enter a level of confidence. To insert a level of confidence, place the confidence level as a percentage (between 0 and 100) in the box beside **Confidence level.** *Note:* To construct a two-sided confidence interval (only type of confidence intervals presented in this text), the selection in the box beside **Alternative** must be **not equal.**

※ To begin constructing confidence intervals of a single population mean using t statistic (σ unknown), select **Stat** on the menu bar. Select **Basic Statistics** from the pulldown menu. From the second pulldown menu, select **1-sample t.** Check **Samples in columns:** if you have raw data and enter

the location of the column containing the observations. Check **Summarized data** if you wish to use the summarized statistics of the sample size, sample mean, and the sample standard deviation rather than raw data. Enter the size of the sample in the box beside **Sample size:.** Enter the sample mean in the box beside **Mean:.** Enter the sample standard deviation in the box beside **Standard deviation.** Click on **Options** if you want to enter a level of confidence. To insert a level of confidence, place the confidence level as a percentage (between 0 and 100) in the box beside **Confidence level.** Note: To construct a two-sided confidence interval (only type of confidence intervals presented in this text), the selection in the box beside **Alternative** must be **not equal.**

※ To begin constructing confidence intervals of a single population proportion using z statistic, select **Stat** on the menu bar. Select **Basic Statistics** from the pulldown menu. From the second pulldown menu, select **1 Proportion.** Check **Samples in columns** if you have raw data and enter the location of the column containing the observations. Note that the data in the column must contain one of only two values (e.g., 1 or 2). Check **Summarized data** if you wish to use the summarized statistics of the number of trials and number of events rather than raw data. Enter the size of the sample in the box beside **Number of trials.** Enter the number of observed events (having the characteristic that you are testing) in the box beside **Number of events.** Click on **Options** if you want to enter a level of confidence. To insert a level of confidence, place the confidence level as a percentage (between 0 and 100) in the box beside **Confidence level.** *Note:* To construct a two-sided confidence interval (only type of confidence intervals presented in this text), the selection in the box beside **Alternative** must be **not equal.**

Statistical Inference: Hypothesis Testing for Single Populations

LEARNING OBJECTIVES

The main objective of Chapter 9 is to help you to learn how to test hypotheses on single populations, thereby enabling you to:

1. Develop both one- and two-tailed null and alternative hypotheses that can be tested in a business setting by examining the rejection and non-rejection regions in light of Type I and Type II errors.

2. Reach a statistical conclusion in hypothesis testing problems about a population mean with a known population standard deviation using the z statistic.

3. Reach a statistical conclusion in hypothesis testing problems about a population mean with an unknown population standard deviation using the t statistic.

4. Reach a statistical conclusion in hypothesis testing problems about a population proportion using the z statistic.

5. Reach a statistical conclusion in hypothesis testing problems about a population variance using the chi-square statistic.

6. Solve for possible Type II errors when failing to reject the null hypothesis.

PhotoAlto/Alamy

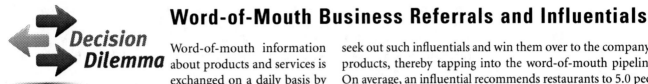

Word-of-Mouth Business Referrals and Influentials

Decision Dilemma

Word-of-mouth information about products and services is exchanged on a daily basis by millions of consumers. It is important for businesses to understand the impact of such "business referrals" because a happy customer can potentially steer dozens of new customers to a business and unhappy customers can direct customers away from a business or product. Word-of-mouth advertising is one of the most credible forms of advertising because the person making the recommendation puts their reputation on the line and that person has nothing to gain but the appreciation of those who are listening. A newer mode of word-of-mouth advertising is the Internet forum or message board, which is an online discussion site. In this format, group members can post messages citing opinions and offering information about a variety of topics. Many consumers now go to such message boards to obtain and share information about various products, services, and companies. According to a study by Mediamark Research of New York City, about 50% of all Americans often seek the advice of others before buying services or products. In addition, almost 40% say that others seek out their advice before purchasing. Maritz Marketing Research of Fenton, Missouri, studied adults in an effort to determine for which products or services they seek advice.

Forty-six percent seek advice when selecting a physician, 44% for a mechanic, and 42% for legal advice. In looking for a restaurant in which to celebrate a special occasion, 38% of all consumers seek out advice and information from others.

Some advice givers are referred to as *influentials*. Influentials are "trend-setting opinion leaders whose activism and expertise make them the natural source for word-of-mouth referrals." This group represents about 10% of all adult Americans. A report issued by Roper Starch Worldwide and cosponsored by *The Atlantic Monthly* stated that influentials tend to be among the first to try new products. They are looking for new restaurants and vacation spots to try, are activists on the job and in their community, and are self-indulgent. Businesses would do well to seek out such influentials and win them over to the company's products, thereby tapping into the word-of-mouth pipeline. On average, an influential recommends restaurants to 5.0 people a year. The following chart shows the average number of recommendations made by influentials per year on other items. These data were compiled and released by Roper Starch Worldwide.

Product or Service	Average Number of Recommendations
Office equipment	5.8
Vacation destination	5.1
TV show	4.9
Retail store	4.7
Clothing	4.5
Consumer electronics	4.5
Car	4.1
Stocks, mutual funds, CDs, etc.	3.4

Managerial and Statistical Questions

1. Each of the figures enumerated in this Decision Dilemma were derived by studies conducted on samples and published as fact. If we want to challenge these figures by conducting surveys of our own, then how would we go about testing these results? How could we test to determine whether these results apply to our market segment today?

2. The Roper Starch Worldwide study listed the mean number of recommendations made by influentials per year for different products or services. If these figures become accepted by industry users, how can we conduct our own tests to determine whether they are actually true? If we randomly sampled some influentials and our mean figures did not match these figures, then could we automatically conclude that their figures are not true? How much difference would we have to obtain to reject their claims? Is there a possibility that we could make an error in conducting such research?

3. Suppose you have theories regarding word-of-mouth advertising, business referrals, or influentials. How would you test the theories to determine whether they are true?

Source: Adapted from Chip Walker, "Word of Mouth," *American Demographics,* (July 1995), pp. 38–45. "Word-of-Mouth Advertising," *Entrepreneur* 2009, located at http://www.entrepreneur.com/encyclopedia/term/82660.html

A foremost statistical mechanism for decision making is the hypothesis test. The concept of hypothesis testing lies at the heart of inferential statistics, and the use of statistics to "prove" or "disprove" claims hinges on it. With **hypothesis testing**, business researchers are able *to structure problems in such a way that they can use statistical evidence to test various theories about business phenomena.* Business applications of statistical hypothesis testing run the gamut from determining whether a production line process is out of control to providing conclusive evidence that a new management leadership approach is significantly more effective than an old one.

Figure III-1 of Unit III Introduction displays a tree diagram taxonomy of inferential techniques, organizing them by usage, number of samples, and type of statistic. While Chapter 8 contains the portion of these techniques that can be used for estimating a mean, a proportion, or a variance for a population with a single sample, Chapter 9 contains techniques used for testing hypotheses about a population mean, a population proportion, and a population variance using a single sample. The entire right side of the tree diagram taxonomy displays various hypothesis-testing techniques. The left-most branch of this right side contains Chapter 9 techniques (for single samples), and this branch is displayed in Figure 9.1. Note that at the bottom of each tree branch in Figure 9.1, the title of the statistical technique along with its respective section number is given for ease of identification and use. If a business researcher is testing a population mean and the population standard deviation is known, then she will use the z test for μ contained in Section 9.2. If the population standard deviation is unknown and therefore the researcher is using the sample standard deviation, then the appropriate technique is the t test for μ contained in Section 9.3. If a business researcher is testing a population proportion, then she will use the z test for p presented in Section 9.4. If the researcher desires to test a population variance from a single sample, then she will use the χ^2 test for σ^2 presented in Section 9.5. Section 9.6 contains techniques for solving for Type II errors.

9.1 INTRODUCTION TO HYPOTHESIS TESTING

In the field of business, decision makers are continually attempting to find answers to questions such as the following:

- What container shape is most economical and reliable for shipping a product?
- Which management approach best motivates employees in the retail industry?
- How can the company's retirement investment financial portfolio be diversified for optimum performance?
- What is the best way to link client databases for fast retrieval of useful information?
- Which indicator best predicts the general state of the economy in the next six months?
- What is the most effective means of advertising in a business-to-business setting?

Business researchers are often called upon to provide insights and information to decision makers to assist them in answering such questions. In searching for answers to questions and in attempting to find explanations for business phenomena, business researchers often develop "hypotheses" that can be studied and explored. **Hypotheses** are *tentative explanations of a principle operating in nature.** In this text, we will explore various types of hypotheses, how to test them, and how to interpret the results of such tests so that useful information can be brought to bear on the business decision-making process.

---

*Paraphrasing of definition published in *Merriam Webster's Collegiate Dictionary*, 10th ed. Springfield, MA: Merriam Webster, Inc., 1983.

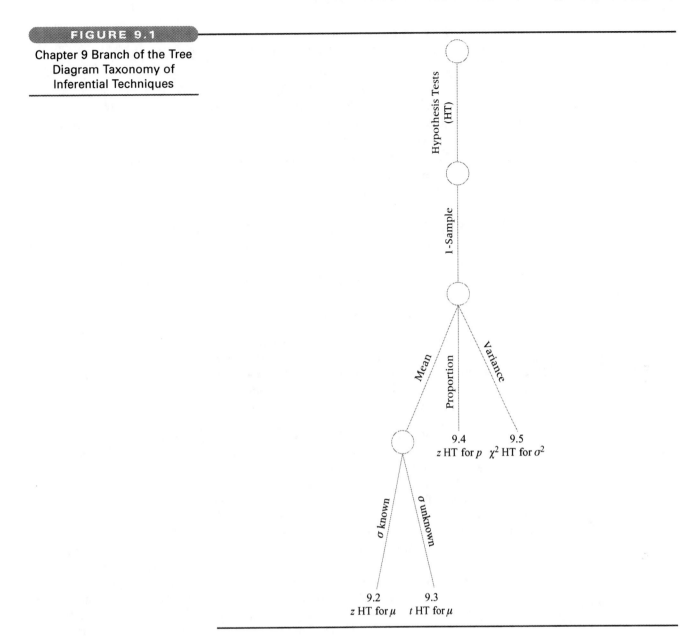

FIGURE 9.1

Chapter 9 Branch of the Tree Diagram Taxonomy of Inferential Techniques

Types of Hypotheses

Three types of hypotheses that will be explored here:

1. *Research* hypotheses
2. *Statistical* hypotheses
3. *Substantive* hypotheses

Although much of the focus will be on testing statistical hypotheses, it is also important for business decision makers to have an understanding of both research and substantive hypotheses.

Research Hypotheses

Research hypotheses are most nearly like hypotheses defined earlier. A **research hypothesis** is *a statement of what the researcher believes will be the outcome of an experiment or a study.* Before studies are undertaken, business researchers often have some idea or theory based on experience or previous work as to how the study will turn out. These ideas, theories, or notions established before an experiment or study is conducted are research hypotheses. Some examples of research hypotheses in business might include:

- Older workers are more loyal to a company.
- Companies with more than $1 billion in assets spend a higher percentage of their annual budget on advertising than do companies with less than $1 billion in assets.
- The implementation of a Six Sigma quality approach in manufacturing will result in greater productivity.
- The price of scrap metal is a good indicator of the industrial production index six months later.
- Airline company stock prices are positively correlated with the volume of OPEC oil production.

Virtually all inquisitive, thinking business people have similar research hypotheses concerning relationships, approaches, and techniques in business. Such hypotheses can lead decision makers to new and better ways to accomplish business goals. However, to formally test research hypotheses, it is generally best to state them as statistical hypotheses.

Statistical Hypotheses

In order to scientifically test research hypotheses, a more formal hypothesis structure needs to be set up using **statistical hypotheses**. Suppose business researchers want to "prove" the research hypothesis that older workers are more loyal to a company. A "loyalty" survey instrument is either developed or obtained. If this instrument is administered to both older and younger workers, how much higher do older workers have to score on the "loyalty" instrument (assuming higher scores indicate more loyal) than younger workers to prove the research hypothesis? What is the "proof threshold"? Instead of attempting to prove or disprove research hypotheses directly in this manner, business researchers convert their research hypotheses to statistical hypotheses and then test the statistical hypotheses using standard procedures.

All statistical hypotheses consist of two parts, a null hypothesis and an alternative hypothesis. These two parts are constructed to contain all possible outcomes of the experiment or study. Generally, the **null hypothesis** *states that the "null" condition exists; that is, there is nothing new happening, the old theory is still true, the old standard is correct, and the system is in control.* The **alternative hypothesis**, on the other hand, *states that the new theory is true, there are new standards, the system is out of control, and/or something is happening.* As an example, suppose flour packaged by a manufacturer is sold by weight; and a particular size of package is supposed to average 40 ounces. Suppose the manufacturer wants to test to determine whether their packaging process is out of control as determined by the weight of the flour packages. The null hypothesis for this experiment is that the average weight of the flour packages is 40 ounces (no problem). The alternative hypothesis is that the average is not 40 ounces (process is out of control).

It is common symbolism to represent the null hypothesis as H_0 and the alternative hypothesis as H_a. The null and alternative hypotheses for the flour example can be restated using these symbols and μ for the population mean as:

$$H_0: \mu = 40 \, oz.$$
$$H_a: \mu \neq 40 \, oz.$$

As another example, suppose a company has held an 18% share of the market. However, because of an increased marketing effort, company officials believe the company's market share is now greater than 18%, and the officials would like to prove it. The null hypothesis is that the market share is still 18% or perhaps it has even dropped below 18%. Converting the 18% to a proportion and using p to represent the population proportion, results in the following null hypothesis:

$$H_0: p \leq .18$$

The alternative hypothesis is that the population proportion is now greater than .18:

$$H_a: p > .18$$

Note that the "new idea" or "new theory" that company officials want to "prove" is stated in the alternative hypothesis. The null hypothesis states that the old market share of 18% is still true.

Generally speaking, new hypotheses that business researchers want to "prove" are stated in the alternative hypothesis. Because many business researchers only undertake an experiment to determine whether their new hypothesis is correct, they are hoping that the alternative hypothesis will be "proven" true. However, if a manufacturer is testing to determine whether his process is out of control as shown in the flour-packaging example, then he is most likely hoping that the alternative hypothesis is not "proven" true thereby demonstrating that the process is still in control.

Note in the market share example that the null hypothesis also contains the less than case ($<$) because between the two hypotheses (null and alternative), all possible outcomes must be included ($<$, $>$, and $=$). One could say that the null and alternative hypotheses are mutually exclusive (no overlap) and collectively exhaustive (all cases included). Thus, whenever a decision is made about which hypothesis is true, logically either one is true or the other but not both. Even though the company officials are not interested in "proving" that their market share is less than 18%, logically it should be included as a possibility. On the other hand, many researchers and statisticians leave out the "less than" ($<$) portion of the null hypothesis on the market share problem because company officials are only interested in "proving" that the market share has increased and the inclusion of the "less than" sign in the null hypothesis is confusing. This approach can be justified in the way that statistical hypotheses are tested. If the equal part of the null hypothesis is rejected because the market share is seemingly greater, then certainly the "less than" portion of the null hypothesis is also rejected because it is further away from "greater than" than is "equal." Using this logic, the null hypothesis for the market share problem can be written as

$$H_0: p = .18$$

rather than

$$H_0: p \leq .18$$

Thus, in this form, the statistical hypotheses for the market share problem can be written as

$$H_0: p = .18$$
$$H_a: p > .18$$

Even though the "less than" sign, $<$, is not included in the null hypothesis, it is implied that it is there. We will adopt such an approach in this book; and thus, all *null* hypotheses presented in this book will be written with an equal sign only ($=$) rather than with a directional sign ($\leq$) or ($\geq$).

Statistical hypotheses are written so that they will produce either a one-tailed or a two-tailed test. The hypotheses shown already for the flour package manufacturing problem are two-tailed:

$$H_0: \mu = 40 \text{ oz.}$$
$$H_a: \mu \neq 40 \text{ oz.}$$

Two-tailed tests always use $=$ and $\neq$ in the statistical hypotheses and are directionless in that the alternative hypothesis allows for either the greater than ($>$) or less than ($<$) possibility. In this particular example, if the process is "out of control," plant officials might not know whether machines are overfilling or underfilling packages and are interested in testing for either possibility.

The hypotheses shown for the market share problem are one-tailed:

$$H_0: p = .18$$
$$H_a: p > .18$$

One-tailed tests are always directional, and the alternative hypothesis uses either the greater than ($>$) or the less than ($<$) sign. A one-tailed test should only be used when the

THINKING CRITICALLY ABOUT STATISTICS IN BUSINESS TODAY

Consumer Attitudes toward Food in the United States

The average American eats 1996.3 pounds of food per year, including over 600 pounds of non-cheese dairy products, 110 pounds of red meat, over 273 pounds of fruit, over 415 pounds of vegetables, 29 pounds of french fries, 23 pounds of pizza, 24 pounds of ice cream, and 53 gallons of soda. On average, a person in the United States consumes 2770 calories of food daily.

About 70% of Americans say that they are concerned about their weight, and around 77% are trying to lose or maintain their weight. About 65% of Americans rate weight loss as their number one way to improve their health. Sixteen percent plan to use an improved diet to maintain their weight. Only 19% of those trying to lose weight actually keep track of their caloric intake. Around half of all Americans are trying to consume more protein, partly because 68% of Americans believe that protein builds muscle. A great percentage of Americans (88%) do their food shopping at supermarkets and grocery stores.

Things to Ponder

1. Think about the abundance of food in the United States, the high percentage of Americans who seem to be concerned about weight, and the various types of food that are being consumed in large quantities. Brainstorm a half dozen or so business opportunities that this might present to American entrepreneurs in terms of products, programs, or services.

2. A high percentage of Americans want to maintain or lose weight. What are some ways that employers/managers can help workers in this regard?

Sources: International Food Information Council (IFIC) Foundation, "2010 Food & Health Survey," Executive Summary & Key Trends, http://www.foodinsight.org/Content/3651/FINAL%202010%20Food%20 and%20Health%20Exec%20Summary%20Final.pdf; "Food Consumption in America," January 30, 2011, http://www.visualeconomics.com/food-consumption-in-america_2010-07-12/.

---

researcher knows for certain that the outcome of an experiment is going to occur only in one direction or the researcher is only interested in one direction of the experiment as in the case of the market share problem. In one-tailed problems, the researcher is trying to "prove" that something is older, younger, higher, lower, more, less, greater, and so on. These words are considered "directional" words in that they indicate the direction of the focus of the research. Without these words, the alternative hypothesis of a one-tailed test cannot be established.

In business research, the conservative approach is to conduct a two-tailed test because sometimes study results can be obtained that are in opposition to the direction that researchers thought would occur. For example, in the market share problem, it might turn out that the company had actually lost market share; and even though company officials were not interested in "proving" such a case, they may need to know that it is true. It is recommended that, if in doubt, business researchers should use a two-tailed test.

Substantive Hypotheses

In testing a statistical hypothesis, a business researcher reaches a conclusion based on the data obtained in the study. If the null hypothesis is rejected and therefore the alternative hypothesis is accepted, it is common to say that a statistically significant result has been obtained. For example, in the market share problem, if the null hypothesis is rejected, the result is that the market share is "significantly greater" than 18%. The word *significant* to statisticians and business researchers merely means that the result of the experiment is unlikely due to chance and a decision has been made to reject the null hypothesis. However, in everyday business life, the word *significant* is more likely to connote "important" or "a large amount." One problem that can arise in testing statistical hypotheses is that particular characteristics of the data can result in a statistically significant outcome that is not a significant business outcome.

As an example, consider the market share study. Suppose a large sample of potential customers is taken, and a sample market share of 18.2% is obtained. Suppose further that a statistical analysis of these data results in statistical significance. We would conclude statistically that the market share is significantly higher than 18%. This finding actually means that it is unlikely that the difference between the sample proportion and the population proportion of .18 is due just to chance. However, to the business decision maker, a market share of 18.2% might not be significantly higher than 18%. Because of the way the word *significant* is used to denote rejection of the null hypothesis rather than an important business difference, business decision makers need to exercise caution in interpreting the outcomes of statistical tests.

In addition to understanding a statistically significant result, business decision makers need to determine what, to them, is a *substantive* result. A **substantive result** is *when the outcome of a statistical study produces results that are important to the decision maker.* The importance to the researcher will vary from study to study. As an example, in a recent year, one healthcare administrator was excited because patient satisfaction had significantly increased (statistically) from one year to the next. However, an examination of the data revealed that on a five-point scale, their satisfaction ratings had gone up from 3.61 to only 3.63. Is going from a 3.61 rating to a 3.63 rating in one year really a substantive increase? On the other hand, increasing the average purchase at a large, high-volume store from $55.45 to $55.50 might be substantive as well as significant if volume is large enough to drive profits higher. Both business researchers and decision makers should be aware that statistically significant results are not always substantive results.

Using the HTAB System to Test Hypotheses

In conducting business research, the process of testing hypotheses involves four major tasks:

- Task 1. Establishing the hypotheses
- Task 2. Conducting the test
- Task 3. Taking statistical action
- Task 4. Determining the business implications

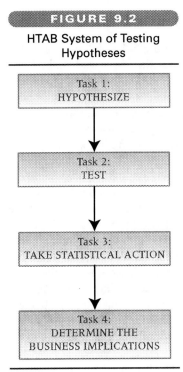

FIGURE 9.2

HTAB System of Testing Hypotheses

Task 1:
HYPOTHESIZE

Task 2:
TEST

Task 3:
TAKE STATISTICAL ACTION

Task 4:
DETERMINE THE BUSINESS IMPLICATIONS

This process, depicted in Figure 9.2, is referred to here as the HTAB system (**H**ypothesize, **T**est, **A**ction, **B**usiness).

Task 1, establishing the hypotheses, encompasses all activities that lead up to the establishment of the statistical hypotheses being tested. These activities might include investigating a business opportunity or problem, developing theories about possible solutions, and establishing research hypotheses. Task 2, conducting the test, involves the selection of the proper statistical test, setting the value of alpha, establishing a decision rule, gathering sample data, and computing the statistical analysis. Task 3, taking statistical action, is making a statistical decision about whether or not to reject the null hypothesis based on the outcome of the statistical test. Task 4, determining the business implications, is deciding what the statistical action means in business terms—that is, interpreting the statistical outcome in terms of business decision making.

Typically, statisticians and researchers present the hypothesis testing process in terms of an eight-step approach:

- Step 1. Establish a null and alternative hypothesis.
- Step 2. Determine the appropriate statistical test.
- Step 3. Set the value of alpha, the Type I error rate.
- Step 4. Establish the decision rule.
- Step 5. Gather sample data.
- Step 6. Analyze the data.
- Step 7. Reach a statistical conclusion.
- Step 8. Make a business decision.

These eight steps fit nicely into the four HTAB tasks as a part of the HTAB paradigm. Figure 9.3 presents the HTAB paradigm incorporating the eight steps into the four HTAB tasks.

Task 1 of the HTAB system, hypothesizing, includes step 1, which is establishing a null and alternative hypothesis. In establishing the null and alternative hypotheses, it is important that the business researcher clearly identify what is being tested and whether the hypotheses are one tailed or two tailed. In hypothesis testing process, it is *always assumed that the null hypothesis is true* at the beginning of the study. In other words, it is assumed that the process is in control (no problem), that the market share has not increased, that older workers are not more loyal to a company than younger workers, and so on. This process is analogous to the U.S. trial system in which the accused is presumed innocent at the beginning of the trial.

FIGURE 9.3

HTAB Paradigm Incorporating
the Eight Steps

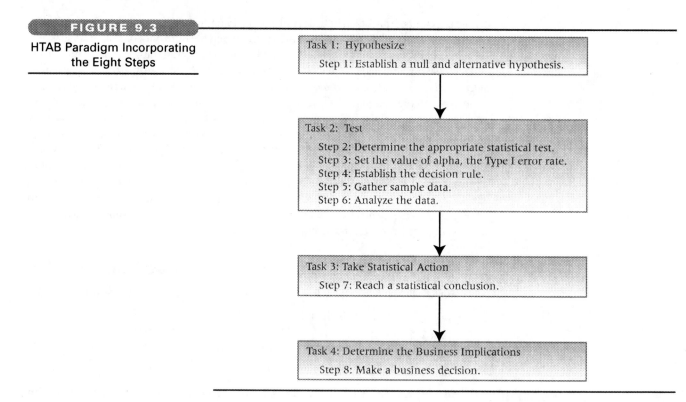

Task 1: Hypothesize

    Step 1: Establish a null and alternative hypothesis.

Task 2: Test

    Step 2: Determine the appropriate statistical test.
    Step 3: Set the value of alpha, the Type I error rate.
    Step 4: Establish the decision rule.
    Step 5: Gather sample data.
    Step 6: Analyze the data.

Task 3: Take Statistical Action

    Step 7: Reach a statistical conclusion.

Task 4: Determine the Business Implications

    Step 8: Make a business decision.

Task 2 of the HTAB system, testing, includes steps 2 through 6. Step 2 is to select the most appropriate statistical test to use for the analysis. In selecting such a test, the business researcher needs to consider the type, number, and level of data being used in the study along with the statistic used in the analysis (mean, proportion, variance, etc.). In addition, business researchers should consider the assumptions underlying certain statistical tests and determine whether they can be met in the study before using such tests.

At step 3, the value of alpha is set. Alpha is the probability of committing a Type I error and will be discussed later. Common values of alpha include .05, .01, .10, and .001.

A decision rule should be established before the study is undertaken (step 4). Using alpha and the test statistic, critical values can be determined. These **critical values** are *used at the decision step to determine whether the null hypothesis is rejected* or not. If the *p*-value method (discussed later) is used, the value of alpha is used as a critical probability value. The process begins by assuming that the null hypothesis is true. Data are gathered and statistics computed. If the evidence is away from the null hypothesis, the business researcher begins to doubt that the null hypothesis is really true. If the evidence is far enough away from the null hypothesis that the critical value is surpassed, the business researcher will reject the null hypothesis and declare that a statistically significant result has been attained. Here again, it is analogous to the U.S. court of law system. Initially, a defendant is assumed to be innocent. Prosecuting attorneys present evidence against the defendant (analogous to data gathered and analyzed in a study). At some point, if enough evidence is presented against the defendant such that the jury no longer believes the defendant is innocent, a critical level of evidence has been reached and the jury finds the defendant guilty. The first four steps in testing hypotheses should *always* be completed *before* the study is undertaken. It is not sound research to gather data first and then try to determine what to do with the data.

Step 5 is to gather sample data. This step might include the construction and implementation of a survey, conducting focus groups, randomly sampling items from an assembly line, or even sampling from secondary data sources (e.g., financial databases). In gathering data, the business researcher is cautioned to recall the proper techniques of random sampling (presented in Chapter 7). Care should be taken in establishing a frame, determining the sampling technique, and constructing the measurement device. A strong effort should be made to avoid all nonsampling errors. After the data are sampled, the test statistic can be calculated (step 6).

Task 3 of the HTAB system, take statistical action, includes step 7. Using the previously established decision rule (in step 4) and the value of the test statistic, the business researcher can draw a statistical conclusion. In *all* hypothesis tests, the business researcher needs to conclude whether the null hypothesis is rejected or is not rejected (step 7).

Task 4 of the HTAB system, determining the business implications, incorporates step 8. After a statistical decision is made, the business researcher or decision maker decides what business implications the study results contain (step 8). For example, if the hypothesis-testing procedure results in a conclusion that train passengers are significantly older today than they were in the past, the manager may decide to cater to these older customers or to draw up a strategy to make ridership more appealing to younger people. It is at this step that the business decision maker must decide whether a statistically significant result is really a substantive result.

Rejection and Nonrejection Regions

Using the critical values established at step 4 of the hypothesis testing process, the possible statistical outcomes of a study can be divided into two groups:

1. Those that cause the rejection of the null hypothesis
2. Those that do not cause the rejection of the null hypothesis.

Conceptually and graphically, statistical outcomes that result in the rejection of the null hypothesis lie in what is termed the **rejection region**. Statistical outcomes that fail to result in the rejection of the null hypothesis lie in what is termed the **nonrejection region**.

As an example, consider the flour-packaging manufacturing example. The null hypothesis is that the average fill for the population of packages is 40 ounces. Suppose a sample of 100 such packages is randomly selected, and a sample mean of 40.01 ounces is obtained. Because this mean is not 40 ounces, should the business researcher decide to reject the null hypothesis? In the hypothesis test process we are using sample statistics (in this case, the sample mean of 40.1 ounces) to make decisions about population parameters (in this case, the population mean of 40 ounces). It makes sense that in taking random samples from a population with a mean of 40 ounces not all sample means will equal 40 ounces. In fact, the central limit theorem (see Chapter 7) states that for large sample sizes, sample means are normally distributed around the population mean. Thus, even when the population mean is 40 ounces, a sample mean might still be 40.1, 38.6, or even 44.2. However, suppose a sample mean of 50 ounces is obtained for 100 packages. This sample mean may be so far from what is reasonable to expect for a population with a mean of 40 ounces that the decision is made to reject the null hypothesis. This promps the question: when is the sample mean so far away from the population mean that the null hypothesis is rejected? The critical values established at step 4 of the hypothesis testing process are used to divide the means that lead to the rejection of the null hypothesis from those that do not. Figure 9.4 displays a normal distribution of sample means around a population mean of 40 ounces. Note the critical values in each end (tail) of the distribution. In each direction beyond the critical values lie

FIGURE 9.4

Rejection and Nonrejection Regions

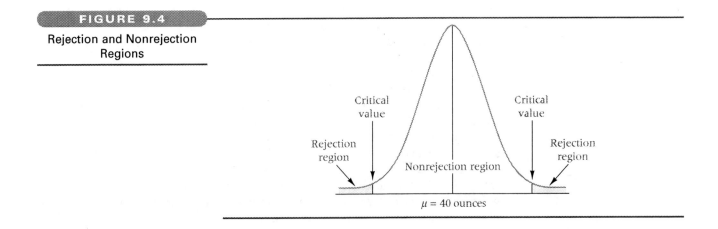

the rejection regions. Any sample mean that falls in that region will lead the business researcher to reject the null hypothesis. Sample means that fall between the two critical values are close enough to the population mean that the business researcher will decide not to reject the null hypothesis. These means are in the nonrejection region.

Type I and Type II Errors

Because the hypothesis testing process uses sample statistics calculated from random data to reach conclusions about population parameters, it is possible to make an incorrect decision about the null hypothesis. In particular, two types of errors can be made in testing hypotheses: Type I error and Type II error.

A **Type I error** is committed by *rejecting a true null hypothesis*. With a Type I error, the null hypothesis is true, but the business researcher decides that it is not. As an example, suppose the flour-packaging process actually is "in control" and is averaging 40 ounces of flour per package. Suppose also that a business researcher randomly selects 100 packages, weighs the contents of each, and computes a sample mean. It is possible, by chance, to randomly select 100 of the more extreme packages (mostly heavy weighted or mostly light weighted) resulting in a mean that falls in the rejection region. The decision is to reject the null hypothesis even though the population mean is actually 40 ounces. In this case, the business researcher has committed a Type I error.

The notion of a Type I error can be used outside the realm of statistical hypothesis testing in the business world. For example, if a manager fires an employee because some evidence indicates that she is stealing from the company and if she really is not stealing from the company, then the manager has committed a Type I error. As another example, suppose a worker on the assembly line of a large manufacturer hears an unusual sound and decides to shut the line down (reject the null hypothesis). If the sound turns out not to be related to the assembly line and no problems are occurring with the assembly line, then the worker has committed a Type I error. In U.S. industries in the 1950s, 1960s, and 1970s, when U.S. products were in great demand, workers were strongly discouraged from making such Type I errors because the production downtime was so expensive. An analogous courtroom example of a Type I error is when an innocent person is sent to jail.

In Figure 9.4, the rejection regions represent the possibility of committing a Type I error. Means that fall beyond the critical values will be considered so extreme that the business researcher chooses to reject the null hypothesis. However, if the null hypothesis is true, any mean that falls in a rejection region will result in a decision that produces a Type I error. The *probability of committing a Type I error* is called **alpha** (α) or **level of significance**. Alpha equals the area under the curve that is in the rejection region beyond the critical value(s). The value of alpha is always set before the experiment or study is undertaken. As mentioned previously, common values of alpha are .05, .01, .10, and .001.

A **Type II error** is committed when a business researcher *fails to reject a false null hypothesis*. In this case, the null hypothesis is false, but a decision is made to not reject it. Suppose in the case of the flour problem that the packaging process is actually producing a population mean of 41 ounces even though the null hypothesis is 40 ounces. A sample of 100 packages yields a sample mean of 40.2 ounces, which falls in the nonrejection region. The business decision maker decides not to reject the null hypothesis. A Type II error has been committed. The packaging procedure is out of control and the hypothesis testing process does not identify it.

Suppose in the business world an employee is stealing from the company. A manager sees some evidence that the stealing is occurring but lacks enough evidence to conclude that the employee is stealing from the company. The manager decides not to fire the employee based on theft. The manager has committed a Type II error. Consider the manufacturing line with the noise. Suppose the worker decides not enough noise is heard to shut the line down, but in actuality, one of the cords on the line is unraveling, creating a dangerous situation. The worker is committing a Type II error. Beginning in the 1980s, U.S. manufacturers started protecting more against Type II errors. They found that in many cases, it was more costly to produce bad product (e.g., scrap/rework costs and loss of market share due to poor quality) than it was to make it right the first time. They

FIGURE 9.5

Alpha, Beta, and Power

State of nature

		Null true	Null false
Action	Fail to reject null	Correct decision	Type II error (β)
	Reject null	Type I error (α)	Correct decision (power)

encouraged workers to "shut down" the line if the quality of work was seemingly not what it should be (risking a Type I error) rather than allowing poor quality product to be shipped. In a court of law, a Type II error is committed when a guilty person is declared innocent.

The probability of committing a Type II error is **beta** (β). Unlike alpha, beta is not usually stated at the beginning of the hypothesis testing procedure. Actually, because beta occurs only when the null hypothesis is not true, the computation of beta varies with the many possible alternative parameters that might occur. For example, in the flour-packaging problem, if the population mean is not 40 ounces, then what is it? It could be 41, 38, or 42 ounces. A value of beta is associated with each of these alternative means.

How are alpha and beta related? First of all, because alpha can only be committed when the null hypothesis is rejected and beta can only be committed when the null hypothesis is not rejected, a business researcher cannot commit both a Type I error and a Type II error at the same time on the same hypothesis test. Generally, alpha and beta are inversely related. If alpha is reduced, then beta is increased, and vice versa. In terms of the manufacturing assembly line, if management makes it harder for workers to shut down the assembly line (reduce Type I error), then there is a greater chance that bad product will be made or that a serious problem with the line will arise (increase Type II error). Legally, if the courts make it harder to send innocent people to jail, then they have made it easier to let guilty people go free. One way to reduce both errors is to increase the sample size. If a larger sample is taken, it is more likely that the sample is representative of the population, which translates into a better chance that a business researcher will make the correct choice. Figure 9.5 shows the relationship between the two types of error. The "state of nature" is how things actually are and the "action" is the decision that the business researcher actually makes. Note that each action alternative contains only one of the errors along with the possibility that a correct decision has been made. **Power**, which is equal to $1 - \beta$, is *the probability of a statistical test rejecting the null hypothesis when the null hypothesis is false.* Figure 9.5 shows the relationship between α, β, and power.

9.2 TESTING HYPOTHESES ABOUT A POPULATION MEAN USING THE *z* STATISTIC (σ KNOWN)

Video

Interactive Applet

One of the most basic hypothesis tests is a test about a population mean. A business researcher might be interested in testing to determine whether an established or accepted mean value for an industry is still true or in testing a hypothesized mean value for a new theory or product. As an example, a computer products company sets up a telephone service to assist customers by providing technical support. The average wait time during weekday hours is 37 minutes. However, a recent hiring effort added technical consultants to the system, and management believes that the average wait time decreased, and they want to prove it. Other business scenarios resulting in hypothesis tests of a single mean might include the following:

- A financial investment firm wants to test to determine whether the average hourly change in the Dow Jones Average over a 10-year period is +0.25.
- A manufacturing company wants to test to determine whether the average thickness of a plastic bottle is 2.4 millimeters.
- A retail store wants to test to determine whether the average age of its customers is less than 40 years.

Formula 9.1 can be used to test hypotheses about a single population mean when σ is known if the sample size is large ($n \geq 30$) for any population and for small samples ($n < 30$) if x is known to be normally distributed in the population.

z TEST FOR A SINGLE MEAN (9.1)	$$z = \frac{\bar{x} - \mu}{\frac{\sigma}{\sqrt{n}}}$$

A survey of CPAs across the United States found that the average net income for sole proprietor CPAs is \$74,914.* Because this survey is now more than 15 years old, an accounting researcher wants to test this figure by taking a random sample of 112 sole proprietor accountants in the United States to determine whether the net income figure changed. The researcher could use the eight steps of hypothesis testing to do so. Assume the population standard deviation of net incomes for sole proprietor CPAs is \$14,530.

HYPOTHESIZE:

At step 1, the hypotheses must be established. Because the researcher is testing to determine whether the figure has changed, the alternative hypothesis is that the mean net income is not \$74,914. The null hypothesis is that the mean still equals \$74,914. These hypotheses follow.

$$H_0: \mu = \$74,914$$
$$H_a: \mu \neq \$74,914$$

TEST:

Step 2 is to determine the appropriate statistical test and sampling distribution. Because the population standard deviation is known (\$14,530) and the researcher is using the sample mean as the statistic, the z test in formula (9.1) is the appropriate test statistic.

$$z = \frac{\bar{x} - \mu}{\frac{\sigma}{\sqrt{n}}}$$

Step 3 is to specify the Type I error rate, or alpha, which is .05 in this problem. Step 4 is to state the decision rule. Because the test is two tailed and alpha is .05, there is $\alpha/2$ or .025 area in each of the tails of the distribution. Thus, the rejection region is in the two ends of the distribution with 2.5% of the area in each. There is a .4750 area between the mean and each of the critical values that separate the tails of the distribution (the rejection region) from the nonrejection region. By using this .4750 area and Table A.5, the critical z value can be obtained.

$$z_{\alpha/2} = \pm 1.96$$

Figure 9.6 displays the problem with the rejection regions and the critical values of z. The decision rule is that if the data gathered produce a z value greater than 1.96 or less than

---

*Adapted from Daniel J. Flaherty, Raymond A. Zimmerman, and Mary Ann Murray, "Benchmarking Against the Best," *Journal of Accountancy* (July 1995), pp. 85–88.

FIGURE 9.6

CPA Net Income Example

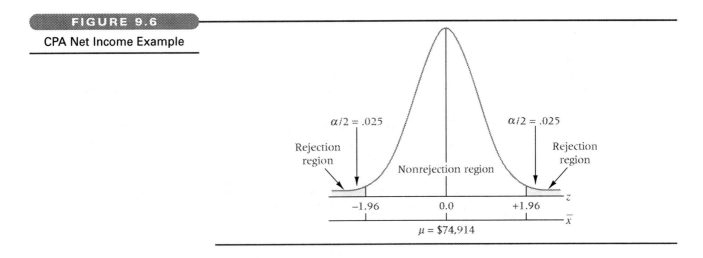

$\alpha/2 = .025$

Rejection region

Nonrejection region

$\alpha/2 = .025$

Rejection region

-1.96 0.0 $+1.96$ z

$\bar{x}$

$\mu = \$74{,}914$

−1.96, the test statistic is in one of the rejection regions and the decision is to reject the null hypothesis. If the observed z value calculated from the data is between −1.96 and +1.96, the decision is to not reject the null hypothesis because the observed z value is in the nonrejection region.

Step 5 is to gather the data. Suppose the 112 CPAs who respond produce a sample mean of $78,695. At step 6, the value of the test statistic is calculated by using $\bar{x} = \$78{,}695$, $n = 112$, $\sigma = \$14{,}530$, and a hypothesized $\mu = \$74{,}914$:

$$z = \frac{78{,}695 - 74{,}914}{\dfrac{14{,}530}{\sqrt{112}}} = 2.75$$

ACTION:

Because this test statistic, $z = 2.75$, is greater than the critical value of z in the upper tail of the distribution, $z = +1.96$, the statistical conclusion reached at step 7 of the hypothesis-testing process is to reject the null hypothesis. *The calculated test statistic* is often referred to as the **observed value**. Thus, the observed value of z for this problem is 2.75 and the critical value of z for this problem is 1.96.

BUSINESS IMPLICATION:

Step 8 is to make a managerial decision. What does this result mean? Statistically, the researcher has enough evidence to reject the figure of $74,914 as the true national average net income for sole proprietor CPAs. Although the researcher conducted a two-tailed test, the evidence gathered indicates that the national average may have increased. The sample mean of $78,695 is $3,781 higher than the national mean being tested. The researcher can conclude that the national average is more than before, but because the $78,695 is only a sample mean, it offers no guarantee that the national average for all sole proprietor CPAs is $3,781 more. If a confidence interval were constructed with the sample data, $78,695 would be the point estimate. Other samples might produce different sample means. Managerially, this statistical finding may mean that CPAs will be more expensive to hire either as full-time employees or as consultants. It may mean that consulting services have gone up in price. For new accountants, it may mean the potential for greater earning power.

Testing the Mean with a Finite Population

If the hypothesis test for the population mean is being conducted with a known finite population, the population information can be incorporated into the hypothesis-testing formula. Doing so can increase the potential for rejecting the null hypothesis. However, remember from Chapter 7 that if the sample size is less than 5% of the population, the finite correction factor does not significantly alter the solution. Formula 9.1 can be amended to include the population information.

FORMULA TO TEST HYPOTHESES ABOUT μ WITH A FINITE POPULATION (9.2)	$$z = \frac{\bar{x} - \mu}{\frac{\sigma}{\sqrt{n}}\sqrt{\frac{N-n}{N-1}}}$$

In the CPA net income example, suppose only 600 sole proprietor CPAs practice in the United States. A sample of 112 CPAs taken from a population of only 600 CPAs is 18.67% of the population and therefore is much more likely to be representative of the population than a sample of 112 CPAs taken from a population of 20,000 CPAs (.56% of the population). The finite correction factor takes this difference into consideration and allows for an increase in the observed value of *z*. The observed *z* value would change to

$$z = \frac{\bar{x} - \mu}{\frac{\sigma}{\sqrt{n}}\sqrt{\frac{N-n}{N-1}}} = \frac{78,695 - 74,914}{\frac{14,530}{\sqrt{112}}\sqrt{\frac{600 - 112}{600 - 1}}} = \frac{3,781}{1,239.2} = 3.05$$

Use of the finite correction factor increased the observed *z* value from 2.75 to 3.05. The decision to reject the null hypothesis does not change with this new information. However, on occasion, the finite correction factor can make the difference between rejecting and failing to reject the null hypothesis.

Using the *p*-Value to Test Hypotheses

Another way to reach a statistical conclusion in hypothesis testing problems is by using the **p-value**, sometimes referred to as **observed significance level**. The *p*-value is growing in importance with the increasing use of statistical computer packages to test hypotheses. No preset value of α is given in the *p*-value method. Instead, the probability of getting a test statistic at least as extreme as the observed test statistic (computed from the data) is computed under the assumption that the null hypothesis is true. Virtually every statistical computer program yields this probability (*p*-value). *The p-value defines the smallest value of alpha for which the null hypothesis can be rejected.* For example, if the *p*-value of a test is .038, the null hypothesis cannot be rejected at $\alpha = .01$ because .038 is the smallest value of alpha for which the null hypothesis can be rejected. However, the null hypothesis can be rejected for $\alpha = .05$.

Suppose a researcher is conducting a one-tailed test with a rejection region in the upper tail and obtains an observed test statistic of $z = 2.04$ from the sample data. Using the standard normal table, Table A.5, we find that the probability of randomly obtaining a *z* value this great or greater by chance is $.5000 - .4793 = .0207$. The *p*-value is .0207. Using this information, the researcher would reject the null hypothesis for $\alpha = .05$ or .10 or any value more than .0207. The researcher would not reject the null hypothesis for any alpha value less than or equal to .0207 (in particular, $\alpha = .01, .001$, etc.).

For a two-tailed test, recall that we split alpha to determine the critical value of the test statistic. With the *p*-value, the probability of getting a test statistic at least as extreme as the observed value is computed. This *p*-value is then compared to $\alpha/2$ for two-tailed tests to determine statistical significance.

Note: The business researcher should be cautioned that some statistical computer packages are programmed to double the observed probability and report that value as the *p*-value when the user signifies that a two-tailed test is being requested. The researcher then compares this *p*-value to alpha values to decide whether to reject the null hypothesis. The researcher must be sure she understands what the computer software package does to the *p*-value for a two-tailed test before she reaches a statistical conclusion.

As an example of using *p*-values with a two-tailed test, consider the CPA net income problem. The observed test statistic for this problem is $z = 2.75$. Using Table A.5, we know that the probability of obtaining a test statistic at least this extreme if the null hypothesis is true is $.5000 - .4970 = .0030$. Observe that in the Minitab output in Figure 9.7 the *p*-value is .0060. Minitab doubles the *p*-value on a two-tailed test so that the researcher can

FIGURE 9.7

Minitab and Excel Output
with *p*-Values

Minitab Output
One-Sample Z

Test of mu = 74914 vs not = 74914
The assumed standard deviation = 14530

N	Mean	SE Mean	95% CI	Z	P
112	78695	1373	(76004, 81386)	2.75	0.006

Excel Output

Sample mean	78695
Standard error	1374
Standard deviation	14530
Count (*n*)	112
Hypothesized value of μ	74914
p-value	0.003

compare the *p*-value to α to reach a statistical conclusion. On the other hand, when Excel yields a *p*-value in its output, it always gives the one-tailed value, which in this case is .003 (see output in Figure 9.7). To reach a statistical conclusion from an Excel-produced *p*-value when doing a two-tailed test, the researcher must compare the *p*-value to $\alpha/2$.

Figure 9.8 summarizes the decisions that can be made using various *p*-values for a one-tailed test. To use this for a two-tailed test, compare the *p*-value in one tail to $\alpha/2$ in a similar manner. Because $\alpha = .10$ is usually the largest value of alpha used by most researchers, if a *p*-value is not less than .10, then the decision is to fail to reject the null hypothesis. In other words, the null hypothesis cannot be rejected if *p*-values are .579 or .106 or .283, etc. If a *p*-value is less than .10 but not less than .05, then the null hypothesis can be rejected for $\alpha = .10$. If it is less than .05, but not less than .01, then the null hypothesis can be rejected for $\alpha = .05$ and so on.

Using the Critical Value Method to Test Hypotheses

Another method of testing hypotheses is the critical value method. In the CPA income example, the null hypothesis was rejected because the computed value of *z* was in the rejection zone. What mean income would it take to cause the observed *z* value to be in the rejection zone? The **critical value method** *determines the critical mean value required for z to be in the rejection region and uses it to test the hypotheses.*

FIGURE 9.8

Rejecting the Null Hypothesis
Using *p*-Values

Range of *p*-Values	Rejection Range
p-value > .10	Cannot reject the null hypothesis for commonly accepted values of alpha
.05 < *p*-value ≤ .10	Reject the null hypothesis for $\alpha = .10$
.01 < *p*-value ≤ .05	Reject the null hypothesis for $\alpha = .05$
.001 < *p*-value ≤ .01	Reject the null hypothesis for $\alpha = .01$
.0001 < *p*-value ≤ .001	Reject the null hypothesis for $\alpha = .001$

FIGURE 9.9

Rejection and Nonrejection
Regions for Critical Value
Method

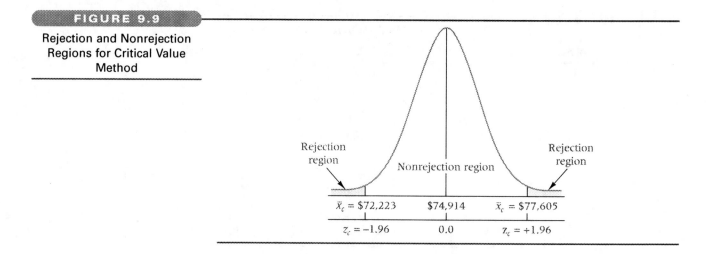

This method also uses formula 9.1. However, instead of an observed z, a critical $\bar{x}$ value, $\bar{x}_c$, is determined. The critical table value of z_c is inserted into the formula, along with μ and σ. Thus,

$$z_c = \frac{\bar{x}_c - \mu}{\dfrac{\sigma}{\sqrt{n}}}$$

Substituting values from the CPA income example gives

$$\pm 1.96 = \frac{\bar{x}_c - 74,914}{\dfrac{14,530}{\sqrt{112}}}$$

or

$$\bar{x}_c = 74,914 \pm 1.96 \frac{14,530}{\sqrt{112}} = 74,914 \pm 2691$$

lower $\bar{x}_c = 72,223$ and upper $\bar{x}_c = 77,605$.

Figure 9.9 depicts graphically the rejection and nonrejection regions in terms of means instead of z scores.

With the critical value method, most of the computational work is done ahead of time. In this problem, before the sample means are computed, the analyst knows that a sample mean value of greater than $77,605 or less than $72,223 must be attained to reject the hypothesized population mean. Because the sample mean for this problem was $78,695, which is greater than $77,605, the analyst rejects the null hypothesis. This method is particularly attractive in industrial settings where standards can be set ahead of time and then quality control technicians can gather data and compare actual measurements of products to specifications.

In an attempt to determine why customer service is important to managers in the United Kingdom, researchers surveyed managing directors of manufacturing plants in Scotland.* One of the reasons proposed was that customer service is a means of retaining customers. On a scale from 1 to 5, with 1 being low and 5 being high, the survey respondents rated this reason more highly than any of the others, with a

---

*William G. Donaldson, "Manufacturers Need to Show Greater Commitment to Customer Service," *Industrial Marketing Management*, vol. 24 (October 1995), pp. 421–430. The 1-to-5 scale has been reversed here for clarity of presentation.

mean response of 4.30. Suppose U.S. researchers believe American manufacturing managers would not rate this reason as highly and conduct a hypothesis test to prove their theory. Alpha is set at .05. Data are gathered and the following results are obtained. Use these data and the eight steps of hypothesis testing to determine whether U.S. managers rate this reason significantly lower than the 4.30 mean ascertained in the United Kingdom. Assume from previous studies that the population standard deviation is 0.574.

3	4	5	5	4	5	5	4	4	4	4
4	4	4	4	5	4	4	4	3	4	4
4	3	5	4	4	5	4	4	4	5	

Solution

HYPOTHESIZE:

STEP 1. Establish hypotheses. Because the U.S. researchers are interested only in "proving" that the mean figure is lower in the United States, the test is one tailed. The alternative hypothesis is that the population mean is lower than 4.30. The null hypothesis states the equality case.

$$H_0: \mu = 4.30$$
$$H_a: \mu < 4.30$$

TEST:

STEP 2. Determine the appropriate statistical test. The test statistic is

$$z = \frac{\bar{x} - \mu}{\dfrac{\sigma}{\sqrt{n}}}$$

STEP 3. Specify the Type I error rate.

$$\alpha = .05$$

STEP 4. State the decision rule. Because this test is a one-tailed test, the critical *z* value is found by looking up .5000 − .0500 = .4500 as the area in Table A.5. The critical value of the test statistic is $z_{.05} = -1.645$. An observed test statistic must be less than −1.645 to reject the null hypothesis. The rejection region and critical value can be depicted as in the following diagram.

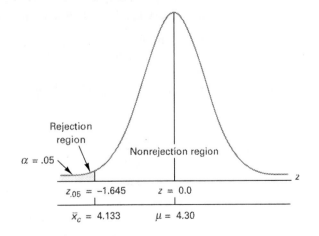

STEP 5. Gather the sample data. The data are shown.

STEP 6. Calculate the value of the test statistic.

$$\bar{x} = 4.156 \qquad \sigma = 0.574$$

$$z = \frac{4.156 - 4.30}{\dfrac{0.574}{\sqrt{32}}} = -1.42$$

ACTION:

STEP 7. State the statistical conclusion. Because the observed test statistic is not less than the critical value and is not in the rejection region, the statistical conclusion is that the null hypothesis cannot be rejected. The same result is obtained using the p-value method. The observed test statistic is $z = -1.42$. From Table A.5, the probability of getting a z value at least this extreme when the null hypothesis is true is $.5000 - .4222 = .0778$. Hence, the null hypothesis cannot be rejected at $\alpha = .05$ because the smallest value of alpha for which the null hypothesis can be rejected is .0778. Had $\alpha = .10$, the decision would have been to reject the null hypothesis.

BUSINESS IMPLICATION:

STEP 8. Make a managerial decision. The test does not result in enough evidence to conclude that U.S. managers think it is less important to use customer service as a means of retaining customers than do UK managers. Customer service is an important tool for retaining customers in both countries according to managers.

Using the critical value method: For what sample mean (or more extreme) value would the null hypothesis be rejected? This critical sample mean can be determined by using the critical z value associated with alpha, $z_{.05} = -1.645$.

$$z_c = \frac{\bar{x}_c - \mu}{\dfrac{\sigma}{\sqrt{n}}}$$

$$-1.645 = \frac{\bar{x}_c - 4.30}{\dfrac{0.574}{\sqrt{32}}}$$

$$\bar{x}_c = 4.133$$

The decision rule is that a sample mean less than 4.133 would be necessary to reject the null hypothesis. Because the mean obtained from the sample data is 4.156, the researchers fail to reject the null hypothesis. The preceding diagram includes a scale with the critical sample mean and the rejection region for the critical value method.

Using the Computer to Test Hypotheses About a Population Mean Using the z Statistic

Both Minitab and Excel can be used to test hypotheses about a single population mean using the z statistic. Figure 9.10 contains output from both Minitab and Excel for Demonstration Problem 9.1. For z tests, Minitab requires knowledge of the population standard deviation. Note that the standard Minitab output includes a statement of the

FIGURE 9.10

Minitab and Excel Output for Demonstration Problem 9.1

Minitab Output

One-Sample Z

Test of mu = 4.3 vs < 4.3
The assumed standard deviation = 0.574

N	Mean	SE Mean	95% CI	Z	P
32	4.156	0.101	(3.957, 4.355)	−1.42	0.078

Excel Output

The p-value for the ratings problem is **0.078339**

one-tailed hypothesis, the observed z value, and the p-value. Because this test is a one-tailed test, the p-value was not doubled. The Excel output contains only the right-tailed p-value of the z statistic. With a negative observed z for Demonstration Problem 9.1, the p-value was calculated by taking $1 - $ (Excel's answer).

9.2 PROBLEMS

9.1 a. Use the data given to test the following hypotheses.

$$H_0: \mu = 25 \qquad H_a: \mu \neq 25$$
$$\bar{x} = 28.1, \ n = 57, \ \sigma = 8.46, \ \alpha = .01$$

b. Use the p-value to reach a statistical conclusion

c. Using the critical value method, what are the critical sample mean values?

9.2 Use the data given to test the following hypotheses. Assume the data are normally distributed in the population.

$$H_0: \mu = 7.48 \qquad H_a: \mu < 7.48$$
$$\bar{x} = 6.91, \ n = 24, \ \sigma = 1.21, \ \alpha = .01$$

9.3 a. Use the data given to test the following hypotheses.

$$H_0: \mu = 1200 \qquad H_a: \mu > 1200$$
$$\bar{x} = 1215, \ n = 113, \ \sigma = 100, \ \alpha = .10$$

b. Use the p-value to obtain the results.

c. Solve for the critical value required to reject the mean.

9.4 The Environmental Protection Agency releases figures on urban air soot in selected cities in the United States. For the city of St. Louis, the EPA claims that the average number of micrograms of suspended particles per cubic meter of air is 82. Suppose St. Louis officials have been working with businesses, commuters, and industries to reduce this figure. These city officials hire an environmental company to take random measures of air soot over a period of several weeks. The resulting data follow. Assume that the population standard deviation is 9.184. Use these data to determine whether the urban air soot in St. Louis is significantly lower than it was when the EPA conducted its measurements. Let $\alpha = .01$. If the null hypothesis is rejected, discuss the substantive hypothesis.

81.6	66.6	70.9	82.5	58.3	71.6	72.4
96.6	78.6	76.1	80.0	73.2	85.5	73.2
68.6	74.0	68.7	83.0	86.9	94.9	75.6
77.3	86.6	71.7	88.5	87.0	72.5	83.0
85.8	74.9	61.7	92.2			

9.5 According to the U.S. Bureau of Labor Statistics, the average weekly earnings of a production worker in 1997 were $424.20. Suppose a labor researcher wants to test to determine whether this figure is still accurate today. The researcher randomly selects 54 production workers from across the United States and obtains a representative earnings statement for one week from each. The resulting sample average is $432.69. Assuming a population standard deviation of $33.90, and a 5% level of significance, determine whether the mean weekly earnings of a production worker have changed.

9.6 According to a study several years ago by the Personal Communications Industry Association, the average wireless phone user earns $62,600 per year. Suppose a researcher believes that the average annual earnings of a wireless phone user are lower now, and he sets up a study in an attempt to prove his theory. He randomly samples 18 wireless phone users and finds out that the average annual salary for this sample is $58,974, with a population standard deviation of $7,810. Use $\alpha = .01$ to test the researcher's theory. Assume wages in this industry are normally distributed.

9.7 A manufacturing company produces valves in various sizes and shapes. One particular valve plate is supposed to have a tensile strength of 5 pounds per millimeter (lbs/mm). The company tests a random sample of 42 such valve plates from a lot of

650 valve plates. The sample mean is a tensile strength of 5.0611 lbs/mm, and the population standard deviation is 0.2803 lbs/mm. Use $\alpha = .10$ and test to determine whether the lot of valve plates has an average tensile strength of 5 lbs/mm.

9.8 According to a report released by CIBC entitled "Women Entrepreneurs: Leading the Charge," the average age for Canadian businesswomen in 2008 was 41. In the report, there was some indication that researchers believed that this mean age will increase. Suppose now, a few years later, business researchers in Canada want to test to determine if, indeed, the mean age of a Canadian businesswoman has increased. The researchers randomly sample 97 Canadian businesswomen and ascertain that the sample mean age is 43.4. From past experience, it is known that the population standard deviation is 8.95. Test to determine if the mean age of a Canadian businesswoman has increased using a 1% level of significance. What is the p-value for this test? What is the decision? If the null hypothesis is rejected, is the result substantive?

9.9 According to HowtoAdvice.com, the average price charged to a customer to have a 12′ by 18′ wall-to-wall carpet shampoo cleaned is about $50. Suppose that a start-up carpet-cleaning company believes that in the region in which they operate, the average price for this service is higher. To test this hypothesis, the carpet-cleaning company randomly contacts 23 customers who have recently had a 12′ by 18′ wall-to-wall carpet shampoo cleaned and asked the customers how much they were charged for the job. Suppose the resulting data are given below and that the population standard deviation price is $3.49. Use a 10% level of significance to test their hypothesis. Assume that such prices are normally distributed in the population. What is the observed value? What is the p-value? What is the decision? If the null hypothesis is rejected, is the result substantive?

$52	52	56	50	50	51	49	49	54	51	51	48
56	52	52	53	56	52	52	56	57	48	53	

9.10 The American Water Works Association estimates that the average person in the United States uses 123 gallons of water per day. Suppose some researchers believe that more water is being used now and want to test to determine whether it is so. They randomly select a sample of Americans and carefully keep track of the water used by each sample member for a day, then analyze the results by using a statistical computer software package. The output is given here. Assume $\alpha = .05$. How many people were sampled? What were the sample mean? Was this a one- or two-tailed test? What was the result of the study? What decision could be stated about the null hypothesis from these results?

```
One-Sample Z: C1

Test of mu = 123 vs > 123
The assumed standard deviation = 27.68


 N   Mean   SE Mean      95% CI          Z    P
40  132.360    4.38 (123.78, 140.94) 2.14 0.016
```

9.3 TESTING HYPOTHESES ABOUT A POPULATION MEAN USING THE *t* STATISTIC (σ UNKNOWN)

Very often when a business researcher is gathering data to test hypotheses about a single population mean, the value of the population standard deviation is unknown and the researcher must use the sample standard deviation as an estimate of it. In such cases, the z test cannot be used.

Chapter 8 presented the *t* distribution, which can be used to analyze hypotheses about a single population mean when σ is unknown if the population is normally distributed for the measurement being studied. In this section, we will examine the *t* test for a single population mean. In general, this *t* test is applicable whenever the researcher is drawing a single random sample to test the value of a population mean (μ), the population standard deviation is unknown, and the population is normally distributed for the measurement of interest. Recall from Chapter 8 that the assumption that the data be normally distributed in the population is rather robust.

The formula for testing such hypotheses follows.

---

t TEST FOR μ (9.3)

$$t = \frac{\bar{x} - \mu}{\dfrac{s}{\sqrt{n}}}$$

$$df = n - 1$$

The U.S. Farmers' Production Company builds large harvesters. For a harvester to be properly balanced when operating, a 25-pound plate is installed on its side. The machine that produces these plates is set to yield plates that average 25 pounds. The distribution of plates produced from the machine is normal. However, the shop supervisor is worried that the machine is out of adjustment and is producing plates that do not average 25 pounds. To test this concern, he randomly selects 20 of the plates produced the day before and weighs them. Table 9.1 shows the weights obtained, along with the computed sample mean and sample standard deviation.

The test is to determine whether the machine is out of control, and the shop supervisor has not specified whether he believes the machine is producing plates that are too heavy or too light. Thus a two-tailed test is appropriate. The following hypotheses are tested.

$$H_0: \mu = 25 \text{ pounds}$$
$$H_a: \mu \neq 25 \text{ pounds}$$

An α of .05 is used. Figure 9.11 shows the rejection regions.

Because $n = 20$, the degrees of freedom for this test are 19 (20 − 1). The *t* distribution table is a one-tailed table but the test for this problem is two tailed, so alpha must be split, which yields $\alpha/2 = .025$, the value in each tail. (To obtain the table *t* value when conducting a two-tailed test, always split alpha and use $\alpha/2$.) The table *t* value for this example is 2.093. Table values such as this one are often written in the following form:

$$t_{.025,19} = 2.093$$

Figure 9.12 depicts the *t* distribution for this example, along with the critical values, the observed *t* value, and the rejection regions. In this case, the decision rule is to reject the

TABLE 9.1

Weights in Pounds of a
Sample of 20 Plates

22.6	22.2	23.2	27.4	24.5
27.0	26.6	28.1	26.9	24.9
26.2	25.3	23.1	24.2	26.1
25.8	30.4	28.6	23.5	23.6
$\bar{x} = 25.51$, $s = 2.1933$, $n = 20$				

FIGURE 9.11

Rejection Regions for the
Machine Plate Example

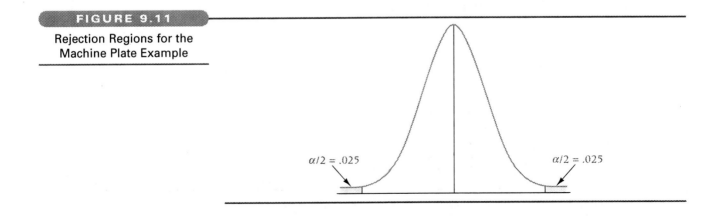

α/2 = .025   α/2 = .025

FIGURE 9.12

Graph of Observed and
Critical *t* Values for the
Machine Plate Example

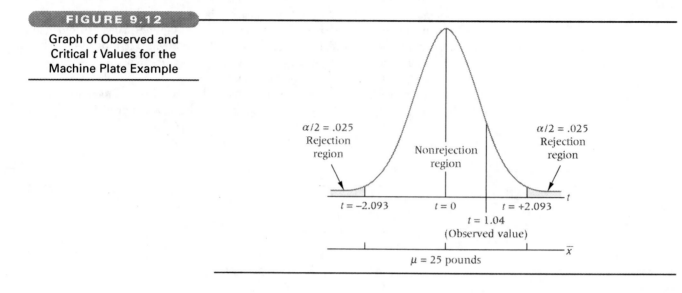

null hypothesis if the observed value of *t* is less than −2.093 or greater than +2.093 (in the tails of the distribution). Computation of the test statistic yields

$$t = \frac{\bar{x} - \mu}{\frac{s}{\sqrt{n}}} = \frac{25.51 - 25.00}{\frac{2.1933}{\sqrt{20}}} = 1.04 \text{ (observed } t \text{ values)}$$

Because the observed *t* value is +1.04, the null hypothesis is not rejected. Not enough evidence is found in this sample to reject the hypothesis that the population mean is 25 pounds.

Figure 9.13 shows Minitab and Excel output for this example. Note that the Minitab output includes the observed *t* value (1.04) and the *p*-value (.311). Since this test is a two-tailed test, Minitab has doubled the one-tailed *p*-value for *t* = 1.04. Thus the *p*-value of .311 can be compared directly to $\alpha = .05$ to reach the conclusion to fail to reject the null hypothesis.

The Excel output contains the observed *t* value (1.04) plus the *p*-value and the critical table *t* value for both a one-tailed and a two-tailed test. Excel also gives the table value of *t* = 2.09 for a two-tailed test, which allows one to verify that the statistical conclusion is to fail to reject the null hypothesis because the observed *t* value is only 1.04, which is less than 2.09.

FIGURE 9.13

Minitab and Excel Output for
the Machine Plate Example

Minitab Output

One-Sample T: Weight

Test of mu = 25 vs not = 25

Variable	N	Mean	StDev	SE Mean	95% CI	T	P
Weight	20	25.510	2.193	0.490	(24.484, 26.536)	1.04	0.311

Excel Output

t-Test: Two-Sample Assuming Unequal Variances

	Weight
Mean	25.51
Variance	4.8104
Observations	20
df	19
t Stat	1.04
P(T<=t)one-tail	0.1557
t Critical one-tail	1.73
P(T<=t)two-tail	0.3114
t Critical two-tail	2.09

DEMONSTRATION PROBLEM 9.2

Figures released by the U.S. Department of Agriculture show that the average size of farms has increased since 1940. In 1940, the mean size of a farm was 174 acres; by 1997, the average size was 471 acres. Between those years, the number of farms decreased but the amount of tillable land remained relatively constant, so now farms are bigger. This trend might be explained, in part, by the inability of small farms to compete with the prices and costs of large-scale operations and to produce a level of income necessary to support the farmers' desired standard of living. Suppose an agribusiness researcher believes the average size of farms has now increased from the 1997 mean figure of 471 acres. To test this notion, she randomly sampled 23 farms across the United States and ascertained the size of each farm from county records. The data she gathered follow. Use a 5% level of significance to test her hypothesis. Assume that number of acres per farm is normally distributed in the population.

445	489	474	505	553	477	454	463	466
557	502	449	438	500	466	477	557	433
545	511	590	561	560				

Solution

HYPOTHESIZE:

STEP 1. The researcher's hypothesis is that the average size of a U.S. farm is more than 471 acres. Because this theory is unproven, it is the alternate hypothesis. The null hypothesis is that the mean is still 471 acres.

$$H_0: \mu = 471$$
$$H_a: \mu > 471$$

TEST:

STEP 2. The statistical test to be used is

$$t = \frac{\overline{x} - \mu}{\frac{s}{\sqrt{n}}}$$

STEP 3. The value of alpha is .05.

STEP 4. With 23 data points, df $= n - 1 = 23 - 1 = 22$. This test is one tailed, and the critical table t value is

$$t_{.05,22} = 1.717$$

The decision rule is to reject the null hypothesis if the observed test statistic is greater than 1.717.

STEP 5. The gathered data are shown.

STEP 6. The sample mean is 498.78 and the sample standard deviation is 46.94. The observed t value is

$$t = \frac{\overline{x} - \mu}{\frac{s}{\sqrt{n}}} = \frac{498.78 - 471}{\frac{46.94}{\sqrt{23}}} = 2.84$$

ACTION:

STEP 7. The observed t value of 2.84 is greater than the table t value of 1.717, so the business researcher rejects the null hypothesis. She accepts the alternative hypothesis and concludes that the average size of a U.S. farm is now more than 471 acres. The following graph represents this analysis pictorially.

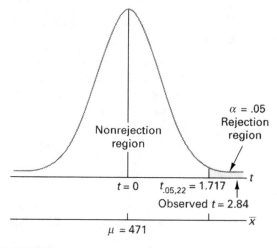

BUSINESS IMPLICATIONS:

STEP 8. Agribusiness researchers can speculate about what it means to have larger farms. If the average size of a farm has increased from 471 acres to almost 500 acres, it may represent a substantive increase.

It could mean that small farms are not financially viable. It might mean that corporations are buying out small farms and that large company farms are on the increase. Such a trend might spark legislative movements to protect the small farm. Larger farm sizes might also affect commodity trading.

Using the Computer to Test Hypotheses About a Population Mean Using the *t* Test

Minitab has the capability of computing a one-sample *t* test for means. Figure 9.14 contains Minitab output for Demonstration Problem 9.2. The output contains the hypotheses being tested, the sample statistics, the observed *t* value (2.84), and the *p*-value (.005). Because the *p*-value is less than $\alpha = .05$, the decision is to reject the null hypothesis.

FIGURE 9.14

Minitab and Excel Output for Demonstration Problem 9.2

Minitab Output

One-Sample T: Acres

Test of mu = 471 vs > 471

					95% Lower		
Variable	N	Mean	StDev	SE Mean	Bound	T	P
Acres	23	498.78	46.94	9.79	481.97	2.84	0.005

Excel Output

t-Test: Two-Sample Assuming Unequal Variances

	Acres
Mean	498.783
Variance	2203.632
Observations	23
df	22
t Stat	2.84
P(*T*<=*t*) one-tail	0.0048
t Critical one-tail	1.72
P(*T*<=*t*) two-tail	0.0096
t Critical two-tail	2.07

Excel does not have a one-sample *t* test function. However, by using the two-sample *t* test for means with unequal variances, the results for a one-sample test can be obtained. This is accomplished by inputting the sample data for the first sample and the value of the parameter being tested (in this case, $\mu = 471$) for the second sample. The output includes the observed *t* value (2.84) and both the table *t* values and *p*-values for one- and two-tailed tests. Because Demonstration Problem 9.2 was a one-tailed test, the *p*-value of .0048, which is the same value obtained using Minitab, is used.

9.3 PROBLEMS

9.11 A random sample of size 20 is taken, resulting in a sample mean of 16.45 and a sample standard deviation of 3.59. Assume *x* is normally distributed and use this information and $\alpha = .05$ to test the following hypotheses.

$$H_0: \mu = 16 \qquad H_a: \mu \neq 16$$

9.12 A random sample of 51 items is taken, with $\bar{x} = 58.42$ and $s^2 = 25.68$. Use these data to test the following hypotheses, assuming you want to take only a 1% risk of committing a Type I error and that *x* is normally distributed.

$$H_0: \mu = 60 \qquad H_a: \mu < 60$$

9.13 The following data were gathered from a random sample of 11 items.

1200	1175	1080	1275	1201	1387
1090	1280	1400	1287	1225	

Use these data and a 5% level of significance to test the following hypotheses, assuming that the data come from a normally distributed population.

$$H_0: \mu = 1160 \qquad H_a: \mu > 1160$$

9.14 The following data (in pounds), which were selected randomly from a normally distributed population of values, represent measurements of a machine part that is supposed to weigh, on average, 8.3 pounds.

8.1	8.4	8.3	8.2	8.5	8.6	8.4	8.3	8.4	8.2
8.8	8.2	8.2	8.3	8.1	8.3	8.4	8.5	8.5	8.7

Use these data and $\alpha = .01$ to test the hypothesis that the parts average 8.3 pounds.

9.15 A hole-punch machine is set to punch a hole 1.84 centimeters in diameter in a strip of sheet metal in a manufacturing process. The strip of metal is then creased and sent on to the next phase of production, where a metal rod is slipped through the hole. It is important that the hole be punched to the specified diameter of 1.84 cm. To test punching accuracy, technicians have randomly sampled 12 punched holes and measured the diameters. The data (in centimeters) follow. Use an alpha of .10 to determine whether the holes are being punched an average of 1.84 centimeters. Assume the punched holes are normally distributed in the population.

1.81	1.89	1.86	1.83
1.85	1.82	1.87	1.85
1.84	1.86	1.88	1.85

9.16 Suppose a study reports that the average price for a gallon of self-serve regular unleaded gasoline is $3.16. You believe that the figure is higher in your area of the country. You decide to test this claim for your part of the United States by randomly calling gasoline stations. Your random survey of 25 stations produces the following prices.

$3.27	$3.29	$3.16	$3.20	$3.37
3.20	3.23	3.19	3.20	3.24
3.16	3.07	3.27	3.09	3.35
3.15	3.23	3.14	3.05	3.35
3.21	3.14	3.14	3.07	3.10

Assume gasoline prices for a region are normally distributed. Do the data you obtained provide enough evidence to reject the claim? Use a 1% level of significance.

9.17 Suppose that in past years the average price per square foot for warehouses in the United States has been $32.28. A national real estate investor wants to determine whether that figure has changed now. The investor hires a researcher who randomly samples 49 warehouses that are for sale across the United States and finds that the mean price per square foot is $31.67, with a standard deviation of $1.29. Assume that prices of warehouse footage are normally distributed in population. If the researcher uses a 5% level of significance, what statistical conclusion can be reached? What are the hypotheses?

9.18 Major cities around the world compete with each other in an effort to attract new businesses. Some of the criteria that businesses use to judge cities as potential locations for their headquarters might include the labor pool; the environment, including work, governmental, and living; the tax structure, the availability of skilled/educated labor, housing, education, medical care; and others. Suppose in a study done several years ago, the city of Atlanta received a mean rating of 3.51 (on a scale of 1 to 5 and assuming an interval level of data) on housing, but that since that time, considerable residential building has occurred in the Atlanta area such that city leaders feel the mean might now be higher. They hire a team of researchers to conduct a survey of businesses around the world to determine how businesses now rate the city on housing (and other variables). Sixty-one businesses take part in the new survey, with a result that Atlanta receives a mean response of 3.72 on housing with a sample standard deviation of 0.65. Assuming that such responses are normally distributed, use a 1% level of significance and these data to test to determine if the mean housing rating for the city of Atlanta by businesses has significantly increased.

9.19 Based on population figures and other general information on the U.S. population, suppose it has been estimated that, on average, a family of four in the United States spends about $1,135 annually on dental expenditures. Suppose further that a regional dental association wants to test to determine if this figure is accurate for their area of the country. To test this, 22 families of four are randomly selected from the population in that area of the country and a log is kept of the family's dental expenditures for one year. The resulting data are given below. Assuming that dental expenditures are normally distributed in the population, use the data and an alpha of .05 to test the dental association's hypothesis.

1008	812	1117	1323	1308	1415
831	1021	1287	851	930	730
699	872	913	944	954	987
1695	995	1003	994		

9.20 According to data released by the World Bank, the mean PM10 (particulate matter) concentration for the city of Kabul, Afghanistan, in 1999 was 46. Suppose that because of efforts to improve air quality in Kabul, increases in modernization, and efforts to establish environmental-friendly businesses, city leaders believe rates of particulate matter in Kabul have decreased. To test this notion, they randomly sample 12 readings over a one-year period with the resulting readings shown below. Do these data present enough evidence to determine that PM10 readings are significantly less now in Kabul? Assume that particulate readings are normally distributed and that $\alpha = .01$.

| 31 | 44 | 35 | 53 | 57 | 47 |
| 32 | 40 | 31 | 38 | 53 | 45 |

9.21 According to a National Public Transportation survey, the average commuting time for people who commute to a city with a population of 1 to 3 million is 19.0 minutes. Suppose a researcher lives in a city with a population of 2.4 million and wants to test this claim in her city. Assume that commuter times are normally distributed in the population. She takes a random sample of commuters and gathers data. The data are analyzed using both Minitab and Excel, and the output is shown here. What are the results of the study? What are the hypotheses?

Minitab Output

One-Sample T

```
Test of mu = 19 vs not = 19

 N    Mean   StDev   SE Mean      95% CI        T     P
26   19.534   4.100    0.804  (17.878, 21.190)  0.66  0.513
```

Excel Output

Mean	19.534
Variance	16.813
Observations	26
df	25
t Stat	0.66
$P(T<=t)$ one-tail	0.256
t Critical one-tail	1.71
$P(T<=t)$ two-tail	0.513
t Critical two-tail	2.06

9.4 TESTING HYPOTHESES ABOUT A PROPORTION

Data analysis used in business decision making often contains proportions to describe such aspects as market share, consumer makeup, quality defects, on-time delivery rate, profitable stocks, and others. Business surveys often produce information expressed in proportion form, such as .45 of all businesses offer flexible hours to employees or .88 of all businesses have Web sites. Business researchers conduct hypothesis tests about such proportions to determine whether they have changed in some way. As an example, suppose a company held a 26% or .26, share of the market for several years. Due to a massive marketing effort and improved product quality, company officials believe that the market share increased, and they want to prove it. Other examples of hypothesis testing about a single population proportion might include:

- A market researcher wants to test to determine whether the proportion of new car purchasers who are female has increased.
- A financial researcher wants to test to determine whether the proportion of companies that were profitable last year in the average investment officer's portfolio is .60.
- A quality manager for a large manufacturing firm wants to test to determine whether the proportion of defective items in a batch is less than .04.

Formula 9.4 for inferential analysis of a proportion was introduced in Section 7.3 of Chapter 7. Based on the central limit theorem, this formula makes possible the testing of hypotheses about the population proportion in a manner similar to that of the formula used to test sample means. Recall that $\hat{p}$ denotes a sample proportion and p denotes the population proportion. To validly use this test, the sample size must be large enough such that $n \cdot p \geq 5$ and $n \cdot q \geq 5$.

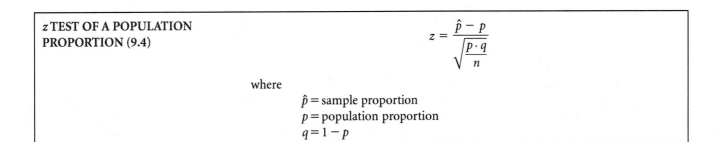

z TEST OF A POPULATION PROPORTION (9.4)

$$z = \frac{\hat{p} - p}{\sqrt{\dfrac{p \cdot q}{n}}}$$

where

$\hat{p}$ = sample proportion
p = population proportion
$q = 1 - p$

FIGURE 9.15

Distribution with Rejection Regions for Flawed-Product Example

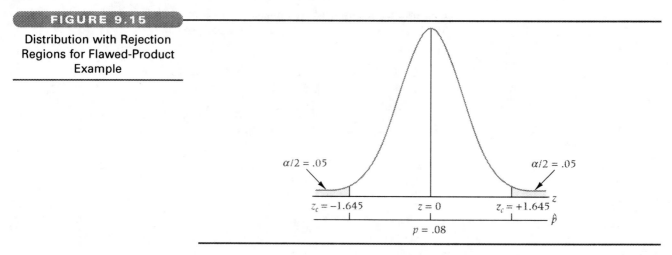

A manufacturer believes exactly 8% of its products contain at least one minor flaw. Suppose a company researcher wants to test this belief. The null and alternative hypotheses are

$$H_0: p = .08$$
$$H_a: p \neq .08$$

This test is two-tailed because the hypothesis being tested is whether the proportion of products with at least one minor flaw is .08. Alpha is selected to be .10. Figure 9.15 shows the distribution, with the rejection regions and $z_{.05}$. Because α is divided for a two-tailed test, the table value for an area of $(1/2)(.10) = .05$ is $z_{.05} = \pm 1.645$.

For the business researcher to reject the null hypothesis, the observed z value must be greater than 1.645 or less than -1.645. The business researcher randomly selects a sample of 200 products, inspects each item for flaws, and determines that 33 items have at least one minor flaw. Calculating the sample proportion gives

$$\hat{p} = \frac{33}{200} = .165$$

The observed z value is calculated as:

$$z = \frac{\hat{p} - p}{\sqrt{\dfrac{p \cdot q}{n}}} = \frac{.165 - .080}{\sqrt{\dfrac{(.08)(.92)}{200}}} = \frac{.085}{.019} = 4.43$$

Note that the denominator of the z formula contains the population proportion. Although the business researcher does not actually know the population proportion, he is testing a population proportion value. Hence he uses the hypothesized population value in the denominator of the formula as well as in the numerator. This method contrasts with the confidence interval formula, where the sample proportion is used in the denominator.

The observed value of z is in the rejection region (observed $z = 4.43 >$ table $z_{.05} = +1.645$), so the business researcher rejects the null hypothesis. He concludes that the proportion of items with at least one minor flaw in the population from which the sample of 200 was drawn is not .08. With $\alpha = .10$, the risk of committing a Type I error in this example is .10.

The observed value of $z = 4.43$ is outside the range of most values in virtually all z tables. Thus if the researcher were using the p-value to arrive at a decision about the null hypothesis, the probability would be .0000, and he would reject the null hypothesis.

The Minitab output shown in Figure 9.16 displays a p-value of .000 for this problem, underscoring the decision to reject the null hypothesis.

FIGURE 9.16

Minitab Output for the Flawed-Product Example

Test and CI for One Proportion

Test of p = 0.08 vs p not = 0.08

Sample	X	N	Sample p	90% CI	Exact P-Value
1	33	200	0.165000	(0.123279, 0.214351)	0.000

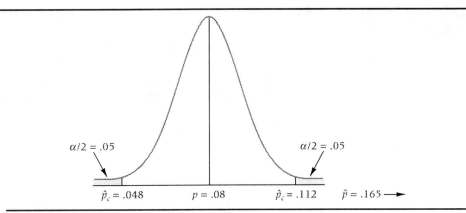

FIGURE 9.17

Distribution Using Critical
Value Method for the
Flawed-Product Example

Suppose the researcher wanted to use the critical value method. He would enter the table value of $z_{.05} = 1.645$ in the z formula for single sample proportions, along with the hypothesized population proportion and n, and solve for the critical value of denoted as $\hat{p}_c$. The result is

$$z_{\alpha/2} = \frac{\hat{p}_c - p}{\sqrt{\dfrac{p \cdot q}{n}}}$$

$$\pm 1.645 = \frac{\hat{p}_c - .08}{\sqrt{\dfrac{(.08)(.92)}{200}}}$$

$$\hat{p}_c = .08 \pm 1.645\sqrt{\frac{(.08)(.92)}{200}} = .08 \pm .032$$

$$= .048 \text{ and } .112$$

Using the critical value method, if the sample proportion is less than .048 or greater than .112, the decision will be to reject the null hypothesis. Since the sample proportion, $\hat{p}$, is .165, which is greater than .112, the decision here is to reject the null hypothesis. The proportion of products with at least one flaw is not .08. Figure 9.17 shows these critical values, the observed value and the rejection regions.

THINKING CRITICALLY ABOUT STATISTICS IN BUSINESS TODAY

Testing Hypotheses about Commuting

How do Americans commute to work? A National Public Transportation survey taken a few years ago indicated that almost 80% of U.S. commuters drive alone to work, more than 11% carpool, and approximately 5% use public transportation. Using hypothesis testing methodology presented in this chapter, researchers can test whether these proportions still hold true today as well as how these figures vary by region. For example, in New York City it is almost certain that the proportion of commuters using public transportation is much higher than 5%. In rural parts of the country where public transportation is unavailable, the proportion of commuters using public transportation would be zero.

What is the average travel time of a commute to work in the United States? According to the National Public Transportation Survey, travel time varies according to the type of transportation used. For example, the average travel time of a commute using a private vehicle is 20 minutes as compared to 42 minutes using public transportation. In part, this difference can be accounted for by the travel speed in miles per hour: private vehicles average 35 miles per hour over a commute compared to 19 miles per hour averaged by public transportation vehicles. It is possible to test any of these means using hypothesis testing techniques presented in this chapter to either validate the figures or to determine whether the figures are no longer true.

Things to Ponder

1. According to the statistics presented here, 80% of U.S. commuters drive alone to work. Why is this so? What are some reasons why Americans drive to work alone? Is it a good thing that Americans drive to work alone? What are some reasons why Americans might not want to drive to work alone?

2. The mean commute time for a private vehicle in the United States is about 20 minutes. Can you think of some reasons why Americans might want to reduce this figure? What are some ways that this figure might be reduced?

DEMONSTRATION PROBLEM 9.3

A survey of the morning beverage market shows that the primary breakfast beverage for 17% of Americans is milk. A milk producer in Wisconsin, where milk is plentiful, believes the figure is higher for Wisconsin. To test this idea, she contacts a random sample of 550 Wisconsin residents and asks which primary beverage they consumed for breakfast that day. Suppose 115 replied that milk was the primary beverage. Using a level of significance of .05, test the idea that the milk figure is higher for Wisconsin.

Solution

HYPOTHESIZE:

STEP 1. The milk producer's theory is that the proportion of Wisconsin residents who drink milk for breakfast is higher than the national proportion, which is the alternative hypothesis. The null hypothesis is that the proportion in Wisconsin does not differ from the national average. The hypotheses for this problem are

$$H_0: p = .17$$
$$H_a: p > .17$$

TEST:

STEP 2. The test statistic is

$$z = \frac{\hat{p} - p}{\sqrt{\dfrac{p \cdot q}{n}}}$$

STEP 3. The Type I error rate is .05.

STEP 4. This test is a one-tailed test, and the table value is $z_{.05} = +1.645$. The sample results must yield an observed z value greater than 1.645 for the milk producer to reject the null hypothesis. The following diagram shows $z_{.05}$ and the rejection region for this problem.

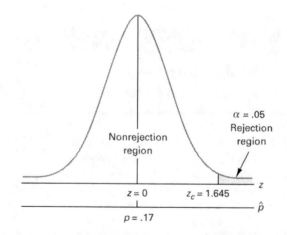

STEP 5. $\qquad n = 550$ and $x = 115$

$$\hat{p} = \frac{115}{550} = .209$$

STEP 6.

$$z = \frac{\hat{p} - p}{\sqrt{\dfrac{p \cdot q}{n}}} = \frac{.209 - .17}{\sqrt{\dfrac{(.17)(.83)}{550}}} = \frac{.039}{.016} = 2.44$$

ACTION:

STEP 7. Because $z = 2.44$ is beyond $z_{.05} = 1.645$ in the rejection region, the milk producer rejects the null hypothesis. The probability of obtaining a $z \geq 2.44$ by chance is .0073. Because this probability is less than $\alpha = .05$, the null hypothesis is also rejected with the p-value. On the basis of the random sample, the producer is ready to conclude that the proportion of Wisconsin residents who drink milk as the primary beverage for breakfast is higher than the national proportion.

BUSINESS IMPLICATIONS:

STEP 8. If the proportion of residents who drink milk for breakfast is higher in Wisconsin than in other parts of the United States, milk producers might have a market opportunity in Wisconsin that is not available in other parts of the country. Perhaps Wisconsin residents are being loyal to home-state products, in which case marketers of other Wisconsin products might be successful in appealing to residents to support their products. The fact that more milk is sold in Wisconsin might mean that if Wisconsin milk producers appealed to markets outside Wisconsin in the same way they do inside the state, they might increase their market share of the breakfast beverage market in other states. Is a proportion of almost .21 really a substantive increase over .17? Certainly in a market of any size at all, an increase of almost 4% of the market share could be worth millions of dollars and in such a case, would be substantive.

A critical proportion can be solved for by

$$z_{.05} = \frac{\hat{p}_c - p}{\sqrt{\dfrac{p \cdot q}{n}}}$$

$$1.645 = \frac{\hat{p}_c - .17}{\sqrt{\dfrac{(.17)(.83)}{550}}}$$

$$\hat{p}_c = .17 + 1.645\sqrt{\frac{(.17)(.83)}{550}} = .17 + .026 = .196$$

With the critical value method, a sample proportion greater than .196 must be obtained to reject the null hypothesis. The sample proportion for this problem is .209, so the null hypothesis is also rejected with the critical value method.

Using the Computer to Test Hypotheses About a Population Proportion

Minitab has the capability of testing hypotheses about a population proportion. Figure 9.18 shows the Minitab output for Demonstration Problem 9.3. Notice that the output includes a restatement of the hypotheses, the sample proportion, and the p-value. From this information, a decision regarding the null hypothesis can be made by comparing the p-value (.010) to α (.050). Because the p-value is less than α, the decision is to reject the null hypothesis.

FIGURE 9.18

Minitab Output for Demonstration Problem 9.3

Test and CI for One Proportion

Test of p = 0.17 vs p > 0.17

Sample	X	N	Sample p	95% Lower Bound	Exact P-Value
1	115	550	0.209091	0.180871	0.010

9.4 PROBLEMS

9.22 Suppose you are testing $H_0: p = .45$ versus $H_a: p > .45$. A random sample of 310 people produces a value of $\hat{p} = .465$. Use $\alpha = .05$ to test this hypothesis.

9.23 Suppose you are testing $H_0: p = .63$ versus $H_a: p < .63$. For a random sample of 100 people, $x = 55$, where x denotes the number in the sample that have the characteristic of interest. Use a .01 level of significance to test this hypothesis.

9.24 Suppose you are testing $H_0: p = .29$ versus $H_a: p \neq .29$. A random sample of 740 items shows that 207 have this characteristic. With a .05 probability of committing a Type I error, test the hypothesis. For the p-value method, what is the probability of the observed z value for this problem? If you had used the critical value method, what would the two critical values be? How do the sample results compare with the critical values?

9.25 The Independent Insurance Agents of America conducted a survey of insurance consumers and discovered that 48% of them always reread their insurance policies, 29% sometimes do, 16% rarely do, and 7% never do. Suppose a large insurance company invests considerable time and money in rewriting policies so that they will be more attractive and easy to read and understand. After using the new policies for a year, company managers want to determine whether rewriting the policies significantly changed the proportion of policyholders who always reread their insurance policy. They contact 380 of the company's insurance consumers who purchased a policy in the past year and ask them whether they always reread their insurance policies. One hundred and sixty-four respond that they do. Use a 1% level of significance to test the hypothesis.

9.26 A study by Hewitt Associates showed that 79% of companies offer employees flexible scheduling. Suppose a researcher believes that in accounting firms this figure is lower. The researcher randomly selects 415 accounting firms and through interviews determines that 303 of these firms have flexible scheduling. With a 1% level of significance, does the test show enough evidence to conclude that a significantly lower proportion of accounting firms offer employees flexible scheduling?

9.27 A survey was undertaken by Bruskin/Goldring Research for Quicken to determine how people plan to meet their financial goals in the next year. Respondents were allowed to select more than one way to meet their goals. Thirty-one percent said that they were using a financial planner to help them meet their goals. Twenty-four percent were using family/friends to help them meet their financial goals followed by broker/accountant (19%), computer software (17%), and books (14%). Suppose another researcher takes a similar survey of 600 people to test these results. If 200 people respond that they are going to use a financial planner to help them meet their goals, is this proportion enough evidence to reject the 31% figure generated in the Bruskin/Goldring survey using $\alpha = .10$? If 158 respond that they are going to use family/friends to help them meet their financial goals, is this result enough evidence to declare that the proportion is significantly higher than Bruskin/Goldring's figure of .24 if $\alpha = .05$?

9.28 Eighteen percent of U.S.-based multinational companies provide an allowance for personal long-distance calls for executives living overseas, according to the Institute for International Human Resources and the National Foreign Trade Council. Suppose a researcher thinks that U.S.-based multinational companies are having a more difficult time recruiting executives to live overseas and that an increasing number of these companies are providing an allowance for personal long-distance calls to these executives to ease the burden of living away from home. To test this hypothesis, a new study is conducted by contacting 376 multinational companies. Twenty-two percent of these surveyed companies are providing an allowance for personal long-distance calls to executives living overseas. Does the test show enough evidence to declare that a significantly higher proportion of multinational companies provide a long-distance call allowance? Let $\alpha = .01$.

9.29 A large manufacturing company investigated the service it received from suppliers and discovered that, in the past, 32% of all materials shipments were received late.

However, the company recently installed a just-in-time system in which suppliers are linked more closely to the manufacturing process. A random sample of 118 deliveries since the just-in-time system was installed reveals that 22 deliveries were late. Use this sample information to test whether the proportion of late deliveries was reduced significantly. Let $\alpha = .05$.

9.30 Where do CFOs get their money news? According to Robert Half International, 47% get their money news from newspapers, 15% get it from communication/colleagues, 12% get it from television, 11% from the Internet, 9% from magazines, 5% from radio, and 1% don't know. Suppose a researcher wants to test these results. She randomly samples 67 CFOs and finds that 40 of them get their money news from newspapers. Does the test show enough evidence to reject the findings of Robert Half International? Use $\alpha = .05$.

9.5   TESTING HYPOTHESES ABOUT A VARIANCE

At times a researcher needs to test hypotheses about a population variance. For example, in the area of statistical quality control, manufacturers try to produce equipment and parts that are consistent in measurement. Suppose a company produces industrial wire that is specified to be a particular thickness. Because of the production process, the thickness of the wire will vary slightly from one end to the other and from lot to lot and batch to batch. Even if the average thickness of the wire as measured from lot to lot is on specification, the variance of the measurements might be too great to be acceptable. In other words, on the average the wire is the correct thickness, but some portions of the wire might be too thin and others unacceptably thick. By conducting hypothesis tests for the variance of the thickness measurements, the quality control people can monitor for variations in the process that are too great.

The procedure for testing hypotheses about a population variance is similar to the techniques presented in Chapter 8 for estimating a population variance from the sample variance. Formula 9.5 used to conduct these tests assumes a normally distributed population.

FORMULA FOR TESTING HYPOTHESES ABOUT A POPULATION VARIANCE (9.5)	$\chi^2 = \dfrac{(n-1)s^2}{\sigma^2}$ $df = n - 1$

Note: *As was mentioned in Chapter 8, the chi-square test of a population variance is extremely sensitive to violations of the assumption that the population is normally distributed.*

As an example, a manufacturing firm has been working diligently to implement a just-in-time inventory system for its production line. The final product requires the installation of a pneumatic tube at a particular station on the assembly line. With the just-in-time inventory system, the company's goal is to minimize the number of pneumatic tubes that are piled up at the station waiting to be installed. Ideally, the tubes would arrive just as the operator needs them. However, because of the supplier and the variables involved in getting the tubes to the line, most of the time there will be some buildup of tube inventory. The company expects that, on the average, about 20 pneumatic tubes will be at the station. However, the production superintendent does not want the variance of this inventory to be greater than 4. On a given day, the number of pneumatic tubes piled up at the workstation is determined eight different times and the following number of tubes are recorded.

23   17   20   29   21   14   19   24

Using these sample data, we can test to determine whether the variance is greater than 4. The hypothesis test is one tailed. Assume the number of tubes is normally distributed. The null hypothesis is that the variance is acceptable—the variance is equal to (or less than) 4. The alternative hypothesis is that the variance is greater than 4.

$$H_0: \sigma^2 = 4$$
$$H_a: \sigma^2 > 4$$

Suppose alpha is .05. Because the sample size is 8, the degrees of freedom for the critical table chi-square value are $8 - 1 = 7$. Using Table A.8, we find the critical chi-square value.

$$\chi^2_{.05,7} = 14.0671$$

Because the alternative hypothesis is greater than 4, the rejection region is in the upper tail of the chi-square distribution. The sample variance is calculated from the sample data to be

$$s^2 = 20.9821$$

The observed chi-square value is calculated as

$$\chi^2 = \frac{(8 - 1)(20.9821)}{4} = 36.72$$

Because this observed chi-square value, $\chi^2 = 36.72$, is greater than the critical chi-square table value, $\chi^2_{.05,7} = 14.0671$, the decision is to reject the null hypothesis. On the basis of this sample of eight data measurements, the population variance of inventory at this workstation is greater than 4. Company production personnel and managers might want to investigate further to determine whether they can find a cause for this unacceptable variance. Figure 9.19 shows a chi-square distribution with the critical value, the rejection region, the nonrejection region, the value of α, and the observed chi-square value.

Using Excel, the p-value of the observed chi-square, 36.72, is determined to be .0000053. Because this value is less than $\alpha = .05$, the conclusion is to reject the null hypothesis using the p-value. In fact, using this p-value, the null hypothesis could be rejected for

$$\alpha = .00001$$

This null hypothesis can also be tested by the critical value method. Instead of solving for an observed value of chi-square, the critical chi-square value for alpha is inserted into formula 9.5 along with the hypothesized value of σ^2 and the degrees of freedom $(n - 1)$. Solving for s^2 yields a critical sample variance value, s_c^2.

$$\chi_c^2 = \frac{(n - 1)s_c^2}{\sigma^2}$$

$$s_c^2 = \frac{\chi_c^2 \cdot \sigma^2}{(n - 1)} = \frac{(14.0671)(4)}{7} = 8.038$$

The critical value of the sample variance is $s_c^2 = 8.038$. Because the observed sample variance actually was 20.9821, which is larger than the critical variance, the null hypothesis is rejected.

FIGURE 9.19

Hypothesis Test Distribution
for Pneumatic Tube Example

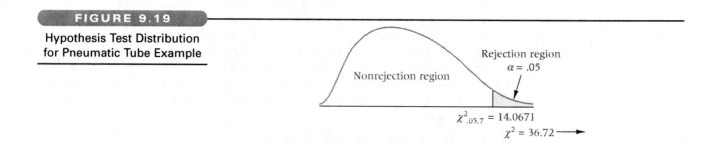

DEMONSTRATION PROBLEM 9.4

A small business has 37 employees. Because of the uncertain demand for its product, the company usually pays overtime on any given week. The company assumed that about 50 total hours of overtime per week is required and that the variance on this figure is about 25. Company officials want to know whether the variance of overtime hours has changed. Given here is a sample of 16 weeks of overtime data (in hours per week). Assume hours of overtime are normally distributed. Use these data to test the null hypothesis that the variance of overtime data is 25. Let $\alpha = .10$.

57	56	52	44
46	53	44	44
48	51	55	48
63	53	51	50

Solution

HYPOTHESIZE:

STEP 1. This test is a two-tailed test. The null and alternative hypotheses are

$$H_0: \sigma^2 = 25$$
$$H_a: \sigma^2 \neq 25$$

TEST:

STEP 2. The test statistic is

$$\chi^2 = \frac{(n-1)s^2}{\sigma^2}$$

STEP 3. Because this test is two tailed, $\alpha = .10$ must be split: $\alpha/2 = .05$

STEP 4. The degrees of freedom are $16 - 1 = 15$. The two critical chi-square values are

$$\chi^2_{(1-.05),15} = \chi^2_{.95,15} = 7.26093$$
$$\chi^2_{.05,15} = 24.9958$$

The decision rule is to reject the null hypothesis if the observed value of the test statistic is less than 7.26093 or greater than 24.9958.

STEP 5. The data are as listed previously.

STEP 6. The sample variance is

$$s^2 = 28.0625$$

The observed chi-square value is calculated as

$$\chi^2 = \frac{(n-1)s^2}{\sigma^2} = \frac{(15)(28.0625)}{25} = 16.84$$

ACTION:

STEP 7. This observed chi-square value is in the nonrejection region because $\chi^2_{.95,15} = 7.26094 < \chi^2_{observed} = 16.84 < \chi^2_{.05,15} = 24.9958$. The company fails to reject the null hypothesis. The population variance of overtime hours per week is 25.

BUSINESS IMPLICATIONS:

STEP 8. This result indicates to the company managers that the variance of weekly overtime hours is about what they expected.

9.5 PROBLEMS

9.31 Test each of the following hypotheses by using the given information. Assume the populations are normally distributed.

a. $H_0: \sigma^2 = 20$

$H_a: \sigma^2 > 20$

$\alpha = .05, n = 15, s^2 = 32$

b. $H_0: \sigma^2 = 8.5$
$H_a: \sigma^2 \neq 8.5$
$\alpha = .10, n = 22, s^2 = 17$

c. $H_a: \sigma^2 = 45$
$H_a: \sigma^2 < 45$
$\alpha = .01, n = 8, s = 4.12$

d. $H_a: \sigma^2 = 5$
$H_a: \sigma^2 \neq 5$
$\alpha = .05, n = 11, s^2 = 1.2$

9.32 Previous experience shows the variance of a given process to be 14. Researchers are testing to determine whether this value has changed. They gather the following dozen measurements of the process. Use these data and $\alpha = .05$ to test the null hypothesis about the variance. Assume the measurements are normally distributed.

52	44	51	58	48	49
38	49	50	42	55	51

9.33 A manufacturing company produces bearings. One line of bearings is specified to be 1.64 centimeters (cm) in diameter. A major customer requires that the variance of the bearings be no more than .001 cm². The producer is required to test the bearings before they are shipped, and so the diameters of 16 bearings are measured with a precise instrument, resulting in the following values. Assume bearing diameters are normally distributed. Use the data and $\alpha = .01$ to test to determine whether the population of these bearings is to be rejected because of too high a variance.

1.69	1.62	1.63	1.70
1.66	1.63	1.65	1.71
1.64	1.69	1.57	1.64
1.59	1.66	1.63	1.65

9.34 A savings and loan averages about $100,000 in deposits per week. However, because of the way pay periods fall, seasonality, and erratic fluctuations in the local economy, deposits are subject to a wide variability. In the past, the variance for weekly deposits has been about $199,996,164. In terms that make more sense to managers, the standard deviation of weekly deposits has been $14,142. Shown here are data from a random sample of 13 weekly deposits for a recent period. Assume weekly deposits are normally distributed. Use these data and $\alpha = .10$ to test to determine whether the variance for weekly deposits has changed.

$93,000	$135,000	$112,000
68,000	46,000	104,000
128,000	143,000	131,000
104,000	96,000	71,000
87,000		

9.35 A company produces industrial wiring. One batch of wiring is specified to be 2.16 centimeters (cm) thick. A company inspects the wiring in seven locations and determines that, on the average, the wiring is about 2.16 cm thick. However, the measurements vary. It is unacceptable for the variance of the wiring to be more than .04 cm². The standard deviation of the seven measurements on this batch of wiring is .34 cm. Use $\alpha = .01$ to determine whether the variance on the sample wiring is too great to meet specifications. Assume wiring thickness is normally distributed.

9.6 SOLVING FOR TYPE II ERRORS

If a researcher reaches the statistical conclusion to fail to reject the null hypothesis, he makes either a correct decision or a Type II error. If the null hypothesis is true, the researcher makes a correct decision. If the null hypothesis is false, then the result is a Type II error.

In business, failure to reject the null hypothesis may mean staying with the status quo, not implementing a new process, or not making adjustments. If a new process, product, theory, or adjustment is not significantly better than what is currently accepted practice, the decision maker makes a correct decision. However, if the new process, product, theory, or adjustment would significantly improve sales, the business climate, costs, or morale, the decision maker makes an error in judgment (Type II). In business, Type II errors can translate to lost opportunities, poor product quality (as a result of failure to discern a problem in the process), or failure to react to the marketplace. Sometimes the ability to react to changes, new developments, or new opportunities is what keeps a business moving and growing. The Type II error plays an important role in business statistical decision making.

Determining the probability of committing a Type II error is more complex than finding the probability of committing a Type I error. The probability of committing a Type I error either is given in a problem or is stated by the researcher before proceeding with the study. A Type II error, β, varies with possible values of the alternative parameter. For example, suppose a researcher is conducting a statistical test on the following hypotheses.

$$H_0: \mu = 12 \text{ ounces}$$

$$H_a: \mu < 12 \text{ ounces}$$

A Type II error can be committed only when the researcher fails to reject the null hypothesis and the null hypothesis is false. In these hypotheses, if the null hypothesis, $\mu = 12$ ounces, is false, what is the true value for the population mean? Is the mean really 11.99 or 11.90 or 11.5 or 10 ounces? For each of these possible values of the population mean, the researcher can compute the probability of committing a Type II error. Often, when the null hypothesis is false, the value of the alternative mean is unknown, so the researcher will compute the probability of committing Type II errors for several possible values. How can the probability of committing a Type II error be computed for a specific alternative value of the mean?

Suppose that, in testing the preceding hypotheses, a sample of 60 cans of beverage yields a sample mean of 11.985 ounces. Assume that the population standard deviation is 0.10 ounces. From $\alpha = .05$ and a one-tailed test, the table $z_{.05}$ value is -1.645. The observed z value from sample data is

$$z = \frac{11.985 - 12.00}{\dfrac{.10}{\sqrt{60}}} = -1.16$$

From this observed value of z, the researcher determines not to reject the null hypothesis. By not rejecting the null hypothesis, the researcher either makes a correct decision or commits a Type II error. What is the probability of committing a Type II error in this problem if the population mean actually is 11.99?

The first step in determining the probability of a Type II error is to calculate a critical value for the sample mean, $\bar{x}_c$. In testing the null hypothesis by the critical value method, this value is used as the cutoff for the nonrejection region. For any sample mean obtained that is less than $\bar{x}_c$ (or greater for an upper-tail rejection region), the null hypothesis is rejected. Any sample mean greater than $\bar{x}_c$ (or less for an upper-tail rejection region) causes the researcher to fail to reject the null hypothesis. Solving for the critical value of the mean gives

$$z_c = \frac{\bar{x}_c - \mu}{\dfrac{\sigma}{\sqrt{n}}}$$

$$-1.645 = \frac{\bar{x}_c - 12}{\dfrac{.10}{\sqrt{60}}}$$

$$\bar{x}_c = 11.979$$

Figure 9.20(a) shows the distribution of values when the null hypothesis is true. It contains a critical value of the mean, $\bar{x}_c = 11.979$ ounces, below which the null hypothesis will be

FIGURE 9.20

Type II Error for Soft Drink
Example with Alternative
Mean = 11.99 Ounces

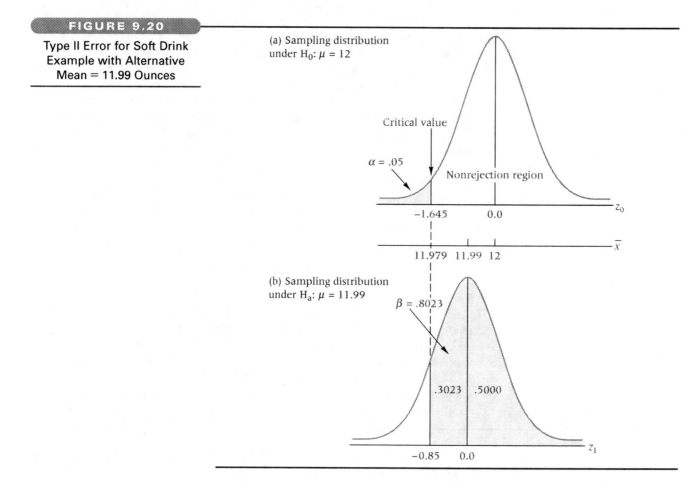

(a) Sampling distribution
under H_0: $\mu = 12$

Critical value

$\alpha = .05$

Nonrejection region

−1.645   0.0 z_0

11.979 11.99 12 $\bar{x}$

(b) Sampling distribution
under H_a: $\mu = 11.99$

$\beta = .8023$

.3023   .5000

−0.85   0.0 z_1

rejected. Figure 9.20(b) shows the distribution when the alternative mean, $\mu_1 = 11.99$ ounces, is true. How often will the business researcher fail to reject the top distribution as true when, in reality, the bottom distribution is true? If the null hypothesis is false, the researcher will fail to reject the null hypotheses whenever $\bar{x}$ is in the nonrejection region, $\bar{x} \geq 11.979$ ounces. If μ actually equals 11.99 ounces, what is the probability of failing to reject $\mu = 12$ ounces when 11.979 ounces is the critical value? The business researcher calculates this probability by extending the critical value ($\bar{x}_c = 11.979$ ounces) from distribution (a) to distribution (b) and solving for the area to the right of $\bar{x}_c = 11.979$.

$$z_1 = \frac{\bar{x}_c - \mu_1}{\frac{\sigma}{\sqrt{n}}} = \frac{11.979 - 11.99}{\frac{.10}{\sqrt{60}}} = -0.85$$

This value of z yields an area of .3023. The probability of committing a Type II error is all the area to the right of $\bar{x}_c = 11.979$ in distribution (b), or $.3023 + .5000 = .8023$. Hence there is an 80.23% chance of committing a Type II error if the alternative mean is 11.99 ounces.

DEMONSTRATION PROBLEM 9.5

Recompute the probability of committing a Type II error for the soft drink example if the alternative mean is 11.96 ounces.

Solution

Everything in distribution (a) of Figure 9.20 stays the same. The null hypothesized mean is still 12 ounces, the critical value is still 11.979 ounces, and $n = 60$. However, distribution (b) of Figure 9.20 changes with $\mu_1 = 11.96$ ounces, as the following diagram shows.

The z formula used to solve for the area of distribution (b), $\mu_1 = 11.96$, to the right of 11.979 is

$$z_1 = \frac{\bar{x}_c - \mu_1}{\dfrac{\sigma}{\sqrt{n}}} = \frac{11.979 - 11.96}{\dfrac{.10}{\sqrt{60}}} = 1.47$$

From Table A.5, only .0708 of the area is to the right of the critical value. Thus the probability of committing a Type II error is only .0708, as illustrated in the following diagram.

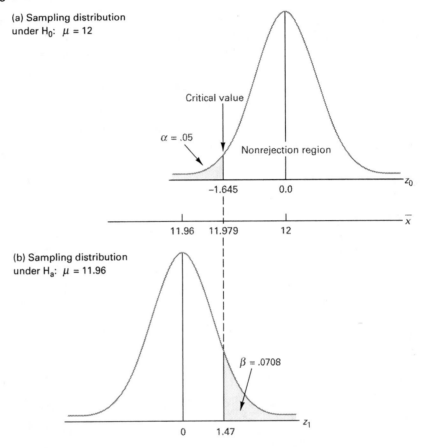

(a) Sampling distribution under H_0: $\mu = 12$

(b) Sampling distribution under H_a: $\mu = 11.96$

DEMONSTRATION PROBLEM 9.6

Suppose you are conducting a two-tailed hypothesis test of proportions. The null hypothesis is that the population proportion is .40. The alternative hypothesis is that the population proportion is not .40. A random sample of 250 produces a sample proportion of .44. With alpha of .05, the table z value for $\alpha/2$ is ± 1.96. The observed z from the sample information is

$$z = \frac{\hat{p} - p}{\sqrt{\dfrac{p \cdot q}{n}}} = \frac{.44 - .40}{.031} = 1.29$$

Thus the null hypothesis is not rejected. Either a correct decision is made or a Type II error is committed. Suppose the alternative population proportion really is .36. What is the probability of committing a Type II error?

Solution

Solve for the critical value of the proportion.

$$z_c = \frac{\hat{p}_c - p}{\sqrt{\dfrac{p \cdot q}{n}}}$$

$$\pm 1.96 = \frac{\hat{p}_c - .40}{\sqrt{\dfrac{(.40)(.60)}{250}}}$$

$$\hat{p}_c = .40 \pm .06$$

The critical values are .34 on the lower end and .46 on the upper end. The alternative population proportion is .36. The following diagram illustrates these results and the remainder of the solution to this problem.

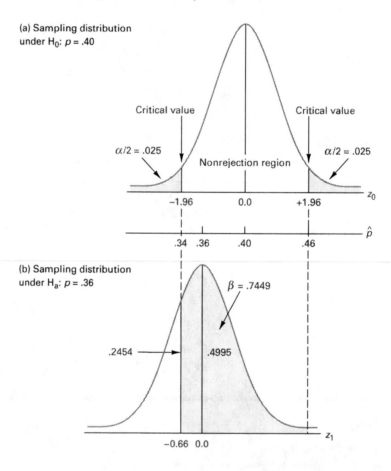

(a) Sampling distribution under H_0: $p = .40$

(b) Sampling distribution under H_a: $p = .36$

Solving for the area between $\hat{p}_c = .34$ and $p_1 = .36$ yields

$$z_1 = \frac{.34 - .36}{\sqrt{\dfrac{(.36)(.64)}{250}}} = -0.66$$

The area associated with $z_1 = -0.66$ is .2454.

The area between .36 and .46 of the sampling distribution under H_a: $p = .36$ (graph (b)) can be solved for by using the following z value.

$$z = \frac{.46 - .36}{\sqrt{\dfrac{(.36)(.64)}{250}}} = 3.29$$

The area from Table A.5 associated with $z = 3.29$ is .4995. Combining this value with the .2454 obtained from the left side of the distribution in graph (b) yields the total probability of committing a Type II error:

$$.2454 + .4995 = .7449$$

With two-tailed tests, both tails of the distribution contain rejection regions. The area between the two tails is the nonrejection region and the region where Type II errors can occur. If the alternative hypothesis is true, the area of the sampling distribution under H_a between the locations where the critical values from H_0 are located is β. In theory, both tails of the sampling distribution under H_a would be non-β area. However, in this problem, the right critical value is so far away from the alternative proportion ($p_1 = .36$) that the area between the right critical value and the alternative proportion is near .5000 (.4995) and virtually no area falls in the upper right tail of the distribution (.0005).

Some Observations About Type II Errors

Type II errors are committed only when the researcher fails to reject the null hypothesis but the alternative hypothesis is true. If the alternative mean or proportion is close to the hypothesized value, the probability of committing a Type II error is high. If the alternative value is relatively far away from the hypothesized value, as in the problem with $\mu = 12$ ounces and $\mu_a = 11.96$ ounces, the probability of committing a Type II error is small. The implication is that when a value is being tested as a null hypothesis against a true alternative value that is relatively far away, the sample statistic obtained is likely to show clearly which hypothesis is true. For example, suppose a researcher is testing to determine whether a company really is filling 2-liter bottles of cola with an average of 2 liters. If the company decides to underfill the bottles by filling them with only 1 liter, a sample of 50 bottles is likely to average a quantity near the 1-liter fill rather than near the 2-liter fill. Committing a Type II error is highly unlikely. Even a customer probably could see by looking at the bottles on the shelf that they are underfilled. However, if the company fills 2-liter bottles with 1.99 liters, the bottles are close in fill volume to those filled with 2.00 liters. In this case, the probability of committing a Type II error is much greater. A customer probably could not catch the underfill just by looking.

In general, if the alternative value is relatively far from the hypothesized value, the probability of committing a Type II error is smaller than it is when the alternative value is close to the hypothesized value. The probability of committing a Type II error decreases as alternative values of the hypothesized parameter move farther away from the hypothesized value. This situation is shown graphically in operating characteristic curves and power curves.

Operating Characteristic and Power Curves

Because the probability of committing a Type II error changes for each different value of the alternative parameter, it is best in managerial decision making to examine a series of possible alternative values. For example, Table 9.2 shows the probabilities of committing a

TABLE 9.2		
β Values and Power Values for the Soft Drink Example		

Alternative Mean	Probability of Committing a Type II Error, β	Power
$\mu_a = 11.999$	.94	.06
$\mu_a = 11.995$	.89	.11
$\mu_a = 11.99$	.80	.20
$\mu_a = 11.98$	.53	.47
$\mu_a = 11.97$	.24	.76
$\mu_a = 11.96$	.07	.93
$\mu_a = 11.95$	.01	.99

Minitab
Operating-Characteristic Curve
for the Soft Drink Example

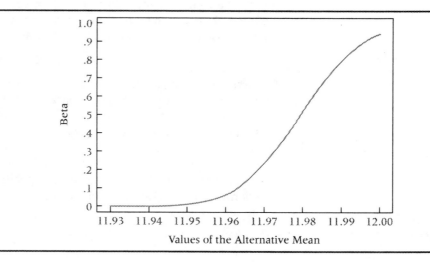

Type II error (β) for several different possible alternative means for the soft drink example discussed in Demonstration Problem 9.5, in which the null hypothesis was H_0: $\mu = 12$ ounces and $\alpha = .05$.

As previously mentioned, power is the probability of rejecting the null hypothesis when it is false and represents the correct decision of selecting the alternative hypothesis when it is true. Power is equal to $1 - \beta$. Note that Table 9.2 also contains the power values for the alternative means and that the β and power probabilities sum to 1 in each case.

These values can be displayed graphically as shown in Figures 9.21 and 9.22. Figure 9.21 is a Minitab-generated **operating characteristic (OC) curve** *constructed by plotting the β values against the various values of the alternative hypothesis.* Notice that when the alternative means are near the value of the null hypothesis, $\mu = 12$, the probability of committing a Type II error is high because it is difficult to discriminate between a distribution with a mean of 12 and a distribution with a mean of 11.999. However, as the values of the alternative means move away from the hypothesized value, $\mu = 12$, the values of β drop. This visual representation underscores the notion that it is easier to discriminate between a distribution with $\mu = 12$ and a distribution with $\mu = 11.95$ than between distributions with $\mu = 12$ and $\mu = 11.999$.

Figure 9.22 is an Excel **power curve** constructed by *plotting the power values $(1 - \beta)$ against the various values of the alternative hypotheses.* Note that the power increases as

Excel Power Curve for the
Soft Drink Example

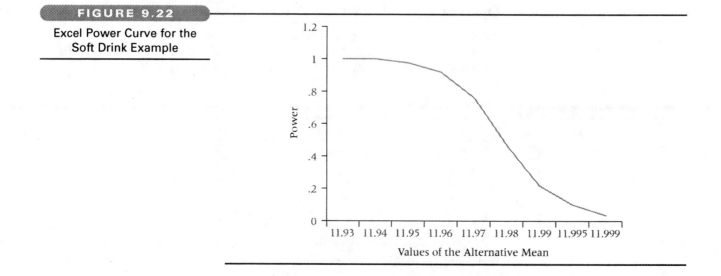

the alternative mean moves away from the value of μ in the null hypotheses. This relationship makes sense. As the alternative mean moves farther and farther away from the null hypothesized mean, a correct decision to reject the null hypothesis becomes more likely.

Effect of Increasing Sample Size on the Rejection Limits

The size of the sample affects the location of the rejection limits. Consider the soft drink example in which we were testing the following hypotheses.

$$H_0: \mu = 12.00 \text{ ounces}$$
$$H_a: \mu < 12.00 \text{ ounces}$$

Sample size was 60 ($n = 60$) and the standard deviation was .10 ($\sigma = .10$). With $\alpha = .05$, the critical value of the test statistic was $z_{.05} = -1.645$. From this information, a critical raw score value was computed:

$$z_c = \frac{\bar{x}_c - \mu}{\dfrac{\sigma}{\sqrt{n}}}$$

$$-1.645 = \frac{\bar{x}_c - 12}{\dfrac{.10}{\sqrt{60}}}$$

$$\bar{x}_c = 11.979$$

Any sample mean obtained in the hypothesis-testing process that is less than 11.979 will result in a decision to reject the null hypothesis.

Suppose the sample size is increased to 100. The critical raw score value is

$$-1.645 = \frac{\bar{x}_c - 12}{\dfrac{.10}{\sqrt{100}}}$$

$$\bar{x}_c = 11.984$$

Notice that the critical raw score value is nearer to the hypothesized value ($\mu = 12$) for the larger sample size than it was for a sample size of 60. Because n is in the denominator of the standard error of the mean ($\sigma/\sqrt{n}$), an increase in n results in a decrease in the standard error of the mean, which when multiplied by the critical value of the test statistic ($z_{\alpha/2}$) results in a critical raw score that is closer to the hypothesized value. For $n = 500$, the critical raw score value for this problem is 11.993.

Increased sample size not only affects the distance of the critical raw score value from the hypothesized value of the distribution, but also can result in reducing β for a given value of α. Examine Figure 9.20. Note that the critical raw score value is 11.979 with alpha equal to .05 for $n = 60$. The value of β for an alternative mean of 11.99 is .8023. Suppose the sample size is 100. The critical raw score value (already solved) is 11.984. The value of β is now .7257. The computation is

$$z = \frac{11.984 - 11.99}{\dfrac{.10}{\sqrt{100}}} = -0.60$$

The area under the standard normal curve for $z = -0.60$ is .2257. Adding $.2257 + .5000$ (from the right half of the H_a sampling distribution) results in a β of .7257. Figure 9.23 shows the sampling distributions with α and β for this problem. In addition, by increasing sample size a business researcher could reduce alpha without necessarily increasing beta. It is possible to reduce the probabilities of committing Type I and Type II errors simultaneously by increasing sample size.

FIGURE 9.23

Type II Error for Soft Drink Example with *n* Increased to 100

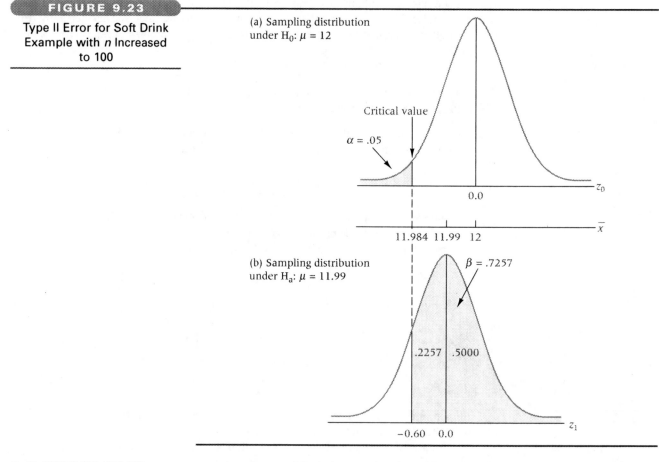

(a) Sampling distribution under H_0: $\mu = 12$

Critical value

$\alpha = .05$

z_0

0.0

$\bar{x}$

11.984 11.99 12

(b) Sampling distribution under H_a: $\mu = 11.99$

$\beta = .7257$

.2257 .5000

z_1

−0.60 0.0

9.6 PROBLEMS

9.36 Suppose a null hypothesis is that the population mean is greater than or equal to 100. Suppose further that a random sample of 48 items is taken and the population standard deviation is 14. For each of the following α values, compute the probability of committing a Type II error if the population mean actually is 99.

a. $\alpha = .10$

b. $\alpha = .05$

c. $\alpha = .01$

d. Based on the answers to parts (a), (b), and (c), what happens to the value of β as α gets smaller?

9.37 For Problem 9.36, use $\alpha = .05$ and solve for the probability of committing a Type II error for the following possible true alternative means.

a. $\mu_a = 98.5$

b. $\mu_a = 98$

c. $\mu_a = 97$

d. $\mu_a = 96$

e. What happens to the probability of committing a Type II error as the alternative value of the mean gets farther from the null hypothesized value of 100?

9.38 Suppose a hypothesis states that the mean is exactly 50. If a random sample of 35 items is taken to test this hypothesis, what is the value of β if the population standard deviation is 7 and the alternative mean is 53? Use $\alpha = .01$.

9.39 An alternative hypothesis is that $p < .65$. To test this hypothesis, a random sample of size 360 is taken. What is the probability of committing a Type II error if $\alpha = .05$ and the alternative proportion is as follows?

a. $p_a = .60$

b. $p_a = .55$

c. $p_a = .50$

9.40 The New York Stock Exchange recently reported that the average age of a female shareholder is 44 years. A broker in Chicago wants to know whether this figure is accurate for the female shareholders in Chicago. The broker secures a master list of shareholders in Chicago and takes a random sample of 58 women. Suppose the average age for shareholders in the sample is 45.1 years, with a population standard deviation of 8.7 years. Test to determine whether the broker's sample data differ significantly enough from the 44-years figure released by the New York Stock Exchange to declare that Chicago female shareholders are different in age from female shareholders in general. Use $\alpha = .05$. If no significant difference is noted, what is the broker's probability of committing a Type II error if the average age of a female Chicago shareholder is actually 45 years? 46 years? 47 years? 48 years? Construct an OC curve for these data. Construct a power curve for these data.

9.41 A Harris poll was taken to determine which of 13 major industries are doing a good job of serving their customers. Among the industries rated most highly by Americans for serving their customers were computer hardware and software companies, car manufacturers, and airlines. The industries rated lowest on serving their customers were tobacco companies, managed care providers, and health insurance companies. Seventy-one percent of those polled responded that airlines are doing a good job serving their customers. Suppose due to rising ticket prices, a researcher feels that this figure is now too high. He takes a poll of 463 Americans, and 324 say that the airlines are doing a good job of serving their customers. Does the survey show enough evidence to declare that the proportion of Americans saying that the airlines are doing a good job of serving their customers is significantly lower than stated in the Harris poll? Let alpha equal .10. If the researcher fails to reject the null hypothesis and if the figure is actually 69% now, what is the probability of committing a Type II error? What is the probability of committing a Type II error if the figure is really 66%? 60%?

Business Referrals

In the Decision Dilemma, many data facts are reported from numerous surveys about consumers seeking advice from others before purchasing items or services. Most of the statistics are stated as though they are facts about the population. For example, one study reports that 46% of all consumers seek advice when selecting a physician. Suppose a business researcher believes that this figure is not true, has changed over time, is not true for a particular region of the country, or is different for a particular type of medicine. Using hypothesis techniques presented in Section 9.4 of this chapter, this figure (46%) can be tested as a population proportion. Because the figures presented in the Decision Dilemma have been published and widely disseminated, the researcher who wants to test them would likely place these figures in the null hypothesis (e.g., $H_0: p = .46$), gather a random sample from whichever population is to be studied, and conduct a hypothesis test.

It was reported by Roper Starch Worldwide that influentials make recommendations about office equipment an average of 5.8 times per year. These and any of the other means reported in this study could be tested. The researcher would need to scien-

tifically identify influentials in the population and randomly select a sample. A research mechanism could be set up whereby the number of referrals by each influential could be recorded for a year and averaged thereby producing a sample mean and a sample standard deviation. Using a selected value of alpha, the sample mean could be statistically tested against the population mean (in this case, $H_0: \mu = 5.8$). The probability of falsely rejecting a true null would be alpha. If the null was actually false ($\mu \neq 5.8$), the probability (β) of failing to reject the false null hypothesis would depend upon what the true number of mean referrals per year was for influentials on office equipment.

If a researcher has theories on influentials and these research theories can be stated as statistical hypotheses, the theory should be formulated as an alternate hypothesis; and the null hypothesis should be that the theory is not true. Samples are randomly selected. If the statistic of choice is a mean, then a z test or t test for a population mean should be used in the analysis dependent on whether or not the population standard deviation is known or unknown. In many studies, the sample standard deviation is used in the analysis instead of the unknown population standard deviation. In these cases, a t test should be used when the assumption that the population data are normally distributed can be made. If the statistic is a proportion, then the z test for a population proportion is appropriate.

ETHICAL CONSIDERATIONS

The process of hypothesis testing encompasses several areas that could potentially lead to unethical activity, beginning with the null and alternative hypotheses. In the hypothesis-testing approach, the preliminary assumption is that the null hypothesis is true. If a researcher has a new theory or idea that he or she is attempting to prove, it is somewhat unethical to express that theory or idea as the null hypothesis. In doing so, the researcher is assuming that what he or she is trying to prove is true and the burden of proof is on the data to reject this idea or theory. The researcher must take great care not to assume that what he or she is attempting to prove is true.

Hypothesis testing through random sampling opens up many possible unethical situations that can occur in sampling, such as identifying a frame that is favorable to the outcome the researcher is seeking or using nonrandom sampling techniques to test hypotheses. In addition, the researcher should be careful to use the proper test statistic for tests of a population mean, particularly when σ is unknown. If t tests are used, or in testing a population variance, the researcher should be careful to apply the techniques only when it can be shown with some confidence that the population is normally distributed. The chi-square test of a population variance has been shown to be extremely sensitive to the assumption that the population is normally distributed. Unethical usage of this technique occurs when the statistician does not carefully check the population distribution shape for compliance with this assumption. Failure to do so can easily result in the reporting of spurious conclusions.

It can be unethical from a business decision-making point of view to knowingly use the notion of statistical significance to claim business significance when the results are not substantive. Therefore, it is unethical to intentionally attempt to mislead the business user by inappropriately using the word *significance*.

SUMMARY

Three types of hypotheses were presented in this chapter: research hypotheses, statistical hypotheses, and substantive hypotheses. Research hypotheses are statements of what the researcher believes will be the outcome of an experiment or study. In order to test hypotheses, business researchers formulate their research hypotheses into statistical hypotheses. All statistical hypotheses consist of two parts, a null hypothesis and an alternative hypothesis. The null and alternative hypotheses are structured so that either one or the other is true but not both. In testing hypotheses, the researcher assumes that the null hypothesis is true. By examining the sampled data, the researcher either rejects or does not reject the null hypothesis. If the sample data are significantly in opposition to the null hypothesis, the researcher rejects the null hypothesis and accepts the alternative hypothesis by default.

Hypothesis tests can be one tailed or two-tailed. Two-tailed tests always utilize $=$ and $\neq$ in the null and alternative hypotheses. These tests are nondirectional in that significant deviations from the hypothesized value that are either greater than or less than the value are in rejection regions. The one-tailed test is directional, and the alternative hypothesis contains $<$ or $>$ signs. In these tests, only one end or tail of the distribution contains a rejection region. In a one-tailed test, the researcher is interested only in deviations from the hypothesized value that are either greater than or less than the value but not both.

Not all statistically significant outcomes of studies are important business outcomes. A substantive result is when the outcome of a statistical study produces results that are important to the decision maker.

When a business researcher reaches a decision about the null hypothesis, the researcher either makes a correct decision or an error. If the null hypothesis is true, the researcher can make a Type I error by rejecting the null hypothesis. The probability of making a Type I error is alpha (α). Alpha is usually set by the researcher when establishing the hypotheses. Another expression sometimes used for the value of α is level of significance.

If the null hypothesis is false and the researcher fails to reject it, a Type II error is committed. Beta (β) is the probability of committing a Type II error. Type II errors must be computed from the hypothesized value of the parameter, α, and a specific alternative value of the parameter being examined. As many possible Type II errors in a problem exist as there are possible alternative statistical values.

If a null hypothesis is true and the researcher fails to reject it, no error is committed, and the researcher makes a correct decision. Similarly, if a null hypothesis is false and it is rejected, no error is committed. Power $(1 - \beta)$ is the probability of a statistical test rejecting the null hypothesis when the null hypothesis is false.

An operating characteristic (OC) curve is a graphical depiction of values of β that can occur as various values of the alternative hypothesis are explored. This graph can be studied to determine what happens to β as one moves away from the value of the null hypothesis. A power curve is used in conjunction with an operating characteristic curve. The power curve is a graphical depiction of the values of power as various values of the alternative hypothesis are examined. The researcher can view the increase in power as values of the alternative hypothesis diverge from the value of the null hypothesis.

Included in this chapter were hypothesis tests for a single mean when σ is known and when σ is unknown, a test of a single population proportion, and a test for a population variance. Three different analytic approaches were presented: (1) standard method, (2) the p-value; and (3) critical value method.

KEY TERMS

Flash
Cards

alpha (α)
alternative hypothesis
beta (β)
critical value

critical value method
hypothesis
hypothesis testing
level of significance
nonrejection region
null hypothesis
observed significance
  level
observed value

one-tailed test
operating characteristic
  (OC) curve
p-value
power
power curve
rejection region

research hypothesis
statistical hypothesis
substantive result
two-tailed test
Type I error
Type II error

FORMULAS

z test for a single mean (9.1)

$$z = \frac{\bar{x} - \mu}{\frac{\sigma}{\sqrt{n}}}$$

Formula to test hypotheses about μ with a finite population (9.2)

$$z = \frac{\bar{x} - \mu}{\frac{\sigma}{\sqrt{n}}\sqrt{\frac{N - n}{N - 1}}}$$

t test for a single mean (9.3)

$$t = \frac{\bar{x} - \mu}{\frac{s}{\sqrt{n}}}$$

$$\text{df} = n - 1$$

z test of a population proportion (9.4)

$$z = \frac{\hat{p} - p}{\sqrt{\frac{p \cdot q}{n}}}$$

Formula for testing hypotheses about a population variance (9.5)

$$\chi^2 = \frac{(n - 1)s^2}{\sigma^2}$$

$$\text{df} = n - 1$$

SUPPLEMENTARY PROBLEMS

CALCULATING THE STATISTICS

9.42 Use the information given and the HTAB system to test the hypotheses. Let $\alpha = .01$.

H_0: $\mu = 36$ H_a: $\mu \neq 36$ $n = 63$ $\bar{x} = 38.4$ $\sigma = 5.93$

9.43 Use the information given and the HTAB system to test the hypotheses. Let $\alpha = .05$. Assume the population is normally distributed.

H_0: $\mu = 7.82$ H_a: $\mu < 7.82$ $n = 17$ $\bar{x} = 17.1$ $s = 1.69$

9.44 For each of the following problems, test the hypotheses. Incorporate the HTAB system with its eight-step process.
  a. H_0: $p = .28$ H_a: $p > .28$ $n = 783$ $x = 230$ $\alpha = .10$
  b. H_0: $p = .61$ H_a: $p \neq .61$ $n = 401$ $\hat{p} = .56$ $\alpha = .05$

9.45 Test the following hypotheses by using the information given and the HTAB system. Let alpha be .01. Assume the population is normally distributed.

H_0: $\sigma^2 = 15.4$ H_a: $\sigma^2 > 15.4$ $n = 18$ $s^2 = 29.6$

9.46 Solve for the value of beta in each of the following problems.
  a. H_0: $\mu = 130$ H_a: $\mu > 130$ $n = 75$ $\sigma = 12$ $\alpha = .01$.
    The alternative mean is actually 135.
  b. H_0: $p = .44$ H_a: $p < .44$ $n = 1095$ $\alpha = .05$.
    The alternative proportion is actually .42.

TESTING YOUR UNDERSTANDING

9.47 According to one survey taken a few years ago, 32% of American households have attempted to reduce their long-distance phone bills by switching long-distance companies. Suppose that business researchers want to test to determine if this figure is still accurate today by taking a new survey of 80 American households who have tried to reduce their long-distance bills. Suppose further that of these 80 households, 25% say they have tried to reduce their bills by switching long-distance companies. Is this result enough evidence to state that a significantly different proportion of American households are trying to reduce long-distance bills by switching companies? Let $\alpha = .01$.

9.48 According to Zero Population Growth, the average urban U.S. resident consumes 3.3 pounds of food per day. Is this figure accurate for rural U.S. residents? Suppose 64 rural U.S. residents are identified by a random procedure and their average consumption per day is 3.60 pounds of food. Assume a population variance of 1.31 pounds of food per day. Use a 5% level of significance to determine whether the Zero Population Growth figure for urban U.S. residents also is true for rural U.S. residents on the basis of the sample data.

9.49 Brokers generally agree that bonds are a better investment during times of low interest rates than during times of high interest rates. A survey of executives during a time of low interest rates showed that 57% of them had some retirement funds invested in bonds. Assume this percentage is constant for bond market investment by executives with retirement funds. Suppose interest rates have risen lately and the proportion of executives with retirement investment money in the bond market may have dropped. To test this idea, a researcher randomly samples 210 executives who have retirement funds. Of these, 93 now have retirement funds invested in bonds. For $\alpha = .10$, does the test show enough evidence to declare that the proportion of executives with retirement fund investments in the bond market is significantly lower than .57?

9.50 Highway engineers in Ohio are painting white stripes on a highway. The stripes are supposed to be approximately 10 feet long. However, because of the machine, the operator, and the motion of the vehicle carrying the equipment, considerable variation occurs among the stripe lengths. Engineers claim that the variance of stripes is not more than 16 inches. Use the sample lengths given here from 12 measured stripes to test the variance claim. Assume stripe length is normally distributed. Let $\alpha = .05$.

Stripe Lengths in Feet

10.3	9.4	9.8	10.1
9.2	10.4	10.7	9.9
9.3	9.8	10.5	10.4

9.51 A computer manufacturer estimates that its line of minicomputers has, on average, 8.4 days of downtime per year. To test this claim, a researcher contacts seven companies that own one of these computers and is allowed to access company computer records. It is determined that, for the sample, the average number of downtime days is 5.6, with a sample standard deviation of 1.3 days. Assuming that number of down-time days is normally distributed, test to determine whether these minicomputers actually average 8.4 days of downtime in the entire population. Let $\alpha = .01$.

9.52 Life insurance experts have been claiming that the average worker in the city of Cincinnati has no more than $25,000 of personal life insurance. An insurance researcher believes that this is not true and sets out to prove that the average worker in Cincinnati has more than $25,000 of personal life insurance. To test this claim, she randomly samples 100 workers in Cincinnati and interviews them about their personal life insurance coverage. She discovers that the average amount of personal life insurance coverage for this sample group is $26,650. The population standard deviation is $12,000.

   a. Determine whether the test shows enough evidence to reject the null hypothesis posed by the salesperson. Assume the probability of committing a Type I error is .05.

   b. If the actual average for this population is $30,000, what is the probability of committing a Type II error?

9.53 A financial analyst watched a particular stock for several months. The price of this stock remained fairly stable during this time. In fact, the financial analyst claims that the variance of the price of this stock did not exceed $4 for the entire period. Recently, the market heated up, and the price of this stock appears more volatile. To determine whether it is more volatile, a sample of closing prices of this stock for eight days is taken randomly. The sample mean price is $36.25, with a sample standard deviation of $7.80. Using a level of significance of .10, test to determine whether the financial analyst's previous variance figure is now too low. Assume stock prices are normally distributed.

9.54 A study of MBA graduates by Universum for the American Graduate Survey 1999 revealed that MBA graduates have several expectations of prospective employers beyond their base pay. In particular, according to the study 46% expect a performance-related bonus, 46% expect stock options, 42% expect a signing bonus, 28% expect profit sharing, 27% expect extra vacation/personal days, 25% expect tuition reimbursement, 24% expect health benefits, and 19% expect guaranteed annual bonuses. Suppose a study was conducted last year to see whether these expectations have changed. If 125 MBA graduates were randomly selected last year, and if 66 expected stock options, does this result provide enough evidence to declare that a significantly higher proportion of MBAs expect stock options? Let $\alpha = .05$. If the proportion really is .50, what is the probability of committing a Type II error?

9.55 Suppose the number of beds filled per day in a medium-sized hospital is normally distributed. A hospital administrator tells the board of directors that, on the average, at least 185 beds are filled on any given day. One of the board members believes that the average is less than 185 and she sets out to test to determine if she is correct. She secures a random sample of 16 days of data (shown below). Use $\alpha = .05$ and the sample data to test the board member's theory. Assume the number of filled beds per day is normally distributed in the population.

Number of Beds Occupied per Day

173	149	166	180
189	170	152	194
177	169	188	160
199	175	172	187

9.56 According to Gartner Inc., the largest share of the worldwide PC market is held by Hewlett-Packard with 19.8%.

Suppose that a market researcher believes that Hewlett Packard holds a higher share of the market in the western region of the United States. To verify this theory, he randomly selects 428 people who purchased a personal computer in the last month in the western region of the United States. Ninety of these purchases were Hewlett-Packard computers. Using a 1% level of significance, test the market researcher's theory. If the market share is really .22 in the southwestern region of the United States, what is the probability of making a Type II error?

9.57 A national publication reported that a college student living away from home spends, on average, no more than $15 per month on laundry. You believe this figure is too low and want to disprove this claim. To conduct the test, you randomly select 17 college students and ask them to keep track of the amount of money they spend during a given month for laundry. The sample produces an average expenditure on laundry of $19.34, with a population standard deviation of $4.52. Use these sample data to conduct the hypothesis test. Assume you are willing to take a 10% risk of making a Type I error and that spending on laundry per month is normally distributed in the population.

9.58 A local company installs natural-gas grills. As part of the installation, a ditch is dug to lay a small natural-gas line from the grill to the main line. On the average, the depth of these lines seems to run about 1 foot. The company claims that the depth does not vary by more than 16 square inches (the variance). To test this claim, a researcher randomly took 22 depth measurements at different locations. The sample average depth was 13.4 inches with a standard deviation of 6 inches. Is this enough evidence to reject the company's claim about the variance? Assume line depths are normally distributed. Let $\alpha = .05$.

9.59 A study of pollutants showed that certain industrial emissions should not exceed 2.5 parts per million. You believe a particular company may be exceeding this average. To test this supposition, you randomly take a sample of nine air tests. The sample average is 3.4 parts per million, with a sample standard deviation of 0.6. Does this result provide enough evidence for you to conclude that the company is exceeding the safe limit? Use $\alpha = .01$. Assume emissions are normally distributed.

9.60 The average cost per square foot for office rental space in the central business district of Philadelphia is $23.58, according to Cushman & Wakefield. A large real estate company wants to confirm this figure. The firm conducts a telephone survey of 95 offices in the central business district of Philadelphia and asks the office managers how much they pay in rent per square foot. Suppose the sample average is $22.83 per square foot. The population standard deviation is $5.11.
  a. Conduct a hypothesis test using $\alpha = .05$ to determine whether the cost per square foot reported by Cushman & Wakefield should be rejected.

  b. If the decision in part (a) is to fail to reject and if the actual average cost per square foot is $22.30, what is the probability of committing a Type II error?

9.61 The American Water Works Association reports that, on average, men use between 10 and 15 gallons of water daily to shave when they leave the water running. Suppose the following data are the numbers of gallons of water used in a day to shave by 12 randomly selected men and the data come from a normal distribution of data. Use these data and a 5% level of significance to test to determine whether the population variance for such water usage is 2.5 gallons.

10	8	13	17	13	15
12	13	15	16	9	7

9.62 Downtime in manufacturing is costly and can result in late deliveries, backlogs, failure to meet orders, and even loss of market share. Suppose a manufacturing plant has been averaging 23 minutes of downtime per day for the past several years, but during the past year, there has been a significant effort by both management and production workers to reduce downtime. In an effort to determine if downtime has been significantly reduced, company productivity researchers have randomly sampled 31 days over the past several months from company records and have recorded the daily downtimes shown below in minutes. Use these data and an alpha of .01 to test to determine if downtime has been significantly reduced. Assume that daily downtimes are normally distributed in the population.

19	22	17	19	32	24	16	18	27	17
24	19	23	27	28	19	17	18	26	22
19	15	18	25	23	19	26	21	16	21
24									

INTERPRETING THE OUTPUT

9.63 According to the U.S. Census Bureau, the average American generates 4.4 pounds of garbage per day. Suppose we believe that because of recycling and a greater emphasis on the environment, the figure is now lower. To test this notion, we take a random sample of Americans and have them keep a log of their garbage for a day. We record and analyze the results by using a statistical computer package. The output follows. Describe the sample. What statistical decisions can be made on the basis of this analysis? Let alpha be .05. Assume that pounds of garbage per day are normally distributed in the population. Discuss any substantive results.

One-Sample Z

```
Test of mu = 4.4 vs < 4.4
The assumed standard deviation = 0.866
                            95%
                            Upper
N    Mean   SE Mean   Bound     Z       P
22   3.969   0.185    4.273   -2.33   0.010
```

9.64 One survey conducted by RHI Management Resources determined that the Lexus is the favorite luxury car for 25% of CFOs. Suppose a financial management association conducts its own survey of CFOs in an effort to determine whether this figure is correct. They use an alpha of .05. Following is the Minitab output with the results of the survey. Discuss the findings, including the hypotheses, one- or two-tailed tests, sample statistics, and the conclusion. Explain from the data why you reached the conclusion you did. Are these results substantive?

Test and CI for One Proportion

Test of p = 0.25 vs p not = 0.25

					Exact
Sample	X	N	Sample p	95% CI	P-Value
1	79	384	0.205729	(0.166399, 0.249663)	0.045

9.65 In a recent year, published statistics by the National Cattlemen's Beef Association claimed that the average retail beef price for USDA All Fresh beef was $2.51. Suppose a survey of retailers is conducted this year to determine whether the price of USDA All Fresh beef has increased. The Excel output of the results of the survey are shown here. Analyze the output and explain what it means in this study. An alpha of .05 was used in this analysis. Assume that beef prices are normally distributed in the population. Comment on any substantive results.

Mean	2.55
Variance	0.0218
Observations	26
df	25
t Stat	1.51
P (T<=t) one-tail	0.072
t Critical one-tail	1.71
P (T<=t) two-tail	0.144
t Critical two-tail	2.06

9.66 The American Express Retail Index states that the average U.S. household will spend $2747 on home improvement projects this year. Suppose a large national home improvement company wants to test that figure in the West, theorizing that the average might be lower in the West. The research firm hired to conduct the study arrives at the results shown here. Analyze the data and explain the results. Comment on any substantive findings.

One-Sample Z

Test of mu = 2747 vs < 2747
The assumed standard deviation = 1557

			95% Upper		
N	Mean	SE Mean	Bound	Z	p
67	2349	190	2662	-2.09	0.018

see www.wiley.com/college/black

ANALYZING THE DATABASES

Database

1. Suppose the average number of employees per industry group in the manufacturing database is believed to be less than 150 (1000s). Test this belief as the alternative hypothesis by using the 140 SIC Code industries given in the database as the sample. Let $\alpha = .10$. Assume that the number of employees per industry group are normally distributed in the population. What did you decide and why?

2. Examine the hospital database. Suppose you want to "prove" that the average hospital in the United States averages more than 700 births per year. Use the hospital database as your sample and test this hypothesis. Let alpha be .01. On average, do hospitals in the United States employ fewer than 900 personnel? Use the hospital database as your sample and an alpha of .10 to test this figure as the alternative hypothesis. Assume that the number of births and number of employees in the hospitals are normally distributed in the population.

3. Consider the financial database. Are the average earnings per share for companies in the stock market less than $2.50? Use the sample of companies represented by this database to test that hypothesis. Let $\alpha = .05$. Test to determine whether the average return on equity for all companies is equal to 21. Use this database as the sample and $\alpha = .10$. Assume that the earnings per share and return on equity are normally distributed in the population.

4. Suppose a researcher wants to test to determine if the average annual food spending for a household in the Midwest region of the U.S. is more than $8000. Use the Midwest region data from the Consumer Food database and a 1% level of significance to test this hypothesis. Assume that annual food spending is normally distributed in the population.

CASE

FRITO-LAY TARGETS THE HISPANIC MARKET

Frito Company was founded in 1932 in San Antonio, Texas, by Elmer Doolin. H. W. Lay & Company was founded in Atlanta, Georgia, by Herman W. Lay in 1938. In 1961, the two companies merged to form Frito-Lay, Inc., with headquarters in Texas. Frito-Lay produced, distributed, and marketed snack foods with particular emphasis on various types of chips. In 1965, the company merged with Pepsi-Cola to form PepsiCo, Inc. Three decades later, Pepsi-Cola combined its domestic and international snack food operations into one business unit called Frito-Lay Company. Today, Frito-Lay brands account for 59% of the U.S. snack chip industry, and there are more than 45,000 Frito-Lay employees in the United States and Canada.

In the late 1990s, despite its overall popularity, Frito-Lay faced a general lack of appeal to Hispanics, a fast-growing U.S. market. In an effort to better penetrate that market, Frito-Lay hired various market researchers to determine why Hispanics were not purchasing their products as often as company officials had hoped and what could be done about the problem. In the studies, market researchers discovered that Hispanics thought Frito-Lay products were too bland, Frito-Lay advertisements were not being widely viewed by Hispanics, and Hispanics tended to purchase snacks in small bags at local grocery stores rather than in the large family-style bags sold at large supermarkets.

Focus groups composed of male teens and male young adults—a group that tends to consume a lot of chips—were formed. The researchers determined that even though many of the teens spoke English at school, they spoke Spanish at home with their family. From this discovery, it was concluded that Spanish advertisements would be needed to reach Hispanics. In addition, the use of Spanish rock music, a growing movement in the Hispanic youth culture, could be effective in some ads.

Researchers also found that using a "Happy Face" logo, which is an icon of Frito-Lay's sister company in Mexico, was effective. Because it reminded the 63% of all Hispanics in the United States who are Mexican American of snack foods from home, the logo increased product familiarity.

As a result of this research, Frito-Lay launched its first Hispanic products in San Antonio, in 1997. Within a few of years, sales of the Doritos brand improved 32% in Hispanic areas. In May 2002, Frito-Lay teamed up with its Mexican affiliate, Sabritas, to launch a new line of products to further appeal to Hispanic customers. Included in these offerings are Sabritas Adobadas tomato and chile potato chips, Sabritones Churrumais fried corn strips with chile and lime seasonings, Crujitos queso and chile flavor puffed corn twists, Fritos Sabrositas lime and chile chips, El Isleno Plantains, and others.

More recently, Frito-Lay has been relying on input and guidance from the Adelante employee network, which is a multicultural Latina/Hispanic professional organization associated with PepsiCo. At Frito-Lay, the organization's mission is to help develop a diverse, inclusive culture accelerating growth opportunities for associates while providing a competitive advantage in an increasingly diverse marketplace. As part of this effort, Adelante has been used to help develop new flavors and advertising programs for Hispanics. Based on information gleaned from Adelante members, new Frito-Lay snack products are being test marketed in several states, and guacamole-flavored Doritos became one of the most successful new-product launches in the company's history.

Discussion

In the research process for Frito-Lay Company, many different numerical questions were raised regarding Frito-Lay products, advertising techniques, and purchase patterns among Hispanics. In each of these areas, statistics—in particular, hypothesis testing—plays a central role. Using the case information and the concepts of statistical hypothesis testing, discuss the following:

1. Many proportions were generated in the focus groups and market research that were conducted for this project, including the proportion of the market that is Hispanic, the proportion of Hispanic grocery shoppers that are women, the proportion of chip purchasers that are teens, and so on. Use techniques presented in this chapter to analyze each of the following and discuss how the results might affect marketing decision makers regarding the Hispanic market.

   a. Suppose that in the past, 94% of all Hispanic grocery shoppers were women. Perhaps due to changing cultural values, we believe that more Hispanic men are now grocery shopping. We randomly sample 689 Hispanic grocery shoppers from around the United States and 606 are women. Does this result provide enough evidence to conclude that a lower proportion of Hispanic grocery shoppers now are women?

   b. What proportion of Hispanics listen primarily to advertisements in Spanish? Suppose one source says that in the past the proportion has been about .83. We want to test to determine whether this figure is true. A random sample of 438 Hispanics is selected, and the Minitab results of testing this hypothesis are shown here. Discuss and explain this output and the implications of this study using $\alpha = .05$.

   Test and CI for One Proportion

   Test of p = 0.83 vs p not = 0.83

Sample	X	N	Sample p	95% CI	Exact P-Value
1	347	438	0.792237	(0.751184, 0.829290)	0.042

2. The statistical mean can be used to measure various aspects of the Hispanic culture and the Hispanic market, including size of purchase, frequency of purchase, age of consumer, size of store, and so on. Use techniques presented in this chapter to analyze each of the following and discuss how the results might affect marketing decisions.

   a. What is the average age of a purchaser of Doritos Salsa Verde? Suppose initial tests indicate that the mean age is 31. Is this figure really correct? To test whether it is, a researcher randomly contacts 24 purchasers of Doritos Salsa Verde with results shown in the following Excel output. Discuss the output in terms of a hypothesis test to determine whether the mean age is actually 31. Let α be .01. Assume that ages of purchasers are normally distributed in the population.

Mean	28.81
Variance	50.2651
Observations	24
df	23
t Stat	−1.52
P (T<=t) one-tail	0.0716
t Critical one-tail	2.50
P (T≠t) two-tail	0.1431
t Critical two-tail	2.81

b. What is the average expenditure of a Hispanic customer on chips per year? Suppose it is hypothesized that the figure is $45 per year. A researcher who knows the Hispanic market believes that this figure is too high and wants to prove her case. She randomly selects 18 Hispanics, has them keep a log of grocery purchases for one year, and obtains the following figures. Analyze the data using techniques from this chapter and an alpha of .05. Assume that expenditures per customer are normally distributed in the population.

$55	37	59	57	27	28
16	46	34	62	9	34
4	25	38	58	3	50

Source: Adapted from "From Bland to Brand," *American Demographics*, (March 1999) p. 57; Ronald J. Alsop, ed., *The Wall Street Journal Almanac 1999.* New York: Ballantine Books, 1998, p. 202; and the 2011 Frito-Lay Web site at http://www.fritolay.com/index.html. The Adelante Group (San Antonio, Texas) January 30, 2011, http://adelante-sa.com/history.htm; "Diversity Finds Its Place: More Organizations Are Dedicating Senior-Level Executives to Drive Diversity Initiatives for Bottom-Line Effect," *HR Magazine*, August 2006, http://findarticles.com/p/articles/mi_m3495/is_8_51/ai_n26968947/; Snack Chat, "Reaching Out to Hispanic Consumers," March 11, 2009, http://www.snacks.com/good_fun_fritolay/2009/03/reaching-out-to-mexican-consumers.html.

USING THE COMPUTER

EXCEL

⁜ Excel has limited capability for conducting hypothesis testing with single samples. By piecing together various Excel commands, it is possible to compute a z test of a single population mean and a t test of a single population mean.

⁜ To conduct a z test of a single population mean, begin with the **Insert Function** (f_x). To access the **Insert Function**, go to the **Formulas** tab on an Excel worksheet (top center tab). The **Insert Function** is on the far left of the menu bar. In the **Insert Function** dialog box at the top, there is a pulldown menu where it says **Or select a category**. From the pulldown menu associated with this command, select **Statistical**. Select **ZTEST** from the **Insert Function's Statistical** menu. In the **ZTEST** dialog box, place the location of the observed values in **Array**. Place the hypothesized value of the mean in **X**. Record the value of the population standard deviation in **Sigma**. The output is the right-tailed p-value for the test statistic. If the z value is negative, subtract 1−Excel output to obtain the p-value for the left tail.

⁜ To perform a t test of a single mean in Excel, one needs to "fool" Excel by using a two-sample t test. To do this, enter the location of the single sample observations as one of the two requested samples and enter the location of the hypothesized mean repeated as many times as there are observations as the other sample.

⁜ Begin this t test by selecting the **Data** tab on the Excel worksheet. From the **Analysis** panel at the right top of the **Data** tab worksheet, click on **Data Analysis**. If your Excel worksheet does not show the **Data Analysis** option, then you can load it as an add-in following directions given in Chapter 2. From the **Data Analysis** pulldown menu, select **t-Test: Two-Sample Assuming Unequal Variances** from the dialog box. Enter the location of the observations from the single sample of data in **Variable 1 Range:**. Enter the location of the repeated hypothesized mean values in **Variable 2 Range:**. Enter the value of zero in **Hypothesized Mean Difference**. Check **Labels** if you have labels. Select **Alpha**. The output includes the observed t value, p-values for both one- and two-tailed tests, and critical t values for both one- and two-tailed tests.

MINITAB

⁜ Minitab has the capability for testing hypotheses about a population mean either when σ is known or it is unknown and for testing hypotheses about a population proportion. The commands, pulldown menus, and dialog boxes are the same as those used to construct confidence intervals shown in Chapter 8.

⁜ To begin a z test of a single population mean, select **Stat** on the menu bar. Select **Basic Statistics** from the pulldown menu. From the second pulldown menu, select **1-sample Z**. Check **Samples in columns** if you have raw data and enter the location of the column containing the observations. Check **Summarized data** if you wish to use the summarized statistics of the sample mean and the sample size rather than raw data. Enter the size of the sample in the box beside **Sample size**. Enter the sample mean in the box beside **Mean**. Enter the value of the population standard deviation in the box beside **Standard deviation**. Enter the value of the hypothesized test mean in the box beside **Test Mean:**. Click on **Options** if you want to enter a value for alpha and/or enter the direction of the alternative hypothesis (greater than, less than, or not equal). Note: **Options** does not allow you to directly enter a value of alpha but rather allows you to insert a level of confidence, which is 1 − alpha for a 2-tailed test. Both the observed z and its associated p-value for the hypothesis test and the confidence interval are given in the output.

⁜ To begin a t test of a single population mean, select **Stat** on the menu bar. Select **Basic Statistics** from the pulldown menu. From the second pulldown menu, select **1-sample t**. Check **Samples in columns** if you have raw data and enter the location of the column containing the observations. Check **Summarized data** if you wish to use the summarized statistics of the sample size, sample mean, and the sample standard deviation rather than raw data. Enter the size of the sample in the box beside **Sample size**. Enter the sample mean in the box beside **Mean**. Enter the sample standard deviation in the box beside **Standard deviation**. Enter the value of the hypothesized test mean in the box beside **Test Mean:**. Click on **Options** if you want to enter a value for alpha and/or enter the direction of the alternative hypothesis (greater than, less than, or not equal). Note: **Options** does not allow you to directly enter a value of alpha but rather allows you to insert a level of confidence, which is 1 – alpha for a two-tailed test. Both the observed t and its associated p-value for the hypothesis test and the confidence interval are given in the output.

▪ To begin a z test of a single population proportion, select **Stat** on the menu bar. Select **Basic Statistics** from the pulldown menu. From the second pulldown menu, select **1 Proportion**. Check **Samples in columns** if you have raw data and enter the location of the column containing the observations. Note that the data in the column must contain one of only two values (e.g., 1 or 2). Check **Summarized data** if you wish to use the summarized statistics of the number of trials and number of events rather than raw data. Enter the size of the sample in the box beside **Number of trials.** Enter the number of observed events (having the characteristic that you are testing) in the box beside **Number of events**. Click on **Options** if you want to enter a value for alpha, and/or enter the direction of the alternative hypothesis (greater than, less than, or not equal). Note: **Options** does not allow you to directly enter a value of alpha but rather allows you to insert a level of confidence, which is 1 – alpha for a two-tailed test. While in **Options,** enter the value of the proportion being tested in the box beside **Test proportion:**. Both p-value associated with the observed z for the hypothesis test and the confidence interval are given in the output.

CHAPTER 10

Statistical Inferences about Two Populations

LEARNING OBJECTIVES

The general focus of Chapter 10 is on testing hypotheses and constructing confidence intervals about parameters from two populations, thereby enabling you to:

1. Test hypotheses and develop confidence intervals about the difference in two means with known population variances using the z statistic.

2. Test hypotheses and develop confidence intervals about the difference in two means of independent samples with unknown population variances using the t test.

3. Test hypotheses and develop confidence intervals about the difference in two dependent populations.

4. Test hypotheses and develop confidence intervals about the difference in two population proportions.

5. Test hypotheses about the difference in two population variances using the F distribution.

Matthew Wiley/Masterfile

Online Shopping

The use of online shopping has grown exponentially in the past decade. The Pew Internet and American Life Project surveyed 2400 American adults and reported that about 50% of adult Americans have purchased an item on the Internet at one time or another. A Nielsen survey of over 26,000 Internet users across the globe reported that more than 85% of the world's online population has used the Internet to make a purchase, increasing the market for online shopping by 40% in the past two years. The highest percentage of Internet users who shop online is 99%, found in South Korea. This figure is followed by 97% in the United Kingdom, Germany, and Japan. The United States is eighth at 94%. A Gallup household survey of 1043 adults taken in a recent year broke down online shopping by household income and type of store. The study reported that while only 16% of households with incomes less than $35,000 made a purchase at an online retailer or on the Internet, 48% of households with more than $100,000 did so, followed by 37% of households in the $75,000 to $99,999 level, 30% in the $50,000 to $74,999 level, and 25% of the $35,000 to $49,999 level. The average amount spent in the past 30 days at an online retailer was $130. Broken down by types of stores, survey results included $166 at electronics stores, $123 at specialty apparel stores, $121 at department stores, $94 at general merchandise stores, $80 at office supply stores, and $63 at discount retailers. The European Interactive Advertising Association (EIAA) conducted a study of over 7000 people across Europe with regard to online shopping. They discovered that, European online shoppers spent an average of €750 and purchased 10 items online over a six-month period. By country, the average number of items purchased over a six-month period were 18 in the United Kingdom; 11 in Denmark; 10 in Germany; 9 in

Sweden; 8 in France; 7 in Norway, the Netherlands, and Italy; 6 in Belgium; and 5 in Spain. In terms of the average amount spent shopping online over a six-month period, shoppers in Norway spent €1406, followed by the United Kingdom, Denmark, Sweden, Belgium, the Netherlands, Germany, France, Italy, and Spain with €1201, €1159, €1013, €790, €681, €521, €509, €454, and €452, respectively.

1. One study reported that the average amount spent by online American shoppers in the past 30 days is $123 at specialty stores and $121 at department stores. These figures are relatively close to each other and were derived from sample information. Suppose a researcher wants to test to determine if there is actually any significant difference in the average amount spent by online American shoppers in the past 30 days at specialty stores vs. department stores. How does she go about conducting such a test?

2. The EIAA study reported that the average number of items purchased over a six-month period for online shoppers was 11 in Denmark and 10 in Germany. These figures were derived from a survey of 7000 people. Is the average number of items purchased over a six-month period for Denmark significantly higher than the average number for Germany? How would one go about determining this?

3. According to the Nielsen survey, 97% of Internet users in Japan shop online. This compares to only 94% in the United States. However, these figures were obtained through a sample of Internet users. If a researcher wants to conduct a similar survey to test to determine if the proportion of Japanese Internet users who shop online is significantly higher than the proportion of American Internet users who shop online, how would he go about doing so?

Sources: http://www.pewinternet.org/Reports/2008/Online-Shopping/04-Online-Shoppers/01-Introduction.aspx; The Gallup poll with results located at http://www.gallup.com/poll/20527/There-Digital-Divide-Online-Shopping.aspx; The Nielsen report at http://th.nielsen.com/site/documents/GlobalOnlineShoppingReportFeb08.pdf; and the EIAA press release at http://www.eiaa.net/news/eiaa-articles-details.asp?id=121&lang=9.

To this point, all discussion of confidence intervals and hypothesis tests has centered on single population parameters. That is, a single sample is randomly drawn from a population, and using data from that sample, a population mean, proportion, or variance is estimated or tested. Chapter 8 presents statistical techniques for constructing confidence intervals to estimate a population mean, a population proportion, or a population variance. Chapter 9 presents statistical techniques for testing hypotheses about a population mean, a population proportion, or a population variance. Often, it is of equal interest to make inferences about two populations. A retail analyst might want to compare per person annual expenditures on shoes in the year 2011 with those in the year 2006 to determine whether a change has occurred over time. A market researcher might want to estimate or test to determine the proportion of market share of one company in two different regions.

In this chapter, we will consider several different techniques for analyzing data that come from two samples. One technique is used with proportions, one is used with variances, and the others are used with means. The techniques for analyzing means are separated into those using the z statistic and those using the t statistic. In four of the five techniques presented in this chapter, the two samples are assumed to be **independent samples**. The samples are independent because *the items or people sampled in each group are in no way related to those in the other group.* Any similarity between items or people in the two samples is coincidental and due to chance. One of the techniques presented in the chapter is for

FIGURE 10.1

Branch of the Tree Diagram Taxonomy of Inferential Techniques: Confidence Intervals

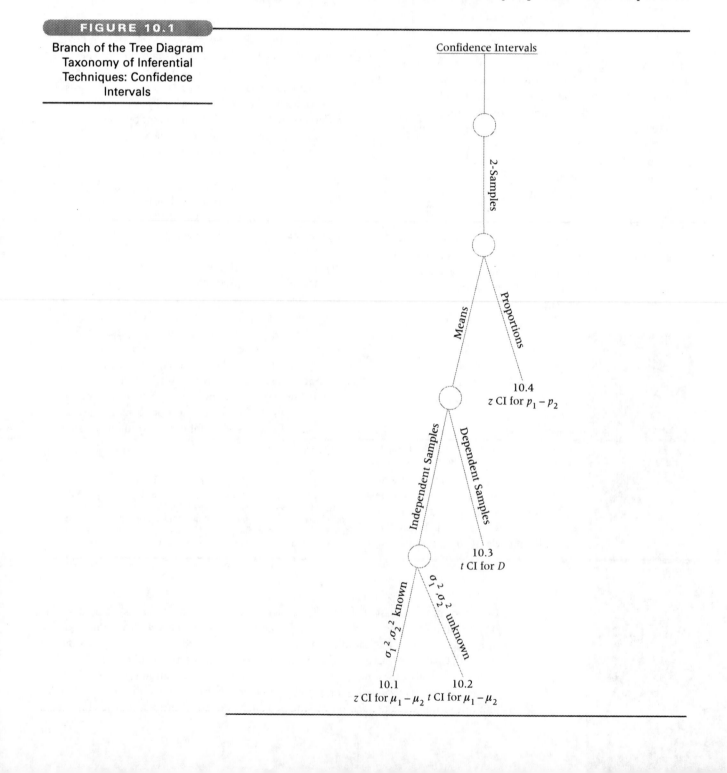

analyzing data from dependent, or related, samples in which items or persons in one sample are matched in some way with items or persons in the other sample. For four of the five techniques, we will examine both hypothesis tests and confidence intervals.

Figure III-1 of the Introduction to Unit III displays a Tree Diagram Taxonomy of Inferential Techniques organizing them by usage, number of samples, and level of data. Chapter 10 contains techniques for constructing confidence intervals and testing hypotheses about the differences in two population means and two population proportions and, in addition, testing hypotheses about two population variances. The entire left side of the tree diagram taxonomy displays various confidence interval estimation techniques. The right-most branch of this side contains Chapter 10 techniques and is displayed in Figure 10.1. The entire right side of the tree diagram taxonomy displays various hypothesis-testing techniques. The central branch of this contains Chapter 10 techniques (2-samples) for testing hypotheses, and this branch is displayed in Figure 10.2. Note that at the bottom of each tree branch in Figures 10.1 and 10.2, the title of the statistical technique along with its respective section number is given for ease of identification and use. If a business

FIGURE 10.2

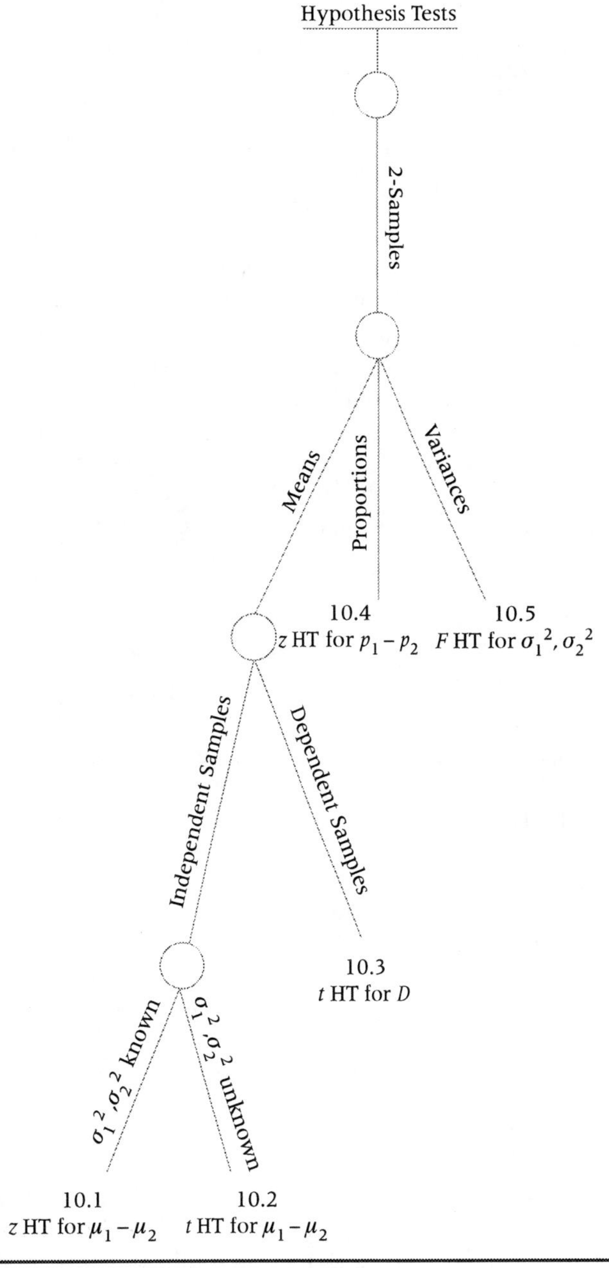

Branch of the Tree Diagram Taxonomy of Inference Techniques: Hypothesis Tests

researcher is constructing confidence intervals or testing hypotheses about the difference in two population means and the population standard deviations or variances are known, then he will use the z test for $\mu_1 - \mu_2$ contained in Section 10.1. If the population standard deviations or variances are unknown, then the appropriate technique is the t test for $\mu_1 - \mu_2$ contained in Section 10.2. If a business researcher is constructing confidence intervals or testing hypotheses about the difference in two related populations, then he will use the t test presented in Section 10.3. If a business researcher is constructing a confidence interval or testing a hypothesis about the difference in two population proportions, then he will use the z test for $p_1 - p_2$ presented in Section 10.4. If the researcher desires to test a hypothesis about two population variances, then he will use the F test presented in Section 10.5.

10.1 HYPOTHESIS TESTING AND CONFIDENCE INTERVALS ABOUT THE DIFFERENCE IN TWO MEANS USING THE z STATISTIC (POPULATION VARIANCES KNOWN)

In some research designs, the sampling plan calls for selecting two independent samples, calculating the sample means and using the difference in the two sample means to estimate or test the difference in the two population means. The object might be to determine whether the two samples come from the same population or, if they come from different populations, to determine the amount of difference in the populations. This type of analysis can be used to determine, for example, whether the effectiveness of two brands of toothpaste differs or whether two brands of tires wear differently. Business research might be conducted to study the difference in the productivity of men and women on an assembly line under certain conditions. An engineer might want to determine differences in the strength of aluminum produced under two different temperatures. Does the average cost of a two-bedroom, one-story house differ between Boston and Seattle? If so, how much is the difference? These and many other interesting questions can be researched by comparing the difference in two sample means.

How does a researcher analyze the difference in two samples by using sample means? The central limit theorem states that the difference in two sample means, $\bar{x}_1 - \bar{x}_2$, is normally distributed for large sample sizes (both n_1 and $n_2 \geq 30$) regardless of the shape of the populations. It can also be shown that

$$\mu_{\bar{x}_1 - \bar{x}_2} = \mu_1 - \mu_2$$

$$\sigma_{\bar{x}_1 - \bar{x}_2} = \sqrt{\frac{\sigma_1^2}{n_1} + \frac{\sigma_2^2}{n_2}}$$

These expressions lead to a z formula for the difference in two sample means.

z FORMULA FOR THE DIFFERENCE IN TWO SAMPLE MEANS (INDEPENDENT SAMPLES AND POPULATION VARIANCES KNOWN) (10.1)	$z = \dfrac{(\bar{x}_1 - \bar{x}_2) - (\mu_1 - \mu_2)}{\sqrt{\dfrac{\sigma_1^2}{n_1} + \dfrac{\sigma_2^2}{n_2}}}$

where

μ_1 = the mean of population 1
μ_2 = the mean of population 2
n_1 = size of sample 1
n_2 = size of sample 2
σ_1^2 = the variance of population 1
σ_2^2 = the variance of population 2

This formula is the basis for statistical inferences about the difference in two means using two random independent samples.

Note: *If the populations are normally distributed on the measurement being studied and if the population variances are known, formula 10.1 can be used for small sample sizes.*

Hypothesis Testing

In many instances, a business researcher wants to test the differences in the mean values of two populations. As an example, a consumer organization might want to test two brands of light bulbs to determine whether one burns longer than the other. A company wanting to relocate might want to determine whether a significant difference separates the average price of a home in Newark, New Jersey, from house prices in Cleveland, Ohio. Formula 10.1 can be used to test the difference between two population means.

As a specific example, suppose we want to conduct a hypothesis test to determine whether the average annual wage for an advertising manager is different from the average annual wage of an auditing manager. Because we are testing to determine whether the means are different, it might seem logical that the null and alternative hypotheses would be

$$H_0: \mu_1 = \mu_2$$
$$H_a: \mu_1 \neq \mu_2$$

where advertising managers are population 1 and auditing managers are population 2. However, statisticians generally construct these hypotheses as

$$H_0: \mu_1 - \mu_2 = \delta$$
$$H_a: \mu_1 - \mu_2 \neq \delta$$

This format allows the business analyst not only to test if the population means are equal but also affords her the opportunity to hypothesize about a particular difference in the means (δ). Generally speaking, most business analysts are only interested in testing whether the difference in the means is different. Thus, δ is set equal to zero, resulting in the following hypotheses, which we will use for this problem and most others.

$$H_0: \mu_1 - \mu_2 = 0$$
$$H_a: \mu_1 - \mu_2 \neq 0$$

Note, however, that a business researcher could be interested in testing to determine if there is, for example, a difference of means equal to, say, 10, in which case, $\delta = 10$.

A random sample of 32 advertising managers from across the United States is taken. The advertising managers are contacted by telephone and asked what their annual salary is. A similar random sample is taken of 34 auditing managers. The resulting salary data are listed in Table 10.1, along with the sample means, the population standard deviations, and the population variances.

TABLE 10.1

Wages for Advertising Managers and Auditing Managers ($1,000)

Advertising Managers		Auditing Managers	
74.256	64.276	69.962	67.160
96.234	74.194	55.052	37.386
89.807	65.360	57.828	59.505
93.261	73.904	63.362	72.790
103.030	54.270	37.194	71.351
74.195	59.045	99.198	58.653
75.932	68.508	61.254	63.508
80.742	71.115	73.065	43.649
39.672	67.574	48.036	63.369
45.652	59.621	60.053	59.676
93.083	62.483	66.359	54.449
63.384	69.319	61.261	46.394
57.791	35.394	77.136	71.804
65.145	86.741	66.035	72.401
96.767	57.351	54.335	56.470
77.242		42.494	67.814
67.056		83.849	71.492

$$n_1 = 32 \qquad n_2 = 34$$
$$\bar{x}_1 = 70.700 \qquad \bar{x}_2 = 62.187$$
$$\sigma_1 = 16.253 \qquad \sigma_2 = 12.900$$
$$\sigma_1^2 = 264.160 \qquad \sigma_2^2 = 166.410$$

FIGURE 10.3

Critical Values and Rejection Regions for the Wage Example

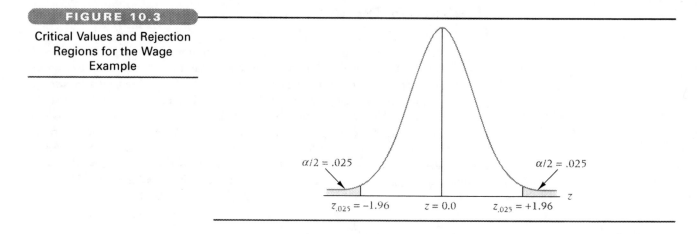

In this problem, the business analyst is testing whether there is a difference in the average wage of an advertising manager and an auditing manager; therefore the test is two tailed. If the business analyst had hypothesized that one was paid more than the other, the test would have been one tailed.

Suppose $\alpha = .05$. Because this test is a two-tailed test, each of the two rejection regions has an area of .025, leaving .475 of the area in the distribution between each critical value and the mean of the distribution. The associated critical table value for this area is $z_{.025} = \pm 1.96$. Figure 10.3 shows the critical table z value along with the rejection regions.

Formula 10.1 and the data in Table 10.1 yield a z value to complete the hypothesis test

$$z = \frac{(70.700 - 62.187) - (0)}{\sqrt{\dfrac{264.160}{32} + \dfrac{166.410}{34}}} = 2.35$$

The observed value of 2.35 is greater than the critical value obtained from the z table, 1.96. The business researcher rejects the null hypothesis and can say that there is a significant difference between the average annual wage of an advertising manager and the average annual wage of an auditing manager. The business researcher then examines the sample means (70.700 for advertising managers and 62.187 for auditing managers) and uses common sense to conclude that advertising managers earn more, on the average, than do auditing managers. Figure 10.4 shows the relationship between the observed z and $z_{\alpha/2}$.

FIGURE 10.4

Location of Observed z Value for the Wage Example

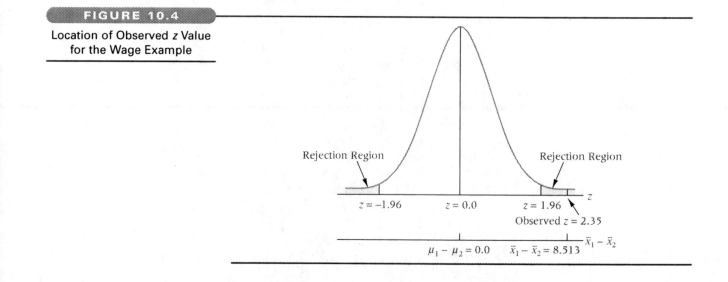

This conclusion could have been reached by using the *p*-value. Looking up the probability of $z \geq 2.35$ in the *z* distribution table in Appendix A.5 yields an area of $.5000 - .4906 = .0094$. This *p*-value (.0094) is less than $\alpha/2 = .025$. The decision is to reject the null hypothesis.

DEMONSTRATION PROBLEM 10.1

A sample of 87 professional working women showed that the average amount paid annually into a private pension fund per person was \$3,352. The population standard deviation is \$1,100. A sample of 76 professional working men showed that the average amount paid annually into a private pension fund per person was \$5,727, with a population standard deviation of \$1,700. A women's activist group wants to "prove" that women do not pay as much per year as men into private pension funds. If they use $\alpha = .001$ and these sample data, will they be able to reject a null hypothesis that women annually pay the same as or more than men into private pension funds? Use the eight-step hypothesis-testing process.

Solution

HYPOTHESIZE:

STEP 1. This test is one tailed. Because the women's activist group wants to prove that women pay less than men into private pension funds annually, the alternative hypothesis should be $\mu_w - \mu_m < 0$, and the null hypothesis is that women pay the same as or more than men, $\mu_w - \mu_m = 0$.

TEST:

STEP 2. The test statistic is

$$z = \frac{(\bar{x}_1 - \bar{x}_2) - (\mu_1 - \mu_2)}{\sqrt{\dfrac{\sigma_1^2}{n_1} + \dfrac{\sigma_2^2}{n_2}}}$$

STEP 3. Alpha has been specified as .001.

STEP 4. By using this value of alpha, a critical $z_{.001} = -3.08$ can be determined. The decision rule is to reject the null hypothesis if the observed value of the test statistic, *z*, is less than −3.08.

STEP 5. The sample data follow.

Women	Men
$\bar{x}_1 = \$3,352$	$\bar{x}_2 = \$5,727$
$\sigma_1 = \$1,100$	$\sigma_2 = \$1,700$
$n_1 = 87$	$n_2 = 76$

STEP 6. Solving for *z* gives

$$z = \frac{(3,352 - 5,727) - (0)}{\sqrt{\dfrac{1,100^2}{87} + \dfrac{1,700^2}{76}}} = \frac{-2,375}{227.9} = -10.42$$

ACTION:

STEP 7. The observed *z* value of −10.42 is deep in the rejection region, well past the table value of $z_c = -3.08$. Even with the small $\alpha = .001$, the null hypothesis is rejected.

BUSINESS IMPLICATIONS:

STEP 8. The evidence is substantial that women, on average, pay less than men into private pension funds annually. The following diagram displays these results.

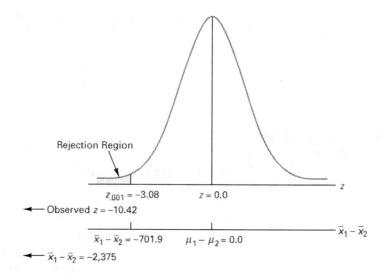

The probability of obtaining an observed z value of -10.42 by chance is virtually zero, because the value is beyond the limits of the z table. By the p-value, the null hypothesis is rejected because the probability is .0000, or less than $\alpha = .001$.

If this problem were worked by the critical value method, what critical value of the difference in the two means would have to be surpassed to reject the null hypothesis for a table z value of -3.08? The answer is

$$(\bar{x}_1 - \bar{x}_2)_c = (\mu_1 - \mu_2) - z\sqrt{\frac{\sigma_1^2}{n_1} + \frac{\sigma_2^2}{n_2}}$$

$$= 0 - 3.08(227.9) = -701.9$$

The difference in sample means would need to be at least 701.9 to reject the null hypothesis. The actual sample difference in this problem was -2375 (3352 − 5727), which is considerably larger than the critical value of difference. Thus, with the critical value method also, the null hypothesis is rejected.

Confidence Intervals

Sometimes being able to estimate the difference in the means of two populations is valuable. By how much do two populations differ in size or weight or age? By how much do two products differ in effectiveness? Do two different manufacturing or training methods produce different mean results? The answers to these questions are often difficult to obtain through census techniques. The alternative is to take a random sample from each of the two populations and study the difference in the sample means.

Algebraically, formula 10.1 can be manipulated to produce a formula for constructing confidence intervals for the difference in two population means.

CONFIDENCE INTERVAL TO ESTIMATE $\mu_1 - \mu_2$ (10.2)	$(\bar{x}_1 - \bar{x}_2) - z\sqrt{\dfrac{\sigma_1^2}{n_1} + \dfrac{\sigma_2^2}{n_2}} \leq \mu_1 - \mu_2 \leq (\bar{x}_1 - \bar{x}_2) + z\sqrt{\dfrac{\sigma_1^2}{n_1} + \dfrac{\sigma_2^2}{n_2}}$

Suppose a study is conducted to estimate the difference between middle-income shoppers and low-income shoppers in terms of the average amount saved on grocery bills per week by using coupons. Random samples of 60 middle-income shoppers and 80 low-income shoppers are taken, and their purchases are monitored for one week. The average amounts saved with coupons, as well as sample sizes and population standard deviations are in the table on the next page.

Middle-Income Shoppers	Low-Income Shoppers
$n_1 = 60$	$n_1 = 80$
$\bar{x}_1 = \$5.84$	$\bar{x}_2 = \$2.67$
$\sigma_1 = \$1.41$	$\sigma_2 = \$0.54$

This information can be used to construct a 98% confidence interval to estimate the difference between the mean amount saved with coupons by middle-income shoppers and the mean amount saved with coupons by low-income shoppers.

The z_c value associated with a 98% level of confidence is 2.33. This value, the data shown, and formula (10.2) can be used to determine the confidence interval.

$$(5.84 - 2.67) - 2.33\sqrt{\frac{1.41^2}{60} + \frac{0.54^2}{80}} \leq \mu_1 - \mu_2 \leq (5.84 - 2.67) + 2.33\sqrt{\frac{1.41^2}{60} + \frac{0.54^2}{80}}$$

$$3.17 - 0.45 \leq \mu_1 - \mu_2 \leq 3.17 + 0.45$$

$$2.72 \leq \mu_1 - \mu_2 \leq 3.62$$

There is a 98% level of confidence that the actual difference in the population mean coupon savings per week between middle-income and low-income shoppers is between $2.72 and $3.62. That is, the difference could be as little as $2.72 or as great as $3.62. The point estimate for the difference in mean savings is $3.17. Note that a zero difference in the population means of these two groups is unlikely, because zero is not in the 98% range.

DEMONSTRATION PROBLEM 10.2

A consumer test group wants to determine the difference in gasoline mileage of cars using regular unleaded gas and cars using premium unleaded gas. Researchers for the group divided a fleet of 100 cars of the same make in half and tested each car on one tank of gas. Fifty of the cars were filled with regular unleaded gas and 50 were filled with premium unleaded gas. The sample average for the regular gasoline group was 21.45 miles per gallon (mpg), and the sample average for the premium gasoline group was 24.60 mpg. Assume that the population standard deviation of the regular unleaded gas population is 3.46 mpg, and that the population standard deviation of the premium unleaded gas population is 2.99 mpg. Construct a 95% confidence interval to estimate the difference in the mean gas mileage between the cars using regular gasoline and the cars using premium gasoline.

Solution

The z value for a 95% confidence interval is 1.96. The other sample information follows.

Regular	Premium
$n_r = 50$	$n_p = 50$
$\bar{x}_r = 21.45$	$\bar{x}_p = 24.60$
$\sigma_r = 3.46$	$\sigma_p = 2.99$

Based on this information, the confidence interval is

$$(21.45 - 24.60) - 1.96\sqrt{\frac{3.46^2}{50} + \frac{2.99^2}{50}} \leq \mu_1 - \mu_2 \leq (21.45 - 24.60) + 1.96\sqrt{\frac{3.46^2}{50} + \frac{2.99^2}{50}}$$

$$-3.15 - 1.27 \leq \mu_1 - \mu_2 \leq -3.15 + 1.27$$

$$-4.42 \leq \mu_1 - \mu_2 \leq -1.88$$

We are 95% confident that the actual difference in mean gasoline mileage between the two types of gasoline is between −1.88 mpg and −4.42 mpg. The point estimate is −3.15 mpg.

z-Test: Two Sample for Means

	Ad Mgr	Aud Mgr
Mean	70.700	62.187
Known Variance	264.160	166.411
Observations	32	34
Hypothesized Mean Difference	0	
z	2.35	
P(Z<=z) one-tail	0.0094	
z Critical one-tail	1.64	
P(Z<=z) two-tail	0.0189	
z Critical two-tail	1.96	

Designating one group as group 1 and another group as group 2 is an arbitrary decision. If the two groups in Demonstration Problem 10.2 were reversed, the confidence interval would be the same, but the signs would be reversed and the inequalities would be switched. Thus the researcher must interpret the confidence interval in light of the sample information. For the confidence interval in Demonstration Problem 10.2, the population difference in mean mileage between regular and premium could be as much as -4.42 mpg. This result means that the premium gasoline could average 4.42 mpg more than regular gasoline. The other side of the interval shows that, on the basis of the sample information, the difference in favor of premium gasoline could be as little as 1.88 mpg.

If the confidence interval were being used to test the hypothesis that there is a difference in the average number of miles per gallon between regular and premium gasoline, the interval would tell us to reject the null hypothesis because the interval does *not* contain zero. When both ends of a confidence interval have the same sign, zero is not in the interval. In Demonstration Problem 10.2, the interval signs are both negative. We are 95% confident that the true difference in population means is negative. Hence, we are 95% confident that there is nonzero difference in means. For such a test, $\alpha = 1 - .95 = .05$. If the signs of the confidence interval for the difference of the sample means are different, the interval includes zero, and finding no significant difference in population means is possible.

Using the Computer to Test Hypotheses About the Difference in Two Population Means Using the z Test

Excel has the capability of testing hypotheses about two population means using a z test, but Minitab does not. Figure 10.5 shows Excel output for the advertising manager and auditing manager wage problem. For z tests, Excel requires knowledge of the population variances. The standard output includes the sample means and population variances, the sample sizes, the hypothesized mean difference (which here, as in most cases, is zero), the observed z value, and the p-values and critical table z values for both a one-tailed and a two-tailed test. Note that the p-value for this two-tailed test is .0189, which is less than $\alpha = .05$ and thus indicates that the decision should be to reject the null hypothesis.

10.1 PROBLEMS

10.1 a. Test the following hypotheses of the difference in population means by using the following data ($\alpha = .10$) and the eight-step process.

$$H_0: \mu_1 - \mu_2 = 0 \qquad H_a: \mu_1 - \mu_2 < 0$$

Sample 1	Sample 2
$\bar{x}_1 = 51.3$	$\bar{x}_2 = 53.2$
$\sigma_1^2 = 52$	$\sigma_2^2 = 60$
$n_1 = 31$	$n_2 = 32$

b. Use the critical value method to find the critical difference in the mean values required to reject the null hypothesis.

c. What is the p-value for this problem?

10.2 Use the following sample information to construct a 90% confidence interval for the difference in the two population means.

Sample 1	Sample 2
$n_1 = 32$	$n_2 = 31$
$\bar{x}_1 = 70.4$	$\bar{x}_2 = 68.7$
$\sigma_1 = 5.76$	$\sigma_2 = 6.1$

10.3 Examine the following data. Assume the variances for the two populations are 22.74 and 26.65 respectively.

a. Use the data to test the following hypotheses ($\alpha = .02$).

$$H_0: \mu_1 - \mu_2 = 0 \qquad H_a: \mu_1 - \mu_2 \neq 0$$

Sample 1							Sample 2					
90	88	80	88	83	94		78	85	82	81	75	76
88	87	91	81	83	88		90	80	76	83	88	77
81	84	84	87	87	93		77	75	79	86	90	75
88	90	91	88	84	83		82	83	88	80	80	74
89	95	97	95	93	97		80	90	74	89	84	79

b. Construct a 98% confidence interval to estimate the difference in population means using these data. How does your result validate the decision you reached in part (a)?

10.4 The Trade Show Bureau conducted a survey to determine why people go to trade shows. The respondents were asked to rate a series of reasons on a scale from 1 to 5, with 1 representing little importance and 5 representing great importance. One of the reasons suggested was general curiosity. The following responses for 50 people from the computers/electronics industry and 50 people from the food/beverage industry were recorded for general curiosity. Use these data and $\alpha = .01$ to determine whether there is a significant difference between people in these two industries on this question. Assume the variance for the computer/electronics population is 1.0188 and the variance for the food/beverage population is 0.9180.

Computers/Electronics					Food/Beverage				
1	2	1	3	2	3	3	2	4	3
0	3	3	2	1	4	5	2	4	3
3	3	1	2	2	3	2	3	2	3
3	2	2	2	2	4	3	3	3	3
1	2	3	2	1	2	4	2	3	3
1	1	3	3	2	2	4	4	4	4
2	1	4	1	4	3	5	3	3	2
2	3	0	1	0	2	0	2	2	5
3	3	2	2	3	4	3	3	2	3
2	1	0	2	3	4	3	3	3	2

10.5 Suppose you own a plumbing repair business and employ 15 plumbers. You are interested in estimating the difference in the average number of calls completed per day between two of the plumbers. A random sample of 40 days of plumber A's work results in a sample average of 5.3 calls, with a population variance of 1.99. A random sample of 37 days of plumber B's work results in a sample mean of 6.5 calls, with a population variance of 2.36. Use this information and a 95% level of confidence to estimate the difference in population mean daily efforts between plumber A and plumber B. Interpret the results. Is it possible that, for these populations of days, the average number of calls completed between plumber A and plumber B do not differ?

10.6 The Bureau of Labor Statistics shows that the average insurance cost to a company per employee per hour is $1.84 for managers and $1.99 for professional specialty workers. Suppose these figures were obtained from 14 managers and 15 professional specialty workers and that their respective population standard deviations are $0.38 and $0.51. Assume that such insurance costs are normally distributed in the population.

a. Calculate a 98% confidence interval to estimate the difference in the mean hourly company expenditures for insurance for these two groups. What is the value of the point estimate?

b. Test to determine whether there is a significant difference in the hourly rates employers pay for insurance between managers and professional specialty workers. Use a 2% level of significance.

10.7 A company's auditor believes the per diem cost in Nashville, Tennessee, rose significantly between 2001 and 2011. To test this belief, the auditor samples 51 business trips from the company's records for 2001; the sample average was $190 per day, with a population standard deviation of $18.50. The auditor selects a second random sample of 47 business trips from the company's records for 2011; the sample average was $198 per day, with a population standard deviation of $15.60. If he uses a risk of committing a Type I error of .01, does the auditor find that the per diem average expense in Nashville has gone up significantly?

10.8 Suppose a market analyst wants to determine the difference in the average price of a gallon of whole milk in Seattle and Atlanta. To do so, he takes a telephone survey of 21 randomly selected consumers in Seattle who have purchased a gallon of milk and asks how much they paid for it. The analyst undertakes a similar survey in Atlanta with 18 respondents. Assume the population variance for Seattle is 0.03, the population variance for Atlanta is 0.015, and that the price of milk is normally distributed. Using the resulting sample information that follows,

a. Compute a 99% confidence interval to estimate the difference in the mean price of a gallon of milk between the two cities.

b. Using a 1% level of significance, test to determine if there is a significant difference in the price of a gallon of milk between the two cities.

Seattle			Atlanta		
$2.55	$2.36	$2.43	$2.25	$2.40	$2.39
2.67	2.54	2.43	2.30	2.33	2.40
2.50	2.54	2.38	2.49	2.29	2.23
2.61	2.80	2.49	2.41	2.48	2.29
2.43	2.61	2.57	2.39	2.59	2.53
2.36	2.56	2.71	2.26	2.38	2.45
2.50	2.64	2.27			

10.9 Employee suggestions can provide useful and insightful ideas for management. Some companies solicit and receive employee suggestions more than others, and company culture influences the use of employee suggestions. Suppose a study is conducted to determine whether there is a significant difference in mean number of suggestions a month per employee between the Canon Corporation and the Pioneer Electronic Corporation. The study shows that the average number of suggestions per month is 1.3 at Canon and 1.0 at Pioneer. Suppose these figures were obtained from random samples of 36 and 45 employees, respectively. If the population standard deviations of suggestions per employee are 0.7 and 0.4 for Canon and Pioneer, respectively, is there a significant difference in the population means? Use $\alpha = .05$.

10.10 Two processes in a manufacturing line are performed manually: operation A and operation B. A random sample of 50 different assemblies using operation A shows that the sample average time per assembly is 8.05 minutes, with a population standard deviation of 1.36 minutes. A random sample of 38 different assemblies using operation B shows that the sample average time per assembly is 7.26 minutes, with a population standard deviation of 1.06 minutes. For $\alpha = .10$, is there enough evidence in these samples to declare that operation A takes significantly longer to perform than operation B?

10.2 HYPOTHESIS TESTING AND CONFIDENCE INTERVALS ABOUT THE DIFFERENCE IN TWO MEANS: INDEPENDENT SAMPLES AND POPULATION VARIANCES UNKNOWN

The techniques presented in Section 10.1 are for use whenever the population variances are known. On many occasions, statisticians test hypotheses or construct confidence intervals about the difference in two population means and the population variances are not known. If the population variances are not known, the *z* methodology is not appropriate. This section presents methodology for handling the situation when the population variances are unknown.

Hypothesis Testing

The hypothesis test presented in this section is a test that compares the means of two samples to determine whether there is a difference in the two population means from which the samples come. This technique is used whenever the population variances are unknown (and hence the sample variances must be used) and the samples are independent (not related in any way). *An assumption underlying this technique is that the measurement or characteristic being studied is normally distributed for both populations.* In Section 10.1, the difference in large sample means was analyzed by formula 10.1:

$$z = \frac{(\bar{x}_1 - \bar{x}_2) - (\mu_1 - \mu_2)}{\sqrt{\dfrac{\sigma_1^2}{n_1} + \dfrac{\sigma_2^2}{n_2}}}$$

If $\sigma_1^2 = \sigma_2^2$, formula 10.1 algebraically reduces to

$$z = \frac{(\bar{x}_1 - \bar{x}_2) - (\mu_1 - \mu_2)}{\sigma\sqrt{\dfrac{1}{n_1} + \dfrac{1}{n_2}}}$$

If σ is unknown, it can be estimated by *pooling* the two sample variances and computing a pooled sample standard deviation.

$$\sigma \approx s_p = \sqrt{\frac{s_1^2(n_1 - 1) + s_2^2(n_2 - 1)}{n_1 + n_2 - 2}}$$

s_p^2 is the weighted average of the two sample variances, s_1^2 and s_2^2. Substituting this expression for σ and changing *z* to *t* produces a formula to test the difference in means.

t FORMULA TO TEST THE DIFFERENCE IN MEANS ASSUMING σ_1^2, σ_2^2, ARE EQUAL (10.3)	$$t = \frac{(\bar{x}_1 - \bar{x}_2) - (\mu_1 - \mu_2)}{\sqrt{\dfrac{s_1^2(n_1 - 1) + s_2^2(n_2 - 1)}{n_1 + n_2 - 2}}\sqrt{\dfrac{1}{n_1} + \dfrac{1}{n_2}}}$$ $$\mathrm{df} = n_1 + n_2 - 2$$

Formula 10.3 is constructed by assuming that the two population variances, σ_1^2 and σ_2^2, are equal. Thus, when using formula 10.3 to test hypotheses about the difference in two means for small independent samples when the population variances are unknown, we must assume that the two samples come from populations in which the variances are essentially equal.

At the Hernandez Manufacturing Company, an application of this test arises. New employees are expected to attend a three-day seminar to learn about the company. At the end of the seminar, they are tested to measure their knowledge about the company. The traditional training method has been lecture and a question-and-answer session. Management decided to experiment with a different training procedure, which processes new employees in two days by using DVDs and having no question-and-answer session. If this procedure works, it could save

TABLE 10.2	Training Method A					Training Method B			
Test Scores for New Employees After Training	56	50	52	44	52	59	54	55	65
	47	47	53	45	48	52	57	64	53
	42	51	42	43	44	53	56	53	57

the company thousands of dollars over a period of several years. However, there is some concern about the effectiveness of the two-day method, and company managers would like to know whether there is any difference in the effectiveness of the two training methods.

To test the difference in the two methods, the managers randomly select one group of 15 newly hired employees to take the three-day seminar (method A) and a second group of 12 new employees for the two-day DVD method (method B). Table 10.2 shows the test scores of the two groups. Using $\alpha = .05$, the managers want to determine whether there is a significant difference in the mean scores of the two groups. They assume that the scores for this test are normally distributed and that the population variances are approximately equal.

HYPOTHESIZE:

STEP 1. The hypotheses for this test follow.

$$H_0: \mu_1 - \mu_2 = 0$$
$$H_a: \mu_1 - \mu_2 \neq 0$$

TEST:

STEP 2. The statistical test to be used is formula 10.3.

STEP 3. The value of alpha is .05.

STEP 4. Because the hypotheses are $=$ and $\neq$, this test is two tailed. The degrees of freedom are 25 ($15 + 12 - 2 = 25$) and alpha is .05. The t table requires an alpha value for one tail only, and, because it is a two-tailed test, alpha is split from .05 to .025 to obtain the table t value: $t_{.025,25} = \pm 2.060$.

The null hypothesis will be rejected if the observed t value is less than -2.060 or greater than $+2.060$.

STEP 5. The sample data are given in Table 10.2. From these data, we can calculate the sample statistics. The sample means and variances follow.

Method A	Method B
$\bar{x}_1 = 47.73$	$\bar{x}_2 = 56.50$
$s_1^2 = 19.495$	$s_2^2 = 18.273$
$n_1 = 15$	$n_2 = 12$

Note: If the equal variances assumption can not be met the following formula should be used.

t FORMULA TO TEST THE DIFFERENCE IN MEANS	$t = \dfrac{(\bar{x}_1 - \bar{x}_2) - (\mu_1 - \mu_2)}{\sqrt{\dfrac{s_1^2}{n_1} + \dfrac{s_2^2}{n_2}}}$ $\qquad$ $df = \dfrac{\left[\dfrac{s_1^2}{n_1} + \dfrac{s_2^2}{n_2}\right]^2}{\dfrac{\left(\dfrac{s_1^2}{n_1}\right)^2}{n_1 - 1} + \dfrac{\left(\dfrac{s_2^2}{n_2}\right)^2}{n_2 - 1}}$

Because this formula requires a more complex degrees-of-freedom component, it may be unattractive to some users. Many statistical computer software packages offer the user a choice of the "pooled" formula or the "unpooled" formula. The "pooled" formula in the computer packages is Formula 10.3, in which equal population variances are assumed. Excel refers to formula 10.3 as a t-Test: Two-Sample Assuming Equal Variances. The formula shown just above is the "unpooled" formula used when population variances cannot be assumed to be equal. Excel refers to this as a t-Test: Two-Sample Assuming Unequal Variances. Again, in each of these formulas, the populations from which the two samples are drawn are assumed to be normally distributed for the phenomenon being measured.

FIGURE 10.6

t Values for the Training
Methods Example

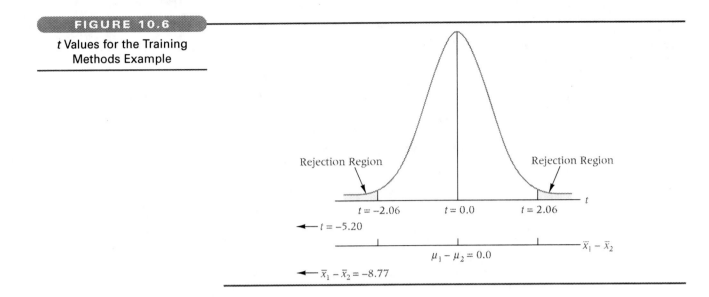

STEP **6.** The observed value of *t* is

$$t = \frac{(47.73 - 56.50) - (0)}{\sqrt{\dfrac{(19.495)(14) + (18.273)(11)}{(15 + 12 - 2)}}\sqrt{\dfrac{1}{15} + \dfrac{1}{12}}} = -5.20$$

ACTION:
STEP **7.** Because the observed value, $t = -5.20$, is less than the lower critical table value, $t = -2.06$, the observed value of *t* is in the rejection region. The null hypothesis is rejected. There is a significant difference in the mean scores of the two tests.

BUSINESS IMPLICATIONS:
STEP **8.** Figure 10.6 shows the critical areas and the observed *t* value. Note that the computed *t* value is −5.20, which is enough to cause the managers of the Hernandez Manufacturing Company to reject the null hypothesis. Their conclusion is that there is a significant difference in the effectiveness of the training methods. Upon examining the sample means, they realize that method B (the two-day DVD method) actually produced an average score that was more than eight points higher than that for the group trained with method A. Given that training method B scores are significantly higher and the fact that the seminar is a day shorter than method A (thereby saving both time and money), it makes business sense to adopt method B as the standard training method.

In a test of this sort, which group is group 1 and which is group 2 is an arbitrary decision. If the two samples had been designated in reverse, the observed *t* value would have been $t = +5.20$ (same magnitude but different sign), and the decision would have been the same.

Using the Computer to Test Hypotheses and Construct Confidence Intervals about the Difference in Two Population Means Using the *t* Test

Both Excel and Minitab have the capability of analyzing *t* tests for the difference in two means. The two computer packages yield similar output. Figure 10.7 contains Excel and Minitab output for the Hernandez Manufacturing Company training methods example. Notice that both outputs contain the same sample means, the degrees of freedom ($df = 25$), the observed *t* value −5.20 and the *p*-value (.000022 on Excel as two-tailed *p* and .000 on Minitab). This *p*-value can be compared directly with $\alpha = .05$ for decision-making purposes (reject the null hypothesis).

FIGURE 10.7

Excel and Minitab Output for
the Training Methods Example

Excel Output

t-Test: Two-Sample Assuming Equal Variances

	Method A	Method B
Mean	47.73	56.50
Variance	19.495	18.273
Observations	15	12
Pooled Variance	18.957	
Hypothesized Mean Difference	0	
df	25	
t Stat	−5.20	
P(T<=t) one-tail	0.000011	
t Critical one-tail	1.71	
P(T<=t) two-tail	0.000022	
t Critical two-tail	2.06	

Minitab Output
Two-Sample T-Test and CI: Method A, Method B

Two-sample T for Method A vs Method B

```
           N   Mean   StDev   SE Mean
Method A   15  47.73  4.42    1.1
Method B   12  56.50  4.27    1.2
```

Difference = mu (Method A) − mu (Method B)

Estimate for difference: −8.77

95% CI for difference: (−12.24, −5.29)

T-Test of difference = 0 (vs not =): T-Value = −5.20 P-Value = 0.000 DF = 25

Both use Pooled StDev = 4.3540

Each package offers other information. Excel displays the sample variances whereas Minitab displays sample standard deviations. Excel displays the pooled variance whereas Minitab displays the pooled standard deviation. Excel prints out *p*-values for both a one-tailed test and a two-tailed test, and the user must select the appropriate value for his or her test. Excel also prints out the critical *t* values for both one- and two-tailed tests. Notice that the critical *t* value for a two-tailed test (2.06) is the same as the critical *t* value obtained by using the *t* table (±2.060). Minitab yields the standard errors of the mean for each sample and the 95% confidence interval. Minitab uses the same command for hypothesis testing and confidence interval estimation for the two-sample case. For this reason, Minitab output for this type of problem always contains both the hypothesis-testing and confidence interval results.

**DEMONSTRATION
PROBLEM 10.3**

**Demonstration
Problem**

Is there a difference in the way Chinese cultural values affect the purchasing strategies of industrial buyers in Taiwan and mainland China? A study by researchers at the National Chiao-Tung University in Taiwan attempted to determine whether there is a significant difference in the purchasing strategies of industrial buyers between Taiwan and mainland China based on the cultural dimension labeled "integration." Integration is being in harmony with one's self, family, and associates. For the study, 46 Taiwanese buyers and 26 mainland Chinese buyers were contacted and interviewed. Buyers were asked to respond to 35 items using a 9-point scale with possible answers ranging from no importance (1) to extreme importance (9). The resulting statistics for the two groups are shown in step 5. Using $\alpha = .01$, test to determine whether there is a significant difference between buyers in Taiwan and buyers in mainland China on integration. Assume that integration scores are normally distributed in the population.

Solution

HYPOTHESIZE:

STEP 1. If a two-tailed test is undertaken, the hypotheses and the table t value are as follows.

$$H_0: \mu_1 - \mu_2 = 0$$
$$H_a: \mu_1 - \mu_2 \neq 0$$

TEST:

STEP 2. The appropriate statistical test is formula 10.3.

STEP 3. The value of alpha is .01.

STEP 4. The sample sizes are 46 and 26. Thus, there are 70 degrees of freedom. With this figure and $\alpha/2 = .005$, critical table t values can be determined.

$$t_{.005,70} = \pm 2.648$$

STEP 5. The sample data follow.

Integration

Taiwanese Buyers	Mainland Chinese Buyers
$n_1 = 46$	$n_2 = 26$
$\bar{x}_1 = 5.42$	$\bar{x}_2 = 5.04$
$s_1^2 = (.58)^2 = .3346$	$s_2^2 = (.49)^2 = .2401$
$df = n_1 + n_2 - 2 = 46 + 26 - 2 = 70$	

STEP 6. The observed t value is

$$t = \frac{(5.42 - 5.04) - (0)}{\sqrt{\dfrac{(.3364)(45) + (.2401)(25)}{46 + 26 - 2}} \sqrt{\dfrac{1}{46} + \dfrac{1}{26}}} = 2.82$$

ACTION:

STEP 7. Because the observed value of $t = 2.82$ is greater than the critical table value of $t = 2.648$, the decision is to reject the null hypothesis.

BUSINESS IMPLICATIONS:

STEP 8. The Taiwan industrial buyers scored significantly higher than the mainland China industrial buyers on integration. Managers should keep in mind in dealing with Taiwanese buyers that they may be more likely to place worth on personal virtue and social hierarchy than do the mainland Chinese buyers.

The following graph shows the critical t values, the rejection regions, the observed t value, and the difference in the raw means.

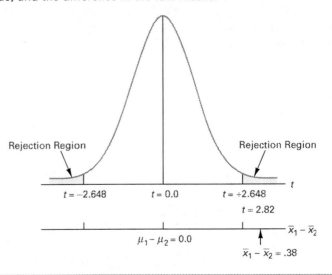

Confidence Intervals

Confidence interval formulas can be derived to estimate the difference in the population means for independent samples when the population variances are unknown. The focus in this section is only on confidence intervals when approximately equal population variances and normally distributed populations can be assumed.

CONFIDENCE INTERVAL TO ESTIMATE $\mu_1 - \mu_2$ ASSUMING THE POPULATION VARIANCES ARE UNKNOWN AND EQUAL (10.4)	$$(\bar{x}_1 - \bar{x}_2) - t\sqrt{\frac{s_1^2(n_1 - 1) + s_2^2(n_2 - 1)}{n_1 + n_2 - 2}}\sqrt{\frac{1}{n_1} + \frac{1}{n_2}} \le \mu_1 - \mu_2 \le$$ $$(\bar{x}_1 - \bar{x}_2) + t\sqrt{\frac{s_1^2(n_1 - 1) + s_2^2(n_2 - 1)}{n_1 + n_2 - 2}}\sqrt{\frac{1}{n_1} + \frac{1}{n_2}}$$ $$df = n_1 + n_2 - 2$$

TABLE 10.3

Conscientiousness Data on Phone Survey Respondents and Average Americans

Phone Survey Respondents	Average Americans
35.38	35.03
37.06	33.90
37.74	34.56
36.97	36.24
37.84	34.59
37.50	34.95
40.75	33.30
35.31	34.73
35.30	34.79
	37.83
$n_1 = 9$	$n_2 = 10$
$\bar{x}_1 = 37.09$	$\bar{x}_2 = 34.99$
$s_1 = 1.727$	$s_2 = 1.253$
$df = 9 + 10 - 2 = 17$	

One group of researchers set out to determine whether there is a difference between "average Americans" and those who are "phone survey respondents."* Their study was based on a well-known personality survey that attempted to assess the personality profile of both average Americans and phone survey respondents. Suppose they sampled nine phone survey respondents and 10 average Americans in this survey and obtained the results on one personality factor, conscientiousness, which are displayed in Table 10.3. Assume that conscientiousness scores are normally distributed in the population.

The table t value for a 99% level of confidence and 17 degrees of freedom is $t_{.005,17} = 2.898$. The confidence interval is

$$(37.09 - 34.99) \pm 2.898\sqrt{\frac{(1.727)^2(8) + (1.253)^2(9)}{9 + 10 - 2}}\sqrt{\frac{1}{9} + \frac{1}{10}}$$

$$2.10 \pm 1.99$$

$$0.11 \le \mu_1 - \mu_2 \le 4.09$$

The researchers are 99% confident that the true difference in population mean personality scores for conscientiousness between phone survey respondents and average Americans is between .11 and 4.09. Zero is not in this interval, so they can conclude that there is a significant difference in the average scores of the two groups. Higher scores indicate more conscientiousness. Therefore, it is possible to conclude from Table 10.3 and this

FIGURE 10.8

Minitab Output for the Phone Survey Respondent and Average American Example

Two-Sample T-Test and CI: Phone Survey Respondent, Average American

```
Two-Sample T for Phone Survey Respondent vs Average American

                            N    Mean   StDev   SE Mean
Phone Survey Respondent     9    37.09   1.73    0.58
Average American           10    34.99   1.25    0.40


Difference = mu (Phone Survey Respondent) - mu (Average American)
Estimate for difference: 2.102
99% CI for difference: (0.112, 4.093)
T-Test of difference = 0 (vs not =): T-Value = 3.06
P-Value = 0.007 DF = 17
Both use Pooled StDev = 1.4949
```

*Source: Data adapted from David Whitlark and Michael Geurts, "Phone Surveys: How Well Do Respondents Represent Average Americans?" *Marketing Research* (Fall 1998), pp. 13–17. Note that the results on this portion of the actual study are about the same as those shown here except that in the actual study the sample sizes were in the 500–600 range.

confidence interval that phone survey respondents are significantly more conscientious than average Americans. These results indicate that researchers should be careful in using phone survey results to reach conclusions about average Americans.

Figure 10.8 contains Minitab output for this problem. Note that the Minitab output includes both the confidence interval (.112 to 4.093) and the observed *t* value (3.06) for hypothesis testing. Because the *p*-value is .007, which is less than .01, the Minitab hypothesis-testing information validates the conclusion reached that there is a significant difference in the scores of the two groups.

DEMONSTRATION PROBLEM 10.4

A coffee manufacturer is interested in estimating the difference in the average daily coffee consumption of regular-coffee drinkers and decaffeinated-coffee drinkers. Its researcher randomly selects 13 regular-coffee drinkers and asks how many cups of coffee per day they drink. He randomly locates 15 decaffeinated-coffee drinkers and asks how many cups of coffee per day they drink. The average for the regular-coffee drinkers is 4.35 cups, with a standard deviation of 1.20 cups. The average for the decaffeinated-coffee drinkers is 6.84 cups, with a standard deviation of 1.42 cups. The researcher assumes, for each population, that the daily consumption is normally distributed, and he constructs a 95% confidence interval to estimate the difference in the averages of the two populations.

Solution

The table *t* value for this problem is $t_{.025,26} = 2.056$. The confidence interval estimate is

$$(4.35 - 6.84) \pm 2.056 \sqrt{\frac{(1.20)^2(12) + (1.42)^2(14)}{13 + 15 - 2}} \sqrt{\frac{1}{13} + \frac{1}{15}}$$

$$-2.49 \pm 1.03$$

$$-3.52 \le \mu_1 - \mu_2 \le -1.46$$

The researcher is 95% confident that the difference in population average daily consumption of cups of coffee between regular- and decaffeinated-coffee drinkers is between 1.46 cups and 3.52 cups. The point estimate for the difference in population means is 2.49 cups, with an error of 1.03 cups.

THINKING CRITICALLY ABOUT STATISTICS IN BUSINESS TODAY

Beverage Consumption: America vs. Europe

How does America compare to Europe in the consumption of beverages? In many categories, including coffee, milk, juice, bottled water, and liquor, consumption is similar. However, according to statistics from the Wine Institute, Americans drink nearly five times as much soda as do Europeans and almost twice as much beer. On the other hand, Europeans drink more than twice as much tea (hot or iced), more than three times as much wine, and over four times as much tap water as do Americans. Statistics show that the average American consumes forty-eight 12 oz. containers of carbonated soda per month compared to only ten for Europeans. On the other hand, Europeans consume an average of sixteen 4 oz. containers of wine per month compared to an average of only five for Americans. According to the study, Americans have a slight edge over Europeans in the consumption of milk, with Americans drinking an average of seventeen 12 oz. containers of milk per month compared to

fifteen for Europeans. This study contained comparisons between Americans and Europeans on 11 different beverages.

Things to Ponder

1. Suppose the figures given in this feature are actually only sample data. Would any of the techniques presented in this chapter be appropriate for conducting hypothesis tests to determine if there is a significant difference between Americans and Europeans on the consumption of various beverages? If so, what additional information would be needed?

2. Can you think of some reasons why Americans consume more carbonated soda pop and beer than Europeans, but less wine, hot or iced tea, or tap water? Do you think that these outcomes may change in time? Why or why not?

Source: "Wine and Other Beverage Consumption in America," http://www.beekmanwine.com/prevtopat.htm, 2011.

10.2 PROBLEMS

10.11 Use the data given and the eight-step process to test the following hypotheses.

$$H_0: \mu_1 - \mu_2 = 0 \qquad H_a: \mu_1 - \mu_2 < 0$$

Sample 1	Sample 2
$n_1 = 8$	$n_2 = 11$
$\bar{x}_1 = 24.56$	$\bar{x}_2 = 26.42$
$s_1^2 = 12.4$	$s_2^2 = 15.8$

Use a 1% level of significance, and assume that x is normally distributed.

10.12 a. Use the following data and $\alpha = .10$ to test the stated hypotheses. Assume x is normally distributed in the populations and the variances of the populations are approximately equal.

$$H_0: \mu_1 - \mu_2 = 0 \qquad H_a: \mu_1 - \mu_2 \neq 0$$

Sample 1	Sample 2
$n_1 = 20$	$n_2 = 20$
$\bar{x}_1 = 118$	$\bar{x}_2 = 113$
$s_1 = 23.9$	$s_2 = 21.6$

b. Use these data to construct a 90% confidence interval to estimate $\mu_1 - \mu_2$.

10.13 Suppose that for years the mean of population 1 has been accepted to be the same as the mean of population 2, but that now population 1 is believed to have a greater mean than population 2. Letting $\alpha = .05$ and assuming the populations have equal variances and x is approximately normally distributed, use the following data to test this belief.

Sample 1		Sample 2	
43.6	45.7	40.1	36.4
44.0	49.1	42.2	42.3
45.2	45.6	43.1	38.8
40.8	46.5	37.5	43.3
48.3	45.0	41.0	40.2

10.14 a. Suppose you want to determine whether the average values for populations 1 and 2 are different, and you randomly gather the following data.

Sample 1						Sample 2					
2	10	7	8	2	5	10	12	8	7	9	11
9	1	8	0	2	8	9	8	9	10	11	10
11	2	4	5	3	9	11	10	7	8	10	10

Test your conjecture, using a probability of committing a Type I error of .01. Assume the population variances are the same and x is normally distributed in the populations.

b. Use these data to construct a 98% confidence interval for the difference in the two population means.

10.15 Suppose a Realtor is interested in comparing the asking prices of midrange homes in Peoria, Illinois, and Evansville, Indiana. The Realtor conducts a small telephone survey in the two cities, asking the prices of midrange homes. A random sample of 21 listings in Peoria resulted in a sample average price of $116,900, with a standard deviation of $2,300. A random sample of 26 listings in Evansville resulted in a sample average price of $114,000, with a standard deviation of $1,750. The Realtor assumes prices of midrange homes are normally distributed and the variance in prices in the two cities is about the same.

    a. What would he obtain for a 90% confidence interval for the difference in mean prices of midrange homes between Peoria and Evansville?

    b. Test whether there is any difference in the mean prices of midrange homes of the two cities for $\alpha = .10$.

10.16 According to an Experiential Education Survey published at JobWeb.com, the average hourly wage of a college student working as a co-op is $15.64 an hour and the average hourly wage of an intern is $15.44. Assume that such wages are normally distributed in the population and that the population variances are equal. Suppose these figures were actually obtained from the data below.

    a. Use these data and $\alpha = .10$ to test to determine if there is a significant difference in the mean hourly wage of a college co-op student and the mean hourly wage of an intern.

    b. Using these same data, construct a 90% confidence interval to estimate the difference in the population mean hourly wages of co-ops and interns.

Co-op Students	Interns
$15.34	$15.10
14.75	14.45
15.88	16.21
16.92	14.91
16.84	13.80
17.37	16.02
14.05	16.25
15.41	15.89
16.74	13.99
14.55	16.48
15.25	15.75
14.64	16.42

10.17 Based on an indication that mean daily car rental rates may be higher for Boston than for Dallas, a survey of eight car rental companies in Boston is taken and the sample mean car rental rate is $47, with a standard deviation of $3. Further, suppose a survey of nine car rental companies in Dallas results in a sample mean of $44 and a standard deviation of $3. Use $\alpha = .05$ to test to determine whether the average daily car rental rates in Boston are significantly higher than those in Dallas. Assume car rental rates are normally distributed and the population variances are equal.

10.18 What is the difference in average daily hotel room rates between Minneapolis and New Orleans? Suppose we want to estimate this difference by taking hotel rate samples from each city and using a 98% confidence level. The data for such a study follow. Use these data to produce a point estimate for the mean difference in the hotel rates for the two cities. Assume the population variances are approximately equal and hotel rates in any given city are normally distributed.

Minneapolis	New Orleans
$n_M = 22$	$n_{NO} = 20$
$\bar{x}_M = \$112$	$\bar{x}_{NO} = \$122$
$s_M = \$11$	$s_{NO} = \$12$

10.19 A study was made to compare the costs of supporting a family of four Americans for a year in different foreign cities. The lifestyle of living in the United States on an annual income of $75,000 was the standard against which living in foreign cities was compared. A comparable living standard in Toronto and Mexico City was attained for about $64,000. Suppose an executive wants to determine whether there is any difference in the average annual cost of supporting her family of four in the manner to which they are accustomed between Toronto and Mexico City. She uses the following data, randomly gathered from 11 families in each city, and an alpha of .01 to test this difference. She assumes the annual cost is normally distributed and the population variances are equal. What does the executive find?

Toronto	Mexico City
$69,000	$65,000
64,500	64,000
67,500	66,000
64,500	64,900
66,700	62,000
68,000	60,500
65,000	62,500
69,000	63,000
71,000	64,500
68,500	63,500
67,500	62,400

Use the data from the previous table to construct a 95% confidence interval to estimate the difference in average annual costs between the two cities.

10.20 Some studies have shown that in the United States, men spend more than women buying gifts and cards on Valentine's Day. Suppose a researcher wants to test this hypothesis by randomly sampling nine men and 10 women with comparable demographic characteristics from various large cities across the United States to be in a study. Each study participant is asked to keep a log beginning one month before Valentine's Day and record all purchases made for Valentine's Day during that one-month period. The resulting data are shown below. Use these data and a 1% level of significance to test to determine if, on average, men actually do spend significantly more than women on Valentine's Day. Assume that such spending is normally distributed in the population and that the population variances are equal.

Men	Women
$107.48	$125.98
143.61	45.53
90.19	56.35
125.53	80.62
70.79	46.37
83.00	44.34
129.63	75.21
154.22	68.48
93.80	85.84
	126.11

10.3 STATISTICAL INFERENCES FOR TWO RELATED POPULATIONS

In the preceding section, hypotheses were tested and confidence intervals constructed about the difference in two population means when the samples are independent. In this section, a method is presented to analyze **dependent samples** or related samples. Some researchers refer to this test as the **matched-pairs** test. Others call it the *t test for related measures* or the *correlated t test*.

What are some types of situations in which the two samples being studied are related or dependent? Let's begin with the before-and-after study. Sometimes as an experimental control mechanism, the same person or object is measured both before and after a treatment. Certainly, the after measurement is *not* independent of the before measurement because the measurements are taken on the same person or object in both cases. Table 10.4 gives data from a hypothetical study in which people were asked to rate a company before and after one week of viewing a 15-minute DVD of the company twice a day. The before scores are one sample and the after scores are a second sample, but each pair of scores is related because the two measurements apply to the same person. The before scores and the after scores are not likely to vary from each other as much as scores gathered from independent samples because individuals bring their biases about businesses and the company to the study. These individual biases affect both the before scores and the after scores in the same way because each pair of scores is measured on the same person.

Other examples of related measures samples include studies in which twins, siblings, or spouses are matched and placed in two different groups. For example, a fashion merchandiser might be interested in comparing men's and women's perceptions of women's clothing. If the men and women selected for the study are spouses or siblings, a built-in relatedness to the measurements of the two groups in the study is likely. Their scores are more apt to be alike or related than those of randomly chosen independent groups of men and women because of similar backgrounds or tastes.

TABLE 10.4

Rating of a Company
(on a Scale from 0 to 50)

Individual	Before	After
1	32	39
2	11	15
3	21	35
4	17	13
5	30	41
6	38	39
7	14	22

Hypothesis Testing

To ensure the use of the proper hypothesis-testing techniques, the researcher must determine whether the two samples being studied are dependent or independent. The approach to analyzing two *related* samples is different from the techniques used to analyze independent samples. Use of the techniques in Section 10.2 to analyze related group data can result in a loss of power and an increase in Type II errors.

The matched-pairs test for related samples requires that the two samples be the same size and that the individual related scores be matched. Formula 10.5 is used to test hypotheses about dependent populations.

t FORMULA TO TEST THE DIFFERENCE IN TWO DEPENDENT POPULATIONS (10.5)	$$t = \frac{\bar{d} - D}{\frac{s_d}{\sqrt{n}}}$$ $$df = n - 1$$

where

n = number of pairs
d = sample difference in pairs
D = mean population difference
s_d = standard deviation of sample difference
$\bar{d}$ = mean sample difference

This *t* test for dependent measures uses the sample difference, *d*, between individual matched sample values as the basic measurement of analysis instead of individual sample values. Analysis of the *d* values effectively converts the problem from a two-sample problem to a single sample of differences, which is an adaptation of the single-sample means formula. This test utilizes the sample mean of differences, and the standard deviation of differences, s_d, which can be computed by using formulas 10.6 and 10.7.

FORMULAS FOR $\bar{d}$ AND s_d
(10.6 AND 10.7)

$$\bar{d} = \frac{\Sigma d}{n}$$

$$s_d = \sqrt{\frac{\Sigma(d - \bar{d})^2}{n - 1}} = \sqrt{\frac{\Sigma d^2 - \dfrac{(\Sigma d)^2}{n}}{n - 1}}$$

An assumption for this test is that the differences of the two populations are normally distributed.

Analyzing data by this method involves calculating a t value with formula 10.5 and comparing it with a critical t value obtained from the table. The critical t value is obtained from the t distribution table in the usual way, with the exception that, in the degrees of freedom $(n - 1)$, n is the number of matched pairs of scores.

Suppose a stock market investor is interested in determining whether there is a significant difference in the P/E (price to earnings) ratio for companies from one year to the next. In an effort to study this question, the investor randomly samples nine companies from the *Handbook of Common Stocks* and records the P/E ratios for each of these companies at the end of year 1 and at the end of year 2. The data are shown in Table 10.5.

These data are related data because each P/E value for year 1 has a corresponding year 2 measurement on the same company. Because no prior information indicates whether P/E ratios have gone up or down, the hypothesis tested is two tailed. Assume $\alpha = .01$. Assume that differences in P/E ratios are normally distributed in the population.

HYPOTHESIZE:

    STEP 1. $H_0: D = 0$

                                 $H_a: D \neq 0$

TEST:

    STEP 2. The appropriate statistical test is

$$t = \frac{\bar{d} - D}{\dfrac{s_d}{\sqrt{n}}}$$

    STEP 3. $\alpha = .01$

    STEP 4. Because $\alpha = .01$ and this test is two tailed, $\alpha/2 = .005$ is used to obtain the table t value. With nine pairs of data, $n = 9$, df $= n - 1 = 8$. The table t value is

TABLE 10.5	Company	Year 1 P/E Ratio	Year 2 P/E Ratio
P/E Ratios for Nine Randomly Selected Companies	1	8.9	12.7
	2	38.1	45.4
	3	43.0	10.0
	4	34.0	27.2
	5	34.5	22.8
	6	15.2	24.1
	7	20.3	32.3
	8	19.9	40.1
	9	61.9	106.5

	TABLE 10.6			
	Company	**Year 1 P/E**	**Year 2 P/E**	**d**
Analysis of P/E Ratio Data	1	8.9	12.7	−3.8
	2	38.1	45.4	−7.3
	3	43.0	10.0	33.0
	4	34.0	27.2	6.8
	5	34.5	22.8	11.7
	6	15.2	24.1	−8.9
	7	20.3	32.3	−12.0
	8	19.9	40.1	−20.2
	9	61.9	106.5	−44.6

$$\bar{d} = -5.033, \quad s_d = 21.599, \quad n = 9$$

$$\text{Observed } t = \frac{-5.033 - 0}{\dfrac{21.599}{\sqrt{9}}} = -0.70$$

$t_{.005,8} = \pm 3.355$. If the observed test statistic is greater than 3.355 or less than −3.355, the null hypothesis will be rejected.

STEP 5. The sample data are given in Table 10.5.

STEP 6. Table 10.6 shows the calculations to obtain the observed value of the test statistic, which is $t = -0.70$.

ACTION:

STEP 7. Because the observed t value is greater than the critical table t value in the lower tail ($t = -0.70 > t = -3.355$), it is in the nonrejection region.

BUSINESS IMPLICATIONS:

STEP 8. There is not enough evidence from the data to declare a significant difference in the average P/E ratio between year 1 and year 2. The graph in Figure 10.9 depicts the rejection regions, the critical values of t, and the observed value of t for this example.

Using the Computer to Make Statistical Inferences about Two Related Populations

Both Minitab and Excel can be used to make statistical inferences about two related populations. Figure 10.10 shows Minitab and Excel output for the P/E Ratio problem. The

	FIGURE 10.9
Graphical Depiction of P/E Ratio Analysis	

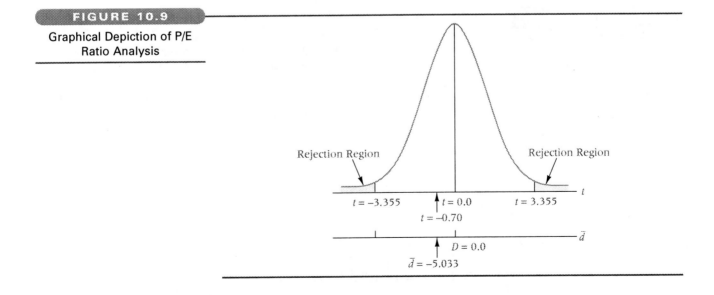

Minitab and Excel Output for
the P/E Ratio Example

Minitab Output

Paired T-Test and CI: Year 1, Year 2

Paired T for Year 1 – Year 2

	N	Mean	StDev	SE Mean
Year 1	9	30.64	16.37	5.46
Year 2	9	35.68	28.94	9.65
Difference	9	−5.03	21.60	7.20

99% CI for mean difference: (−29.19, 19.12)
T-Test of mean difference = 0 (vs not = 0):
T-Value = −0.70 P-Value = 0.504

Excel Output

t-Test: Paired Two Sample for Means

	Year 1	Year 2
Mean	30.64	35.68
Variance	268.135	837.544
Observations	9	9
Pearson Correlation	0.674	
Hypothesized Mean Difference	0	
df	8	
t Stat	−0.70	
P(T<=t) one-tail	0.252	
t Critical one-tail	2.90	
P(T<=t) two-tail	0.504	
t Critical two-tail	3.36	

Minitab output contains summary data for each sample and the difference of the two samples along with a confidence interval of the difference, a restating of the tested hypotheses, the observed t value, and the p-value. Because the p-value (0.504) is greater than the value of alpha (.01), the decision is to fail to reject the null hypothesis.

The Excel output contains the hypothesized mean difference, the observed t value (−0.70), and the critical t values and their associated p-values for both a one-tailed and a two-tailed test. The p-value for a two-tailed test is the same as that produced by Minitab, indicating that the decision is to fail to reject the null hypothesis.

**DEMONSTRATION
PROBLEM 10.5**

Let us revisit the hypothetical study discussed earlier in the section in which consumers are asked to rate a company both before and after viewing a video on the company twice a day for a week. The data from Table 10.4 are displayed again here. Use an alpha of .05 to test to determine whether there is a significant increase in the ratings of the company after the one-week video treatment. Assume that differences in ratings are normally distributed in the population.

Individual	Before	After
1	32	39
2	11	15
3	21	35
4	17	13
5	30	41
6	38	39
7	14	22

Solution

Because the same individuals are being used in a before-and-after study, it is a related measures study. The desired effect is to increase ratings, which means the hypothesis test is one tailed.

HYPOTHESIZE:

STEP 1.

$$H_0: D = 0$$
$$H_a: D < 0$$

Because the researchers want to "prove" that the ratings increase from Before to After and because the difference is computed by subtracting After ratings from the Before ratings, the desired alternative hypothesis is $D < 0$.

TEST:

STEP 2. The appropriate test statistic is formula (10.5).

STEP 3. The Type I error rate is .05.

STEP 4. The degrees of freedom are $n - 1 = 7 - 1 = 6$. For $\alpha = .05$, the table t value is $t_{.05,6} = -1.943$. The decision rule is to reject the null hypothesis if the observed value is less than -1.943.

STEP 5. The sample data and some calculations follow.

Individual	Before	After	d
1	32	39	−7
2	11	15	−4
3	21	35	−14
4	17	13	+4
5	30	41	−11
6	38	39	−1
7	14	22	−8
$\bar{d} = -5.857$		$s_d = 6.0945$	

STEP 6. The observed t value is:

$$t = \frac{-5.857 - 0}{\frac{6.0945}{\sqrt{7}}} = -2.54$$

Computer analysis of this problem reveals that the p-value is 0.022.

ACTION:

STEP 7. Because the observed value of -2.54 is less than the critical, table value of -1.943 and the p-value (0.022) is less than alpha (.05), the decision is to reject the null hypothesis.

BUSINESS IMPLICATIONS:

STEP 8. There is enough evidence to conclude that, on average, the ratings have increased significantly. This result might be used by managers to support a decision to continue using the videos or to expand the use of such videos in an effort to increase public support for their company.

The following graph depicts the observed value, the rejection region, and the critical t value for the problem.

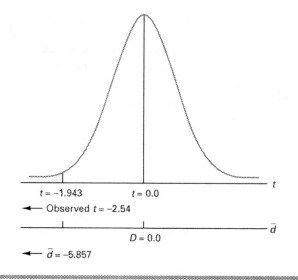

$t = -1.943$ $t = 0.0$

← Observed $t = -2.54$

$D = 0.0$ $\bar{d}$

← $\bar{d} = -5.857$

Confidence Intervals

Sometimes a researcher is interested in estimating the mean difference in two populations for related samples. A confidence interval for D, the mean population difference of two related samples, can be constructed by algebraically rearranging formula (10.5), which was used to test hypotheses about D. Again the assumption is that the differences are normally distributed in the population.

CONFIDENCE INTERVAL FORMULA TO ESTIMATE THE DIFFERENCE IN RELATED POPULATIONS, D (10.8)	$$\bar{d} - t\frac{s_d}{\sqrt{n}} \leq D \leq \bar{d} + t\frac{s_d}{\sqrt{n}}$$ $$\mathrm{df} = n - 1$$

The following housing industry example demonstrates the application of formula 10.8. The sale of new houses apparently fluctuates seasonally. Superimposed on the seasonality are economic and business cycles that also influence the sale of new houses. In certain parts of the country, new-house sales increase in the spring and early summer and drop off in the fall. Suppose a national real estate association wants to estimate the average difference in the number of new-house sales per company in Indianapolis between 2010 and 2011. To do so, the association randomly selects 18 real estate firms in the Indianapolis area and obtains their new-house sales figures for May 2010 and May 2011. The numbers of sales per company are shown in Table 10.7. Using these data, the association's analyst estimates the average difference in the number of sales per real estate company in Indianapolis for May 2010 and May 2011 and constructs a 99% confidence interval. The analyst assumes that differences in sales are normally distributed in the population.

The number of pairs, n, is 18, and the degrees of freedom are 17. For a 99% level of confidence and these degrees of freedom, the table t value is $t_{.005,17} = 2.898$. The values for $\bar{d}$, and s_d are shown in Table 10.8.

The point estimate of the difference is $\bar{d} = -3.389$. The 99% confidence interval is

$$\bar{d} - t\frac{s_d}{\sqrt{n}} \leq D \leq \bar{d} + t\frac{s_d}{\sqrt{n}}$$

$$-3.389 - 2.898\frac{3.274}{\sqrt{18}} \leq D \leq -3.389 + 2.898\frac{3.274}{\sqrt{18}}$$

$$-3.389 - 2.236 \leq D \leq -3.389 + 2.236$$

$$-5.625 \leq D \leq -1.153$$

Realtor	May 2010	May 2011
1	8	11
2	19	30
3	5	6
4	9	13
5	3	5
6	0	4
7	13	15
8	11	17
9	9	12
10	5	12
11	8	6
12	2	5
13	11	10
14	14	22
15	7	8
16	12	15
17	6	12
18	10	10

TABLE 10.7

Number of New House Sales in Indianapolis

The analyst estimates with a 99% level of confidence that the average difference in new-house sales for a real estate company in Indianapolis between 2010 and 2011 in May is somewhere between −5.625 and −1.153 houses. Because 2011 sales were subtracted from 2010 sales, the minus signs indicate more sales in 2011 than in 2010. Note that both ends of the confidence interval contain negatives. This result means that the analyst can be 99% confident that zero difference is not the average difference. If the analyst were using this confidence interval to test the hypothesis that there is no significant mean difference in average new-house sales per company in Indianapolis between May 2010 and May 2011, the null hypothesis would be rejected for $\alpha = .01$. The point estimate for this example is −3.389 houses, with an error of 2.236 houses. Figure 10.11 is the Minitab computer output for the confidence interval.

TABLE 10.8

Differences in Number of New House Sales, 2010–2011

Realtor	May 2010	May 2011	d
1	8	11	−3
2	19	30	−11
3	5	6	−1
4	9	13	−4
5	3	5	−2
6	0	4	−4
7	13	15	−2
8	11	17	−6
9	9	12	−3
10	5	12	−7
11	8	6	+2
12	2	5	−3
13	11	10	+1
14	14	22	−8
15	7	8	−1
16	12	15	−3
17	6	12	−6
18	10	10	0

$\bar{d} = -3.389$ and $s_d = 3.274$

FIGURE 10.11

Minitab Output for the New
House Sales Example

```
Paired T-Test and CI: 2010, 2011

Paired T for 2010 - 2011

                N       Mean    StDev    SE Mean
2010           18       8.44     4.64     1.09
2011           18      11.83     6.54     1.54
Difference     18      -3.389    3.274    0.772

99% CI for mean difference: (-5.626, -1.152)
T-Test of mean difference = 0 (vs not = 0):
T-Value = -4.39 P-Value = 0.000
```

10.3 PROBLEMS

10.21 Use the data given and a 1% level of significance to test the following hypotheses. Assume the differences are normally distributed in the population.

$$H_0: D = 0 \qquad H_a: D > 0$$

Pair	Sample 1	Sample 2
1	38	22
2	27	28
3	30	21
4	41	38
5	36	38
6	38	26
7	33	19
8	35	31
9	44	35

10.22 Use the data given to test the following hypotheses ($\alpha = .05$). Assume the differences are normally distributed in the population.

$$H_0: D = 0 \qquad H_a: D \neq 0$$

Individual	Before	After
1	107	102
2	99	98
3	110	100
4	113	108
5	96	89
6	98	101
7	100	99
8	102	102
9	107	105
10	109	110
11	104	102
12	99	96
13	101	100

10.23 Construct a 98% confidence interval to estimate D from the following sample information. Assume the differences are normally distributed in the population.

$$\bar{d} = 40.56, \qquad s_d = 26.58, \qquad n = 22$$

10.24 Construct a 90% confidence interval to estimate D from the following sample information. Assume the differences are normally distributed in the population.

Client	Before	After
1	32	40
2	28	25
3	35	36
4	32	32
5	26	29
6	25	31
7	37	39
8	16	30
9	35	31

10.25 Because of uncertainty in real estate markets, many homeowners are considering remodeling and constructing additions rather than selling. Probably the most expensive room in the house to remodel is the kitchen, with an average cost of about $23,400. In terms of resale value, is remodeling the kitchen worth the cost? The following cost and resale figures are published by *Remodeling* magazine for 11 cities. Use these data to construct a 99% confidence interval for the difference between cost and added resale value of kitchen remodeling. Assume the differences are normally distributed in the population.

City	Cost	Resale
Atlanta	$20,427	$25,163
Boston	27,255	24,625
Des Moines	22,115	12,600
Kansas City, MO	23,256	24,588
Louisville	21,887	19,267
Portland, OR	24,255	20,150
Raleigh-Durham	19,852	22,500
Reno	23,624	16,667
Ridgewood, NJ	25,885	26,875
San Francisco	28,999	35,333
Tulsa	20,836	16,292

10.26 The vice president of marketing brought to the attention of sales managers that most of the company's manufacturer representatives contacted clients and maintained client relationships in a disorganized, haphazard way. The sales managers brought the reps in for a three-day seminar and training session on how to use an organizer to schedule visits and recall pertinent information about each client more effectively. Sales reps were taught how to schedule visits most efficiently to maximize their efforts. Sales managers were given data on the number of site visits by sales reps on a randomly selected day both before and after the seminar. Use the following data to test whether significantly more site visits were made after the seminar ($\alpha = .05$). Assume the differences in the number of site visits are normally distributed.

Rep	Before	After
1	2	4
2	4	5
3	1	3
4	3	3
5	4	3
6	2	5
7	2	6
8	3	4
9	1	5

10.27 Eleven employees were put under the care of the company nurse because of high cholesterol readings. The nurse lectured them on the dangers of this condition and put them on a new diet. Shown are the cholesterol readings of the 11 employees both before the new diet and one month after use of the diet began. Construct a 98% confidence interval to estimate the population mean difference of cholesterol readings for people who are involved in this program. Assume differences in cholesterol readings are normally distributed in the population.

Employee	Before	After
1	255	197
2	230	225
3	290	215
4	242	215
5	300	240
6	250	235
7	215	190
8	230	240
9	225	200
10	219	203
11	236	223

10.28 Lawrence and Glover published the results of a study in the *Journal of Managerial Issues* in which they examined the effects of accounting firm mergers on auditing delay. Auditing delay is the time between a company's fiscal year-end and the date of the auditor's report. The hypothesis is that with the efficiencies gained through mergers the length of the audit delay would decrease. Suppose to test their hypothesis, they examined the audit delays on 27 clients of Big Six firms from both before and after the Big Six firm merger (a span of five years). Suppose further that the mean difference in audit delay for these clients from before merger to after merger was a decrease in 3.71 days and the standard deviation of difference was five days. Use these data and $\alpha = .01$ to test whether the audit delays after the merger were significantly lower than before the merger. Assume that the differences in auditing delay are normally distributed in the population.

10.29 A nationally known supermarket decided to promote its own brand of soft drinks on TV for two weeks. Before the ad campaign, the company randomly selected 21 of its stores across the United States to be part of a study to measure the campaign's effectiveness. During a specified half-hour period on a certain Monday morning, all the stores in the sample counted the number of cans of its own brand of soft drink sold. After the campaign, a similar count was made. The average difference was an increase of 75 cans, with a standard deviation of difference of 30 cans. Using this information, construct a 90% confidence interval to estimate the population average difference in soft drink sales for this company's brand before and after the ad campaign. Assume the differences in soft drink sales for the company's brand are normally distributed in the population.

10.30 Is there a significant difference in the gasoline mileage of a car for regular unleaded and premium unleaded? To test this question, a researcher randomly selected 15 drivers for a study. They were to drive their cars for one month on regular unleaded and for one month on premium unleaded gasoline. The participants drove their own cars for this experiment. The average sample difference was 2.85 miles per gallon in favor of the premium unleaded, and the sample standard deviation of difference was 1.9 miles per gallon. For $\alpha = .01$, does the test show enough evidence for the researcher to conclude that there is a significant difference in mileage between regular unleaded and premium unleaded gasoline? Assume the differences in gasoline mileage figures are normally distributed in the population.

10.4 STATISTICAL INFERENCES ABOUT TWO POPULATION PROPORTIONS, $p_1 - p_2$

Sometimes a researcher wishes to make inferences about the difference in two population proportions. This type of analysis has many applications in business, such as comparing the market share of a product for two different markets, studying the difference in the proportion of female customers in two different geographic regions, or comparing the proportion of defective products from one period to another. In making inferences about the difference in two population proportions, the statistic normally used is the difference in the sample proportions: $\hat{p}_1 - \hat{p}_2$. This statistic is computed by taking random samples and determining $\hat{p}$ for each sample for a given characteristic, then calculating the difference in these sample proportions.

The central limit theorem states that for large samples (each of $n_1 \cdot \hat{p}_1$, $n_1 \cdot \hat{q}_1$, $n_2 \cdot \hat{p}_2$, and $n_2 \cdot \hat{q}_2 > 5$, where $\hat{q} = 1 - \hat{p}$), the difference in sample proportions is normally distributed with a mean difference of

$$\mu_{\hat{p}_1 - \hat{p}_2} = p_1 - p_2$$

and a standard deviation of the difference of sample proportions of

$$\sigma_{\hat{p}_1 - \hat{p}_2} = \sqrt{\frac{p_1 \cdot q_1}{n_1} + \frac{p_2 \cdot q_2}{n_2}}$$

From this information, a z formula for the difference in sample proportions can be developed.

z FORMULA FOR THE DIFFERENCE IN TWO POPULATION PROPORTIONS (10.9)	$$z = \frac{(\hat{p}_1 - \hat{p}_2) - (p_1 - p_2)}{\sqrt{\dfrac{p_1 \cdot q_1}{n_1} + \dfrac{p_2 \cdot q_2}{n_2}}}$$

where

$\hat{p}_1$ = proportion from sample 1
$\hat{p}_2$ = proportion from sample 2
n_1 = size of sample 1
n_2 = size of sample 2
p_1 = proportion from population 1
p_2 = proportion from population 2
$q_1 = 1 - p_1$
$q_2 = 1 - p_2$

Hypothesis Testing

Formula 10.9 is the formula that can be used to determine the probability of getting a particular difference in two sample proportions when given the values of the population proportions. In testing hypotheses about the difference in two population proportions, particular values of the population proportions are not usually known or assumed. Rather, the hypotheses are about the difference in the two population proportions $(p_1 - p_2)$. Note that formula 10.9 requires knowledge of the values of p_1 and p_2. Hence, a modified version of formula 10.9 is used when testing hypotheses about $p_1 - p_2$. This formula utilizes a pooled value obtained from the sample proportions to replace the population proportions in the denominator of formula (10.9).

The denominator of formula 10.9 is the standard deviation of the difference in two sample proportions and uses the population proportions in its calculations. However, the population proportions are unknown, so an estimate of the standard deviation of the difference in two sample proportions is made by using sample proportions as point estimates of the population proportions. The sample proportions are combined by using a weighted average to produce $\bar{p}$, which, in conjunction with $\bar{q}$ and the sample sizes, produces a point estimate of the standard deviation of the difference in sample proportions. The result is formula 10.10, which we shall use to test hypotheses about the difference in two population proportions.

z FORMULA TO TEST THE DIFFERENCE IN POPULATION PROPORTIONS (10.10)	$$z = \frac{(\hat{p}_1 - \hat{p}_2) - (p_1 - p_2)}{\sqrt{(\bar{p} \cdot \bar{q})\left(\dfrac{1}{n_1} + \dfrac{1}{n_2}\right)}}$$

where $\bar{p} = \dfrac{x_1 + x_2}{n_1 + n_2} = \dfrac{n_1 \hat{p}_1 + n_2 \hat{p}_2}{n_1 + n_2}$ and $\bar{q} = 1 - \bar{p}$

Testing the difference in two population proportions is useful whenever the researcher is interested in comparing the proportion of one population that has a certain characteristic with the proportion of a second population that has the same characteristic. For example, a researcher might be interested in determining whether the proportion of people driving new cars (less than one year old) in Houston is different from the proportion in Denver. A study could be conducted with a random sample of Houston drivers and a random sample of Denver drivers to test this idea. The results could be used to compare the new-car potential of the two markets and the propensity of drivers in these areas to buy new cars.

As another example, do consumers and CEOs have different perceptions of ethics in business? A group of researchers attempted to determine whether there was a difference in the proportion of consumers and the proportion of CEOs who believe that fear of getting caught or losing one's job is a strong influence of ethical behavior. In their study, they found that 57% of consumers said that fear of getting caught or losing one's job was a strong influence on ethical behavior, but only 50% of CEOs felt the same way.

Suppose these data were determined from a sample of 755 consumers and 616 CEOs. Does this result provide enough evidence to declare that a significantly higher proportion of consumers than of CEOs believe fear of getting caught or losing one's job is a strong influence on ethical behavior?

HYPOTHESIZE:

STEP 1. Suppose sample 1 is the consumer sample and sample 2 is the CEO sample. Because we are trying to prove that a higher proportion of consumers than of CEOs believe fear of getting caught or losing one's job is a strong influence on ethical behavior, the alternative hypothesis should be $p_1 - p_2 > 0$. The following hypotheses are being tested.

$$H_0: p_1 - p_2 = 0$$
$$H_a: p_1 - p_2 > 0$$

where

p_1 is the proportion of consumers who select the factor

p_2 is the proportion of CEOs who select the factor

TEST:

STEP 2. The appropriate statistical test is formula 10.10.

STEP 3. Let $\alpha = .10$.

STEP 4. Because this test is a one-tailed test, the critical table z value is $z_c = 1.28$. If an observed value of z of more than 1.28 is obtained, the null hypothesis will be rejected. Figure 10.12 shows the rejection region and the critical value for this problem.

STEP 5. The sample information follows.

Consumers	CEOs
$n_1 = 755$	$n_2 = 616$
$\hat{p}_1 = .57$	$\hat{p}_2 = .50$

FIGURE 10.12

Rejection Region for the Ethics
Example

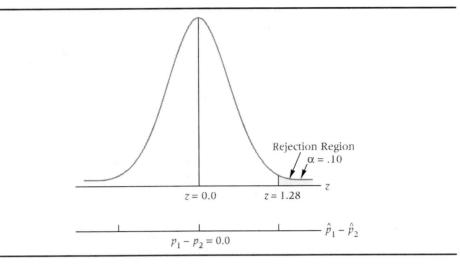

STEP **6.**

$$\bar{p} = \frac{n_1\hat{p}_1 + n_2\hat{p}_2}{n_1 + n_2} = \frac{(755)(.57) + (616)(.50)}{755 + 616} = .539$$

If the statistics had been given as raw data instead of sample proportions, we would have used the following formula.

$$\bar{p} = \frac{x_1 + x_2}{n_1 + n_2}$$

The observed z value is

$$z = \frac{(.57 - .50) - (0)}{\sqrt{(.539)(.461)\left(\dfrac{1}{755} + \dfrac{1}{616}\right)}} = 2.59$$

ACTION:

STEP **7.** Because $z = 2.59$ is greater than the critical table z value of 1.28 and is in the rejection region, the null hypothesis is rejected.

BUSINESS IMPLICATIONS:

STEP **8.** A significantly higher proportion of consumers than of CEOs believe fear of getting caught or losing one's job is a strong influence on ethical behavior. CEOs might want to take another look at ways to influence ethical behavior. If employees are more like consumers than CEOs, CEOs might be able to use fear of getting caught or losing one's job as a means of ensuring ethical behavior on the job. By transferring the idea of ethical behavior to the consumer, retailers might use fear of being caught and prosecuted to retard shoplifting in the retail trade.

**DEMONSTRATION
PROBLEM 10.6**

A study of female entrepreneurs was conducted to determine their definition of success. The women were offered optional choices such as happiness/self-fulfillment, sales/profit, and achievement/challenge. The women were divided into groups according to the gross sales of their businesses. A significantly higher proportion of female entrepreneurs in the $100,000 to $500,000 category than in the less than $100,000 category seemed to rate sales/profit as a definition of success.

Suppose you decide to test this result by taking a survey of your own and identify female entrepreneurs by gross sales. You interview 100 female entrepreneurs with gross sales of less than $100,000, and 24 of them define sales/profit as success. You then interview 95 female entrepreneurs with gross sales of $100,000 to $500,000, and 39 cite sales/profit as a definition of success. Use this information to test to determine whether there is a significant difference in the proportions of the two groups that define success as sales/profit. Use $\alpha = .01$.

Solution

HYPOTHESIZE:

STEP 1. You are testing to determine whether there is a difference between two groups of entrepreneurs, so a two-tailed test is required. The hypotheses follow.

$$H_0: p_1 - p_2 = 0$$
$$H_a: p_1 - p_2 \neq 0$$

STEP 2. The appropriate statistical test is formula 10.10.

STEP 3. Alpha has been specified as .01.

STEP 4. With $\alpha = .01$, you obtain a critical z value from Table A.5 for $\alpha/2 = .005$, $z_{.005} = \pm 2.575$. If the observed z value is more than 2.575 or less than -2.575, the null hypothesis is rejected.

STEP 5. The sample information follows.

Less than $100,000	$100,000 to $500,000
$n_1 = 100$	$n_2 = 95$
$x_1 = 24$	$x_2 = 39$
$\hat{p}_1 = \dfrac{24}{100} = .24$	$\hat{p}_2 = \dfrac{39}{95} = .41$

where

$$\bar{p} = \frac{x_1 + x_2}{n_1 + n_2} = \frac{24 + 39}{100 + 95} = \frac{63}{195} = .323$$

$x =$ the number of entrepreneurs who define sales/profits as success

STEP 6. The observed z value is

$$z = \frac{(\hat{p}_1 - \hat{p}_2) - (p_1 - p_2)}{\sqrt{(\bar{p} \cdot \bar{q})\left(\dfrac{1}{n_1} + \dfrac{1}{n_2}\right)}} = \frac{(.24 - .41) - (0)}{\sqrt{(.323)(.677)\left(\dfrac{1}{100} + \dfrac{1}{95}\right)}} = \frac{-.17}{.067} = -2.54$$

ACTION:

STEP 7. Although this observed value is near the rejection region, it is in the non-rejection region. The null hypothesis is not rejected. The test did not show enough evidence here to reject the null hypothesis and declare that the responses to the question by the two groups are different statistically. Note that alpha was small and that a two-tailed test was conducted. If a one-tailed test had been used, z_c would have been $z_{.01} = -2.33$, and the null hypothesis would have been rejected. If alpha had been .05, z_c would have been $z_{.025} = \pm 1.96$, and the null hypothesis would have been rejected. This result underscores the crucial importance of selecting alpha and determining whether to use a one-tailed or two-tailed test in hypothesis testing.

The following diagram shows the critical values, the rejection regions, and the observed value for this problem.

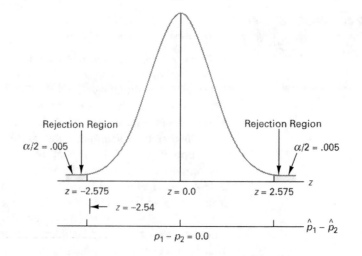

BUSINESS IMPLICATIONS:

STEP 8. We cannot statistically conclude that a greater proportion of female entrepreneurs in the higher gross sales category define success as sales/profit. One of the payoffs of such a determination is to find out what motivates the people with whom we do business. If sales/profits motivate people, offers or promises of greater sales and profits can be a means of attracting their services, their interest, or their business. If sales/profits do not motivate people, such offers would not generate the kind of response wanted and we would need to look for other ways to motivate them.

Confidence Intervals

Sometimes in business research the investigator wants to estimate the difference in two population proportions. For example, what is the difference, if any, in the population proportions of workers in the Midwest who favor union membership and workers in the South who favor union membership? In studying two different suppliers of the same part, a large manufacturing company might want to estimate the difference between suppliers in the proportion of parts that meet specifications. These and other situations requiring the estimation of the difference in two population proportions can be solved by using confidence intervals.

The formula for constructing confidence intervals to estimate the difference in two population proportions is a modified version of formula 10.9. Formula 10.9 for two proportions requires knowledge of each of the population proportions. Because we are attempting to estimate the difference in these two proportions, we obviously do not know their value. To overcome this lack of knowledge in constructing a confidence interval formula, we substitute the sample proportions in place of the population proportions and use these sample proportions in the estimate, as follows.

$$z = \frac{(\hat{p}_1 - \hat{p}_2) - (p_1 - p_2)}{\sqrt{\dfrac{\hat{p}_1 \cdot \hat{q}_1}{n_1} + \dfrac{\hat{p}_2 \cdot \hat{q}_2}{n_2}}}$$

Solving this equation for $p_1 - p_2$ produces the formula for constructing confidence intervals for $p_1 - p_2$.

CONFIDENCE INTERVAL TO ESTIMATE $p_1 - p_2$ (10.11)	$(\hat{p}_1 - \hat{p}_2) - z\sqrt{\dfrac{\hat{p}_1 \cdot \hat{q}_1}{n_1} + \dfrac{\hat{p}_2 \cdot \hat{q}_2}{n_2}} \leq p_1 - p_2 \leq (\hat{p}_1 - \hat{p}_2) + z\sqrt{\dfrac{\hat{p}_1 \cdot \hat{q}_1}{n_1} + \dfrac{\hat{p}_2 \cdot \hat{q}_2}{n_2}}$

To see how this formula is used, suppose that in an attempt to target its clientele, managers of a supermarket chain want to determine the difference between the proportion of morning shoppers who are men and the proportion of after–5 P.M. shoppers who are men. Over a period of two weeks, the chain's researchers conduct a systematic random sample survey of 400 morning shoppers, which reveals that 352 are women and 48 are men. During this same period, a systematic random sample of 480 after–5 P.M. shoppers reveals that 293 are women and 187 are men. Construct a 98% confidence interval to estimate the difference in the population proportions of men.

The sample information is shown here.

Morning Shoppers	After–5 P.M. Shoppers
$n_1 = 400$	$n_2 = 480$
$x_1 = 48$ men	$x_2 = 187$ men
$\hat{p}_1 = .12$	$\hat{p}_2 = .39$
$\hat{q}_1 = .88$	$\hat{q}_2 = .61$

FIGURE 10.13

Minitab Output for the
Shopping Example

```
          TEST AND CI FOR TWO PROPORTIONS

Sample   X    N    Sample p
1        48   400  0.120000
2        187  480  0.389583
Difference = p(1) - p(2)
Estimate for difference: -0.269583
98% CI for difference: (-0.333692, -0.205474)
Test for difference = 0 (vs not = 0):
Z = -9.78   P-Value = 0.000
Fisher's exact test: P-Value = 0.000
```

For a 98% level of confidence, $z = 2.33$. Using formula 10.11 yields

$$(.12 - .39) - 2.33\sqrt{\frac{(.12)(.88)}{400} + \frac{(.39)(.61)}{480}} \leq p_1 - p_2$$

$$\leq (.12 - .39) + 2.33\sqrt{\frac{(.12)(.88)}{400} + \frac{(.39)(.61)}{480}}$$

$$-.27 - .064 \geq p_1 - p_2 \geq -.27 + .064$$

$$-.334 \geq p_1 - p_2 \geq -.206$$

There is a 98% level of confidence that the difference in population proportions is between $-.334$ and $-.206$. Because the after–5 P.M. shopper proportion was subtracted from the morning shoppers, the negative signs in the interval indicate a higher proportion of men in the after–5 P.M. shoppers than in the morning shoppers. Thus the confidence level is 98% that the difference in proportions is at least .206 and may be as much as .334.

Using the Computer to Analyze the Difference in Two Proportions

Minitab has the capability of testing hypotheses or constructing confidence intervals about the difference in two proportions. Figure 10.13 shows Minitab output for the shopping example. Notice that the output contains a summary of sample information along with the difference in sample proportions, the confidence interval, the computer z value for a hypothesis test, and the p-value. The confidence interval shown here is the same as the one we just computed except for rounding differences.

10.4 PROBLEMS

10.31 Using the given sample information, test the following hypotheses.

    a. $H_0: p_1 - p_2 = 0$ $H_a: p_1 - p_2 \neq 0$

Sample 1	Sample 2
$n_1 = 368$	$n_2 = 405$
$x_1 = 175$	$x_2 = 182$ Let $\alpha = .05$.

Note that x is the number in the sample having the characteristic of interest.

b. $H_0: p_1 - p_2 = 0$ $H_a: p_1 - p_2 > 0$

Sample 1	Sample 2
$n_1 = 649$	$n_2 = 558$
$\hat{p}_1 = .38$	$\hat{p}_2 = .25$ Let $\alpha = .10$.

10.32 In each of the following cases, calculate a confidence interval to estimate $p_1 - p_2$.

   a. $n_1 = 85$, $n_2 = 90$, $\hat{p}_1 = .75$, $\hat{p}_2 = .67$; level of confidence = 90%

   b. $n_1 = 1100$, $n_2 = 1300$, $\hat{p}_1 = .19$, $\hat{p}_2 = .17$; level of confidence = 95%

   c. $n_1 = 430$, $n_2 = 399$, $x_1 = 275$, $x_2 = 275$; level of confidence = 85%

   d. $n_1 = 1500$, $n_2 = 1500$, $x_1 = 1050$, $x_2 = 1100$; level of confidence = 80%

10.33 According to a study conducted for Gateway Computers, 59% of men and 70% of women say that weight is an extremely/very important factor in purchasing a laptop computer. Suppose this survey was conducted using 374 men and 481 women. Do these data show enough evidence to declare that a significantly higher proportion of women than men believe that weight is an extremely/very important factor in purchasing a laptop computer? Use a 5% level of significance.

10.34 Does age make a difference in the amount of savings a worker feels is needed to be secure at retirement? A study by CommSciences for Transamerica Asset Management found that .24 of workers in the 25–33 age category feel that $250,000 to $500,000 is enough to be secure at retirement. However, .35 of the workers in the 34–52 age category feel that this amount is enough. Suppose 210 workers in the 25–33 age category and 176 workers in the 34–52 age category were involved in this study. Use these data to construct a 90% confidence interval to estimate the difference in population proportions on this question.

10.35 Companies that recently developed new products were asked to rate which activities are most difficult to accomplish with new products. Options included such activities as assessing market potential, market testing, finalizing the design, developing a business plan, and the like. A researcher wants to conduct a similar study to compare the results between two industries: the computer hardware industry and the banking industry. He takes a random sample of 56 computer firms and 89 banks. The researcher asks whether market testing is the most difficult activity to accomplish in developing a new product. Some 48% of the sampled computer companies and 56% of the sampled banks respond that it is the most difficult activity. Use a level of significance of .20 to test whether there is a significant difference in the responses to the question from these two industries.

10.36 A large production facility uses two machines to produce a key part for its main product. Inspectors have expressed concern about the quality of the finished product. Quality control investigation has revealed that the key part made by the two machines is defective at times. The inspectors randomly sampled 35 units of the key part from each machine. Of those produced by machine A, five were defective. Seven of the 35 sampled parts from machine B were defective. The production manager is interested in estimating the difference in proportions of the populations of parts that are defective between machine A and machine B. From the sample information, compute a 98% confidence interval for this difference.

10.37 According to a CCH Unscheduled Absence survey, 9% of small businesses use telecommuting of workers in an effort to reduce unscheduled absenteeism. This proportion compares to 6% for all businesses. Is there really a significant difference between small businesses and all businesses on this issue? Use these data and an alpha of .10 to test this question. Assume that there were 780 small businesses and 915 other businesses in this survey.

10.38 Many Americans spend time worrying about paying their bills. A survey by Fleishman-Hilliard Research for MassMutual discovered that 60% of Americans with kids say that paying bills is a major concern. This proportion compares to 52% of Americans without kids. Suppose 850 Americans with kids and 910 without kids were contacted for this study. Use these data to construct a 95% confidence interval to estimate the difference in population proportions between Americans with kids and Americans without kids on this issue.

10.5 TESTING HYPOTHESES ABOUT TWO POPULATION VARIANCES

Video

Sometimes we are interested in studying the variance of a population rather than a mean or proportion. Section 9.5 discussed how to test hypotheses about a single population variance, but on some occasions business researchers are interested in testing hypotheses about the difference in two population variances. In this section, we examine how to conduct such tests. When would a business researcher be interested in the variances from two populations?

In quality control, analysts often examine both a measure of central tendency (mean or proportion) and a measure of variability. Suppose a manufacturing plant made two batches of an item, produced items on two different machines, or produced items on two different shifts. It might be of interest to management to compare the variances from two batches or two machines to determine whether there is more variability in one than another.

Variance is sometimes used as a measure of the risk of a stock in the stock market. The greater the variance, the greater the risk. By using techniques discussed here, a financial researcher could determine whether the variances (or risk) of two stocks are the same.

In testing hypotheses about two population variances, the sample variances are used. It makes sense that if two samples come from the same population (or populations with equal variances), the ratio of the sample variances, s_1^2/s_2^2, should be about 1. However, because of sampling error, sample variances even from the same population (or from two populations with equal variances) will vary. This *ratio of two sample variances* formulates what is called an **F value**.

$$F = \frac{s_1^2}{s_2^2}$$

These ratios, if computed repeatedly for pairs of sample variances taken from a population, are distributed as an **F distribution**. The F distribution will vary by the sizes of the samples, which are converted to degrees of freedom.

With the F distribution, there are degrees of freedom associated with the numerator (of the ratio) and the denominator. An assumption underlying the F distribution is that the populations from which the samples are drawn are normally distributed for x. *The F test of two population variances is extremely sensitive to violations of the assumption that the populations are normally distributed.* The statistician should carefully investigate the shape of the distributions of the populations from which the samples are drawn to be certain the populations are normally distributed. The formula used to test hypotheses comparing two population variances follows.

F TEST FOR TWO POPULATION VARIANCES (10.12)	$$F = \frac{s_1^2}{s_2^2}$$ $$\mathrm{df}_{\mathrm{numerator}} = v_1 = n_1 - 1$$ $$\mathrm{df}_{\mathrm{denominator}} = v_2 = n_2 - 1$$

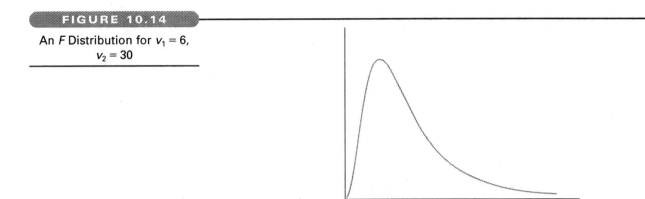

FIGURE 10.14

An *F* Distribution for $v_1 = 6$, $v_2 = 30$

Table A.7 contains *F* distribution table values for $\alpha = .10, .05, .025, .01$, and $.005$. Figure 10.14 shows an *F* distribution for $v_1 = 6$ and $v_2 = 30$. Notice that the distribution is nonsymmetric, which can be a problem when we are conducting a two-tailed test and want to determine the critical value for the lower tail. Table A.7 contains only *F* values for the upper tail. However, the *F* distribution is not symmetric nor does it have a mean of zero as do the *z* and *t* distributions; therefore, we cannot merely place a minus sign on the upper-tail critical value and obtain the lower-tail critical value (in addition, the *F* ratio is always positive—it is the ratio of two variances). This dilemma can be solved by using formula 10.13, which essentially states that the critical *F* value for the lower tail $(1 - \alpha)$ can be solved for by taking the inverse of the *F* value for the upper tail (α). The degrees of freedom numerator for the upper-tail critical value is the degrees of freedom denominator for the lower-tail critical value, and the degrees of freedom denominator for the upper-tail critical value is the degrees of freedom numerator for the lower-tail critical value.

FORMULA FOR DETERMINING THE CRITICAL VALUE FOR THE LOWER-TAIL *F* (10.13)

$$F_{1-\alpha, v_2, v_1} = \frac{1}{F_{\alpha, v_1, v_2}}$$

A hypothesis test can be conducted using two sample variances and formula 10.12. The following example illustrates this process.

Suppose a machine produces metal sheets that are specified to be 22 millimeters thick. Because of the machine, the operator, the raw material, the manufacturing environment, and other factors, there is variability in the thickness. Two machines produce these sheets. Operators are concerned about the consistency of the two machines. To test consistency, they randomly sample 10 sheets produced by machine 1 and 12 sheets produced by machine 2. The thickness measurements of sheets from each machine are given in the table on the following page. Assume sheet thickness is normally distributed in the population. How can we test to determine whether the variance from each sample comes from the same population variance (population variances are equal) or from different population variances (population variances are not equal)?

HYPOTHESIZE:

STEP 1. Determine the null and alternative hypotheses. In this case, we are conducting a two-tailed test (variances are the same or not), and the following hypotheses are used.

$$H_0: \sigma_1^2 = \sigma_2^2$$
$$H_a: \sigma_1^2 \neq \sigma_2^2$$

TEST:

STEP 2. The appropriate statistical test is

$$F = \frac{s_1^2}{s_2^2}$$

TABLE 10.9

A Portion of the *F* Distribution Table

Percentage Points of the *F* Distribution

$\alpha = 0.025$

v_2	v_1 1	2	3	4	5	6	7	8	9	
				Numerator Degrees of Freedom						
1	647.8	799.5	864.2	899.6	921.8	937.1	948.2	956.7	963.3	
2	38.51	39.00	39.17	39.25	39.30	39.33	39.36	39.37	39.39	
3	17.44	16.04	15.44	15.10	14.88	14.73	14.62	14.54	14.47	
4	12.22	10.65	9.98	9.60	9.36	9.20	9.07	8.98	8.90	
5	10.01	8.43	7.76	7.39	7.15	6.98	6.85	6.76	6.68	
6	8.81	7.26	6.60	6.23	5.99	5.82	5.70	5.60	5.52	$F_{.025,9,11}$
7	8.07	6.54	5.89	5.52	5.29	5.12	4.99	4.90	4.82	
8	7.57	6.06	5.42	5.05	4.82	4.65	4.53	4.43	4.36	
9	7.21	5.71	5.08	4.72	4.48	4.32	4.20	4.10	4.03	
10	6.94	5.46	4.83	4.47	4.24	4.07	3.95	3.85	3.78	
11	6.72	5.26	4.63	4.28	4.04	3.88	3.76	3.66	3.59	
12	6.55	5.10	4.47	4.12	3.89	3.73	3.61	3.51	3.44	
13	6.41	4.97	4.35	4.00	3.77	3.60	3.48	3.39	3.31	
14	6.30	4.86	4.24	3.89	3.66	3.50	3.38	3.29	3.21	
15	6.20	4.77	4.15	3.80	3.58	3.41	3.29	3.20	3.12	
16	6.12	4.69	4.08	3.73	3.50	3.34	3.22	3.12	3.05	
17	6.04	4.62	4.01	3.66	3.44	3.28	3.16	3.06	2.98	
18	5.98	4.56	3.95	3.61	3.38	3.22	3.10	3.01	2.93	
19	5.92	4.51	3.90	3.56	3.33	3.17	3.05	2.96	2.88	
20	5.87	4.46	3.86	3.51	3.29	3.13	3.01	2.91	2.84	
21	5.83	4.42	3.82	3.48	3.25	3.09	2.97	2.87	2.80	
22	5.79	4.38	3.78	3.44	3.22	3.05	2.93	2.84	2.76	
23	5.75	4.35	3.75	3.41	3.18	3.02	2.90	2.81	2.73	
24	5.72	4.32	3.72	3.38	3.15	2.99	2.87	2.78	2.70	
25	5.69	4.29	3.69	3.35	3.13	2.97	2.85	2.75	2.68	
26	5.66	4.27	3.67	3.33	3.10	2.94	2.82	2.73	2.65	
27	5.63	4.24	3.65	3.31	3.08	2.92	2.80	2.71	2.63	
28	5.61	4.22	3.63	3.29	3.06	2.90	2.78	2.69	2.61	
29	5.59	4.20	3.61	3.27	3.04	2.88	2.76	2.67	2.59	
30	5.57	4.18	3.59	3.25	3.03	2.87	2.75	2.65	2.57	
40	5.42	4.05	3.46	3.13	2.90	2.74	2.62	2.53	2.45	
60	5.29	3.93	3.34	3.01	2.79	2.63	2.51	2.41	2.33	
120	5.15	3.80	3.23	2.89	2.67	2.52	2.39	2.30	2.22	
∞	5.02	3.69	3.12	2.79	2.57	2.41	2.29	2.19	2.11	

Denominator Degrees of Freedom

STEP 3. Let $\alpha = .05$.

STEP 4. Because we are conducting a two-tailed test, $\alpha/2 = .025$. Because $n_1 = 10$ and $n_2 = 12$, the degrees of freedom numerator for the upper-tail critical value is $v_1 = n_1 - 1 = 10 - 1 = 9$ and the degrees of freedom denominator for the upper-tail critical value is $v_2 = n_2 - 1 = 12 - 1 = 11$. The critical F value for the upper tail obtained from Table A.7 is

$$F_{.025,9,11} = 3.59$$

Table 10.9 is a copy of the F distribution for a one-tailed $\alpha = .025$ (which yields equivalent values for two-tailed $\alpha = .05$ where the upper tail contains .025 of the area). Locate $F_{.025,9,11} = 3.59$ in the table. The lower-tail critical value can be calculated from the upper-tail value by using formula 10.13.

$$F_{.975,11,9} = \frac{1}{F_{.025,9,11}} = \frac{1}{3.59} = .28$$

The decision rule is to reject the null hypothesis if the observed F value is greater than 3.59 or less than .28.

STEP 5. Next we compute the sample variances. The data are shown here.

Machine 1		Machine 2	
22.3	21.9	22.0	21.7
21.8	22.4	22.1	21.9
22.3	22.5	21.8	22.0
21.6	22.2	21.9	22.1
21.8	21.6	22.2	21.9
		22.0	22.1
$s_1^2 = .11378$		$s_2^2 = .02023$	
$n_1 = 10$		$n_2 = 12$	

STEP 6.

$$F = \frac{s_1^2}{s_2^2} = \frac{.11378}{.02023} = 5.62$$

The ratio of sample variances is 5.62.

ACTION:

STEP 7. The observed F value is 5.62, which is greater than the upper-tail critical value of 3.59. As Figure 10.15 shows, this F value is in the rejection region. Thus, the decision is to reject the null hypotheses. The population variances are not equal.

FIGURE 10.15

Minitab Graph of F Values and Rejection Region for the Sheet Metal Example

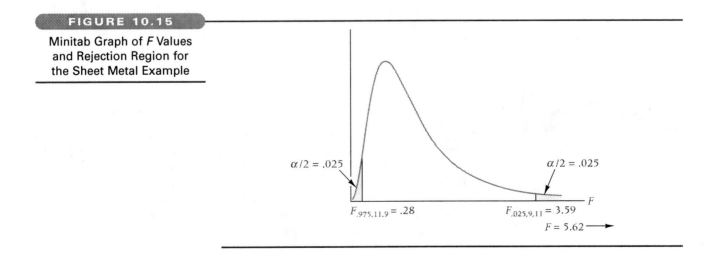

FIGURE 10.16

Minitab and Excel Output for
the Sheet Metal Example

Minitab Output

Test for Equal Variances: Machine 1, Machine 2

95% Bonferroni confidence intervals for
standard deviations

	N	Lower	StDev	Upper
Machine 1	10	0.220642	0.337310	0.679225
Machine 2	12	0.096173	0.142223	0.262900

F-Test (Normal Distribution)
Test statistic = 5.62, p-value = 0.009

EXCEL Output

F- Test Two-Sample for Variances

	Machine 1	Machine 2
Mean	22.04	21.98
Variance	0.11378	0.02023
Observations	10	12
df	9	11
F	5.62	
P(F<=f) one-tail	0.0047	
F Critical one-tail	2.90	

BUSINESS IMPLICATIONS:

STEP 8. An examination of the sample variances reveals that the variance from machine 1 measurements is greater than that from machine 2 measurements. The operators and process managers might want to examine machine 1 further; an adjustment may be needed or some other reason may be causing the seemingly greater variations on that machine.

Using the Computer to Test Hypotheses About Two Population Variances

Both Excel and Minitab have the capability of directly testing hypotheses about two population variances. Figure 10.16 shows Minitab and Excel output for the sheet metal example. The Minitab output contains the observed F value and its associated p-value. The Excel output contains the two sample means, the two sample variances, the observed F value, the p-value for a one-tailed test, and the critical F value for a one-tailed test. Because the sheet metal example is a two-tailed test, compare the p-value of .0047 to $\alpha/2 = .025$. Because this value (.0047) is less than $\alpha/2 = .025$, the decision is to reject the null hypothesis.

DEMONSTRATION PROBLEM 10.7

According to Runzheimer International, a family of four in Manhattan with $60,000 annual income spends more than $22,000 a year on basic goods and services. In contrast, a family of four in San Antonio with the same annual income spends only $15,460 on the same items. Suppose we want to test to determine whether the variance of money spent per year on the basics by families across the United States is greater than the variance of money spent on the basics by families in Manhattan—that is, whether the amounts spent by families of four in Manhattan are more homogeneous than the amounts spent by such families nationally. Suppose a random sample of eight Manhattan families produces the figures in the table, which are given along with those reported from a random sample of seven families across the United States. Complete a hypothesis-testing procedure to determine whether the variance of values taken from across the United States can be shown to be greater than the variance of values obtained from families in Manhattan. Let $\alpha = .01$. Assume the amount spent on the basics is normally distributed in the population.

Amount Spent on Basics by Family of Four with $60,000 Annual Income

Across United States	Manhattan
$18,500	$23,000
19,250	21,900
16,400	22,500
20,750	21,200
17,600	21,000
21,800	22,800
14,750	23,100
	21,300

Solution

HYPOTHESIZE:

STEP 1. This is a one-tailed test with the following hypotheses.

$$H_0: \sigma_1^2 = \sigma_2^2$$
$$H_a: \sigma_1^2 > \sigma_2^2$$

Note that what we are trying to prove—that the variance for the U.S. population is greater than the variance for families in Manhattan—is in the alternative hypothesis.

TEST:

STEP 2. The appropriate statistical test is

$$F = \frac{s_1^2}{s_2^2}$$

STEP 3. The Type I error rate is .01.

STEP 4. This test is a one-tailed test, so we will use the F distribution table in Appendix A.7 with $\alpha = .01$. The degrees of freedom for $n_1 = 7$ and $n_2 = 8$ are $v_1 = 6$ and $v_2 = 7$. The critical F value for the upper tail of the distribution is

$$F_{.01,6,7} = 7.19.$$

The decision rule is to reject the null hypothesis if the observed value of F is greater than 7.19.

STEP 5. The following sample variances are computed from the data.

$$s_1^2 = 5,961,428.6$$
$$n_1 = 7$$
$$s_2^2 = 737,142.9$$
$$n_2 = 8$$

STEP 6. The observed F value can be determined by

$$F = \frac{s_1^2}{s_2^2} = \frac{5,961,428.6}{737,142.9} = 8.09$$

ACTION:

STEP 7. Because the observed value of $F = 8.09$ is greater than the table critical F value of 7.19, the decision is to reject the null hypothesis.

BUSINESS IMPLICATIONS:

STEP 8. The variance for families in the United States is greater than the variance of families in Manhattan. Families in Manhattan are more homogeneous in amount spent on basics than families across the United States. Marketing managers need to understand this homogeneity as they attempt to find niches in the Manhattan population. Manhattan may not contain as many subgroups as can be found across the United States. The task of locating market niches may be easier in Manhattan than in the rest of the country because fewer possibilities are likely. The following Minitab graph shows the rejection region as well as the critical and observed values of F.

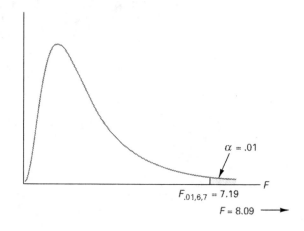

$\alpha = .01$

$F_{.01,6,7} = 7.19$

$F = 8.09 \longrightarrow$

Note: *Some authors recommend the use of this F test to determine whether the data being analyzed by a t test for two population means are meeting the assumption of equal population variances. However, some statistical researchers suggest that for equal sample sizes, the t test is insensitive to the equal variance assumption, and therefore the F test is not needed in that situation. For unequal sample sizes, the F test of variances is "not generally capable of detecting assumption violations that lead to poor performance" with the t test.* This text does not present the application of the F test to determine whether variance assumptions for the t test have been met.*

10.5 PROBLEMS

10.39 Test the following hypotheses by using the given sample information and $\alpha = .01$. Assume the populations are normally distributed.

$$H_0: \sigma_1^2 = \sigma_2^2 \qquad H_a: \sigma_1^2 < \sigma_2^2$$
$$n_1 = 10, \qquad n_2 = 11, \qquad s_1^2 = 562, \qquad s_2^2 = 1013$$

10.40 Test the following hypotheses by using the given sample information and $\alpha = .05$. Assume the populations are normally distributed.

$$H_0: \sigma_1^2 = \sigma_2^2 \qquad H_a: \sigma_1^2 \neq \sigma_2^2$$
$$n_1 = 5, \qquad n_2 = 19, \qquad s_1 = 4.68, \qquad s_2 = 2.78$$

10.41 Suppose the data shown here are the results of a survey to investigate gasoline prices. Ten service stations were selected randomly in each of two cities and the figures represent the prices of a gallon of unleaded regular gasoline on a given day. Use the F test to determine whether there is a significant difference in the variances of the prices of unleaded regular gasoline between these two cities. Let $\alpha = .01$. Assume gasoline prices are normally distributed.

*Carol A. Markowski and Edward P. Markowski, "Conditions for the Effectiveness of a Preliminary Test of Variance," *The American Statistician,* vol. 44 (November 1990), pp. 322–326.

City 1			City 2		
3.43	3.32	3.38	3.33	3.30	3.44
3.40	3.39	3.38	3.42	3.46	3.37
3.39	3.38	3.28	3.39	3.39	3.38
	3.34			3.36	

10.42 How long are resale houses on the market? One survey by the Houston Association of Realtors reported that in Houston, resale houses are on the market an average of 112 days. Of course, the length of time varies by market. Suppose random samples of 13 houses in Houston and 11 houses in Chicago that are for resale are traced. The data shown here represent the number of days each house was on the market before being sold. Use the given data and a 1% level of significance to determine whether the population variances for the number of days until resale are different in Houston than in Chicago. Assume the numbers of days resale houses are on the market are normally distributed.

Houston		Chicago	
132	126	118	56
138	94	85	69
131	161	113	67
127	133	81	54
99	119	94	137
126	88	93	
134			

10.43 One recent study showed that the average annual amount spent by an East Coast household on frankfurters was $23.84 compared with an average of $19.83 for West Coast households. Suppose a random sample of 11 East Coast households showed that the standard deviation of these purchases (frankfurters) was $7.52, whereas a random sample of 15 West Coast households resulted in a standard deviation of $6.08. Do these samples provide enough evidence to conclude that the variance of annual frankfurter purchases for East Coast households is greater than the variance of annual frankfurter purchases for West Coast households? Let alpha be .05. Assume amounts spent per year on frankfurters are normally distributed. Suppose the data did show that the variance among East Coast households is greater than that among West Coast households. What might this variance mean to decision makers in the frankfurter industry?

10.44 According to the General Accounting Office of the U.S. government, the average age of a male federal worker is 43.6 years and that of a male worker in the nonfederal sector is 37.3 years. Is there any difference in the variation of ages of men in the federal sector and men in the nonfederal sector? Suppose a random sample of 15 male federal workers is taken and the variance of their ages is 91.5. Suppose also a random sample of 15 male nonfederal workers is taken and the variance of their ages is 67.3. Use these data and $\alpha = .01$ to answer the question. Assume ages are normally distributed.

Online Shopping

Various techniques in Chapter 10 can be used to analyze the online shopping data presented in the Decision Dilemma if the data are actually only sample statistics. The Pew Internet and American Life Project surveyed 2400 American adults. However, suppose only 245 of these shopped at specialty stores, spending an average of $123, and 212 shopped at department stores, spending an average of $121. Suppose further that the population standard deviation of such spending at specialty stores is $35 and the population standard deviation of such spending at department stores is $32. Using the z test presented in Section 10.1, we can test to determine if there is a significant difference in the average amounts spent by online shoppers in the past 30 days between these two types of stores. Let alpha equal .05. This is a two-tailed test in which the null hypothesis is that there is no difference between the mean amounts for the two types of stores, and the alternative hypothesis is that there is a difference. The critical z value for this test is ±1.96. Applying formula 10.1 to the data, an observed z value of 0.64 is obtained. Because this observed value is less than the critical value of ±1.96, the decision is to fail to reject the null hypothesis. This is confirmed by the p-value, which is .2611. If the reported averages of $123 and $121 were sample averages obtained from samples of 245 and 212, respectively, with these population standard deviations, there is likely no real difference in the population mean amounts spent at specialty stores and department stores.

The EIAA study reported that the mean number of items purchased over a six-month period for online shoppers was 11 in Denmark and 10 in Germany. However, these were sample means obtained from a survey of 7000 people. Is the mean of 11 obtained for Denmark really significantly higher than the mean of 10 obtained from Germany? Suppose that 843 Danish people participated in this study, as did 1064 Germans. In addition, suppose that the sample standard deviation of number of items was 2.7 for Denmark and 3.1 for Germany. If we want to test to determine if the mean number of Denmark is significantly higher than the mean number for Germany, the null hypothesis is that there is no difference and the alternative hypothesis is that the mean for Denmark is higher than the mean for Germany (a one-tailed test). Let alpha equal .01. Since the population variances are unknown and the samples are independent, we can use formula 10.3 in Section 10.2 of this chapter to perform the analysis. The degrees of freedom for this analysis are 1905 (843 + 1064 − 2). The critical table t value is approximately 2.326. The observed t value computed using formula 10.3 is t = 7.40, which is significant because it is bigger than the critical table value. Thus, even though the difference in the mean

number of items between Denmark and Germany purchased over a six-month period for online shoppers is only 1, given the large sample sizes and the sample standard deviations, there is sufficient evidence to conclude that a significantly greater number of items are purchased by people in Denmark than by people in Germany. Whether a difference of 1 is substantive is a matter of interpretation by online businesses and business researchers.

The Nielsen survey of 26,000 Internet users from around the world revealed that 97% of Japan's Internet users shop online compared to 94% in the United States. Since these two values are taken from a sample of users, they are actually sample proportions. Suppose a business researcher wants to use these figures to test to determine if the proportion of Japanese Internet users who shop online is significantly higher than the proportion of American Internet users who shop online. The null hypothesis is that there is no difference in the population proportions. The alternate hypothesis is that the population proportion for Japan is higher than the population proportion for the United States. Suppose the .97 sample proportion came from 561 Japanese participants in the Nielsen survey and that the .94 sample proportion came from 685 American participants in the survey. Using a 5% level of significance, we can test these hypotheses using formula 10.9 from Section 10.4 of Chapter 10. Since this is a one-tailed z test with an alpha of .05, the critical table z value is 1.645. Using formula 10.9 to analyze the data, we obtain an observed z value of 2.50. Because this observed value is greater than the critical table value, the decision is to reject the null hypothesis. This conclusion is confirmed by examining the p-value, which is .0062 and is less than .05. Thus, our analysis indicates that a significantly higher proportion of Japanese Internet users shop online than do Americans. An important business question might be, is .03 (the difference between .97 and .94) really a substantive or important difference? A 3% difference can sometimes be a lot in the business world. On the other hand, 94% of American Internet users shopping online is still an extremely high proportion.

ETHICAL CONSIDERATIONS

The statistical techniques presented in this chapter share some of the pitfalls of confidence interval methodology and hypothesis-testing techniques mentioned in preceding chapters. Included among these pitfalls are assumption violations. Remember, if small sample sizes are used in analyzing means, the z tests are valid only when the population is normally distributed and the population variances are known. If the population variances are unknown, a t test can be used if the population is normally distributed and if the population variances can be assumed to be equal. The z tests and confidence intervals for two population

proportions also have a minimum sample-size requirement that should be met. In addition, it is assumed that both populations are normally distributed when the F test is used for two population variances.

Use of the t test for two independent populations is not unethical when the populations are related, but it is likely to result in a loss of power. As with any hypothesis-testing procedure, in determining the null and alternative hypotheses, make certain you are not assuming true what you are trying to prove.

SUMMARY

Business research often requires the analysis of two populations. Three types of parameters can be compared: means, proportions, and variances. Except for the F test for population variances, all techniques presented contain both confidence intervals and hypothesis tests. In each case, the two populations are studied through the use of sample data randomly drawn from each population.

The population means are analyzed by comparing two sample means. When sample sizes are large ($n \geq 30$) and population variances are known, a z test is used. When sample sizes are small, the population variances are known, and the populations are normally distributed, the z test is used to analyze the population

means. If the population variances are unknown, and the populations are normally distributed, the t test of means for independent samples is used. For populations that are related on some measure, such as twins or before-and-after, a t test for dependent measures (matched pairs) is used. The difference in two population proportions can be tested or estimated using a z test.

The population variances are analyzed by an F test when the assumption that the populations are normally distributed is met. The F value is a ratio of the two variances. The F distribution is a distribution of possible ratios of two sample variances taken from one population or from two populations containing the same variance.

KEY TERMS

Flash Cards

dependent samples
F distribution

F value
independent samples

matched-pairs test
related measures

FORMULAS

z test for the difference in two independent sample means

$$z = \frac{(\bar{x}_1 - \bar{x}_2) - (\mu_1 - \mu_2)}{\sqrt{\dfrac{\sigma_1^2}{n_1} + \dfrac{\sigma_2^2}{n_2}}}$$

Confidence interval for estimating the difference in two independent population means using z

$$(\bar{x}_1 - \bar{x}_2) - z\sqrt{\frac{\sigma_1^2}{n_1} + \frac{\sigma_2^2}{n_2}} \leq \mu_1 - \mu_2 \leq (\bar{x}_1 - \bar{x}_2)$$
$$+ z\sqrt{\frac{\sigma_1^2}{n_1} + \frac{\sigma_2^2}{n_2}}$$

t test for two independent sample means, and population variances unknown but assumed to be equal (assume also that the two populations are normally distributed)

$$t = \frac{(\bar{x}_1 - \bar{x}_2) - (\mu_1 - \mu_2)}{\sqrt{\dfrac{s_1^2(n_1 - 1) + s_2^2(n_2 - 1)}{n_1 + n_2 - 2}}\sqrt{\dfrac{1}{n_1} + \dfrac{1}{n_2}}}$$
$$df = n_1 + n_2 - 2$$

Confidence interval for estimating the difference in two independent means, and population variances unknown but assumed to be equal (assume also that two populations are normally distributed)

$$(\bar{x}_1 - \bar{x}_2) \pm t\sqrt{\frac{s_1^2(n_1 - 1) + s_2^2(n_2 - 1)}{n_1 + n_2 - 2}}\sqrt{\frac{1}{n_1} + \frac{1}{n_2}}$$
$$df = n_1 + n_2 - 2$$

t test for the difference in two related samples (the differences are normally distributed in the population)

$$t = \frac{\bar{d} - D}{\dfrac{s_d}{\sqrt{n}}}$$
$$df = n - 1$$

Formulas for $\bar{d}$ and s_d

$$\bar{d} = \frac{\Sigma d}{n}$$

$$s_d = \sqrt{\frac{\Sigma(d - \bar{d})^2}{n - 1}} = \sqrt{\frac{\Sigma d^2 - \dfrac{(\Sigma d)^2}{n}}{n - 1}}$$

Confidence interval formula for estimating the difference in related samples (the differences are normally distributed in the population)

$$\bar{d} - t\frac{s_d}{\sqrt{n}} \leq D \leq \bar{d} + t\frac{s_d}{\sqrt{n}}$$
$$df = n - 1$$

z formula for testing the difference in population proportions

$$z = \frac{(\hat{p}_1 - \hat{p}_2) - (p_1 - p_2)}{\sqrt{(\bar{p} \cdot \bar{q})\left(\dfrac{1}{n_1} + \dfrac{1}{n_2}\right)}}$$

where $\bar{p} = \dfrac{x_1 + x_2}{n_1 + n_2} = \dfrac{n_1\hat{p}_1 + n_2\hat{p}_2}{n_1 + n_2}$ and $\bar{q} = 1 - \bar{p}$

Confidence interval to estimate $p_1 - p_2$

$$(\hat{p}_1 - \hat{p}_2) - z\sqrt{\frac{\hat{p}_1 \cdot \hat{q}_1}{n_1} + \frac{\hat{p}_2 \cdot \hat{q}_2}{n_2}} \le p_1 - p_2$$

$$\le (\hat{p}_1 - \hat{p}_2) + z\sqrt{\frac{\hat{p}_1 \cdot \hat{q}_1}{n_1} + \frac{\hat{p}_2 \cdot \hat{q}_2}{n_2}}$$

F test for two population variances (assume the two populations are normally distributed)

$$F = \frac{s_1^2}{s_2^2}$$

$$df_{numerator} = v_1 = n_1 - 1$$

$$df_{denominator} = v_2 = n_2 - 1$$

Formula for determining the critical value for the lower-tail F

$$F_{1-\alpha, v_2, v_1} = \frac{1}{F_{\alpha, v_1, v_2}}$$

SUPPLEMENTARY PROBLEMS

CALCULATING THE STATISTICS

10.45 Test the following hypotheses with the data given. Let $\sigma = .10$.

$H_0: \mu_1 - \mu_2 = 0$ $H_a: \mu_1 - \mu_2 \ne 0$

Sample 1	Sample 2
$\bar{x}_1 = 138.4$	$\bar{x}_2 = 142.5$
$\sigma_1 = 6.71$	$\sigma_2 = 8.92$
$n_1 = 48$	$n_2 = 39$

10.46 Use the following data to construct a 98% confidence interval to estimate the difference between μ_1 and μ_2.

Sample 1	Sample 2
$\bar{x}_1 = 34.9$	$\bar{x}_2 = 27.6$
$\sigma_1^2 = 2.97$	$\sigma_2^2 = 3.50$
$n_1 = 34$	$n_2 = 31$

10.47 The following data come from independent samples drawn from normally distributed populations. Use these data to test the following hypotheses. Let the Type I error rate be .05.

$H_0: \mu_1 - \mu_2 = 0$

$H_a: \mu_1 - \mu_2 > 0$

Sample 1	Sample 2
$\bar{x}_1 = 2.06$	$\bar{x}_2 = 1.93$
$s_1^2 = .176$	$s_2^2 = .143$
$n_1 = 12$	$n_2 = 15$

10.48 Construct a 95% confidence interval to estimate $\mu_1 - \mu_2$ by using the following data. Assume the populations are normally distributed.

Sample 1	Sample 2
$\bar{x}_1 = 74.6$	$\bar{x}_2 = 70.9$
$s_1^2 = 10.5$	$s_2^2 = 11.4$
$n_1 = 18$	$n_2 = 19$

10.49 The following data have been gathered from two related samples. The differences are assumed to be normally distributed in the population. Use these data and alpha of .01 to test the following hypotheses.

$H_0: D = 0$

$H_a: D < 0$

$n = 21, \bar{d} = -1.16, s_d = 1.01$

10.50 Use the following data to construct a 99% confidence interval to estimate D. Assume the differences are normally distributed in the population.

Respondent	Before	After
1	47	63
2	33	35
3	38	36
4	50	56
5	39	44
6	27	29
7	35	32
8	46	54
9	41	47

10.51 Test the following hypotheses by using the given data and alpha equal to .05.

$H_0: p_1 - p_2 = 0$

$H_a: p_1 - p_2 \ne 0$

Sample 1	Sample 2
$n_1 = 783$	$n_2 = 896$
$x_1 = 345$	$x_2 = 421$

10.52 Use the following data to construct a 99% confidence interval to estimate $p_1 - p_2$.

Sample 1	Sample 2
$n_1 = 409$	$n_2 = 378$
$\hat{p}_1 = .71$	$\hat{p}_2 = .67$

10.53 Test the following hypotheses by using the given data. Let alpha $= .05$

$H_0: \sigma_1^2 = \sigma_2^2$

$H_a: \sigma_1^2 \ne \sigma_2^2$

$n_1 = 8, n_2 = 10, s_1^2 = 46, s_2^2 = 37$

TESTING YOUR UNDERSTANDING

10.54 Suppose a large insurance company wants to estimate the difference between the average amount of term life insurance purchased per family and the average amount of whole life insurance purchased per family. To obtain an estimate, one of the company's actuaries randomly selects 27 families who have term life insurance only and 29 families who have whole life policies only. Each sample is taken from families in which the leading provider is younger than 45 years of age. Use the data obtained to construct a 95% confidence interval to estimate the difference in means for these two groups. Assume the amount of insurance is normally distributed.

Term	Whole Life
$\bar{x}_T = \$75,000$	$\bar{x}_W = \$45,000$
$s_T = \$22,000$	$s_W = \$15,500$
$n_T = 27$	$n_W = 29$

10.55 A study is conducted to estimate the average difference in bus ridership for a large city during the morning and afternoon rush hours. The transit authority's researcher randomly selects nine buses because of the variety of routes they represent. On a given day the number of riders on each bus is counted at 7:45 A.M. and at 4:45 P.M., with the following results.

Bus	Morning	Afternoon
1	43	41
2	51	49
3	37	44
4	24	32
5	47	46
6	44	42
7	50	47
8	55	51
9	46	49

Use the data to compute a 90% confidence interval to estimate the population average difference. Assume ridership is normally distributed.

10.56 There are several methods used by people to organize their lives in terms of keeping track of appointments, meetings, and deadlines. Some of these include using a desk calendar, using informal notes of scrap paper, keeping them "in your head," using a day planner, and keeping a formal "to do" list. Suppose a business researcher wants to test the hypothesis that a greater proportion of marketing managers keep track of such obligations "in their head" than do accountants. To test this, a business researcher samples 400 marketing managers and 450 accountants. Of those sampled, 220 marketing managers keep track "in their head" while 216 of the accountants do so. Using a 1% level of significance, what does the business researcher find?

10.57 A study was conducted to compare the salaries of accounting clerks and data entry operators. One of the hypotheses to be tested is that the variability of salaries among accounting clerks is the same as the variability of salaries of data entry operators. To test this hypothesis, a random sample of 16 accounting clerks was taken, resulting in a sample mean salary of $26,400 and a sample standard deviation of $1,200. A random sample of 14 data entry operators was taken as well, resulting in a sample mean of $25,800 and a sample standard deviation of $1,050. Use these data and $\alpha = .05$ to test to determine whether the population variance of salaries is the same for accounting clerks as it is for data entry operators. Assume that salaries of data entry operators and accounting clerks are normally distributed in the population.

10.58 A study was conducted to develop a scale to measure stress in the workplace. Respondents were asked to rate 26 distinct work events. Each event was to be compared with the stress of the first week on the job, which was awarded an arbitrary score of 500. Sixty professional men and 41 professional women participated in the study. One of the stress events was "lack of support from the boss." The men's sample average rating of this event was 631 and the women's sample average rating was 848. Suppose the population standard deviations for men and for women both were about 100. Construct a 95% confidence interval to estimate the difference in the population mean scores on this event for men and women.

10.59 A national grocery store chain wants to test the difference in the average weight of turkeys sold in Detroit and the average weight of turkeys sold in Charlotte. According to the chain's researcher, a random sample of 20 turkeys sold at the chain's stores in Detroit yielded a sample mean of 17.53 pounds, with a standard deviation of 3.2 pounds. Her random sample of 24 turkeys sold at the chain's stores in Charlotte yielded a sample mean of 14.89 pounds, with a standard deviation of 2.7 pounds. Use a 1% level of significance to determine whether there is a difference in the mean weight of turkeys sold in these two cities. Assume the population variances are approximately the same and that the weights of turkeys sold in the stores are normally distributed.

10.60 A tree nursery has been experimenting with fertilizer to increase the growth of seedlings. A sample of 35 two-year-old pine trees are grown for three more years with a cake of fertilizer buried in the soil near the trees' roots. A second sample of 35 two-year-old pine trees are grown for three more years under identical conditions (soil, temperature, water) as the first group, but not fertilized. Tree growth is measured over the three-year period with the following results.

Trees with Fertilizer	Trees Without Fertilizer
$n_1 = 35$	$n_2 = 35$
$\bar{x}_1 = 38.4$ inches	$\bar{x}_2 = 23.1$ inches
$\sigma_1 = 9.8$ inches	$\sigma_2 = 7.4$ inches

Do the data support the theory that the population of trees with the fertilizer grew significantly larger during the period in which they were fertilized than the non-fertilized trees? Use $\alpha = .01$.

10.61 One of the most important aspects of a store's image is the perceived quality of its merchandise. Other factors include merchandise pricing, assortment of products, convenience of location, and service. Suppose image perceptions of shoppers of specialty stores and shoppers of discount stores are being compared. A random sample of shoppers is taken at each type of store, and the shoppers are asked whether the quality of merchandise is a determining factor in their perception of the store's image. Some 75% of the 350 shoppers at the specialty stores say Yes, but only 52% of the 500 shoppers at the discount store say Yes. Use these data to test to determine if there is a significant difference between the proportion of shoppers at specialty stores and the proportion of shoppers at discount stores who say that quality of merchandise is a determining factor in their perception of a store's image. Let alpha equal .10.

10.62 Is there more variation in the output of one shift in a manufacturing plant than in another shift? In an effort to study this question, plant managers gathered productivity reports from the 8 A.M. to 4 P.M. shift for eight days. The reports indicated that the following numbers of units were produced on each day for this shift.

5528	4779	5112	5380
4918	4763	5055	5106

Productivity information was also gathered from seven days for the 4 P.M. to midnight shift, resulting in the following data.

4325	4016	4872	4559
3982	4754	4116	

Use these data and $\alpha = .01$ to test to determine whether the variances of productivity for the two shifts are the same. Assume productivity is normally distributed in the population.

10.63 What is the average difference between the price of name-brand soup and the price of store-brand soup? To obtain an estimate, an analyst randomly samples eight stores. Each store sells its own brand and a national name brand. The prices of a can of name-brand tomato soup and a can of the store-brand tomato soup follow.

Store	Name Brand	Store Brand
1	54¢	49¢
2	55	50
3	59	52
4	53	51
5	54	50
6	61	56
7	51	47
8	53	49

Construct a 90% confidence interval to estimate the average difference. Assume that the differences in prices of tomato soup are normally distributed in the population.

10.64 As the prices of heating oil and natural gas increase, consumers become more careful about heating their homes. Researchers want to know how warm homeowners keep their houses in January and how the results from Wisconsin and Tennessee compare. The researchers randomly call 23 Wisconsin households between 7 P.M. and 9 P.M. on January 15 and ask the respondent how warm the house is according to the thermostat. The researchers then call 19 households in Tennessee the same night and ask the same question. The results follow.

Wisconsin				Tennessee			
71	71	65	68	73	75	74	71
70	61	67	69	74	73	74	70
75	68	71	73	72	71	69	72
74	68	67	69	74	73	70	72
69	72	67	72	69	70	67	
70	73	72					

For $\alpha = .01$, is the average temperature of a house in Tennessee significantly higher than that of a house in Wisconsin on the evening of January 15? Assume the population variances are equal and the house temperatures are normally distributed in each population.

10.65 In manufacturing, does worker productivity drop on Friday? In an effort to determine whether it does, a company's personnel analyst randomly selects from a manufacturing plant five workers who make the same part. He measures their output on Wednesday and again on Friday and obtains the following results.

Worker	Wednesday Output	Friday Output
1	71	53
2	56	47
3	75	52
4	68	55
5	74	58

The analyst uses $\alpha = .05$ and assumes the difference in productivity is normally distributed. Do the samples provide enough evidence to show that productivity drops on Friday?

10.66 A manufacturer uses two machines to drill holes in pieces of sheet metal used in engine construction. The workers who attach the sheet metal to the engine become inspectors in that they reject sheets so poorly drilled that they cannot be attached. The production manager is interested in knowing whether one machine produces more defective drillings than the other machine. As an experiment, employees mark the sheets so that the manager can determine which machine was used to drill the holes. A random sample of 191 sheets of metal drilled by machine 1 is taken, and 38 of the sheets are defective. A random sample of 202 sheets of metal drilled by machine 2 is taken, and 21 of the sheets are defective. Use $\alpha = .05$ to determine whether there is a significant difference in the proportion of sheets drilled with defective holes between machine 1 and machine 2.

10.67 Is there a difference in the proportion of construction workers who are under 35 years of age and the proportion of telephone repair people who are under 35 years of age? Suppose a study is conducted in Calgary, Alberta, using random samples of 338 construction workers and 281 telephone repair people. The sample of construction workers includes 297 people under 35 years of age and the sample of telephone repair people includes 192 people under that age. Use these data to construct a 90% confidence interval to estimate the difference in proportions of people under 35 years of age among construction workers and telephone repair people.

10.68 Executives often spend so many hours in meetings that they have relatively little time to manage their individual areas of operation. What is the difference in mean time spent in meetings by executives of the aerospace industry and executives of the automobile industry? Suppose random samples of 33 aerospace executives and 35 automobile executives are monitored for a week to determine how much time they spend in meetings. The results follow.

Aerospace	Automobile
$n_1 = 33$	$n_2 = 35$
$\bar{x}_1 = 12.4$ hours	$\bar{x}_2 = 4.6$ hours
$\sigma_1 = 2.9$ hours	$\sigma_2 = 1.8$ hours

Use the data to estimate the difference in the mean time per week executives in these two industries spend in meetings. Use a 99% level of confidence.

10.69 Various types of retail outlets sell toys during the holiday season. Among them are specialty toy stores, large discount toy stores, and other retailers that carry toys as only one part of their stock of goods. Is there any difference in the dollar amount of a customer purchase between a large discount toy store and a specialty toy store if they carry relatively comparable types of toys? Suppose in December a random sample of 60 sales slips is selected from a large discount toy outlet and a random sample of 40 sales slips is selected from a specialty toy store. The data gathered from these samples follow.

Large Discount Toy Store	Specialty Toy Store
$\bar{x}_D = \$47.20$	$\bar{x}_S = \$27.40$
$\sigma_D = \$12.45$	$\sigma_S = \$9.82$

Use $\alpha = .01$ and the data to determine whether there is a significant difference in the average size of purchases at these stores.

10.70 One of the thrusts of quality control management is to examine the process by which a product is produced. This approach also applies to paperwork. In industries where large long-term projects are undertaken, days and even weeks may elapse as a change order makes its way through a maze of approvals before receiving final approval. This process can result in long delays and stretch schedules to the breaking point. Suppose a quality control consulting group claims that it can significantly reduce the number of days required for such paperwork to receive approval. In an attempt to "prove" its case, the group selects five jobs for which it revises the paperwork system. The following data show the number of days required for a change order to be approved before the group intervened and the number of days required for a change order to be approved after the group instituted a new paperwork system.

Before	After
12	8
7	3
10	8
16	9
8	5

Use $\alpha = .01$ to determine whether there was a significant drop in the number of days required to process paperwork to approve change orders. Assume that the differences in days are normally distributed.

10.71 For the two large newspapers in your city, you are interested in knowing whether there is a significant difference in the average number of pages in each dedicated solely to advertising. You randomly select 10 editions of newspaper A and 6 editions of newspaper B (excluding weekend editions). The data follow. Use $\alpha = .01$ to test whether there is a significant difference in averages. Assume the number of pages of advertising per edition is normally distributed and the population variances are approximately equal.

A		B	
17	17	8	14
21	15	11	10
11	19	9	6
19	22		
26	16		

INTERPRETING THE OUTPUT

10.72 A study by Colliers International presented the highest and the lowest global rental rates per year per square foot of office space. Among the cities with the lowest rates were Perth, Australia; Edmonton, Alberta, Canada; and Calgary, Alberta, Canada with rates of $8.81, $9.55, and $9.69, respectively. At the high end were Hong Kong; Mumbai, India; and Tokyo, Japan, with rates over $100. Suppose a researcher conducted her own survey of businesses renting office space to determine whether one city is significantly more expensive than another. The data are tallied and analyzed by using Minitab. The results follow. Discuss the output. Assume that rental rates are normally distributed in the population. What cities were studied? How large were the samples? What were the sample statistics? What was the value of alpha? What were the hypotheses, and what was the conclusion?

```
Two-Sample T-Test and CI

Sample      N    Mean    StDev    SE Mean
Hong Kong   19   130.4   12.9     3.0
Mumbai      23   128.4   13.9     2.9


Difference = mu (Hong Kong) - mu (Mumbai)
Estimate for difference: 2.00
98% CI for difference: (-8.11, 12.11)
T-Test of difference = 0 (vs not =):
T-Value = 0.48 P-Value = 0.634 DF = 40
Both use Pooled StDev = 13.4592
```

10.73 Why do employees "blow the whistle" on other employees for unethical or illegal behavior? One study conducted by the AICPA reported the likelihood that employees would blow the whistle on another employee for such things as unsafe working conditions, unsafe products, and poorly managed operations. On a scale from 1 to 7, with 1 denoting highly improbable and 7 denoting highly probable, unnecessary purchases received a 5.72 in the study. Suppose this study was administered at a company and then all employees were subjected to a one-month series of seminars on reasons to blow the whistle on fellow employees. One month later the study was administered again to the same employees at the company in an effort to determine whether the treatment had any effect. The following Excel output shows the results of the study. What were the sample sizes? What might the hypotheses have been? If $\alpha = .05$, what conclusions could be made? Which of the statistical tests presented in this chapter is likely to have been used? Assume that differences in scores are normally distributed.

t-Test: Paired Two Sample for Means

	Variable 1	Variable 2
Mean	3.991	5.072
Variance	1.898	0.785
Observations	14	14
Pearson Correlation	−0.04585	
Hypothesized Mean Difference	0	
df	13	
t Stat	−2.47	
P(T<=t) one-tail	0.0102	
t Critical one-tail	1.77	
P(T<=t) two-tail	0.00204	
t Critical two-tail	2.16	

10.74 A large manufacturing company produces computer printers that are distributed and sold all over the United States. Due to lack of industry information, the company has a difficult time ascertaining its market share in different parts of the country. They hire a market research firm to estimate their market share in a northern city and a southern city. They would also like to know whether there is a difference in their market shares in these two cities; if so, they want to estimate how much. The market research firm randomly selects printer customers from different locales across both cities and determines what brand of computer printer they purchased. The following Minitab output shows the results from this study. Discuss the results including sample sizes, estimation of the difference in proportions, and any significant differences determined. What were the hypotheses tested?

```
Test and CI for Two Proportions

Sample          X     N     Sample P
Northern City   147   473   0.310782
Southern City   104   385   0.270130


Difference = p (Northern City) - p (Southern City
Estimate for difference: 0.0406524
99% CI for difference: (-0.0393623, 0.120667)
Test for difference = 0 (vs not = 0):
Z = 1.31 P-Value = 0.191
```

10.75 A manufacturing company produces plastic pipes that are specified to be 10 inches long and 1/8 inch thick with an opening of 3/4 inch. These pipes are molded on two different machines. To maintain consistency, the company periodically randomly selects pipes for testing. In one specific test, pipes were randomly sampled from each machine and the lengths were measured. A statistical test was computed using Excel in an effort to determine whether the variance for machine 1 was significantly greater than the variance for machine 2. The results are shown here. Discuss the outcome of this test along with some of the other information given in the output.

F-Test Two-Sample for Variances

	Variable 1	Variable 2
Mean	10.03	9.97
Variance	0.02920	0.01965
Observations	26	28
df	25	27
F	1.49	
P(F<=f) one-tail	0.15766	
F Critical one-tail	1.92	

ANALYZING THE DATABASES

Database

1. Test to determine whether there is a significant difference between mean Value Added by the Manufacturer and the mean Cost of Materials in manufacturing. Use the Manufacturing database as the sample data and let alpha be .01.

2. Use the Manufacturing database to test to determine whether there is a significantly greater variance among the values of End-of-Year Inventories than among Cost of Materials. Let $\alpha = .05$.

3. Is there a difference between the average Number of Admissions at a general medical hospital and a psychiatric hospital? Use the Hospital database to test this hypothesis with $\alpha = .10$. The variable Service in the Hospital database differentiates general medical hospitals (coded 1) and psychiatric hospitals (coded 2). Now test to determine whether there is a difference between these two types of hospitals on the variables Beds and Total Expenses.

4. Use the Financial database to test whether there is a significant difference in the proportion of companies whose earnings per share are more than $2.00 and the proportion of companies whose dividends per share are between $1.00 and $2.00. Let $\alpha = .05$.

5. Using the appropriate technique selected from this chapter and the Consumer Food database, test to determine if there is a significant difference between households in a metro area and households outside metro areas in annual food spending. Let $\alpha = .01$.

CASE

SEITZ CORPORATION: PRODUCING QUALITY GEAR-DRIVEN AND LINEAR-MOTION PRODUCTS

The Seitz Corporation, a QS 9000 certified organization based in Torrington, Connecticut, is a leading designer and manufacturer of thermoplastic motion control systems and components and an industry leader in plastics and gear trains. Founded in 1949 by the late Karl F. Seitz, the company began as a small tool-making business and grew slowly. In the late 1960s, the company expanded its services to include custom injection molding. As their customer base grew to include leading printer manufacturers, Seitz developed and patented a proprietary line of perforated-form handling tractors. Utilizing its injection-molding technology, the company engineered an all-plastic tractor called Data Motion, which replaced costly metal versions. By the late 1970s, business was booming, and Data Motion had become the worldwide industry leader.

In the 1980s, foreign competition entered the business equipment market, and many of Seitz's customers relocated or closed shop. The ripple effect hit Seitz as sales declined and profits eroded. Employment at the company dropped from a high of 313 in 1985 to only 125 in 1987. Drastic changes had to be made at Seitz.

To meet the challenge in 1987, Seitz made a crucial decision to change the way it did business. The company implemented a formal five-year plan with measurable goals called "World-Class Excellence Through Total Quality." Senior managers devoted many hours to improving employee training and involvement. New concepts were explored and integrated into the business plan. Teams and programs were put into place to immediately correct deficiencies in Seitz's systems that were revealed in customer satisfaction surveys. All employees from machine operators to accountants were taught that quality means understanding customers' needs and fulfilling them correctly the first time.

Once the program started, thousands of dollars in cost savings and two new products generating almost $1 million in sales resulted. Annual sales grew from $10.8 million in 1987 to $19 million in 1990. Seitz's customer base expanded from 312 in 1987 to 550 at the end of 1990.

In the decade of the 1990s, Seitz continued its steady growth. By 1999, Seitz was shipping products to 28 countries, and customers included Xerox, Hewlett Packard, Canon, U.S. Tsubaki, and many more worldwide. By 1998, sales topped the $30 million mark. In January 2000, the company established the Seitz Motion Control Systems Co., Ltd., in Changzhou, China, about 150 miles northwest of Shanghai, to provide product and tooling design engineering, sourcing and supply chain management services, and contract manufacturing. The Seitz Corporation headquarters is located in Torrington, Connecticut in an 80,000 square foot facility with over 150 associates, 50 molding machines ranging in size from 35 tons to 770 tons, an in-house tooling department, and a corporate staff. While the primary core competency of the Seitz Corporation is rotary and linear motion control, making them an industry leader in plastics and gear trains, Seitz offers a full range of product design and tooling services.

Discussion

1. Seitz's list of several hundred business-to-business customers continues to grow. Managers would like to know whether the average dollar amount of sales per transaction per customer has changed from last year to this year. Suppose company accountants sampled 20 customers randomly from last year's records and determined that the mean sales per customer was $2,300, with a standard deviation of $500. They sampled 25 customers randomly

from this year's files and determined that the mean sales per customer for this sample was $2,450, with a standard deviation of $540. Analyze these data and summarize your findings for managers. Explain how this information can be used by decision makers. Assume that sales per customer are normally distributed.

2. One common approach to measuring a company's quality is through the use of customer satisfaction surveys. Suppose in a random sample, Seitz's customers are asked whether the plastic tractor produced by Seitz has outstanding quality (Yes or No). Assume Seitz produces these tractors at two different plant locations and that the tractor customers can be divided according to where their tractors were manufactured. Suppose a random sample of 45 customers who bought tractors made at plant 1 results in 18 saying the tractors have excellent quality and a random sample of 51 customers who bought tractors made at plant 2 results in 12 saying the tractors have excellent quality. Use a confidence interval to express the estimated difference in population proportions of excellent ratings between the two groups of customers. Does it seem to matter which plant produces the tractors in terms of the quality rating received from customers? What would you report from these data?

3. Suppose the customer satisfaction survey included a question on the overall quality of Seitz measured on a scale from 0 to 10 where higher numbers indicate greater quality. Company managers monitor the figures from year to year to help determine whether Seitz is improving customers' perceptions of its quality. Suppose random samples of the responses from 2010 customers and 2011 customers are taken and analyzed on this question, and the following Minitab analysis of the data results. Help managers interpret this analysis so that comparisons can be made between 2010 and 2011. Discuss the samples, the statistics, and the conclusions.

```
Two-Sample T-Test and CI: 2010, 2011

Two-sample T for 2010 vs 2011
          N     Mean    StDev   SE Mean
2010      75    6.466   0.352   0.041
2011      93    6.604   0.398   0.041

Difference = mu (2010) - mu (2011)
Estimate for difference: -0.1376
95% CI for difference: (-0.2535, -0.0217)
T-Test of difference = 0 (vs not = 0):
T-Value = -2.34 P-Value = 0.020 DF = 166
Both use Pooled StDev = 0.3782
```

4. Suppose Seitz produces pulleys that are specified to be 50 millimeters (mm) in diameter. A large batch of pulleys is made in week 1 and another is made in week 5. Quality control people want to determine whether there is a difference in the variance of the diameters of the two batches. Assume that a sample of six pulleys from the week 1 batch results in the following diameter measurements (in mm): 51, 50, 48, 50, 49, 51. Assume that a sample of seven pulleys from the week 5 batch results in the following diameter measurements (in mm): 50, 48, 48, 51, 52, 50, 52. Conduct a test to determine whether the variance in diameters differs between these two populations. Why would the quality control people be interested in such a test? What results of this test would you relate to them? What about the means of these two batches? Analyze these data in terms of the means and report on the results. Assume that pulley diameters are normally distributed in the population.

Source: Adapted from "Seitz Corporation," *Strengthening America's Competitiveness: Resource Management Insights for Small Business Success,*" published by Warner Books on behalf of Connecticut Mutual Life Insurance Company and the U.S. Chamber of Commerce in association with the Blue Chip Enterprise Initiative, 1991. Case update based on Seitz Corporation 2011, http://www.seitzcorp.com/about.htm.

USING THE COMPUTER

EXCEL

- Excel has the capability of performing any of the statistical techniques presented in this chapter with the exception of testing the difference in two population proportions.

- Each of the tests presented here in Excel is accessed through the **Data Analysis** feature.

- To conduct a z test for the difference in two means, begin by selecting the **Data** tab on the Excel worksheet. From the **Analysis** panel at the right top of the **Data** tab worksheet, click on **Data Analysis**. If your Excel worksheet does not show the **Data Analysis** option, then you can load it as an add-in following directions given in Chapter 2. From the **Data Analysis** pulldown menu, select **z-Test: Two Sample**

for Means from the dialog box. Enter the location of the observations from the first group in **Variable 1 Range**. Enter the location of the observations from the second group in **Variable 2 Range**. Enter the hypothesized value for the mean difference in **Hypothesized Mean Difference**. Enter the known variance of population 1 in **Variable 1 Variance (known)**. Enter the known variance of population 2 in **Variable 2 Variance (known)**. Check **Labels** if you have labels. Select **Alpha**.

- To conduct a *t* test for the difference in two means, begin by selecting the **Data** tab on the Excel worksheet. From the **Analysis** panel at the right top of the **Data** tab worksheet, click on **Data Analysis**. If your Excel worksheet does not show the **Data Analysis** option, then you can load it as an add-in following directions given in Chapter 2. From the **Data Analysis** pulldown menu, select **t-Test: Two-Sample Assuming Equal Variances** from the dialog box if you are assuming that the population variances are equal. Select **t-Test: Two-Sample Assuming Unequal Variances** from the dialog box if you are assuming that the population variances are not equal. Input is the same for either test. Enter the location of the observations from the first group in **Variable 1 Range**. Enter the location of the observations from the second group in **Variable 2 Range**. Enter the hypothesized value for the mean difference in **Hypothesized Mean Difference**. Check **Labels** if you have labels. Select **Alpha**.

▨ To conduct a *t* test for related populations, begin by selecting the **Data** tab on the Excel worksheet. From the **Analysis** panel at the right top of the **Data** tab worksheet, click on **Data Analysis**. If your Excel worksheet does not show the **Data Analysis** option, then you can load it as an add-in following directions given in Chapter 2. From the **Data Analysis** pulldown menu, select **t-Test: Paired Two-Sample for Means** from the dialog box. Enter the location of the observations from the first group in **Variable 1 Range**. Enter the location of the observations from the second group in **Variable 2 Range**. Enter the hypothesized value for the mean difference in **Hypothesized Mean Difference**. Check **Labels** if you have labels. Select **Alpha**.

▨ To conduct an *F* test for two population variances, begin by selecting the **Data** tab on the Excel worksheet. From the **Analysis** panel at the right top of the **Data** tab worksheet, click on **Data Analysis**. If your Excel worksheet does not show the **Data Analysis** option, then you can load it as an add-in following directions given in Chapter 2. From the **Data Analysis** pulldown menu, select **F-Test: Two-Sample for Variances** from the dialog box. Enter the location of the observations from the first group in **Variable 1 Range**. Enter the location of the observations from the second group in **Variable 2 Range**. Check **Labels** if you have labels. Select **Alpha**.

MINITAB

▨ With the exception of the two-sample *z* test and confidence interval, Minitab has the capability to perform any of the statistical techniques presented in this chapter.

▨ To begin a *t* test for the difference in two means or confidence intervals about the difference of two means from independent populations and population variances unknown, select **Stat** on the menu bar. Select **Basic Statistics** from the pulldown menu. From the second pulldown menu, select **2-Sample t**. Check **Samples in one column** if the data are "stacked" in one column: 1.) Place the location of the column with the stacked observations in the box labeled **Samples**. 2.) Place the location of the column containing the group identifiers in the box labeled **Subscripts**. Check **Samples in different columns** if the data are located in two separate columns (unstacked):

1.) Place the location of one column of observations in **First**, and 2.) Place the location of the other column of observations in **Second**. Check **Summarized data** if you want to enter statistics on the two samples rather than the raw data: 1.) In the row beside **First**, enter the values of the sample size, the sample mean, and the sample standard deviation for the first sample in **Sample size**, **Mean**, and **Standard deviation**, respectively, and 2.) In the row beside **Second**, enter the values of the sample size, the sample mean, and the sample standard deviation for the second sample in **Sample size**, **Mean**, and **Standard deviation**, respectively. Check the box beside **Assume equal variances** if you want to use the equal variances model. Leave it blank if you do not want to assume equal variances. Click on **Options** if you want to enter a confidence level, the mean difference being tested, and/or the direction of the alternative hypothesis (greater than, less than, or not equal). Both the observed *t* for the hypothesis test and the confidence interval are given in the output.

▨ To begin *t* tests or confidence intervals about the difference in two related populations, select **Stat** on the menu bar. Select **Basic Statistics** from the pulldown menu. From the second pulldown menu, select **Paired t**. Check **Samples in columns** if the data are in columns: 1.) Place the location of one sample of observations in the box beside **First sample**, and 2.) Place the location of the other sample of observations in the box beside **Second sample**. Check **Summarized data (differences)** if you want to enter sample statistics on the pairs of data rather than the raw data. Enter the values of the sample size, the sample mean, and the sample standard deviation for the pairs in the boxes beside **Sample size, Mean**, and **Standard deviation**, respectively. Click on **Options** if you want to enter a confidence level, the test mean difference, and/or the direction of the alternative hypothesis (greater than, less than, or not equal). Both the observed *t* for the hypothesis test and the confidence interval are given in the output.

▨ To begin a *z* test or confidence interval about the difference in two population proportions, select **Stat** on the menu bar. Select **Basic Statistics** from the pulldown menu. From the second pulldown menu, select **2 Proportions**. Check **Samples in one column** if the dichotomous data are in one column and the group identifiers are in another column: 1.) Place the location of the raw data in the box beside **Samples**, and 2.) Place the location of the group identifiers in the box beside **Subscripts**. Check **Samples in different columns** if the dichotomous data are located in two separate columns (unstacked): 1.) Place the location of one column of observations in **First**, and 2.) Place the location of the other column of observations in **Second**. Check **Summarized data (differences)** if you want to enter the values of *x* and *n* for each group rather than the raw data: 1.) Enter the sample sizes for each sample under **Trials** in the boxes beside **First** and **Second** denoting the two samples, and 2.) Enter the number of items that possessed the desired characteristics (*x*) for each sample under **Events** in the boxes beside **First** and **Second** denoting the two samples. Click on **Options** if you want to enter a confidence level, the test difference in population proportions, and/or the direction of the alternative hypothesis (greater than, less than, or not equal). You can check the box beside **Use pooled estimate of p for test** if you want to use a pooled estimate of p in conducting the z test for population proportions. Both the observed z for the hypothesis test and the confidence interval are given in the output.

▓ To begin an F test about the difference in two population variances, select **Stat** on the menu bar. Select **Basic Statistics** from the pulldown menu. From the second pulldown menu, select **2 Variances**. Check **Samples in one column** if the data are in one column and the group identifiers are in another column: 1.) Place the location of the raw data in the box beside **Samples**, and 2.) Place the

location of the group identifiers in the box beside **Subscripts**. Check **Samples in different columns** if the data are located in two separate columns (unstacked): 1.) Place the location of one column of observations in **First**, and 2.) Place the location of the other column of observations in **Second**. Check **Summarized data** if you want to enter the values of the sample size and the sample variance for each group rather than the raw data: 1.) Enter the sample sizes for each sample under **Sample size:** in the boxes beside **First** and **Second** designating the two samples. 2.) Enter the values of the respective sample variance for each sample under **Variance** in the boxes beside **First** and **Second** designating the two samples. Click on **Options** if you want to enter a confidence level or your own title. Both the observed F for the hypothesis test and the confidence interval are given in the output.

CHAPTER 11

Analysis of Variance and Design of Experiments

LEARNING OBJECTIVES

The focus of this chapter is the design of experiments and the analysis of variance, thereby enabling you to:

1. Describe an experimental design and its elements, including independent variables—both treatment and classification—and dependent variables.

2. Test a completely randomized design using a one-way analysis of variance.

3. Use multiple comparison techniques, including Tukey's honestly significant difference test and the Tukey-Kramer procedure, to test the difference in two treatment means when there is overall significant difference between treatments.

4. Test a randomized block design which includes a blocking variable to control for confounding variables.

5. Test a factorial design using a two-way analysis of variance, noting the advantages and applications of such a design and accounting for possible interaction between two treatment variables.

Jeff Greenberg/PhotoEdit

Job and Career Satisfaction of Foreign Self-Initiated Expatriates

Because of worker shortages in some industries, in a global business environment, firms around the world sometimes must compete with each other for workers. This is especially true in industries and job designations where specialty skills are required. In order to fill such needs, companies sometimes turn to self-initiated expatriates. Self-initiated expatriates are defined to be workers who are hired as individuals on a contractual basis to work in a foreign country—in contrast to individuals who are given overseas transfers by a parent organization; that is, they are "guest workers" as compared to "organizational expatriates." Some examples could be computer experts from India, China, and Japan being hired by Silicon Valley companies; American engineers working with Russian companies to extract oil and gas; or financial experts from England who are hired by Singapore companies to help manage the stock market. How satisfied are self-initiated expatriates with their jobs and their careers?

In an attempt to answer that question, suppose a study was conducted by randomly sampling self-initiated expatriates in five industries: information technology (IT), finance, education, healthcare, and consulting. Each is asked to rate his or her present job satisfaction on a 7-point Likert scale, with 7 being very satisfied and 1 being very unsatisfied. Suppose the data shown below are a portion of the study.

IT	Finance	Education	Healthcare	Consulting
5	3	2	3	6
6	4	3	2	7
5	4	3	4	5
7	5	2	3	6
	4	2	5	
		3		

Suppose in addition, self-initiated expatriates are asked to report their overall satisfaction with their career on the same 7-point scale. The ratings are broken down by the respondent's experience in the host country and age and the resultant data are shown below.

		Time in Host Country			
		<1 year	1–2 years	3–4 years	≥5 years
Age	30–39	3	4	3	6
		2	5	4	4
		3	3	5	5
	40–49	4	3	4	4
		3	4	4	6
		2	3	5	5
	Over 50	4	4	5	6
		3	4	4	5
		4	5	5	6

Managerial and Statistical Questions

1. Is there a difference in the job satisfaction ratings of self-initiated expatriates by industry? If we were to use the *t* test for the difference of two independent population means presented in Chapter 10 to analyze these data, we would need to do 10 different *t* tests since there are five different industries. Is there a better, more parsimonious way to analyze this data? Can the analysis be done simultaneously using one technique?

2. The second table in the Decision Dilemma displays career satisfaction data broken down two different ways, age and time in country. How does a researcher analyze such data when there are two different types of groups or classifications? What if one variable, such as age, acts on another variable, such as time in the country, such that there is an interaction? That is, time in the country might matter more in one category than in another. Can this effect be measured and if so, how?

Source: Concepts adapted from Chay Hoon Lee, "A Study of Underemployment Among Self-Initiated Expatriates," *Journal of World Business* vol. 40, no. 2 (May 2005), pp. 172–187.

Sometimes business research entails more complicated hypothesis-testing scenarios than those presented to this point in the text. Instead of comparing the wear of tire tread for two brands of tires to determine whether there is a significant difference between the brands, as we could have done by using Chapter 10 techniques, a tire researcher may choose to compare three, four, or even more brands of tires at the same time. In addition, the researcher may want to include different levels of quality of tires in the experiment, such as low-quality, medium-quality, and high-quality tires. Tests may be conducted under

409

FIGURE 11.1

Branch of the Tree Diagram
Taxonomy of Inference
Techniques

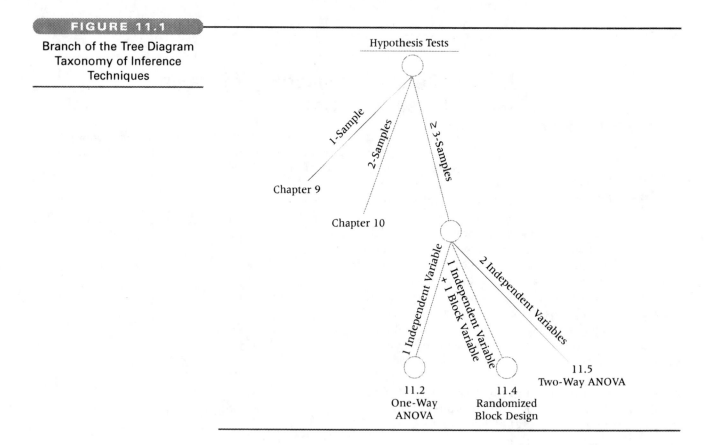

varying conditions of temperature, precipitation, or road surface. Such experiments involve selecting and analyzing more than two samples of data.

Figure III-1 of the Introduction to Unit III displays the Tree Diagram Taxonomy of Inferential Techniques, organizing the techniques by usage and number of samples. The entire right side of the tree diagram taxonomy contains various hypothesis-testing techniques. Techniques for testing hypotheses using a *single* sample are presented in Chapter 9; and techniques for testing hypotheses about the differences in two populations using *two* samples are presented in Chapter 10. The far right branch of the tree diagram taxonomy contains techniques for analyzing *three or more* samples. This branch, shown in Figure 11.1, represents the techniques presented in Chapter 11.

11.1 INTRODUCTION TO DESIGN OF EXPERIMENTS

An **experimental design** is *a plan and a structure to test hypotheses in which the researcher either controls or manipulates one or more variables.* It contains independent and dependent variables. In an experimental design, an **independent variable** may be either a treatment variable or a classification variable. A **treatment variable** is *a variable the experimenter controls or modifies in the experiment.* A **classification variable** is *some characteristic of the experimental subject that was present prior to the experiment and is not a result of the experimenter's manipulations or control.* Independent variables are sometimes also referred to as **factors.** Wal-Mart executives might sanction an in-house study to compare daily sales volumes for a given size store in four different demographic settings: (1) inner-city stores (large city), (2) suburban stores (large city), (3) stores in a medium-sized city, and (4) stores in a small town. Managers might also decide to compare sales on the five different weekdays (Monday through Friday). In this study, the independent variables are store demographics and day of the week.

A finance researcher might conduct a study to determine whether there is a significant difference in application fees for home loans in five geographic regions of the

United States and might include three different types of lending organizations. In this study, the independent variables are geographic region and types of lending organizations. Or suppose a manufacturing organization produces a valve that is specified to have an opening of 6.37 centimeters. Quality controllers within the company might decide to test to determine how the openings for produced valves vary among four different machines on three different shifts. This experiment includes the independent variables of type of machine and work shift.

Whether an independent variable can be manipulated by the researcher depends on the concept being studied. Independent variables such as work shift, gender of employee, geographic region, type of machine, and quality of tire are classification variables with conditions that existed prior to the study. The business researcher cannot change the characteristic of the variable, so he or she studies the phenomenon being explored under several conditions of the various aspects of the variable. As an example, the valve experiment is conducted under the conditions of all three work shifts.

However, some independent variables can be manipulated by the researcher. For example, in the well-known Hawthorne studies of the Western Electric Company in the 1920s in Illinois, the amount of light in production areas was varied to determine the effect of light on productivity. In theory, this independent variable could be manipulated by the researcher to allow any level of lighting. Other examples of independent variables that can be manipulated include the amount of bonuses offered workers, level of humidity, and temperature. These are examples of treatment variables.

Each independent variable has two or more levels, or classifications. **Levels**, or **classifications**, of independent variables are *the subcategories of the independent variable used by the researcher in the experimental design.* For example, the different demographic settings listed for the Wal-Mart study are four levels, or classifications, of the independent variable store demographics: (1) inner-city store, (2) suburban store, (3) store in a medium-sized city, and (4) store in small town. In the valve experiment, four levels or classifications of machines within the independent variable machine type are used: machine 1, machine 2, machine 3, and machine 4.

The other type of variable in an experimental design is a **dependent variable**. A dependent variable is *the response to the different levels of the independent variables.* It is the measurement taken under the conditions of the experimental design that reflect the effects of the independent variable(s). In the Wal-Mart study, the dependent variable is the dollar amount of daily total sales. For the study on loan application fees, the fee charged for a loan application is probably the dependent variable. In the valve experiment, the dependent variable is the size of the opening of the valve.

Experimental designs in this chapter are analyzed statistically by a group of techniques referred to as **analysis of variance**, or **ANOVA**. The analysis of variance concept begins with the notion that individual items being studied, such as employees, machine-produced products, district offices, hospitals, and so on, are not all the same. Note the measurements for the openings of 24 valves randomly selected from an assembly line that are given in Table 11.1. The mean opening is 6.34 centimeters (cm). Only one of the 24 valve openings is actually the mean. Why do the valve openings vary? The total sum of squares of deviation of these valve openings around the mean is .3915 cm^2. Why is this value not zero? Using various types of experimental designs, we can explore some possible reasons for this variance with analysis of variance techniques. As we explore each of the experimental designs and their associated analysis, note that the statistical technique is attempting to "break down" the total variance among the objects being studied into possible causes. In

TABLE 11.1				
Valve Opening Measurements (in cm) for 24 Valves Produced on an Assembly Line	6.26	6.19	6.33	6.26	6.50
	6.19	6.44	6.22	6.54	6.23
	6.29	6.40	6.23	6.29	6.58
	6.27	6.38	6.58	6.31	6.34
	6.21	6.19	6.36	6.56	

$\bar{x} = 6.34$. Total Sum of Squares Deviation = SST = $\sum(x_i - \bar{x})^2 = .3915$

the case of the valve openings, this variance of measurements might be due to such variables as machine, operator, shift, supplier, and production conditions, among others.

Many different types of experimental designs are available to researchers. In this chapter, we will present and discuss three specific types of experimental designs: completely randomized design, randomized block design, and factorial experiments.

11.1 PROBLEMS

11.1 Some New York Stock Exchange analysts believe that 24-hour trading on the stock exchange is the wave of the future. As an initial test of this idea, the New York Stock Exchange opened two after-hour "crossing sections" in the early 1990s and studied the results of these extra-hour sessions for one year.

    a. State an independent variable that could have been used for this study.

    b. List at least two levels, or classifications, for this variable.

    c. Give a dependent variable for this study.

11.2 Southwest Airlines is able to keep fares low, in part because of relatively low maintenance costs on its airplanes. One of the main reasons for the low maintenance costs is that Southwest flies only one type of aircraft, the Boeing 737. However, Southwest flies three different versions of the 737. Suppose Southwest decides to conduct a study to determine whether there is a significant difference in the average annual maintenance costs for the three types of 737s used.

    a. State an independent variable for such a study.

    b. What are some of the levels or classifications that might be studied under this variable?

    c. Give a dependent variable for this study.

11.3 A large multinational banking company wants to determine whether there is a significant difference in the average dollar amounts purchased by users of different types of credit cards. Among the credit cards being studied are MasterCard, Visa, Discover, and American Express.

    a. If an experimental design were set up for such a study, what are some possible independent variables?

    b. List at least three levels, or classifications, for each independent variable.

    c. What are some possible dependent variables for this experiment?

11.4 Is there a difference in the family demographics of people who stay at motels? Suppose a study is conducted in which three categories of motels are used: economy motels, modestly priced chain motels, and exclusive motels. One of the dependent variables studied might be the number of children in the family of the person staying in the motel. Name three other dependent variables that might be used in this study.

11.2 THE COMPLETELY RANDOMIZED DESIGN (ONE-WAY ANOVA)

One of the simplest experimental designs is the completely randomized design. In the **completely randomized design**, *subjects are assigned randomly to treatments.* The completely randomized design contains only one independent variable, with two or more treatment levels, or classifications. If only two treatment levels, or classifications, of the independent variable are present, the design is the same one used to test the difference in means of two independent populations presented in Chapter 10, which used the t test to analyze the data.

In this section, we will focus on completely randomized designs with three or more classification levels. Analysis of variance, or ANOVA, will be used to analyze the data that result from the treatments.

FIGURE 11.2

Completely Randomized
Design

A completely randomized design could be structured for a tire-quality study in which tire quality is the independent variable and the treatment levels are low, medium, and high quality. The dependent variable might be the number of miles driven before the tread fails state inspection. A study of daily sales volumes for Wal-Mart stores could be undertaken by using a completely randomized design with demographic setting as the independent variable. The treatment levels, or classifications, would be inner-city stores, suburban stores, stores in medium-sized cities, and stores in small towns. The dependent variable would be sales dollars.

As an example of a completely randomized design, suppose a researcher decides to analyze the effects of the machine operator on the valve opening measurements of valves produced in a manufacturing plant, like those shown in Table 11.1. The independent variable in this design is machine operator. Suppose further that four different operators operate the machines. These four machine operators are the levels of treatment, or classification, of the independent variable. The dependent variable is the opening measurement of the valve. Figure 11.2 shows the structure of this completely randomized design. Is there a significant difference in the mean valve openings of 24 valves produced by the four operators? Table 11.2 contains the valve opening measurements for valves produced under each operator.

TABLE 11.2

Valve Openings by Operator

1	2	3	4
6.33	6.26	6.44	6.29
6.26	6.36	6.38	6.23
6.31	6.23	6.58	6.19
6.29	6.27	6.54	6.21
6.40	6.19	6.56	
	6.50	6.34	
	6.19	6.58	
	6.22		

One-Way Analysis of Variance

In the machine operator example, is it possible to analyze the four samples by using a t test for the difference in two sample means? These four samples would require $_4C_2 = 6$ individual t tests to accomplish the analysis of two groups at a time. Recall that if $\alpha = .05$ for a particular test, there is a 5% chance of rejecting a null hypothesis that is true (i.e., committing a Type I error). If enough tests are done, eventually one or more null hypotheses will be falsely rejected by chance. Hence, $\alpha = .05$ is valid only for one t test. In this problem, with six t tests, the error rate compounds, so when the analyst is finished with the problem there is a much greater than .05 chance of committing a Type I error. Fortunately, a technique has been developed that analyzes all the sample means at one time and thus precludes the buildup of error rate: analysis of variance (ANOVA). A completely randomized design is analyzed by a **one-way analysis of variance**.

In general, if k samples are being analyzed, the following hypotheses are being tested in a one-way ANOVA.

$$H_0: \mu_1 = \mu_2 = \mu_3 = \ldots = \mu_k$$

H_a: At least one of the means is different from the others.

The null hypothesis states that the population means for all treatment levels are equal. Because of the way the alternative hypothesis is stated, if even one of the population means is different from the others, the null hypothesis is rejected.

Testing these hypotheses by using one-way ANOVA is accomplished by partitioning the total variance of the data into the following two variances.

1. The variance resulting from the treatment (columns)
2. The error variance, or that portion of the total variance unexplained by the treatment

FIGURE 11.3

Partitioning Total Sum of
Squares of Variation

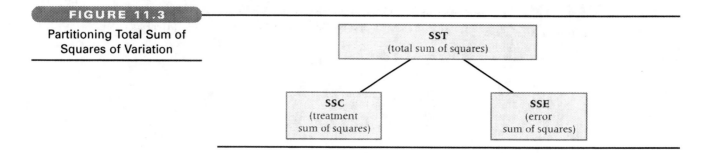

As part of this process, the total sum of squares of deviation of values around the mean can be divided into two additive and independent parts.

$$SST \quad = \quad SSC \quad + \quad SSE$$

$$\sum_{i=1}^{n_j} \sum_{j=1}^{C} (x_{ij} - \bar{x})^2 = \sum_{j=1}^{C} n_j(\bar{x}_j - \bar{x})^2 + \sum_{i=1}^{n_j} \sum_{j=1}^{C} (x_{ij} - \bar{x}_j)^2$$

where

SST $=$ total sum of squares
SSC $=$ sum of squares column (treatment)
SSE $=$ sum of squares error
i $=$ particular member of a treatment level
j $=$ a treatment level
C $=$ number of treatment levels
n_j $=$ number of observations in a given treatment level
$\bar{x}$ $=$ grand mean
$\bar{x}_j$ $=$ mean of a treatment group or level
x_{ij} $=$ individual value

This relationship is shown in Figure 11.3. Observe that the total sum of squares of variation is partitioned into the sum of squares of treatment (columns) and the sum of squares of error.

The formulas used to accomplish one-way analysis of variance are developed from this relationship. The double summation sign indicates that the values are summed within a treatment level and across treatment levels. Basically, ANOVA compares the relative sizes of the *treatment* variation and the *error* variation (within-group variation). The error variation is unaccounted-for variation and can be viewed at this point as variation due to individual differences within treatment groups. If a significant difference in treatments is present, the treatment variation should be large relative to the error variation.

Figure 11.4 displays the data from the machine operator example in terms of treatment level. Note the variation of values (x) *within* each treatment level. Now examine the variation between levels 1 through 4 (the difference in the machine operators). In particular, note

FIGURE 11.4

Location of Mean Value
Openings by Operator

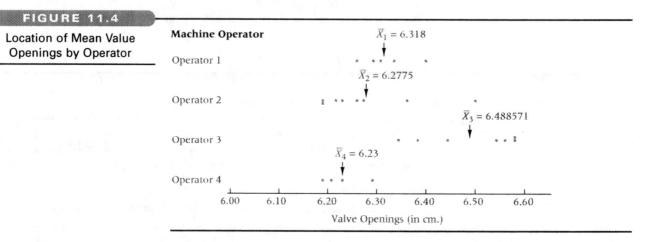

that values for treatment level 3 seem to be located differently from those of levels 2 and 4. This difference also is underscored by the mean values for each treatment level:

$$\bar{x}_1 = 6.318 \quad \bar{x}_2 = 6.2775 \quad \bar{x}_3 = 6.488571 \quad \bar{x}_4 = 6.23$$

Analysis of variance is used to determine statistically whether the variance between the treatment level means is greater than the variances within levels (error variance). Several important assumptions underlie analysis of variance:

1. Observations are drawn from normally distributed populations.
2. Observations represent random samples from the populations.
3. Variances of the populations are equal.

These assumptions are similar to those for using the *t* test for independent samples in Chapter 10. It is assumed that the populations are normally distributed and that the population variances are equal. These techniques should be used only with random samples.

An ANOVA is computed with the three sums of squares: total, treatment (columns), and error. Shown here are the formulas to compute a one-way analysis of variance. The term SS represents sum of squares, and the term MS represents mean square. SSC is the sum of squares columns, which yields the sum of squares between treatments. It measures the variation between columns or between treatments since the independent variable treatment levels are presented as columns. SSE is the sum of squares of error, which yields the variation within treatments (or columns). Some say that it is a measure of the individual differences unaccounted for by the treatments. SST is the total sum of squares and is a measure of all variation in the dependent variable. As shown previously, SST contains both SSC and SSE and can be partitioned into SSC and SSE. MSC, MSE, and MST are the mean squares of column, error, and total, respectively. Mean square is an average and is computed by dividing the sum of squares by the degrees of freedom. Finally, the *F* value is determined by dividing the treatment variance (MSC) by the error variance (MSE). As discussed in Chapter 10, the *F* is a ratio of two variances. In the ANOVA situation, the **F value** is *a ratio of the treatment variance to the error variance.*

FORMULAS FOR COMPUTING A ONE-WAY ANOVA

$$SSC = \sum_{j=1}^{C} n_j (\bar{x}_j - \bar{x})^2$$

$$SSE = \sum_{i=1}^{n_j} \sum_{j=1}^{C} (x_{ij} - \bar{x}_j)^2$$

$$SST = \sum_{i=1}^{n_j} \sum_{j=1}^{C} (x_{ij} - \bar{x})^2$$

$$df_C = C - 1$$

$$df_E = N - C$$

$$df_T = N - 1$$

$$MSC = \frac{SSC}{df_C}$$

$$MSE = \frac{SSE}{df_E}$$

$$F = \frac{MSC}{MSE}$$

where

i = a particular member of a treatment level
j = a treatment level
C = number of treatment levels
n_j = number of observations in a given treatment level
$\bar{x}$ = grand mean
$\bar{x}_j$ = column mean
x_{ij} = individual value

Performing these calculations for the machine operator example yields the following.

Machine Operator

1	2	3	4
6.33	6.26	6.44	6.29
6.26	6.36	6.38	6.23
6.31	6.23	6.58	6.19
6.29	6.27	6.54	6.21
6.40	6.19	6.56	
	6.50	6.34	
	6.19	6.58	
	6.22		

T_j: $T_1 = 31.59$ $T_2 = 50.22$ $T_3 = 45.42$ $T_4 = 24.92$ $T = 152.15$
n_j: $n_1 = 5$ $n_2 = 8$ $n_3 = 7$ $n_4 = 4$ $N = 24$
$\bar{x}_j$: $\bar{x}_1 = 6.318$ $\bar{x}_2 = 6.2775$ $\bar{x}_3 = 6.488571$ $\bar{x}_4 = 6.23$ $\bar{x} = 6.339583$

$$
\begin{aligned}
SSC = \sum_{j=1}^{C} n_j(\bar{x}_j - \bar{x})^2 &= [5(6.318 - 6.339583)^2 + 8(6.2775 - 6.339583)^2 \\
&\quad + 7(6.488571 - 6.339583)^2 + 4(6.23 - 6.339583)^2] \\
&= 0.00233 + 0.03083 + 0.15538 + 0.04803 \\
&= 0.23658
\end{aligned}
$$

$$
\begin{aligned}
SSE = \sum_{i=1}^{n_j}\sum_{j=1}^{C}(x_{ij} - \bar{x}_j)^2 &= [(6.33 - 6.318)^2 + (6.26 - 6.318)^2 + (6.31 - 6.318)^2 \\
&\quad + (6.29 - 6.318)^2 + (6.40 - 6.318)^2 + (6.26 - 6.2775)^2 \\
&\quad + (6.36 - 6.2775)^2 + \ldots + (6.19 - 6.23)^2 + (6.21 - 6.23)^2 \\
&= 0.15492
\end{aligned}
$$

$$
\begin{aligned}
SST = \sum_{i=1}^{n_j}\sum_{j=1}^{C}(x_{ij} - \bar{x})^2 &= [(6.33 - 6.339583)^2 + (6.26 - 6.339583)^2 \\
&\quad + (6.31 - 6.339583)^2 + \ldots + (6.19 - 6.339583)^2 \\
&\quad + (6.21 - 6.339583)^2 \\
&= 0.39150
\end{aligned}
$$

$$df_C = C - 1 = 4 - 1 = 3$$
$$df_E = N - C = 24 - 4 = 20$$
$$df_T = N - 1 = 24 - 1 = 23$$
$$MSC = \frac{SSC}{df_C} = \frac{.23658}{3} = .078860$$
$$MSE = \frac{SSE}{df_E} = \frac{.15492}{20} = .007746$$
$$F = \frac{.078860}{.007746} = 10.18$$

From these computations, an analysis of variance chart can be constructed, as shown in Table 11.3. The observed F value is 10.18. It is compared to a critical value from the F table to determine whether there is a significant difference in treatment or classification.

Source of Variance	df	SS	MS	F
Between	3	0.23658	0.078860	10.18
Error	20	0.15492	0.007746	
Total	23	0.39150		

TABLE 11.4

An Abbreviated *F* Table
for $\alpha = .05$

		NUMERATOR DEGREES OF FREEDOM							
	1	**2**	**3**	**4**	**5**	**6**	**7**	**8**	**9**
19	4.38	3.52	3.13	2.90	2.74	2.63	2.54	2.48	2.42
20	4.35	3.49	3.10	2.87	2.71	2.60	2.51	2.45	2.39
21	4.32	3.47	3.07	2.84	2.68	2.57	2.49	2.42	2.37

(Denominator Degrees of Freedom)

Reading the *F* Distribution Table

The **F distribution** table is in Table A.7. Associated with every *F* value in the table are two unique df values: degrees of freedom in the numerator (df_C) and degrees of freedom in the denominator (df_E). To look up a value in the *F* distribution table, the researcher must know both degrees of freedom. Because each *F* distribution is determined by a unique pair of degrees of freedom, many *F* distributions are possible. Space constraints limit Table A.7 to *F* values for only $\alpha = .005, .01, .025, .05,$ and $.10$. However, statistical computer software packages for computing ANOVAs usually give a probability for the *F* value, which allows a hypothesis-testing decision for any alpha based on the *p*-value method.

In the one-way ANOVA, the df_C values are the treatment (column) degrees of freedom, $C - 1$. The df_E values are the error degrees of freedom, $N - C$. Table 11.4 contains an abbreviated *F* distribution table for $\alpha = .05$. For the machine operator example, $df_C = 3$ and $df_E = 20$, $F_{.05,3,20}$ from Table 11.4 is 3.10. This value is the critical value of the *F* test. Analysis of variance tests are always one-tailed tests with the rejection region in the upper tail. The decision rule is to reject the null hypothesis if the observed *F* value is greater than the critical *F* value ($F_{.05,3,20} = 3.10$). For the machine operator problem, the observed *F* value of 10.18 is larger than the table *F* value of 3.10. The null hypothesis is rejected. Not all means are equal, so there is a significant difference in the mean valve openings by machine operator. Figure 11.5 is a Minitab graph of an *F* distribution showing the critical *F* value for this example and the rejection region. Note that the *F* distribution begins at zero and contains no negative values because the *F* value is the ratio of two variances, and variances are always positive.

Using the Computer for One-Way ANOVA

Many researchers use the computer to analyze data with a one-way ANOVA. Figure 11.6 shows the Minitab and Excel output of the ANOVA computed for the machine operator example. The output includes the analysis of variance table presented in Table 11.3. Both Minitab and Excel ANOVA tables display the observed *F* value, mean squares, sum of squares, degrees of freedom, and a value of *p*. The value of *p* is the probability of an *F* value of 10.18 occurring by chance in an ANOVA with this structure (same degrees of freedom)

FIGURE 11.5

Minitab Graph of *F* Values for
the Machine Operator
Example

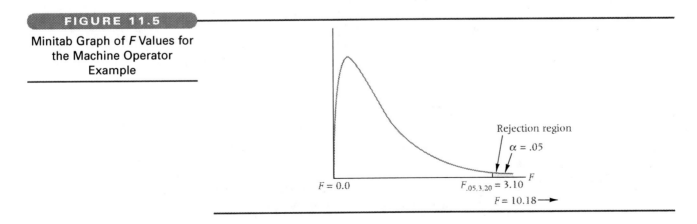

FIGURE 11.6

Minitab and Excel Analysis of the Machine Operator Problem

Minitab Output

One-way ANOVA: Operator 1, Operator 2, Operator 3, Operator 4

```
Source   DF      SS       MS       F       P
Factor    3   0.23658  0.07886  10.18   0.000
Error    20   0.15492  0.00775
Total    23   0.39150
```

S = 0.08801 R-Sq = 60.43% R-Sq(adj) = 54.49%

```
                                   Individual 95% CIs For Mean Based on
                                   Pooled StDev
Level        N    Mean   StDev  ---------+---------+---------+---------+---
Operator 1   5   6.3180  0.0526            (-----*-----)
Operator 2   8   6.2775  0.1053         (----*-----)
Operator 3   7   6.4886  0.1006                            (--- * ---)
Operator 4   4   6.2300  0.0432  (-------*-------)
                                   ---------+---------+---------+---------+---
Pooled StDev = 0.0880                     6.24      6.36      6.48      6.60
```

Excel Output

Anova: Single Factor

SUMMARY

Groups	Count	Sum	Average	Variance
Operator 1	5	31.59	6.31800	0.00277
Operator 2	8	50.22	6.27750	0.01108
Operator 3	7	45.42	6.48857	0.01011
Operator 4	4	24.92	6.23000	0.00187

ANOVA

Source of Variation	SS	df	MS	F	P-value	F crit
Between Groups	0.23658	3	0.07886	10.18	0.000279	3.10
Within Groups	0.15492	20	0.00775			
Total	0.39150	23				

even if there is no difference between means of the treatment levels. Using the p-value method of testing hypotheses presented in Chapter 9, we can easily see that because this p-value is only .000279, the null hypothesis would be rejected using $\alpha = .05$. Most computer output yields the value of p, so there is no need to look up a table value of F against which to compare the observed F value. The Excel output also includes the critical table F value for this problem, $F_{.05,3,20} = 3.10$.

The second part of the Minitab output in Figure 11.6 contains the size of samples and sample means for each of the treatment levels. Displayed graphically are the 95% confidence levels for the population means of each treatment level group. These levels are computed by using a pooled standard deviation from all the treatment level groups. The researcher can visually observe the confidence intervals and make a subjective determination about the relative difference in the population means. More rigorous statistical techniques for testing the differences in pairs of groups are given in Section 11.3.

Comparison of *F* and *t* Values

Analysis of variance can be used to test hypotheses about the difference in two means. Analysis of data from two samples by both a t test and an ANOVA shows that the observed F value equals the observed t value squared.

$$F = t^2 \qquad \text{for df}_C = 1$$

The t test of independent samples actually is a special case of one-way ANOVA when there are only two treatment levels ($df_C = 1$). The t test is computationally simpler than ANOVA for two groups. However, some statistical computer software packages do not contain a t test. In these cases, the researcher can perform a one-way ANOVA and then either take the square root of the F value to obtain the value of t or use the generated probability with the p-value method to reach conclusions.

DEMONSTRATION PROBLEM 11.1

A company has three manufacturing plants, and company officials want to determine whether there is a difference in the average age of workers at the three locations. The following data are the ages of five randomly selected workers at each plant. Perform a one-way ANOVA to determine whether there is a significant difference in the mean ages of the workers at the three plants. Use $\alpha = .01$ and note that the sample sizes are equal.

Solution

HYPOTHESIZE:

STEP 1. The hypotheses follow.

$$H_0: \mu_1 = \mu_2 = \mu_3$$

H_a: At least one of the means is different from the others.

TEST:

STEP 2. The appropriate test statistic is the F test calculated from ANOVA.

STEP 3. The value of α is .01.

STEP 4. The degrees of freedom for this problem are $3 - 1 = 2$ for the numerator and $15 - 3 = 12$ for the denominator. The critical F value is $F_{.01,2,12} = 6.93$.

Because ANOVAs are always one tailed with the rejection region in the upper tail, the decision rule is to reject the null hypothesis if the observed value of F is greater than 6.93.

STEP 5.

Plant (Employee Ages)

1	2	3
29	32	25
27	33	24
30	31	24
27	34	25
28	30	26

STEP 6.

$$T_j:\quad T_1 = 141 \quad T_2 = 160 \quad T_3 = 124 \quad T = 425$$
$$n_j:\quad n_1 = 5 \quad n_2 = 5 \quad n_3 = 5 \quad N = 15$$
$$\bar{x}_j:\quad \bar{x}_1 = 28.2 \quad \bar{x}_2 = 32.0 \quad \bar{x}_3 = 24.8 \quad \bar{x} = 28.33$$

$$SSC = 5(28.2 - 28.33)^2 + 5(32.0 - 28.33)^2 + 5(24.8 - 28.33)^2 = 129.73$$
$$SSE = (29 - 28.2)^2 + (27 - 28.2)^2 + \ldots + (25 - 24.8)^2 + (26 - 24.8)^2 = 19.60$$
$$SST = (29 - 28.33)^2 + (27 - 28.33)^2 + \ldots + (25 - 28.33)^2$$
$$+ (26 - 28.33)^2 = 149.33$$
$$df_C = 3 - 1 = 2$$
$$df_E = 15 - 3 = 12$$
$$df_T = 15 - 1 = 14$$

Source of Variance	SS	df	MS	F
Between	129.73	2	64.865	39.72
Error	19.60	12	1.633	
Total	149.33	14		

ACTION:

STEP 7. The decision is to reject the null hypothesis because the observed F value of 39.72 is greater than the critical table F value of 6.93.

BUSINESS IMPLICATIONS:

STEP 8. There is a significant difference in the mean ages of workers at the three plants. This difference can have hiring implications. Company leaders should understand that because motivation, discipline, and experience may differ with age, the differences in ages may call for different managerial approaches in each plant.

The chart shown below displays the dispersion of the ages of workers from the three samples, along with the mean age for each plant sample. Note the difference in group means. The significant F value says that the differences between the mean ages are relatively greater than the differences of ages within each group.

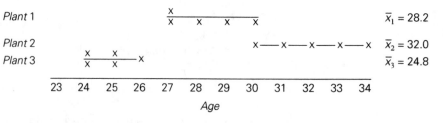

Following are the Minitab and Excel output for this problem.

Minitab Output

```
One-way ANOVA: Plant 1, Plant 2, Plant 3
```

Source	DF	SS	MS	F	P
Factor	2	129.73	64.87	39.71	0.000
Error	12	19.60	1.63		
Total	14	149.33			

```
S = 1.278  R-Sq = 86.88%  R-Sq(adj) = 84.69%
                                Individual 95% CIs For Mean
                                Based on Pooled StDev
Level      N    Mean    StDev   --+---------+---------+---------+----
Plant 1    5   28.200   1.304                  (---*---)
Plant 2    5   32.000   1.581                             (---*---)
Plant 3    5   24.800   0.837    (---*---)
                                --+---------+---------+---------+----
Pooled StDev = 1.278            25.0     27.5      30.0      32.5
```

Excel Output

Anova: Single Factor

SUMMARY

Groups	Count	Sum	Average	Variance
Plant 1	5	141	28.2	1.7
Plant 2	5	160	32	2.5
Plant 3	5	124	24.8	0.7

ANOVA

Source of Variation	SS	df	MS	F	P-value	F crit
Between Groups	129.73333	2	64.8667	39.71	0.0000051	3.89
Within Groups	19.6	12	1.6333			
Total	149.33333	14				

11.2 PROBLEMS

11.5 Compute a one-way ANOVA on the following data.

1	2	3
2	5	3
1	3	4
3	6	5
3	4	5
2	5	3
1		5

Determine the observed F value. Compare the observed F value with the critical table F value and decide whether to reject the null hypothesis. Use $\alpha = .05$.

11.6 Compute a one-way ANOVA on the following data.

1	2	3	4	5
14	10	11	16	14
13	9	12	17	12
10	12	13	14	13
	9	12	16	13
	10		17	12
				14

Determine the observed F value. Compare the observed F value with the critical table F value and decide whether to reject the null hypothesis. Use $\alpha = .01$.

11.7 Develop a one-way ANOVA on the following data.

1	2	3	4
113	120	132	122
121	127	130	118
117	125	129	125
110	129	135	125

Determine the observed F value. Compare it to the critical F value and decide whether to reject the null hypothesis. Use a 1% level of significance.

11.8 Compute a one-way ANOVA on the following data.

1	2
27	22
31	27
31	25
29	23
30	26
27	27
28	23

Determine the observed F value. Compare it to the critical table F value and decide whether to reject the null hypothesis. Perform a t test for independent measures on the data. Compare the t and F values. Are the results different? Use $\alpha = .05$.

11.9 Suppose you are using a completely randomized design to study some phenomenon. There are five treatment levels and a total of 55 people in the study. Each treatment level has the same sample size. Complete the following ANOVA.

Source of Variance	SS	df	MS	F
Treatment	583.39			
Error	972.18			
Total	1555.57			

11.10 Suppose you are using a completely randomized design to study some phenomenon. There are three treatment levels and a total of 17 people in the study. Complete the following ANOVA table. Use $\alpha = .05$ to find the table F value and use the data to test the null hypothesis.

Source of Variance	SS	df	MS	F
Treatment	29.64			
Error	68.42			
Total				

11.11 A milk company has four machines that fill gallon jugs with milk. The quality control manager is interested in determining whether the average fill for these machines is the same. The following data represent random samples of fill measures (in quarts) for 19 jugs of milk filled by the different machines. Use $\alpha = .01$ to test the hypotheses. Discuss the business implications of your findings.

Machine 1	Machine 2	Machine 3	Machine 4
4.05	3.99	3.97	4.00
4.01	4.02	3.98	4.02
4.02	4.01	3.97	3.99
4.04	3.99	3.95	4.01
	4.00	4.00	
	4.00		

11.12 That the starting salaries of new accounting graduates would differ according to geographic regions of the United States seems logical. A random selection of accounting firms is taken from three geographic regions, and each is asked to state the starting salary for a new accounting graduate who is going to work in auditing. The data obtained follow. Use a one-way ANOVA to analyze these data. Note that the data can be restated to make the computations more reasonable (example: $\$42,500 = 4.25$). Use a 1% level of significance. Discuss the business implications of your findings.

South	Northeast	West
$40,500	$51,000	$45,500
41,500	49,500	43,500
40,000	49,000	45,000
41,000	48,000	46,500
41,500	49,500	46,000

11.13 A management consulting company presents a three-day seminar on project management to various clients. The seminar is basically the same each time it is given. However, sometimes it is presented to high-level managers, sometimes to midlevel managers, and sometimes to low-level managers. The seminar facilitators believe evaluations of the seminar may vary with the audience. Suppose the following data are some randomly selected evaluation scores from different levels of managers who attended the seminar. The ratings are on a scale from 1 to 10, with 10 being the highest. Use a one-way ANOVA to determine whether there is a significant difference in the evaluations according to manager level. Assume $\alpha = .05$. Discuss the business implications of your findings.

High Level	Midlevel	Low Level
7	8	5
7	9	6
8	8	5
7	10	7
9	9	4
	10	8
	8	

11.14 Family transportation costs are usually higher than most people believe because those costs include car payments, insurance, fuel costs, repairs, parking, and public transportation. Twenty randomly selected families in four major cities are asked to use their records to estimate a monthly figure for transportation cost. Use the data obtained and ANOVA to test whether there is a significant difference in monthly transportation costs for families living in these cities. Assume that $\alpha = .05$. Discuss the business implications of your findings.

Atlanta	New York	Los Angeles	Chicago
$850	$450	$1050	$740
680	725	900	650
750	500	1150	875
800	375	980	750
875	700	800	800

11.15 Shown here is the Minitab output for a one-way ANOVA. Analyze the results. Include the number of treatment levels, the sample sizes, the F value, the overall statistical significance of the test, and the values of the means.

One-Way Analysis of Variance
Analysis of Variance

Source	df	SS	MS	F	p
Factor	3	1701	567	2.95	0.040
Error	61	11728	192		
Total	64	13429			

Individual 95% CIs For Mean Based on Pooled StDev

Level	N	Mean	StDev
C1	18	226.73	13.59
C2	15	238.79	9.41
C3	21	232.58	12.16
C4	11	239.82	20.96

Pooled StDev = 13.87

11.16 Business is very good for a chemical company. In fact, it is so good that workers are averaging more than 40 hours per week at each of the chemical company's five plants. However, management is not certain whether there is a difference between the five plants in the average number of hours worked per week per worker. Random samples of data are taken at each of the five plants. The data are analyzed using Excel. The results follow. Explain the design of the study and determine whether there is an overall significant difference between the means at $\alpha = .05$? Why or why not? What are the values of the means? What are the business implications of this study to the chemical company?

Anova: Single Factor

SUMMARY

Groups	Count	Sum	Average	Variance
Plant 1	11	636.5577	57.87	63.5949
Plant 2	12	601.7648	50.15	62.4813
Plant 3	8	491.7352	61.47	47.4772
Plant 4	5	246.0172	49.20	65.6072
Plant 5	7	398.6368	56.95	140.3540

ANOVA

Source of Variation	SS	df	MS	F	P-value	F crit
Between Groups	900.086	4	225.022	3.10	0.0266	2.62
Within Groups	2760.136	38	72.635			
Total	3660.223	42				

MULTIPLE COMPARISON TESTS

Analysis of variance techniques are particularly useful in testing hypotheses about the differences of means in multiple groups because ANOVA utilizes only one single overall test. The advantage of this approach is that the probability of committing a Type I error, α, is controlled. As noted in Section 11.2, if four groups are tested two at a time, it takes six t tests ($_4C_2$) to analyze hypotheses between all possible pairs. In general, if k groups are tested two at a time, $_kC_2 = k(k-1)/2$ paired comparisons are possible.

Suppose alpha for an experiment is .05. If two different pairs of comparisons are made in the experiment using alpha of .05 in each, there is a .95 probability of not making a Type I error in each comparison. This approach results in a .9025 probability of not making a Type I error in either comparison (.95 × .95), and a .0975 probability of committing a Type I error in at least one comparison (1 − .9025). Thus, the probability of committing a Type I error for this experiment is not .05 but .0975. In an experiment where the means of four groups are being tested two at a time, six different tests are conducted. If each is analyzed using $\alpha = .05$, the probability that no Type I error will be committed in any of the six tests is .95 × .95 × .95 × .95 × .95 × .95 = .735 and the probability of committing at least one Type I error in the six tests is 1 − .735 = .265. If an ANOVA is computed on all groups simultaneously using $\alpha = .05$, the value of alpha is maintained in the experiment.

Sometimes the researcher is satisfied with conducting an overall test of differences in groups such as the one ANOVA provides. However, when it is determined that there is an overall difference in population means, it is often desirable to go back to the groups and determine from the data which pairs of means are significantly different. Such pairwise analyses can lead to the buildup of the Type I experimental error rate, as mentioned. Fortunately, several techniques, referred to as **multiple comparisons**, have been developed to handle this problem.

Multiple comparisons are to be used only when an overall significant difference between groups has been obtained by using the F value of the analysis of variance. Some of these techniques protect more for Type I errors and others protect more for Type II errors. Some multiple comparison techniques require equal sample sizes. There seems to be some difference of opinion in the literature about which techniques are most appropriate. Here we will consider only a posteriori or post hoc pairwise comparisons.

A posteriori or **post hoc** pairwise comparisons are made *after the experiment when the researcher decides to test for any significant differences in the samples based on a significant overall F value.* In contrast, **a priori** comparisons are made when the researcher *determines before the experiment which comparisons are to be made.* The error rates for these two types of comparisons are different, as are the recommended techniques. In this text, we only consider pairwise (two-at-a-time) multiple comparisons. Other types of comparisons are possible but belong in a more advanced presentation. The two multiple comparison tests discussed here are Tukey's HSD test for designs with equal sample sizes and the Tukey-Kramer procedure for situations in which sample sizes are unequal. Minitab yields computer output for each of these tests.

Tukey's Honestly Significant Difference (HSD) Test: The Case of Equal Sample Sizes

Tukey's honestly significant difference (HSD) test, sometimes known as Tukey's T method, is a popular test for pairwise a posteriori multiple comparisons. This test, developed by John W. Tukey and presented in 1953, is somewhat limited by the fact that it requires equal sample sizes.

Tukey's HSD test takes into consideration the number of treatment levels, the value of mean square error, and the sample size. Using these values and a table value, q, the HSD determines the critical difference necessary between the means of any two treatment levels for the means to be significantly different. Once the HSD is computed, the researcher can examine the absolute value of any or all differences between pairs of means from treatment levels to determine whether there is a significant difference. The formula to compute a Tukey's HSD test follows.

TUKEY'S HSD TEST	
	$$HSD = q_{\alpha,C,N-C}\sqrt{\frac{MSE}{n}}$$

where:

MSE = mean square error

n = sample size

$q_{\alpha,C,N-C}$ = critical value of the studentized range distribution from Table A.10

In Demonstration Problem 11.1, an ANOVA test was used to determine that there was an overall significant difference in the mean ages of workers at the three different plants, as evidenced by the F value of 39.72. The sample data for this problem follow.

	PLANT		
	1	**2**	**3**
	29	32	25
	27	33	24
	30	31	24
	27	34	25
	28	30	26
Group Means	28.2	32.0	24.8
n_j	5	5	5

Because the sample sizes are equal in this problem, Tukey's HSD test can be used to compute multiple comparison tests between groups 1 and 2, 2 and 3, and 1 and 3. To compute the HSD, the values of MSE, n, and q must be determined. From the solution presented in Demonstration Problem 11.1, the value of MSE is 1.633. The sample size, n_j, is 5. The value of q is obtained from Table A.10 by using

Number of Populations = Number of Treatment Means = C

along with $df_E = N - C$.

In this problem, the values used to look up q are

$$C = 3$$
$$df_E = N - C = 12$$

Table A.10 has a q table for $\alpha = .05$ and one for $\alpha = .01$. In this problem, $\alpha = .01$. Shown in Table 11.5 is a portion of Table A.10 for $\alpha = .01$.

For this problem, $q_{.01,3,12} = 5.04$. HSD is computed as

$$HSD = q\sqrt{\frac{MSE}{n}} = 5.04\sqrt{\frac{1.633}{5}} = 2.88$$

TABLE 11.5

q Values for $\alpha = .01$

Degrees of Freedom	Number of Populations				
	2	3	4	5	...
1	90	135	164	186	
2	14	19	22.3	24.7	
3	8.26	10.6	12.2	13.3	
4	6.51	8.12	9.17	9.96	
.					
.					
.					
11	4.39	5.14	5.62	5.97	
12	4.32	5.04	5.50	5.84	

<table>
<tr><td>

TABLE 11.6

Minitab Output for
Tukey's HSD

</td><td>

```
Tukey 99% Simultaneous Confidence Intervals
All Pairwise Comparisons

Individual confidence level = 99.62%

Plant 1 subtracted from:

            Lower  Center  Upper
Plant 2    0.914   3.800   6.686
Plant 3   -6.286  -3.400  -0.514

Plant 2 subtracted from:

            Lower  Center  Upper
Plant 3  -10.086  -7.200  -4.314
```

</td></tr>
</table>

Using this value of HSD, the business researcher can examine the differences between the means from any two groups of plants. Any of the pairs of means that differ by more than 2.88 are significantly different at $\alpha = .01$. Here are the differences for all three possible pairwise comparisons.

$$|\bar{x}_1 - \bar{x}_2| = |28.2 - 32.0| = 3.8$$
$$|\bar{x}_1 - \bar{x}_3| = |28.2 - 24.8| = 3.4$$
$$|\bar{x}_2 - \bar{x}_3| = |32.0 - 24.8| = 7.2$$

All three comparisons are greater than the value of HSD, which is 2.88. Thus, the mean ages between any and all pairs of plants are significantly different.

Using the Computer to Do Multiple Comparisons

Table 11.6 shows the Minitab output for computing a Tukey's HSD test. The computer output contains the confidence intervals for the differences in pairwise means for pairs of treatment levels. If the confidence interval includes zero, there is no significant difference in the pair of means. (If the interval contains zero, there is a possibility of no difference in the means.) Note in Table 11.6 that all three pairs of confidence intervals contain the same sign throughout the interval. For example, the confidence interval for estimating the difference in means from 1 and 2 is $0.914 \leq \mu_1 - \mu_2 \leq 6.686$. This interval does not contain zero, so we are confident that there is more than a zero difference in the two means. The same holds true for levels 1 and 3 and levels 2 and 3.

**DEMONSTRATION
PROBLEM 11.2**

A metal-manufacturing firm wants to test the tensile strength of a given metal under varying conditions of temperature. Suppose that in the design phase, the metal is processed under five different temperature conditions and that random samples of size five are taken under each temperature condition. The data follow.

**Tensile Strength of Metal Produced Under Five
Different Temperature Settings**

1	2	3	4	5
2.46	2.38	2.51	2.49	2.56
2.41	2.34	2.48	2.47	2.57
2.43	2.31	2.46	2.48	2.53
2.47	2.40	2.49	2.46	2.55
2.46	2.32	2.50	2.44	2.55

A one-way ANOVA is performed on these data by using Minitab, with the resulting analysis shown here.

```
One-way ANOVA: Tensile Strength versus Temp. Setting
Source          DF      SS         MS        F       P
Temp. Setting    4   0.108024   0.027006  43.70   0.000
Error           20   0.012360   0.000618
Total           24   0.120384

S = 0.02486  R-Sq = 89.73%  R-Sq(adj) = 87.68%
```

Note from the ANOVA table that the F value of 43.70 is statistically significant at $\alpha = .01$. There is an overall difference in the population means of metal produced under the five temperature settings. Use the data to compute a Tukey's HSD to determine which of the five groups are significantly different from the others.

Solution

From the ANOVA table, the value of MSE is .000618. The sample size, n_j, is 5. The number of treatment means, C, is 5 and the df_E are 20. With these values and $\alpha = .01$, the value of q can be obtained from Table A.10.

$$q_{.01,5,20} = 5.29$$

HSD can be computed as

$$\text{HSD} = q\sqrt{\frac{\text{MSE}}{n}} = 5.29\sqrt{\frac{.000618}{5}} = .0588$$

The treatment group means for this problem follow.

$$\text{Group 1} = 2.446$$
$$\text{Group 2} = 2.350$$
$$\text{Group 3} = 2.488$$
$$\text{Group 4} = 2.468$$
$$\text{Group 5} = 2.552$$

Computing all pairwise differences between these means (in absolute values) produces the following data.

	Group				
	1	**2**	**3**	**4**	**5**
1	—	.096	.042	.022	.106
2	.096	—	.138	.118	.202
3	.042	.138	—	.020	.064
4	.022	.118	.020	—	.084
5	.106	.202	.064	.084	—

Comparing these differences to the value of HSD = .0588, we can determine that the differences between groups 1 and 2 (.096), 1 and 5 (.106), 2 and 3 (.138), 2 and 4 (.118), 2 and 5 (.202), 3 and 5 (.064), and 4 and 5 (.084) are significant at $\alpha = .01$.

Not only is there an overall significant difference in the treatment levels as shown by the ANOVA results, but there is a significant difference in the tensile strength of metal between seven pairs of levels. By studying the magnitudes of the individual treatment levels' means, the steel-manufacturing firm can determine which temperatures result in the greatest tensile strength. The Minitab output for this Tukey's HSD is shown on the next page. Note that the computer analysis shows significant differences between pairs 1 and 2, 1 and 5, 2 and 3, 2 and 4, 2 and 5, 3 and 5, and 4 and 5 because these confidence intervals do not contain zero. These results are consistent with the manual calculations.

```
Tukey 99% Simultaneous Confidence Intervals
All Pairwise Comparisons among Levels of Temp. Setting

Individual confidence level = 99.87%

Temp. Setting = 1 subtracted from:
Temp.
Setting      Lower       Center      Upper   -----+-------+------+-------+-
2          -0.15481     -0.09600   -0.03719       (-- * --)
3          -0.01681      0.04200    0.10081                 (-- * --)
4          -0.03681      0.02200    0.08081             (-- * --)
5           0.04719      0.10600    0.16481                   (-- * --)
                                            -----+-------+------+-------+-
                                            -0.15     0.00    0.15     0.30

Temp. Setting = 2 subtracted from:
Temp.
Setting      Lower       Center      Upper   -----+-------+------+-------+-
3           0.07919      0.13800    0.19681                     (-- * --)
4           0.05919      0.11800    0.17681                   (-- * --)
5           0.14319      0.20200    0.26081                         (-- * --)
                                            -----+-------+------+-------+-
                                            -0.15     0.00    0.15     0.30

Temp. Setting = 3 subtracted from:
Temp.
Setting      Lower       Center      Upper   -----+-------+------+-------+-
4          -0.07881     -0.02000    0.03881             (-- * --)
5           0.00519      0.06400    0.12281                 (-- * --)
                                            -----+-------+------+-------+-
                                            -0.15     0.00    0.15     0.30

Temp. Setting = 4 subtracted from:
Temp.
Setting      Lower       Center      Upper   -----+-------+------+-------+-
5           0.02519      0.08400    0.14281                   (-- * --)
                                            -----+-------+------+-------+-
                                            -0.15     0.00    0.15     0.30
```

Tukey-Kramer Procedure: The Case of Unequal Sample Sizes

Tukey's HSD was modified by C. Y. Kramer in the mid-1950s to handle situations in which the sample sizes are unequal. The modified version of HSD is sometimes referred to as the **Tukey-Kramer procedure**. The formula for computing the significant differences with this procedure is similar to that for the equal sample sizes, with the exception that the mean square error is divided in half and weighted by the sum of the inverses of the sample sizes under the root sign.

TUKEY-KRAMER FORMULA

$$q_{\alpha,C,N-C}\sqrt{\frac{MSE}{2}\left(\frac{1}{n_r} + \frac{1}{n_s}\right)}$$

where

MSE = mean square error

n_r = sample size for rth sample

n_s = sample size for sth sample

$q_{\alpha,\,C,\,N-C}$ = critical value of the studentized range distribution from Table A.10

TABLE 11.7

Means and Sample Sizes for the Valves Produced by Four Operators

Operator	Sample Size	Mean
1	5	6.3180
2	8	6.2775
3	7	6.4886
4	4	6.2300

As an example of the application of the Tukey-Kramer procedure, consider the machine operator example in Section 11.2. A one-way ANOVA was used to test for any difference in the mean valve openings produced by four different machine operators. An overall F of 10.18 was computed, which was significant at $\alpha = .05$. Because the ANOVA hypothesis test is significant and the null hypothesis is rejected, this problem is a candidate for multiple comparisons. Because the sample sizes are not equal, Tukey's HSD cannot be used to determine which pairs are significantly different. However, the Tukey-Kramer procedure can be applied. Shown in Table 11.7 are the means and sample sizes for the valve openings for valves produced by the four different operators.

TABLE 11.8

Results of Pairwise
Comparisons for the Machine
Operators Example Using the
Tukey-Kramer Procedure

Pair	Critical Difference	Actual Difference
1 and 2	.1405	.0405
1 and 3	.1443	.1706*
1 and 4	.1653	.0880
2 and 3	.1275	.2111*
2 and 4	.1509	.0475
3 and 4	.1545	.2586*

*Significant at $\alpha = .05$.

The mean square error for this problem, MSE, is shown in Table 11.3 as .007746. The four operators in the problem represent the four levels of the independent variable, machine operator. Thus, $C = 4$, $N = 24$, and $N - C = 20$. The value of alpha in the problem is .05. With this information, the value of q is obtained from Table A.10 as

$$q_{.05,4,20} = 3.96$$

The distance necessary for the difference in the means of two samples to be statistically significant must be computed by using the Tukey-Kramer procedure for each pair because the sample sizes differ. In this problem with $C = 4$, there are $C(C - 1)/2$ or six possible pairwise comparisons. The computations follow.

For operators 1 and 2,

$$3.96\sqrt{\frac{.007746}{2}\left(\frac{1}{5} + \frac{1}{8}\right)} = .1405$$

The difference between the means of operator 1 and operator 2 is

$$6.3180 - 6.2775 = .0405.$$

Because this result is less than the critical difference of .1405, there is no significant difference between the average valve openings of valves produced by machine operators 1 and 2.

Table 11.8 reports the critical differences for each of the six pairwise comparisons as computed by using the Tukey-Kramer procedure, along with the absolute value of the

TABLE 11.9

Minitab Multiple Comparisons
in the Machine Operator
Example Using the
Tukey-Kramer Procedure

```
Tukey 95% Simultaneous Confidence Intervals
All Pairwise Comparisons

Individual confidence level = 98.89%

Operator 1 subtracted from:

              Lower      Center      Upper
Operator 2   -0.18099   -0.04050    0.09999
Operator 3    0.02627    0.17057    0.31487
Operator 4   -0.25332   -0.08800    0.07732

             -----+---------+---------+---------+-
Operator 2                  (----*----)
Operator 3                        (----*----)
Operator 4            (----*-----)
             -----+---------+---------+---------+-
                 -0.25      0.00      0.25      0.50


Operator 2 subtracted from:
              Lower      Center      Upper
Operator 3    0.08353    0.21107    0.33862
Operator 4   -0.19841   -0.04750    0.10341

             -----+---------+---------+---------+-
Operator 3                        (---.*---)
Operator 4             (---.*---)
             -----+---------+---------+---------+-
                 -0.25      0.00      0.25      0.50

Operator 3 subtracted from:

              Lower      Center      Upper
Operator 4   -0.41304   -0.25857   -0.10411

             -----+---------+---------+---------+-
Operator 4   (-----*----)
             -----+---------+---------+---------+-
                 -0.25      0.00      0.25      0.50
```

actual distances between the means. Any actual distance between means that is greater than the critical distance is significant. As shown in the table, the means of three pairs of samples, operators 1 and 3, operators 2 and 3, and operators 3 and 4 are significantly different.

Table 11.9 shows the Minitab output for this problem. Minitab uses the Tukey-Kramer procedure for unequal values of n. As before with the HSD test, Minitab produces a confidence interval for the differences in means for pairs of treatment levels. If the confidence interval includes zero, there is no significant difference in the pairs of means. If the signs over the interval are the same (zero is not in the interval), there is a significant difference in the means. Note that the signs over the intervals for pairs (1, 3), (2, 3) and (3, 4) are the same, indicating a significant difference in the means of those two pairs. This conclusion agrees with the results determined through the calculations reported in Table 11.8.

11.3 PROBLEMS

11.17 Suppose an ANOVA has been performed on a completely randomized design containing six treatment levels. The mean for group 3 is 15.85, and the sample size for group 3 is eight. The mean for group 6 is 17.21, and the sample size for group 6 is seven. MSE is .3352. The total number of observations is 46. Compute the significant difference for the means of these two groups by using the Tukey-Kramer procedure. Let $\alpha = .05$.

11.18 A completely randomized design has been analyzed by using a one-way ANOVA. There are four treatment groups in the design, and each sample size is six. MSE is equal to 2.389. Using $\alpha = .05$, compute Tukey's HSD for this ANOVA.

11.19 Using the results of problem 11.5, compute a critical value by using the Tukey-Kramer procedure for groups 1 and 2. Use $\alpha = .05$. Determine whether there is a significant difference between these two groups.

11.20 Use the Tukey-Kramer procedure to determine whether there is a significant difference between the means of groups 2 and 5 in problem 11.6. Let $\alpha = .01$.

11.21 Using the results from problem 11.7, compute a Tukey's HSD to determine whether there are any significant differences between group means. Let $\alpha = .01$.

11.22 Using problem 11.8, compute Tukey's HSD and determine whether there is a significant difference in means by using this methodology. Let $\alpha = .05$.

11.23 Use the Tukey-Kramer procedure to do multiple comparisons for problem 11.11. Let $\alpha = .01$. State which pairs of machines, if any, produce significantly different mean fills.

11.24 Use Tukey's HSD test to compute multiple comparisons for the data in problem 11.12. Let $\alpha = .01$. State which regions, if any, are significantly different from other regions in mean starting salary figures.

11.25 Using $\alpha = .05$, compute critical values using the Tukey-Kramer procedure for the pairwise groups in problem 11.13. Determine which pairs of groups are significantly different, if any.

11.26 Do multiple comparisons on the data in problem 11.14 using Tukey's HSD test and $\alpha = .05$. State which pairs of cities, if any, have significantly different mean costs.

11.27 Problem 11.16 analyzed the number of weekly hours worked per person at five different plants. An F value of 3.10 was obtained with a probability of .0266. Because the probability is less than .05, the null hypothesis is rejected at $\alpha = .05$. There is an overall difference in the mean weekly hours worked by plant. Which pairs of plants have significant differences in the means, if any? To answer this question, a Minitab computer analysis was done. The data follow. Study the output in light of problem 11.16 and discuss the results.

```
Tukey 95% Simultaneous Confidence Intervals
All Pairwise Comparisons

Individual confidence level = 99.32%

Plant 1 subtracted from:

          Lower    Center   Upper    -----+-------+-------+-------+-
Plant 2  -17.910   -7.722   2.466         (----*-----)
Plant 3   -7.743    3.598  14.939                (-----*-----)
Plant 4  -21.830   -8.665   4.499      (-------*-------)
Plant 5  -12.721   -0.921  10.880          (-----*-----)
                                       -----+-------+-------+-------+-
                                          -15       0      15      30

Plant 2 subtracted from:

          Lower    Center   Upper    -----+-------+-------+-------+-
Plant 3    0.180   11.320  22.460                   (------*----)
Plant 4  -13.935   -0.944  12.048           (------*------)
Plant 5   -4.807    6.801  18.409               (-----*------)
                                       -----+-------+-------+-------+-
                                          -15       0      15      30

Plant 3 subtracted from:

          Lower    Center   Upper    -----+-------+-------+-------+-
Plant 4  -26.178  -12.263   1.651    (-------*--------)
Plant 5  -17.151   -4.519   8.113       (------*------)
                                       -----+-------+-------+-------+-
                                          -15       0      15      30

Plant 4 subtracted from:

          Lower    Center   Upper    -----+-------+-------+-------+-
Plant 5   -6.547    7.745  22.036                (------*------)
                                       -----+-------+-------+-------+-
                                          -15       0      15      30
```

THINKING CRITICALLY ABOUT STATISTICS IN BUSINESS TODAY

Does National Ideology Affect a Firm's Definition of Success?

One researcher, G. C. Lodge, proposed that companies pursue different performance goals based on the ideology of their home country. L. Thurow went further by suggesting that such national ideologies drive U.S. firms to be short-term profit maximizers, Japanese firms to be growth maximizers, and European firms to be a mix of the two.

Three other researchers, J. Katz, S. Werner, and L. Brouthers, decided to test these suggestions by studying 114 international banks from the United States, the European Union (EU), and Japan listed in the Global 1000. Specifically, there were 34 banks from the United States, 45 banks from the European Union, and 35 banks from Japan in the study. Financial and market data were gathered and averaged on each bank over a five-year period to limit the effect of single-year variations.

The banks were compared on general measures of success such as profitability, capitalization, growth, size, risk, and earnings distribution by specifically examining 11 measures. Eleven one-way analyses of variance designs were computed, one for each dependent variable. These included return on equity, return on assets, yield, capitalization, assets, market value, growth, Tobin's Q, price-to-earnings ratio, payout ratio, and risk. The independent variable in each ANOVA was country, with three levels: U.S., EU, and Japan.

In all 11 ANOVAs, there was a significant difference between banks in the three countries ($\alpha = .01$) supporting the theme of different financial success goals for different national cultures. Because of the overall significant difference attained in the ANOVAs, each analysis of variance was followed by a multiple comparison test to determine which, if any, of the pairs were significantly different. These comparisons revealed that U.S. and EU banks maintained significantly higher levels than Japanese banks on return on equity, return on assets, and yield. This result underscores the notion that U.S. and EU banks have more of a short-term profit orientation than do Japanese banks. There was a significant difference in banks from each of the three countries on amount of capitalization. U.S. banks had the highest level of capitalization followed by EU banks and then Japanese banks. This result may reflect the cultural attitude about how much capital is needed to ensure a sound economy, with U.S. banks maintaining higher levels of capital.

The study found that Japanese banks had significantly higher levels on growth, Tobin's Q, and price-to-earnings ratio than did the other two national entities. This result confirms the hypothesis that Japanese firms are more interested in growth. In addition, Japanese banks had a significantly higher asset size and market value of equity than did U.S. banks. The researchers had hypothesized that EU banks would have a greater portfolio risk than that of U.S. or Japanese banks. They found that EU banks did have significantly higher risk and paid out significantly higher dividends than did either Japanese or U.S. banks.

Things to Ponder

1. If you represent an American company wanting to do business in Japan, what are some points from this study that might guide you in your endeavor?

2. What did you learn about EU banks in this study that may set them apart from U.S. banks?

Source: Adapted from Jeffrey P. Katz, Steve Werner, and Lance Brouthers, "Does Winning Mean the Same Thing Around the World? National Ideology and the Performance of Global Competitors," *Journal of Business Research,* vol. 44, no. 2 (February 1999), pp. 117–126.

11.4 THE RANDOMIZED BLOCK DESIGN

▶ Video

A second research design is the **randomized block design**. The randomized block design is similar to the completely randomized design in that it focuses on one independent variable (treatment variable) of interest. However, the randomized block design also includes a second variable, referred to as a blocking variable, that can be used to control for confounding or concomitant variables.

Confounding variables, or **concomitant variables**, are *variables that are not being controlled by the researcher in the experiment but can have an effect on the outcome of the treatment being studied.* For example, Demonstration Problem 11.2 showed how a completely randomized design could be used to analyze the effects of temperature on the tensile strengths of metal. However, other variables not being controlled by the researcher in this experiment may affect the tensile strength of metal, such as humidity, raw materials, machine, and shift. One way to control for these variables is to include them in the experimental design. The randomized block design has the capability of adding one of these variables into the analysis as a blocking variable. A **blocking variable** is *a variable that the researcher wants to control but is not the treatment variable of interest.*

One of the first people to use the randomized block design was Sir Ronald A. Fisher. He applied the design to the field of agriculture, where he was interested in studying the growth patterns of varieties of seeds for a given type of plant. The seed variety was his independent variable. However, he realized that as he experimented on different plots of ground, the "block" of ground might make some difference in the experiment. Fisher designated several different plots of ground as blocks, which he controlled as a second variable. Each of the seed varieties was planted on each of the blocks. The main thrust of his study was to compare the seed varieties (independent variable). He merely wanted to control for the difference in plots of ground (blocking variable).

In Demonstration Problem 11.2, examples of blocking variables might be machine number (if several machines are used to make the metal), worker, shift, or day of the week. The researcher probably already knows that different workers or different machines will produce at least slightly different metal tensile strengths because of individual differences. However, designating the variable (machine or worker) as the blocking variable and computing a randomized block design affords the potential for a more powerful analysis. In other experiments, some other possible variables that might be used as blocking variables include sex of subject, age of subject, intelligence of subject, economic level of subject, brand, supplier, or vehicle.

A special case of the randomized block design is the repeated measures design. The **repeated measures design** is a randomized block design in which each block level is an individual item or person, and that person or item is measured across all treatments. Thus, where a block level in a randomized block design is night shift and items produced under different treatment levels on the night shift are measured, in a repeated measures design, a block level might be an individual machine or person; items produced by that person or machine are then randomly chosen across all treatments. Thus, a repeated measure of the person or machine is made across all treatments. This repeated measures design is an extension of the *t* test for dependent samples presented in Section 10.3.

The sum of squares in a completely randomized design is

$$SST = SSC + SSE$$

In a randomized block design, the sum of squares is

$$SST = SSC + SSR + SSE$$

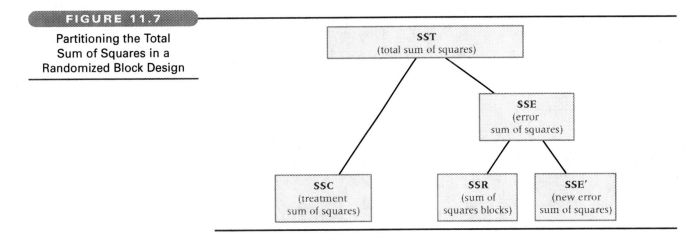

FIGURE 11.7

Partitioning the Total Sum of Squares in a Randomized Block Design

where

SST = sum of squares total
SSC = sum of squares columns (treatment)
SSR = sum of squares rows (blocking)
SSE = sum of squares error

SST and SSC are the same for a given analysis whether a completely randomized design or a randomized block design is used. For this reason, the SSR (blocking effects) comes out of the SSE; that is, some of the error variation in the completely randomized design is accounted for in the blocking effects of the randomized block design, as shown in Figure 11.7. By reducing the error term, it is possible that the value of F for treatment will increase (the denominator of the F value is decreased). However, if there is not sufficient difference between levels of the blocking variable, the use of a randomized block design can lead to a less powerful result than would a completely randomized design computed on the same problem. Thus, the researcher should seek out blocking variables that he or she believes are significant contributors to variation among measurements of the dependent variable. Figure 11.8 shows the layout of a randomized block design.

In each of the intersections of independent variable and blocking variable in Figure 11.8, one measurement is taken. In the randomized block design, one measurement is given for each treatment level under each blocking level.

The null and alternate hypotheses for the treatment effects in the randomized block design are

$$H_0: \mu_{\cdot 1} = \mu_{\cdot 2} = \mu_{\cdot 3} = \ldots = \mu_{\cdot C}$$

H_a: At least one of the treatment means is different from the others.

For the blocking effects, they are

$$H_0: \mu_{1 \cdot} = \mu_{2 \cdot} = \mu_{3 \cdot} = \ldots = \mu_{R \cdot}$$

H_a: At least one of the blocking means is different from the others.

FIGURE 11.8

A Randomized Block Design

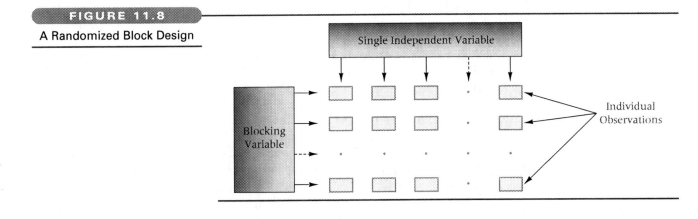

Essentially, we are testing the null hypothesis that the population means of the treatment groups are equal. If the null hypothesis is rejected, at least one of the population means does not equal the others.

The formulas for computing a randomized block design follow.

FORMULAS FOR COMPUTING A RANDOMIZED BLOCK DESIGN

$$SSC = n \sum_{j=1}^{C} (\bar{x}_j - \bar{x})^2$$

$$SSR = C \sum_{i=1}^{n} (\bar{x}_i - \bar{x})^2$$

$$SSE = \sum_{i=1}^{n} \sum_{j=1}^{C} (x_{ij} - \bar{x}_j - \bar{x}_i + \bar{x})^2$$

$$SST = \sum_{i=1}^{n} \sum_{j=1}^{C} (x_{ij} - \bar{x})^2$$

where

i = block group (row)
j = treatment level (column)
C = number of treatment levels (columns)
n = number of observations in each treatment level (number of blocks or rows)
x_{ij} = individual observation
$\bar{x}_j$ = treatment (column) mean
$\bar{x}_i$ = block (row) mean
$\bar{x}$ = grand mean
N = total number of observations

$$df_C = C - 1$$
$$df_R = n - 1$$
$$df_E = (C - 1)(n - 1) = N - n - C + 1$$

$$MSC = \frac{SSC}{C - 1}$$

$$MSR = \frac{SSR}{n - 1}$$

$$MSE = \frac{SSE}{N - n - C + 1}$$

$$F_{treatments} = \frac{MSC}{MSE}$$

$$F_{blocks} = \frac{MSR}{MSE}$$

The observed F value for treatments computed using the randomized block design formula is tested by comparing it to a table F value, which is ascertained from Appendix A.7 by using α, df_C (treatment), and df_E (error). If the observed F value is greater than the table value, the null hypothesis is rejected for that alpha value. Such a result would indicate that not all population treatment means are equal. At this point, the business researcher has the option of computing multiple comparisons if the null hypothesis has been rejected.

Some researchers also compute an F value for blocks even though the main emphasis in the experiment is on the treatments. The observed F value for blocks is compared to a critical table F value determined from Appendix A.7 by using α, df_R (blocks), and df_E (error). If the F value for blocks is greater than the critical F value, the null hypothesis that all block population means are equal is rejected. This result tells the business researcher that including the blocking in the design was probably worthwhile and that a significant amount of variance was drawn off from the error term, thus increasing the power of the treatment test. In this text, we have omitted F_{blocks} from the normal presentation and problem solving. We leave the use of this F value to the discretion of the reader.

As an example of the application of the randomized block design, consider a tire company that developed a new tire. The company conducted tread-wear tests on the tire to determine whether there is a significant difference in tread wear if the average speed with which the automobile is driven varies. The company set up an experiment in which the independent variable was speed of automobile. There were three treatment levels: slow speed (car is driven 20 miles per hour), medium speed (car is driven 40 miles per hour), and high speed (car is driven 60 miles per hour). Company researchers realized that several possible variables could confound the study. One of these variables was supplier. The company uses five suppliers to provide a major component of the rubber from which the tires are made. To control for this variable experimentally, the researchers used supplier as a blocking variable. Fifteen tires were randomly selected for the study, three from each supplier. Each of the three was assigned to be tested under a different speed condition. The data are given here, along with treatment and block totals. These figures represent tire wear in units of 10,000 miles.

	Speed			Block Means
Supplier	Slow	Medium	Fast	$\bar{x}_i$
1	3.7	4.5	3.1	3.77
2	3.4	3.9	2.8	3.37
3	3.5	4.1	3.0	3.53
4	3.2	3.5	2.6	3.10
5	3.9	4.8	3.4	4.03
Treatment Means $\bar{x}_j$	3.54	4.16	2.98	$\bar{x} = 3.56$

To analyze this randomized block design using $\alpha = .01$, the computations are as follows.

$$C = 3$$
$$n = 5$$
$$N = 15$$

$$SSC = n \sum_{j=1}^{C} (\bar{x}_j - \bar{x})^2$$
$$= 5[(3.54 - 3.56)^2 + (4.16 - 3.56)^2 + (2.98 - 3.56)^2]$$
$$= 3.484$$

$$SSR = C \sum_{i=1}^{n} (\bar{x}_i - \bar{x})^2$$
$$= 3[(3.77 - 3.56)^2 + (3.37 - 3.56)^2 + (3.53 - 3.56)^2 + (3.10 - 3.56)^2 + (4.03 - 3.56)^2]$$
$$= 1.541$$

$$SSE = \sum_{i=1}^{n} \sum_{j=1}^{C} (x_{ij} - \bar{x}_j - \bar{x}_i + \bar{x})^2$$
$$= (3.7 - 3.54 - 3.77 + 3.56)^2 + (3.4 - 3.54 - 3.37 + 3.56)^2$$
$$+ \cdots + (2.6 - 2.98 - 3.10 + 3.56)^2 + (3.4 - 2.98 - 4.03 + 3.56)^2$$
$$= .143$$

$$SST = \sum_{i=1}^{n} \sum_{j=1}^{C} (x_{ij} - \bar{x})^2$$

$$= (3.7 - 3.56)^2 + (3.4 - 3.56)^2 + \cdots + (2.6 - 3.56)^2 + (3.4 - 3.56)^2$$

$$= 5.176$$

$$MSC = \frac{SSC}{C - 1} = \frac{3.484}{2} = 1.742$$

$$MSR = \frac{SSR}{n - 1} = \frac{1.541}{4} = .38525$$

$$MSE = \frac{SSE}{N - n - C + 1} = \frac{.143}{8} = .017875$$

$$F = \frac{MSC}{MSE} = \frac{1.742}{.017875} = 97.45$$

Source of Variation	SS	df	MS	F
Treatment	3.484	2	1.742	97.45
Block	1.541	4	.38525	
Error	.143	8	.017875	
Total	5.176	14		

For alpha of .01, the critical F value is

$$F_{.01,2,8} = 8.65$$

Because the observed value of F for treatment (97.45) is greater than this critical F value, the null hypothesis is rejected. At least one of the population means of the treatment levels is not the same as the others; that is, there is a significant difference in tread wear for cars driven at different speeds. If this problem had been set up as a completely randomized design, the SSR would have been a part of the SSE. The degrees of freedom for the blocking effects would have been combined with degrees of freedom of error. Thus, the value of SSE would have been $1.541 + .143 = 1.684$, and df_E would have been $4 + 8 = 12$. These would then have been used to recompute $MSE = 1.684/12 = .140$. The value of F for treatments would have been

$$F = \frac{MSC}{MSE} = \frac{1.742}{0.140} = 12.44$$

Thus, the F value for treatment with the blocking was 97.45 and *without* the blocking was 12.44. By using the random block design, a much larger observed F value was obtained.

Using the Computer to Analyze Randomized Block Designs

Both Minitab and Excel have the capability of analyzing a randomized block design. The computer output from each of these software packages for the tire tread wear example is displayed in Table 11.10. The randomized block design analysis is done on Minitab by using the same process as the two-way ANOVA, which will be discussed in Section 11.5.

The Minitab output includes F values and their associated p-values for both the treatment and the blocking effects. As with most standard ANOVA tables, the sum of squares, mean squares, and degrees of freedom for each source of variation are included.

Excel treats a randomized block design like a two-way ANOVA (Section 11.5) that has only one observation per cell. The Excel output includes sums, averages, and variances for each row and column. The Excel ANOVA table displays the observed F values for the treatment (columns) and the blocks (rows). An important inclusion in the Excel output is the p-value for each F, along with the critical (table) F values.

TABLE 11.10

Minitab and Excel Output for the Tread Wear Example

Minitab Output

Two-way ANOVA: Mileage versus Supplier, Speed

```
Source    DF     SS       MS      F       P
Supplier   4  1.54933  0.38733  21.72  0.000
Speed      2  3.48400  1.74200  97.68  0.000
Error      8  0.14267  0.01783
Total     14  5.17600
S = 0.1335  R-Sq = 97.24%  R-Sq(adj) = 95.18%
```

Excel Output

Anova: Two-Factor Without Replication

SUMMARY	Count	Sum	Average	Variance
1	3	11.3	3.767	0.4933
2	3	10.1	3.367	0.3033
3	3	10.6	3.533	0.3033
4	3	9.3	3.100	0.2100
5	3	12.1	4.033	0.5033
Slow	5	17.7	3.54	0.073
Medium	5	20.8	4.16	0.258
Fast	5	14.9	2.98	0.092

ANOVA

Source of Variation	SS	df	MS	F	P-value	F crit
Rows	1.549333	4	0.387333	21.72	0.0002357	7.01
Columns	3.484000	2	1.742000	97.68	0.0000024	8.65
Error	0.142667	8	0.017833			
Total	5.176000	14				

DEMONSTRATION PROBLEM 11.3

Suppose a national travel association studied the cost of premium unleaded gasoline in the United States during the summer of 2011. From experience, association directors believed there was a significant difference in the average cost of a gallon of premium gasoline among urban areas in different parts of the country. To test this belief, they placed random calls to gasoline stations in five different cities. In addition, the researchers realized that the brand of gasoline might make a difference. They were mostly interested in the differences between cities, so they made city their treatment variable. To control for the fact that pricing varies with brand, the researchers included brand as a blocking variable and selected six different brands to participate. The researchers randomly telephoned one gasoline station for each brand in each city, resulting in 30 measurements (five cities and six brands). Each station operator was asked to report the current cost of a gallon of premium unleaded gasoline at that station. The data are shown here. Test these data by using a randomized block design analysis to determine whether there is a significant difference in the average cost of premium unleaded gasoline by city. Let $\alpha = .01$.

Geographic Region

Brand	Miami	Philadelphia	Minneapolis	San Antonio	Oakland	$\bar{x}_i$
A	3.47	3.40	3.38	3.32	3.50	3.414
B	3.43	3.41	3.42	3.35	3.44	3.410
C	3.44	3.41	3.43	3.36	3.45	3.418
D	3.46	3.45	3.40	3.30	3.45	3.412
E	3.46	3.40	3.39	3.39	3.48	3.424
F	3.44	3.43	3.42	3.39	3.49	3.434
$\bar{x}_j$	3.450	3.4167	3.4067	3.3517	3.4683	$\bar{x} = 3.4187$

Solution

HYPOTHESIZE:

STEP 1. The hypotheses follow.

For treatments,

$H_0: \mu_{.1} = \mu_{.2} = \mu_{.3} = \mu_{.4} = \mu_{.5}$

H_a: At least one of the treatment means is different from the others.

For blocks,

$H_0: \mu_{1.} = \mu_{2.} = \mu_{3.} = \mu_{4.} = \mu_{5.} = \mu_{6.}$

H_a: At least one of the blocking means is different from the others.

TEST:

STEP 2. The appropriate statistical test is the F test in the ANOVA for randomized block designs.

STEP 3. Let $\alpha = .01$.

STEP 4. There are four degrees of freedom for the treatment ($C - 1 = 5 - 1 = 4$), five degrees of freedom for the blocks ($n - 1 = 6 - 1 = 5$), and 20 degrees of freedom for error [$(C - 1)(n - 1) = (4)(5) = 20$]. Using these, $\alpha = .01$, and Table A.7, we find the critical F values.

$$F_{.01,4,20} = 4.43 \text{ for treatments}$$

$$F_{.01,5,20} = 4.10 \text{ for blocks}$$

The decision rule is to reject the null hypothesis for treatments if the observed F value for treatments is greater than 4.43 and to reject the null hypothesis for blocking effects if the observed F value for blocks is greater than 4.10.

STEP 5. The sample data including row and column means and the grand mean are given in the preceding table.

STEP 6.

$$SSC = n\sum_{j=1}^{C}(\bar{x}_j - \bar{x})^2$$

$$= 6[(3.450 - 3.4187)^2 + (3.4167 - 3.4187)^2 + (3.4067 - 3.4187)^2$$

$$+ (3.3517 - 3.4187)^2 + (3.4683 - 3.4187)^2]$$

$$= .04846$$

$$SSR = C\sum_{i=1}^{n}(\bar{x}_i - \bar{x})^2$$

$$= 5[(3.414 - 3.4187)^2 + (3.410 - 3.4187)^2 + (3.418 - 3.4187)^2$$

$$+ (3.412 - 3.4187)^2 + (3.424 - 3.4187)^2 + (3.434 - 3.4187)^2]$$

$$= .00203$$

$$SSE = \sum_{i=1}^{n}\sum_{j=1}^{C}(x_{ij} - \bar{x}_j - \bar{x}_i + \bar{x})^2$$

$$= (3.47 - 3.450 - 3.414 + 3.4187)^2 + (3.43 - 3.450 - 3.410 + 3.4187)^2 + \ldots$$

$$+ (3.48 - 3.4683 - 3.424 + 3.4187)^2 + (3.49 - 3.4683 - 3.434 + 3.4187)^2 = .01281$$

$$SST = \sum_{i=1}^{n}\sum_{j=1}^{C}(x_{ij} - \bar{x})^2$$

$$= (3.47 - 3.4187)^2 + (3.43 - 3.4187)^2 + \ldots + (3.48 - 3.4187)^2 + (3.49 - 3.4187)^2$$

$$= .06330$$

$$MSC = \frac{SSC}{C - 1} = \frac{.04846}{4} = .01212$$

$$MSR = \frac{SSR}{n - 1} = \frac{.00203}{5} = .00041$$

$$MSE = \frac{SSE}{(C-1)(n-1)} = \frac{.01281}{20} = .00064$$

$$F = \frac{MSC}{MSE} = \frac{.01212}{.00064} = 18.94$$

Source of Variance	SS	df	MS	F
Treatment	.04846	4	.01212	18.94
Block	.00203	5	.00041	
Error	.01281	20	.00064	
Total	.06330	29		

ACTION:

STEP 7. Because $F_{treat} = 18.94 > F_{.01,4,20} = 4.43$, the null hypothesis is rejected for the treatment effects. There is a significant difference in the average price of a gallon of premium unleaded gasoline in various cities.

A glance at the MSR reveals that there appears to be relatively little blocking variance. The result of determining an F value for the blocking effects is

$$F = \frac{MSR}{MSE} = \frac{.00041}{.00064} = 0.64$$

The value of F for blocks is not significant at $\alpha = .01$ ($F_{.01,5,20} = 4.10$). This result indicates that the blocking portion of the experimental design did not contribute significantly to the analysis. If the blocking effects (SSR) are added back into SSE and the df_R are included with df_E, the MSE becomes .00059 instead of .00064. Using the value .00059 in the denominator for the treatment F increases the observed treatment F value to 20.54. Thus, including nonsignificant blocking effects in the original analysis caused a loss of power.

Shown here are the Minitab and Excel ANOVA table outputs for this problem.

Minitab Output

```
Two-way ANOVA: Gas Prices versus Brand, City

Source DF        SS         MS       F      P
Brand    5  0.0020267  0.0004053   0.63  0.677
City     4  0.0485133  0.0121283  18.94  0.000
Error   20  0.0128067  0.0006403
Total   29  0.0633467
```

Excel Output

Anova: Two-Factor Without Replication

ANOVA						
Source of Variation	SS	df	MS	F	P-value	F crit
Rows	0.002027	5	0.000405	0.63	0.6768877	4.10
Columns	0.048513	4	0.012128	18.94	0.0000014	4.43
Error	0.012807	20	0.000640			
Total	0.063347	29				

BUSINESS IMPLICATIONS:

STEP 8. The fact that there is a significant difference in the price of gasoline in different parts of the country can be useful information to decision makers. For example, companies in the ground transportation business are greatly affected by increases in the cost of fuel. Knowledge of price differences in fuel can help these companies plan strategies and routes. Fuel price differences can sometimes be indications of cost-of-living differences or distribution problems, which can affect a company's relocation decision or cost-of-living increases given to employees who transfer to the higher-priced locations. Knowing that the price of gasoline varies around the country can generate interest among market researchers who might want to study why the differences are there and what drives them. This information can sometimes result in a better understanding of the marketplace.

11.4 PROBLEMS

11.28 Use ANOVA to analyze the data from the randomized block design given here. Let $\alpha = .05$. State the null and alternative hypotheses and determine whether the null hypothesis is rejected.

		Treatment Level			
		1	*2*	*3*	*4*
	1	23	26	24	24
	2	31	35	32	33
Block	3	27	29	26	27
	4	21	28	27	22
	5	18	25	27	20

11.29 The following data were gathered from a randomized block design. Use $\alpha = .01$ to test for a significant difference in the treatment levels. Establish the hypotheses and reach a conclusion about the null hypothesis.

		Treatment Level		
		1	*2*	*3*
	1	1.28	1.29	1.29
Block	2	1.40	1.36	1.35
	3	1.15	1.13	1.19
	4	1.22	1.18	1.24

11.30 A randomized block design has a treatment variable with six levels and a blocking variable with 10 blocks. Using this information and $\alpha = .05$, complete the following table and reach a conclusion about the null hypothesis.

Source of Variance	SS	df	MS	F
Treatment	2,477.53			
Blocks	3,180.48			
Error	11,661.38			
Total				

11.31 A randomized block design has a treatment variable with four levels and a blocking variable with seven blocks. Using this information and $\alpha = .01$, complete the following table and reach a conclusion about the null hypothesis.

Source of Variance	SS	df	MS	F
Treatment	199.48			
Blocks	265.24			
Error	306.59			
Total				

11.32 Safety in motels and hotels is a growing concern among travelers. Suppose a survey was conducted by the National Motel and Hotel Association to determine U.S. travelers' perception of safety in various motel chains. The association chose four different national chains from the economy lodging sector and randomly selected 10 people who had stayed overnight in a motel in each of the four chains in the past two years. Each selected traveler was asked to rate each motel chain on a scale from 0 to 100 to indicate how safe he or she felt at that motel. A score of 0 indicates completely unsafe and a score of 100 indicates perfectly safe. The scores follow. Test this randomized block design to determine whether there is a significant difference in the safety ratings of the four motels. Use $\alpha = .05$

Traveler	Motel 1	Motel 2	Motel 3	Motel 4
1	40	30	55	45
2	65	50	80	70
3	60	55	60	60
4	20	40	55	50
5	50	35	65	60
6	30	30	50	50
7	55	30	60	55
8	70	70	70	70
9	65	60	80	75
10	45	25	45	50

11.33 In recent years, the debate over the U.S. economy has been constant. The electorate seems somewhat divided as to whether the economy is in a recovery or not. Suppose a survey was undertaken to ascertain whether the perception of economic recovery differs according to political affiliation. People were selected for the survey from the Democratic Party, the Republican Party, and those classifying themselves as independents. A 25-point scale was developed in which respondents gave a score of 25 if they felt the economy was definitely in complete recovery, a 0 if the economy was definitely not in a recovery, and some value in between for more uncertain responses. To control for differences in socioeconomic class, a blocking variable was maintained using five different socioeconomic categories. The data are given here in the form of a randomized block design. Use $\alpha = .01$ to determine whether there is a significant difference in mean responses according to political affiliation.

	Political Affiliation		
Socioeconomic Class	Democrat	Republican	Independent
Upper	11	5	8
Upper middle	15	9	8
Middle	19	14	15
Lower middle	16	12	10
Lower	9	8	7

11.34 As part of a manufacturing process, a plastic container is supposed to be filled with 46 ounces of saltwater solution. The plant has three machines that fill the containers. Managers are concerned that the machines might not be filling the containers with the same amount of saltwater solution, so they set up a randomized block design to test this concern. A pool of five machine operators operates each of the three machines at different times. Company technicians randomly select five containers filled by each machine (one container for each of the five operators). The measurements are gathered and analyzed. The Minitab output from this analysis follows. What was the structure of the design? How many blocks were there? How many treatment classifications? Is there a statistical difference in the treatment means? Are the blocking effects significant? Discuss the implications of the output.

```
Two-way ANOVA: Measurement versus Machine, Operator
Source     DF      SS      MS      F      P
Machine     2    78.30   39.15   6.72   .019
Operator    4     5.09    1.27   0.22   .807
Error       8    46.66    5.83
Total      14   130.06
```

11.35 The comptroller of a company is interested in determining whether the average length of long-distance calls by managers varies according to type of telephone. A randomized block design experiment is set up in which a long-distance call by each of five managers is sampled for four different types of telephones: cellular, computer, regular, and cordless. The treatment is type of telephone and the blocks are the managers. The results of analysis by Excel are shown here. Discuss the results and any implications they might have for the company.

Anova: Two-Factor Without Replication

ANOVA

Source of Variation	SS	df	MS	F	P-value	F crit
Managers	11.3346	4	2.8336	12.74	0.00028	3.26
Phone Type	10.6043	3	3.5348	15.89	0.00018	3.49
Error	2.6696	12	0.2225			
Total	24.6085	19				

11.5 A FACTORIAL DESIGN (TWO-WAY ANOVA)

Video

Some experiments are designed so that *two or more treatments* (independent variables) *are explored simultaneously.* Such experimental designs are referred to as **factorial designs**. In factorial designs, *every level of each treatment is studied under the conditions of every level of all other treatments.* Factorial designs can be arranged such that three, four, or *n* treatments or independent variables are studied simultaneously in the same experiment. As an example, consider the valve opening data in Table 11.1. The mean valve opening for the 24 measurements is 6.34 centimeters. However, every valve but one in the sample measures something other than the mean. Why? Company management realizes that valves at this firm are made on different machines, by different operators, on different shifts, on different days, with raw materials from different suppliers. Business researchers who are interested in finding the sources of variation might decide to set up a factorial design that incorporates all five of these independent variables in one study. In this text, we explore the factorial designs with two treatments only.

Advantages of the Factorial Design

If two independent variables are analyzed by using a completely randomized design, the effects of each variable are explored separately (one per design). Thus, it takes two completely randomized designs to analyze the effects of the two independent variables. By using a factorial design, the business researcher can analyze both variables at the same time in one design, saving the time and effort of doing two different analyses and minimizing the experiment-wise error rate.

Some business researchers use the factorial design as a way to control confounding or concomitant variables in a study. By building variables into the design, the researcher attempts to control for the effects of multiple variables *in* the experiment. With the completely randomized design, the variables are studied in isolation. With the factorial design, there is potential for increased power over the completely randomized design because the additional effects of the second variable are removed from the error sum of squares.

The researcher can explore the possibility of interaction between the two treatment variables in a two-factor factorial design if multiple measurements are taken under every combination of levels of the two treatments. Interaction will be discussed later.

Factorial designs with two treatments are similar to randomized block designs. However, whereas randomized block designs focus on one treatment variable and control for a blocking effect, a two-treatment factorial design focuses on the effects of both variables. Because the randomized block design contains only one measure for each (treatment-block) combination, interaction cannot be analyzed in randomized block designs.

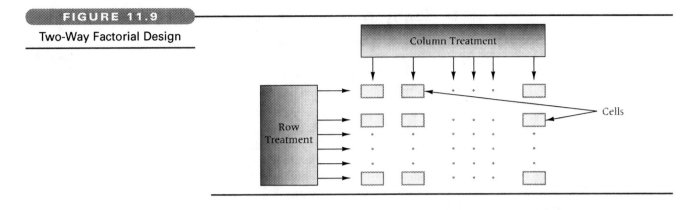

FIGURE 11.9

Two-Way Factorial Design

Factorial Designs with Two Treatments

The structure of a two-treatment factorial design is featured in Figure 11.9. Note that there are two independent variables (two treatments) and that there is an intersection of each level of each treatment. These intersections are referred to as *cells*. One treatment is arbitrarily designated as *row* treatment (forming the rows of the design) and the other treatment is designated as *column* treatment (forming the columns of the design). Although it is possible to analyze factorial designs with unequal numbers of items in the cells, the analysis of unequal cell designs is beyond the scope of this text. All factorial designs discussed here have cells of equal size.

Treatments (independent variables) of factorial designs must have at least two levels each. The simplest factorial design is a 2×2 factorial design, where each treatment has two levels. If such a factorial design were diagrammed in the manner of Figure 11.9, it would include two rows and two columns, forming four cells.

In this section, we study only factorial designs with $n > 1$ measurements for each combination of treatment levels (cells). This approach allows us to attempt to measure the interaction of the treatment variables. As with the completely randomized design and the randomized block design, a factorial design contains only one dependent variable.

Applications

Many applications of the factorial design are possible in business research. For example, the natural gas industry can design an experiment to study usage rates and how they are affected by temperature and precipitation. Theorizing that the outside temperature and type of precipitation make a difference in natural gas usage, industry researchers can gather usage measurements for a given community over a variety of temperature and precipitation conditions. At the same time, they can make an effort to determine whether certain types of precipitation, combined with certain temperature levels, affect usage rates differently than other combinations of temperature and precipitation (interaction effects).

Stock market analysts can select a company from an industry such as the construction industry and observe the behavior of its stock under different conditions. A factorial design can be set up by using volume of the stock market and prime interest rate as two independent variables. For volume of the market, business researchers can select some days when the volume is up from the day before, some days when the volume is down from the day before, and some other days when the volume is essentially the same as on the preceding day. These groups of days would constitute three levels of the independent variable, market volume. Business researchers can do the same thing with prime rate. Levels can be selected such that the prime rate is (1) up, (2) down, and (3) essentially the same. For the dependent variable, the researchers would measure how much the company's stock rises or falls on those randomly selected days (stock change). Using the factorial design, the business researcher can determine whether stock changes are different under various levels of market volume, whether stock changes are different under various levels of the prime interest rate, and whether stock changes react differently under various combinations of volume and prime rate (interaction effects).

Statistically Testing the Factorial Design

Analysis of variance is used to analyze data gathered from factorial designs. For factorial designs with two factors (independent variables), a **two-way analysis of variance (two-way ANOVA)** is used to test hypotheses statistically. The following hypotheses are tested by a two-way ANOVA.

Row effects:	H_0: Row means all are equal.
	H_a: At least one row mean is different from the others.
Column effects:	H_0: Column means are all equal.
	H_a: At least one column mean is different from the others.
Interaction effects:	H_0: The interaction effects are zero.
	H_a: An interaction effect is present.

Formulas for computing a two-way ANOVA are given in the following box. These formulas are computed in a manner similar to computations for the completely randomized design and the randomized block design. F values are determined for three effects:

1. Row effects
2. Column effects
3. Interaction effects

The row effects and the column effects are sometimes referred to as the main effects. Although F values are determined for these main effects, an F value is also computed for interaction effects. Using these observed F values, the researcher can make a decision about the null hypotheses for each effect.

Each of these observed F values is compared to a table F value. The table F value is determined by α, df_{num}, and df_{denom}. The degrees of freedom for the numerator (df_{num}) are determined by the effect being studied. If the observed F value is for columns, the degrees of freedom for the numerator are $C - 1$. If the observed F value is for rows, the degrees of freedom for the numerator are $R - 1$. If the observed F value is for interaction, the degrees of freedom for the numerator are $(R - 1) \cdot (C - 1)$. The number of degrees of freedom for the denominator of the table value for each of the three effects is the same, the error degrees of freedom, $RC(n - 1)$. The table F values (critical F) for a two-way ANOVA follow.

TABLE F VALUES FOR A TWO-WAY ANOVA	Row effects: $\quad F_{\alpha, R-1, RC(n-1)}$ Column effects: $\quad F_{\alpha, C-1, RC(n-1)}$ Interaction effects: $\quad F_{\alpha, (R-1)(C-1), RC(n-1)}$

FORMULAS FOR COMPUTING A TWO-WAY ANOVA	$\displaystyle SSR = nC \sum_{i=1}^{R} (\bar{x}_i - \bar{x})^2$ $\displaystyle SSC = nR \sum_{j=1}^{C} (\bar{x}_j - \bar{x})^2$ $\displaystyle SSI = n \sum_{i=1}^{R} \sum_{j=1}^{C} (\bar{x}_{ij} - \bar{x}_i - \bar{x}_j + \bar{x})^2$ $\displaystyle SSE = \sum_{i=1}^{R} \sum_{j=1}^{C} \sum_{k=1}^{n} (x_{ijk} - \bar{x}_{ij})^2$ $\displaystyle SST = \sum_{i=1}^{R} \sum_{j=1}^{C} \sum_{k=1}^{n} (x_{ijk} - \bar{x})^2$

$$df_R = R - 1$$
$$df_C = C - 1$$
$$df_I = (R - 1)(C - 1)$$
$$df_E = RC(n - 1)$$
$$df_T = N - 1$$

$$MSR = \frac{SSR}{R - 1}$$

$$MSC = \frac{SSC}{C - 1}$$

$$MSI = \frac{SSI}{(R - 1)(C - 1)}$$

$$MSE = \frac{SSE}{RC(n - 1)}$$

$$F_R = \frac{MSR}{MSE}$$

$$F_C = \frac{MSC}{MSE}$$

$$F_I = \frac{MSI}{MSE}$$

where

n = number of observations per cell
C = number of column treatments
R = number of row treatments
i = row treatment level
j = column treatment level
k = cell member
x_{ijk} = individual observation
$\overline{x}_{ij}$ = cell mean
$\overline{x}_i$ = row mean
$\overline{x}_j$ = column mean
$\overline{x}$ = grand mean

Interaction

As noted before, along with testing the effects of the two treatments in a factorial design, it is possible to test for the interaction effects of the two treatments whenever multiple measures are taken in each cell of the design. **Interaction** occurs *when the effects of one treatment vary according to the levels of treatment of the other effect.* For example, in a study examining the impact of temperature and humidity on a manufacturing process, it is possible that temperature and humidity will interact in such a way that the effect of temperature on the process varies with the humidity. Low temperatures might not be a significant manufacturing factor when humidity is low but might be a factor when humidity is high. Similarly, high temperatures might be a factor with low humidity but not with high humidity.

As another example, suppose a business researcher is studying the amount of red meat consumed by families per month and is examining economic class and religion as two independent variables. Class and religion might interact in such a way that with certain religions, economic class does not matter in the consumption of red meat, but with other religions, class does make a difference.

In terms of the factorial design, interaction occurs when the pattern of cell means in one row (going across columns) varies from the pattern of cell means in other rows. This

FIGURE 11.10

A 2 × 3 Factorial Design with Interaction

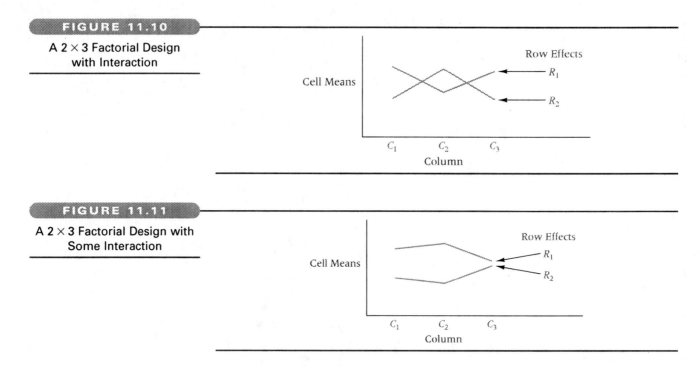

FIGURE 11.11

A 2 × 3 Factorial Design with Some Interaction

variation indicates that the differences in column effects depend on which row is being examined. Hence, an interaction of the rows and columns occurs. The same thing can happen when the pattern of cell means within a column is different from the pattern of cell means in other columns.

Interaction can be depicted graphically by plotting the cell means within each row (and can also be done by plotting the cell means within each column). The means within each row (or column) are then connected by a line. If the broken lines for the rows (or columns) are parallel, no interaction is indicated.

Figure 11.10 is a graph of the means for each cell in each row in a 2 × 3 (2 rows, 3 columns) factorial design with interaction. Note that the lines connecting the means in each row cross each other. In Figure 11.11 the lines converge, indicating the likely presence of some interaction. Figure 11.12 depicts a 2 × 3 factorial design with no interaction.

When the interaction effects are significant, the main effects (row and column) are confounded and should not be analyzed in the usual manner. In this case, it is not possible to state unequivocally that the row effects or the column effects are significantly different because the difference in means of one main effect varies according to the level of the other main effect (interaction is present). Some specific procedures are recommended for examining main effects when significant interaction is present. However, these techniques are beyond the scope of material presented here. Hence, in this text, whenever interaction effects are present (F_{inter} is significant), the researcher should *not* attempt to interpret the main effects (F_{row} and F_{col}).

As an example of a factorial design, consider the fact that at the end of a financially successful fiscal year, CEOs often must decide whether to award a dividend to stockholders

FIGURE 11.12

A 2 × 3 Factorial Design with No Interaction

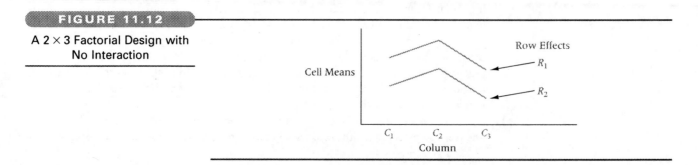

or to make a company investment. One factor in this decision would seem to be whether attractive investment opportunities are available.* To determine whether this factor is important, business researchers randomly select 24 CEOs and ask them to rate how important "availability of profitable investment opportunities" is in deciding whether to pay dividends or invest. The CEOs are requested to respond to this item on a scale from 0 to 4, where 0 = no importance, 1 = slight importance, 2 = moderate importance, 3 = great importance, and 4 = maximum importance. The 0–4 response is the dependent variable in the experimental design.

The business researchers are concerned that where the company's stock is traded (New York Stock Exchange, American Stock Exchange, and over-the-counter) might make a difference in the CEOs' response to the question. In addition, the business researchers believe that how stockholders are informed of dividends (annual reports versus presentations) might affect the outcome of the experiment. Thus, a two-way ANOVA is set up with "where the company's stock is traded" and "how stockholders are informed of dividends" as the two independent variables. The variable "how stockholders are informed of dividends" has two treatment levels, or classifications.

1. Annual/quarterly reports
2. Presentations to analysts

The variable "where company stock is traded" has three treatment levels, or classifications.

1. New York Stock Exchange
2. American Stock Exchange
3. Over-the-counter

This factorial design is a 2×3 design (2 rows, 3 columns) with four measurements (ratings) per cell, as shown in the following table.

		Where Company Stock Is Traded			
		New York Stock Exchange	American Stock Exchange	Over the Counter	$\overline{X}_i =$
How Stockholders Are Informed of Dividends	Annual Quarterly Reports	2 1 2 1 $\overline{X}_{11} = 1.5$	2 3 3 2 $\overline{X}_{12} = 2.5$	4 3 4 3 $\overline{X}_{13} = 3.5$	2.5
	Presentations to Analysts	2 3 1 2 $\overline{X}_{21} = 2.0$	3 3 2 4 $\overline{X}_{22} = 3.0$	4 4 3 4 $\overline{X}_{23} = 3.75$	2.9167
	$\overline{X}_j =$	1.75	2.75	3.625	

$$\overline{X} = 2.7083$$

These data are analyzed by using a two-way analysis of variance and $\alpha = .05$.

$$SSR = nC\sum_{i=1}^{R}(\overline{x}_i - \overline{x})^2$$
$$= 4(3)[(2.5 - 2.7083)^2 + (2.9167 - 2.7083)^2] = 1.0418$$

---

*Adapted from H. Kent Baker, "Why Companies Pay No Dividends," *Akron Business and Economic Review*, vol. 20 (Summer 1989), pp. 48–61.

$$SSC = nR \sum_{j=1}^{C} (\bar{x}_j - \bar{x})^2$$

$$= 4(2)[(1.75 - 2.7083)^2 + (2.75 - 2.7083)^2 + (3.625 - 2.7083)^2] = 14.0833$$

$$SSI = n \sum_{i=1}^{R} \sum_{j=1}^{C} (\bar{x}_{ij} - \bar{x}_i - \bar{x}_j + \bar{x})^2$$

$$= 4[(1.5 - 2.5 - 1.75 + 2.7083)^2 + (2.5 - 2.5 - 2.75 + 2.7083)^2$$
$$+ (3.5 - 2.5 - 3.625 + 2.7083)^2 + (2.0 - 2.9167 - 1.75 + 2.7083)^2$$
$$+ (3.0 - 2.9167 - 2.75 + 2.7083)^2 + (3.75 - 2.9167 - 3.625 + 2.7083)^2] = .0833$$

$$SSE = \sum_{i=1}^{R} \sum_{j=1}^{C} \sum_{k=1}^{n} (x_{ijk} - \bar{x}_{ij})^2$$

$$= (2 - 1.5)^2 + (1 - 1.5)^2 + \cdots + (3 - 3.75)^2 + (4 - 3.75)^2 = 7.7500$$

$$SST = \sum_{i=1}^{R} \sum_{j=1}^{C} \sum_{k=1}^{n} (x_{ijk} - \bar{x})^2$$

$$= (2 - 2.7083)^2 + (1 - 2.7083)^2 + \cdots + (3 - 2.7083)^2 + (4 - 2.7083)^2 = 22.9583$$

$$MSR = \frac{SSR}{R - 1} = \frac{1.0418}{1} = 1.0418$$

$$MSC = \frac{SSC}{C - 1} = \frac{14.0833}{2} = 7.0417$$

$$MSI = \frac{SSI}{(R - 1)(C - 1)} = \frac{.0833}{2} = .0417$$

$$MSE = \frac{SSE}{RC(n - 1)} = \frac{7.7500}{18} = .4306$$

$$F_R = \frac{MSR}{MSE} = \frac{1.0418}{.4306} = 2.42$$

$$F_C = \frac{MSC}{MSE} = \frac{7.0417}{.4306} = 16.35$$

$$F_I = \frac{MSI}{MSE} = \frac{.0417}{.4306} = 0.10$$

Source of Variation	SS	df	MS	F
Row	1.0418	1	1.0418	2.42
Column	14.0833	2	7.0417	16.35*
Interaction	.0833	2	.0417	0.10
Error	7.7500	18	.4306	
Total	22.9583	23		

*Denotes significance at $\alpha = .05$.

The critical F value for the interaction effects at $\alpha = .05$ is

$$F_{.05,2,18} = 3.55.$$

The observed F value for interaction effects is 0.10. Because this value is less than the critical table value (3.55), no significant interaction effects are evident. Because no significant interaction effects are present, it is possible to examine the main effects.

The critical F value of the row effects at $\alpha = .05$ is $F_{.05,1,18} = 4.41$. The observed F value of 2.42 is less than the table value. Hence, no significant row effects are present.

The critical F value of the column effects at $\alpha = .05$ is $F_{.05,2,18} = 3.55$. This value is coincidentally the same as the critical table value for interaction because in this problem the degrees of freedom are the same for interaction and column effects. The observed F value for columns (16.35) is greater than this critical value. Hence, a significant difference in row effects is evident at $\alpha = .05$.

A significant difference is noted in the CEOs' mean ratings of the item "availability of profitable investment opportunities" according to where the company's stock is traded. A cursory examination of the means for the three levels of the column effects (where stock is traded) reveals that the lowest mean was from CEOs whose company traded stock on the New York Stock Exchange. The highest mean rating was from CEOs whose company traded

---

FIGURE 11.13

Minitab and Excel Output for the CEO Dividend Problem

Minitab Output

```
Two-way ANOVA: Rating versus How Reported, Where Traded

Source          DF       SS        MS        F        P
How Reported     1    1.0417   1.04167    2.42    0.137
Where Traded     2   14.0833   7.04167   16.35    0.000
Interaction      2    0.0833   0.04167    0.10    0.908
Error           18    7.7500   0.43056
Total           23   22.9583

S = 0.6562    R-Sq = 66.24%    R-Sq(adj) = 56.87%
```

```
                          Individual 95% CIs For Mean Based on Pooled StDev
How  Reported   Mean     +——— + —— + —— + ——
1              2.50000   (————*————)
2              2.91667                (————*————)
                         +—— + —— + —— + ——
                        2.10   2.45   2.80   3.15
```

```
                          Individual 95% CIs For Mean Based on Pooled StDev
Where  Traded   Mean     — + —— + —— + —— + ——
1              1.750     (———*———)
2              2.750                (———*———)
3              3.625                          (———*———)
                         — + —— + —— + —— + ——
                        1.60   2.40   3.20   4.00
```

Excel Output

ANOVA: Two-Factor With Replication

SUMMARY	NYSE	ASE	OTC	Total
A.Q. Reports				
Count	4	4	4	12
Sum	6	10	14	30
Average	1.5	2.5	3.5	2.5
Variance	0.3333	0.3333	0.3333	1
Pres. to Analysts				
Count	4	4	4	12
Sum	8	12	15	35
Average	2	3	3.75	2.9167
Variance	0.6667	0.6667	0.25	0.9924
Total				
Count	8	8	8	
Sum	14	22	29	
Average	1.75	2.75	3.625	
Variance	0.5	0.5	0.2679	

ANOVA

Source of Variation	SS	df	MS	F	P-value	F crit
Sample	1.0417	1	1.0417	2.42	0.13725	4.41
Columns	14.0833	2	7.0417	16.35	0.00009	3.55
Interaction	0.0833	2	0.0417	0.10	0.90823	3.55
Within	7.7500	18	0.4306			
Total	22.9583	23				

stock over-the-counter. Using multiple comparison techniques, the business researchers can statistically test for differences in the means of these three groups.

Because the sample sizes within each column are equal, Tukey's HSD test can be used to compute multiple comparisons. The value of MSE is .431 for this problem. In testing the column means with Tukey's HSD test, the value of n is the number of items in a column, which is eight. The number of treatments is $C = 3$ for columns and $N - C = 24 - 3 = 21$.

With these two values and $\alpha = .05$, a value for q can be determined from Table A.10:

$$q_{.05,3,21} = 3.58$$

From these values, the honestly significant difference can be computed:

$$\text{HSD} = q\sqrt{\frac{\text{MSE}}{n}} = 3.58\sqrt{\frac{.431}{8}} = .831$$

The mean ratings for the three columns are

$$\bar{x}_1 = 1.75, \bar{x}_2 = 2.75, \bar{x}_3 = 3.625$$

The absolute value of differences between means are as follows:

$$|\bar{x}_1 - \bar{x}_2| = |1.75 - 2.75| = 1.00$$
$$|\bar{x}_1 - \bar{x}_3| = |1.75 - 3.625| = 1.875$$
$$|\bar{x}_2 - \bar{x}_3| = |2.75 - 3.625| = .875$$

All three differences are greater than .831 and are therefore significantly different at $\alpha = .05$ by the HSD test. Where a company's stock is traded makes a difference in the way a CEO responds to the question.

Using a Computer to Do a Two-Way ANOVA

A two-way ANOVA can be computed by using either Minitab or Excel. Figure 11.13 displays the Minitab and Excel output for the CEO example. The Minitab output contains an ANOVA table with each of the three F values and their associated p-values. In addition, there are individual 95% confidence intervals for means of both row and column effects. These intervals give the researcher a visual idea of differences between means. A more formal test of multiple comparisons of the column means is done with Minitab by using Tukey's HSD test. This output is displayed in Figure 11.14. Observe that in all three comparisons the signs on each end of the particular confidence interval are the same (and thus zero is not included); hence there is a significant difference in the means in each of the three pairs.

FIGURE 11.14

Tukey's Pairwise Comparisons for Column Means

```
Tukey 95% Simultaneous Confidence Intervals
All Pairwise Comparisons among levels of where Traded

Individual confidence level = 98.00%
Where Traded = 1 subtracted from:

Where
Traded    Lower   Center   Upper  ----+-------+-------+-------+----
2        0.1818   1.0000  1.8182              (----*-----)
3        1.0568   1.8750  2.6932                    (-----*-----)
                                      ----+-------+-------+-------+----
                                       -1.2     0.0     1.2     2.4

Where Traded = 2 subtracted from:

Where
Traded    Lower   Center   Upper  ----+-------+-------+-------+----
3        0.0568   0.8750  1.6932              (-----*-----)
                                      ----+-------+-------+-------+----
                                       -1.2     0.0     1.2     2.4
```

The Excel output for two-way ANOVA with replications on the CEO dividend example is included in Figure 11.13. The Excel output contains cell, column, and row means along with observed F values for rows (sample), columns, and interaction. The Excel output also contains p-values and critical F values for each of these F's. Note that the output here is virtually identical to the findings obtained by the manual calculations.

DEMONSTRATION PROBLEM 11.4

Some theorists believe that training warehouse workers can reduce absenteeism.* Suppose an experimental design is structured to test this belief. Warehouses in which training sessions have been held for workers are selected for the study. The four types of warehouses are (1) general merchandise, (2) commodity, (3) bulk storage, and (4) cold storage. The training sessions are differentiated by length. Researchers identify three levels of training sessions according to the length of sessions: (1) 1–20 days, (2) 21–50 days, and (3) more than 50 days. Three warehouse workers are selected randomly for each particular combination of type of warehouse and session length. The workers are monitored for the next year to determine how many days they are absent. The resulting data are in the following 4×3 design (4 rows, 3 columns) structure. Using this information, calculate a two-way ANOVA to determine whether there are any significant differences in effects. Use $\alpha = .05$.

Solution

HYPOTHESIZE:

STEP 1. The following hypotheses are being tested.

For row effects:

H_0: $\mu_1. = \mu_2. = \mu_3. = \mu_4.$
H_a: At least one of the row means is different from the others.

For column effects:

H_0: $\mu._1 = \mu._2 = \mu._3$
H_a: At least one of the column means is different from the others.

For interaction effects:

H_0: The interaction effects are zero.
H_a: There is an interaction effect.

TEST:

STEP 2. The two-way ANOVA with the F test is the appropriate statistical test.
STEP 3. $\alpha = .05$
STEP 4.

$$df_{rows} = 4 - 1 = 3$$
$$df_{columns} = 3 - 1 = 2$$
$$df_{interaction} = (3)(2) = 6$$
$$df_{error} = (4)(3)(2) = 24$$

For row effects, $F_{.05,3,24} = 3.01$; for column effects, $F_{.05,2,24} = 3.40$; and for interaction effects, $F_{.05,6,24} = 2.51$. For each of these effects, if any observed F value is greater than its associated critical F value, the respective null hypothesis will be rejected.

---

*Adapted from Paul R. Murphy and Richard F. Poist, "Managing the Human Side of Public Warehousing: An Overview of Modern Practices," *Transportation Journal*, vol. 31 (Spring 1992), pp. 54–63.

STEP 5.

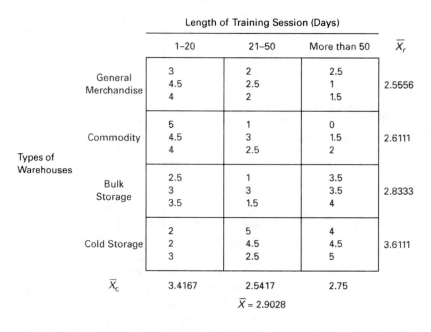

		Length of Training Session (Days)			
		1–20	21–50	More than 50	$\overline{X}_r$
Types of Warehouses	General Merchandise	3 4.5 4	2 2.5 2	2.5 1 1.5	2.5556
	Commodity	5 4.5 4	1 3 2.5	0 1.5 2	2.6111
	Bulk Storage	2.5 3 3.5	1 3 1.5	3.5 3.5 4	2.8333
	Cold Storage	2 2 3	5 4.5 2.5	4 4.5 5	3.6111
	$\overline{X}_c$	3.4167	2.5417	2.75	

$$\overline{\overline{X}} = 2.9028$$

STEP 6. The Minitab and Excel (ANOVA table only) output for this problem follows

Minitab Output

```
Two-way ANOVA: Absences versus Type of Ware, Length
      Source        DF         SS        MS       F        P
      Type of ware   3     6.4097   2.13657    3.46    0.032
      Length         2     5.0139   2.50694    4.06    0.030
      Interaction    6    33.1528   5.52546    8.94    0.000
      Error         24    14.8333   0.61806
      Total         35    59.4097
```

Excel Output

ANOVA

Source of Variation	SS	df	MS	F	P-value	F crit
Types of Warehouses	6.40972	3	2.13657	3.46	0.03221	3.01
Length of Training Session	5.01389	2	2.50694	4.06	0.03037	3.40
Interaction	33.15278	6	5.52546	8.94	0.00004	2.51
Within	14.83333	24	0.61806			
Total	59.40972	35				

ACTION:
STEP 7. Looking at the source of variation table, we must first examine the interaction effects. The observed F value for interaction is 8.94 for both Excel and Minitab. The observed F value for interaction is greater than the critical F value. The interaction effects are statistically significant at $\alpha = .05$. The p-value for interaction shown in Excel is .000035. The interaction effects are significant at $\alpha = .0001$. The business researcher should not bother to examine the main effects because the significant interaction confounds the main effects.

BUSINESS IMPLICATIONS:
STEP 8. The significant interaction effects indicate that certain warehouse types in combination with certain lengths of training session result in different absenteeism rates than do other combinations of levels for these two variables. Using the cell means shown here, we can depict the interactions graphically.

		Length of Training Session (Days)		
		1–20	21–50	More than 50
Type of Warehouse	General Merchandise	3.8	2.2	1.7
	Commodity	4.5	2.2	1.2
	Bulk Storage	3.0	1.8	3.7
	Cold Storage	2.3	4.0	4.5

Minitab produces the following graph of the interaction.

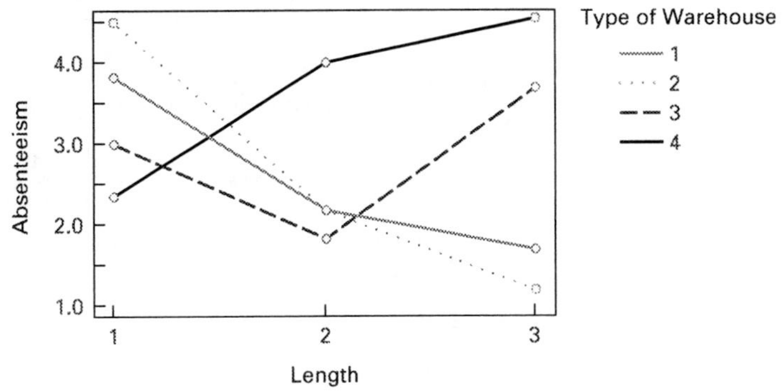

Note the intersecting and crossing lines, which indicate interaction. Under the short-length training sessions, 1, cold-storage workers had the lowest rate of absenteeism and workers at commodity warehouses had the highest. However, for medium-length sessions, 2, cold-storage workers had the highest rate of absenteeism and bulk-storage had the lowest. For the longest training sessions, 3, commodity warehouse workers had the lowest rate of absenteeism, even though these workers had the highest rate of absenteeism for short-length sessions. Thus, the rate of absenteeism for workers at a particular type of warehouse depended on length of session. There was an interaction between type of warehouse and length of session. This graph could be constructed with the row levels along the bottom axis instead of column levels.

11.5 PROBLEMS

11.36 Describe the following factorial design. How many independent and dependent variables are there? How many levels are there for each treatment? If the data were known, could interaction be determined from this design? Compute all degrees of freedom. Each data value is represented by an *x*.

	Variable 1			
Variable 2	x_{111} x_{112} x_{113}	x_{121} x_{122} x_{123}	x_{131} x_{132} x_{133}	x_{141} x_{142} x_{143}
	x_{211} x_{212} x_{213}	x_{221} x_{222} x_{223}	x_{231} x_{232} x_{233}	x_{241} x_{242} x_{243}

11.37 Describe the following factorial design. How many independent and dependent variables are there? How many levels are there for each treatment? If the data were known, could interaction be determined from this design? Compute all degrees of freedom. Each data value is represented by an x.

Variable 1

x_{111}	x_{121}	x_{131}
x_{112}	x_{122}	x_{132}
x_{211}	x_{221}	x_{231}
x_{212}	x_{222}	x_{232}

Variable 2

x_{311}	x_{321}	x_{331}
x_{312}	x_{322}	x_{332}
x_{411}	x_{421}	x_{431}
x_{412}	x_{422}	x_{432}

11.38 Complete the following two-way ANOVA table. Determine the critical table F values and reach conclusions about the hypotheses for effects. Let $\alpha = .05$.

Source of Variance	SS	df	MS	F
Row	126.98	3		
Column	37.49	4		
Interaction	380.82			
Error	733.65	60		
Total				

11.39 Complete the following two-way ANOVA table. Determine the critical table F values and reach conclusions about the hypotheses for effects. Let $\alpha = .05$.

Source of Variance	SS	df	MS	F
Row	1.047	1		
Column	3.844	3		
Interaction	0.773			
Error	____	__		
Total	12.632	23		

11.40 The data gathered from a two-way factorial design follow. Use the two-way ANOVA to analyze these data. Let $\alpha = .01$.

Treatment 1

		A	B	C
	A	23	21	20
		25	21	22
Treatment 2				
	B	27	24	26
		28	27	27

11.41 Suppose the following data have been gathered from a study with a two-way factorial design. Use $\alpha = .05$ and a two-way ANOVA to analyze the data. State your conclusions.

Treatment 2

		A	B	C	D
	A	1.2 1.3 1.3 1.5	2.2 2.1 2.0 2.3	1.7 1.8 1.7 1.6	2.4 2.3 2.5 2.4
Treatment 1					
	B	1.9 1.6 1.7 2.0	2.7 2.5 2.8 2.8	1.9 2.2 1.9 2.0	2.8 2.6 2.4 2.8

11.42 Children are generally believed to have considerable influence over their parents in the purchase of certain items, particularly food and beverage items. To study this notion further, a study is conducted in which parents are asked to report how many food and beverage items purchased by the family per week are purchased mainly because of the influence of their children. Because the age of the child may have an effect on the study, parents are asked to focus on one particular child in the family for the week, and to report the age of the child. Four age categories are selected for the children: 4–5 years, 6–7 years, 8–9 years, and 10–12 years. Also, because the number of children in the family might make a difference, three different sizes of families are chosen for the study: families with one child, families with two children, and families with three or more children. Suppose the following data represent the reported number of child-influenced buying incidents per week. Use the data to compute a two-way ANOVA. Let $\alpha = .05$.

		Number of Children in Family		
		1	2	3 or more
	4–5	2	1	1
		4	2	1
Age of	6–7	5	3	2
Child		4	1	1
(years)	8–9	8	4	2
		6	5	3
	10–12	7	3	4
		8	5	3

11.43 A shoe retailer conducted a study to determine whether there is a difference in the number of pairs of shoes sold per day by stores according to the number of competitors within a 1-mile radius and the location of the store. The company researchers selected three types of stores for consideration in the study: stand-alone suburban stores, mall stores, and downtown stores. These stores vary in the numbers of competing stores within a 1-mile radius, which have been reduced to four categories: 0 competitors, 1 competitor, 2 competitors, and 3 or more competitors. Suppose the following data represent the number of pairs of shoes sold per day for each of these types of stores with the given number of competitors. Use $\alpha = .05$ and a two-way ANOVA to analyze the data.

		Number of Competitors			
		0	1	2	3 or more
	Stand-Alone	41	38	59	47
		30	31	48	40
		45	39	51	39
Store	Mall	25	29	44	43
Location		31	35	48	42
		22	30	50	53
	Downtown	18	22	29	24
		29	17	28	27
		33	25	26	32

11.44 Study the following analysis of variance table that was produced by using Minitab. Describe the design (number of treatments, sample sizes, etc.). Are there any significant effects? Discuss the output.

```
Two-way ANOVA:DV versus RowEffect, ColEffect
Source          DF        SS         MS        F        P
RowEffect        2      92.31     46.156    13.23    0.000
ColEffect        4     998.80    249.700    71.57    0.000
Interaction      8     442.13     55.267    15.84    0.000
Error           30     104.67      3.489
Total           44    1637.91
```

11.45 Consider the valve opening data displayed in Table 11.1. Suppose the data represent valves produced on four different machines on three different shifts and that the quality controllers want to know whether there is any difference in the mean measurements of valve openings by shift or by machine. The data are given here, organized by machine and shift. In addition, Excel has been used to analyze the data with a two-way ANOVA. What are the hypotheses for this problem? Study the output in terms of significant differences. Discuss the results obtained. What conclusions might the quality controllers reach from this analysis?

		Valve Openings (cm)		
		Shift 1	Shift 2	Shift 3
	1	6.56	6.38	6.29
		6.40	6.19	6.23
	2	6.54	6.26	6.19
Machine		6.34	6.23	6.33
	3	6.58	6.22	6.26
		6.44	6.27	6.31
	4	6.36	6.29	6.21
		6.50	6.19	6.58

ANOVA: Two-Factor with Replication

ANOVA

Source of Variation	SS	df	MS	F	P-value	F crit
Sample	0.00538	3	0.00179	0.14	0.9368	3.49
Columns	0.19731	2	0.09865	7.47	0.0078	3.89
Interaction	0.03036	6	0.00506	0.38	0.8760	3.00
Within	0.15845	12	0.01320			
Total	0.39150	23				

11.46 Finish the computations in the Minitab ANOVA table shown below and on the next page and determine the critical table F values. Interpret the analysis. Examine the associated Minitab graph and interpret the results. Discuss this problem, including the structure of the design, the sample sizes, and decisions about the hypotheses.

```
Two-way ANOVA: depvar versus row, column
Source          DF        SS         MS
Row              2      0.296      0.148
Column           2      1.852      0.926
Interaction      4      4.370      1.093
Error           18     14.000      0.778
Total           26     20.519
```

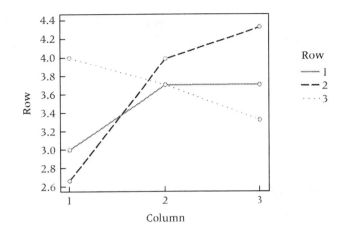

Is there a difference in the job satisfaction ratings of self-initiated expatriates by industry? The data presented in the Decision Dilemma to study this question represent responses on a seven-point Likert scale by 24 self-initiated expatriates from five different industries. The Likert scale score is the dependent variable. There is only one independent variable, industry, with five classification levels: IT, finance, education, healthcare, and consulting. If a series of t tests for the difference of two means from independent populations were used to analyze these data, there would be $_5C_2$ or 10 different t tests on this one problem. Using $\alpha = .05$ for each test, the probability of at least one of the 10 tests being significant by chance when the null hypothesis is true is $1 - (.95)^{10} = .4013$. That is, performing 10 t tests on this problem could result in an overall probability of committing a Type I error equal to .4013, not .05. In order to control the overall error, a one-way ANOVA is used on this completely randomized design to analyze these data by producing a single value of F and holding the probability of committing a Type I error at .05. Both Excel and Minitab have the capability of analyzing these data, and Minitab output for this problem is shown below.

```
One-way ANOVA: IT, Finance, Education, Healthcare, Consulting
Source    DF      SS       MS      F      P
Factor     4    43.175   10.794   15.25  0.000
Error     19    13.450    0.708
Total     23    56.625
S = 0.8414   R-Sq = 76.25%  R-Sq(adj) = 71.25%

                                 Individual 95% CIs For Mean Based on
                                 Pooled StDev
Level         N     Mean    StDev  ----+--------+------+-------+-
IT            4    5.7500   0.9574                    (----*----)
Finance       5    4.0000   0.7071           (----*----)
Education     6    2.5000   0.5477  (----*----)
Healthcare    5    3.4000   1.1402      (---*----)
Consulting    4    6.0000   0.8165                      (----*---)
                                   ----+--------+------+-------+-
                                     3.0      4.5    6.0     7.5
```

With an F value of 15.25 and a p-value of 0.000, the results of the one-way ANOVA show that there is an overall significant difference in job satisfaction between the five industries. Examining the Minitab confidence intervals shown graphically suggests that there might be a significant difference between some pairs of industries. Because there was an overall significant difference in the industries, it is appropriate to use Tukey's HSD test to determine which of the pairs of industries are significantly different. Tukey's test controls for the overall error so that the problem mentioned previously arising from computing ten t tests is avoided. The Minitab output for Tukey's test is:

```
Tukey 95% Simultaneous Confidence Intervals
All Pairwise Comparisons

Individual confidence level = 99.27%

IT subtracted from:
             Lower    Center   Upper    -----+--------+------+--------+-
Finance     -3.4462  -1.7500  -0.0538        (----*----)
Education   -4.8821  -3.2500  -1.6179   (----*----)
Healthcare  -4.0462  -2.3500  -0.6538    (-----*----)
Consulting  -1.5379   0.2500   2.0379           (-----*----)
                                        -----+--------+------+--------+-
                                           -3.0     0.0    3.0     6.0

Finance subtracted from:
             Lower    Center   Upper    -----+--------+------+--------+-
Education   -3.0311  -1.5000   0.0311    (----*----)
Healthcare  -2.1991  -0.6000   0.9991       (----*----)
Consulting   0.3038   2.0000   3.6962            (----*----)
                                        -----+--------+------+--------+-
                                           -3.0     0.0    3.0     6.0

Education subtracted from:
             Lower    Center   Upper    -----+--------+------+--------+-
Healthcare  -0.6311   0.9000   2.4311           (----*----)
Consulting   1.8679   3.5000   5.1321                 (---*---)
                                        -----+--------+------+--------+-
                                           -3.0     0.0    3.0     6.0

Healthcare subtracted from:
             Lower    Center   Upper    -----+--------+------+--------+-
Consulting   0.9038   2.6000   4.2962                (----*----)
                                        -----+--------+------+--------+-
                                           -3.0     0.0    3.0     6.0
```

Any confidence interval in which the sign of the value for the lower end of the interval is the same as the sign of the value for the upper end indicates that zero is not in the interval and that there is a significant difference between the pair in that case. Examining the Minitab output reveals that IT and Finance, IT and Education, IT and Healthcare, Finance and Consulting, Education and Consulting, and Healthcare and Consulting all are significantly different pairs of industries.

In analyzing career satisfaction, self-initiated expatriates were sampled from three age categories and four categories of time in the host country. This experimental design is a two-way factorial design with age and time in the host country as independent variables and individual scores on the seven-point Likert scale being the dependent variable. There are three classification levels under the independent variable Age: 30–39, 40–49, and over 50, and there are four classifications under the independent variable Time in Host Country: <1 year, 1 to 2 years, 3 to 4 years, and 5 or more years. Because there is more than one score per cell, interaction can be analyzed. A two-way ANOVA with replication is run in Excel to analyze the data and the result is shown below.

Excel Output:

ANOVA

Source of Variation	SS	df	MS	F	P-value	F crit
Age	3.5556	2	1.7778	2.91	0.07392	3.40
Time in Host Country	20.9722	3	6.9907	11.44	0.00007	3.01
Interaction	1.1111	6	0.1852	0.30	0.92918	2.51
Within	14.6667	24	0.6111			
Total	40.3056	35				

An examination of this output reveals no significant interaction effects (p-value of 0.929183). Since there are no significant interaction effects, it is appropriate to examine the main effects. Because of a p-value of 0.000075, there is a significant difference in Time in Host Country using an alpha of 0.0001.

Multiple comparison analysis could be done to determine which, if any, pairs of Time in Host Country are significantly different. The p-value for Age is 0.073920 indicating that there is a significant difference between Age classifications at alpha 0.10 but not at alpha of 0.05.

ETHICAL CONSIDERATIONS

In theory, any phenomenon that affects the dependent variable in an experiment should be either entered into the experimental design or controlled in the experiment. Researchers will sometimes report statistical findings from an experiment and fail to mention the possible concomitant variables that were neither controlled by the experimental setting nor controlled by the experimental design. The findings from such studies are highly questionable and often lead to spurious conclusions. Scientifically, the researcher needs to conduct the experiment in an environment such that as many concomitant variables are controlled as possible. To the extent that they are not controlled, the researcher has an ethical responsibility to report that fact in the findings.

Other ethical considerations enter into conducting research with experimental designs. Selection of treatment levels should be done with fairness or even randomness in cases where the treatment has several possibilities for levels. A researcher can build in skewed views of the treatment effects by erroneously selecting treatment levels to be studied. Some researchers believe that reporting significant main effects from a factorial design when there are confounding interaction effects is unethical or at least misleading.

Another ethical consideration is the leveling of sample sizes. Some designs, such as the two-way factorial design or completely randomized design with Tukey's HSD, require equal sample sizes. Sometimes unequal sample sizes arise either through the selection process or through attrition. A number of techniques for approaching this problem are not presented in this book. It remains highly unethical to make up data values or to eliminate values arbitrarily to produce equal sample sizes.

SUMMARY

Sound business research requires that the researcher plan a design for the experiment before a study is undertaken. The design of the experiment should encompass the treatment variables to be studied, manipulated, and controlled. These variables are often referred to as the independent variables. It is possible to study several independent variables and several levels, or classifications, of each of those variables in one design. In addition, the researcher selects one measurement to be taken from sample items under the conditions of the experiment. This measurement is referred to as the dependent variable because if the treatment effect is significant, the measurement of the dependent variable will "depend" on the independent variable(s) selected. This chapter explored three types of experimental designs: completely randomized design, randomized block design, and the factorial experimental designs.

The completely randomized design is the simplest of the experimental designs presented in this chapter. It has only one independent, or treatment, variable. With the completely randomized design, subjects are assigned randomly to treatments. If the treatment variable has only two levels, the design becomes identical to the one used to test the difference in means of independent populations presented in Chapter 10. The data from a completely randomized design are analyzed by a one-way analysis of variance (ANOVA). A one-way ANOVA produces an F value that can be compared to table F values in Appendix A.7 to determine whether the ANOVA F value is statistically significant. If it is, the null hypothesis that all population means are equal is rejected and at least one of the means is different from the others. Analysis of variance does not tell the researcher which means, if any, are significantly different from others. Although the researcher can visually examine means to determine which ones are greater and lesser, statistical techniques called multiple comparisons must be used to determine statistically whether pairs of means are significantly different.

Two types of multiple comparison techniques are presented and used in this chapter: Tukey's HSD test and the Tukey-Kramer procedure. Tukey's HSD test requires that equal sample sizes be used. It utilizes the mean square of error from the ANOVA, the sample size, and a q value that is obtained from Table A.10 to solve for the least difference between a pair of means that would be significant (HSD). The absolute value of the difference in sample means is compared to the HSD value to determine statistical significance. The Tukey-Kramer procedure is used in the case of unequal sample sizes.

A second experimental design is the randomized block design. This design contains a treatment variable (independent variable) and a blocking variable. The independent variable is the main variable of interest in this design. The blocking variable is a variable the researcher is interested in controlling rather than studying. A special case of randomized block design is the repeated measures design, in which the blocking variable represents subjects or items for which repeated measures are taken across the full range of treatment levels.

In randomized block designs, the variation of the blocking variable is removed from the error variance. This approach can potentially make the test of treatment effects more powerful. If the blocking variable contains no significant differences, the blocking can make the treatment effects test less powerful. Usually an F is computed only for the treatment effects in a randomized block design. Sometimes an F value is computed for blocking effects to determine whether the blocking was useful in the experiment.

A third experimental design is the factorial design. A factorial design enables the researcher to test the effects of two or more independent variables simultaneously. In complete factorial designs, every treatment level of each independent variable is studied under the conditions of every other treatment level for all independent variables. This chapter focused only on factorial designs with two independent variables. Each independent variable can have two or more treatment levels. These two-way factorial designs are analyzed by two-way analysis of variance (ANOVA). This analysis produces an F value for each of the two treatment effects and for interaction. Interaction is present when the results of one treatment vary significantly according to the levels of the other treatment. At least two measurements per cell must be present in order to compute interaction. If the F value for interaction is statistically significant, the main effects of the experiment are confounded and should not be examined in the usual manner.

KEY TERMS

Flash Cards

a posteriori
a priori
analysis of variance (ANOVA)

blocking variable
classification variable
classifications
completely randomized design
concomitant variables
confounding variables
dependent variable
experimental design

F distribution
F value
factorial design
factors
independent variable
interaction
levels
multiple comparisons
one-way analysis of variance

post hoc
randomized block design
repeated measures design
treatment variable
Tukey-Kramer procedure
Tukey's HSD test
two-way analysis of variance

FORMULAS

Formulas for computing a one-way ANOVA

$$SSC = \sum_{j=1}^{C} n_j(\bar{x}_j - \bar{x})^2$$

$$SSE = \sum_{i=1}^{n_j} \sum_{j=1}^{C} (x_{ij} - \bar{x}_j)^2$$

$$SST = \sum_{i=1}^{n_j} \sum_{j=1}^{C} (x_{ij} - \bar{x})^2$$

$$df_C = C - 1$$

$$df_E = N - C$$

$$df_T = N - 1$$

$$MSC = \frac{SSC}{df_C}$$

$$MSE = \frac{SSE}{df_E}$$

$$F = \frac{MSC}{MSE}$$

Tukey's HSD test

$$HSD = q_{\alpha,C,N-C}\sqrt{\frac{MSE}{n}}$$

Tukey-Kramer formula

$$q_{\alpha,C,N-C}\sqrt{\frac{MSE}{2}\left(\frac{1}{n_r} + \frac{1}{n_s}\right)}$$

Formulas for computing a randomized block design

$$SSC = n\sum_{j=1}^{C} (\bar{x}_j - \bar{x})^2$$

$$SSR = C\sum_{i=1}^{n} (\bar{x}_i - \bar{x})^2$$

$$SSE = \sum_{i=1}^{n} \sum_{j=1}^{C} (x_{ij} - \bar{x}_j - \bar{x}_i + \bar{x})^2$$

$$SST = \sum_{i=1}^{n} \sum_{j=1}^{C} (x_{ij} - \bar{x})^2$$

$$df_C = C - 1$$

$$df_R = n - 1$$

$$df_E = (C-1)(n-1) = N - n - C + 1$$

$$MSC = \frac{SSC}{C - 1}$$

$$MSR = \frac{SSR}{n - 1}$$

$$MSE = \frac{SSE}{N - n - C + 1}$$

$$F_{treatments} = \frac{MSC}{MSE}$$

$$F_{blocks} = \frac{MSR}{MSE}$$

Formulas for computing a two-way ANOVA

$$SSR = nC \sum_{i=1}^{R} (\bar{x}_i - \bar{x})^2$$

$$SSC = nR \sum_{j=1}^{C} (\bar{x}_j - \bar{x})^2$$

$$SSI = n \sum_{i=1}^{R} \sum_{j=1}^{C} (\bar{x}_{ij} - \bar{x}_i - \bar{x}_j + \bar{x})^2$$

$$SSE = \sum_{i=1}^{R} \sum_{j=1}^{C} \sum_{k=1}^{n} (x_{ijk} - \bar{x}_{ij})^2$$

$$SST = \sum_{i=1}^{R} \sum_{j=1}^{C} \sum_{k=1}^{n} (x_{ijk} - \bar{x})^2$$

$$df_R = R - 1$$

$$df_C = C - 1$$

$$df_I = (R - 1)(C - 1)$$

$$df_E = RC(n - 1)$$

$$df_T = N - 1$$

$$MSR = \frac{SSR}{R - 1}$$

$$MSC = \frac{SSC}{C - 1}$$

$$MSI = \frac{SSI}{(R - 1)(C - 1)}$$

$$MSE = \frac{SSE}{RC(n - 1)}$$

$$F_R = \frac{MSR}{MSE}$$

$$F_C = \frac{MSC}{MSE}$$

$$F_I = \frac{MSI}{MSE}$$

SUPPLEMENTARY PROBLEMS

CALCULATING THE STATISTICS

11.47 Compute a one-way ANOVA on the following data. Use $\alpha = .05$. If there is a significant difference in treatment levels, use Tukey's HSD to compute multiple comparisons. Let $\alpha = .05$ for the multiple comparisons.

	Treatment		
1	*2*	*3*	*4*
10	9	12	10
12	7	13	10
15	9	14	13
11	6	14	12

11.48 Complete the following ANOVA table.

Source of Variance	SS	df	MS	F
Treatment				
Error	249.61	19		
Total	317.80	25		

11.49 You are asked to analyze a completely randomized design that has six treatment levels and a total of 42 measurements. Complete the following table, which contains some information from the study.

Source of Variance	SS	df	MS	F
Treatment	210			
Error	655			
Total				

11.50 Compute a one-way ANOVA of the following data. Let $\alpha = .01$. Use the Tukey-Kramer procedure to conduct multiple comparisons for the means.

	Treatment	
1	*2*	*3*
7	11	8
12	17	6
9	16	10
11	13	9
8	10	11
9	15	7
11	14	10
10	18	
7		
8		

11.51 Examine the structure of the following experimental design. Determine which of the three designs presented in the chapter would be most likely to characterize this structure. Discuss the variables and the levels of variables. Determine the degrees of freedom.

	Methodology		
Person	*Method 1*	*Method 2*	*Method 3*
1	x_{11}	x_{12}	x_{13}
2	x_{21}	x_{22}	x_{23}
3	x_{31}	x_{32}	x_{33}
4	x_{41}	x_{42}	x_{43}
5	x_{51}	x_{52}	x_{53}
6	x_{61}	x_{62}	x_{63}

11.52 Complete the following ANOVA table and determine whether there is any significance in treatment effects. Let $\alpha = .05$.

Source of Variance	SS	df	MS	F
Treatment	20,994	3		
Blocking		9		
Error	33,891			
Total	71,338			

11.53 Analyze the following data, gathered from a randomized block design using $\alpha = .05$. If there is a significant difference in the treatment effects, use Tukey's HSD test to do multiple comparisons.

		Treatment			
		A	B	C	D
	1	17	10	9	21
	2	13	9	8	16
Blocking	3	20	17	18	22
Variable	4	11	6	5	10
	5	16	13	14	22
	6	23	19	20	28

11.54 A two-way ANOVA has been computed on a factorial design. Treatment 1 has five levels and treatment 2 has two levels. Each cell contains four measures. Complete the following ANOVA table. Use $\alpha = .05$ to test to determine significance of the effects. Comment on your findings.

Source of Variance	SS	df	MS	F
Treatment 1	29.13			
Treatment 2	12.67			
Interaction	73.49			
Error	110.38			
Total				

11.55 Compute a two-way ANOVA on the following data ($\alpha = .01$).

		Treatment 1		
		A	B	C
		5	2	2
	A	3	4	3
		6	4	5
		11	9	13
	B	8	10	12
Treatment 2		12	8	10
		6	7	4
	C	4	6	6
		5	7	8
		9	8	8
	D	11	12	9
		9	9	11

TESTING YOUR UNDERSTANDING

11.56 A company conducted a consumer research project to ascertain customer service ratings from its customers. The customers were asked to rate the company on a scale from 1 to 7 on various quality characteristics. One question was the promptness of company response to a repair problem. The following data represent customer responses to this question. The customers were divided by geographic region and by age. Use analysis of variance to analyze the responses. Let $\alpha = .05$. Compute multiple comparisons where they are appropriate. Graph the cell means and observe any interaction.

		Geographic Region			
		Southeast	West	Midwest	Northeast
		3	2	3	2
	21–35	2	4	3	3
		3	3	2	2
		5	4	5	6
Age	36–50	5	4	6	4
		4	6	5	5
		3	2	3	3
	Over 50	1	2	2	2
		2	3	3	1

11.57 A major automobile manufacturer wants to know whether there is any difference in the average mileage of four different brands of tires (A, B, C, and D), because the manufacturer is trying to select the best supplier in terms of tire durability. The manufacturer selects comparable levels of tires from each company and tests some on comparable cars. The mileage results follow.

A	B	C	D
31,000	24,000	30,500	24,500
25,000	25,500	28,000	27,000
28,500	27,000	32,500	26,000
29,000	26,500	28,000	21,000
32,000	25,000	31,000	25,500
27,500	28,000		26,000
	27,500		

Use $\alpha = .05$ to test whether there is a significant difference in the mean mileage of these four brands. Assume tire mileage is normally distributed.

11.58 Agricultural researchers are studying three different ways of planting peanuts to determine whether significantly different levels of production yield will result. The researchers have access to a large peanut farm on which to conduct their tests. They identify six blocks of land. In each block of land, peanuts are planted in each of the three different ways. At the end of the growing season, the peanuts are harvested and the average number of pounds per acre is determined for peanuts planted under each method in each block. Using the following data and $\alpha = .01$, test to determine whether there is a significant difference in yields among the planting methods.

Block	Method 1	Method 2	Method 3
1	1310	1080	850
2	1275	1100	1020
3	1280	1050	780
4	1225	1020	870
5	1190	990	805
6	1300	1030	910

11.59 The Construction Labor Research Council lists a number of construction labor jobs that seem to pay approximately the same wages per hour. Some of these are bricklaying, iron working, and crane operation. Suppose a labor researcher takes a random sample of workers from each of these types of construction jobs and from across the country and asks what are their hourly wages. If this survey yields the following data, is there a significant difference in mean hourly wages for these three jobs? If there is a significant difference, use the Tukey-Kramer procedure to determine which pairs, if any, are also significantly different. Let $\alpha = .05$.

	Job Type	
Bricklaying	**Iron Working**	**Crane Operation**
19.25	26.45	16.20
17.80	21.10	23.30
20.50	16.40	22.90
24.33	22.86	19.50
19.81	25.55	27.00
22.29	18.50	22.95
21.20		25.52
		21.20

11.60 Why are mergers attractive to CEOs? One of the reasons might be a potential increase in market share that can come with the pooling of company markets. Suppose a random survey of CEOs is taken, and they are asked to respond on a scale from 1 to 5 (5 representing strongly agree) whether increase in market share is a good reason for considering a merger of their company with another. Suppose also that the data are as given here and that CEOs have been categorized by size of company and years they have been with their company. Use a two-way ANOVA to determine whether there are any significant differences in the responses to this question. Let $\alpha = .05$.

		Company Size ($ million per year in sales)			
		0–5	**6–20**	**21–100**	**>100**
		2	2	3	3
		3	1	4	4
	0–2	2	2	4	4
		2	3	5	3
Years		2	2	3	3
with the		1	3	2	3
Company	3–5	2	2	4	3
		3	3	4	4
		2	2	3	2
		1	3	2	3
	Over 5	1	1	3	2
		2	2	3	3

11.61 Are some office jobs viewed as having more status than others? Suppose a study is conducted in which eight unemployed people are interviewed. The people are asked to rate each of five positions on a scale from 1 to 10 to indicate the status of the position, with 10 denoting most status and 1 denoting least status. The resulting data are given below. Use $\alpha = .05$ to analyze the repeated measures randomized block design data.

		Job			
	Mail Clerk	**Data Entry**	**Recep- tionist**	**Secre- tary**	**Admin. Asst.**
Respondent 1	4	5	3	7	6
2	2	4	4	5	4
3	3	3	2	6	7
4	4	4	4	5	4
5	3	5	1	3	5
6	3	4	2	7	7
7	2	2	2	4	4
8	3	4	3	6	6

INTERPRETING THE OUTPUT

11.62 Analyze the following Minitab output. Describe the design of the experiment. Using $\alpha = .05$ determine whether there are any significant effects; if so, explain why. Discuss any other ramifications of the output.

```
One-way ANOVA: Dependent Variable versus Factor
Analysis of Variance
Source       DF      SS      MS      F      p
Factor        3    876.6   292.2   3.01   0.045
Error        32   3107.5    97.1
Total        35   3984.1
                          Individual 95% CIs for
                          Mean Based on Pooled
                          StDev
Level   N   Mean    StDev  -+----+----+----+--
C1      8   307.73  5.98   (----*----)
C2      7   313.20  9.71        (----*----)
C3     11   308.60  9.78    (----*----)
C4     10   319.74  12.18              (---*---)
                          -+----+----+----+--
Pooled StDev = 9.85      301.0 308.0 315.0 322.0
```

11.63 Following is Excel output for an ANOVA problem. Describe the experimental design. The given value of alpha was .05. Discuss the output in terms of significant findings.

Anova: Two-Factor Without Replication

ANOVA						
Source of Variation	SS	df	MS	F	P-value	F crit
Rows	48.278	5	9.656	3.16	0.057	3.33
Columns	10.111	2	5.056	1.65	0.230	4.10
Error	30.556	10	3.056			
Total	88.944	17				

11.64 Study the following Minitab output and graph. Discuss the meaning of the output.

```
Two-Way ANOVA: Dependent Variable Versus
Row Effects, Column Effects
Source          DF     SS      MS      F      p
Row Eff          4    4.70    1.17   0.98   0.461
Col. Eff         1    3.20    3.20   2.67   0.134
Interaction      4   22.30    5.57   4.65   0.022
Error           10   12.00    1.20
Total           19   42.20
```

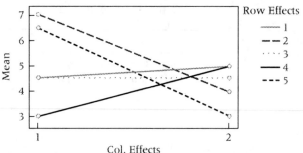

11.65 Interpret the following Excel output. Discuss the structure of the experimental design and any significant effects. Alpha is .05.

Anova: Two-Factor with Replication

ANOVA						
Source of Variation	SS	df	MS	F	P-value	F crit
Sample	2913.889	3	971.296	4.30	0.0146	3.01
Columns	240.389	2	120.194	0.53	0.5940	3.40
Interaction	1342.944	6	223.824	0.99	0.4533	2.51
Within	5419.333	24	225.806			
Total	9916.556	35				

11.66 Study the following Minitab output. Determine whether there are any significant effects and discuss the results. What kind of design was used and what was the size of it?

```
Two-Way Analysis of Variance
Source        df        SS        MS
Blocking       4     41.44     10.36
Treatment      4    143.93     35.98
Error         16    117.82      7.36
Total         24    303.19
```

11.67 Discuss the following Minitab output.

```
One-Way Analysis of Variance
Source          df       SS      MS       F       P
Treatment        3    138.0    46.0    3.51   0.034
Error           20    262.2    13.1
Total           23    400.3
Individual 95% CIs For Mean Based on Pooled
StDev
Level   N    Mean     StDev ----+----+----+----+
1       6   53.778    5.470  (----*----)
2       6   54.665    1.840  (----*----)
3       6   59.911    3.845              (----*----)
4       6   57.293    2.088        (----*----)
                             ----+----+----+----+
Pooled StDev = 3.621         52.5  56.0  59.5  63.0


Tukey's pairwise comparisons
Family error rate = 0.0500
Individual error rate = 0.0111
Critical value = 3.96
Intervals for (column level mean) - (row level
mean)
           1         2         3
2       -6.741
         4.967
3      -11.987   -11.100
        -0.279     0.608
4       -9.369    -8.482    -3.236
         2.339     3.225     8.472
```

ANALYZING THE DATABASES

see www.wiley.com/college/black

Database

1. Do various financial indicators differ significantly according to type of company? Use a one-way ANOVA and the financial database to answer this question. Let Type of Company be the independent variable with seven levels (Apparel, Chemical, Electric Power, Grocery, Healthcare Products, Insurance, and Petroleum). Compute three one-way ANOVAs, one for each of the following dependent variables: Earnings Per Share, Dividends Per Share, and Average P/E Ratio. On each ANOVA, if there is a significant overall difference between Type of Company, compute multiple comparisons to determine which pairs of types of companies, if any, are significantly different.

2. In the Manufacturing database, the Value of Industrial Shipments has been recoded into four classifications (1–4) according to magnitude of value. Let this value be the independent variable with four levels of classifications. Compute a one-way ANOVA to determine whether there is any significant difference in classification of the Value of Industrial Shipments on the Number of Production Workers (dependent variable). Perform the same analysis using End-of-Year Inventories as the dependent variable. Now change the independent variable to Industry Group, of which there are 20, and perform first a one-way ANOVA using Number of Production Workers as the dependent variable and then a one-way ANOVA using End-of-Year Inventory as the dependent variable.

3. The hospital database contains data on hospitals from seven different geographic regions. Let this variable be the independent variable. Determine whether there is a significant difference in Admissions for these geographic regions using a one-way ANOVA. Perform the same analysis using Births as the dependent variable. Control is a variable with four levels of classification denoting the type of control the hospital is under (such as federal government or for-profit). Use this variable as the independent variable and test to determine whether there is a significant difference in the Admissions of a hospital by Control. Perform the same test using Births as the dependent variable.

4. The Consumer Food database contains data on Annual Food Spending, Annual Household Income, and Non-Mortgage Household Debt broken down by Region and Location. Using Region as an independent variable with four classification levels (four regions of the U.S.), perform three different one-way ANOVA's—one for each of the three dependent variables (Annual Food Spending, Annual Household Income, Non-Mortgage Household Debt). Did you find any significant differences by region? If so, conduct multiple comparisons to determine which regions, if any, are significantly different.

CASE

THE CLARKSON COMPANY: A DIVISION OF TYCO INTERNATIONAL

In 1950, J. R. Clarkson founded a family-owned industrial valve design and manufacturing company in Sparks, Nevada. For almost a half century, the company, known as the Clarkson Company, worked on advancing metal and mineral processing. The Clarkson Company became known for its knife-gate and control valves, introduced in the 1970s, that are able to halt and isolate sections of slurry flow. By the late 1990s, the company had become a key supplier of knife-gate valves, helping to control the flow in many of the piping systems around the world in different industries, including mining, energy, and wastewater treatment.

The knife-gate valve uses a steel gate like a blade that lowers into a slurry flow to create a bubble-tight seal. While conventional metal gates fill with hardened slurry and fail easily thereby requiring high maintenance, Clarkson's design introduced an easily replaceable snap-in elastomer sleeve that is durable, versatile, and handles both high pressure and temperature variation. Pipeline operators value Clarkson's elastomer sleeve because traditional seals have cost between $75 and $500 to replace, and considerable revenue is lost when a slurry system is stopped for maintenance repairs. Clarkson's product lasts longer and is easier to replace.

In the late 1990s, the Clarkson Company was acquired by Tyco Valves & Controls, a division of Tyco International, Ltd. Tyco Valves & Controls, located in Reno, Nevada, and having ISO 9000 certification, continues to produce, market, and distribute products under the Clarkson brand name, including the popular knife-gate valve.

Discussion

1. The successful Clarkson knife-gate valve contains a wafer that is thin and light. Yet, the wafer is so strong it can operate with up to 150 pounds-per-square-inch (psi) of pressure on it, making it much stronger than those of competing brands. Suppose Tyco engineers have developed a new wafer that is even stronger. They want to set up an experimental design to test the strength of the wafer but they want to conduct the tests under three different temperature conditions, 70°, 110°, and 150°. In addition, suppose Tyco uses two different suppliers (company A and company B) of the synthetic materials that are used to manufacture the wafers. Some wafers are made primarily of raw materials supplied by company A, and some are made primarily of raw materials from company B. Thus, the engineers have set up a 2 × 3 factorial design with temperature and supplier as the independent variables and pressure (measured in psi) as the dependent variable. Data are gathered and are shown here. Analyze the data and discuss the business implications of the findings. If you were conducting the study, what would you report to the engineers?

	Temperature		
	70°	**110°**	**150°**
	163	157	146
Supplier A	159	162	137
	161	155	140
	158	159	150
Supplier B	154	157	142
	164	160	155

2. Pipeline operators estimate that it costs between $75 and $500 in U.S. currency to replace each seal, thus making the Clarkson longer-lasting valves more attractive. Tyco

does business with pipeline companies around the world. Suppose in an attempt to develop marketing materials, Tyco marketers are interested in determining whether there is a significant difference in the cost of replacing pipeline seals in different countries. Four countries— Canada, Colombia, Taiwan, and the United States—are chosen for the study. Pipeline operators from equivalent operations are selected from companies in each country. The operators keep a cost log of seal replacements. A random sample of the data follows. Use these data to help Tyco determine whether there is a difference in the cost of seal replacements in the various countries. Explain your answer and tell how Tyco might use the information in their marketing materials.

Canada	Colombia	Taiwan	United States
$215	$355	$170	$230
205	280	190	190
245	300	235	225
270	330	195	220
290	360	205	215
260	340	180	245
225	300	190	230

3. In the late 1980s, the Clarkson Company installed a manufacturing resource planning system. Using this and other quality improvement approaches, the company was able to reduce lead-time from six to eight weeks to less than two weeks. Suppose that Tyco now uses a similar system and wants to test to determine whether lead-times differ significantly according to the type of valve it is manufacturing. As a control of the experiment, they are including in the study, as a blocking variable, the day of the week the valve was ordered. One lead-time was selected per valve per day of the week. The data are given here in weeks. Analyze the data and discuss your findings.

	Type of Valve					
	Safety	Butterfly	Clack	Slide	Poppet	Needle
Monday	1.6	2.2	1.3	1.8	2.5	0.8
Tuesday	1.8	2.0	1.4	1.5	2.4	1.0
Wednesday	1.0	1.8	1.0	1.6	2.0	0.8
Thursday	1.8	2.2	1.4	1.6	1.8	0.6
Friday	2.0	2.4	1.5	1.8	2.2	1.2

Source: Adapted from "J. R. Clarkson Co., From Afterthought to Forethought," Real-World Lessons for America's Small Businesses: Insights from the Blue Chip Enterprise Initiative. Published by *Nation's Business* magazine on behalf of Connecticut Mutual Life Insurance Company and the U.S. Chamber of Commerce in association with the Blue Chip Enterprise Initiative, 1992; the Clarkson Co., Company Profile, Thomas Register Industry Answer Results, available at http://www.thomasregister.com; "The Clarkson Company Saves Time and Money Improving Piping Valves," ALGOR, pp. 1–4, available at http://www.algor.com; "Controlling the Flow," *Mechanical Engineering*, December 1998, pp. 1–5, available at http://www.memagazine.org. Tyco Valves & Controls Web site at www.tycovalves.com, and http://www.tycoflowcontrol.com/valves/products/slurry_valves/knife_gate_valves/2011.

USING THE COMPUTER

EXCEL

* Excel has the capability of performing a completely randomized design (one-way ANOVA), a randomized block design, and a two-way factorial design (two-way ANOVA).

* Each of the tests presented here in Excel is accessed through the **Data Analysis** feature.

* To conduct a one-way ANOVA, begin by selecting the **Data** tab on the Excel worksheet. From the **Analysis** panel at the right top of the **Data** tab worksheet, click on **Data Analysis**. If your Excel worksheet does not show the **Data Analysis** option, then you can load it as an add-in following directions given in Chapter 2. From the **Data Analysis** pulldown menu, select **Anova: Single Factor**. Click and drag over the data and enter in **Input Range**. Check **Labels in the First Row** if you included labels in the data. Insert the value of alpha in **Alpha**.

* To conduct a randomized block design, load the treatment observations into columns. Data may be loaded either with or without labels. Select the **Data** tab on the Excel worksheet. From the **Analysis** panel at the right top of the **Data** tab worksheet, click on **Data Analysis**. If your Excel worksheet does not show the **Data Analysis** option, then you

can load it as an add-in following directions given in Chapter 2. From the **Data Analysis** pulldown menu, select **Anova: Two-Factor Without Replication**. Click and drag over the data under **Input Range**. Check **Labels in the First Row** if you have included labels in the data. Insert the value of alpha in **Alpha**.

* To conduct a two-way ANOVA, load the treatment observations into columns. Excel is quite particular about how the data are entered for a two-way ANOVA. Data must be loaded in rows and columns as with most two-way designs. However, two-way ANOVA in Excel requires labels for both rows and columns; and if labels are not supplied, Excel will incorrectly use some of the data for labels. Since cells will have multiple values, there need only be a label for each new row (cell). Select the **Data** tab on the Excel worksheet. From the **Analysis** panel at the right top of the **Data** tab worksheet, click on **Data Analysis**. If your Excel worksheet does not show the **Data Analysis** option, then you can load it as an add-in following directions given in Chapter 2. From the **Data Analysis** pulldown menu, select **Anova: Two-Factor With Replication**. Click and drag over the data under **Input Range**. Enter the number of values per cell in **Rows per sample**. Insert the value of alpha in **Alpha**.

MINITAB

- Minitab also has the capability to perform a completely randomized design (one-way ANOVA), a randomized block design, and a two-way factorial design along with multiple comparisons.

- There are two ways to compute a one-way ANOVA in Minitab, stacking all observations in one column with group identifiers in another column, or entering the observations unstacked in separate columns.

- To begin a one-way ANOVA with **Unstacked Data**, select **Stat** from the menu bar. Select **ANOVA** from the pulldown menu. Select **One-Way** (**Unstacked**). In the slot, **Responses (in separate columns)**, list the columns containing the data. For multiple comparisons, select **Comparisons** and make your selection from the dialog box that appears. The multiple comparison options are Tukey's, Fisher's, Dunnett's, or Hsu's MCB tests. In the multiple comparison dialog box, you can insert the family error rate in the box on the right as a whole number.

- To begin a one-way ANOVA with **Stacked Data**, select **Stat** from the menu bar. Select **ANOVA** from the pulldown menu. Select **One-Way**. In the slot **Response**, list the column containing the observations. In the slot **Factor**, list the column containing the group identifiers. For multiple comparisons, select **Comparisons** and make your selection from the dialog box that appears. The multiple comparison options are Tukey's, Fisher's, Dunnett's, or Hsu's MCB tests. In the multiple comparison dialog box, you can insert the family error rate in the box on the right as a whole number.

- There are two ways to compute a randomized block design or a two-way ANOVA in Minitab, using the **Two-Way** procedure or using the **Balanced ANOVA** procedure. Both the randomized block design and the two-way ANOVA are analyzed in the same way and are presented together here.

- To begin using the **Two-Way** procedure, select **Stat** from the menu bar. Select **ANOVA** from the pulldown menu. Select **Two-Way**. The observations should be "stacked," that is, listed in one column. Place the location of these observations in the **Response** box. The group identifiers for the row effects should be listed in another column. Place the location of the row identifiers in **Row factor**. The group identifiers for the column effects should be listed in another column. Place the location of the column identifiers in **Column factor**.

- To begin using the **Balanced ANOVA** procedure, select **Stat** from the menu bar. Select **ANOVA** from the pulldown menu. Select **Balanced ANOVA** from the pulldown menu. Place the location of the observations in the **Responses** box. Place the columns containing the group identifiers to be analyzed in the **Model** box. To compute a two-way ANOVA with interaction, place the location of the column containing the row effects identifiers and the location of the column containing column effects identifiers in the **Model** box. To test for interaction also place a third term in the **Model** box that is the product of the row and column effects. For example, if the row effects are X and the column effects are Y, place a X*Y in the **Model** box along with X and Y.

REGRESSION ANALYSIS AND FORECASTING

In the first three units of the text, you were introduced to basic statistics, distributions, and how to make inferences through confidence interval estimation and hypothesis testing. In Unit IV, we explore relationships between variables through regression analysis and learn how to develop models that can be used to predict one variable by another variable or even multiple variables. We will examine a cadre of statistical techniques that can be used to forecast values from time-series data and how to measure how well the forecast is.

CHAPTER 12

Simple Regression Analysis and Correlation

LEARNING OBJECTIVES

The overall objective of this chapter is to give you an understanding of bivariate linear regression analysis, thereby enabling you to:

1. Calculate the Pearson product-moment correlation coefficient to determine if there is a correlation between two variables.
2. Explain what regression analysis is and the concepts of independent and dependent variable.
3. Calculate the slope and y-intercept of the least squares equation of a regression line and from those, determine the equation of the regression line.
4. Calculate the residuals of a regression line and from those determine the fit of the model, locate outliers, and test the assumptions of the regression model.
5. Calculate the standard error of the estimate using the sum of squares of error, and use the standard error of the estimate to determine the fit of the model.
6. Calculate the coefficient of determination to measure the fit for regression models, and relate it to the coefficient of correlation.
7. Use the t and F tests to test hypotheses for both the slope of the regression model and the overall regression model.
8. Calculate confidence intervals to estimate the conditional mean of the dependent variable and prediction intervals to estimate a single value of the dependent variable.
9. Determine the equation of the trend line to forecast outcomes for time periods in the future, using alternate coding for time periods if necessary.
10. Use a computer to develop a regression analysis, and interpret the output that is associated with it.

© Antonella Carri/Age Fotostock America, Inc.

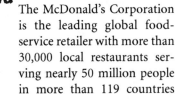

Decision Dilemma

Predicting International Hourly Wages by the Price of a Big Mac

The McDonald's Corporation is the leading global food-service retailer with more than 30,000 local restaurants serving nearly 50 million people in more than 119 countries each day. This global presence, in addition to its consistency in food offerings and restaurant operations, makes McDonald's a unique and attractive setting for economists to make salary and price comparisons around the world. Because the Big Mac hamburger is a standardized hamburger produced and sold in virtually every McDonald's around the world, the *Economist*, a weekly newspaper focusing on international politics and business news and opinion, as early as 1986 was compiling information about Big Mac prices as an indicator of exchange rates. Building on this idea, researchers Ashenfelter and Jurajda proposed comparing wage rates across countries and the price of a Big Mac hamburger. Shown below are Big Mac prices and net hourly wage figures (in U.S. dollars) for 27 countries. Note that net hourly wages are based on a weighted average of 12 professions.

Country	Big Mac Price (U.S. $)	Net Hourly Wage (U.S. $)
Philippines	2.19	1.40
Poland	2.60	4.10
Russia	2.33	5.90
Singapore	3.08	5.90
South Africa	2.45	5.10
South Korea	2.82	6.10
Sweden	6.56	13.50
Switzerland	6.19	22.60
Thailand	2.17	2.60
Turkey	3.89	4.30
UAE	2.99	10.10
United States	3.73	16.50

Managerial and Statistical Questions

1. Is there a relationship between the price of a Big Mac and the net hourly wages of workers around the world? If so, how strong is the relationship?

2. Is it possible to develop a model to predict or determine the net hourly wage of a worker around the world by the price of a Big Mac hamburger in that country? If so, how good is the model?

3. If a model can be constructed to determine the net hourly wage of a worker around the world by the price of a Big Mac hamburger, what would be the predicted net hourly wage of a worker in a country if the price of a Big Mac hamburger was $3.00?

Sources: McDonald's Web site, at http://www.mcdonalds.com/corp/about. html; Michael R. Pakko and Patricia S. Pollard, "Burgernomics: A Big Mac Guide to Purchasing Power Parity," research publication by the St. Louis Federal Reserve Bank, at http://research.stlouisfed.org/publications/review/ 03/11/pakko.pdf; Orley Ashenfelter and Stepán Jurajda, "Cross-Country Comparisons of Wage Rates: The Big Mac Index," unpublished manuscript, Princeton University and CERGEEI/Charles University, October 2001; Nicholas Vardy, "The 'Big Mac' Index for 2010," at http://nickvardy.com/2010/ 07/29/the-big-mac-index-for-2010/; "Prices and Earnings," 2009 edition, UBS, at http://www.ubs.com/1/e/media_overview/media_global/releases? newsId=170250.

Country	Big Mac Price (U.S. $)	Net Hourly Wage (U.S. $)
Argentina	1.78	3.30
Australia	3.84	14.00
Brazil	4.91	4.30
Britain	3.48	13.90
Canada	4.00	12.80
Chile	3.34	3.10
China	1.95	3.00
Czech Republic	3.43	5.10
Denmark	4.90	17.70
Hungary	3.33	3.00
Indonesia	2.51	1.30
Japan	3.67	15.70
Malaysia	2.19	3.10
Mexico	2.50	1.80
New Zealand	3.59	8.40

(*continued*)

In business, the key to decision making often lies in the understanding of the relationships between two or more variables. For example, a company in the distribution business may determine that there is a relationship between the price of crude oil and the company's transportation costs. Financial experts, in studying the behavior of the bond market, might find it useful to know if the interest rates on bonds are related to the prime interest rate set by the Federal Reserve. A marketing executive might want to know how strong the relationship is between advertising dollars and sales dollars for a product or a company.

In this chapter, we will study the concept of correlation and how it can be used to estimate the relationship between two variables. We will also explore simple regression analysis through which mathematical models can be developed to predict one variable by another. We will examine tools for testing the strength and predictability of regression models, and we will learn how to use regression analysis to develop a forecasting trend line.

12.1 CORRELATION

Interactive Applet

TABLE 12.1

Data for the Economics Example

Day	Interest Rate	Futures Index
1	7.43	221
2	7.48	222
3	8.00	226
4	7.75	225
5	7.60	224
6	7.63	223
7	7.68	223
8	7.67	226
9	7.59	226
10	8.07	235
11	8.03	233
12	8.00	241

Correlation is *a measure of the degree of relatedness of variables.* It can help a business researcher determine, for example, whether the stocks of two airlines rise and fall in any related manner. For a sample of pairs of data, correlation analysis can yield a numerical value that represents the degree of relatedness of the two stock prices over time. In the transportation industry, is a correlation evident between the price of transportation and the weight of the object being shipped? If so, how strong are the correlations? In economics, how strong is the correlation between the producer price index and the unemployment rate? In retail sales, are sales related to population density, number of competitors, size of the store, amount of advertising, or other variables?

Several measures of correlation are available, the selection of which depends mostly on the level of data being analyzed. Ideally, researchers would like to solve for ρ, the population coefficient of correlation. However, because researchers virtually always deal with sample data, this section introduces a widely used sample **coefficient of correlation**, r. This measure is applicable only if both variables being analyzed have at least an interval level of data. Chapter 17 presents a correlation measure that can be used when the data are ordinal.

The statistic r is the **Pearson product-moment correlation coefficient**, named after Karl Pearson (1857–1936), an English statistician who developed several coefficients of correlation along with other significant statistical concepts. The term r is a *measure of the linear correlation of two variables.* It is a number that ranges from -1 to 0 to $+1$, representing the strength of the relationship between the variables. An r value of $+1$ denotes a perfect positive relationship between two sets of numbers. An r value of -1 denotes a perfect negative correlation, which indicates an inverse relationship between two variables: as one variable gets larger, the other gets smaller. An r value of 0 means no linear relationship is present between the two variables.

PEARSON PRODUCT-MOMENT CORRELATION COEFFICIENT (12.1)	$$r = \frac{\Sigma(x - \bar{x})(y - \bar{y})}{\sqrt{\Sigma(x - \bar{x})^2 \, \Sigma(y - \bar{y})^2}} = \frac{\Sigma xy - \frac{(\Sigma x \, \Sigma y)}{n}}{\sqrt{\left[\Sigma x^2 - \frac{(\Sigma x)^2}{n}\right]\left[\Sigma y^2 - \frac{(\Sigma y)^2}{n}\right]}}$$

Figure 12.1 depicts five different degrees of correlation: (a) represents strong negative correlation, (b) represents moderate negative correlation, (c) represents moderate positive correlation, (d) represents strong positive correlation, and (e) contains no correlation.

What is the measure of correlation between the interest rate of federal funds and the commodities futures index? With data such as those shown in Table 12.1, which represent the values for interest rates of federal funds and commodities futures indexes for a sample of 12 days, a correlation coefficient, r, can be computed.

FIGURE 12.1

Five Correlations

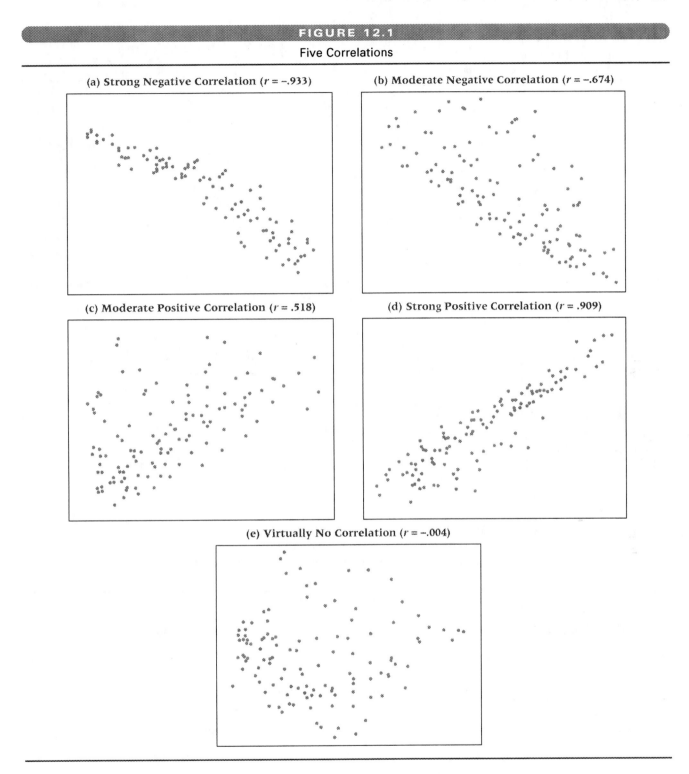

(a) Strong Negative Correlation ($r = -.933$)

(b) Moderate Negative Correlation ($r = -.674$)

(c) Moderate Positive Correlation ($r = .518$)

(d) Strong Positive Correlation ($r = .909$)

(e) Virtually No Correlation ($r = -.004$)

Examination of the formula for computing a Pearson product-moment correlation coefficient (12.1) reveals that the following values must be obtained to compute r: Σx, Σx^2, Σy, Σy^2, Σxy, and n. In correlation analysis, it does not matter which variable is designated x and which is designated y. For this example, the correlation coefficient is computed as shown in Table 12.2. The r value obtained ($r = .815$) represents a relatively strong positive relationship between interest rates and commodities futures index over this 12-day period. Figure 12.2 shows both Excel and Minitab output for this problem.

TABLE 12.2

Computation of r for the Economics Example

Day	Interest Rate x	Futures Index y	x^2	y^2	xy
1	7.43	221	55.205	48,841	1,642.03
2	7.48	222	55.950	49,284	1,660.56
3	8.00	226	64.000	51,076	1,808.00
4	7.75	225	60.063	50,625	1,743.75
5	7.60	224	57.760	50,176	1,702.40
6	7.63	223	58.217	49,729	1,701.49
7	7.68	223	58.982	49,729	1,712.64
8	7.67	226	58.829	51,076	1,733.42
9	7.59	226	57.608	51,076	1,715.34
10	8.07	235	65.125	55,225	1,896.45
11	8.03	233	64.481	54,289	1,870.99
12	8.00	241	64.000	58,081	1,928.00
	$\Sigma x = 92.93$	$\Sigma y = 2{,}725$	$\Sigma x^2 = 720.220$	$\Sigma y^2 = 619{,}207$	$\Sigma xy = 21{,}115.07$

$$r = \frac{(21{,}115.07) - \dfrac{(92.93)(2725)}{12}}{\sqrt{\left[(720.22) - \dfrac{(92.93)^2}{12}\right]\left[(619{,}207) - \dfrac{(2725)^2}{12}\right]}} = .815$$

FIGURE 12.2

Excel and Minitab Output for the Economics Example

Excel Output

	Interest Rate	Futures Index
Interest Rate	1	
Futures Index	0.815	1

Minitab Output

Correlations: Interest Rate, Futures Index
Pearson correlation of Interest Rate and Futures Index = 0.815
p-Value = 0.001

12.1 PROBLEMS

12.1 Determine the value of the coefficient of correlation, r, for the following data.

X	4	6	7	11	14	17	21
Y	18	12	13	8	7	7	4

12.2 Determine the value of r for the following data.

X	158	296	87	110	436
Y	349	510	301	322	550

12.3 In an effort to determine whether any correlation exists between the price of stocks of airlines, an analyst sampled six days of activity of the stock market. Using the following prices of Delta stock and Southwest stock, compute the coefficient of correlation. Stock prices have been rounded off to the nearest tenth for ease of computation.

Delta	Southwest
47.6	15.1
46.3	15.4
50.6	15.9
52.6	15.6
52.4	16.4
52.7	18.1

12.4 The following data are the claims (in $ millions) for BlueCross BlueShield benefits for nine states, along with the surplus (in $ millions) that the company had in assets in those states.

State	Claims	Surplus
Alabama	$1,425	$277
Colorado	273	100
Florida	915	120
Illinois	1,687	259
Maine	234	40
Montana	142	25
North Dakota	259	57
Oklahoma	258	31
Texas	894	141

Use the data to compute a correlation coefficient, r, to determine the correlation between claims and surplus.

12.5 The National Safety Council released the following data on the incidence rates for fatal or lost-worktime injuries per 100 employees for several industries in three recent years.

Industry	Year 1	Year 2	Year 3
Textile	.46	.48	.69
Chemical	.52	.62	.63
Communication	.90	.72	.81
Machinery	1.50	1.74	2.10
Services	2.89	2.03	2.46
Nonferrous metals	1.80	1.92	2.00
Food	3.29	3.18	3.17
Government	5.73	4.43	4.00

Compute r for each pair of years and determine which years are most highly correlated.

12.2 INTRODUCTION TO SIMPLE REGRESSION ANALYSIS

Regression analysis is *the process of constructing a mathematical model or function that can be used to predict or determine one variable by another variable or other variables.* The most elementary regression model is called **simple regression** or **bivariate regression** involving two variables in which one variable is predicted by another variable. In simple regression, *the variable to be predicted* is called the **dependent variable** and is designated as *y*. The *predictor* is called the **independent variable**, or *explanatory variable*, and is designated as *x*. In simple regression analysis, only a straight-line relationship between two variables is examined. Nonlinear relationships and regression models with more than one independent variable can be explored by using multiple regression models, which are presented in Chapters 13 and 14.

Can the cost of flying a commercial airliner be predicted using regression analysis? If so, what variables are related to such cost? A few of the many variables that can potentially contribute are type of plane, distance, number of passengers, amount of luggage/freight, weather conditions, direction of destination, and perhaps even pilot skill. Suppose a study is conducted using only Boeing 737s traveling 500 miles on comparable routes during the same season of the year. Can the number of passengers predict the cost of flying such routes? It seems logical that more passengers result in more weight and more baggage, which could, in turn, result in increased fuel consumption and other costs. Suppose the data displayed in Table 12.3 are the costs and associated number of passengers for twelve 500-mile commercial airline flights using Boeing 737s during the same season of the year. We will use these data to develop a regression model to predict cost by number of passengers.

Usually, the first step in simple regression analysis is to construct a **scatter plot** (or scatter diagram), discussed in Chapter 2. Graphing the data in this way yields preliminary information about the shape and spread of the data. Figure 12.3 is an Excel scatter plot of the data in Table 12.3. Figure 12.4 is a close-up view of the scatter plot produced by

TABLE 12.3
Airline Cost Data

Number of Passengers	Cost ($1,000)
61	4.280
63	4.080
67	4.420
69	4.170
70	4.480
74	4.300
76	4.820
81	4.700
86	5.110
91	5.130
95	5.640
97	5.560

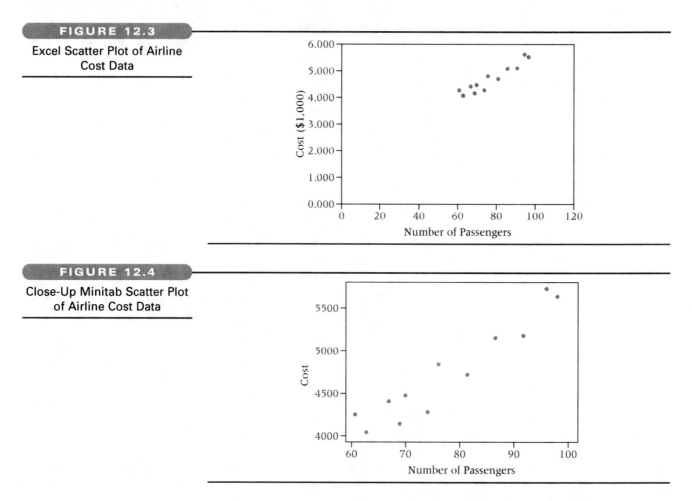

FIGURE 12.3

Excel Scatter Plot of Airline Cost Data

FIGURE 12.4

Close-Up Minitab Scatter Plot of Airline Cost Data

Minitab. Try to imagine a line passing through the points. Is a linear fit possible? Would a curve fit the data better? The scatter plot gives some idea of how well a regression line fits the data. Later in the chapter, we present statistical techniques that can be used to determine more precisely how well a regression line fits the data.

12.3 DETERMINING THE EQUATION OF THE REGRESSION LINE

Interactive Applet

The first step in determining the equation of the regression line that passes through the sample data is to establish the equation's form. Several different types of equations of lines are discussed in algebra, finite math, or analytic geometry courses. Recall that among these equations of a line are the two-point form, the point-slope form, and the slope-intercept form. In regression analysis, researchers use the slope-intercept equation of a line. In math courses, the slope-intercept form of the equation of a line often takes the form

$$y = mx + b$$

where

m = slope of the line
b = y intercept of the line

In statistics, the slope-intercept form of the equation of the regression line through the population points is

$$\hat{y} = \beta_0 + \beta_1 x$$

where

$\hat{y}$ = the predicted value of y
β_0 = the population y intercept
β_1 = the population slope

For any specific dependent variable value, y_i,

$$y_i = \beta_0 + \beta_1 x_i + \epsilon_i$$

where

$x_i =$ the value of the independent variable for the ith value
$y_i =$ the value of the dependent variable for the ith value
$\beta_0 =$ the population y intercept
$\beta_1 =$ the population slope
$\epsilon_i =$ the error of prediction for the ith value

Unless the points being fitted by the regression equation are in perfect alignment, the regression line will miss at least some of the points. In the preceding equation, ϵ_i represents the error of the regression line in fitting these points. If a point is on the regression line, $\epsilon_i = 0$.

These mathematical models can be either deterministic models or probabilistic models. **Deterministic models** are *mathematical models that produce an "exact" output for a given input.* For example, suppose the equation of a regression line is

$$y = 1.68 + 2.40x$$

For a value of $x = 5$, the exact predicted value of y is

$$y = 1.68 + 2.40(5) = 13.68$$

We recognize, however, that most of the time the values of y will not equal exactly the values yielded by the equation. Random error will occur in the prediction of the y values for values of x because it is likely that the variable x does not explain all the variability of the variable y. For example, suppose we are trying to predict the volume of sales (y) for a company through regression analysis by using the annual dollar amount of advertising (x) as the predictor. Although sales are often related to advertising, other factors related to sales are not accounted for by amount of advertising. Hence, a regression model to predict sales volume by amount of advertising probably involves some error. For this reason, in regression, we present the general model as a probabilistic model. A **probabilistic model** is *one that includes an error term that allows for the y values to vary for any given value of x.*

A deterministic regression model is

$$y = \beta_0 + \beta_1 x$$

The probabilistic regression model is

$$y = \beta_0 + \beta_1 x + \epsilon$$

$\beta_0 + \beta_1 x$ is the deterministic portion of the probabilistic model, $\beta_0 + \beta_1 x + \epsilon$. In a deterministic model, all points are assumed to be on the line and in all cases ϵ is zero.

Virtually all regression analyses of business data involve sample data, not population data. As a result, β_0 and β_1 are unattainable and must be estimated by using the sample statistics, b_0 and b_1. Hence the equation of the regression line contains the sample y intercept, b_0, and the sample slope, b_1.

EQUATION OF THE SIMPLE REGRESSION LINE	$$\hat{y} = b_0 + b_1 x$$
	where
	$b_0 =$ the sample intercept
	$b_1 =$ the sample slope

To determine the equation of the regression line for a sample of data, the researcher must determine the values for b_0 and b_1. This process is sometimes referred to as least squares analysis. **Least squares analysis** is *a process whereby a regression model is developed by producing the minimum sum of the squared error values.* On the basis of this premise and calculus, a particular set of equations has been developed to produce components of the regression model.*

*Derivation of these formulas is beyond the scope of information being discussed here but is presented in WileyPLUS.

FIGURE 12.5

Minitab Plot of a Regression Line

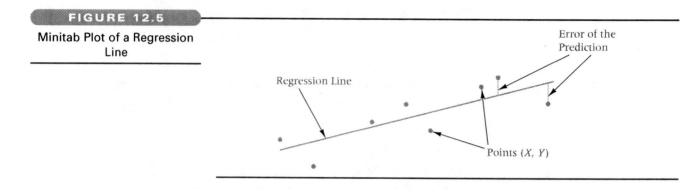

Examine the regression line fit through the points in Figure 12.5. Observe that the line does not actually pass through any of the points. The vertical distance from each point to the line is the error of the prediction. In theory, an infinite number of lines could be constructed to pass through these points in some manner. The least squares regression line is the regression line that results in the smallest sum of errors squared.

Formula 12.2 is an equation for computing the value of the sample slope. Several versions of the equation are given to afford latitude in doing the computations.

SLOPE OF THE REGRESSION LINE (12.2)

$$b_1 = \frac{\Sigma(x - \bar{x})(y - \bar{y})}{\Sigma(x - \bar{x})^2} = \frac{\Sigma xy - n\bar{x}\bar{y}}{\Sigma x^2 - n\bar{x}^2} = \frac{\Sigma xy - \dfrac{(\Sigma x)(\Sigma y)}{n}}{\Sigma x^2 - \dfrac{(\Sigma x)^2}{n}}$$

The expression in the numerator of the slope formula 12.2 appears frequently in this chapter and is denoted as SS_{xy}.

$$SS_{xy} = \Sigma(x - \bar{x})(y - \bar{y}) = \Sigma xy - \frac{(\Sigma x)(\Sigma y)}{n}$$

The expression in the denominator of the slope formula 12.2 also appears frequently in this chapter and is denoted as SS_{xx}.

$$SS_{xx} = \Sigma(x - \bar{x})^2 = \Sigma x^2 - \frac{(\Sigma x)^2}{n}$$

With these abbreviations, the equation for the slope can be expressed as in Formula 12.3.

ALTERNATIVE FORMULA FOR SLOPE (12.3)

$$b_1 = \frac{SS_{xy}}{SS_{xx}}$$

Formula 12.4 is used to compute the sample y intercept. The slope must be computed before the y intercept.

y INTERCEPT OF THE REGRESSION LINE (12.4)

$$b_0 = \bar{y} - b_1\bar{x} = \frac{\Sigma y}{n} - b_1\frac{(\Sigma x)}{n}$$

Formulas 12.2, 12.3, and 12.4 show that the following data are needed from sample information to compute the slope and intercept: Σx, Σy, Σx^2, and, Σxy, unless sample means are used. Table 12.4 contains the results of solving for the slope and intercept and determining the equation of the regression line for the data in Table 12.3.

The least squares equation of the regression line for this problem is

$$\hat{y} = 1.57 + .0407x$$

TABLE 12.4

Solving for the Slope and the y Intercept of the Regression Line for the Airline Cost Example

Number of Passengers	Cost ($1,000)		
x	y	x^2	xy
61	4.280	3,721	261.080
63	4.080	3,969	257.040
67	4.420	4,489	296.140
69	4.170	4,761	287.730
70	4.480	4,900	313.600
74	4.300	5,476	318.200
76	4.820	5,776	366.320
81	4.700	6,561	380.700
86	5.110	7,396	439.460
91	5.130	8,281	466.830
95	5.640	9,025	535.800
97	5.560	9,409	539.320
$\Sigma x = 930$	$\Sigma y = 56.690$	$\Sigma x^2 = 73,764$	$\Sigma xy = 4462.220$

$$SS_{xy} = \Sigma xy - \frac{(\Sigma x)(\Sigma y)}{n} = 4462.22 - \frac{(930)(56.69)}{12} = 68.745$$

$$SS_{xx} = \Sigma x^2 - \frac{(\Sigma x)^2}{n} = 73,764 - \frac{(930)^2}{12} = 1689$$

$$b_1 = \frac{SS_{xy}}{SS_{xx}} = \frac{68.745}{1689} = .0407$$

$$b_0 = \frac{\Sigma y}{n} - b_1\frac{\Sigma x}{n} = \frac{56.69}{12} - (.0407)\frac{930}{12} = 1.57$$

$$\hat{y} = 1.57 + .0407x$$

The slope of this regression line is .0407. Because the x values were recoded for the ease of computation and are actually in $1,000 denominations, the slope is actually $40.70. One interpretation of the slope in this problem is that for every unit increase in x (every person added to the flight of the airplane), there is a $40.70 increase in the cost of the flight. The y-intercept is the point where the line crosses the y-axis (where x is zero). Sometimes in regression analysis, the y-intercept is meaningless in terms of the variables studied. However, in this problem, one interpretation of the y-intercept, which is 1.570 or $1,570, is that even if there were no passengers on the commercial flight, it would still cost $1,570. In other words, there are costs associated with a flight that carries no passengers.

Superimposing the line representing the least squares equation for this problem on the scatter plot indicates how well the regression line fits the data points, as shown in the Excel graph in Figure 12.6. The next several sections explore mathematical ways of testing how well the regression line fits the points.

FIGURE 12.6

Excel Graph of Regression Line for the Airline Cost Example

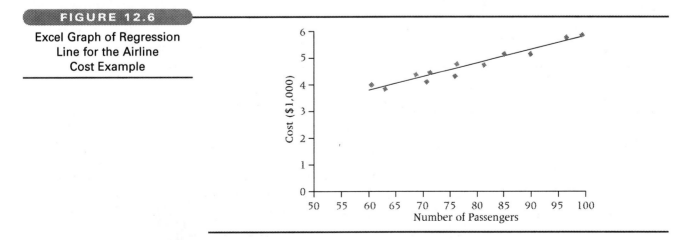

DEMONSTRATION PROBLEM 12.1

A specialist in hospital administration stated that the number of FTEs (full-time employees) in a hospital can be estimated by counting the number of beds in the hospital (a common measure of hospital size). A healthcare business researcher decided to develop a regression model in an attempt to predict the number of FTEs of a hospital by the number of beds. She surveyed 12 hospitals and obtained the following data. The data are presented in sequence, according to the number of beds.

Number of Beds	FTEs	Number of Beds	FTEs
23	69	50	138
29	95	54	178
29	102	64	156
35	118	66	184
42	126	76	176
46	125	78	225

Solution

The following Minitab graph is a scatter plot of these data. Note the linear appearance of the data.

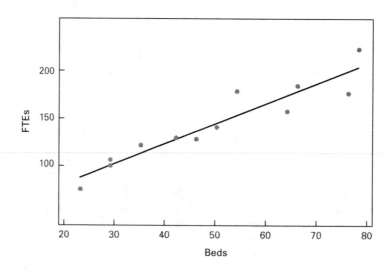

Next, the researcher determined the values of Σx, Σy, Σx^2, and Σxy.

Hospital	Number of Beds x	FTEs y	x^2	xy
1	23	69	529	1,587
2	29	95	841	2,755
3	29	102	841	2,958
4	35	118	1,225	4,130
5	42	126	1,764	5,292
6	46	125	2,116	5,750
7	50	138	2,500	6,900
8	54	178	2,916	9,612
9	64	156	4,096	9,984
10	66	184	4,356	12,144
11	76	176	5,776	13,376
12	78	225	6,084	17,550
	$\Sigma x = 592$	$\Sigma y = 1,692$	$\Sigma x^2 = 33,044$	$\Sigma xy = 92,038$

Using these values, the researcher solved for the sample slope (b_1) and the sample y-intercept (b_0).

$$SS_{xy} = \Sigma xy - \frac{(\Sigma x)(\Sigma y)}{n} = 92{,}038 - \frac{(592)(1692)}{12} = 8566$$

$$SS_{xx} = \Sigma x^2 - \frac{(\Sigma x)^2}{n} = 33{,}044 - \frac{(592)^2}{12} = 3838.667$$

$$b_1 = \frac{SS_{xy}}{SS_{xx}} = \frac{8566}{3838.667} = 2.232$$

$$b_0 = \frac{\Sigma y}{n} - b_1 \frac{\Sigma x}{12} = \frac{1692}{12} - (2.232)\frac{592}{12} = 30.888$$

The least squares equation of the regression line is

$$\hat{y} = 30.888 + 2.232x$$

The slope of the line, $b_1 = 2.232$, means that for every unit increase of x (every bed), y (number of FTEs) is predicted to increase by 2.232. Even though the y-intercept helps the researcher sketch the graph of the line by being one of the points on the line (0, 30.888), it has limited usefulness in terms of this solution because $x = 0$ denotes a hospital with no beds. On the other hand, it could be interpreted that a hospital has to have at least 31 FTEs to open its doors even with no patients—a sort of "fixed cost" of personnel.

12.3 PROBLEMS

12.6 Sketch a scatter plot from the following data, and determine the equation of the regression line.

x	12	21	28	8	20
y	17	15	22	19	24

12.7 Sketch a scatter plot from the following data, and determine the equation of the regression line.

x	140	119	103	91	65	29	24
y	25	29	46	70	88	112	128

12.8 A corporation owns several companies. The strategic planner for the corporation believes dollars spent on advertising can to some extent be a predictor of total sales dollars. As an aid in long-term planning, she gathers the following sales and advertising information from several of the companies for 2011 ($ millions).

Advertising	Sales
12.5	148
3.7	55
21.6	338
60.0	994
37.6	541
6.1	89
16.8	126
41.2	379

Develop the equation of the simple regression line to predict sales from advertising expenditures using these data.

12.9 Investment analysts generally believe the interest rate on bonds is inversely related to the prime interest rate for loans; that is, bonds perform well when lending rates are down and perform poorly when interest rates are up. Can the bond rate be predicted by the prime interest rate? Use the following data to construct a least squares regression line to predict bond rates by the prime interest rate.

Bond Rate	Prime Interest Rate
5%	16%
12	6
9	8
15	4
7	7

12.10 Is it possible to predict the annual number of business bankruptcies by the number of firm births (business starts) in the United States? The following data published by the U.S. Small Business Administration, Office of Advocacy, are pairs of the number of business bankruptcies (1000s) and the number of firm births (10,000s) for a six-year period. Use these data to develop the equation of the regression model to predict the number of business bankruptcies by the number of firm births. Discuss the meaning of the slope.

Business Bankruptcies (1000)	Firm Births (10,000)
34.3	58.1
35.0	55.4
38.5	57.0
40.1	58.5
35.5	57.4
37.9	58.0

12.11 It appears that over the past 45 years, the number of farms in the United States declined while the average size of farms increased. The following data provided by the U.S. Department of Agriculture show five-year interval data for U.S. farms. Use these data to develop the equation of a regression line to predict the average size of a farm by the number of farms. Discuss the slope and *y*-intercept of the model.

Year	Number of Farms (millions)	Average Size (acres)
1950	5.65	213
1955	4.65	258
1960	3.96	297
1965	3.36	340
1970	2.95	374
1975	2.52	420
1980	2.44	426
1985	2.29	441
1990	2.15	460
1995	2.07	469
2000	2.17	434
2005	2.10	444

12.12 Can the annual new orders for manufacturing in the United States be predicted by the raw steel production in the United States? Shown on the next page are the annual new orders for 10 years according to the U.S. Census Bureau and the raw steel production for the same 10 years as published by the American Iron & Steel Institute. Use these data to develop a regression model to predict annual new orders by raw steel production. Construct a scatter plot and draw the regression line through the points.

Raw Steel Production (100,000s of net tons)	New Orders ($ trillions)
99.9	2.74
97.9	2.87
98.9	2.93
87.9	2.87
92.9	2.98
97.9	3.09
100.6	3.36
104.9	3.61
105.3	3.75
108.6	3.95

12.4 RESIDUAL ANALYSIS

How does a business researcher test a regression line to determine whether the line is a good fit of the data other than by observing the fitted line plot (regression line fit through a scatter plot of the data)? One particularly popular approach is to use the *historical data* (x and y values used to construct the regression model) to test the model. With this approach, the values of the independent variable (x values) are inserted into the regression model and a predicted value ($\hat{y}$) is obtained for each x value. These predicted values ($\hat{y}$) are then compared to the actual y values to determine how much error the equation of the regression line produced. *Each difference between the actual y values and the predicted y values is the error of the regression line at a given point, $y - \hat{y}$, and is referred to as the* **residual**. It is the sum of squares of these residuals that is minimized to find the least squares line.

Table 12.5 shows $\hat{y}$ values and the residuals for each pair of data for the airline cost regression model developed in Section 12.3. The predicted values are calculated by inserting an x value into the equation of the regression line and solving for $\hat{y}$. For example, when $x = 61$, $\hat{y} = 1.57 + .0407(61) = 4.053$, as displayed in column 3 of the table. Each of these predicted y values is subtracted from the actual y value to determine the error, or residual. For example, the first y value listed in the table is 4.280 and the first predicted value is 4.053, resulting in a residual of $4.280 - 4.053 = .227$. The residuals for this problem are given in column 4 of the table.

Note that the sum of the residuals is approximately zero. Except for rounding error, the sum of the residuals is *always zero*. The reason is that a residual is geometrically the vertical distance from the regression line to a data point. The equations used to solve for the slope

TABLE 12.5
Predicted Values and Residuals for the Airline Cost Example

Number of Passengers x	Cost ($1,000) y	Predicted Value $\hat{y}$	Residual $y - \hat{y}$
61	4.280	4.053	.227
63	4.080	4.134	−.054
67	4.420	4.297	.123
69	4.170	4.378	−.208
70	4.480	4.419	.061
74	4.300	4.582	−.282
76	4.820	4.663	.157
81	4.700	4.867	−.167
86	5.110	5.070	.040
91	5.130	5.274	−.144
95	5.640	5.436	.204
97	5.560	5.518	.042

$$\Sigma(y - \hat{y}) = -.001$$

FIGURE 12.7

Close-Up Minitab Scatter Plot with Residuals for the Airline Cost Example

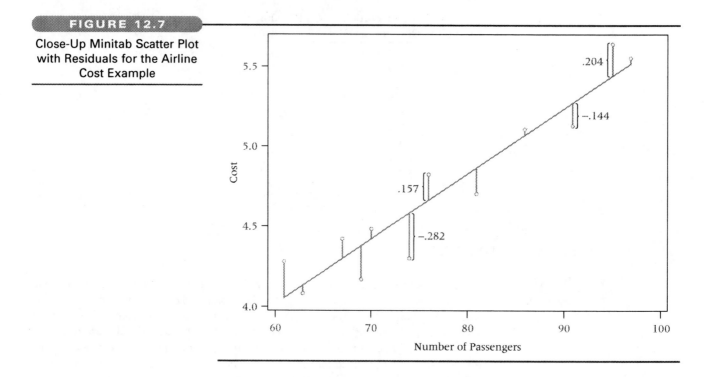

and intercept place the line geometrically in the middle of all points. Therefore, vertical distances from the line to the points will cancel each other and sum to zero. Figure 12.7 is a Minitab-produced scatter plot of the data and the residuals for the airline cost example.

An examination of the residuals may give the researcher an idea of how well the regression line fits the historical data points. The largest residual for the airline cost example is −.282, and the smallest is .040. Because the objective of the regression analysis was to predict the cost of flight in $1,000s, the regression line produces an error of $282 when there are 74 passengers and an error of only $40 when there are 86 passengers. This result presents the *best* and *worst* cases for the residuals. The researcher must examine other residuals to determine how well the regression model fits other data points.

Sometimes residuals are used to locate outliers. **Outliers** are *data points that lie apart from the rest of the points.* Outliers can produce residuals with large magnitudes and are usually easy to identify on scatter plots. Outliers can be the result of misrecorded or miscoded data, or they may simply be data points that do not conform to the general trend. The equation of the regression line is influenced by every data point used in its calculation in a manner similar to the arithmetic mean. Therefore, outliers sometimes can unduly influence the regression line by "pulling" the line toward the outliers. The origin of outliers must be investigated to determine whether they should be retained or whether the regression equation should be recomputed without them.

Residuals are usually plotted against the x-axis, which reveals a view of the residuals as x increases. Figure 12.8 shows the residuals plotted by Excel against the x-axis for the airline cost example.

FIGURE 12.8

Excel Graph of Residuals for the Airline Cost Example

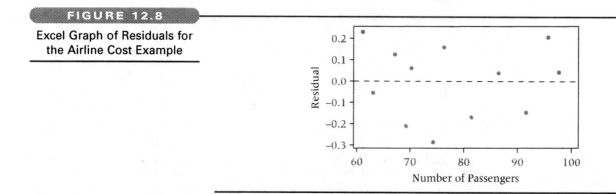

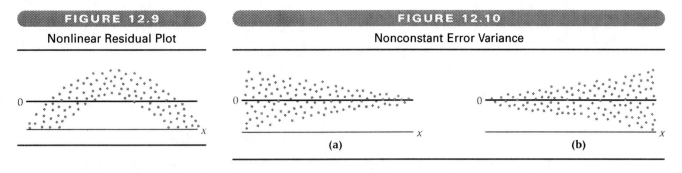

FIGURE 12.9

Nonlinear Residual Plot

FIGURE 12.10

Nonconstant Error Variance

(a)

(b)

Using Residuals to Test the Assumptions of the Regression Model

One of the major uses of residual analysis is to test some of the assumptions underlying regression. The following are the assumptions of simple regression analysis.

1. The model is linear.
2. The error terms have constant variances.
3. The error terms are independent.
4. The error terms are normally distributed.

A particular method for studying the behavior of residuals is the residual plot. The **residual plot** is *a type of graph in which the residuals for a particular regression model are plotted along with their associated value of x as an ordered pair* $(x, y - \hat{y})$. Information about how well the regression assumptions are met by the particular regression model can be gleaned by examining the plots. Residual plots are more meaningful with larger sample sizes. For small sample sizes, residual plot analyses can be problematic and subject to over-interpretation. Hence, because the airline cost example is constructed from only 12 pairs of data, one should be cautious in reaching conclusions from Figure 12.8. The residual plots in Figures 12.9, 12.10, and 12.11, however, represent large numbers of data points and therefore are more likely to depict overall trends accurately.

If a residual plot such as the one in Figure 12.9 appears, the assumption that the model is linear does not hold. Note that the residuals are negative for low and high values of *x* and are positive for middle values of *x*. The graph of these residuals is parabolic, not linear. The residual plot does not have to be shaped in this manner for a nonlinear relationship to exist. Any significant deviation from an approximately linear residual plot may mean that a nonlinear relationship exists between the two variables.

The assumption of *constant error variance* sometimes is called **homoscedasticity**. If *the error variances are not constant* (called **heteroscedasticity**), the residual plots might look like one of the two plots in Figure 12.10. Note in Figure 12.10(a) that the error variance is greater for small values of *x* and smaller for large values of *x*. The situation is reversed in Figure 12.10(b).

If the error terms are not independent, the residual plots could look like one of the graphs in Figure 12.11. According to these graphs, instead of each error term being independent of the one next to it, the value of the residual is a function of the residual value next to it. For example, a large positive residual is next to a large positive residual and a small negative residual is next to a small negative residual.

The graph of the residuals from a regression analysis that meets the assumptions—a *healthy residual graph*—might look like the graph in Figure 12.12. The plot is relatively linear; the variances of the errors are about equal for each value of *x*, and the error terms do not appear to be related to adjacent terms.

FIGURE 12.11

Graphs of Nonindependent Error Terms

(a)

(b)

FIGURE 12.12

Healthy Residual Graph

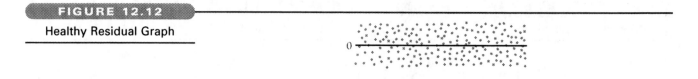

Using the Computer for Residual Analysis

Some computer programs contain mechanisms for analyzing residuals for violations of the regression assumptions. Minitab has the capability of providing graphical analysis of residuals. Figure 12.13 displays Minitab's residual graphic analyses for a regression model developed to predict the production of carrots in the United States per month by the total production of sweet corn. The data were gathered over a time period of 168 consecutive months (see WileyPLUS for the agricultural database).

These Minitab residual model diagnostics consist of three different plots. The graph on the upper right is a plot of the residuals versus the fits. Note that this residual plot "flares-out" as x gets larger. This pattern is an indication of heteroscedasticity, which is a violation of the assumption of constant variance for error terms. The graph in the upper left is a normal probability plot of the residuals. A straight line indicates that the residuals are normally distributed. Observe that this normal plot is relatively close to being a straight line, indicating that the residuals are nearly normal in shape. This normal distribution is confirmed by the graph on the lower left, which is a histogram of the residuals. The histogram groups residuals in classes so the researcher can observe where groups of the residuals lie without having to rely on the residual plot and to validate the notion that the residuals are approximately normally distributed. In this problem, the pattern is indicative of at least a mound-shaped distribution of residuals.

FIGURE 12.13

Minitab Residual Analyses

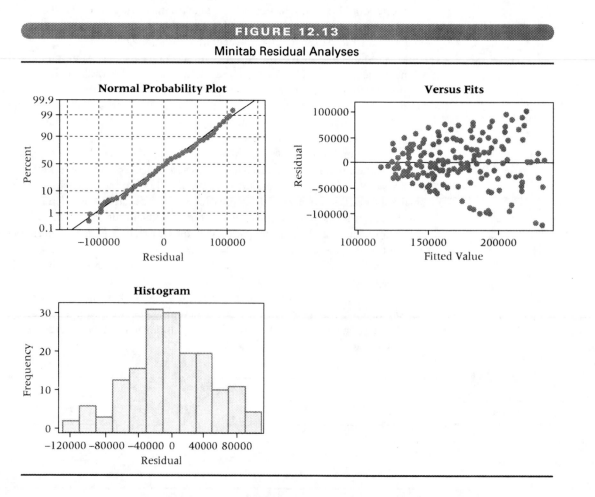

DEMONSTRATION PROBLEM 12.2

Compute the residuals for Demonstration Problem 12.1 in which a regression model was developed to predict the number of full-time equivalent workers (FTEs) by the number of beds in a hospital. Analyze the residuals by using Minitab graphic diagnostics.

Solution

The data and computed residuals are shown in the following table.

Hospital	Number of Beds x	FTES y	Predicted Value $\hat{y}$	Residuals $y - \hat{y}$
1	23	69	82.22	−13.22
2	29	95	95.62	−.62
3	29	102	95.62	6.38
4	35	118	109.01	8.99
5	42	126	124.63	1.37
6	46	125	133.56	−8.56
7	50	138	142.49	−4.49
8	54	178	151.42	26.58
9	64	156	173.74	−17.74
10	66	184	178.20	5.80
11	76	176	200.52	−24.52
12	78	225	204.98	20.02
				$\Sigma(y - \hat{y}) = -.01$

Note that the regression model fits these particular data well for hospitals 2 and 5, as indicated by residuals of −.62 and 1.37 FTEs, respectively. For hospitals 1, 8, 9, 11, and 12, the residuals are relatively large, indicating that the regression model does

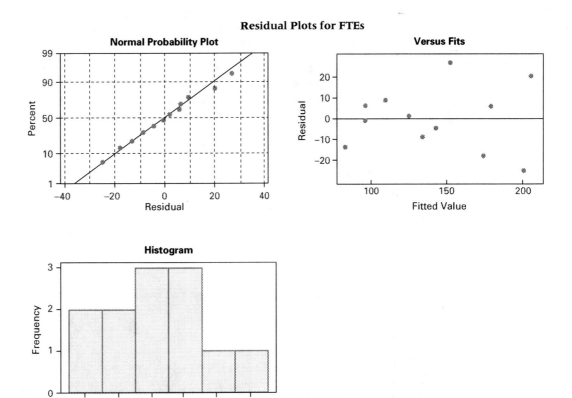

not fit the data for these hospitals well. The Residuals Versus the Fitted Values graph indicates that the residuals seem to increase as *x* increases, indicating a potential problem with heteroscedasticity. The normal plot of residuals indicates that the residuals are nearly normally distributed. The histogram of residuals shows that the residuals pile up in the middle, but are somewhat skewed toward the larger positive values.

12.4 PROBLEMS

12.13 Determine the equation of the regression line for the following data, and compute the residuals.

x	15	8	19	12	5
y	47	36	56	44	21

12.14 Solve for the predicted values of *y* and the residuals for the data in Problem 12.6. The data are provided here again:

x	12	21	28	8	20
y	17	15	22	19	24

12.15 Solve for the predicted values of *y* and the residuals for the data in Problem 12.7. The data are provided here again:

x	140	119	103	91	65	29	24
y	25	29	46	70	88	112	128

12.16 Solve for the predicted values of *y* and the residuals for the data in Problem 12.8. The data are provided here again:

Advertising	12.5	3.7	21.6	60.0	37.6	6.1	16.8	41.2
Sales	148	55	338	994	541	89	126	379

12.17 Solve for the predicted values of *y* and the residuals for the data in Problem 12.9. The data are provided here again:

Bond Rate	5%	12%	9%	15%	7%
Prime Interest Rate	16%	6%	8%	4%	7%

12.18 In problem 12.10, you were asked to develop the equation of a regression model to predict the number of business bankruptcies by the number of firm births. Using this regression model and the data given in problem 12.10 (and provided here again), solve for the predicted values of *y* and the residuals. Comment on the size of the residuals.

Business Bankruptcies (1,000)	Firm Births (10,000)
34.3	58.1
35.0	55.4
38.5	57.0
40.1	58.5
35.5	57.4
37.9	58.0

12.19 The equation of a regression line is

$$\hat{y} = 50.506 - 1.646x$$

and the data are as follows.

x	5	7	11	12	19	25
y	47	38	32	24	22	10

Solve for the residuals and graph a residual plot. Do these data seem to violate any of the assumptions of regression?

12.20 Wisconsin is an important milk-producing state. Some people might argue that because of transportation costs, the cost of milk increases with the distance of markets from Wisconsin. Suppose the milk prices in eight cities are as follows.

Cost of Milk (per gallon)	Distance from Madison (miles)
$2.64	1,245
2.31	425
2.45	1,346
2.52	973
2.19	255
2.55	865
2.40	1,080
2.37	296

Use the prices along with the distance of each city from Madison, Wisconsin, to develop a regression line to predict the price of a gallon of milk by the number of miles the city is from Madison. Use the data and the regression equation to compute residuals for this model. Sketch a graph of the residuals in the order of the x values. Comment on the shape of the residual graph.

12.21 Graph the following residuals, and indicate which of the assumptions underlying regression appear to be in jeopardy on the basis of the graph.

x	$y - \hat{y}$
213	−11
216	−5
227	−2
229	−1
237	+6
247	+10
263	+12

12.22 Graph the following residuals, and indicate which of the assumptions underlying regression appear to be in jeopardy on the basis of the graph.

x	$y - \hat{y}$
10	+6
11	+3
12	−1
13	−11
14	−3
15	+2
16	+5
17	+8

12.23 Study the following Minitab Residuals Versus Fits graphic for a simple regression analysis. Comment on the residual evidence of lack of compliance with the regression assumptions.

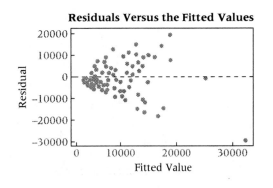

Residuals Versus the Fitted Values

12.5 STANDARD ERROR OF THE ESTIMATE

Residuals represent errors of estimation for individual points. With large samples of data, residual computations become laborious. Even with computers, a researcher sometimes has difficulty working through pages of residuals in an effort to understand the error of the regression model. An alternative way of examining the error of the model is the standard error of the estimate, which provides a single measurement of the regression error.

Because the sum of the residuals is zero, attempting to determine the total amount of error by summing the residuals is fruitless. This zero-sum characteristic of residuals can be avoided by squaring the residuals and then summing them.

Table 12.6 contains the airline cost data from Table 12.3, along with the residuals and the residuals squared. The *total of the residuals squared* column is called the **sum of squares of error (SSE)**.

SUM OF SQUARES OF ERROR	$SSE = \Sigma(y - \hat{y})^2$

In theory, infinitely many lines can be fit to a sample of points. However, formulas 12.2 and 12.4 produce a line of best fit for which the SSE is the smallest for any line that can be fit to the sample data. This result is guaranteed, because formulas 12.2 and 12.4 are derived from calculus to minimize SSE. For this reason, the regression process used in this chapter is called *least squares* regression.

A computational version of the equation for computing SSE is less meaningful in terms of interpretation than $\Sigma(y - \hat{y})^2$ but it is usually easier to compute. The computational formula for SSE follows.

COMPUTATIONAL FORMULA FOR SSE	$SSE = \Sigma y^2 - b_0 \Sigma y - b_1 \Sigma xy$

For the airline cost example,

$$\Sigma y^2 = \Sigma[(4.280)^2 + (4.080)^2 + (4.420)^2 + (4.170)^2 + (4.480)^2 + (4.300)^2 + (4.820)^2$$
$$+ (4.700)^2 + (5.110)^2 + (5.130)^2 + (5.640)^2 + (5.560)^2] = 270.9251$$
$$b_0 = 1.5697928$$

TABLE 12.6

Determining SSE for the Airline Cost Example

Number of Passengers x	Cost ($1,000) y	Residual $y - \hat{y}$	$(y - \hat{y})^2$
61	4.280	.227	.05153
63	4.080	−.054	.00292
67	4.420	.123	.01513
69	4.170	−.208	.04326
70	4.480	.061	.00372
74	4.300	−.282	.07952
76	4.820	.157	.02465
81	4.700	−.167	.02789
86	5.110	.040	.00160
91	5.130	−.144	.02074
95	5.640	.204	.04162
97	5.560	.042	.00176
		$\Sigma(y - \hat{y}) = -.001$	$\Sigma(y - \hat{y})^2 = .31434$

Sum of squares of error = SSE = .31434

$$b_1 = .0407016*$$

$$\Sigma y = 56.69$$

$$\Sigma xy = 4462.22$$

$$\text{SSE} = \Sigma y^2 - b_0 \Sigma y - b_1 \Sigma xy$$

$$= 270.9251 - (1.5697928)(56.69) - (.0407016)(4462.22) = .31405$$

The slight discrepancy between this value and the value computed in Table 12.6 is due to rounding error.

The sum of squares error is in part a function of the number of pairs of data being used to compute the sum, which lessens the value of SSE as a measurement of error. A more useful measurement of error is the standard error of the estimate. The **standard error of the estimate**, denoted s_e, is *a standard deviation of the error of the regression model* and has a more practical use than SSE. The standard error of the estimate follows.

STANDARD ERROR OF THE ESTIMATE	$s_e = \sqrt{\dfrac{\text{SSE}}{n-2}}$

The standard error of the estimate for the airline cost example is

$$s_e = \sqrt{\frac{\text{SSE}}{n-2}} = \sqrt{\frac{.31434}{10}} = .1773$$

How is the standard error of the estimate used? As previously mentioned, the standard error of the estimate is a standard deviation of error. Recall from Chapter 3 that if data are approximately normally distributed, the empirical rule states that about 68% of all values are within $\mu \pm 1\sigma$ and that about 95% of all values are within $\mu \pm 2\sigma$. One of the assumptions for regression states that for a given x the error terms are normally distributed. Because the error terms are normally distributed, s_e is the standard deviation of error, and the average error is zero, approximately 68% of the error values (residuals) should be within $0 \pm 1s_e$ and 95% of the error values (residuals) should be within $0 \pm 2s_e$. By having knowledge of the variables being studied and by examining the value of s_e, the researcher can often make a judgment about the fit of the regression model to the data by using s_e. How can the s_e value for the airline cost example be interpreted?

The regression model in that example is used to predict airline cost by number of passengers. Note that the range of the airline cost data in Table 12.3 is from 4.08 to 5.64 ($4,080 to $5,640). The regression model for the data yields an s_e of .1773. An interpretation of s_e is that the standard deviation of error for the airline cost example is $177.30. If the error terms were normally distributed about the given values of x, approximately 68% of the error terms would be within $\pm\$177.30$ and 95% would be within $\pm2(\$177.30) = \pm\$354.60$. Examination of the residuals reveals that 8 out of 12 (67%) of the residuals are within $\pm 1s_e$ and 100% of the residuals are within $2s_e$. The standard error of the estimate provides a single measure of error, which, if the researcher has enough background in the area being analyzed, can be used to understand the magnitude of errors in the model. In addition, some researchers use the standard error of the estimate to identify outliers. They do so by looking for data that are outside $\pm 2s_e$ or $\pm 3s_e$.

DEMONSTRATION PROBLEM 12.3

Compute the sum of squares of error and the standard error of the estimate for Demonstration Problem 12.1, in which a regression model was developed to predict the number of FTEs at a hospital by the number of beds.

---

*Note: In previous sections, the values of the slope and intercept were rounded off for ease of computation and interpretation. They are shown here with more precision in an effort to reduce rounding error.

Solution

Hospital	Number of Beds x	FTES y	Residuals $y - \hat{y}$	$(y - \hat{y})^2$
1	23	69	−13.22	174.77
2	29	95	−.62	0.38
3	29	102	6.38	40.70
4	35	118	8.99	80.82
5	42	126	1.37	1.88
6	46	125	−8.56	73.27
7	50	138	−4.49	20.16
8	54	178	26.58	706.50
9	64	156	−17.74	314.71
10	66	184	5.80	33.64
11	76	176	−24.52	601.23
12	78	225	20.02	400.80
	$\Sigma x = 592$	$\Sigma y = 1692$	$\Sigma(y - \hat{y}) = -.01$	$\Sigma(y - \hat{y})^2 = 2448.86$

SSE = 2448.86

$$S_e = \sqrt{\frac{SSE}{n - 2}} = \sqrt{\frac{2448.86}{10}} = 15.65$$

The standard error of the estimate is 15.65 FTEs. An examination of the residuals for this problem reveals that 8 of 12 (67%) are within $\pm 1 s_e$ and 100% are within $\pm 2 s_e$. Is this size of error acceptable? Hospital administrators probably can best answer that question.

12.5 PROBLEMS

12.24 Determine the sum of squares of error (SSE) and the standard error of the estimate (s_e) for Problem 12.6. Determine how many of the residuals computed in Problem 12.14 (for Problem 12.6) are within one standard error of the estimate. If the error terms are normally distributed, approximately how many of these residuals should be within $\pm 1 s_e$?

12.25 Determine the SSE and the s_e for Problem 12.7. Use the residuals computed in Problem 12.15 (for Problem 12.7) and determine how many of them are within $\pm 1 s_e$ and $\pm 2 s_e$. How do these numbers compare with what the empirical rule says should occur if the error terms are normally distributed?

12.26 Determine the SSE and the s_e for Problem 12.8. Think about the variables being analyzed by regression in this problem and comment on the value of s_e.

12.27 Determine the SSE and s_e for Problem 12.9. Examine the variables being analyzed by regression in this problem and comment on the value of s_e.

12.28 In problem 12.10, you were asked to develop the equation of a regression model to predict the number of business bankruptcies by the number of firm births. For this regression model, solve for the standard error of the estimate and comment on it.

12.29 Use the data from problem 12.19 and determine the s_e.

12.30 Determine the SSE and the s_e for Problem 12.20. Comment on the size of s_e for this regression model, which is used to predict the cost of milk.

12.31 Determine the equation of the regression line to predict annual sales of a company from the yearly stock market volume of shares sold in a recent year. Compute the standard error of the estimate for this model. Does volume of shares sold appear to be a good predictor of a company's sales? Why or why not?

Company	Annual Sales ($ billions)	Annual Volume (millions of shares)
Merck	10.5	728.6
Altria	48.1	497.9
IBM	64.8	439.1
Eastman Kodak	20.1	377.9
Bristol-Myers Squibb	11.4	375.5
General Motors	123.8	363.8
Ford Motors	89.0	276.3

12.6 COEFFICIENT OF DETERMINATION

A widely used measure of fit for regression models is the **coefficient of determination**, or r^2. The coefficient of determination is *the proportion of variability of the dependent variable (y) accounted for or explained by the independent variable (x).*

The coefficient of determination ranges from 0 to 1. An r^2 of zero means that the predictor accounts for none of the variability of the dependent variable and that there is no regression prediction of y by x. An r^2 of 1 means perfect prediction of y by x and that 100% of the variability of y is accounted for by x. Of course, most r^2 values are between the extremes. The researcher must interpret whether a particular r^2 is high or low, depending on the use of the model and the context within which the model was developed.

In exploratory research where the variables are less understood, low values of r^2 are likely to be more acceptable than they are in areas of research where the parameters are more developed and understood. One NASA researcher who uses vehicular weight to predict mission cost searches for the regression models to have an r^2 of .90 or higher. However, a business researcher who is trying to develop a model to predict the motivation level of employees might be pleased to get an r^2 near .50 in the initial research.

The dependent variable, y, being predicted in a regression model has a variation that is measured by the sum of squares of y (SS_{yy}):

$$SS_{yy} = \Sigma(y - \bar{y})^2 = \Sigma y^2 - \frac{(\Sigma y)^2}{n}$$

and is the sum of the squared deviations of the y values from the mean value of y. This variation can be broken into two additive variations: the *explained variation,* measured by the sum of squares of regression (SSR), and the *unexplained variation,* measured by the sum of squares of error (SSE). This relationship can be expressed in equation form as

$$SS_{yy} = SSR + SSE$$

If each term in the equation is divided by SS_{yy}, the resulting equation is

$$1 = \frac{SSR}{SS_{yy}} + \frac{SSE}{SS_{yy}}$$

The term r^2 is the proportion of the y variability that is explained by the regression model and represented here as

$$r^2 = \frac{SSR}{SS_{yy}}$$

Substituting this equation into the preceding relationship gives

$$1 = r^2 + \frac{SSE}{SS_{yy}}$$

Solving for r^2 yields formula 12.5.

COEFFICIENT OF DETERMINATION (12.5)

$$r^2 = 1 - \frac{SSE}{SS_{yy}} = 1 - \frac{SSE}{\Sigma y^2 - \frac{(\Sigma y)^2}{n}}$$

Note: $0 \leq r^2 \leq 1$

The value of r^2 for the airline cost example is solved as follows:

$$SSE = .31434$$

$$SS_{yy} = \Sigma y^2 - \frac{(\Sigma y)^2}{n} = 270.9251 - \frac{(56.69)^2}{12} = 3.11209$$

$$r^2 = 1 - \frac{SSE}{SS_{yy}} = 1 - \frac{.31434}{3.11209} = .899$$

That is, 89.9% of the variability of the cost of flying a Boeing 737 airplane on a commercial flight is explained by variations in the number of passengers. This result also means that 11.1% of the variance in airline flight cost, y, is unaccounted for by x or unexplained by the regression model.

The coefficient of determination can be solved for directly by using

$$r^2 = \frac{SSR}{SS_{yy}}$$

It can be shown through algebra that

$$SSR = b_1^2 SS_{xx}$$

From this equation, a computational formula for r^2 can be developed.

COMPUTATIONAL FORMULA FOR r^2

$$r^2 = \frac{b_1^2 SS_{xx}}{SS_{yy}}$$

For the airline cost example, $b_1 = .0407016$, $SS_{xx} = 1689$, and $SS_{yy} = 3.11209$. Using the computational formula for r^2 yields

$$r^2 = \frac{(.0407016)^2 (1689)}{3.11209} = .899$$

DEMONSTRATION PROBLEM 12.4

Compute the coefficient of determination (r^2) for Demonstration Problem 12.1, in which a regression model was developed to predict the number of FTEs of a hospital by the number of beds.

Solution

$$SSE = 2448.86$$

$$SS_{yy} = 260,136 - \frac{(1692)^2}{12} = 21,564$$

$$r^2 = 1 - \frac{SSE}{SS_{yy}} = 1 - \frac{2448.86}{21,564} = .886$$

This regression model accounts for 88.6% of the variance in FTEs, leaving only 11.4% unexplained variance.

Using $SS_{xx} = 3838.667$ and $b_1 = 2.232$ from Demonstration Problem 12.1, we can solve for r^2 with the computational formula:

$$r^2 = \frac{b_1^2 SS_{xx}}{SS_{yy}} = \frac{(2.232)^2 (3838.667)}{21,564} = .886$$

Relationship Between r and r^2

Is r, the coefficient of correlation (introduced in Section 12.1), related to r^2, the coefficient of determination in linear regression? The answer is yes: r^2 equals $(r)^2$. The coefficient of determination is the square of the coefficient of correlation. In Demonstration Problem 12.1, a regression model was developed to predict FTEs by number of hospital beds. The r^2 value for the model was .886. Taking the square root of this value yields $r = .941$, which is the correlation between the sample number of beds and FTEs. A word of caution here: Because r^2 is always positive, solving for r by taking $\sqrt{r^2}$ gives the correct magnitude of r but may give the wrong sign. The researcher must examine the sign of the slope of the regression line to determine whether a positive or negative relationship exists between the variables and then assign the appropriate sign to the correlation value.

12.6 PROBLEMS

12.32 Compute r^2 for Problem 12.24 (Problem 12.6). Discuss the value of r^2 obtained.

12.33 Compute r^2 for Problem 12.25 (Problem 12.7). Discuss the value of r^2 obtained.

12.34 Compute r^2 for Problem 12.26 (Problem 12.8). Discuss the value of r^2 obtained.

12.35 Compute r^2 for Problem 12.27 (Problem 12.9). Discuss the value of r^2 obtained.

12.36 In problem 12.10, you were asked to develop the equation of a regression model to predict the number of business bankruptcies by the number of firm births. For this regression model, solve for the coefficient of determination and comment on it.

12.37 The Conference Board produces a Consumer Confidence Index (CCI) that reflects people's feelings about general business conditions, employment opportunities, and their own income prospects. Some researchers may feel that consumer confidence is a function of the median household income. Shown here are the CCIs for nine years and the median household incomes for the same nine years published by the U.S. Census Bureau. Determine the equation of the regression line to predict the CCI from the median household income. Compute the standard error of the estimate for this model. Compute the value of r^2. Does median household income appear to be a good predictor of the CCI? Why or why not?

CCI	Median Household Income ($1,000)
116.8	37.415
91.5	36.770
68.5	35.501
61.6	35.047
65.9	34.700
90.6	34.942
100.0	35.887
104.6	36.306
125.4	37.005

12.7 HYPOTHESIS TESTS FOR THE SLOPE OF THE REGRESSION MODEL AND TESTING THE OVERALL MODEL

Testing the Slope

A hypothesis test can be conducted on the sample slope of the regression model to determine whether the population slope is significantly different from zero. This test is another way to determine how well a regression model fits the data. Suppose a researcher decides that it is not worth the effort to develop a linear regression model to predict y from x. An alternative approach might be to average the y values and use $\bar{y}$ as the predictor of y for all values of x. For the airline cost example, instead of using number of passengers as the predictor, the researcher would use the average value of airline cost, $\bar{y}$, as the predictor. In this case the average value of y is

$$\bar{y} = \frac{56.69}{12} = 4.7242, \text{ or } \$4{,}724.20$$

Using this result as a model to predict y, if the number of passengers is 61, 70, or 95—or any other number—the predicted value of y is still 4.7242. Essentially, this approach fits the line of $\bar{y} = 4.7242$ through the data, which is a horizontal line with a slope of zero. Would a regression analysis offer anything more than the $\bar{y}$ model? Using this nonregression model (the $\bar{y}$ model) as a worst case, the researcher can analyze the regression line to determine whether it adds a more significant amount of predictability of y than does the $\bar{y}$ model. Because the slope of the $\bar{y}$ line is zero, one way to determine whether the regression line adds significant predictability is to test the population slope of the regression line to find out whether the slope is different from zero. As the slope of the regression line diverges from zero, the regression model is adding predictability that the $\bar{y}$ line is not generating. For this reason, testing the slope of the regression line to determine whether the slope is different from zero is important. If the slope is not different from zero, the regression line is doing nothing more than the $\bar{y}$ line in predicting y.

How does the researcher go about testing the slope of the regression line? Why not just examine the observed sample slope? For example, the slope of the regression line for the airline cost data is .0407. This value is obviously not zero. The problem is that this slope is obtained from a sample of 12 data points; and if another sample was taken, it is likely that a different slope would be obtained. For this reason, the population slope is statistically tested using the sample slope. The question is: If all the pairs of data points for the population were available, would the slope of that regression line be different from zero? Here the sample slope, b_1, is used as evidence to test whether the population slope is different from zero. The hypotheses for this test follow.

$$H_0\text{: } \beta_1 = 0$$
$$H_a\text{: } \beta_1 \neq 0$$

Note that this test is two tailed. The null hypothesis can be rejected if the slope is either negative or positive. A negative slope indicates an inverse relationship between x and y. That is, larger values of x are related to smaller values of y, and vice versa. Both negative and positive slopes can be different from zero. To determine whether there is a significant *positive* relationship between two variables, the hypotheses would be one tailed, or

$$H_0\text{: } \beta_1 = 0$$
$$H_a\text{: } \beta_1 > 0$$

To test for a significant *negative* relationship between two variables, the hypotheses also would be one tailed, or

$$H_0\text{: } \beta_1 = 0$$
$$H_a\text{: } \beta_1 < 0$$

In each case, testing the null hypothesis involves a t test of the slope.

t TEST OF SLOPE

$$t = \frac{b_1 - \beta_1}{s_b}$$

where

$$s_b = \frac{s_e}{\sqrt{SS_{xx}}}$$

$$s_e = \sqrt{\frac{SSE}{n-2}}$$

$$SS_{xx} = \Sigma x^2 - \frac{(\Sigma x)^2}{n}$$

β_1 = the hypothesized slope

df = $n - 2$

The test of the slope of the regression line for the airline cost regression model for $\alpha = .05$ follows. The regression line derived for the data is

$$\hat{y} = 1.57 + .0407x$$

The sample slope is .0407 = b_1. The value of s_e is .1773, $\Sigma x = 930$, $\Sigma x^2 = 73,764$, and $n = 12$. The hypotheses are

$$H_0: \beta_1 = 0$$
$$H_a: \beta_1 \neq 0$$

The df = $n - 2 = 12 - 2 = 10$. As this test is two tailed, $\alpha/2 = .025$. The table *t* value is $t_{.025,10} = \pm2.228$. The observed *t* value for this sample slope is

$$t = \frac{.0407 - 0}{.1773 \bigg/ \sqrt{73,764 - \dfrac{(930)^2}{12}}} = 9.43$$

As shown in Figure 12.14, the *t* value calculated from the sample slope falls in the rejection region and the *p*-value is .00000014. The null hypothesis that the population slope is zero is rejected. This linear regression model is adding significantly more predictive information to the $\bar{y}$ model (no regression).

It is desirable to reject the null hypothesis in testing the slope of the regression model. In rejecting the null hypothesis of a zero population slope, we are stating that the regression model is adding something to the explanation of the variation of the dependent variable that the average value of *y* model does not. Failure to reject the null hypothesis in this test causes the researcher to conclude that the regression model has no predictability of the dependent variable, and the model, therefore, has little or no use.

FIGURE 12.14

t Test of Slope from Airline Cost Example

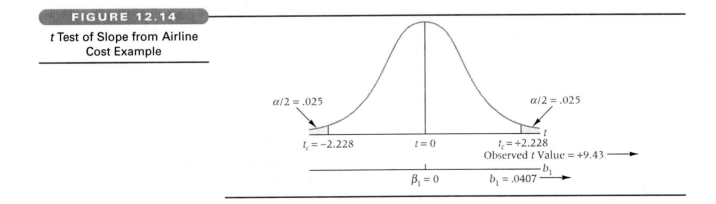

THINKING CRITICALLY ABOUT STATISTICS IN BUSINESS TODAY

Are Facial Characteristics Correlated with CEO Traits?

Researchers John R. Graham, Campbell R. Harvey, and Manju Puri, all of the Fuqua School of Business at Duke, conducted a study using almost 2,000 participants in an effort to determine if facial characteristics are related to various CEO traits. In one experiment of the study, the researchers showed pictures of 138 CEOs to 230 study participants who were asked to rate each CEO picture in terms of four attributes: competence, attractiveness, trustworthiness, and likeability. The results of the study showed that all four traits are positively correlated. That is, if a CEO (based on the picture) was rated as high on competence, he was also rated high on each of attractiveness, trustworthiness, and likeability. The largest correlation was between trustworthiness and likeability, and the smallest correlation was between trustworthiness and attractiveness. These ratings on each of the four traits were also analyzed to determine if there was a correlation with total sales of the CEO's firm and with CEO income. The results showed that there was a small positive correlation between CEO ratings on competence and company sales. There was also a small positive correlation between CEO ratings on competence and their income. In another experiment, 138 CEOs were rated on being "baby-faced." Analysis of the study data showed that there was a positive correlation between CEOs baby-faced rating and likability. That is, the more a CEO appeared to be baby-faced, the higher they were rated in likeability. However, there was a negative correlation between CEOs baby-faced rating and competence.

Things to Ponder

1. Similar studies have been conducted in the area of political science to determine the electability of people running for office. What do you think is the real impact of studies like this in business?

2. The authors of the study suggest that baby-faced people tend to have large, round eyes, high eyebrows and a small chin thereby giving the perception of a baby-faced appearance. In this study, baby-faced CEOs were rated more highly on one attribute and low on another attribute. Based on these results, what advice would you give to a "baby-faced" business manager who aspires to be a CEO?

Source: John R. Graham, Campbell R. Harvey, and Manju Puri. "A Corporate Beauty Contest," working paper (15906) in the NBER Working Paper Series, National Bureau of Economic Research, at http://www.nber.org/papers/w15906, April 2010.

DEMONSTRATION PROBLEM 12.5

Test the slope of the regression model developed in Demonstration Problem 12.1 to predict the number of FTEs in a hospital from the number of beds to determine whether there is a significant positive slope. Use $\alpha = .01$.

Solution

The hypotheses for this problem are

$$H_0: \beta_1 = 0$$
$$H_a: \beta_1 > 0$$

The level of significance is .01. With 12 pairs of data, df = 10. The critical table t value is $t_{.01,10} = 2.764$. The regression line equation for this problem is

$$\hat{y} = 30.888 + 2.232x$$

The sample slope, b_1, is 2.232, and $s_e = 15.65$, $\Sigma x = 592$, $\Sigma x^2 = 33{,}044$, and $n = 12$. The observed t value for the sample slope is

$$t = \frac{2.232 - 0}{15.65 \Big/ \sqrt{33{,}044 - \dfrac{(592)^2}{12}}} = 8.84$$

The observed t value (8.84) is in the rejection region because it is greater than the critical table t value of 2.764 and the p-value is .0000024. The null hypothesis is rejected. The population slope for this regression line is significantly different from zero in the positive direction. This regression model is adding significant predictability over the $\bar{y}$ model.

Testing the Overall Model

It is common in regression analysis to compute an F test to determine the overall significance of the model. Most computer software packages include the F test and its associated ANOVA table as standard regression output. In multiple regression (Chapters 13 and 14), this test determines whether at least one of the regression coefficients (from multiple predictors) is different from zero. Simple regression provides only one predictor and only one regression coefficient to test. Because the regression coefficient is the slope of the regression line, the F test for overall significance is testing the same thing as the t test in simple regression. The hypotheses being tested in simple regression by the F test for overall significance are

$$H_0: \beta_1 = 0$$
$$H_a: \beta_1 \neq 0$$

In the case of simple regression analysis, $F = t^2$. Thus, for the airline cost example, the F value is

$$F = t^2 = (9.43)^2 = 88.92$$

The F value is computed directly by

$$F = \frac{SS_{reg}/df_{reg}}{SS_{err}/df_{err}} = \frac{MS_{reg}}{MS_{err}}$$

where

$$df_{reg} = k$$
$$df_{err} = n - k - 1$$
$$k = \text{the number of independent variables}$$

The values of the sum of squares (SS), degrees of freedom (df), and mean squares (MS) are obtained from the analysis of variance table, which is produced with other regression statistics as standard output from statistical software packages. Shown here is the analysis of variance table produced by Minitab for the airline cost example.

```
Analysis of Variance
Source             DF        SS        MS        F         p
Regression          1    2.7980    2.7980     89.09     0.000
Residual Error     10    0.3141    0.0314
Total              11    3.1121
```

The F value for the airline cost example is calculated from the analysis of variance table information as

$$F = \frac{2.7980/1}{.3141/10} = \frac{2.7980}{.03141} = 89.08$$

The difference between this value (89.08) and the value obtained by squaring the t statistic (88.92) is due to rounding error. The probability of obtaining an F value this large or larger by chance if there is no regression prediction in this model is .000 according to the ANOVA output (the p-value). This output value means it is highly unlikely that the population slope is zero and also unlikely that there is no prediction due to regression from this model given the sample statistics obtained. Hence, it is highly likely that this regression model adds significant predictability of the dependent variable.

Note from the ANOVA table that the degrees of freedom due to regression are equal to 1. Simple regression models have only one independent variable; therefore, $k = 1$. The degrees of freedom error in simple regression analysis is always $n - k - 1 = n - 1 - 1 = n - 2$. With the degrees of freedom due to regression (1) as the numerator degrees of freedom and the degrees of freedom due to error $(n - 2)$ as the denominator degrees of freedom, Table A.7 can be used to obtain the critical F value $(F_{\alpha,1,n-2})$ to help make the hypothesis testing decision about the overall regression model if the p-value of F is not given in the computer output. This critical F value is always found in the right tail of the distribution. In simple regression, the relationship between the critical t value to test the slope and the critical F value of overall significance is

$$t_{\alpha/2,n-2}^2 = F_{\alpha,1,n-2}$$

For the airline cost example with a two-tailed test and $\alpha = .05$, the critical value of $t_{.025,10}$ is ± 2.228 and the critical value of $F_{.05,1,10}$ is 4.96.

$$t_{.025,10}^2 = (\pm 2.228)^2 = 4.96 = F_{.05,1,10}$$

12.7 PROBLEMS

12.38 Test the slope of the regression line determined in Problem 12.6. Use $\alpha = .05$.

12.39 Test the slope of the regression line determined in Problem 12.7. Use $\alpha = .01$.

12.40 Test the slope of the regression line determined in Problem 12.8. Use $\alpha = .10$.

12.41 Test the slope of the regression line determined in Problem 12.9. Use a 5% level of significance.

12.42 Test the slope of the regression line developed in Problem 12.10. Use a 5% level of significance.

12.43 Study the following analysis of variance table, which was generated from a simple regression analysis. Discuss the F test of the overall model. Determine the value of t and test the slope of the regression line.

```
Analysis of Variance
Source        DF        SS        MS       F       p
Regression     1      116.65    116.65    8.26    0.021
Error          8      112.95     14.12
Total          9      229.60
```

12.8 ESTIMATION

One of the main uses of regression analysis is as a prediction tool. If the regression function is a good model, the researcher can use the regression equation to determine values of the dependent variable from various values of the independent variable. For example, financial brokers would like to have a model with which they could predict the selling price of a stock on a certain day by a variable such as unemployment rate or producer price index. Marketing managers would like to have a site location model with which they could predict the sales volume of a new location by variables such as population density or number of competitors. The airline cost example presents a regression model that has the potential to predict the cost of flying an airplane by the number of passengers.

In simple regression analysis, a point estimate prediction of y can be made by substituting the associated value of x into the regression equation and solving for y. From the airline cost example, if the number of passengers is $x = 73$, the predicted cost of the airline flight can be computed by substituting the x value into the regression equation determined in Section 12.3:

$$\hat{y} = 1.57 + .0407x = 1.57 + .0407(73) = 4.5411$$

The point estimate of the predicted cost is 4.5411 or \$4,541.10.

Confidence Intervals to Estimate the Conditional Mean of y: $\mu_{y|x}$

Although a point estimate is often of interest to the researcher, the regression line is determined by a sample set of points; and if a different sample is taken, a different line will result, yielding a different point estimate. Hence computing a *confidence interval* for the estimation is often useful. Because for any value of *x* (independent variable) there can be many values of *y* (dependent variable), one type of **confidence interval** is *an estimate of the average value of y for a given x*. This average value of *y* is denoted $E(y_x)$—the expected value of *y* and can be computed using formula (12.6).

CONFIDENCE INTERVAL TO ESTIMATE $E(y_x)$ FOR A GIVEN VALUE OF x (12.6)	$$\hat{y} \pm t_{\alpha/2, n-2} s_e \sqrt{\frac{1}{n} + \frac{(x_0 - \bar{x})^2}{SS_{xx}}}$$ where $$x_0 = \text{a particular value of } x$$ $$SS_{xx} = \Sigma x^2 - \frac{(\Sigma x)^2}{n}$$

The application of this formula can be illustrated with construction of a 95% confidence interval to estimate the average value of *y* (airline cost) for the airline cost example when *x* (number of passengers) is 73. For a 95% confidence interval, $\alpha = .05$ and $\alpha/2 = .025$. The df $= n - 2 = 12 - 2 = 10$. The table *t* value is $t_{.025,10} = 2.228$. Other needed values for this problem, which were solved for previously, are

$$s_e = .1773 \quad \Sigma x = 930 \quad \bar{x} = 77.5 \quad \Sigma x^2 = 73,764$$

For $x_0 = 73$, the value of $\hat{y}$ is 4.5411. The computed confidence interval for the average value of *y*, $E(y_{73})$, is

$$4.5411 \pm (2.228)(.1773) \sqrt{\frac{1}{12} + \frac{(73 - 77.5)^2}{73,764 - \frac{(930)^2}{12}}} = 4.5411 \pm .1220$$

$$4.4191 \leq E(y_{73}) \leq 4.6631$$

That is, with 95% confidence the average value of *y* for *x* = 73 is between 4.4191 and 4.6631.

Table 12.7 shows confidence intervals computed for the airline cost example for several values of *x* to estimate the average value of *y*. Note that as *x* values get farther from the mean *x* value (77.5), the confidence intervals get wider; as the *x* values get closer to the mean, the confidence intervals narrow. The reason is that the numerator of the second term under the radical sign approaches zero as the value of *x* nears the mean and increases as *x* departs from the mean.

Prediction Intervals to Estimate a Single Value of *y*

A second type of interval in regression estimation is a **prediction interval** to *estimate a single value of y for a given value of x.*

TABLE 12.7		
Confidence Intervals to Estimate the Average Value of *y* for Some *x* Values in the Airline Cost Example		

x	Confidence Interval	
62	4.0934 ± .1876	3.9058 to 4.2810
68	4.3376 ± .1461	4.1915 to 4.4837
73	4.5411 ± .1220	4.4191 to 4.6631
85	5.0295 ± .1349	4.8946 to 5.1644
90	5.2330 ± .1656	5.0674 to 5.3986

PREDICTION INTERVAL TO ESTIMATE y FOR A GIVEN VALUE OF x (12.7)	$\hat{y} \pm t_{\alpha/2,n-2}\, s_e \sqrt{1 + \dfrac{1}{n} + \dfrac{(x_0 - \bar{x})^2}{SS_{xx}}}$

where

$$x_0 = \text{a particular value of } x$$

$$SS_{xx} = \Sigma x^2 - \frac{(\Sigma x)^2}{n}$$

Formula 12.7 is virtually the same as formula 12.6, except for the additional value of 1 under the radical. This additional value widens the prediction interval to estimate a single value of y from the confidence interval to estimate the average value of y. This result seems logical because the average value of y is toward the middle of a group of y values. Thus the confidence interval to estimate the average need not be as wide as the prediction interval produced by formula 12.7, which takes into account all the y values for a given x.

A 95% prediction interval can be computed to estimate the single value of y for $x = 73$ from the airline cost example by using formula 12.7. The same values used to construct the confidence interval to estimate the average value of y are used here.

$$t_{.025,10} = 2.228, \; s_e = .1773, \; \Sigma x = 930, \; \bar{x} = 77.5, \; \Sigma x^2 = 73{,}764$$

For $x_0 = 73$, the value of $\hat{y} = 4.5411$. The computed prediction interval for the single value of y is

$$4.5411 \pm (2.228)(.1773)\sqrt{1 + \frac{1}{12} + \frac{(73 - 77.5)^2}{73{,}764 - \dfrac{(930)^2}{12}}} = 4.5411 \pm .4134$$

$$4.1277 \le y \le 4.9545$$

Prediction intervals can be obtained by using the computer. Shown in Figure 12.15 is the computer output for the airline cost example. The output displays the predicted value for $x = 73$ ($\hat{y} = 4.5411$), a 95% confidence interval for the average value of y for $x = 73$, and a 95% prediction interval for a single value of y for $x = 73$. Note that the resulting values are virtually the same as those calculated in this section.

Figure 12.16 displays Minitab confidence intervals for various values of x for the average y value and the prediction intervals for a single y value for the airline example. Note that the intervals flare out toward the ends, as the values of x depart from the average x value. Note also that the intervals for a single y value are always wider than the intervals for the average y value for any given value of x.

An examination of the prediction interval formula to estimate y for a given value of x explains why the intervals flare out.

$$\hat{y} \pm t_{\alpha/2,n-2}\, s_e \sqrt{1 + \frac{1}{n} + \frac{(x_0 - \bar{x})^2}{SS_{xx}}}$$

As we enter different values of x_0 from the regression analysis into the equation, the only thing that changes in the equation is $(x_0 - \bar{x})^2$. This expression increases as individual values of x_0 get farther from the mean, resulting in an increase in the width of the interval. The interval is narrower for values of x_0 nearer $\bar{x}$ and wider for values of x_0 further from $\bar{x}$. A comparison of formulas 12.6 and 12.7 reveals them to be identical except that formula 12.7—to compute a prediction interval to estimate y for a given value of x—contains a 1 under the radical sign. This distinction ensures that formula 12.7 will yield wider intervals than 12.6 for otherwise identical data.

FIGURE 12.15

Minitab Output for
Prediction Intervals

Fit	StDev Fit	95.0% CI	95.0 PI
4.5410	0.0547	(4.4191, 4.6629)	(4.1278, 4.9543)

FIGURE 12.16

Minitab Intervals
for Estimation

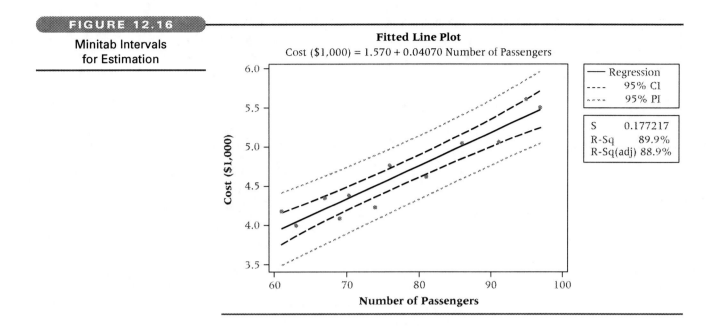

Fitted Line Plot
Cost ($1,000) = 1.570 + 0.04070 Number of Passengers

Caution: *A regression line is determined from a sample of points. The line, the r^2, the s_e, and the confidence intervals change for different sets of sample points. That is, the linear relationship developed for a set of points does not necessarily hold for values of x outside the domain of those used to establish the model. In the airline cost example, the domain of x values (number of passengers) varied from 61 to 97. The regression model developed from these points may not be valid for flights of say 40, 50, or 100 because the regression model was not constructed with x values of those magnitudes. However, decision makers sometimes extrapolate regression results to values of x beyond the domain of those used to develop the formulas (often in time-series sales forecasting). Understanding the limitations of this type of use of regression analysis is essential.*

DEMONSTRATION PROBLEM 12.6

Construct a 95% confidence interval to estimate the average value of y (FTEs) for Demonstration Problem 12.1 when $x = 40$ beds. Then construct a 95% prediction interval to estimate the single value of y for $x = 40$ beds.

Solution

For a 95% confidence interval, $\alpha = .05$ $n = 12$, and df $= 10$. The table t value is $t_{.025,10} = 2.228$; $s_e = 15.65$, $\Sigma x = 592$, $\bar{x} = 49.33$, and $\Sigma x^2 = 33{,}044$. For $x_0 = 40$, $\hat{y} = 120.17$. The computed confidence interval for the average value of y is

$$120.17 \pm (2.228)(15.65) \sqrt{\frac{1}{12} + \frac{(40 - 49.33)^2}{33{,}044 - \frac{(592)^2}{12}}} = 120.17 \pm 11.35$$

$$108.82 \leq E(y_{40}) \leq 131.52$$

With 95% confidence, the statement can be made that the average number of FTEs for a hospital with 40 beds is between 108.82 and 131.52.

The computed prediction interval for the single value of y is

$$120.17 \pm (2.228)(15.65) \sqrt{1 + \frac{1}{12} + \frac{(40 - 49.33)^2}{33{,}044 - \frac{(592)^2}{12}}} = 120.17 \pm 36.67$$

$$83.5 \leq y \leq 156.84$$

With 95% confidence, the statement can be made that a single number of FTEs for a hospital with 40 beds is between 83.5 and 156.84. Obviously this interval is much wider than the 95% confidence interval for the average value of y for $x = 40$.

The following Minitab graph depicts the 95% interval bands for both the average *y* value and the single *y* values for all 12 *x* values in this problem. Note once again the flaring out of the bands near the extreme values of *x*.

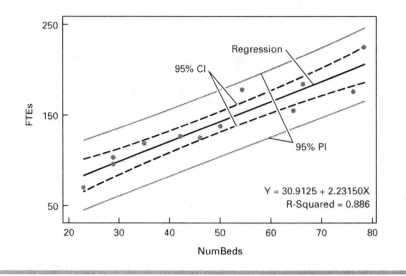

12.8 PROBLEMS

12.44 Construct a 95% confidence interval for the average value of *y* for Problem 12.6. Use $x = 25$.

12.45 Construct a 90% prediction interval for a single value of *y* for Problem 12.7; use $x = 100$. Construct a 90% prediction interval for a single value of *y* for Problem 14.2; use $x = 130$. Compare the results. Which prediction interval is greater? Why?

12.46 Construct a 98% confidence interval for the average value of *y* for Problem 12.8; use $x = 20$. Construct a 98% prediction interval for a single value of *y* for Problem 14.3; use $x = 20$. Which is wider? Why?

12.47 Construct a 99% confidence interval for the average bond rate in Problem 12.9 for a prime interest rate of 10%. Discuss the meaning of this confidence interval.

12.9 USING REGRESSION TO DEVELOP A FORECASTING TREND LINE

Business researchers often use historical data with measures taken over time in an effort to forecast what might happen in the future. A particular type of data that often lends itself well to this analysis is **time-series data** defined as *data gathered on a particular characteristic over a period of time at regular intervals*. Some examples of time-series data are 10 years of weekly Dow Jones Industrial Averages, twelve months of daily oil production, or monthly consumption of coffee over a two-year period. To be useful to forecasters, time-series measurements need to be made in regular time intervals and arranged according to time of occurrence. As an example, consider the time-series sales data over a 10-year time period for the Huntsville Chemical Company shown in Table 12.8. Note that the measurements (sales) are taken over time and that the sales figures are given on a yearly basis. Time-series data can also be reported daily, weekly, monthly, quarterly, semi-annually, or for other defined time periods.

TABLE 12.8

Ten-Year Sales Data for
Huntsville Chemicals

Year	Sales ($ millions)
2002	7.84
2003	12.26
2004	13.11
2005	15.78
2006	21.29
2007	25.68
2008	23.80
2009	26.43
2010	29.16
2011	33.06

It is generally believed that time-series data contain any one or combination of four elements: trend, cyclicality, seasonality, and irregularity. While each of these four elements will be discussed in greater deal in Chapter 15, Time-Series Forecasting and Index Numbers, here we examine **trend** and define it as *the long-term general direction of data.* Observing the scatter plot of the Huntsville Chemical Company's sales data shown in Figure 12.17, it is apparent that there is positive trend in the data. That is, there appears to be a long-term upward general direction of sales over time. How can trend be expressed in mathematical terms? In the field of forecasting, it is common to attempt to fit a trend line through time-series data by determining the equation of the trend line and then using the equation of the trend line to predict future data points. How does one go about developing such a line?

Determining the Equation of the Trend Line

Developing the equation of a linear trend line in forecasting is actually a special case of simple regression where the y or dependent variable is the variable of interest that a business analyst wants to forecast and for which a set of measurements has been taken over a period of time. For example, with the Huntsville Chemicals Company data, if company forecasters want to predict sales for the year 2014 using these data, sales would be the dependent variable in the simple regression analysis. In linear trend analysis, the time period is used as the x, the independent or predictor variable, in the analysis to determine the equation of the trend line. In the case of the Huntsville Chemicals Company, the x variable represents the years 2002–2011.

Using sales as the y variable and time (year) as the x variable, the equation of the trend line can be calculated in the usual way as shown in Table 12.9 and is determined to be: $\hat{y} = -5,333.91 + 2.6687\,x$. The slope, 2.6687, means that for every yearly increase in time, sales increases by an average of $2.6687 (million). The intercept would represent company sales in the year 0 which, of course, in this problem has no meaning since the Huntsville Chemical Company was not in existence in the year 0. Figure 12.18 is a Minitab display of the Huntsville sales data with the fitted trend line. Note that the output contains the equation of the trend line along with the values of s (standard error of the estimate) and R-Sq (r^2). As is typical with data that have a relatively strong trend, the r^2 value (.963) is quite high.

FIGURE 12.17

Minitab Scatter Plot of
Huntsville Chemicals Data

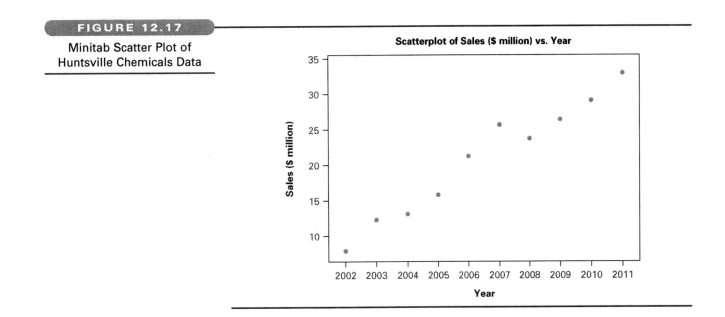

Scatterplot of Sales ($ million) vs. Year

TABLE 12.9			
Year x	**Sales** y	x^2	xy
2002	7.84	4,008,004	15,695.68
2003	12.26	4,012,009	24,556.78
2004	13.11	4,016,016	26,272.44
2005	15.78	4,020,025	31,638.90
2006	21.29	4,024,036	42,707.74
2007	25.68	4,028,049	51,539.76
2008	23.80	4,032,064	47,790.40
2009	26.43	4,036,081	53,097.87
2010	29.16	4,040,100	58,611.60
2011	33.06	4,044,121	66,483.66
$\Sigma x = 20,065$	$\Sigma y = 208.41$	$\Sigma x^2 = 40,260,505$	$\Sigma xy = 418,394.83$

Determining the Equation of the Trend Line for the Huntsville Chemical Company Sales Data

$$b_1 = \frac{\sum xy - \frac{(\sum x)(\sum y)}{n}}{\sum x^2 - \frac{(\sum x)^2}{n}} = \frac{(418,394.83) - \frac{(20,065)(208.41)}{10}}{40,260,505 - \frac{(20,065)^2}{10}} = \frac{220.17}{82.5} = 2.6687$$

$$b_0 = \frac{\sum y}{n} - b_1 \frac{\sum x}{n} = \frac{208.41}{10} - (2.6687)\frac{20,065}{10} = -5,333.91$$

Equation of the Trend Line: $\hat{y} = -5,333.91 + 2.6687x$

Forecasting Using the Equation of the Trend Line

The main use of the equation of a trend line by business analysts is for forecasting outcomes for time periods in the future. Recall the caution from Section 12.8 that using a regression model to predict y values for x values outside the domain of those used to develop the model may not be valid. Despite this caution and understanding the potential drawbacks, business forecasters nevertheless extrapolate trend lines beyond the most current time periods of the data and attempt to predict outcomes for time periods in the future. To forecast for future time periods using a trend line, insert the time period of interest into the equation of the

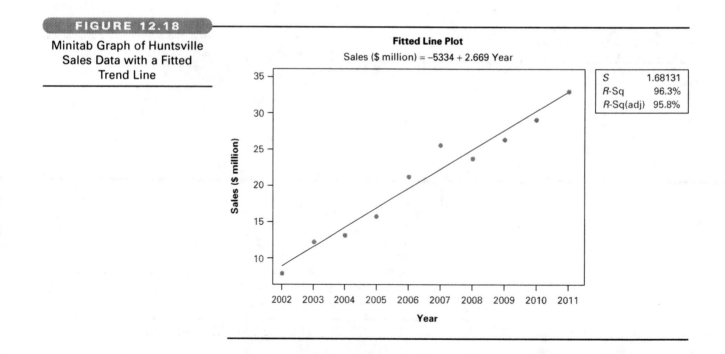

FIGURE 12.18

Minitab Graph of Huntsville Sales Data with a Fitted Trend Line

FIGURE 12.19

Minitab Output for Trend
Line and Forecasts

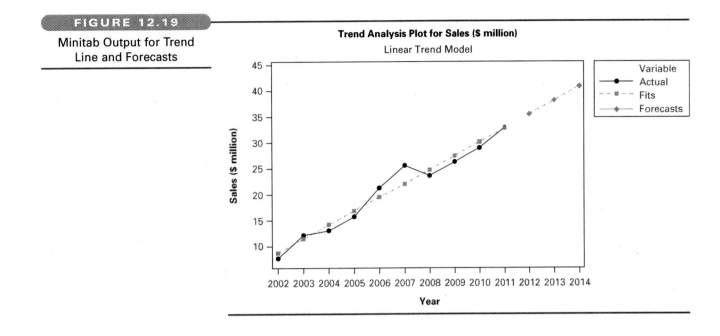

trend line and solve for $\hat{y}$. For example, suppose forecasters for the Huntsville Chemicals Company want to predict sales for the year 2014 using the equation of the trend line developed from their historical time series data. Replacing x in the equation of the sales trend line with 2014, results in a forecast of $40.85 (million):

$$\hat{y}(2014) = -5,333.91 + 2.6687(2014) = 40.85$$

Figure 12.19 shows Minitab output for the Huntsville Chemicals Company data with the trend line through the data and graphical forecasts for the next three periods (2012, 2013, and 2014). Observe from the graph that the forecast for 2014 is about $41 (million).

Alternate Coding for Time Periods

If you manually calculate the equation of a trend line when the time periods are years, you notice that the calculations can get quite large and cumbersome (observe Table 12.9). However, if the years are consecutive, they can be recoded using many different possible schemes and still produce a meaningful trend line equation (albeit a different y intercept value). For example, instead of using the years 2002–2011, suppose we use the years 1 to 10. That is, 2002 = 1 (first year), 2003 = 2, 2004 = 3, and so on, to 2011 = 10. This recoding scheme produces the trend line equation of: $\hat{y} = 6.1632 + 2.6687x$ as shown in Table 12.10. Notice that the slope of the trend line is the same whether the years 2002 through 2011 are used or the recoded years of 1 through 10, but the y intercept (6.1632) is different. This needs to be taken into consideration when using the equation of the trend line for forecasting. Since the new trend equation was derived from recoded data, forecasts will also need to be made using recoded data. For example, using the recoded system of 1 through 10 to represent "years," the year 2014 is recoded as 13 (2011 = 10, 2012 = 11, 2013 = 12, and 2014 = 13). Inserting this value into the trend line equation results in a forecast of $40.86, the same as the value obtained using raw years as time.

$$\hat{y} = 6.1632 + 2.6687x = 6.1632 + 2.6687(13) = \$40.86 \text{ (million)}.$$

Similar time recoding schemes can be used in the calculating of trend line equations when the time variable is something other than years. For example, in the case of monthly time series data, the time periods can be recoded as:

January = 1, February = 2, March = 3,..., December = 12.

	TABLE 12.10	Year	Sales		
	Using Recoded Data to Calculate the Trend Line Equation	x	y	x^2	xy
		1	7.84	1	7.84
		2	12.26	4	24.52
		3	13.11	9	39.33
		4	15.78	16	63.12
		5	21.29	25	106.45
		6	25.68	36	154.08
		7	23.80	49	166.60
		8	26.43	64	211.44
		9	29.16	81	262.44
		10	33.06	100	330.60

$\Sigma x = 55$ $\quad\quad \Sigma y = 208.41$ $\quad\quad \Sigma x^2 = 385$ $\quad\quad \Sigma xy = 1{,}366.42$

$$b_1 = \frac{\Sigma xy - \frac{(\Sigma x)(\Sigma y)}{n}}{\Sigma x^2 - \frac{(\Sigma x)^2}{n}} = \frac{(1{,}366.42) - \frac{(55)(208.41)}{10}}{385 - \frac{(55)^2}{10}} = \frac{220.165}{82.5} = 2.6687$$

$$b_0 = \frac{\Sigma y}{n} - b_1 \frac{\Sigma x}{n} = \frac{208.41}{10} - (2.6687)\frac{55}{10} = 6.1632$$

Equation of the Trend Line: $\quad \hat{y} = 6.1632 + 2.6687x$

In the case of quarterly data over a two-year period, the time periods can be recoded with a scheme such as:

Time Period		Recoded Time Period
Year 1:	Quarter 1	1
	Quarter 2	2
	Quarter 3	3
	Quarter 4	4
Year 2:	Quarter 1	5
	Quarter 2	6
	Quarter 3	7
	Quarter 4	8

DEMONSTRATION PROBLEM 12.7

Shown below are monthly food and beverage sales in the United States during a recent year over an eight-month period ($ million). Develop the equation of a trend line through these data and use the equation to forecast sales for October.

Month	Sales ($ million)
January	32,569
February	32,274
March	32,583
April	32,304
May	32,149
June	32,077
July	31,989
August	31,977

Solution

Shown here is a Minitab-produced scatter diagram of these time series data:

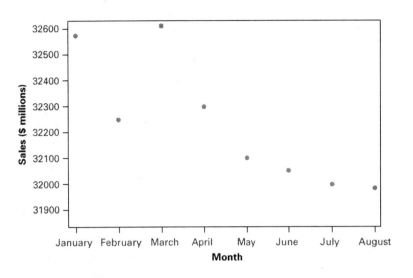

The months of January through August can be coded using the numbers of 1 through 8, respectively. Using these numbers as the time period values (*x*) and sales as the dependent variable (*y*), the following output was obtained from Minitab:

```
Regression Analysis: Sales versus Month

The regression equation is
Sales = 32628 - 86.2 Month
Predictor         Coef    SE Coef         T         P
Constant       32628.2       93.3    349.80     0.000
Month           -86.21      18.47     -4.67     0.003
S = 119.708   R-Sq = 78.4%   R-Sq(adj) = 74.8%
```

The equation of the trend line is: $\hat{y} = 32{,}628.2 - 86.21x$. A slope of -86.21 indicates that there is a downward trend of food and beverage sales over this period of time at a rate of \$86.21 (million) per month. The *y* intercept of 32,628.2 represents what the trend line would estimate the sales to have been in period 0 or December of the previous year. The sales figure for October can be forecast by inserting $x = 10$ into this model and obtaining:

$$\hat{y}(10) = 32{,}628.2 - 86.21(10) = 31{,}766.1.$$

12.9 PROBLEMS

12.48 Determine the equation of the trend line for the data shown below on U.S. exports of fertilizers to Indonesia over a five-year period provided by the U.S Census Bureau. Using the trend line equation, forecast the value for the year 2013.

Year	Fertilizer ($ millions)
2007	11.9
2008	17.9
2009	22.0
2010	21.8
2011	26.0

12.49 Shown below are rental and leasing revenue figures for office machinery and equipment in the United States over a seven-year period according to the U.S. Census Bureau. Use these data to construct a trend line and forecast the rental and leasing revenue for the year 2012 using these data.

Year	Rental and Leasing ($ millions)
2004	5,860
2005	6,632
2006	7,125
2007	6,000
2008	4,380
2009	3,326
2010	2,642

12.50 After a somewhat uncertain start, e-commerce sales in the United States have been growing for the past several years. Shown below are quarterly e-commerce sales figures ($ billions) released by the Census Bureau for the United States over a three-year period. Use these data to determine the equation of a trend line for e-commerce sales during this time and use the trend "model" to forecast e-commerce sales for the third quarter of the year 2012.

Year	Quarter	Sales ($ billions)
2008	1	11.93
	2	12.46
	3	13.28
	4	15.08
2009	1	16.08
	2	16.82
	3	17.60
	4	18.66
2010	1	19.73
	2	21.11
	3	22.21
	4	22.94

12.10 INTERPRETING THE OUTPUT

Although manual computations can be done, most regression problems are analyzed by using a computer. In this section, computer output from both Minitab and Excel will be presented and discussed.

At the top of the Minitab regression output, shown in Figure 12.20, is the regression equation. Next is a table that describes the model in more detail. "Coef" stands for coefficient of the regression terms. The coefficient of Number of Passengers, the x variable, is 0.040702. This value is equal to the slope of the regression line and is reflected in the regression equation. The coefficient shown next to the constant term (1.5698) is the value of the constant, which is the y intercept and also a part of the regression equation. The "T" values are a t test for the slope and a t test for the intercept or constant. (We generally do not interpret the t test for the constant.) The t value for the slope, $t = 9.44$ with an associated probability of .000, is the same as the value obtained manually in section 12.7. Because the probability of the t value is given, the p-value method can be used to interpret the t value.

FIGURE 12.20

Minitab Regression Analysis
of the Airline Cost Example

Regression Analysis: Cost ($1,000) versus Number of Passengers

```
The regression equation is
Cost ($1,000) = 1.57 + 0.0407 Number of Passengers


Predictor                    Coef    SE Coef     T      P
Constant                   1.5698    0.3381    4.64   0.001
Number of Passengers  0.040702    0.004312    9.44   0.000


S = 0.177217  R-Sq = 89.9%    R-Sq(adj) = 88.9%


Analysis of Variance

Source            DF      SS      MS       F      P
Regression         1   2.7980  2.7980   89.09  0.000
Residual Error    10   0.3141  0.0314
Total             11   3.1121

        Number of    Cost
Obs    Passengers  ($1,000)    Fit    SE Fit   Residual
  1        61.0     4.2800   4.0526   0.0876    0.2274
  2        63.0     4.0800   4.1340   0.0808   -0.0540
  3        67.0     4.4200   4.2968   0.0683    0.1232
  4        69.0     4.1700   4.3782   0.0629   -0.2082
  5        70.0     4.4800   4.4189   0.0605    0.0611
  6        74.0     4.3000   4.5817   0.0533   -0.2817
  7        76.0     4.8200   4.6631   0.0516    0.1569
  8        81.0     4.7000   4.8666   0.0533   -0.1666
  9        86.0     5.1100   5.0701   0.0629    0.0399
 10        91.0     5.1300   5.2736   0.0775   -0.1436
 11        95.0     5.6400   5.4364   0.0912    0.2036
 12        97.0     5.5600   5.5178   0.0984    0.0422
```

The next row of output is the standard error of the estimate s_e, S = 0.177217; the coefficient of determination, r^2, R-Sq = 89.9%; and the adjusted value of r^2, R-Sq(adj) = 88.9%. (Adjusted r^2 will be discussed in Chapter 13.) Following these items is the analysis of variance table. Note that the value of $F = 89.09$ is used to test the overall model of the regression line. The final item of the output is the predicted value and the corresponding residual for each pair of points.

Although the Excel regression output, shown in Figure 12.21 for Demonstration Problem 12.1, is somewhat different from the Minitab output, the same essential regression features are present. The regression equation is found under Coefficients at the bottom of ANOVA. The slope or coefficient of x is 2.2315 and the y-intercept is 30.9125. The standard error of the estimate for the hospital problem is given as the fourth statistic under Regression Statistics at the top of the output, Standard Error = 15.6491. The r^2 value is given as 0.886 on the second line. The t test for the slope is found under t Stat near the bottom of the ANOVA section on the "Number of Beds" (x variable) row, $t = 8.83$. Adjacent to the t Stat is the P-value, which is the probability of the t statistic occurring by chance if the null hypothesis is true. For this slope, the probability shown is 0.000005. The ANOVA table is in the middle of the output with the F value having the same probability as the t statistic, 0.000005, and equaling t^2. The predicted values and the residuals are shown in the Residual Output section.

Excel Regression Output for
Demonstration Problem 12.1

SUMMARY OUTPUT

Regression Statistics

Multiple R	0.942
R Square	0.886
Adjusted R Square	0.875
Standard Error	15.6491
Observations	12

ANOVA

	df	SS	MS	F	Significance F
Regression	1	19115.06322	19115.06	78.05	0.000005
Residual	10	2448.94	244.89		
Total	11	21564			

	Coefficients	Standard Error	t Stat	P-value
Intercept	30.9125	13.2542	2.33	0.041888
Number of Beds	2.2315	0.2526	8.83	0.000005

RESIDUAL OUTPUT

Observation	Predicted FTEs	Residuals
1	82.237	−13.237
2	95.626	−0.626
3	95.626	6.374
4	109.015	8.985
5	124.636	1.364
6	133.562	−8.562
7	142.488	−4.488
8	151.414	26.586
9	173.729	−17.729
10	178.192	5.808
11	200.507	−24.507
12	204.970	20.030

Predicting International Hourly Wages by the Price of a Big Mac

In the Decision Dilemma, questions were raised about the relationship between the price of a Big Mac hamburger and net hourly wages around the world and if a model could be developed to predict net hourly wages by the price of a Big Mac. Data were given for a sample of 27 countries. In exploring the possibility that there is a relationship between these two variables, a Pearson product-moment correlation coefficient, r, was computed to be .717. This r value indicates that there is a relatively high correlation between the two variables and that developing a regression model to predict one variable by the other has potential. Designating net hourly wages as the y or dependent variable and the price of a Big Mac as the x or predictor variable, the follow-ing regression output was obtained for these data using Excel.

Regression Statistics

Multiple R	0.717
R Square	0.514
Adjusted R Square	0.495
Standard Error	4.213
Observations	27

ANOVA

	df	SS	MS	F	Significance F
Regression	1	469.657	469.657	26.46	0.00003
Residual	25	443.775	17.751		
Total	26	913.432			

	Coefficients	Standard Error	t Stat	P-Value
Intercept	−4.154	2.448	−1.70	.10210
Big Mac Price	3.547	0.690	5.14	.00003

Taken from this output, the regression model is:

Net Hourly Wage = −4.154 + 3.547 (Price of Big Mac)

While the *y*-intercept has virtually no practical meaning in this analysis, the slope indicates that for every dollar increase in the price of a Big Mac, there is an incremental increase of $3.547 in net hourly wages for a country. It is worth underscoring here that just because there is a relationship between two variables, it does not mean there is a cause-and-effect relationship. That is, McDonald's cannot raise net hour wages in a country just by increasing the cost of a Big Mac!

Using this regression model, the net hourly wage for a country with a $3.00 Big Mac can be predicted by substituting x = 3 into the model:

Net Hourly Wage = −4.154 + 3.547(3) = $6.49

That is, the model predicts that the net hourly wage for a country is $6.49 when the price of a Big Mac is $3.00.

How good a fit is the regression model to the data? Observe from the Excel output that the *F* value for testing the overall significance of the model (26.46) is highly significant with a *p*-value of .00003, and that the *t* statistic for testing to determine if the slope is significantly different from zero is 5.14 with a *p*-value of .00003. In simple regression, the *t* sta-

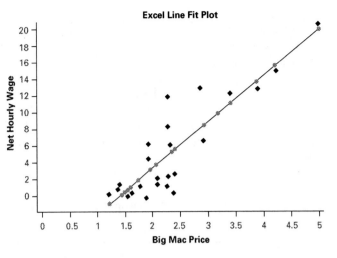

tistic is the square root of the *F* value and these statistics relate essentially the same information—that there are significant regression effects in the model. The r^2 value is 51.4%, indicating that the model has moderate predictability. The standard error of the model, s = 4.21, indicates that if the error terms are approximately normally distributed, about 68% of the predicted net hourly wages would fall within ±$4.21.

Shown here is an Excel-produced line fit plot. Note from the plot that there generally appears be a linear relationship between the variables but that many of the data points fall considerably away from the fitted regression line, indicating that the price of a Big Mac only partially accounts for net hourly wages.

ETHICAL CONSIDERATIONS

Regression analysis offers several opportunities for unethical behavior. One way is to present a regression model in isolation from information about the fit of the model. That is, the regression model is represented as a valid tool for prediction without any regard for how well it actually fits the data. While it is true that least squares analysis can produce a line of best fit through virtually any set of points, it does not necessarily follow that the regression model is a good predictor of the dependent variable. For example, sometimes business consultants sell regression models to companies as forecasting tools or market predictors without disclosing to the client that the r^2 value is very low, the slope of the regression line is not significant, the residuals are large, and the standard error of the estimate is large. This is unethical behavior.

Another unethical use of simple regression analysis is stating or implying a cause-and-effect relationship between two variables just because they are highly correlated and produce a high r^2 in regression. The Decision Dilemma presents a good example of this with the regression analysis

of the price of a Big Mac hamburger and the net hourly wages in a country. While the coefficient of determination is 51.4% and there appears to be a modest fit of the regression line to the data, that does not mean that increasing the price of a Big Mac in a given country will increase the country's net hourly wages. Often, two correlated variables are related to a third variable that drives the two of them but is not included in the regression analysis. In the Decision Dilemma example, both Big Mac prices and net hourly wages may be related to exchange rates or a country's economic condition.

A third way that business analysts can act unethically in using regression analysis is to knowingly violate the assumptions underlying regression. Regression analysis requires equal error variance, independent error terms, and error terms that are normally distributed. Through the use of residual plots and other statistical techniques, a business researcher can test these assumptions. To present a regression model as fact when the assumptions underlying it are being grossly violated is unethical behavior.

It is important to remember that since regression models are developed from sample data, when an x value is entered into a simple regression model, the resulting prediction is only a point estimate. While business people do often use regression models as predicting tools, it should be kept in mind that the prediction value is an estimate not a guaranteed outcome. By utilizing or at least pointing out confidence intervals and prediction intervals, such as those presented in Section 12.8, the business researcher places the predicted point estimate within the context of inferential estimation and is thereby acting more ethically.

And lastly, another ethical problem that arises in regression analysis is using the regression model to predict values of the independent variable that are outside the domain of values used to develop the model. The airline cost model used in this chapter was built with between 61 and 97 passengers. A linear relationship appeared to be evident between flight costs and number of passengers over this domain. This model is not guaranteed to fit values outside the domain of 61 to 97 passengers, however. In fact, either a nonlinear relationship or no relationship may be present between flight costs and number of passengers if values from outside this domain are included in the model-building process. It is a mistake and probably unethical behavior to make claims for a regression model outside the perview of the domain of values for which the model was developed.

SUMMARY

Correlation measures the degree of relatedness of variables. The most well-known measure of correlation is the Pearson product-moment coefficient of correlation, r. This value ranges from -1 to 0 to $+1$. An r value of $+1$ is perfect positive correlation and an r value of -1 is perfect negative correlation. Positive correlation means that as one variable increases in value, the other variable tends to increase. Negative correlation means that as one variable increases in value, the other variable tends to decrease. For r values near zero, little or no correlation is present.

Regression is a procedure that produces a mathematical model (function) that can be used to predict one variable by other variables. Simple regression is bivariate (two variables) and linear (only a line fit is attempted). Simple regression analysis produces a model that attempts to predict a y variable, referred to as the dependent variable, by an x variable, referred to as the independent variable. The general form of the equation of the simple regression line is the slope-intercept equation of a line. The equation of the simple regression model consists of a slope of the line as a coefficient of x and a y-intercept value as a constant.

After the equation of the line has been developed, several statistics are available that can be used to determine how well the line fits the data. Using the historical data values of x, predicted values of y (denoted as $\hat{y}$) can be calculated by inserting values of x into the regression equation. The predicted values can then be compared to the actual values of y to determine how well the regression equation fits the known data. The difference between a specific y value and its associated predicted y value is called the residual or error of prediction. Examination of the residuals can offer insight into the magnitude of the errors produced by a model. In addition, residual analysis can be used to help determine whether the assumptions underlying the regression analysis have been met. Specifically, graphs of the residuals can reveal (1) lack of linearity, (2) lack of homogeneity of error variance, and (3) independence of error terms. Geometrically, the residuals are the vertical distances from the y values to the regression line. Because the equation that yields the regression line is derived in such a way that the line is in the geometric middle of the points, the sum of the residuals is zero.

A single value of error measurement called the standard error of the estimate, s_e, can be computed. The standard error of the estimate is the standard deviation of error of a model. The value of s_e can be used as a single guide to the magnitude of the error produced by the regression model as opposed to examining all the residuals.

Another widely used statistic for testing the strength of a regression model is r^2, or the coefficient of determination. The coefficient of determination is the proportion of total variance of the y variable accounted for or predicted by x. The coefficient of determination ranges from 0 to 1. The higher the r^2 is, the stronger is the predictability of the model.

Testing to determine whether the slope of the regression line is different from zero is another way to judge the fit of the regression model to the data. If the population slope of the regression line is not different from zero, the regression model is not adding significant predictability to the dependent variable. A t statistic is used to test the significance of the slope. The overall significance of the regression model can be tested using an F statistic. In simple regression, because only one predictor is present, this test accomplishes the same thing as the t test of the slope and $F = t^2$.

One of the most prevalent uses of a regression model is to predict the values of y for given values of x. Recognizing that the predicted value is often not the same as the actual value, a confidence interval has been developed to yield a range within which the mean y value for a given x should fall. A prediction interval for a single y value for a given x value also is specified. This second interval is wider because it allows for the wide diversity of individual values, whereas the confidence interval for the mean y value reflects only the range of average y values for a given x.

Time-series data are data that are gathered over a period of time at regular intervals. Developing the equation of a forecasting trend line for time-series data is a special case of simple regression analysis where the time factor is the predictor variable. The time variable can be in units of years, months, weeks, quarters, and others.

KEY TERMS

	confidence interval	outliers	simple regression
	dependent variable	prediction interval	standard error of the
	deterministic model	probabilistic model	estimate (s_e)
	heteroscedasticity	regression analysis	sum of squares of error
	homoscedasticity	residual	(SSE)
coefficient of	independent variable	residual plot	
determination (r^2)	least squares analysis	scatter plot	

FORMULAS

Pearson's product-moment correlation coefficient

$$r = \frac{\Sigma(x - \bar{x})(y - \bar{y})}{\sqrt{\Sigma(x - \bar{x})^2 \, \Sigma(y - \bar{y})^2}}$$

$$= \frac{\Sigma xy - \dfrac{(\Sigma x \Sigma y)}{n}}{\sqrt{\left[\Sigma x^2 - \dfrac{(\Sigma x)^2}{n}\right]\left[\Sigma y^2 - \dfrac{(\Sigma y)^2}{n}\right]}}$$

Equation of the simple regression line

$$\hat{y} = \beta_0 + \beta_1 x$$

Sum of squares

$$SS_{xx} = \Sigma x^2 - \frac{(\Sigma x)^2}{n}$$

$$SS_{yy} = \Sigma y^2 - \frac{(\Sigma y)^2}{n}$$

$$SS_{xy} = \Sigma xy - \frac{\Sigma x \Sigma y}{n}$$

Slope of the regression line

$$b_1 = \frac{\Sigma(x - \bar{x})(y - \bar{y})}{\Sigma(x - \bar{x})^2} = \frac{\Sigma xy - n\bar{x}\bar{y}}{\Sigma x^2 - n\bar{x}^2}$$

$$= \frac{\Sigma xy - \dfrac{(\Sigma x)(\Sigma y)}{n}}{\Sigma x^2 - \dfrac{(\Sigma x)^2}{n}}$$

y-intercept of the regression line

$$b_0 = \bar{y} - b_1 \bar{x} = \frac{\Sigma y}{n} - b_1 \frac{(\Sigma x)}{n}$$

Sum of squares of error

$$SSE = \Sigma(y - \hat{y})^2 = \Sigma y^2 - b_0 \Sigma y - b_1 \Sigma xy$$

Standard error of the estimate

$$s_e = \sqrt{\frac{SSE}{n - 2}}$$

Coefficient of determination

$$r^2 = 1 - \frac{SSE}{SS_{yy}} = 1 - \frac{SSE}{\Sigma y^2 - \dfrac{(\Sigma y)^2}{n}}$$

Computational formula for r^2

$$r^2 = \frac{b_1^2 SS_{xx}}{SS_{yy}}$$

t test of slope

$$t = \frac{b_1 - \beta_1}{s_b}$$

$$s_b = \frac{s_e}{\sqrt{SS_{xx}}}$$

Confidence interval to estimate $E(y_x)$ for a given value of x

$$\hat{y} \pm t_{\alpha/2, \, n-2} s_e \sqrt{\frac{1}{n} + \frac{(x_0 - \bar{x})^2}{SS_{xx}}}$$

Prediction interval to estimate y for a given value of x

$$\hat{y} \pm t_{\alpha/2, \, n-2} s_e \sqrt{1 + \frac{1}{n} + \frac{(x_0 - \bar{x})^2}{SS_{xx}}}$$

SUPPLEMENTARY PROBLEMS

CALCULATING THE STATISTICS

12.51 Determine the Pearson product-moment correlation coefficient for the following data.

x	1	10	9	6	5	3	2
y	8	4	4	5	7	7	9

12.52 Use the following data for parts (a) through (f).

x	5	7	3	16	12	9
y	8	9	11	27	15	13

a. Determine the equation of the least squares regression line to predict y by x.

b. Using the x values, solve for the predicted values of y and the residuals.

c. Solve for s_e.

d. Solve for r^2.

e. Test the slope of the regression line. Use $\alpha = .01$.

f. Comment on the results determined in parts (b) through (e), and make a statement about the fit of the line.

12.53 Use the following data for parts (a) through (g).

x	53	47	41	50	58	62	45	60
y	5	5	7	4	10	12	3	11

a. Determine the equation of the simple regression line to predict y from x.

b. Using the x values, solve for the predicted values of y and the residuals.

c. Solve for SSE.

d. Calculate the standard error of the estimate.

e. Determine the coefficient of determination.

f. Test the slope of the regression line. Assume $\alpha = .05$. What do you conclude about the slope?

g. Comment on parts (d) and (e).

12.54 If you were to develop a regression line to predict y by x, what value would the coefficient of determination have?

x	213	196	184	202	221	247
y	76	65	62	68	71	75

12.55 Determine the equation of the least squares regression line to predict y from the following data.

x	47	94	68	73	80	49	52	61
y	14	40	34	31	36	19	20	21

a. Construct a 95% confidence interval to estimate the mean y value for $x = 60$.

b. Construct a 95% prediction interval to estimate an individual y value for $x = 70$.

c. Interpret the results obtained in parts (a) and (b).

12.56 Determine the equation of the trend line through the following cost data. Use the equation of the line to forecast cost for year 7.

Year	Cost ($ millions)
1	56
2	54
3	49
4	46
5	45

TESTING YOUR UNDERSTANDING

12.57 A manager of a car dealership believes there is a relationship between the number of salespeople on duty and the number of cars sold. Suppose the following sample is used to develop a simple regression model to predict the number of cars sold by the number of salespeople. Solve for r^2 and explain what r^2 means in this problem.

Week	Number of Cars Sold	Number of Salespeople
1	79	6
2	64	6
3	49	4
4	23	2
5	52	3

12.58 Executives of a video rental chain want to predict the success of a potential new store. The company's researcher begins by gathering information on number of rentals and average family income from several of the chain's present outlets.

Rentals	Average Family Income ($1,000)
710	65
529	43
314	29
504	47
619	52
428	50
317	46
205	29
468	31
545	43
607	49
694	64

Develop a regression model to predict the number of rentals per day by the average family income. Comment on the output.

12.59 It seems logical that restaurant chains with more units (restaurants) would have greater sales. This assumption is mitigated, however, by several possibilities: some units may be more profitable than others, some units may be larger, some units may serve more meals, some units may serve more expensive meals, and so on. The data shown here were published by Technomic. Perform a simple regression analysis to predict a restaurant chain's sales by its number of units. How strong is the relationship?

Chain	Sales ($ billions)	Number of Units (1000)
McDonald's	17.1	12.4
Burger King	7.9	7.5
Taco Bell	4.8	6.8
Pizza Hut	4.7	8.7
Wendy's	4.6	4.6
KFC	4.0	5.1
Subway	2.9	11.2
Dairy Queen	2.7	5.1
Hardee's	2.7	2.9

12.60 Shown here are the total employment labor force figures for the country of Romania over a 13-year period published in LABORSTA. Develop the equation of a trend line through these data and use the equation to predict the total employment labor force of Romania for the year 2013.

Year	Total Employment (1000s)
1996	10,935
1997	11,050
1998	10,845
1999	10,776
2000	10,764
2001	10,697
2002	9,234
2003	9,223
2004	9,158
2005	9,147
2006	9,313
2007	9,353
2008	9,369

12.61 How strong is the correlation between the inflation rate and 30-year treasury yields? The following data published by Fuji Securities are given as pairs of inflation rates and treasury yields for selected years over a 35-year period.

Inflation Rate	30-Year Treasury Yield
1.57%	3.05%
2.23	3.93
2.17	4.68
4.53	6.57
7.25	8.27
9.25	12.01
5.00	10.27
4.62	8.45

Compute the Pearson product-moment correlation coefficient to determine the strength of the correlation between these two variables. Comment on the strength and direction of the correlation.

12.62 According to the National Marine Fisheries Service, the current landings in millions of pounds of fish by U.S. fleets are more than one and one-half times what they were in the 1970s. In other words, fishing has not faded as an industry. However, the growth of this industry has varied by region as shown in the following data. Some regions have remained relatively constant, the South Atlantic region has dropped in pounds caught, and the Pacific-Alaska region has grown almost threefold.

Fisheries	1977	2009
New England	581	646
Mid-Atlantic	213	200
Chesapeake	668	473
South Atlantic	345	113
Gulf of Mexico	1476	1420
Pacific-Alaska	1776	4972

Develop a simple regression model to predict the 2009 landings by the 1977 landings. According to the model, if a region had 700 landings in 1977, what would the predicted number be for 2009? Construct a confidence interval for the average y value for the 700 landings. Use the t statistic to test to determine whether the slope is significantly different from zero. Use $\alpha = .05$.

12.63 People in the aerospace industry believe the cost of a space project is a function of the weight of the major object being sent into space. Use the following data to develop a regression model to predict the cost of a space project by the weight of the space object. Determine r^2 and s_e.

Weight (tons)	Cost ($ millions)
1.897	$ 53.6
3.019	184.9
0.453	6.4
0.988	23.5
1.058	33.4
2.100	110.4
2.387	104.6

12.64 The following data represent a breakdown of state banks and all savings organizations in the United States every 5 years over a 60-year span according to the Federal Reserve System.

Time Period	State Banks	All Savings
1	1342	2330
2	1864	2667
3	1912	3054
4	1847	3764
5	1641	4423
6	1405	4837
7	1147	4694
8	1046	4407
9	997	4328
10	1070	3626
11	1009	2815
12	1042	2030
13	992	1779

Develop a regression model to predict the total number of state banks by the number of all savings organizations. Comment on the strength of the model. Develop a time-series trend line for All Savings using the time periods given. Forecast All Savings for period 15 using this equation.

12.65 Is the amount of money spent by companies on advertising a function of the total revenue of the company?

Shown are revenue and advertising cost data for seven companies published by *Advertising Age* and *Fortune* magazine.

Company	Advertising ($ millions)	Revenues ($ billions)
Wal-Mart	1,073	408.2
Procter & Gamble	4,898	79.7
AT&T	3,345	123.0
General Motors	3,296	104.6
Verizon	2,822	107.8
Ford Motor	2,577	118.3
Hewlett-Packard	829	114.6

Use the data to develop a regression line to predict the amount of advertising by revenues. Compute s_e and r^2. Assuming $\alpha = .05$, test the slope of the regression line. Comment on the strength of the regression model.

12.66 Can the consumption of water in a city be predicted by air temperature? The following data represent a sample of a day's water consumption and the high temperature for that day.

Water Use (millions of gallons)	Temperature (degrees Fahrenheit)
219	103°
56	39
107	77
129	78
68	50
184	96
150	90
112	75

Develop a least squares regression line to predict the amount of water used in a day in a city by the high temperature for that day. What would be the predicted water usage for a temperature of 100°? Evaluate the regression model by calculating s_e, by calculating r^2, and by testing the slope. Let $\alpha = .01$.

INTERPRETING THE OUTPUT

12.67 Study the following Minitab output from a regression analysis to predict y from x.

a. What is the equation of the regression model?
b. What is the meaning of the coefficient of x?
c. What is the result of the test of the slope of the regression model? Let $\alpha = .10$. Why is the t ratio negative?
d. Comment on r^2 and the standard error of the estimate.
e. Comment on the relationship of the F value to the t ratio for x.
f. The correlation coefficient for these two variables is $-.7918$. Is this result surprising to you? Why or why not?

```
Regression Analysis: Y versus X
The regression equation is
Y = 67.2 - 0.0565 X

Predictor    Coef     SE Coef     T       p
Constant    67.231     5.046    13.32   0.000
X          -0.05650   0.01027   -5.50   0.000

S = 10.32   R-Sq = 62.7%   R-Sq(adj) = 60.6%

Analysis of Variance
Source          DF     SS      MS      F      P
Regression       1   3222.9  3222.9  30.25  0.000
Residual Error  18   1918.0   106.6
Total           19   5141.0
```

12.68 Study the following Excel regression output for an analysis attempting to predict the number of union members in the United States by the size of the labor force for selected years over a 30-year period from data published by the U.S. Bureau of Labor Statistics. Analyze the computer output. Discuss the strength of the model in terms of proportion of variation accounted for, slope, and overall predictability. Using the equation of the regression line, attempt to predict the number of union members when the labor force is 110,000. Note that the model was developed with data already recoded in 1,000 units. Use the data in the model as is.

SUMMARY OUTPUT

Regression Statistics	
Multiple R	0.798
R Square	0.636
Adjusted R Square	0.612
Standard Error	258.632
Observations	17

ANOVA

	df	SS	MS	F	Significance F
Regression	1	1756035.529	1756036	26.25	0.00012
Residual	15	1003354.471	66890.3		
Total	16	2759390			

	Coefficients	Standard Error	t Stat	P-value
Intercept	20704.3805	879.6067	23.54	0.00000
Total Employment	-0.0390	0.0076	-5.12	0.00012

12.69 Study the following Minitab residual diagnostic graphs. Comment on any possible violations of regression assumptions.

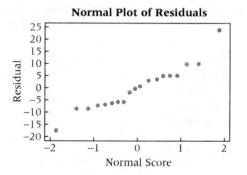

Normal Plot of Residuals

Histogram of Residuals

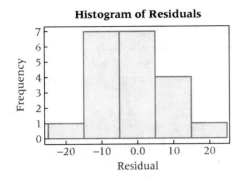

Residuals Versus the Fitted Values

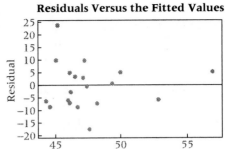

ANALYZING THE DATABASES

see www.wiley.com/college/black and WileyPLUS

Database

1. Develop a regression model from the Consumer Food database to predict Annual Food Spending by Annual Household Income. Discuss the model and its strength on the basis of statistics presented in this chapter. Now develop a regression model to predict Non-Mortgage Household Debt by Annual Household Income. Discuss this model and its strengths. Compare the two models. Does it make sense that Annual Food Spending and Non-Mortgage Household Debt could each be predicted by Annual Household Income? Why or why not?

2. Using the Hospital database, develop a regression model to predict the number of Personnel by the number of Births. Now develop a regression model to predict number of Personnel by number of Beds. Examine the regression output. Which model is stronger in predicting number of Personnel? Explain why, using techniques presented in this chapter. Use the second regression model to predict the number of Personnel in a hospital that has 110 beds.

Construct a 95% confidence interval around this prediction for the average value of *y*.

3. Analyze all the variables except Type in the Financial database by using a correlation matrix. The seven variables in this database are capable of producing 21 pairs of correlations. Which are most highly correlated? Select the variable that is most highly correlated with P/E ratio and use it as a predictor to develop a regression model to predict P/E ratio. How did the model do?

4. Construct a correlation matrix for the six U.S. and international stock indicators. Describe what you find. That is, what indicators seem to be most strongly related to other indicators? Now focus on the three international stock indicators. Which pair of these stock indicators is most correlated? Develop a regression model to predict the DJIA by the Nikkei 225. How strong is the model? Develop a regression model to predict the DJIA by the Hang Seng. How strong is the model? Develop a regression model to predict the DJIA by the Mexico IPC. How strong is the model? Compare the three models.

CASE

DELTA WIRE USES TRAINING AS A WEAPON

The Delta Wire Corporation was founded in 1978 in Clarksdale, Mississippi. The company manufactures high-carbon specialty steel wire for global markets and at present employs about 100 people. For the past few years, sales increased each year.

A few years ago, however, things did not look as bright for Delta Wire because it was caught in a potentially disastrous bind. With the dollar declining in value, foreign competition was becoming a growing threat to Delta's market position. In addition to the growing foreign competition, industry quality requirements were becoming tougher each year.

Delta officials realized that some conditions, such as the value of the dollar, were beyond their control. However, one

area that they could improve upon was employee education. The company worked with training programs developed by the state of Mississippi and a local community college to set up its own school. Delta employees were introduced to statistical process control and other quality assurance techniques. Delta reassured its customers that the company was working hard on improving quality and staying competitive. Customers were invited to sit in on the educational sessions. Because of this effort, Delta has been able to weather the storm and continues to sustain a leadership position in the highly competitive steel wire industry.

Delta continued its training and education program. In the 1990s, Delta instituted a basic skills training program that eventually led to a decrease in nonconforming material from 6% to 2% and a productivity increase from 70,000 to 90,000 pounds per week. In addition, this initiative resulted in a "best in class" award from Goodyear, its largest customer.

Although acquired by Bekaert of Belgium in January of 2006, the Delta Wire Corporation, a major supplier of bead wire for tire reinforcement and other specialized wire products for the North American market, continues to operate in its current capacity. Bekaert wants to support Delta Wire's market share growth and ensure adequate product availability to its customers.

Discussion

1. Delta Wire prides itself on its efforts in the area of employee education. Employee education can pay off in many ways. Discuss some of them. One payoff can be the renewed interest and excitement generated toward the job and the company. Some people theorize that because of a more positive outlook and interest in implementing things learned, the more education received by a worker, the less likely he or she is to miss work days. Suppose the following data represent the number of days of sick leave taken by 20 workers last year along with the number of contact hours of employee education/training they each received in the past year. Use the techniques learned in this chapter to analyze the data. Include both regression and correlation techniques. Discuss the strength of the relationship and any models that are developed.

Employee	Hours of Education	Sick Days	Employee	Hours of Education	Sick Days
1	24	5	11	8	8
2	16	4	12	60	1
3	48	0	13	0	9
4	120	1	14	28	3
5	36	5	15	15	8
6	10	7	16	88	2
7	65	0	17	120	1
8	36	3	18	15	8
9	0	12	19	48	0
10	12	8	20	5	10

2. Many companies find that the implementation of total quality management eventually results in improved sales. Companies that fail to adopt quality efforts lose market share in many cases or go out of business. One measure of the effect of a company's quality improvement efforts is customer satisfaction. Suppose Delta Wire hired a research firm to measure customer satisfaction each year. The research firm developed a customer satisfaction scale in which totally satisfied customers can award a score as high as 50 and totally unsatisfied

customers can award scores as low as 0. The scores are measured across many different industrial customers and averaged for a yearly mean customer score. Do sales increase with increases in customer satisfaction scores? To study this notion, suppose the average customer satisfaction score each year for Delta Wire is paired with the company's total sales of that year for the last 15 years, and a regression analysis is run on the data. Assume the following Minitab and Excel outputs are the result. Suppose you were asked by Delta Wire to analyze the data and summarize the results. What would you find?

MINITAB OUTPUT

```
Regression Analysis: Sales Versus Satisfaction

The regression equation is
Sales = 1.73 + 0.162 CustSat

Predictor      Coef     StDev      T       p
Constant     1.7332    0.4364    3.97   0.002
CustSat      0.16245   0.01490  10.90   0.000

S = 0.4113    R-Sq = 90.1%  R-Sq(adj) = 89.4%

Analysis of Variance

Source          DF   SS       MS      F       p
Regression       1   20.098   20.098  118.80  0.000
Residual Error  13   2.199    0.169
Total           14   22.297
```

EXCEL OUTPUT

SUMMARY OUTPUT

Regression Statistics

Multiple R	0.949
R Square	0.901
Adjusted R Square	0.894
Standard Error	0.411
Observations	15

ANOVA

	df	SS	MS	F	Significance F
Regression	1	20.098	20.098	118.8	0.000
Residual	13	2.199	0.169		
Total	14	22.297			

	Coefficients	Standard Error	t Stat	P-value
Intercept	1.733	0.436	3.97	0.0016
Sick Days	0.162	0.015	10.90	0.0000

3. Delta Wire increased productivity from 70,000 to 90,000 pounds per week during a time when it instituted a basic skills training program. Suppose this program was implemented over an 18-month period and that the following data are the number of total cumulative basic skills hours of training and the per week productivity figures taken once a month over this time. Use techniques from this chapter to analyze the data and make a brief report to Delta about the predictability of productivity from cumulative hours of training.

Cumulative Hours of Training	Productivity (in pounds per week)
0	70,000
100	70,350
250	70,500
375	72,600
525	74,000
750	76,500
875	77,000
1,100	77,400
1,300	77,900
1,450	77,200
1,660	78,900
1,900	81,000
2,300	82,500

Cumulative Hours of Training	Productivity (in pounds per week)
2,600	84,000
2,850	86,500
3,150	87,000
3,500	88,600
4,000	90,000

(*continued*)

Source: Adapted from "Delta Wire Corporation," *Strengthening America's Competitiveness: Resource Management Insights for Small Business Success.* Published by Warner Books on behalf of Connecticut Mutual Life Insurance Company and the U.S. Chamber of Commerce in association with the Blue Chip Enterprise Initiative, 1991, International Monetary Fund; Terri Bergman, "TRAINING: The Case for Increased Investment," *Employment Relations Today,* Winter 1994–1995, pp. 381–391, available at http://www.ed.psu.edu/nwac/document/train/invest.html. Bekaert Web site, at: http://www.bekaert.com/corporate/press/2006/31-jan-2006.htm.

USING THE COMPUTER

EXCEL

※ Excel has the capability of doing simple regression analysis. For a more inclusive analysis, use the **Data Analysis** tool. For a more "a la carte" approach, use Excel's **Insert Function**.

※ To use the **Data Analysis** tool for a more inclusive analysis, begin by selecting the **Data** tab on the Excel worksheet. From the **Analysis** panel at the right top of the **Data** tab worksheet, click on **Data Analysis**. If your Excel worksheet does not show the **Data Analysis** option, then you can load it as an add-in following directions given in Chapter 2. From the **Data Analysis** pulldown menu, select **Regression**. In the **Regression** dialog box, input the location of the *y* values in **Input Y Range**. Input the location of the *x* values in **Input X Range**. Input **Labels** and input **Confidence Level**. To pass the line through the origin, check **Constant is Zero**. To print out the raw residuals, check **Residuals**. To print out residuals converted to *z* scores, check **Standardized Residuals**. For a plot of the residuals, check **Residual Plots**. For a plot of the line through the points, check **Line Fit Plots**. Standard output includes r, r^2, s_e, and an ANOVA table with the F test, the slope and intercept, t statistics with associated *p*-values, and any optionally requested output such as graphs or residuals.

※ To use the **Insert Function** (f_x) go to the **Formulas** tab on an Excel worksheet (top center tab). The **Insert Function** is on the far left of the menu bar. In the **Insert Function** dialog box at the top, there is a pulldown menu where it says **Or select a category**. From the pulldown menu associated with this command, select **Statistical**. Select **INTERCEPT** from the **Insert Function's Statistical** menu to solve for the *y*-intercept, **RSQ** to solve for r^2, **SLOPE** to solve for the slope, and **STEYX** to solve for the standard error of the estimate.

MINITAB

※ Minitab has a relatively thorough capability to perform regression analysis. To begin, select **Stat** from the menu bar. Select **Regression** from the **Stat** pulldown menu. Select **Regression** from the **Regression** pulldown menu. Place the column name or column location of the *y* variable in **Response**. Place the column name or column location of the *x* variable in **Predictors**. Select **Graphs** for options relating to residual plots. Use this option and check **Four in one** to produce the residual diagnostic plots shown in the chapter. Select **Options** for confidence intervals and prediction intervals. Select **Results** for controlling the regression analysis output. Select **Storage** to store fits and/or residuals.

※ To obtain a fitted-line plot, select **Stat** from the menu bar. Select **Regression** from the **Stat** pulldown menu. Select **Fitted Line Plot** from the **Regression** pulldown menu. In the Fitted Line Plot dialog box, place the column name or column location of the *y* variable in **Response(Y)**.

Place the column name or column location of the *x* variable in **Predictor(X)**. Check **Type of Regression Model** as **Linear** (Chapter 12), **Quadratic**, or **Cubic**.

Select **Graphs** for options relating to residual plots. Use this option and check **Four in one** to produce the residual diagnostic plots shown in the chapter.

Select **Options** for confidence intervals and prediction intervals.

Select **Storage** to store fits and/or residuals.

CHAPTER 13

Multiple Regression Analysis

LEARNING OBJECTIVES

This chapter presents the potential of multiple regression analysis as a tool in business decision making and its applications, thereby enabling you to:

1. Explain how, by extending the simple regression model to a multiple regression model with two independent variables, it is possible to determine the multiple regression equation for any number of unknowns.

2. Examine significance tests of both the overall regression model and the regression coefficients.

3. Calculate the residual, standard error of the estimate, coefficient of multiple determination, and adjusted coefficient of multiple determination of a regression model.

4. Use a computer to find and interpret multiple regression outputs.

Michael Krasowitz/Photographer's Choice/Getty Images

Are You Going to Hate Your New Job?

Getting a new job can be an exciting and energizing event in your life.

But what if you discover after a short time on the job that you hate your job? Is there any way to determine ahead of time whether you will love or hate your job? Sue Shellenbarger of *The Wall Street Journal* discusses some of the things to look for when interviewing for a position that may provide clues as to whether you will be happy on that job.

Among other things, work cultures vary from hip, free-wheeling start-ups to old-school organizational-driven domains. Some organizations place pressure on workers to feel tense and to work long hours while others place more emphasis on creativity and the bottom line. Shellenbarger suggests that job interviewees pay close attention to how they are treated in an interview. Are they just another cog in the wheel or are they valued as an individual? Is a work-life balance apparent within the company? Ask what a typical workday is like at that firm. Inquire about the values that undergird the management by asking questions such as "What is your proudest accomplishment?" Ask about flexible schedules and how job training is managed. For example, does the worker have to go to job training on their own time?

A "Work Trends" survey undertaking by the John J. Heldrich Center for Workforce Development at Rutgers University and the Center for Survey Research and Analysis at the University of Connecticut posed several questions to employees in a survey to ascertain their job satisfaction. Some of the themes included in these questions were relationship with your supervisor, overall quality of the work environment, total hours worked each week, and opportunities for advancement at the job.

Suppose another researcher gathered survey data from 19 employees on these questions and also asked the employees to rate their job satisfaction on a scale from 0 to 100 (with 100 being perfectly satisfied). Suppose the following data represent the results of this survey. Assume that relationship with supervisor is rated on a scale from 0 to 50 (0 represents poor relationship and 50 represents an excellent relationship), overall quality of the work environment is rated on a scale from 0 to 100 (0 represents poor work environment and 100 represents an excellent work environment), and opportunities for advancement is rated on a scale from 0 to 50 (0 represents no opportunities and 50 represents excellent opportunities).

Job Satisfaction	Relationship with Supervisor	Overall Quality of Work Environment	Total Hours Worked per Week	Opportunities for Advancement
55	27	65	50	42
20	12	13	60	28
85	40	79	45	7
65	35	53	65	48
45	29	43	40	32
70	42	62	50	41
35	22	18	75	18
60	34	75	40	32
95	50	84	45	48
65	33	68	60	11
85	40	72	55	33
10	5	10	50	21
75	37	64	45	42
80	42	82	40	46
50	31	46	60	48
90	47	95	55	30
75	36	82	70	39
45	20	42	40	22
65	32	73	55	12

Managerial and Statistical Questions

1. Several variables are presented that may be related to job satisfaction. Which variables are stronger predictors of job satisfaction? Might other variables not mentioned here be related to job satisfaction?

2. Is it possible to develop a mathematical model to predict job satisfaction using the data given? If so, how strong is the model? With four independent variables, will we need to develop four different simple regression models and compare their results?

Source: Adapted from Sue Shellenbarger, "How to Find Out if You're Going to Hate a New Job Before You Agree to Take It," *The Wall Street Journal*, June 13, 2002, p. D1.

Simple regression analysis (discussed in Chapter 12) is bivariate linear regression in which one **dependent variable**, y, is predicted by one **independent variable**, x. Examples of simple regression applications include models to predict retail sales by population density, Dow Jones averages by prime interest rates, crude oil production by energy consumption, and CEO compensation by quarterly sales. However, in many cases, other independent variables, taken in conjunction with these variables, can make the regression model a better fit in predicting the dependent variable. For example, sales could be predicted by the size of store and number of competitors in addition to population density. A model to predict the Dow Jones average of 30 industrials could include, in addition to the prime interest rate, such predictors as yesterday's volume, the bond interest rate, and the producer price index. A model to predict CEO compensation could be developed by using variables such as company earnings per share, age of CEO, and size of company in addition to quarterly sales. A model could perhaps be developed to predict the cost of outsourcing by such variables as unit price, export taxes, cost of money, damage in transit, and other factors. Each of these examples contains only one dependent variable, y, as with simple regression analysis. However, multiple independent variables, x (predictors) are involved. *Regression analysis with two or more independent variables or with at least one nonlinear predictor* is called **multiple regression** analysis.

13.1 THE MULTIPLE REGRESSION MODEL

Multiple regression analysis is similar in principle to simple regression analysis. However, it is more complex conceptually and computationally. Recall from Chapter 12 that the equation of the probabilistic simple regression model is

$$y = \beta_0 + \beta_1 x + \epsilon$$

where

y = the value of the dependent variable
β_0 = the population y intercept
β_1 = the population slope
ϵ = the error of prediction

Extending this notion to multiple regression gives the general equation for the probabilistic multiple regression model.

$$y = \beta_0 + \beta_1 x_1 + \beta_2 x_2 + \beta_3 x_3 + \cdots + \beta_k x_k + \epsilon$$

where

y = the value of the dependent variable
β_0 = the regression constant
β_1 = the partial regression coefficient for independent variable 1
β_2 = the partial regression coefficient for independent variable 2
β_3 = the partial regression coefficient for independent variable 3
β_k = the partial regression coefficient for independent variable k
k = the number of independent variables

In multiple regression analysis, the dependent variable, y, is sometimes referred to as the **response variable**. The **partial regression coefficient** of an independent variable, β_i, *represents the increase that will occur in the value of y from a one-unit increase in that independent variable if all other variables are held constant.* The "full" (versus partial) regression coefficient of an independent variable is a coefficient obtained from the bivariate model (simple regression) in which the independent variable is the sole predictor of y. The partial regression coefficients occur because more than one predictor is included in a model. The partial regression coefficients are analogous to β_1, the slope of the simple regression model in Chapter 12.

In actuality, the partial regression coefficients and the regression constant of a multiple regression model are population values and are unknown. In virtually all research, these values are estimated by using sample information. Shown here is the form of the equation for estimating y with sample information.

$$\hat{y} = b_0 + b_1 x_1 + b_2 x_2 + b_3 x_3 + \cdots + b_k x_k$$

where

$\hat{y}$ = the predicted value of y
b_0 = the estimate of the regression constant
b_1 = the estimate of regression coefficient 1
b_2 = the estimate of regression coefficient 2
b_3 = the estimate of regression coefficient 3
b_k = the estimate of regression coefficient k
k = the number of independent variables

Multiple Regression Model with Two Independent Variables (First-Order)

The simplest multiple regression model is one constructed with two independent variables, where the highest power of either variable is 1 (first-order regression model). The regression model is

$$y = \beta_0 + \beta_1 x_1 + \beta_2 x_2 + \in$$

The constant and coefficients are estimated from sample information, resulting in the following model.

$$\hat{y} = b_0 + b_1 x_1 + b_2 x_2$$

Figure 13.1 is a three-dimensional graph of a series of points (x_1, x_2, y) representing values from three variables used in a multiple regression model to predict the sales price of a house by the number of square feet in the house and the age of the house. Simple regression models yield a line that is fit through data points in the xy plane. In multiple regression analysis, the resulting model produces a **response surface**. In the multiple regression model shown here with two independent first-order variables, the response surface is a **response plane**. The response plane for such a model is fit in a three-dimensional space (x_1, x_2, y).

If such a response plane is fit into the points shown in Figure 13.1, the result is the graph in Figure 13.2. Notice that most of the points are not on the plane. As in simple regression, an error in the fit of the model in multiple regression is usually present. The distances shown in the graph from the points to the response plane are the errors of fit, or residuals $(y - \hat{y})$. Multiple regression models with three or more independent variables involve more than three dimensions and are difficult to depict geometrically.

Observe in Figure 13.2 that the regression model attempts to fit a plane into the three-dimensional plot of points. Notice that the plane intercepts the y axis. Figure 13.2 depicts

---

FIGURE 13.1

Points in a Sample Space

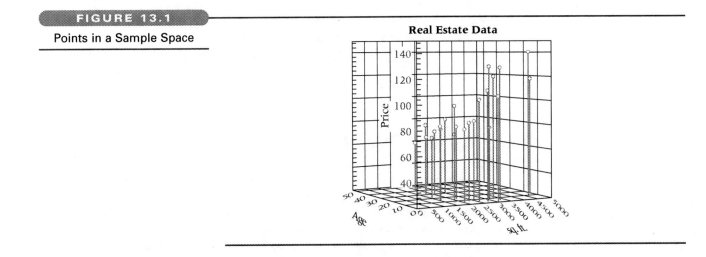

FIGURE 13.2

Response Plane for a First-Order Two-Predictor Multiple Regression Model

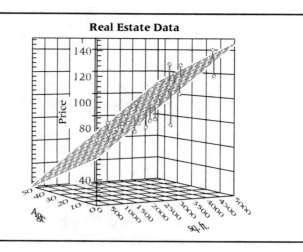

Real Estate Data

some values of y for various values of x_1 and x_2. The error of the response plane ($\in$) in predicting or determining the y values is the distance from the points to the plane.

Determining the Multiple Regression Equation

The simple regression equations for determining the sample slope and intercept given in Chapter 12 are the result of using methods of calculus to minimize the sum of squares of error for the regression model. The procedure for developing these equations involves solving two simultaneous equations with two unknowns, b_0 and b_1. Finding the sample slope and intercept from these formulas requires the values of Σx, Σy, Σxy, and Σx^2.

The procedure for determining formulas to solve for multiple regression coefficients is similar. The formulas are established to meet an objective of *minimizing the sum of squares of error for the model*. Hence, the regression analysis shown here is referred to as **least squares analysis**. Methods of calculus are applied, resulting in $k + 1$ equations with $k + 1$ unknowns (b_0 and k values of b_i) for multiple regression analyses with k independent variables. Thus, a regression model with six independent variables will generate seven simultaneous equations with seven unknowns (b_0, b_1, b_2, b_3, b_4, b_5, b_6).

For multiple regression models with two independent variables, the result is three simultaneous equations with three unknowns (b_0, b_1, and b_2).

$$b_0 n + b_1 \Sigma x_1 + b_2 \Sigma x_2 = \Sigma y$$
$$b_0 \Sigma x_1 + b_1 \Sigma x_1^2 + b_2 \Sigma x_1 x_2 = \Sigma x_1 y$$
$$b_0 \Sigma x_2 + b_1 \Sigma x_1 x_2 + b_2 \Sigma x_2^2 = \Sigma x_2 y$$

The process of solving these equations by hand is tedious and time-consuming. Solving for the regression coefficients and regression constant in a multiple regression model with two independent variables requires Σx_1, Σx_2, Σy, Σx_1^2, Σx_2^2, $\Sigma x_1 x_2$, $\Sigma x_1 y$, and $\Sigma x_2 y$. In actuality, virtually all business researchers use computer statistical software packages to solve for the regression coefficients, the regression constant, and other pertinent information. In this chapter, we will discuss computer output and assume little or no hand calculation. The emphasis will be on the interpretation of the computer output.

A Multiple Regression Model

A real estate study was conducted in a small Louisiana city to determine what variables, if any, are related to the market price of a home. Several variables were explored, including the number of bedrooms, the number of bathrooms, the age of the house, the number of square feet of living space, the total number of square feet of space, and the number of garages. Suppose the researcher wants to develop a regression model to predict the market price of a home by two variables, "total number of square feet in the house" and "the age of the house." Listed in Table 13.1 are the data for these three variables.

TABLE 13.1		
Real Estate Data		

Market Price ($1,000)	Total Number of Square Feet	Age of House (Years)
y	x_1	x_2
63.0	1605	35
65.1	2489	45
69.9	1553	20
76.8	2404	32
73.9	1884	25
77.9	1558	14
74.9	1748	8
78.0	3105	10
79.0	1682	28
83.4	2470	30
79.5	1820	2
83.9	2143	6
79.7	2121	14
84.5	2485	9
96.0	2300	19
109.5	2714	4
102.5	2463	5
121.0	3076	7
104.9	3048	3
128.0	3267	6
129.0	3069	10
117.9	4765	11
140.0	4540	8

A number of statistical software packages can perform multiple regression analysis, including Excel and Minitab. The output for the Minitab multiple regression analysis on the real estate data is given in Figure 13.3. (Excel output is shown in Demonstration Problem 13.1.)

The Minitab output for regression analysis begins with "The regression equation is." From Figure 13.3, the regression equation for the real estate data in Table 13.1 is

$$\hat{y} = 57.4 + .0177x_1 - .666x_2$$

The regression constant, 57.4, is the y-intercept. The y-intercept is the value of $\hat{y}$ if both x_1 (number of square feet) and x_2 (age) are zero. In this example, a practical understanding of the y-intercept is meaningless. It makes little sense to say that a house containing no square feet ($x_1 = 0$) and no years of age ($x_2 = 0$) would cost $57,400. Note in Figure 13.2 that the response plane crosses the y-axis (price) at 57.4.

FIGURE 13.3	
Minitab Output of Regression for the Real Estate Example	

```
Regression Analysis: Price versus Square Feet, Age

The regression equation is
Price = 57.4 + 0.0177 Square Feet - 0.666 Age

Predictor          Coef     SE Coef        T       P
Constant          57.35       10.01     5.73   0.000
Square Feet     0.017718    0.003146     5.63   0.000
Age              -0.6663      0.2280    -2.92   0.008

S = 11.9604   R-Sq = 74.1%      R-Sq(adj) = 71.5%

Analysis of Variance

Source            DF       SS       MS       F       P
Regression         2   8189.7   4094.9   28.63   0.000
Residual Error    20   2861.0    143.1
Total             22  11050.7
```

The coefficient of x_1 (total number of square feet in the house) is .0177, which means that a one-unit increase in square footage would result in a predicted increase of .0177 · ($1,000) = $17.70 in the price of the home if age were held constant. All other variables being held constant, the addition of 1 square foot of space in the house results in a predicted increase of $17.70 in the price of the home.

The coefficient of x_2 (age) is −.666. The negative sign on the coefficient denotes an inverse relationship between the age of a house and the price of the house: the older the house, the lower the price. In this case, if the total number of square feet in the house is kept constant, a one-unit increase in the age of the house (1 year) will result in −.666 · ($1,000) = −$666, a predicted $666 drop in the price.

In examining the regression coefficients, it is important to remember that the independent variables are often measured in different units. It is usually not wise to compare the regression coefficients of predictors in a multiple regression model and decide that the variable with the largest regression coefficient is the best predictor. In this example, the two variables are in different units, square feet and years. Just because x_2 has the larger coefficient (.666) does not necessarily make x_2 the strongest predictor of y.

This regression model can be used to predict the price of a house in this small Louisiana city. If the house has 2500 square feet total and is 12 years old, $x_1 = 2500$ and $x_2 = 12$. Substituting these values into the regression model yields

$$\hat{y} = 57.4 + .0177x_1 - .666x_2$$
$$= 57.4 + .0177(2500) - .666(12) = 93.658$$

The predicted price of the house is $93,658. Figure 13.2 is a graph of these data with the response plane and the residual distances.

DEMONSTRATION PROBLEM 13.1

Demonstration Problem

Since 1980, the prime interest rate in the United States has varied from less than 5% to over 15%. What factor in the U.S. economy seems to be related to the prime interest rate? Two possible predictors of the prime interest rate are the annual unemployment rate and the savings rate in the United States. Shown below are data for the annual prime interest rate for the even-numbered years over a 28-year period in the United States along with the annual unemployment rate and the annual average personal saving (as a percentage of disposable personal income). Use these data to develop a multiple regression model to predict the annual prime interest rate by the unemployment rate and the average personal saving. Determine the predicted prime interest rate if the unemployment rate is 6.5 and the average personal saving is 5.0.

Year	Prime Interest Rate	Unemployment Rate	Personal Saving
1982	14.85	9.7	11.2
1984	12.04	7.5	10.8
1986	8.33	7.0	8.2
1988	9.32	5.5	7.3
1990	10.01	5.6	7.0
1992	6.25	7.5	7.7
1994	7.15	6.1	4.8
1996	8.27	5.4	4.0
1998	8.35	4.5	4.3
2000	9.23	4.0	2.3
2002	4.67	5.8	2.4
2004	4.34	5.5	2.1
2006	7.96	4.6	0.7
2008	5.09	5.8	1.8
2010	3.25	9.6	5.8

Solution

The following output shows the results of analyzing the data by using the regression portion of Excel.

SUMMARY OUTPUT

Regression Statistics	
Multiple R	0.774
R Square	0.599
Adjusted R Square	0.533
Standard Error	2.083
Observations	15

ANOVA

	df	SS	MS	F	Significance F
Regression	2	78.0034	39.0017	8.98	0.0041
Residual	12	52.0893	4.3408		
Total	14	130.0927			

	Coefficients	Standard Error	t Stat	P-value
Intercept	9.2585	2.244	4.13	0.0014
Unemployment Rates	−1.0486	0.455	−2.30	0.0399
Personal Savings	0.9815	0.236	4.16	0.0013

The regression equation is

$$\hat{y} = 9.2585 - 1.0486x_1 + 0.9815x_2$$

where:

$\hat{y}$ = prime interest rate
x_1 = unemployment rate
x_2 = personal saving

The model indicates that for every one-unit (1%) increase in the unemployment rate, the predicted prime interest rate decreases by 1.0486%, if personal saving is held constant. The model also indicates that for every one-unit (1%) increase in personal saving, the predicted prime interest rate increases by 0.9815%, if unemployment is held constant.

If the unemployment rate is 6.5 and the personal saving rate is 5.0, the predicted prime interest rate is 6.56%:

$$\hat{y} = 9.2585 - 1.0486(6.5) + 0.9815(5.0) = 7.35$$

13.1 PROBLEMS

13.1 Use a computer to develop the equation of the regression model for the following data. Comment on the regression coefficients. Determine the predicted value of y for $x_1 = 200$ and $x_2 = 7$.

y	x_1	x_2
12	174	3
18	281	9
31	189	4
28	202	8
52	149	9
47	188	12
38	215	5
22	150	11
36	167	8
17	135	5

13.2 Use a computer to develop the equation of the regression model for the following data. Comment on the regression coefficients. Determine the predicted value of y for $x_1 = 33$, $x_2 = 29$, and $x_3 = 13$.

y	x_1	x_2	x_3
114	21	6	5
94	43	25	8
87	56	42	25
98	19	27	9
101	29	20	12
85	34	45	21
94	40	33	14
107	32	14	11
119	16	4	7
93	18	31	16
108	27	12	10
117	31	3	8

13.3 Using the following data, determine the equation of the regression model. How many independent variables are there? Comment on the meaning of these regression coefficients.

Predictor	Coefficient
Constant	121.62
x_1	−.174
x_2	6.02
x_3	.00026
x_4	.0041

13.4 Use the following data to determine the equation of the multiple regression model. Comment on the regression coefficients.

Predictor	Coefficient
Constant	31,409.5
x_1	.08425
x_2	289.62
x_3	−.0947

13.5 Is there a particular product that is an indicator of per capita personal consumption for countries around the world? Shown on the next page are data on per capita personal consumption, paper consumption, fish consumption, and gasoline consumption for 11 countries. Use the data to develop a multiple regression model to predict per capita personal consumption by paper consumption, fish consumption, and gasoline consumption. Discuss the meaning of the partial regression weights.

Country	Per Capita Personal Consumption ($ U.S.)	Paper Consumption (kg per person)	Fish Consumption (lbs per person)	Gasoline Consumption (liters per person)
Bangladesh	836	1	23	2
Greece	3,145	85	53	394
Italy	21,785	204	48	368
Japan	37,931	250	141	447
Kenya	276	4	12	16
Norway	1,913	156	113	477
Philippines	2,195	19	65	43
Portugal	3,154	116	133	257
United Kingdom	19,539	207	44	460
United States	109,521	308	47	1,624
Venezuela	622	27	40	528

13.6 Jensen, Solberg, and Zorn investigated the relationship of insider ownership, debt, and dividend policies in companies. One of their findings was that firms with high insider ownership choose lower levels of both debt and dividends. Shown here is a sample of data of these three variables for 11 different industries. Use the data to develop the equation of the regression model to predict insider ownership by debt ratio and dividend payout. Comment on the regression coefficients.

Industry	Insider Ownership	Debt Ratio	Dividend Payout
Mining	8.2	14.2	10.4
Food and beverage	18.4	20.8	14.3
Furniture	11.8	18.6	12.1
Publishing	28.0	18.5	11.8
Petroleum refining	7.4	28.2	10.6
Glass and cement	15.4	24.7	12.6
Motor vehicle	15.7	15.6	12.6
Department store	18.4	21.7	7.2
Restaurant	13.4	23.0	11.3
Amusement	18.1	46.7	4.1
Hospital	10.0	35.8	9.0

 SIGNIFICANCE TESTS OF THE REGRESSION MODEL AND ITS COEFFICIENTS

Multiple regression models can be developed to fit almost any data set if the level of measurement is adequate and enough data points are available. Once a model has been constructed, it is important to test the model to determine whether it fits the data well and whether the assumptions underlying regression analysis are met. Assessing the adequacy of the regression model can be done in several ways, including testing the overall significance of the model, studying the significance tests of the regression coefficients, computing the residuals, examining the standard error of the estimate, and observing the coefficient of determination. In this section, we examine significance tests of the regression model and of its coefficients.

Testing the Overall Model

With simple regression, a *t* test of the slope of the regression line is used to determine whether the population slope of the regression line is different from zero—that is, whether the independent variable contributes significantly in linearly predicting the dependent variable.

The hypotheses for this test, presented in Chapter 12 are

$$H_0: \beta_1 = 0$$

$$H_a: \beta_1 \neq 0$$

For multiple regression, an analogous test makes use of the F statistic. The overall significance of the multiple regression model is tested with the following hypotheses.

$$H_0: \beta_1 = \beta_2 = \beta_3 = \ldots = \beta_k = 0$$

H_a: At least one of the regression coefficeients is $\neq 0$.

If we fail to reject the null hypothesis, we are stating that the regression model has no significant predictability for the dependent variable. A rejection of the null hypothesis indicates that at least one of the independent variables is adding significant predictability for y.

This F test of overall significance is often given as a part of the standard multiple regression output from statistical software packages. The output appears as an analysis of variance (ANOVA) table. Shown here is the ANOVA table for the real estate example taken from the Minitab output in Figure 13.3.

Analysis of Variance

Source	DF	SS	MS	F	p
Regression	2	8189.7	4094.9	28.63	0.000
Residual Error	20	2861.0	143.1		
Total	22	11050.7			

The F value is 28.63; because $p = .000$, the F value is significant at $\alpha = .001$. The null hypothesis is rejected, and there is at least one significant predictor of house price in this analysis.

The F value is calculated by the following equation.

$$F = \frac{MS_{reg}}{MS_{err}} = \frac{SS_{reg}/df_{reg}}{SS_{err}/df_{err}} = \frac{SSR/k}{SSE/(N - k - 1)}$$

where

MS = mean square
SS = sum of squares
df = degrees of freedom
k = number of independent variables
N = number of observations

Note that in the ANOVA table for the real estate example, $df_{reg} = 2$. The degrees of freedom formula for regression is the number of regression coefficients plus the regression constant minus 1. The net result is the number of regression coefficients, which equals the number of independent variables, k. The real estate example uses two independent variables, so $k = 2$. Degrees of freedom error in multiple regression equals the total number of observations minus the number of regression coefficients minus the regression constant, or $N - k - 1$. For the real estate example, $N = 23$; thus, $df_{err} = 23 - 2 - 1 = 20$.

As shown in Chapter 11, $MS = SS/df$. The F ratio is formed by dividing MS_{reg} by MS_{err}. In using the F distribution table to determine a critical value against which to test the observed F value, the degrees of freedom numerator is df_{reg} and the degrees of freedom denominator is df_{err}. The table F value is obtained in the usual manner, as presented in Chapter 11. With $\alpha = .01$ for the real estate example, the table value is

$$F_{.01,2,20} = 5.85$$

Comparing the observed F of 28.63 to this table value shows that the decision is to reject the null hypothesis. This same conclusion was reached using the p-value method from the computer output.

If a regression model has only one linear independent variable, it is a simple regression model. In that case, the F test for the overall model is the same as the t test for significance of the population slope. The F value displayed in the regression ANOVA table is related to the t test for the slope in the simple regression case as follows.

$$F = t^2$$

In simple regression, the F value and the t value give redundant information about the overall test of the model.

Most researchers who use multiple regression analysis will observe the value of F and its p-value rather early in the process. If F is not significant, then no population regression coefficient is significantly different from zero, and the regression model has no predictability for the dependent variable.

Significance Tests of the Regression Coefficients

In multiple regression, individual significance tests can be computed for each regression coefficient using a t test. Each of these t tests is analogous to the t test for the slope used in Chapter 12 for simple regression analysis. The hypotheses for testing the regression coefficient of each independent variable take the following form:

$$H_0: \beta_1 = 0$$
$$H_a: \beta_1 \neq 0$$

$$H_0: \beta_2 = 0$$
$$H_a: \beta_2 \neq 0$$

$$\vdots$$

$$H_0: \beta_k = 0$$
$$H_a: \beta_k \neq 0$$

Most multiple regression computer packages yield observed t values to test the individual regression coefficients as standard output. Shown here are the t values and their associated probabilities for the real estate example as displayed with the multiple regression output in Figure 13.3.

Variable	T	P
Square feet	5.63	.000
Age	−2.92	.008

At $\alpha = .05$, the null hypothesis is rejected for both variables because the probabilities (p) associated with their t values are less than .05. If the t ratios for any predictor variables are not significant (fail to reject the null hypothesis), the researcher might decide to drop that variable(s) from the analysis as a nonsignificant predictor(s). Other factors can enter into this decision. In Chapter 14, we will explore techniques for model building in which some variable sorting is required.

The degrees of freedom for each of these individual tests of regression coefficients are $n - k - 1$. In this particular example because there are $k = 2$ predictor variables, the degrees of freedom are $23 - 2 - 1 = 20$. With $\alpha = .05$ and a two-tailed test, the critical table t value is

$$t_{.025,20} = \pm 2.086$$

Notice from the t ratios shown here that if this critical table t value had been used as the hypothesis test criterion instead of the p-value method, the results would have been the same. Testing the regression coefficients not only gives the researcher some insight into the fit of the regression model, but it also helps in the evaluation of how worthwhile individual independent variables are in predicting y.

13.2 PROBLEMS

13.7 Examine the Minitab output shown here for a multiple regression analysis. How many predictors were there in this model? Comment on the overall significance of the regression model. Discuss the t ratios of the variables and their significance.

```
The regression equation is
```

$$Y = 4.096 - 5.111X_1 + 2.662X_2 + 1.557X_3 + 1.141X_4 + 1.650$$
$$X_5 - 1.248X_6 + 0.436X_7 + 0.962X_8 + 1.289X_9$$

Predictor	Coef	Stdev	T	p
Constant	4.096	1.2884	3.24	.006
X_1	-5.111	1.8700	2.73	.011
X_2	2.662	2.0796	1.28	.212
X_3	1.557	1.2811	1.22	.235
X_4	1.141	1.4712	0.78	.445
X_5	1.650	1.4994	1.10	.281
X_6	-1.248	1.2735	0.98	.336
X_7	0.436	0.3617	1.21	.239
X_8	0.962	1.1896	0.81	.426
X_9	1.289	1.9182	0.67	.508

$S = 3.503$ $R\text{-sq} = 40.8\%$ $R\text{-sq(adj.)} = 20.3\%$

Analysis of Variance

Source	DF	SS	MS	F	p
Regression	9	219.746	24.416	1.99	.0825
Error	26	319.004	12.269		
Total	35	538.750			

13.8 Displayed here is the Minitab output for a multiple regression analysis. Study the ANOVA table and the t ratios and use these to discuss the strengths of the regression model and the predictors. Does this model appear to fit the data well? From the information here, what recommendations would you make about the predictor variables in the model?

```
The regression equation is
```

$$Y = 34.7 + 0.0763\,X_1 + 0.00026X_2 - 1.12\,X_3$$

Predictor	Coef	Stdev	T	p
Constant	34.672	5.256	6.60	.000
X_1	0.07629	0.02234	3.41	.005
X_2	0.000259	0.001031	0.25	.805
X_3	-1.1212	0.9955	-1.13	.230

$S = 9.722$ $R\text{-sq} = 51.5\%$ $R\text{-sq(adj)} = 40.4\%$

Analysis of Variance

Source	DF	SS	MS	F	p
Regression	3	1306.99	435.66	4.61	.021
Error	13	1228.78	94.52		
Total	16	2535.77			

13.9 Using the data in Problem 13.5, develop a multiple regression model to predict per capita personal consumption by the consumption of paper, fish, and gasoline. Discuss the output and pay particular attention to the F test and the t tests.

13.10 Using the data from Problem 13.6, develop a multiple regression model to predict insider ownership from debt ratio and dividend payout. Comment on the strength of the model and the predictors by examining the ANOVA table and the t tests.

13.11 Develop a multiple regression model to predict y from x_1, x_2, and x_3 using the following data. Discuss the values of F and t.

y	x_1	x_2	x_3
5.3	44	11	401
3.6	24	40	219
5.1	46	13	394
4.9	38	18	362
7.0	61	3	453
6.4	58	5	468
5.2	47	14	386
4.6	36	24	357
2.9	19	52	206
4.0	31	29	301
3.8	24	37	243
3.8	27	36	228
4.8	36	21	342
5.4	50	11	421
5.8	55	9	445

13.12 Use the following data to develop a regression model to predict y from x_1 and x_2. Comment on the output. Develop a regression model to predict y from x_1 only. Compare the results of this model with those of the model using both predictors. What might you conclude by examining the output from both regression models?

y	x_1	x_2
28	12.6	134
43	11.4	126
45	11.5	143
49	11.1	152
57	10.4	143
68	9.6	147
74	9.8	128
81	8.4	119
82	8.8	130
86	8.9	135
101	8.1	141
112	7.6	123
114	7.8	121
119	7.4	129
124	6.4	135

13.13 Study the following Excel multiple regression output. How many predictors are in this model? How many observations? What is the equation of the regression line? Discuss the strength of the model in terms F. Which predictors, if any, are significant? Why or why not? Comment on the overall effectiveness of the model.

SUMMARY OUTPUT

Regression Statistics	
Multiple R	0.842
R Square	0.710
Adjusted R Square	0.630
Standard Error	109.430
Observations	15

ANOVA

	df	SS	MS	F	Significance F
Regression	3	321946.82	107315.6	8.96	0.0027
Residual	11	131723.20	11974.8		
Total	14	453670.00			

	Coefficients	Standard Error	t Stat	P-value
Intercept	657.053	167.46	3.92	0.0024
x Variable 1	5.7103	1.792	3.19	0.0087
x Variable 2	−0.4169	0.322	−1.29	0.2222
x Variable 3	−3.4715	1.443	−2.41	0.0349

13.3 RESIDUALS, STANDARD ERROR OF THE ESTIMATE, AND R^2

Three more statistical tools for examining the strength of a regression model are the residuals, the standard error of the estimate, and the coefficient of multiple determination.

Residuals

The **residual**, or error, of the regression model is *the difference between the y value and the predicted value, $\hat{y}$.*

$$\text{Residual} = y - \hat{y}$$

The residuals for a multiple regression model are solved for in the same manner as they are with simple regression. First, a predicted value, $\hat{y}$, is determined by entering the value for each independent variable for a given set of observations into the multiple regression equation and solving for $\hat{y}$. Next, the value of $y - \hat{y}$ is computed for each set of observations. Shown here are the calculations for the residuals of the first set of observations from Table 13.1. The predicted value of y for $x_1 = 1605$ and $x_2 = 35$ is

$$\hat{y} = 57.4 + .0177(1605) - .666(35) = 62.499$$

Actual value of $y = 63.0$
Residual $= y - \hat{y} = 63.0 - 62.499 = 0.501$

All residuals for the real estate data and the regression model displayed in Table 13.1 and Figure 13.3 are displayed in Table 13.2.

An examination of the residuals in Table 13.2 can reveal some information about the fit of the real estate regression model. The business researcher can observe the residuals and decide whether the errors are small enough to support the accuracy of the model. The house price figures are in units of $1,000. Two of the 23 residuals are more than 20.00, or more than $20,000 off in their prediction. On the other hand, two residuals are less than 1, or $1,000 off in their prediction.

Residuals are also helpful in locating outliers. **Outliers** are *data points that are apart, or far, from the mainstream of the other data.* They are sometimes data points that were mistakenly recorded or measured. Because every data point influences the regression model, outliers can exert an overly important influence on the model based on their distance from other points. In examining the residuals in Table 13.2 for outliers, the eighth residual listed

TABLE 13.2

Residuals for the Real Estate Regression Model

y	$\hat{y}$	$y - \hat{y}$
63.0	62.499	.501
65.1	71.485	−6.385
69.9	71.568	−1.668
76.8	78.639	−1.839
73.9	74.097	−.197
77.9	75.653	2.247
74.9	83.012	−8.112
78.0	105.699	−27.699
79.0	68.523	10.477
83.4	81.139	2.261
79.5	88.282	−8.782
83.9	91.335	−7.435
79.7	85.618	−5.918
84.5	95.391	−10.891
96.0	85.456	10.544
109.5	102.774	6.726
102.5	97.665	4.835
121.0	107.183	13.817
104.9	109.352	−4.452
128.0	111.230	16.770
129.0	105.061	23.939
117.9	134.415	−16.515
140.0	132.430	7.570

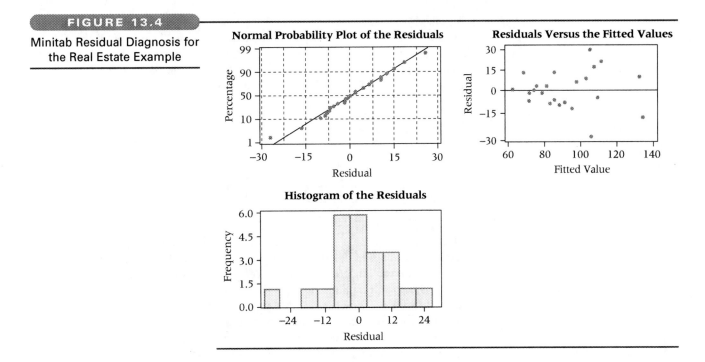

FIGURE 13.4

Minitab Residual Diagnosis for the Real Estate Example

is −27.699. This error indicates that the regression model was not nearly as successful in predicting house price on this particular house as it was with others (an error of more than $27,000). For whatever reason, this data point stands somewhat apart from other data points and may be considered an outlier.

Residuals are also useful in testing the assumptions underlying regression analysis. Figure 13.4 displays Minitab diagnostic techniques for the real estate example. In the top right is a graph of the residuals. Notice that residual variance seems to increase in the right half of the plot, indicating potential heteroscedasticity. As discussed in Chapter 12, one of the assumptions underlying regression analysis is that the error terms have homoscedasticity or homogeneous variance. That assumption might be violated in this example. The normal plot of residuals is nearly a straight line, indicating that the assumption of normally distributed error terms probably has not been violated.

SSE and Standard Error of the Estimate

One of the properties of a regression model is that the residuals sum to zero. As pointed out in Chapter 12, this property precludes the possibility of computing an "average" residual as a single measure of error. In an effort to compute a single statistic that can represent the error in a regression analysis, the zero-sum property can be overcome by *squaring the residuals and then summing the squares*. Such an operation produces the sum of squares of error (SSE).

The formula for computing the sum of squares error (SSE) for multiple regression is the same as it is for simple regression.

$$SSE = \Sigma(y - \hat{y})^2$$

For the real estate example, SSE can be computed by squaring and summing the residuals displayed in Table 13.2.

$$
\begin{aligned}
SSE = &[(.501)^2 + (-6.385)^2 + (-1.668)^2 + (-1.839)^2 \\
&+ (-.197)^2 + (2.247)^2 + (-8.112)^2 + (-27.699)^2 \\
&+ (10.477)^2 + (2.261)^2 + (-8.782)^2 + (-7.435)^2 \\
&+ (-5.918)^2 + (-10.891)^2 + (10.544)^2 + (6.726)^2 \\
&+ (4.835)^2 + (13.817)^2 + (-4.452)^2 + (16.770)^2 \\
&+ (23.939)^2 + (-16.515)^2 + (7.570)^2] \\
= &\ 2861.0
\end{aligned}
$$

SSE can also be obtained directly from the multiple regression computer output by selecting the value of SS (sum of squares) listed beside error. Shown here is the ANOVA portion of the output displayed in Figure 13.3, which is the result of a multiple regression analysis model developed to predict house prices. Note that the SS for error shown in the ANOVA table equals the value of $\Sigma(y - \hat{y})^2$ just computed (2861.0).

```
                                   SSE
                                  /
Analysis of Variance             /

Source        DF      SS       / MS        F        P
Regression    2      8189.7   /  4094.9   28.63    .000
Error         20    (2861.0)     143.1
Total         22    11050.7
```

SSE has limited usage as a measure of error. However, it is a tool used to solve for other, more useful measures. One of those is the **standard error of the estimate, s_e,** which is essentially *the standard deviation of residuals (error) for the regression model.* As explained in Chapter 12, an assumption underlying regression analysis is that the error terms are approximately normally distributed with a mean of zero. With this information and by the empirical rule, approximately 68% of the residuals should be within $\pm 1 s_e$ and 95% should be within $\pm 2 s_e$. This property makes the standard error of the estimate a useful tool in estimating how accurately a regression model is fitting the data.

The standard error of the estimate is computed by dividing SSE by the degrees of freedom of error for the model and taking the square root.

$$s_e = \sqrt{\frac{SSE}{n - k - 1}}$$

where

$n =$ number of observations
$k =$ number of independent variables

The value of s_e can be computed for the real estate example as follows.

$$s_e = \sqrt{\frac{SSE}{n - k - 1}} = \sqrt{\frac{2861}{23 - 2 - 1}} = 11.96$$

The standard error of the estimate, s_e, is usually given as standard output from regression analysis by computer software packages. The Minitab output displayed in Figure 13.3 contains the standard error of the estimate for the real estate example.

$$S = 11.96$$

By the empirical rule, approximately 68% of the residuals should be within $\pm 1 s_e = \pm 1(11.96) = \pm 11.96$. Because house prices are in units of $1,000, approximately 68% of the predictions are within $\pm 11.96(\$1,000)$, or $\pm\$11,960$. Examining the output displayed in Table 13.2, 18/23, or about 78%, of the residuals are within this span. According to the empirical rule, approximately 95% of the residuals should be within $\pm 2 s_e$ or $\pm 2(11.96) = \pm 23.92$. Further examination of the residual values in Table 13.2 shows that 21 of 23, or 91%, fall within this range. The business researcher can study the standard error of the estimate and these empirical rule–related ranges and decide whether the error of the regression model is sufficiently small to justify further use of the model.

Coefficient of Multiple Determination (R^2)

The **coefficient of multiple determination (R^2)** is analogous to the coefficient of determination (r^2) discussed in Chapter 12. R^2 represents *the proportion of variation of the dependent variable, y, accounted for by the independent variables in the regression model.* As with r^2, the range of possible values for R^2 is from 0 to 1. An R^2 of 0 indicates no relationship between the predictor variables in the model and y. An R^2 of 1 indicates that 100% of the variability of y has been accounted for by the predictors. Of course, it is desirable for R^2 to be high, indicating the strong predictability of a regression model. The coefficient of multiple determination can be calculated by the following formula:

$$R^2 = \frac{SSR}{SS_{yy}} = 1 - \frac{SSE}{SS_{yy}}$$

R^2 can be calculated in the real estate example by using the sum of squares regression (SSR), the sum of squares error (SSE), and sum of squares total (SS_{yy}) from the ANOVA portion of Figure 13.3.

```
                                            SS_yy
                                     SSE
                              SSR
Analysis of Variance
─────────────────────────────────────────────────────────────
Source        DF    SS            MS      F       p
Regression     2   (8189.7)     4094.9   28.63   .000
Error         20   (2861.0)      143.1
Total         22  (11050.7)
─────────────────────────────────────────────────────────────
```

$$R^2 = \frac{SSR}{SS_{yy}} = \frac{8189.7}{11050.7} = .741$$

or

$$R^2 = 1 - \frac{SSE}{SS_{yy}} = 1 - \frac{2861.0}{11050.7} = .741$$

In addition, virtually all statistical software packages print out R^2 as standard output with multiple regression analysis. A reexamination of Figure 13.3 reveals that R^2 is given as

$$R\text{-sq} = 74.1\%$$

This result indicates that a relatively high proportion of the variation of the dependent variable, house price, is accounted for by the independent variables in this regression model.

Adjusted R^2

As additional independent variables are added to a regression model, the value of R^2 cannot decrease, and in most cases it will increase. In the formulas for determining R^2,

$$R^2 = \frac{SSR}{SS_{yy}} = 1 - \frac{SSE}{SS_{yy}}$$

The value of SS_{yy} for a given set of observations will remain the same as independent variables are added to the regression analysis because SS_{yy} is the sum of squares for the dependent variable. Because additional independent variables are likely to increase SSR at least by some amount, the value of R^2 will probably increase for any additional independent variables.

However, sometimes additional independent variables add no *significant* information to the regression model, yet R^2 increases. R^2 therefore may yield an inflated figure. Statisticians have developed an **adjusted R^2** *to take into consideration both the additional information each new independent variable brings to the regression model and the changed degrees of freedom of regression.* Many standard statistical computer packages now compute and report adjusted R^2 as part of the output. The formula for computing adjusted R^2 is

$$\text{Adjusted } R^2 = 1 - \frac{SSE/(n - k - 1)}{SS_{yy}/(n - 1)}$$

The value of adjusted R^2 for the real estate example can be solved by using information from the ANOVA portion of the computer output in Figure 13.3.

THINKING CRITICALLY ABOUT STATISTICS IN BUSINESS TODAY

Assessing Property Values Using Multiple Regression

According to county assessor sources, Colorado state statute requires that all county assessors in the state value residential real property solely by a market approach. Furthermore, in the statute, it is stated that such a market approach will be based on a representative body of sales sufficient to set a pattern. No specifics on market analysis methods are given in the statutes, but there are several commonly used methods, including multiple regression. In the multiple regression approach, an attempt is made to develop a model to predict recent sales (dependent variable) by such property characteristics (independent variables) as location, lot size, building square feet, construction quality, property type (single family, condominium, townhouse), garage size, basement type, and other features. One county Web site states that "regression does not require strict similarity between property sales because it estimates the value contribution (coefficient) for each attribute. . . ." In producing a sound multiple regression model to predict property values, several models are developed, refined, and compared using the typical indicators of a good fit, such as R^2, standard error of

the estimate, F test for the overall model, and p-values associated with the t tests of significance for predictors. The final multiple regression model is then used in the estimation of property values by the appraiser, who enters into the regression model (equation) the specific measure of each independent (predictor) variable for a given property, resulting in a predicted appraised property value for tax purposes. The models are updated for currency and based on data that are never more than two years old.

Things to Ponder

1. How does the multiple regression method improve the validity of property value assessments over typical standard methods? Do you think it is more fair and equitable? If so, why?

2. Can you think of other similar possible applications of multiple regression in business?

Source: Douglas County, Colorado, Assessor's Office, at http:/www.douglas.co.us/assessor/Multiple_Regression.html, March 20, 2011, and Gunnison County Assessor's Office, at http://www.gunnisoncounty.org/assessor_assessment_process.html, March 20, 2011.

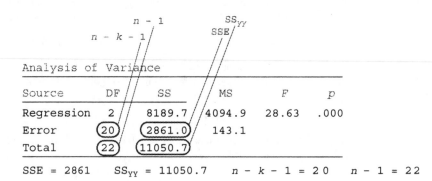

$$\text{SSE} = 2861 \qquad \text{SS}_{YY} = 11050.7 \qquad n - k - 1 = 20 \qquad n - 1 = 22$$

$$\text{Adj. } R^2 = 1 - \left[\frac{2861/20}{11050.7/22}\right] = 1 - .285 = .715$$

The standard Minitab regression output in Figure 13.3 contains the value of the adjusted R^2 already computed. For the real estate example, this value is shown as

$$R\text{-sq (adj.)} = 71.5\%$$

A comparison of R^2 (.741) with the adjusted R^2 (.715) for this example shows that the adjusted R^2 reduces the overall proportion of variation of the dependent variable accounted for by the independent variables by a factor of .026, or 2.6%. The gap between the R^2 and adjusted R^2 tends to increase as nonsignificant independent variables are added to the regression model. As n increases, the difference between R^2 and adjusted R^2 becomes less.

13.3 PROBLEMS

13.14 Study the Minitab output shown in Problem 13.7. Comment on the overall strength of the regression model in light of S, R^2, and adjusted R^2.

13.15 Study the Minitab output shown in Problem 13.8. Comment on the overall strength of the regression model in light of S, R^2, and adjusted R^2.

13.16 Using the regression output obtained by working Problem 13.5, comment on the overall strength of the regression model using S, R^2, and adjusted R^2.

13.17 Using the regression output obtained by working Problem 13.6, comment on the overall strength of the regression model using S, R^2, and adjusted R^2.

13.18 Using the regression output obtained by working Problem 13.11, comment on the overall strength of the regression model using S, R^2, and adjusted R^2.

13.19 Using the regression output obtained by working Problem 13.12, comment on the overall strength of the regression model using S, R^2, and adjusted R^2.

13.20 Study the Excel output shown in Problem 13.13. Comment on the overall strength of the regression model in light of S, R^2, and adjusted R^2.

13.21 Study the Minitab residual diagnostic output that follows. Discuss any potential problems with meeting the regression assumptions for this regression analysis based on the residual graphics.

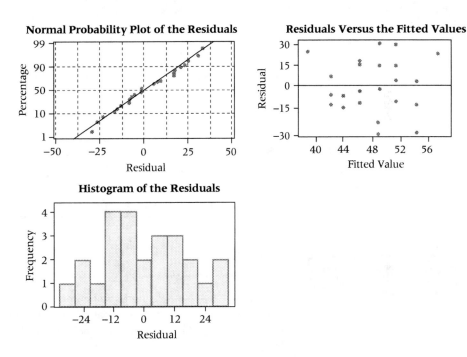

13.4 INTERPRETING MULTIPLE REGRESSION COMPUTER OUTPUT

A Reexamination of the Multiple Regression Output

Figure 13.5 shows again the Minitab multiple regression output for the real estate example. Many of the concepts discussed thus far in the chapter are highlighted. Note the following items:

1. The equation of the regression model
2. The ANOVA table with the F value for the overall test of the model
3. The t ratios, which test the significance of the regression coefficients
4. The value of SSE
5. The value of s_e
6. The value of R^2
7. The value of adjusted R^2

FIGURE 13.5

Annotated Version of the
Minitab Output of Regression
for the Real Estate Example

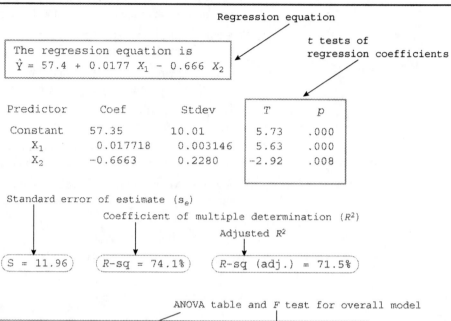

Regression equation

t tests of
regression coefficients

The regression equation is
$\hat{Y} = 57.4 + 0.0177 \, X_1 - 0.666 \, X_2$

Predictor	Coef	Stdev	T	p
Constant	57.35	10.01	5.73	.000
X_1	0.017718	0.003146	5.63	.000
X_2	-0.6663	0.2280	-2.92	.008

Standard error of estimate (s_e)

Coefficient of multiple determination (R^2)

Adjusted R^2

S = 11.96   R-sq = 74.1%   R-sq (adj.) = 71.5%

ANOVA table and *F* test for overall model

Analysis of Variance

Source	DF	SS	MS	F	p
Regression	2	8189.7	4094.9	28.63	.000
Error	20	2861.0	143.1		
Total	22	11050.7			

**DEMONSTRATION
PROBLEM 13.2**

Discuss the Excel multiple regression output for Demonstration Problem 13.1. Comment on the *F* test for the overall significance of the model, the *t* tests of the regression coefficients, and the values of s_e, R^2, and adjusted R^2.

Solution

This multiple regression analysis was done to predict the prime interest rate using the predictors of unemployment and personal saving. The equation of the regression model was presented in the solution of Demonstration Problem 13.1. Shown here is the complete multiple regression output from the Excel analysis of the data.

The value of *F* for this problem is 12.21, with a *p*-value of .0013, which is significant at $\alpha = .01$. On the basis of this information, the null hypothesis is rejected for the overall test of significance. At least one of the predictor variables is statistically significant from zero, and there is significant predictability of the prime interest rate by this model.

An examination of the *t* ratios reveals that personal savings is a significant predictor at $\alpha = .001$ ($t = 4.86$ with a *p*-value of .0004) and that unemployment rates is a significant predictor at $\alpha = .05$ ($t = -2.85$ with a *p*-value of .0147). The positive signs on the regression coefficient and the *t* value for personal savings indicate that as personal savings increase, the prime interest rate tends to get higher. On the other hand, the negative signs on the regression coefficient and the *t* value for unemployment rates indicate that as the unemployment rate increases, the prime interest rate tends to decrease.

The standard error of the estimate is $s_e = 1.890$, indicating that approximately 68% of the residuals are within ± 1.890. An examination of the Excel-produced residuals shows that actually 11 out of 15, or 73.3%, fall in this interval. Approximately 95%

of the residuals should be within $\pm2(1.890) = \pm3.780$, and an examination of the Excel-produced residuals shows that 14 out of 15, or 93.3%, of the residuals are within this interval.

R^2 for this regression analysis is .671, or 67.1%. The adjusted R^2 is .616, indicating that there is some inflation in the R^2 value. Overall, there is modest predictability in this model.

SUMMARY OUTPUT

Regression Statistics

Multiple R	0.819
R Square	0.671
Adjusted R Square	0.616
Standard Error	1.890
Observations	15

ANOVA

	df	SS	MS	F	Significance F
Regression	2	87.2388	43.6194	12.21	0.0013
Residual	12	42.8539	3.5712		
Total	14	130.0927			

	Coefficients	Standard Error	t Stat	P-value
Intercept	7.4196	1.943	3.82	0.0024
Unemployment Rates	−1.2092	0.425	−2.85	0.0147
Personal Savings	1.3993	0.288	4.86	0.0004

RESIDUAL OUTPUT

Observation	Predicted Prime Interest Rate	Residuals
1	10.9430	3.9070
2	12.6236	−0.5836
3	9.5901	−1.2601
4	10.4243	−1.1043
5	9.7437	0.2663
6	8.5657	−2.3157
7	7.3200	−0.1700
8	7.7466	0.5234
9	9.3946	−1.0446
10	6.6409	2.5891
11	5.3040	−0.6340
12	5.5268	−1.1868
13	5.2158	2.7442
14	6.1435	−1.0535
15	3.9276	−0.6776

13.4 PROBLEMS

13.22 Study the Minitab regression output that follows. How many predictors are there? What is the equation of the regression model? Using the key statistics discussed in this chapter, discuss the strength of the model and the predictors.

```
Regression Analysis: Y versus X₁, X₂, X₃, X₄

The regression equation is
Y = - 55.9 + 0.0105 X₁ - 0.107 X₂  + 0.579 X₃ - 0.870 X₄
Predictor      Coef    SE Coef       T       P
 Constant     -55.93     24.22    -2.31   0.025
       X₁     0.01049   0.02100    0.50   0.619
       X₂    -0.10720   0.03503   -3.06   0.003
       X₃     0.57922   0.07633    7.59   0.000
       X₄    -0.8695    0.1498    -5.81   0.000
S = 9.025   R-Sq = 80.2%   R-Sq(adj) = 78.7%
```

Analysis of Variance

Source	DF	SS	MS	F	p
Regression	2	18088.5	4522.1	55.52	0.000
Residual Error	55	4479.7	81.4		
Total	59	22568.2			

13.23 Study the Excel regression output that follows. How many predictors are there? What is the equation of the regression model? Using the key statistics discussed in this chapter, discuss the strength of the model and its predictors.

SUMMARY OUTPUT

Regression Statistics

Multiple R	0.814
R Square	0.663
Adjusted R Square	0.636
Standard Error	51.761
Observations	28

ANOVA

	df	SS	MS	F	Significance F
Regression	2	131567.02	65783.51	24.55	0.0000013
Residual	25	66979.65	2679.19		
Total	27	198546.68			

	Coefficients	Standard Error	t Stat	P-value
Intercept	203.3937	67.518	3.01	0.0059
X_1	1.1151	0.528	2.11	0.0448
X_2	−2.2115	0.567	−3.90	0.0006

Are You Going to Hate Your New Job?

In the Decision Dilemma, several variables are considered in attempting to determine whether a person will like his or her new job. Four predictor (independent) variables are given with the data set: relationship with supervisor, overall quality of work environment, total hours worked per week, and opportunities for advancement. Other possible variables might include openness of work culture, amount of pressure, how the interviewee is treated during the interview, availability of flexible scheduling, size of office, amount of time allotted for lunch, availability of management, interesting work, and many others.

Using the data that are given, a multiple regression model can be developed to predict job satisfaction from the four independent variables. Such an analysis allows the business researcher to study the entire data set in one model rather than

constructing four different simple regression models, one for each independent variable. In the multiple regression model, job satisfaction is the dependent variable. There are 19 observations. The Excel regression output for this problem follows.

The test for overall significance of the model produced an F of 87.79 with a p-value of .000000001 (significant at $\alpha = .00000001$). The R^2 of .962 and adjusted R^2 of .951 indicate very strong predictability in the model. The standard error of the estimate, 5.141, can be viewed in light of the job satisfaction values that ranged from 10 to 95 and the residuals, which are not shown here. Fourteen of the 19 residuals (73.7%) are within the standard error of the estimate. Examining the t statistics and their associated p-values reveals that two independent variables, relationship with supervisor ($t = 5.33$, p-value = .0001), and overall quality of work environment ($t = 2.73$, p-value = .0162) are significant predictors at $\alpha = .05$. Judging by their large p-values, it appears that total hours worked per week and opportunities for advancement are not good predictors of job satisfaction.

SUMMARY OUTPUT

Regression Statistics

Multiple R	0.981
R Square	0.962
Adjusted R Square	0.951
Standard Error	5.141
Observations	19

ANOVA

	df	SS	MS	F	Significance F
Regression	4	9282.569	2320.642	87.79	0.000000001
Residual	14	370.062	26.433		
Total	18	9652.632			

	Coefficients	Standard Error	t Stat	P-value
Intercept	−1.469	8.116	−0.18	0.8590
Relationship with Supervisor	1.391	0.261	5.33	0.0001
Overall Quality of Work Environment	0.317	0.116	2.73	0.0162
Total Hours Worked per Week	0.043	0.121	0.36	0.7263
Opportunities for Advancement	−0.094	0.102	−0.92	0.3711

ETHICAL CONSIDERATIONS

Multiple regression analysis can be used either intentionally or unintentionally in questionable or unethical ways. When degrees of freedom are small, an inflated value of R^2 can be obtained, leading to overenthusiastic expectations about the predictability of a regression model. To prevent this type of reliance, a researcher should take into account the nature of the data, the variables, and the value of the adjusted R^2.

Another misleading aspect of multiple regression can be the tendency of researchers to assume cause-and-effect relationships between the dependent variable and predictors. Just because independent variables produce a significant R^2 does not necessarily mean those variables are causing the deviation of the *y* values. Indeed, some other force not in the model may be driving both the independent variables and the dependent variable over the range of values being studied.

Some people use the estimates of the regression coefficients to compare the worth of the predictor variables; the larger the coefficient, the greater is its worth. At least two problems can be found in this approach. The first is that most variables are measured in different units. Thus, regression coefficient weights are partly a function of the unit of measurement of the variable. Second, if multicollinearity (discussed in Chapter 14) is present, the interpretation of the regression coefficients is questionable. In addition, the presence of multicollinearity raises several issues about the interpretation of other regression output. Researchers who ignore this problem are at risk of presenting spurious results.

Another danger in using regression analysis is in the extrapolation of the model to values beyond the range of values used to derive the model. A regression model that fits data within a given range does not necessarily fit data outside that range. One of the uses of regression analysis is in the area of forecasting. Users need to be aware that what has occurred in the past is not guaranteed to continue to occur in the future. Unscrupulous and sometimes even well-intentioned business decision makers can use regression models to project conclusions about the future that have little or no basis. The receiver of such messages should be cautioned that regression models may lack validity outside the range of values in which the models were developed.

SUMMARY

Multiple regression analysis is a statistical tool in which a mathematical model is developed in an attempt to predict a dependent variable by two or more independent variables or in which at least one predictor is nonlinear. Because doing multiple regression analysis by hand is extremely tedious and time-consuming, it is almost always done on a computer.

The standard output from a multiple regression analysis is similar to that of simple regression analysis. A regression equation is produced with a constant that is analogous to the *y*-intercept in simple regression and with estimates of the regression coefficients that are analogous to the estimate of the slope in simple regression. An *F* test for the overall model is computed to determine whether at least one of the regression coefficients is significantly different from zero. This F value is usually displayed in an ANOVA table, which is part of the regression output. The ANOVA table also contains the sum of squares of error and sum of squares of regression, which are used to compute other statistics in the model.

Most multiple regression computer output contains t values, which are used to determine the significance of the regression coefficients. Using these t values, statisticians can make decisions about including or excluding variables from the model.

Residuals, standard error of the estimate, and R^2 are also standard computer regression output with multiple regression. The coefficient of determination for simple regression models is denoted r^2, whereas for multiple regression it is R^2. The interpretation of residuals, standard error of the estimate, and R^2 in multiple regression is similar to that in simple regression. Because R^2 can be inflated with nonsignificant variables in the mix, an adjusted R^2 is often computed. Unlike R^2, adjusted R^2 takes into account the degrees of freedom and the number of observations.

KEY TERMS

 Flash Cards

adjusted R^2
coefficient of multiple
  determination (R^2)

dependent variable
independent variable
least squares analysis
multiple regression
outliers

partial regression coefficient
R^2
residual
response plane
response surface

response variable
standard error of the
  estimate (s_e)
sum of squares of error (SSE)

FORMULAS

The F value

$$F = \frac{MS_{reg}}{MS_{err}} = \frac{SS_{reg}/df_{reg}}{SS_{err}/df_{err}} = \frac{SSR/k}{SSE/(N - k - 1)}$$

Sum of squares of error

$$SSE = \Sigma(y - \hat{y})^2$$

Standard error of the estimate

$$s_e = \sqrt{\frac{SSE}{n - k - 1}}$$

Coefficient of multiple determination

$$R^2 = \frac{SSR}{SS_{yy}} = 1 - \frac{SSE}{SS_{yy}}$$

Adjusted R^2

$$\text{Adjusted } R^2 = 1 - \frac{SSE/(n - k - 1)}{SS_{yy}/(n - 1)}$$

SUPPLEMENTARY PROBLEMS

CALCULATING THE STATISTICS

13.24 Use the following data to develop a multiple regression model to predict y from x_1 and x_2. Discuss the output, including comments about the overall strength of the model, the significance of the regression coefficients, and other indicators of model fit.

y	x_1	x_2
198	29	1.64
214	71	2.81
211	54	2.22
219	73	2.70
184	67	1.57
167	32	1.63
201	47	1.99
204	43	2.14
190	60	2.04
222	32	2.93
197	34	2.15

13.25 Given here are the data for a dependent variable, y, and independent variables. Use these data to develop a regression model to predict y. Discuss the output.

y	x_1	x_2	x_3
14	51	16.4	56
17	48	17.1	64
29	29	18.2	53
32	36	17.9	41
54	40	16.5	60
86	27	17.1	55
117	14	17.8	71
120	17	18.2	48
194	16	16.9	60
203	9	18.0	77
217	14	18.9	90
235	11	18.5	67

TESTING YOUR UNDERSTANDING

13.26 The U.S. Bureau of Mines produces data on the price of minerals. Shown here are the average prices per year for several minerals over a decade. Use these data and multiple regression to produce a model to predict the average price of gold from the other variables. Comment on the results of the process.

Gold ($ per oz.)	Copper (cents per lb.)	Silver ($ per oz.)	Aluminum (cents per lb.)
161.1	64.2	4.4	39.8
308.0	93.3	11.1	61.0
613.0	101.3	20.6	71.6
460.0	84.2	10.5	76.0
376.0	72.8	8.0	76.0
424.0	76.5	11.4	77.8
361.0	66.8	8.1	81.0
318.0	67.0	6.1	81.0
368.0	66.1	5.5	81.0
448.0	82.5	7.0	72.3
438.0	120.5	6.5	110.1
382.6	130.9	5.5	87.8

13.27 The Shipbuilders Council of America in Washington, D.C., publishes data about private shipyards. Among the variables reported by this organization are the employment figures (per 1000), the number of naval vessels under construction, and the number of repairs or conversions done to commercial ships (in $ millions). Shown here are the data for these three variables over a seven-year period. Use the data to develop a regression model to predict private shipyard employment from number of naval vessels under construction and repairs or conversions of commercial ships. Comment on the regression model and its strengths and its weaknesses.

	Commercial Ship	
Employment	**Naval Vessels**	**Repairs or Conversions**
133.4	108	431
177.3	99	1335
143.0	105	1419
142.0	111	1631
130.3	100	852
120.6	85	847
120.4	79	806

13.28 The U.S. Bureau of Labor Statistics produces consumer price indexes for several different categories. Shown here are the percentage changes in consumer price indexes over a period of 20 years for food, shelter, apparel, and fuel oil. Also displayed are the percentage changes in consumer price indexes for all commodities. Use these data and multiple regression to develop a

model that attempts to predict all commodities by the other four variables. Comment on the result of this analysis.

All Commodities	Food	Shelter	Apparel	Fuel Oil
.9	1.0	2.0	1.6	3.7
.6	1.3	.8	.9	2.7
.9	.7	1.6	.4	2.6
.9	1.6	1.2	1.3	2.6
1.2	1.3	1.5	.9	2.1
1.1	2.2	1.9	1.1	2.4
2.6	5.0	3.0	2.5	4.4
1.9	.9	3.6	4.1	7.2
3.5	3.5	4.5	5.3	6.0
4.7	5.1	8.3	5.8	6.7
4.5	5.7	8.9	4.2	6.6
3.6	3.1	4.2	3.2	6.2
3.0	4.2	4.6	2.0	3.3
7.4	14.5	4.7	3.7	4.0
11.9	14.3	9.6	7.4	9.3
8.8	8.5	9.9	4.5	12.0
4.3	3.0	5.5	3.7	9.5
5.8	6.3	6.6	4.5	9.6
7.2	9.9	10.2	3.6	8.4
11.3	11.0	13.9	4.3	9.2

13.29 The U.S. Department of Agriculture publishes data annually on various selected farm products. Shown here are the unit production figures (in millions of bushels) for three farm products for 10 years during a 20-year period. Use these data and multiple regression analysis to predict corn production by the production of soybeans and wheat. Comment on the results.

Corn	Soybeans	Wheat
4152	1127	1352
6639	1798	2381
4175	1636	2420
7672	1861	2595
8876	2099	2424
8226	1940	2091
7131	1938	2108
4929	1549	1812
7525	1924	2037
7933	1922	2739

13.30 The American Chamber of Commerce Researchers Association compiles cost-of-living indexes for selected metropolitan areas. Shown here are cost-of-living indexes for 25 different cities on five different items for a recent year. Use the data to develop a regression model to predict the grocery cost-of-living index by the indexes of housing, utilities, transportation, and healthcare. Discuss the results, highlighting both the significant and nonsignificant predictors.

City	Grocery Items	Housing	Utilities	Transportation	Healthcare
Albany	108.3	106.8	127.4	89.1	107.5
Albuquerque	96.3	105.2	98.8	100.9	102.1
Augusta, GA	96.2	88.8	115.6	102.3	94.0
Austin	98.0	83.9	87.7	97.4	94.9
Baltimore	106.0	114.1	108.1	112.8	111.5
Buffalo	103.1	117.3	127.6	107.8	100.8
Colorado Springs	94.5	88.5	74.6	93.3	102.4
Dallas	105.4	98.9	108.9	110.0	106.8
Denver	91.5	108.3	97.2	105.9	114.3
Des Moines	94.3	95.1	111.4	105.7	96.2
El Paso	102.9	94.6	90.9	104.2	91.4
Indianapolis	96.0	99.7	92.1	102.7	97.4
Jacksonville	96.1	90.4	96.0	106.0	96.1
Kansas City	89.8	92.4	96.3	95.6	93.6
Knoxville	93.2	88.0	91.7	91.6	82.3
Los Angeles	103.3	211.3	75.6	102.1	128.5
Louisville	94.6	91.0	79.4	102.4	88.4
Memphis	99.1	86.2	91.1	101.1	85.5
Miami	100.3	123.0	125.6	104.3	137.8
Minneapolis	92.8	112.3	105.2	106.0	107.5
Mobile	99.9	81.1	104.9	102.8	92.2
Nashville	95.8	107.7	91.6	98.1	90.9
New Orleans	104.0	83.4	122.2	98.2	87.0
Oklahoma City	98.2	79.4	103.4	97.3	97.1
Phoenix	95.7	98.7	96.3	104.6	115.2

INTERPRETING THE OUTPUT

13.31 Shown here are the data for y and three predictors, x_1, x_2, and x_3. A multiple regression analysis has been done on these data; the Minitab results are given. Comment on the outcome of the analysis in light of the data.

y	x_1	x_2	x_3
94	21	1	204
97	25	0	198
93	22	1	184
95	27	0	200
90	29	1	182
91	20	1	159
91	18	1	147
94	25	0	196
98	26	0	228
99	24	0	242
90	28	1	162
92	23	1	180
96	25	0	219

Regression Analysis: Y versus X_1, X_2, X_3
The regression equation is
Y = 87.9 − 0.256 X_1 − 2.71 X_2 + 0.0706 X_3

Predictor	Coef	SE Coef	T	P
Constant	87.890	3.445	25.51	0.000
X1	−0.25612	0.08317	−3.08	0.013
X2	−2.7137	0.7306	−3.71	0.005
X3	0.07061	0.01353	5.22	0.001

S = 0.850311   R-Sq = 94.1%   R-Sq(adj) = 92.1%

Analysis of Variance

Source	DF	SS	MS	F	p
Regression	3	103.185	34.395	47.57	0.000
Residual Error	9	6.507	0.723		
Total	12	109.692			

13.32 Minitab residual diagnostic output from the multiple regression analysis for the data given in Problem 13.30 follows. Discuss any potential problems with meeting the regression assumptions for this regression analysis based on the residual graphics.

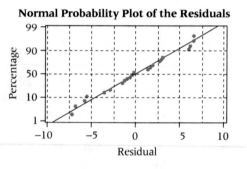

Normal Probability Plot of the Residuals

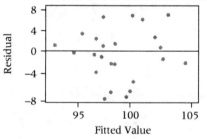

Residuals Versus the Fitted Values

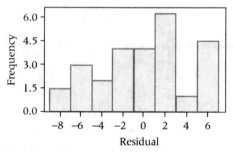

Histogram of the Residuals

ANALYZING THE DATABASES

1. Use the Manufacturing database to develop a multiple regression model to predict Cost of Materials by Number of Employees, New Capital Expenditures, Value Added by Manufacture, and End-of-Year Inventories. Discuss the results of the analysis.

2. Develop a regression model using the Financial database. Use Total Revenues, Total Assets, Return on Equity, Earnings Per Share, Average Yield, and Dividends Per Share to predict the average P/E ratio for a company. How strong is the model? Which variables seem to be the best predictors?

3. Using the International Stock Market database, develop a multiple regression model to predict the Nikkei by the DJIA, the Nasdaq, the S&P 500, the Hang Seng, the FTSE 100, and the IPC. Discuss the outcome, including the model, the strength of the model, and the strength of the predictors.

4. Develop a multiple regression model to predict Annual Food Spending by Annual Household Income and Non-Mortgage Household Debt using the Consumer Food database. How strong is the model? Which of the two predictors seems to be stronger? Why?

CASE

STARBUCKS INTRODUCES DEBIT CARD

Starbucks is a resounding restaurant success story. Beginning with its first coffee house in 1971, Starbucks has grown to more than 11,000 U.S. locations. Opening up its first international outlet in the mid 1990s, Starbucks now operates in more than 50 countries outside of North America. Besides selling beverages, pastries, confections, and coffee-related accessories and equipment at its retail outlets, Starbucks also purchases and roasts high-quality coffee beans in several locations. The company's objective is to become the most recognized and respected brand in the world. Starbucks maintains a strong environmental orientation and is committed to taking a leadership position environmentally. In addition, the company has won awards for corporate social responsibility through its community-building programs, its strong commitment to its origins (coffee producers, family, community), and the Starbucks Foundation, which is dedicated to creating hope, discovery, and opportunity in the communities where Starbucks resides.

In November 2001, Starbucks launched its prepaid (debit) Starbucks Card. The card, which holds between $5 and $500, can be used at virtually any Starbucks location. The card was so popular when it first was released that many stores ran out. By mid-2002, Starbucks had activated more than 5 million of these cards. The Starbucks Card has surpassed the $2.5 billion mark for total activations and reloads since its introduction. As customers "reload" the cards, it appears they are placing more money on them than the initial value of the card.

Starbucks has gone on to promote their Starbucks Card as a flexible marketing tool that can be used by individuals as a gift of thanks and appreciation for friendship or service and can be used by companies to reward loyal customers and as an incentive to employees.

Discussion

1. Starbucks enjoyed considerable success with its debit cards, which they sell for $5 to $500. Suppose Starbucks management wants to study the reasons why some people purchase debit cards with higher prepaid amounts than do other people. Suppose a study of 25 randomly selected prepaid

card purchasers is taken. Respondents are asked the amount of the prepaid card, the customer's age, the number of days per month the customer makes a purchase at Starbucks, the number of cups of coffee the customer drinks per day, and the customer's income. The data follow. Using these data, develop a multiple regression model to study how well the amount of the prepaid card can be predicted by the other variables and which variables seem to be more promising in doing the prediction. What sales implications might be evident from this analysis?

Amount of Prepaid Card ($)	Age	Days per Month at Starbucks	Cups of Coffee per Day	Income ($1,000)
5	25	4	1	20
25	30	12	5	35
10	27	10	4	30
5	42	8	5	30
15	29	11	8	25
50	25	12	5	60
10	50	8	3	30
15	45	6	5	35
5	32	16	7	25
5	23	10	1	20
20	40	18	5	40
35	35	12	3	40
40	28	10	3	50
15	33	12	2	30
200	40	15	5	80
15	37	3	1	30
40	51	10	8	35
5	20	8	4	25
30	26	15	5	35
100	38	19	10	45
30	27	12	3	35
25	29	14	6	35
25	34	10	4	45
50	30	6	3	55
15	22	8	5	30

2. Suppose marketing wants to be able to profile frequent visitors to a Starbucks store. Using the same data set already provided, develop a multiple regression model to predict Days per month at Starbucks by Age, Income, and Number of cups of coffee per day. How strong is the model? Which particular independent variables seem to have more promise in predicting how many days per month a customer visits Starbucks? What marketing implications might be evident from this analysis?

3. Over the past decade or so, Starbucks has grown quite rapidly. As they add stores and increase the number of drinks, their sales revenues increase. In reflecting about this growth, think about some other variables that might be related to the increase in Starbucks sales revenues. Some data for the past seven years on the number of Starbucks stores (worldwide), approximate sales revenue (in $ millions), number of different drinks sold, and average weekly earnings of U.S. production workers are given here. Most figures are approximate. Develop a multiple regression model to predict sales revenue by number of drinks sold, number of stores, and average weekly earnings. How strong is the model? What are the key predictors, if any? How might this analysis help Starbucks management in attempting to determine what drives sales revenues?

Sales Year	Revenue	Number of Stores	Number of Drinks	Average Weekly Earnings
1	400	676	15	386
2	700	1015	15	394
3	1000	1412	18	407
4	1350	1886	22	425
5	1650	2135	27	442
6	2200	3300	27	457
7	2600	4709	30	474

Source: Adapted from Shirley Leung, "Starbucks May Indeed Be a Robust Staple," *The Wall Street Journal*, July 26, 2002, p. B4; James Peters, "Starbucks' Growth Still Hot; Gift Card Jolts Chain's Sales," *Nation's Restaurant News*, February 11, 2002, pp. 1–2. Starbuck's Web site (February, 2008) at: http://www/starbucks.com/aboutus/Company_Factsheet.pdf.

USING THE COMPUTER

EXCEL

▨ Excel has the capability of doing multiple regression analysis. The commands are essentially the same as those for simple regression except that the x range of data may include several columns. Excel will determine the number of predictor variables from the number of columns entered in to **Input X Range**.

▨ Begin by selecting the **Data** tab on the Excel worksheet. From the **Analysis** panel at the right top of the **Data** tab worksheet, click on **Data Analysis**. If your Excel worksheet does not show the **Data Analysis** option, then you can load it as an add-in following directions given in Chapter 2. From the **Data Analysis** pulldown menu, select **Regression**. In the **Regression** dialog box, input the location of the y values in **Input Y Range**. Input the location of the x values in **Input X Range**. Input **Labels** and input **Confidence Level**. To pass the line through the origin, check **Constant is Zero**. To printout the raw residuals, check **Residuals**. To printout residuals converted to z scores, check **Standardized Residuals**. For a plot of the residuals, check **Residual Plots**. For a plot of the line through the points check **Line Fit Plots**.

▨ Standard output includes R, R^2, s_e, and an ANOVA table with the F test, the slope and intercept, t statistics with associated p-values, and any optionally requested output, such as graphs or residuals.

MINITAB

▨ Multiple regression analysis can be performed by Minitab using the following commands. Select **Stat** from the menu bar. Select **Regression** from the **Stat** pulldown menu. Select **Regression** from the **Regression** pulldown menu. Place the column name or column location of the y variable in **Response**. Place the column name(s) or column location(s) of the x variable(s) in **Predictors**. Select **Graphs** for options relating to residual plots. Use this option and check **Four in one** to produce the residual diagnostic plots shown in the chapter. Select **Options** for confidence intervals and prediction intervals. Select **Results** for controlling the regression analysis output. Select **Storage** to store fits and/or residuals.

▨ To obtain a fitted-line plot, select **Stat** from the menu bar. Select **Regression** from the **Stat** pulldown menu. Select **Fitted Line Plot** from the **Regression** pulldown menu. In the Fitted Line Plot dialog box, place the column name or column location of the y variable in **Response(Y)**. Place the column name(s) or column location(s) of the x variable(s) in **Response(X)**. Check **Type of Regression Model** as **Linear**, **Quadratic**, or **Cubic**. Select **Graphs** for options relating to residual plots. Use this option and check **Four in one** to produce the residual diagnostic plots shown in the chapter. Select **Options** for confidence intervals and prediction intervals. Select **Storage** to store fits and/or residuals.

TABLE A.1
Random Numbers

12651	61646	11769	75109	86996	97669	25757	32535	07122	76763
81769	74436	02630	72310	45049	18029	07469	42341	98173	79260
36737	98863	77240	76251	00654	64688	09343	70278	67331	98729
82861	54371	76610	94934	72748	44124	05610	53750	95938	01485
21325	15732	24127	37431	09723	63529	73977	95218	96074	42138
74146	47887	62463	23045	41490	07954	22597	60012	98866	90959
90759	64410	54179	66075	61051	75385	51378	08360	95946	95547
55683	98078	02238	91540	21219	17720	87817	41705	95785	12563
79686	17969	76061	83748	55920	83612	41540	86492	06447	60568
70333	00201	86201	69716	78185	62154	77930	67663	29529	75116
14042	53536	07779	04157	41172	36473	42123	43929	50533	33437
59911	08256	06596	48416	69770	68797	56080	14223	59199	30162
62368	62623	62742	14891	39247	52242	98832	69533	91174	57979
57529	97751	54976	48957	74599	08759	78494	52785	68526	64618
15469	90574	78033	66885	13936	42117	71831	22961	94225	31816
18625	23674	53850	32827	81647	80820	00420	63555	74489	80141
74626	68394	88562	70745	23701	45630	65891	58220	35442	60414
11119	16519	27384	90199	79210	76965	99546	30323	31664	22845
41101	17336	48951	53674	17880	45260	08575	49321	36191	17095
32123	91576	84221	78902	82010	30847	62329	63898	23268	74283
26091	68409	69704	82267	14751	13151	93115	01437	56945	89661
67680	79790	48462	59278	44185	29616	76531	19589	83139	28454
15184	19260	14073	07026	25264	08388	27182	22557	61501	67481
58010	45039	57181	10238	36874	28546	37444	80824	63981	39942
56425	53996	86245	32623	78858	08143	60377	42925	42815	11159
82630	84066	13592	60642	17904	99718	63432	88642	37858	25431
14927	40909	23900	48761	44860	92467	31742	87142	03607	32059
23740	22505	07489	85986	74420	21744	97711	36648	35620	97949
32990	97446	03711	63824	07953	85965	87089	11687	92414	67257
05310	24058	91946	78437	34365	82469	12430	84754	19354	72745
21839	39937	27534	88913	49055	19218	47712	67677	51889	70926
08833	42549	93981	94051	28382	83725	72643	64233	97252	17133
58336	11139	47479	00931	91560	95372	97642	33856	54825	55680
62032	91144	75478	47431	52726	30289	42411	91886	51818	78292
45171	30557	53116	04118	58301	24375	65609	85810	18620	49198
91611	62656	60128	35609	63698	78356	50682	22505	01692	36291
55472	63819	86314	49174	93582	73604	78614	78849	23096	72825
18573	09729	74091	53994	10970	86557	65661	41854	26037	53296
60866	02955	90288	82136	83644	94455	06560	78029	98768	71296
45043	55608	82767	60890	74646	79485	13619	98868	40857	19415
17831	09737	79473	75945	28394	79334	70577	38048	03607	06932
40137	03981	07585	18128	11178	32601	27994	05641	22600	86064
77776	31343	14576	97706	16039	47517	43300	59080	80392	63189
69605	44104	40103	95635	05635	81673	68657	09559	23510	95875
19916	52934	26499	09821	97331	80993	61299	36979	73599	35055
02606	58552	07678	56619	65325	30705	99582	53390	46357	13244
65183	73160	87131	35530	47946	09854	18080	02321	05809	04893
10740	98914	44916	11322	89717	88189	30143	52687	19420	60061
98642	89822	71691	51573	83666	61642	46683	33761	47542	23551
60139	25601	93663	25547	02654	94829	48672	28736	84994	13071

TABLE A.2
Binomial Probability Distribution

n = 1

Probability

x	.1	.2	.3	.4	.5	.6	.7	.8	.9
0	.900	.800	.700	.600	.500	.400	.300	.200	.100
1	.100	.200	.300	.400	.500	.600	.700	.800	.900

n = 2

Probability

x	.1	.2	.3	.4	.5	.6	.7	.8	.9
0	.810	.640	.490	.360	.250	.160	.090	.040	.010
1	.180	.320	.420	.480	.500	.480	.420	.320	.180
2	.010	.040	.090	.160	.250	.360	.490	.640	.810

n = 3

Probability

x	.1	.2	.3	.4	.5	.6	.7	.8	.9
0	.729	.512	.343	.216	.125	.064	.027	.008	.001
1	.243	.384	.441	.432	.375	.288	.189	.096	.027
2	.027	.096	.189	.288	.375	.432	.441	.384	.243
3	.001	.008	.027	.064	.125	.216	.343	.512	.729

n = 4

Probability

x	.1	.2	.3	.4	.5	.6	.7	.8	.9
0	.656	.410	.240	.130	.063	.026	.008	.002	.000
1	.292	.410	.412	.346	.250	.154	.076	.026	.004
2	.049	.154	.265	.346	.375	.346	.265	.154	.049
3	.004	.026	.076	.154	.250	.346	.412	.410	.292
4	.000	.002	.008	.026	.063	.130	.240	.410	.656

n = 5

Probability

x	.1	.2	.3	.4	.5	.6	.7	.8	.9
0	.590	.328	.168	.078	.031	.010	.002	.000	.000
1	.328	.410	.360	.259	.156	.077	.028	.006	.000
2	.073	.205	.309	.346	.313	.230	.132	.051	.008
3	.008	.051	.132	.230	.313	.346	.309	.205	.073
4	.000	.006	.028	.077	.156	.259	.360	.410	.328
5	.000	.000	.002	.010	.031	.078	.168	.328	.590

n = 6

Probability

x	.1	.2	.3	.4	.5	.6	.7	.8	.9
0	.531	.262	.118	.047	.016	.004	.001	.000	.000
1	.354	.393	.303	.187	.094	.037	.010	.002	.000
2	.098	.246	.324	.311	.234	.138	.060	.015	.001
3	.015	.082	.185	.276	.313	.276	.185	.082	.015
4	.001	.015	.060	.138	.234	.311	.324	.246	.098
5	.000	.002	.010	.037	.094	.187	.303	.393	.354
6	.000	.000	.001	.004	.016	.047	.118	.262	.531

(*Continued*)

n = 7

x	Probability								
	.1	.2	.3	.4	.5	.6	.7	.8	.9
0	.478	.210	.082	.028	.008	.002	.000	.000	.000
1	.372	.367	.247	.131	.055	.017	.004	.000	.000
2	.124	.275	.318	.261	.164	.077	.025	.004	.000
3	.023	.115	.227	.290	.273	.194	.097	.029	.003
4	.003	.029	.097	.194	.273	.290	.227	.115	.023
5	.000	.004	.025	.077	.164	.261	.318	.275	.124
6	.000	.000	.004	.017	.055	.131	.247	.367	.372
7	.000	.000	.000	.002	.008	.028	.082	.210	.478

n = 8

x	Probability								
	.1	.2	.3	.4	.5	.6	.7	.8	.9
0	.430	.168	.058	.017	.004	.001	.000	.000	.000
1	.383	.336	.198	.090	.031	.008	.001	.000	.000
2	.149	.294	.296	.209	.109	.041	.010	.001	.000
3	.033	.147	.254	.279	.219	.124	.047	.009	.000
4	.005	.046	.136	.232	.273	.232	.136	.046	.005
5	.000	.009	.047	.124	.219	.279	.254	.147	.033
6	.000	.001	.010	.041	.109	.209	.296	.294	.149
7	.000	.000	.001	.008	.031	.090	.198	.336	.383
8	.000	.000	.000	.001	.004	.017	.058	.168	.430

n = 9

x	Probability								
	.1	.2	.3	.4	.5	.6	.7	.8	.9
0	.387	.134	.040	.010	.002	.000	.000	.000	.000
1	.387	.302	.156	.060	.018	.004	.000	.000	.000
2	.172	.302	.267	.161	.070	.021	.004	.000	.000
3	.045	.176	.267	.251	.164	.074	.021	.003	.000
4	.007	.066	.172	.251	.246	.167	.074	.017	.001
5	.001	.017	.074	.167	.246	.251	.172	.066	.007
6	.000	.003	.021	.074	.164	.251	.267	.176	.045
7	.000	.000	.004	.021	.070	.161	.267	.302	.172
8	.000	.000	.000	.004	.018	.060	.156	.302	.387
9	.000	.000	.000	.000	.002	.010	.040	.134	.387

n = 10

x	Probability								
	.1	.2	.3	.4	.5	.6	.7	.8	.9
0	.349	.107	.028	.006	.001	.000	.000	.000	.000
1	.387	.268	.121	.040	.010	.002	.000	.000	.000
2	.194	.302	.233	.121	.044	.011	.001	.000	.000
3	.057	.201	.267	.215	.117	.042	.009	.001	.000
4	.011	.088	.200	.251	.205	.111	.037	.006	.000
5	.001	.026	.103	.201	.246	.201	.103	.026	.001
6	.000	.006	.037	.111	.205	.251	.200	.088	.011
7	.000	.001	.009	.042	.117	.215	.267	.201	.057
8	.000	.000	.001	.011	.044	.121	.233	.302	.194
9	.000	.000	.000	.002	.010	.040	.121	.268	.387
10	.000	.000	.000	.000	.001	.006	.028	.107	.349

TABLE A.2

Binomial Probability
Distribution (*Continued*)

n = 11

Probability

x	.1	.2	.3	.4	.5	.6	.7	.8	.9
0	.314	.086	.020	.004	.000	.000	.000	.000	.000
1	.384	.236	.093	.027	.005	.001	.000	.000	.000
2	.213	.295	.200	.089	.027	.005	.001	.000	.000
3	.071	.221	.257	.177	.081	.023	.004	.000	.000
4	.016	.111	.220	.236	.161	.070	.017	.002	.000
5	.002	.039	.132	.221	.226	.147	.057	.010	.000
6	.000	.010	.057	.147	.226	.221	.132	.039	.002
7	.000	.002	.017	.070	.161	.236	.220	.111	.016
8	.000	.000	.004	.023	.081	.177	.257	.221	.071
9	.000	.000	.001	.005	.027	.089	.200	.295	.213
10	.000	.000	.000	.001	.005	.027	.093	.236	.384
11	.000	.000	.000	.000	.000	.004	.020	.086	.314

n = 12

Probability

x	.1	.2	.3	.4	.5	.6	.7	.8	.9
0	.282	.069	.014	.002	.000	.000	.000	.000	.000
1	.377	.206	.071	.017	.003	.000	.000	.000	.000
2	.230	.283	.168	.064	.016	.002	.000	.000	.000
3	.085	.236	.240	.142	.054	.012	.001	.000	.000
4	.021	.133	.231	.213	.121	.042	.008	.001	.000
5	.004	.053	.158	.227	.193	.101	.029	.003	.000
6	.000	.016	.079	.177	.226	.177	.079	.016	.000
7	.000	.003	.029	.101	.193	.227	.158	.053	.004
8	.000	.001	.008	.042	.121	.213	.231	.133	.021
9	.000	.000	.001	.012	.054	.142	.240	.236	.085
10	.000	.000	.000	.002	.016	.064	.168	.283	.230
11	.000	.000	.000	.000	.003	.017	.071	.206	.377
12	.000	.000	.000	.000	.000	.002	.014	.069	.282

n = 13

Probability

x	.1	.2	.3	.4	.5	.6	.7	.8	.9
0	.254	.055	.010	.001	.000	.000	.000	.000	.000
1	.367	.179	.054	.011	.002	.000	.000	.000	.000
2	.245	.268	.139	.045	.010	.001	.000	.000	.000
3	.100	.246	.218	.111	.035	.006	.001	.000	.000
4	.028	.154	.234	.184	.087	.024	.003	.000	.000
5	.006	.069	.180	.221	.157	.066	.014	.001	.000
6	.001	.023	.103	.197	.209	.131	.044	.006	.000
7	.000	.006	.044	.131	.209	.197	.103	.023	.001
8	.000	.001	.014	.066	.157	.221	.180	.069	.006
9	.000	.000	.003	.024	.087	.184	.234	.154	.028
10	.000	.000	.001	.006	.035	.111	.218	.246	.100
11	.000	.000	.000	.001	.010	.045	.139	.268	.245
12	.000	.000	.000	.000	.002	.011	.054	.179	.367
13	.000	.000	.000	.000	.000	.001	.010	.055	.254

(*Continued*)

TABLE A.2

Binomial Probability
Distribution (*Continued*)

n = 14

x	.1	.2	.3	.4	.5	.6	.7	.8	.9
0	.229	.044	.007	.001	.000	.000	.000	.000	.000
1	.356	.154	.041	.007	.001	.000	.000	.000	.000
2	.257	.250	.113	.032	.006	.001	.000	.000	.000
3	.114	.250	.194	.085	.022	.003	.000	.000	.000
4	.035	.172	.229	.155	.061	.014	.001	.000	.000
5	.008	.086	.196	.207	.122	.041	.007	.000	.000
6	.001	.032	.126	.207	.183	.092	.023	.002	.000
7	.000	.009	.062	.157	.209	.157	.062	.009	.000
8	.000	.002	.023	.092	.183	.207	.126	.032	.001
9	.000	.000	.007	.041	.122	.207	.196	.086	.008
10	.000	.000	.001	.014	.061	.155	.229	.172	.035
11	.000	.000	.000	.003	.022	.085	.194	.250	.114
12	.000	.000	.000	.001	.006	.032	.113	.250	.257
13	.000	.000	.000	.000	.001	.007	.041	.154	.356
14	.000	.000	.000	.000	.000	.001	.007	.044	.229

n = 15

x	.1	.2	.3	.4	.5	.6	.7	.8	.9
0	.206	.035	.005	.000	.000	.000	.000	.000	.000
1	.343	.132	.031	.005	.000	.000	.000	.000	.000
2	.267	.231	.092	.022	.003	.000	.000	.000	.000
3	.129	.250	.170	.063	.014	.002	.000	.000	.000
4	.043	.188	.219	.127	.042	.007	.001	.000	.000
5	.010	.103	.206	.186	.092	.024	.003	.000	.000
6	.002	.043	.147	.207	.153	.061	.012	.001	.000
7	.000	.014	.081	.177	.196	.118	.035	.003	.000
8	.000	.003	.035	.118	.196	.177	.081	.014	.000
9	.000	.001	.012	.061	.153	.207	.147	.043	.002
10	.000	.000	.003	.024	.092	.186	.206	.103	.010
11	.000	.000	.001	.007	.042	.127	.219	.188	.043
12	.000	.000	.000	.002	.014	.063	.170	.250	.129
13	.000	.000	.000	.000	.003	.022	.092	.231	.267
14	.000	.000	.000	.000	.000	.005	.031	.132	.343
15	.000	.000	.000	.000	.000	.000	.005	.035	.206

TABLE A.2

Binomial Probability
Distribution (*Continued*)

n = 16

x	.1	.2	.3	.4	.5	.6	.7	.8	.9
0	.185	.028	.003	.000	.000	.000	.000	.000	.000
1	.329	.113	.023	.003	.000	.000	.000	.000	.000
2	.275	.211	.073	.015	.002	.000	.000	.000	.000
3	.142	.246	.146	.047	.009	.001	.000	.000	.000
4	.051	.200	.204	.101	.028	.004	.000	.000	.000
5	.014	.120	.210	.162	.067	.014	.001	.000	.000
6	.003	.055	.165	.198	.122	.039	.006	.000	.000
7	.000	.020	.101	.189	.175	.084	.019	.001	.000
8	.000	.006	.049	.142	.196	.142	.049	.006	.000
9	.000	.001	.019	.084	.175	.189	.101	.020	.000
10	.000	.000	.006	.039	.122	.198	.165	.055	.003
11	.000	.000	.001	.014	.067	.162	.210	.120	.014
12	.000	.000	.000	.004	.028	.101	.204	.200	.051
13	.000	.000	.000	.001	.009	.047	.146	.246	.142
14	.000	.000	.000	.000	.002	.015	.073	.211	.275
15	.000	.000	.000	.000	.000	.003	.023	.113	.329
16	.000	.000	.000	.000	.000	.000	.003	.028	.185

n = 17

x	.1	.2	.3	.4	.5	.6	.7	.8	.9
0	.167	.023	.002	.000	.000	.000	.000	.000	.000
1	.315	.096	.017	.002	.000	.000	.000	.000	.000
2	.280	.191	.058	.010	.001	.000	.000	.000	.000
3	.156	.239	.125	.034	.005	.000	.000	.000	.000
4	.060	.209	.187	.080	.018	.002	.000	.000	.000
5	.017	.136	.208	.138	.047	.008	.001	.000	.000
6	.004	.068	.178	.184	.094	.024	.003	.000	.000
7	.001	.027	.120	.193	.148	.057	.009	.000	.000
8	.000	.008	.064	.161	.185	.107	.028	.002	.000
9	.000	.002	.028	.107	.185	.161	.064	.008	.000
10	.000	.000	.009	.057	.148	.193	.120	.027	.001
11	.000	.000	.003	.024	.094	.184	.178	.068	.004
12	.000	.000	.001	.008	.047	.138	.208	.136	.017
13	.000	.000	.000	.002	.018	.080	.187	.209	.060
14	.000	.000	.000	.000	.005	.034	.125	.239	.156
15	.000	.000	.000	.000	.001	.010	.058	.191	.280
16	.000	.000	.000	.000	.000	.002	.017	.096	.315
17	.000	.000	.000	.000	.000	.000	.002	.023	.167

(*Continued*)

TABLE A.2

Binomial Probability
Distribution (*Continued*)

n = 18

Probability

x	.1	.2	.3	.4	.5	.6	.7	.8	.9
0	.150	.018	.002	.000	.000	.000	.000	.000	.000
1	.300	.081	.013	.001	.000	.000	.000	.000	.000
2	.284	.172	.046	.007	.001	.000	.000	.000	.000
3	.168	.230	.105	.025	.003	.000	.000	.000	.000
4	.070	.215	.168	.061	.012	.001	.000	.000	.000
5	.022	.151	.202	.115	.033	.004	.000	.000	.000
6	.005	.082	.187	.166	.071	.015	.001	.000	.000
7	.001	.035	.138	.189	.121	.037	.005	.000	.000
8	.000	.012	.081	.173	.167	.077	.015	.001	.000
9	.000	.003	.039	.128	.185	.128	.039	.003	.000
10	.000	.001	.015	.077	.167	.173	.081	.012	.000
11	.000	.000	.005	.037	.121	.189	.138	.035	.001
12	.000	.000	.001	.015	.071	.166	.187	.082	.005
13	.000	.000	.000	.004	.033	.115	.202	.151	.022
14	.000	.000	.000	.001	.012	.061	.168	.215	.070
15	.000	.000	.000	.000	.003	.025	.105	.230	.168
16	.000	.000	.000	.000	.001	.007	.046	.172	.284
17	.000	.000	.000	.000	.000	.001	.013	.081	.300
18	.000	.000	.000	.000	.000	.000	.002	.018	.150

n = 19

Probability

x	.1	.2	.3	.4	.5	.6	.7	.8	.9
0	.135	.014	.001	.000	.000	.000	.000	.000	.000
1	.285	.068	.009	.001	.000	.000	.000	.000	.000
2	.285	.154	.036	.005	.000	.000	.000	.000	.000
3	.180	.218	.087	.017	.002	.000	.000	.000	.000
4	.080	.218	.149	.047	.007	.001	.000	.000	.000
5	.027	.164	.192	.093	.022	.002	.000	.000	.000
6	.007	.095	.192	.145	.052	.008	.001	.000	.000
7	.001	.044	.153	.180	.096	.024	.002	.000	.000
8	.000	.017	.098	.180	.144	.053	.008	.000	.000
9	.000	.005	.051	.146	.176	.098	.022	.001	.000
10	.000	.001	.022	.098	.176	.146	.051	.005	.000
11	.000	.000	.008	.053	.144	.180	.098	.017	.000
12	.000	.000	.002	.024	.096	.180	.153	.044	.001
13	.000	.000	.001	.008	.052	.145	.192	.095	.007
14	.000	.000	.000	.002	.022	.093	.192	.164	.027
15	.000	.000	.000	.001	.007	.047	.149	.218	.080
16	.000	.000	.000	.000	.002	.017	.087	.218	.180
17	.000	.000	.000	.000	.000	.005	.036	.154	.285
18	.000	.000	.000	.000	.000	.001	.009	.068	.285
19	.000	.000	.000	.000	.000	.000	.001	.014	.135

TABLE A.2

Binomial Probability
Distribution (*Continued*)

n = 20

Probability

x	.1	.2	.3	.4	.5	.6	.7	.8	.9
0	.122	.012	.001	.000	.000	.000	.000	.000	.000
1	.270	.058	.007	.000	.000	.000	.000	.000	.000
2	.285	.137	.028	.003	.000	.000	.000	.000	.000
3	.190	.205	.072	.012	.001	.000	.000	.000	.000
4	.090	.218	.130	.035	.005	.000	.000	.000	.000
5	.032	.175	.179	.075	.015	.001	.000	.000	.000
6	.009	.109	.192	.124	.037	.005	.000	.000	.000
7	.002	.055	.164	.166	.074	.015	.001	.000	.000
8	.000	.022	.114	.180	.120	.035	.004	.000	.000
9	.000	.007	.065	.160	.160	.071	.012	.000	.000
10	.000	.002	.031	.117	.176	.117	.031	.002	.000
11	.000	.000	.012	.071	.160	.160	.065	.007	.000
12	.000	.000	.004	.035	.120	.180	.114	.022	.000
13	.000	.000	.001	.015	.074	.166	.164	.055	.002
14	.000	.000	.000	.005	.037	.124	.192	.109	.009
15	.000	.000	.000	.001	.015	.075	.179	.175	.032
16	.000	.000	.000	.000	.005	.035	.130	.218	.090
17	.000	.000	.000	.000	.001	.012	.072	.205	.190
18	.000	.000	.000	.000	.000	.003	.028	.137	.285
19	.000	.000	.000	.000	.000	.000	.007	.058	.270
20	.000	.000	.000	.000	.000	.000	.001	.012	.122

n = 25

Probability

x	.1	.2	.3	.4	.5	.6	.7	.8	.9
0	.072	.004	.000	.000	.000	.000	.000	.000	.000
1	.199	.024	.001	.000	.000	.000	.000	.000	.000
2	.266	.071	.007	.000	.000	.000	.000	.000	.000
3	.226	.136	.024	.002	.000	.000	.000	.000	.000
4	.138	.187	.057	.007	.000	.000	.000	.000	.000
5	.065	.196	.103	.020	.002	.000	.000	.000	.000
6	.024	.163	.147	.044	.005	.000	.000	.000	.000
7	.007	.111	.171	.080	.014	.001	.000	.000	.000
8	.002	.062	.165	.120	.032	.003	.000	.000	.000
9	.000	.029	.134	.151	.061	.009	.000	.000	.000
10	.000	.012	.092	.161	.097	.021	.001	.000	.000
11	.000	.004	.054	.147	.133	.043	.004	.000	.000
12	.000	.001	.027	.114	.155	.076	.011	.000	.000
13	.000	.000	.011	.076	.155	.114	.027	.001	.000
14	.000	.000	.004	.043	.133	.147	.054	.004	.000
15	.000	.000	.001	.021	.097	.161	.092	.012	.000
16	.000	.000	.000	.009	.061	.151	.134	.029	.000
17	.000	.000	.000	.003	.032	.120	.165	.062	.002
18	.000	.000	.000	.001	.014	.080	.171	.111	.007
19	.000	.000	.000	.000	.005	.044	.147	.163	.024
20	.000	.000	.000	.000	.002	.020	.103	.196	.065
21	.000	.000	.000	.000	.000	.007	.057	.187	.138
22	.000	.000	.000	.000	.000	.002	.024	.136	.226
23	.000	.000	.000	.000	.000	.000	.007	.071	.266
24	.000	.000	.000	.000	.000	.000	.001	.024	.199
25	.000	.000	.000	.000	.000	.000	.000	.004	.072

TABLE A.3

Poisson Probabilities

					λ					
x	**.005**	**.01**	**.02**	**.03**	**.04**	**.05**	**.06**	**.07**	**.08**	**.09**
0	.9950	.9900	.9802	.9704	.9608	.9512	.9418	.9324	.9231	.9139
1	.0050	.0099	.0196	.0291	.0384	.0476	.0565	.0653	.0738	.0823
2	.0000	.0000	.0002	.0004	.0008	.0012	.0017	.0023	.0030	.0037
3	.0000	.0000	.0000	.0000	.0000	.0000	.0000	.0001	.0001	.0001

x	**.1**	**.2**	**.3**	**.4**	**.5**	**.6**	**.7**	**.8**	**.9**	**1.0**
0	.9048	.8187	.7408	.6703	.6065	.5488	.4966	.4493	.4066	.3679
1	.0905	.1637	.2222	.2681	.3033	.3293	.3476	.3595	.3659	.3679
2	.0045	.0164	.0333	.0536	.0758	.0988	.1217	.1438	.1647	.1839
3	.0002	.0011	.0033	.0072	.0126	.0198	.0284	.0383	.0494	.0613
4	.0000	.0001	.0003	.0007	.0016	.0030	.0050	.0077	.0111	.0153
5	.0000	.0000	.0000	.0001	.0002	.0004	.0007	.0012	.0020	.0031
6	.0000	.0000	.0000	.0000	.0000	.0000	.0001	.0002	.0003	.0005
7	.0000	.0000	.0000	.0000	.0000	.0000	.0000	.0000	.0000	.0001

x	**1.1**	**1.2**	**1.3**	**1.4**	**1.5**	**1.6**	**1.7**	**1.8**	**1.9**	**2.0**
0	.3329	.3012	.2725	.2466	.2231	.2019	.1827	.1653	.1496	.1353
1	.3662	.3614	.3543	.3452	.3347	.3230	.3106	.2975	.2842	.2707
2	.2014	.2169	.2303	.2417	.2510	.2584	.2640	.2678	.2700	.2707
3	.0738	.0867	.0998	.1128	.1255	.1378	.1496	.1607	.1710	.1804
4	.0203	.0260	.0324	.0395	.0471	.0551	.0636	.0723	.0812	.0902
5	.0045	.0062	.0084	.0111	.0141	.0176	.0216	.0260	.0309	.0361
6	.0008	.0012	.0018	.0026	.0035	.0047	.0061	.0078	.0098	.0120
7	.0001	.0002	.0003	.0005	.0008	.0011	.0015	.0020	.0027	.0034
8	.0000	.0000	.0001	.0001	.0001	.0002	.0003	.0005	.0006	.0009
9	.0000	.0000	.0000	.0000	.0000	.0000	.0001	.0001	.0001	.0002

x	**2.1**	**2.2**	**2.3**	**2.4**	**2.5**	**2.6**	**2.7**	**2.8**	**2.9**	**3.0**
0	.1225	.1108	.1003	.0907	.0821	.0743	.0672	.0608	.0550	.0498
1	.2572	.2438	.2306	.2177	.2052	.1931	.1815	.1703	.1596	.1494
2	.2700	.2681	.2652	.2613	.2565	.2510	.2450	.2384	.2314	.2240
3	.1890	.1966	.2033	.2090	.2138	.2176	.2205	.2225	.2237	.2240
4	.0992	.1082	.1169	.1254	.1336	.1414	.1488	.1557	.1622	.1680
5	.0417	.0476	.0538	.0602	.0668	.0735	.0804	.0872	.0940	.1008
6	.0146	.0174	.0206	.0241	.0278	.0319	.0362	.0407	.0455	.0504
7	.0044	.0055	.0068	.0083	.0099	.0118	.0139	.0163	.0188	.0216
8	.0011	.0015	.0019	.0025	.0031	.0038	.0047	.0057	.0068	.0081
9	.0003	.0004	.0005	.0007	.0009	.0011	.0014	.0018	.0022	.0027
10	.0001	.0001	.0001	.0002	.0002	.0003	.0004	.0005	.0006	.0008
11	.0000	.0000	.0000	.0000	.0000	.0001	.0001	.0001	.0002	.0002
12	.0000	.0000	.0000	.0000	.0000	.0000	.0000	.0000	.0000	.0001

TABLE A.3

Poisson Probabilities
(*Continued*)

					λ					
x	3.1	3.2	3.3	3.4	3.5	3.6	3.7	3.8	3.9	4.0
0	.0450	.0408	.0369	.0334	.0302	.0273	.0247	.0224	.0202	.0183
1	.1397	.1304	.1217	.1135	.1057	.0984	.0915	.0850	.0789	.0733
2	.2165	.2087	.2008	.1929	.1850	.1771	.1692	.1615	.1539	.1465
3	.2237	.2226	.2209	.2186	.2158	.2125	.2087	.2046	.2001	.1954
4	.1733	.1781	.1823	.1858	.1888	.1912	.1931	.1944	.1951	.1954
5	.1075	.1140	.1203	.1264	.1322	.1377	.1429	.1477	.1522	.1563
6	.0555	.0608	.0662	.0716	.0771	.0826	.0881	.0936	.0989	.1042
7	.0246	.0278	.0312	.0348	.0385	.0425	.0466	.0508	.0551	.0595
8	.0095	.0111	.0129	.0148	.0169	.0191	.0215	.0241	.0269	.0298
9	.0033	.0040	.0047	.0056	.0066	.0076	.0089	.0102	.0116	.0132
10	.0010	.0013	.0016	.0019	.0023	.0028	.0033	.0039	.0045	.0053
11	.0003	.0004	.0005	.0006	.0007	.0009	.0011	.0013	.0016	.0019
12	.0001	.0001	.0001	.0002	.0002	.0003	.0003	.0004	.0005	.0006
13	.0000	.0000	.0000	.0000	.0001	.0001	.0001	.0001	.0002	.0002
14	.0000	.0000	.0000	.0000	.0000	.0000	.0000	.0000	.0000	.0001

x	4.1	4.2	4.3	4.4	4.5	4.6	4.7	4.8	4.9	5.0
0	.0166	.0150	.0136	.0123	.0111	.0101	.0091	.0082	.0074	.0067
1	.0679	.0630	.0583	.0540	.0500	.0462	.0427	.0395	.0365	.0337
2	.1393	.1323	.1254	.1188	.1125	.1063	.1005	.0948	.0894	.0842
3	.1904	.1852	.1798	.1743	.1687	.1631	.1574	.1517	.1460	.1404
4	.1951	.1944	.1933	.1917	.1898	.1875	.1849	.1820	.1789	.1755
5	.1600	.1633	.1662	.1687	.1708	.1725	.1738	.1747	.1753	.1755
6	.1093	.1143	.1191	.1237	.1281	.1323	.1362	.1398	.1432	.1462
7	.0640	.0686	.0732	.0778	.0824	.0869	.0914	.0959	.1002	.1044
8	.0328	.0360	.0393	.0428	.0463	.0500	.0537	.0575	.0614	.0653
9	.0150	.0168	.0188	.0209	.0232	.0255	.0281	.0307	.0334	.0363
10	.0061	.0071	.0081	.0092	.0104	.0118	.0132	.0147	.0164	.0181
11	.0023	.0027	.0032	.0037	.0043	.0049	.0056	.0064	.0073	.0082
12	.0008	.0009	.0011	.0013	.0016	.0019	.0022	.0026	.0030	.0034
13	.0002	.0003	.0004	.0005	.0006	.0007	.0008	.0009	.0011	.0013
14	.0001	.0001	.0001	.0001	.0002	.0002	.0003	.0003	.0004	.0005
15	.0000	.0000	.0000	.0000	.0001	.0001	.0001	.0001	.0001	.0002

(*Continued*)

Poisson distribut.

Poisson Probabilities
(*Continued*)

					λ					
x	5.1	5.2	5.3	5.4	5.5	5.6	5.7	5.8	5.9	6.0
0	.0061	.0055	.0050	.0045	.0041	.0037	.0033	.0030	.0027	.0025
1	.0311	.0287	.0265	.0244	.0225	.0207	.0191	.0176	.0162	.0149
2	.0793	.0746	.0701	.0659	.0618	.0580	.0544	.0509	.0477	.0446
3	.1348	.1293	.1239	.1185	.1133	.1082	.1033	.0985	.0938	.0892
4	.1719	.1681	.1641	.1600	.1558	.1515	.1472	.1428	.1383	.1339
5	.1753	.1748	.1740	.1728	.1714	.1697	.1678	.1656	.1632	.1606
6	.1490	.1515	.1537	.1555	.1571	.1584	.1594	.1601	.1605	.1606
7	.1086	.1125	.1163	.1200	.1234	.1267	.1298	.1326	.1353	.1377
8	.0692	.0731	.0771	.0810	.0849	.0887	.0925	.0962	.0998	.1033
9	.0392	.0423	.0454	.0486	.0519	.0552	.0586	.0620	.0654	.0688
10	.0200	.0220	.0241	.0262	.0285	.0309	.0334	.0359	.0386	.0413
11	.0093	.0104	.0116	.0129	.0143	.0157	.0173	.0190	.0207	.0225
12	.0039	.0045	.0051	.0058	.0065	.0073	.0082	.0092	.0102	.0113
13	.0015	.0018	.0021	.0024	.0028	.0032	.0036	.0041	.0046	.0052
14	.0006	.0007	.0008	.0009	.0011	.0013	.0015	.0017	.0019	.0022
15	.0002	.0002	.0003	.0003	.0004	.0005	.0006	.0007	.0008	.0009
16	.0001	.0001	.0001	.0001	.0001	.0002	.0002	.0002	.0003	.0003
17	.0000	.0000	.0000	.0000	.0000	.0001	.0001	.0001	.0001	.0001

x	6.1	6.2	6.3	6.4	6.5	6.6	6.7	6.8	6.9	7.0
0	.0022	.0020	.0018	.0017	.0015	.0014	.0012	.0011	.0010	.0009
1	.0137	.0126	.0116	.0106	.0098	.0090	.0082	.0076	.0070	.0064
2	.0417	.0390	.0364	.0340	.0318	.0296	.0276	.0258	.0240	.0223
3	.0848	.0806	.0765	.0726	.0688	.0652	.0617	.0584	.0552	.0521
4	.1294	.1249	.1205	.1162	.1118	.1076	.1034	.0992	.0952	.0912
5	.1579	.1549	.1519	.1487	.1454	.1420	.1385	.1349	.1314	.1277
6	.1605	.1601	.1595	.1586	.1575	.1562	.1546	.1529	.1511	.1490
7	.1399	.1418	.1435	.1450	.1462	.1472	.1480	.1486	.1489	.1490
8	.1066	.1099	.1130	.1160	.1188	.1215	.1240	.1263	.1284	.1304
9	.0723	.0757	.0791	.0825	.0858	.0891	.0923	.0954	.0985	.1014
10	.0441	.0469	.0498	.0528	.0558	.0588	.0618	.0649	.0679	.0710
11	.0244	.0265	.0285	.0307	.0330	.0353	.0377	.0401	.0426	.0452
12	.0124	.0137	.0150	.0164	.0179	.0194	.0210	.0227	.0245	.0263
13	.0058	.0065	.0073	.0081	.0089	.0099	.0108	.0119	.0130	.0142
14	.0025	.0029	.0033	.0037	.0041	.0046	.0052	.0058	.0064	.0071
15	.0010	.0012	.0014	.0016	.0018	.0020	.0023	.0026	.0029	.0033
16	.0004	.0005	.0005	.0006	.0007	.0008	.0010	.0011	.0013	.0014
17	.0001	.0002	.0002	.0002	.0003	.0003	.0004	.0004	.0005	.0006
18	.0000	.0001	.0001	.0001	.0001	.0001	.0001	.0002	.0002	.0002
19	.0000	.0000	.0000	.0000	.0000	.0000	.0001	.0001	.0001	.0001

TABLE A.3

Poisson Probabilities
(*Continued*)

					λ					
x	7.1	7.2	7.3	7.4	7.5	7.6	7.7	7.8	7.9	8.0
0	.0008	.0007	.0007	.0006	.0006	.0005	.0005	.0004	.0004	.0003
1	.0059	.0054	.0049	.0045	.0041	.0038	.0035	.0032	.0029	.0027
2	.0208	.0194	.0180	.0167	.0156	.0145	.0134	.0125	.0116	.0107
3	.0492	.0464	.0438	.0413	.0389	.0366	.0345	.0324	.0305	.0286
4	.0874	.0836	.0799	.0764	.0729	.0696	.0663	.0632	.0602	.0573
5	.1241	.1204	.1167	.1130	.1094	.1057	.1021	.0986	.0951	.0916
6	.1468	.1445	.1420	.1394	.1367	.1339	.1311	.1282	.1252	.1221
7	.1489	.1486	.1481	.1474	.1465	.1454	.1442	.1428	.1413	.1396
8	.1321	.1337	.1351	.1363	.1373	.1381	.1388	.1392	.1395	.1396
9	.1042	.1070	.1096	.1121	.1144	.1167	.1187	.1207	.1224	.1241
10	.0740	.0770	.0800	.0829	.0858	.0887	.0914	.0941	.0967	.0993
11	.0478	.0504	.0531	.0558	.0585	.0613	.0640	.0667	.0695	.0722
12	.0283	.0303	.0323	.0344	.0366	.0388	.0411	.0434	.0457	.0481
13	.0154	.0168	.0181	.0196	.0211	.0227	.0243	.0260	.0278	.0296
14	.0078	.0086	.0095	.0104	.0113	.0123	.0134	.0145	.0157	.0169
15	.0037	.0041	.0046	.0051	.0057	.0062	.0069	.0075	.0083	.0090
16	.0016	.0019	.0021	.0024	.0026	.0030	.0033	.0037	.0041	.0045
17	.0007	.0008	.0009	.0010	.0012	.0013	.0015	.0017	.0019	.0021
18	.0003	.0003	.0004	.0004	.0005	.0006	.0006	.0007	.0008	.0009
19	.0001	.0001	.0001	.0002	.0002	.0002	.0003	.0003	.0003	.0004
20	.0000	.0000	.0001	.0001	.0001	.0001	.0001	.0001	.0001	.0002
21	.0000	.0000	.0000	.0000	.0000	.0000	.0000	.0000	.0001	.0001

x	8.1	8.2	8.3	8.4	8.5	8.6	8.7	8.8	8.9	9.0
0	.0003	.0003	.0002	.0002	.0002	.0002	.0002	.0002	.0001	.0001
1	.0025	.0023	.0021	.0019	.0017	.0016	.0014	.0013	.0012	.0011
2	.0100	.0092	.0086	.0079	.0074	.0068	.0063	.0058	.0054	.0050
3	.0269	.0252	.0237	.0222	.0208	.0195	.0183	.0171	.0160	.0150
4	.0544	.0517	.0491	.0466	.0443	.0420	.0398	.0377	.0357	.0337
5	.0882	.0849	.0816	.0784	.0752	.0722	.0692	.0663	.0635	.0607
6	.1191	.1160	.1128	.1097	.1066	.1034	.1003	.0972	.0941	.0911
7	.1378	.1358	.1338	.1317	.1294	.1271	.1247	.1222	.1197	.1171
8	.1395	.1392	.1388	.1382	.1375	.1366	.1356	.1344	.1332	.1318
9	.1256	.1269	.1280	.1290	.1299	.1306	.1311	.1315	.1317	.1318
10	.1017	.1040	.1063	.1084	.1104	.1123	.1140	.1157	.1172	.1186
11	.0749	.0776	.0802	.0828	.0853	.0878	.0902	.0925	.0948	.0970
12	.0505	.0530	.0555	.0579	.0604	.0629	.0654	.0679	.0703	.0728
13	.0315	.0334	.0354	.0374	.0395	.0416	.0438	.0459	.0481	.0504
14	.0182	.0196	.0210	.0225	.0240	.0256	.0272	.0289	.0306	.0324
15	.0098	.0107	.0116	.0126	.0136	.0147	.0158	.0169	.0182	.0194
16	.0050	.0055	.0060	.0066	.0072	.0079	.0086	.0093	.0101	.0109
17	.0024	.0026	.0029	.0033	.0036	.0040	.0044	.0048	.0053	.0058
18	.0011	.0012	.0014	.0015	.0017	.0019	.0021	.0024	.0026	.0029
19	.0005	.0005	.0006	.0007	.0008	.0009	.0010	.0011	.0012	.0014
20	.0002	.0002	.0002	.0003	.0003	.0004	.0004	.0005	.0005	.0006
21	.0001	.0001	.0001	.0001	.0001	.0002	.0002	.0002	.0002	.0003
22	.0000	.0000	.0000	.0000	.0001	.0001	.0001	.0001	.0001	.0001

(*Continued*)

TABLE A.3

Poisson Probabilities
(*Continued*)

					λ					
x	9.1	9.2	9.3	9.4	9.5	9.6	9.7	9.8	9.9	10.0
0	.0001	.0001	.0001	.0001	.0001	.0001	.0001	.0001	.0001	.0000
1	.0010	.0009	.0009	.0008	.0007	.0007	.0006	.0005	.0005	.0005
2	.0046	.0043	.0040	.0037	.0034	.0031	.0029	.0027	.0025	.0023
3	.0140	.0131	.0123	.0115	.0107	.0100	.0093	.0087	.0081	.0076
4	.0319	.0302	.0285	.0269	.0254	.0240	.0226	.0213	.0201	.0189
5	.0581	.0555	.0530	.0506	.0483	.0460	.0439	.0418	.0398	.0378
6	.0881	.0851	.0822	.0793	.0764	.0736	.0709	.0682	.0656	.0631
7	.1145	.1118	.1091	.1064	.1037	.1010	.0982	.0955	.0928	.0901
8	.1302	.1286	.1269	.1251	.1232	.1212	.1191	.1170	.1148	.1126
9	.1317	.1315	.1311	.1306	.1300	.1293	.1284	.1274	.1263	.1251
10	.1198	.1210	.1219	.1228	.1235	.1241	.1245	.1249	.1250	.1251
11	.0991	.1012	.1031	.1049	.1067	.1083	.1098	.1112	.1125	.1137
12	.0752	.0776	.0799	.0822	.0844	.0866	.0888	.0908	.0928	.0948
13	.0526	.0549	.0572	.0594	.0617	.0640	.0662	.0685	.0707	.0729
14	.0342	.0361	.0380	.0399	.0419	.0439	.0459	.0479	.0500	.0521
15	.0208	.0221	.0235	.0250	.0265	.0281	.0297	.0313	.0330	.0347
16	.0118	.0127	.0137	.0147	.0157	.0168	.0180	.0192	.0204	.0217
17	.0063	.0069	.0075	.0081	.0088	.0095	.0103	.0111	.0119	.0128
18	.0032	.0035	.0039	.0042	.0046	.0051	.0055	.0060	.0065	.0071
19	.0015	.0017	.0019	.0021	.0023	.0026	.0028	.0031	.0034	.0037
20	.0007	.0008	.0009	.0010	.0011	.0012	.0014	.0015	.0017	.0019
21	.0003	.0003	.0004	.0004	.0005	.0006	.0006	.0007	.0008	.0009
22	.0001	.0001	.0002	.0002	.0002	.0002	.0003	.0003	.0004	.0004
23	.0000	.0001	.0001	.0001	.0001	.0001	.0001	.0001	.0002	.0002
24	.0000	.0000	.0000	.0000	.0000	.0000	.0000	.0001	.0001	.0001

TABLE A.4

The e^{-x} Table

x	e^{-x}	x	e^{-x}	x	e^{-x}	x	e^{-x}
0.0	1.0000	3.0	0.0498	6.0	0.00248	9.0	0.00012
0.1	0.9048	3.1	0.0450	6.1	0.00224	9.1	0.00011
0.2	0.8187	3.2	0.0408	6.2	0.00203	9.2	0.00010
0.3	0.7408	3.3	0.0369	6.3	0.00184	9.3	0.00009
0.4	0.6703	3.4	0.0334	6.4	0.00166	9.4	0.00008
0.5	0.6065	3.5	0.0302	6.5	0.00150	9.5	0.00007
0.6	0.5488	3.6	0.0273	6.6	0.00136	9.6	0.00007
0.7	0.4966	3.7	0.0247	6.7	0.00123	9.7	0.00006
0.8	0.4493	3.8	0.0224	6.8	0.00111	9.8	0.00006
0.9	0.4066	3.9	0.0202	6.9	0.00101	9.9	0.00005
1.0	0.3679	4.0	0.0183	7.0	0.00091	10.0	0.00005
1.1	0.3329	4.1	0.0166	7.1	0.00083		
1.2	0.3012	4.2	0.0150	7.2	0.00075		
1.3	0.2725	4.3	0.0136	7.3	0.00068		
1.4	0.2466	4.4	0.0123	7.4	0.00061		
1.5	0.2231	4.5	0.0111	7.5	0.00055		
1.6	0.2019	4.6	0.0101	7.6	0.00050		
1.7	0.1827	4.7	0.0091	7.7	0.00045		
1.8	0.1653	4.8	0.0082	7.8	0.00041		
1.9	0.1496	4.9	0.0074	7.9	0.00037		
2.0	0.1353	5.0	0.0067	8.0	0.00034		
2.1	0.1225	5.1	0.0061	8.1	0.00030		
2.2	0.1108	5.2	0.0055	8.2	0.00027		
2.3	0.1003	5.3	0.0050	8.3	0.00025		
2.4	0.0907	5.4	0.0045	8.4	0.00022		
2.5	0.0821	5.5	0.0041	8.5	0.00020		
2.6	0.0743	5.6	0.0037	8.6	0.00018		
2.7	0.0672	5.7	0.0033	8.7	0.00017		
2.8	0.0608	5.8	0.0030	8.8	0.00015		
2.9	0.0550	5.9	0.0027	8.9	0.00014		

TABLE A.5

Areas of the Standard Normal Distribution

The entries in this table are the probabilities that a standard normal random variable is between 0 and z (the shaded area).

z	0.00	0.01	0.02	0.03	0.04	0.05	0.06	0.07	0.08	0.09
0.0	.0000	.0040	.0080	.0120	.0160	.0199	.0239	.0279	.0319	.0359
0.1	.0398	.0438	.0478	.0517	.0557	.0596	.0636	.0675	.0714	.0753
0.2	.0793	.0832	.0871	.0910	.0948	.0987	.1026	.1064	.1103	.1141
0.3	.1179	.1217	.1255	.1293	.1331	.1368	.1406	.1443	.1480	.1517
0.4	.1554	.1591	.1628	.1664	.1700	.1736	.1772	.1808	.1844	.1879
0.5	.1915	.1950	.1985	.2019	.2054	.2088	.2123	.2157	.2190	.2224
0.6	.2257	.2291	.2324	.2357	.2389	.2422	.2454	.2486	.2517	.2549
0.7	.2580	.2611	.2642	.2673	.2704	.2734	.2764	.2794	.2823	.2852
0.8	.2881	.2910	.2939	.2967	.2995	.3023	.3051	.3078	.3106	.3133
0.9	.3159	.3186	.3212	.3238	.3264	.3289	.3315	.3340	.3365	.3389
1.0	.3413	.3438	.3461	.3485	.3508	.3531	.3554	.3577	.3599	.3621
1.1	.3643	.3665	.3686	.3708	.3729	.3749	.3770	.3790	.3810	.3830
1.2	.3849	.3869	.3888	.3907	.3925	.3944	.3962	.3980	.3997	.4015
1.3	.4032	.4049	.4066	.4082	.4099	.4115	.4131	.4147	.4162	.4177
1.4	.4192	.4207	.4222	.4236	.4251	.4265	.4279	.4292	.4306	.4319
1.5	.4332	.4345	.4357	.4370	.4382	.4394	.4406	.4418	.4429	.4441
1.6	.4452	.4463	.4474	.4484	.4495	.4505	.4515	.4525	.4535	.4545
1.7	.4554	.4564	.4573	.4582	.4591	.4599	.4608	.4616	.4625	.4633
1.8	.4641	.4649	.4656	.4664	.4671	.4678	.4686	.4693	.4699	.4706
1.9	.4713	.4719	.4726	.4732	.4738	.4744	.4750	.4756	.4761	.4767
2.0	.4772	.4778	.4783	.4788	.4793	.4798	.4803	.4808	.4812	.4817
2.1	.4821	.4826	.4830	.4834	.4838	.4842	.4846	.4850	.4854	.4857
2.2	.4861	.4864	.4868	.4871	.4875	.4878	.4881	.4884	.4887	.4890
2.3	.4893	.4896	.4898	.4901	.4904	.4906	.4909	.4911	.4913	.4916
2.4	.4918	.4920	.4922	.4925	.4927	.4929	.4931	.4932	.4934	.4936
2.5	.4938	.4940	.4941	.4943	.4945	.4946	.4948	.4949	.4951	.4952
2.6	.4953	.4955	.4956	.4957	.4959	.4960	.4961	.4962	.4963	.4964
2.7	.4965	.4966	.4967	.4968	.4969	.4970	.4971	.4972	.4973	.4974
2.8	.4974	.4975	.4976	.4977	.4977	.4978	.4979	.4979	.4980	.4981
2.9	.4981	.4982	.4982	.4983	.4984	.4984	.4985	.4985	.4986	.4986
3.0	.4987	.4987	.4987	.4988	.4988	.4989	.4989	.4989	.4990	.4990
3.1	.4990	.4991	.4991	.4991	.4992	.4992	.4992	.4992	.4993	.4993
3.2	.4993	.4993	.4994	.4994	.4994	.4994	.4994	.4995	.4995	.4995
3.3	.4995	.4995	.4995	.4996	.4996	.4996	.4996	.4996	.4996	.4997
3.4	.4997	.4997	.4997	.4997	.4997	.4997	.4997	.4997	.4997	.4998
3.5	.4998									
4.0	.49997									
4.5	.499997									
5.0	.4999997									
6.0	.499999999									

TABLE A.6

Critical Values from the *t* Distribution

	Values of α for one-tailed test and α/2 for two-tailed test					
df	$t_{.100}$	$t_{.050}$	$t_{.025}$	$t_{.010}$	$t_{.005}$	$t_{.001}$
1	3.078	6.314	12.706	31.821	63.656	318.289
2	1.886	2.920	4.303	6.965	9.925	22.328
3	1.638	2.353	3.182	4.541	5.841	10.214
4	1.533	2.132	2.776	3.747	4.604	7.173
5	1.476	2.015	2.571	3.365	4.032	5.894
6	1.440	1.943	2.447	3.143	3.707	5.208
7	1.415	1.895	2.365	2.998	3.499	4.785
8	1.397	1.860	2.306	2.896	3.355	4.501
9	1.383	1.833	2.262	2.821	3.250	4.297
10	1.372	1.812	2.228	2.764	3.169	4.144
11	1.363	1.796	2.201	2.718	3.106	4.025
12	1.356	1.782	2.179	2.681	3.055	3.930
13	1.350	1.771	2.160	2.650	3.012	3.852
14	1.345	1.761	2.145	2.624	2.977	3.787
15	1.341	1.753	2.131	2.602	2.947	3.733
16	1.337	1.746	2.120	2.583	2.921	3.686
17	1.333	1.740	2.110	2.567	2.898	3.646
18	1.330	1.734	2.101	2.552	2.878	3.610
19	1.328	1.729	2.093	2.539	2.861	3.579
20	1.325	1.725	2.086	2.528	2.845	3.552
21	1.323	1.721	2.080	2.518	2.831	3.527
22	1.321	1.717	2.074	2.508	2.819	3.505
23	1.319	1.714	2.069	2.500	2.807	3.485
24	1.318	1.711	2.064	2.492	2.797	3.467
25	1.316	1.708	2.060	2.485	2.787	3.450
26	1.315	1.706	2.056	2.479	2.779	3.435
27	1.314	1.703	2.052	2.473	2.771	3.421
28	1.313	1.701	2.048	2.467	2.763	3.408
29	1.311	1.699	2.045	2.462	2.756	3.396
30	1.310	1.697	2.042	2.457	2.750	3.385
40	1.303	1.684	2.021	2.423	2.704	3.307
50	1.299	1.676	2.009	2.403	2.678	3.261
60	1.296	1.671	2.000	2.390	2.660	3.232
70	1.294	1.667	1.994	2.381	2.648	3.211
80	1.292	1.664	1.990	2.374	2.639	3.195
90	1.291	1.662	1.987	2.368	2.632	3.183
100	1.290	1.660	1.984	2.364	2.626	3.174
150	1.287	1.655	1.976	2.351	2.609	3.145
200	1.286	1.653	1.972	2.345	2.601	3.131
∞	1.282	1.645	1.960	2.326	2.576	3.090

TABLE A.7

Percentage Points of the F Distribution

		$\alpha = .10$							
v_2	v_1	Numerator Degrees of Freedom							
	1	2	3	4	5	6	7	8	9
1	39.86	49.50	53.59	55.83	57.24	58.20	58.91	59.44	59.86
2	8.53	9.00	9.16	9.24	9.29	9.33	9.35	9.37	9.38
3	5.54	5.46	5.39	5.34	5.31	5.28	5.27	5.25	5.24
4	4.54	4.32	4.19	4.11	4.05	4.01	3.98	3.95	3.94
5	4.06	3.78	3.62	3.52	3.45	3.40	3.37	3.34	3.32
6	3.78	3.46	3.29	3.18	3.11	3.05	3.01	2.98	2.96
7	3.59	3.26	3.07	2.96	2.88	2.83	2.78	2.75	2.72
8	3.46	3.11	2.92	2.81	2.73	2.67	2.62	2.59	2.56
9	3.36	3.01	2.81	2.69	2.61	2.55	2.51	2.47	2.44
10	3.29	2.92	2.73	2.61	2.52	2.46	2.41	2.38	2.35
11	3.23	2.86	2.66	2.54	2.45	2.39	2.34	2.30	2.27
12	3.18	2.81	2.61	2.48	2.39	2.33	2.28	2.24	2.21
13	3.14	2.76	2.56	2.43	2.35	2.28	2.23	2.20	2.16
14	3.10	2.73	2.52	2.39	2.31	2.24	2.19	2.15	2.12
15	3.07	2.70	2.49	2.36	2.27	2.21	2.16	2.12	2.09
16	3.05	2.67	2.46	2.33	2.24	2.18	2.13	2.09	2.06
17	3.03	2.64	2.44	2.31	2.22	2.15	2.10	2.06	2.03
18	3.01	2.62	2.42	2.29	2.20	2.13	2.08	2.04	2.00
19	2.99	2.61	2.40	2.27	2.18	2.11	2.06	2.02	1.98
20	2.97	2.59	2.38	2.25	2.16	2.09	2.04	2.00	1.96
21	2.96	2.57	2.36	2.23	2.14	2.08	2.02	1.98	1.95
22	2.95	2.56	2.35	2.22	2.13	2.06	2.01	1.97	1.93
23	2.94	2.55	2.34	2.21	2.11	2.05	1.99	1.95	1.92
24	2.93	2.54	2.33	2.19	2.10	2.04	1.98	1.94	1.91
25	2.92	2.53	2.32	2.18	2.09	2.02	1.97	1.93	1.89
26	2.91	2.52	2.31	2.17	2.08	2.01	1.96	1.92	1.88
27	2.90	2.51	2.30	2.17	2.07	2.00	1.95	1.91	1.87
28	2.89	2.50	2.29	2.16	2.06	2.00	1.94	1.90	1.87
29	2.89	2.50	2.28	2.15	2.06	1.99	1.93	1.89	1.86
30	2.88	2.49	2.28	2.14	2.05	1.98	1.93	1.88	1.85
40	2.84	2.44	2.23	2.09	2.00	1.93	1.87	1.83	1.79
60	2.79	2.39	2.18	2.04	1.95	1.87	1.82	1.77	1.74
120	2.75	2.35	2.13	1.99	1.90	1.82	1.77	1.72	1.68
∞	2.71	2.30	2.08	1.94	1.85	1.77	1.72	1.67	1.63

Denominator Degrees of Freedom

TABLE A.7

Percentage Points of the *F* Distribution (*Continued*)

					$\alpha = .10$					v_1	
				Numerator Degrees of Freedom							
10	12	15	20	24	30	40	60	120	∞		v_2
60.19	60.71	61.22	61.74	62.00	62.26	62.53	62.79	63.06	63.33	1	
9.39	9.41	9.42	9.44	9.45	9.46	9.47	9.47	9.48	9.49	2	
5.23	5.22	5.20	5.18	5.18	5.17	5.16	5.15	5.14	5.13	3	
3.92	3.90	3.87	3.84	3.83	3.82	3.80	3.79	3.78	3.76	4	
3.30	3.27	3.24	3.21	3.19	3.17	3.16	3.14	3.12	3.10	5	
2.94	2.90	2.87	2.84	2.82	2.80	2.78	2.76	2.74	2.72	6	
2.70	2.67	2.63	2.59	2.58	2.56	2.54	2.51	2.49	2.47	7	
2.54	2.50	2.46	2.42	2.40	2.38	2.36	2.34	2.32	2.29	8	
2.42	2.38	2.34	2.30	2.28	2.25	2.23	2.21	2.18	2.16	9	
2.32	2.28	2.24	2.20	2.18	2.16	2.13	2.11	2.08	2.06	10	
2.25	2.21	2.17	2.12	2.10	2.08	2.05	2.03	2.00	1.97	11	
2.19	2.15	2.10	2.06	2.04	2.01	1.99	1.96	1.93	1.90	12	
2.14	2.10	2.05	2.01	1.98	1.96	1.93	1.90	1.88	1.85	13	
2.10	2.05	2.01	1.96	1.94	1.91	1.89	1.86	1.83	1.80	14	
2.06	2.02	1.97	1.92	1.90	1.87	1.85	1.82	1.79	1.76	15	
2.03	1.99	1.94	1.89	1.87	1.84	1.81	1.78	1.75	1.72	16	
2.00	1.96	1.91	1.86	1.84	1.81	1.78	1.75	1.72	1.69	17	
1.98	1.93	1.89	1.84	1.81	1.78	1.75	1.72	1.69	1.66	18	
1.96	1.91	1.86	1.81	1.79	1.76	1.73	1.70	1.67	1.63	19	
1.94	1.89	1.84	1.79	1.77	1.74	1.71	1.68	1.64	1.61	20	
1.92	1.87	1.83	1.78	1.75	1.72	1.69	1.66	1.62	1.59	21	
1.90	1.86	1.81	1.76	1.73	1.70	1.67	1.64	1.60	1.57	22	
1.89	1.84	1.80	1.74	1.72	1.69	1.66	1.62	1.59	1.55	23	
1.88	1.83	1.78	1.73	1.70	1.67	1.64	1.61	1.57	1.53	24	
1.87	1.82	1.77	1.72	1.69	1.66	1.63	1.59	1.56	1.52	25	
1.86	1.81	1.76	1.71	1.68	1.65	1.61	1.58	1.54	1.50	26	
1.85	1.80	1.75	1.70	1.67	1.64	1.60	1.57	1.53	1.49	27	
1.84	1.79	1.74	1.69	1.66	1.63	1.59	1.56	1.52	1.48	28	
1.83	1.78	1.73	1.68	1.65	1.62	1.58	1.55	1.51	1.47	29	
1.82	1.77	1.72	1.67	1.64	1.61	1.57	1.54	1.50	1.46	30	
1.76	1.71	1.66	1.61	1.57	1.54	1.51	1.47	1.42	1.38	40	
1.71	1.66	1.60	1.54	1.51	1.48	1.44	1.40	1.35	1.29	60	
1.65	1.60	1.55	1.48	1.45	1.41	1.37	1.32	1.26	1.19	120	
1.60	1.55	1.49	1.42	1.38	1.34	1.30	1.24	1.17	1.00	∞	

Denominator Degrees of Freedom

(*Continued*)

TABLE A.7

Percentage Points of the F Distribution (Continued)

v_2 \ v_1	$\alpha = .05$ Numerator Degrees of Freedom								
	1	2	3	4	5	6	7	8	9
1	161.45	199.50	215.71	224.58	230.16	233.99	236.77	238.88	240.54
2	18.51	19.00	19.16	19.25	19.30	19.33	19.35	19.37	19.38
3	10.13	9.55	9.28	9.12	9.01	8.94	8.89	8.85	8.81
4	7.71	6.94	6.59	6.39	6.26	6.16	6.09	6.04	6.00
5	6.61	5.79	5.41	5.19	5.05	4.95	4.88	4.82	4.77
6	5.99	5.14	4.76	4.53	4.39	4.28	4.21	4.15	4.10
7	5.59	4.74	4.35	4.12	3.97	3.87	3.79	3.73	3.68
8	5.32	4.46	4.07	3.84	3.69	3.58	3.50	3.44	3.39
9	5.12	4.26	3.86	3.63	3.48	3.37	3.29	3.23	3.18
10	4.96	4.10	3.71	3.48	3.33	3.22	3.14	3.07	3.02
11	4.84	3.98	3.59	3.36	3.20	3.09	3.01	2.95	2.90
12	4.75	3.89	3.49	3.26	3.11	3.00	2.91	2.85	2.80
13	4.67	3.81	3.41	3.18	3.03	2.92	2.83	2.77	2.71
14	4.60	3.74	3.34	3.11	2.96	2.85	2.76	2.70	2.65
15	4.54	3.68	3.29	3.06	2.90	2.79	2.71	2.64	2.59
16	4.49	3.63	3.24	3.01	2.85	2.74	2.66	2.59	2.54
17	4.45	3.59	3.20	2.96	2.81	2.70	2.61	2.55	2.49
18	4.41	3.55	3.16	2.93	2.77	2.66	2.58	2.51	2.46
19	4.38	3.52	3.13	2.90	2.74	2.63	2.54	2.48	2.42
20	4.35	3.49	3.10	2.87	2.71	2.60	2.51	2.45	2.39
21	4.32	3.47	3.07	2.84	2.68	2.57	2.49	2.42	2.37
22	4.30	3.44	3.05	2.82	2.66	2.55	2.46	2.40	2.34
23	4.28	3.42	3.03	2.80	2.64	2.53	2.44	2.37	2.32
24	4.26	3.40	3.01	2.78	2.62	2.51	2.42	2.36	2.30
25	4.24	3.39	2.99	2.76	2.60	2.49	2.40	2.34	2.28
26	4.23	3.37	2.98	2.74	2.59	2.47	2.39	2.32	2.27
27	4.21	3.35	2.96	2.73	2.57	2.46	2.37	2.31	2.25
28	4.20	3.34	2.95	2.71	2.56	2.45	2.36	2.29	2.24
29	4.18	3.33	2.93	2.70	2.55	2.43	2.35	2.28	2.22
30	4.17	3.32	2.92	2.69	2.53	2.42	2.33	2.27	2.21
40	4.08	3.23	2.84	2.61	2.45	2.34	2.25	2.18	2.12
60	4.00	3.15	2.76	2.53	2.37	2.25	2.17	2.10	2.04
120	3.92	3.07	2.68	2.45	2.29	2.18	2.09	2.02	1.96
∞	3.84	3.00	2.60	2.37	2.21	2.10	2.01	1.94	1.88

Denominator Degrees of Freedom

TABLE A.7
Percentage Points of the F Distribution (Continued)

					$\alpha = .05$					v_1	
				Numerator Degrees of Freedom							
10	12	15	20	24	30	40	60	120	∞		v_2
241.88	243.90	245.90	248.00	249.10	250.10	251.10	252.20	253.30	254.30	1	
19.40	19.41	19.43	19.45	19.45	19.46	19.47	19.48	19.49	19.50	2	
8.79	8.74	8.70	8.66	8.64	8.62	8.59	8.57	8.55	8.53	3	
5.96	5.91	5.86	5.80	5.77	5.75	5.72	5.69	5.66	5.63	4	
4.74	4.68	4.62	4.56	4.53	4.50	4.46	4.43	4.40	4.36	5	
4.06	4.00	3.94	3.87	3.84	3.81	3.77	3.74	3.70	3.67	6	
3.64	3.57	3.51	3.44	3.41	3.38	3.34	3.30	3.27	3.23	7	
3.35	3.28	3.22	3.15	3.12	3.08	3.04	3.01	2.97	2.93	8	
3.14	3.07	3.01	2.94	2.90	2.86	2.83	2.79	2.75	2.71	9	
2.98	2.91	2.85	2.77	2.74	2.70	2.66	2.62	2.58	2.54	10	
2.85	2.79	2.72	2.65	2.61	2.57	2.53	2.49	2.45	2.40	11	
2.75	2.69	2.62	2.54	2.51	2.47	2.43	2.38	2.34	2.30	12	
2.67	2.60	2.53	2.46	2.42	2.38	2.34	2.30	2.25	2.21	13	
2.60	2.53	2.46	2.39	2.35	2.31	2.27	2.22	2.18	2.13	14	
2.54	2.48	2.40	2.33	2.29	2.25	2.20	2.16	2.11	2.07	15	
2.49	2.42	2.35	2.28	2.24	2.19	2.15	2.11	2.06	2.01	16	
2.45	2.38	2.31	2.23	2.19	2.15	2.10	2.06	2.01	1.96	17	
2.41	2.34	2.27	2.19	2.15	2.11	2.06	2.02	1.97	1.92	18	
2.38	2.31	2.23	2.16	2.11	2.07	2.03	1.98	1.93	1.88	19	
2.35	2.28	2.20	2.12	2.08	2.04	1.99	1.95	1.90	1.84	20	
2.32	2.25	2.18	2.10	2.05	2.01	1.96	1.92	1.87	1.81	21	
2.30	2.23	2.15	2.07	2.03	1.98	1.94	1.89	1.84	1.78	22	
2.27	2.20	2.13	2.05	2.01	1.96	1.91	1.86	1.81	1.76	23	
2.25	2.18	2.11	2.03	1.98	1.94	1.89	1.84	1.79	1.73	24	
2.24	2.16	2.09	2.01	1.96	1.92	1.87	1.82	1.77	1.71	25	
2.22	2.15	2.07	1.99	1.95	1.90	1.85	1.80	1.75	1.69	26	
2.20	2.13	2.06	1.97	1.93	1.88	1.84	1.79	1.73	1.67	27	
2.19	2.12	2.04	1.96	1.91	1.87	1.82	1.77	1.71	1.65	28	
2.18	2.10	2.03	1.94	1.90	1.85	1.81	1.75	1.70	1.64	29	
2.16	2.09	2.01	1.93	1.89	1.84	1.79	1.74	1.68	1.62	30	
2.08	2.00	1.92	1.84	1.79	1.74	1.69	1.64	1.58	1.51	40	
1.99	1.92	1.84	1.75	1.70	1.65	1.59	1.53	1.47	1.39	60	
1.91	1.83	1.75	1.66	1.61	1.55	1.50	1.43	1.35	1.25	120	
1.83	1.75	1.67	1.57	1.52	1.46	1.39	1.32	1.22	1.00	∞	

Denominator Degrees of Freedom

(Continued)

TABLE A.7

Percentage Points of the F Distribution (Continued)

$\alpha = .025$

v_2	Numerator Degrees of Freedom								
v_1	1	2	3	4	5	6	7	8	9
1	647.79	799.48	864.15	899.60	921.83	937.11	948.20	956.64	963.28
2	38.51	39.00	39.17	39.25	39.30	39.33	39.36	39.37	39.39
3	17.44	16.04	15.44	15.10	14.88	14.73	14.62	14.54	14.47
4	12.22	10.65	9.98	9.60	9.36	9.20	9.07	8.98	8.90
5	10.01	8.43	7.76	7.39	7.15	6.98	6.85	6.76	6.68
6	8.81	7.26	6.60	6.23	5.99	5.82	5.70	5.60	5.52
7	8.07	6.54	5.89	5.52	5.29	5.12	4.99	4.90	4.82
8	7.57	6.06	5.42	5.05	4.82	4.65	4.53	4.43	4.36
9	7.21	5.71	5.08	4.72	4.48	4.32	4.20	4.10	4.03
10	6.94	5.46	4.83	4.47	4.24	4.07	3.95	3.85	3.78
11	6.72	5.26	4.63	4.28	4.04	3.88	3.76	3.66	3.59
12	6.55	5.10	4.47	4.12	3.89	3.73	3.61	3.51	3.44
13	6.41	4.97	4.35	4.00	3.77	3.60	3.48	3.39	3.31
14	6.30	4.86	4.24	3.89	3.66	3.50	3.38	3.29	3.21
15	6.20	4.77	4.15	3.80	3.58	3.41	3.29	3.20	3.12
16	6.12	4.69	4.08	3.73	3.50	3.34	3.22	3.12	3.05
17	6.04	4.62	4.01	3.66	3.44	3.28	3.16	3.06	2.98
18	5.98	4.56	3.95	3.61	3.38	3.22	3.10	3.01	2.93
19	5.92	4.51	3.90	3.56	3.33	3.17	3.05	2.96	2.88
20	5.87	4.46	3.86	3.51	3.29	3.13	3.01	2.91	2.84
21	5.83	4.42	3.82	3.48	3.25	3.09	2.97	2.87	2.80
22	5.79	4.38	3.78	3.44	3.22	3.05	2.93	2.84	2.76
23	5.75	4.35	3.75	3.41	3.18	3.02	2.90	2.81	2.73
24	5.72	4.32	3.72	3.38	3.15	2.99	2.87	2.78	2.70
25	5.69	4.29	3.69	3.35	3.13	2.97	2.85	2.75	2.68
26	5.66	4.27	3.67	3.33	3.10	2.94	2.82	2.73	2.65
27	5.63	4.24	3.65	3.31	3.08	2.92	2.80	2.71	2.63
28	5.61	4.22	3.63	3.29	3.06	2.90	2.78	2.69	2.61
29	5.59	4.20	3.61	3.27	3.04	2.88	2.76	2.67	2.59
30	5.57	4.18	3.59	3.25	3.03	2.87	2.75	2.65	2.57
40	5.42	4.05	3.46	3.13	2.90	2.74	2.62	2.53	2.45
60	5.29	3.93	3.34	3.01	2.79	2.63	2.51	2.41	2.33
120	5.15	3.80	3.23	2.89	2.67	2.52	2.39	2.30	2.22
∞	5.02	3.69	3.12	2.79	2.57	2.41	2.29	2.19	2.11

Denominator Degrees of Freedom

TABLE A.7
Percentage Points of the *F* Distribution (*Continued*)

				$\alpha = .025$						v_1	
				Numerator Degrees of Freedom							
10	12	15	20	24	30	40	60	120	∞		v_2
968.63	976.72	984.87	993.08	997.27	1001.40	1005.60	1009.79	1014.04	1018.00	1	
39.40	39.41	39.43	39.45	39.46	39.46	39.47	39.48	39.49	39.50	2	
14.42	14.34	14.25	14.17	14.12	14.08	14.04	13.99	13.95	13.90	3	
8.84	8.75	8.66	8.56	8.51	8.46	8.41	8.36	8.31	8.26	4	
6.62	6.52	6.43	6.33	6.28	6.23	6.18	6.12	6.07	6.02	5	
5.46	5.37	5.27	5.17	5.12	5.07	5.01	4.96	4.90	4.85	6	
4.76	4.67	4.57	4.47	4.41	4.36	4.31	4.25	4.20	4.14	7	
4.30	4.20	4.10	4.00	3.95	3.89	3.84	3.78	3.73	3.67	8	
3.96	3.87	3.77	3.67	3.61	3.56	3.51	3.45	3.39	3.33	9	
3.72	3.62	3.52	3.42	3.37	3.31	3.26	3.20	3.14	3.08	10	
3.53	3.43	3.33	3.23	3.17	3.12	3.06	3.00	2.94	2.88	11	
3.37	3.28	3.18	3.07	3.02	2.96	2.91	2.85	2.79	2.72	12	
3.25	3.15	3.05	2.95	2.89	2.84	2.78	2.72	2.66	2.60	13	
3.15	3.05	2.95	2.84	2.79	2.73	2.67	2.61	2.55	2.49	14	
3.06	2.96	2.86	2.76	2.70	2.64	2.59	2.52	2.46	2.40	15	
2.99	2.89	2.79	2.68	2.63	2.57	2.51	2.45	2.38	2.32	16	
2.92	2.82	2.72	2.62	2.56	2.50	2.44	2.38	2.32	2.25	17	
2.87	2.77	2.67	2.56	2.50	2.44	2.38	2.32	2.26	2.19	18	
2.82	2.72	2.62	2.51	2.45	2.39	2.33	2.27	2.20	2.13	19	
2.77	2.68	2.57	2.46	2.41	2.35	2.29	2.22	2.16	2.09	20	
2.73	2.64	2.53	2.42	2.37	2.31	2.25	2.18	2.11	2.04	21	
2.70	2.60	2.50	2.39	2.33	2.27	2.21	2.14	2.08	2.00	22	
2.67	2.57	2.47	2.36	2.30	2.24	2.18	2.11	2.04	1.97	23	
2.64	2.54	2.44	2.33	2.27	2.21	2.15	2.08	2.01	1.94	24	
2.61	2.51	2.41	2.30	2.24	2.18	2.12	2.05	1.98	1.91	25	
2.59	2.49	2.39	2.28	2.22	2.16	2.09	2.03	1.95	1.88	26	
2.57	2.47	2.36	2.25	2.19	2.13	2.07	2.00	1.93	1.85	27	
2.55	2.45	2.34	2.23	2.17	2.11	2.05	1.98	1.91	1.83	28	
2.53	2.43	2.32	2.21	2.15	2.09	2.03	1.96	1.89	1.81	29	
2.51	2.41	2.31	2.20	2.14	2.07	2.01	1.94	1.87	1.79	30	
2.39	2.29	2.18	2.07	2.01	1.94	1.88	1.80	1.72	1.64	40	
2.27	2.17	2.06	1.94	1.88	1.82	1.74	1.67	1.58	1.48	60	
2.16	2.05	1.94	1.82	1.76	1.69	1.61	1.53	1.43	1.31	120	
2.05	1.94	1.83	1.71	1.64	1.57	1.48	1.39	1.27	1.00	∞	

Denominator Degrees of Freedom

(*Continued*)

TABLE A.7

Percentage Points of the F Distribution (Continued)

v_2	v_1 $\alpha = .01$ Numerator Degrees of Freedom								
	1	2	3	4	5	6	7	8	9
1	4052.18	4999.34	5403.53	5624.26	5763.96	5858.95	5928.33	5980.95	6022.40
2	98.50	99.00	99.16	99.25	99.30	99.33	99.36	99.38	99.39
3	34.12	30.82	29.46	28.71	28.24	27.91	27.67	27.49	27.34
4	21.20	18.00	16.69	15.98	15.52	15.21	14.98	14.80	14.66
5	16.26	13.27	12.06	11.39	10.97	10.67	10.46	10.29	10.16
6	13.75	10.92	9.78	9.15	8.75	8.47	8.26	8.10	7.98
7	12.25	9.55	8.45	7.85	7.46	7.19	6.99	6.84	6.72
8	11.26	8.65	7.59	7.01	6.63	6.37	6.18	6.03	5.91
9	10.56	8.02	6.99	6.42	6.06	5.80	5.61	5.47	5.35
10	10.04	7.56	6.55	5.99	5.64	5.39	5.20	5.06	4.94
11	9.65	7.21	6.22	5.67	5.32	5.07	4.89	4.74	4.63
12	9.33	6.93	5.95	5.41	5.06	4.82	4.64	4.50	4.39
13	9.07	6.70	5.74	5.21	4.86	4.62	4.44	4.30	4.19
14	8.86	6.51	5.56	5.04	4.69	4.46	4.28	4.14	4.03
15	8.68	6.36	5.42	4.89	4.56	4.32	4.14	4.00	3.89
16	8.53	6.23	5.29	4.77	4.44	4.20	4.03	3.89	3.78
17	8.40	6.11	5.19	4.67	4.34	4.10	3.93	3.79	3.68
18	8.29	6.01	5.09	4.58	4.25	4.01	3.84	3.71	3.60
19	8.18	5.93	5.01	4.50	4.17	3.94	3.77	3.63	3.52
20	8.10	5.85	4.94	4.43	4.10	3.87	3.70	3.56	3.46
21	8.02	5.78	4.87	4.37	4.04	3.81	3.64	3.51	3.40
22	7.95	5.72	4.82	4.31	3.99	3.76	3.59	3.45	3.35
23	7.88	5.66	4.76	4.26	3.94	3.71	3.54	3.41	3.30
24	7.82	5.61	4.72	4.22	3.90	3.67	3.50	3.36	3.26
25	7.77	5.57	4.68	4.18	3.85	3.63	3.46	3.32	3.22
26	7.72	5.53	4.64	4.14	3.82	3.59	3.42	3.29	3.18
27	7.68	5.49	4.60	4.11	3.78	3.56	3.39	3.26	3.15
28	7.64	5.45	4.57	4.07	3.75	3.53	3.36	3.23	3.12
29	7.60	5.42	4.54	4.04	3.73	3.50	3.33	3.20	3.09
30	7.56	5.39	4.51	4.02	3.70	3.47	3.30	3.17	3.07
40	7.31	5.18	4.31	3.83	3.51	3.29	3.12	2.99	2.89
60	7.08	4.98	4.13	3.65	3.34	3.12	2.95	2.82	2.72
120	6.85	4.79	3.95	3.48	3.17	2.96	2.79	2.66	2.56
∞	6.63	4.61	3.78	3.32	3.02	2.80	2.64	2.51	2.41

Denominator Degrees of Freedom

TABLE A.7
Percentage Points of the F Distribution (Continued)

10	12	15	20	24	30	40	60	120	∞	v_1
										v_2
6055.93	6106.68	6156.97	6208.66	6234.27	6260.35	6286.43	6312.97	6339.51	6366.00	1
99.40	99.42	99.43	99.45	99.46	99.47	99.48	99.48	99.49	99.50	2
27.23	27.05	26.87	26.69	26.60	26.50	26.41	26.32	26.22	26.13	3
14.55	14.37	14.20	14.02	13.93	13.84	13.75	13.65	13.56	13.46	4
10.05	9.89	9.72	9.55	9.47	9.38	9.29	9.20	9.11	9.02	5
7.87	7.72	7.56	7.40	7.31	7.23	7.14	7.06	6.97	6.88	6
6.62	6.47	6.31	6.16	6.07	5.99	5.91	5.82	5.74	5.65	7
5.81	5.67	5.52	5.36	5.28	5.20	5.12	5.03	4.95	4.86	8
5.26	5.11	4.96	4.81	4.73	4.65	4.57	4.48	4.40	4.31	9
4.85	4.71	4.56	4.41	4.33	4.25	4.17	4.08	4.00	3.91	10
4.54	4.40	4.25	4.10	4.02	3.94	3.86	3.78	3.69	3.60	11
4.30	4.16	4.01	3.86	3.78	3.70	3.62	3.54	3.45	3.36	12
4.10	3.96	3.82	3.66	3.59	3.51	3.43	3.34	3.25	3.17	13
3.94	3.80	3.66	3.51	3.43	3.35	3.27	3.18	3.09	3.00	14
3.80	3.67	3.52	3.37	3.29	3.21	3.13	3.05	2.96	2.87	15
3.69	3.55	3.41	3.26	3.18	3.10	3.02	2.93	2.84	2.75	16
3.59	3.46	3.31	3.16	3.08	3.00	2.92	2.83	2.75	2.65	17
3.51	3.37	3.23	3.08	3.00	2.92	2.84	2.75	2.66	2.57	18
3.43	3.30	3.15	3.00	2.92	2.84	2.76	2.67	2.58	2.49	19
3.37	3.23	3.09	2.94	2.86	2.78	2.69	2.61	2.52	2.42	20
3.31	3.17	3.03	2.88	2.80	2.72	2.64	2.55	2.46	2.36	21
3.26	3.12	2.98	2.83	2.75	2.67	2.58	2.50	2.40	2.31	22
3.21	3.07	2.93	2.78	2.70	2.62	2.54	2.45	2.35	2.26	23
3.17	3.03	2.89	2.74	2.66	2.58	2.49	2.40	2.31	2.21	24
3.13	2.99	2.85	2.70	2.62	2.54	2.45	2.36	2.27	2.17	25
3.09	2.96	2.81	2.66	2.58	2.50	2.42	2.33	2.23	2.13	26
3.06	2.93	2.78	2.63	2.55	2.47	2.38	2.29	2.20	2.10	27
3.03	2.90	2.75	2.60	2.52	2.44	2.35	2.26	2.17	2.06	28
3.00	2.87	2.73	2.57	2.49	2.41	2.33	2.23	2.14	2.03	29
2.98	2.84	2.70	2.55	2.47	2.39	2.30	2.21	2.11	2.01	30
2.80	2.66	2.52	2.37	2.29	2.20	2.11	2.02	1.92	1.80	40
2.63	2.50	2.35	2.20	2.12	2.03	1.94	1.84	1.73	1.60	60
2.47	2.34	2.19	2.03	1.95	1.86	1.76	1.66	1.53	1.38	120
2.32	2.18	2.04	1.88	1.79	1.70	1.59	1.47	1.32	1.00	∞

$\alpha = .01$ — Numerator Degrees of Freedom

Denominator Degrees of Freedom

(Continued)

TABLE A.7

Percentage Points of the F Distribution (Continued)

v_2	\ v_1				$\alpha = .005$				
				Numerator Degrees of Freedom					
	1	2	3	4	5	6	7	8	9
1	16212.46	19997.36	21614.13	22500.75	23055.82	23439.53	23715.20	23923.81	24091.45
2	198.50	199.01	199.16	199.24	199.30	199.33	199.36	199.38	199.39
3	55.55	49.80	47.47	46.20	45.39	44.84	44.43	44.13	43.88
4	31.33	26.28	24.26	23.15	22.46	21.98	21.62	21.35	21.14
5	22.78	18.31	16.53	15.56	14.94	14.51	14.20	13.96	13.77
6	18.63	14.54	12.92	12.03	11.46	11.07	10.79	10.57	10.39
7	16.24	12.40	10.88	10.05	9.52	9.16	8.89	8.68	8.51
8	14.69	11.04	9.60	8.81	8.30	7.95	7.69	7.50	7.34
9	13.61	10.11	8.72	7.96	7.47	7.13	6.88	6.69	6.54
10	12.83	9.43	8.08	7.34	6.87	6.54	6.30	6.12	5.97
11	12.23	8.91	7.60	6.88	6.42	6.10	5.86	5.68	5.54
12	11.75	8.51	7.23	6.52	6.07	5.76	5.52	5.35	5.20
13	11.37	8.19	6.93	6.23	5.79	5.48	5.25	5.08	4.94
14	11.06	7.92	6.68	6.00	5.56	5.26	5.03	4.86	4.72
15	10.80	7.70	6.48	5.80	5.37	5.07	4.85	4.67	4.54
16	10.58	7.51	6.30	5.64	5.21	4.91	4.69	4.52	4.38
17	10.38	7.35	6.16	5.50	5.07	4.78	4.56	4.39	4.25
18	10.22	7.21	6.03	5.37	4.96	4.66	4.44	4.28	4.14
19	10.07	7.09	5.92	5.27	4.85	4.56	4.34	4.18	4.04
20	9.94	6.99	5.82	5.17	4.76	4.47	4.26	4.09	3.96
21	9.83	6.89	5.73	5.09	4.68	4.39	4.18	4.01	3.88
22	9.73	6.81	5.65	5.02	4.61	4.32	4.11	3.94	3.81
23	9.63	6.73	5.58	4.95	4.54	4.26	4.05	3.88	3.75
24	9.55	6.66	5.52	4.89	4.49	4.20	3.99	3.83	3.69
25	9.48	6.60	5.46	4.84	4.43	4.15	3.94	3.78	3.64
26	9.41	6.54	5.41	4.79	4.38	4.10	3.89	3.73	3.60
27	9.34	6.49	5.36	4.74	4.34	4.06	3.85	3.69	3.56
28	9.28	6.44	5.32	4.70	4.30	4.02	3.81	3.65	3.52
29	9.23	6.40	5.28	4.66	4.26	3.98	3.77	3.61	3.48
30	9.18	6.35	5.24	4.62	4.23	3.95	3.74	3.58	3.45
40	8.83	6.07	4.98	4.37	3.99	3.71	3.51	3.35	3.22
60	8.49	5.79	4.73	4.14	3.76	3.49	3.29	3.13	3.01
120	8.18	5.54	4.50	3.92	3.55	3.28	3.09	2.93	2.81
∞	7.88	5.30	4.28	3.72	3.35	3.09	2.90	2.74	2.62

Denominator Degrees of Freedom

TABLE A.7
Percentage Points of the F Distribution (*Continued*)

				$\alpha = .005$						v_1
				Numerator Degrees of Freedom						
10	12	15	20	24	30	40	60	120	∞	v_2
24221.84	24426.73	24631.62	24836.51	24937.09	25041.40	25145.71	25253.74	25358.05	25465.00	1
199.39	199.42	199.43	199.45	199.45	199.48	199.48	199.48	199.49	199.50	2
43.68	43.39	43.08	42.78	42.62	42.47	42.31	42.15	41.99	41.83	3
20.97	20.70	20.44	20.17	20.03	19.89	19.75	19.61	19.47	19.32	4
13.62	13.38	13.15	12.90	12.78	12.66	12.53	12.40	12.27	12.14	5
10.25	10.03	9.81	9.59	9.47	9.36	9.24	9.12	9.00	8.88	6
8.38	8.18	7.97	7.75	7.64	7.53	7.42	7.31	7.19	7.08	7
7.21	7.01	6.81	6.61	6.50	6.40	6.29	6.18	6.06	5.95	8
6.42	6.23	6.03	5.83	5.73	5.62	5.52	5.41	5.30	5.19	9
5.85	5.66	5.47	5.27	5.17	5.07	4.97	4.86	4.75	4.64	10
5.42	5.24	5.05	4.86	4.76	4.65	4.55	4.45	4.34	4.23	11
5.09	4.91	4.72	4.53	4.43	4.33	4.23	4.12	4.01	3.90	12
4.82	4.64	4.46	4.27	4.17	4.07	3.97	3.87	3.76	3.65	13
4.60	4.43	4.25	4.06	3.96	3.86	3.76	3.66	3.55	3.44	14
4.42	4.25	4.07	3.88	3.79	3.69	3.59	3.48	3.37	3.26	15
4.27	4.10	3.92	3.73	3.64	3.54	3.44	3.33	3.22	3.11	16
4.14	3.97	3.79	3.61	3.51	3.41	3.31	3.21	3.10	2.98	17
4.03	3.86	3.68	3.50	3.40	3.30	3.20	3.10	2.99	2.87	18
3.93	3.76	3.59	3.40	3.31	3.21	3.11	3.00	2.89	2.78	19
3.85	3.68	3.50	3.32	3.22	3.12	3.02	2.92	2.81	2.69	20
3.77	3.60	3.43	3.24	3.15	3.05	2.95	2.84	2.73	2.61	21
3.70	3.54	3.36	3.18	3.08	2.98	2.88	2.77	2.66	2.55	22
3.64	3.47	3.30	3.12	3.02	2.92	2.82	2.71	2.60	2.48	23
3.59	3.42	3.25	3.06	2.97	2.87	2.77	2.66	2.55	2.43	24
3.54	3.37	3.20	3.01	2.92	2.82	2.72	2.61	2.50	2.38	25
3.49	3.33	3.15	2.97	2.87	2.77	2.67	2.56	2.45	2.33	26
3.45	3.28	3.11	2.93	2.83	2.73	2.63	2.52	2.41	2.29	27
3.41	3.25	3.07	2.89	2.79	2.69	2.59	2.48	2.37	2.25	28
3.38	3.21	3.04	2.86	2.76	2.66	2.56	2.45	2.33	2.21	29
3.34	3.18	3.01	2.82	2.73	2.63	2.52	2.42	2.30	2.18	30
3.12	2.95	2.78	2.60	2.50	2.40	2.30	2.18	2.06	1.93	40
2.90	2.74	2.57	2.39	2.29	2.19	2.08	1.96	1.83	1.69	60
2.71	2.54	2.37	2.19	2.09	1.98	1.87	1.75	1.61	1.43	120
2.52	2.36	2.19	2.00	1.90	1.79	1.67	1.53	1.36	1.00	∞

TABLE A.8

The Chi-Square Table

Values of χ^2 for Selected Probabilities

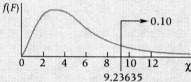

Example: df (Number of degrees of freedom) = 5, the tail above $\chi^2 = 9.23635$ represents 0.10 or 10% of area under the curve.

Degrees of Freedom	Area in Upper Tail									
	.995	.99	.975	.95	.9	.1	.05	.025	.01	.005
1	0.0000393	0.0001571	0.0009821	0.0039322	0.0157907	2.7055	3.8415	5.0239	6.6349	7.8794
2	0.010025	0.020100	0.050636	0.102586	0.210721	4.6052	5.9915	7.3778	9.2104	10.5965
3	0.07172	0.11483	0.21579	0.35185	0.58438	6.2514	7.8147	9.3484	11.3449	12.8381
4	0.20698	0.29711	0.48442	0.71072	1.06362	7.7794	9.4877	11.1433	13.2767	14.8602
5	0.41175	0.55430	0.83121	1.14548	1.61031	9.2363	11.0705	12.8325	15.0863	16.7496
6	0.67573	0.87208	1.23734	1.63538	2.20413	10.6446	12.5916	14.4494	16.8119	18.5475
7	0.98925	1.23903	1.68986	2.16735	2.83311	12.0170	14.0671	16.0128	18.4753	20.2777
8	1.34440	1.64651	2.17972	2.73263	3.48954	13.3616	15.5073	17.5345	20.0902	21.9549
9	1.73491	2.08789	2.70039	3.32512	4.16816	14.6837	16.9190	19.0228	21.6660	23.5893
10	2.15585	2.55820	3.24696	3.94030	4.86518	15.9872	18.3070	20.4832	23.2093	25.1881
11	2.60320	3.05350	3.81574	4.57481	5.57779	17.2750	19.6752	21.9200	24.7250	26.7569
12	3.07379	3.57055	4.40378	5.22603	6.30380	18.5493	21.0261	23.3367	26.2170	28.2997
13	3.56504	4.10690	5.00874	5.89186	7.04150	19.8119	22.3620	24.7356	27.6882	29.8193
14	4.07466	4.66042	5.62872	6.57063	7.78954	21.0641	23.6848	26.1189	29.1412	31.3194
15	4.60087	5.22936	6.26212	7.26093	8.54675	22.3071	24.9958	27.4884	30.5780	32.8015
16	5.14216	5.81220	6.90766	7.96164	9.31224	23.5418	26.2962	28.8453	31.9999	34.2671
17	5.69727	6.40774	7.56418	8.67175	10.08518	24.7690	27.5871	30.1910	33.4087	35.7184
18	6.26477	7.01490	8.23074	9.39045	10.86494	25.9894	28.8693	31.5264	34.8052	37.1564
19	6.84392	7.63270	8.90651	10.11701	11.65091	27.2036	30.1435	32.8523	36.1908	38.5821
20	7.43381	8.26037	9.59077	10.85080	12.44260	28.4120	31.4104	34.1696	37.5663	39.9969
21	8.03360	8.89717	10.28291	11.59132	13.23960	29.6151	32.6706	35.4789	38.9322	41.4009
22	8.64268	9.54249	10.98233	12.33801	14.04149	30.8133	33.9245	36.7807	40.2894	42.7957
23	9.26038	10.19569	11.68853	13.09051	14.84795	32.0069	35.1725	38.0756	41.6383	44.1814
24	9.88620	10.85635	12.40115	13.84842	15.65868	33.1962	36.4150	39.3641	42.9798	45.5584
25	10.51965	11.52395	13.11971	14.61140	16.47341	34.3816	37.6525	40.6465	44.3140	46.9280
26	11.16022	12.19818	13.84388	15.37916	17.29188	35.5632	38.8851	41.9231	45.6416	48.2898
27	11.80765	12.87847	14.57337	16.15139	18.11389	36.7412	40.1133	43.1945	46.9628	49.6450
28	12.46128	13.56467	15.30785	16.92788	18.93924	37.9159	41.3372	44.4608	48.2782	50.9936
29	13.12107	14.25641	16.04705	17.70838	19.76774	39.0875	42.5569	45.7223	49.5878	52.3355
30	13.78668	14.95346	16.79076	18.49267	20.59924	40.2560	43.7730	46.9792	50.8922	53.6719
40	20.70658	22.16420	24.43306	26.50930	29.05052	51.8050	55.7585	59.3417	63.6908	66.7660
50	27.99082	29.70673	32.35738	34.76424	37.68864	63.1671	67.5048	71.4202	76.1538	79.4898
60	35.53440	37.48480	40.48171	43.18797	46.45888	74.3970	79.0820	83.2977	88.3794	91.9518
70	43.27531	45.44170	48.75754	51.73926	55.32894	85.5270	90.5313	95.0231	100.4251	104.2148
80	51.17193	53.53998	57.15315	60.39146	64.27784	96.5782	101.8795	106.6285	112.3288	116.3209
90	59.19633	61.75402	65.64659	69.12602	73.29108	107.5650	113.1452	118.1359	124.1162	128.2987
100	67.32753	70.06500	74.22188	77.92944	82.35813	118.4980	124.3221	129.5613	135.8069	140.1697

TABLE A.9
Critical Values for the Durbin-Watson Test

Entries in the table give the critical values for a one-tailed Durbin-Watson test for autocorrelation. For a two-tailed test, the level of significance is doubled.

	Significant Points of d_L and d_U: $\alpha = .05$ Number of Independent Variables									
k	1		2		3		4		5	
n	d_L	d_U	d_L	d_U	d_L	d_U	d_L	d_U	d_L	d_U
15	1.08	1.36	0.95	1.54	0.82	1.75	0.69	1.97	0.56	2.21
16	1.10	1.37	0.98	1.54	0.86	1.73	0.74	1.93	0.62	2.15
17	1.13	1.38	1.02	1.54	0.90	1.71	0.78	1.90	0.67	2.10
18	1.16	1.39	1.05	1.53	0.93	1.69	0.82	1.87	0.71	2.06
19	1.18	1.40	1.08	1.53	0.97	1.68	0.86	1.85	0.75	2.02
20	1.20	1.41	1.10	1.54	1.00	1.68	0.90	1.83	0.79	1.99
21	1.22	1.42	1.13	1.54	1.03	1.67	0.93	1.81	0.83	1.96
22	1.24	1.43	1.15	1.54	1.05	1.66	0.96	1.80	0.86	1.94
23	1.26	1.44	1.17	1.54	1.08	1.66	0.99	1.79	0.90	1.92
24	1.27	1.45	1.19	1.55	1.10	1.66	1.01	1.78	0.93	1.90
25	1.29	1.45	1.21	1.55	1.12	1.66	1.04	1.77	0.95	1.89
26	1.30	1.46	1.22	1.55	1.14	1.65	1.06	1.76	0.98	1.88
27	1.32	1.47	1.24	1.56	1.16	1.65	1.08	1.76	1.01	1.86
28	1.33	1.48	1.26	1.56	1.18	1.65	1.10	1.75	1.03	1.85
29	1.34	1.48	1.27	1.56	1.20	1.65	1.12	1.74	1.05	1.84
30	1.35	1.49	1.28	1.57	1.21	1.65	1.14	1.74	1.07	1.83
31	1.36	1.50	1.30	1.57	1.23	1.65	1.16	1.74	1.09	1.83
32	1.37	1.50	1.31	1.57	1.24	1.65	1.18	1.73	1.11	1.82
33	1.38	1.51	1.32	1.58	1.26	1.65	1.19	1.73	1.13	1.81
34	1.39	1.51	1.33	1.58	1.27	1.65	1.21	1.73	1.15	1.81
35	1.40	1.52	1.34	1.58	1.28	1.65	1.22	1.73	1.16	1.80
36	1.41	1.52	1.35	1.59	1.29	1.65	1.24	1.73	1.18	1.80
37	1.42	1.53	1.36	1.59	1.31	1.66	1.25	1.72	1.19	1.80
38	1.43	1.54	1.37	1.59	1.32	1.66	1.26	1.72	1.21	1.79
39	1.43	1.54	1.38	1.60	1.33	1.66	1.27	1.72	1.22	1.79
40	1.44	1.54	1.39	1.60	1.34	1.66	1.29	1.72	1.23	1.79
45	1.48	1.57	1.43	1.62	1.38	1.67	1.34	1.72	1.29	1.78
50	1.50	1.59	1.46	1.63	1.42	1.67	1.38	1.72	1.34	1.77
55	1.53	1.60	1.49	1.64	1.45	1.68	1.41	1.72	1.38	1.77
60	1.55	1.62	1.51	1.65	1.48	1.69	1.44	1.73	1.41	1.77
65	1.57	1.63	1.54	1.66	1.50	1.70	1.47	1.73	1.44	1.77
70	1.58	1.64	1.55	1.67	1.52	1.70	1.49	1.74	1.46	1.77
75	1.60	1.65	1.57	1.68	1.54	1.71	1.51	1.74	1.49	1.77
80	1.61	1.66	1.59	1.69	1.56	1.72	1.53	1.74	1.51	1.77
85	1.62	1.67	1.60	1.70	1.57	1.72	1.55	1.75	1.52	1.77
90	1.63	1.68	1.61	1.70	1.59	1.73	1.57	1.75	1.54	1.78
95	1.64	1.69	1.62	1.71	1.60	1.73	1.58	1.75	1.56	1.78
100	1.65	1.69	1.63	1.72	1.61	1.74	1.59	1.76	1.57	1.78

This table is reprinted by permission of *Biometrika* trustees from J. Durbin and G. S. Watson, "Testing for Serial Correlation in Least Square Regression II," *Biometrika*, vol. 38, 1951, pp. 159–78.

(*Continued*)

TABLE A.9

Critical Values for the
Durbin-Watson Test
(*Continued*)

Significant Points of d_L and d_U: $\alpha = .01$
Number of Independent Variables

k	1		2		3		4		5	
n	d_L	d_U	d_L	d_U	d_L	d_U	d_L	d_U	d_L	d_U
15	0.81	1.07	0.70	1.25	0.59	1.46	0.49	1.70	0.39	1.96
16	0.84	1.09	0.74	1.25	0.63	1.44	0.53	1.66	0.44	1.90
17	0.87	1.10	0.77	1.25	0.67	1.43	0.57	1.63	0.48	1.85
18	0.90	1.12	0.80	1.26	0.71	1.42	0.61	1.60	0.52	1.80
19	0.93	1.13	0.83	1.26	0.74	1.41	0.65	1.58	0.56	1.77
20	0.95	1.15	0.86	1.27	0.77	1.41	0.68	1.57	0.60	1.74
21	0.97	1.16	0.89	1.27	0.80	1.41	0.72	1.55	0.63	1.71
22	1.00	1.17	0.91	1.28	0.83	1.40	0.75	1.54	0.66	1.69
23	1.02	1.19	0.94	1.29	0.86	1.40	0.77	1.53	0.70	1.67
24	1.04	1.20	0.96	1.30	0.88	1.41	0.80	1.53	0.72	1.66
25	1.05	1.21	0.98	1.30	0.90	1.41	0.83	1.52	0.75	1.65
26	1.07	1.22	1.00	1.31	0.93	1.41	0.85	1.52	0.78	1.64
27	1.09	1.23	1.02	1.32	0.95	1.41	0.88	1.51	0.81	1.63
28	1.10	1.24	1.04	1.32	0.97	1.41	0.90	1.51	0.83	1.62
29	1.12	1.25	1.05	1.33	0.99	1.42	0.92	1.51	0.85	1.61
30	1.13	1.26	1.07	1.34	1.01	1.42	0.94	1.51	0.88	1.61
31	1.15	1.27	1.08	1.34	1.02	1.42	0.96	1.51	0.90	1.60
32	1.16	1.28	1.10	1.35	1.04	1.43	0.98	1.51	0.92	1.60
33	1.17	1.29	1.11	1.36	1.05	1.43	1.00	1.51	0.94	1.59
34	1.18	1.30	1.13	1.36	1.07	1.43	1.01	1.51	0.95	1.59
35	1.19	1.31	1.14	1.37	1.08	1.44	1.03	1.51	0.97	1.59
36	1.21	1.32	1.15	1.38	1.10	1.44	1.04	1.51	0.99	1.59
37	1.22	1.32	1.16	1.38	1.11	1.45	1.06	1.51	1.00	1.59
38	1.23	1.33	1.18	1.39	1.12	1.45	1.07	1.52	1.02	1.58
39	1.24	1.34	1.19	1.39	1.14	1.45	1.09	1.52	1.03	1.58
40	1.25	1.34	1.20	1.40	1.15	1.46	1.10	1.52	1.05	1.58
45	1.29	1.38	1.24	1.42	1.20	1.48	1.16	1.53	1.11	1.58
50	1.32	1.40	1.28	1.45	1.24	1.49	1.20	1.54	1.16	1.59
55	1.36	1.43	1.32	1.47	1.28	1.51	1.25	1.55	1.21	1.59
60	1.38	1.45	1.35	1.48	1.32	1.52	1.28	1.56	1.25	1.60
65	1.41	1.47	1.38	1.50	1.35	1.53	1.31	1.57	1.28	1.61
70	1.43	1.49	1.40	1.52	1.37	1.55	1.34	1.58	1.31	1.61
75	1.45	1.50	1.42	1.53	1.39	1.56	1.37	1.59	1.34	1.62
80	1.47	1.52	1.44	1.54	1.42	1.57	1.39	1.60	1.36	1.62
85	1.48	1.53	1.46	1.55	1.43	1.58	1.41	1.60	1.39	1.63
90	1.50	1.54	1.47	1.56	1.45	1.59	1.43	1.61	1.41	1.64
95	1.51	1.55	1.49	1.57	1.47	1.60	1.45	1.62	1.42	1.64
100	1.52	1.56	1.50	1.58	1.48	1.60	1.46	1.63	1.44	1.65

TABLE A.10

Critical Values of the Studentized Range (*q*) Distribution

$\alpha = .05$

Degrees of Freedom	2	3	4	5	6	7	8	9	10	11	12	13	14	15	16	17	18	19	20
1	18.0	27.0	32.8	37.1	40.4	43.1	45.4	47.4	49.1	50.6	52.0	53.2	54.3	55.4	56.3	57.2	58.0	58.8	59.6
2	6.08	8.33	9.80	10.9	11.7	12.4	13.0	13.5	14.0	14.4	14.7	15.1	15.4	15.7	15.9	16.1	16.4	16.6	16.8
3	4.50	5.91	6.82	7.50	8.04	8.48	8.85	9.18	9.46	9.72	9.95	10.2	10.3	10.5	10.7	10.8	11.0	11.1	11.2
4	3.93	5.04	5.76	6.29	6.71	7.05	7.35	7.60	7.83	8.03	8.21	8.37	8.52	8.66	8.79	8.91	9.03	9.13	9.23
5	3.64	4.60	5.22	5.67	6.03	6.33	6.58	6.80	6.99	7.17	7.32	7.47	7.60	7.72	7.83	7.93	8.03	8.12	8.21
6	3.46	4.34	4.90	5.30	5.63	5.90	6.12	6.32	6.49	6.65	6.79	6.92	7.03	7.14	7.24	7.34	7.43	7.51	7.59
7	3.34	4.16	4.68	5.06	5.36	5.61	5.82	6.00	6.16	6.30	6.43	6.55	6.66	6.76	6.85	6.94	7.02	7.10	7.17
8	3.26	4.04	4.53	4.89	5.17	5.40	5.60	5.77	5.92	6.05	6.18	6.29	6.39	6.48	6.57	6.65	6.73	6.80	6.87
9	3.20	3.95	4.41	4.76	5.02	5.24	5.43	5.59	5.74	5.87	5.98	6.09	6.19	6.28	6.36	6.44	6.51	6.58	6.64
10	3.15	3.88	4.33	4.65	4.91	5.12	5.30	5.46	5.60	5.72	5.83	5.93	6.03	6.11	6.19	6.27	6.34	6.40	6.47
11	3.11	3.82	4.26	4.57	4.82	5.03	5.20	5.35	5.49	5.61	5.71	5.81	5.90	5.98	6.06	6.13	6.20	6.27	6.33
12	3.08	3.77	4.20	4.51	4.75	4.95	5.12	5.27	5.39	5.51	5.61	5.71	5.80	5.88	5.95	6.02	6.09	6.15	6.21
13	3.06	3.73	4.15	4.45	4.69	4.88	5.05	5.19	5.32	5.43	5.53	5.63	5.71	5.79	5.86	5.93	5.99	6.05	6.11
14	3.03	3.70	4.11	4.41	4.64	4.83	4.99	5.13	5.25	5.36	5.46	5.55	5.64	5.71	5.79	5.85	5.91	5.97	6.03
15	3.01	3.67	4.08	4.37	4.59	4.78	4.94	5.08	5.20	5.31	5.40	5.49	5.57	5.65	5.72	5.78	5.85	5.90	5.96
16	3.00	3.65	4.05	4.33	4.56	4.74	4.90	5.03	5.15	5.26	5.35	5.44	5.52	5.59	5.66	5.73	5.79	5.84	5.90
17	2.98	3.63	4.02	4.30	4.52	4.70	4.86	4.99	5.11	5.21	5.31	5.39	5.47	5.54	5.61	5.67	5.73	5.79	5.84
18	2.97	3.61	4.00	4.28	4.49	4.67	4.82	4.96	5.07	5.17	5.27	5.35	5.43	5.50	5.57	5.63	5.69	5.74	5.79
19	2.96	3.59	3.98	4.25	4.47	4.65	4.79	4.92	5.04	5.14	5.23	5.31	5.39	5.46	5.53	5.59	5.65	5.70	5.75
20	2.95	3.58	3.96	4.23	4.45	4.62	4.77	4.90	5.01	5.11	5.20	5.28	5.36	5.43	5.49	5.55	5.61	5.66	5.71
24	2.92	3.53	3.90	4.17	4.37	4.54	4.68	4.81	4.92	5.01	5.10	5.18	5.25	5.32	5.38	5.44	5.49	5.55	5.59
30	2.89	3.49	3.85	4.10	4.30	4.46	4.60	4.72	4.82	4.92	5.00	5.08	5.15	5.21	5.27	5.33	5.38	5.43	5.47
40	2.86	3.44	3.79	4.04	4.23	4.39	4.52	4.63	4.73	4.82	4.90	4.98	5.04	5.11	5.16	5.22	5.27	5.31	5.36
60	2.83	3.40	3.74	3.98	4.16	4.31	4.44	4.55	4.65	4.73	4.81	4.88	4.94	5.00	5.06	5.11	5.15	5.20	5.24
120	2.80	3.36	3.68	3.92	4.10	4.24	4.36	4.47	4.56	4.64	4.71	4.78	4.84	4.90	4.95	5.00	5.04	5.09	5.13
∞	2.77	3.31	3.63	3.86	4.03	4.17	4.29	4.39	4.47	4.55	4.62	4.68	4.74	4.80	4.85	4.89	4.93	4.97	5.01

(*Continued*)

TABLE A.10

Critical Values of the Studentized Range (q) Distribution (Continued)

$\alpha = .01$

Degrees of Freedom	2	3	4	5	6	7	8	9	10	11	12	13	14	15	16	17	18	19	20
									Number of Populations										
1	90.0	135.	164.	186.	202.	216.	227.	237.	246.	253.	260.	266.	272.	277.	282.	286.	290.	294.	298.
2	14.0	19.0	22.3	24.7	26.6	28.2	29.5	30.7	31.7	32.6	33.4	34.1	34.8	35.4	36.0	36.5	37.0	37.5	37.9
3	8.26	10.6	12.2	13.3	14.2	15.0	15.6	16.2	16.7	17.1	17.5	17.9	18.2	18.5	18.8	19.1	19.3	19.5	19.8
4	6.51	8.12	9.17	9.96	10.6	11.1	11.5	11.9	12.3	12.6	12.8	13.1	13.3	13.5	13.7	13.9	14.1	14.2	14.4
5	5.70	6.97	7.80	8.42	8.91	9.32	9.67	9.97	10.2	10.5	10.7	10.9	11.1	11.2	11.4	11.6	11.7	11.8	11.9
6	5.24	6.33	7.03	7.56	7.97	8.32	8.61	8.87	9.10	9.30	9.49	9.65	9.81	9.95	10.1	10.2	10.3	10.4	10.5
7	4.95	5.92	6.54	7.01	7.37	7.68	7.94	8.17	8.37	8.55	8.71	8.86	9.00	9.12	9.24	9.35	9.46	9.55	9.65
8	4.74	5.63	6.20	6.63	6.96	7.24	7.47	7.68	7.87	8.03	8.18	8.31	8.44	8.55	8.66	8.76	8.85	8.94	9.03
9	4.60	5.43	5.96	6.35	6.66	6.91	7.13	7.32	7.49	7.65	7.78	7.91	8.03	8.13	8.23	8.32	8.41	8.49	8.57
10	4.48	5.27	5.77	6.14	6.43	6.67	6.87	7.05	7.21	7.36	7.48	7.60	7.71	7.81	7.91	7.99	8.07	8.15	8.22
11	4.39	5.14	5.62	5.97	6.25	6.48	6.67	6.84	6.99	7.13	7.25	7.36	7.46	7.56	7.65	7.73	7.81	7.88	7.95
12	4.32	5.04	5.50	5.84	6.10	6.32	6.51	6.67	6.81	6.94	7.06	7.17	7.26	7.36	7.44	7.52	7.59	7.66	7.73
13	4.26	4.96	5.40	5.73	5.98	6.19	6.37	6.53	6.67	6.79	6.90	7.01	7.10	7.19	7.27	7.34	7.42	7.48	7.55
14	4.21	4.89	5.32	5.63	5.88	6.08	6.26	6.41	6.54	6.66	6.77	6.87	6.96	7.05	7.12	7.20	7.27	7.33	7.39
15	4.17	4.83	5.25	5.56	5.80	5.99	6.16	6.31	6.44	6.55	6.66	6.76	6.84	6.93	7.00	7.07	7.14	7.20	7.26
16	4.13	4.78	5.19	5.49	5.72	5.92	6.08	6.22	6.35	6.46	6.56	6.66	6.74	6.82	6.90	6.97	7.03	7.09	7.15
17	4.10	4.74	5.14	5.43	5.66	5.85	6.01	6.15	6.27	6.38	6.48	6.57	6.66	6.73	6.80	6.87	6.94	7.00	7.05
18	4.07	4.70	5.09	5.38	5.60	5.79	5.94	6.08	6.20	6.31	6.41	6.50	6.58	6.65	6.72	6.79	6.85	6.91	6.96
19	4.05	4.67	5.05	5.33	5.55	5.73	5.89	6.02	6.14	6.25	6.34	6.43	6.51	6.58	6.65	6.72	6.78	6.84	6.89
20	4.02	4.64	5.02	5.29	5.51	5.69	5.84	5.97	6.09	6.19	6.29	6.37	6.45	6.52	6.59	6.65	6.71	6.76	6.82
24	3.96	4.54	4.91	5.17	5.37	5.54	5.69	5.81	5.92	6.02	6.11	6.19	6.26	6.33	6.39	6.45	6.51	6.56	6.61
30	3.89	4.45	4.80	5.05	5.24	5.40	5.54	5.65	5.76	5.85	5.93	6.01	6.08	6.14	6.20	6.26	6.31	6.36	6.41
40	3.82	4.37	4.70	4.93	5.11	5.27	5.39	5.50	5.60	5.69	5.77	5.84	5.90	5.96	6.02	6.07	6.12	6.17	6.21
60	3.76	4.28	4.60	4.82	4.99	5.13	5.25	5.36	5.45	5.53	5.60	5.67	5.73	5.79	5.84	5.89	5.93	5.98	6.02
120	3.70	4.20	4.50	4.71	4.87	5.01	5.12	5.21	5.30	5.38	5.44	5.51	5.56	5.61	5.66	5.71	5.75	5.79	5.83
∞	3.64	4.12	4.40	4.60	4.76	4.88	4.99	5.08	5.16	5.23	5.29	5.35	5.40	5.45	5.49	5.54	5.57	5.61	5.65

TABLE A.11

Critical Values of R for the Runs Test: Lower Tail

n_1 \ n_2	\multicolumn{19}{c}{$\alpha = .025$}

n_1 \ n_2	2	3	4	5	6	7	8	9	10	11	12	13	14	15	16	17	18	19	20
2											2	2	2	2	2	2	2	2	2
3					2	2	2	2	2	2	2	2	2	3	3	3	3	3	3
4				2	2	2	3	3	3	3	3	3	3	3	4	4	4	4	4
5			2	2	3	3	3	3	3	4	4	4	4	4	4	4	5	5	5
6		2	2	3	3	3	3	4	4	4	4	5	5	5	5	5	5	6	6
7		2	2	3	3	3	4	4	5	5	5	5	5	6	6	6	6	6	6
8		2	3	3	3	4	4	5	5	5	6	6	6	6	6	7	7	7	7
9		2	3	3	4	4	5	5	5	6	6	6	7	7	7	7	8	8	8
10		2	3	3	4	5	5	5	6	6	7	7	7	7	8	8	8	8	9
11		2	3	4	4	5	5	6	6	7	7	7	8	8	8	9	9	9	9
12	2	2	3	4	4	5	6	6	7	7	7	8	8	8	9	9	9	10	10
13	2	2	3	4	5	5	6	6	7	7	8	8	9	9	9	10	10	10	10
14	2	2	3	4	5	5	6	7	7	8	8	9	9	9	10	10	10	11	11
15	2	3	3	4	5	6	6	7	7	8	8	9	9	10	10	11	11	11	12
16	2	3	4	4	5	6	6	7	8	8	9	9	10	10	11	11	11	12	12
17	2	3	4	4	5	6	7	7	8	9	9	10	10	11	11	11	12	12	13
18	2	3	4	5	5	6	7	8	8	9	9	10	10	11	11	12	12	13	13
19	2	3	4	5	6	6	7	8	8	9	10	10	11	11	12	12	13	13	13
20	2	3	4	5	6	6	7	8	9	9	10	10	11	12	12	13	13	13	14

Source: Adapted from F. S. Swed and C. Eisenhart, *Ann. Math. Statist.*, vol. 14, 1943, pp. 83–86.

TABLE A.12

Critical Values of R for the Runs Test: Upper Tail

n_1 \ n_2	\multicolumn{19}{c}{$\alpha = .025$}

n_1 \ n_2	2	3	4	5	6	7	8	9	10	11	12	13	14	15	16	17	18	19	20
2																			
3																			
4				9	9														
5			9	10	10	11	11												
6			9	10	11	12	12	13	13	13	13								
7				11	12	13	13	14	14	14	14	15	15	15					
8				11	12	13	14	14	15	15	16	16	16	16	17	17	17	17	17
9					13	14	14	15	16	16	16	17	17	18	18	18	18	18	18
10					13	14	15	16	16	17	17	18	18	18	19	19	19	20	20
11					13	14	15	16	17	17	18	19	19	19	20	20	20	21	21
12					13	14	16	16	17	18	19	19	20	20	21	21	21	22	22
13						15	16	17	18	19	19	20	20	21	21	22	22	23	23
14						15	16	17	18	19	20	20	21	22	22	23	23	23	24
15						15	16	18	18	19	20	21	22	22	23	23	24	24	25
16							17	18	19	20	21	21	22	23	23	24	25	25	25
17							17	18	19	20	21	22	23	23	24	25	25	26	26
18							17	18	19	20	21	22	23	24	25	25	26	26	27
19							17	18	20	21	22	23	23	24	25	26	26	27	27
20							17	18	20	21	22	23	24	25	25	26	27	27	28

TABLE A.13

p-Values for Mann-Whitney *U* Statistic Small Samples ($n_1 \leq n_2$)

$n_2 = 3$	U_0	n_1 1	2	3		
	0	.25	.10	.05		
	1	.50	.20	.10		
	2		.40	.20		
	3		.60	.35		
	4			.50		

$n_2 = 4$	U_0	n_1 1	2	3	4	
	0	.2000	.0667	.0286	.0143	
	1	.4000	.1333	.0571	.0286	
	2	.6000	.2667	.1143	.0571	
	3		.4000	.2000	.1000	
	4		.6000	.3143	.1714	
	5			.4286	.2429	
	6			.5714	.3429	
	7				.4429	
	8				.5571	

$n_2 = 5$	U_0	n_1 1	2	3	4	5
	0	.1667	.0476	.0179	.0079	.0040
	1	.3333	.0952	.0357	.0159	.0079
	2	.5000	.1905	.0714	.0317	.0159
	3		.2857	.1250	.0556	.0278
	4		.4286	.1964	.0952	.0476
	5		.5714	.2857	.1429	.0754
	6			.3929	.2063	.1111
	7			.5000	.2778	.1548
	8				.3651	.2103
	9				.4524	.2738
	10				.5476	.3452
	11					.4206
	12					.5000

Computed by M. Pagano, Dept. of Statistics, University of Florida. Reprinted by permission from William Mendenhall and James E. Reinmuth, *Statistics for Management and Economics,* 5th ed. Copyright © 1986 by PWS-KENT Publishers, Boston.

TABLE A.13

p-Values for Mann-Whitney *U* Statistic Small Samples ($n_1 \leq n_2$) (*Continued*)

$n_2 = 6$	U_0	1	2	3	4	5	6
				n_1			
	0	.1429	.0357	.0119	.0048	.0022	.0011
	1	.2857	.0714	.0238	.0095	.0043	.0022
	2	.4286	.1429	.0476	.0190	.0087	.0043
	3	.5714	.2143	.0833	.0333	.0152	.0076
	4		.3214	.1310	.0571	.0260	.0130
	5		.4286	.1905	.0857	.0411	.0206
	6		.5714	.2738	.1286	.0628	.0325
	7			.3571	.1762	.0887	.0465
	8			.4524	.2381	.1234	.0660
	9			.5476	.3048	.1645	.0898
	10				.3810	.2143	.1201
	11				.4571	.2684	.1548
	12				.5429	.3312	.1970
	13					.3961	.2424
	14					.4654	.2944
	15					.5346	.3496
	16						.4091
	17						.4686
	18						.5314

$n_2 = 7$	U_0	1	2	3	4	5	6	7
					n_1			
	0	.1250	.0278	.0083	.0030	.0013	.0006	.0003
	1	.2500	.0556	.0167	.0061	.0025	.0012	.0006
	2	.3750	.1111	.0333	.0121	.0051	.0023	.0012
	3	.5000	.1667	.0583	.0212	.0088	.0041	.0020
	4		.2500	.0917	.0364	.0152	.0070	.0035
	5		.3333	.1333	.0545	.0240	.0111	.0055
	6		.4444	.1917	.0818	.0366	.0175	.0087
	7		.5556	.2583	.1152	.0530	.0256	.0131
	8			.3333	.1576	.0745	.0367	.0189
	9			.4167	.2061	.1010	.0507	.0265
	10			.5000	.2636	.1338	.0688	.0364
	11				.3242	.1717	.0903	.0487
	12				.3939	.2159	.1171	.0641
	13				.4636	.2652	.1474	.0825
	14				.5364	.3194	.1830	.1043
	15					.3775	.2226	.1297
	16					.4381	.2669	.1588
	17					.5000	.3141	.1914
	18						.3654	.2279
	19						.4178	.2675
	20						.4726	.3100
	21						.5274	.3552
	22							.4024
	23							.4508
	24							.5000

(*Continued*)

TABLE A.13

p-Values for Mann-Whitney *U*
Statistic Small Samples
($n_1 \leq n_2$) (*Continued*)

$n_2 = 8$	U_0	1	2	3	4	5	6	7	8
	0	.1111	.0222	.0061	.0020	.0008	.0003	.0002	.0001
	1	.2222	.0444	.0121	.0040	.0016	.0007	.0003	.0002
	2	.3333	.0889	.0242	.0081	.0031	.0013	.0006	.0003
	3	.4444	.1333	.0424	.0141	.0054	.0023	.0011	.0005
	4	.5556	.2000	.0667	.0242	.0093	.0040	.0019	.0009
	5		.2667	.0970	.0364	.0148	.0063	.0030	.0015
	6		.3556	.1394	.0545	.0225	.0100	.0047	.0023
	7		.4444	.1879	.0768	.0326	.0147	.0070	.0035
	8		.5556	.2485	.1071	.0466	.0213	.0103	.0052
	9			.3152	.1414	.0637	.0296	.0145	.0074
	10			.3879	.1838	.0855	.0406	.0200	.0103
	11			.4606	.2303	.1111	.0539	.0270	.0141
	12			.5394	.2848	.1422	.0709	.0361	.0190
	13				.3414	.1772	.0906	.0469	.0249
	14				.4040	.2176	.1142	.0603	.0325
	15				.4667	.2618	.1412	.0760	.0415
	16				.5333	.3108	.1725	.0946	.0524
	17					.3621	.2068	.1159	.0652
	18					.4165	.2454	.1405	.0803
	19					.4716	.2864	.1678	.0974
	20					.5284	.3310	.1984	.1172
	21						.3773	.2317	.1393
	22						.4259	.2679	.1641
	23						.4749	.3063	.1911
	24						.5251	.3472	.2209
	25							.3894	.2527
	26							.4333	.2869
	27							.4775	.3227
	28							.5225	.3605
	29								.3992
	30								.4392
	31								.4796
	32								.5204

TABLE A.13

p-Values for Mann-Whitney *U* Statistic Small Samples ($n_1 \leq n_2$) (*Continued*)

$n_2 = 9$ U_0	1	2	3	4	5	6	7	8	9
0	.1000	.0182	.0045	.0014	.0005	.0002	.0001	.0000	.0000
1	.2000	.0364	.0091	.0028	.0010	.0004	.0002	.0001	.0000
2	.3000	.0727	.0182	.0056	.0020	.0008	.0003	.0002	.0001
3	.4000	.1091	.0318	.0098	.0035	.0014	.0006	.0003	.0001
4	.5000	.1636	.0500	.0168	.0060	.0024	.0010	.0005	.0002
5		.2182	.0727	.0252	.0095	.0038	.0017	.0008	.0004
6		.2909	.1045	.0378	.0145	.0060	.0026	.0012	.0006
7		.3636	.1409	.0531	.0210	.0088	.0039	.0019	.0009
8		.4545	.1864	.0741	.0300	.0128	.0058	.0028	.0014
9		.5455	.2409	.0993	.0415	.0180	.0082	.0039	.0020
10			.3000	.1301	.0559	.0248	.0115	.0056	.0028
11			.3636	.1650	.0734	.0332	.0156	.0076	.0039
12			.4318	.2070	.0949	.0440	.0209	.0103	.0053
13			.5000	.2517	.1199	.0567	.0274	.0137	.0071
14				.3021	.1489	.0723	.0356	.0180	.0094
15				.3552	.1818	.0905	.0454	.0232	.0122
16				.4126	.2188	.1119	.0571	.0296	.0157
17				.4699	.2592	.1361	.0708	.0372	.0200
18				.5301	.3032	.1638	.0869	.0464	.0252
19					.3497	.1942	.1052	.0570	.0313
20					.3986	.2280	.1261	.0694	.0385
21					.4491	.2643	.1496	.0836	.0470
22					.5000	.3035	.1755	.0998	.0567
23						.3445	.2039	.1179	.0680
24						.3878	.2349	.1383	.0807
25						.4320	.2680	.1606	.0951
26						.4773	.3032	.1852	.1112
27						.5227	.3403	.2117	.1290
28							.3788	.2404	.1487
29							.4185	.2707	.1701
30							.4591	.3029	.1933
31							.5000	.3365	.2181
32								.3715	.2447
33								.4074	.2729
34								.4442	.3024
35								.4813	.3332
36								.5187	.3652
37									.3981
38									.4317
39									.4657
40									.5000

(*Continued*)

TABLE A.13

p-Values for Mann-Whitney U Statistic Small Samples ($n_1 \le n_2$) (*Continued*)

		n_1									
$n_2 = 10$	U_0	1	2	3	4	5	6	7	8	9	10
	0	.0909	.0152	.0035	.0010	.0003	.0001	.0001	.0000	.0000	.0000
	1	.1818	.0303	.0070	.0020	.0007	.0002	.0001	.0000	.0000	.0000
	2	.2727	.0606	.0140	.0040	.0013	.0005	.0002	.0001	.0000	.0000
	3	.3636	.0909	.0245	.0070	.0023	.0009	.0004	.0002	.0001	.0000
	4	.4545	.1364	.0385	.0120	.0040	.0015	.0006	.0003	.0001	.0001
	5	.5455	.1818	.0559	.0180	.0063	.0024	.0010	.0004	.0002	.0001
	6		.2424	.0804	.0270	.0097	.0037	.0015	.0007	.0003	.0002
	7		.3030	.1084	.0380	.0140	.0055	.0023	.0010	.0005	.0002
	8		.3788	.1434	.0529	.0200	.0080	.0034	.0015	.0007	.0004
	9		.4545	.1853	.0709	.0276	.0112	.0048	.0022	.0011	.0005
	10		.5455	.2343	.0939	.0376	.0156	.0068	.0031	.0015	.0008
	11			.2867	.1199	.0496	.0210	.0093	.0043	.0021	.0010
	12			.3462	.1518	.0646	.0280	.0125	.0058	.0028	.0014
	13			.4056	.1868	.0823	.0363	.0165	.0078	.0038	.0019
	14			.4685	.2268	.1032	.0467	.0215	.0103	.0051	.0026
	15			.5315	.2697	.1272	.0589	.0277	.0133	.0066	.0034
	16				.3177	.1548	.0736	.0351	.0171	.0086	.0045
	17				.3666	.1855	.0903	.0439	.0217	.0110	.0057
	18				.4196	.2198	.1099	.0544	.0273	.0140	.0073
	19				.4725	.2567	.1317	.0665	.0338	.0175	.0093
	20				.5275	.2970	.1566	.0806	.0416	.0217	.0116
	21					.3393	.1838	.0966	.0506	.0267	.0144
	22					.3839	.2139	.1148	.0610	.0326	.0177
	23					.4296	.2461	.1349	.0729	.0394	.0216
	24					.4765	.2811	.1574	.0864	.0474	.0262
	25					.5235	.3177	.1819	.1015	.0564	.0315
	26						.3564	.2087	.1185	.0667	.0376
	27						.3962	.2374	.1371	.0782	.0446
	28						.4374	.2681	.1577	.0912	.0526
	29						.4789	.3004	.1800	.1055	.0615
	30						.5211	.3345	.2041	.1214	.0716
	31							.3698	.2299	.1388	.0827
	32							.4063	.2574	.1577	.0952
	33							.4434	.2863	.1781	.1088
	34							.4811	.3167	.2001	.1237
	35							.5189	.3482	.2235	.1399
	36								.3809	.2483	.1575
	37								.4143	.2745	.1763
	38								.4484	.3019	.1965
	39								.4827	.3304	.2179
	40								.5173	.3598	.2406
	41									.3901	.2644
	42									.4211	.2894
	43									.4524	.3153
	44									.4841	.3421
	45									.5159	.3697
	46										.3980
	47										.4267
	48										.4559
	49										.4853
	50										.5147

TABLE A.14

Critical Values of *T* for the
Wilcoxon Matched-Pairs
Signed Rank Test (Small
Samples)

1-SIDED	2-SIDED	n = 5	n = 6	n = 7	n = 8	n = 9	n = 10
$\alpha = .05$	$\alpha = .10$	1	2	4	6	8	11
$\alpha = .025$	$\alpha = .05$		1	2	4	6	8
$\alpha = .01$	$\alpha = .02$			0	2	3	5
$\alpha = .005$	$\alpha = .01$				0	2	3

1-SIDED	2-SIDED	n = 11	n = 12	n = 13	n = 14	n = 15	n = 16
$\alpha = .05$	$\alpha = .10$	14	17	21	26	30	36
$\alpha = .025$	$\alpha = .05$	11	14	17	21	25	30
$\alpha = .01$	$\alpha = .02$	7	10	13	16	20	24
$\alpha = .005$	$\alpha = .01$	5	7	10	13	16	19

1-SIDED	2-SIDED	n = 17	n = 18	n = 19	n = 20	n = 21	n = 22
$\alpha = .05$	$\alpha = .10$	41	47	54	60	68	75
$\alpha = .025$	$\alpha = .05$	35	40	46	52	59	66
$\alpha = .01$	$\alpha = .02$	28	33	38	43	49	56
$\alpha = .005$	$\alpha = .01$	23	28	32	37	43	49

1-SIDED	2-SIDED	n = 23	n = 24	n = 25	n = 26	n = 27	n = 28
$\alpha = .05$	$\alpha = .10$	83	92	101	110	120	130
$\alpha = .025$	$\alpha = .05$	73	81	90	98	107	117
$\alpha = .01$	$\alpha = .02$	62	69	77	85	93	102
$\alpha = .005$	$\alpha = .01$	55	61	68	76	84	92

1-SIDED	2-SIDED	n = 29	n = 30	n = 31	n = 32	n = 33	n = 34
$\alpha = .05$	$\alpha = .10$	141	152	163	175	188	201
$\alpha = .025$	$\alpha = .05$	127	137	148	159	171	183
$\alpha = .01$	$\alpha = .02$	111	120	130	141	151	162
$\alpha = .005$	$\alpha = .01$	100	109	118	128	138	149

1-SIDED	2-SIDED	n = 35	n = 36	n = 37	n = 38	n = 39	
$\alpha = .05$	$\alpha = .10$	214	228	242	256	271	
$\alpha = .025$	$\alpha = .05$	195	208	222	235	250	
$\alpha = .01$	$\alpha = .02$	174	186	198	211	224	
$\alpha = .005$	$\alpha = .01$	160	171	183	195	208	

1-SIDED	2-SIDED	n = 40	n = 41	n = 42	n = 43	n = 44	n = 45
$\alpha = .05$	$\alpha = .10$	287	303	319	336	353	371
$\alpha = .025$	$\alpha = .05$	264	279	295	311	327	344
$\alpha = .01$	$\alpha = .02$	238	252	267	281	297	313
$\alpha = .005$	$\alpha = .01$	221	234	248	262	277	292

1-SIDED	2-SIDED	n = 46	n = 47	n = 48	n = 49	n = 50	
$\alpha = .05$	$\alpha = .10$	389	408	427	446	466	
$\alpha = .025$	$\alpha = .05$	361	379	397	415	434	
$\alpha = .01$	$\alpha = .02$	329	345	362	380	398	
$\alpha = .005$	$\alpha = .01$	307	323	339	356	373	

From E. Wilcoxon and R. A. Wilcox, "Some Rapid Approximate Statistical Procedures," 1964. Reprinted
by permission of Lederle Labs, a division of the American Cyanamid Co.

TABLE A.15

Factors for Control Charts

| Number of Items In Sample | AVERAGES | | | RANGES | |
| | Factors for Control Limits | | Factors for Central Line | Factors for Control Limits | |
n	A_2	A_3	d_2	D_3	D_4
2	1.880	2.659	1.128	0	3.267
3	1.023	1.954	1.693	0	2.575
4	0.729	1.628	2.059	0	2.282
5	0.577	1.427	2.326	0	2.115
6	0.483	1.287	2.534	0	2.004
7	0.419	1.182	2.704	0.076	1.924
8	0.373	1.099	2.847	0.136	1.864
9	0.337	1.032	2.970	0.184	1.816
10	0.308	0.975	3.078	0.223	1.777
11	0.285	0.927	3.173	0.256	1.744
12	0.266	0.886	3.258	0.284	1.716
13	0.249	0.850	3.336	0.308	1.692
14	0.235	0.817	3.407	0.329	1.671
15	0.223	0.789	3.472	0.348	1.652

Adapted from American Society for Testing and Materials, *Manual on Quality Control of Materials,* 1951, Table B2, p. 115. For a more detailed table and explanation, see Acheson J. Duncan, *Quality Control and Industrial Statistics,* 3d ed. Homewood, IL.: Richard D. Irwin, 1974, Table M, p. 927.

Answers to Selected Odd-Numbered Quantitative Problems

Chapter 1

1.7. a. ratio
  b. ratio
  c. ordinal
  d. nominal
  e. ratio
  f. ratio
  g. nominal
  h. ratio

1.9. a. 900 electric contractors
  b. 35 electric contractors
  c. average score for 35 participants
  d. average score for all 900 electric contractors

Chapter 2

No answers given

Chapter 3

3.1. 4, 4

3.3. 41.7

3.5. 19, 27, 17, 25, 30

3.7. 31.77, 28, 21

3.9. 32250, 286000, 8100, 79962.5, 293000, 842376

3.11. a. 8
  b. 2.041
  c. 6.204
  d. 2.491
  e. 4
  f. 0.69, −0.92, −0.11, 1.89, −1.32, −0.52, 0.29

3.13. a. 4.598
  b. 4.598

3.15. 58, 631.295, 242.139

3.17. a. .75
  b. .84
  c. .609
  d. .902

3.19. a. 2.667
  b. 11.060
  c. 3.326
  d. 5
  e. −0.85
  f. 37.65%

3.21. Between 113 and 137
  Between 101 and 149
  Between 89 and 161

3.23. 2.236

3.25. 95%, 2.5%, .15%, 16%

3.27. 4.64, 3.59, 1

3.29. 185.694, 13.627

3.31. a. 44.9
  b. 39
  c. 44.82
  d. 187.2
  e. 13.7

3.33. a. 38
  b. 25
  c. 32.857
  d. 251
  e. 15.843

3.35. skewed right

3.37. 0.726

3.39. no outliers. negatively skewed

3.41. 2.5, 2, 2, 7, 1, 3, 2

3.43. 472.19, 307.6, 188.6, 338.75, 918.5, 168.5, 469.5, 2130.1, 301

3.45. a. 414422, 417250

    b. 230640, 92580

    c. 5186094518.72, 72014.54

    d. −1.17, 0.31

    e. −0.12

3.47. a. 33.412, 32.5

    b. 58.483, 7.647

3.49. 10.78%, 6.43%

3.51. a. 392 to 446, 365 to 473, 338 to 500

    b. 79.7%

    c. −0.704

3.53. skewed right

3.55. 21.93, 18.14

Chapter 4

4.1. 15, .60

4.3. {4, 8, 10, 14, 16, 18, 20, 22, 26, 28, 30}

4.5. 20, combinations, .60

4.7. 38,760

4.9. a. .7167

    b. .5000

    c. .65

    d. .5167

4.11. not solvable

4.13. a. .86

    b. .31

    c. .14

4.15. a. .2807

    b. .0526

    c. .0000

    d. .0000

4.17. a. .0122

    b. .0144

4.19. a. .57

    b. .3225

    c. .4775

    d. .5225

    e. .6775

    f. .0475

4.21. a. .039

    b. .571

    c. .129

4.23. a. .2286

    b. .2297

    c. .3231

    d. .0000

4.25. not independent

4.27. a. .4054

    b. .3261

    c. .4074

    d. .32

4.29. a. .03

    b. .2875

    c. .3354

    d. .9759

4.31. .0538, .5161, .4301

4.33. .7941, .2059

4.35. a. .4211

    b. .6316

    c. .2105

    d. .1250

    e. .5263

    f. .0000

    g. .6667

    h. .0000

4.37. a. .28

    b. .04

    c. .86

    d. .32

    e. .1739

    f. .66

4.39. a. .5410

    b. .7857

    c. .70

    d. .09

    e. .2143

4.41. a. .39

    b. .40

    c. .48

    d. not independent

    e. not mutually exclusive

4.43. a. .3483

    b. .5317

    c. .4683

    d. .0817

4.45. a. .2625

    b. .74375

    c. .60

    d. .25625

    e. .0875

4.47. a. .20

    b. .6429

    c. .40

    d. .60

    e. .40

    f. .3333

4.49. a. .469

    b. .164

    c. .2360

    d. .1934

    e. .754

4.51. a. .2130
b. .4370
c. .2240
d. .6086
e. .3914
f. .8662

4.53. a. .276
b. .686
c. .816
d. .59
e. .4023

Chapter 5

5.1. 2.666, 1.8364, 1.3552

5.3. 0.956, 1.1305

5.5. a. .0036
b. .1147
c. .3822
d. .5838

5.7. a. 14, 2.05
b. 24.5, 3.99
c. 50, 5

5.9. a. .0815
b. .0008
c. .227

5.11. a. .585
b. .009
c. .013

5.13. a. .1032
b. .0000
c. .0352
d. .3480

5.15. a. .0538
b. .1539
c. .4142
d. .0672
e. .0244
f. .3702

5.17. a. 6.3, 2.51
b. 1.3, 1.14
c. 8.9, 2.98
d. 0.6, .775

5.19. 3.5
a. .0302
b. .1424
c. .0817
d. .42
e. .1009

5.21. a. .5488
b. .3293
c. .1220

d. .8913
e. .1912

5.23. a. .3012
b. .0000
c. .0336

5.25. a. .0104
b. .0000
c. .1653
d. .9636

5.27. a. .5091
b. .2937
c. .4167
d. .0014

5.29. a. .0529
b. .0294
c. .4235

5.31. a. .1333
b. .0238
c. .1143

5.33. .0474

5.35. a. .124
b. .849
c. .090
d. .000

5.37. a. .1607
b. .7626
c. .3504
d. .5429

5.39. a. .1108
b. .017
c. 5
d. .1797
e. .125
f. .0000
g. .056
h. $x = 8(.180), \mu = 8$

5.41. a. .2644
b. .0694
c. .0029
d. .7521

5.43. a. 5
b. .0244

5.45. a. .0687
b. .020
c. .1032
d. 2.28

5.47. .174

5.49. a. .3012
b. .1203
c. .7065

5.51. a. .0002
b. .0595
c. .2330

5.53. a. .0907
b. .0358
c. .1517
d. .8781

5.55. a. .265
b. .0136
c. .0067

5.57. a. .3584
b. .8333
c. .0981

5.59. a. .0474
b. .1605
c. .9547

Chapter 6

6.1. a. 1/40
b. 220, 11.547
c. .25
d. .3750
e. .6250

6.3. 2.97, 0.098, .2941

6.5. 222.857, .0013, .2267, .0000, .1684

6.7. a. .8944
b. .0122
c. .2144

6.9. a. .1788
b. .0329
c. .1476

6.11. a. 188.25
b. 244.65
c. 163.81
d. 206.11

6.13. 454.55

6.15. 22.984

6.17. a. $P(x \leq 16.5 \mid \mu = 21$ and $\sigma = 2.51)$
b. $P(10.5 \leq x \leq 20.5 \mid \mu = 12.5$ and $\sigma = 2.5)$
c. $P(21.5 \leq x \leq 22.5 \mid \mu = 24$ and $\sigma = 3.10)$
d. $P(x > 14.5 \mid \mu = 7.2$ and $\sigma = 1.99)$

6.19. a. .1170, .120
b. .4090, .415
c. .1985, .196
d. fails test

6.21. .0495

6.23. a. .1922
b. .6808

c. .0064
d. .0695

6.27. a. .0012
b. .8700
c. .0011
d. .9918

6.29. a. .0000
b. .0000
c. .0872
d. .41 minutes

6.31. $\mu = 246.31$
a. .5194
b. .2305

6.33. 15, 15, .1254

6.35. a. .1587
b. .0013
c. .6915
d. .9270
e. .0000

6.37. a. .0202
b. .9817
c. .1849
d. .4449

6.39. .0000

6.41. a. .0537
b. .0013
c. .1535

6.43. .5319, 41.5, .0213

6.45. a. .3050
b. .6413
c. .2985
d. .0045

6.47. a. .0129
b. .0951
c. .9934
d. .5713

6.49. a. .0025
b. .8944
c. .3482

6.51. a. .0655
b. .6502
c. .9993

6.53. $11428.57

6.55. a. .5488
b. .2592
c. 1.67 months

6.57. 1940, 2018.75, 2269

6.59. .0516, 1.07%

Chapter 7

7.7. 825

7.13. a. .0548
 b. .7881
 c. .0082
 d. .8575
 e. .1664

7.15. 11.11

7.17. a. .9772
 b. .2385
 c. .1469
 d. .1230

7.19. .0000

7.21. a. .1894
 b. .0559
 c. .0000
 d. 16.4964

7.23. a. .1492
 b. .9404
 c. .6985
 d. .1445
 e. .0000

7.25. .26

7.27. a. .1977
 b. .2843
 c. .9881

7.29. a. .1020
 b. .7568
 c. .7019

7.31. 55, 45, 90, 25, 35

7.37. a. .3156
 b. .00003
 c. .1736

7.41. a. .0021
 b. .9265
 c. .0281

7.43. a. .0314
 b. .2420
 c. .2250
 d. .1469
 e. .0000

7.45. a. .8534
 b. .0256
 c. .0007

7.49. a. .6787
 b. .0571
 c. .0059

7.51. .9147

Chapter 8

8.1. a. $24.11 \leq \mu \leq 25.89$
 b. $113.17 \leq \mu \leq 126.03$
 c. $3.136 \leq \mu \leq 3.702$
 d. $54.55 \leq \mu \leq 58.85$

8.3. $45.92 \leq \mu \leq 48.08$

8.5. 66, $62.75 \leq \mu \leq 69.25$

8.7. 5.3, $5.13 \leq \mu \leq 5.47$

8.9. $2.852 \leq \mu \leq 3.760$

8.11. $23.036 \leq \mu \leq 26.030$

8.13. $42.18 \leq \mu \leq 49.06$

8.15. $120.6 \leq \mu \leq 136.2$, 128.4

8.17. $15.631 \leq \mu \leq 16.545$, 16.088

8.19. $2.26886 \leq \mu \leq 2.45346$, 2.36116, .0923

8.21. $36.77 \leq \mu \leq 62.83$

8.23. $7.53 \leq \mu \leq 14.66$

8.25. a. $.386 \leq p \leq .634$
 b. $.777 \leq p \leq .863$
 c. $.456 \leq p \leq .504$
 d. $.246 \leq p \leq .394$

8.27. $.38 \leq p \leq .56$
 $.36 \leq p \leq .58$
 $.33 \leq p \leq .61$

8.29. a. $.4287 \leq p \leq .5113$
 b. $.2488 \leq p \leq .3112$

8.31. a. .266
 b. $.247 \leq p \leq .285$

8.33. $.5935 \leq p \leq .6665$

8.35. a. $18.46 \leq \sigma^2 \leq 189.73$
 b. $0.64 \leq \sigma^2 \leq 7.46$
 c. $645.45 \leq \sigma^2 \leq 1923.10$
 d. $12.61 \leq \sigma^2 \leq 31.89$

8.37. $9.71 \leq \sigma^2 \leq 46.03$, 18.49

8.39. $14,084,038.51 \leq \sigma^2 \leq 69,553,848.45$

8.41. a. 2522
 b. 601
 c. 268
 d. 16,577

8.43. 106

8.45. 1,083

8.47. 97

8.49. 12.03, $11.78 \leq \mu \leq 12.28$, $11.72 \leq \mu \leq 12.34$,
 $11.58 \leq \mu \leq 12.48$

8.51. $29.133 \leq \sigma^2 \leq 148.235$, $25.911 \leq \sigma^2 \leq 182.529$

8.53. $9.19 \leq \mu \leq 12.34$

8.55. $2.307 \leq \sigma^2 \leq 15.374$

8.57. $36.231 \leq \mu \leq 38.281$

8.59. $.542 \leq p \leq .596, .569$

8.61. $5.892 \leq \mu \leq 7.542$

8.63. $.726 \leq p \leq .814$

8.65. $34.11 \leq \mu \leq 53.29, 101.44 \leq \sigma^2 \leq 821.35$

8.67. $-0.20 \leq \mu \leq 5.16, 2.48$

8.69. 543

8.71. $.0026 \leq \sigma^2 \leq .0071$

Chapter 9

9.1. a. $z = 2.77$, reject
   b. .0028
   c. 22.115, 27.885

9.3. a. $z = 1.59$, reject
   b. .0559
   c. 1212.04

9.5. $z = 1.84$, fail to reject

9.7. $z = 1.46$, fail to reject

9.9. $z = 2.98, .0014$, reject

9.11. $t = 0.56$, fail to reject

9.13. $t = 2.44$, reject

9.15. $t = 1.59$, fail to reject

9.17. $t = -3.31$, reject

9.19. $t = -2.02$, fail to reject

9.21. fail to reject

9.23. $z = -1.66$, fail to reject

9.25. $z = -1.89$, fail to reject

9.27. $z = 1.22$, fail to reject,
   $z = 1.34$, fail to reject

9.29. $z = -3.11$, reject

9.31. a. $\chi^2 = 22.4$, fail to reject
   b. $\chi^2 = 42$, reject
   c. $\chi^2 = 2.64$, fail to reject
   d. $\chi^2 = 2.4$, reject

9.33. $\chi^2 = 21.7$, fail to reject

9.35. $\chi^2 = 17.34$, reject

9.37. a. $\beta = .8159$
   b. $\beta = .7422$
   c. $\beta = .5636$
   d. $\beta = .3669$

9.39. a. $\beta = .3632$
   b. $\beta = .0122$
   c. $\beta = .0000$

9.41. $z = -0.48$, fail to reject, .6293, .1492, .0000

9.43. $t = -1.98$, reject

9.45. $\chi^2 = 32.675$, fail to reject

9.47. $z = -1.34$, fail to reject

9.49. $z = -3.72$, reject

9.51. $t = -5.70$, reject

9.53. $\chi^2 = 106.47$, reject

9.55. $t = -2.80$, reject

9.57. $z = 3.96$, reject

9.59. $t = 4.50$, reject

9.61. $\chi^2 = 45.866$, reject

Chapter 10

10.1. a. $z = -1.01$, fail to reject
   b. -2.41
   c. .1562

10.3. a. $z = 5.48$, reject
   b. $4.04 \leq \mu_1 - \mu_2 \leq 10.02$

10.5. $-1.86 \leq \mu_1 - \mu_2 \leq -0.54$

10.7. $z = -2.32$, fail to reject

10.9. $z = -2.29$, reject

10.11. $t = -1.05$, fail to reject

10.13. $t = -4.64$, reject

10.15. a. $1905.38 \leq \mu_1 - \mu_2 \leq 3894.62$
   b. $t = -4.91$, reject

10.17. $t = 2.06$, reject

10.19. $t = 4.95$, reject, $2258.05 \leq \mu_1 - \mu_2 \leq 5541.95$

10.21. $t = 3.31$, reject

10.23. $26.29 \leq D \leq 54.83$

10.25. $-3415.6 \leq D \leq 6021.2$

10.27. $6.58 \leq D \leq 49.60$

10.29. $63.71 \leq D \leq 86.29$

10.31. a. $z = 0.75$, fail to reject
   b. $z = 4.83$, reject

10.33. $z = -3.35$, reject

10.35. $z = -0.94$, fail to reject

10.37. $z = 2.35$, reject

10.39. $F = 1.80$, fail to reject

10.41. $F = 0.81$, fail to reject

10.43. $F = 1.53$, fail to reject

10.45. $z = -2.38$, reject

10.47. $t = 0.85$, fail to reject

10.49. $t = -5.26$, reject

10.51. $z = -1.20$, fail to reject

10.53. $F = 1.24$, fail to reject

10.55. $-3.201 \leq D \leq 2.313$

10.57. $F = 1.31$, fail to reject

10.59. $t = 2.97$, reject

10.61. $z = 6.78$, reject

10.63. $3.553 \leq D \leq 5.447$

10.65. $t = 6.71$, reject

10.67. $.142 \le p_1 - p_2 \le .250$

10.69. $z = 8.86$, reject

10.71. $t = 4.52$, reject

Chapter 11

11.5. $F = 11.07$, reject

11.7. $F = 13.00$, reject

11.9. 4, 50, 54, 145.8975, 19.4436, $F = 7.50$, reject

11.11. $F = 10.10$, reject

11.13. $F = 11.76$, reject

11.15. 4 levels; sizes 18, 15, 21, and 11; $F = 2.95$, $p = .04$; means = 226.73, 238.79, 232.58, and 239.82.

11.17. HSD = 0.896, groups 3 & 6 significantly different

11.19. HSD = 1.586, groups 1 & 2 significantly different

11.21. HSD = 10.27, groups 1 & 3 significantly different

11.23. $\text{HSD}_{1,3} = .0381$, groups 1 & 3 significantly different

11.25. $\text{HSD}_{1,3} = 1.764$, $\text{HSD}_{2,3} = 1.620$, groups 1 & 3 and 2 & 3 significantly different

11.29. $F = 1.48$, fail to reject

11.31. $F = 3.90$, fail to reject

11.33. $F = 15.37$, reject

11.37. 2, 1, 4 row levels, 3 column levels, yes
$\text{df}_{\text{row}} = 3$, $\text{df}_{\text{col.}} = 2$, $\text{df}_{\text{int.}} = 6$, $\text{df}_{\text{error}} = 12$, $\text{df}_{\text{total}} = 23$

11.39. $\text{MS}_{\text{row}} = 1.047$, $\text{MS}_{\text{col.}} = 1.281$, $\text{MS}_{\text{int.}} = 0.258$, $\text{MS}_{\text{error}} = 0.436$,
$F_{\text{row}} = 2.40$, $F_{\text{col.}} = 2.94$, $F_{\text{int.}} = 0.59$,
fail to reject any hypothesis

11.41. $F_{\text{row}} = 87.25$, reject; $F_{\text{col.}} = 63.67$, reject; $F_{\text{int.}} = 2.07$,
fail to reject

11.43. $F_{\text{row}} = 34.31$, reject; $F_{\text{col.}} = 14.20$, reject;
$F_{\text{int.}} = 3.32$, reject

11.45. no significant interaction or row effects; significant column effects.

11.47. $F = 8.82$, reject; HSD = 3.33 groups 1 & 2, 2 & 3, and 2 & 4 significantly different.

11.49. $\text{df}_{\text{treat.}} = 5$, $\text{MS}_{\text{treat.}} = 42.0$, $\text{df}_{\text{error}} = 36$,
$\text{MS}_{\text{error}} = 18.194$, $F = 2.31$

11.51. 1 treatment variable, 3 levels; 1 blocking variable, 6 levels;
$\text{df}_{\text{treat.}} = 2$, $\text{df}_{\text{block}} = 5$, $\text{df}_{\text{error}} = 10$

11.53. $F_{\text{treat.}} = 31.51$, reject; $F_{\text{blocks}} = 43.20$, reject;
HSD = 8.757, no pairs significant

11.55. $F_{\text{rows}} = 38.21$, reject; $F_{\text{col.}} = 0.23$, fail to reject;
$F_{\text{inter}} = 1.30$, fail to reject

11.57. $F = 7.38$, reject

11.59. $F = 0.46$, fail to reject

11.61. $F_{\text{treat.}} = 13.64$, reject

Chapter 12

12.1. -0.927

12.3. 0.645

12.5. 0.975, 0.985, 0.957

12.7. $\hat{y} = 144.414 - 0.898x$

12.9. $\hat{y} = 15.460 - 0.715x$

12.11. $\hat{y} = 600.186 - 72.328x$

12.13. $\hat{y} = 13.625 + 2.303x, -1.1694, 3.9511, -1.3811, 2.7394, -4.1401$

12.15. 18.6597, 37.5229, 51.8948, 62.6737, 86.0281, 118.3648, 122.8561; 6.3403, -8.5229, -5.8948, 7.3263, 1.9720, -6.3648, 5.1439

12.17. 4.0259, 11.1722, 9.7429, 12.6014, 10.4576; 0.9741, 0.8278, -0.7429, 2.3986, -3.4575

12.19. 4.7244, -0.9836, -0.3996, -6.7537, 2.7683, 0.6442;
No apparent violations

12.21. The error terms appear to be non independent

12.23. Violation of the homoscedasticity assumption

12.25. SSE = 272.0, $s_e = 7.376$, 6 out of 7 and 7 out of 7

12.27. SSE = 19.8885, $s_e = 2.575$

12.29. $s_e = 4.391$

12.31. $\hat{y} = 118.257 - 0.1504x$, $s_e = 40.526$

12.33. $r^2 = .972$

12.35. $r^2 = .685$

12.37. $\hat{y} = -599.3674 + 19.2204x$, $s_e = 13.539$, $r^2 = .688$

12.39. $t = -13.18$, reject

12.41. $t = -2.56$, fail to reject

12.43. F is significant at $\alpha = .05$, $t = 2.874$, reject at $\alpha = .05$

12.45. $38.523 \le y \le 70.705$, $10.447 \le y \le 44.901$

12.47. $0.97 \le E(y_{10}) \le 15.65$

12.49. $\hat{y} = 1367819.18 - 678.9643x$, $\hat{y}(2012) = 1743.01$

12.51. $r = -.94$

12.53. a. $\hat{y} = -11.335 + 0.355x$

b. 7.48, 5.35, 3.22, 6.415, 9.225, 10.675, 4.64, 9.965, -2.48, -0.35, 3.78, -2.415, 0.745, 1.325, -1.64, 1.035

c. SSE = 32.4649

d. $s_e = 2.3261$

e. $r^2 = .608$

f. $t = 3.05$, reject

12.55. a. $20.92 \le E(y_{60}) \le 26.8$

b. $20.994 \le y \le 37.688$

12.57. $r^2 = .826$

12.59. $\hat{y} = -0.863565 + 0.92025x$; $r^2 = .405$

12.61. $r = .8998$

12.63. $\hat{y} = -39.0071 + 66.36277x$, $r^2 = .906$, $s_e = 21.13$

12.65. $\hat{y} = 3757.2796 - 7.06396x$, $s_e = 1254.27$, $r^2 = .3322$,
$t = -1.58$, fail to reject

Chapter 13

13.1. $\hat{y} = 25.03 - 0.0497x_1 + 1.928x_2$, 28.586

13.3. $\hat{y} = 121.62 - 0.174x_1 + 6.02x_2 + 0.00026x_3 + 0.0041x_4$, 4

13.5. Per capita consumption $= -7{,}629.627 + 116.2549$ paper consumption $- 120.0904$ fish consumption $+ 45.73328$ gasoline consumption

13.7. 9, fail to reject null overall at $\alpha = .05$, only $t = 2.73$ for x_1, significant at $\alpha = .05$, $s_e = 3.503$, $R^2 = .408$, adj. $R^2 = .203$

13.9. Per capita consumption $= -7{,}629.627 + 116.2549$ paper consumption $- 120.0904$ fish consumption $+ 45.73328$ gasoline consumption; $F = 14.319$ with p-value $= .0023$; $t = 2.67$ with p-value $= .032$ for gasoline consumption. The p-values of the t statistics for the other two predictors are insignificant.

13.11. $\hat{y} = 3.981 + 0.07322x_1 - 0.03232x_2 - 0.003886x_3$, $F = 100.47$ significant at $\alpha = .001$, $t = 3.50$ for x_1 significant at $\alpha = .01$, $s_e = 0.2331$, $R^2 = .965$, adj. $R^2 = .955$

13.13. 3 predictors, 15 observations, $\hat{y} = 657.053 + 5.710x_1 - 0.417x_2 - 3.471x_3$, $R^2 = .842$, adjusted $R^2 = .630$, $s_e = 109.43$, $F = 8.96$ with $p = .0027$, x_1 significant at $\alpha = .01$, x_3 significant at $\alpha = .05$

13.15. $s_e = 9.722$, $R^2 = .515$, adjusted $R^2 = .404$

13.17. $s_e = 6.544$, $R^2 = .005$, adjusted $R^2 = .000$

13.19. model with x_1, x_2: $s_e = 6.333$, $R^2 = .963$, adjusted $R^2 = .957$ model with x_1: $s_e = 6.124$, $R^2 = .963$, adjusted $R^2 = .960$

13.21. heterogeneity of variance

13.23. 2, $\hat{y} = 203.3937 + 1.1151x_1 - 2.2115x_2$, $F = 24.55$, reject, $R^2 = .663$, adjusted $R^2 = .636$

13.25. $\hat{y} = 362 - 4.75x_1 - 13.9x_2 + 1.87x_3$; $F = 16.05$, reject; $s_e = 37.07$; $R^2 = .858$; adjusted $R^2 = .804$; x_1 only significant predictor

13.27. Employment $= 71.03 + 0.4620$ Naval Vessels $+ 0.02082$ Commercial $F = 1.22$, fail to reject; $R^2 = .379$; adjusted $R^2 = .068$; no significant predictors

13.29. Corn $= -2718 + 6.26$ Soybeans $- 0.77$ Wheat; $F = 14.25$, reject; $s_e = 862.4$; $R^2 = .803$; adjusted $R^2 = .746$; Soybeans was a significant predictor

A

a posteriori After the experiment; pairwise comparisons made by the researcher *after* determining that there is a significant overall F value from ANOVA; also called *post hoc.*

a priori Determined before, or prior to, an experiment.

adjusted R^2 A modified value of R^2 in which the degrees of freedom are taken into account, thereby allowing the researcher to determine whether the value of R^2 is inflated for a particular multiple regression model.

after-process quality control A type of quality control in which product attributes are measured by inspection after the manufacturing process is completed to determine whether the product is acceptable.

all possible regressions A multiple regression search procedure in which all possible multiple linear regression models are determined from the data using all variables.

alpha (α) The probability of committing a Type I error; also called the level of significance.

alternative hypothesis The hypothesis that complements the null hypothesis; usually it is the hypothesis that the researcher is interested in proving.

analysis of variance (ANOVA) A technique for statistically analyzing the data from a completely randomized design; uses the F test to determine whether there is a significant difference in two or more independent groups.

arithmetic mean The average of a group of numbers.

autocorrelation A problem that arises in regression analysis when the data occur over time and the error terms are correlated; also called serial correlation.

autoregression A multiple regression forecasting technique in which the independent variables are time-lagged versions of the dependent variable.

averaging models Forecasting models in which the forecast is the average of several preceding time periods.

B

backward elimination A step-by-step multiple regression search procedure that begins with a full model containing all predictors. A search is made to determine if there are any nonsignificant independent variables in the model. If there are no nonsignificant predictors, then the backward process ends with the full model. If there are nonsignificant predictors, then the predictor with the smallest absolute value of t is eliminated and a new model

is developed with the remaining variables. This procedure continues until only variables with significant t values remain in the model.

bar graph A bar graph is a chart that contains two or more categories along one axis and a series of bars, one for each category, along the other axis. Usually the length of the bar represents the magnitude of the measure for each category. A bar graph is qualitative and may be either horizontal or vertical.

Bayes' rule An extension of the conditional law of probabilities discovered by Thomas Bayes that can be used to revise probabilities.

benchmarking A quality control method in which a company attempts to develop and establish total quality management from product to process by examining and emulating the best practices and techniques used in their industry.

beta (β) The probability of committing a Type II error.

bimodal Data sets that have two modes.

binomial distribution Widely known discrete distribution in which there are only two possibilities on any one trial.

blocking variable A variable that the researcher wants to control but is not the treatment variable of interest.

bounds The error portion of the confidence interval that is added and/or subtracted from the point estimate to form the confidence interval.

box-and-whisker plot A diagram that utilizes the upper and lower quartiles along with the median and the two most extreme values to depict a distribution graphically; sometimes called a box plot.

C

***c* chart** A quality control chart for attribute compliance that displays the number of nonconformances per item or unit.

categorical data Non numerical data that are frequency counts of categories from one or more variables.

cause-and-effect diagram A tool for displaying possible causes for a quality problem and the interrelationships among the causes; also called a fishbone diagram or an Ishikawa diagram.

census A process of gathering data from the whole population for a given measurement of interest.

centerline The middle horizontal line of a control chart, often determined either by a product or service specification or by computing an expected value from sample information.

central limit theorem A theorem that states that regardless of the shape of a population, the distributions of sample means and proportions are normal if sample sizes are large.

Chebyshev's theorem   A theorem stating that at least $1 - 1/k^2$ values will fall within $\pm k$ standard deviations of the mean regardless of the shape of the distribution.

check sheet   Simple forms consisting of multiple categories and columns for recording tallies for displaying the frequency of outcomes for some quality-related event or activity.

chi-square distribution   A continuous distribution determined by the sum of the squares of k independent random variables.

chi-square goodness-of-fit test   A statistical test used to analyze probabilities of multinomial distribution trials along a single dimension; compares expected, or theoretical, frequencies of categories from a population distribution to the observed, or actual, frequencies from a distribution.

chi-square test of independence   A statistical test used to analyze the frequencies of two variables with multiple categories to determine whether the two variables are independent.

class mark   Another name for class midpoint; the midpoint of each class interval in grouped data.

class midpoint   For any given class interval of a frequency distribution, the value halfway across the class interval; the average of the two class endpoints.

classical method of assigning probabilities   Probabilities assigned based on rules and laws.

classification variable   The independent variable of an experimental design that was present prior to the experiment and is not the result of the researcher's manipulations or control.

classifications   The subcategories of the independent variable used by the researcher in the experimental design; also called levels.

cluster (or area) sampling   A type of random sampling in which the population is divided into nonoverlapping areas or clusters and elements are randomly sampled from the areas or clusters.

coefficient of correlation (r)   A statistic developed by Karl Pearson to measure the linear correlation of two variables.

coefficient of determination (r^2)   The proportion of variability of the dependent variable accounted for or explained by the independent variable in a regression model.

coefficient of multiple determination (R^2)   The proportion of variation of the dependent variable accounted for by the independent variables in the regression model.

coefficient of skewness   A measure of the degree of skewness that exists in a distribution of numbers; compares the mean and the median in light of the magnitude of the standard deviation.

coefficient of variation (CV)   The ratio of the standard deviation to the mean, expressed as a percentage.

collectively exhaustive events   A list containing all possible elementary events for an experiment.

combinations   Used to determine the number of possible ways n things can happen from N total possibilities when sampling without replacement.

complement of a union   The only possible case other than the union of sets X and Y; the probability that neither X nor Y is in the outcome.

complementary events   Two events, one of which comprises all the elementary events of an experiment that are not in the other event.

completely randomized design   An experimental design wherein there is one treatment or independent variable with two or more treatment levels and one dependent variable. This design is analyzed by analysis of variance.

concomitant variables   Variables that are not being controlled by the researcher in the experiment but can have an effect on the outcome of the treatment being studied; also called confounding variables.

conditional probability   The probability of the occurrence of one event given that another event has occurred.

confidence interval   A range of values within which the analyst can declare, with some confidence, the population parameter lies.

confounding variables   Variables that are not being controlled by the researcher in the experiment but can have an effect on the outcome of the treatment being studied; also called concomitant variables.

contingency analysis   Another name for the chi-square test of independence.

contingency table   A two-way table that contains the frequencies of responses to two questions; also called a raw values matrix.

continuous distributions   Distributions constructed from continuous random variables.

continuous random variables   Variables that take on values at every point over a given interval.

control chart   A quality control graph that contains an upper control limit, a lower control limit, and a centerline; used to evaluate whether a process is or is not in a state of statistical control.

convenience sampling   A nonrandom sampling technique in which items for the sample are selected for the convenience of the researcher.

correction for continuity   A correction made when a binomial distribution problem is approximated by the normal distribution because a discrete distribution problem is being approximated by a continuous distribution.

correlation   A measure of the degree of relatedness of two or more variables.

covariance   The variance of x and y together.

critical value   The value that divides the nonrejection region from the rejection region.

cross tabulation   A process for producing a two-dimensional table that displays the frequency counts for two variables simultaneously.

critical value method   A method of testing hypotheses in which the sample statistic is compared to a critical value in order to reach a conclusion about rejecting or failing to reject the null hypothesis.

cumulative frequency   A running total of frequencies through the classes of a frequency distribution.

cycles   Patterns of highs and lows through which data move over time periods usually of more than a year.

cyclical effects   The rise and fall of time-series data over periods longer than 1 year.

D

data   Recorded measurements.

decision alternatives   The various choices or options available to the decision maker in any given problem situation.

decision analysis   A category of quantitative business techniques particularly targeted at clarifying and enhancing the decision-making process.

decision making under certainty   A decision-making situation in which the states of nature are known.

decision making under risk   A decision-making situation in which it is uncertain which states of nature will occur but the probability of each state of nature occurring has been determined.

decision making under uncertainty A decision-making situation in which the states of nature that may occur are unknown and the probability of a state of nature occurring is also unknown.

decision table A matrix that displays the decision alternatives, the states of nature, and the payoffs for a particular decision-making problem; also called a payoff table.

decision trees A flowchart-like depiction of the decision process that includes the various decision alternatives, the various states of nature, and the payoffs.

decomposition Breaking down the effects of time-series data into the four component parts of trend, cyclical, seasonal, and irregular.

degrees of freedom A mathematical adjustment made to the size of the sample; used along with α to locate values in statistical tables.

dependent samples Two or more samples selected in such a way as to be dependent or related; each item or person in one sample has a corresponding matched or related item in the other samples. Also called related samples.

dependent variable In regression analysis, the variable that is being predicted.

descriptive statistics Statistics that have been gathered on a group to describe or reach conclusions about that same group.

deseasonalized data Time-series data in which the effects of seasonality have been removed.

Design for Six Sigma A quality scheme, an offshoot of Six Sigma, that places an emphasis on designing a product or process right the first time thereby allowing organizations the opportunity to reach even higher sigma levels through Six Sigma.

deterministic model Mathematical models that produce an "exact" output for a given input.

deviation from the mean The difference between a number and the average of the set of numbers of which the number is a part.

discrete distributions Distributions constructed from discrete random variables.

discrete random variables Random variables in which the set of all possible values is at most a finite or a countably infinite number of possible values.

disproportionate stratified random sampling A type of stratified random sampling in which the proportions of items selected from the strata for the final sample do not reflect the proportions of the strata in the population.

dot plot A dot plot is a relatively simple statistical chart used to display continuous quantitative data where each data value is plotted along the horizontal axis and is represented on the chart by a dot.

dummy variable Another name for a qualitative or indicator variable; usually coded as 0 or 1 and represents whether or not a given item or person possesses a certain characteristic.

Durbin-Watson test A statistical test for determining whether significant autocorrelation is present in a time-series regression model.

E

elementary events Events that cannot be decomposed or broken down into other events.

empirical rule A guideline that states the approximate percentage of values that fall within a given number of standard deviations of a mean of a set of data that are normally distributed.

EMV'er A decision maker who bases his or her decision on the expected monetary value of the decision alternative.

error of an individual forecast The difference between the actual value and the forecast of that value.

error of estimation The difference between the statistic computed to estimate a parameter and the parameter.

event An outcome of an experiment.

expected monetary value (EMV) A value of a decision alternative computed by multiplying the probability of each state of nature by the state's associated payoff and summing these products across the states of nature.

expected value The long-run average of occurrences; sometimes referred to as the mean value.

expected value of perfect information The difference between the payoff that would occur if the decision maker knew which states of nature would occur and the expected monetary payoff from the best decision alternative when there is no information about the occurrence of the states of nature.

expected value of sample information The difference between the expected monetary value with information and the expected monetary value without information.

experiment A process that produces outcomes.

experimental design A plan and a structure to test hypotheses in which the researcher either controls or manipulates one or more variables.

exponential distribution A continuous distribution closely related to the Poisson distribution that describes the times between random occurrences.

exponential smoothing A forecasting technique in which a weighting system is used to determine the importance of previous time periods in the forecast.

F

***F* distribution** A distribution based on the ratio of two random variances; used in testing two variances and in analysis of variance.

***F* value** The ratio of two sample variances, used to reach statistical conclusions regarding the null hypothesis; in ANOVA, the ratio of the treatment variance to the error variance.

factorial design An experimental design in which two or more independent variables are studied simultaneously and every level of each treatment is studied under the conditions of every level of all other treatments. Also called a factorial experiment.

factors Another name for the independent variables of an experimental design.

Failure Mode and Effects Analysis (FMEA) A systematic way for identifying the effects of potential product or process failure. It includes methodology for eliminating or reducing the chance of a failure occurring.

finite correction factor A statistical adjustment made to the z formula for sample means; adjusts for the fact that a population is finite and the size is known.

first-differences approach A method of transforming data in an attempt to reduce or remove autocorrelation from a time-series regression model; results in each data value being subtracted from each succeeding time period data value, producing a new, transformed value.

fishbone diagram A display of possible causes of a quality problem and the interrelationships among the causes. The problem is diagrammed along the main line of the "fish" and possible causes are diagrammed as line segments angled off in such a way as to give the appearance of a fish skeleton. Also called an Ishikawa diagram or a cause-and-effect diagram.

five-number summary   The five numbers that determine a box-and-whisker plot. These include the median, the lower quartile, the upper quartile, the smallest value, and the largest value.

flowchart   A schematic representation of all the activities and interactions that occur in a process.

forecasting   The art or science of predicting the future.

forecasting error   A single measure of the overall error of a forecast for an entire set of data.

forward selection   A multiple regression search procedure that is essentially the same as stepwise regression analysis except that once a variable is entered into the process, it is never deleted.

frame   A list, map, directory, or some other source that is being used to represent the population in the process of sampling.

frequency distribution   A summary of data presented in the form of class intervals and frequencies.

frequency polygon   A graph constructed by plotting a dot for the frequencies at the class midpoints and connecting the dots.

Friedman test   A nonparametric alternative to the randomized block design.

G

grouped data   Data that have been organized into a frequency distribution.

H

heteroscedasticity   The condition that occurs when the error variances produced by a regression model are not constant.

histogram   A type of vertical bar chart constructed by graphing line segments for the frequencies of classes across the class intervals and connecting each to the x axis to form a series of rectangles.

homoscedasticity   The condition that occurs when the error variances produced by a regression model are constant.

Hurwicz criterion   An approach to decision making in which the maximum and minimum payoffs selected from each decision alternative are used with a weight, α, between 0 and 1 to determine the alternative with the maximum weighted average. The higher the value of α, the more optimistic is the decision maker.

hypergeometric distribution   A distribution of probabilities of the occurrence of x items in a sample of n when there are A of that same item in a population of N.

hypothesis   A tentative explanation of a principle operating in nature.

hypothesis testing   A process of testing hypotheses about parameters by setting up null and alternative hypotheses, gathering sample data, computing statistics from the samples, and using statistical techniques to reach conclusions about the hypotheses.

I

independent events   Events such that the occurrence or nonoccurrence of one has no effect on the occurrence of the others.

independent samples   Two or more samples in which the selected items are related only by chance.

independent variable   In regression analysis, the predictor variable.

index number   A ratio, often expressed as a percentage, of a measure taken during one time frame to that same measure taken during another time frame, usually denoted as the base period.

indicator variable   Another name for a dummy or qualitative variable; usually coded as 0 or 1 and represents whether or not a given item or person possesses a certain characteristic.

inferential statistics   Statistics that have been gathered from a sample and used to reach conclusions about the population from which the sample was taken.

in-process quality control   A quality control method in which product attributes are measured at various intervals throughout the manufacturing process.

interaction   When the effects of one treatment in an experimental design vary according to the levels of treatment of the other effect(s).

interquartile range   The range of values between the first and the third quartile.

intersection   The portion of the population that contains elements that lie in both or all groups of interest.

interval estimate   A range of values within which it is estimated with some confidence the population parameter lies.

interval level data   Next to highest level of data. These data have all the properties of ordinal level data, but in addition, intervals between consecutive numbers have meaning.

irregular fluctuations   Unexplained or error variation within time-series data.

Ishikawa diagram   A tool developed by Kaoru Ishikawa as a way to display possible causes of a quality problem and the interrelationships of the causes; also called a fishbone diagram or a cause-and-effect diagram.

J

joint probability   The probability of the intersection occurring, or the probability of two or more events happening at once.

joint probability table   A two-dimensional table that displays the marginal and intersection probabilities of a given problem.

judgment sampling   A nonrandom sampling technique in which items selected for the sample are chosen by the judgment of the researcher.

just-in-time inventory system   An inventory system in which little or no extra raw materials or parts for production are stored.

K

Kruskal-Wallis test   The nonparametric alternative to one-way analysis of variance; used to test whether three or more samples come from the same or different populations.

kurtosis   The amount of peakedness of a distribution.

L

lambda (λ)   Denotes the long-run average of a Poisson distribution.

Laspeyres price index   A type of weighted aggregate price index in which the quantity values used in the calculations are from the base year.

lean manufacturing   A quality-management philosophy that focuses on the reduction of wastes and the elimination of unnecessary steps in an operation or process.

least squares analysis   The process by which a regression model is developed based on calculus techniques that attempt to produce a minimum sum of the squared error values.

leptokurtic   Distributions that are high and thin.

level of significance   The probability of committing a Type I error; also known as alpha.

levels   The subcategories of the independent variable used by the researcher in the experimental design; also called classifications.

logistic regression   A methodology often used to develop a regression-type model for predicting a dichotomous dependent variable. This method utilizes an "s-curve" type function to develop a math model from one or more variables, which can yield the probability of belonging to one group or the other.

lower control limit (LCL)   The bottom-end line of a control chart, usually situated approximately three standard deviations of the statistic below the centerline; data points below this line indicate quality control problems.

M

Mann-Whitney U test   A nonparametric counterpart of the t test used to compare the means of two independent populations.

manufacturing quality   A view of quality in which the emphasis is on the manufacturer's ability to target consistently the requirements for the product with little variability.

marginal probability   A probability computed by dividing a subtotal of the population by the total of the population.

matched-pairs test   A t test to test the differences in two related or matched samples; sometimes called the t test for related measures or the correlated t test.

maximax criterion   An optimistic approach to decision making under uncertainty in which the decision alternative is chosen according to which alternative produces the maximum overall payoff of the maximum payoffs from each alternative.

maximin criterion   A pessimistic approach to decision making under uncertainty in which the decision alternative is chosen according to which alternative produces the maximum overall payoff of the minimum payoffs from each alternative.

mean   The long-run average of occurrences; also called the expected value.

mean absolute deviation (MAD)   The average of the absolute values of the deviations around the mean for a set of numbers.

mean square error (MSE)   The average of all errors squared of a forecast for a group of data.

measurement   When a standard process is used to assign numbers to particular attributes or characteristics of a variable.

measures of central tendency   One type of measure that is used to yield information about the center of a group of numbers.

measures of shape   Tools that can be used to describe the shape of a distribution of data.

measures of variability   Statistics that describe the spread or dispersion of a set of data.

median   The middle value in an ordered array of numbers.

mesokurtic   Distributions that are normal in shape—that is, not too high or too flat.

metric data   Interval and ratio level data; also called quantitative data.

minimax regret   A decision-making strategy in which the decision maker determines the lost opportunity for each decision alternative and selects the decision alternative with the minimum of lost opportunity or regret.

mn counting rule   A rule used in probability to count the number of ways two operations can occur if the first operation has m possibilities and the second operation has n possibilities.

mode   The most frequently occurring value in a set of data.

moving average   When an average of data from previous time periods is used to forecast the value for ensuing time periods and this average is modified at each new time period by including more recent values not in the previous average and dropping out values from the more distant time periods that were in the average. It is continually updated at each new time period.

multicollinearity   A problematic condition that occurs when two or more of the independent variables of a multiple regression model are highly correlated.

multimodal   Data sets that contain more than two modes.

multiple comparisons   Statistical techniques used to compare pairs of treatment means when the analysis of variance yields an overall significant difference in the treatment means.

multiple regression   Regression analysis with one dependent variable and two or more independent variables or at least one nonlinear independent variable.

mutually exclusive events   Events such that the occurrence of one precludes the occurrence of the other.

N

naïve forecasting models   Simple models in which it is assumed that the more recent time periods of data represent the best predictions or forecasts for future outcomes.

nominal level data   The lowest level of data measurement; used only to classify or categorize.

nonlinear regression model   Multiple regression models in which the models are nonlinear, such as polynomial models, logarithmic models, and exponential models.

nonmetric data   Nominal and ordinal level data; also called qualitative data.

nonparametric statistics   A class of statistical techniques that make few assumptions about the population and are particularly applicable to nominal and ordinal level data.

nonrandom sampling   Sampling in which not every unit of the population has the same probability of being selected into the sample.

nonrandom sampling techniques   Sampling techniques used to select elements from the population by any mechanism that does not involve a random selection process.

nonrejection region   Any portion of a distribution that is not in the rejection region. If the observed statistic falls in this region, the decision is to fail to reject the null hypothesis.

nonsampling errors   All errors other than sampling errors.

normal distribution   A widely known and much-used continuous distribution that fits the measurements of many human characteristics and many machine-produced items.

null hypothesis   The hypothesis that assumes the status quo—that the old theory, method, or standard is still true; the complement of the alternative hypothesis.

O

observed significance level   Another name for the p-value method of testing hypotheses.

observed value   A statistic computed from data gathered in an experiment that is used in the determination of whether or not to reject the null hypothesis.

ogive   A cumulative frequency polygon; plotted by graphing a dot at each class endpoint for the cumulative or decumulative frequency value and connecting the dots.

one-tailed test A statistical test wherein the researcher is interested only in testing one side of the distribution.

one-way analysis of variance The process used to analyze a completely randomized experimental design. This process involves computing a ratio of the variance between treatment levels of the independent variable to the error variance. This ratio is an F value, which is then used to determine whether there are any significant differences between the means of the treatment levels.

operating-characteristic (OC) curve In hypothesis testing, a graph of Type II error probabilities for various possible values of an alternative hypotheses.

opportunity loss table A decision table constructed by subtracting all payoffs for a given state of nature from the maximum payoff for that state of nature and doing this for all states of nature; displays the lost opportunities or regret that would occur for a given decision alternative if that particular state of nature occurred.

ordinal level data Next-higher level of data from nominal level data; can be used to order or rank items, objects, or people.

outliers Data points that lie apart from the rest of the points.

P

p chart A quality control chart for attribute compliance that graphs the proportion of sample items in noncompliance with specifications for multiple samples.

p-value method A method of testing hypotheses in which there is no preset level of α. The probability of getting a test statistic at least as extreme as the observed test statistic is computed under the assumption that the null hypothesis is true. This probability is called the p-value, and it is the smallest value of α for which the null hypothesis can be rejected.

Paasche price index A type of weighted aggregate price index in which the quantity values used in the calculations are from the year of interest.

parameter A descriptive measure of the population.

parametric statistics A class of statistical techniques that contain assumptions about the population and that are used only with interval and ratio level data.

Pareto analysis A quantitative tallying of the number and types of defects that occur with a product or service, often recorded in a Pareto chart.

Pareto chart A vertical bar chart in which the number and types of defects for a product or service are graphed in order of magnitude from greatest to least.

partial regression coefficient The coefficient of an independent variable in a multiple regression model that represents the increase that will occur in the value of the dependent variable from a one-unit increase in the independent variable if all other variables are held constant.

payoff table A matrix that displays the decision alternatives, the states of nature, and the payoffs for a particular decision-making problem; also called a decision table.

payoffs The benefits or rewards that result from selecting a particular decision alternative.

percentiles Measures of central tendency that divide a group of data into 100 parts.

pie chart A circular depiction of data where the area of the whole pie represents 100% of the data being studied and slices represent a percentage breakdown of the sublevels.

platykurtic Distributions that are flat and spread out.

point estimate An estimate of a population parameter constructed from a statistic taken from a sample.

Poisson distribution A discrete distribution that is constructed from the probability of occurrence of rare events over an interval; focuses only on the number of discrete occurrences over some interval or continuum.

poka-yoke Means "mistake proofing" and uses devices, methods, or inspections in order to avoid machine error or simple human error.

population A collection of persons, objects, or items of interest.

post hoc After the experiment; pairwise comparisons made by the researcher *after* determining that there is a significant overall F value from ANOVA; also called a *posteriori*.

power The probability of rejecting a false null hypothesis.

power curve A graph that plots the power values against various values of the alternative hypothesis.

prediction interval A range of values used in regression analysis to estimate a single value of y for a given value of x.

probabilistic model A model that includes an error term that allows for various values of output to occur for a given value of input.

process A series of actions, changes, or functions that bring about a result.

product quality A view of quality in which quality is measurable in the product based on the fact that there are perceived differences in products and quality products possess more attributes.

proportionate stratified random sampling A type of stratified random sampling in which the proportions of the items selected for the sample from the strata reflect the proportions of the strata in the population.

Q

quadratic regression model A multiple regression model in which the predictors are a variable and the square of the variable.

qualitative variable Another name for a dummy or indicator variable; represents whether or not a given item or person possesses a certain characteristic and is usually coded as 0 or 1.

quality When a product delivers what is stipulated in its specifications.

quality circle A small group of workers consisting of supervisors and six to 10 employees who meet frequently and regularly to consider quality issues in their department or area of the business.

quality control The collection of strategies, techniques, and actions taken by an organization to ensure the production of quality products.

quartiles Measures of central tendency that divide a group of data into four subgroups or parts.

quota sampling A nonrandom sampling technique in which the population is stratified on some characteristic and then elements selected for the sample are chosen by nonrandom processes.

R

R chart A plot of sample ranges used in quality control.

R^2 The coefficient of multiple determination; a value that ranges from 0 to 1 and represents the proportion of the dependent variable in a multiple regression model that is accounted for by the independent variables.

random sampling Sampling in which every unit of the population has the same probability of being selected for the sample.

random variable   A variable that contains the outcomes of a chance experiment.

randomized block design   An experimental design in which there is one independent variable of interest and a second variable, known as a blocking variable, that is used to control for confounding or concomitant variables.

range   The difference between the largest and the smallest values in a set of numbers.

ratio level data   Highest level of data measurement; contains the same properties as interval level data, with the additional property that zero has meaning and represents the absence of the phenomenon being measured.

rectangular distribution   A relatively simple continuous distribution in which the same height is obtained over a range of values; also referred to as the uniform distribution.

reengineering   A radical approach to total quality management in which the core business processes of a company is redesigned.

regression analysis   The process of constructing a mathematical model or function that can be used to predict or determine one variable by any other variable.

rejection region   If a computed statistic lies in this portion of a distribution, the null hypothesis will be rejected.

related measures   Another name for matched pairs or paired data in which measurements are taken from pairs of items or persons matched on some characteristic or from a before-and-after design and then separated into different samples.

relative frequency   The proportion of the total frequencies that fall into any given class interval in a frequency distribution.

relative frequency of occurrence   Assigning probability based on cumulated historical data.

repeated measures design   A randomized block design in which each block level is an individual item or person, and that person or item is measured across all treatments.

research hypothesis   A statement of what the researcher believes will be the outcome of an experiment or a study.

residual   The difference between the actual y value and the y value predicted by the regression model; the error of the regression model in predicting each value of the dependent variable.

residual plot   A type of graph in which the residuals for a particular regression model are plotted along with their associated values of x.

response plane   A plane fit in a three-dimensional space and that represents the response surface defined by a multiple regression model with two independent first-order variables.

response surface   The surface defined by a multiple regression model.

response variable   The dependent variable in a multiple regression model; the variable that the researcher is trying to predict.

risk avoider   A decision maker who avoids risk whenever possible and is willing to drop out of a game when given the chance even when the payoff is less than the expected monetary value.

risk taker   A decision maker who enjoys taking risk and will not drop out of a game unless the payoff is more than the expected monetary value.

robust   Describes a statistical technique that is relatively insensitive to minor violations in one or more of its underlying assumptions.

runs test   A nonparametric test of randomness used to determine whether the order or sequence of observations in a sample is random.

S

sample   A portion of the whole.

sample proportion   The quotient of the frequency at which a given characteristic occurs in a sample and the number of items in the sample.

sample-size estimation   An estimate of the size of sample necessary to fulfill the requirements of a particular level of confidence and to be within a specified amount of error.

sample space   A complete roster or listing of all elementary events for an experiment.

sampling error   Error that occurs when the sample is not representative of the population.

scatter plot (chart)   A plot or graph of the pairs of data from a simple regression analysis.

search procedures   Processes whereby more than one multiple regression model is developed for a given database, and the models are compared and sorted by different criteria, depending on the given procedure.

seasonal effects   Patterns of data behavior that occur in periods of time of less than 1 year, often measured by the month.

serial correlation   A problem that arises in regression analysis when the error terms of a regression model are correlated due to time-series data; also called autocorrelation.

set notation   The use of braces to group numbers that have some specified characteristic.

simple average   The arithmetic mean or average for the values of a given number of time periods of data.

simple average model   A forecasting averaging model in which the forecast for the next time period is the average of values for a given number of previous time periods.

simple index number   A number determined by computing the ratio of a quantity, price, or cost for a particular year of interest to the quantity price or cost of a base year, expressed as a percentage.

simple random sampling   The most elementary of the random sampling techniques; involves numbering each item in the population and using a list or roster of random numbers to select items for the sample.

simple regression   Bivariate, linear regression.

Six Sigma   A total quality-management approach that measures the capability of a process to perform defect-free work, where a defect is defined as anything that results in customer dissatisfaction.

skewness   The lack of symmetry of a distribution of values.

smoothing techniques   Forecasting techniques that produce forecasts based on leveling out the irregular fluctuation effects in time-series data.

snowball sampling   A nonrandom sampling technique in which survey subjects who fit a desired profile are selected based on referral from other survey respondents who also fit the desired profile.

Spearman's rank correlation   A measure of the correlation of two variables; used when only ordinal level or ranked data are available.

standard deviation   The square root of the variance.

standard error of the estimate (s_e)   A standard deviation of the error of a regression model.

standard error of the mean   The standard deviation of the distribution of sample means.

standard error of the proportion   The standard deviation of the distribution of sample proportions.

standardized normal distribution *z* distribution; a distribution of *z* scores produced for values from a normal distribution with a mean of 0 and a standard deviation of 1.

states of nature The occurrences of nature that can happen after a decision has been made that can affect the outcome of the decision and over which the decision maker has little or no control.

stationary Time-series data that contain no trend, cyclical, or seasonal effects.

statistic A descriptive measure of a sample.

statistical hypothesis A formal hypothesis structure set up with a null and an alternative hypothesis to scientifically test research hypotheses.

statistics A science dealing with the collection, analysis, interpretation, and presentation of numerical data.

stem-and-leaf plot A plot of numbers constructed by separating each number into two groups, a stem and a leaf. The leftmost digits are the stems and the rightmost digits are the leaves.

stepwise regression A step-by-step multiple regression search procedure that begins by developing a regression model with a single predictor variable and adds and deletes predictors one step at a time, examining the fit of the model at each step until there are no more significant predictors remaining outside the model.

stratified random sampling A type of random sampling in which the population is divided into various nonoverlapping strata and then items are randomly selected into the sample from each stratum.

subjective probability A probability assigned based on the intuition or reasoning of the person determining the probability.

substantive result Occurs when the outcome of a statistical study produces results that are important to the decision maker.

sum of squares of error (SSE) The sum of the residuals squared for a regression model.

sum of squares of *x* The sum of the squared deviations about the mean of a set of values.

systematic sampling A random sampling technique in which every *k*th item or person is selected from the population.

T

***t* distribution** A distribution that describes the sample data when the standard deviation is unknown and the population is normally distributed.

***t* value** The computed value of *t* used to reach statistical conclusions regarding the null hypothesis in small-sample analysis.

team building When a group of employees are organized as an entity to undertake management tasks and perform other functions such as organizing, developing, and overseeing projects.

time-series data Data gathered on a given characteristic over a period of time at regular intervals.

total quality management (TQM) A program that occurs when all members of an organization are involved in improving quality; all goals and objectives of the organization come under the purview of quality control and are measured in quality terms.

transcendent quality A view of quality that implies that a product has an innate excellence, uncompromising standards, and high achievement.

treatment variable The independent variable of an experimental design that the researcher either controls or modifies.

trend Long-run general direction of a business climate over a period of several years.

Tukey-Kramer procedure A modification of the Tukey HSD multiple comparison procedure; used when there are unequal sample sizes.

Tukey's four-quadrant approach A graphical method using the four quadrants for determining which expressions of Tukey's ladder of transformations to use.

Tukey's honestly significant difference (HSD) test In analysis of variance, a technique used for pairwise *a posteriori* multiple comparisons to determine if there are significant differences between the means of any pair of treatment levels in an experimental design. This test requires equal sample sizes and uses a *q* value along with the mean square error in its computation.

Tukey's ladder of transformations A process used for determining ways to recode data in multiple regression analysis to achieve potential improvement in the predictability of the model.

two-stage sampling Cluster sampling done in two stages: A first round of samples is taken and then a second round is taken from within the first samples.

two-tailed test A statistical test wherein the researcher is interested in testing both sides of the distribution.

two-way analysis of variance (two-way ANOVA) The process used to statistically test the effects of variables in factorial designs with two independent variables.

Type I error An error committed by rejecting a true null hypothesis.

Type II error An error committed by failing to reject a false null hypothesis.

U

ungrouped data Raw data, or data that have not been summarized in any way.

uniform distribution A relatively simple continuous distribution in which the same height is obtained over a range of values; also called the rectangular distribution.

union A new set of elements formed by combining the elements of two or more other sets.

union probability The probability of one event occurring or the other event occurring or both occurring.

unweighted aggregate price index number The ratio of the sum of the prices of a market basket of items for a particular year to the sum of the prices of those same items in a base year, expressed as a percentage.

upper control limit (UCL) The top-end line of a control chart, usually situated approximately three standard deviations of the statistic above the centerline; data points above this line indicate quality-control problems.

user quality A view of quality in which the quality of the product is determined by the user.

utility The degree of pleasure or displeasure a decision maker has in being involved in the outcome selection process given the risks and opportunities available.

V

value quality A view of quality having to do with price and costs and whether the consumer got his or her money's worth.

variable A characteristic of any entity being studied that is capable of taking on different values.

variance The average of the squared deviations about the arithmetic mean for a set of numbers.

variance inflation factor A statistic computed using the R^2 value of a regression model developed by predicting one independent variable of a regression analysis by other independent variables; used to determine whether there is multicollinearity among the variables.

W

weighted aggregate price index number A price index computed by multiplying quantity weights and item prices and summing the products to determine a market basket's worth in a given year and then determining the ratio of the market basket's worth in the year of interest to the same value computed for a base year, expressed as a percentage.

weighted moving average A moving average in which different weights are applied to the data values from different time periods.

Wilcoxon matched-pairs signed rank test A nonparametric alternative to the t test for two related or dependent samples.

X

$\bar{x}$ chart A quality control chart for measurements that graphs the sample means computed for a series of small random samples over a period of time.

Z

z distribution A distribution of z scores; a normal distribution with a mean of 0 and a standard deviation of 1.

z score The number of standard deviations a value (x) is above or below the mean of a set of numbers when the data are normally distributed.

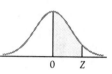

The entries in this table are the probabilities that a standard normal random variable is between 0 and Z (the shaded area).

Z	0.00	0.01	0.02	0.03	0.04	0.05	0.06	0.07	0.08	0.09
0.0	.0000	.0040	.0080	.0120	.0160	.0199	.0239	.0279	.0319	.0359
0.1	.0398	.0438	.0478	.0517	.0557	.0596	.0636	.0675	.0714	.0753
0.2	.0793	.0832	.0871	.0910	.0948	.0987	.1026	.1064	.1103	.1141
0.3	.1179	.1217	.1255	.1293	.1331	.1368	.1406	.1443	.1480	.1517
0.4	.1554	.1591	.1628	.1664	.1700	.1736	.1772	.1808	.1844	.1879
0.5	.1915	.1950	.1985	.2019	.2054	.2088	.2123	.2157	.2190	.2224
0.6	.2257	.2291	.2324	.2357	.2389	.2422	.2454	.2486	.2517	.2549
0.7	.2580	.2611	.2642	.2673	.2704	.2734	.2764	.2794	.2823	.2852
0.8	.2881	.2910	.2939	.2967	.2995	.3023	.3051	.3078	.3106	.3133
0.9	.3159	.3186	.3212	.3238	.3264	.3289	.3315	.3340	.3365	.3389
1.0	.3413	.3438	.3461	.3485	.3508	.3531	.3554	.3577	.3599	.3621
1.1	.3643	.3665	.3686	.3708	.3729	.3749	.3770	.3790	.3810	.3830
1.2	.3849	.3869	.3888	.3907	.3925	.3944	.3962	.3980	.3997	.4015
1.3	.4032	.4049	.4066	.4082	.4099	.4115	.4131	.4147	.4162	.4177
1.4	.4192	.4207	.4222	.4236	.4251	.4265	.4279	.4292	.4306	.4319
1.5	.4332	.4345	.4357	.4370	.4382	.4394	.4406	.4418	.4429	.4441
1.6	.4452	.4463	.4474	.4484	.4495	.4505	.4515	.4525	.4535	.4545
1.7	.4554	.4564	.4573	.4582	.4591	.4599	.4608	.4616	.4625	.4633
1.8	.4641	.4649	.4656	.4664	.4671	.4678	.4686	.4693	.4699	.4706
1.9	.4713	.4719	.4726	.4732	.4738	.4744	.4750	.4756	.4761	.4767
2.0	.4772	.4778	.4783	.4788	.4793	.4798	.4803	.4808	.4812	.4817
2.1	.4821	.4826	.4830	.4834	.4838	.4842	.4846	.4850	.4854	.4857
2.2	.4861	.4864	.4868	.4871	.4875	.4878	.4881	.4884	.4887	.4890
2.3	.4893	.4896	.4898	.4901	.4904	.4906	.4909	.4911	.4913	.4916
2.4	.4918	.4920	.4922	.4925	.4927	.4929	.4931	.4932	.4934	.4936
2.5	.4938	.4940	.4941	.4943	.4945	.4946	.4948	.4949	.4951	.4952
2.6	.4953	.4955	.4956	.4957	.4959	.4960	.4961	.4962	.4963	.4964
2.7	.4965	.4966	.4967	.4968	.4969	.4970	.4971	.4972	.4973	.4974
2.8	.4974	.4975	.4976	.4977	.4977	.4978	.4979	.4979	.4980	.4981
2.9	.4981	.4982	.4982	.4983	.4984	.4984	.4985	.4985	.4986	.4986
3.0	.4987	.4987	.4987	.4988	.4988	.4989	.4989	.4989	.4990	.4990
3.1	.4990	.4991	.4991	.4991	.4992	.4992	.4992	.4992	.4993	.4993
3.2	.4993	.4993	.4994	.4994	.4994	.4994	.4994	.4995	.4995	.4995
3.3	.4995	.4995	.4995	.4996	.4996	.4996	.4996	.4996	.4996	.4997
3.4	.4997	.4997	.4997	.4997	.4997	.4997	.4997	.4997	.4997	.4998
3.5	.4998									
4.0	.49997									
4.5	.499997									
5.0	.4999997									
6.0	.499999999									